www.wadsworth.com

wadsworth.com is the World Wide Web site for Wadsworth and is your direct source to dozens of on-line resources.

At *wadsworth.com* you can find out about supplements, demonstration software, and student resources. You can also send email to many of our authors and preview new publications and exciting new technologies.

wadsworth.com
Changing the way the world learns®

Life-Span Human Development

Fourth Edition

Carol K. Sigelman
The George Washington University

Elizabeth A. Rider
Elizabethtown College

THOMSON

WADSWORTH

Australia • Canada • Mexico • Singapore • Spain • United Kingdom • United States

THOMSON
★
WADSWORTH

Psychology Publisher: Edith Beard Brady

Development Editor: Sherry Symington

Assistant Editor: Rebecca Heider

Editorial Assistant: Maritess A. Tse

Technology Project Manager: Michelle Vardeman

Marketing Manager: Lori Grebe

Marketing Assistant: Michael Silverstein

Advertising Project Manager: Tami Strang

Project Manager, Editorial Production: Lisa Weber

Print/Media Buyer: Karen Hunt

Permissions Editor: Joohee Lee

Production Service: Cecile Joyner, The Cooper Company

Text and Cover Designer: Jennifer Dunn

Photo Researcher: Terri Wright

Copy Editor: Peggy Tropp

Illustrators: John and Judy Waller

Indexer: Kay Banning

Cover Images: © CORBIS (baby); Digital Image © 2002 Getty Images/PhotoDisc (all others)

Cover Printer: Lehigh Press

Compositor: Graphic World, Inc.

Printer: Quebecor/World, Versailles

For more information about our products, contact us at:
Thomson Learning Academic Resource Center
1-800-423-0563
For permission to use material from this text, contact us by:
Phone: 1-800-730-2214
Fax: 1-800-730-2215
Web: http://www.thomsonrights.com

Library of Congress Control Number: 2002103356

ISBN 0-534-55350-8

Wadsworth/Thomson Learning
10 Davis Drive
Belmont, CA 94002-3098
USA

Asia
Thomson Learning
60 Albert Street, #15-01
Albert Complex
Singapore 189969

Australia
Nelson Thomson Learning
102 Dodds Street
South Melbourne, Victoria 3205
Australia

Canada
Nelson Thomson Learning
1120 Birchmount Road
Toronto, Ontario M1K 5G4
Canada

Europe/Middle East/Africa
Thomson Learning
Berkshire House
168-173 High Holborn
London WC1V 7AA
United Kingdom

Latin America
Thomson Learning
Seneca, 53
Colonia Polanco
11560 Mexico D.F.
Mexico

Spain
Paraninfo Thomson Learning
Calle/Magallanes, 25
28015 Madrid, Spain

To the students who have inspired us

Brief Contents

Contents

CHAPTER 4

Prenatal Development and Birth 80

CHAPTER 5

The Physical Self 106

CHAPTER 12

Gender Roles and Sexuality 311

Male and Female 312

The Infant 315

The Child 316

The Adolescent 318

The Adult 327

Sexuality over the Life Span 330

CHAPTER 13

Social Cognition and Moral Development 339

Social Cognition 340

Perspectives on Moral Development 346

Attachment and Social Relationships 369

Preface

Welcome to the fourth edition of *Life-Span Human Development!* This new edition has many exciting changes, yet retains the core features that have been praised by both instructors and students over the years. Elizabeth A. Rider is our new co-author and has brought her considerable talents and expertise in cognitive development and gender psychology to the book. We have retained our unique integrated topical/chronological approach yet have fine-tuned the chapter organization to offer stronger coverage of key topics and controversies and to better meet the needs of the life-span course.

Unique Integrated Topical/Chronological Approach

The most distinctive feature of this book remains its *integrated topical/chronological approach.* Almost all other life-span development textbooks adopt a chronological or "age/stage" approach, carving the life span into age ranges and describing the prominent characteristics of individuals within each age range. In contrast, this book uses a topical approach for the overall organization of the book, blended with a chronological approach within chapters. Each chapter focuses on a domain of development such as physical growth, cognition, or personality and traces developmental trends and influences in that domain from infancy to old age. Each chapter calls attention to age groups through major sections on infancy, childhood, adolescence, and adulthood.

Why Topical?

Why have we bucked the tide? Like many other instructors, we have typically favored topically organized textbooks when teaching child, adolescent, or adult development courses. As a result, it seemed only natural to use that same topical approach in introducing students to the whole life span. Besides, chronologically organized texts often have to repeat themselves as they remind readers of where development left off in an earlier age period (covered several chapters ago).

More importantly, a topic-by-topic organization conveys the flow of development—the systematic, and often dramatic, transformations that take place, as well as the developmental continuities. The topical approach also helps us to emphasize developmental *processes*—how nature and nurture interact over the life span to effect change—as well as the sizable differences among individuals.

Finally, a predominantly topical approach is more compatible with a *life-span perspective,* which views any period of life from the perspective of what comes before and what is yet to come. In chronologically organized textbooks, many topics are discussed only in connection with the age group to which they seem most relevant—for example, attachment in relation to infancy or sexuality in relation to adolescence and adulthood.

A topical organization makes one ask intriguing questions that one might otherwise not ask. For example, consider these questions regarding the topic of attachment:

- *What do infants' attachments to their parents have in common with attachments between childhood friends or adult romantic partners?*
- *Do securely attached infants later have a greater capacity to form and sustain friendships or romantic partnerships than infants whose early social experiences are less favorable?*
- *What are the consequences at different points in the life span of lacking someone to whom one is closely attached?*

Attachments are obviously important throughout the life span, and a topical organization helps make that clear.

Why Chronological?

While we have adopted a topical approach because we consider it the best way to introduce the how and why of human development, we also appreciate the strengths of the chronological approach, particularly its ability to portray the whole person in each period of the life span. For this reason, we have integrated the age/stage approach within the topical organization, aiming to have the best of both worlds.

Each topical chapter contains major sections on infancy, childhood, adolescence, and adulthood. The existence of these sections is proof that chapters have indeed traced development in each of the domains covered across the *whole* life span. These age/stage sections call attention to the distinctive qualities of each phase of life and make it easier for students to find material on an age period of particular interest to them. Of course, each chapter emphasizes a particular period of the life span more or less, depending on the topic.

Adaptability of the Integrated Topical/Chronological Approach

Even though links between chapters are noted throughout the book, instructors who are teaching short courses or who are otherwise pressed for time can omit a chapter here or there without fear of rendering other chapters incomprehensible. For example:

- a cognitively-oriented course might omit one or more of the socially-oriented chapters (11, 12, 14, 15, 16, and 17)

- a socially-oriented course might omit one or more of the cognitive chapters (6, 7, 8, 9, and 10).

Moreover, this approach allows instructors enough flexibility to cover infancy, childhood, and adolescence in the first portion of the course, if they prefer, and save the material on adulthood for the end.

INTERRELATIONSHIPS IN DEVELOPMENT

Our unique topical/chronological approach is also especially effective for highlighting the interrelationships among physical, cognitive, and psychosocial development at any age. We want students to understand that human development is an incredibly complex process that grows out of transactions between a changing person and a changing world, out of dynamic relationships among biological, psychological, and social influences. No matter what the contributor to development—a gene, a temperament, a parent, a culture—it does not act alone. We also want students to appreciate that these influences continue to act throughout our lifetimes.

Rigorous and Readable, Research Oriented and "Real"

Why has *Life-Span Human Development* continued to receive high praise from both faculty and students over the years? Our primary goals provide a clue: we have worked to create a text that is rigorous yet readable, both research-oriented and "real" to students.

This edition of *Life-Span Human Development* continues in this tradition and tackles complex theoretical controversies such as the nature/nurture issue and incorporates the best of both classic and contemporary research from multiple disciplines.

We also appreciate that solid scholarship is of little good to students unless they want to read it and can understand it. We maintain that even the most complex issues in human development can be made understandable through clear and straightforward writing.

To make the material more "real" to students, we have focused on including examples, analogies, and discussions of research that highlight the relevance of the course to student's lives. In this edition we have incorporated much additional material that is relevant to the work of students in their roles as parents, teachers, psychologists, nurses, day-care workers, and other human service professionals. We have focused on helping students see that major theories of human development do not just guide researchers but can help anyone analyze issues that we all face—including such practical matters as raising children, working with troubled adolescents, or coping with Alzheimer's disease in the family.

Organization of the Text

CORE CONCEPTS: CHAPTERS 1 TO 4

The book begins by orienting students to the scientific study of life-span development (Chapter 1) and to the central issues and theoretical perspectives that have dominated the field

(Chapter 2). It then explores developmental processes in some depth, examining genetic influences (Chapter 3) and early environmental influences (Chapter 4) on development. These chapters show how genes contribute to maturational changes and individual differences throughout the life span and how people are also the products of their prenatal and postnatal environments. If students gain nothing else from their study of human development, we hope they gain a deeper understanding of the nature–nurture issue and of the many interacting forces acting on the developing person.

DEVELOPMENT OF BASIC HUMAN CAPACITIES: CHAPTERS 5 TO 10

Chapters on the growth and aging of body and nervous system (Chapter 5) and on the development of sensory and perceptual capacities (Chapter 6) launch our examination of the development of basic human capacities. Chapter 7 covers Piaget's perspective on cognitive development and the quite different perspective offered by Lev Vygotsky; Chapter 8 views memory and problem solving from an information-processing perspective; Chapter 9 highlights the psychometric approach to cognition, exploring individual differences in intelligence and creativity; and Chapter 10 explores language development and the roles of language and cognition in educational achievement.

DEVELOPMENT OF SELF IN SOCIETY: CHAPTERS 11 TO 17

The next three chapters concern the development of the self—changes in self-conceptions and personality, including vocational identity (Chapter 11), in gender roles and sexuality (Chapter 12), and in social cognition and morality (Chapter 13). The self is set more squarely in a social context as we trace life-span changes in attachment relationships (Chapter 14) and in roles and relationships within the family (Chapter 15). Finally, we offer a life-span perspective on developmental problems and disorders (Chapter 16) and examine why people die and how they cope with death (Chapter 17).

"BIG PICTURE" PERSPECTIVE: EPILOGUE

We have included an epilogue that summarizes major developments in each of seven periods of the life span as well as broad themes in life-span development that are emphasized throughout the book. This conclusion focuses attention on the whole person and serves as a handy reference throughout the course for students who want "the big picture." Some instructors prefer to assign this at the beginning of their courses to help ground students, while others use it both to start the course and to stimulate discussion at the end.

New to This Edition

In this edition, we emphasize more than ever the complexities of interactions between nature and nurture in human development. We have expanded the coverage of genes, hormones, and other biological forces while also adding to the discussions of social and cultural influences. For example, we expanded coverage of the development of the brain, including its growth spurt in adolescence, and we now discuss in Chapter 11, *Self and Personality*, and subsequent chapters how development differs in individualistic and collectivist cultures.

As always, the book has been thoroughly updated from start to finish; it conveys the most recent discoveries and insights developmentalists have to offer. We take pride in having written a well-researched and well-referenced book that professors and students can use as a resource. Finally, we have done some judicious pruning to allow us to deepen our coverage of selected topics. In pursuing these goals, we have added some exciting new topics and greatly expanded and updated coverage of other topics. A sampling:

CHAPTER 1. UNDERSTANDING LIFE-SPAN HUMAN DEVELOPMENT

- Improved coverage of changes in adolescence, middle adulthood, and old age
- Attention to the complex issues researchers face
- New example (in a boxed feature) of naturalistic research on male and female aggression in different cultures

CHAPTER 2. THEORIES OF HUMAN DEVELOPMENT

- Introduction of Lev Vygotsky as a featured theorist in relation to Contextual and Systems Theories
- Inclusion of sufficient material on learning theories to allow students to analyze parent and teacher actions in terms of classical and operant conditioning and observational learning

CHAPTER 3. GENES, ENVIRONMENT AND DEVELOPMENT

- New coverage of sex differences in parental investment in child rearing from an evolutionary perspective
- The latest from the Human Genome Project
- Coverage of a major behavior genetics study by Reiss and colleagues
- The latest on gene therapy and issues surrounding cloning
- More on controversies surrounding behavior genetics research

CHAPTER 4. PRENATAL DEVELOPMENT AND BIRTH

- The latest research on prenatal development and teratogens
- Expanded coverage of birthing practices
- More on the father's experience of birth
- The latest on issues related to low-birth weight
- New reproductive technologies

CHAPTER 5. THE PHYSICAL SELF

- Substantial changes in the organization of material on early brain development, including a separate section on brain plasticity
- New research on use of infant walkers and the emergence of motor skills
- New section on the psychological implications of physical changes for older adults

- New boxed feature on adolescent risk taking in relation to brain development during adolescence
- New boxed feature with the latest research on teens and sleep

CHAPTER 6. PERCEPTION

- Added material on the use of evoked potentials in testing hearing, and on issues in assessing hearing impairment across the life span
- Reorganized and updated coverage of the perceptual capacities of adults

CHAPTER 7. COGNITION

- Removal of coverage of language to Chapter 10 to allow students to focus on cognition
- Expanded coverage of Vygotsky's perspective, including a comparison of his theory to that of Piaget

CHAPTER 8. MEMORY AND INFORMATION PROCESSING

- With material on basic learning processes moved, a sharper focus on developments in memory and information processing
- New section on autobiographical memory, with reference to scripts and eyewitness memory
- A new discussion of what is and is not "normal" forgetting in old age

CHAPTER 9. INTELLIGENCE AND CREATIVITY

- New information on modern intelligence tests including the Kaufman Assessment Battery for Children, Feuerstein's Learning Potential Assessment Device, and the Cognitive Assessment System

CHAPTER 10. LANGUAGE AND EDUCATION

- Whole new chapter on language development and educational achievement, highlighting relationships between language skills, reading, and academic achievement
- Trends in science and math education
- A section on integrating school and work during adolescence
- New material on adult literacy and continuing education
- An exploration of controversies regarding the value of computers in the classroom.
- Further discussion of Vygotsky's theory
- Integrated discussion of the educational implications of the theories and research in Chapters 6, 7, 8, and 9

CHAPTER 11. SELF AND PERSONALITY

- A thoroughly reworked chapter on self and personality that incorporates material on vocational development, midlife crisis, and theories of successful aging previously covered in a chapter on Achievement
- Emphasis on the concept of "goodness of fit" between person and environment in relation to both personality development and vocational development

- New section on definitions of the self in individualistic and collectivist cultures

CHAPTER 12. GENDER ROLES AND SEXUALITY

- Clarification of which gender differences are real and which are mythical
- The latest research on gender-role development

CHAPTER 13. SOCIAL COGNITION AND MORAL DEVELOPMENT

- Expansion of coverage of theory of mind, including cross-cultural research
- In-depth coverage of the roots of youth violence in the wake of a rash of school shootings

CHAPTER 14. ATTACHMENT AND SOCIAL RELATIONSHIPS

- Controversy surrounding Judith Harris's argument that peers are more important than parents in the socialization of children
- Differences in attachment in individualistic and collectivist cultures
- New research on the effects of early social deprivation and secure attachment on the stress response system and emotion regulation later in life and new research on developmental outcomes of Romanian orphans
- New research on dating in adolescence

CHAPTER 15. THE FAMILY

- Updates on trends in family life
- Expanded coverage of economic hardship and poverty

CHAPTER 16. DEVELOPMENTAL PSYCHOPATHOLOGY

- Expanded coverage of the developmental psychopathology perspective
- The latest research on the use of stimulant drugs to treat ADHD
- New breakthroughs in research on Alzheimer's disease

CHAPTER 17. THE FINAL CHALLENGE: DEATH AND DYING

- Recent challenges to our assumptions about how people grieve
- The latest in theories of why we die and how life might be extended

EPILOGUE: FITTING THE PIECES TOGETHER

- Reworked summary of major developments in each of seven periods of the life span
- Discussion of broad themes in life-span development

Chapter Organization

The chapters of this book follow a consistent format and contain:

Chapter outline that orients students to what lies ahead.

Introductory material that stimulates interest, lays out the plan for the chapter, and introduces key concepts, theories, and issues relevant to the area of development to be explored.

Developmental sections (Chapters 5–17) that describe key changes and continuities, as well as the mechanisms underlying them, during four developmental periods: infancy, childhood, adolescence, and adulthood.

"Explorations" boxed features that allow more in-depth investigation of research on a topic (for example, cross-cultural research on sex differences in aggression, preventing and treating genetic conditions, the performance of aging drivers, language acquisition among deaf children, the development of ethnic identity, cultural and ethnic differences in parenting, and gender differences in depression).

"Applications" boxed features that examine how knowledge has been used to optimize development in a domain of development (for instance, to treat genetic defects, improve cognitive functioning and memory skills across the life span, combat youth violence, help social isolates, prevent family violence, and lengthen life).

Summary points that overview the chapter's main themes to aid students in reviewing the material.

Key terms, a list of the new terms introduced in the chapter, in the order in which they were introduced. The terms are printed in boldface, defined when they are first presented in a chapter, and included in the glossary at the end of the book.

Critical thinking questions that challenge students to think about or apply the chapter material in new ways.

On the Web, a list of web sites where students can go for further information on chapter topics, along with key terms to promote research using InfoTrac College Edition (an online library available with the book). Also, students are directed to the resources available on the Wadsworth Psychology Web Site (http://www.wadsworth.com/psychology), as well as those available on the Wadsworth Life-Span CD-ROM.

Referencing

Finally, a word on referencing. Each chapter cites the authors and dates of publication for a large number of books and articles, which are fully referenced in the chapter-by-chapter bibliographies at the end of the book. Some students may wonder why they are there. It is because we are committed to the value of systematic research, because we must give credit where credit is due, and because we want students and their professors to have the resources they need to pursue their interests in human development.

Supplements

Life-Span Human Development, Fourth Edition, is accompanied by a wide array of supplements prepared for both the instructor and student to create the best learning environment inside as well as outside the classroom. All the continuing supplements for *Life-Span Human Development,* Fourth Edition, have been thoroughly revised and updated, and several are new to this edition. Especially noteworthy are the new media and Internet-based supplements. We invite you to examine and take full advantage of the teaching and learning tools available to you.

For the Instructor

Instructor's Manual with Test Bank. Revised by Bradley J. Caskey of the University of Wisconsin, River Falls, this manual contains chapter-specific outlines, a list of print, video, and online resources, and student learning objectives. The manual has a special emphasis on active learning with suggested student activities and projects for each chapter. The test bank, in both print and computerized form, consists of 100 multiple-choice questions and 15 true-false questions for each chapter, all with page references. Each multiple-choice item is categorized based on type (factual or conceptual). Also included are 10 essay questions for each chapter of the text.

ExamView® Computerized Testing. Create, deliver, and customize printed and online tests and study guides in minutes with this easy-to-use assessment and tutorial system. ExamView includes a Quick Test Wizard and an Online Test Wizard to guide instructors step by step through the process of creating tests. The test appears on screen exactly as it will print or display online. Using ExamView's complete word processing capabilities, instructors can enter an unlimited number of new questions or edit questions included with ExamView.

CLASSROOM PRESENTATION TOOLS
FOR THE INSTRUCTOR

Multimedia Manager for Developmental Psychology 2003: A Microsoft® PowerPoint® Link Tool. With the one-stop digital library and presentation tool, instructors can assemble, edit, and present custom lectures with ease. The Multimedia Manager contains a selection of digital media from Wadsworth's latest titles in developmental psychology, including figures and tables. Also included are animations, CNN video clips and pre-assembled Microsoft PowerPoint lecture slides based on each specific text. Instructors can use the material or add their own material for a truly customized lecture presentation.

CNN®Today Developmental Psychology Video Series, Volumes 1–3. Lifespan Development Video Series, Volumes 1–2. Illustrate the relevance of developmental psychology to everyday life with this exclusive series of videos for the lifespan course. Jointly created by Wadsworth and CNN, each video consists of approximately 45 minutes of footage originally broadcast on CNN and specifically selected to illustrate important developmental psychology concepts. The videos are divided into short two- to seven-minute segments, perfect for

use as lecture launchers or as illustrations of key developmental psychology concepts. Special adoption conditions apply.

Wadsworth Developmental Psychology Video Library. Bring developmental psychology concepts to life with videos from Wadsworth's Developmental Psychology Video Library, which includes thought-provoking offerings from Films for Humanities, as well as other excellent educational video sources. This extensive collection illustrates important developmental psychology concepts covered in many life-span courses. Certain adoption conditions apply.

For the Student

Study Guide. Written by co-author Elizabeth A. Rider of Elizabethtown College, the Study Guide is designed to promote active learning through a guided review of the important principles and concepts in the text. The study materials for each chapter include a comprehensive multiple-choice self-test and exercises that challenge students to think about and to apply what they have learned.

Life-Span CD-ROM. This interactive CD-ROM stimulates student to learn about key theories and important concepts through the use of narrative, video, animations, quizzes, and web links. The material is organized into four major areas: physical development; language, learning and cognitive development; social and emotional development; and ecological systems theory and dynamic systems theory.

Coverage of the theorists includes:

- Brief biography
- Brief description of theory
- Video segments with audio introduction and written script guiding user to key components to observe
- Multiple choice quiz to help students test their knowledge
- Embedded applications that present a scenario followed by questions that stimulate students to think critically
- Research Online: link to book's web site

Coverage of broader concepts includes narrative accompanied by video, challenge questions, quizzes, applications, and links to the book's web site.

Internet-Based Supplements

WebTutor™ Advantage on WebCT and Blackboard. This Web-based software for students and instructors takes a course beyond the classroom to an anywhere, anytime environment. Students gain access to a full array of study tools, including chapter outlines, chapter-specific quizzing material, interactive games, and videos. With WebTutor Advantage, instructors can provide virtual office hours, post syllabi, track student progress with the quizzing material, and even customize content to meet students' needs. Instructors can also use the communication tools to set up threaded discussions and conduct "real-time" chats. "Out of the box" or customized, WebTutor Advantage provides a powerful tool for instructors and students alike.

InfoTrac® College Edition. With InfoTrac College Edition, instructors can stimulate discussions and supplement lectures with the latest developments in developmental psychology. Available as a free options with newly purchased texts, InfoTrac College Edition gives instructors and students four months of free access to an extensive database of reliable, full-length articles (not just abstracts) from hundreds of top academic journals and popular periodicals. In-text exercises suggest search terms to make the most of this resource.

Wadsworth Psychology Web Site at http://www.wadsworth.com/psychology. This Web site provides instructors and students with a wealth of *free* information and resources, such as:

- Journals
- Associations
- Conference listings
- Psych-in-the-News
- Hot topics
- Book-specific student resources

Additional instructor resources include:

- Research and Teaching Showcase
- Resources for Instructors Archives
- Book-specific instructor resources

Acknowledgments

A project of this magnitude cannot be carried out without the efforts of many people. We are very grateful to the many reviewers of the manuscript for their constructive criticism and useful suggestions.

Reviewers of the first edition included Fredda Blanchard-Fields of Louisiana State University, Janet Fritz of Colorado State University, John Klein of Castleton State College, Rosanne Lorden of Eastern Kentucky University, Robin Palkovitz of the University of Delaware, Suzanne Pasch of the University of Wisconsin at Milwaukee, and Katherine Van Giffen of California State University at Long Beach.

Reviewers of the second edition were David Beach of the University of Wisconsin-Parkside, Charles Harris of James Madison University, Malia Huchendorf of Normandale Community College, Vivian Jenkins of the University of Southern Indiana, Nancy Macdonald of the University of South Carolina-Sumter, Jim O'Neill of Wayne State University, Marjorie Reed of Oregon State University, and Ruth Wilson of Idaho State University.

Reviewers of the third edition were Bob Bornstein, Miami University-Oxford; Donna Brent, Hartwick College; Mary Ann Bush, Western Michigan University; Shelley Drazen, Binghamton University (SUNY); Suzanne Krinsky, University of Southern Colorado; Becky White Loewy, San Francisco State University; Russell Miars, Portland State University;

Elizabeth Rider, Elizabethtown College; Eileen Rogers, University of Texas-San Antonio; Timothy Shearon, Albertson College of Idaho; Polly Trnavsky, Appalachian State University; and Catherine Weir, Colorado College. Catherine Weir also deserves thanks for her substantive contributions to the revision of several chapters.

Reviewers of this edition were Denise Ann Bodman of Arizona State University, Kim G. Brenneman of Eastern Mennonite University, Mary Ann Bush of Western Michigan University, Yiwei Chen of Bowling Green State University, Michelle R. Dunlap of Connecticut College, Marion Eppler of East Carolina University, Dan Florell of Eastern Kentucky University, James N. Forbes of Angelo State University, Claire Ford of Bridgewater State College, Charles Harris of James Madison University, Karen Hartlep of California State University—Bakersfield, Debra L. Hollister of Valencia Community College, Stephen Hoyer of Pittsburg State University, David P. Hurford of Pittsburg State University, Wayne G. Joosse of Calvin College, Bridget C. Kelsey of the University of Oklahoma, Brett Laursen of Florida Atlantic University, Sherry Loch of Paradise Valley Community College, Becky White Loewy of San Francisco State University, Robert F. Marcus of the University of Maryland, Ann K. Mullis of Florida State University, Ronald L. Mullis of Florida State University, Mark Rafter of College of the Canyons, Mark Runco of California State University—Fullerton, Tim Shearon of Albertson College, and Luis Terrazas of California State University—San Marcos.

We would like to thank David Shaffer of the University of Georgia for all that his work did to make the first and second editions of this book a success. And for all that they did to assist with the writing of this edition, we are appreciative of our student assistants Joe Gasper, Megan Halladay, Lauren Swenson, and Julie Zhang.

Credit for excellent supplementary materials goes to Bradley J. Caskey of the University of Wisconsin, River Falls, who revised the Instructors Manual and Test Bank; co-author Elizabeth Rider, who wrote the Student Guide; and Kathy Trotter of Chattanooga State Technical Community College and Michie Swartwood of SUNY, Cortland, who wrote the material for the Life-Span CD-ROM that accompanies this book.

Producing this book required the joint efforts of Wadsworth and The Cooper Company. We thank Edith Beard Brady, Publisher, and Sherry Symington, Development Editor, of Wadsworth for ensuring a smooth transfer of this book from Brooks/Cole to Wadsworth and for doing so much to make this edition the most visually appealing and pedagogically effective edition yet. We thank Cecile Joyner for her characteristically outstanding management of the book's production and unfailing good cheer; Peggy Tropp for her capable copy editing; Jennifer Dunn for her creative work on the graphic design; and Terri Wright for photo researching. All of these pros were a joy to work with, and the book is much better because of them. We are grateful, as well, for the able assistance of Lisa Weber, Production Project Manager; Stephen Rapley, Creative Director; Michelle Vardeman, Technology Project Manager; Rebecca Heider, Assistant Editor; and Maritess Tse, Editorial

Assistant. We also appreciate the strong support of Tami Strang, Advertising Project Manager; Lori Grebe, Marketing Manager; and Laurel Anderson, Marketing Assistant.

We are also deeply indebted to the sponsoring editors who preceded Edith—to C. Deborah Laughton, who insisted that this project be undertaken in the first place, and to Vicki Knight, who skillfully shepherded the first edition through its final stages and oversaw the second edition until placing it in the capable hands of Jim Brace-Thompson. Finally, Lee Sigelman has coped superbly once again with a distracted and unamusing partner, and Corby Rider has learned creative ways to help rather than hinder his mom's work.

Carol K. Sigelman
Elizabeth A. Rider

About the Authors

CAROL K. SIGELMAN is associate vice president for research and graduate studies and professor of psychology at The George Washington University. She has also been on the faculty at Texas Tech University, Eastern Kentucky University (where she won the Outstanding Teacher Award), and the University of Arizona. She has taught courses in child, adolescent, adult, and life-span development and has published research on such topics as the communication skills of individuals with developmental disabilities, the development of stigmatizing reactions to children and adolescents who are different, and children's emerging understandings of diseases and psychological disorders. Through a grant from the National Institute of Child Health and Human Development, she studied children's intuitive theories of AIDS and developed and evaluated a curriculum to correct their misconceptions and convey the facts of HIV infection. Through a grant from the National Institute on Drug Abuse, she and her colleagues have conducted similar research on how well children and adolescents of different ages understand the effects of alcohol and drugs on body, brain, and behavior. For fun, she bikes with her husband or walks her cat Doughy.

ELIZABETH A. RIDER is associate dean of the faculty and associate professor of psychology at Elizabethtown College in Pennsylvania. She has also been on the faculty at University of North Carolina—Asheville. She earned her undergraduate degree from Gettysburg College and her doctorate from Vanderbilt University. She has taught courses on child and life-span development, women and gender issues, applied developmental psychology, and genetic and environmental influences on development. She has published research on children's and adults' spatial perception, orientation, and wayfinding. Through a grant from the Pennsylvania State System for Higher Education, she studied factors associated with academic success. Her text on the psychology of women, *Our Voices*, was published by Wadsworth in 2000. When she's not working, her life revolves around her son and his activities.

Understanding Life-Span Human Development

Joel Gordon

WHEN ROBERT DOLE RAN for president in 1996 at the age of 73, Ella Miller, nearing age 116, did not think he was too old. In fact, although she voted for Clinton, she figured age was an advantage for Dole: "I think he's just beginning to be a man. I've learned more since I've become old" (Tousignant, 1996, p. B5). She attributed her long life to the fact that she never worries: "I try to make life more jolly than sad" (Tousignant, 1996, p. B5). She has also learned that "life is love—if you don't love, you don't make it" (Washington & Milloy, 1996, p. 64).

Imagine living through the entire 20th century and all its dramatic changes. Born in Tennessee in 1880, 15 years after the Civil War, 2 years before Franklin Delano Roosevelt was born, and years before the automobile, much less the Internet, Mrs. Miller was the eldest daughter of former slaves. She had only two dresses as a child, and she recalls seeing her first airplane and thinking it was going to fall on her (Tousignant, 1995). She received no formal education. She married but had no children. After her husband, Isaac, died at the age of 70, she worked as a domestic helper for two elderly women until she retired (at age 107!). One of the growing number of **centenarians** (persons age 100 or older) in the United States, Mrs. Miller lived with her niece, remained active, spoke to elementary school children about life in the late 1800s, and stocked up on candy and cookies whenever she went grocery shopping—until she died in 2000 of heart failure at the age of 119, as old as humans get ("Ella Galbraith Miller," 2000).

James A. Parcell / *The Washington Post*

Centenarian Ella Miller, daughter of former slaves, at age 115

This book is about the development of humans like Ella Miller and you, from conception to death. Among the many, many fascinating and important questions it addresses are these: What does the world look like to newborn infants? Does the divorce of a child's parents have lasting effects on the child's personality or later relationships with the other sex? Why do some college students have more trouble than others deciding on a major or committing themselves to a serious relationship? Do most adults really experience a midlife crisis in which they question what they have done with their lives? How do people typically change as they age, and how does retirement affect them? It also takes on more fundamental questions: How do genetic and environmental influences contribute to human development? And how in the world does a single fertilized egg cell evolve into an adult human being?

Do any of these questions intrigue you? Probably so, for we are all developing persons very much interested in ourselves and the other developing people around us. Most college students want to understand how they and those they know have been affected by their experiences, how they have changed over the years, and where they may be heading. Many students also have very practical motivations for learning about human development—for example, a desire to be a better parent or to work more effectively as a psychologist, nurse, teacher, or other human service professional.

This introductory chapter lays the groundwork for the remainder of the book by addressing some basic questions about the nature of life-span human development and describing ways to study it.

What Is Development?

Let's begin by asking what it means to say that human beings "develop" over the life span and by defining some other key terms.

A Working Definition

Development can be defined as *systematic changes and continuities in the individual that occur between conception and death,* or from "womb to tomb." Development entails many changes, and by describing these changes as *systematic,* we imply that they are orderly, patterned, and relatively enduring—not fleeting and unpredictable like mood swings. Development also involves *continuities,* ways in which we remain the same or continue to reflect our pasts.

The systematic changes and continuities of interest to students of human development fall into three broad domains:

1. **Physical development:** the growth of the body and its organs, the functioning of physiological systems, the appearance of physical signs of aging, changes in motor abilities, and so on.

2. **Cognitive development:** changes and continuities in perception, language, learning, memory, problem solving, and other mental processes.
3. **Psychosocial development:** change and carryover in personal and interpersonal aspects of development such as motives, emotions, personality traits, interpersonal skills and relationships, and roles played in the family and in the larger society.

Even though developmentalists often specialize in one or another of these three aspects of development, they appreciate that humans are *whole* beings and that changes in one area affect the others. The baby who develops the ability to crawl, for example, now has new opportunities to develop her mind by exploring the contents of shelves and cabinets and to hone her social skills by trailing her parents from room to room.

How do you picture typical changes from birth to old age? Many people picture tremendous positive gains in capacity from infancy to young adulthood, little change at all during early adulthood and middle age, and a loss of capacities in the later years. This stereotyped view of the life span is largely, although not entirely, false. It has some truth with respect to biological development, for example. Traditionally, biologists have defined **growth** as the physical changes that occur from conception to maturity. We do indeed become biologically mature and physically competent during the early part of the life span. **Biological aging** is the deterioration of organisms (including human beings) that leads inevitably to their death. Biologically, then, development does involve growth in early life, stability in early and middle adulthood, and the declines associated with aging in later life.

Most developmental scientists today have rejected this simple model of the life span, however. They recognize that developmental change at any age involves both gains and losses. They appreciate, too, that we do not always get better or worse but instead just become different than we were (as when a child who once feared loud noises comes to fear hairy monsters under the bed instead). Development clearly means more than positive changes that occur in infancy, childhood, and adolescence, and **aging** involves more than biological aging. It refers to a wide range of changes, *positive and negative,* in the mature organism. Because both positive and negative changes—gains and losses—occur in every phase of the life span, we should not associate child development only with gains or aging only with losses (Baltes, Lindenberger, & Staudinger, 1998). For example, rates of depression increase from early childhood to early adulthood (Gotlib & Hammen, 1992), but expertise and wisdom often grow from early adulthood to middle and later adulthood (Baltes et al., 1998). In short, *development involves gains, losses, just plain changes, and samenesses in each phase of the life span.*

Developmental Processes

Two important processes underlie developmental change: maturation and learning. **Maturation** is the biological unfolding of the individual according to a plan contained in the *genes* (the hereditary material passed from parents to child at conception). Just as seeds systematically become mature plants, human beings "unfold" within the womb (assuming that they receive the necessary nourishment from their environment). Their genetic "program" then makes it likely that they will walk and utter their first words at about 1 year of age, achieve sexual maturity at age 12 to 14, and gray in their 40s and 50s. Maturational changes in the brain contribute to cognitive changes such as increased memory skills and psychosocial changes such as increased understanding of other people's feelings. Genetically influenced maturational processes guide all of us through many of the same developmental changes at about the same points in our lives.

The child is not the only developing person in this photo. Younger members of the family contribute to the ongoing development of their older relatives.

The second critical developmental process is **learning**—the process through which *experience* brings about relatively permanent changes in thoughts, feelings, or behavior. A certain degree of physical maturation is clearly necessary before a child can dribble a basketball, but careful instruction and long, hard hours of practice are just as clearly required if the child is ever to excel in basketball. Throughout the life span, we learn from our experiences and change in response to the **environment**—all the external physical and social conditions and events that can affect us, from crowded living quarters to stimulating social interactions. As we will see time and time again, developmental changes are generally the products of a complex interplay between "nature" (genetic endowment and maturation) and "nurture" (environmental influences and learning).

In summary, development is a multifaceted and complex process. It involves gains, losses, and other changes and continuities in physical, cognitive, and psychosocial functioning, brought about by both nature and nurture, both maturation and learning. As we shall now see, development also occurs in a historical and cultural context that influences how the life span and its phases are viewed.

How Do We View the Life Span?

What periods of the life span do you distinguish? Table 1.1 lists the periods that many of today's developmentalists regard as distinct. You will want to keep them in mind as you read this book, for we will constantly be speaking of infants, preschoolers, school-age children, adolescents, and young, middle-aged, and older adults. Note, however, that the given ages are only approximate. Age is only a rough indicator of level of development, and there are many differences among individuals of the same age. This is especially true of elderly adults, whom some people stereotype as "all alike."

Table 1.1   An Overview of Periods of the Life Span

Period of Life	Age Range
Prenatal period	Conception to birth
Infancy	First 2 years of life
Preschool period	2 to 5 or 6 years (some prefer to describe as "toddlers" children who have begun to walk and are age 1 to 3)
Middle childhood	6 to 12 or so (until the onset of puberty)
Adolescence	12 or so to 20 or so (when the individual is relatively independent of parents and assumes adult roles)
Early adulthood	20 to 40 years
Middle adulthood	40 to 65 years
Late adulthood	65 years and older

Age Grades, Age Norms, and the Social Clock

Table 1.1 represents only one view of the periods of the life span. Age—like gender, race, and other significant human characteristics—means different things in different societies. Each society has its own ways of dividing the life span and of treating the individuals who fall into different age groups. Each socially defined age group in a society—called an **age grade,** or age stratum—is assigned different statuses, roles, privileges, and responsibilities. We, for example, grant "adults" (18-year-olds, by law) a voting privilege that we do not grant to children, and we give retail discounts to older adults but not to young or middle-aged adults. Just as high schools have "elite" seniors and "lowly" freshmen, whole societies are layered into age grades.

Once it has established age grades, each society also defines what people should and should not be doing at different points in the life span. According to Bernice Neugarten and her colleagues (Neugarten, Moore, & Lowe, 1965), these expectations, or **age norms,** are society's way of telling people how to act their age. In our culture, for example, most people agree that 6-year-olds are too young to date or drink beer but are old enough to attend school. We also agree that adults should leave home between the ages of 18 and 25, marry at around age 25, and retire at around age 65 (Neugarten et al., 1965; Settersten, 1998). By contrast, in less industrialized countries, where couples typically have children in their teens and often become ill, disabled, and unable to work in middle age, quite different age norms may prevail. Age norms also change as societies change (Shanahan, 2000).

Why are age norms important? First, they influence people's decisions about how to lead their lives. They are the basis for what Neugarten (1968) termed the **social clock**—a sense of when things should be done and when one is ahead of or behind the schedule dictated by age norms. Prompted by the social clock, for example, an unmarried 25-year-old may feel that he should get married before it is too late or a childless 35-year-old might fear that she will miss her chance at parenthood unless she has a baby soon. Second, age norms affect how easily people adjust to life transitions. Normal life events such as having children typically affect us more negatively when they occur "off time" than when they occur "on time," at socially appropriate ages (McLanahan & Sorensen, 1985). It can be challenging indeed to experience puberty as either an 8-year-old or an 18-year-old or to become a new parent at 13 or 48!

With this background, let us briefly examine how age grades and age norms have evolved through history and how they vary from culture to culture today.

Historical Changes

Every human lives and develops in a historical context. Being a developing person today, therefore, differs from being a developing person when Ella Miller lived or in even earlier periods. Moreover, the quick historical tour that we are about to take should convince you that the phases of the life span that we recognize today were not always perceived as distinct.

CHILDHOOD

Phillippe Ariès (1962) conducted an ambitious historical analysis and concluded that, before 1600, European societies had no concept of childhood as we know it. Until then, he believed, children were viewed as miniature adults. In medieval Europe (A.D. 500–1500), for example, 6-year-olds were dressed in miniature versions of adult clothing and expected to work alongside adults at home, at a shop, or in the fields (Ariès, 1962). Moreover, a 10-year-old convicted of stealing could be hanged (Kean, 1937).

It is now clear that it is an exaggeration to say that pre-17th-century adults held a "miniature adult" view of childhood (Cunningham, 1996). Parents throughout history seem to have recognized that children are different from adults. However, before the 17th and 18th centuries, people in Western societies *did* pressure children to grow up, adopt adult roles, and contribute economically to the family's survival as soon as possible. During the 17th and 18th centuries, our modern concept of childhood gradually came into being. Children came to be seen as more distinctly childlike—as innocent beings who should be protected, given a proper moral and religious education, and taught skills such as reading and writing so they would eventually become good workers (Cunningham, 1996).

Some historians have also concluded that children were treated much more brutally in the past than now (deMause, 1974). One mother in colonial America, for example, described struggling with her 4-month-old infant: "I whipped him til he was actually black and blue, and until I *could not* whip him any more, and he never gave up one single inch" (deMause, 1974, p. 41). Was this really brutality, though? Punishment that

Although medieval children were pressured to abandon their childish ways as soon as possible and were dressed like miniature adults, it is doubtful that they were really viewed as miniature adults.

"All right, so I missed your soccer game. But didn't my assistant send you a lovely fruit basket?"

Has our society become one that expects children to grow up quickly and largely on their own?

would clearly be judged abusive from our modern perspective was more accepted in Puritan America. It was administered out of concern for the child's moral and social upbringing rather than to be cruel (Vinovskis, 1996). Today, we do not accept abusive behavior in the name of strict discipline, but our society is hardly rid of child abuse (see Chapter 15).

Overall, then, it is inaccurate to conclude that until the 17th century, parents regarded children as nothing but miniature adults and treated them with exceptional brutality. Yet the historical trend *has* been toward a greater appreciation of the uniqueness of childhood, the importance of good parenting and education, and the need to protect the rights and well-being of children. The historical context of child development continues to change. Some observers argue that our society has been reverting to a medieval view of childhood—asking children to grow up very quickly with all too little help from their parents and expecting them to cope with terrorists, drugs dealers, gun violence, and other social ills (Elkind, 1992; Hersch, 1998). Might we be exposing children to too many "adult" issues and situations too early in life? Maybe. But also consider that children in colonial America often slept in the same room with their parents and probably learned a bit about human sexuality in the process, or consider that the age of consent for sexual relations was 12 or younger as late as the end of the 19th century (Coontz, 2000). Historians have discovered that the experience of childhood is not clearly better or worse than it was in past eras, though it is clearly different.

ADOLESCENCE

If the modern concept of childhood arose only during the 17th and 18th centuries, perhaps it is not surprising that **adolescence**—the transitional period between childhood and adulthood that begins with puberty and ends when the individual has acquired adult competencies and responsibilities—came to be viewed as a distinct period of the life span in Western societies only at the end of the 19th century and beginning of the 20th century (Hine, 1999; Kett, 1977). At first, developing industries needed cheap labor and could make do with children and, later, immigrants. But as industry advanced, it needed an *educated* labor force, so laws were passed restricting child labor and making schooling compulsory. By the middle of the 20th century, adolescence had become a distinct life stage in which youth spent their days in school, separated from the adult world and living in their own peer culture (Furstenberg, 2000). As adolescents began to attend college in large numbers after World War II, the age of entry into the adult world was postponed still further (Furstenberg, 2000; Keniston, 1970).

ADULTHOOD

How is adulthood today different from adulthood in past eras? For one thing, more people are living longer. In ancient Rome, the average age of death was 20 to 30 years old; in the late 17th century, it was 35 to 40 years (Dublin & Lotka, 1936). These figures, which are *averages,* are low mainly because so many more infants died in the past. However, even those lucky

enough to make it through early childhood had relatively low odds, by modern standards, of living to be 65 or older.

The average life expectancy has continued to increase dramatically during this century. In about 1900, the average life expectancy for a newborn born in the United States was 49 years. By 1998, the life expectancy had climbed to 80 for a white female, 75 for a black female, 75 for a white male, and 68 for a black male (U.S. Census Bureau, 2000). Ella Miller beat the odds by living to 119.

The makeup of the U.S. population also changed significantly in the 20th century. In 1900, about 4% of the population was 65 and older. By the mid-1990s, the percentage was close to 13% and climbing (Hobbs, 2001). In 1950, there were more than four youths for every one elderly adult in the world's population; in another 50 years, older adults will outnumber youth (Longman, 1999). Census takers are closely watching the **baby boom generation**—the huge number of people born between 1946 and 1964—move into middle age. By 2030, when most Baby Boomers will have retired from work, an estimated 20% of the U.S. population—one of five Americans—will be 65 or older (Hobbs, 2001). No wonder we hear a lot about the challenges to society that an aging population will present.

What are some of the implications of these changes? As 20th-century parents began to bear fewer children and live long enough to see their children "empty the nest," Western societies began to recognize *middle age* as a distinct period between early adulthood and old age (Moen & Wethington, 1999). As the Baby Boomers move through middle age, this period has attracted more scholarly attention than ever (see Willis & Reid, 1999). Interestingly, middle age has been stereotyped as either a time of midlife crisis and turmoil or a time of stability and little developmental change at all. It is now understood to be a time of good health, stable relationships, many responsibilities, and high satisfaction for most people. It is also a time when people cope quite successfully with changes such as menopause and other signs of aging and achieve peak levels of cognitive functioning (Squires, 1999; Willis & Schaie, 1999).

The experience of old age also changed during the 20th century, with the introduction of Social Security, Medicare, and other such programs for the elderly (Cole, 1992). In earlier centuries, people who survived to old age literally worked until they dropped; now, unless they are poor like Ella Miller, they retire in their 60s. As a result, we have come to define old age as the retirement phase of life. Today's elderly adults are also healthier and more active than the elderly adults of the past; indeed, Kenneth Manton estimates that today's 85-year-old is about as healthy as a 65-year-old was just 25 years ago (Trafford, 1996).

In sum, age—whether it is 7, 17, or 70—has meant something quite different in each historical era. And most likely, the experience of being 7, 17, or 70 will be quite different in the 21st century than it was in the 20th. As the Explorations box on page 7 illustrates, human development also differs from culture to culture and subculture to subculture. The broader message is clear: We must view development in its historical, cultural, and subcultural context. We must bear in mind that

Cultural and Subcultural Differences in Life-Span Development

AP/Wide World Photos

Each January 15 in Japan, 20-year-olds are officially pronounced adults in a national celebration. Young women receive kimonos, young men receive suits, and all are reminded of their responsibilities to society. Young adults also gain the right to drink, smoke, and vote. The modern ceremony grew out of an ancient one in which young samurai became recognized as warriors (Reid, 1993). The age-grading system in Japanese culture clearly marks the beginning of adulthood.

It is not difficult to demonstrate that human development differs from culture to culture. Just as life expectancies have differed from historical period to historical period, they differ from nation to nation today. According to a new World Health Organization estimate of how long an infant born today is likely to live in reasonably good health, Japan leads the pack, with a disease- and disability-corrected life expectancy of 74.5 (Brown, 2000). The United States ranks 24th among the 191 countries studied, with a "healthy" life expectancy of 70.0. By contrast, newborns in Sierra Leone can expect only 25.9 years of good health on average, largely because infant mortality rates are very high in this and other less developed countries (Brown, 2000).

Just as the life span has been viewed differently in different historical eras, different societies today also have their own ways of dividing it into socially meaningful periods, or age grades (Fry, 1999). In Western industrialized societies, the life span is often visualized as a straight line extending from birth to death. In some cultures, however, the recognized phases include a period before birth as well as an afterlife, or the life span may be pictured as a circle that includes reincarnation, or some other way of being "recycled" and born again (Fry, 1985). Anthropologist Jennie Keith (1985) reports that the St. Lawrence Eskimo simply

distinguish between boys and men (or girls and women), whereas the Arusha people of East Africa have *six* socially meaningful ages for males: youths, junior warriors, senior warriors, junior elders, senior elders, and retired elders. The cultures Keith, Christine Fry, and their colleagues have studied recognize anywhere from one to ten distinct stages of life, averaging five (Fry, 1999).

The meaning of age also varies from subculture to subculture within a society. Our society is diverse socioeconomically, racially, and ethnically, and African American, Hispanic American, Native American, Asian American, and European American children are likely to have different developmental experiences. Within each of these broad racial and ethnic groups, of course, there are also immense variations associated with such factors as specific national origin, length of time in North America, degree of integration into mainstream society, language usage, and socioeconomic status.

Scholars who conduct cross-cultural research appreciate that they must work hard to keep their own cultural values from biasing their perceptions of other cultures. Scholars who study racial and ethnic diversity within the United States and other industrialized countries also need to remember this important lesson. Too often, they have judged minority group children and adults according to white middle-class standards and have found them to be "deficient" (Ogbu, 1981; Phinney, 2000). More and more researchers today appreciate the importance of understanding the distinctive contexts in which children from various racial and ethnic backgrounds develop.

Consider just one example. Linda Burton (1996), studying age norms in a low-income African American community, found that it is considered appropriate for a young woman to become a mother at 16 and a grandmother at 34—earlier than in most middle-class communities, white or black. Teenage mothers in this community looked to their own mothers and, especially, their grandmothers to help them care for their children. Much the same norms prevail among low-income European Americans in rural Appalachia. It may seem unusual from a middle-class perspective for children to be born to mothers so young and then to be raised largely by people other than their mothers and fathers. Yet it is not unusual at all in cultures around the world for child care responsibilities to be shared like this with grandmothers and other relatives (Wilson, 1989). Nor is there any evidence that such care is damaging to development. Only through research can we determine what remains the same and what changes in human development across the many contexts in which it occurs.

each social group settles on its own definitions of the life span, the age grades within it, and the norms appropriate to each age range, and that each experiences its own set of life events. One of the most fascinating challenges in the study of human development is to understand which aspects of development are universal and which aspects vary considerably from context to context.

What Is the Science of Life-Span Development?

If development consists of systematic changes and continuities from conception to death, the science of development consists of the study of those changes and continuities. In this section we consider the goals of the science of life-span development and the development of this science over time.

Goals of Study

Three broad goals guide the study of life-span development: the description, explanation, and optimization of human development (Baltes, Reese, & Lipsitt, 1980). To achieve the goal of *description,* developmental scholars characterize the behavior of human beings of different ages and trace how it changes with age. They describe both *normal development* and *individual differences,* or variations, in development. Although "average" trends in human development across the life span can be described, it is clear that no two of us (even identical twins) develop along precisely the same pathways. Some babies are considerably more alert and active than others. Some 80-year-olds are out on the dance floor; others are home in bed.

Description is the starting point in any science, but ultimately scientists want to achieve their second goal, *explanation.* Developmentalists seek to understand (1) why humans develop as they typically do, and (2) why some individuals develop differently than others. To do so, they study the contributions of nature and nurture, genes and environment, to development.

The third goal is *optimization* of human development. How can human beings be helped to develop in positive directions? How can their capacities be enhanced, how can developmental difficulties be prevented, and how can any developmental problems that do emerge be overcome? Pursuing the goal of optimizing development might involve evaluating ways to stimulate intellectual growth in preschool programs, to prevent alcohol abuse among college students, or to support elderly adults after the death of a spouse.

In summary, the scope of this book, like the scope of the science of human development, is large. We want to show you what developmentalists have learned about normal human development from conception to death and about individual differences in that development. Moreover, we seek to describe, explain, and optimize development.

Origins

Just as human development itself has changed through the ages, attempts to understand development have evolved over time. Although philosophers have long expressed their views on the nature of human beings and the proper methods of raising children, it was not until the late 19th century that the first scientific investigations of development were undertaken. A number of scholars began to carefully observe the growth and development of their own children and to publish their findings in the form of **baby biographies.** Perhaps the most influential of these baby biographers was Charles Darwin (1809–1882), who made daily records of his son's development (Darwin, 1877; see also Charlesworth, 1992). Darwin's curiosity about child development stemmed from his interest in evolution. Quite simply, he believed that infants share many characteristics with their nonhuman ancestors and that understanding the development of the individual embryo and child can offer insights into the evolution of the species. Darwin's evolutionary perspective strongly influenced early theories of human development, which emphasized universal, biologically based maturational changes (Cairns, 1998; Parke et al., 1994).

Baby biographies left much to be desired as works of science, however. Because different baby biographers emphasized very different aspects of their children's behavior, baby biographies were difficult to compare. Then, too, parents are not entirely objective observers of their own children, and early baby biographers may also have let their assumptions about evolution and development bias their observations. Finally, each baby biography was based on a single child— often the child of a distinguished family. Conclusions based on a single case may not hold true for other children.

Bettmann/CORBIS

G. Stanley Hall is widely recognized as the founder of the scientific study of human development.

We can give Charles Darwin and other eminent baby biographers much credit for making human development a legitimate topic of study and influencing early views of it. Still, the man who is most often cited as the founder of developmental psychology is G. Stanley Hall, the first president of the American Psychological Association (1846–1924). Well aware of the shortcomings of baby biographies, Hall attempted to collect more objective data on large samples of individuals. He developed a now all-too-familiar research tool, the questionnaire, to explore "the contents of children's minds" (Hall, 1891). By asking children questions about every conceivable topic, he discovered that children's understanding of the world grows rapidly during childhood and that the "logic" of young children is often not very logical at all.

Hall went on to write an influential book, *Adolescence* (1904). Strongly influenced by Darwin's evolutionary theory, Hall drew parallels between adolescence and the turbulent period in the evolution of human society during which barbarism gave way to modern civilization. Adolescence, then, was a tempestuous period of the life span, a time of emotional ups and downs and rapid changes—a time of what Hall called **storm and stress.** Thus it is Hall we have to thank for the notion that most teenagers are emotionally unstable—a largely inaccurate notion, as it turns out (Arnett, 1999). Later, this remarkable pioneer turned his attention to the end of the life span in *Senescence* (1922), an analysis of how society treats (or really, mistreats) its older members. Although his methods were limited by modern standards, and although his ideas about evolution and its relation to periods of human development were flawed, he deserves much credit for stimulating scientific research on life-span human development and for raising many important questions about it (Cairns, 1998).

Today's Life-Span Perspective

G. Stanley Hall viewed all phases of the life span as worthy of study. However, the science of human development began to break up into age-group specialty areas during the 20th century. Some researchers focused on infant or child development, others specialized in adolescence, and still others formed the specialization called **gerontology,** the study of aging and old age.

Starting in the 1960s and 1970s, a true **life-span perspective** on human development began to reemerge. Paul Baltes (1987) has laid out seven key assumptions of the life-span perspective (see Baltes et al., 1998, for an elaboration). These are tremendously important themes that you will see echoed again and again throughout this book.

1. Development is a lifelong process. Today's developmentalists appreciate that human development is not just "kid stuff," that we change throughout the life span. They also believe that development in any one period of life is best seen in the context of the whole life span. For instance, our understanding of adolescent development is bound to be richer if we concern ourselves with what led up to it and where it is leading.

2. Development is multidirectional. To G. Stanley Hall and many other early scholars, development was viewed as a universal process leading always toward more "mature" functioning. Today's developmentalists recognize that humans of any age can be experiencing growth in one set of capacities, decline in another set, and no change at all in still another.

3. Development involves both gain and loss. As we noted earlier, development at every age involves both growth and decline. Gaining a capacity for logical thought as a school-age child may mean losing some of the capacity for fanciful, imaginative thinking one had as a preschooler, for example.

4. Development is characterized by lifelong plasticity. Plasticity refers to the capacity to change in response to positive or negative experiences. Developmental scholars have long known that child development can be damaged by a deprived environment and optimized by an enriched one. It is now understood that this plasticity continues into later life—that the aging process can be altered considerably depending on the individual's experiences. For example, elderly adults who have been losing intellectual abilities can, with the help of special training and practice, regain some of those abilities (Baltes et al., 1998).

5. Development is shaped by its historical/cultural context. This theme, which has been discussed already, is illustrated well by the pioneering work of Glen Elder and his colleagues. Elder traced the impact of the Great Depression of the 1930s on the later life courses and development of children and adolescents growing up at the time (Elder, 1998; Elder, Liker, & Cross, 1984). Although many families survived the hardships of the Great Depression very nicely, this economic crisis was harder on individuals who were children rather than adolescents at the time, especially if their out-of-work fathers became less affectionate and less consistent in disciplining them. When this was the case, children displayed behavior problems and had low aspirations and poor records in school. As adults, the men had erratic careers and unstable marriages, and the women were seen by their own children as ill tempered. Clearly the trajectories our lives take can be affected for many years by the social context in which we grow up.

6. Development is multiply influenced. G. Stanley Hall and other early scholars believed that development is due to genetically programmed maturational processes. Learning theorists have argued just as strongly that how we develop is the result of our unique learning experiences. It may be human nature to look for simple explanations of complex phenomena. For example, many of us try to explain inexplicable events such as school shootings in terms of one cause or another, whether it is a gene for aggression, permissive parenting, the availability of guns, or too much violence in the media (Wachs, 2000). Development is not so simple, however. Today's developmental scientists appreciate that human development is the product of many interacting causes—both inside and outside the person, both biological and environmental. It is the product of ongoing interactions between a changing person and his or her changing world.

7. Understanding development requires multiple disciplines. Because human development is influenced by everything from biochemical reactions to historical events, it is impossible for any one discipline to have all the answers. A full understanding of human development will come only when many disciplines, each with its own perspectives and tools of study, join forces. Anthropologists, biologists, historians, psychologists, sociologists, and many others have something to contribute. Some universities have established interdisciplinary human development programs that bring members of different disciplines together in order to forge more integrated perspectives on development.

In summary, by adopting a life-span perspective on human development in this book, we will be assuming that development (1) occurs throughout the life span rather than just in childhood, (2) can take many different directions, (3) involves gains and losses at every age, (4) is characterized by plasticity at every age, (5) is affected by its historical and cultural context, (6) is influenced by multiple causal factors interacting with one another, and (7) can best be understood if scholars from multiple disciplines join forces to understand it.

How Is Developmental Research Conducted?

How do developmental scholars gain understanding of this complex phenomenon called life-span development? Through the same scientific method used in any physical or social science. Let us review for you, briefly, some basic concepts of scientific research and then turn to research strategies devised specifically for describing, explaining, and optimizing development.

The Scientific Method

There is nothing mysterious about the **scientific method.** It is both a method and an *attitude*—a belief that investigators should allow their systematic observations (or *data*) to determine the merits of their thinking. For example, for every "expert" who believes that psychological differences between males and females are largely biological in origin, there is likely to be another expert who just as firmly insists that boys and girls differ because they are raised differently. Whom shall we believe? It is in the spirit of the scientific method to believe the data—that is, the findings of research. The scientist is willing to abandon a pet theory if the data contradict it. Ultimately, then, the scientific method can help the scientific community and society at large weed out flawed ideas.

The scientific method involves a process of generating ideas and testing them by making observations. Often, casual observations provide preliminary ideas for a **theory**—a set of concepts and propositions intended to describe and explain some aspect of experience. Jean Piaget, for instance, observed his own children's development and used these observations as the basis for his influential theory of cognitive development (see Chapter 7).

Theories generate specific predictions, or **hypotheses,** regarding a particular set of observations. Consider, for example, a theory claiming that psychological differences between the sexes are largely due to differences in the ways that parents and other adults treat boys and girls. Based on this theory, a researcher might hypothesize that if parents grant boys and girls the same freedoms, the two sexes will be similarly independent, whereas if parents let boys do more things than they let girls do, boys will be more independent than girls. Suppose that the study designed to test this hypothesis indicates that boys are more independent than girls no matter how their parents treat them. Then the hypothesis would be disconfirmed by the findings, and the researcher would want to rethink this theory of sex-linked differences. If other hypotheses based on this theory were also inconsistent with the facts, the theory would have to be significantly revised or abandoned entirely in favor of a better theory.

This, then, is the heart of the scientific method: Theories generate hypotheses that are tested through observation of behavior, and new observations indicate which theories are worth keeping and which are not (see Figure 1.1).

Data Collection

No matter what aspect of human development we are interested in—whether it is the formation of bonds between infants and their parents, adolescent drug use, or memory skills in elderly adults—we must find an appropriate way to measure what interests us. Let's look briefly at some of the pros and cons of the two major methods of data collection used by de-

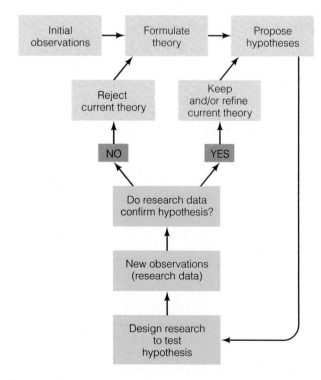

Figure 1.1 The scientific method in action

velopmental researchers: self-report measures and behavioral observations.

SELF-REPORTS

Interviews, written questionnaires, and tests and scales designed to measure abilities or personality traits all involve asking people questions. These self-report measures are often *standardized,* meaning that they ask the same questions in precisely the same order for everyone so that the responses of different individuals can be directly compared.

Although self-report methods are widely used to study human development, they have their shortcomings. First, they typically cannot be used with infants, very young children, or other individuals who cannot read or understand speech very well. Second, because individuals of different ages may not understand questions in the same way, age differences in responses may reflect age differences in comprehension or interpretation rather than age differences in the quality of interest to the researcher. Developmental researchers always face the challenge of ensuring that their data-gathering tools measure the same thing at all ages they intend to study.

Third and finally, respondents may try to present themselves in a positive or socially desirable light. The interview findings in Figure 1.2, for example, suggest that older adults fear death less than younger adults do. But could it be that elderly adults were simply more reluctant to admit to a stranger that they were afraid? Might some other method of data collection have revealed a higher level of death anxiety among older adults than this single, direct question did? Very possibly.

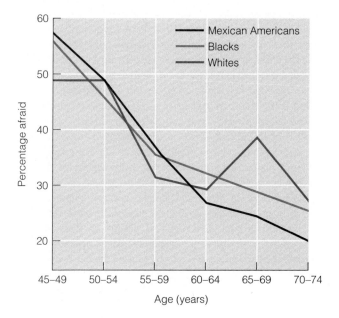

Figure 1.2 How afraid are you of death? Would you say you are: not at all afraid?/somewhat afraid?/or very afraid? Vern Bengston, Jose Cuellar, and Pauline Ragan (1977) asked this question in interviews with adults in Los Angeles. The graph shows the percentage of adults of each age who said they were "very afraid" or "somewhat afraid" of death.

SOURCE: From Bengston, Cuellar, & Ragan (1977)

BEHAVIORAL OBSERVATIONS

Naturalistic observation involves observing people in their common, everyday (that is, natural) surroundings (see Pellegrini, 1996). Ongoing behavior is observed in homes, schools, playgrounds, workplaces, nursing homes, or wherever people are going about their lives. The Explorations box on page 12 describes a study that used naturalistic observation to determine whether the sex differences in aggressive behavior evident in U.S. society can be detected in other cultures as well.

Naturalistic observation has been used to study child development more often than adult development, largely because infants and young children often cannot be studied through self-report techniques that demand verbal skills. The greatest advantage of naturalistic observation is that it is the only technique that can tell us what children or adults actually do in everyday life. Yet naturalistic observation also has its limitations. First, some behaviors (for example, heroic efforts to help other people) occur too infrequently and unexpectedly to be observed in this manner. Second, it is difficult to pinpoint the causes of the behavior, or of any developmental trends in the behavior, because in a natural setting many events are usually happening at the same time, any of which may be affecting people's behavior. Finally, the mere presence of an observer can sometimes make people behave differently than they otherwise would. Children may "ham it up" when they have an audience; parents may be on their best behavior. For this reason, researchers sometimes videotape the proceedings from a hidden location or spend time in the setting before they collect their "real" data so that the individuals they are observing become used to their presence and behave more naturally.

To achieve greater control over the conditions under which they gather behavioral data, researchers often use **structured observation;** that is, they create special conditions designed to elicit the behavior of interest. For example, a researcher might bring children individually to a laboratory room and stage an emergency in which a loud crash and scream are heard from the adjoining room. The researcher might then observe whether each child intervenes and, if so, in what way and how quickly. Structured observation permits the study of behaviors that are rarely observable in natural settings. By exposing all research participants to the same stimuli, this approach also increases the investigator's ability to compare the effect of a stimulus on different individuals. Concerns about this method center on whether conclusions based on behavior in specially designed settings will generalize to behavior in natural settings.

These, then, are the most commonly used techniques of collecting data about human development: self-report measures (interviews, questionnaires, and tests) and behavioral observation (both naturalistic and structured). Because each method has its limitations, our knowledge is advanced the most when *multiple* methods are used to study the same aspect of human development and these different methods lead to similar conclusions. The results of multiple studies addressing the same question can be synthesized to produce overall conclusions through the research method of **meta-**

Are Boys More Aggressive Than Girls in Every Culture?

In the United States, there is consistent evidence that boys are more likely than girls to engage in physically aggressive behavior and that men commit more violent crimes than women (Hyde, 1984; Knight, Fabes, & Higgins, 1996). Does this sex difference reflect biological differences between the sexes, or could it reflect cultural influences peculiar to the United States, such as the large amount of violence on American television or differences in the way Americans raise girls and boys? One way to shed light on this nature/nurture question is to determine whether sex differences in physical aggression are also evident in societies quite different from our own.

This is what Robert Munroe and his colleagues (2000) sought to do in a study of aggression among 3- to 9-year-old children in four nonindustrialized societies from diverse parts of the globe: Belize, Kenya, Nepal, and American Samoa. In each society, 24 girls and 24 boys were studied. Residents of the communities studied were trained to do naturalistic observations of children's social interactions. Using preset schedules, they tracked children down wher-ever they were in the community and immediately recorded the context and the child's behavior any time the child was with at least two other individuals. Each child was observed about 35 times; more than 6,000 specific observations were collected in all. Three types of social behavior were defined as aggressive: assaulting (hitting, kicking, or otherwise at-tacking someone), horseplay (roughhousing), and symbolic aggression (making insulting and threatening gestures and statements). In coding these and nine other social behav-iors, pairs of observers agreed at least 79% of the time on the type of social act they had observed.

Boys did indeed exhibit at least somewhat more aggres-sion than girls in all four societies studied. Overall, about 10% of boys' social behaviors, compared with 6% of girls', were ag-gressive. Boys were especially likely to behave aggressively when they were with a relatively large number of other boys. Girls too were most aggressive when they were in a group with a large proportion of boys. Munroe and his colleagues note that male play groups in which young males compete for dominance are observed in other primates species besides humans and may reflect our evolutionary past.

At the same time, cultural differences in aggression—and in sex differences in aggression—were evident in this study. The two most patrilineal cultures (cultures in which families are organized around male kin groups) were Kenya and Nepal. These proved to be the cultures in which aggressive behavior was most frequent (10–11% of social acts, as op-posed to 4–6% in Belize and American Samoa). Moreover, sex differences in aggression were clearest in these patrilin-eal cultures. The Black Carib of Belize, by contrast, are known for their low rates of aggression in adulthood; they proved to be the least aggressive group of children studied and the group in which boys and girls differed least.

As is often the case when we ask whether nature or nur-ture is more important in development, the findings suggest that both matter. Boys appear to be more aggressive than girls in most societies, but cultural and situational influences on the behavior of males and females are also important. And, as in other studies relying on naturalistic observation as a method of data gathering, it is difficult to determine which of many biological and social influences operating in the natural environment are actually causing the behavior we observe.

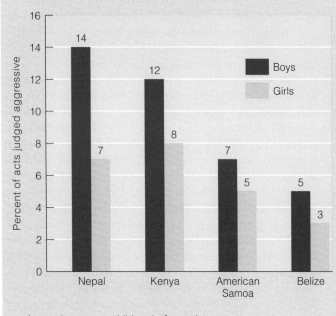

Aggression among children in four cultures.

Source: Based on means reported in Munroe et al. (2000).

analysis (Glass, McGaw, & Smith, 1981; Lipsey, 2001). For ex-ample, in an effort to determine whether males consistently behave more aggressively than females, Janet Hyde (1984) conducted a meta-analysis in which she averaged the mean scores on various measures of aggression obtained by males and females in 143 different studies. She concluded that males were indeed reliably more aggressive than females but that the size of this sex difference was quite small.

General Research Methods

Once developmental scientists have figured out what they want to measure and how to measure it, they can test their hypotheses about the factors responsible for development. The most powerful research method for explaining behavior and identifying the causes of developmental changes in behavior is the experiment. When experiments cannot be conducted, correlational research techniques may suggest answers to important "why" questions.

THE EXPERIMENTAL METHOD

In an **experiment,** an investigator manipulates or alters some aspect of the environment in order to see what effect this has on behavior. Consider an experiment conducted by Lynette Friedrich and Aletha Stein (1973) some years ago to study the effects of different kinds of television programs on the social behavior of preschool children. These researchers divided children in a nursery school into three groups: One group was exposed to violent cartoons like *Superman* and *Batman* (aggressive treatment condition), another group watched episodes of *Mister Rogers' Neighborhood* portraying many helpful and cooperative acts (prosocial treatment condition), and a third group saw programs featuring circuses and farm scenes with neither aggressive nor altruistic themes (neutral control condition).

The goal of an experiment is to see whether the different treatments that form the **independent variable**—the variable being manipulated so that its causal effects can be assessed—have differing effects on the behavior being studied, the **dependent variable** in the experiment. The independent variable in Friedrich and Stein's experiment was the type of television children watched (aggressive, prosocial, or neutral). One of the dependent variables that Friedrich and Stein chose to study, using a complicated observation system, was the number of aggressive behaviors children displayed toward other children in the nursery school. Behavior was observed before each child spent a month watching daily episodes of one of the three kinds of television programs and was recorded again after that period to see if it had changed.

Many studies demonstrate that observational learning of aggression occurs among children who watch a lot of violence on television.

What were the findings? The children who watched violent programs became more aggressive than children who watched prosocial or neutral programs—but only if they were already relatively aggressive. Thus, this experiment demonstrated a clear cause-and-effect relationship, although only for some children, between the kind of behavior children watched on television and their own subsequent behavior.

This study has the three critical features shared by any true experiment:

1. Manipulation of the independent variable. The investigator must arrange for different groups to have different experiences so that the effects of those experiences can be assessed. If an investigator merely compares children who already watch a lot of violent television and children who watch very little, he or she cannot establish that violent television watching *causes* increased aggression.

2. Random assignment of individuals to treatment conditions. Random assignment of participants to experimental conditions (for example, by drawing names from a jar) is a way of ensuring that the treatment groups are similar in all respects at the outset (in previous tendencies to be aggressive or helpful, socioeconomic status, and all other individual characteristics that could affect their social behavior). Only if experimental groups are similar in all respects initially can we be confident that any differences among groups at the end of the experiment were caused by differences in the experimental treatments they received.

3. Experimental control. In a true experiment with proper **experimental control,** all other factors besides the independent variable are controlled or held constant so that they cannot contribute to differences among the treatment groups. Friedrich and Stein ensured that children in the three treatment conditions were treated similarly *except for* the type of television they watched. It would have ruined the experiment, for example, if the children exposed to violent programs had to watch them in a small, crowded room where tempers might flare, while children in the other two groups watched in larger, less crowded rooms. The variable of interest, type of TV watched, would then be *confounded,* or entangled, with degree of crowding in the room, and we would be unable to separate the effects of one from the other.

The greatest strength of the experimental method is its ability to establish unambiguously that one thing *causes* another—that manipulating the independent variable causes a change in the dependent variable. When experiments are properly conducted, they do indeed contribute to our ability to *explain* human development, and sometimes help us to *optimize* it as well.

Does the experimental method have any limitations? Absolutely! First, the findings of laboratory experiments do not always hold true in the real world, especially if the situations created in laboratory experiments are artificial and unlike the situations that people encounter in everyday life. Urie Bronfenbrenner (1979), who has been critical of the fact that so many developmental studies are contrived experiments, once charged that developmental psychology had become "the science of the strange behavior of children in strange situations with strange adults" (p. 19). Experiments often show us what *can* cause development but not necessarily what actually *does* most strongly shape development in natural settings (McCall, 1977).

A second limitation of the experimental method is that it cannot be used to address many significant questions about human development for ethical reasons. How would you conduct a true experiment to determine how older women are affected by their husbands' deaths, for example? You would need to identify a sample of elderly women, randomly assign them to either the experimental group or the control group, and then manipulate the independent variable by leaving the control group participants alone but killing the husband of each woman in the experimental group! Ethical principles obviously demand that developmentalists use methods other than true experimental ones to study questions about the impact of widowhood and many, many other important questions about development.

Researchers sometimes study the effects of a program or intervention on development through a **quasi-experiment**—an experiment-like study that evaluates the effects of different treatments but does not randomly assign individuals to treatment groups. A gerontologist, for example, might conduct a quasi-experiment to compare the adjustment of widows who choose to participate in a support group for widows and those who do not. When individuals are not randomly assigned to treatment groups, though, uncontrolled differences between the groups studied could influence the results (for example, the widows who seek help might be more sociable than those who do not). As a result, the researcher is not able to make strong statements about what caused what, as in a true experiment.

THE CORRELATIONAL METHOD

Largely because of ethical issues, most developmental research today is correlational rather than experimental in nature. The **correlational method** generally involves determining whether two or more variables are related in a systematic way. The researcher does not randomly assign participants to treatment conditions, manipulate the independent variable, or control other factors, as in an experiment. Instead, the researcher takes people as he or she finds them and attempts to determine whether there are relationships between their experiences, characteristics, and developmental outcomes.

How would a correlational study of the effects of television on children's aggressive behavior differ from Friedrich and Stein's experiment on this topic? In a correlational study by Jerome and Dorothy Singer (1981), parents were asked to complete detailed logs describing the TV viewing habits of their preschool children: how much they watched and what they watched during a year's time. On four occasions, observers rated how aggressive the children were in interactions with other children in their nursery schools. In this manner, the researchers gathered data on the two variables of interest to them: amount of exposure to violent TV and level of aggression.

The Singers were then able to determine the strength of the relationship between these two variables by calculating a **correlation coefficient**—a measure of the extent to which individuals' scores on one variable are systematically associated with their scores on another variable. A correlation coefficient (symbolized r) can range in value from $+1.00$ to -1.00. A positive correlation between TV viewing and aggression would indicate that as the number of hours of TV children watch increases, so does the number of aggressive acts they commit (see Figure 1.3). A large positive correlation (say $+.90$) indicates a stronger positive relationship than a smaller one (say $r = .30$). A negative correlation would result if the heaviest TV viewers were quite consistently the *least* aggressive children and the lightest viewers were the *most* aggressive children. A correlation near .00 would be obtained if there were no relationship between the two variables—if it were impossible to predict how aggressive a child is based on knowing his or her TV viewing habits.

Like many other researchers, Singer and Singer found a moderately strong positive correlation ($r = +.33$) between watching a lot of action and adventure programs and behaving aggressively in the nursery school. Does this correlational study firmly establish that watching action-packed programs *causes* children to become more aggressive, though? Can you think of any alternative explanations for the correlation between TV watching and aggression?

One possibility is that *the direction of the cause–effect relationship is reversed*. It may not be that exposure to violent TV causes children to become aggressive; instead, aggressive children may be more likely than other children to seek out blood and gore on TV. A second possibility is that *the association be-*

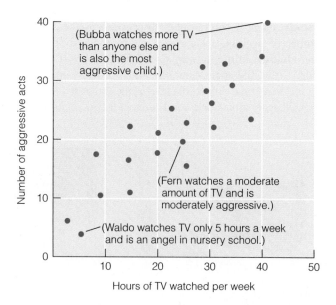

Figure 1.3 Plot of a hypothetical correlation between the amount of TV children watch and the number of aggressive acts they display. Each dot represents a specific child who watches a particular amount of TV and commits a particular number of aggressive acts. Here the correlation is large and positive: The more TV a child watches, the more aggressive he or she is.

tween the two variables is actually due to some third variable. An example of such a "third variable" might be parental rejection. Some children might have parents who are harsh and rejecting, and they might watch a lot more TV than most children to avoid unpleasant interactions with their parents. They may be aggressive because they are angry and upset about being rejected. If so, TV watching did not cause these children to become more aggressive than their peers. Rather, a third variable—parental rejection—is the cause of both their aggressive ways and their TV viewing habits.

Thus, the correlational method has one major limitation: *It cannot unambiguously establish a causal relationship between one variable and another the way an experiment can.* Correlational studies can *suggest* that a causal relationship exists, however. Indeed, Singer and Singer (1981) used complex statistical techniques to show that watching violent television probably did contribute to aggression in children and that several alternative explanations for the relationship between TV viewing and aggression could probably be ruled out. Similarly, Daniel Anderson and his colleagues (2001) found a correlation between viewing violent TV in preschool and engaging in aggressive behavior in adolescence, although only among children who focused on TV characters in their play and conversations. This study controlled statistically for "third variables" such as low parent education that could be expected to contribute to both watching violent TV and being highly aggressive. Nonetheless, neither the Singer study nor the Anderson study could establish a *definite* cause–effect link because of their correlational nature.

Despite this key limitation, the correlational method is extremely valuable. First, as already noted, many problems can be addressed only through the correlational method (or with quasi-experiments) because it would be unethical to conduct certain experiments. Second, correlational studies allow us to learn about how multiple factors operating in the "real world" conspire to influence development. Because life-span development is influenced by multiple factors rather than one factor at a time, experiments are not enough. Today's developmental researchers rely on complex correlational designs and statistical methods to understand relationships among potential causal factors such as life experiences and personal characteristics, as well as their joint contributions to good or poor developmental outcomes (Wachs, 2000). See Table 1.2 for a comparison of experimental and correlational methods.

Overall, our ability to understand why humans develop as they do is advanced the most when the results of different kinds of studies *converge*—when experiments demonstrate a clear cause-and-effect relationship under controlled conditions *and* correlational studies reveal that this same relationship seems to be operating in everyday life, even in the context of other possible causes. A variety of studies have now demonstrated that the link between watching violence on television and behaving aggressively is real (Bushman & Huesmann, 2001; Jason, Kennedy Hanaway, & Brackshaw, 1999).

Developmental Research Designs

Along with the experimental and correlational methods used by all kinds of researchers to study relationships between variables, developmental researchers need specialized research designs to study how people change and remain the same as they get older. To achieve the goal of describing development, researchers have relied extensively on two types of research designs: the cross-sectional design and the longitudinal design. A third design, the sequential study, has come into use in an attempt to overcome the limitations of the other two techniques. Let's first define the original two approaches and then explore their strengths and weaknesses.

CROSS-SECTIONAL AND LONGITUDINAL DESIGNS

In a **cross-sectional design,** the performances of people of different age groups on a measure of interest are compared. A researcher interested in the development of vocabulary might gather samples of speech from a number of 2-, 3-, and 4-year-olds; calculate the mean (or average) number of distinct words used per child for each age group; and compare these means to describe how the vocabulary sizes of children of ages 2, 3, and 4 differ. The cross-sectional study provides information about *age differences*. By seeing how different age groups

Table 1.2 Comparison of the Experimental Method and the Correlational Method

Experimental Method	Correlational Method
Manipulation of an independent variable (investigator exposes participants to different experiences)	Studies people who have already had different experiences
Random assignment to treatment groups to ensure similarity of groups	Assignment by "nature" to groups (groups may not be similar in all respects)
Experimental control of extraneous variables	Lack of control over extraneous variables
Can establish a cause–effect relationship between independent variable and dependent variable	Can suggest but not firmly establish that one variable causes another
May not be possible for ethical reasons	Can be used to study issues that cannot be studied experimentally
May be artificial (findings from contrived experimental settings may not generalize well to the "real world")	Can study multiple influences operating in natural settings (findings may generalize better to the "real world")

differ, we can attempt to draw conclusions about how performance changes with age.

In a **longitudinal design,** the performance of one group of individuals is assessed repeatedly over time. The language development study just described would be longitudinal rather than cross-sectional if we identified a group of 2-year-olds, measured their vocabulary sizes, waited a year until they were age 3 and measured their vocabularies again, did the same thing a year later when they were age 4, and then compared their mean scores at the three ages. In any longitudinal study, whether it covers only a few months in infancy or 20 or 50 years, the same individuals are studied *as they develop.* Thus, the longitudinal design provides information about *age changes* rather than age differences.

Now, what difference does it make whether we choose the cross-sectional or the longitudinal design to describe development? Suppose a team of researchers were interested in whether attitudes about the roles of men and women in society typically become more traditional or more liberated over the adult years. Suppose they conducted a longitudinal study by administering the gender-role questionnaire three times to a group of men and women: in 1960 (when the men and women were 30); in 1980 (when they were 50), and in 2000 (when they were 70). But in 2000, another research team conducted a cross-sectional study of this same question, comparing the gender-role attitudes of adults 30, 50, and 70 years old. Figure 1.4 illustrates these two alternative designs, and Figure 1.5 portrays hypothetical age trends that they might generate.

What is going on here? The cross-sectional study seems to be indicating that as people get older, their attitudes about gender roles become more traditional. The longitudinal study suggests precisely the opposite: As people get older, their attitudes about gender roles seem to become more liberated. How could a cross-sectional study and a longitudinal study on the same topic lead to such different conclusions?

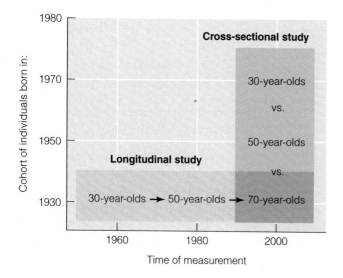

Figure 1.4 Cross-sectional and longitudinal studies of development from age 30 to age 70

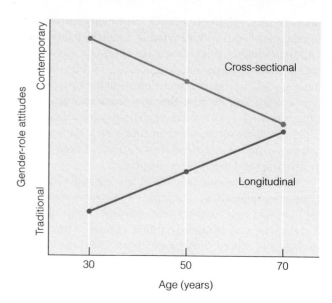

Figure 1.5 Conflicting findings of hypothetical cross-sectional and longitudinal studies of gender-role attitudes. How could the two studies produce different age trends?

AGE, COHORT, AND TIME OF MEASUREMENT EFFECTS

To unravel this mystery, one must realize that the findings of developmental studies can be influenced by three factors: *age effects, cohort effects,* and *time of measurement effects.* **Age effects** are the effects of getting older. Note that the whole purpose of our developmental study is to describe how attitudes about gender roles change as a function of *age.* **Cohort effects** are the effects of being born in one particular historical context rather than another (for example, of being born during the Great Depression of the 1930s rather than in the 1920s). Any *cohort* is a group of people born at the same time, either in the same year or within a specified, limited span of years. People who are in their 70s today not only are older than people in their 30s, but they belong to a different cohort or generation and have had different formative experiences. Finally, **time of measurement effects** in developmental research are the effects of historical events and trends occurring during the time when the data are being collected (for example, effects of World War II or of the creation of the World Wide Web). Time of measurement effects are not unique to a particular cohort but can affect anyone alive at the time. Once one is aware that age, cohort, and time of measurement can all influence developmental research findings, one can appreciate that both the cross-sectional and the longitudinal designs have their problems.

STRENGTHS AND WEAKNESSES OF THE CROSS-SECTIONAL DESIGN

In the cross-sectional study of gender attitudes, the three age groups being compared represent three different cohorts of people. The 70-year-olds were born in 1930, the 50-year-olds in 1950, and the 30-year-olds in 1970. How might the formative experiences of these three groups have differed in ways that could affect their attitudes about gender roles? The oldest group grew up in an era when traditional attitudes about gender roles were strongly held: Women were to stay at home and raise the children; men were to work and bring home the bacon. Possibly, then, older adults' unliberated responses to the questionnaire in 2000 reflect views they learned early in life and maintained for the rest of their lives. Perhaps their views did not actually *become* more traditional as they got older. And perhaps the 30-year-old cohort, which grew up when the women's movement was in full swing, formed relatively liberated gender-role attitudes early in life and will retain those liberated attitudes as they get older. Perhaps, then, what initially looked like a developmental trend toward greater traditionality (an age effect) is actually only a cohort effect resulting from differences in the formative experiences of the different generations studied.

The cross-sectional study *does* tell us how people of different ages (cohorts) differ, and this can be useful information. But the cross-sectional technique does not necessarily tell us how people actually develop as they get older. Do 70-year-olds have more conservative gender-role attitudes than 30-year-olds because they are older, or because they are members of a different cohort raised in a more traditional historical period? We cannot tell. *Age effects and cohort effects are confounded, or entangled.*

The problem of cohort effect, then, is the central problem in cross-sectional research, and it is a very real problem in studies designed to describe how adults develop over the years. As we shall see in Chapter 9, cross-sectional studies of performance on intelligence tests once appeared to indicate that we lose our intellectual faculties starting in middle age. Yet the older adults in these studies grew up in a time when many people did not graduate from high school. Did these older people lose intellectual abilities in old age, or did they merely perform less well than younger cohorts because they received less education in their youth? What cross-sectional studies often detect is a cohort effect, not a true developmental trend or age effect.

Despite this central problem, developmentalists still commonly use the cross-sectional design. Why? Because it has the great advantage of being quick and easy: We can go out this year, sample individuals of different ages, and be done with it. Moreover, this design should yield valid conclusions if the cohorts studied are likely to have had similar growing-up experiences—as when 3- and 4-year-olds rather than 30- and 40-year-olds are compared. When researchers attempt to make inferences about development over the span of many years, however, cohort effects become a serious problem.

The second major limitation of the cross-sectional design is that it tells us nothing about the development of individuals. Because each person is observed at only one point in time, we learn nothing about how each person actually changes with age. We cannot see, for example, whether different people show divergent patterns of change in their gender-role attitudes over time, or whether individuals who are especially liberated in their attitudes as 30-year-olds are also especially liberated at 70. To address issues like these, we need longitudinal research.

STRENGTHS AND WEAKNESSES OF THE LONGITUDINAL DESIGN

Because the longitudinal design actually traces changes in individuals as they age, it can tell us whether most people change in the same direction or whether different individuals travel different developmental paths. It can indicate whether the characteristics and behaviors measured remain consistent over time—for example, whether the bright or aggressive or dependent young person retains those same traits in later life. And it can tell us whether experiences early in life predict traits and behaviors later in life. The cross-sectional design can do none of this.

What, then, are the limitations of the longitudinal design? In our longitudinal study of gender-role attitudes, adults were first assessed at age 30 and then reassessed at age 50 and age 70. The study centered on *one cohort* of individuals: people who were members of the 1930 birth cohort. These people were raised in a particular historical context and then experienced changes in their social environment as they aged. Thus, we must consider possible time of measurement effects on the gender-role attitudes they expressed.

These adults were 30 in 1960, and their responses to the gender-role attitudes survey were undoubtedly influenced by the prevailing traditional views of that time. By the time they were interviewed as 70-year-olds, it was 2000, and times had changed immensely because of the women's movement and other social changes. Why, then, are their responses in 2000 more liberal than their responses in 1960? It may not be because gender-role attitudes *typically* become more liberal as people get older but because major societal changes occurred from one time of measurement to the next during the time frame of our study.

Gender-role attitudes did in fact become more liberal in the United States from the 1970s to the 1990s. For example, in 1977, more than half of survey respondents said it was more important for a wife to help her husband's career than to have her own; by 1996, only about one in five agreed (Brewster & Padavic,

Lewis W. Hine/CORBIS

How might your childhood have been different if you had worked in the coal mines like these boys? Each cohort or generation develops somewhat differently as a result of their particular experiences.

2000). Perhaps we would obtain entirely different "developmental" trends if we did our hypothetical longitudinal study in an era in which sexism suddenly became popular again!

In the longitudinal study, then, *age effects and time of measurement effects are confounded.* We cannot tell for sure whether the age-related changes observed are true developmental trends or whether they reflect historical events occurring during the study (either at a particular point of assessment or between assessments). The problem, then, is that we may not be able to *generalize* what we find in a longitudinal study to people developing in different eras than the ones in the study.

The longitudinal design has other disadvantages. One is fairly obvious: This approach is costly and time-consuming, particularly if it is used to trace development over a long span of time and at many points in time. Second, because knowledge is constantly changing, measures that seemed good at the start of the study may seem dated or incomplete by the end. Third, participants drop out of long-term studies; they may move, lose interest, or, especially in studies of aging, die during the course of the study. The result is a smaller and often less representative sample on which to base conclusions. Fourth and finally, researchers must be on guard for the effects of repeated testing; sometimes simply taking a test improves performance on that test the next time around.

Are both the cross-sectional and longitudinal designs hopelessly flawed, then? That would be overstating their weaknesses. As we have noted, cross-sectional studies are very efficient and informative, especially when the cohorts studied are not widely different in age or formative experiences. Meanwhile, longitudinal studies are extremely valuable for what they can reveal about the actual changes in performance that occur as individuals get older—even though it must be recognized that the cohort studied may not develop in precisely the same way that an earlier or later cohort does. Still, in an attempt to overcome the limitations of both cross-sectional and longitudinal designs, developmentalists have devised a new and more powerful method of describing developmental change: the sequential design.

SEQUENTIAL DESIGNS: THE BEST OF BOTH WORLDS

Sequential designs combine the cross-sectional approach and the longitudinal approach in a single study (Schaie, 1994). A sequential study of gender-role attitudes might compare the attitudes of different age groups of adults (say 30-, 50-, and 70-year-olds), as in a cross-sectional design, and then repeatedly assessing the attitudes of the individuals in these different cohorts as they get older (say every 5 years), as in a longitudinal design. Sequential designs, by combining the cross-sectional and longitudinal approaches, improve on both. They can tell us (1) which age-related trends are truly developmental in nature and reflect how most people, regardless of cohort, can be expected to change over time (*age effects*); (2) which age trends differ from cohort to cohort

Table 1.3 Summary of the Cross-Sectional, Longitudinal, and Sequential Development Designs

	Cross-Sectional Method	Longitudinal Method	Sequential Method
PROCEDURE	Observes people of different ages (or cohorts) at one point in time	Observes people of one age group repeatedly over time	Combines cross-sectional and longitudinal approaches; observe different cohorts on multiple occasions
INFORMATION GAINED	Describes age differences	Describes age changes	Describes age differences and age changes
ADVANTAGES	Demonstrates age differences in behavior; hints at developmental trends	Actually indicates how individuals are alike and different in the way they change over time	Helps separate the effects of age, cohort, and time of measurement
	Takes little time to conduct; is inexpensive	Can reveal links between early behavior or experiences and later behavior	Indicates whether developmental changes experienced by one generation or cohort are similar to those experienced by other cohorts
DISADVANTAGES	Age trends may reflect cohort effects (differences between cohorts) rather than true developmental change	Age trends may reflect historical (time of measurement) effects during the study rather than true developmental change	Often complex and time-consuming
	Provides no information about change in individuals over time	Relatively time-consuming and expensive	Despite being the strongest method, may still leave questions about whether a developmental change is generalizable
		Measures devised may later prove inadequate	
		Participants drop out	
		Participants can be affected by repeated testing	

and suggest that each generation is affected by its distinct growing-up experiences (*cohort effects*); and (3) which trends suggest that historical events occurring during a specific time period have similar effects on all the cohorts alive at the time (*time of measurement effects*). In short, sequential designs can at least begin to untangle the effects of age, cohort, and time of measurement and to indicate which age trends are truly developmental in nature. Yet they are extremely complex, expensive, and not always able to provide definitive answers. See Table 1.3 for a summary of the three basic developmental designs.

What Issues Arise in Studying Development?

Designing good developmental research is not easy. Researchers must first draw on theories and previous research to form a clear notion of what questions they want to answer and what hypotheses they want to test. They must then define the variables that interest them and decide how to measure them accurately. And of course they must decide on a research design, weighing the pros and cons of the experimental and correlational methods if they wish to study influences on development, and choosing a cross-sectional, longitudinal, or sequential design if they are trying to describe age-related changes. Researchers must also grapple with many other issues. Here we will highlight just two: choosing the individuals to be studied and protecting their rights.

Choosing Samples

A research **sample** is simply a group of individuals chosen for study. Researchers study a sample and hope to generalize their findings to a larger **population**—a well-defined group such as American high school students or Canadian nursing home residents. In many kinds of research, the ideal sample is a **random sample**—a sample formed by identifying all members of the larger population of interest and then, by a random means (such as drawing names blindly), selecting a portion of that population to participate in the study. Random sampling increases confidence that the sample studied is representative or typical of the larger population of interest and therefore that conclusions based on studying the sample will hold true of the whole population.

In actual practice, developmentalists often draw their samples—sometimes random, sometimes not—from their local communities. Thus, a researcher might survey a random sample of students at a local high school about their drug use but then be unable to make statements about American teenagers in general if, for example, the school is in a high-income suburb where drug use patterns are different than they might be in a low-income inner-city area. As a result, researchers must be careful to describe the characteristics of the sample they studied and to avoid overgeneralizing their findings to populations that might be socioeconomically or culturally different from their research sample.

When developmental researchers conduct cross-sectional studies of younger and older adults, they face an additional challenge. If they randomly sample younger and older adults, they will usually find that the older adults have had less education than the younger ones. If the older adults then perform worse than the younger ones on cognitive tests, is this age difference the result of aging processes, or is it just a cohort effect associated with age group differences in education? Many researchers cope with this problem by selecting for study younger and older adults with equivalent years of education—for example, college graduates only. Then, any performance differences between the age groups would not be the result of differences in the amount of education they received. But notice that the samples chosen are no longer representative of their age groups and that conclusions about college-educated older people might not hold true for the large number of older adults who did *not* graduate from college. Again, researchers need to describe their samples carefully and acknowledge that their findings might not generalize to different cultural or socioeconomic groups. What we learn about human development depends on whom we sample.

Protecting the Rights of Research Participants

Developmental researchers sometimes also face thorny issues involving **research ethics**—the standards of conduct that investigators are ethically bound to honor in order to protect their research participants from physical or psychological harm (see Sales & Folkman, 2000). For example, is it ethical to deceive children by telling them that they performed poorly on a test in order to create in them a temporary sense of failure? Is it an invasion of a family's privacy to ask adolescents questions about conversations they have had with their parents about sex?

Developmental findings established through the study of a sample of European American children do not always hold true in a sample of African American or Hispanic children. It is important to study development in a wide range of subcultural settings.

Such issues have led the American Psychological Association (1982), the Society for Research in Child Development (1990), the federal government, and many other agencies to establish guidelines for ethical research with human beings. Federal regulations require universities and other organizations that conduct research with humans to have Institutional Review Boards that determine whether proposed research projects conform to ethical standards and approve them only if they do. The federal government has tightened its oversight of research in recent years as a result of past abuses (Fisher, 1999; Sales & Folkman, 2000).

Deciding whether a proposed study is on safe ethical ground involves weighing the possible benefits of the research (gains in knowledge and potential *benefits* to humanity or to the participants themselves) against the potential *risks* to participants. If the potential benefits greatly outweigh the potential risks, and if there are no other, less risky, procedures that could produce these same benefits, the investigation is likely to be viewed as ethical. The investigator's ethical responsibilities boil down to respecting the rights of research participants by (1) allowing them to make informed and uncoerced decisions about taking part in research, (2) debriefing them afterward (especially if they are not told everything in advance or are deceived), (3) protecting them from harm, and (4) treating any information they provide as confidential.

1. Informed consent. Researchers generally should inform potential participants of all aspects of the research that might affect their decision to participate so that they can make a voluntary decision based on knowledge of what the research involves. But are young children or mentally impaired children or adults capable of understanding what they are being asked to do and of giving their *informed* consent? Probably not. Therefore, researchers who study such "vulnerable" populations should obtain informed consent from both the individual (if possible) and someone who can act on the individual's behalf—for example, the parent or guardian of a child, or the legal representative of a nursing home resident. Investigators must not pressure anyone to participate and must respect any participant's right to refuse to participate in the first place, to drop out at any point during the study, and to refuse to have his or her data used by the investigator.

2. Debriefing. Researchers generally tell participants about the purposes of the study in advance, but in some cases doing so would ruin the study. If we told college students in advance that we were studying cheating and then gave them an opportunity to cheat on a test, do you think anyone would cheat? Instead, we might set up a situation in which students believe they can cheat without being detected and then *debrief* them afterward, explaining the true purpose of the study. We would also have an obligation to make sure that participants do not leave feeling upset about the fact that they cheated.

3. Protection from harm. Researchers are bound not to harm research participants either physically or psychologically. Infants may cry if they are left in a room with a stranger, adolescents may be embarrassed if they are asked personal questions, and the investigator must try to anticipate such consequences (Koocher & Keith-Spiegel, 1994). If harm to the participants seems likely, the researcher should consider another way of answering the research question. If participants do become upset or are harmed in any way, the researcher must take steps to undo the damage.

4. Confidentiality. Researchers also have an ethical responsibility to keep confidential the information they collect. It would be unacceptable, for example, to tell a child's teacher that the child performed poorly on an intelligence test or to tell an adult's employer that he or she revealed a drinking problem in an interview. Only if participants give explicit permission to have information about them shared with someone else, or if the law requires disclosure of information (as when child abuse is suspected), should that information be passed on.

Clearly, developmental researchers have some serious issues to weigh if they want their research to be not only well designed but ethically responsible. All things considered, understanding life-span human development is an incredibly complex undertaking. It would be downright impossible if researchers merely conducted study after study without any guiding ideas. *Theories* of human development provide those guiding ideas; they are the subject of Chapter 2.

Summary Points

1. Life-span human development consists of systematic changes and continuities in the individual occurring between conception and death. Developmental changes involve growth and aging, and gains, losses, and just plain changes in the physical, cognitive, and psychosocial domains. They are the result of both nature and nurture—genetically programmed maturation as well as learning and other environmental influences.

2. Concepts of the life span and its distinctive periods (or age grades and their corresponding age norms and social clocks) have changed greatly over history and vary greatly from culture to culture today. Until the 17th and 18th centuries, children were expected to assume adult roles very early and were less often seen as innocents to be protected. In Western cultures, adolescence did not come to be viewed as a distinct phase of the life span until the late 19th century. A lengthening of the average life span and a decline in birth rates in the 20th century have led to a middle-aged "empty nest" phase and an old age characterized by retirement.

3. The science of life-span development has three goals: the description, explanation, and optimization of development. It got its start in the late 19th century with baby biographies written by Charles Darwin and others interested in the evolution of the species and with G. Stanley Hall's questionnaires. Although many developmentalists specialize in studying one age group or another, today's developmentalists are increasingly adopting a life-span perspective

that views development as a lifelong, multidirectional process that involves gain and loss, is characterized by considerable plasticity, is shaped by its historical/cultural context, has many causes, and is best viewed from a multidisciplinary perspective.

4. The scientific method involves formulating theories based on observations, using theories to generate specific hypotheses, testing these hypotheses by collecting new observations in research investigations, and using the data so obtained to evaluate the worth of theories.

5. The most widely used data collection techniques in studies of development are self-report measures (interviews, questionnaires, tests) and behavioral observations (either naturalistic or structured/contrived). Results from multiple studies can be synthesized through meta-analysis.

6. To achieve the goal of explaining (and often of optimizing) development, researchers rely on experiments. An independent variable is manipulated to see what effects this has on a dependent variable. Participants are randomly assigned to treatment groups, and extraneous factors are experimentally controlled. Properly conducted, an experiment can firmly establish cause-and-effect relationships, whereas quasi-experiments, in which participants are not randomly assigned to treatment groups, cannot.

7. The correlational method also cannot yield firm conclusions about cause and effect, because of difficulties in determining the direction of causal influence and ruling out third variables that influence the relationship between two variables. However, it is widely used to study relationships among people's characteristics, experiences, and behavior and does not raise as many ethical issues as experimentation.

8. Developmental researchers rely principally on cross-sectional and longitudinal research designs to describe development. The cross-sectional design, which compares different age groups (cohorts) at a single time of measurement, is easy to conduct but may be misleading if an age trend is due to generational differences in life experiences (cohort effects) rather than to true developmental change (age effects). In the longitudinal design, one group (cohort) is assessed repeatedly as its members develop. However, participants in a longitudinal study may change over the years, not as a function of age itself but in response to historical events (time of measurement effects). To counteract the limitations of cross-sectional and longitudinal designs, researchers have devised sequential designs combining the two approaches.

9. Developmental researchers must decide whether to randomly sample the population of interest or to use some other sampling approach to ensure that the different age groups they compare in cross-sectional studies are similar in everything but age. They must also adhere to standards of ethical research practice, with attention to informed consent, debriefing, protection from harm, and confidentiality.

Critical Thinking

1. Given the age grades and age norms that prevail in our society, how would you compare the advantages and disadvantages of being an adolescent as opposed to a young adult? of being an elderly adult as opposed to a young adult?

2. You are interested in developmental changes in adolescents' attitudes toward premarital sex from age 12 to age 20. Design both a cross-sectional and a longitudinal study of this question, and weigh the advantages and disadvantages of the two designs.

3. What effect does adequacy of prenatal nutrition have on a child's IQ test performance at age 5? Suggest both an experimental design and a correlational design to study this question. What features make the two designs different, and what are their pros and cons? Hint: Don't forget to consider ethical issues.

4. You want to do research in which you interview elderly women shortly after the death of their husbands about their emotional reactions to widowhood. Based on the material on ethical issues in developmental research, what ethical issues would you be concerned about? What steps would you take to make your study as ethical as possible?

Key Terms

centenarian	naturalistic observation
development	structured observation
growth	meta-analysis
biological aging	experiment
aging	independent variable
maturation	dependent variable
learning	random assignment
environment	experimental control
age grade	quasi-experiment
age norms	correlational method
social clock	correlation coefficient
adolescence	cross-sectional design
baby boom generation	longitudinal design
baby biographies	age effects
storm and stress	cohort effects
gerontology	time of measurement effects
life-span perspective	sequential design
plasticity	sample
scientific method	population
theory	random sample
hypothesis	research ethics

On the Web

Web Sites to Explore

Census Data

The Web site of the U.S. Bureau of the Census, http://www.census.gov, provides a wealth of statistical information about the population of the United States, including information about different age groups.

Life-Span Developmental Psychology Resources and Child and Adolescent Development Resources

For a large menu of resources on life-span human development and child and adolescent development, try "Developmental Psychology Links." It links you to professional organizations such as the Society for Research on Child Development and to journals in the field, as well as to selected Web resources on infancy and childhood, adolescence, and aging. http://www.socialpsychology.org/develop.htm#lifespan

Gerontology Resources

For a comprehensive directory of Web resources on statistics, professional organizations, and literature on aging, Alzheimer's disease, other forms of dementia, and death and dying, try exploring the "Gerontology/Aging Resources" links listed on this site: http://www.umdnj.edu/libweb/gerontol.htm

Search Online with InfoTrac College Edition

For additional information, explore InfoTrac College Edition, your online library. Go to http://www.infotrac-college.com and use the pass code that came on the card with your book.

You might find it interesting to search for Generation X. How is this generation or cohort defined, and how is it believed to differ as a cohort from the Baby Boom generation? Or try searching for the terms *cross-sectional* and *longitudinal*. Find an article that reports the results of each of these two types of developmental research designs.

Visit Our Web Site
Go to http://www.wadsworth.com/psychology, where you will find online resources directly linked to your book.

Life-Span CD-ROM

Go to the Wadsworth Life-Span CD-ROM for further study of the concepts in this chapter. The CD-ROM also includes quizzes and additional activities to expand your learning experience.

Theories of Human Development

SHERRY IS AN ATTRACTIVE 15-year-old whose relationship with Robert has become the center of her life. She gets by in school, but most of what goes on in the classroom bores her. Her relationship with her parents has been a bit strained lately, partly because her mother does not want her to spend so much time with Robert. Robert, age 16, is also struggling at school while juggling his part-time job, family responsibilities, and time with Sherry. And these two teenagers have a more serious problem: Sherry is pregnant. The sex "just happened" one night after a party and continued thereafter. Neither Sherry nor Robert wanted a baby.

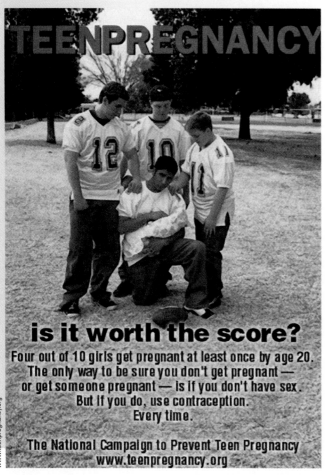

www.teenpregnancy.org

Teenage pregnancy is one of many facts about human development waiting to be explained by theories. This ad is designed to prevent it. Do you think it will be effective?

Having children is a normal part of human development, but how can we explain unwanted teenage pregnancies like this one from a developmental perspective? What is your theory? What explanations do the leading theories of human development offer? More practically, what can be done to reduce the high rate of teenage pregnancy in U.S. society? In 1995, 49% of females and 55% of males ages 15 to 19 had had sex (U.S. Census Bureau, 2000).

Although the teenage pregnancy rate has actually dropped since it peaked in 1991, almost 1 in 10 females ages 15 to 19 becomes pregnant each year, and just over half of these pregnant teenagers give birth (Ventura et al., 2000). The consequences sometimes include an interrupted education, low income, and a difficult start for both new parent and new child (Brooks-Gunn & Furstenberg, 1989; Coley & Chase-Lansdale, 1998). Meanwhile, sexually transmitted diseases, including AIDS, are epidemic among adolescents; yet all too many continue to engage in risky sex (Hogan, Sun, & Cornwell, 2000). What practical solutions to the problems of unwanted teenage pregnancy and sexually transmitted disease might different developmental theorists offer? We will attempt to answer these questions in this chapter, to illustrate that different theories of human development offer different lenses through which to view the same phenomena of human development.

The Nature of Theories

As noted in Chapter 1, a *theory* is a set of ideas proposed to describe and explain certain phenomena. Theories of human development should give us insights into many developmental phenomena, including teenage pregnancy. Indeed, the beauty of theories is that they can organize our thinking about a wide range of specific facts or events.

In science, it is not enough simply to catalog fact after fact without organizing this information around some set of concepts and propositions. We would soon be swamped by meaningless data—trivia experts who lack "the big picture." A theory of human development provides needed organization, offering a lens through which we can interpret any number of specific facts or observations. A theory also guides the collection of new facts or observations, making clear (1) what is most important to study, (2) what can be hypothesized or predicted about it, and (3) how it should be studied. Because different theorists often have very different views on these critical matters, what is learned in any science depends a good deal on which theoretical perspectives become dominant, which in turn depends on which theories best account for the facts.

All of us hold some basic beliefs about human development—for example, about the importance of genes versus good parenting in healthy development. Reading this chapter should make you more aware of your own assumptions about human development and how they compare to those of the major theorists. Scientific theories are expected to be more rigorous than our everyday theories, though. A good developmental theory should be

- **Internally consistent.** Its different parts and propositions should tie together and should not generate contradictory hypotheses or predictions.
- **Falsifiable.** It should be capable of generating specific hypotheses that can be tested through research and that can then be confirmed or disconfirmed. If a theory is

vague or generates contradictory hypotheses about development, it cannot guide research, cannot be adequately evaluated, and therefore will not be very useful in advancing our knowledge.

- **Supported by data.** A good theory should help us better describe, predict, and explain human development.

Theories that fail to meet these evaluation criteria—theories that are not internally consistent, falsifiable, and supported by data—need to be revised or, ultimately, discarded altogether.

In this chapter, we examine four major theoretical viewpoints:

1. The *psychoanalytic* viewpoint developed by Sigmund Freud and revised by Erik Erikson and other followers
2. The *cognitive developmental* viewpoint associated with Jean Piaget
3. The *learning* perspective developed by B. F. Skinner, Albert Bandura, and others
4. The *contextual/systems* approach to human development across the life span, exemplified by Urie Bronfenbrenner and Lev Vygotsky

Each theory makes particular assumptions or statements about the nature of human development. To aid us in comparing theories, we'll first examine some of the basic developmental issues on which theorists—and people in general—often disagree.

Basic Issues in Human Development

What are developing humans like? How does development come about? What courses does it follow? Let's look at five major developmental issues (see also P. H. Miller, 2002; Parke et al., 1994). We invite you to clarify your own stands on major developmental issues by completing the brief questionnaire in the Explorations box below. The Explorations box on page 47 at the end of the chapter indicates how the major developmental theorists might answer the questions, so you can compare your own assumptions to theirs. In other boxes, we have taken the liberty of commenting for the theorists, whether they

Where Do You Stand on Major Developmental Issues?

Choose one answer for each question, and write down the corresponding letter or fill it in at the end of the box. Compare your results with those in the Explorations box on page 47 at the end of this chapter.

1. Children are
   a. creatures whose basically negative or selfish impulses must be controlled.
   b. neither inherently good nor inherently bad.
   c. creatures who are born with many positive and few negative tendencies.
2. Biological influences (heredity, maturational forces) and environmental influences (culture, parenting styles, learning experiences) are thought to contribute to development. Overall,
   a. biological factors contribute far more than environmental factors.
   b. biological factors contribute somewhat more than environmental factors.
   c. biological and environmental factors are equally important.
   d. environmental factors contribute somewhat more than biological factors.
   e. environmental factors contribute far more than biological factors.
3. People are basically
   a. active beings who are the prime determiners of their own abilities and traits.

   b. passive beings whose characteristics are molded either by social influences (parents and other significant people, outside events) or by biological changes beyond their control.
4. Development proceeds
   a. through stages, so that the individual changes rather abruptly into a quite different kind of person than he or she was in an earlier stage.
   b. in a variety of ways, some stagelike, some gradual or continuous.
   c. continuously—in small increments without abrupt changes or distinct stages.
5. When we compare the development of different individuals, we see
   a. many similarities; children and adults develop along universal paths and experience similar changes at similar ages.
   b. many differences; different people often undergo different sequences of change and have widely different timetables of development.

Question				
1	2	3	4	5

Your pattern of answers:

are dead or alive, imagining how each would view teenage pregnancy. You might want to anticipate what each theorist will say before you read each of these boxes, to see if you can successfully apply the theories to a specific problem. It is our hope that as you grasp the major theories, you will be in a position to draw on their concepts and propositions to make sense of your own and other people's development.

Assumptions about Human Nature

Are people inherently good, inherently bad, or neither? Well before modern theories of human development were proposed, philosophers of the 17th and 18th centuries were taking stands on the nature of human beings. Thomas Hobbes (1588–1679), for one, portrayed children as inherently selfish and bad and believed that it was society's responsibility to teach them to behave in civilized ways. By contrast, Jean Jacques Rousseau (1712–1778) argued that children were innately good, that they were born with an intuitive understanding of right and wrong, and that they would develop in positive directions as long as society did not interfere with their natural tendencies. In the middle was the English philosopher John Locke (1632–1704), who maintained that an infant is a **tabula rasa,** or "blank slate," waiting to be written on by his or her experiences. Locke believed, that is, that children were neither innately good nor innately bad, but could develop in any number of directions depending on their experiences.

These different visions of human nature are all represented in one or more modern theories of development and have radically different implications for how one should raise children. In teaching children to share, for example, should one assume that their innate selfish tendencies must be battled every step of the way, or that they are predisposed to be helpful and caring, or that they have the potential to become either selfish beasts or selfless wonders depending on how they are brought up?

Nature and Nurture

Is development primarily the product of nature (biological forces) or nurture (environmental forces)? Perhaps no controversy in the study of human development has been more heated than the **nature/nurture issue.** On the nature side of the debate have been those who emphasize the influence of individual heredity, universal maturational processes guided by the genes, and biologically based predispositions that are the product of our evolutionary history. A strong believer in nature would claim that all normal children achieve the same developmental milestones at similar times because of maturational forces and that differences among children or adults are largely due to differences in their genetic makeup. On the nurture side of the debate have been those who emphasize *environment*—conditions and events outside the person. Nurture includes the influences of learning experiences, child-rearing methods, societal changes, and culture. A strong believer in nurture would argue, as John Locke did, that human development can take many different forms depending on the individual's experiences over a lifetime.

Activity and Passivity

Are people active in their own development, or are they passively shaped by forces outside themselves? With respect to this **activity/passivity issue,** some theorists believe that children are curious, active creatures who orchestrate their own development by exploring the world around them and shaping their own environments. The girl who asks her mother for dolls at the toy store and the boy who clamors instead for toy trucks are actively contributing to their own gender-role development.

Other theorists view humans as passive beings who are largely the products of forces beyond their control—usually environmental influences but possibly strong biological forces. From this vantage point, children's academic failings might be blamed on the failure of their parents and teachers to provide them with the proper learning experiences, and the problems of socially isolated older adults might be attributed to societal neglect of the elderly rather than to deficiencies within the individual. Theorists disagree about just how active individuals are in creating their own environments and, in the process, producing their own development.

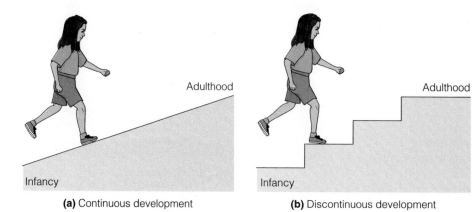

(a) Continuous development   **(b)** Discontinuous development

Figure 2.1 The course of development as described by continuity and discontinuity (stage) theorists

Continuity and Discontinuity

Do you believe that humans change gradually, in ways that leave them not so different than they were before, or do you believe they change abruptly and dramatically? One aspect of the **continuity/discontinuity issue** concerns whether the changes we undergo over the life span are gradual or abrupt. *Continuity* theorists view human development as a process that occurs in small steps, without sudden changes. In contrast, *discontinuity* theorists picture the course of development as more like a series of stairsteps, each of which elevates the individual to a new (and presumably more advanced) level of functioning. When an adolescent rapidly gains six inches in height and grows a beard, the change seems quite discontinuous. See Figure 2.1.

A second aspect of the continuity/discontinuity issue concerns whether changes are *quantitative* or *qualitative* in nature. Quantitative changes are changes in *degree* and indicate continuity: A person gains wrinkles, or knows more vocabulary words, or interacts with friends more or less frequently. By contrast, qualitative changes are changes in *kind* and suggest discontinuity. They are changes that make the individual fundamentally different in some way than he or she was before. The transformation of a caterpillar into a butterfly, of a nonverbal infant into a speaking toddler, or of a prepubertal child into a sexually mature adolescent are examples of qualitative changes. Continuity theorists typically hold that developmental changes are gradual and quantitative, whereas discontinuity theorists hold that they are more abrupt and qualitative.

Discontinuity theorists often propose that we progress through **developmental stages.** A stage is a distinct phase of the life cycle characterized by a particular set of abilities, motives, emotions, or behaviors that form a coherent pattern. Each stage is viewed as qualitatively different from the stage before or the stage after. Thus, the preschool child may be said to solve problems in an entirely different manner than the infant, adolescent, or adult.

Universality and Context-Specificity

Finally, do we all follow the same developmental path, or do different people follow different paths? Developmental theorists often disagree on the **universality/context-specificity issue**—on the extent to which developmental changes are common to everyone (*universal*) or different from person to person (*context specific*). Stage theorists typically believe that the stages they propose are universal. For example, a stage theorist might claim that virtually all children enter a new stage in their intellectual development at about the time they start school, or that most adults, sometime around the age of 40, experience a "midlife crisis" in which they raise major questions about their lives. From this perspective, development proceeds in certain universal directions.

But other theorists believe that human development is far more varied than this. Paths of development followed in one culture may be very different from paths followed in another culture. For example, preschool children in the United States sometimes believe that dreams are real but give up this belief as they get older. By contrast, children raised in the Atayal culture of Taiwan were observed to become more convinced with age that dreams are real, most likely because that is what adults in their culture believe (Kohlberg, 1966). Even within a single culture, sequences of developmental change may differ from subcultural group to subcultural group, from family to family, or from individual to individual.

These, then, are some of the major issues about human development that different theories resolve in different ways: the goodness/badness of human nature, nature/nurture, activity/passivity, continuity/discontinuity, and universality/context-specificity issues (see Table 2.1). Now let's begin our survey of the theories, starting with a brief look at Freud's well-known psychoanalytic perspective.

Freud: Psychoanalytic Theory

It is difficult to think of a theorist who has had a greater impact on Western thought than Sigmund Freud, the Viennese physician who lived from 1856 to 1939. This revolutionary thinker challenged prevailing notions of human nature and human development by proposing that we are driven by motives and emotions of which we are largely unaware and that we are shaped by our earliest experiences in life (see Hall, 1954). His name is a household word, and his **psychoanalytic theory** continues to influence thinking about human

Table 2.1	Issues in Human Development
Issue	**Description**
Nature/Nurture	Is development primarily the product of genes, biology, and maturation—or of experience, learning, and social influences?
Activity/Passivity	Do humans actively shape their own environments and contribute to their own development—or are they passively shaped by forces beyond their control?
Continuity/Discontinuity	Do humans change gradually and in quantitative ways—or do they progress through qualititively different stages and change dramatically into quite different beings than they were before?
Universality/Context-Specificity	Is development similar from person to person and from culture to culture—or do pathways of development vary considerably depending on the social contexts in which humans develop?

Sigmund Freud's psychoanalytic theory was one of the first, and certainly one of the most influential, theories of how the personality develops from childhood to adulthood.

development, even though it is far less influential today than it once was and only about 2 percent of psychotherapists currently practice traditional Freudian psychoanalysis (McDonald, 1998). Because you have undoubtedly been introduced to this theory before, we'll cover it only briefly.

Instincts and Unconscious Motives

Central to Freudian psychoanalytic theory is the notion that human beings have basic biological urges or drives that must be satisfied. Freud viewed the newborn as a "seething cauldron," an inherently selfish creature "driven" by **instincts,** or inborn biological forces that motivate behavior. These biological instincts are the source of the psychic (or mental) energy that fuels human behavior and that is channeled in new directions over the course of human development.

Freud strongly believed in **unconscious motivation**— the power of instincts and other inner forces to influence our behavior without our awareness. A teenage boy, for example, may not realize that his devotion to body building could be a way of channeling his sexual or aggressive urges. Freud came to rely on such therapy techniques as hypnosis, free association (a quick spilling out of ideas), and dream analysis because he believed that only these techniques could uncover underlying unconscious motives. So, we immediately see that Freud's theory is highly biological in emphasis: Biological instincts—forces that often provide an unconscious motivation for our actions—are said to guide human development.

Id, Ego, and Superego

According to Freud (1933), each individual has a fixed amount of psychic energy that can be used to satisfy basic urges or instincts and to grow psychologically. As the child develops, this psychic energy is divided among three components of the personality: the id, the ego, and the superego.

At birth, all psychic energy resides in the **id**—the impulsive, irrational part of the personality whose entire mission is to satisfy the instincts. It obeys the "pleasure principle," seeking immediate gratification, even when biological needs cannot be realistically or appropriately met. If you think about it, young infants do seem to be "all id" in many ways. When they are hungry or wet, they simply fuss and cry until their needs are met. They are not known for their patience!

The second component of the personality is the **ego,** the rational side of the individual that operates according to the "reality principle" and tries to find realistic ways of gratifying the instincts. According to Freud (1933), the ego begins to emerge during infancy when psychic energy is diverted from the id to energize cognitive processes such as perception, learning, and problem solving. The hungry toddler may be able to do more than merely cry when she is hungry; she may be able to draw on the resources of the ego to hunt down Dad, lead him to the kitchen, and say "cookie." However, toddlers' egos are still relatively immature; they want what they want NOW. As the ego matures further, children become more and more able to postpone their pleasures until a more appropriate time and to devise logical and realistic strategies for meeting their needs.

The third part of the Freudian personality is the **superego,** the individual's internalized moral standards. The superego develops from the ego and strives for *perfection* rather than for pleasure or realism (Freud, 1933). It begins to develop as 3- to 6-year-old children *internalize* (take on as their own) the moral standards and values of their parents. Once the superego emerges, children have a parental voice in their heads that keeps them from violating society's rules in the interest of gratifying their selfish desires and makes them feel guilty or ashamed if they do. The superego insists that we find socially acceptable or ethical outlets for the id's undesirable impulses.

Conflict among the id, ego, and superego is inevitable, Freud claimed. In the mature, healthy personality, a dynamic balance operates: The id communicates its basic needs, the ego restrains the impulsive id long enough to find realistic ways to satisfy these needs, and the superego decides whether the ego's problem-solving strategies are morally acceptable. The ego is clearly "in the middle"; it must somehow strike a balance between the opposing demands of the id and the superego, all the while accommodating to the realities of the external world.

According to Freud (1940/1964), psychological problems often arise when the individual's limited amount of psychic energy is unevenly distributed among the id, the ego, and the superego. For example, people diagnosed as antisocial personalities, or sociopaths, who routinely lie and cheat to get their way, may have very strong ids and normal egos but very weak superegos, never having learned to respect the rights of other people. In contrast, the married woman who cannot undress in front of her husband may be controlled by an overly strong

Table 2.2 The Stage Theories of Freud and Erikson

Freud's Psychosexual Theory		Erikson's Psychosocial Theory	
Stage/Age Range	**Description**	**Stage/Age Range**	**Description**
Oral stage (birth to 1 year)	Libido is focused on the mouth as a source of pleasure. Obtaining oral gratification from a mother figure is critical to later development.	Trust versus mistrust (birth to 1 year)	Infants must learn to trust their caregivers to meet their needs. Responsive parenting is critical.
Anal stage (1 to 3 years)	Libido is focused on the anus. Toilet training creates conflicts between the child's biological urges and society's demands.	Autonomy versus shame and doubt (1 to 3 years)	Children must learn to be autonomous—to assert their wills and do things for themselves—or they will doubt their abilities.
Phallic stage (3 to 6 years)	Libido centers on the genitals. Resolution of the Oedipus or Electra complex results in identification with the same-sex parent and development of the superego.	Initiative versus guilt (3 to 6 years)	Preschoolers develop initiative by devising and carrying out bold plans, but they must learn not to impinge on the rights of others.
Latency period (6 to 12 years)	Libido is quiet; psychic energy is invested in schoolwork and play with same-sex friends.	Industry versus inferiority (6 to 12 years)	Children must master important social and academic skills and keep up with their peers or they will feel inferior.
Genital stage (12 years and older)	Puberty reawakens the sexual instincts as youths seek to establish mature sexual relationships and pursue the biological goal of reproduction.	Identity versus role confusion (12 to 20 years)	Adolescents ask who they are and must establish social and vocational identities or else remain confused about the roles they should play as adults.
		Intimacy versus isolation (20 to 40 years)	Young adults seek to form a shared identity with another person but may fear intimacy and experience loneliness and isolation.
		Generativity versus stagnation (40 to 65 years)	Middle-aged adults must feel that they are producing something that will outlive them, either as parents or as workers, or they will become stagnant and self-centered.
		Integrity versus despair (65 and older)	Older adults must come to view their lives as meaningful in order to face death without worries and regrets.

superego, perhaps because she was made to feel deeply ashamed about any interest she took in her body as a young girl. Analysis of the dynamics operating among the three parts of the personality provided Freud and his followers with an important means of describing and understanding individual differences in personality and the origins of psychological disorders.

Psychosexual Development

Freud (1940/1964) maintained that as the child matures biologically, the psychic energy of the sex instinct, which he called **libido,** shifts from one part of the body to another, seeking to gratify different biological needs. In the process, the child moves through five **psychosexual stages:** oral, anal, phallic, latency, and genital. These stages are outlined in Table 2.2.

Freud emphasized the role of nature over that of nurture in development. He believed that inborn biological instincts drive behavior and that biological maturation guides all children through the five psychosexual stages. Yet he also viewed

nurture—especially early experiences within the family—as an important contributor to individual differences in adult personality. At each psychosexual stage, the id's impulses and social demands come into conflict. Harsh child-rearing methods can heighten this conflict and the child's anxiety.

To defend itself against anxiety, the ego, without being aware of it, adopts **defense mechanisms** (Freud, 1940/1964). Consider the defense mechanism of **fixation**—a kind of arrested development in which part of the libido remains tied to an early stage. A baby boy who was rarely allowed to linger at the breast, was screamed at for mouthing and chewing paychecks and other fascinating objects left lying around the house, or was otherwise deprived of oral gratification might become fixated at the oral stage. He would then seek to satisfy unmet oral needs and to avoid the potentially even more agonizing conflicts of the anal stage. He might display this oral fixation by becoming a chronic thumb sucker and, later in life, by chain-smoking, talking incessantly (as college professors are prone to do), or becoming too dependent on other people.

Similarly, the girl who is harshly punished for toileting accidents may become fixated at the anal stage and turn into an inhibited or stingy adult. Or she may deal with her anxiety through another important defense mechanism, **regression,** which involves retreating to an earlier, less traumatic, stage of development. The 3-year-old who has been punished for a toileting accident may revert to infantile behavior—cooing like a baby, demanding juice from a baby bottle, wanting to be snuggled. Similarly, the man who has had a terrible day at work may want his wife to act like his mother and "baby" him. In this way, Freud argued, *early experiences may have long-term effects on personality development.*

The *phallic stage* from age 3 to age 6 is an especially treacherous time, according to Freud. Youngsters develop an incestuous desire for the parent of the other sex. (The boy's *Oedipus complex* and the girl's *Electra complex* are discussed in Chapter 12.). If all goes well, they will resolve the emotional conflict they experience by identifying with the same-sex parent and in the process incorporating that parent's values into the superego. After the lull of the latency period (Table 2.2), during which sexual urges are tame and 6- to 12-year-olds invest psychic energy in schoolwork and play, adolescents reaching puberty enter the final stage of psychosexual development, the *genital stage.* During this phase, they may have difficulty accepting their new sexuality, may reexperience some of the conflicting feelings toward their parents that they felt during the phallic stage, and may distance themselves from their parents in order to defend against these anxiety-producing feelings. During adulthood, humans may develop a greater capacity to love and typically satisfy the mature sex instinct by having children. However, Freud believed that psychosexual development stops with adolescence and that the individual remains in the genital stage throughout adulthood.

In short, Freud insisted that the past lives on. Early childhood experiences may haunt us in later life and influence our adult personalities, interests, and behaviors. Parents significantly affect a child's success in passing through the biologically programmed psychosexual stages. They can err by overindulging the child's urges, but more commonly they create lasting and severe inner conflicts and anxieties by denying an infant oral gratification, using harsh toilet-training practices with a toddler, or punishing the preschooler who is fascinated by naked bodies. Heavy reliance on fixation, regression, and other defense mechanisms may then become necessary just to keep the ego intact and functioning. In the Explorations box below, we imagine what Freud might have said about the causes of teenage pregnancy and about the case of Sherry and Robert described at the start of the chapter. What might you say if you were Freud?

Strengths and Weaknesses

Many developmentalists fault Freud for proposing a theory that is ambiguous, internally inconsistent, difficult to pin down and test, and therefore not very falsifiable (Fonagy & Target, 2000). Testing hypotheses that require studying unconscious motivations and the workings of the unseen id, ego, and superego has been challenging indeed. Freud himself offered little hard evidence to support his theory. Moreover, when the theory *has* been tested, many of its specific ideas have not been supported (Crews, 1996; Fisher & Greenberg, 1977). As a result, it has been judged "a theory in search of some facts" (MacMillan, 1991, p. 548).

For example, Freud initially uncovered evidence that many of his patients had been sexually or physically abused during childhood. Because he could not believe it, he claimed

Explorations

Freud on Teenage Pregnancy

I welcome this opportunity to return to life to comment on the problem of teenage pregnancy. As you know, I was always fascinated by sex! We must realize that teenagers experience intense emotional conflicts during the genital stage of psychosexual development. Their new sexual urges are anxiety provoking and may reawaken the sexual conflicts of earlier psychosexual stages.

I would need to find out more about the early childhood experiences and psychic conflicts of Sherry and Robert to pinpoint the specific causes of their behavior, but it occurs to me that they may not have strong enough egos and superegos to keep their selfish ids in check [Babikian & Goldman, 1971; Hart & Hilton, 1988]. Perhaps they sought immediate gratification of their sexual urges with no thought of future consequences and no sense of guilt. Possibly these teenagers were motivated by inner conflicts that had their roots in infancy or the preschool years. For instance, many pregnant girls come from homes without fathers [Hogan, Sun, & Cornwell, 2000]. Perhaps Sherry never fully resolved her phallic stage issues and was unconsciously seeking to possess her father by possessing Robert. Robert, of course, might have been seeking to gratify his unconscious desire for his mother through Sherry. Teenagers often distance themselves from their parents as a defense against reawakened feelings of love for the other-sex parent.

In short, teenage pregnancy is likely to result from difficulty managing sexual urges because of personality problems that are rooted in early childhood experiences.

instead that children wished for and fantasized about, but did not actually experience, seduction by their parents (Gleaves & Hernandez, 1999; Masson, 1984). This claim has received little support (Crews, 1996). Meanwhile, we now know that child sexual abuse is widespread and can indeed contribute to lasting psychological difficulties (see Chapter 12).

Despite the fact that many of Freud's specific ideas have been difficult to test or have not been supported by research, many of his *general* insights have stood up well. They have profoundly influenced later theories of human development and continue to influence the treatment of psychological disorders (Fonagy & Target, 2000). First, Freud called attention to the unconscious and often conflicting motives and mental processes underlying human behavior. Second, he was one of the first to highlight the importance for later development of early experiences in the family. Third and finally, he pointed out the important role of emotions in development. Developmentalists have often slighted emotional development, focusing instead on observable behavior or on rational thought processes.

Erikson: Neo-Freudian Psychoanalytic Theory

Still another sign of Freud's immense influence is the fact that he inspired so many disciples and descendants to contribute in their own right to our understanding of human development. Among these well-known *neo-Freudians* were Alfred Adler, who suggested that siblings (and rivalries between siblings) are significant in development; Carl Jung, who claimed that adults experience a kind of "midlife crisis" (see Chapter 11) and then become freer to express both the "masculine" and "feminine" sides of their personalities; Karen Horney, who challenged Freud's ideas about sex differences; Harry Stack Sullivan, who argued that close friendships in childhood set the stage for intimate relationships later in life (see Chapter 14); and Freud's daughter Anna, who developed techniques of psychoanalysis appropriate for children.

But the neo-Freudian who most influenced thinking about life-span development was Erik Erikson (1902–1994; see Chapter 11 for more detail). Erikson studied with Anna Freud and emigrated from Germany to the United States when Hitler rose to power (see Friedman, 1999). Like Freud, Erikson (1963, 1968, 1982) concerned himself with the inner dynamics of personality and proposed that the personality evolves through systematic stages. Erikson's point of view differed from Freud's in the following ways:

1. Erikson placed less emphasis on sexual urges as the drivers of development and more emphasis on social influences such as peers, teachers, schools, and the broader culture.
2. Erikson placed less emphasis on the irrational, selfish id and more on the rational ego and its adaptive powers.

3. Erikson held a more positive view of human nature, seeing us as active in our development, largely rational, and able to overcome the effects of harmful early experiences.
4. Erikson maintained that human development continues during adulthood.

Psychosocial Development

Erikson believed that human beings everywhere face eight major psychosocial crises, or conflicts, during their lives. (Erikson's stages are next to Freud's in Table 2.2.) Whether the conflict of a particular stage is successfully resolved or not, the individual is pushed by both biological maturation and social demands into the next stage. However, the unsuccessful resolution of a conflict will influence how subsequent stages play out.

The first conflict, **trust versus mistrust,** revolves around whether or not an infant becomes able to rely on other people to be responsive to his or her needs. To develop a sense of trust, infants must be able to count on their primary caregivers to feed them, relieve their discomfort, come when beckoned, and return their smiles and babbles. Whereas Freud focused on the significance of a caregiver's feeding practices, Erikson believed that the caregiver's *general responsiveness* was critical to later development. If caregivers neglect, reject, or respond inconsistently to the infant, he or she will mistrust others. A healthy balance between the terms of the conflict must be struck for development to proceed optimally. Trust should outweigh mistrust, but an element of skepticism is needed as well: An infant who is overindulged may become too trusting (a gullible "sucker").

During the so-called "terrible twos," toddlers must learn to trust *themselves* enough to assert their wills. This is the

Erik Erikson built on Freudian theory and proposed that people experience eight psychosexual crises over the life span.

psychosocial conflict of **autonomy versus shame and doubt.** Toddlers are determined to do things themselves to demonstrate their independence and their control over their parents. They say "me, me, me" and "no, no, no," loudly proclaiming that they have wills of their own. If their parents humiliate or punish them when they have toileting accidents or spill their milk, they may end up doubting their competence or even believing that they are fundamentally bad people.

Four- and five-year-olds who have achieved a sense of autonomy enter Erikson's stage of **initiative versus guilt,** in which they develop a sense of purpose by devising bold plans but must also learn not to step on other people in the process. In the preschool years of imaginative play, children acquire new motor skills, devise plans to build sand castles and to conquer monsters in their fantasy play, and take great pride in accomplishing their goals. A sense of initiative, Erikson believed, paves the way for success in elementary school, when children face the conflict of **industry versus inferiority.** To gain a sense of industry, children must master the important cognitive and social skills—reading, writing, cooperative teamwork, and so on—that are necessary to win the approval of both adults and peers.

Erikson (1968) is best known for characterizing adolescence as a time of "identity crisis," a critical period in the lifelong process of forming one's identity as a person. During this psychosocial stage of **identity versus role confusion,** adolescents attempt to define who they are (in terms of career, religion, sexual identity, and so on), where they are heading, and how they fit into society. As part of their search, they often change their minds and experiment with new looks, new majors, and new group memberships.

Whereas Freud's stages stopped with adolescence, Erikson outlined three key psychosocial conflicts during the adult years. Young adulthood, Erikson believed, is a time for dealing with the psychosocial conflict of **intimacy versus isolation.** The young adult who has not resolved the issue of identity versus role confusion may be threatened by the idea of entering a committed, long-term relationship and being "tied down," or may become overdependent on a partner as a source of identity. In middle age, adults become concerned with the issue of **generativity versus stagnation.** They struggle to gain a sense that they have produced something that will outlive them, whether by raising happy, healthy children or by doing something meaningful through their work or volunteer activities. If all goes well, they will genuinely care about the welfare of future generations, as opposed to being "in a rut," absorbed with their own problems.

Finally, elderly adults confront the psychosocial conflict of **integrity versus despair.** They try to find a sense of meaning in their lives that will help them face the inevitability of death. If they are successful, they are able to look back over their lives and say that there is little they would change. If they are not successful, they may dwell on past injustices and paths not taken and have difficulty preparing for death.

Erikson on Teenage Pregnancy

I am not quite as obsessed by sex as my inspiration, Dr. Freud, but I can agree with him on some things. I agree that emotional conflicts rooted in early experience can affect later behavior. For example, if either Robert or Sherry had unresponsive caregivers when they were infants, they could have had difficulty resolving my psychosocial conflict of *trust versus mistrust.* Adolescents who never developed a strong sense of trust in other people may fear being abandoned and may try to use sex as a way to keep that from happening. The importance of unresolved emotional conflicts can be seen in the fact that depressed young women are more likely than nondepressed ones to become involved in early sexual activity [Whitbeck et al., 1999].

Ah, but why focus on infancy? I agree with Sigmund that accepting one's self as a sexual being is an important task of adolescence, but that's just one aspect of the broader adolescent psychosocial conflict of *identity versus role confusion.* Adolescents are changing rapidly, physically and cognitively, and they are being asked by society to establish who they are as individuals and as members of society. Many adolescents seek a sense of identity by experimenting with different roles and behaviors to see what suits them. They try drugs, dye their hair orange, join radical groups, change majors every semester, and, yes, have sex—all to forge a firm sense of identity. I should know: I was the tall, blond stepson of a Jewish doctor and wandered all over Europe after high school, trying out a career as an artist and a number of other possibilities before I ended up studying child psychoanalysis under Anna Freud and finally found my calling in my mid-20s [Friedman, 1999].

So, perhaps Sherry and Robert were simply searching for their identities when they began their sexual relationship. Or maybe they tried to find an easy resolution to their role confusion through each other—by latching onto an identity as the other's boyfriend or girlfriend [Erikson, 1968]. If Sherry and Robert are finding an identity prematurely through each other, I must be pessimistic about their future. I maintain—and research bears me out—that one must know oneself before one can love someone else; that is, one must find one's true *identity* and end *role confusion* before one can resolve the conflict between *intimacy* and *isolation* [Orlofsky, 1993].

Erikson clearly did not agree with Freud that the personality is essentially "set in stone" during early childhood. Yet he, like Freud and other psychoanalytic theorists, believed that people everywhere progress through systematic stages of development, undergoing similar personality changes at similar ages. As individuals successfully resolve the central conflict of each stage of psychosocial development, they gain new personality strengths (or "ego virtues")—for example, trust of self and other people in infancy, a greater concern for future generations in middle adulthood. Individual differences in personality presumably reflect the different experiences individuals have as they struggle to cope with the challenges of each life stage. Both biological maturation and the demands of the social environment influence the individual's progress through Erikson's stage sequence. By way of illustration, the Explorations box on page 32 expresses what Erikson might have said about teenage pregnancy.

Strengths and Weaknesses

Many people find Erikson's emphasis on our rational, adaptive nature and on an interaction of biological and social influences easier to accept than Freud's emphasis on unconscious, irrational motivations based in biological needs. Erikson also seems to have captured some central developmental issues in his eight stages. He has had an especially great impact on thinking about and research on adolescent identity formation and changes in the self during adulthood (see Chapter 11). At the same time, Erikson's theory has many of the same shortcomings as Freud's. It is sometimes vague and difficult to test. And although it provides a useful *description* of human personality development, it does not provide an adequate *explanation* of how this development comes about.

Important psychoanalytic theorists such as Erikson continue to shape our understanding of human development. However, many developmentalists have rejected the whole psychoanalytic perspective in favor of theories that are more precise and testable.

Learning Theories

Give me a dozen healthy infants, well formed, and my own specified world to bring them up in and I'll guarantee to take any one at random and train him to become any type of specialist I might select—doctor, lawyer, artist, merchant, chief, and yes, even beggar-man and thief, regardless of his talents, penchants, tendencies, abilities, vocations, and race of his ancestors. (Watson, 1925, p. 82)

There is a bold statement! It reflects a belief that nurture is everything and that nature, or genetic endowment, counts for nothing. It was made by John B. Watson, a strong believer in the importance of learning in human development and one of the pioneers of learning theory perspectives on human development.

Watson: Classical Conditioning

Watson's (1913) **behaviorism** rested on his belief that conclusions about human development and functioning should be based on observations of overt behavior rather than on speculations about cognitive and emotional processes that are unobservable. Watson rejected psychoanalytic theory and devoted a good deal of his time to trying to explain Freud's fascinating discoveries about human beings in terms of basic learning principles (Rilling, 2000). He maintained that learned associations between external stimuli and observable responses are the building blocks of both normal and abnormal human development. Like John Locke, Watson believed that children have no inborn tendencies and that how they turn out depends entirely on the environment in which they grow up and the ways in which their parents and other significant people in their lives treat them.

In one attempt to make his point, Watson and colleague Rosalie Raynor (1920) set out to demonstrate that fears can be learned—that they are not necessarily inborn, as was commonly thought at the time. They used the principles of **classical conditioning,** a simple form of learning in which a stimulus that initially had no effect on the individual comes to elicit a response through its association with a stimulus that already elicits the response. The Russian physiologist Ivan Pavlov discovered classical conditioning. In a famous experiment, he demonstrated that dogs, who have an innate (unlearned) tendency to salivate at the sight of food, could learn to salivate at the sound of a bell if, during a training period, the bell was regularly sounded just before they were given food.

Watson and Raynor presented a gentle white rat to a now-famous infant named Albert, who showed no fear of it whatsoever. However, every time the rat was brought forth, Watson would slip behind Albert and bang a steel rod with a hammer.

John B. Watson was the father of behaviorism.

In this situation, the loud noise served as an **unconditioned stimulus (UCS)**—that is, a built-in, unlearned stimulus for fear—which in turn is an unlearned or **unconditioned response (UCR)** to loud noises (as babies are naturally upset by them). During conditioning, the stimuli of the white rat and the loud noise were presented together several times. Afterward, Watson presented the white rat to Albert without banging the steel rod; Albert now whimpered and cried in response to the white rat alone. His behavior had changed as a result of his experience. Specifically, an initially neutral stimulus, the white rat, had become a **conditioned stimulus (CS)** for a **conditioned response (CR),** fear, as shown in Figure 2.2. This learned response generalized to other furry items such as a rabbit and a Santa Claus mask. By today's standards, Watson's experiment would be viewed as unethical, but he had made his point: Emotional responses can be learned. Fortunately, fears that are learned through classical conditioning can be unlearned if the feared stimulus is paired with an unconditioned stimulus for happy emotions (Cover Jones, 1924).

Classical conditioning is undoubtedly involved when infants learn to love their parents, who at first may be neutral stimuli but who become associated with the positive sensations of receiving milk, being rocked, and being comforted. And classical conditioning helps explain why adults find that certain songs on the radio, scents, or articles of clothing "turn them on." A wide range of emotional associations and attitudes are acquired through classical conditioning.

According to the learning theory perspective, then, it is a mistake to assume that children advance through a series of distinct stages guided by biological maturation, as Freud, Erikson, and other stage theorists have argued. Instead, learning theorists view development as nothing more than learning. It is a continuous process of behavior change that is context-specific and can differ enormously from person to person. Watson's basic view was advanced further by B. F. Skinner.

Skinner: Operant Conditioning

B. F. Skinner (1905–1990), whose name is as well known as that of any American psychologist, had a long, distinguished career at Harvard University. Through his research with animals, Skinner (1953) gained understanding of another very important form of learning, **operant** (or instrumental) **conditioning,** in which a learner's behavior becomes either more or less probable depending on the consequences it produces. A learner first behaves in some way and then comes to associate this action with the positive or negative consequences that follow it. The basic principle behind operant conditioning makes a good deal of sense: We tend to repeat behaviors that have pleasant consequences and cut down on behaviors that have unpleasant consequences. Through operant conditioning, we learn new skills and a range of habits, both good and bad.

In the language of operant conditioning, *reinforcement* occurs when a consequence *strengthens* a response, or makes it

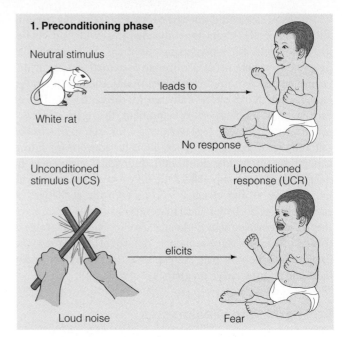

1. Preconditioning phase

Neutral stimulus

White rat — leads to → No response

Unconditioned stimulus (UCS)

Loud noise — elicits → Fear

Unconditioned response (UCR)

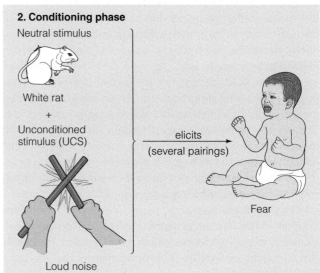

2. Conditioning phase

Neutral stimulus

White rat
+
Unconditioned stimulus (UCS)

Loud noise

— elicits (several pairings) → Fear

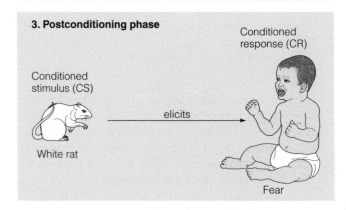

3. Postconditioning phase

Conditioned stimulus (CS)

White rat — elicits → Fear

Conditioned response (CR)

Figure 2.2 The three phases of classical conditioning

more likely to occur in the future. If a preschool child cleans her room and then receives a hug and then cleans her room more frequently in the future, the hug provided **positive reinforcement** for room cleaning. *Positive* here means that some-

B. F. Skinner's operant learning theory emphasized the role of the environment in controlling behavior.

thing has been *added* to the situation, and *reinforcement* means that the behavior is strengthened. Thus a positive reinforcer is an event that, when introduced following a behavior, makes that behavior more probable in the future. (Note that it is the actual effect on the child's behavior that defines a consequence as reinforcing, not the fact that you *think* the child might find a hug reinforcing.) Behaviorists have found that it is best to provide continuous positive reinforcement when a new skill or habit is first being learned, reinforcing every occurrence. Then, to maintain the behavior over long periods, it is best to shift to a type of partial reinforcement schedule in which only some occurrences of the behavior are reinforced and the pattern is unpredictable. Then the learner is likely to continue performing even if reinforcement stops coming.

Negative reinforcement (which is *not* a fancy term for punishment) occurs when a behavioral tendency is strengthened because something negative or unpleasant is *removed* from the situation, or is escaped or avoided, after the behavior occurs. Have you been in a car in which an obnoxious buzzer

sounds until you fasten your seatbelt? The idea is that your "buckling up" behavior will become a habit through *negative reinforcement:* buckling up allows you to escape the unpleasant buzzer. No candy or hugs follow the buckling up, so it is negative rather than positive reinforcement that makes you likely to buckle up. Many of our bad habits allow us to escape or avoid unpleasantness and were learned through negative reinforcement. Teenagers may learn to lie to avoid long lectures from their parents or to drink because it allows them to escape feelings of anxiety at parties. In each case, a behavior is strengthened through negative reinforcement—through the removal or elimination of something unpleasant.

Contrast reinforcement, whether it is positive or negative, with punishment: Whereas reinforcement increases the strength of the behavior that preceded it, punishment decreases the strength of, or weakens, that behavior. Two forms of punishment parallel the two forms of reinforcement. **Positive punishment** occurs when an unpleasant event is added to the situation following a behavior (for example, a cashier is criticized for coming up short of cash at the end of the day). **Negative punishment** occurs when something pleasant is removed from the situation following the behavior (the amount she was short is deducted from her pay). Both positive and negative punishment decrease the likelihood that the punished behavior will be repeated.

The four possible consequences of a behavior are summarized in Figure 2.3. In addition, some behavior is simply ignored; that is, it has no particular consequence. Behavior that is ignored, or no longer reinforced, tends to become less frequent through a process called **extinction.** Indeed, a good alternative to punishing a child's misbehavior is to ignore it while reinforcing desirable behavior that is incompatible with it. All too often, the well-behaved child is ignored and the misbehaving child gets the attention—attention that actually serves as positive reinforcement for the misbehavior!

Skinner and other behavioral theorists have emphasized the power of positive reinforcement in raising children and have generally discouraged the use of physical punishment in child rearing. By contrast, many parents believe that punishment of bad behavior is necessary in raising children; indeed,

	Pleasant stimulus	Unpleasant stimulus
Administered	**Positive reinforcement, adding a pleasant stimulus** (strengthens the behavior) Dad gives in to the whining and lets Moosie play Nintendo, making whining more likely in the future.	**Positive punishment, adding an unpleasant stimulus** (weakens the behavior) Dad calls Moosie a "baby." Moosie does not like this at all and is less likely to whine in the future.
Withdrawn	**Negative punishment, withdrawing a pleasant stimulus** (weakens the behavior) Dad confiscates Moosie's favorite Nintendo game to discourage whining in the future.	**Negative reinforcement, withdrawing an unpleasant stimulus** (strengthens the behavior) Dad stops joking with Lulu. Moosie gets very jealous when Dad pays attention to Lulu, so his whining enables him to bring this unpleasant state of affairs to an end.

Figure 2.3 Possible consequences of whining behavior. Moosie comes into the TV room and sees his father talking and joking with his sister, Lulu, as the two watch a football game. Soon Moosie begins to whine, louder and louder, that he wants them to turn off the television so he can play Nintendo games. If you were Moosie's father, how would you react? Here are four possible consequences of Moosie's behavior. Consider both the type of consequence—whether it is a pleasant or aversive stimulus—and whether it is administered ("added to" the situation) or withdrawn. Notice that reinforcers strengthen whining behavior, or make it more likely in the future, whereas punishers weaken it.

80% of American adults agree that children sometimes need a "good, hard spanking" (Flynn, 1994). What does research tell us? Although it is generally best to use more positive approaches before resorting to punishment, punishment *can* be effective if it (1) is administered immediately after the act (not hours later when the child is being an angel), (2) is administered consistently after each offense, (3) is not overly harsh, (4) is accompanied by explanations, (5) is administered by an otherwise affectionate person, and (6) is combined with efforts to reinforce more acceptable behavior (Domjan, 1993; Perry & Parke, 1975). Regular physical punishment can have undesirable side effects, however—for example, making children resentful and anxious and teaching them that hitting is an appropriate way to solve problems (Straus, 1994).

In sum, B. F. Skinner, like John B. Watson, believed that the course of human development depends on the individual's learning experiences. One boy's aggressive behavior may be reinforced over time because he gets his way with other children and because his parents encourage his "macho" behavior. Another boy may quickly learn that aggression is prohibited and punished. The two may develop in entirely different directions based on their different histories of reinforcement and punishment.

Most developmentalists appreciate that Skinner's operant-conditioning principles can help explain many aspects of human development. Yet some theorists believe that Skinner placed too much emphasis on a single type of learning and too little emphasis on the role of cognitive processes such as attention, memory, and reflection in learning. For this reason, today's developmental scholars are more attracted to Albert Bandura's cognitive brand of learning theory than to Skinner's.

Bandura: Social Learning Theory

Albert Bandura's (1977, 1986, 1989, 2000) "social cognitive theory," most often referred to as **social learning theory,** claims that humans are cognitive beings whose active processing of information from the environment plays a major role in their learning and development. Bandura argues that human learning is very different from rat learning because humans have far more sophisticated cognitive capabilities. He agrees with Skinner that operant conditioning is an important type of learning, but he notes that humans *think* about the connections between their behavior and its consequences, anticipate what consequences are likely to follow from their future behavior, and often are more affected by what they *believe* will happen than by the consequences they actually encounter. For example, a woman may continue to pursue an engineering degree despite many punishments and few immediate rewards because she *anticipates* a greater reward when she completes her studies. We are not just passively shaped by the external consequences of our behavior; we actively think about past and present experiences and anticipate the future. We also reinforce or punish ourselves with mental pats on the back and self-criticism.

Bandura's cognitive emphasis is very clear in his highlighting of **observational learning** as the most important mechanism through which human behavior changes. Observational learning is simply learning that results from observing the behavior of other people (called *models*). By imitating other people, a child may learn how to speak a language and tackle math problems, as well as how to swear, snack between meals, and smoke. It is regarded as a more cognitive form of learning than conditioning because learners must pay attention, construct and remember mental representations (images, verbal summaries) of what they saw, retrieve them from memory at a later time, and use them to guide behavior.

In a classic experiment, Bandura (1965) set out to demonstrate that children could learn a response that was neither elicited by a conditioned stimulus (as in classical conditioning) nor performed and then strengthened by a reinforcer (as in operant conditioning). He had nursery school children watch a short film in which an adult *model* attacked an inflatable "Bobo" doll, hitting the doll with a mallet while shouting "Sockeroo," throwing rubber balls at the doll while shouting "Bang, bang, bang," and so on. Some children saw the model praised, others saw him punished, and still others saw no consequences follow his violent attack. After the film ended, children were observed in a playroom with the Bobo doll and many of the props the model had used to work Bobo over.

What did children learn from this adventure in observational learning? Children who saw the model rewarded and children in the no-consequences condition imitated more of the model's aggressive acts than did children who had seen the model punished for aggression. But interestingly, when children who had seen the model punished were asked to re-

Albert Bandura highlighted the role of cognition in human learning. He is on the faculty at Stanford University.

produce all of the model's behavior they could remember, they showed that they had learned just as much as the other children. Apparently, then, children can learn from observation without imitating (performing) the learned responses. Whether they will perform what they learn depends in part on a process called **vicarious reinforcement,** in which a learner becomes more or less likely to perform a behavior based on the consequences experienced *by the model* he or she observes.

Watson and Skinner may have believed that humans are passively shaped by the environment to become whatever those around them groom them to be, but Bandura does not. Because he views humans as active, cognitive beings, he holds that human development occurs through a continuous reciprocal interaction among the person, the person's behavior, and the environment—a perspective he calls **reciprocal determinism.** As Bandura sees it, "People are partly the products of their environments, but by selecting, creating, and transforming their environmental circumstances they are producers of environments as well" (Bandura, 2000, p. 75). Their personal characteristics and behaviors affect the people around them, just as these people are influencing their personal characteristics and future behaviors.

Like Watson and Skinner, though, Bandura is skeptical of the idea of universal stages of human development. He maintains that development is context-specific and can proceed along many different paths. It is also continuous, occurring gradually through a lifetime of learning. Bandura does acknowledge that children's cognitive learning capacities mature over time, so that they can remember more about what they have seen and can imitate a greater variety of novel behaviors. Yet he also believes that children of the same age will not be much alike at all if their learning experiences have differed considerably.

Obviously there is a fundamental disagreement between stage theorists like Freud and Erikson and learning theorists like Bandura. Learning theorists do not give us a general description of the normal course of human development, because they insist that there is no such description to give. Instead, they offer a rich account of the *mechanisms* through which behavior can change over time. They ask us to use principles of learning that are universal in their applicability to understand how each individual changes with age in unique ways (Goldhaber, 2000). These learning principles can certainly help us understand teenage pregnancy; we imagine what Bandura would say about it in the Explorations box on page 38.

Strengths and Weaknesses

Watson's and Skinner's behavioral learning theories and Bandura's modern social learning theory have contributed immensely to our understanding of development and continue to be influential. Learning theories are very precise and testable. Carefully controlled experiments have shown how we might learn everything from altruism to alcoholism. Moreover, the learning principles involved in classical conditioning, operant conditioning, and observational learning operate across the entire life span and can be used to understand behavior at any age. Finally, learning theories have very practical applications; they have been the basis for many highly effective techniques for optimizing development and treating developmental problems. Parents and teachers can certainly be more effective when they systematically reinforce the

One is never too old to learn by observing others.

et me begin by building on the work of a learning theorist who preceded me. B. F. Skinner would undoubtedly get right to the heart of it and say that teenagers have sex because sex is reinforcing—and that they become pregnant because using contraception is not! One team of researchers put it well: "It is quite likely that if teenagers had to take a pill to become pregnant, early childbearing would quickly vanish as a social problem" [Furstenberg et al., 1981].

This is true enough, but my social cognitive brand of learning theory offers additional insights into teenage pregnancy. Sherry and Robert have been discovering a great deal about sexual behavior through observational learning. Today's adolescents live in a social world filled with messages about sex from their peers, the media, and to a lesser extent, their parents. They actively process this information for future use. If they learn that their friends are sexually active, and if they also think that their friends find sex more reinforcing than costly, they are likely to do what their friends are doing [Benda & DiBlasio, 1994]. Adolescents also watch sex on TV all the time—often exploitive sex, with hardly a mention of birth control or such consequences as HIV infection or the stresses of teenage parenthood. Adolescents today have far more opportunities to learn sexually irresponsible behavior than to learn sexually responsible behavior through observation.

Finally, let me emphasize that people's *expectations* about the consequences of their actions are often more important than the actual reinforcers and punishers operating in their lives. If Robert, for example, *believes* that using a condom will decrease his sexual enjoyment, or if Sherry *believes* that Robert will get mad if she asks him to use a condom, those beliefs will surely decrease the chances that they will use protection. In subcultures in which adolescents expect early parenthood to bring many benefits and few problems, we should not be surprised to see many young parents [Unger, Molina, & Teran, 2000].

---

behavior they hope to instill in children and when they serve as role models of desirable behavior. And many psychotherapists today use behavioral and social/cognitive learning techniques to treat psychological problems.

At the same time, learning theories, even Bandura's social learning theory, leave something to be desired as explanations of human development. Consider the following demonstration. Paul Weisberg (1963) reinforced 3-month-old infants with smiles and gentle rubs on the chin whenever they happened to make babbling sounds like "bababa." He found that these infants babbled more often than did infants who received the same social stimulation randomly rather than only after each babbling sound they made. But does this mean that infants normally begin to babble *because* babbling is reinforced by their caregivers? Not necessarily. All normal infants, even deaf ones, babble at about 4 months of age. Moreover, no matter what experiences we provide to a newborn, he or she will not be maturationally ready to babble. We must suspect, then, that the maturation of the neural and muscular control required for babbling has more than a little to do with the onset of babbling during infancy.

This example really highlights two criticisms of learning theories as theories of human development. First, learning theorists rarely demonstrate that learning is actually responsible for commonly observed developmental changes; they show through their experiments only that learning *might have* resulted in developmental change. Some critics wish that learning theorists would provide a fuller account of normal changes across the life span. Second, early learning theorists, and even Bandura, probably put too little emphasis on biological influences on development such as genetic endowment and maturational processes that affect how we respond to learning experiences.

After learning theories dominated the study of development in the 1950s and 1960s, many scientists began to look for a theory that was more clearly "developmental"—that showed how humans beings change systematically as they get older. They found what they wanted in the remarkable work of Jean Piaget.

Cognitive Developmental Theory

No theorist has contributed more to our understanding of children's minds than Jean Piaget (1896–1980), a Swiss scholar who began to study children's intellectual development during the 1920s. This remarkable man developed quickly himself, publishing his first scientific paper (a letter to the editor about an albino sparrow) at the tender age of 11. Eventually, Piaget blended his interest in zoology and the adaptation of animals to their environments with his interest in philosophy.

He then devoted his career to the study of how humans acquire knowledge and use it to adapt to their world.

Piaget's lifelong interest in cognitive development emerged while he worked at the Alfred Binet laboratories in Paris on the first standardized intelligence (IQ) test. IQ tests estimate a person's intelligence based on the number and types of questions that he or she answers correctly. Piaget soon became interested in children's *wrong* answers and noticed that children of about the same age gave the same kinds of wrong answers. By questioning them to find out how they were thinking about the problems presented to them, he began to realize that young children do not simply know less than older children do; instead, *they think in a qualitatively different way.* Eventually Piaget developed a full-blown theory to account for changes in thinking from infancy to adolescence.

Piaget's Constructivism

Influenced by his background in biology, Piaget (1950) viewed intelligence as a process that helps an organism adapt to its environment. The infant who can grasp a cookie and bring it to her mouth is behaving adaptively, as is the adolescent who can solve algebra problems or fix a flat tire. As children mature, they acquire ever more complex "cognitive structures," or organized patterns of thought or action, that aid them in adapting to their environments.

How do children develop more complex cognitive structures and increase their understanding of the world? Piaget insisted that children are not born with innate ideas about reality, as some philosophers have claimed. Nor are they simply filled with information by adults, as learning theorists have tended to claim. Instead, Piaget took a position called **constructivism,** claiming that children actively construct new understandings of the world based on their experiences. Some preschool children, for example, develop on their own the idea

Swiss psychologist Jean Piaget revolutionized the field of human development with his theory of cognitive growth.

that the sun is alive because it moves across the sky, that children get diseases because they tell lies or otherwise misbehave, and that babies come from the baby store.

How do children construct more accurate understandings of the world? By being the curious and active explorers that they are: by watching what is going on around them, by seeing what happens when they experiment on the objects they encounter, and by recognizing instances in which their current understandings are inadequate to explain events. Children use their current understandings of the world to help them solve problems, but they also revise their understandings to make them fit the facts of reality better (Piaget, 1952). It is the *interaction* between biological maturation (most importantly, a developing brain) and experience (especially discrepancies between the child's understanding and reality) that is responsible for the child's progress from one stage of cognitive development to a new, qualitatively different, stage.

Stages of Cognitive Development

Piaget proposed four major periods of cognitive development: the *sensorimotor stage* (birth to age 2), the *preoperational stage* (ages 2 to 7), the *concrete operations stage* (ages 7 to 11), and the *formal operations stage* (ages 11 to 12 or later). These stages form what Piaget called an *invariant sequence;* that is, all children progress through them in exactly the order in which they are listed, with no skipping of stages and no regression to earlier stages. The ages given are only guidelines.

The key features of each stage are summarized in Table 2.3; we will discuss them in depth in Chapter 7. The core message is that humans of different ages think in very different ways.

Infants in the **sensorimotor stage** deal with the world directly through their *perceptions* (senses) and *actions* (motor abilities). They are unable to use symbols (gestures, images, or words representing real objects and events) to help them mentally devise solutions to problems. However, they learn a great deal about the world and acquire tools for solving problems through their sensory and motor experiences.

The preschooler who has entered the **preoperational stage** of cognitive development now has the capacity for symbolic thought but is not yet capable of logical problem solving. The 4- or 5-year-old can use words as symbols to talk about a problem and can mentally imagine doing something before actually doing it. However, lacking the tools of logical thought, preoperational children must rely on their perceptions and as a result are easily fooled by appearances. For example, they tend to think that large objects will sink in water, even if they are light. According to Piaget, they are also egocentric thinkers who have difficulty adopting perspectives other than their own. As a result, they may cling to incorrect ideas simply because they *want* them to be true.

School-age children who have advanced to the **concrete operations stage** are more logical than preschoolers. They use a trial-and-error approach to problem solving and do well on

Table 2.3 Jean Piaget's Four Stages of Cognitive Development

Stage/Age Range	Description
Sensorimotor (birth to 2)	Infants use their senses and motor actions to explore and understand the world. At the start they have only innate reflexes, but they develop ever more "intelligent" actions and, by the end, are capable of symbolic thought using images or words and can therefore plan solutions to problems mentally.
Preoperational (2 to 7)	Preschoolers use their capacity for symbolic thought in developing language, engaging in pretend play, and solving problems. But their thinking is not yet logical; they are egocentric (unable to take others' perspectives) and easily fooled by perceptions.
Concrete operations (7 to 11 or later)	School-age children acquire logical operations that allow them to mentally classify and otherwise act on concrete objects in their heads. They can solve practical, real-world problems through a trial-and-error approach.
Formal operations (11 to 12 or later)	Adolescents can think about abstract concepts and purely hypothetical possibilities and can trace the long-range consequences of possible actions. With age and experience, they can form hypotheses and systematically test them through the scientific method.

Bob Daemmrich/Stock, Boston

Piaget believed that children are naturally curious explorers who try to make sense of their surroundings.

problems that involve thinking about the "real" world of concrete objects. These children can perform a number of important logical actions, or *operations,* in their heads on concrete objects (hence, the term *concrete operations*). For example, they can mentally categorize or add and subtract objects. They can also draw sound general conclusions based on their ob-

servations. However, they have difficulty dealing with abstract and hypothetical problems.

Adolescents who have reached the **formal operations stage** are able to think more abstractly and hypothetically than school-age children. They can define "justice" abstractly, in terms of fairness, rather than concretely, in terms of the cop on the corner or the judge in the courtroom. They can formulate hypotheses or predictions in their heads, plan in advance how to systematically test their ideas experimentally, and imagine the consequences of their tests. It often takes some years beyond age 11 or 12 before adolescents can adopt a thoroughly systematic and scientific method of solving problems and can think logically about the implications of purely hypothetical ideas. Then they may be able to devise grand theories about what's wrong with parents, the school system, or the federal government!

Obviously, children's cognitive capacities change dramatically between infancy and adolescence as they progress through Piaget's four stages of cognitive development. Young children simply do not think as we do. And certain characteristics of adolescents' thinking can get them into trouble, as illustrated in the Explorations box on page 41, where we imagine what Piaget might say about the causes of teenage pregnancy.

Strengths and Weaknesses

Like Freud, Piaget was a true pioneer whose work has left a deep and lasting imprint on thinking about human development. You will see his influence throughout this text, for the same mind that "constructs" understanding of the physical world also comes, with age, to understand sex differences, moral values, emotions, death, and a range of other important aspects of the human experience. Indeed, Piaget's cognitive developmental perspective dominated the study of child development for two or three decades, until the *information-processing approach* to studying cognition took command in the 1980s (P. H. Miller, 2002). This approach emphasizes processes such as attention, memory, decision making, and the like and will be the focus of Chapter 8. More recently, the sociocultural perspective on cognitive development offered by

Piaget on Teenage Pregnancy

Teenagers must *decide* whether or not to have sex and whether or not to use birth control. These decisions demand cognitive abilities, and that's where my theory comes in. Now, you might think that an adolescent who has reached my stage of formal operations would be ready to consider all the possible consequences of his or her actions and make sound decisions. This is true. But different children achieve formal-operational thinking at different rates. I noticed that Sherry and Robert were not doing particularly well in school. Perhaps they are slow developers still functioning in the stage of concrete operations or have just begun to show early signs of formal-operational thought but do not yet have the more advanced cognitive skills required to consider all the implications of the alternatives they face when making a decision.

I also find that adolescents just entering the stage of formal operations often get carried away with their new cognitive powers. They sometimes begin to feel that they are unique and not subject to the laws of nature that apply to everyone else: "Other teenagers may get pregnant, but it won't happen to me" [see Chapter 7]. Studies show that many teenagers fail to anticipate that they will need contraception, act impulsively, misunderstand their risks of becoming pregnant, do not think about the future consequences of their behavior, and are just plain misinformed about sex and birth control [Cobliner, 1974; Gordon, 1990; Morrison, 1985]. In one study, 13- to 15-year-olds averaged only 40% right on a test about reproduction, contraception, and sexually transmitted diseases; more than 60% did not know that urinating after sex will not prevent pregnancy, for example [Carrera et al., 2000].

I conclude, then, that the cognitive limitations and knowledge gaps of many teenagers have quite a bit to do with today's high rate of teenage pregnancy. These adolescents are not necessarily in the throes of personality conflicts, as Dr. Freud would have you believe. Nor are they deprived of the proper learning experiences, as Drs. Skinner and Bandura argue. They may simply be cognitively immature and uninformed.

a contemporary of Piaget, Lev Vygotsky, has received a good deal of attention, as we'll see when we look at contextual and systems theory.

Despite the rise of rival theories, though, most developmentalists today accept Piaget's basic beliefs that thinking changes in qualitative ways during childhood, that children are active in their own development, and that development occurs through an interaction of nature and nurture. Piaget's description of intellectual development has been put to the test and has been largely, though not wholly, supported. Finally, Piaget's ideas have influenced education and child rearing by encouraging teachers and parents to pitch their educational programs to the child's level of understanding and to stimulate children to discover new concepts through their own firsthand experiences.

Still, Piaget has come in for his share of criticism (Lourenco & Machado, 1996; also see Chapter 7). For example, critics fault Piaget for saying too little about the influences of motivation and emotion on thought processes. They question whether Piaget's stages really hang together as coherent modes of thinking or whether children instead acquire different cognitive skills at different rates. They also challenge the idea that all humans in every culture develop through the same stages, toward the same endpoints. They began to notice, for example, that people may not make it to the last of Piaget's stages unless they are exposed to formal education. As a result, developmentalists began to seek theoretical perspectives that allowed for more diversity in the pathways that

human development could take, while still retaining Piaget's theme that nature and nurture interact to produce developmental change.

Contextual and Systems Theories

Contextual/systems theories of development hold that changes over the life span arise from the ongoing transactions and mutual influence between a changing organism and a changing world (see, for example, Riegel, 1979; Dent-Read & Zukow-Goldring, 1997; Wachs, 2000). Changes in the person produce changes in his or her environment; changes in the environment produce changes in the person. It is impossible to think about the individual in isolation from the physical and social contexts with which he or she interacts because they are all part of a larger system (Wachs, 2000). It is also too simple to think that development always leads in one direction toward some mature endpoint, as stage theorists do.

Some contextual/systems theories have arisen from work in the fields of psychobiology and evolutionary biology (see Gottlieb, 2000; Gottlieb, Wahlsten, & Lickliter, 1998). As we will see in Chapter 3, this work demonstrates that development is the product of complex interplays between nature and nurture, biology and environment. Psychobiological and evolutionary theories help us appreciate that each person's development takes place in the context of our evolutionary history as a species. That is, we share certain genes with other humans because those genes enabled our ancestors to adapt to the environments in which they found themselves. A psychobiological/evolutionary perspective also helps us appreciate that the development of the individual arises from complex interactions over time between genetic and environmental influences—interactions in which genes affect the environment and environment affects the ways in which genes are expressed.

Other contextual/systems theorists have become intrigued by the fact that human development takes different forms in different social contexts and different historical eras. They view development as the product of the person's interactions with his or her social world. Here we'll consider two noted contextual/systems theorists who have helped us understand the social ecology of human development: Lev Vygotsky and Urie Bronfenbrenner.

Vygotsky: A Sociocultural Perspective

Lev Vygotsky (1934/1962, 1930–1935/1978) was a Russian psychologist who was an active scholar when Piaget was formulating his theory and who took issue with some of Piaget's views. He died at the age of 38, before he could fully develop his own theory, but his perspective has gained great acceptance among developmental scientists in the past two decades, especially among those who have been looking for alternatives to Piaget's theory.

Vygotsky challenged Piaget's view that humans develop through universal stages of cognitive development. Instead,

RIA-NOVOSTI/SOVFOTO

Lev Vygotsky

his **sociocultural perspective** maintains that cognitive development is shaped by the sociocultural context in which it occurs and grows out of the child's interactions with members of his or her culture. Each culture provides its members with certain tools of thought—most notably a language, but also tools such as pencils, art media, mathematical systems, and computers. The ways in which people in a particular culture approach and solve problems are passed down from generation to generation through oral and written communication. Hence culture, especially as it is embodied in language, shapes the nature of thinking. As a result, cognitive development is not the same universally; it varies across social and historical contexts depending on what tools of thinking the culture makes available.

In Vygotsky's view, then, cognitive development is a social process. Piaget may have seen children as independent explorers developing their minds through their experiments with the world of objects, but Vygotsky saw children as social beings who develop their minds through their interactions with parents, teachers, and other more knowledgeable members of the culture. If, for example, Mom coaches Ben as he constructs his first paper airplane and talks about how he should go about folding the paper, Ben may well repeat her words to himself later when he tries to construct a plane by himself. Through such social dialogues, children learn how skilled problem solvers in their society go about tackling problems and gradually internalize the language used by their mentors so that it becomes part of their own thinking. Adults continue to learn this way—through dialogues between themselves and other members of their culture.

Notice that the socialization process of interest to Vygotsky is similar to Bandura's observational learning. But in Vygotsky's view, children do not just imitate models. Instead, they and their social partners are true partners in development, "co-constructing" knowledge as they collaborate on problem-solving tasks. In the process, what begins as social interaction using the tool of language becomes individual thought. As we will see when we return to Piaget and Vygotsky in Chapter 7, Vygotsky's ideas have had a strong impact on education, serving as a basis for educational approaches in which children are tutored or coached by more knowledgeable individuals or collaborate to solve problems. Yet Vygotsky may have been so intrigued by social processes in development that he paid too little attention to biological influences and to differences among individuals who develop within the same cultural context. Bronfenbrenner's bioecological approach aims to give both biological and environmental influences their due.

Bronfenbrenner: The Bioecological Approach

Much like Lev Vygotsky, Urie Bronfenbrenner became disturbed early in his career that many developmentalists studied human development out of context, expecting it to be universal and failing to appreciate how much it could vary from culture to culture, from neighborhood to neighborhood, and from home to home. Later in his career, after stimulating many developmentalists to study contextual influences on development, he complained that too many developmentalists now studied "context without development" (Bronfenbrenner, 1995). They had forgotten to look closely at biological and psychological changes in the individual who interacts with his or her environment. What Bronfenbrenner really sought was a middle ground in which both biological and environmental influences on development are appreciated.

Gradually, Bronfenbrenner formulated his **bioecological approach** (formerly ecological approach) to development, making clear his emphasis on nature *and* nurture (Bronfenbrenner, 1979, 1989; Bronfenbrenner & Evans, 2000; Bronfenbrenner & Morris, 1998). According to this model, the developing person is embedded in a series of environmental systems that interact with one another and with the individual to influence development. The relationship between person and environment is one of *reciprocal influence;* person and environment form a dynamic, ever-changing system.

A woman, for example, may take cocaine during pregnancy, and this may make her newborn extraordinarily fussy. Environment has affected development. But a fussy baby is likely to affect the environment—for example, by irritating his mother. Mother now expresses her tenseness and irritability in her interactions with him, and this makes him all the more irritable and fussy, which of course aggravates his mother even more, which of course makes him even more cranky.

Bronfenbrenner analyzes these kinds of ongoing transactions between a changing person and a changing environment using a systems approach. He describes four environmental systems that influence, and are influenced by, the developing person over time:

- The **microsystem** is the immediate environment in which the person functions. The primary microsystem for a firstborn infant is likely to be the family—perhaps infant, mother, and father reciprocally influencing one another. The infant may also experience other microsystems such as a day care center or grandmother's house. Within any microsystem, infants contribute to their own development by affecting their companions, who in turn influence them in new ways.
- The **mesosystem** consists of the interrelationships or linkages between two or more microsystems. For example, a marital conflict in the family (one microsystem) could make a child withdraw from staff members and other children at the day care center (another microsystem) so that his or her experience there becomes less intellectually stimulating. A loving home environment, by contrast, is likely to allow a child to benefit more from experiences in the day care center, or later in school.
- The **exosystem** consists of linkages involving social settings that the individual does not experience directly but that can still influence his or her development. For example, children interacting with their parents at home can be affected by their parents' work experiences and social interactions outside the home. Mothers may have difficulty providing a stimulating home environment when they have few friends to turn to for information and support and when their husbands are away from home a great deal (Cotterell, 1986). Similarly, children's experiences in school can be affected by their exosystem— by a plant closing in their community that results in a cut in the school system's budget.
- The **macrosystem** is the larger cultural context in which the microsystem, mesosystem, and exosystem are embedded. The shared understandings that we call culture include views about the nature of human beings at different points in the life span, about what children need to be taught to function in society, and about how one should lead one's life as an adult. As we emphasized in Chapter 1, development is shaped by the historical and cultural context in which it occurs.

The environmental systems proposed by Bronfenbrenner—each of them shaping and being shaped by the developing person—are sketched in Figure 2.4. Each of us functions in particular microsystems linked to one another through the mesosystem and embedded in the larger contexts of the exosystem and the macrosystem. We develop, and settings such as the family or the broader culture also evolve and change. Moreover, we move into new settings, as when a child progresses from preschool to elementary school to junior high school and becomes involved in new peer groups and social organizations. As our environments change and as we change them, we ourselves change.

However they define the forces that interact to shape development, contextual and systems theorists such as Vygotsky

Cornell University

Urie Bronfenbrenner developed a bioecological approach to development, in which both biological and environmental influences are taken into account.

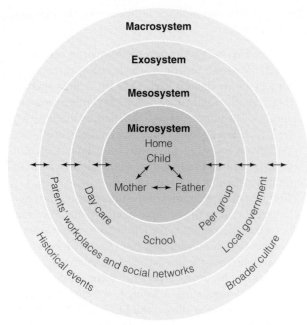

Figure 2.4 Bronfenbrenner's bioecological model of development pictures the environment as a series of nested structures. The microsystem refers to relations between the developing person and the immediate environment, the mesosystem to connections among the individual's immediate settings, the exosystem to settings that affect but do not contain the individual, and the macrosystem to the broader cultural context of development. Both person and environment are continuously changing.

SOURCE: Adapted from Kopp & Krakow (1982)

and Bronfenbrenner believe that person and environment are both in continual flux, and that changes in one inevitably produce changes in the other because they are part of a larger system. We cannot ignore the fact that people develop in a changing cultural and historical context—something that Piaget and other stage theorists tended to do. Nor can we focus all of our attention on environmental influences and ignore the fact that humans are biological organisms whose genes contribute to their development and that they actively shape their environments—something that early learning theorists tended to do. Some thoughts Urie Bronfenbrenner might have about contributors to teenage pregnancy are presented in the Explorations box on page 45.

Strengths and Weaknesses

Contextual and systems perspectives on development began to emerge in response to some of the deficiencies of earlier stage theories and learning theories of development. These perspectives are complex, but that is because life-span human development is complex. We can applaud Vygotsky, Bronfenbrenner, and like-minded theorists for emphasizing some very important truths about human development. Development *is* the product of both biological and environmental forces interacting within a complex system. And we cannot always predict how it will turn out unless we look

more closely at the ongoing transactions between the person and the environment. As Dale Goldhaber (2000, p. 324) notes, "the quest for universal, and at times idealized, images of development tends to make us forget about the particulars—even the 'messiness'—of individual lives."

The life-span developmental perspective introduced in Chapter 1 is contextual in its orientation. But perhaps you have noticed that the contextual/systems perspective does not give us a very clear picture of the course of human development. Indeed, there is no full-blown contextual/systems theory as yet. Up to this point, Bronfenbrenner and others have mainly alerted us to the need to examine how individual factors, ranging from genes to personality traits, and environmental factors, ranging from prenatal nutrition to culture, interact over time to produce developmental change. We could, therefore, criticize contextual/systems theory for being only partially formulated at this point.

But a more serious criticism can also be made: The contextual/systems perspective may never provide any coherent developmental theory. Why? Suppose we really take seriously the idea that development can take a wide range of forms depending on a wide range of influences both within and outside the person. How can we ever state generalizations about development that will hold up for most people? Must we develop separate theories for different subgroups of people—one theory for black women born in 1950 and living in Kenya, another for white men born in 1960 and living in the southeastern United States, and so on? If change over a lifetime depends on the ongoing transactions between a unique person and a unique environment, is each life span unique? The problem is this: "For the contextualist, often the only generalization that holds is, 'It depends.'" (Goldhaber, 2000, p. 33).

In light of these concerns, some theorists propose that we combine the contextual/systems perspective with the best features of stage theories that propose universal paths of development (Lerner & Kauffman, 1985). We might then see humans as moving in orderly directions in some aspects of their development, yet we could also try to understand how that developmental course differs in different social contexts. We might view developmental attainments such as formal-operational thinking not as inevitable achievements but as attainments that are more or less *probable* depending on the individual's genetic endowment and life experiences.

Theories in Perspective

That completes our survey of some of the grand and emerging theories of human development. These theories can be grouped into even grander categories based on the broad assumptions they make about human development (Pepper, 1942; Reese & Overton, 1970; also see Goldhaber, 2000).

Freud, Erikson, Piaget, and other stage theorists form one broad group and have much in common. They believe that

I believe that Sherry and Robert are faced with a pregnancy due to the workings of multiple, interacting forces within themselves and within the environmental systems in which they are developing. According to my bioecological theory, teenage pregnancy is unlikely to be rooted in one simple cause, such as a weak superego or limited cognitive development. We must analyze carefully the ongoing interactions between these changing young people and the changing world in which they are developing.

We know, of course, that Sherry and Robert, like other adolescents, are experiencing rapid physical, hormonal, cognitive, and psychosocial change—and that they are actively influencing those around them, including each other [Corcoran, 1999; B. C. Miller, Benson, & Galbraith, 2001]. In turn, they are being influenced by the individuals in their *microsystems*. The microsystem of central interest here is the romantic relationship between the two of them. We know that an adolescent's sexual partner strongly influences his or her sexual behavior and use of contraceptives [Thompson & Spanier, 1978]. Other microsystems also affect and are affected by these young people—certainly their families and their peer groups, as well as schools, churches, and so on.

Consider what I call the *mesosystem*, linkages between microsystems. Could troubles in the microsystems of their families be causing Sherry and Robert to be overly dependent on each other in the microsystem of their relationship? Or might Robert and Sherry have been influenced by the

exosystem—by forces in their community that they do not directly experience? Rates of teenage pregnancy and childbirth are in fact higher in some sociocultural contexts than in others. They are especially high among African American and Latina adolescents living in low-income urban areas where educational and vocational opportunities are limited [South, 1999].

Finally, consider the broadest of my four environmental systems, the *macrosystem*. In some cultures, early childbearing is the norm, and teenage pregnancy is therefore not considered a problem. In our own society, it *is* considered a problem. The United States has undergone a number of important changes that have altered the adolescent experience— for example, greater sexual permissiveness and more single-parent families and working mothers (and therefore less guidance of teenagers) [Bronfenbrenner et al., 1998]. Sherry and Robert have undoubtedly been influenced by these broad social changes. This may be why, even though our teenage pregnancy rate has been declining for a number of years, it is still 9 times higher than the teenage pregnancy rates in most Western European nations and has not declined as rapidly as rates in those countries have [Meschke, Bartholomae, & Zentall, 2000; Singh & Darroch, 2000].

So, a multitude of interacting factors contribute to our high adolescent pregnancy rate, from the biological to the cultural. If my bioecological perspective on development seems complex, that's because human development is complex!

---

development is guided in certain universal directions by forces springing from within the individual. Humans need a supportive environment in order to develop in healthy directions, but mainly they unfold—much as a rose unfolds from its humble beginnings as a seed—according to a master plan carried in their genes. They evolve through distinct or discontinuous stages that are universal and lead to the same final state of maturity. Parents who subscribe to the stage theory perspective on development are likely to be supportive but not pushy in their efforts to enhance their children's development. They would tend to trust their children to seek out the learning opportunities they most need at a given stage in their growth. They would respond to their children's changing needs and interests but would not feel compelled to structure all their children's learning experiences for them.

By contrast, learning theorists such as Watson, Skinner, and Bandura emphasize the role of the environment more than the role of the person in development. Parents who subscribe to a learning theory model of human development are not likely to trust genetically guided maturational forces

to ensure that their children develop in healthy directions. Such parents may assume that their children will not develop at all (or at least will never be Harvard material!) unless they are systematically exposed to the proper learning experiences. They are likely to take deliberate steps to shape desirable behaviors and eliminate undesirable ones in their offspring.

Finally, contextual and systems theorists emphasize *both* person and environment as components of a larger system. Humans contribute actively to the developmental process (as stage theorists like Piaget maintain), but the environment is an active participant in the developmental drama as well (as learning theorists maintain). The potential exists for both qualitative (stagelike) change and quantitative change. Development can proceed along many different paths depending on the intricate interplay of internal and external influences. Parents who adopt a contextual/systems model of development, such as Vygotsky's sociocultural perspective or Bronfenbrenner's bioecological model, are likely to appreciate that their children are influencing them just as much as they are influencing their children.

Using Developmental Theories to Prevent Teenage Pregnancy

Each of the developmental theories explored in this chapter suggests an approach to preventing and treating developmental problems. Psychoanalytic theorists tend to locate the problem within the person. Freud might want to identify and target for intervention teenagers who have especially strong ids and weak egos and superegos or who are experiencing extremes of anxiety and strained relationships with their parents. Erikson might identify teenagers who are having significant problems resolving the crisis of identity versus role confusion. High-risk teenagers might then be treated through psychoanalysis; the aim would be to help them resolve the inner conflicts that might get them in trouble. This approach might well work with teenagers who are indeed psychologically disturbed. The only problem is that most pregnant girls are not (Furstenberg et al., 1981).

Adopting Piaget's cognitive developmental perspective might make us pessimistic that young teenagers can learn to engage in long-term planning and rational decision making about sexual issues until they are solidly into the formal operations stage of cognitive development. However, if we could identify the kinds of faulty cognitive structures or misunderstandings that young adolescents have about their risks of pregnancy and about contraceptive methods, we could attempt to correct their mistaken ideas using concrete examples and simple explanations. The solution to teenage pregnancy, then, would be improved sex education courses—courses that provide teenagers with accurate information and help them think clearly about the long-term consequences of their sexual decisions.

Most researchers concerned about teenage sexuality and pregnancy agree that improved sex education is an important part of the solution. Only if sex education programs are carefully designed and put emphasis on teaching decision-making and communication skills do they succeed not only in imparting information but also in increasing use of contraception and reducing pregnancy rates (Franklin & Corcoran, 2000). So perhaps we need to consider solutions that locate the problem in the environment rather than in the individual's psychological weaknesses or cognitive deficiencies.

Learning theorists strongly believe that changing the environment will change the person. In support of this belief, it appears that the most effective approach to teenage pregnancy prevention is to make contraceptives readily available to teens through community clinics and teach them how to use them (Franklin & Corcoran, 2000). This approach reflects a Skinnerian philosophy of encouraging the behavior one wants by making it more reinforcing and less punishing. Drawing on Albert Bandura's social learning theory, it might also be beneficial to provide teenagers with more role models of responsible sexual behavior. Through the right observational learning experiences, teenagers might develop more sexually responsible habits and learn that the consequences of safer sex are likely to be more desirable than the consequences of early parenthood (Unger, Molina, & Teran, 2000).

Contextual and systems theorists such as Bronfenbrenner would insist that changing *both* the person and the environment—changing the whole bioecological system—may be necessary. Quick fixes are unlikely to work. The solution may ultimately require changing the broader social context in which today's adolescents are developing. Teenage pregnancy in poverty areas may not be reduced significantly until poor parents face fewer stresses, schools are safe and stimulating, jobs are available, and more disadvantaged young people gain hope that they can climb out of poverty if they pursue an education and postpone parenthood (Furstenberg, Brooks-Gunn, & Morgan, 1987; Singh & Darroch, 2000). At the same time, adolescents can be helped to understand the pros and cons of different life choices and to appreciate that they have the power to shape their own development.

We see, then, that the theoretical position one takes has a profound impact on how one goes about attempting to optimize development. Yet, as we have also seen, each theory may have only a partial solution to the problem being addressed. In all likelihood, multiple approaches will be needed to address complex problems such as the high rate of teenage pregnancy—and certainly to achieve the larger goal of understanding human development.

They are likely to view themselves as *partners* with their children in the development process.

It is because different theories rest on very different basic assumptions that they offer such different pictures of human development and its causes. Theorists who view the world through different lenses are likely to disagree even when the same "facts" are set before them because they tend to offer different interpretations of those facts. This is the very nature of science. Our understanding of human development has changed, and will continue to change, as one prevailing view gives way to another. From the beginning of the study of human development at the turn of the 20th century through the heyday of Freud's psychoanalytic theory, a stage theory perspective prevailed, emphasizing biological forces and plac-

Compare Yourself with the Theorists

In the Exploration box on page 25 at the start of this chapter, you were asked to indicate your position on basic issues in human development by answering five questions. If you transcribe your answers below, you can compare your stands to those of the theorists described in this chapter (and also review the theories). With whom do you seem to agree the most?

	Question				
	1	2	3	4	5

Your pattern of answers:

Psychoanalytic Theory: Freud's Version

	a	b	b	a	a

Freud held that biologically based sexual instincts motivate behavior and steer development through five psychosexual stages leading from the oral stage to the genital stage. He believed that (1) the child's urges are basically selfish and aggressive; (2) biological changes are the driving force behind psychosexual stages (though he believed that parents influence how well these stages are negotiated); (3) children are passively influenced by forces beyond their control; (4) development is stagelike rather than continuous; and (5) the psychosexual stages are universal.

Psychoanalytic Theory: Erikson's Version

	c	c	a	a	a

Erikson theorized that humans progress through eight psychosocial conflicts, from trust versus mistrust to integrity versus despair, as they mature biologically and attempt to adapt to their social environment. He held that (1) we are born with basically good qualities; (2) nature and nurture are about equally important; (3) people are active in their own development; (4) development is stagelike; and (5) the eight psychosocial stages are universal, though they may be expressed differently in different cultures.

Learning Theory: Skinner's Version

	b	e	b	c	b

Skinner maintained that development is the result of learning from the consequences of one's behavior through operant conditioning. In his view, (1) children are inherently neither good nor bad; (2) nurture or environment is far more important than nature; (3) people are passively shaped by environmental events; (4) development is gradual and continuous, as habits increase or decrease in strength in response to reinforcers and punishers; and (5) development is context-specific and can proceed in many different directions and change directions depending on the individual's learning experiences.

Learning Theory: Bandura's Version

	b	d	a	c	b

Bandura's social learning theory states that humans change through cognitive forms of learning, especially observational learning. He argues that (1) children are inherently neither good nor bad; (2) nurture is more important than nature; (3) people influence their environments and thus are active in their own development; (4) development is continuous rather than stagelike; and (5) development can proceed in many directions and change directions depending on life experiences.

Piaget's Cognitive Developmental Theory

	c	b	a	a	a

Piaget described four distinct stages in the development of intelligence (sensorimotor, preoperational, concrete operational, and formal operational) that result as children attempt to make sense of their experience. He suggested that (1) we are born with positive tendencies such as curiosity; (2) maturation interacting with experience guides all children through the same sequence of stages, although at different rates; (3) we are active in our own development as we "construct" more sophisticated understandings; (4) development is stagelike; and (5) everyone progresses through the same sequence of stages.

Contextual/Systems Theories

	b	c	a	b	b

Bronfenbrenner, Vygotsky, and similar contextual/systems theorists believe that development results from the transactions between a changing person and a changing environment. These theorists appear to believe that (1) humans are inherently neither good nor bad; (2) nature and nurture, interacting continually, make us what we are; (3) people are active in their own development; (4) development probably involves some continuity and some discontinuity, some stagelike changes and some gradual ones; and (5) although some aspects of development may be universal, development also varies widely from individual to individual and can change directions depending on experience.

b, e, b, c, b

ing individual development in the context of evolution (Cairns, 1998; Parke et al., 1994). In the 1950s and 1960s, learning theories came to the fore, and attention shifted away from biology toward the environment. Then, with the rising influence of cognitive psychology and Jean Piaget's theory of cognitive development in the late 1960s and 1970s, a stage theory model emphasizing the interaction of nature and nurture gained prominence. In the 1980s and 1990s, we gained a fuller appreciation of the roles of both genetic and cultural/historical influences on development (Cairns, 1998).

So, where are we today? The broad perspective on key developmental issues taken by contextual/systems theorists such as Vygotsky and Bronfenbrenner is the perspective that most 21st-century developmentalists have adopted. The field has moved beyond the extreme, black-or-white positions taken by many of its pioneers. We now appreciate that human beings have the potential to develop in good *and* bad directions, that human development is always the product of nature *and* nurture, that humans *and* their environments are active in the developmental process, that development is both continuous *and* discontinuous in form, and that development has both universal aspects *and* aspects particular to certain cultures, times, and individuals. In short, the assumptions and theories that guide the study of human development have become increasingly complex as the incredible complexity of human development has become more apparent. Perhaps as a result, "grand" theories of development, such as the ones discussed in this chapter, are not as influential today, and researchers are guided more by "minitheories" that are more specific in focus (Parke et al., 1994).

As we noted at the start of the chapter, one of the main functions of theories in any science is to guide attempts to contribute to knowledge through research. Thus Freud stimulated researchers to study inner personality conflicts, Skinner inspired them to analyze how behavior changes when its environmental consequences change, and Piaget inspired them to explore children's thinking about every imaginable topic. Different theories stimulate different kinds of research and yield different kinds of facts.

Theories also guide practice. As we have seen, each theory of human development represents a particular way of defining developmental issues and problems. Often how you define a problem determines how you attempt to solve it. To illustrate this point, let's take one last look at teenage pregnancy. As we have seen, different theorists hold radically different opinions about the causes of teenage pregnancy. How do you think each would go about trying to *reduce* the rate of teenage pregnancy? The Applications box on page 46 offers some ideas.

We hope you are convinced that theories are not just useless ideas. Developmental researchers need theories to guide their work, and every parent, teacher, human service professional, and observer of human beings is guided by some set of basic assumptions about how human beings develop and why they develop as they do. We hope that reading this chapter will stimulate you to think about your own theory of human development. One way to start is by completing the exercise that appears in the Explorations box on page 47 and seeing which theorists' views are most compatible with your own.

You need not choose one theory and reject others. Indeed, because different theories often highlight different aspects of development, one may be more relevant to a particular issue or to a particular age group than another. Many developmentalists today are theoretical **eclectics** who rely on many theories, recognizing that none of the major theories of human development can explain everything but that each has something to contribute to our understanding. In many ways, the emerging contextual/systems perspective on development is the broadest point of view yet proposed. There is no reason why many of the insights offered by Erikson, Piaget, Bandura, and others cannot be incorporated within this perspective to help us understand changing people in their changing worlds.

Summary Points

1. A theory is a set of ideas proposed to describe and explain certain phenomena; it provides a perspective that helps organize a wide range of facts and is valuable to the extent that it is internally consistent, falsifiable, and supported by data.

2. Theories of human development address issues concerning assumptions about human nature, nature/nurture, activity/passivity, continuity/discontinuity, and universality/context-specificity in development.

3. According to Freud's psychoanalytic theory, humans are driven by inborn instincts of which they are largely unconscious. The id, which is purely instinctual, rules the infant; the rational ego emerges during infancy; and the superego, or conscience, takes form in the preschool years. Five psychosexual stages—oral, anal, phallic, latency, and genital—unfold as the sex instinct matures; each is characterized by conflicts that create the need for ego defense mechanisms and have lasting effects on the personality.

4. According to Erikson's neo-Freudian version of psychoanalytic theory, development is a lifelong process involving eight psychosocial stages, beginning with trust versus mistrust in infancy and concluding with integrity versus despair in old age. Compared to Freud, Erikson emphasized biological urges less and social influences more; emphasized id less and ego more; held a more positive, optimistic view of human nature; and theorized about the entire life span.

5. Learning theorists hold that we change gradually through learning experiences and that we can develop in many different

directions. Behaviorist John Watson advocated attention to overt behavior and environmental influences on development and demonstrated the role of classical conditioning in the development of emotional responses. B. F. Skinner advanced the behavioral perspective by demonstrating the importance of operant conditioning and reinforcement and punishment in learning skills and habits. Albert Bandura's social learning theory differs from behavioral learning theories in emphasizing cognitive processes, observational learning, and a reciprocal determinism of person and environment.

6. Jean Piaget's cognitive developmental theory stresses universal, invariant stages in which children actively construct increasingly complex understandings by interacting with their environments. These stages are sensorimotor, preoperational, concrete-operational, and formal-operational.

7. The emerging contextual/systems perspective on development—illustrated by Vygotsky's sociocultural perspective (with its emphasis on how culture shapes the development of thought as children collaborate with more experienced problem solvers) and Bronfenbrenner's bioecological theory (with its micro-, meso-, exo-, and macrosystems)—emphasizes that a changing person and a changing environment interact as part of a larger system.

8. Theories can be grouped into families based on the assumptions that underlie them. During the 20th century, stage theories emphasizing forces within the person and universal maturational processes gave way to learning theories emphasizing environmental factors, which in turn gave way to Piaget's influential cognitive developmental stage theory and, most recently, to contextual and systems theories that emphasize the dynamic interaction between person and environment.

9. Theories of human development guide not only research but also practice; psychoanalytic, cognitive developmental, learning, and contextual/systems theorists would each propose different approaches to the problem of teenage pregnancy.

10. From an eclectic perspective, no single theoretical viewpoint offers a totally adequate account of human development, but each contributes in important ways to our understanding.

Critical Thinking

1. Jasper, age 6, has just started first grade and suddenly has a case of school phobia. Every morning he complains of headaches, tummy aches, and foot aches and begs his mother to let him stay home. His mother let him stay home almost all of last week and very much wants to understand why Jasper does not want to go to school. Help her out by indicating what particular psychoanalytic, learning, cognitive developmental, and contextual/systems theorists might propose as an explanation of school phobia.

2. Matilda, age 78, fell and broke her hip recently and has become overly dependent on her daughter for help ever since, even though she can actually get around quite well. How might particular psychoanalytic, learning, cognitive developmental, and contextual/systems theorists explain her old-age dependency?

3. Play the role of Urie Bronfenbrenner, bioecological theorist, commenting on the theories of Sigmund Freud, Jean Piaget, and B. F. Skinner. How would you assess the best contributions of each? What is missing from or wrong with each perspective from a bioecological point of view?

4. You have decided to become an eclectic and to take from each of the four major perspectives in this chapter (psychoanalytic, learning, cognitive developmental, and contextual/systems theory) only *one* truly great insight into human development. What four ideas would you choose, and why?

Key Terms

tabula rasa

nature/nurture issue

activity/passivity issue

continuity/discontinuity issue

developmental stage

universality/context-specificity issue

psychoanalytic theory

instinct

unconscious motivation

id

ego

superego

libido

psychosexual stages

defense mechanisms

fixation

regression

trust versus mistrust

autonomy versus shame and doubt

initiative versus guilt

industry versus inferiority

identity versus role confusion

intimacy versus isolation

generativity versus stagnation

integrity versus despair

behaviorism

classical conditioning

unconditioned stimulus (UCS)

unconditioned response (UCR)

conditioned stimulus (CS)

conditioned response (CR)

operant conditioning

positive reinforcement

negative reinforcement

positive punishment

negative punishment

extinction

social learning theory

observational learning

vicarious reinforcement

reciprocal determinism

constructivism

sensorimotor stage

preoperational stage

concrete operations stage

formal operations stage

contextual/systems theories

sociocultural perspective

bioecological approach

microsystem

mesosystem

exosystem

macrosystem

eclectic

On the Web

Web Sites to Explore

Freud
This site of the Abraham A. Brill Library of the New York Psychoanalytic Institute (see especially its section "Sigmund Freud on the Internet") offers biographical information and excerpts from a few of the writings of the founder of psychoanalytic theory. http://www.nypsa.org

Piaget
The Jean Piaget Society provides biographical information, links to other Piaget resources on the Web, and lists of suggested readings for those who would like to learn more about Piaget's research and writings. http://www.piaget.org

Bronfenbrenner
Although most of the theorists discussed in this chapter are no longer alive, you'll be interested to know that Urie Bronfenbrenner, emeritus professor at Cornell, has his own Web site, in which he outlines his current interests and lists his recent publications. His

recent interests range from the "growing chaos" in children's environments today to developmental processes in middle adulthood and old age.

http://www.human.cornell.edu/faculty/facultybio.cfm?netid5ub11

Search Online with InfoTrac College Edition

For additional information, explore InfoTrac College Education, your online library. Go to

http://www.infotrac-college.com

and use the pass code that came on the card with your book.

For example, try searching for Freud. How is he viewed today? See if you can locate two or more reviews of books about him and find out. You can see what is being written today about Piaget, Erikson, Bandura, or Vygotsky as well.

Visit Our Web Site

Go to http://www.wadsworth.com/psychology, where you will find online resources directly linked to your book.

Life-Span CD-ROM

Go to the Wadsworth Life-Span CD-ROM for further study of the concepts in this chapter. The CD-ROM also includes quizzes and additional activities to expand your learning experience.

CHAPTER t h r e e

Genes, Environment, and Development

IMAGINE MEETING A LONG-LOST identical twin face-to-face for the first time. This is a fantasy that many people have, but it has been a reality for many of the participants in a study of twins separated at birth being conducted at the University of Minnesota by Dr. Thomas Bouchard, Jr., and his associates (Bouchard, 1984; Bouchard et al., 1990). Although the research team expected to observe similarities in the ways twins responded to a 50-hour battery of tests, they probably were not prepared for the number of eerie coincidences that were revealed when these twins were reunited.

A newspaper story about Jim Lewis and Jim Springer inspired Bouchard to undertake his study in the first place (Wright, 1995). Together again after spending all but the first four weeks of their 39 years apart, these identical twins had both married women named Linda—and then women named Betty. They named their first sons James Alan and James Allan, had dogs named Toy, and liked Miller Lite beer and Salem cigarettes.

Barbara Herbert and Daphne Goodship, also reunited after 39 years apart, both wore a beige dress and a brown velvet jacket when they met for the first time in London. They shared a habit of "squidging" (pushing up their noses), had fallen down the stairs at age 15, laughed more than anyone they knew, and never voted.

Oscar Stohr and Jack Yufe, one adopted by a Catholic Czechoslovakian who had been loyal to the Nazis in World War II, the other raised in the Caribbean by his Jewish father and taught to despise Nazism, quickly discovered that they shared a passion for spicy food, a habit of flushing the toilet both before and after using it, a tendency to read magazines from back to front, and an enjoyment of sneezing loudly to scare people (Wright, 1995).

Identical twins share some remarkable similarities, even when separated early in life, but differ as well.

Perhaps the influence of **genes** on development must be taken seriously! But so must the influence of environment. What exactly are the roles of heredity and environment in shaping our many physical and psychological characteristics? That is the puzzle we grapple with in this chapter. Many people are environmentalists at heart, believing that there is no such thing as a "bad seed," that proper parenting and a stimulating environment can make any child develop well, and that most of the psychological differences between people reflect their experiences over a lifetime. Reading this chapter should increase your appreciation of genetic contributions to development while also giving you new insights into the importance of environmental influences.

We begin by considering some ways in which genes make human beings alike in their characteristics and in their development. Then the chapter turns to what we inherit at conception and how this genetic endowment can influence our traits. Then it explores how genes and environment make individuals different from one another in intelligence, personality, and other characteristics. Finally, we draw some general conclusions about heredity and environment from a life-span perspective. Let's start by focusing on the characteristics that all humans share.

Species Heredity, Evolution, and Human Development

Most discussions of heredity focus on its role in creating differences among people. Some individuals inherit blue eyes, others brown eyes; some inherit blood type O, others blood type A or B. But isn't it remarkable that just about every one of us has two eyes and that we all have blood coursing through our veins? And that virtually all of us develop in similar ways at similar ages—walking and talking at about 1 year, maturing sexually at 12 to 14, watching our skin wrinkle in our 40s and 50s? These similarities are not coincidental. They are due to **species heredity**—the genetic endowment that members of a particular species have in common, including genes that govern maturation and aging processes. Humans can feel guilty but cannot fly; birds can fly but cannot feel guilty. Each species has its own distinct species heredity. The fact that humans all over the world share both a human species heredity and a characteristically human environment explains why some patterns of development and aging are universal. Where did we get this common species heredity? That's a question evolutionary theory can help answer.

Darwin's Theory of Evolution

The theory of evolution proposed by Charles Darwin (1809–1882), and clarified and modified ever since, attempts to explain how the characteristics of a species change over time and how new species can evolve from earlier ones (Darwin, 1859). It has been tremendously important to our

Christopher Brown/Stock, Boston

understanding of why humans develop as they do. The main arguments of Darwin's theory are these:

1. There is genetic variation in a species. Some members of the species have different genes (and different genetically influenced characteristics and behaviors) than others. If all members of the species were genetically identical, there would be no way for the genetic makeup of the species to change over time.

2. Some genes aid in adaptation more than others do. Suppose that some members of a species have genes that make them strong and intelligent, whereas others have genes that make them weak and dull. Those with the genes for strength and intelligence would likely be better able to adapt to their environment—for example, to win fights for survival or to figure out how to obtain food.

3. Those genes that aid their bearers in adapting to the environment will be passed on to future generations more frequently than those genes that do not. This is the principle of **natural selection**—the idea that nature "selects," or allows to survive and reproduce, those members of a species whose genes permit them to adapt to their environment. By contrast, those genes that somehow reduce the chances that an individual will survive and reproduce will become rarer and rarer over time because they will not be passed on to many offspring. Through natural selection, then, the genetic makeup of a whole species can slowly change over time.

Consider a classic example of evolution. H. B. D. Kettlewell (1959) carefully studied moths in England. There is genetic variation among moths that makes some of them dark in color and others light in color. By placing light and dark moths in a number of different sites, Kettlewell found that in rural areas light-colored moths were most likely to survive but that in industrial areas dark moths were most likely to survive. The explanation? In rural areas, light-colored moths blend in well with light-colored trees and are therefore better protected from predators. Natural selection favors them. However, in sooty industrial areas, light-colored moths are easy pickings against the darkened trees, whereas dark moths are well disguised. When industry came to England, the proportion of dark moths increased; as pollution was brought under control in some highly industrialized areas, the proportion of light-colored moths increased again (Bishop & Cooke, 1975).

Or consider this more recent example, which illustrates how rapidly natural selection can occur. Within only about 10 years, fruit flies imported to the United States from Europe had developed longer wings if they settled in the cold of British Columbia than if they settled near Los Angeles (Huey, cited in Pennisi, 2000). The same difference in wing length distinguishes northern and southern European members of this variety of fruit fly. For reasons not yet clear, longer wings, and the heavier bodies that go with them, prove adaptive in colder climates, whereas shorter wings prove adaptive in warmer weather.

Notice, then, that evolutionary theory is not just about genes. It is about the *interaction between genes and environment.* A particular genetic makeup may enhance survival in one kind of environment but prove maladaptive in another.

Which genes are advantageous, and therefore become more common in future generations, depends on what traits the environment demands.

According to evolutionary theory, then, humans, like any other species, are as they are and develop as they do partly because they have a shared species heredity that has evolved through natural selection. Perhaps the most significant legacy of biological evolution is a powerful brain that allows humans to learn from their experiences, to invent new ways of adapting to their environments, and to master a complex language so that they can teach what they know to future generations (Scarr & Kidd, 1983). This brain has enabled humans to change over the course of history through a second kind of evolution—*cultural* evolution—for example, by inventing and passing on to children ways of building shelters, classifying kin, or any of the countless practices that appear in every human society (de Waal, 1999).

Modern Evolutionary Perspectives

Darwin's evolutionary theory was very influential when the scientific study of human development began and is appreciated anew today. It has been the foundation for the work of ethologists, evolutionary psychologists, psychobiologists, and other scholars who attempt to understand relationships between biology and behavior and theorize about the significance of evolution for individual human development. Many of them are adopting the contextual/systems perspective described in Chapter 2 (Gottlieb, 2000).

Ethology is a field of study that seeks to understand the evolved behavior of various species in their natural environments (see Archer, 1992; Hinde, 1983). The closely related disciplines of **evolutionary psychology** and sociobiology test predictions about human behavior derived from evolutionary theory (D. M. Buss, 1999; E. O. Wilson, 1975). Developmental psychobiologists seek to understand how complex interactions between biological and environmental factors, which take place in the context of our evolutionary history, shape the development of the individual. Research in all these areas has made developmentalists appreciate the value of looking at human development from an evolutionary perspective and asking how what we do may have proven adaptive for our evolutionary ancestors.

Noted ethologists Konrad Lorenz and Niko Tinbergen posed many interesting questions about how many apparently innate animal behaviors might be adaptive in the sense that they contribute to species survival. Because behavior is adaptive only in relation to a particular environment, ethologists prefer naturalistic observation as a method of study. So, for example, they have recorded birdsongs in the wild, analyzed their features carefully, explored how male birds learn the songs characteristic of their species, and attempted to understand how songs aid birds in reproducing and surviving.

Ethologists suggest that humans, too, display species-specific behaviors that are the products of our evolutionary history. In Chapter 13, we will encounter an influential ethological theory that views the formation of close attachments between human infants and their caregivers as evolved behavior that increases the odds that the young will survive. Like baby birds following behind their mothers, human infants cry for, cling to, and follow after their caregivers. Other ethologists have observed that preschool children, like many other primates, form "dominance hierarchies," or pecking orders, in which each group member has a ranking. These social hierarchies serve the adaptive function of reducing aggression; they tell an individual to submit to a dominant member of the group rather than starting what is likely to be a losing battle (Strayer, 1980).

From an evolutionary perspective, the most important goal in life, whether conscious or unconscious, is to ensure that a next generation is born and survives. Aspects of family life of interest to developmentalists, such as mate selection, childbearing, and parenting behavior, contribute to this goal. Evolutionary psychologists have shown how solutions to problems faced by our ancestors thousands of years ago may have become built into our species heredity and expressed in universal patterns of behavior (Buss, 1999).

Consider the fact that mothers typically spend more time and energy than fathers raising children. In a review of re-

search on paternal investment in child rearing, David Geary (2000) notes that this is the case in more than 95% of mammals and that human fathers are actually more invested in child rearing than most mammal dads. Why aren't fathers more involved? Part of the reason is undoubtedly the biology of mammals; mothers have the capacity to nourish their offspring in the womb and then to nourish them after birth through nursing. Other factors come into play, however, in determining which of two reproductive strategies most males of a species adopt. The choices are a *parental investment strategy,* in which parents invest their energies in rearing and protecting a small number of offspring, or a *mating strategy,* in which they mate with multiple partners and invest little energy in raising the many offspring that result.

Research indicates that involvement of mammal fathers in parenting tends to be greater when the father's efforts can indeed increase the survival and welfare of his offspring, when he can be quite certain that he is the father of the children, and when his opportunities to mate with other females are limited (Geary, 2000). The promiscuous mating strategy tends to be favored, then, when offspring are likely to survive and flourish

Similarities between animals and humans make us suspect that many aspects of human development are the product of evolution.

even without the father's help, when fathers cannot be sure who fathered their mate's children, and when fathers can easily find other partners. Why do some humans rely primarily on the parental investment strategy and others on the mating strategy? It has been hypothesized that human children learn by observing their parents which reproductive strategy is most adaptive in their particular environment (Belsky, Steinberg, & Draper, 1991; Ketelaar & Ellis, 2000).

Notice, then, that evolutionary psychologists do not claim that humans are robots simply acting out instinctive behaviors dictated by their genes. Instead, they believe that humans have evolved in ways that allow them to learn which patterns of social behavior are most biologically adaptive in their culture, subculture, and particular circumstances (Archer, 1992; Belsky et al., 1991). Some of their claims are controversial and are not yet solidly supported. Yet many developmental scientists now agree that it is important to place human development in its evolutionary context and ask how common patterns of human behavior and development as well as common sex differences might have evolved.

While evolutionary biologists and psychologists are examining the evolutionary roots of human behavior, a growing number of developmental psychobiologists are studying in elaborate detail how biological influences such as genes and hormones interact with experience to guide normal development (see Gandelman, 1992; Gottlieb, Wahlsten, & Lickliter, 1998). Consider one very revealing finding about a behavior everyone assumed to be innate—the tendency of young mallard ducklings to prefer their mothers' vocal calls to those of other birds such as chickens. Gilbert Gottlieb (1991) has shown that duckling embryos that were exposed to chicken calls before hatching and then prevented from vocalizing at birth actually come to prefer the call of a chicken to that of a mallard mother! The ducklings' prenatal experiences apparently overrode their genetic predisposition. Genes do not *determine* anything, then. They are partners with the environment in directing individuals, including humans, along certain universal developmental pathways (Gandelman, 1992; Gottlieb et al., 1998). The message here is critical: *Even seemingly instinctive, inborn patterns of behavior will not emerge unless the individual has both (1) normal genes (species heredity), and (2) normal early experiences.*

So ethologists, evolutionary psychologists, and psychobiologists have much to tell us about why humans are as they are and how genes and environment contribute to normal patterns of human development. Let's now turn to the ways in which humans are *different* and to the contributions of their different genetic makeups and environments to these differences.

Individual Heredity

To understand heredity, we must start at **conception,** the moment when an egg is fertilized by a sperm. Once we have established what is inherited at conception, we can examine how genes translate into traits.

The Genetic Code

A few hours after sperm penetrates ovum, the sperm cell begins to disintegrate, releasing its genetic material. The nucleus of the ovum releases its own genetic material, and a new cell nucleus is created from the genetic material provided by mother and father. This new cell, called a **zygote** and only the size of a pinhead, is the beginning of a human being. Conception has occurred.

The genetic material contained in the new zygote is 46 threadlike bodies called **chromosomes,** which function as 23 pairs. Both members of a chromosome pair influence the same characteristics. Each chromosome is made up of thousands of *genes,* the basic units of heredity. It used to be estimated that we have about 100,000 genes, but now scientists believe we have more like 30,000 (Weiss, 2001c). Each gene is a stretch of DNA, the "double helix" molecule that provides a chemical code for development. Specifically, genes provide instructions for the production of particular amino acids, which in turn form proteins, the building blocks of all bodily tissues and of essential substances such as hormones, neurotransmitters, and enzymes. The **Human Genome Project,** a massive, government-sponsored effort to decipher the human genetic code, is greatly advancing our understanding of genetics, as the Explorations box on page 56 shows.

A sperm cell and an ovum each contribute 23 chromosomes to the zygote. Thus, of each chromosome pair—and of each pair of genes located on corresponding sites on a chromosome pair—one member came from the father and one member came from the mother. Sperm and ova each have only 23 chromosomes because they are produced through the specialized process of cell division called **meiosis.** A reproductive germ cell in the ovaries of a female or the testes of a male contains 46 chromosomes. It splits to form two 46-chromosome cells, and then these two cells split again to form four cells, each with 23 chromosomes. The end product is one egg (and three nonfunctional bodies) in a female or four sperm in a male. Each resulting sperm cell or ovum thus has only one member of each of the parent's 23 pairs of chromosomes.

The single-celled zygote formed at conception becomes a multiple-celled organism through the more usual process of cell division, **mitosis.** During mitosis, a cell (and each of its 46 chromosomes) simply divides to produce two identical cells, each containing the same 46 chromosomes. As the zygote moves through the fallopian tube toward its prenatal home in the uterus, it first divides into two cells, and the two then become four, the four become eight, and so on. Except for sperm and ova, all our cells contain copies of the 46 chromosomes provided at conception. Mitosis continues throughout life, creating new cells that enable us to grow and replacing old cells that are damaged.

GENETIC UNIQUENESS AND RELATEDNESS

To understand how we are both different from and like others genetically, consider more closely the 46 chromosomes that contain the blueprint for the development of a new individual. When a pair of parental chromosomes separates during

Reading the Human Genome

On June 26, 2000, Francis Collins, head of the Human Genome Project within the National Institutes of Health, and J. Craig Ventner, head of Celera Genomics Corporation, a private company that launched its own furious effort to unscramble the genetic code, jointly announced the completion of a draft version of the human genome. What does this achievement really mean? In a massive 10-year effort, researchers at several universities and companies in the United States and England have mapped the sequence of the chemical units or "letters" that make up the strands of DNA in human chromosomes. They still needed to do some "spell checking" when they made their announcement, but they had a pretty good "draft" of the human genome (Weiss & Gillis, 2000). The drudgery of this monstrous task was done by supercomputers and robots the size of small cars working alongside human technicians. The raw material analyzed was DNA samples from a few humans of diverse racial backgrounds.

The four basic units of the genetic code are the bases A (adenine), C (cytosine), G (guanine), and T (thymine). It is estimated that the human genome has 3.1 billion of these chemical letters. Interesting only 3–4% of the human genome—1 inch out of an estimated 6 feet of DNA—is believed to consist of genes, each of which is a specific sequence of from 1,000 to 100,000 bases (Weiss, 2000). The rest is largely "junk" DNA whose function is as yet unknown but which may play a role in protecting us from stress or in helping to turn genes on and off (Weiss, 2001c). About 999 of 1,000 bases are identical in all humans; it is the remaining 1 of 1,000 that makes us different (Fischer, 2000b).

Once a gene associated with a disease or disorder is located on a particular chromosome amid the junk DNA surrounding it, much remains to be done before any useful applications of this information are possible. Researchers will clone, or copy, the gene's DNA sequence to allow them to study it. They may first try to devise a test for the gene, next try to determine the functions of the gene's products so that they can begin to understand how the disease or disorder comes about, and only then attempt to develop a means of preventing or curing the dysfunction associated with the gene (Hawley & Mori, 1999). As James Watson, co-discoverer of the double helix structure of DNA, has put it, "We have the book, and now we've got to learn how to read it" (Weiss & Gillis, 2000, p. A12). It has been estimated that researchers currently know the functions of only about 4% of the bases, so there is much more "reading" to be done (Weiss & Gillis, 2000). However, progress will rapid now that the genome has been largely described.

It may take decades for the potential of this basic genetic research to be realized, but we seem headed for a time when DNA testing will be common. It will be used to help doctors determine how patients will respond to medications, so that medications that will not work or could have dangerous side effects can be avoided and dosages can be tailored to the individual (Fischer, 2000b). We may come to understand that what we currently know as a particular disease or psychological disorder is actually a number of distinct conditions, each with a different genetic underpinning and each requiring a different treatment. Finally, we are likely to gain the ability to correct genetic "spelling errors" associated with diseases and disorders through gene therapy, as discussed at the end of the chapter (Fischer, 2000b).

(continued)

meiosis, which of the two chromosomes will end up in a particular sperm or ovum is a matter of chance. And, because each chromosome pair separates independently of all other pairs, and since each reproductive cell contains 23 pairs of chromosomes, a single parent can produce 2^{23}—more than 8 million—different sperm or ova. Any couple could theoretically have 64 trillion babies without producing two children with identical genes!

In fact, the genetic uniqueness of children of the same parents is even greater than this because of a quirk of meiosis known as **crossing over.** When pairs of chromosomes line up before they separate, they cross each other and parts of them are exchanged, much as if you were to exchange a couple of fingers with a friend during a handshake. Crossing over increases still further the number of distinct sperm or ova that an individual can produce. In short, it is incredibly unlikely that there ever was or ever will be another human exactly like you genet-

ically. The one exception is **identical twins** (or identical triplets, and so on), which result when one fertilized ovum divides to form two or more genetically identical individuals, as happens in about 1 of every 250 births (Plomin, 1990).

How genetically alike are parent and child, or brother and sister? You and either your mother or your father have 50% of your genes in common, because you received half of your chromosomes (and genes) from each parent. But if you have followed our mathematics, you will see that siblings may have many genes in common or very few, depending on what happens during meiosis. Because siblings receive half of their genes from the same mother and half from the same father, their genetic resemblance to each other is 50%, the same genetic resemblance as that of parent and child. The critical difference is that they share half of their genes *on the average;* some siblings share more and others fewer. Indeed, we've all

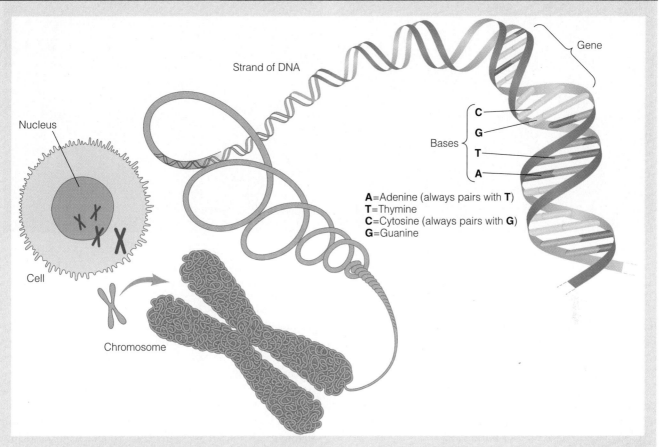

The chromosomes in each cell consist of strands of DNA made up of sequences of the bases A, T, C, and G, some of which are functional units called genes.

SOURCE: Adapted from "For DNA, a defining moment. With code revealed, challenge will be to find its meaning and use," *The Washington Post*, May 23, 2000, p. A16.

known some siblings who are almost like twins, and others who could not be more different if they tried.

Fraternal twins result when two ova are released at approximately the same time and each is fertilized by a different sperm, as happens in about 1 of every 125 births. Fraternal twins are no more alike genetically than brothers and sisters born at different times and need not even be of the same sex. Grandparent and grandchild, as well as half-brothers and half-sisters, have 25% of their genes in common on the average. Thus, everyone except an identical twin is genetically unique, but each of us also shares genes in common with kin that contribute to family resemblances.

DETERMINATION OF SEX

Of the 23 pairs of chromosomes that each individual inherits, 22 (called *autosomes*) are similar in males and females. The 23rd pair are the sex chromosomes. A male child has one long chromosome called an **X chromosome** because of its shape, and a short, stubby companion with fewer genes called a **Y chromosome.** Females have two X chromosomes. The illustration shows chromosomes that have been photographed through a powerful microscope and then arranged in pairs and rephotographed in a pattern called a **karyotype.**

Because the mother has only X chromosomes, and the father's sperm cell has either an X or a Y chromosome (depending on how the sex chromosomes sort out during meiosis), it is the father who determines a child's gender. If an ovum with its one X chromosome is fertilized by a sperm bearing a Y chromosome, the product is an XY zygote, a genetic male. A single gene on the Y chromosome then sets in motion the biological events that result in male sexual organs (Hawley & Mori, 1999). If a sperm carrying an X chromosome reaches

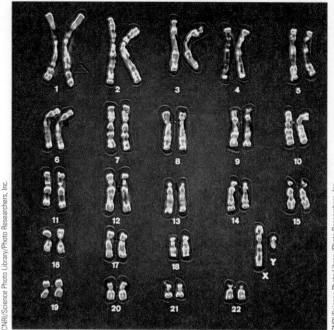
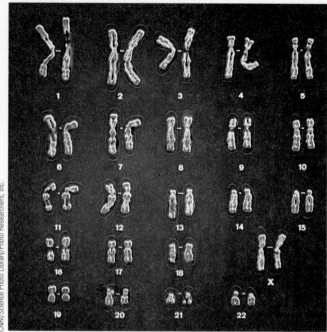

The male karyotype (left) shows the 22 pairs of autosomal chromosomes and the 2 sex chromosomes—an elongated X and a shorter Y chromosome. The photographic arrangement of a female's chromosomes (right) shows two X chromosomes.

the ovum first, the result is an XX zygote, a genetic female. Perhaps if these facts had been known in earlier eras, women would not have been criticized, tortured, divorced, and even beheaded for failing to bear male heirs.

So, a genetically unique boy or girl has roughly 30,000 genes on 46 chromosomes. How do these genes influence the individual's characteristics and development? It is still a mystery, but we now have parts of the answer.

Translation of the Genetic Code

As we have seen, genes provide instructions for development by calling for the production of chemical substances. For example, genes set in motion a process that results in the laying down of a pigment called melanin in the iris of the eye. Some people's genes call for much of this pigment, and the result is brown eyes; other people's genes call for less of it, and the result is blue eyes. Genetically coded proteins also guide the formation of cells that become neurons in the brain, influencing potential intelligence in the process.

Genes influence and in turn are influenced by the biochemical environment surrounding them during development (Aldridge, 1996; Gottlieb, 2000). For example, a particular cell can become part of an eyeball or part of a kneecap depending on what cells are next to it during embryonic development. No one, however, completely understands the remarkable process that transforms a single cell into millions of diverse cells—blood cells, nerve cells, skin cells, and so on—all organized into a living human being. Nor does anyone fully understand how genes help bring about certain developments at certain points in the life span. Some genes clearly direct the

production of proteins that are responsible for how the body's organs are constructed and how they function. Other genes apparently have the task of *regulating* the first set of genes. Current thinking is that specific gene pairs with specific messages to send are turned on or off by regulator genes at different times over the course of development (Plomin et al., 2001). Thus, regulator genes might activate genes responsible for the growth spurt we experience as adolescents and shut down the action in adulthood.

Environmental factors clearly influence how the messages specified by the genes are carried out. Consider the genes that influence height. Some people inherit genes calling for exceptional height and others inherit genes calling for a short stature. But **genotype,** the genetic makeup a person inherits, is different from **phenotype,** the actual characteristic or trait the person eventually has (for example, a height of 5 feet 8 inches). An individual whose genotype calls for exceptional height may or may not be tall. A child who is severely malnourished from the prenatal period on may have the genetic potential to be a basketball center but may well end up too short to make the team. *Environmental influences combine with genetic influences to determine how a genotype is translated into a particular phenotype—the way a person actually looks, thinks, feels, and behaves.*

Mechanisms of Inheritance

Another way to approach the riddle of how genes influence us is to consider the major mechanisms of inheritance—how parents' genes influence their children's traits. There are three main mechanisms of inheritance: single gene-pair inheritance, sex-linked inheritance, and polygenic (or multiple gene) inheritance.

SINGLE GENE-PAIR INHERITANCE

Through **single gene-pair inheritance,** some human characteristics are influenced by only one pair of genes—one from the mother, one from the father. Although he knew nothing of genes, a 19th-century monk named Gregor Mendel contributed greatly to our knowledge of single gene-pair inheritance and earned his place as the father of genetics by crossbreeding different strains of peas and carefully observing the outcomes (see Henig, 2000, for a biography). He noticed a predictable pattern to the way in which two alternative characteristics would appear in the offspring of cross-breedings—for example, smooth seeds or wrinkled seeds, green pods or yellow pods. He called some characteristics (for example, smooth seeds) *dominant* because they appeared more often in later generations than their opposite traits, which he called *recessive.*

As an illustration of the principles of Mendelian heredity, consider the remarkable fact that about three-fourths of us can curl our tongues upward into a tubelike shape, whereas one-fourth of us cannot. It happens that there is a gene associated with tongue curling, a **dominant gene.** The absence of tongue-curling ability is associated with a **recessive gene.** The person who inherits one "tongue-curl" gene ∪ and one "no-curl" gene ─

would be able to curl his or her tongue (that is, would have a tongue-curling phenotype) because the tongue-curl gene dominates or overpowers the recessive, no-curl gene. See Figure 3.1.

Let's label the dominant, tongue-curl gene ∪ and the recessive, no-curl gene ─. We can now calculate the odds that parents with different genotypes for tongue curling will have children who can or cannot curl their tongues. A father will contribute one or the other of his two genes to a sperm, and the mother will contribute one or the other of her two genes to an ovum. Each child inherits one of the mother's genes and one of the father's.

Dominant genes triumph over recessive genes. If a father with the genotype ∪∪ (a tongue-curler) and a mother with the genotype ─ ─ (lacking the ability to curl her tongue) have children, each and every child they produce will necessarily have one gene for tongue curling and one for a lack of tongue curling (genotype ∪─), and each will be a tongue curler. Because the tongue-curl gene dominates, we can say that this couple has a 100% chance of having a tongue-curling child. Notice that two different genotypes—∪∪ and ∪─—both make for the same phenotype: an acrobatic tongue.

A tongue-curling man and a tongue-curling woman can surprise everyone and have a child who lacks this amazing talent. These two parents both have the ∪─ genotype. If the father's recessive gene and the mother's recessive gene happen to

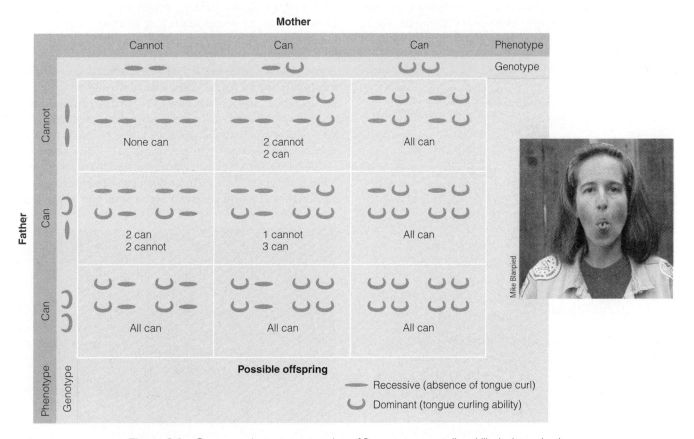

Figure 3.1 Can you curl your tongue as shown? Because tongue-curling ability is determined by a dominant gene, if you can curl your tongue, then either your mother or your father can, because one of them must have the dominant gene for tongue curling. If you cannot, one or both of them might still be able to curl their tongues. All possibilities are shown in the figure.

unite in the zygote, they will have a non-tongue-curling child (with the genotype − −). The chances are 25%—one out of four—that this couple will have such a child. Of course, the laws of conception are very much like the laws of cards. This couple could either beat the odds and have a whole family of non-tongue-curling children or have no − − children at all. Since people who cannot curl their tongues must have the − − genotype, two non-tongue-curling parents will have only non-tongue-curling (− −) children.

Table 3.1 lists a number of other examples of dominant and recessive traits associated with single gene-pair inheritance. In truth, some of the physical characteristics in this table (such as eye color and hair color and curliness) are influenced by something besides a single pair of genes. However, it turns out that many genetically linked diseases and defects are entirely due to two recessive genes, one inherited from each parent.

Consider an example of special significance to the African American community: **sickle-cell disease.** Individuals with this disease have sickle-shaped blood cells that tend to cluster together and distribute less oxygen through the circulatory system than normal cells do. Individuals with sickle-cell disease have great difficulty breathing and exerting themselves, experience very painful swelling of their joints, and often die by adolescence from heart or kidney failure. About 9% of African Americans in the United States have the genotype we'll call *Ss;* they carry one gene *(S)* that calls for round blood cells and one *(s)* that calls for sickle-shaped blood cells (Thompson, 1975).

Such people are called **carriers** because, although they do not have the disease, they can transmit the gene for it to their children. The child who inherits two recessive sickle-cell genes *(ss)* has sickle-cell disease. An *Ss* father and an *Ss* mother (two carriers) have a 25% chance of having a child with sickle-cell disease *(ss)*. For this and other genetic problems traceable to a pair of recessive genes, a couple will not be at risk for having a child with the defect unless both are carriers of the troublemaking gene.

An important feature of the sickle-cell trait is that the dominant gene associated with round blood cells shows **incomplete dominance**—that is, it does not totally mask all the effects of the recessive sickle-cell gene. Thus, carriers of the sickle-cell gene actually have many round blood cells and some sickle-shaped cells (see photo). When they are at high altitudes, are given anesthesia, or are otherwise deprived of oxygen, carriers may experience symptoms of sickle-cell disease—painful swelling of the joints and severe fatigue.

In still other cases of single gene-pair heredity, two genes influence a trait but neither dominates the other. This is called **codominance** because the phenotype of the person with two distinct genes in a pair is an exact compromise between the two genes. For example, an AB blood type is a blend of A and B blood types, and black/white interracial marriages often produce children with light-brown skin, a compromise between genes calling for heavily pigmented skin and genes calling for lightly pigmented skin. Single gene-pair inheritance is obviously a bit more complex than it looks at first glance.

SEX-LINKED INHERITANCE

Some traits are called **sex-linked characteristics** because they are influenced by single genes located on the sex chromosomes rather than on the other 22 pairs of chromosomes. Indeed, we could say "X-linked" rather than "sex-linked" because the vast majority of these attributes are associated with genes located only on X chromosomes.

Why do far more males than females display red–green color blindness? The inability to distinguish red from green is caused by a recessive gene that appears only on X chromo-

Table 3.1	**Examples of Dominant and Recessive Traits**
Dominant Traits	**Recessive Traits**
Brown eyes	Gray, green, hazel, or blue eyes
Dark hair	Blond hair
Nonred hair	Red hair
Curly hair	Straight hair
Normal vision	Nearsightedness
Farsightedness	Normal vision
Roman nose	Straight nose
Broad lips	Thin lips
Extra digits	Five digits
Double-jointedness	Normal joints
Pigmented skin	Albinism
Type A blood	Type O blood
Type B blood	Type O blood
Normal hearing	Congenital deafness
Normal blood cells	Sickle-cell disease*
Huntington's disease*	Normal physiology
Normal physiology	Cystic fibrosis*
Normal physiology	Phenylketonuria (PKU)*
Normal physiology	Tay-Sachs disease*

*This condition is discussed elsewhere in the chapter.
SOURCES: Data from Burns and Bottino (1989) and McKusick (1990)

Photo Researchers, Inc.

"Sickled" (elongated) and normal (round) blood cells from a carrier of the sickle-cell gene.

somes. Recall that Y chromosomes are shorter than X chromosomes and have fewer genes. If a boy inherits the recessive color-blindness gene on his X chromosome, there is no color-vision gene on the Y chromosome that could dominate the color-blindness gene. He will be color blind. By contrast, a girl who inherits the gene usually has a normal color-vision gene on her other X chromosome that dominates the color-blindness gene (see Figure 3.2). She would have to inherit two of the recessive color-blindness genes (one from each parent) to be color blind herself. Which parent gives a boy who is color blind his color-blindness gene? Definitely his mother, for she is the source of his X chromosome. **Hemophilia,** a deficiency in the blood's ability to clot, is also far more common among males than females because it, too, is associated with a gene on X chromosomes. Other sex-linked traits include the Duchenne type of muscular dystrophy and certain forms of deafness and night blindness.

POLYGENIC INHERITANCE

So far we have considered only the influence of single genes or gene pairs on human traits. Every week, it seems, we read in the newspaper that researchers have identified "the gene" for cancer, bedwetting, happiness, or some other phenomenon. However, most important human characteristics are influenced by *multiple* pairs of genes (interacting with the environment, of course) rather than by a single pair of genes; that is, they are **polygenic traits.** Examples of polygenic traits include height and weight, intelligence, temperament, susceptibility to cancer and depression, and many others (Plomin et al., 2001).

When a trait is influenced by multiple genes, we see many degrees of the trait depending on which combinations of genes individuals inherit. The trait (for example, intelligence) tends to be distributed in the population according to the familiar bell-shaped or normal curve. We see many people near

the mean or average of the distribution, fewer at the extremes. This is exactly the way intelligence and most other measurable human traits are distributed. At this point, we do not know exactly how many gene pairs influence intelligence or other polygenic traits. What we can say is that unknown numbers and combinations of genes, interacting with environmental forces, create a wide range of individual differences in most important human traits.

Mutations

We have now surveyed the three major mechanisms by which the genes inherited at conception influence traits: single gene-pair, sex-linked, and polygenic inheritance. Occasionally, however, a new gene appears as if out of nowhere; it is not passed on by a parent. A **mutation** is a change in the structure or arrangement of one or more genes that produces a new phenotype. Evidence from the Human Genome Project now indicates that sperm are more likely to contain mutations than ova, making fathers the major source of genetic disorders but, at the same time, the source of new genes that may have adaptive value for the species (Weiss, 2001b).

Experts believe that the recessive gene for the sex-linked disorder hemophilia was first introduced into the royal families of Europe by Queen Victoria. Since no cases of hemophilia could be found in the Queen's ancestry, the gene may have been a mutation that she passed on to her offspring (Massie & Massie, 1975). New cases of hemophilia, then, can be due either to spontaneous mutations or to sex-linked inheritance. The odds that mutations will occur are increased by environmental hazards such as radiation, toxic industrial waste, and agricultural chemicals in food (Burns & Bottino, 1989).

Some mutations have beneficial effects and become more and more common in a population through the process of natural selection. The sickle-cell gene is a good example. It probably arose originally as a mutation but became more prevalent in Africa, Central America, and other tropical areas over many generations because it protected those who had it from malaria and allowed them to live longer and produce more children than people without the protective gene. Unfortunately, the sickle-cell gene does more harm than good in environments where malaria is no longer a problem. Or consider **cystic fibrosis,** a disease that causes a buildup of sticky mucus in the lungs, makes breathing difficult, and shortens the lives of affected children. It develops when an individual inherits two recessive genes. Carriers of this gene were apparently protected from the epidemics of diarrhea that killed many Europeans in earlier centuries, which may explain why about 1 in 2,000 Caucasians develop cystic fibrosis (Hawley & Mori, 1999). Thus, mutations can be either beneficial or harmful, depending on their nature and on the environment in which their bearers live.

Chromosome Abnormalities

Genetic endowment can also influence human characteristics through **chromosome abnormalities,** in which a child

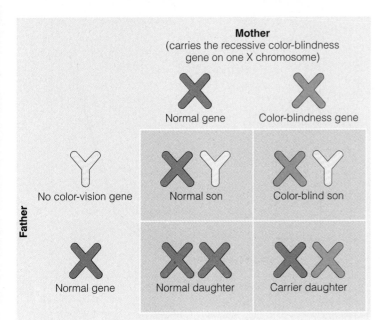

Figure 3.2 The workings of sex-linked inheritance of red–green color blindness

Children with Down syndrome can live rich lives if they receive appropriate educational opportunities and support.

receives too many or too few chromosomes (or abnormal chromosomes) at conception. Most such abnormalities are due to errors in chromosome division during meiosis. Through an accident of nature, an ovum or sperm cell may be produced with more or fewer than the usual 23 chromosomes. In most cases, a zygote with the wrong number of chromosomes is spontaneously aborted, but approximately 1 child in 200 is born with either more or, very rarely, fewer chromosomes than the normal 46 (Plomin, 1986).

One very familiar chromosome abnormality is **Down syndrome,** also known as *trisomy 21* because it is associated with three rather than two 21st chromosomes. Children with Down syndrome have distinctive eyelid folds, short stubby limbs, and thick tongues (see photo). Their levels of intellectual functioning vary widely, but they are typically mentally retarded to some degree and therefore develop and learn at a slower pace than most children.

What determines who has a Down syndrome child and who does not? Sheer chance, partly. The errors in cell division responsible for Down syndrome can occur in any mother—or father. However, the odds also increase dramatically as the age of the parent increases. The chances of having a baby with the syndrome are about 1 in 1,000 for mothers under 30 but climb to about 1 in 140 for mothers age 40 or older (see Figure 3.3). Mothers who have already borne one Down syndrome child have an even higher risk, presumably because they are more susceptible to producing defective eggs than most women are (Shafer & Kuller, 1996). A father's age also has a bearing on the odds of a Down syndrome birth, though not as much as the mother's age (Hawley & Mori, 1999).

Why is the older woman at high risk for producing a child with chromosome abnormalities? First, ova begin to form during the prenatal period and degenerate over the years (Hawley & Mori, 1999). By contrast, the process of meiosis that produces sperm does not begin until puberty and takes only about 75 days per sperm (Hawley & Mori, 1999). Second,

older women have had more opportunities to be exposed to environmental hazards that can damage ova, such as radiation, drugs, chemicals, and viruses (Strigini et al., 1990). Similarly, the risk of Down syndrome is greater if the father has been exposed to environmental hazards such as radiation that can damage his chromosomes (Strigini et al., 1990).

Most other chromosome abnormalities involve cases in which a child receives either too many or too few sex chromosomes. Like Down syndrome, these *sex chromosome abnormalities* can be attributed mainly to errors in meiosis that become increasingly likely in older parents and parents whose chromosomes have been damaged by environmental hazards. One well-known example is **Turner syndrome,** in which a female (about 1 in 3,000) is born with a single X chromosome (XO) in each of her cells. These girls remain small and often have stubby fingers and toes, a "webbed" neck, a broad chest, and underdeveloped breasts. They are unable to reproduce, typically favor traditionally feminine activities, and often have lower than average spatial and mathematical reasoning abilities (Downey et al., 1991).

Another example is **Klinefelter syndrome,** in which a male (1 in 200) is born with one or more extra X chromosomes (XXY). Klinefelter males tend to be tall and generally masculine in appearance, but they are sterile and at puberty develop feminine sex characteristics such as enlarged breasts. Most have normal general intelligence test scores, but many

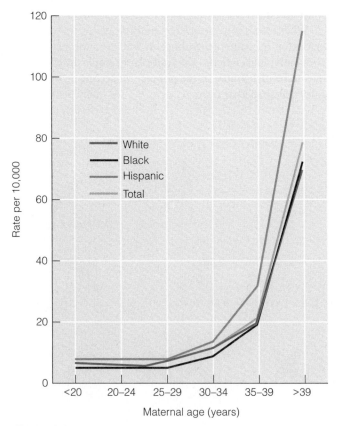

Figure 3.3 The rate of Down syndrome births increases steeply as the mother's age increases.

SOURCE: "Down Syndrome Prevalence at Birth" (1994)

are below average in language skills and school achievement (Mandoki et al., 1991).

We have now outlined the fundamentals of heredity. Each person has a unique genetic makeup, or genotype, contained in his or her 23 pairs of chromosomes. Combinations of the parents' genes are passed on at conception and influence people's traits (phenotypes) through the mechanisms of single gene-pair, sex-linked, and polygenic inheritance. A minority of individuals are also powerfully affected by genetic mutations or chromosome abnormalities.

Genetic Diagnosis and Counseling

Diagnostic testing services and counseling are available to parents who fear they may have a child with a genetic defect. To set parents-to-be at ease, let's begin by noting that about 97% of babies will *not* have genetic defects (Shiloh, 1996). However, there are a couple of thousand genetic defects associated with a single gene or gene pair, several kinds of chromosome disorders, and many polygenic susceptibilities to diseases and disorders such as schizophrenia.

Genetic counseling is a service that offers relevant information to people who suspect that they or their unborn children are at risk for some genetically based problem. Today's genetic counselors have access to more information than ever about the nature, detection, and treatment of genetic defects. It is now possible in a matter of minutes to analyze a sample of DNA obtained from inside a person's cheek for the presence of specific genes associated with diseases and disorders (Plomin, 2000). More than 800 such genetic tests—the number is growing every day—have been devised (Couzin, 1999a). To illustrate the issues in modern genetic diagnosis and counseling, we will focus on two disorders: Tay-Sachs disease and Huntington's disease.

TAY-SACHS DISEASE

Tay-Sachs disease is a condition caused by a single pair of recessive genes that causes degeneration of the nervous system and usually kills its victims in early childhood (Roche & Kuller, 1996). The problem is that a genetically caused metabolic defect results in an accumulation of fat in the child's brain. Tay-Sachs disease strikes most frequently among Jewish people of Eastern European ancestry and among French Canadians. If a Jewish couple concerned about Tay-Sachs sought the advice of a genetic counselor, he or she might obtain a complete family history from each partner—one that includes information about the diseases and causes of death of relatives, any previous problems in childbearing, and the countries of origin of relatives.

For some defects and disorders, especially those influenced by multiple gene pairs, family histories of this sort are the only basis for calculating the odds that a problem may occur. However, simple blood tests can determine whether prospective parents carry the gene for Tay-Sachs disease, as well as for sickle-cell disease, hemophilia, and countless other conditions. Suppose our couple learns from a blood test that they are both carriers of the recessive gene for Tay-Sachs disease. A genetic counselor would explain that there is a 1-in-4 chance that any

child they conceive would inherit a recessive gene from each of them and therefore have Tay-Sachs disease, and a 2-in-4 chance that any child would, like the parents themselves, be a carrier. After providing the couple with this information, the genetic counselor would inform them about prenatal screening procedures that can detect many genetic abnormalities (including Tay-Sachs disease) in the fetus. Three widely used techniques—amniocentesis, chorionic villus biopsy, and ultrasound—are described in the Explorations box on page 64.

For the parents whose tests reveal a normal fetus, the anxiety of undergoing the tests and waiting for the results gives way to relief. For those who learn that their fetus has a serious defect, the experience can be agonizing, especially if their religious or personal beliefs argue against the option of abortion. In the case of Tay-Sachs disease, a couple must choose between terminating the pregnancy and watching their baby deteriorate and die; no cure for this condition has yet been discovered.

HUNTINGTON'S DISEASE

Occasionally a genetic defect is associated with a single dominant gene. **Huntington's disease** is a famous (and terrifying) example that typically strikes in middle age and results in a steady deterioration of the nervous system. Among the effects are motor disturbances such as slurred speech, an erratic, seemingly drunken walk, grimaces, and jerky movements; personality changes such as increased moodiness and irritability; and dementia or loss of cognitive abilities (Bishop & Waldholz, 1990; Wheeler, 1999). Any child of a parent with Huntington's disease is almost sure to develop the disease if he or she receives the dominant Huntington's gene rather than its normal counterpart gene at conception; the risk is therefore 1 out of 2, or 50%. Fortunately, the gene is very rare; only about 5 people in 100,000 develop the disease (Hawley & Mori, 1999).

In 1983, James Gusella and his colleagues were able to apply a then new technique of locating specific genes on the chromosomes to trace the gene for Huntington's disease to chromosome 4. Nancy Wexler, a psychologist whose mother had developed Huntington's and who therefore stands a 50-50 chance of developing it herself, helped by assembling a team to collect blood samples from a large family in Venezuela in which Huntington's disease ran rampant (Bishop & Waldholz, 1990). Gusella and his team were then able to pinpoint how the genetic "fingerprints" of family members who had Huntington's differed from those of family members who did not.

The discovery of the location of the Huntington's gene led to the development of a test to enable the relatives of Huntington's victims to find out whether or not they had inherited the gene so that they would not have to spend a good part of their lives fearing the worst. Interestingly, it is estimated that only about 15% of people at risk for Huntington's choose to take the Huntington's test (Couzin, 1999a). However, many who do take it feel better knowing one way or the other what the future holds (Wiggins et al., 1992). Also, if one member of a couple has the gene and the couple wishes to have children, in vitro fertilization

Prenatal Detection of Abnormalities

Pregnant women today, especially those over 35 or 40, turn to a variety of medical techniques to tell them in advance whether their babies are likely to be normal. The easiest and most commonly used of these methods is **ultrasound**—the use of sound waves to scan the womb and create a visual image of the fetus on a monitor screen. Ultrasound can indicate how many fetuses are in the womb and whether they are alive, but it can detect only those genetic defects that produce visible physical abnormalities. Prospective parents often enjoy "meeting" their child and

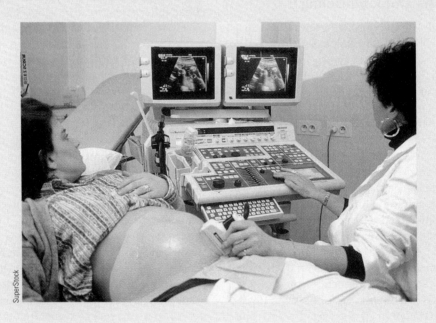

SuperStock

procedures can be used to test fertilized eggs for the presence of the gene and implant only eggs without the gene in the mother's uterus (Hawley & Mori, 1999). Unfortunately, we still do not understand exactly what the function of the Huntington's gene is and cannot prevent brain deterioration in affected individuals (Difiglia, 2000). Progress in preventing and treating genetic disorders is being made very rapidly, however, as we will see later. Meanwhile, we are ready to explore the extent to which important psychological differences among humans are influenced by their hereditary endowments and their experiences.

Studying Genetic and Environmental Influences

Behavioral genetics is the scientific study of the extent to which genetic and environmental differences among people or animals are responsible for differences in their traits

(Plomin et al., 2001). It is impossible to say that a given person's intelligence test score is the result of, say, 80%, 50%, or 20% heredity and the rest environment. The individual would have no intelligence at all without *both* a genetic makeup and experiences. It *is* possible for behavioral geneticists to estimate the **heritability** of measured intelligence (IQ) and of other traits or behaviors. Heritability has a very specific meaning: *the proportion of all the variability in the trait within a large sample of people that can be linked to genetic differences among those individuals.* To say that measured intelligence is "heritable," then, is to say that differences in tested IQ within a group of people are to some degree attributable to the fact that these individuals have different genetic endowments. It is critical to understand that estimates of heritability differ from study to study depending on who is studied and how (Maccoby, 2000).

It may seem from the name that behavioral geneticists tell us only about genetic contributions to development, but their work tells us about the relative contributions of both genetic and environmental factors to differences among people. How do they gather evidence?

can find out (when the pregnancy is far enough along) whether their child is going to be a girl or a boy. Ultrasound is now widely used even when abnormalities are not suspected. It is safer than X-rays and is generally considered very safe overall, although its possible long-term effects are still being evaluated (Hawley & Mori, 1999).

To detect chromosome abnormalities such as Down syndrome, **amniocentesis** is commonly used. A needle is inserted into the abdomen, and a sample of amniotic fluid is withdrawn. Fetal cells that have been shed can be analyzed to determine the sex of fetus, the presence of a wide range of chromosomal abnormalities, and, through DNA analysis, the presence of many genetic defects. Despite a risk of miscarriage in about 1 of 200 cases, amniocentesis is considered quite safe and is often recommended for older mothers (Hawley & Mori, 1999). Its main disadvantage used to be that it could not be performed before about the 16th week of pregnancy. However, improvements in technique such as the use of ultrasound to guide the needle have made amniocentesis safer and possible as early as the 10th to 12th week of pregnancy (Hawley & Mori, 1999). It is not very painful, although one mother described it as like "someone sticking a turkey baster through my belly button" (Hawley & Mori, 1999).

Chorionic villus sampling (CVS) involves inserting a catheter through the mother's vagina and cervix into the membrane called the chorion that surrounds the fetus, then extracting tiny hair cells from the chorion that contain genetic material from the fetus. Sample cells can then be analyzed for the same genetic defects that can be detected using amniocentesis. The difference is that chorionic villus sampling can be performed earlier, as early as the sixth week of pregnancy, allowing parents more time to consider the pros and cons of continuing the pregnancy if an abnormality is detected (Carlson, 1994; Hawley & Mori, 1999). Because use of CVS early in pregnancy can be risky, and because it does not always provide clear results, its use has declined (Hawley & Mori, 1999).

All of these prenatal diagnostic techniques should be used with caution. Yet the small risks entailed should not keep women from agreeing to ultrasound, amniocentesis, or even CVS when there is reason to suspect a problem. Most couples can look forward to immense relief when they are told that their baby is just fine. Techniques of prenatal diagnosis are also becoming safer and safer all the time. And researchers have been perfecting a technique that allows them to extract from a maternal blood sample some of the small number of fetal cells that pass into the mother's blood, avoiding risk to the fetus entirely (Beardsley, 1997).

Experimental Breeding

To study the relative influence of genes and environment on animal behavior, behavioral geneticists sometimes design breeding experiments, much like those Gregor Mendel conducted to discover the workings of heredity in plants. For example, **selective breeding** involves attempting to breed animals for a particular trait in order to determine whether it is a heritable trait. In a classic study, R. C. Tryon (1940) tested a large number of rats for the ability to run a complex maze. Rats that made few errors were labeled "maze bright"; those that made many errors were termed "maze dull." Then, across several generations, Tryon mated bright rats with bright rats and dull rats with dull rats. If differences in experience rather than differences in genetic makeup had accounted for maze performance differences in the first generation of rats studied, selective breeding would have had no impact. Instead, across generations, the differences in learning performance between the maze-bright and maze-dull groups of rats became increasingly larger. Tryon showed that maze-learning ability in rats is influenced by genetic makeup.

Selective breeding studies have also shown that genes contribute to such attributes as activity level, emotionality, aggressiveness, and sex drive in rats, mice, and chickens (Plomin et al., 2001). Because people don't take kindly to the idea of being selectively bred by experimenters, such research cannot be done with humans. Instead, research on genetic influence in humans relies on determining the extent to which people who are genetically similar are also psychologically similar.

Twin, Adoption, and Family Studies

Twins have long been recognized as very important sources of evidence about the effects of heredity. A simple type of *twin study* involves determining whether identical twins reared together are more similar to each other in traits of interest than fraternal twins reared together. If genes matter, identical twins should be more similar, for they have 100% of their genes in common, whereas fraternal twins share only 50% on the average. You might be thinking that identical twins are also treated more similarly than fraternal twins and thus share a more similar environment. This is true, and yet there is little relationship between how similarly twins are treated and how similar they turn out to be psychologically (Loehlin, 1992).

Today, most sophisticated twin studies include not only identical and fraternal twin pairs raised together but also identical and fraternal twins reared apart—four groups in all, differing in both the extent to which they share the same genes and the extent to which they share the same home environment (Bouchard & Pedersen, 1999). Identical twins separated near birth and brought up in very different environments—like the twins introduced at the beginning of the chapter—are particularly fascinating and informative in their own right, of course, because any similarities between them cannot be attributed to common family experiences.

However, the twin method is not without its critics. For example, it asks whether twins who share 100% of their genes are more similar to one another than twins who share 50% of their genes, but it does not allow us to determine whether pairs of individuals who share exactly the same environment are more similar than pairs who share 50% of their experiences in common (Turkheimer, 2000). As a result, the twin method may be more suited to identifying genetic influences on human differences than environmental ones. Also, some critics still suspect that the more similar environments of identical twins contribute to their similarities. They charge, for example, that behavior geneticists underestimate the role of prenatal influences and the possibility that identical twins are more psychologically similar than other siblings, even if they are separated after birth, because they shared the same womb (Devlin, Daniels, & Roeder, 1997).

A second commonly used method is the *adoption study*. Are children adopted early in life similar to their biological parents, whose genes they share, or are they similar to their adoptive parents, whose environment they share? If adopted children resemble their biological parents in intelligence or personality, even though those parents did not raise them, genes must be influential. If they resemble their adoptive parents, even though they are genetically unrelated to them, a good case can be made for environmental influence. Like the twin method, the adoption method is useful in estimating the relative contributions of heredity and environment to individual differences. Yet it, too, has been criticized. Researchers must be careful to correct for the tendency of adoption agencies to place children in homes similar to those they were adopted from. And because adoptive homes are generally above-average environments, adoption studies may underestimate the impact on human differences of wide variations in the environments families provide for their children (Stoolmiller, 1999).

Finally, more and more researchers are conducting complex *family studies* that include pairs of siblings who have different degrees of genetic similarity—for example, identical twins, fraternal twins, full biological siblings, half siblings, and unrelated siblings who live together in stepfamilies (Reiss et al., 2000; Segal, 2000). They are also measuring qualities of these family members' experiences to determine how similar or different the environments of siblings are. Researchers are even beginning to look at all of this longitudinally so that they can assess the extent to which both genes and environment contribute to *continuity and change* in traits as individuals develop (Reiss et al., 2000).

Estimating Influences

Behavioral geneticists rely on certain mathematical calculations to tell them whether or not a trait is genetically influenced and to estimate the degree to which heredity and environment account for individual differences in the trait. When they study traits that a person either has or does not have (for example, a smoking habit or diabetes), researchers calculate and compare **concordance rates**—the percentage of pairs of people studied (for example, pairs of identical twins or adoptive parents and children) in which, if one member of a pair displays the trait of interest, the other does too. If concordance rates are higher for more genetically related than for less genetically related pairs of people, the trait is heritable.

Suppose we are interested in whether homosexuality is genetically influenced. We might locate gay men who have twins, either identical or fraternal, locate their twin siblings, and find out whether they too are gay. In one study of this type (Bailey & Pillard, 1991), the concordance rate for identical twins was 52% (29 of the 56 co-twins of gay men were also gay), whereas the concordance rate for fraternal twins was 22% (12 of 54 co-twins were also gay). This finding and others suggest that genetic makeup contributes to both men's and women's sexual orientation, although not all studies find the concordance between identical twins to be this high (Bailey, Dunne, & Martin, 2000). But notice that identical twins are *not* perfectly concordant. Environmental factors must also affect sexual orientation. After all, Bailey and Pillard found that, in 48% of the identical twin pairs, one twin was gay but the other was not, despite their identical genes.

When a trait can be present in varying degrees, as is true of height or intelligence, *correlation coefficients* rather than concordance rates are calculated (see Chapter 1). In a behavioral genetics study of IQ scores, a correlation would indicate whether the IQ score of one twin is systematically related to the IQ score of the other, such that if one twin is bright, the other is bright, and if one is not-so-bright, the other is not-so-bright. The larger the correlation for a group of twins, the closer the resemblance between members of twin pairs.

To better appreciate the logic of behavioral genetics studies, consider what Robert Plomin and his colleagues (Plomin et al., 1988) found when they assessed aspects of personality among twins in Sweden whose ages averaged 59. One of their measures assessed an aspect of emotionality— the tendency to be angry or quick-tempered. The scale was given to many pairs of identical twins and fraternal twins, some pairs raised together, others separated near birth and raised apart. Correlations reflecting the degree of similarity between twins are presented in Table 3.2. From such data, behavioral geneticists can estimate the contributions of three factors to individual differences in emotionality: *genes, shared environmental influences,* and *nonshared environmental influences.*

1. Genes. In our example, genetic influences are clearly evident, for identical twins are consistently more similar in emotionality than fraternal twins are. The correlation of +.33 for identical twins reared apart, in and of itself, also testifies to the importance of genetic makeup. If identical twins grow up in different families, any similarity in their psychological traits must be due to their genetic similarity. These data suggest that emotionality is heritable; about a third of the variation in emotionality in this sample can be linked to variations in genetic endowment.

2. Shared environmental influences. Individuals living in the same home environment experience **shared environmental influences** that work to make them similar to one another—for example, a common parenting style or access to the same toys, peers, schools, and neighborhood. Do you see evidence of shared environmental influences in the correlations in Table 3.2? Notice that both identical and fraternal twins are slightly more similar in emotionality if they are raised together (.37 exceeds .33, .17 exceeds .09) than if they are raised apart. However, these correlations tell us that shared environmental influences are weak: Twins are almost as similar when they grew up in different homes as when they grew up in the same home.

3. Nonshared environmental influences. Experiences that are unique to the individual—that are *not* shared by other members of the family—are referred to as **nonshared environmental influences.** Whether they involve being treated differently by parents, having different friends, undergoing different life crises, or even being affected differently by the same events, they make members of the same family different

If you have brothers or sisters, do you think your parents treated you better or worse than they treated your siblings? If so, what might have been the effects of these nonshared environmental influences on your development?

from one another (Rowe, 1994). Is there evidence of nonshared environmental influence in Table 3.2? Notice that identical twins raised together are not perfectly similar, even though they share 100% of their genes *and* the same family environment; a correlation of +.37 is much lower than a perfect correlation of +1.00. The differences between identical twins raised together must be due to differences in their unique, or nonshared, experiences. Perhaps identical twins are treated differently somehow by their parents, friends, and teachers, or perhaps one twin experiences more stress than the other, and this results in differences in their degrees of emotionality. Anyone who has a brother or sister can attest to the fact that different children in the same family are not always treated identically by their parents. They do not have the same experiences outside the home either.

Consider once more the four possible correlations in Table 3.2. If *genes* were all that mattered, the correlations for identical twins would be +1.00 (regardless of whether they were raised together or apart) and the correlations for fraternal twins would be .50 (because, on average, they share 50% of their genes). If shared environmental influences were all that mattered, we would see correlations of +1.00 for both identical and fraternal twins raised together but no similarity at all (correlations of .00) between twins raised in different environments. Finally, if nonshared environmental influences, or unique experiences, were all that mattered, members of twin pairs—whether identical or fraternal, raised together or apart—would be no more alike than pairs of strangers plucked at random from a street corner. Their characteristics would depend entirely on their idiosyncratic experiences in life, and all the correlations in the table would be .00.

Table 3.2 **Correlations from a Twin Study of the Heritability of Angry Emotionality**

	Raised Together	Raised Apart
Identical twin pairs	.37	.33
Fraternal twin pairs	.17	.09

NOTE: By dissecting this table, we can assess the contributions of genes, shared environment, and nonshared environment to individual differences in angry emotionality.

Genes: Are identical twins more similar than fraternal twins? Yes, .37 is greater than .17, and .33 is greater than .09, so greater genetic similarity is associated with greater similarity in emotionality.

Shared environment: Are twins who grow up together more similar than twins raised apart? Only a small effect of shared environment is evident in this example: .37 is slightly greater than .33, and .17 is slightly greater than .09.

Nonshared environment: Are identical twins raised in the same home dissimilar, despite sharing 100% of their genes and an environment? Yes, a correlation of .37 is far less than a perfect correlation of 1.00. If identical twins raised in the same home are not identical on the trait of interest, the differences between them must be due to their unique, nonshared experiences.

SOURCE: Plomin et al. (1988)

Keep these predictions in mind as we see what researchers have discovered through twin, adoption, and family studies about the actual contributions of genes, shared environment, and nonshared environment to the many similarities and differences among human beings. Keep in mind, too, that some developmentalists, because they believe that genetic and environmental influences are completely intertwined, fault the methods used by behavioral geneticists and their whole approach of trying to separate the contributions of genes and environment (Lewontin, Rose, & Kamin, 1984; Gottlieb, 2000). We will return to these criticisms later.

Accounting for Individual Differences

Information from twin and adoption studies has dramatically changed and challenged the way we think about human development, as we will see throughout this book. Our examples here are drawn from behavioral genetics studies of intellectual abilities, temperament and personality, and psychological disorders (see Plomin et al., 2001; Rose, 1995; Rowe, 1994, for reviews).

Intellectual Abilities

How do genes and environment contribute to differences in intellectual functioning, and how do their relative contributions change over the life span? Consider the average correlations among the IQ scores of different types of relatives presented in Table 3.3. These averages are from a review by Thomas Bouchard and Matthew McGue (1981) of studies involving 526 correlations based on 113,942 pairs of children, adolescents, and adults. Clearly, these correlations rise when people are closely related genetically and are highest when they are identical twins. Overall, the heritability of IQ scores is about .50, meaning that genetic differences account for about 50% of the variation in IQ scores and environmental differences account for the other half of the variation in the samples studied (Plomin, 1990).

Can you also detect the workings of environment? Notice that (1) pairs of family members reared together are somewhat more similar in IQ than pairs reared apart; (2) fraternal twins, who should have especially similar family experiences because they grow up at the same time, are often more alike than siblings born at different times; and (3) the IQs of adopted children are related to those of their adoptive parents. All of these findings suggest that *shared environmental influences* tend to make individuals who live together more alike than if they lived separately. Notice too, though, that genetically identical twins reared together are not perfectly similar. This is evidence that their unique or *nonshared* experiences have made them different from each other.

Do the contributions of genes and environment to differences in intellectual ability change over the life span? You

might think that genetic influences would decrease as we accumulate experience, but genetic endowment actually appears to *gain* importance from infancy to adulthood as a source of individual differences in intellectual performance (McCartney, Harris, & Bernieri, 1990; McGue et al., 1993). Consider a longitudinal study of the intellectual development of identical and fraternal twins from infancy to adolescence conducted by Ronald Wilson (1978, 1983). Identical twins scored no more similarly than fraternal twins on a measure of infant mental development during the first year of life; thus, evidence of heritability was lacking in infancy. Generally, neither differences in genetic makeup nor differences in experience account very well for behavioral and psychological differences among infants, perhaps because powerful maturational forces keep redirecting infants back to the same species-wide developmental pathway (McCall, 1981).

However, in Wilson's study, the influence of individual heredity began to show itself at about 18 months of age. Now the correlation of the mental development scores of siblings was higher for identical twins than for fraternal twins. Identical twins even experienced more similar spurts in intellectual development than fraternal twins. The identical twins in this study stayed highly similar throughout childhood and into adolescence. The correlation between their IQ scores averaged about .85. Meanwhile, fraternal twins were most similar in IQ at about age 3 and became less similar over the years. By age 15, the correlation between their IQ scores had dropped to .54. As a result, the heritability of IQ scores in this sample increased from the infant years to adolescence.

A similar message comes from adoption studies. Genetically unrelated children of the same age who live in the same family, although not as similar in IQ as genetically related children, have similar IQs; the correlation between their scores in one recent study was .26 (Segal, 2000). Moreover, the intel-

Table 3.3 Average Correlations between the Intelligence Scores of Different Pairs of Individuals

	Raised Together	Raised Apart
Identical twins	.86	.72
Fraternal twins	.60	.52
Biological siblings	.47	.24
Biological parent and child	.42	.22
Half siblings	.31	—
Adopted siblings	.34	—
Adoptive parent and adopted child	.19	—
Unrelated siblings (same age, same home)	.26	—

SOURCES: All but two of these averages were calculated by Bouchard and McGue (1981) from studies of both children and adults. The correlation for fraternal twins reared apart is based on data reported by Pedersen, McClearn, Plomin, and Friberg (1985), that for unrelated children in the same home on data reported by Segal (2000).

lectual performance of adopted children is correlated with that of their biological parents *and* their adoptive parents, suggesting effects of both genetic makeup and shared family environment. By adolescence, however, the resemblance to biological parents is still evident, while adopted children's scores no longer correlate with those of their adoptive parents (Scarr & Weinberg, 1978).

Overall, most studies indicate that the heritability of intelligence test performance increases with age, as does the importance of nonshared environmental influences, but that shared environmental influences become less significant with age (Patrick, 2000; Plomin et al., 2001). Why might this be? Siblings may well be exposed to similar (shared) learning experiences when they are young, but as they get older, partly because of their different genetic makeups, they may seek out and have different (nonshared) life experiences. They may elicit different reactions from their parents, join different peer groups, encounter different teachers, and so on (Dunn & Plomin, 1990). Identical twins continue to perform more similarly on IQ tests than fraternal twins do in adulthood. Although some studies suggest that heritability decreases somewhat in old age, genetic influences on individual differences in intellectual performance are clearly evident in later life (Finkel et al., 1998; Plomin et al., 1994).

Overall, Matt McGue and his colleagues (1993) conclude the following:

1. The estimated heritability of IQ scores increases from 40–50% in childhood to 80% in adulthood, after children have left home and shared environmental influences are therefore not as strong.
2. Variation due to shared environment decreases from 30% in childhood to near zero in adulthood because family members have fewer experiences in common.
3. The most important environmental influences in the long run appear to be *nonshared* ones that make the IQ scores of brothers and sisters in the same family different from one another.

Some people interpret evidence of the heritability of IQ scores as proof that we cannot improve people's intellectual development by enriching their environment. That's just not true! Yes, the IQs of adopted children are ultimately correlated more strongly with the IQs of their biological parents than with the IQs of their adoptive parents. However, the *level* of intellectual performance that adopted children reach can increase dramatically (by 20 points on an IQ test) if they are adopted into more intellectually stimulating homes than those provided by their biological parents (Scarr & Weinberg, 1983). Similarly, comprehensive early intervention programs for children from disadvantaged homes can significantly raise their IQ scores (Campbell et al., 2001). Most likely, then, stimulating environments help children realize more fully the genetically based potentials each of them has. It is critical for parents, teachers, and others concerned with optimizing development to understand that qualities that are genetically influenced can still be altered.

Temperament and Personality

As parents well know, different babies have different personalities. In trying to describe infant personality, researchers have focused on aspects of **temperament**—a set of tendencies to respond in predictable ways, such as sociability, activity level, and emotional reactivity, that serve as the building blocks of later personality (see Chapter 11 for a fuller discussion of temperament.) Behavior genetics research indicates that genes do indeed contribute to individual differences in temperament in infancy and beyond (Plomin et al., 2001; Rowe, 1994).

For example, Arnold Buss and Robert Plomin (1984) reported average correlations of around .50 to .60 between the temperament scores of identical twins. The corresponding correlations for fraternal twins were not much greater than zero. Think about that: A zero correlation is what you would expect if they were strangers living in different homes rather than fraternal twins who, on average, share half their genes, the same home, and often the same bedroom! It does not seem to matter whether we look at fraternal twin pairs or ordinary siblings or unrelated children adopted into the same family; *living in the same home does not make children more similar in personality* (Dunn & Plomin, 1990).

Similar conclusions have been reached about the contributions of genes and environment to adult personality (see Loehlin et al., 1998, and Chapter 11). Overall, it has been estimated that, of all the differences among adults on major dimensions of personality, about 40% of the variation may be due to genetic differences (Loehlin, 1985). Only 5% of the variation reflects the effects of shared family environment. Indeed, identical twins are about as similar in personality when they are raised apart as when they grow up in the same home (Bouchard et al., 1990). The remaining 55% of the variability in adult personalities is due to nonshared environmental influences.

Herein lies a very significant message: The family environment is important in personality development, but not because it has a standard effect on all family members that makes them alike. True, there are some areas of socialization in which parents treat all their children similarly and contribute to similarities among them. For example, parents may influence their children to adopt attitudes and interests similar to their own, at least while they are living at home, although genes appear to play a larger role and shared environment a smaller role once children grow up and leave home (Eaves et al., 1997; Plomin et al., 2001). Shared environment also helps to make adolescent siblings similar in the extent to which they smoke, drink, and commit delinquent acts (McGue, Sharma, & Benson, 1996; Rowe, 1994). Indeed, siblings are often partners in crime!

Yet behavior geneticists have discovered that the family environment often plays a more important role in creating differences among family members than in creating similarities (Reiss et al., 2000; Rowe, 1994). When it comes to many personality traits, nonshared environmental influences interacting with genetic influences seem to be most significant. Even a shared family event—for example, a divorce—is likely

The temperament of infants is genetically influenced.

to have different effects on different members of the family (Rowe & Jacobson, 1999). One child may become more shy and inhibited; another may become an outgoing party animal.

Researchers who used to assume that parents molded all their children's personalities in similar directions are now trying to figure out why siblings have such very different personalities, despite sharing 50% their genes on average and growing up in the same home. It is increasingly clear that siblings are treated differently by their parents, experience their relationships with one another differently, and often have very different experiences with peers, teachers, and other people outside the home as well (Dunn & Plomin, 1990; Manke et al., 1995; Reiss et al., 2000). But can we show that differences in experience are responsible for differences in personality? In one study, whichever twin reported greater maternal strictness was likely to be more depressed than his or her co-twin (Baker & Daniels, 1990) Correlational studies of this sort have not revealed many solid and consistent links between differences in experiences and differences in personality, however. Moreover, it is not yet clear whether the relationships that have been found demonstrate that nonshared experiences shape personality or that personality influences the experiences one has (Turkheimer & Waldron, 2000). It probably works both ways, as suggested by the concept of *reciprocal determinism.*

Still, these and other studies suggest the value of studying multiple children in the same families and looking more closely at nonshared environmental influences and their implications for development. This is a tremendously important insight. As Judith Harris (1998) has argued in her controversial but influential book, *The Nurture Assumption,* developmentalists have assumed for too long that parents treat all their children much the same, steer them along similar developmental paths, and are hugely influential. That is, develop-

mentalists have believed strongly that shared environmental influences within the family matter most in the developmental process. Increasingly, it seems more useful to ask how genetic differences and differences in experiences, both inside and outside the home, might explain differences in the development of brothers and sisters.

Psychological Disorders

As we will see throughout this book, both genes and environment contribute to psychological disorders across the life span—to alcohol and drug abuse, depression, attention deficit hyperactivity disorder, eating disorders, criminal behavior, and every other psychological disorder that has been studied (Plomin et al., 2001; State et al., 2000). Consider just one example. **Schizophrenia** is a serious mental illness that involves disturbances in logical thinking, emotional expression, and social behavior and that typically emerges in late adolescence or early adulthood. In the 1950s and 1960s, experts were convinced that it was caused by mothers who were cold and inconsistent in their parenting style (Rowe & Jacobson, 1999). Now we know that genes contribute substantially to this disorder. The average concordance rate for schizophrenia among identical twins is 48%; that is, if one twin has the disorder, in 48% of the pairs studied, the other does too (Gottesman, 1991). By comparison, the concordance rate for fraternal twins is only 17%. In addition, children who have at least one biological parent who is schizophrenic have an increased risk of schizophrenia *even if they are adopted away early in life* (Heston, 1970). The increased risk these children face has more to do with their genes than with being brought up by a schizophrenic adult.

It is easy to conclude, mistakenly, that any child of a schizophrenic is doomed to become a schizophrenic. But here are the facts: Whereas about 1% of people in the general population develop schizophrenia, about 13% of children who have a schizophrenic parent become schizophrenic (Gottesman, 1991). Although this figure does indicate that children of schizophrenics are at greater risk for schizophrenia than other children, 86–90% of the children of one schizophrenic parent do *not* develop the disorder. Even if you are the child of two schizophrenics or an identical twin whose co-twin develops the disorder, the odds are only about one in two that you too will become schizophrenic.

Clearly, then, environmental factors also contribute significantly to this mental illness. People do not inherit psychological disorders; they inherit *predispositions* to develop disorders. Assuming that a person has inherited a genetic susceptibility to schizophrenia, it may take one or more stressful experiences to trigger the illness. Prenatal exposure to infectious diseases is one suspected contributor. Rates of schizophrenia are higher for individuals born during the winter flu season and in crowded urban areas, where illnesses spread easily from person to person, than among people born at other times of the year and in rural areas (Mortensen et al., 1999). Also, identical twins who share the same placenta and therefore exchange blood (and possibly viruses) are more concordant for schizophrenia than are identical twins who have their own separate placentas and blood supplies (Davis, Phelps, & Bracha, 1999). Much evidence also tells us that children who are at genetic risk for psychological disorders such as schizophrenia, because a biological parent has the disorder, are at risk of having the disorder if they are brought up by harsh and unsupportive parents but often turn out perfectly normal if they are raised in a good home environment (Maccoby, 2000).

In short, we now know that children may inherit predispositions to develop a number of problems and disorders and that their experiences interact with their genetic makeup to determine how well adjusted they turn out to be. One implication is clear: It is overly simple and often wrong to assume that any behavior problem a child displays must be the result of bad parenting.

The Heritability of Different Traits

You may have the impression by now that individual differences in all human traits are significantly influenced by genes. Although there is truth to this, some traits are more heritable than others. Figure 3.4 presents some of the correlations obtained in the Minnesota Twin Study between the traits of identical twins raised apart and reunited later in life, and it makes our point.

Observable physical characteristics, from eye color to height, are very strongly associated with individual genetic

endowment. Even weight is heritable; adopted children resemble their biological parents but not their adoptive parents in weight (Grilo & Pogue-Geile, 1991). Certain aspects of physiology, such as measured brain activity and reactions to alcohol, are highly heritable, too (Lykken, Tellegen, & Iacono, 1982; Neale & Martin, 1989). In addition, about half of the variation among people in susceptibility to diseases and death appears to be tied to genetic differences (Yashin, Iachine, & Harris, 1999; and see Chapter 17). If physical and physiological characteristics are strongly heritable, general intelligence is moderately heritable. Somewhat less influenced by genes are aspects of temperament and personality and susceptibility to many psychological disorders. Finally, genetic endowment only modestly influences attitudes and interests (Rowe, 1994).

Now and then, researchers discover that genes are largely irrelevant and that environment is the critical factor in influencing a trait. For example, in an interesting study of maternal behavior and stress responses in rats, baby rats were raised by their own mothers or by adopted mothers (Francis et al., 1999). The mothers were either relaxed, stress-resistant rats who licked their pups frequently or reserved, fearful mothers who groomed their offspring less frequently. Whether the pups could withstand stressful experiences and whether they were nurturing toward their own offspring later in life were not affected by whether the pups were born to relaxed or reserved biological mothers. Instead, stress resistance and competent mothering were associated with being raised by an outgoing, relaxed mother.

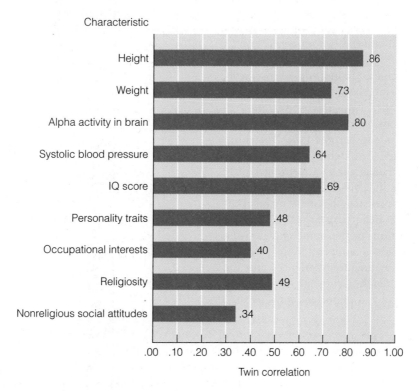

Figure 3.4 Correlations between the traits of identical twins raised apart in the Minnesota Twin Study

SOURCE: Bouchard et al. (1990)

In the human instance, performance on tests of creativity provides a good example of a trait that does not seem to be very influenced by genes. Identical twins are not much more alike than fraternal twins, suggesting that genes do not matter much. However, twins of both sorts are similar to one another, suggesting that the shared environment is somehow important in nurturing creativity (Plomin et al., 2001; Reznikoff et al., 1973).

In sum, heredity influences physical traits more than psychological ones, and a few traits such as creativity very little. However, a broad range of psychological traits are heritable to some extent, with genes accounting for up to half of the variation in a group and environmental factors accounting for the other half or more of the variation (Plomin et al., 2001; Wachs, 2000).

Heredity and Environment Conspiring

What should we conclude overall about the influences of genes and environment and about the ways in which these two great forces in development conspire to make us what we are? Genes do not just orchestrate our growth before birth and then leave us alone. Instead, they are "turning on" and "turning off" in patterned ways throughout the life span, helping to shape the attributes and behavior patterns that we carry with us through our lives. A shared species heredity makes us similar in the ways we develop and age. Unique individual genetic makeups cause us to develop and age in our own ways. No less important are environmental influences, from conception to death.

From infancy through childhood and adolescence, children's unique genetic blueprints show themselves more and more in their behavior. Identical twins start similar and remain similar, but fraternal twins, like brothers and sisters generally, go their own ways and become more and more dissimilar. Shared environmental influences—the forces that make children in the same family alike—are stronger early in life than they are later in life. Nonshared environmental influences—those unique experiences that make members of the family different—remain important throughout the life span. In short, as we move out of the home and into the larger world, we seem to become, more and more, products of our unique genes and our unique experiences. But the two do not operate independently. Genes and environment are interrelated in interesting and important ways, as we'll now see.

Gene/Environment Interactions

As we have seen throughout this chapter, behavioral geneticists try to establish how much of the variation we observe in human traits such as intelligence can be attributed to individual differences in genetic makeup and how much can be attributed to individual differences in experience. Useful as that research is, it does not take us very far in understanding the complex interplay between genes and environment over the life span (Turkheimer, 2000). As Ann Anastasi (1958) asserted many years ago, instead of asking *how much* is due to genes and how much is due to environment, we should be asking *how* heredity and environment work together to make us what we are.

It is clear that genes do not determine anything; instead, they provide us with potentials that are realized or not depending on the quality of our experiences. Figure 3.5 illustrates this view. We see evidence that genetic endowment matters: Children with high genetic potential to be intelligent will generally outperform children with below-average potential on IQ tests. It is equally clear that environment matters: Regardless of their genetic potential, children generally obtain higher IQ scores if they are brought up in enriched, intellectually stimulating environments than if they are raised in restricted, intellectually impoverished ones.

The most important message in the figure, however, is embodied in the concept of **gene/environment interaction:** How our genotypes are expressed depends on what kind of environment we experience, and how we respond to the environment depends on what kind of genes we have. In Figure 3.5, we see that growing up in a deprived environment can make children with the genetic potential to be geniuses perform as poorly as children with far less genetic potential, but that this high-potential genotype will be expressed as highly intelligent behavior if children are brought up in stimulating environments. We also see that children with high genetic potential benefit more from a stimulating environment than other children do.

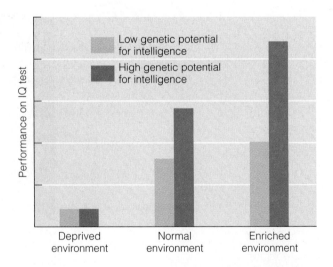

Figure 3.5 Genes may provide certain potentials, but whether these potentials are realized or not depends on the quality of the environment.

Gene/Environment Correlations

Appreciating that genes and environment interact is a good start, but heredity and environment are even more intimately intertwined than the concept of gene/environment interaction implies. Each person's genetic makeup influences the kinds of experiences that he or she seeks out and actually has, and these experiences then strengthen or weaken genetically based tendencies.

Sandra Scarr and Kathleen McCartney (1983), drawing on the theorizing of Plomin, DeFries, and Loehlin (1977), have proposed three kinds of **gene/environment correlations,** or ways in which one's genes and one's environment are systematically interrelated: passive, evocative, and active. The concept of gene/environment *interactions* tells us that people with different genes react differently to the environments they encounter. By contrast, the concept of gene/environment *correlations* says that people with different genes encounter different environments (Loehlin, 1992). As an illustration, let's imagine one child with a genetic potential to be highly sociable and a second child whose genes make for shyness.

PASSIVE GENE/ENVIRONMENT CORRELATIONS

The kind of home environment that parents provide for their children is influenced in part by the parents' own genotypes. Since parents provide children not only with a home environment but with their genes, it turns out that the rearing environments to which children are exposed are correlated with (and are likely to suit) their genotypes.

If the son of a basketball player turns out to be a good basketball player, is it due to genetic endowment or experience? We can't say because genes and environment are correlated. Through passive gene–environment correlation, the children of athletes not only inherit their parents' genes for athleticism but grow up in sports-oriented family environments.

For instance, sociable parents not only transmit their "sociable" genes to their children but also, because they have "sociable" genes, create a very social home environment, inviting their friends over frequently, taking their children to many social events, and so on. These children inherit genes for sociability, but they also experience an environment that matches their genes and that may make them even more sociable than they would otherwise be. By contrast, the child with shy parents is likely to receive genes for shyness *and* a correlated environment—one without much social stimulation.

EVOCATIVE GENE/ENVIRONMENT CORRELATIONS

A child's genotype also evokes certain kinds of reactions from other people. The smiley, sociable baby is likely to get more smiles and social stimulation than the withdrawn, shy baby does. Similarly, the sociable child may be sought out more often as a playmate by other children, the sociable adolescent may be invited to more parties, and the sociable adult may be given more job assignments involving public relations. In short, genetic makeup may affect the reactions of other people to a child and, hence, the kind of social environment that the child will experience.

ACTIVE GENE/ENVIRONMENT CORRELATIONS

Finally, a child's genotype influences the kinds of environments he or she actively *seeks*. The individual with a genetic predisposition to be extraverted is likely to seek out parties, invite friends to the house, join organizations, and otherwise build a "niche" that is highly socially stimulating. The child with genes for shyness may actively avoid large group activities and instead develop solitary interests.

Scarr and McCartney suggest that the balance of passive, evocative, and active genotype/environment correlations shifts during development. Because infants are at home a good deal, their environment is largely influenced by their parents through passive genetic influences. Evocative influences continue to operate in much the same way throughout life; our characteristic traits consistently prompt characteristic reactions in other people. As children develop, however, they become increasingly able to build their own niches, so active gene influences become more important. Scarr and McCartney believe that this is one reason why fraternal twins, siblings, and adopted children in the same family become less alike as they get older. They share an early home environment, but because they are genetically different, they increasingly build different niches (nonshared environments) as they get older and more independent. Identical twins, by contrast, may stay alike, even when separated, because their similar genes make them continue to seek out similar experiences.

GENETIC INFLUENCE ON THE ENVIRONMENT

Is there any evidence supporting Scarr and McCartney's contention that one's genes are correlated with, and possibly influence, one's experiences in life? Yes, there is. Behavioral geneticists are discovering that measures of environment are themselves heritable! What this means is that identical twins are more similar than fraternal twins, and biological siblings are more similar than adoptive siblings, in the environments they experience and in their perceptions of these environments. For example, genes influence sibling similarity in

- Both objective and perceived aspects of parenting style, such as warmth and the quality of the parent–child relationship (Plomin & Bergeman, 1991; Reiss et al., 2000)
- Time spent watching television (Plomin et al., 1990)
- Number of stressful life events experienced (Kendler et al., 1993)

- Responses to surveys asking them how their experiences differ—that is, surveys supposedly assessing nonshared environmental influences (Pike et al., 2000)

If our genetically influenced personality traits affect how others treat us and what experiences we seek and have, these findings make perfect sense. However, such findings also challenge some of our most fundamental assumptions about human development. After all, what they really say is that what we regard as purely "environmental" influences on development actually reflect, in part, the workings of heredity (Reiss et al., 2000; Rowe, 1994). Robert Plomin (1990) offers

Prevention and Treatment of Genetic Conditions

Ultimately, genetic researchers want to understand how genes associated with diseases and disorders work their damage and how their effects can be prevented, cured, or at least minimized. One of the greatest success stories in genetic research involves **phenylketonuria,** or **PKU,** a disorder caused by a pair of recessive genes. Affected children lack a critical enzyme needed to metabolize phenylalanine, a component of many foods (including milk). As phenylalanine accumulates in the body, it is converted to a harmful acid that attacks the nervous system and causes children to be mentally retarded and hyperactive.

PKU was discovered in 1934 by a Norwegian doctor, Asbjorn Folling, who was approached by a mother of two children with mental retardation who suspected that the strange smell of her children's urine might be a clue to their condition (Centerwall & Centerwall, 2000). In the mid-1950s, scientists developed a special diet low in phenylalanine, and in 1961, they developed a simple blood test that could detect PKU soon after birth, before any damage had been done. Today, newborn infants are routinely screened for PKU, and affected children are immediately placed on the special (and, unfortunately, quite distasteful) diet, which must be followed very strictly throughout childhood (Miller, 1995). Here, then, genetic research led to the prevention of one of the many causes of mental retardation. And here we also have a wonderful example of the interaction between genes and environment: A child will develop the condition and become mentally retarded only if he or she inherits the PKU genes *and* eats a normal (rather than special) diet.

Gene Therapy
Aided by information generated by the Human Genome Project, researchers are now actively experimenting with new forms of **gene therapy**—interventions that involve substituting normal genes for the genes associated with a disease or disorder, or otherwise altering a person's genetic

makeup. In some experiments, viruses are used to carry normal replacement genes into an individual's cells (Aldridge, 1996; Hawley & Mori, 1999). In mice and other animals, it is possible to inject cells that have been engineered to contain a particular gene into embryos so that the cells multiply as the embryo develops (Hawley & Mori, 1999). In one such experiment, a strain of mice called Doogie (after the gifted young doctor on the television series *Doogie Howser, M.D.*) was created in this manner (Tang et al., 1999). An extra copy of a gene that produces a protein that stimulates the production of connections among neurons during learning was inserted into mouse embryo cells (Tang et al., 1999). The resulting "Doogie" mice ended up with more of this protein, and they performed much better than control mice on a battery of learning tasks.

There are, of course, more genes than one involved in learning and memory. However, might the discovery of "Doogie" genes in humans someday lead to the use of gene therapy to improve cognitive functioning in humans? If so, would it be used to help mentally retarded children and elderly adults with Alzheimer's disease, or would it be used by wealthy parents to boost their children's IQ scores? So far, gene therapy experiments with humans have generally failed due to a host of problems (Hawley & Mori, 1999). The death of Jesse Gelsinger, a young man from Arizona who was the first person to die in a gene therapy trial, is illustrative. His immune system attacked the viruses that were to carry normal genes into his malfunctioning liver and destroyed not only the virus but his own organs (Fischer, 2000a). This 1999 tragedy resulted in stricter controls on gene therapy research.

Although effective gene therapies undoubtedly *will* be developed, it is simpleminded to think that gene therapies will prevent or cure most diseases and disorders when we know that most conditions are the product of genes and environment interacting. Preventing or curing polygenic dis-a good example: Suppose we find that parents who read to their children have brighter children than parents who do not read to their children. In the not-so-distant past, most developmentalists would have interpreted this finding rather uncritically as evidence that parents make important contributions to their children's intellectual development. Without denying the importance of parents, suppose we offer this alternative interpretation: Parents and children whose genes predispose them to be highly intelligent are more likely to seek out opportunities to read than parents and children who are less intellectually inclined. If this is the case, can we be so sure that reading to children *causes* them to be brighter? Would we be able to show that reading to children is benefi-

cial even when the parents and children involved are genetically unrelated?

One more example: If we observe that aggressive children tend to have parents who are negative and hostile toward them, can we be sure that these children's aggression is due to the experiences they have had growing up with negative parents? Isn't it possible that they inherited genes from their irritable and aggressive parents that predisposed them to be irritable and aggressive themselves? Might they have had a good chance of becoming aggressive even if they had been adopted early in life by warm and supportive parents? In one study (O'Connor et al., 1998), it turned out that adopted children whose biological parents were antisocial were treated more

orders such as schizophrenia will be especially hard, as it will require a better understanding how multiple genes *and* multiple environmental risk factors contribute to the disorder. No "quick fix" like the PKU diet will be possible. In the meantime, many potentially devastating effects of genetic and chromosomal abnormalities can at least be minimized or controlled, if not cured. For example, children with Turner syndrome or Klinefelter syndrome can be given sex hormones to make their appearance more gender-typical, and individuals with sickle-cell disease can be given transfusions of blood containing the normal red blood cells they lack.

Cloning

Someday, genetic research may be applied to allow a man or woman who cannot have a child to have one who has his or her own genetic endowment—or to create particularly healthy, intelligent, and well-adjusted members of the species. **Cloning** is the process of converting a single cell from one animal into a new animal that is a genetic duplicate of the first. In 1997, Keith Campbell, a Scottish cell biologist, reported that he had cloned a sheep named Dolly (Begley, 1997). A mammary cell from one ewe was inserted into another ewe's ovum (from which the nucleus had been removed), divided through mitosis, was implanted in a surrogate mother ewe, and ultimately became Dolly. Cloning has now succeeded with other species, including cows, which may be cloned in Japan to yield the perfect beefsteak (Normile, 1998). And on November 25, 2001, it was announced that the first cloned human embryos had been produced, though they grew no larger than six cells (Weiss, 2001b).

It's not yet clear whether clones will develop normally throughout their lives, however. Dolly, the cloned lamb, showed signs of premature cell aging. Cloned cows appear to develop health problems as they get older, possibly be-

cause they do not have the diversity of genes that comes from having a mother and a father rather than a mother only, or possibly because embryos are damaged somehow during the cloning process (Couzin, 1999b). More warnings come from research with mice. Although clones created from embryonic stem cells—the as-yet undifferentiated cells that are much in the news because of controversy over their use in medical research—have identical genes, they differ widely with respect to which of these genes are turned on and which are turned off (Humpherys et al., 2001; Weiss, 2001a). This suggests that clones of the same cell could develop in very different, and not all positive, directions—bad news for those who hope that specialized cloned cells developed from embryonic stem cells can be used to treat various diseases.

Despite unanswered questions about animal cloning and ethical concerns, human cloning will probably be pursued. Do you think a cloned human would really be identical in all ways to the person from whom he or she was cloned? If you have internalized the message of Chapter 3, your answer should be, "No, because nature and nurture interact to make us what we are." Even though clones and their "parents" have identical genes, we now know that these genes may not show identical patterns of activity. Moreover, clones would be highly unlikely to have identical experiences throughout their lives. As a result, they would differ in many ways, just as identical twins do—a point that many people do not appreciate about cloning.

Nonetheless, the prospect of human cloning horrifies many people: Will women be able to bear children without benefit of men—or even without benefit of sperm banks? Will Hitlers produce little Hitlers to carry on their evil work, as in the film *The Boys from Brazil?* The pace of breakthroughs in genetic research will only increase, and we as a society must grapple with the issues these advances raise.

negatively by their adoptive parents than children whose biological parents were not antisocial—a good example of evocative gene/environment correlation and the influence of children on their parents. This gene/environment correlation was partly the product of genetic influence, but it was also the product of environmental influence, for negative behavior on the part of adoptive parents, once evoked by the child, made its own contributions to children's antisocial behavior problems, beyond the effects of the child's genes.

Perhaps the most convincing evidence of the importance of gene/environment correlations comes from an ambitious study by David Reiss, Jenae Neiderhiser, E. Mavis Hetherington, and Robert Plomin, summarized in their book, *The Relationship Code* (2000). The sample for this study consisted of 720 pairs of same-sex adolescents who differed in their degree of biological relationship from identical twins to biological siblings to unrelated step-siblings. The researchers measured environmental factors such as parent–child and sibling interaction as well as adolescent adjustment variables such as self-esteem, sociability, depression, and antisocial behavior.

The main message of this major study is that family processes are important, but not for the reasons developmentalists have traditionally assumed. Family processes, Reiss and his colleagues argue, may be important mainly as a mechanism through which the genetic code is expressed. Repeatedly, the study revealed that genes shared by parents and children partly or even largely accounted for relationships between children's experiences and their developmental outcomes—for example, between negative parenting tactics and antisocial behavior by adolescents. In 44 of 52 instances in which significant relationships between measures of the family environment and adolescent adjustment were detected, genes influenced *both* family environment and adolescent adjustment and accounted for most of the relationship between the two (Reiss & Neiderhiser, 2000).

This research suggests that genes and environment conspire to shape development. Genes influence how parents, peers, and others treat children. These environmental influences—usually nonshared ones that differ from sibling to sibling—then influence the individual's development, often working to reinforce genetically based predispositions (Lytton, 2000; Reiss et al., 2000; Wachs, 2000). Behavioral geneticists, who often emphasize the importance of genes, and socialization researchers, who stress the role of experiences in development, are both right, then. The practical implication is that caregivers who are sensitive to a child's genetically based predispositions will be in a good position to strengthen the child's adaptive tendencies and suppress or work around the maladaptive ones.

In sum, both genes and environment are at work over the entire life span, although the relative contributions of these two forces change with age from infancy to adolescence. But we are missing the full story unless we appreciate both gene/environment interactions and gene/environment correlations. Genes help determine not only how we respond to experiences (through gene/environment interactions), but also what experiences we have (through gene/environment correlations). Now you can understand why today's developmentalists regard it as foolish to ask whether nature *or* nurture is

responsible for human development. We are shaped by an incredibly complex interplay of genetic and environmental influences from conception to death.

Controversies Surrounding Genetic Research

It is clear that society as a whole will have to grapple with the complex and troubling ethical issues that have arisen as geneticists have gained the capacity to identify the carriers and potential victims of diseases and disorders, to give parents information that might prompt them to abort a pregnancy, and to experiment with techniques for altering the genetic code through gene therapy and cloning (see the Applications box on page 74). Some observers are concerned that genetic testing will be used by insurance companies to deny coverage to individuals who are at risk for diseases and disorders—or by employers to discriminate against them. Others worry about **eugenics**—attempts to improve the human race by altering the genetic makeup of a population. In the early 1900s in the United States, awareness that criminality, mental retardation, mental illness, and similar problems ran in families led to laws banning marriage by affected individuals. Laws were even passed to require involuntary sterilization of individuals who might pass their "defective" genes on to others, and tough immigration laws were passed to keep supposedly "feeble-minded" foreigners (who naturally scored poorly on intelligence tests administered in English) out of the country (Hawley & Mori, 1999). And then, of course, there was the Nazis' crusade to breed a super race. For these and other reasons, genetic research is controversial, and will remain so.

Meanwhile, behavior genetics research is controversial among developmental scientists. On the one hand, it has given us some very important insights into human development: that genes are important, that the unique experiences of siblings are more influential than those they share, that children influence parents just as parents influence children. Nonetheless, many respected researchers continue to question the validity of some of the behavior genetics research surveyed in this chapter. They believe that techniques for calculating heritability attribute too much importance to genes and too little to environment (Maccoby, 2000). They doubt that the influences of genes and environment on individual differences can ever be cleanly separated and maintain that parents have far more important effects on their children's development than some behavior geneticists acknowledge (Collins et al., 2000). They also emphasize that behavior genetics research tells us little about the long and involved process through which genotypes are actually translated into phenotypes—the real mystery (Gottlieb, 2000).

Still, parents may be in a better position to be good parents if they better understand their children's genetically based predispositions and how to respond appropriately to them. Of course, providing children with optimal experiences depends on knowing which environments stimulate healthy development and which do not. It is fitting, then, that our next chapter takes a closer look at early environmental influences on development.

It's no surprise that identical twins look alike and that parents dress them alike. The surprise in this photo is that the identical twins—without any instructions—unconsciously put their hands in similar positions.

Summary Points

1. As humans, we share a species heredity that is the product of the natural selection of traits over the course of evolution and that makes some aspects of our development and aging universal. Ethologists, evolutionary psychologists, and psychobiologists believe that normal development must be understood as the product of both species-wide genes and exposure to normal experiences.

2. Each human also has an individual heredity provided at conception, when sperm and ovum, each having retained 23 chromosomes at meiosis, unite to form a single-cell zygote that contains 46 chromosomes (23 from each parent) with some 30,000 genes that are rapidly being mapped by the Human Genome Project. The result is that each child of the same parents (other than identical twins) is genetically unique.

3. A child's sex is determined by the sex (X and Y) chromosomes. Genetic males have an X and a Y chromosome, whereas genetic females have two X chromosomes, meaning that the father determines the child's sex.

4. The genetic basis for development is not completely understood, but we do know that genes provide an instructional "code" that influences how cells are formed and how they function and that regulator genes turn these genes "on" and "off" throughout the life span. Environmental factors influence how one's genotype (genetic makeup) is translated into a phenotype (actual traits).

5. There are three main mechanisms of inheritance: single gene-pair inheritance, sex-linked inheritance, and polygenic (multiple-gene) inheritance. Most important human traits are influenced by polygenic inheritance. Some children are also affected by noninherited changes in gene structure (mutations); others, because of errors in meiosis, have chromosome abnormalities (such as Down syndrome) or sex chromosome abnormalities (such as Turner and Klinefelter syndromes).

6. Genetic conditions such as Tay-Sachs disease and Huntington's disease can have profound effects on development. Genetic counseling can help people calculate the risks that their unborn children may have a genetic disorder. Blood tests can identify the carriers of many single gene-pair disorders, and abnormalities in the fetus can be detected through amniocentesis, chorionic villus sampling, and ultrasound. As knowledge of the genetic code increases, many more genetic disorders are likely to become predictable, detectable, and treatable, like PKU. However, applications of gene therapy with humans have not yet been successful and, along with the prospect of cloning, raise serious ethical issues.

7. Behavioral genetics is the study of genetic and environmental contributions to individual differences in psychological traits and behaviors. Human behavioral geneticists, by conducting twin, adoption, and other family studies, describe resemblances between pairs of people using concordance rates and correlation coefficients. They then estimate the heritability of traits (the proportion of variation in a trait in a group that is linked to genetic differences among those individuals), as well as the contributions of shared and nonshared environmental influences.

8. Performance on measures of intelligence is a heritable trait. Infant mental development is strongly influenced by a species-wide maturational plan, but over the course of childhood and adolescence, individual differences in mental ability more strongly reflect both individual genetic makeup and environmental influences.

9. Aspects of temperament, such as emotionality, are also genetically influenced. Members of the same family often develop very different personalities owing to nonshared aspects of their experiences, whereas shared environmental influences are minimal.

10. Many psychological disorders and problems, including schizophrenia, have a genetic basis, but environmental factors have a good deal of influence on whether or not a genetic predisposition to develop a problem is realized.

11. Overall, physical and physiological characteristics are more strongly influenced by individual genetic endowment than are intellectual abilities and, in turn, personality traits. Certain traits (creativity and some social attitudes) appear to be more strongly influenced by environmental factors than genetic ones.

12. Overall, both genes and nonshared environmental influences are influential over the entire life span, whereas shared environmental influences that make members of the same family alike are often modest in size and become less important with age. Gene/environment interactions mean that environment influences how genes are expressed and that genes influence how people react to the environment. Moreover, passive, evocative, and active gene/environment correlations suggest that we experience and seek out environments that match and further reinforce our genetic predispositions.

Critical Thinking

1. Hairy Ear Syndrome (we made it up) is caused by a single dominant gene, H. Using diagrams like those in Figures 3.1 and 3.2, figure out the odds that Herb (who has the genotype Hh) and Harriet (who also has the genotype Hh) will have a child with Hairy Ear. Now repeat the exercise, but assume that Hairy Ear is caused by a recessive gene, h, and that both parents again have an Hh genotype.

2. Suppose you are interested in physical aggression and want to find out how much genetic endowment influences how physically aggressive adolescents are. Sketch out two studies that could be conducted to answer this question, and indicate what they would be able to tell us about the contributions of genes, shared environment, and nonshared environment to aggressive tendencies.

3. Researchers have found evidence that children who are physically punished by their parents tend to behave more aggressively around their peers than children who are not. What explanation for this finding might a social learning theorist like Albert Bandura propose? What alternative explanations does research on behavioral genetics, including work on gene/environment correlations, suggest?

4. Alan's biological mother developed schizophrenia and was placed in a mental hospital when he was only a year old. He grew up with his father and stepmother (neither of whom had psychological disorders) from then on. Based on the material in this chapter, what would you tell Alan about his chances of becoming schizophrenic if you were a genetic counselor?

Key Terms

gene	polygenic trait
species heredity	mutation
natural selection	cystic fibrosis
ethology	chromosome abnormalities
evolutionary psychology	Down syndrome
conception	Turner syndrome
zygote	Klinefelter syndrome
chromosome	genetic counseling
Human Genome Project	Tay-Sachs disease
meiosis	Huntington's disease
mitosis	ultrasound

crossing over	amniocentesis
identical twins	chorionic villus sampling (CVS)
fraternal twins	behavioral genetics
X chromosome	heritability
Y chromosome	selective breeding
karyotype	concordance rate
genotype	shared environmental influences
phenotype	nonshared environmental influences
single gene-pair inheritance	temperament
dominant gene	schizophrenia
recessive gene	gene/environment interaction
sickle-cell disease	gene/environment correlation
carrier	phenylketonuria (PKU)
incomplete dominance	gene therapy
codominance	cloning
sex-linked characteristic	eugenics
hemophilia	

On the Web

Web Sites to Explore

The Human Genome Project
The Human Genome Project is an international research effort aimed at characterizing the makeup of all 46 human chromosomes by mapping sequences of their DNA. For a look at how this is done, as well as the latest in efforts to understand and prevent genetic defects and diseases, check out the National Human Genome Research Institute site within the National Institutes of Health. www.nhgri.nih.gov

Genetic Education and Counseling
The Genetic Education Center at the University of Kansas Medical Center also has a wealth of good materials on the Human Genome Project and on genetic disorders and conditions. It is aimed at educators and genetic counselors. Among its features are a glossary of genetic terms; a page on the ethical, legal, and social implications of genetic research; and up-to-date information about the Human Genome Project. www.kumc.edu/gec

The Human Genome Sequence Map
A draft of the Human Genome Sequence Map is available at the National Center for Biotechnology Information. Although the information presented on this site is sophisticated and geared toward scientists, a tour of the draft Human Genome will give you a great sense of the complexity of this project.
www.ncbi.nlm.nih.gov/genome/guide/

Huntington's Disease
For a closer look at this devastating and deadly disease caused by a single dominant gene, visit the Web site of the Huntington's Disease Advocacy Center. Personal stories of people who have lived with Huntington's, as well as recent news and research findings, are provided. Under the link to "Answers to HD Questions," the etiology of Huntington's disease is explained. http://www.hdac.org/

Search Online with InfoTrac College Edition

For additional information, explore InfoTrac College Education, your online library. Go to http://www.infotrac-college.com and use the pass code that came on the card with your book.

For example, try searching for amniocentesis, and find out the latest about the risks involved in this technique. Alternatively, search for one of the genetic disorders discussed in this chapter—for example, sickle-cell disease, Huntington's disease, or cystic fibrosis—and see what's new in diagnosis and treatment.

Visit Our Web Site
Go to http://www.wadsworth.com/psychology, where you will find online resources directly linked to your book.

Life-Span CD-ROM

Go to the Wadsworth Life-Span CD-ROM for further study of the concepts in this chapter. The CD-ROM also includes quizzes and additional activities to expand your learning experience.

CHAPTER four

Prenatal Development and Birth

IN 1990, ABC'S *TURNING POINT* aired a report called "The Lost Souls," exposing the deplorable conditions in Romania's orphanages (Global Focus, 1999). We learned that as many as 30 babies and young children might be cared for by a single caregiver. As a result, diapers were changed infrequently, infants were fed in assembly-line fashion, and "baths" consisted of being rinsed off with a hose (Rutter, 1996). The children received very little, if any, social interaction or cognitive stimulation. When adopted, many of them had medical problems, were developmentally delayed, and exhibited emotional and behavior abnormalities (see also Chapter 13 on the effects of early deprivation).

To what extent are infants influenced by their early environmental experiences?

How did their early environments affect these children? Would their early experiences continue to affect their development, or could later enriched experiences compensate for early deprivation? The answers to these questions reveal the complexities of environmental influences. In general, we know that children who spent less time in these dismal orphanages—who were adopted before age 2—fared better in the long run than those who spent more time in such impoverished conditions. Still, many of these young adoptees have persistent problems. In a 5-year study of 46 Romanian children adopted by families in British Columbia, one-third were found to have significant developmental, social, and behavioral problems, and another third had mild or moderate problems, suggesting that early experiences have long-term effects (Ames, 1997; see also Rutter, 1998). Yet one-third of the Romanian adoptees were doing well, suggesting that some children are able to flourish in new environments despite early deprivation.

Obviously, environmental influences on development—bad and good—demand our serious attention. In Chapter 3, we stressed that genes and environments interact throughout the life span to make us what we are. If a common genetic heritage can make different human beings alike in some respects, so can similar environments. If unique genes make one person different from another, so do unique experiences.

The concept of **environment** is really rather complex. It encompasses both physical and social forces outside the organism that influence the person's development (Bronfenbrenner & Crouter, 1983). The physical environment includes everything from the molecules that reach the fetus's bloodstream before birth to the architecture of one's home to the climate outside it. The social environment includes all the people who can influence and be influenced by the developing person, as well as the broader culture. Early theorists tended to view the environment as a set of forces that shape the individual, as though a person were just a lump of clay to be molded. Now we understand that people shape their physical and social environments and are, in turn, affected by the environments they have helped create. In other words, the relationship between person and environment is one of *reciprocal influence.*

For example, if a woman uses cocaine during pregnancy, her newborn may be extraordinarily fussy: Environment has affected development. But a fussy baby is likely to affect the environment by irritating his mother, who now expresses her tenseness in her interactions with him, which makes him all the fussier, which of course aggravates his mother even more, which of course makes him even crankier. These sorts of transactions between person and environment begin at the moment of conception (Smotherman & Robinson, 1996).

Environment, then, is (1) both physical and social, (2) at work prenatally and postnatally, and (3) involved in reciprocal transactions with the developing person. In this chapter, we examine some of the environmental factors that are critical to very early development: before birth, when a mother's condition, disease status, and drug exposure can be critical; during the period surrounding birth, when delivery techniques and opportunities to interact can be important; and in early infancy, when influences within the family and larger culture further shape development. We will, of course, consider environmental influences on development throughout this text. Our main mission in this chapter is to find out to what extent early environmental influences, interacting with genetic influences, make or break later development.

David Young-Wolff/PhotoEdit

Development in the Prenatal Environment

Perhaps at no time in the life span does development occur faster, or is the environment more important, than between conception and birth. To understand how the **prenatal environment**—the physical environment of the womb—can affect development, we must first understand the maturational milestones that normally occur before birth. Then it will be clearer why development can be thrown far off course by certain damaging influences at certain times.

Prenatal Stages

Midway in the menstrual cycle, every 28 days or so, females ovulate: An ovum (egg cell) ripens, leaves the ovary, and begins its journey through the fallopian tube to the uterus. Usually the egg disintegrates and leaves the body as part of the menstrual flow. However, if the woman has intercourse with a fertile man during ovulation, the 300 to 450 million sperm cells in his seminal fluid swim, tadpole-style, in all directions. Of the 5,000 to 20,000 sperm that survive the long journey into the fallopian tubes, *one* may meet and penetrate the ovum on its descent from the ovary. (See Figure 4.1) A biochemical reaction occurs that repels other sperm and keeps them from penetrating the already fertilized egg. As explained in Chapter 3, *conception*, the beginning of life, occurs when the genetic material of the sperm and egg unite to form a single-celled *zygote*. The process may sound simple enough but, as we see in the Explorations box on page 83, many couples cannot conceive a child, much as they want to, and seek medical help.

The zygote contains the 46 chromosomes that are the genetic blueprint for the individual's development. It takes about 266 days (about 9 months) for the zygote to become a fetus of some 200 billion cells that is ready to be born. This prenatal development is divided into three periods: (1) the germinal period, (2) the period of the embryo, and (3) the period of the fetus.

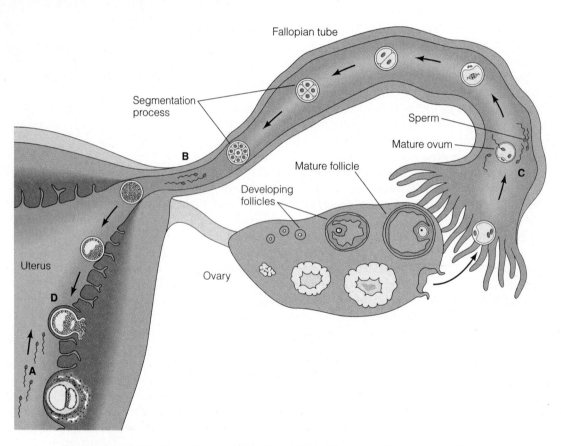

Figure 4.1   Fertilization and implantation. At A, millions of sperm cells have entered the vagina and are finding their way into the uterus. At B, some of the spermatozoa are moving up the fallopian tube (there is a similar tube on the other side) toward the ovum. At C, fertilization occurs. The fertilized ovum drifts down the tube, dividing and forming new cells as it goes, until it implants itself in the wall of the uterus (D) by the seventh or eighth day after fertilization.

Reproductive Technologies: New Conceptions of Conception

Many couples have no trouble conceiving children, but approximately 8% experience difficulties conceiving a child, despite desperately wanting one. Infertility is equally likely to be traced to the man as the woman and can result from a variety of causes. For example, adolescents and adults who have contracted sexually transmitted diseases may become infertile as a result (E. P. Steinberg et al., 1998). Many of these couples turn to "assisted reproduction technologies" (ART) to try to have a child. Some couples are helped in relatively simple ways. A man may be advised to wear looser pants and underwear (because an unusually high temperature in the testes interferes with sperm production). A woman may be asked to take her temperature in order to determine when she ovulates and is therefore most likely to become pregnant.

When simpler methods fail, some couples move on to more elaborate (and expensive) technologies. These typically start with or include prescription drugs for the woman to stimulate her ovaries to produce more eggs. Although this is the least invasive and least expensive of the ARTs, it has recently come under fire because of its connection to multiple births (Gleicher et al., 2000). Several highly visible cases of multiple births—the McCaughey septuplets in 1997 and Nkem Chukwu's octuplets in December 1998—resulted after the mothers had taken "fertility drugs." Chukwu's eight babies all weighed less than 2 pounds at birth (the smallest one—just over 10 ounces—died soon after birth) and racked up medical bills of about $400,000 each before going home (Nichols, 1999). To reduce the chances of such risky higher-order multiple births, many physicians suggest "selective reduction" in which some embryos are aborted to improve the outcome for the remaining embryos. Both Chukwu and the McCaugheys refused this option for personal/religious reasons.

Another ART is **artificial insemination,** which involves injecting sperm, from a woman's partner or from a donor, into her uterus. In **in vitro fertilization (IVF),** several eggs are first removed from a woman's ovary, then fertilized by sperm in a petri dish in the laboratory, and finally transferred to the woman's uterus in hopes that one will implant on the wall of the uterus. The first such "test tube baby" was Baby Louise, born in England in 1978. Many variations of IVF are possible, depending on who provides the eggs and sperm. The couple wanting to have a child (the would-be biological mother and father) could donate both eggs and sperm. At the other extreme, an infant conceived through IVF could wind up with five "parents": a sperm donor, an egg donor, a surrogate mother in whom the fertilized egg is implanted, and a caregiving mother and father (Beck, 1994)! Couples who seek IVF had better bring their checkbooks, as it costs at least $10,000 a try and is successful only about one time out of five (Kowalski, 2000).

What are the implications for the new family of using IVF and other reproductive technologies? Infertile couples may experience many heartbreaks in their quest for parenthood if try after try fails. But what if they succeed? To find out, Chun-Shin Hahn and Janet DiPietro (2001) compared mother–child pairs in which the children were conceived through IVF with mother–child pairs in which the children were conceived the usual way. The children were ages 3 to 7 at the time of the study, and mothers as well as teachers completed a variety of measures assessing developmental outcomes of the children.

The two groups of mothers were remarkably similar in their parenting behaviors, and the two groups of children were also quite similar in their behaviors. Teachers thought that the IVF mothers were more openly affectionate with their children. And IVF mothers reported greater protectiveness toward their children, possibly because they had tried so hard and paid so much to become parents and undoubtedly wanted their children very much. In other research, parents reported caring just as much for children conceived with the help of someone else's sperm or egg (and therefore genetically unrelated to them) as children conceived through IVF using their own sperm and egg (Golombok et al., 1995).

Thus, children conceived through today's reproductive technologies do not appear to be handicapped by their unique start in life, but they also do not seem to benefit from their parents' greater emotional involvement with them. Ultimately, how one is conceived may be inconsequential relative to how one is raised.

THE GERMINAL PERIOD

The **germinal period** lasts 8 to 14 days. First the zygote divides many times through mitosis, forming the **blastula,** a hollow ball of cells about the size of the head of a pin. When the blastula reaches the uterus, it implants tendrils from its outer layer into the blood vessels of the uterine wall. This is quite an accomplishment; only about half of all fertilized ova are successfully implanted in the uterus. In addition, not all implanted embryos survive the early phases of prenatal development. Approximately 15% of recognized pregnancies result in miscarriage, and many other, unrecognized pregnancies presumably end in miscarriage as well (Molnar, Oliver, & Geyman, 2000).

THE EMBRYONIC PERIOD

The **period of the embryo** lasts from implantation, two weeks after conception, to the end of the eighth week of prenatal development. During this short time, every major organ takes shape, in at least a primitive form, in a process called **organogenesis.**

Soon after implantation, the embryo secretes a hormone that prevents the mother from menstruating; this helps ensure its survival. (The presence of this hormone in a woman's urine is evidence of pregnancy in a common test.) Meanwhile, the layers of the embryo differentiate, forming structures that sustain development (Sadler, 1996). The outer layer becomes both the **amnion,** a watertight membrane that fills with fluid that cushions and protects the embryo, and the **chorion,** a membrane that surrounds the amnion and attaches rootlike extensions called *villi* to the uterine lining to gather nourishment for the embryo. The chorion eventually becomes the lining of the **placenta,** a tissue that is fed by blood vessels from the mother and is connected to the embryo by means of the **umbilical cord.** Through the placenta and umbilical cord, the embryo receives oxygen and nutrients from the mother and eliminates carbon dioxide and metabolic wastes into the mother's bloodstream. A membrane called the *placental barrier* allows these small molecules to pass through (along with more dangerous substances to be discussed shortly), but it prevents the quite large blood cells of embryo and mother from mingling.

Meanwhile, the inner layers of the germinal cell mass are differentiating into an embryo. Influenced by both their genetic blueprint and their environment of neighboring cells, cells migrate to their appropriate locations, cluster into groups, take on specialized functions, and become distinct organ systems (Aldridge, 1996). Development proceeds at a breathtaking pace. By only the fourth week after conception, a tiny heart has not only formed but has begun to beat. The eyes, ears, nose, and mouth rapidly take shape in the second month, and buds appear that will become arms and legs. During the second month, a very primitive nervous system also makes newly formed muscles contract. At only 60 days after conception, at the close of the period of the embryo, the organism is a little over an inch long and has a distinctly human appearance.

The important process of sexual differentiation begins during the seventh and eighth prenatal weeks. First, undifferentiated tissue becomes either male testes or female ovaries: If the embryo inherited a Y chromosome at conception, a gene on it calls for the construction of testes; in a genetic female with two X chromosomes, ovaries form instead. The testes of a male embryo secrete **testosterone,** the primary male sex hormone that stimulates the development of a male internal reproductive system, as well as another hormone that inhibits the development of a female internal reproductive system. In the absence of these hormones, the embryo develops the internal reproductive system of a female. Clearly, the period of the embryo is dramatic and highly important, for it is when the structures that make us human evolve. Yet most pregnant women, either because they do not yet know they are pregnant or do not appreciate the value of early prenatal care, do not go to a doctor until *after* the eighth week of prenatal development, too late to prevent the damage that can be caused by an unhealthy lifestyle (Sadler, 1996).

THE FETAL PERIOD

The **period of the fetus** lasts from the ninth week of pregnancy until birth. Organ systems that formed during the period of the embryo continue to grow and begin to function.

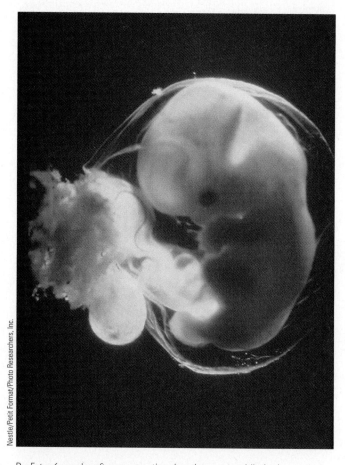

By 5 to 6 weeks after conception, head, torso, and limbs have formed, a tiny heart has begun to beat, and the umbilical cord (lower center) has taken shape to transport nutrients. By the end of the period of the embryo (8 weeks), all major organs have formed.

Harmful agents will no longer cause major malformations because organs have already formed, but they can stunt the growth of the fetus and interfere with the wiring of its rapidly developing nervous system.

In the third month of pregnancy, distinguishable external sex organs appear, the bones and muscles develop, and the fetus becomes quite frisky: By the end of the third month (that is, by the end of the first third of pregnancy, or trimester), it moves its arms, kicks its legs, makes fists, and even turns somersaults. The fetus is only about 3 inches long, but it can swallow, digest food, and urinate. All this "behaving" contributes to the proper development of the nervous system, digestive system, and other systems of the body (Smotherman & Robinson, 1996).

During the *second trimester* (the fourth, fifth, and sixth months), more refined activities appear (including thumb sucking), and by the end of this period the sensory organs are functioning: Premature infants as young as 25 weeks respond to loud noises and bright lights (Allen & Capute, 1986).

At about 24 to 25 weeks of age, midway through the fifth month, the fetus reaches the **age of viability,** when survival outside the uterus is possible *if* the brain and respiratory system are well enough developed (Lorenz, 2000). The age of viability is earlier today than at any time in the past because medical techniques for keeping fragile babies alive have improved considerably over the past few decades. Still, somewhere between 42% and 83% of infants born this early do not survive, and of those who do, many experience chronic health or neurological problems (Hack & Fanaroff, 1999).

During the *third trimester* (the seventh, eighth, and ninth months), the fetus gains weight at a rapid rate. This time is also critical in the development of the brain, as is the entire prenatal period (see Chapter 5). Early in pregnancy, the basic architecture of the nervous system is laid down. During the second half of pregnancy, neurons not only multiply at an astonishing rate, but they increase in size and develop an insulating cover, *myelin,* that improves their ability to transmit signals rapidly. Most important, guided by both a genetic

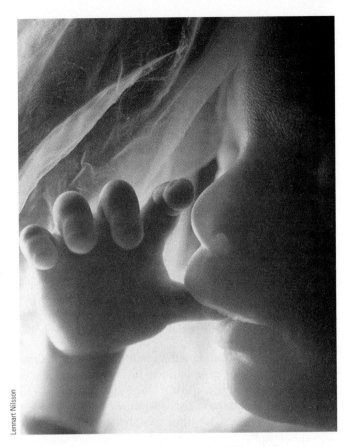

As it nears the end of the gestational period (38–40 weeks for a full-term infant), the fetus engages in many behaviors observed in newborns (here, it sucks its thumb).

blueprint and early sensory experience, neurons connect with one another and organize into working groups that control vision, memory, motor behavior, and other functions. For good reason, we should be very concerned about damage to the developing human during the first trimester, when the brain and other organs are forming. However, we should not overlook the significance of the second and third trimesters, which are critical to normal brain functioning and therefore to normal development (Diaz, 1997).

As the brain develops, the behavior of the fetus becomes more and more like the organized and adaptive behavior we see in the newborn. For example, Janet DiPietro and her colleagues (1996b) repeatedly assessed heart rates, activity levels, and behavioral states such as sleeping and waking in 34 fetuses from the 20th week of pregnancy through the 39th week of pregnancy. During this period, fetal heart rates became more variable and more responsive to such stimuli as a vibrator placed on the mother's abdomen. Fetuses moved, on average, about once a minute and were active 20–30% of the time.

In addition, heart rate activity and movement became increasingly organized into coherent patterns of waking and sleeping known as **infant states.** As Figure 4.2 shows, at 20 weeks of age, fetuses spent only about 17% of their time in one or another organized infant state such as quiet sleep, active sleep, or active waking. By the end of the prenatal period, they were in one distinct state or another at least 85% of the

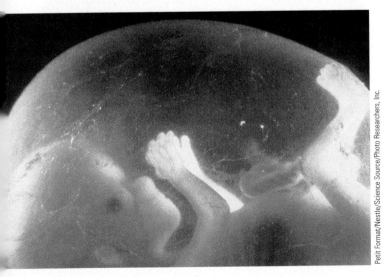

By 16 weeks, the fetus has a distinctly human appearance.

time. They spent most of their time snoozing, especially in active sleep. Whereas in the 20th week of pregnancy they were almost never active and awake, by the 32nd week they spent 11–16% of their time in an active, waking state. The patterns detected in this and other studies suggest that important changes in the nervous system occur 28 to 32 weeks after conception, when premature infants are typically well equipped to survive. As the nervous system becomes more organized, so does behavior.

Interestingly, different fetuses displayed consistent differences in their patterns of heart rate and movement, and the researchers detected correlations between measures of fetal physiology and behavior and measures of infant temperament (DiPietro et al., 1996a). For example, active fetuses tended to be active, difficult, and unpredictable babies, and fetuses whose states were better organized were also better regulated at 3 months of age, as indicated by fewer wakings during the night. The message is clear: Newborn behavior does not just spring from nowhere; it emerges long before birth. *There is a good deal of continuity between prenatal behavior and postnatal behavior.*

By the middle of the ninth month, the fetus is so large that its most comfortable position in cramped quarters is head down with limbs curled in (the "fetal position"). The mother's uterus contracts at irregular intervals during the last month of pregnancy. When these contractions are strong, frequent, and regular, the mother is in the first stage of labor and the prenatal period is drawing to a close. Under normal circumstances, birth will occur in a matter of hours.

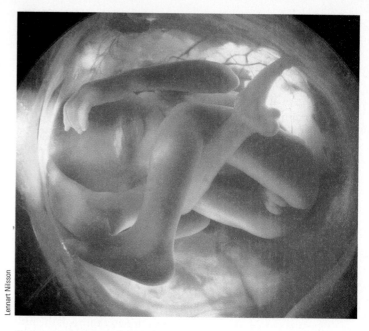

During the fetal period, growth is substantial and there is little room for the fetus to move around in the womb. This fetus is curled up in the classic "fetal position" in its tight quarters.

The developing embryo-then-fetus is a vulnerable little creature. How can its development be optimized? What hazards does it face? "Experts" throughout history have offered a number of odd ideas about the effects of the prenatal physical environment on growth. For example, it was once believed that pregnant women could enhance their chances of bearing sons if they exercised (thereby stimulating the muscle development of their fetuses!) and that sexual activity during pregnancy would cause the child to be sexually precocious (MacFarlane, 1977). And until the early 1940s, it was widely—and very wrongly—believed that the placenta was a marvelous screen that protected the embryo and fetus from nicotine, viruses, and all kinds of other hazards. Today, we understand that transactions between the organism and its environment begin at conception. When all is right, the prenatal environment provides just the stimulation and support needed for the fetus to mature physically and to develop a repertoire of behaviors that allow it to seek more stimulation, which in turn contributes to the development of still more sophisticated behavior (Smotherman & Robinson, 1996). The Applications box on page 87 explores how parents can set the stage for a healthy pregnancy. When the prenatal environment is abnormal, development can be steered far off track, as we will now see by examining possible effects of a mother's physical and emotional condition, the diseases she has, the drugs she takes, and the environmental toxins she encounters.

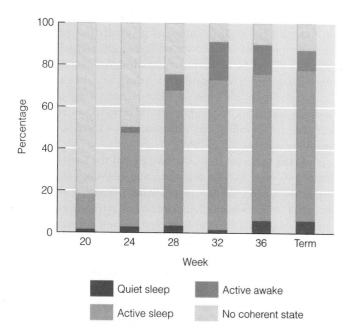

Figure 4.2 Percentage of time the fetus spends in different states from the 20th week until the end of pregnancy. Time in one coherent state or another increases with age, and most time is spent in a state of active sleep.
SOURCE: DiPietro et al. (1996b)

The Mother's State

The quality of the prenatal environment a mother provides is influenced by such factors as her age, emotional state, and nutritional status.

Getting Life Off to a Good Start

The more we learn about important environmental influences on human development, the better able we are to optimize the environment and therefore to optimize development. Although the nature and quality of an individual's environment matters throughout the life span, it seems sensible to do as much as possible to get a baby's life off to a good start.

For starters, it would be good for babies if more of them were planned and wanted. Moreover, a woman should begin making positive changes in her lifestyle, such as giving up smoking, before she even thinks about becoming pregnant. Once a woman is pregnant, she should seek good prenatal care as quickly as possible so that she will learn how to optimize the well-being of both herself and her unborn child and so that any problems during the pregnancy can be managed appropriately. The guidelines for pregnant women are not that complicated, though they are often violated. They boil down to such practices as eating an adequate diet, protecting oneself against diseases, and avoiding drugs. Research suggests that special intervention programs such as home visits to mothers who smoke to encourage healthy habits and provide social support can prevent damage to their children (Olds, Henderson, & Tatelbaum, 1994).

Today, many couples also enroll in classes that prepare them for childbirth. These classes started in the 1940s to help reduce the fear and pain experienced by many women during labor and delivery. The **Lamaze method** of prepared childbirth teaches women to associate childbirth with pleasant feelings and to ready themselves for the process by learning exercises, breathing and pushing methods, and relaxation techniques that make childbirth easier (Lamaze, 1958). Parents typically attend Lamaze classes for six to eight weeks before the delivery. The father or another supportive person becomes a coach who helps the mother train her muscles and perfect her breathing for the event that lies ahead. Couples who participate in childbirth preparation classes report a greater sense of control during labor and delivery, and this sense of control is associated with higher levels of satisfaction with the childbirth experience (Hart & Foster, 1997). Unfortunately, following their delivery, many women believe that their prenatal classes didn't go as far as they could have in providing practice with the coping strategies useful for a smooth delivery (Spiby et al., 1999).

AGE

The safest time to bear a child appears to be from about age 16 to age 35 (Amini et al., 1996; Gilbert, Nesbitt, & Danielsen, 1999; Orvus et al., 1999). Very young mothers have higher than normal rates of birth complications, premature deliveries, and low-birth-weight babies. The reproductive system of the young teen (15 years or younger) may not be physically mature enough to sustain a fetus, making this group most vulnerable to having a low-birth-weight baby (Reichman & Pagnini, 1997). However, the greater problem appears to be that teenagers often do not seek prenatal care, and they are more likely to face adverse socioeconomic conditions than mothers in their 20s (Reichman & Pagnini, 1997).

As for mothers over 35 or so, they are twice as likely to lose a fetus than younger mothers (Fretts & Usher, 1997). In the past, many fetal deaths in older women were caused by congenital abnormalities. With today's extensive prenatal testing of women over 35, however, fewer babies are dying from congenital problems, in part because many such fetuses are identified early and aborted. Still, fetal death rates remain higher for older women for reasons that are not well understood (Fretts & Usher, 1997). Keep in mind that despite the increased risk of fetal death among older women, the vast majority of older women have normal pregnancies and healthy babies.

EMOTIONAL CONDITION

Does it matter how the mother feels about being pregnant or how her life is going while she is pregnant? Although most women are happy about conceiving a child, the fact remains that many pregnancies are unintended. Even mothers who want their babies are likely to experience some symptoms of anxiety and depression during their pregnancies. How might the fetus be affected by these negative emotions, as well as by more severe emotional stresses?

When a woman becomes emotionally aroused, her glands secrete powerful hormones such as adrenaline (also called epinephrine) that may cross the placental barrier and enter the fetus's bloodstream. At the very least, these hormones temporarily increase the fetus's motor activity. A temporarily stressful experience such as falling or receiving a scare will generally not damage mother or fetus. It is only when a mother experiences *prolonged and severe* emotional stress and anxiety during her pregnancy (as a result, for example, of the death of her husband or another child or a cancer diagnosis) that damage may be done (Hansen, Lou, & Olsen, 2001). The most likely effects are increased fetal heart rate and stunted prenatal growth, which can result in low birth weight, premature birth, and birth complications (Lobel, 1994; Monk et al., 2000; Paarlberg et al., 1995). Babies of highly stressed mothers tend to be small, hyperactive, irritable, and irregular in their feeding, sleeping, and bowel habits (Sameroff & Chandler, 1975; Vaughan et al., 1987).

How might maternal stress stunt fetal growth and contribute to the offspring's irritability and anxiety? The mechanisms are not yet clear. The link between stressful experiences and small, premature babies may involve stress hormones, changes in the immune system, reduced blood flow through the arteries in the uterus, or even a poor diet (Paarlberg et al., 1995; Teixeira, Fisk & Glover, 1999). Whatever the mechanism, it is clear that not all stressed mothers have babies who are small and arrive early. In one revealing study (McCubbin et al., 1996), pregnant mothers were brought to the laboratory and asked to take a somewhat stressful arithmetic test. Those whose blood pressures rose the most dramatically during this mild stress test were more likely than other women to deliver premature babies with low birth weights. Thus, the *presence* of stress in a woman's life may not be as important as her *responsiveness* to stress in determining outcomes. Research by Marci Lobel and her colleagues (2000) seems to confirm this. They found that women with optimistic outlooks were less likely to view their lives as stressful and less likely to have babies with low birth weight. In contrast, pessimistic women were more likely to consistently view their lives as stressful and more likely to deliver low-birth-weight babies.

The link between maternal stress and active, irritable behavior in infants is also hard to explain. Hypotheses include the idea that stress directly causes behavioral problems, that the baby of an emotional mother may simply be genetically predisposed to have a "difficult" temperament, and that a mother's emotional tensions may affect her care of the baby *after* birth. Since experimentation is impossible, establishing causal links is difficult. Still, mothers who experience severe stress during pregnancy should probably seek therapeutic help. In one study, the babies of stressed mothers who received counseling weighed more at birth than the babies of stressed mothers who did not get help (Rothberg & Lits, 1991).

Stress and anxiety are not the only maternal states to consider. Maternal depression during pregnancy may lead to motor delays in newborns (Lundy et al., 1999). Depression affects levels of neurotransmitters (brain chemicals) in both mothers and their newborns. Researchers have found a connection between these changes in neurotransmitter levels and certain immature motor responses of newborns. We don't yet know, however, whether these effects persist over time.

NUTRITIONAL CONDITION

At the turn of the last century, doctors advised mothers to gain a mere 10 to 15 pounds while pregnant (Luke, Johnson & Petrie, 1993). With better understanding of nutrition and pregnancy, doctors in this century are more likely to recommend a healthy, high-protein, high-calorie diet with a total weight gain 25 to 30 pounds (Rossner, 1998; Reifsnider & Gill, 2000). And it is certainly not unusual for some mothers-to-be to gain even more weight during pregnancy. We now know that inadequate prenatal nutrition can be harmful. Severe maternal malnutrition, which occurs during famine, stunts prenatal growth and produces small, underweight babies (Stein et al., 1975; Susser & Stein, 1994). The effects of malnutrition depend on when it occurs. During the first trimester, malnutrition can disrupt the formation of the spinal cord, result in fewer brain cells, and even cause stillbirth (Susser & Stein, 1994). During the third trimester, it is most likely to result in smaller neurons, a smaller brain, and a smaller child overall.

The offspring of malnourished mothers sometimes show cognitive deficits as infants and children. Poor prenatal nutrition may also put some children at risk for certain diseases in adulthood, especially hypertension, coronary heart disease, and diabetes (Barker, 1994; Goldberg & Prentice, 1994). Some research (Stanner et al., 1997) challenges this, however, and in many cases prenatal malnutrition does not have serious long-term effects on development (Golub et al., 1996). Much depends on whether a child receives an adequate diet and good care *post*natally (Wachs, 1995). Dietary supplements, especially when combined with stimulating day care, can go a long way toward heading off the potentially damaging effects of prenatal malnutrition. Best, of course, is good nourishment before *and* after birth.

Teratogens

A **teratogen** is any disease, drug, or other environmental agent that can harm a developing fetus (for example, by causing deformities, blindness, brain damage, or even death). The list of teratogens has grown frighteningly long over the years, and the environment contains many more potential teratogens whose effects on development have not yet been assessed. Before considering the effects of some major teratogens, however, let's emphasize that more than 90% of babies are normal and that many of those born with defects have mild, temporary, or reversible problems (Baird et al., 1988).

Let's start with a few generalizations about the effects of teratogens, which we will then illustrate with examples (Abel, 1989; Friedman & Polifka, 1996; Spreen et al., 1984):

- The effects of a teratogenic agent are worst during the critical period when an organ system grows most rapidly.
- Not all embryos and fetuses are affected, or affected equally, by a teratogen.
- Susceptibility to harm is determined by the unborn child's genetic makeup as well as by the mother's, and by the quality of the prenatal environment.
- The higher the exposure to a teratogen, the more likely it is that serious damage will occur.
- The effects of a teratogen often depend on the quality of the postnatal environment.

Let's look more closely at the first generalization, which is particularly important. A period of rapid growth is a **critical period** for an organ system—a time during which the developing organism is especially sensitive to environmental influences, positive or negative. As you'll recall, organogenesis takes place during the period of the embryo (weeks 3 to 8 of prenatal development). As Figure 4.3 shows, it is during this time—before a woman is even likely to know she is pregnant—that most organ systems are most vulnerable to damage. Moreover, each organ has a critical period that corresponds to its own time of most rapid development (for example, weeks 3 to 6 for the heart, 4 to 7 for the arms). Once an organ or body part is fully formed, it is usually less susceptible to damage. However, because some organ systems—above all, the nervous system—can be damaged throughout pregnancy, *sensitive periods* might be a better term than critical periods.

DISEASES

The principles of teratology can be illustrated by surveying just a few of the many diseases that can disrupt prenatal development.

Rubella. A woman affected by **rubella** (German measles) during pregnancy may bear a child with one or more of a variety of defects, including blindness, deafness, heart defects, and mental retardation. Rubella is most dangerous during the first trimester, a critical period in which the eyes, ears, heart, and brain are rapidly forming. Yet not all babies whose mothers had rubella, even during the most critical period of prenatal development, will have problems. Birth defects occur in 60% to 85% of babies whose mothers had the disease in the first eight weeks of pregnancy, in about 50% of those infected in the third month, and in only 16% of those

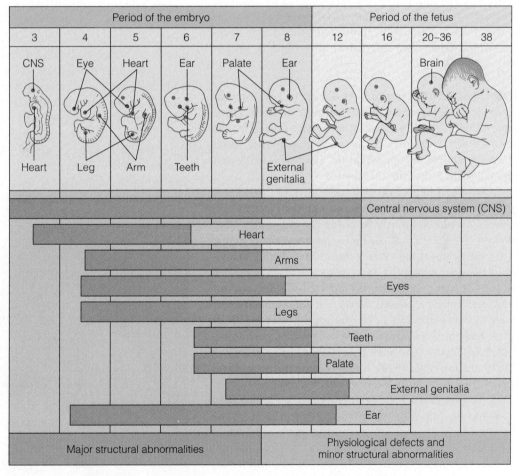

Figure 4.3 The critical periods of prenatal development. Teratogens are more likely to produce major structural abnormalities during the third through the eighth prenatal week. Note, however, that many organs and body parts remain sensitive to teratogenic agents throughout the nine-month prenatal period.

SOURCE: Adapted from Moore (1988)

infected in weeks 13 to 20 (Kelley-Buchanan, 1988). Consistent with the critical-period principle, damage to the nervous system, eyes, and heart is most likely during that part of the first eight weeks of pregnancy when each of these organs is forming, whereas deafness is more likely when the mother contracts rubella in weeks 6 to 13 of the pregnancy. Today, doctors stress that a woman should not try to become pregnant unless she has been immunized against rubella or has already had it.

Syphilis. Now consider another teratogen, the sexually transmitted disease **syphilis.** Syphilis during pregnancy can cause miscarriage or stillbirth (Genc & Ledger, 2000). Babies born alive to mothers who have syphilis, like those born to mothers who have rubella, often suffer from blindness, deafness, heart problems, or brain damage. This illustrates the principle that different teratogens, here syphilis and rubella, can be responsible for the same problem. However, whereas rubella is most damaging early in pregnancy, syphilis is most damaging in the middle and later stages of pregnancy. This is because syphilitic organisms cannot cross the placental barrier until the 18th prenatal week, providing a window of opportunity for treating the mother-to-be who finds out she has the disease. Even with appropriate treatment—penicillin—some infants are infected or die (Genc & Ledger, 2000).

AIDS. The sexually transmitted disease of greatest concern in recent decades is **acquired immune deficiency syndrome (AIDS),** the life-threatening disease caused by the virus HIV. AIDS destroys the immune system and makes victims susceptible to "opportunistic" infections that eventually kill them unless they are treated with multiple drugs. HIV-infected mothers can transmit the virus to their babies (1) prenatally, if the virus passes through the placenta; (2) perinatally, when blood may be exchanged between mother and child as the umbilical cord separates from the placenta; or (3) postnatally, if the virus is transmitted during breastfeeding (Thorne & Newell, 2000). Somewhere between 13% and 48% of babies born to HIV-infected mothers are infected (see Thorne & Newell, 2000). The rate is much lower if these mothers take AZT or zibovudine to treat the HIV or if their newborns are given a new drug called nevirapine, which helps block transmission of HIV at birth (D. Brown, 2000; Lindegren et al., 1999). Bottle-feeding further reduces the rate of HIV transmission from affected mothers to their infants (Brown, 2000). Infected infants now live longer than they did at the outset of the AIDS epidemic, thanks to the development of appropriate treatments—64% are alive at age 6, and many survive into adolescence (French Pediatric HIV Infection Study Group, 1997). Fortunately, mother-to-child transmission of HIV in the United States has decreased more than 40% since peaking in 1992 (Key & DeNoon, 1998; Lindegren et al., 1999). A number of maternal conditions that may affect prenatal development are listed in Table 4.1.

DRUGS

More than half of pregnant women take at least one prescription or over-the-counter drug during pregnancy (Kacew, 1999; Schnoll, 1986). Under a doctor's close supervision, medications used to treat ailments and medical conditions are usually safe for mother and fetus. However, certain individuals exposed to certain drugs in certain doses at certain times during the prenatal period are damaged for life.

Thalidomide. In the late 1950s, a West German drug company sold large quantities of **thalidomide,** a popular over-the-counter tranquilizer that was said to relieve morning sickness (the periodic nausea many women experience during the first trimester of pregnancy). Presumably, the drug was perfectly safe, for it had no ill effects in tests on pregnant rats. Tragically, however, the drug did have adverse effects on humans. Indeed, more than any other drug, thalidomide alerted the world to the dangers of taking drugs during pregnancy.

Thousands of women who used thalidomide during the first two months of pregnancy gave birth to babies with all or parts of their limbs missing, with the feet or hands attached directly to the torso like flippers, or with deformed eyes, ears, noses, and hearts (Rodier, 2000). It soon became clear that there are critical periods for different deformities. If the mother had taken thalidomide 20 to 22 days postconception (34–36 days after the first day of a woman's last menstrual period), her baby was likely to be born without ears. If she had taken it on the 22nd through 27th day postconception, the baby often had missing or small thumbs; if thalidomide was taken between the 27th and 33rd days after conception, the child was likely to have stunted legs or no legs. And if the mother waited until the 35th or 36th day after conception before using thalidomide, her baby was usually not affected. Thus, thalidomide had very specific effects on development,

This mother uses her leg to hug her daughter because she was born without arms. *Her* mother took the drug thalidomide early in pregnancy when arm buds were forming.

Table 4.1 Maternal Diseases and Conditions That May Affect an Embryo, Fetus, or Newborn

Sexually Transmitted Diseases

Acquired immune deficiency syndrome (AIDS)	If transmitted from mother to child, destroys defenses against disease and may lead to death. Mothers can acquire it through sexual contact or contact with contaminated blood (see text).
Chlamydia	Can lead to premature birth or low birth weight or cause eye inflammation or pneumonia in newborns. This most common STD is easily treatable.
Gonorrhea	Attacks the eyes of the child during birth; blindness is prevented by administering silver nitrate eyedrops to newborns.
Herpes simplex (genital herpes)	May cause eye and brain damage or death in the first trimester. Mothers with active herpes are advised to undergo cesarean deliveries to avoid infecting their babies during delivery, as 85% of infants born with herpes acquire the virus during birth.
Syphilis	Untreated, can cause miscarriage or serious birth defects, such as blindness and mental retardation (see text).

Other maternal conditions or diseases

Chicken pox	Can cause spontaneous abortion, premature delivery, and slow growth; fewer than 2% of exposed fetuses develop limb, facial, or skeletal malformations.
Cytomegalovirus	Common infection with mild flu-like symptoms in adults. About 25% of infected newborns develop hearing or vision loss, mental retardation, or other impairments; 10% develop severe neurological problems, even death.
Influenza (flu)	The more powerful strains can cause spontaneous abortions or neural abnormalities early in pregnancy.
Rubella	May cause vision and hearing loss, mental retardation, heart defects, cerebral palsy, and microcephaly (see text).
Toxemia	Affecting about 5% of mothers in the third trimester, its mildest form, *preeclampsia,* causes high blood pressure and rapid weight gain in the mother. Untreated, preeclampsia may become *eclampsia* and cause maternal convulsions and coma and death of mother and/or unborn child. Surviving infants may be brain damaged.
Toxoplasmosis	This illness, caused by a parasite present in raw meat and cat feces, leads to blindness, deafness, and mental retardation in approximately 40% of infants born to infected mothers.

SOURCES: Based in part on information from Batshaw (1997); Ratcliffe, Byrd, & Sakornbut (1996); Simpson & Creehan (1996); and Winn & Hobbins (2000)

depending on what structures were developing when the drug was taken.

Thalidomide, banned for many years, is once again being prescribed by physicians, this time for treatment of conditions associated with leprosy, AIDS, tuberculosis, and some forms of cancer (Wright, 2000). Given its tragic past association with birth defects, the manufacturers of thalidomide have stamped each pill with a drawing of a pregnant woman inside a circle with a diagonal line through it (the universal "no" symbol) and have included a picture of a baby with the characteristic stunted limbs on the packaging accompanying the pills. Critics, however, worry that these measures will not be enough to prevent future birth defects.

Tobacco. Despite warnings on cigarette packages that smoking may be damaging to fetuses, about 14% of pregnant women smoke during pregnancy (Pollack, Lantz, & Fruhna, 2000). Some studies report that as many as 30% of pregnant women smoke an average of 9 cigarettes per day (Wisborg et al., 2000). Women who smoke report higher rates of miscarriage than nonsmokers (Mishra, Dobson, & Schofield, 2000). The babies of mothers who smoke tend to grow more slowly

in the womb and are likely to be born prematurely and small (Haug et al., 2000; Nordentoft et al., 1996). In some, the growth of the limbs is stunted because smoking restricts blood flow to the fetus (Källén, 1997). The more the mother smokes, the stronger the growth retardation. "Passive smoking" may be risky as well; birth weights are lower when both parents smoke than when mothers only smoke (Haug et al., 2000). But if fathers smoke and mothers do not, the risk of low birth weight is no greater than when neither parent smokes. Often the small babies of smokers experience catch-up growth after they are born and reach normal size by late infancy, but the more their mothers smoke, the less likely it is that their growth will catch up completely (Streissguth et al., 1994).

The babies of smokers are also more susceptible than other babies to respiratory infections and breathing difficulties (Diaz, 1997). The more a woman smokes during pregnancy, the greater the odds of **sudden infant death syndrome (SIDS),** in which a sleeping baby suddenly stops breathing and dies (Wisborg et al., 2000). Some studies also link maternal smoking to at least mild cognitive difficulties and to behavior problems such as impulsivity (Diaz, 1997). However, there is disagreement about whether these psychological effects endure beyond childhood. Finally, some disturbing research with animals suggests that chronic prenatal exposure to nicotine—a legal substance—has more negative effects on central nervous system development than sporadic exposure to the illegal drug cocaine (Slotkin, 1998).

In sum, maternal smoking during pregnancy is unwise, as it slows fetal growth and contributes to respiratory and, possibly, cognitive difficulties. These effects may be due not only to nicotine and other chemicals in cigarettes but also to toxic by-products of smoking such as carbon monoxide that reduce the flow of blood and oxygen to the fetus.

Alcohol.   Alcohol consumed by the mother readily crosses the placenta, where it can directly affect fetal development and disrupt hormone functions of the placenta (Gabriel et al., 1998). As we'll see in the next chapter, alcohol disrupts the normal process of neuronal development. Several outcomes of prenatal alcohol exposure are possible, depending on the severity of the effects. The most severe is a cluster of symptoms dubbed **fetal alcohol syndrome (FAS),** with noticeable physical symptoms such as a small head and distinctive facial abnormalities (see photo on this page). Children with FAS are smaller and lighter than normal, and their physical growth lags behind that of their age mates (Day et al., 1999).

Children with FAS also show signs of central nervous system damage. As newborns, they are likely to display excessive irritability, hyperactivity, seizures, or tremors. The majority of children with fetal alcohol syndrome score well below average on intelligence tests throughout childhood and adolescence, and many are mentally retarded (Streissguth et al., 1999; Streissguth, Randels, & Smith, 1991). Hyperactive behavior and attention deficits are also common among these children. Longitudinal research indicates that more than 90% of them have mental health problems later in life; they are likely to get

© David H. Wells/CORBIS

This boy has the widely spaced eyes, flattened nose, and underdeveloped lip that are characteristic of fetal alcohol syndrome.

into trouble at school, break the law, and lose jobs (Autti-Rämö, 2000; Colburn, 1996).

As many as 30% of pregnant women drink some alcohol during pregnancy; 12% admit to "risk drinking" (7 or more drinks per week or 5 drinks on one occasion); and up to 4% abuse alcohol (Stratton, Howe, & Battaglia, 1996; Wisborg et al., 2000). As a result, 3 in 1,000 babies in the United States are born with FAS and suffer its symptoms all their lives. Children who were exposed prenatally to alcohol but don't have all the characteristics of FAS are referred to as "partial FAS" babies; they typically have the facial abnormalities associated with FAS (Stratton et al., 1996). Similarly, children with "alcohol-related birth defects" and "alcohol-related neurodevelopmental disorder" do not have all the features of FAS, but have some physical, behavioral, and/or cognitive problems (Stratton et al., 1996).

How much drinking does it take to harm an unborn baby? In keeping with the dosage principle of teratology, mothers who consume larger quantities of alcohol are at greater risk for having children with alcohol-related complications (Streissguth et al., 1999). The pattern of drinking is also important. Binge drinking (consuming five or more drinks during a single session) has more negative effects on fetal development than consuming the same number of drinks across multiple sessions (Jacobson & Jacobson, 1999). Consuming five drinks in one evening results in higher blood alcohol levels for both mother and fetus than consuming one drink on each of five evenings. Finally, in keeping with the first principle of teratogens, the effects of alcohol depend on what systems are developing at the time of exposure. The facial abnormalities associated with FAS result from consumption during the first trimester, when the face and skull bones are forming. During the second and third trimesters, there is much fetal growth as well as rapid brain development; thus, alcohol consumption during this latter part of pregnancy is likely to stunt growth and brain development.

No amount of drinking seems to be entirely safe (Rolater, 2000). Even a mother who drinks less than an ounce a day is at risk to have a sluggish or placid newborn whose mental development is slightly below average (Jacobson et al., 1993). What's more, there is no well-defined critical period before or after which fetal alcohol effects cannot occur; drinking late in pregnancy can be as risky as drinking soon after conception (Jacobson et al., 1993).

Why do some babies of drinking mothers suffer ill effects while others do not? The chances of damage depend in part on the mother's physiology—for example, on how efficiently she metabolizes alcohol and, therefore, how much is passed on to the fetus (Abel, 1989). Complicating the situation is the fact that problem drinkers often have other problems that can aggravate the effects of alcohol on the fetus or cause damage in their own right—among them, malnutrition, use of drugs other than alcohol, cigarette smoking, and lack of prenatal care (Stratton et al., 1996). In addition, the embryo's genetic makeup and physical condition influence its ability to resist and recover from damage. So, for example, one fraternal twin may show all the physical abnormalities associated with FAS while the other twin, though exposed to the same prenatal environment, may show almost none; by contrast, identical twins respond very similarly when they are exposed to alcohol prenatally (Streissguth & Dehaene, 1993). As our third principle of teratology states, both the child's characteristics and the mother's influence the extent to which a given teratogen proves damaging.

Finally, we should note that it is not just the mother's use of alcohol that can adversely affect development. An emerging body of research indicates that a father's use of alcohol can also influence fetal development, possibly by altering the viability of sperm or creating mutations in the sperm's genetic material (Cicero, 1994). The precise mechanism by which alcohol affects sperm is not yet well understood, but it is increasingly clear that a father's abuse of alcohol, like a mother's, is a risk factor in development.

Cocaine. Although there is no "cocaine syndrome" with characteristic physical abnormalities like those associated with fetal alcohol syndrome, cocaine use can indeed damage the fetus (Van Beveren et al., 2000). It can cause spontaneous abortion in the first trimester of pregnancy and premature detachment of the placenta or fetal strokes later in pregnancy (Diaz, 1997). Cocaine also contributes to fetal malnourishment, retarded growth, and low birth weight (Chiriboga et al., 1999). At birth, a small proportion of babies born to cocaine users experience withdrawal-like symptoms such as tremors and extreme irritability, as well as respiratory difficulties (Diaz, 1997).

Cocaine-exposed infants show deficits on several measures of information processing (Singer et al., 1999) and sensory motor skills during their first year (Arendt et al., 1998). Fortunately, most problems caused by prenatal cocaine exposure do not persist into childhood (Tronick & Beeghly, 1999). For problems that do persist, it's unclear whether they are due to the prenatal exposure to cocaine or to other prenatal or postnatal risk factors they may experience as the children of substance-abusing parents. For instance, many pregnant women who use cocaine also smoke during pregnancy (Dempsey et al., 1998). Some adverse developmental consequences attributed to cocaine may actually result from exposure to cigarette smoke (Dempsey et al., 2000). Other research shows that cocaine-using mothers are less attentive to their babies and engage in fewer interactions with them at 3 and 6 months than non-drug-using mothers or mothers who use drugs other than cocaine (Mayes et al., 1997).

Table 4.2 catalogs a number of other substances and their known or suspected effects on the child. What should we make of these findings? We now understand that drugs do not damage all fetuses exposed to them in a simple, direct way. Instead, complex transactions between an individual with a certain genetic makeup and his or her prenatal, perinatal, and postnatal environments influence whether or not prenatal drug exposure does lasting damage (van Beveren et al., 2000).

Table 4.2 Some Drugs Taken by the Mother That Affect the Fetus or Newborn

Alcohol	Small head, facial abnormalities, heart defects, low birth weight, and intellectual retardation (see text).
Antiepileptic drugs	Drugs such as Dilantin, used to treat seizures, increase the incidence of cleft lip and palate.
Aspirin	Occasional low dose okay, but used in large quantities may cause neonatal bleeding and gastrointestinal discomfort. Large amounts of aspirin *may* be associated with low birth weight, lower intelligence test scores, and mild motor skill deficits (Barr et al., 1990; Vorhees & Mollnow, 1987).
Chemotherapy drugs	Cross the placenta and attack rapidly dividing cells; can increase malformations and lead to miscarriage.
Marijuana	Heavy use of marijuana has been linked to premature birth, low birth weight, and mild behavioral abnormalities such as irritability at birth, but does not cause physical abnormalities or have long-lasting effects on most children (Fried, O'Connell, & Watkinson, 1992).
Narcotics	Addiction to heroin, codeine, methadone, or morphine increases the risk of premature delivery and low birth weight. The newborn is often addicted and experiences potentially fatal withdrawal symptoms, such as vomiting and convulsions. Longer-term cognitive deficits are sometimes evident.
Sex hormones	Birth control pills containing female hormones have been known to produce heart defects and cardiovascular problems, but today's pill formulas are safer. Progesterone in drugs used to prevent miscarriage may masculinize the fetus. Diethylstilbestrol (DES), once also prescribed to prevent miscarriage, increased the risk of cervical cancer and created infertility and pregnancy problems in exposed daughters (DESAction, 2000; Kaufman et al., 2000).
Stimulants	Caffeine use has been linked to miscarriages (Cnattingius et al., 2000), higher heart rates (Schuetze & Zeskind, 1997), and abnormal reflexes and irritability at birth (Jacobson, Fein, et al., 1984), but does not seem to have longer-lasting effects on development (Barr & Streissguth, 1991). Cocaine use can cause premature delivery, spontaneous abortion, low birth weight, and may result in later learning and behavior problems (Keller & Snyder-Keller, 2000; also see text). Amphetamine use has been linked to aggressive behavior and low school achievement (Billing et al., 1994).
Tobacco	Babies of smokers tend to be small and premature, have respiratory problems, and sometimes show intellectual deficits or behavior problems later in development (see text).

SOURCES: Based in part on information from Batshaw (1997); Diaz (1997); Friedman & Polifka (1996); and Winn & Hobbins (2000)

Still, women who are planning to become pregnant or who are pregnant should avoid all drugs unless they are prescribed by a physician and essential to health.

ENVIRONMENTAL HAZARDS

Radiation.   A mother can control what she ingests, but sometimes she cannot avoid a hazardous external environment. After atomic bombs were dropped on Hiroshima and Nagasaki in 1945, not one pregnant woman who was within one-half mile of the blasts gave birth to a live child, and 75% of those who were within a mile and a quarter of the blasts had stillborn infants or seriously handicapped children who died soon after birth (Apgar & Beck, 1974); surviving children of these mothers had a higher than normal rate of mental retardation (Vorhees & Mollnow, 1987). Even clinical doses of radiation, like those used in X-rays and cancer treatment, are capable of causing mutations, spontaneous abortions, and a variety of birth defects, especially if the mother is exposed during the first trimester of pregnancy. For this reason, expectant mothers are routinely advised to avoid X-rays unless they are essential to their own survival, and women who work with X-ray equipment must take proper precautions. Despite some concern about it, by the way, a woman who works in front of a computer screen all day does not appear to place her fetus at risk (Parazzini et al., 1993).

Pollutants.   Pollutants in the air we breathe and the water we drink include "heavy metals," such as lead, which are discharged by smelting operations and other industries and may be present in paint, dust, or water pipes in old houses. Children who were exposed to lead prenatally show impaired intellectual functioning as infants in proportion to the amount of lead in their umbilical cords (Bellinger et al., 1987; also see Figure 4.4). This finding holds true even after controlling for other differences among children, such as socioeconomic status.

A *father's* exposure to environmental toxins can also affect a couple's children. A father's prolonged exposure to radiation, anesthetic gases used in operating rooms, pesticides, or other environmental toxins—like his use of alcohol—can damage the genetic material in his sperm and cause genetic defects in his children (Stone, 1992; Strigini et al., 1990). Clearly, there is a critical need for more research aimed at identifying a huge number of chemicals, wastes, and other environmental hazards that may affect unborn children. One expert estimates that there are 70,000 synthetic chemicals "out there" that children may be exposed to, and fewer than 20% of these have been evaluated for toxicity (Morris, 1999).

SUMMING UP

The message is clear: The chemistry of the prenatal environment often determines whether an embryo or fetus survives and how it looks and functions after birth. A variety of teratogens can affect development, although as we have learned, the influence of teratogens varies. Effects are worst when organ systems are growing most rapidly; not all embryos or fetuses are equally affected by the same teratogen; harmful effects depend on the genetic makeup of both the mother and her unborn child and on the quality of the prenatal environment; effects are more serious with greater exposure to teratogens; and the effects of teratogens often depend on the quality of the postnatal environment. By becoming familiar with the information touched on here, and by keeping up with new knowledge, parents-to-be can do much to increase the already high odds that their unborn child will be normal as it approaches its next challenge: the birth process.

The Perinatal Environment

The **perinatal environment** is the environment surrounding birth; it includes influences such as drugs given to the mother during labor, delivery practices, and the social environment shortly after birth. Like the prenatal environment, the perinatal environment can greatly affect human development (Gatten et al., 1994).

In most Western cultures, there has been a dramatic shift in birthing practices. In 1930, 80% of births took place at home; by 1990, this figure had plummeted to 1% (Zander & Chamberlain, 1999). This change in birth setting was accompanied by a shift from thinking about birth as a natural family event that occurred at home to thinking that birth is a medical problem to be solved with high technology (Ackermann-Liebrich et al., 1996). Despite the medicalized setting of most of today's birth, many couples want to give birth in a more relaxed atmosphere that gives them the peace of mind provided by nearby modern technology along with a comfortable homelike feeling. Many hospitals have responded by restructuring their labor and delivery rooms and practices to give parents greater flexibility and control when it comes time to deliver.

Increasingly, a laboring woman has a partner, relative, or friend with her during labor and delivery; women find the support provided by this familiar person helpful and reassur-

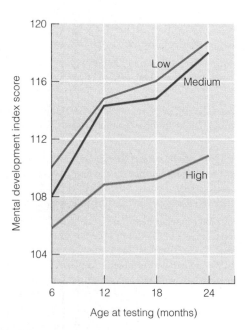

Figure 4.4   Mental development scores of infants with low, medium, or high levels of lead in their umbilical cords before birth
SOURCE: Bellinger et al. (1987)

ing (Somers-Smith, 1999). Some women have the support of a *doula*—an individual trained to provide continuous physical and emotional support throughout the childbirth process. Such support tends to shorten labor and reduce the need for pain medication and assisted delivery (such as use of forceps or vacuum; Scott, Klaus, & Klaus, 1999). Mothers with doula support also report more positive feelings about the birth experience, fewer symptoms of postnatal depression, and greater likelihood of breast-feeding than nonsupported mothers (Scott et al., 1999). Clearly, then, the context surrounding labor and delivery is important: Women who receive more support during childbirth have more positive experiences.

Childbirth is a three-stage process. See Figure 4.5. The first stage of labor begins as the mother experiences regular *contractions* of the uterus and ends when her cervix has fully dilated (widened) so that the fetus's head can pass through. This stage of labor lasts an average of 8 to 14 hours for first-born children, compared to only 3 to 8 hours for later-borns, but may last as long as 30 hours. It ends when the cervix has dilated to 10 centimeters. The second stage of labor is *delivery,* which begins as the fetus's head passes through the cervix into the vagina and ends when the baby emerges from the mother's body. This is the time when the mother is often told to "bear down" (push) with each contraction to assist her baby through the birth canal. A quick delivery may take less than a half hour; a long one may take several hours. Finally, the third stage of the birth process is the delivery of the placenta, which lasts only a few minutes.

Stage 1

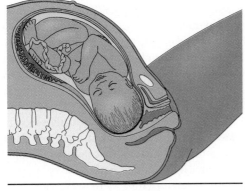

(a) Dilation of the cervix begins

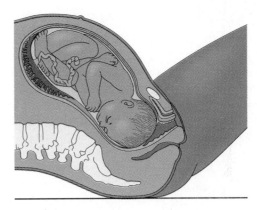

(b) Contractions are greatest and cervix opens completely

Stage 2

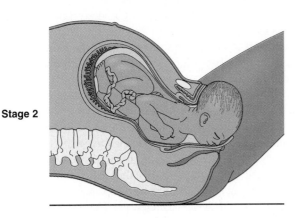

(c) Baby's head appears

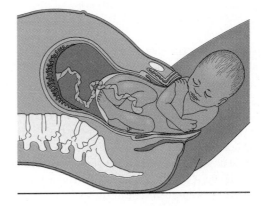

(d) Baby passes through the vagina

Stage 3

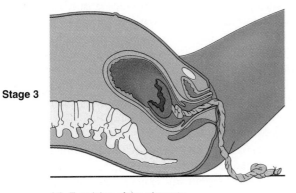

(d) Expulsion of the placenta

Figure 4.5 The three stages of labor. Stage 1: (a) Contractions of the uterus cause dilation and effacement of the cervix. (b) Transition is reached when the frequency and strength of the contractions are at their peak and the cervix opens completely. Stage 2: (c) The mother pushes with each contraction, forcing the baby down the birth canal, and the head appears. (d) Near the end of Stage 2, the shoulders emerge and are followed quickly by the rest of the baby's body. Stage 3: (e) With a few final pushes, the placenta is delivered.

Although most births in Western cultures take place in hospitals, this woman is giving birth at home with her husband actively involved.

When the birth process is completed, the mother (and often the father too, if he is present) is typically physically exhausted, relieved to be through the ordeal of giving birth, and exhilarated all at once. Meanwhile, the fetus has been thrust from its carefree but cramped existence into a strange new world.

Possible Hazards

In the large majority of births, the entire process goes smoothly, and parents and newborn quickly begin their relationship. Occasionally, however, problems arise.

ANOXIA

One clear hazard during the birth process is **anoxia,** or oxygen shortage (also called asphyxia). Anoxia can occur for any number of reasons—for example, because the umbilical cord becomes pinched or tangled during birth, because sedatives given to the mother reach the fetus and interfere with the baby's breathing, because mucus lodged in the baby's throat prevents normal breathing, or even because the mother is older (Gilbert et al., 1999). Anoxia is dangerous primarily because brain cells die if they are starved of oxygen for more than a few minutes. Severe anoxia can cause mental retardation or **cerebral palsy,** a neurological disability associated with difficulty controlling muscle movements (Anslow, 1998; Carter, 1998). Milder cases of anoxia make some infants irritable at birth or delay their motor and cognitive development. However, many victims, especially those whose environments after birth are optimal, function perfectly normally later in childhood (Sameroff & Chandler, 1975). Children who experience relatively brief anoxia usually suffer no ill effects, but children with prolonged anoxia often have permanent disabilities (Sorenson & Borch, 1999).

The chances of anoxia have been greatly reduced by the use of fetal monitoring procedures during labor and delivery. Doctors are now alert to the risk of anoxia if the fetus is not positioned in the usual head-down position. If the baby is born feet or buttocks first (a **breech presentation**), delivery becomes more complex and takes longer, although the vast majority of breech babies are normal. A vaginal delivery is nearly impossible for the one fetus in a hundred lying sideways in the uterus. The fetus must be turned to assume a head-first position or be delivered by **cesarean section,** a surgical procedure in which an incision is made in the mother's abdomen and uterus so that the baby can be removed. And that leads us to the potential hazards associated with delivery procedures and technologies themselves.

COMPLICATED DELIVERY

In some cases, mothers may need assistance with delivery, possibly because labor has proceeded too long with little to show for it, or because of concern about the well-being of the baby or mother. There is much debate in the medical literature about whether delivery is better assisted with forceps or vacuum extraction (Johanson & Menon, 2000; O'Grady, Pope, & Patel, 2000). For many years, doctors frequently used *forceps* (an instrument resembling an oversized pair of salad tongs). However, forceps on the soft skull of the newborn sometimes caused serious problems, including cranial bleeding and brain damage. Alternatively, doctors may use *vacuum extraction* ("suction") to assist with difficult deliveries. This procedure has fewer risks associated with it, although it is not risk free. In a vacuum extraction, a cup is inserted through the opening of the birth canal and attached to the baby's head. Suction is applied to make the cup adhere to the baby's scalp and, during each contraction and with the mother bearing down, the doctor uses the traction created by the suction to help deliver the baby. From the mother's point of view, vacuum extraction is less traumatic than forceps. For the baby, there is likely to be swelling of the scalp and some marking where the cup was attached. More serious injuries are possible if the vacuum is not properly used.

As for the cesarean section, it too has been controversial. Use of this alternative to normal vaginal delivery has prevented the death of many babies—for example, when the baby is too large or the mother is too small to permit normal delivery, when a fetus out of position cannot be repositioned, or when fetal monitoring reveals that a birth complication is likely. Medical advances have made cesarean sections about as safe as vaginal deliveries, and few ill effects on mothers and infants have been observed (Kochanevich-Wallace et al., 1988). Mothers who have "C-sections" do take longer to recover from the birth process, and they are less satisfied with the birth process and less positive toward and involved with their babies, at least during the first month after birth (DiMatteo et al., 1996). Nonetheless, the development of babies born by cesarean appears to be perfectly normal (Durik, Hyde, & Clark, 2000).

Many observers have questioned why cesarean deliveries have become so much more common than they used to be, to the point that they accounted for almost 25% of births in the United States in 1988 (Clarke & Taffel, 1996). The U.S. government had set a goal of reducing the rate of cesareans to 15% by the year 2000, but managed to reduce it only slightly

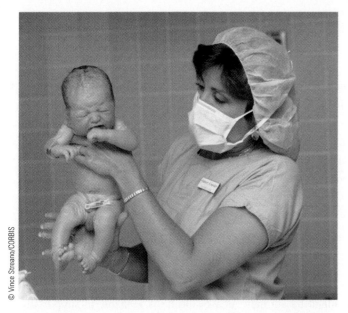

Most newborns have not yet acquired the "cuteness" of somewhat older babies. Instead, they are often red, wrinkled, and swollen in places, and they may be covered with amniotic fluid, blood, fine downy hair (lanugo), and a white greasy substance called vernix. Their heads may even be misshapen from coming through the birth canal or from the use of forceps or suction during delivery.

to 21% of all deliveries (Ventura et al., 2001). It is also understood now that mothers who have one cesarean birth need not have all their subsequent babies by cesarean, as was believed only a short time ago (Harrington et al., 1997). Nonetheless, some obstetricians continue to rely heavily on this procedure because it protects them from the costly malpractice suits that might arise from complications in vaginal deliveries (Castro, 1999). Some doctors may also find that cesareans are more convenient and generate more revenue than vaginal deliveries (H. S. Brown, 1996). Overall, birth by cesarean delivery can be lifesaving in some cases and is unlikely to disrupt normal development but is also more common than it needs to be in our society.

MEDICATIONS

Concerns have also been raised about medications given to mothers during the birth process—analgesics and anesthetics to reduce their pain, sedatives to relax them, and stimulants to induce or intensify uterine contractions (Simpson & Creehan, 1996). Sedative drugs that act on the entire body cross the placenta and can affect the baby. Babies whose mothers receive large doses of obstetrical medication are generally sluggish and irritable, are difficult to feed or cuddle during the first few days of life, and smile infrequently (Elbourne & Wiseman, 2000). In short, they act as though they are drugged. Think about it: Doses of medication large enough to affect mothers can have much greater impacts on newborns who weigh only 7 pounds and have immature circulatory and excretory systems that cannot get rid of drugs for days or even weeks.

Regional analgesics, such as epidurals and spinal blocks, reduce sensation in specific parts of the body. Because they do not cross the placenta, they have fewer ill effects on babies and are preferred by many physicians. Epidurals are also rated by mothers as more effective for pain control than other forms of analgesics (Macario et al., 2000; Sheiner et al., 2000). But along with these advantages, we must weigh disadvantages, including longer labor times with epidurals (Halpern et al., 1998).

So, should mothers avoid obstetric medications at all costs? That advice is perhaps too strong. For example, some women are at risk of experiencing birth complications because of their size or body shape or because their babies are large. For such women, sedatives in appropriate doses can actually *reduce* the chances of complications such as anoxia (Myers & Myers, 1979).

It is also important to recognize that there are many drugs, some safer than others. For example, sedatives such as Demerol disrupt the newborn's functioning and responsiveness to stimuli more than local anesthetics that deaden the pelvic area only (Emory, Schlackman, & Fiano, 1996). How much of a drug is taken, when it is taken, and by which mother it is taken are also important. More alert to the potentially negative effects of medications given during labor and delivery, doctors today are more likely than doctors of the past to use drugs only when clearly necessary and to use the least toxic drugs in the lowest effective doses at the safest times (Simpson & Creehan, 1996). Thus, taking obstetric medications is not as risky a business today as it once was, but it is still a decision that requires weighing the pros and cons carefully.

IDENTIFYING HIGH-RISK NEWBORNS

In the end, a small minority of infants are in great jeopardy at birth because of genetic defects, prenatal hazards, or perinatal damage. It is essential to these infants' survival and well-being that they be identified as early as possible. Newborns are routinely screened using the **Apgar test,** which provides a quick assessment of the newborn's heart rate, respiration, color, muscle tone, and reflexes (Apgar & James, 1962; also see Table 4.3). The simple test is given immediately and 5 minutes after birth. It yields scores of 0, 1, or 2 for each of the five factors, which are then added to yield a total score that can range from 0 to 10. Infants who score 7 or higher are in good shape. However, infants scoring 4 or lower are at risk—their heartbeats are sluggish or nonexistent, their muscles are limp, and their breathing, if they are breathing, is shallow and irregular. These babies will immediately experience a different postnatal environment than the normal baby experiences, for they require medical intervention in intensive care units to survive, as we will see at the end of the chapter.

The birth of a baby is a dramatic experience for the whole family. However, it was not so long ago that most hospitals barred fathers from the delivery room and snatched babies away from their mothers soon after delivery to place them in nurseries. Let us look briefly at the birth experience from a family perspective.

Table 4.3 The Apgar Test

	Score		
Characteristic	0	1	2
Heart rate	Absent	Slow (under 100 beats per minute)	Over 100 beats per minute
Respiratory effort	Absent	Slow or irregular	Good; baby is crying
Muscle tone	Flaccid; limp	Weak; some flexion	Strong; active motion
Color	Blue or pale	Body pink, extremities blue	Completely pink
Reflex irritability	No response	Frown, grimace, or weak cry	Vigorous cry

The Mother's Experience

What is it really like to give birth to a child? In a study of Swedish mothers (Waldenström et al., 1996), most mothers admitted they experienced severe pain and a good deal of anxiety, including feelings of outright panic. Yet most also emerged from the delivery room feeling very good about their achievement and their ability to cope ("I did it!"). Overall, 77% felt the experience was positive, and 10% said it was negative. And, despite longer labors and more medication, first-time mothers did not perceive labor and delivery much differently than experienced mothers did.

What factors influence a mother's experience? Psychological factors such as the mother's attitude toward her pregnancy, her knowledge and expectations about the birth process, her sense of control over childbirth, and the social support she receives from her partner or someone else are important determinants of her experience of delivery and of her new baby (Waldenström et al., 1996; Wilcock, Kobayashi, & Murray, 1997). Social support can be especially important. When the father, or another supportive person whose main role is to comfort the mother, is present during labor and delivery, women experience less pain, use less medication, are less likely to have cesarean sections, and are likely to feel better about the whole birth process (Hodnett & Osborn, 1989; Kennell et al., 1991).

CULTURAL FACTORS

The experience of childbearing is shaped by the cultural context in which it occurs. For example, different cultures have different views of the desirability of having children. In some, a large family is a status symbol, whereas in the People's Republic of China, a "one-child policy" discourages multiple childbearing in hopes of slowing population growth and raising the standard of living. As a result of this policy, the average number of children a Chinese woman bears dropped from 4.8 in 1970 to 1.8 in 1994 (Post, 1994). The ratio of boys to girls has also changed; many parents want their one child to be a boy who can support them in old age and therefore abort female fetuses that have been identified through ultrasound tests or abandon their female babies after they are born (Post, 1994).

Practices surrounding birth also differ widely (Chalmers, 1996; S. Steinberg, 1996). Among the Pokot people of Kenya,

for example, cultural beliefs and rituals help to ensure strong social support of the mother and a successful birth (O'Dempsey, 1988). The whole community celebrates the coming birth, and the father-to-be stops hunting lest he be killed by animals. As a result, he is available to support his wife. A midwife, aided by female relatives, delivers the baby. The placenta is buried in the goat enclosure, and the baby is washed in cold water and given a mixture of hot ash and boiled herbs so that it will vomit the amniotic fluid that it has swallowed. Mothers are given plenty of time to recover. They go into seclusion for a month and devote themselves entirely to their babies for three months.

In Uttar Predesh in northern India, by contrast, the blood associated with childbirth is viewed as polluting, and the whole event as shameful (Jeffery & Jeffery, 1993). A *dai*, a poorly paid attendant hired by the woman's mother-in-law, delivers the baby. The *dai* typically hates her menial, disgusting job, provides no pain relievers, discourages the mother from crying out in pain, and offers little emotional support. The mother is kept in the house for several days and in the family compound for weeks so that she will not pollute others. Because the baby is also believed to be polluted, its hair is shaved off.

Many observers charge that childbirth in highly industrialized Western societies has become too "medicalized" and that we should go back to the traditional ways observed in less developed countries. Yet as the Indian example illustrates, not all "traditional" practices are in the best interests of parents and babies (Jeffery & Jeffery, 1993). Also, Western societies do a far better job than developing countries of preventing mother and infant mortality. In some areas of sub-Saharan Africa, for example, about 15% of babies die during childbirth or in the first year of life (Caldwell, 1996). In Western, industrial societies, infant mortality rates have dropped from almost 20% in the late 18th century to 3–4% recently (Murphy, 2000). Unfortunately, infant mortality is twice as high for black infants compared to white infants (Guyer et al., 2000). The secret to a more optimal birth experience may be to blend beneficial traditional practices such as offering emotional support to new mothers with modern medical know-how (Chalmers, 1996).

POSTNATAL DEPRESSION

Some new mothers suffer from depression following the birth of their baby. As many as 60% of all new mothers report feeling tearful, irritable, moody, anxious, and depressed within the first few days after birth (Najman et al., 2000). This condition—the baby blues—is relatively mild, passes quickly, and is probably linked to the steep drops in levels of female hormones that normally occur after delivery, as well as to the stresses associated with delivering a child and taking on the responsibilities of parenthood.

A second, and far more serious, condition is **postnatal depression**—an episode of clinical depression that lasts for a matter of months rather than days in a woman who has just given birth. It affects approximately 1 in 10 new mothers (Cooper & Murray, 1998). Only very rarely does a woman who has never had significant emotional problems become clinically depressed for the first time after giving birth. Most of the affected women have histories of depression, and many were depressed during pregnancy as well. Also, women who are vulnerable to depression are more likely to actually become depressed if they are experiencing other life stresses on top of the stresses of becoming a mother (O'Hara et al., 1991). Lack of social support—especially a poor relationship with one's partner—also increases the odds (Gotlib et al., 1991).

Postnatal depression has significant implications for the parent–infant relationship. One study compared the children of 58 mothers who experienced postnatal depression to the children of 42 nondepressed mothers over a 5-year period (Murray et al., 1999). The children of the depressed mothers were less securely attached to their mothers during infancy and were less responsive during interactions with their mothers at age 5. Mothers who had been postnatally depressed reported greater behavior problems by their children. In school, the children of depressed mothers were more likely to engage in rather elementary forms of physical play and less likely to engage in higher-level creative play. Finally, children of depressed mothers had a tendency to respond negatively when another child approached them in a friendly manner.

How might maternal depression in the weeks and months following delivery affect children's behavior as long as 5 years later? Mothers who are depressed tend to be less responsive to their babies and feel some hostility toward their babies. They are also tired, distracted, and often lack the energy needed to be fully engaged with their infant. Even though mothers typically recover from postnatal depression, research suggests that these early attitudes about their baby and the resulting pattern of early mother–child interactions set the stage for ongoing interaction problems that affect the child's behavior (Murray et al., 1999). Thus, for their own sake and for the sake of their infants, mothers experiencing more than a mild case of the "maternity blues" should seek professional help in overcoming their depression.

The Father's Experience

Until the 1970s, fathers in Western culture were routinely excluded from the birth process. Today, however, many men are present for their child's birth. Like mothers, fathers experience the birth process as a significant event in their lives that involves a mix of positive and negative emotions. Also like mothers, fathers tend to be anxious during pregnancy and birth. In several studies, new fathers admitted that they felt scared, unprepared, helpless, and frustrated during labor (Chandler & Field, 1997; Chapman, 2000; Hallgren et al., 1999). They found labor to be more work than they had expected and sometimes felt excluded as the nurses took over. For Tim, whose wife Angie dilated only 2 centimeters in 12 hours, then received drugs to induce labor, and eventually had to have a cesarean delivery, the process was even more agonizing. Despite the stresses, though, negative emotions usually give way to relief, pride, and joy when the baby finally arrives (Chandler & Field, 1997). Indeed, most fathers find early contact with their babies special. As one father put it, "when my wife handed Anna to me, I was completely unprepared for the intense experience of fatherhood. I was overwhelmed by my feeling of belonging to and with this new child" (Reed, 1996, p. 52).

In the weeks and months following delivery, transition to fatherhood is somewhat rocky (Barclay & Lupton, 1999). Despite its rewards, many men find that caring for an infant is a demanding job, with many unanticipated lifestyle alterations.

The Postnatal Environment: Culture and Early Socialization

After the prenatal environment and the perinatal environment, we experience the postnatal environment—for a lifetime. In chapters to come, we will have much to say about a wide range of environmental influences on life-span development: parents, peers, schools, workplaces, and so on. Here we simply want to make the point that human development is influenced by the broader social context in which it occurs—by cultural factors (or what Urie Bronfenbrenner, as discussed in Chapter 2, calls the *macrosystem*). In the Applications box on page 100, we discuss ways to optimize development of young infants.

Parents are products of their broader culture, and they in turn transmit that culture to their offspring. **Socialization** is the process by which individuals acquire the beliefs, values, and behaviors judged important in their society. By socializing the young, society controls their undesirable behavior, prepares them to adapt to the environment in which they must function, and ensures that cultural traditions will be carried on by future generations. The socialization process begins at birth. Robert LeVine (1974, p. 230; also see LeVine, 1988) maintains that parents everywhere share three very broad goals for their children:

- **Survival goal:** to promote the physical survival and health of the child, ensuring that the child lives long enough to have children of his or her own

Applications

Optimizing Early Development

So now that you have a baby, what do you do? New parents are often uncertain about how to relate to their babies and may find the period after birth stressful. T. Berry Brazelton (1979) has devised a way to help parents appreciate their baby's competencies and feel competent themselves as parents. He developed a newborn assessment technique, the Brazelton Neonatal Behavioral Assessment Scale, that assesses the strength of infant reflexes as well as the infant's responses to 26 situations (for example, reactions to cuddling, general irritability, and orienting to the examiner's face and voice). Brazelton uses this test to teach parents to understand their babies as individuals and to appreciate many of the pleasing competencies that they possess. During "Brazelton training," parents observe the test being administered and also learn how to administer it themselves to elicit smiles and other heartwarming responses from their babies.

In some studies, mothers of high-risk (and sometimes difficult) infants who receive Brazelton training become more responsive in their face-to-face interactions with their babies than mothers who do not, and their infants score higher on developmental tests (Britt & Myers, 1994; Widmayer & Field, 1980). Compared to untrained mothers, trained mothers report that their infants are more predictable, suggesting that trained mothers are more sensitive to their babies' signals (Fowles, 1999). Although this brief intervention appears to be a good way to help parents and babies get off to a good start, it cannot accomplish miracles and sometimes has little impact (Britt & Myers, 1994).

Giving the seriously premature and low-birth-weight infant a good start requires more effort. Neonatal intensive care units, with their high-tech life-sustaining machines and computerized monitoring systems, have greatly improved the odds that babies who are at high risk will survive the perinatal period. Consider John Henry, born 16 weeks early, weighing 1 pound 10½ ounces ("John Henry's NICU Story," 2000). His eyes were fused shut, he needed a ventilator to breathe, he had a heart defect that would require surgery, and he contracted numerous infections that put his tiny life in grave jeopardy. Defying the odds, John Henry went home after 4½ months in the neonatal intensive care unit, weighing 7½ pounds. At age 5, John Henry looked and behaved much like other boys his age. Yet only 20 years ago, when "high-tech" neonatal care did not exist, John Henry probably would not have lived.

Much is still being learned about how to optimize the rather abnormal environment in which infants like John Henry spend the first several weeks of life. Since "preemies" are not still fetuses and yet are not quite normal newborns, it is not clear whether they should be handled like babies or given womblike accommodations befitting fetuses (Smotherman & Robinson, 1996). Not long ago, these babies simply lay in their isolettes, receiving little stimulation and contact at all. They were, in effect, deprived of the sensory stimulation that they would have received either in the womb or in a normal home environment. Today, their perinatal sensory environment is much improved, thanks to research on the effects of neonatal sensory stimulation programs.

Many sensory stimulation programs have centered on the "body senses" because much bodily stimulation is provided in the womb. Preterm infants have been stroked, held upright, rocked, and even put on waterbeds (Schaefer, Hatcher, & Barglow, 1980). Preterm infants who receive just three 15-minute stimulation sessions a day (having their bodies massaged and their limbs flexed) over 10 days gain anywhere from 31% to 47% more weight per day, show more mature behaviors on the Brazelton scale, and are able to leave the hospital 5 days earlier than control infants (Field, 2001; Scafidi et al., 1986, 1990). It appears that fairly simple and inexpensive environmental changes and special stimulation programs can help the high-risk infant develop normally.

Finally, high-risk infants can benefit from programs that teach their parents how to provide responsive care and appropriate intellectual stimulation to them once they are home. Home visits to advise parents, combined with a stimulating day care program for low-birth-weight toddlers, can teach mothers how to be better teachers of their young children and stimulate these children's cognitive development. In an ambitious project called the Infant Health and Development Program, premature and low-birth-weight infants at eight sites have benefited from such early intervention (Bradley et al., 1994; Brooks-Gunn et al., 1993; McCarton et al., 1997). The program involved weekly home visits during the first year of life and then biweekly home visits and attendance by the infant at a special day care center for half a day every day from age 1 to age 3. Mothers were given child care education and support as well. The program appears to help parents provide a more growth-enhancing home environment—for example, to give their babies appropriate toys and learning materials and to interact with them in stimulating ways.

The intervention helped these high-risk babies, especially the heavier ones, achieve more cognitive growth by age 3 than they would otherwise achieve. However, an impressive 14-point boost in IQ scores at age 3 for heavier low-birth-weight children who received the intervention had dropped to a 4-point advantage at age 8 (McCarton et al., 1997). Children who weighed 2,000 grams (4 lbs 6 oz) or less at birth did not get much benefit. We have more to learn, then, about what it takes to keep the development of at-risk children on a positive track after the perinatal period comes to a close. However, everything we do know about life-span environmental forces suggests that supportive parents and programs can do a great deal to optimize every child's development.

- **Economic goal:** to foster the skills and traits that the child will need for economic self-maintenance as an adult
- **Self-actualization goal:** to foster capacities for maximizing other cultural values (for example, morality, religion, achievement, wealth, prestige, and a sense of personal satisfaction)

LeVine also maintains that these universal goals of parenting form a hierarchy. Until parents are confident that their children will survive, higher-order goals such as teaching them to talk, count, or follow moral rules can wait. And only when parents and other caregivers believe that their children have acquired many of the basic attributes that will eventually contribute to their economic self-sufficiency will they encourage such goals as self-actualization or self-fulfillment.

Because different peoples must adapt to different environments, they sometimes emphasize different parenting goals, and their child care and child-rearing practices differ accordingly. In societies where infant mortality is high, the survival goal of parenting is naturally top priority. Babies may not even be named or viewed as persons until they seem likely to survive (Nsamenang, 1992). Parents keep infants close 24 hours a day to protect them. Among the !Kung, a hunting and gathering society of the Kalahari Desert in southern Africa, for example, babies are carried upright in slings during the day,

In many cultures, parents attempt to achieve the survival goal of parenting by keeping their babies close at all times.

and they sleep in the same bed with their mothers at night (Konner, 1981). They are breast-fed, suckling several times an hour as desired, and may not be weaned until the ripe old age of 4. In general, infants in hunter–gatherer societies are indulged considerably, at least until their survival is assured.

Infant care practices are considerably different in modern, industrialized societies where infant mortality is lower. Babies typically sleep apart from their parents; they breast-feed, if at all, for only a few months before being switched to the bottle and then to solid food; and they generally must learn to accommodate their needs to their parents' schedules (Konner, 1981). Mayan mothers in Guatemala, who sleep in the same bed with their babies until they are toddlers, express shock at the American practice of leaving infants alone in their own bedrooms (Morelli et al., 1992).

Parenting practices in the early postnatal period are influenced not only by the extent to which infant survival is in doubt but also by specific cultural belief systems. Amy Richman and her associates (1988) have observed mothers interacting with their babies in five societies, two agrarian and three industrial. Figure 4.6 shows some striking differences between how Gusii mothers in Kenya and white middle-class mothers in Boston interact with their 9- to 10-month-old infants (see also Richman, Miller, & LeVine, 1992). Gusii mothers hold their infants and make physical contact to soothe them far more than American mothers do, but they look at and talk to their babies less.

Why the differences? Like so many parents in non-Western societies with high infant mortality rates, Gusii mothers emphasize the survival goal of parenting, keeping their offspring comfortable and safe by holding them close. In addition, the Gusii believe that babies cannot understand speech until about age 2. No wonder, then, that they rarely converse with their young charges. And because cultural norms in their society demand that they avert their gaze during conversations, they rarely make eye contact with their babies either, even during lengthy breast-feeding sessions. In Boston, by contrast, playpens and infant seats are available as substitutes for mothers' arms, and their use probably reflects the value American parents place on teaching their children to be autonomous. Moreover, American mothers believe that babies *can* understand speech and that they should get an early start on developing language skills in order to succeed in school. As a result, American mothers chat away while they interact with their babies.

Although we do not know much at all about long-term effects of cultural differences in parenting practices, it is clear that infants respond to the parenting they receive. Thus, for example, Charles Super and Sara Harkness (1981) report that Kipsigis babies in Kenya wake every three to four hours to feed, whereas by 6 months of age, American babies sleep eight or nine hours straight at night. Dutch babies sleep about ten hours straight (Russell, 1995). In Boston, where mothers establish regular schedules for their infants and want their babies to be alert and responsive to their stimulation during the day but quiet at night, a baby who cannot learn to sleep through the night is quickly labeled a "problem baby" (Super

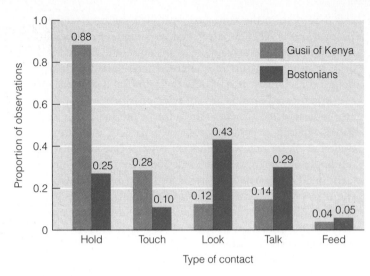

Figure 4.6 Compared to parents in Boston, Gusii parents in Kenya hold and touch their infants more but look at and talk to them less.

Source: Richman et al. (1988)

& Harkness, 1981). Dutch parents are even more insistent that babies follow regular schedules, which helps explain why Dutch babies sleep even longer at night than U.S. babies (Russell, 1995). In Kenya, by contrast, a baby who wakes at night is not viewed as difficult at all. Because mothers and infants sleep together, it is perfectly acceptable for babies to rouse their mothers now and then during the night to feed. Of special significance for development, then, may be the *goodness of fit* between an infant's behavior and the culture's demands. The baby whose temperament is well matched to its cultural "niche" is likely to have an easier experience of infancy than the baby who is not temperamentally suited to meet cultural demands. More generally, development can and does proceed normally in a wide range of cultures but it is also colored by the specific cultural context in which it occurs.

Risk and Resilience

To what extent is harm done in the prenatal or perinatal period long-lasting, and to what extent can postnatal experiences make up for it? We have encountered many examples in this chapter of what can go wrong before or during birth. Some damaging effects are clearly irreversible: The thalidomide baby will never grow normal arms or legs, and the child who is mentally retarded owing to fetal alcohol syndrome will always be mentally retarded. Yet many of us turned out fine despite the fact that our mothers, unaware of many risk factors that concern us today, smoked and drank during their pregnancies or received heavy doses of medication during delivery or experienced serious illness. So, even though many factors place a fetus at risk and increase the likelihood of prob-

lems after birth, not all at-risk infants end up with problems (Fraser, 1997). Is it also possible that some babies who are exposed and who are clearly affected recover from their deficiencies later in life?

Indeed it is, and we now have longitudinal follow-up studies to tell us so (Kopp & Kahler, 1989). For instance, some children whose mothers smoked during pregnancy experience no long-term physical, social, or intellectual problems (Lefkowitz, 1981). Similarly, some adult men whose mothers experienced severe malnutrition during pregnancy show no deficits later in life (Stein & Susser, 1976; Stein et al., 1975).

And then we have the results of major longitudinal studies of babies who were "at risk" at birth—for example, who had low birth weights, had been exposed to prenatal hazards, or suffered poor health (Baker & Mednick, 1984; Werner, 1989b; Werner & Smith, 1982, 1992). These studies indicate that babies at risk—particularly those whose problems at birth are severe—have more intellectual and social problems as children and as adolescents than normal babies do. And yet many of these at-risk babies outgrow their problems with time. Emmy Werner has now studied a group of at-risk babies born in 1955 on the island of Kauai in Hawaii for 30 years (Werner, 1989a, 1989b). One-third of these at-risk children showed remarkable **resilience** by getting themselves back on a normal course of development. Through this self-righting capacity, they were able to mature into competent, successful adults with no evident learning, social, or vocational problems. Thus, despite being "at risk" for poor outcomes, they achieved positive results. Two major findings emerge from this research:

- The effects of prenatal and perinatal stress decrease over time.
- The outcomes of early risk depend on the quality of the postnatal environment.

The postnatal environments of these successful at-risk children included two types of **protective factors** that helped the children overcome their disadvantage:

- **Personal resources.** Possibly due to their genetic makeup, some children have qualities such as intelligence, sociability, and communication skills that help them to choose or create more nurturing and stimulating environments and to cope with challenges. For example, parents noted that these children were "easygoing" and affectionate as infants, which elicited positive caregiving responses.
- **A supportive postnatal environment.** Some children at risk receive the social support they need, within or outside the family. Most important, they are able to find at least one person who loves them unconditionally.

Both personal resources and supportive postnatal environments can help prevent developmental problems and allow resilient children to thrive despite early disadvantages. With this as background, let's look more closely at one particular group of at-risk babies: those with low birth weight.

Approximately 8% of babies born in the United States are low birth weight (less than 2,500 grams, or 5½ pounds). Some of these babies are born at term, but many are born preterm (less than 37 weeks gestation). The survival and health of these small infants is a concern, particularly for infants who are born with *very* low birth weight (Paneth, 1995). Indeed, although low-birth-weight infants account for about 8% of all births, they account for 65% of all infant deaths (Murphy, 2000). As Table 4.4 illustrates, the younger (and smaller) these babies are at birth, the lower their chances of survival.

Low birth weight is strongly linked to low socioeconomic status. According to Hughes and Simpson (1995), "women who live in poverty, who have low levels of education, who work in low-wage jobs, and who have few other social resources are more likely to suffer adverse birth outcomes than are more advantaged women" (p. 87). Most programs attempting to prevent low birth weight specifically target the health conditions associated with poverty, such as poor nutrition and inadequate prenatal health care (Hughes & Simpson, 1995). Unfortunately, such programs have not been terribly successful because they do not address many of the entrenched behaviors and beliefs that accompany socioeconomic disadvantage in the United States.

Low birth weight is also associated with multiple births, which have increased substantially over the past several decades largely because of increased use of ovulation-stimulating drugs to treat infertility (Guyer et al., 1999). In 1980, there were 37 higher-order multiple births (three or more) for every 100,000 births; by 1997, this figure had jumped to 173 multiples for every 100,000 births. Among single-birth infants, approximately 5% are low birth weight, but among twins, nearly half are low birth weight, and among higher-order multiples, 86% are low birth weight (Cohen et al., 1999).

The good news is that most low-birth-weight babies born since the advent of neonatal intensive care in the 1960s function within the normal range of development (Hack, Klein, & Taylor, 1995). However, compared to normal-birth-weight children, low-birth-weight children are at greater risk for blindness, deafness, poor academic achievement, autism, and health problems. Respiratory difficulties are likely because premature babies have not yet produced enough **surfactant,** a substance that prevents the air sacs of the lungs from sticking together and therefore aids breathing. The most common

neurological problem for low-birth-weight infants is cerebral palsy, with rates of cerebral palsy increasing as birth weight decreases.

Although the long-term prognosis for low-birth-weight babies is now good, many children born with *very* low birth weight (less than 1,500 grams) continue to experience neurosensory impairments and academic problems throughout their childhood and teen years (Saigal et al., 2000). The fate of premature and low-birth-weight babies depends to a considerable extent on two factors. The first is their biological condition—their health and neurological status in particular (Koller et al., 1997). The second is the quality of the postnatal environment they experience. For instance, in a study of more than 8,000 infants, Dennis Hogan and Jennifer Park (2000) found that the disadvantages of low birth weight were amplified for children of minority status growing up in poverty with a single parent. In contrast, low-birth-weight babies whose families had high socioeconomic status, although they start out with delays, completely catch up to the average child by age 6 (Wilson, 1985). It seems that premature, low-birth-weight babies can achieve normal levels of intellectual functioning during childhood when they live in middle-class homes, when their mothers are relatively educated, and most important, *when their mothers, rich or poor, are attentive and responsive when interacting with them* (Brooks-Gunn et al., 1993; Miceli et al., 2000).

Studies like these raise a larger issue about the importance of early experience. Some developmentalists take seriously the concept of critical (or sensitive) periods in early development. Others stress the resilience of human beings, their ability to rebound from early disadvantages and to respond to environmental influences throughout their lives rather than only during so-called critical periods. Which is it?

We have encountered evidence in favor of both positions. Hazards during the important prenatal and perinatal periods *can* leave lasting scars, and yet many children show remarkable resilience. Isn't this the lesson we learn from the Romanian orphans described at the beginning of the chapter? Some were permanently affected by extreme deprivation during sensitive periods of development early in life. But many showed considerable resilience when their environment improved. There *do* seem to be some points in the life span, especially early on, in which both positive and negative

Table 4.4 **Survival and Health of Premature Babies by Gestational Age (Number of Completed Weeks Since Last Menstruation)**

	<23 Weeks	23 Weeks	24 Weeks	25 Weeks
Percentage of Babies Who Survive	0–15%	2–35%	17–58%	35–85%
Percentage of Survivors with Chronic Lung Disease	89%	57–70%	33–89 %	16–71%
Percentage of Survivors with Severe Neurodevelopmental Disability[1]	69%	30%	17–45%	12–35%

SOURCE: Data from Hack & Fanaroff (1999)
[1]Includes cerebral palsy, mental retardation, blindness or severe myopia, and deafness.

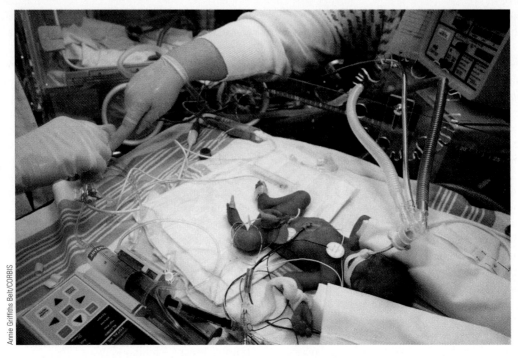

Modern technology permits survival of younger and smaller babies, but many experts believe we have reached the lowest limits of viability at 23–24 weeks gestation.

environmental forces have especially strong impacts. Yet at the same time, *environment matters throughout life.* Certainly, it would be a mistake to assume that all children who have problems at birth are doomed. In short, early experience by itself can, but rarely does, make or break development; later experience counts too, sometimes enough to turn a negative course of development completely around.

As Chapter 3 and Chapter 4 have testified, both nature and nurture contribute to life-span human development. Certain genes and early environments can have profound negative impacts on development. Yet the vast majority of us come into existence with an amazingly effective genetic program to guide our development. Most of us, whether we grow up in Kenya or Japan or the United States, also receive the ben-

efits of a normal human environment, an environment that joins forces with this genetic program to promote normal development (Gottlieb, 1996). Sometimes early insults cannot be undone, but other times only very adverse conditions over a long period of time—conditions like those experienced by some of the Romanian orphans—can keep us from developing normally. Even then, we often show a good deal of resilience if given half a chance.

We will encounter numerous examples in the remainder of this text of the positive and negative impacts that environmental forces can have on development throughout the life span. We will also want to bear in mind that each person's genetic endowment affects what experiences he or she has and how he or she is affected by them.

Summary Points

1. The environment of human development includes all events or conditions outside the person that affect or are affected by the person's development, including both the physical and the social environment.

2. Environmental influences on development begin at conception as the zygote begins its passage through three stages of prenatal development: (1) the germinal period, (2) the period of the embryo, and (3) the period of the fetus.

3. The prenatal physical environment is most supportive when a mother is between 16 and 35, is not stressed, and is well nourished.

A variety of teratogens, such as diseases and drugs, can significantly affect development. Five principles help us understand the effects of teratogens: Effects are worst when organ systems are growing most rapidly; not all embryos or fetuses are equally affected by the same teratogen; harmful effects depend on the genetic makeup of both the mother and her unborn child as well as the quality of the prenatal environment; effects are more serious with greater exposure to teratogens; and the effects of teratogens often depend on the quality of the postnatal environment.

4. The perinatal environment (the environment surrounding birth) is also important. Childbirth is a three-step process consisting of labor, delivery, and afterbirth (expulsion of the placenta). Despite

recent concerns about overuse, cesarean sections are still common. Perinatal risks to the baby include anoxia and the effects of medications given to the mother.

5. Most new parents are anxious during labor and delivery but find the experience a positive one. Support for new mothers varies across cultures.

6. Part of the postnatal environment is the cultural context. Survival, economic, and self-actualization goals of parenting are universal, but parents in cultures with high infant mortality must concentrate on infant survival and therefore keep their infants with them around the clock. Some babies are temperamentally more suited to their cultural niche than others and respond better to socialization efforts.

7. Some problems created by prenatal and perinatal hazards are long-lasting, but many babies at risk show remarkable resilience and outgrow their problems, especially if they have personal resources such as sociability and intelligence and grow up in stimulating and supportive postnatal environments where someone loves them.

8. Ways of getting human lives off to a good start today include prenatal care, Lamaze classes, alternative birth centers, neonatal intensive care units, and training for parents of high-risk infants.

Critical Thinking

1. Thinking about the material in Chapter 3 and Chapter 4, develop a plan for preventing mental retardation that involves consideration of both genetic and environmental contributors (prenatal, perinatal, and postnatal) to significantly limited intellectual development.

2. Some people argue that women who abuse alcohol or other drugs during pregnancy should be charged with abuse or attempted murder, or actual murder if they have a miscarriage. Using material from this chapter on teratogens and the prenatal environment, argue both sides of this issue.

3. Thinking about the material on birth and the perinatal environment, arrange the perfect birth experience for you and your baby, and justify its features. Where would you be, who would be there, and what would be done?

4. Write a newsletter for parents-to-be. Your goal is to provide practical advice on the unborn baby's environment and compare this to what the environment outside the womb will be like for the baby after it is born.

Key Terms

environment	testosterone
prenatal environment	period of the fetus
germinal period	age of viability
blastula	infant states
artificial insemination	Lamaze method
in vitro fertilization (IVF)	teratogen
period of the embryo	critical period
organogenesis	rubella
amnion	syphilis
chorion	acquired immune deficiency syndrome (AIDS)
placenta	
umbilical cord	thalidomide

sudden infant death syndrome (SIDS)	Apgar test
fetal alcohol syndrome (FAS)	postnatal depression
perinatal environment	socialization
anoxia	resilience
cerebral palsy	protective factors
breech presentation	surfactant
cesarean section	

On the Web

Web Sites to Explore

Premature Infants

The American Association for Premature Infants helps inform and support families with a premature infant.
http://www.aapi-online.org

The Visible Embryo

Here are two sites where you can find out precisely what's going on during the 40 weeks of pregnancy.
http://www.visembryo.com/baby/index.html
http://embryo.soad.umich.edu/index.html

Fetal Alcohol Syndrome

This site is maintained by the Centers for Disease Control and Prevention (CDC) and contains basic information about FAS.
http://www.cdc.gov/nceh/cddh/fas/fasfact.htm

Best Bet on Pregnancy and Birth

"ParentsPlace" features practical advice from a midwife about everything from conceiving a child to handling morning sickness and weight gain and giving birth. Also discusses a number of teratogens.
http://www.parentsplace.com/genobject.cgi/readroom/pregnant.html

Search Online with InfoTrac College Edition

For additional information, explore InfoTrac College Education, your online library. Go to
http://www.infotrac-college.com
and use the passcode that came on the card with your book.

- Using the key words "alcohol" and "birth," locate an article that looks at the long-term effects of prenatal alcohol use on development. What variables seem to influence the long-term outcome of children exposed prenatally to alcohol?

- Read the latest research about prematurity by doing an advanced search (use "PowerTrac") with "premature birth" as a key word combined with the current year's date. Has there been any progress on survival rates or outcomes for babies born severely premature (earlier than 24–25 weeks)?

Visit Our Web Site

Go to http://www.wadsworth.com/psychology, where you will find online resources directly linked to your book.

Life-Span CD-ROM

Go to the Wadsworth Life-Span CD-ROM for further study of the concepts in this chapter. The CD-ROM also includes quizzes and additional activities to expand your learning experience.

The Physical Self

© Laura Dwight/CORBIS

As the first quote indicates, there are definitely physical changes across the life span. But contrary to many popular views, aging is not simply a matter of declining health and deteriorating physical abilities. As the comments from Rose and Jean demonstrate, many older adults remain actively involved in life. When physical changes do occur, their effects depend a great deal on how these changes are interpreted by the individual.

In this chapter, we examine many of the physical systems that underlie human functioning. These include the endocrine and nervous systems, with emphasis on the development and aging of the brain. We will also examine the reproductive system as it matures during adolescence and changes during adulthood. And we will watch the physical self in action, as motor skills develop during childhood and physical fitness and motor behavior change during adulthood. We will identify influences on physical development and aging, so that we can better understand why some children develop—and some older adults age—more rapidly than others.

The human body is marvelously complex, with many parts working together to make the full range of behavior possible. As we saw in Chapter 4, all the major organs take shape during the first eight weeks of the prenatal period. Each bodily system has an orderly course of development (Tanner, 1990). For example, the nervous system develops very rapidly, completing most of its important growth by the end of infancy. The reproductive system, by contrast, is slower to develop than most of the organs and systems and does not grow rapidly. In order to understand physical growth and sexual maturation, we must understand the endocrine (hormonal) system. And if we want to know why adults are physically and mentally more competent than infants, we must understand the nervous system.

The Endocrine System

How *does* the human body grow? All humans have a distinctly human genetic makeup that makes them develop physically in similar directions and at similar rates. Individual heredity also influences the individual's rate of physical development and final size—in interaction, of course, with environmental factors such as diet.

But how are genetic messages translated into action? It is here that the endocrine system plays its role. **Endocrine glands** secrete chemicals called *hormones* directly into the bloodstream. Perhaps the most critical of the endocrine glands is the **pituitary gland,** the so-called master gland located at the base of the brain. Directly controlled by the *hypothalamus* of the brain, it triggers the release of hormones from all other endocrine glands by sending hormonal messages to those glands. Moreover, the pituitary produces **growth hormone,** which triggers the production of specialized hormones that directly regulate growth. Children who lack growth hormone are unlikely to exceed 4 feet (or 130 cm) in height as adults, but can now be treated successfully with synthetic growth hormones (Vance, Mauras, & Wood, 1999). By contrast, administering human growth hormone to children who are simply short and do not have an endocrine problem is likely to do no good and can even backfire. Hormone treatment tends to induce an early and short puberty, and these children are either early in attaining the height they would have reached anyway or actually end up smaller than they would otherwise have been (Rosenfeld, 1997).

The *thyroid gland* also plays a key role in physical growth and development, as well as in the development of the nervous system. Babies born to mothers who had a thyroid deficiency during pregnancy have lower IQ scores as children (Haddow et al., 1999). Thyroid deficiency during infancy can also lead to mental retardation and slow growth if unnoticed and untreated (Robertson, 1993). Children who develop a thyroid deficiency later in life will not suffer brain damage, as most of their brain growth has already occurred, but their physical growth will slow down drastically.

In Chapter 4, we encountered still another critical role of the endocrine system. A male fetus will not develop male reproductive organs unless (1) a gene on his Y chromosome triggers the development of the testes (which are endocrine glands), and (2) the testes secrete the most important of the male hormones, **testosterone.** Male sex hormones become highly important again during adolescence. When people speak of adolescence as a time of "raging hormones," they are quite right. The testes of a male secrete large quantities of testosterone and other male hormones (called **androgens**). These hormones stimulate the production of growth hormone, which in turn triggers the adolescent growth spurt. Androgens are also responsible for the development of the male sex organs and contribute to sexual motivation during adulthood (Tanner, 1990).

Meanwhile, in adolescent girls, the ovaries (also endocrine glands) produce larger quantities of the primary female hormone, **estrogen,** and of progesterone. Estrogen increases dramatically at puberty, stimulating the production of growth hormone and the adolescent growth spurt, much as testosterone does in males. It is also responsible for the development of the breasts, pubic hair, and female sex organs, as well as for the control of menstrual cycles throughout a

Table 5.1   Hormonal Influences on Growth and Development

Endocrine Gland	Hormones Produced	Effects on Growth and Development
Pituitary	Growth hormone	Regulates growth from birth through adolescence; triggers adolescent growth spurt
	Activating hormones	Signal other endocrine glands (such as ovaries and testes) to secrete their hormones
Thyroid	Thyroxine	Affects growth and development of the brain and helps to regulate growth of the body during childhood
Testes	Testosterone	Responsible for development of the male reproductive system during the prenatal period; directs male sexual development during adolescence
Ovaries	Estrogen Progesterone	Responsible for regulation of menstrual cycle; estrogen directs female sexual development during adolescence
Adrenal glands	Adrenal androgens	Play a supportive role in the development of muscle and bone; contribute to sexual motivation

woman's reproductive years. Finally, the *adrenal glands* secrete androgen-like hormones that contribute to the maturation of the bones and muscles in both sexes. There is also evidence that the maturation of the adrenal glands during middle childhood results in sexual attraction well before puberty in both boys and girls (McClintock & Herdt, 1996) and relates to sexual interest in adulthood (Arlt et al., 1999). The roles of different endocrine glands in physical growth and development are summarized in Table 5.1.

In adulthood, endocrine glands continue to secrete hormones, under the direction of the hypothalamus and the pituitary, to regulate bodily processes. For example, thyroid hormones help the body's cells metabolize (break down) foods into usable nutrients, and the adrenal glands help the body cope with stress. Throughout the life span, then, the endocrine system works together with the nervous system to keep the body on an even keel. Yet changes occur; for example, declines in levels of sex hormones are associated with menopause. And, as we will see in Chapter 17, some theorists believe that changes in the functioning of the endocrine glands late in life bring about aging and death.

In short, the endocrine system, in collaboration with the nervous system, is centrally involved in growth during childhood, physical and sexual maturation during adolescence, functioning over the entire life span, and aging later in life.

The Nervous System

None of the physical or mental achievements that we regard as human would be possible without a functioning nervous system. Briefly, the nervous system consists of the brain and spinal cord (central nervous system) and neural tissue that extends into all parts of the body (peripheral nervous system). Its basic unit is a **neuron** (see Figure 5.1). Although neurons come in many shapes and sizes, they have some common features. Branching, bushy *dendrites* receive signals from other neurons, and the long *axon* of a neuron transmits signals—to another neuron or, in some cases, directly to a muscle cell. The axon of one neuron makes a connection with another neuron at a tiny gap called a **synapse.** By releasing *neurotransmitters*

stored at the ends of its axons, one neuron can either stimulate or inhibit the action of another neuron. The axons of many neurons become covered by a fatty sheath called **myelin,** which acts like insulation to speed the transmission of neural impulses. Myelination begins prenatally but continues for many years, proceeding from the spinal cord to hindbrain, midbrain, and forebrain.

Now imagine a brain with as many as 100 billion neurons, each communicating through synapses to thousands of others. How does this brain develop to make adults more physically and mentally capable than young infants? Is it that adults have more neurons than infants do? More synapses connecting neurons or a more organized pattern of connections? And what actually happens to the brain in later life?

Early Brain Development

In the weeks following conception, brain development is phenomenal. The beginnings of a brain are apparent after only three to four weeks, when the *neural plate* folds up to form the *neural tube* (see Figure 5.2). The bottom of the tube becomes the spinal cord. "Lumps" emerge at the top of the tube and form the forebrain, midbrain, and hindbrain (see Figure 5.3). The so-called primitive or lower portions of the brain develop earliest. They regulate such biological functions as digestion, respiration, and elimination; they also control sleep–wake states and permit simple motor reactions. These are the parts of the brain that make life possible.

In perhaps 1 out of 1,000 pregnancies, the neural tube fails to fully close (Eliot, 1999). When this happens at the bottom of the tube, it can lead to *spina bifida,* in which part of the spinal cord is not fully encased in the protective covering of the spinal column. Failure to close at the top of the neural tube can lead to *anencephaly,* in which the main portion of the brain above the brainstem fails to develop, or *encephalocele,* in which a portion of the brain protrudes from the skull. Neural tube defects are more common when the mother is deficient in folic acid, again illustrating the importance to development of good maternal nutrition (Hall, 2000).

By three months after conception, the midbrain and hindbrain are well on their way to being developed, but the forebrain still has a long way to go. The **cerebral cortex**—the outer

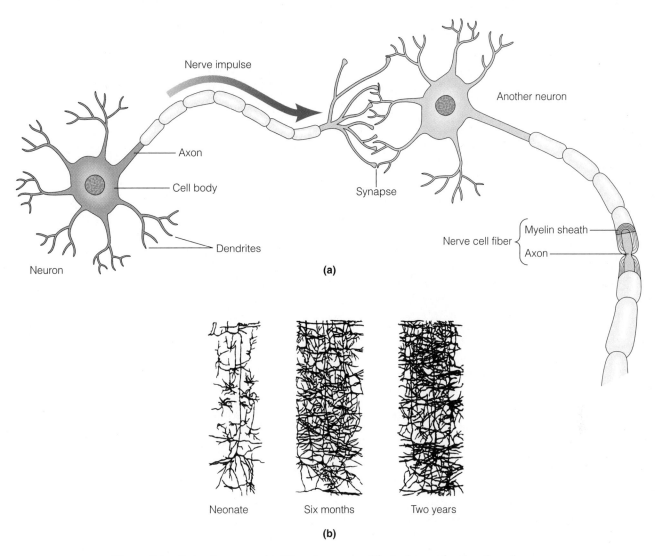

Figure 5.1 Parts of a neuron. (a) Although neurons differ in size and function, they all contain three main parts: the dendrites, which receive messages from adjacent neurons; the cell body; and the axon, which sends messages across the synapse to other neurons. (b) The formation of dendrites leading to new connections among existing neurons, as well as the myelination of neural pathways, accounts for much of the increase in brain weight during a baby's first two years.

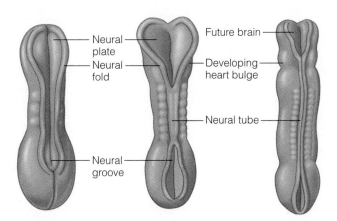

Figure 5.2 The nervous system emerges from the neural plate, which thickens and folds to form the neural groove. When the edges of the groove meet, the neural tube is formed. All of this takes place between 18 and 26 days after conception.

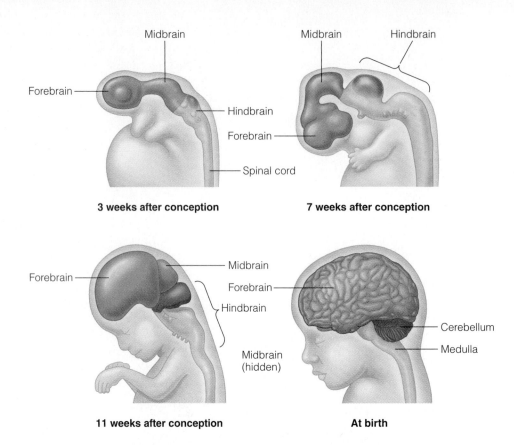

3 weeks after conception

7 weeks after conception

11 weeks after conception

At birth

Figure 5.3   The brain at four stages of development, showing hindbrain, midbrain, and fore-brain.

portion of the forebrain—is still smooth and undifferentiated. Gradually, the two hemispheres that make up the cerebral cortex become larger and more convoluted, making for a characteristically human brain. The cortex continues to develop well after birth and becomes organized into areas that control voluntary body movements, perception, and higher intellectual functions such as learning, thinking, and speaking.

Let's look closely at the processes involved in early brain development. These include the proliferation of brain cells, their migration to particular regions of the brain, their differentiation as specialized neurons, the formation of synapses that link neurons in functioning networks, and finally, com-petition and pruning processes that reduce the number of neurons and connections (see Table 5.2) (Janowsky & Carper, 1996; Johnson, 1997).

PROLIFERATION

Neurons are produced at a staggering rate during the prenatal period; by one estimate, the number of neurons increases by 250,000 every minute throughout all of pregnancy, with a concentrated period of proliferation occurring between 10 and 20 weeks after conception (Aylward, 1997). As a result of this rapid proliferation, the young infant has somewhere around 100 billion neurons. Another period of proliferation

Table 5.2   Summary of Nervous System Development

Process	Peak Occurrence
Formation of neural tube	3–4 weeks after conception
Proliferation (mass production) of nerve cells	2–4 months after conception
Migration of neurons from neural tube to final location	3–5 months after conception
Organization:	5 months after conception to 5 years after birth
Differentiation	
Connections—growth of axons and dendrites; formation of synapses	
Competition and pruning	
Myelination	End of prenatal period through adolescence

SOURCES: Adapted from Aylward (1997) and Lundy-Ekman (1998)

takes place after birth, but this produces an increase in *glial cells,* not nerve cells (Aylward, 1997). Glial cells function primarily as support cells for neurons. Until recently, it was widely believed that new neurons were produced only during the prenatal period; however, recent evidence indicates that new neurons are generated in the hippocampus of the adult brain (Eriksson et al., 1998). Nonetheless, the rate of neuronal proliferation is much greater during the prenatal period than at any time postnatally. Thus, number of neurons cannot explain why adults are cognitively more adept than babies.

MIGRATION

Once formed, neurons migrate from their place of origin to particular locations within the brain where they will become part of specialized functioning units. The impetus for migration is influenced by both genetic instructions and the biochemical environment in which brain cells find themselves. Neurons travel along the surface of glial cells and detach at programmed destinations in the developing brain. Neurons migrate to the closest or innermost parts of the brain first and to the farthest or outermost parts last. A great deal of neuronal migration occurs between 8 and 15 weeks after conception (Aylward, 1997). Unfortunately, teratogens such as alcohol can interfere with the migration process, causing developmental defects (Nowakowski, 1987). Like the proliferation of neurons, the migration of neurons is largely complete by birth and therefore cannot explain cognitive development thereafter.

ORGANIZATION

Organization is a complex process involving differentiation of neurons, synapse formation, and finally, competition among and pruning of neurons. During the differentiation or specialization process, neurons grow axons, extend dendrites, and produce the neurotransmitters that will be involved in communicating with other neurons (Nowakowski & Hayes, 1999). The type of neurotransmitter(s) produced by a brain cell and the ultimate destination of its axon and dendrites depend on where the cell ended up following migration. Every neuron starts out with the potential to become any specific type of neuron; what it actually becomes—how it differentiates— depends on where it migrates. Thus, if a neuron that would normally migrate to the visual cortex of an animal's brain is transplanted into the area of the cortex that controls hearing, it will differentiate as an auditory neuron instead of a visual neuron (Johnson, 1997).

As they become specialized in function, neurons form connections with other neurons through the process of **synaptogenesis.** Like the production of neurons, the formation of synapses occurs at a staggering rate. Indeed, the last three months of prenatal life and the first two years after birth are called the period of the **brain growth spurt.** Neuronal proliferation, synapse formation, and the production of myelin all occur very rapidly during this period.

At the same time, however, neurons are also dying and newly formed synapses are disappearing. What's happening? Researchers estimate that proliferation produces 40–50% more neurons than the mature brain really needs (Aylward, 1997). Many of these neurons die soon after they are created. Cells in the brain are highly responsive to the effects of experience, both normal and abnormal, both growth-producing and damaging. During the sensitive period of the brain growth spurt, the brain needs stimulation in order to develop normally and can be permanently damaged without it (Aylward, 1997). The genetic code supplies only a rough sketch of the wiring of the brain; it is up to experience, during sensitive periods for brain development early in life, to finalize and fine-tune the neural circuitry. For example, by moving around in the womb, the fetus contributes to the formation of synaptic connections among neurons (Ackerman, 1992). As neurons extend their axons to other neurons and form synapses, these synapses enter into a kind of competition for resources and space. The neural connections most often activated by the infant's early experiences will survive; faulty synapses and those that are used infrequently are pruned out, much as unused paths through a park disappear.

PLASTICITY

As we have just seen, the development of the brain early in life is not due entirely to the unfolding of a maturational program; it is the product of both a genetic program and early experience. Assuming that the infant has normal opportunities to explore and experience the world, the result will be a normal brain and normal development. However, the lack of normal experiences can interfere with normal brain development. Classic studies conducted by David Hubel and Torsten Wiesel showed that depriving newborn kittens of normal visual experience by suturing one eye closed for eight weeks resulted in a lack of normal connections between that eye and the visual cortex—and blindness even after the eye had been reopened (Hubel & Wiesel, 1970). Even as little as one week of deprivation during the critical period of the first eight weeks of life can lead to permanent vision loss in the kitten (Kandel & Jessell, 1991). By contrast, depriving an adult cat's eye of light does no permanent damage. In humans, the critical period for the visual cortex appears to extend for six years; children who have cataracts or for some other reason are unable to see during their first six years also suffer permanent damage to their vision (R. F. Thompson, 1993). Similarly, children with *strabismus* (short, jerky movements of the two eyeballs resulting in an inability to integrate the images from both eyes into a single image) initially have good visual acuity in both eyes. But if the condition is not corrected early, children typically lose vision in the eye that they "tune out" in order to focus on a single image from the other eye (Kandel & Jessell, 1991).

This research shows that the immature brain has great **plasticity;** that is, it is responsive to the individual's unique experiences and can develop in a variety of ways (Johnson, 1997, 1999). On the negative side, the developing brain is highly vulnerable to damage if it is exposed to drugs or diseases (recall the discussion of teratogens in Chapter 4) or if it is deprived of sensory and motor experiences. On the positive side, though, this highly adaptable brain can often recover successfully from injuries. Neurons that are not yet fully committed to their specialized functions can often take over the functions of neurons that are damaged (Rakic, 1991). Moreover, the immature brain is especially able to benefit from stimulating experiences. Rats that grow up in enriched environments with plenty of sensory stimulation develop larger, better-functioning brains with more synapses than rats that grow up in barren cages (Greenough, Black, & Wallace, 1987; Nilsson et al., 1999). Brain plasticity is greatest early in development. However, the organization of synapses within the nervous system continues to change in response to experience throughout the life span. Animals put through their paces in mazes grow bushier dendrites, but their brains lose some of their complexity if the animals are then moved to less stimulating quarters (R. F. Thompson, 1993).

In short, the critical period for brain development—the time when it proceeds most rapidly—is during the late prenatal period and early infancy. The processes of proliferation, migration, differentiation, synaptogenesis, and pruning all contribute to the final product. The developing brain is characterized by a good deal of plasticity: Normal genes may provide rough guidelines as to how the brain should be configured, but early experience determines the specific architecture of the brain.

Later Brain Development

Although the brain is proportionately the largest and most developed part of the body at birth, much development still takes place after birth. At birth, the brain weighs about 25% of its adult total; by age 2, it reaches 75% of its adult weight; and by the age of 5, the brain has achieved 90% of its adult weight. The myelination of neurons continues throughout childhood, and the different areas of the brain become more specialized.

One important feature of the developing organization of the brain is the **lateralization,** or asymmetry, of the two hemispheres of the cerebral cortex. Instead of developing identically, the functions controlled by the two hemispheres diverge (Springer & Deutsch, 1997). In most people, the left cerebral hemisphere controls the right side of the body and is adept at the *sequential processing* needed for analytic reasoning as well as for processing language. The right hemisphere generally controls the left side of the body and is skilled at *simultaneous processing* of information needed for understanding spatial information and processing visual-motor information. Although it is an oversimplification, the left hemisphere is often called the "thinking" side of the brain, whereas the right hemisphere is called the "emotional" brain.

But having two hemispheres of the brain is not the same as having two brains. The hemispheres "communicate" and work together through the *corpus callosum,* "the superhighway of neurons connecting the halves of the brain" (Gazzaniga, 1998, p. 50). And even though one hemisphere might be more active than the other during certain tasks, they both play a role in all activities. For example, the left hemisphere is considered the seat of language because it controls word content, grammar, and syntax, but the right hemisphere processes melody, pitch, sound intensity, and the affective content of language (Gazzaniga, 2000; Hellige, 1993).

If one hemisphere is damaged, it may be possible for the other hemisphere to "take over" the functions lost. For example, in a small sample of children who had their left hemispheres removed to try to reduce or eliminate severe seizures, all regained normal use of language (Vining et al., 1997; see also DeBode & Curtiss, 2000). The sample included two children who were 12 and 13 years old at the time of surgery—fairly old in terms of brain development. Thus, although the left hemisphere processes language in most people (perhaps 92%), the right hemisphere may also be able to fill this function (Knecht et al., 2000; see also Gazzaniga, 1998).

When exactly does the brain become lateralized? Signs of brain lateralization are clearly evident at birth. Newborns are more likely to turn their heads to the right than to the left (A. M. Thompson & Smart, 1993), and one-quarter show a clear right hand preference in their grasp reflex (Tan & Tan, 1999). And from the first days of life, speech sounds stimulate slightly more electrical activity in the left side of the cerebral cortex than in the right (Molfese, 1977). This evidence suggests that young brains are already organized in a lateralized fashion. Still, preference for one side of the body over the other becomes more stable and systematic throughout childhood (Coren, Porac, & Duncan, 1981).

Signs of lateralization so early in life suggest that it has a genetic basis. Further support for the role of genes comes from family studies of handedness. Overall, about 9 in 10 people rely on their right hands (or left hemispheres) to write and perform other motor activities. In families where both parents are right-handed, the odds of having a left-handed child are only 2 in 100. These odds increase to 17 in 100 when one parent is left-handed and to 46 in 100 when both parents are left-handed (Springer & Deutsch, 1997). This suggests a genetic basis to handedness, although it could also indicate that children become left-handed because of experiences provided by left-handed parents. However, experience would not account for head-turning preferences in young infants nor the differential activation of the left and right hemispheres observed in newborns when listening to speech sounds. Thus, nature rather than nurture seems to better account for much of the lateralization of the brain.

Overall, then, the brain appears to be structured very early so that the two hemispheres of the cortex will be capable of specialized functioning. As we develop, the large majority of us come to rely more on the left hemisphere to carry out language activities and more on the right hemisphere to do such things as perceive spatial relationships. We also come to rely more consistently on one hemisphere, usually the left, to control many of our physical activities.

When does the brain complete its development? In the past, the answer to this question might have been adolescence, childhood, or even infancy. Today, however, the answer is that brain development is never truly complete; the brain changes across the life span. Nonetheless, there are periods when the brain experiences "growth spurts" (P. M. Thompson et al., 2000). These growth spurts seem to occur at just the times in infancy, childhood, and adolescence when Jean Piaget and others believe major cognitive breakthroughs occur (see, for example, Epstein, 2001; Kwon & Lawson, 2000; Somsen et al., 1997). For example, teenagers are more likely than children to ask hypothetical "what if" questions and to reason about weighty abstractions such as truth and justice. Reorganization of the brain may be responsible for such breakthroughs in adolescent thinking. For example, maturation of the prefrontal lobes during adolescence enables students to focus on task-relevant material while blocking out task-irrelevant information (Casey, Giedd & Thomas, 2000; Kwon & Lawson, 2000).

Other changes in the brain also take place between ages 12 and 20. By about age 16 the brain reaches its full adult weight (Tanner, 1990). Myelination of certain pathways, including those that allow us to concentrate for lengthy periods of time, continues during adolescence, which may help explain why infants, toddlers, school-age children, and even young adolescents have shorter attention spans than do older adolescents and adults (Tanner, 1990). New evidence indicates that myelination continues well into adulthood, which may

Can Brain Development Explain Why Adolescents Take More Risks Than Adults?

Adolescents are notorious for taking chances that most adults would not take. They often display poor judgment and decision making when it comes to alcohol, drug, and cigarette use, as well as with regard to their sexual activities and driving. In Kansas City, for example, ten adolescents died in 1999–2000 in automobile accidents that resulted from "hill-hopping"—getting a car airborne as it crests the top of a hill (M. R. Williams, 2000). Other risky behaviors during adolescence include (National Center for Health Statistics, 2000b):

- Frequent smoking (reported by 17% of adolescents)
- Drinking alcohol (about 50%)
- Drinking and driving (13%)
- Riding with a driver who has been drinking (33%)
- Using marijuana (27%)
- Carrying weapons (17%)
- Having unprotected sex (42%)

Various explanations have been offered for adolescents' risk taking, including their need to separate from parents and the influence of the peer group. Linda Spear's research (2000b) suggests that brain development also contributes to risky behavior. She has found that the prefrontal cortex—that part of the brain involved in control of emotions and decision making—decreases in size and undergoes a reorganization of neuronal connections during adolescence (see also Casey, Giedd, & Thomas, 2000). Other research points to changes in the limbic system of the brain—another structure involved in emotional responsivity—during adolescence (Baird et al., 1999). Such brain changes may be responsible for the adolescent's risky behaviors, particularly when combined with social factors such as peer pressure.

Neurotransmitters (brain chemicals) may help explain the link between brain activity and adolescents' risky be-

Benelux Press/Index Stock Imagery/PictureQuest

havior. Animal research reveals that one chemical, dopamine, reaches peak levels during adolescence in the prefrontal cortex and limbic system before dropping and then leveling off (Lewis et al., 1998). This chemical is involved in novelty seeking as well as in determining the motivational value of activities (Spear, 2000a). If this holds true for human adolescents, then their risky behaviors may reflect a combination of their seeking new experiences and the changing incentive value of stimuli—both influenced by changes in brain chemistry during adolescence. So far, the research with humans does seem to support this brain–behavior connection. The adolescent brain, then, is still a work in progress, and some risk taking by teenagers may be par for the course until further brain developments refine their good judgment and decision making.

explain why adults are better able than teenagers to integrate thoughts and emotions (Benes, 1998). The speed at which the nervous system processes information also continues to increase during adolescence (Kail, 1991).

Finally, although 12-year-olds, even those who are intellectually gifted, are often "clever," they are rarely what one would call "wise." They can solve many problems correctly, but they are not as skilled as older adolescents or adults at showing foresight or adopting broad perspectives on problems (Segalowitz, Unsal, & Dywan, 1992). Although changes in the brain during adolescence are less dramatic than those earlier in life, it is quite likely that some of the cognitive growth we observe during the teenage years becomes possible only because of further brain development. For instance, when coupled with appropriate physical and social experiences, maturation of the brain contributes to the development of scientific reasoning ability. Changes in the brain during adolescence may also account for some of the risky behaviors associated with this period (see the Explorations box on page 113).

The Aging Brain

Many people fear that aging means losing one's brain cells and ultimately becoming "senile." As we'll see in Chapter 16, *Alzheimer's disease* (and other conditions that cause serious brain damage and dementia) are *not* part of normal aging; they do not affect the majority of older people. Normal aging *is* associated with gradual and relatively mild *degeneration* within the nervous system—a loss of neurons, diminished functioning of many remaining neurons, and potentially harmful changes in the tissues surrounding and supporting neurons (Selkoe, 1992). Just as brain weight and volume increase over the childhood years, they decrease over the adult years, especially after age 50 (Courchesne et al., 2000; Resnick, 2000). As people age, more and more of their neurons atrophy or shrivel, transmit signals less effectively, and ultimately die (Bondareff, 1985). Elderly adults may end up with 5–30% fewer neurons, depending on the brain site studied, than they had in young adulthood (Selkoe, 1992). Neuron loss is greater in the areas of the brain that control sensory and motor activities than in either the association areas of the cortex (involved in thought) or the brain stem and lower brain (involved in basic life functions such as breathing; Whitbourne, 2001).

Other signs of brain degeneration besides neuron loss include (1) declines in the levels of important neurotransmitters; (2) the formation of "senile plaques," hard areas in the tissue surrounding neurons that may interfere with neuronal functioning and are seen in abundance in people with Alzheimer's disease; and (3) reduced blood flow to the brain, which may starve neurons of the oxygen and nutrients they need in order to function (Bondareff, 1985). One of the main implications of such degeneration, as we will see later, is that older brains typically process information more slowly than younger brains do.

On the positive side, research shows that the brain can change in response to experience and develop new capabilities

Mental "exercise" in later life is likely to contribute to neural growth in the aging brain and compensate for neural degeneration.

throughout the life span (Black, Isaacs, & Greenough, 1991; Johnson, 1997). Neurons can form new synapses and further extend their dendrites (Kolb & Whishaw, 1998), thus filling in gaps left by dying neurons. This self-repair demonstrates at least some degree of *plasticity* in the aging brain, just as in the young brain.

What does it mean for older adults that both degeneration and plasticity—both losses and gains—characterize the aging brain? In some people, degeneration may win out, and declines in intellectual performance will occur. In other people, plasticity may prevail; their brains may form new and adaptive neural connections faster than they are lost so that performance on some tasks may actually *improve* with age (at least until very old age). As we'll see in Chapters 7, 8, and 9, older adults vary widely in how effectively they learn, remember, and think, as well as in how well their intellectual abilities hold up as they age (C. K. Morse, 1993). On average, though, plasticity and growth may make up for degeneration until people are in their 70s and 80s. One key to maintaining or even improving performance in old age is to avoid the many diseases that can interfere with nervous system functioning. Another key is to remain intellectually active—to create an "enriched environment" for one's brain. Certainly, we can reject the view that aging involves nothing but a slow death of neural tissue. Old brains *can* learn new tricks!

Having looked at the development of the endocrine system and the nervous system, we are now in a position to examine the development and aging of the physical self. We concentrate on the body (its size, composition, and functioning) and the use of body and brain in physical activities such as locomotion and finely controlled movements.

The Infant

Tremendous amounts of growth and physical development occur during the two years of infancy. Understanding the newborn's capacities and limitations brings a fuller appreciation of the dramatic changes that take place between birth and adulthood.

Newborn Capabilities

Newborns used to be viewed as helpless little organisms ill prepared to cope with the world outside the womb. We now know that they are indeed equipped to begin life. What *are* the capabilities of the newborn? Among the most important are reflexes, functioning senses, a capacity to learn, and organized, individualized patterns of waking and sleeping.

REFLEXES

One of the newborn's greatest strengths is a full set of useful **reflexes.** A reflex is an unlearned and involuntary response to a stimulus, as when the eye automatically blinks in response to a puff of air. Reflexes can be contrasted with the newborn's spontaneous arm waving, leg kicking, and thrashing— movements that have no obvious stimulus. Table 5.3 lists some reflexes that can be readily observed in all normal newborns. These seemingly simple reactions are actually quite varied and complex patterns of behavior.

Some reflexes are called *survival reflexes* because they have clear adaptive value. Examples include the breathing reflex (useful for obvious reasons), the eye-blink reflex (which protects against bright lights or foreign particles), and the sucking reflex (needed to obtain food). The so-called *primitive reflexes* are not clearly useful; in fact, many are believed to be remnants of our evolutionary history that have outlived their purpose. The *Babinski reflex* is a good example. Why would it be adaptive for infants to fan their toes when the bottoms of their feet are stroked? We don't know. Other primitive reflexes may have some adaptive value, at least in some cultures. For example, the grasping reflex may help infants who are carried in slings or on their mothers' hips to hang on. Finally, some primitive reflexes—for example, the stepping reflex—are forerunners of useful voluntary behaviors that develop later in infancy (Fentress & McLeod, 1986). Expression of primitive reflexes at age 6 weeks, however, is not related to the expression of later motor behaviors (Bartlett, 1997). Thus, infants who demonstrate a strong primitive grasping reflex at 6 weeks are not necessarily the infants who demonstrate a strong voluntary grasp later in infancy.

Primitive reflexes typically disappear during the early months of infancy. For instance, the grasping reflex becomes very weak by 4 months. These primitive reflexes are controlled by the lower, "subcortical" areas of the brain and are lost as the higher centers of the cerebral cortex develop and make voluntary motor behaviors possible. Even though many primitive reflexes are not very useful to infants, they have proven to be extremely useful in diagnosing infants' neurological problems. If such reflexes are *not* present at birth—or if they last too long in infancy—we know that something is wrong with a baby's nervous system. The existence of reflexes at birth tells us that infants come to life ready to respond to stimulation in adaptive ways. The *disappearance* of certain reflexes tells us that the nervous system is developing normally and that experience is having an impact on both brain and behavior.

BEHAVIORAL STATES

Another sign that newborns are equipped for life is their ability to establish *organized and individualized patterns of daily activity.* Settling into an organized sleep–wake pattern is an indication that the baby is integrating biological, physiological, and psychosocial information (Sadeh, Raviv, & Gruber, 2000). Infants must move from short sleep–wake cycles distributed throughout the day and night to a pattern that includes longer sleep periods at night with longer wake periods during the day. Newborns have no clear sense of night or day and may wake every one to four hours regardless of time of day. Three-month-old infants are beginning to establish a predictable sleep–wake cycle, and three-quarters of 6-month-olds have settled into a fairly consistent pattern (Minard, Freudigman, & Thoman, 1999). They spend more time asleep at night and awake during the day, and many sleep through the night, much to the delight of their tired parents. Newborns spend fully half of their sleeping hours in active sleep, also called **REM sleep** (for the rapid eye movements that occur during it). Infants older than 6 months spend only 25–30% of their total sleep in REM sleep, which more closely resembles the 20% that adults spend in REM sleep.

Why do young infants sleep so much and spend so much more time in REM sleep than adults? Daphne Maurer and Charles Maurer (1988) suggest that infants use sleep to regulate sensory stimulation. Being bombarded by too much stimulation can "overload" the immature nervous system. To reduce the stimulation, infants tend to become less active, more quiet, and shift into sleep. This may explain why infants are notoriously fussy at the end of a busy day—often at dinnertime when parents are tired and hoping for some peace. The infant's nervous system can be overstimulated from the flood of stimulation it received during the day. Somehow, the arousal needs to be reduced—perhaps by crying and then sleeping. Adults sometimes marvel at how infants can sleep through the loudest noises and the brightest lights, but being able to do so may serve a valuable function.

Research on infant states also makes it clear that newborns have a good deal of individuality (Thoman & Whitney, 1990). In a study by Brown (1964), one newborn was observed to be in an alert waking state only 4% of the time, whereas another was alert 37% of the time. Similarly, one newborn cried only 17% of the time, but another spent fully 39% of its time crying. Premature babies spend more time in transitions from one state to another, and the time they spend in any particular state is shorter than it is for full-term infants (Wyly, 1997). Such variations among infants have obvious implications for parents. It is likely to be far more pleasant to be with a baby who is often alert and rarely cries than it is to interact with a baby who is rarely attentive and frequently fussy. As we saw in Chapter 3, both genetic endowment and environment contribute to these kinds of differences in infant temperament.

Life gets easier for parents (in some ways) as infants get older. As Table 5.4 shows, infants gradually spend more time awake and less time eating, fussing, and crying. Although their sleep times do not change much, their sleep patterns do: They

Table 5.3   Major Reflexes Present in Full-Term Newborns

Reflexes	Developmental Course	Significance
SURVIVAL REFLEXES		
Breathing reflex	Permanent	Provides oxygen and expels carbon dioxide
Eye-blink reflex	Permanent	Protects eyes from bright light or foreign objects
Pupillary reflex: Constriction of pupils to bright light; dilation to dark or dimly lit surroundings	Permanent	Protects against bright light; adapts visual system to low illumination
Rooting reflex: Turning of cheek in direction of a tactile (touch) stimulus	Weakens by 2 months; disappears by 5 months	Orients child to breast or bottle
Sucking reflex: Sucking on objects placed (or taken) into mouth	Is gradually modified by experience over the first few months of life; disappears by 7 months	Allows child to take in nutrients
Swallowing reflex	Is permanent but modified by experience	Allows child to take in nutrients and protects against choking
PRIMITIVE REFLEXES		
Babinski reflex: Fanning and then curling toes when bottom of foot is stroked	Disappears between 12 and 18 months of life	Presence at birth and disappearance in first year indicate normal neurological development
Grasping reflex: Curling of fingers around objects (such as a finger) that touch baby's palm	Disappears in first 3–4 months; is replaced by a voluntary grasp	Presence at birth and later disappearance indicate normal neurological development
Moro reflex: Loud noise or sudden change in position of baby's head will cause baby to throw arms outward, arch back, and then bring arms toward each other as if to hold onto something	Disappears by 4 months; however, child continues to react to unexpected noises or a loss of bodily support by showing a startle reflex (which does not disappear)	Presence at birth and later disappearance (or evolution into the startle reflex) indicate normal neurological development
Swimming reflex: Infant immersed in water will display active movements of arms and legs and involuntary hold breath (thus staying afloat for some time)	Disappears in first 4–6 months	Presence at birth and later disappearance indicate normal neurological development
Stepping reflex: Infants held upright so that their feet touch a flat surface will step as if to walk	Disappears in first 8 weeks unless infant has regular opportunities to practice it	Presence at birth and later disappearance indicate normal neurological development

NOTE: Preterm infants may show little or no evidence of primitive reflexes at birth, and their survival reflexes are likely to be irregular or immature. However, the missing reflexes will typically appear soon after birth and will disappear a little later than they do in full-term infants.

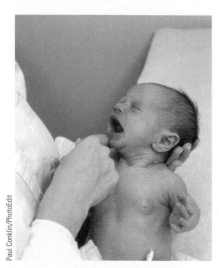

Rooting reflex

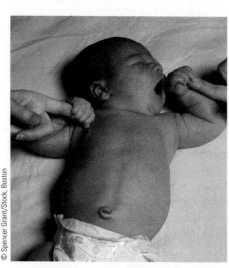

Grasping reflex

Stepping reflex

sleep for longer periods at night and take fairly predictable naps during the day.

SENSING AND LEARNING

As we saw in Chapter 4, the sensory systems are developing before birth, and all of the senses are functioning reasonably well at birth. Newborns do indeed see and hear, and they respond to tastes, smells, and touches in predictable ways too. For instance, newborns can visually track slow-moving objects; they can turn in the direction of sounds; they can turn away from unpleasant odors; they are responsive to touch; and they show preferences for sweet tastes (Wyly, 1997). We'll explore these sensory capabilities further in Chapter 6.

Another strength of newborns is their *ability to learn* from their experiences. They can, for example, learn to suck faster if sucking produces a pleasant-tasting sugary liquid rather than plain water (Lipsitt, 1990). In other words, they can change their behavior according to its consequences. This is an example of the process of operant conditioning, which was introduced in Chapter 2.

Newborn infants are indeed competent and ready for life. They have a wide range of reflexes, functioning senses, a capacity to learn, and an organized and unique pattern of waking and sleeping. But when you think about newborns in comparison to adults, it's also clear that newborns are quite limited beings. Their brains are not nearly as developed as they will be by the end of infancy. Their capacity to move *voluntarily and intentionally* is limited, and although their senses are working, they cannot interpret stimuli as well as an older individual can. They can learn, but they are slow learners compared to older children, often requiring many learning trials before they form an association between stimulus and response. And they clearly lack important social and communication skills. In short, newborns have both strengths and limitations—strengths that can serve as building blocks for later development, limitations that tell us much remains to be accomplished.

Principles of Growth

Newborns are typically about 20 inches long and weigh 7 to 7½ pounds. Boys are longer than girls at birth and during the first two years of life, although not during the preschool years (Hauspie et al., 1996). Weight and length at birth can mislead us about eventual weight and height, though, because the growth of some fetuses is stunted by a poor prenatal environment (Hauspie et al., 1996). In the first few months of life, infants grow rapidly, gaining nearly an ounce of weight a day and an inch in length each month. By age 2, they have already attained about half of their eventual adult height and weigh 27 to 30 pounds. Although we usually think of growth as a slow and steady process, daily measurements of infant length show that babies grow in fits and starts (Lampl, Veldhuis, & Johnson, 1992). They may grow a couple of centimeters one day and then not grow at all for a few weeks before experiencing another little growth spurt. In the end, 90–95% of an infant's days are growth free, and yet their occasional bursts of physical growth add up to substantial increases in size.

Infants who receive inadequate nutrition—whether from lack of resources, neglect, or feeding problems—show *growth retardation* (Tanner, 1990). However, when provided with adequate nutrition, they grow much faster than normal. This **catch-up growth** after a period of malnutrition or illness reflects the body's struggle to get back on the growth course that it is genetically programmed to follow.

Bones and muscles also develop quickly during infancy. At birth, most of the infant's bones are soft, pliable, and difficult to break. They are too small and flexible to allow newborns to sit up or balance themselves when pulled to a standing position. The soft cartilage-like tissues of the young infant gradually ossify (harden) into bony material as calcium and other minerals are deposited into them. In addition, more bones develop, and they become more closely interconnected. As for muscles, young infants are relative weaklings. They have all the muscle cells they will ever have, but their strength will increase as their muscles grow larger.

You have probably noticed that young infants seem to be all head compared to older children and adults. That is because growth follows the **cephalocaudal principle,** occurring in a head-to-tail direction. This pattern is clear in Figure 5.4: The head is far ahead of the rest of the body during the prenatal period and accounts for about 25% of the newborn's length. But the head accounts for only 12% of an adult's height. During the first year after birth, the trunk grows the fastest; in the second year, the legs are the fastest growing part of the body.

While infants are growing from the head downward, they are also growing and developing muscles from the center outward to the extremities. This **proximodistal principle** of growth can be seen during the prenatal period, when the chest and internal organs form before the arms, hands, and fingers. During the first year of life, the trunk is rapidly filling out while the arms remain short and stubby until they undergo their own period of rapid development.

A third important principle of growth and development is the **orthogenetic principle.** This means that development starts out global and undifferentiated and moves toward increasing differentiation and hierarchical integration (Werner, 1957). Consider a human who starts out as a single, undifferentiated cell at conception. As growth proceeds, that single cell

Table 5.4	Percentage of Day (24-hour period) Spent in Various Behavioral States at 2, 6, 12, and 40 Weeks. Note especially the increase in time awake.			
BEHAVIOR	2 Weeks	6 Weeks	12 Weeks	40 Weeks
Sleeping	59%	56%	57%	55%
Awake	14	19	25	34
Feeding	17	15	11	8
Fussing	5	6	5	3
Crying	4	3	2	<1

Columns may not add to 100% because of rounding.

SOURCE: Adapted from St. James-Roberts & Plewis (1996)

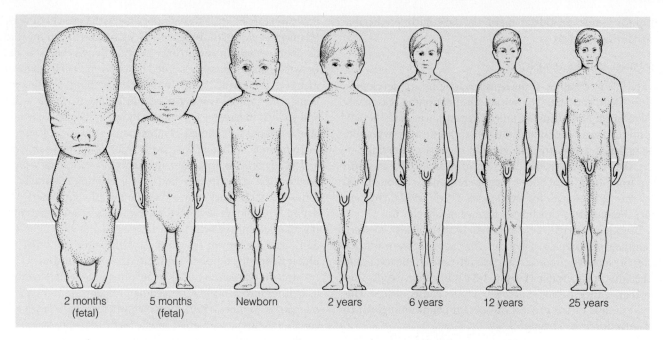

Figure 5.4 Changes in the proportions of the human body from the fetal period through adulthood. The head represents 50% of body length at 2 months after conception but only 12–13% of adult height. By contrast, the legs constitute only about 12–13% of the length of a 2-month-old fetus but 50% of an adult's height.

becomes billions of highly specialized cells (neurons, blood cells, liver cells, and so on). These differentiated cells become organized, or integrated, into functioning systems such as the brain or the digestive system.

Overall, then, physical growth is orderly, obeying the cephalocaudal, proximodistal, and orthogenetic principles. As we will see shortly, motor development follows these same principles. The rapid physical and muscular growth that occurs during infancy, combined with the development of the nervous system, helps make possible the tremendous advances in motor development that we see during these two years.

Physical Behavior

The motor behaviors of newborns are far more organized and sophisticated than they appear at first glance, but newborns are not ready to dance or thread needles. By age 2, however, immobile infants have become toddlers, walking up and down stairs by themselves and using their hands to accomplish simple self-care tasks and to operate toys. How do the motor skills involved in walking and manipulating objects develop?

LOCOMOTOR DEVELOPMENT

Table 5.5 shows the age at which half of U.S. infants master particular motor milestones. This average age of mastery is called the **developmental norm** for a skill. Developmental norms like these must be interpreted carefully. They depend on the group studied (children walk earlier today than they used to and walk earlier in some cultures than in others), and they hide a good deal of variation among children, even in the sequence in which skills are mastered (von Hofsten, 1993).

Table 5.5 Age Norms (in months)* for Important Motor Milestones during the First Year (based on Anglo-American, Hispanic, and African American children in the United States). Can you see the cephalocaudal and proximodistal principles of development at work?

2 months	Lifts head up when lying on stomach
3 months	Rolls over from stomach to back; holds head steady when being carried
4 months	Grasps a cube or other small object
5 months	Sits without support toward end of month
6 months	Stands holding onto something
7 months	Rolls over from back to stomach; may begin to crawl or creep; shows thumb opposition
8 months	Pulls self up to standing position
9 months	Walks holding onto furniture; bangs two objects together
10 months	Plays clapping games (for example, pat-a-cake)
11 months	Stands alone
12 months	Walks well alone; drinks from a cup

SOURCES: Bayley (1993); Frankenburg et al. (1992)
*Age at which 50% of infants have demonstrated the skill. Keep in mind that there are large individual differences in when infants display various developmental milestones.

Finally, most children who master a skill earlier or later than the developmental norm are still within the normal range of development. Parents should not be alarmed if their child is a month or two "behind" the norm; only significantly delayed achievement of new skills is cause for concern.

Can you recognize the workings of the cephalocaudal and proximodistal principles of development in the milestones in Table 5.5? Early motor development follows the *cephalocaudal principle* because the neurons between the brain and the muscles myelinate in a head-to-tail manner. Thus, infants can lift their heads before they can control their trunks enough to sit, and they can sit before they can control their legs to walk. The *proximodistal principle* of development is also evident in early motor development. Activities involving the trunk are mastered before activities involving the arms and legs, and activities involving the arms and legs are mastered before activities involving the hands and fingers or feet and toes. Therefore, infants can roll over before they can walk or bring their arms together to grasp a bottle, and children generally master **gross motor skills** (skills such as kicking the legs or drawing large circles that involve large muscles and whole body or limb movements) before mastering **fine motor skills** (skills such as picking Cheerios off the breakfast table or writing letters of the alphabet that involve precise movements of the hands and fingers or feet and toes). As the nerves and muscles mature in a downward and outward direction, infants gradually gain control over the lower and the peripheral parts of their bodies.

The *orthogenetic principle* is also evident in early motor development. A very young infant is likely to hurl his whole body as a unit at a bottle of milk held close by (*global response*). An older infant gains the ability to move specific parts of her body separately (*differentiation*); she may be able to extend one arm toward the bottle without extending the other arm, move the hand but not the arm to grasp it, and so on, making distinct, differentiated movements. Finally, the still older infant is able to coordinate separate movements in a functional sequence—reaching for, grasping, and pulling in the bottle while opening the mouth to receive it and closing the mouth when the prize is captured (*integration*).

Crawling. Life changes dramatically for infants and their parents when the infants first begin to crawl or creep, normally at around 7 months of age. Different infants find different ways to navigate at first; one may slither on her belly in a kind of combat crawl, another may use only his forearms to pull ahead, another may chug along backwards. However, most infants end up crawling on their hands and knees at about 10 months of age, and they all seem to figure out that the best way to keep their balance is to move the arm and leg that are diagonal to one another at the same time (Freedland & Bertenthal, 1994).

With their new mobility, infants are better able to explore the objects around them and to interact with other people. Experience moving through the spatial world contributes to cognitive, social, and emotional development (see Bertenthal, Campos, & Kermoian, 1994). For example, crawlers, as well as noncrawlers who are made mobile with the aid of special walkers, are more able to search for and find hidden objects

Young toddlers have difficulty maintaining their balance because of their large, heavy heads and torsos and their weak muscles.

than are infants of the same age who are not mobile. Crawling also contributes to more frequent social interactions with parents and to the emergence of a healthy fear of heights.

Walking. Although parents must be on their toes when their infants first begin walking, at about 1 year of age, they take great delight in witnessing this new milestone in motor development, as do infants themselves. According to Esther Thelen (1984, 1995), the basic motor patterns required for walking are present at birth. They are evident in the newborn's stepping reflex and in the spontaneous kicking that infants do when they are lying down. Indeed, Thelen noticed that the stepping reflex and early kicking motions were actually identical. She began to question the traditional understanding that early reflexes, controlled by subcortical areas of the brain, are inhibited once the cortex takes control of movements. Thelen showed that it simply requires more strength to make the walking motion standing up (as in the stepping reflex) than to make it lying down (as in kicking). She demonstrated that babies who no longer showed the stepping motion when placed on a table *did* show it when suspended in water so that less muscle power was needed to move their chunky legs. The upshot? Infants need more than a more mature nervous system in order to walk; they must also develop more muscle and become less top-heavy. Even when they do begin to walk, they lack good balance, partly because of their big heads and short legs. Steps are short; legs are wide apart; and hips, knees, and ankles are flexed. There is much teetering and falling, and a smooth gait and good balance will not be achieved for some time. Thelen's point is that we would walk funny too if we, like infants, were "fat, weak, and unstable" (Thelen, 1984, p. 246).

How do infant "walkers" affect the emergence of walking? Do they enhance walking, perhaps by allowing infants to exercise their legs without having to support the full weight of their bodies? To answer these questions, Andrea Siegel and Roger Burton (1999) studied three groups of infants: One group used no walkers; a second group used older-model walkers that had large leg openings and allowed the infants to see their legs and feet; and a third group used newer-model walkers designed to be safer than the older model with small leg openings and large opaque trays. These newer walkers helped prevent infants from slipping out of the seat, but they blocked the infants' view of their legs and feet. Infants who did not use either type of walker sat up, crawled, and walked earlier than infants with the old-style walkers, and they in turn walked earlier than infants with newer walkers. Why? Infants in the newer walkers with the opaque trays did not receive sensory feedback about their movements; they could not see how their movements altered the positions of their legs relative to other body parts and to the stationary environment. As we'll see later in this section, infants need feedback to learn how to coordinate their body movements with the demands of the environment.

Walker use also affected scores on the Bayley, a measure of motor and mental development. As Figure 5.5 shows, infants in the newer walkers scored significantly lower on motor development than the other two groups and scored significantly lower on mental development than infants in the no-walker group. The newer walkers restrict visual-motor experiences at a time when infants are seeking new levels of interaction with their environment. Emerging skills of crawling, reaching, and grasping are restricted, which limits what infants can learn about their environment. These infants likely catch up in mental development to their no-walker peers once they stop using walkers, usually around 10 months of age when they are capable of climbing out of these contraptions.

MANIPULATING OBJECTS

When we look at what infants can do with their hands, we also find a progression from reflexive activity to more voluntary, coordinated behavior. As we have seen, newborns come equipped with a grasping reflex. It weakens at 2 to 4 months

of age, and for a time infants cannot aim their grasps very well. They take swipes at objects, and even make contact more than you'd expect by chance, but they often miss. And rather than opening their hands to grasp what they are reaching for, they make a fist (Bower, 1982; von Hofsten, 1993).

By the middle of the first year, infants can once again grasp objects well, although they use a rather clumsy, clamp-like grasp in which they press the palm and outer fingers together. As they gain postural control of their trunks and heads and visual control of their eyes, they become increasingly skillful at reaching for and manipulating objects with their hands (Bertenthal & von Hofsten, 1998). The workings of the proximodistal principle of development can be seen when infants who could control their arms and then their hands finally become able to control the individual fingers enough to use a **pincer grasp.** Involving only the thumb and the forefinger (or another finger), the pincer grasp appears at about 9 to 12 months (Halverson, 1931).

By 16 months of age, infants can scribble with a crayon, and by the end of the second year they can copy a simple horizontal or vertical line and even build towers of five or more blocks. They are rapidly gaining control of specific, *differentiated* movements and then *integrating* those movements into whole, coordinated actions. They use their new locomotor and manipulation skills to get to know and adapt to the world around them. By cornering bugs and stacking Cheerios, they develop their minds.

EMERGENCE OF MOTOR SKILLS

How do these skills emerge? Esther Thelen (1996) observed infants throughout their first year and discovered that they spent a great deal of time engaged in **rhythmic stereotypies.** The infants moved their bodies in repetitive ways—rocking, swaying, bouncing, mouthing objects, and banging their arms up and down. Thelen found that infants performed these rhythmic stereotypies shortly before a new skill emerged, but not after the skill had become well established. Thus, infants might rock back and forth while on their hands and knees, but once they were crawling, they no longer rocked.

Thelen and Smith (1994) propose a **dynamic systems approach** to explain such motor developments. According to this view, developments take place over time through a "self-organizing" process in which children use the sensory feedback they receive when they try out different movements to modify their motor behavior in adaptive ways (Smith & Thelen, 1993). In this view, motor milestones such as crawling and walking are the learned outcomes of a process of interaction with the environment in which infants do the best they can with what they have to achieve their goals (Thelen, 1995). Neural maturation, physical growth, muscle strength, balance, and other characteristics of the child interact with gravity, floor surfaces, and characteristics of the specific task to influence what children can and cannot learn to do with their bodies. Recall the infants who couldn't see their legs or feet in the newer walkers. It took them longer to achieve certain motor milestones than infants who could see their legs and learn how their movements affected their relationship to the environment.

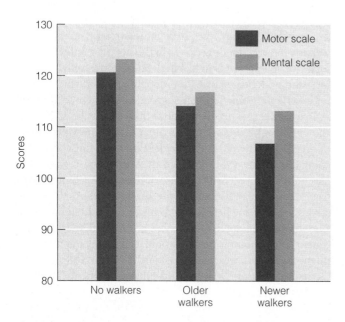

Figure 5.5 Scores on the Bayley Scales of Mental and Psychomotor Development for infants who use no walkers, older (can see their feet) walkers, or newer (feet are not visible) walkers

SOURCE: Siegel & Burton (1999)

These 3-year-olds may think they're playing, but stringing beads also exercises their eye–hand coordination and fine motor skills.

Consistent with the dynamic systems approach, Karen Adolph and Anthony Avolio (2000) found that young toddlers could adjust their walking to changes in both body dimensions and the slope of a walkway. The researchers had infants walk on slopes of different degrees while outfitted with a vest that had removable "saddlebags" that could be weighted to simulate changes in their body dimensions (see Figure 5.6). The weights added mass and shifted the infants' center of gravity, akin to what happens when infants grow bigger. Would infants be able to compensate for the changes in their body and the environment? Yes—they adjusted their motor skills to adapt to rapid "growth" of their bodies as well as to changes in the environment (see also Adolph, 1997). Like adults carrying a heavy load on their shoulders, infants bent their knees and kept their upper bodies stiffly upright to maintain their balance with heavier loads. Infants also seemed to recognize when the walkway was too steep to travel safely—they either avoided it or scooted down on their bottoms or on their hands and knees.

According to the dynamic systems perspective, toddlers walk not because their genetic code programs them to do so but because they *learn* that walking works pretty well, given their biomechanical properties and the characteristics of the environments they must navigate (Thelen, 1995). In the dynamic systems approach, nature (maturation) and nurture (sensory and motor experience) are both essential and largely inseparable. Feedback from the senses and from motor actions is integrated with the ever-changing abilities of the infant. Having learned how to adjust one motor skill (such as crawling) to successfully navigate environmental conditions, however, does not mean that infants will generalize this knowledge to other motor skills (such as walking) (Adolph & Avolio, 2000). Different motor skills present different challenges.

Figure 5.6 Adolph and Avolio's walkway with adjustable slope. Infants are outfitted with weighted saddlebags to alter their body mass and center of gravity. While an experimenter stays beside infants to ensure safety, parents stand at the end of the walkway and encourage their child to walk toward them.
SOURCE: Adolph & Avolio (2000)

Crawling infants, for instance, must learn to avoid such dangers as bumping their head into table legs. Walking infants face other challenges, such as not toppling over when turning around. To master these challenges, infants need opportunities to gather feedback from each motor activity.

An important contribution of the dynamic systems approach to motor development is its integration of action with thought. The motor behaviors that we have been discussing are not separate and distinct from the child's knowledge. As Thelen and Smith (1994) phrase it, "knowing is a *product* of our dynamic system" (p. 310, emphasis in original). Thus, there is far more to motor development than is implied by

norms indicating when we might expect to see infants sit up, stand alone, or walk independently. The emergence of motor skills is complex and is closely connected to perceptual-cognitive developments (Bushnell & Boudreau, 1993).

The Child

Development of the body and of motor behavior during childhood is slower than it was during infancy, but it is steady. One need only compare the bodies and the physical feats of

Promoting Lifelong Health with Physical Activity

It's clear that physical activity has beneficial effects on physical functioning across the life span. For instance, children who participate in a systematic exercise program are more physically fit than children who follow a more sedentary lifestyle (see Tuckman, 1999, for review). Similarly, exercise by older adults can improve cardiovascular and respiratory functioning, slow bone loss, and strengthen muscles. In one study, older athletes (average age of 69 years) were compared to older nonathletes on a number of physiological measures following exercise. The athletes showed better oxygen uptake capacity and greater cardiovascular stamina than the nonathletes (Jungblut et al., 2000). In another study, elderly adults who did low-intensity exercise and weight lifting for a year became stronger and more flexible and experienced less pain as a result (Sharpe et al., 1997). Exercise also reduces the number of sick days, doctor visits, and hospitalizations of older adults (German et al., 1995). Overall, it is estimated that regular exercise by older adults can delay the onset of physical disabilities by up to seven years (Vita et al., 1998).

The benefits of exercise go beyond physical fitness; physical activity may also enhance cognitive and psychological functioning. In a review of studies on children's participation in physical activity and their academic performance, Roy Shepard (1997) concluded that increased physical activity was associated with improved academic skills. But these data are largely correlational, and many factors may mediate the connection between physical activity and academic performance. For instance, Mark Tremblay and colleagues (Tremblay, Inman, & Willms, 2000) found that regular participation in physical activity did *not* strongly influence 12-year-olds' academic performance, but it did positively affect their self-esteem. Students who are healthier and feel better about themselves may ultimately perform better in the classroom.

Older adults also reap multiple benefits from participating in exercise programs. Exercise can make aging adults feel less stressed and happier, and it can enhance cognitive

Bob Daemmrich/Stock, Boston

functioning (Haber, 1994; King, Taylor, & Haskell, 1993; Rowe & Kahn, 1998). Physical activity is also associated with lower incidence of depression among older adults (Lampinen, Heikkinen, & Ruoppila, 2000).

the 2-year-old and the 10-year-old to be impressed by how much change occurs over childhood.

Steady Growth

From age 2 until puberty, children gain about 2 to 3 inches in height and 5 to 6 pounds in weight every year (National Center for Health Statistics, 2000a). During middle childhood (ages 6–11), children may *seem* to grow very little, probably because the gains are small in proportion to the child's size (4–4½ feet tall and 60–80 pounds) and therefore harder to detect. The cephalocaudal and proximodistal principles of growth continue to operate. As the lower parts of the body and the extremities fill out, the child takes on more adultlike body proportions. The bones are continuing to grow and harden, and the muscles are becoming stronger.

Physical Behavior

Infants and toddlers are quite capable of controlling their movements in relation to a *stationary* world, but children master the ability to move capably in a *changing* environment (Sayre & Gallagher, 2001). They must learn to modify their movements to adapt to changes in the environment. This

Unfortunately, we live in an era that inadvertently promotes physical inactivity. The average child watches 3 hours of television every day (Huston et al., 1999), and schools have reduced recess time and physical education requirements (Tremblay, Pella, & Taylor, 1996). Time riding in cars and sitting at the computer has increased while walking and physical activity time has decreased. As a result, as many as 30% of American children are estimated to be overweight (Wolfe et al., 1994), and being an overweight child or adolescent usually means becoming an overweight adult (Boodman, 1995). Children who watch more than 5 hours of television a day are about five times more likely to be overweight than children who watch 0 to 2 hours a day, perhaps because they get little exercise and eat the junk foods they see advertised on TV (Gortmaker et al., 1996). Weight loss programs are likely to be more successful with child "couch potatoes" than with adult ones, though; self-control may not be as necessary if parents can control their children's eating habits for them (Wilson, 1994).

Teenagers face increased risks of obesity because their metabolism rates slow down as they mature physically. Individuals who are overweight as adolescents—even those who slim down as adults—run a greater-than-average risk of coronary heart disease and a host of other health problems some 55 years later (Must et al., 1992). Middle-aged adults also run a special risk of gaining weight, especially if they become less physically active but keep eating as much as they did as younger adults (Haber, 1994).

Obesity—being 20% or more above the "ideal" weight for your height, age, and sex—is clearly a threat to health, and rates of obesity have been increasing in our society at all ages, even among children (Dwyer & Stone, 2000). Obese people do not live as long as their normal-weight peers, and they are at greater risk for such problems as heart and kidney disease, high blood pressure, diabetes, liver problems, and even arthritis. Obesity is usually the product of both nature and nurture: Heredity is perhaps the most important factor (Grilo & Pogue-Geile, 1991), but poor eating habits, inactivity, and even parenting beliefs also contribute (Gable & Lutz, 2000). One intriguing finding comes from a recent study comparing obese and nonobese children on a number of factors, including eating habits and activities (Gable & Lutz, 2000). Surprisingly, the two groups did *not* differ in their consumption of high-fat, high-sugar, junk foods. They *did* differ in their activities: Obese children watched more television, participated in fewer extracurricular activities, and engaged in less active play. So perhaps parents should worry less about the junk food their children consume—as long as it is not excessive or a substitute for healthy foods—and focus more on getting their children involved in physical activities.

Exercise is clearly beneficial to physical and mental health over the life span. What exercise cannot do is halt the inevitable aging process. Even frequent joggers gain weight and add inches to their waists as they enter middle age (P. T. Williams, 1997). True, people who exercise generally weigh less and have slimmer waists than those who do not, but a 30-year-old man who runs 20–30 miles a week until he is 50 would add almost 2 inches to his waist anyway; he would have to run farther and farther each year to avoid it. To try to beat aging, then, it is not enough to remain active; one must become *more* active over the years (Williams, 1997).

As this discussion shows, physical and psychological development are intimately intertwined throughout the life span. Changes in the body require psychological adjustments and bring psychological change. Newly mobile infants benefit cognitively and emotionally from access to a larger physical and social world; adolescents alter their body images in response to physical and sexual maturation; and aging adults change in response to disease and disability. At the same time, psychological and social factors influence reactions to these physical changes.

Children are not as coordinated in preschool as they will be a few years later.

allows them to bring their hands together at just the right time to catch a ball and avoid bumping into moving people when walking through a crowded mall. They also refine many motor skills. For example, young children throw a ball only with the arm, but older children learn to step forward as they throw. Thus, older children can throw a ball farther than younger ones can, not just because they are bigger and stronger but also because they can integrate multiple body movements—raising their arm, turning their body, stepping forward with one foot, and pushing their body forward with the other foot (Sayre & Gallagher, 2001).

The toddler in motion appears awkward compared to the older child, who takes steps in more fluid and rhythmic strides and is better able to avoid obstacles. And children quickly become able to do more than just walk. By age 3, they can walk or run in a straight line, though they cannot easily turn or stop while running. Kindergarten children can integrate two motor skills—hopping on one foot with walking or running—into mature skipping (Loovis & Butterfield, 2000). With each passing year, school-age children can run a little faster, jump a little higher, and throw a ball a little farther (Keough & Sugden, 1985). Their motor skills are also very responsive to practice. In one study, children improved their arm movements 25–30% with practice—an impressive accomplishment compared to the 10% improvement shown by adults who practiced (Thomas, Yan, & Stelmach, 2000). We see some gender differences in mo-

tor skills, with boys slightly ahead in throwing, kicking, and running, but these differences seem to arise from practice and different expectations for males and females (Thomas & French, 1985). The Applications box on page 122 explores some of the benefits of physical activity for children as well as adults.

From age 3 to 5, eye–hand coordination and control of the small muscles are improving rapidly, giving children more and more sophisticated use of their hands. Three-year-olds find it difficult to button their shirts, tie their shoes, or copy simple designs. By age 5, children can accomplish all of these feats and can also cut a straight line with scissors or copy letters and numbers with a crayon. By age 8 or 9, they can use household tools such as screwdrivers and have become skilled performers at games that require eye–hand coordination. Handwriting quality and speed also improve steadily from age 6 to age 15 (van Galen, 1993).

Finally, older children have quicker reactions than young children do. When dogs suddenly run in front of their bikes, they can do something about it. In studies of **reaction time,** a stimulus, such as a light, suddenly appears, and the subject's task is to respond to it as quickly as possible—for example, by pushing a button. These studies reveal that reaction time improves steadily throughout childhood (Eaton & Ritchot, 1995; Yan et al., 2000). As children get older, they can carry out any number of cognitive processes more quickly as well (Kail, 1991; van Galen, 1993). This speeding up of neural responses with age contributes in important ways to steady improvements in memory and other cognitive skills from infancy to adolescence (see Chapter 8).

In short, no matter what aspect of physical growth and motor behavior we consider, we see steady and impressive improvement over the childhood years. But these changes are not nearly so dramatic as those that will occur during the adolescent years, as the child becomes an adult.

The Adolescent

Adolescents are intensely focused on their physical self, and rightly so—dramatic physical changes are taking place during this period.

Physical Growth and Sexual Maturation

Consider your own transformation from child to adult. You rapidly grew taller during the **adolescent growth spurt** and took on the body size and proportions of an adult. Moreover, you experienced **puberty**—the processes of biological change that result in an individual's attaining sexual maturity and becoming capable of producing a child. Let's take a look at both of these processes.

THE GROWTH SPURT

As noted earlier in the chapter, the growth spurt is triggered by an increase in the level of growth hormones circulating through the body during adolescence. Boys and girls grow at different rates, as do different body parts. Girls' peak rate of growth for height is just under 12 years; for boys it is 13.4 years (Geithner et al., 1999). Peak rate of growth for weight is 12.5 years for girls and 13.9 for boys. Thus, boys lag behind girls by one to two years. Both sexes return to a slower rate of growth after the peak of their growth spurts. Like infants, adolescents may grow in spurts rather than continuously (Lampl et al., 1992). Girls achieve their adult height by around 16 years, while boys are still growing at 18, 19, even 20 years of age (National Center for Health Statistics, 2000a).

Muscles also develop rapidly in both sexes, with boys normally gaining a higher proportion of muscle mass than girls do. Total body weight increases in both sexes, but it is distributed differently: Girls gain extra fat, primarily in the breasts, hips, and buttocks; boys develop broader shoulders.

SEXUAL MATURATION

Long before the physical signs of puberty are evident, the body is changing to prepare for sexual maturity. The adrenal glands increase production of adrenal androgens as early as age 6 to 8, which contributes in small part to such secondary sex characteristics as pubic and axillary (underarm) hair (see Spear, 2000a). But the more obvious signs of sexual maturity emerge with increased production of gonadal hormones (those produced by the testes or ovaries): androgens in males and estrogen and progesterone in females. The gonadal hormones are primarily responsible for the development of secondary sexual characteristics and sexual maturity.

For girls, the most dramatic event in the sexual maturation process is **menarche**—the first menstruation—normally between the ages of 11 and 15, with an average of 12½ in the United States (see Figure 5.7). Menstruation is the process of shedding the lining of the uterus that has been prepared to support a fertilized egg. However, young girls often begin to menstruate before they have begun to ovulate, so they *may* not actually be capable of reproducing for several years after menarche (see Spear, 2000a).

Physical and sexual maturation among girls in the United States appears to occur a good deal earlier than norms based on older studies indicate, and it proceeds at different rates in different ethnic groups. Marcia Herman-Giddens and her colleagues (1997) discovered that African American girls begin to experience pubertal changes a year or more earlier than European American girls. At the age of 8, for example, 48% of African American girls, compared to only 15% of European American girls, had begun to develop breasts, pubic hair, or both. African American girls reached menarche at an average age of 12.1, European American girls at 12.9. Wide variation was evident in both racial groups, however; a few girls (1% of whites, 3% of blacks) showed signs of breast or pubic hair development at age 3, while a few had not begun to mature even at age 12!

For the average boy, the sexual maturation process begins at about age 11 to 11½ with an initial enlargement of the testes and scrotum (the saclike structure that encloses the testes). Unpigmented, straight pubic hair appears soon thereafter, and about six months later, the penis grows rapidly at about the

same time that the adolescent growth spurt begins (Tanner, 1990; and see Figure 5.7). The marker of sexual maturation that is most like menarche in girls is **semenarche,** or a boy's first ejaculation—the emission of seminal fluid in a "wet dream" or while masturbating. It typically occurs at about age 13. Just as girls often do not ovulate until some time after menarche, boys often do not produce viable sperm until some time after their first ejaculation.

Somewhat later, boys begin to sprout facial hair, first at the corners of the upper lip and finally on the chin and jawline. As the voice lowers, many boys have the embarrassing experience of hearing their voices "crack" uncontrollably up and down between a squeaky soprano and a deep baritone, sometimes within a single sentence. Boys may not see the first signs of a hairy chest until their late teens or early twenties, if at all.

VARIATIONS IN TIMING

As noted above, there are large individual differences in the timing of physical and sexual maturation. An early-maturing girl may develop breast buds at age 8 and reach menarche at age 10, whereas a late-developing boy may not begin to experience a growth of his penis until age 14½ or a height spurt until age 16. Within a middle school, then, one will find a wide assortment of bodies, ranging from those that are entirely childlike to those that are fully adultlike. No wonder adolescents are self-conscious about their appearance.

What determines an adolescent's rate of development? Genes are part of the answer: Identical twins typically experience changes at similar times, and early or late maturation tends to run in families (Tanner, 1990). In both sexes, the

Although there are large individual differences, girls typically mature earlier than boys, which sometimes leads to girls' towering over the boys in their classes.

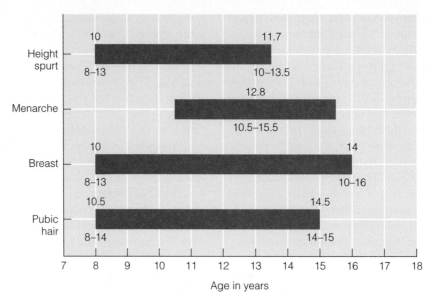

(a) Females

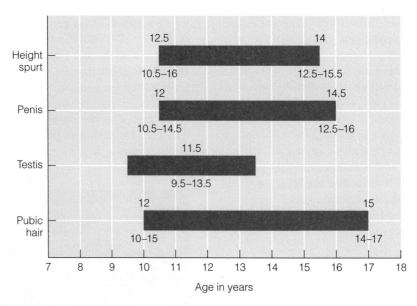

(b) Males

Figure 5.7 Sequence of events in the sexual maturation of females (A) and males (B). The numbers represent the variation among individuals in the ages at which each aspect of maturation begins or ends. For example, we see that the growth of the penis may begin as early as age 10½ or as late as age 14½.

Source: Adapted from Marshall & Tanner (1990); Malina & Bouchard (1991)

changes involved in physical and sexual maturation are triggered when the hypothalamus of the brain stimulates activity in the endocrine system (see the discussion at the beginning of this chapter). Boys and girls have similar levels of both male and female sex hormones during childhood. By the time sexual maturation is complete, however, males have larger quantities of male hormones (androgens, including testosterone) circulating in their blood than females do, whereas females have larger quantities of female hormones (estrogen, progesterone, and others).

Physical and sexual maturation, then, are processes set in motion by the genes and executed by hormones. But environment also plays its part in the timing of maturation. This is dramatically illustrated by the **secular trend**—the historical trend in industrialized societies toward earlier maturation and greater body size. In 1840, for example, the average age of menarche was $16\frac{1}{2}$ years, a full four years later than it is today (Rees, 1993). Today, one can still find cultures where sexual maturity is reached much later than it is in Western nations. For example, in one region of Saudi Arabia the average age of menarche is 15.1, and in one part of New Guinea the average girl does not reach menarche until age 18 (Dosoky & Amoudi, 1997; Tanner, 1990).

What explains the secular trend? Better nutrition and advances in medical care seem to be the major factors (Tanner, 1990). Today's children are more likely than their parents or grandparents to reach their genetic potential for maturation and growth because they are better fed and less likely to experience growth-retarding illnesses. Even within our own relatively affluent society, poorly nourished adolescents—both boys and girls—mature later than well-nourished ones do. Girls who are tall and overweight as children tend to mature earlier than other girls (St. George, Williams, & Silva, 1994). By contrast, girls who engage regularly in strenuous physical activity and girls who suffer from *anorexia nervosa* (the life-threatening eating disorder that involves dieting to the point of starvation) may begin menstruating very late or stop menstruating after they have begun (Hopwood et al., 1990; Rosetta, 1993).

Recent research by Bruce Ellis and Judy Garber (2000) shows that family and marital stress also affects the timing of puberty in girls. Girls whose mothers were depressed were likely to experience early puberty, as were girls who had a stepfather or mother's boyfriend present in the home. In particular, girls who were relatively young when an unrelated male moved into the house and whose mothers and stepfathers or boyfriends had a more conflicted, stressful relationship were likely to experience early sexual maturity. In other research, though, Croatian girls living under the stressful conditions of war showed *delayed* sexual maturation (Prebeg & Bralic, 2000). And girls from lower socioeconomic backgrounds lag several months behind their higher socioeconomic counterparts, possibly because of less adequate nutrition and health care (Dosoky & Amoudi, 1997). Truly, then, physical and sexual maturation are the products of an *interaction* between heredity and environment, with some environments delaying maturation and others hastening it.

PSYCHOLOGICAL IMPLICATIONS

What psychological effects do the many changes associated with puberty really have on adolescents? In many cultures, girls approaching or experiencing puberty tend to become concerned about their appearance and worry about how others will respond to them. One adolescent girl may think she is too tall, another that she is too short. One may try to pad her breasts; another may hunch her shoulders to hide hers. Not surprisingly, research confirms that individual reactions to menarche vary widely, with many girls reporting a mixture of positive and negative feelings as well as some confusion about the process (Koff & Rierdan, 1995; Moore, 1995). Unfortunately, cultural views about menstruation are often negative, and girls internalize these negative myths about what to expect. As a result, some develop poor body images because

they are bothered by the weight gains that typically accompany menarche (see Seiffge-Krenke,1998).

What about boys? Their body images are more positive than those of girls, and they are more likely to welcome their weight gain (Richards et al., 1990). But they hope to be tall, hairy, and handsome, and they may become preoccupied with their physical and athletic prowess. Whereas menarche is a memorable event for girls, boys are often unaware of some of the physical changes they are experiencing (Zani, 1991). They notice their first ejaculation, but they rarely tell anyone about it and often were not prepared for it (Stein & Reiser, 1994). Although males express a mix of positive and negative reactions to becoming sexually mature, they generally react more positively to semenarche than girls do to menarche; 62% of boys regard semenarche positively, whereas only 23% of girls view menarche positively (see Seiffge-Krenke, 1998).

Pubertal changes may prompt changes in family relations. Adolescents physically distance themselves from their parents by engaging in less body contact, especially with fathers, and they go to great lengths to avoid being seen naked by their parents (Schulz, 1991 in Seiffge-Krenke, 1998). Likewise, parents seem to restructure the parent–child relationship, placing greater distance between them. Perhaps as a result of the physical barriers that are erected between adolescents and their parents, teens become more independent and less close to their parents (Steinberg, 1989). They are also more likely to experience conflicts with their parents, especially with their mothers—more often about minor issues such as unmade beds, late hours, and loud music than about core values. Hormone changes in early adolescence may contribute to this increased conflict with parents, as well as to moodiness, bouts of depression, lower or more variable energy levels, and restlessness (Buchanan, Eccles, & Becker, 1992). However, cultural beliefs about family relations and about the significance of becoming an adult also influence parent–child interactions during adolescence. For example, many Mexican American boys and their parents appear to become *closer* rather than more distant during the peak of pubertal changes (Molina & Chassin, 1996).

Even when parent–child relationships are disrupted during early adolescence, they become warmer again once the pubertal transition is completed. Parents—mothers and fathers alike—can help adolescents adjust successfully to puberty by maintaining close relationships and helping adolescents accept themselves (Swarr & Richards, 1996). Overall, we should not imagine that the physical and hormonal changes of puberty cause psychological changes in the individual in a direct and straightforward way. Instead, biological changes interact with psychological characteristics of the person and changes in the social environment to influence how adolescence is experienced (Magnusson, 1995; Paikoff & Brooks-Gunn, 1991).

EARLY VERSUS LATE DEVELOPMENT

If "timely" maturation has psychological implications, what is it like to be "off time"—to be an especially early or late developer? The answer depends on whether we are talking about males or females and also on whether we examine their adjustment during adolescence or later on.

Consider the short-term impact of being an early-developing or late-developing boy. Early-developing boys are judged to be socially competent, attractive, and self-assured, and they enjoy greater social acceptance by their peers (Bulcroft, 1991). The only negative aspect of being an early-maturing boy is earlier involvement in substance use and other problem behaviors (Tschann et al., 1994). By comparison, late maturation in boys has several disadvantages. Late-maturing boys tend to be more anxious and less sure of themselves, and are rated as less athletic (Jones, 1965; Livson &

Peskin, 1980). As a group, they even score lower than other students do, at least in early adolescence, on school achievement tests (Dubas, Graber, & Petersen, 1991).

Now consider early- and late-maturing girls. Traditionally, physical prowess has not been as important in girls' peer groups as in boys', so an early-developing girl may not gain much status from being larger and more muscled. In addition, since girls develop about two years earlier than boys do, a girl may be subjected to ridicule for a time—the only one in her grade who is developed and thus the target of some teasing. Perhaps for some of these reasons, early maturation appears to be more of a disadvantage than an advantage for girls. Many

Are Today's Teens Sleep Deprived?

© Paul A. Souders/CORBIS

Impaired by sleep loss, individuals start a task feeling fine. Minutes later, however, heads begin to nod, and the rate of deterioration accelerates. Instead of being able to sustain attention for a 45-minute lecture in a classroom, for example, a student might be able to manage only 3 to 5 minutes. (National Academy of Sciences, 2000, p. 15)

How much sleep do teens need, and what happens when they don't get enough? Young adolescents (13 years) sleep, on average, 7 hours and 42 minutes, and older adolescents (19 years) sleep about 7 hours per night (Wolfson & Carskadon, 1998). However, it's estimated that teens *need* somewhere between 8 and 9 hours of sleep—indicating a shortfall of between 1 and 2 hours of sleep every night (Carskadon, et al., 1980). Indeed, only 15% of adolescents

get the recommended 8 or more hours of sleep during the week (Wolfson & Carskadon, 1998). Unlike children, adolescents have variable sleep patterns, with later sleep and wake times on the weekend than during the week.

Everybody has days when they feel tired, but teenagers are especially likely to be at risk for daytime sleepiness and the consequences associated with fatigue. Changes in the sleep–wake cycle, melatonin production, and circadian rhythms during adolescence mean that the "natural" time for falling asleep is 11:00 or later. Although psychosocial factors may contribute to the later bedtimes (for example, talking late into the night with friends), biological factors—puberty in particular—seem primarily responsible (Carskadon, Vieira, & Acebo, 1993). Not surprisingly, then, teens report later and later bedtimes from age 10 to age 17 (Wolfson & Carskadon, 1998). Teens who go to bed at 11:00 should not wake up until around 8:00 in the morning if they are to get the recommended amount of sleep. However, most teens (84%) find themselves getting out of bed before 7:00, and 1 in 4 gets up by 6:00, to get to school on time. High schools typically start earlier than middle or elementary schools, often by 7:30, usually to accommodate bus schedules. Thus, just when their biological clocks are pushing back sleep times at night, schools are getting teens up earlier in the morning!

What are the consequences of not getting enough sleep?

1. Sleepiness. Even when teens get what seems like an adequate amount of sleep, they report greater sleepiness during the day and are quicker to fall asleep than younger children who get the same amount of sleep. Sleepiness is associated with decreased motivation or trouble initiating and maintaining activity, especially on "boring" tasks (Dahl, 1999). Tired teens may be able to successfully navigate their way through a favorite class or read a particularly good

studies report an association between early maturation and lower self-esteem among girls (see, for example, Forys & Rider, 2000; J. M. Williams & Currie, 2000). The early-maturing girl tends to be *less* popular than her prepubertal classmates, and she is more likely to report symptoms of depression and anxiety, especially if she had psychological problems as a child (Gallant & Derry, 1995; Graber, et al., 1997; Hayward et al., 1997). Early-maturing girls often end up socializing with an older peer group; consequently, they are more likely to become involved in the "teen scene" of dating, drinking, having sex, and engaging in minor troublemaking (Simmons & Blyth, 1987; Stattin & Magnusson, 1990; Tschann et al., 1994).

Late-maturing girls (like late-maturing boys) may experience some anxiety as they wait to mature, but they are not nearly as disadvantaged as late-maturing boys. Indeed, whereas later-developing boys tend to perform poorly on school achievement tests, later-developing girls outperform other students (Dubas et al., 1991). Perhaps late-developing girls focus on academic skills at a time when other girls have shifted some of their focus to extracurricular activities.

Do differences between early and late developers persist into later adolescence and adulthood? Typically, they fade with time. By late high school, for example, differences in academic performance between early and late maturers have

book, but these same teens may have trouble completing an assignment in their least favorite subject or studying for an exam. Teens who have had their sleep restricted display increased sleepiness in proportion to the number of nights that their sleep is reduced. But surprisingly—at least to many adults—these same teens "perk up" in the evenings and show high levels of energy that discourage them from going to bed early (National Academy of Sciences, 2000).

2. Emotional lability, or "moodiness." Teens who sleep less at night or who stay up later on the weekends than their peers report higher levels of depression, irritability, and lack of tolerance for frustration (Dahl, 1999; Wolfson & Carskadon, 1998). They may also have difficulty controlling their emotional responses, which leads to greater expression of aggression or anger (Dahl, 1999).

3. Attention and academic performance problems. Students who don't get enough sleep have trouble concentrating in school, experience short-term memory problems, and may doze off in class (National Institutes of Health, 1997). They also earn lower grades, but it is not yet clear from the correlational data whether inadequate sleep causes the lower grades (Wolfson & Carskadon, 1998). Some tasks may be more affected by sleep deprivation than others; dual tasks and tasks requiring creative or abstract thinking seem to be more vulnerable than single tasks requiring concrete thinking (Dahl, 1999).

4. Increased number of accidents. In addition to causing lapses of attention, sleep deprivation also slows reaction times. Together, these increase the likelihood of accidents, which may help explain why adolescents have higher rates of car accidents than any other age group. Becoming drowsy or falling asleep behind the wheel of a car contributes to more than 100,000 accidents every year, and more than half of these accidents involve young drivers (National Sleep Foundation, 2000). Another million car crashes every year are caused by driver inattention, a correlate of sleepiness.

A few schools have responded to such findings by pushing back their start times. For example, the Minneapolis School District dramatically shifted from a 7:15 start to an 8:40 start in 1997 (Wahlstrom, 1999). Following this change, students reported getting an additional hour of sleep each weekday; teachers reported that students were more alert during the first few class periods; and absenteeism and tardiness decreased (Wahlstrom & Bemis, 1998).

Despite the potential benefits of starting high school later, a myriad of factors work against widespread adoption of this change. These include money for additional buses, unless other schools in the same district switch to an earlier start time or they all start later. One district switched its high school and elementary school schedules so that the elementary students were the ones starting early. But this raised concerns about the younger children being placed at risk by going to school when it may still be dark in the morning and having more unsupervised time after an earlier school dismissal. Other sticky issues include athletic and extracurricular activities scheduled for after school and the after-school work schedules of many adolescents. And not all teachers have been thrilled with later start times because of the correspondingly later end times.

Schools may not be able to change their start times, but adolescents can learn more about their sleep needs and the effects of sleep deprivation. Adhering to a regular bedtime and wake time on the weekends as well as on schooldays can help maintain healthy sleep habits. Unfortunately, "sleeping in" on the weekends alters the sleep–wake cycle and makes it more difficult to get up early for work or school on Monday morning. So, next time you find yourself dozing off in class or at work, don't jump to the conclusion that the work you're doing is boring. It may be that your sleep–wake cycle is out of sync with the schedule imposed on you by the school or work world.

already disappeared (Dubas et al., 1991), and early-maturing girls are no longer less popular than other girls (Hayward et al., 1997). However, there may be lasting effects of some of the risky behaviors engaged in by early-maturing girls (such as sex and drinking). And some research shows that early-maturing girls have a greater likelihood than all other groups of experiencing lifetime adjustment problems, including both anxiety and depression (Graber et al., 1997). Some of the advantages of being an early-maturing boy may carry over into adulthood, but early-maturing boys also seem to be more rigid and conforming than late-maturing ones, who may learn some lessons about coping in creative ways from their struggles as adolescents (Jones, 1965).

Overall, then, late-maturing boys and early-maturing girls are especially likely to find the adolescent period disruptive. However, psychological differences between early- and late-maturing adolescents become smaller and more mixed in quality by adulthood. It is also important to note that differences between early and late maturers are relatively small and that many other factors besides the timing of maturation influence whether this period of life goes smoothly or not. For example, girls who make the transition from elementary to middle school at the same time they experience puberty exhibit greater adjustment problems than girls who do not experience a school transition and pubertal changes at the same time (Simmons & Blyth, 1987).

Finally, and perhaps most important, timing-of-puberty effects depend on the *adolescent's perception* of whether pubertal events are experienced early, on time, or late (Seiffge-Krenke, 1998). Thus, one girl may believe she is a "late bloomer" when she doesn't menstruate until age 14. But another girl who exercises strenuously may believe that menarche at age 14 is perfectly normal because delayed menarche is typical of serious athletes. Peer and family member reactions to an adolescent's pubertal changes are also instrumental in determining the adolescent's adjustment. This may help explain the difference in adjustment between early-maturing boys and early-maturing girls. Parents may be more concerned and negative about their daughter's emerging sexuality than they are about their son's. These attitudes may be inadvertently conveyed to teens, affecting their experience of puberty and their self-concept.

Physical Behavior

The dramatic physical growth that occurs during adolescence makes teenagers stronger and more physically competent than children. Rapid muscle development over the adolescent years makes both boys and girls noticeably stronger than they were as children (Faust, 1977). Their performance of large-muscle activities continues to improve: An adolescent can throw a ball farther, cover more ground in the standing long jump, and run much faster than a child can (Keough & Sugden, 1985). However, as the adolescent years progress, the physical performance of boys continues to improve, whereas that of girls often levels off or even declines (Thomas & French, 1985).

It is easy to see that larger muscles enable boys to outperform girls in activities that require strength. But biological differences cannot entirely explain sex differences in physical performance (Smoll & Schutz, 1990). Gender-role socialization may be partly responsible (Herkowitz, 1978). As girls mature sexually and physically, they are often encouraged to be less "tomboyish" and to become more interested in traditionally "feminine" (often more sedentary) activities. Studies of world records in track, swimming, and cycling suggest that as gender roles have changed in the past few decades, women have been improving their performances, and the male–female gap in physical performance has narrowed dramatically (Sparling, O'Donnell, & Snow, 1998; Whipp & Ward, 1992). A small gender gap remains in some areas of physical activity, largely related to biological difference—greater muscle mass in males, greater body fat in females, differences in oxygen transport capacity (Sparling, et al., 1998). But as today's girls participate more often in sports and other strenuous physical activities, their performance on tests of large-muscle activity is likely to remain stable or improve during adolescence, rather than declining as it did in previous generations. Then *both* young women and young men will be likely to enter adulthood in peak physical condition.

Before leaving this section on adolescents, take a look at the Explorations box on page 128, which examines whether today's teens are sleep deprived.

The Adult

The body of the mature adolescent or young adult is at its prime in many ways. It is strong and fit; its organs are functioning efficiently. But it is aging, as it has been all along. Physical aging occurs slowly and steadily over the entire life span. It begins to have noticeable effects on physical appearance and functioning in middle age and has had an even more significant impact by the time old age is reached, though more in some people than in others. We'll now examine the physical aging process.

Physical Appearance and Structure

Only minor changes in physical appearance occur in the 20s and 30s, but many people do notice signs that they are aging as they reach their 40s. Skin becomes wrinkled, dry, and loose, especially among people who have spent more time in the sun. Hair thins and often turns gray from loss of pigment-producing cells. And to most people's dismay, they put on extra weight throughout much of adulthood as their metabolism declines but their eating and exercise habits do not adjust accordingly (Kart, Metress, & Metress, 1992). Some people, influenced by societal stereotypes to equate "old" with "unattractive," find these changes difficult to accept.

The body shows additional effects of aging in old age. After gaining weight throughout early and middle adulthood, people typically begin to lose weight starting in their 60s (Haber, 1994). Loss of weight in old age is usually coupled with a loss of muscle over the entire span of adulthood. However, it is not age per se that reduces muscle mass, but the sedentary lifestyle adopted by many older adults (Harper, 1999). When Abby King and colleagues (2000) surveyed nearly 3,000 women in middle and older adulthood, they found that only 9% met the criteria for being regularly active. And as age increased, level of activity decreased. Age is not the only culprit, though, in making adults less active; low level of education, poor neighborhood characteristics, and personal factors (such as caregiving responsibilities and lack of energy) also influence whether or not adults exercise (King et al., 2000).

Aging is also associated with decreased bone density which, along with reduced muscle mass and joint changes, can lead to shortened stature, stooped posture, fractures, and pain. Most older adults are not bothered by the slight decrease in their height (about ½ inch for men and 1 inch for women by age 70), but they *are* troubled by joint pain and fractures because these changes can impair mobility and detract from the quality of life.

Extreme bone loss in later life results from **osteoporosis,** a disease in which a serious loss of minerals leaves the bones fragile and easily fractured. It involves pain and can actually result in death if the victim falls and fractures a hip. As many as one-third of elderly adults who fracture a hip die within one year (Rose & Maffulli, 1999). Osteoporosis is a special problem for older women, who never had as much bone mass as men to start with and whose bones tend to thin rapidly after menopause (see Henderson & Goltzman, 2000). European and Asian women with light frames, those who smoke, and those with a family history of osteoporosis are especially at risk. Women with osteoporosis may eventually develop the so-called dowager's hump, a noticeably rounded upper back. One long-term victim lost almost 6 inches in height by age 70 (far more than the average loss of 1 inch) and ended up with her ribcage sitting on her hipbones (Franklin, 1995).

What can be done to prevent osteoporosis? For starters, dietary habits can influence a person's risk for osteoporosis. Many individuals do not get enough calcium to develop strong bones when they are young or to maintain bone health as they get older (Kart et al., 1992). Weight-bearing exercises such as walking or jogging can help prevent osteoporosis, as can the estrogen replacement therapy that some women take following menopause (see later section; Kart et al., 1992). It is increasingly evident that good bone health starts in childhood and adolescence (Krucoff, 2000). Girls and young women who are physically active and eat a healthy diet develop higher bone density that protects them from bone loss in later life.

The joints are also aging over the adult years. The cushioning between bones wears out, and the joints become stiffer. Many older adults experience pain or discomfort from arthritis, or joint inflammation. The most common joint problem among older adults is **osteoarthritis,** which results from gradual deterioration of the cartilage that cushions the bones from rubbing against one another. For some older adults, joint disease is deforming and painful, and limits their activities. The older person who can no longer fasten buttons, stoop to pick up dropped items, or even get into and out of the bathtub may easily feel incompetent and dependent (Whitbourne, 2001).

Functioning and Health

Aging also involves a gradual decline in the efficiency of most bodily systems from the 20s on (Christofalo, 1988; Whitbourne, 2001). Most systems increase to a peak sometime between childhood and early adulthood and decline slowly thereafter. No matter what physical function we look at—the capacity of the heart or lungs to meet the demands of exercise, the ability of the body to control its temperature, the ability of the immune system to fight disease, or strength—the gradual effects of aging are evident. For example, Monique Samson and her colleagues (2000) assessed handgrip strength in healthy men and women between the ages of 20 and 80. Women showed only small decreases in muscle strength prior to age 55 but much larger decreases after 55. Men showed steady loss of muscle strength across all ages studied.

It should be noted, however, that individual differences in physiological functioning grow larger with age (Harris et al., 1992). Aerobic capacity and other physiological measures vary more widely among 70-year-olds than among 20-year-olds. In other words, even though the average old person is less physiologically fit than the average young person, *not all older people have poor physiological functioning,*

Another fact of physical aging is a decline in the **reserve capacity** of many organ systems—that is, their ability to respond to demands for extraordinary output, as in emergencies (Goldberg & Hagberg, 1990). For example, old and young do not differ much in resting heart rates, but older adults, unless they are completely disease-free, will have lower *maximal* heart rates (Lakatta, 1990). This means that older adults who do not feel very old at all as they go about their normal routines may feel very old indeed if they try to run up mountains.

By the time people are 65 or older, it is hard to find many of them who do not have something wrong with their bodies. Acute illnesses such as colds and infections actually become less frequent from childhood on, but chronic diseases and disorders become more common. National health surveys indicate that many of the 70-and-older age group have at least one chronic impairment—whether a sensory loss, arthritis, hypertension, or a degenerative disease (Federal Interagency

Some older adults have a good deal of reserve capacity and can perform strenuous activities even in their 80s or 90s.

Forum, 2000). Arthritis alone affects 50% of elderly men and 64% of elderly women; in addition, about 45% have hypertension (high blood pressure), and about 22% have heart disease (Federal Interagency Forum, 2000). Among older adults who live in poverty, many of whom are minority group members, health problems and difficulties in day-to-day functioning are even more common and also more severe (Clark & Maddox, 1992; Hobbs, 1996). Still, as Table 5.6 shows, a majority of adults maintain the physical capabilities that allow them to function successfully.

Psychological Implications

We live in a society that values youth while devaluing old age and the physical changes that often accompany it. What are the psychological implications of growing older under these conditions? Negative stereotypes about older adults abound— they are sickly, frail, forgetful, unattractive, dependent, or otherwise incompetent. Such stereotypes can lead to **ageism,** or prejudice against elderly people. Most elderly adults have internalized these negative views, but believe they apply to *other* older adults and not to themselves.

Laura Hurd (1999) interviewed women between 50 and 90 years of age who attended programs at a "senior center." She found that the women actively worked to distance themselves from the "old" category and to remain in the "not old" category. These categories were defined not by age, but by what individuals can and cannot do. Generally, the women believed that they were not old because they had the physical and mental abilities to avoid nursing home care. In particular, they believed that remaining active—both physically and socially—was key to avoid becoming old. Women who considered themselves "not old" believed that men and women who were old had given in to the stereotypes of aging by being inactive and solitary.

As we've seen, many older adults, even those who consider themselves "not old," do have chronic diseases and impairments. Still, 72% of people 65 and older say they are in excellent, very good, or good health (Federal Interagency Forum, 2000). Moreover, relatively few say they need assistance with daily activities, though the figure climbs with age from 9% of those age 65–69 to 50% of those 85 and older (Hobbs, 1996). Although having a chronic disease or disability does tend to lower an older person's sense of well-being, many people with arthritis, diabetes, and other difficulties are no less content

with their lives than anyone else (Kempen, Ormel, & Relyveld, 1997). Clearly, the majority of older people are able to retain their sense of well-being and ability to function independently despite an increased likelihood of impairments.

The Reproductive System

During most of adulthood, the sex hormones that start to be secreted during adolescence help to ensure interest in sexual behavior and the ability to have children, but they also have psychological implications and affect the experience of aging. Hormone levels fluctuate somewhat on a day-to-day basis in men (Harman & Talbert, 1985), and men with high levels of testosterone tend to be more sexually active and aggressive than other men (Schiavi et al., 1991; Archer, 1991), Otherwise, it is not clear that changes in men's hormone levels are tied to changes in their moods and behavior.

By contrast, hormone levels in women shift drastically each month as they progress through their menstrual cycles. These shifts have psychological implications for some women. Estrogen and progesterone levels rise to a peak at midcycle, when a woman is ovulating, and decline as she approaches her menstrual period. The cyclic changes in hormones may lead to such symptoms as bloating, moodiness, breast tenderness, and headaches during the days just before the menstrual flow, symptoms collectively referred to as **premenstrual syndrome** (PMS). Among women 21 to 64 years of age, 41% report that they experience premenstrual syndrome and another 17% report at least some symptoms prior to menstruation (Singh et al., 1998). Many adolescent women (88%) report moderate or severe symptoms (Cleckner-Smith, Doughty, & Grossman, 1998).

However, there is some debate about the validity of PMS. In research where women are simply asked to complete mood surveys every day and don't know that their menstrual cycles are being studied, most report little premenstrual mood change at all (Englander-Golden et al., 1986). This suggests that expectations and not hormones play a role in many cases of PMS. Only a minority of women—probably fewer than 5%—experience significant PMS. Changes in estrogen and progesterone levels may be responsible for the severe PMS these women experience (Schmidt et al., 1998). Women with severe PMS may find relief when treated with antidepressant drugs such as Prozac (Dimmock et al., 2000). For women with milder forms of PMS, treatment with calcium and vitamin D may alleviate symptoms because estrogen levels can alter how well these substances are absorbed by the body (Thys-Jacob, 2000). Clearly, individuals vary in how they experience menstrual cycles.

We now know that genetic endowment influences the extent to which a woman experiences both premenstrual and menstrual distress (Condon, 1993; Kendler et al., 1992). Social factors also enter in. Learned societal stereotypes of what women "should" experience at different phases of the menstrual cycle appear to influence what women do experience and report (Ainscough, 1990; Englander-Golden et al., 1986). Most likely, then, biological, psychological, social, and cultural factors all contribute to a woman's experience of the menstrual cycle during her adult life (McFarlane & Williams, 1990).

Table 5.6 Older Adults' Physical Skills

	Men	Women
Percentage of Adults 70 and Older Who Can:		
Walk ¼ mile	88	82
Climb 10 stairs without resting	92	88
Stoop, crouch, or kneel	90	84
Reach up over head	97	86

SOURCE: Federal Interagency Forum on Aging-Related Statistics (2000)

Cultural Differences in the Experience of Menopause

The physical changes involved in menopause are universal, but the psychological experience of it is not. Consider hot flashes, which are the most frequent complaint of menopausal women. Nearly three-quarters of American and Canadian women report experiencing at least one hot flash during the menopausal period, but only 1 in 5 Japanese women recall having had any (Lock, 1993; Shaw, 1997). Even within the United States, Japanese and Chinese women report fewer menopausal symptoms than African American, European American, and Hispanic women (Gold et al., 2000). In Zimbabwe, women experience the same symptoms as reported by women in Western cultures, but they view these as part of a normal and healthy stage of life and not as an unhealthy sign of loss (McMaster, Pitts, & Poyah, 1997). Thus, they tend not to seek treatment or complain about their "symptoms."

Marcha Flint (1982) surveyed women of a high and socially advantaged caste in India and found that women who had not reached menopause actually looked forward to it, and women who had reached it were pleased that they had. Why? According to Flint, menopause brought social rewards to these Indian women. They were freed from the taboos associated with menstruation that had kept them veiled and segregated from male society as younger women. They could now mingle with men other than their husbands and fathers and even drink the local brew with the fellows. Moreover, they still had meaningful work roles and were seen as wise by virtue of their years. In North American society, by comparison, aging often means a loss of status for older women, and menopause is regarded as a medical condition of aging to be treated with hormones.

Not all women share this negative and medicalized view of menopause, even when the broader culture around them embraces this view. Some American women, for instance, report that menopause is insignificant relative to other things going on in their lives (Winterich & Umberson, 1999).

Others regard menopause as a normal life transition, even an opportunity to embark on new life options (Adler et al., 2000). So once again, we see that biological, psychological, and social factors all play a part in how a seemingly common event is interpreted differently by different individuals.

AP/Wide World Photos

MENOPAUSE

Like other systems of the body, the reproductive system ages. The ending of a woman's menstrual periods in midlife is called **menopause**. The average woman experiences menopause at age 51, and the usual age range is from 42 to 58. The process actually takes place very gradually over a period of 5–10 years, as periods become either more or less frequent, and less regular (McKinlay, Brambilla, & Posner, 1992; see also Barbach, 2000; Matthews, 1992). Levels of estrogen and other female hormones decline, so that the woman who has been through menopause has a hormone mix that is less "feminine" and more "masculine" than that of the premenopausal woman. When menopause is completed, a woman is no longer ovulating, no longer menstruating, and no longer capable of conceiving a child.

The age at which a woman reaches menopause is somewhat related to both the age at which she reached menarche and the age at which her mother reached menopause (Varea et al., 2000). Although life expectancy has increased and the age of menarche has decreased over history as part of the secular trend, the age of menopause does not appear to have changed much and is similar from culture to culture (Brody et al., 2000). What *has* changed is that women are now living long enough to experience a considerable period of postmenopausal life.

Society holds rather stereotypic views of menopausal women. They are regarded as irritable, emotional, depressed, and unstable. How much truth is there to this stereotype? Not much. About two-thirds of women in our society do experience **hot flashes**—sudden experiences of warmth and sweating, usually centered around the face and upper body, that occur at unpredictable times, last for a few seconds or minutes, and are often followed by a cold shiver (Robinson, 1996). Many also experience *vaginal dryness* and irritation or pain during intercourse as a result. Still other women experience no symptoms at all.

What about the psychological symptoms—irritability and depression? Once again, we discover wide variation among menopausal women—and not much truth to the negative stereotypes. In a particularly well designed study, Karen Matthews and her associates (Matthews, 1992; Matthews et al., 1990) studied 541 initially premenopausal women over a three-year period, comparing those who subsequently experienced menopause with women of similar ages who did not become menopausal. The typical woman entering menopause initially experienced some physical symptoms such as hot flashes. Some women also reported mild depression and temporary emotional distress, probably in reaction to their physical symptoms, but only about 10% could be said to have become seriously depressed in response to menopause. Typically, menopause had no effect whatsoever on women's levels of anxiety, anger, perceived stress, or job dissatisfaction. When women *do* experience severe psychological problems during the menopausal transition, they often had those problems well before the age of menopause (Greene, 1984).

Women who have been through menopause generally claim that it had little effect on them or that it even improved their lives; they're usually more positive about it than women who have not been through it yet (Gannan & Ekstrom, 1993; Wilbur, Miller, & Montgomery, 1995). For most women, menopause brings no changes one way or the other in sexual interest and activity, although sexual activity does gradually decline in both women and men over the adult years (Laumann, Paik, & Rosen, 1999). In short, despite all the negative stereotypes, menopause seems to be "no big deal" for most women.

Why do some women experience more severe menopausal symptoms than others do? Again, part of the answer may lie with biology. Women who have a history of menstrual problems (such as PMS) report more menopausal symptoms, both physical and psychological (C. A. Morse et al., 1998). Thus, some women may experience greater biological changes. But psychological and social factors of the sort that influence women's reactions to sexual maturation and to their menstrual cycles also influence the severity of menopausal symptoms. For example, women who expect menopause to be a negative experience are likely to get what they expect (Matthews, 1992). There is also a good deal of variation across cultures in how menopause is experienced (see the Explorations box on page 133). It appears that the impact of menopause is colored by the meaning it has for the woman, as influenced by her society's prevailing views of menopause and by her own personal characteristics.

In U.S. society, **hormone replacement therapy** (**HRT**) (taking estrogen and progestin to compensate for hormone loss at menopause) is increasingly recommended to women who are beginning to experience menopausal changes. This hormone treatment relieves physical symptoms of menopause such as hot flashes and vaginal dryness, and prevents or slows osteoporosis (Matthews, 1992). It may protect against the increased risk of coronary heart disease associated with the loss of estrogen (Grodstein et al., 2000), it may relieve depression (Zweifel & O'Brien, 1997), and it may even lower the odds of Alzheimer's disease (Cyr et al., 2000; Foy et al., 2000). Not everyone agrees with the philosophy of treating a natural change associated with aging as though it were a medical condition, however, and there is some evidence that HRT is associated with an increased risk of breast cancer among some women (Schairer et al., 2000).

THE MALE CLIMACTERIC

Despite popular references to the "male menopause" (see, for example, Diamond, 1997), men cannot experience menopause, since they do not menstruate. They also do not experience the sharp drop in hormones that accompanies menopause in women (Gould, Petty, & Jacobs, 2000). Thus, attempts to equate the changes that occur in men's reproductive functioning to those that occur in women are misleading (Metz & Miner, 1998). What men *do* experience is more accurately characterized by the concept of **climacteric,** which refers to the loss of reproductive capacity in either sex in later life. Women experience their climacteric as a fairly discrete event—cessation of menstruation—and within a relatively narrow age range, around age 50. Men, however, may lose the ability to father children at this same time, much later, or even never: Men in their 90s have been known to father children. The sperm produced by older men may not be as active as those produced by younger men. Levels of testosterone also decrease very gradually over the adult years in most men, to the point that 80-year-old men have about 50% of the testosterone that they had at age 20 (Gray et al., 1991). Among 50- to 70-year-old men, half complain of *erectile dysfunction* (ED) despite having sufficient levels of testosterone; a majority of these cases of ED are due to medical conditions such as diabetes and not to less hormone production (Gould et al., 2000).

In sum, the changes associated with the climacteric in men are more gradual, more variable, and less complete than those in women. As a result, men experience fewer psychological correlates. Frequency of sexual activity does decline as men age. However, this trend cannot be blamed entirely on decreased hormone levels, because sexual activity often declines even when testosterone levels remain high (Gould et al., 2000; see also Chapter 12 on sexuality).

For both sexes, then, changes in the reproductive system are a normal part of aging. Neither women nor men seem to suffer much as their ability to have children wanes or disappears. Sexual activity becomes less frequent, but it remains an important part of life for most older adults.

Physical Behavior

How well can older adults carry out physical activities in daily life? Obviously, those who have severe arthritis may have difficulty merely walking or dressing themselves without pain, but here we focus on two more typical changes in physical behavior over the adult years: a slowing of behavior and a decreased ability to engage in strenuous activities.

SLOWING DOWN

You may have noticed, as you breeze by them on the sidewalk, that older adults often walk more slowly than young people do. Indeed, research suggests that the amount of time stoplights provide for pedestrians to cross the street is not enough for the 99% of people age 72 or older who walk at a pace slower than 4 feet per second (Langlois et al., 1997). Some older adults also walk as if they were treading on a slippery surface—with short, shuffling steps and not much arm movement (Murray, Kory, & Clarkson, 1969). Why is this?

Difficulty with balance is one likely culprit. The sensory systems involved in balance do not function as well in old age as they did in earlier years (Ochs et al., 1985). Indeed, balance is often used as an indicator of older adults' functional mobility—their ability to stand, sit, walk, and turn (Shumway-Cook, Brauer, & Woollacott, 2000). Individuals with poor balance may compensate by walking more slowly. More generally, older adults who have fallen or fear they will fall make many adaptive changes in their walk to protect themselves (Newstead et al., 2000).

An older person's slow pace of walking may also be due to loss of strength and reduced cardiovascular functioning (Buchner, 1997). The pace at which adults of any age choose to walk and the fastest pace at which they can walk are associated with their cardiovascular capacity and their muscle mass (Cunningham et al., 1982). Older people with strong hearts and muscles may walk very briskly, but those who have cardiovascular limitations may slow down.

On average, older adults perform many motor actions more slowly and with less coordination than younger adults do (Morgan et al., 1994; Stelmach & Nahom, 1992). The underlying reason is a slowing of the brain. Gerontologist James Birren has argued that *the* central change that comes about as we age is a slowing of the nervous system (Birren & Fisher, 1995). It affects not only motor behavior but mental functioning as well, and it affects a majority of elderly people to at least some degree. We have already seen that young children have slow reaction times. Speed on a variety of perceptual-motor tasks then improves and peaks among young adults, only to gradually decrease among middle-aged and older adults (Earles & Salthouse, 1995; Yan, Thomas, & Stelmach, 1998). In a study comparing younger adults (18–24 years) to older adults (62–72 years) on five motor tasks, the older adults performed more slowly on all five (Francis & Spirduso, 2000). The older adults were especially slow on fine motor tasks requiring object manipulation, such as inserting pegs in holes. They also have more trouble when tasks are novel and when they are complex—for example, when any one of several stimuli might appear on a screen and each requires a different response (Sliwinski et al., 1994; Spirduso & MacRae, 1990). On average, older adults take $1\frac{1}{2}$ to 2 times longer to respond than young adults do on a wide range of cognitive tasks that require speedy answers (Lima, Hale, & Myerson, 1991).

We should not expect all old people to be slow in all situations, however. The reaction times of older adults vary a great deal (Yan et al., 1998, 2000). Physically fit older people and those who are free from cardiovascular diseases have quicker reactions than their peers who lead sedentary lives or have diseases, although they are still likely to be slower than they were when they were younger (Earles & Salthouse, 1995; Spirduso & MacRae, 1990). Aerobic exercise or experience playing video games can also speed the reactions of older adults (Dustman et al., 1989, 1992). In addition, experience can help elderly people compensate for a slower nervous system so that they can continue to perform well on familiar motor tasks (Salthouse, 1984).

The slowing of the nervous system and of motor performance is one important fact of aging. Another is that many people become out of shape. Typically, adults decrease their involvement in vigorous physical activity as they get older—females earlier than males (Ruchlin & Lachs, 1999). By late adulthood, they may find that they get tired just climbing stairs or carrying groceries; running a marathon is out of the question. Because of declines in reserve capacity, aging bodies are at a greater disadvantage when they must perform tasks requiring maximal strength, speed, or endurance than when they are asked to perform normal daily activities (Goldberg & Hagberg, 1990). The average older person tires more quickly and needs more time to recover after vigorous activity than the average younger person.

Yet once again, diversity is greater among older adults than among younger ones. *Some* older people can perform vigorous physical activities with distinction. Michael Stones and Albert Kozma (1985) cite the examples of the 70-year-old woman who competed in the 1972 Olympic equestrian events and the 98-year-old man who could run a marathon (26 miles) in $7\frac{1}{2}$ hours!

DISEASE, DISUSE, AND ABUSE

As we've seen, many aspects of physical functioning decline over the adult years in many individuals. But an important question arises: When we look at the performance of older people, are we seeing the effects of aging alone or the effects of something else? The "something else" could be disease, disuse of the body, abuse of the body—or all three.

We've seen that most older people have at least some chronic *disease* or impairment, such as arthritis or heart disease. How would an elderly person function if he or she could manage to stay completely disease-free? James Birren and his colleagues (1963) addressed just this question in a classic study of men aged 65 to 91. Extensive medical examinations were conducted to identify two groups of elderly men: (1) those who were almost perfectly healthy and had *no* signs of disease at all and (2) those who had slight traces of disease-in-the-making but no clinically diagnosable diseases. Several aspects of physical and intellectual functioning were assessed in these men, and the participants were compared to young men.

The most remarkable finding was that the healthier group of older men hardly differed at all from the younger men! They were equal even in their capacity for physical exercise, and they actually beat the younger men on measures of intelligence requiring general information or knowledge of vocabulary words. Their main limitations were the slower brain activity and reaction times that seem to be so basic to the aging process. Overall, *aging itself in the absence of disease had little effect on physical and psychological functioning.* However, the men with slight traces of impending disease *were* deficient on several measures. Diseases that have progressed to the point of symptoms have even more serious consequences for performance.

So it is possible that disease, rather than aging itself, accounts for many declines in functioning in later life (see also Houx, Vreeling, & Jolles, 1991). We must note, however, that Birren and his colleagues had a tough time finding the perfectly healthy older people they studied. Most older people experience *both* aging and disease, and it is difficult to separate the effects of the two. Although aging and disease are distinct, increased vulnerability to disease is one part—and an important part—of normal aging.

Disuse of the body also contributes to steeper declines in physical functioning in some adults than in others (Wagner et al., 1992). Masters and Johnson (1966) proposed a "use it or lose it" maxim to describe the fact that sexual functioning deteriorates if a person engages in little or no sexual activity. The same maxim can be applied to other systems of the body. Muscles atrophy if they are not used, and the heart functions less well if a person leads a sedentary life. Changes like these in some aging adults are much like the changes observed in people of any age who are confined to bed for a long time (Goldberg & Hagberg, 1990). The brain also needs "mental exercise" in order to display plasticity and to continue to function effectively in old age (Black et al., 1991). In short, most systems of the body seem to thrive on *use,* but too many people become inactive as they age (Ruchlin & Lachs, 1999).

Finally, *abuse* of the body contributes to declines in functioning in some people. Excessive alcohol consumption, a high-fat diet, and smoking are all clear examples (Haber, 1994). Additionally, although elderly adults are not often recreational drug abusers, many do take several prescribed medications. Drugs typically affect older adults more powerfully than they do younger adults; they can also interact with one another and with the aging body's chemistry to impair functioning (Cherry & Morton, 1989; Lamy, 1986).

Overall, then, poor functioning in old age may represent any combination of the effects of aging, disease, disuse, and abuse. We may not be able to do much to change basic aging processes, but we can certainly change our lifestyles to optimize the odds of a long and healthy old age.

Summary Points

1. Each of the many systems of the human body develops and ages at its own rate, guided by a genetic program set into action by the brain and hormones released by the endocrine system. Endocrine glands such as the pituitary, thyroid, testes, and ovaries regulate behavior by secreting hormones directly into the bloodstream.

2. The nervous system consists of billions of neurons that communicate by means of neurotransmitter chemicals. The brain emerges from the neural plate within weeks after conception. Neurons then proliferate, differentiate, and organize themselves into interconnected groups. The plasticity of the infant brain allows it to select certain neural connections over others in response to normal early experiences, as well as to benefit from enriching stimulation.

3. During childhood, neural transmission speeds up, and lateralization of various brain functions, though present at birth, becomes more evident in behavior. During adolescence, the brain, especially the prefrontal cortex, continues to develop, permitting sustained attention and strategic planning.

4. The aging brain exhibits both degeneration and plasticity. Neurons atrophy and die, levels of neurotransmitters decrease, and blood flow to the brain decreases; but the aging brain forms new synapses to compensate for neural loss and reorganizes itself in response to learning experiences.

5. Newborns have a wide range of reflexes (both survival and primitive reflexes), working senses, a capacity to learn, and organized sleeping and waking states; they are competent but also limited creatures.

6. Infants grow physically according to the cephalocaudal ("head-to-tail"), proximodistal (center outwards), and orthogenetic (global and undifferentiated to differentiated and integrated) principles. Bones harden, and muscles strengthen.

7. As the motor areas of the brain's cortex mature, motor milestones are achieved in a predictable cephalocaudal and proximodistal order, and differentiated responses are integrated into meaningful sequences of movement. Maturation is a factor in early motor development, but normal opportunities to interact with the environment and learn motor behaviors are also necessary, according to the dynamic systems approach.

8. During childhood, the body steadily grows, and both large muscle and small muscle control and reaction time improve. Children learn to coordinate their movements within a changing environment.

9. The adolescent growth spurt and pubertal changes make adolescence a time of dramatic physical change. Girls reach menarche (first menstruation) at an average age of 12½; boys experience semenarche (first ejaculation) a bit later. Rates of maturation vary widely, in part because of genetic makeup and in part because of nutrition and health status.

10. Most adolescent girls and boys react to the maturation process with mixed feelings, worry about their physical appearance and capabilities, and experience heightened conflict with parents in early adolescence. Early maturation tends to give boys an advantage over their peers, but appears to be disadvantageous for girls. Most differences between early and later maturers fade over time, however.

11. Physical capabilities of boys improve but those of many girls level off or even decline during adolescence, perhaps because of gender stereotypes.

12. Most systems of the body reach a peak of functioning between childhood and early adulthood and decline gradually thereafter; decreases in reserve capacity are especially noticeable. However, individual differences in physiological functioning become greater with age. Older adults lose bone density, which may lead to fractures or osteoporosis. Good bone health starts in childhood with adequate calcium and is maintained with regular physical activity.

13. During the reproductive years of adulthood, some women experience mood swings during the menstrual cycle, but few women are incapacitated by premenstrual syndrome. Men's hormone levels also fluctuate, though not in monthly cycles.

14. Women reach menopause and lose their reproductive capacity at about age 50; most experience hot flashes and vaginal dryness, but few experience severe psychological symptoms. The reproductive systems of men age more gradually and less completely during the male climacteric.

15. As people age, they experience a slowing of their nervous systems, reaction times, and motor behavior; their capacity for vigorous activity is also reduced.

16. Aging, disease, disuse, and abuse of the body all affect performance in later life. Perfectly healthy older people function much like younger people except for their slower reactions, but the development of chronic diseases is a fact of aging for most people.

17. Physical activity is important throughout the life span and is positively correlated with both physical and mental health. Many children and adults are overweight, not only because of genetic factors, but because they do not engage in adequate levels of activity.

Critical Thinking

1. We now know that the architecture of the brain is created in response to early experience rather than laid down by the genes. In what ways might a brain "fine-tuned" by experience be superior to a brain whose structure is entirely determined at birth?

2. Recall a time when you learned a new motor skill—for example, how to roller-blade or hit a golf ball. Can you apply the dynamic systems approach to understand how your skill developed over time and what influenced its development?

3. Many (indeed, most) of the stereotypes of the physical aging process are negative and quite depressing. What in this chapter gives you reason to be more optimistic about aging, and why? Cite specific concepts and research findings.

4. Suppose you set as your goal reaching the age of 100 in superb physical condition. Describe and justify a plan for achieving your goal, and then indicate why you might not make it despite your best efforts.

Key Terms

endocrine gland	brain growth spurt
pituitary gland	plasticity
growth hormone	lateralization
testosterone	reflex
androgens	REM sleep
estrogen	catch-up growth
neuron	cephalocaudal principle
synapse	proximodistal principle
myelin	orthogenetic principle
cerebral cortex	developmental norm
synaptogenesis	gross motor skills

fine motor skills	osteoporosis
pincer grasp	ostheoarthritis
rhythmic stereotypies	reserve capacity
dynamic systems approach	ageism
reaction time	premenstrual syndrome (PMS)
adolescent growth spurt	menopause
puberty	hot flashes
menarche	hormone replacement therapy (HRT)
semenarche	climacteric
secular trend	

On the Web

Web Sites to Explore

Health
Here are two sites that provide extensive information on health issues. The first is somewhat more scholarly and includes recent resources on each topic; the second one is sponsored by the same group that produces the Discovery Channel for television.
http://www.medlineplus.gov/
http://www.discoveryhealth.com

Sleep
Here is scholarly information on sleep needs, habits, and problems.
http://www.sleepfoundation.org

Early Brain Development
This site examines brain development from the prenatal period through the first three postnatal years. Includes topics such as critical periods, environmental influences, and risk factors.
http://www.zerotothree.org/brainwonders

Search Online with InfoTrac College Edition

For additional information, explore InfoTrac College Education, your online library. Go to
http://www.infotrac-college.com
and use the passcode that came on the card with your book.

For example, do a keyword search for "brain development" and organize the results into two general categories: (1) factors affecting early brain growth and (2) consequences of aging on the brain. Focus on articles that have been published in the past two years. Are the findings consistent with the material in the text? Do they extend any of the points made in the chapter? Briefly summarize the most current findings from brain research.

Visit Our Web Site
Go to **http://www.wadsworth.com/psychology**, where you will find online resources directly linked to your book.

Life-Span CD-ROM

Go to the Wadsworth Life-Span CD-ROM for further study of the concepts in this chapter. The CD-ROM also includes quizzes and additional activities to expand your learning experience.

Perception

EQUIPPED WITH AN IMMATURE nervous system, a baby arrives into a clamorous world of stimuli that come both from within and without her growing body. In the early months of life, a normally developing child begins the task of making order out of the sensations that stream unbidden and unchanneled through her maturing senses. First she must attain control over her body's motions and internal sensations and over her own attention . . . these abilities to process sights, sounds, and other sensations and to organize responses in a calm, focused manner support mastery of further basic skills of development. (Greenspan, 1997, p. 45)

Psychologists have long distinguished between sensation and perception. **Sensation** is the process by which sensory receptor neurons detect information and transmit it to the brain. From birth, infants sense the environment. They detect light, sound, odor-bearing molecules in the air, and other stimuli. But do they make "sense" of it? **Perception**

is the interpretation of sensory input: recognizing what you see, understanding what is said to you, knowing that the odor you have detected is a sizzling steak, and so on. It is affected by one's history of learning experiences. Does the newborn really perceive the world, then, or merely sense it? And what happens to sensory and perceptual capacities as we age? Perhaps we should start with a more basic question: Why should you care about the development of sensation and perception?

Sensation and perception are at the very heart of human functioning. Everything you do depends on your perceiving the world around you. You certainly would have a tough time as a student if you could neither read the printed word nor understand speech. Indeed, you would not be able to walk to class without the aid of the body senses that control movement. Possibly one of the reasons that sensation and perception may not seem important is that they occur so effortlessly for most people. And as long as the sensory–perceptual systems are in good working order, we tend to take them for granted. But as soon as there is a "glitch" in the system, we become painfully aware of the limitations imposed when, for example, we lose our vision or sense of smell.

There is another reason to be interested in sensation and perception. They have been at the center of a debate among philosophers and, more recently, developmental scientists about how we gain knowledge of reality.

Issues of Nature and Nurture

Is the ability to perceive the world around us solely dependent on innate biological factors, or is this ability acquired through experience and learning? Philosophers were raising this nature–nurture issue about perception long before anyone had conducted research on the perceptual capabilities of young infants. **Empiricists** such as the 17th-century British philosopher John Locke (1690/1939) took the nurture side of the nature–nurture issue; they believed that the infant enters the world as a *tabula rasa* (blank slate) who knows nothing except what he or she learns through the senses. Empiricists think infants perceive the world very differently than adults do; only by accumulating perceptual experience do they learn how to interpret sensory stimuli in meaningful ways.

Nativists take the nature side of the nature–nurture issue and argue that we come into the world equipped with knowledge that allows us to perceive a meaningful world from the start. For example, Rene Descartes (1638/1965) and Immanuel Kant (1781/1958) believed that we are born with an understanding of the spatial world. Presumably, infants don't need to *learn* that receding objects will appear smaller or that approaching objects will seem larger; perceptual understandings like these are innate or at least mature very rapidly. According to nativists, these abilities have been built into the human nervous system through the course of evolution, making the infant perceiver quite similar to the adult perceiver.

Many of today's developmental theorists take less extreme stands on the nature–nurture issue. They understand

Al Cook/Stock, Boston

In what ways are the perceptual experiences of infants and adults similar, and in what ways are they different because of the adult's greater experience with the world?

that human beings' innate biological endowment, maturational processes, and experience all contribute to perceptual development. Yet they still grapple with nature–nurture issues, and some still take a strong stand on either the nature or the nurture side of the debate. Some have concluded that the infant is equipped to interpret sensory experience much as adults do almost from birth (Spelke, 1994), whereas others argue that the perceptual areas of the brain and perceptual skills evolve gradually as the infant responds to sights, sounds, and other stimuli (Smith & Katz, 1996). Researchers who study perceptual development attempt to determine which perceptual capacities are evident so early in life as to seem innate and which take longer to emerge and appear to be learned. They also attempt to identify the kinds of experiences that are required for normal perceptual development, sometimes by studying children who have been deprived of certain experiences. Their work is some of the most exciting in all of developmental psychology.

Nature–nurture issues also arise in the study of declines in sensory and perceptual abilities in later life. Are these declines universal, suggesting that they are the product of fundamental aging processes? Or do they differ a good deal from person to person and result from factors other than aging, such as disease, or exposure to ultraviolet rays, loud noise, and other environmental influences known to damage the senses? Just as we must pin down the contributions of nature and nurture to early perceptual development, we must clarify their roles in perceptual aging.

So, let us get into it. We will look very closely at sensation and perception in infancy, for this is when most fundamental perceptual capacities emerge. We will also see how much more "intelligent" the senses become during childhood and adolescence and question the image of old age as a time of little more than sensory decline. Finally, we will look more closely at how nature and nurture contribute to perceptual development across the life span.

The Infant

The pioneering American psychologist William James (1890) claimed that sights, sounds, and other sensory inputs formed a "blooming, buzzing confusion" to the young infant. James was actually noting that impressions from the several senses are fused rather than separable, but his statement has since been quoted to represent the view that the world of the young infant is hopelessly confusing.

Today, the accepted view is that young infants have far greater perceptual abilities than anyone ever suspected. Their senses are functioning even before birth, and in the early months of life they show many signs that they are perceiving a coherent rather than a chaotic world. Why the change in views? It is not that babies have gotten any smarter. It is that researchers have gotten smarter. They have developed more sophisticated methods of studying exactly what infants can and cannot do. Infants, after all, cannot tell us directly what they perceive, so the trick has been to develop ways to let their behavior speak for them.

Assessing Perceptual Abilities

As researchers have devised more and more ingenious ways of testing the perceptual capacities of young infants, they have uncovered more and more sophisticated capacities at younger and younger ages. The main methods used to study infant perception are the habituation, preferential looking, evoked potentials, and operant conditioning techniques (see Gibson & Pick, 2000; Kellman & Banks, 1998).

HABITUATION

Infants—and humans of all ages, for that matter—lose interest in a stimulus that is presented over and over again. This process of *learning to be bored* is called **habituation.** Suppose we repeatedly present the same visual stimulus to an infant; eventually the infant gets bored and looks away—habituates. If this infant regains interest when a somewhat different stimulus is substituted, we know that the two stimuli—for example, different visual designs, tones, or touches—have been discriminated from each other (Gibson & Pick, 2000).

PREFERENTIAL LOOKING

Alternatively, we can present an infant with two stimuli at the same time and measure the length of time the infant spends looking at each. A preference for one over the other, like responding to a novel stimulus in the habituation paradigm, indicates that the infant discriminates the two stimuli (see Figure 6.1). And if the infant looks equally long at the two stimuli? Then it's unclear what we can conclude; the infant may well discriminate the stimuli but simply not like one better than the other. It's also possible that infants have a preference but do not display it with preferential looking (see Rovee-Collier, 2001). They may reveal this preference when tested with an alternative method such as interacting with the preferred object.

EVOKED POTENTIALS

We can get an idea of how the brain responds to stimulation by measuring its electrical activity with small metal disks (electrodes) attached to the skin's surface. The infant simply sits back in a comfortable seat and watches or listens to various stimuli. The electrodes and computer do the work of recording the brain's response to these stimuli so that we can "see" what is going on inside the brain.

OPERANT CONDITIONING

As we learned in Chapter 2, humans will repeat a response that has a pleasant consequence; that is, they are capable of learning through *operant conditioning.* Young infants are not easily conditioned, but they can learn to suck faster or slower or to turn their head to the side when a certain stimulus is presented if they are reinforced for that response. Suppose that we want to determine whether infants can distinguish two speech sounds. First, the infants might be conditioned over

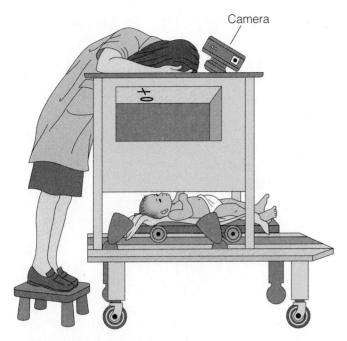

Camera

Figure 6.1 Researchers must devise special ways to assess infants' perceptual abilities. Here, an experimenter and camera record how much time the infant looks at each stimulus. The visual preference test was pioneered by Robert Fantz in the early 1960s.

SOURCE: Schiffman (2000)

several trials to turn their heads every time they hear Sound 1—perhaps by being shown an interesting toy or being given a taste of milk. Then, Sound 2 would be presented; if the infant turns his head, that suggests that the two sounds are perceived as equivalent; if the infant does *not* turn his head, we can conclude that the two sounds have been discriminated.

Methods for studying infant perception have their limitations. For example, infants can fail to respond to some difference between stimuli for reasons that have nothing to do with an inability to discriminate between them (Rosser, 1994). Still, these techniques, along with others, have revealed a good deal about what infants perceive and what they do not, as we will now see.

Vision

Most of us tend to think of vision as our most indispensable sense. Because vision is indeed important, we'll examine its early development in some detail before turning to the other major senses.

BASIC CAPACITIES

The eye functions by taking in stimulation in the form of light and converting it to electrochemical signals to the brain. How well does the newborn's visual system work? Quite well, in fact. From the first minutes after birth, the infant can detect changes in brightness and can visually track a slow-moving picture or object, though not as sensitively as adults (see Muir, Humphrey, & Humphrey, 1994). The ability to discriminate degrees of brightness develops rapidly. By only 2 months of age, infants can distinguish a white bar that differs only 5% in

luminance from a solid white background (Peeples & Teller, 1975).

Very young infants also see the world in color, not in black and white, as some early observers had thought (Adams, Maurer, & Davis, 1986). How do we know this? Suppose we accustom an infant to a blue disk using the habituation technique. What will happen if we now present either a blue disk of a different shade or a green disk? Four-month-old infants will show little interest in a disk of a different blue but will be very attentive to a green disk—even when the light reflected from these two stimuli differs in wavelength from the original blue stimulus by exactly the same amount (H. R. Schiffman, 2000; Teller, Peeples, & Sekel, 1978). Four-month-olds appear to discriminate colors and categorize portions of the continuum of wavelengths of light into the same basic color categories (red, blue, green, and yellow) that adults do. Color vision is present at birth, but newborns often cannot discriminate color differences because their receptors are not yet mature. By 2 to 3 months of age, though, color vision is mature (Schiffman, 2000; Teller et al., 1978).

Are objects clear or blurry to young infants? This is a matter of **visual acuity,** or the ability to perceive detail. By adult standards, the newborn's visual acuity is terrible, but it improves rapidly during the first six months (Schiffman, 2000). You have undoubtedly heard of 20/20 vision, as measured by the familiar Snellen eye chart with the big E at the top. Infants cannot be asked to read eye charts. However, they do prefer to look at a patterned stimulus rather than a blank one—unless it is so fine-grained that it looks no different than a blank. By presenting increasingly fine-grained striped disks paired with blank disks to infants using the preferential looking technique, we can find the point at which their perception of the stripes is lost and translate this into an estimate of visual acuity.

Estimates of newborns' acuity range from 20/600 to as poor as 20/1200 (Schiffman, 2000). At best, this means that an adult with normal vision can see at 600 feet what the infant sees clearly at only 20 feet. Objects are blurry to the young infant unless they are about 8 inches from the face or are bold patterns with sharp light–dark contrasts—the face of a parent, for example (Aslin, 1988). The young infant's world is also blurred because of limitations in **visual accommodation**—the ability of the lens of the eye to change shape in order to bring objects at different distances into focus. It is likely to take six months to a year before the infant can see as well as an adult (Schiffman, 2000).

In short, the eyes of the young infant are not working at peak levels, but they are certainly working. Newborns can perceive light and dark, focus on nearby objects, distinguish colors, and see patterns that are not too finely detailed (Hainline & Abramov, 1992). But does all this visual stimulation make any sense?

PATTERN PERCEPTION

It is one thing to say that young infants can see, but it is another to say that they can *discriminate* different patterns of visual stimulation. Can they detect the difference between two objects or two faces? In the early 1960s, Robert Fantz (1961, 1963,

1965) conducted a number of pioneering studies to determine whether infants can discriminate various forms or patterns. He found that babies less than 2 days old could indeed discriminate visual forms. They preferred to look at patterned stimuli such as faces or concentric circles rather than at unpatterned disks. They also seemed to have a special interest in the human face, for they looked at faces longer than at other patterned stimuli such as a bull's-eye or newsprint. However, young infants looked only a little bit longer at a face drawing than at a stimulus with facial features in a scrambled array (Fantz, 1961; see Walker-Andrews, 1997). Here, then, was evidence that human faces are of interest to very young infants not because they are perceived as meaningful faces, but because they have certain physical properties that create interest, whether those properties show up in a real face or a scrambled face.

So the search began for the properties of patterns that "turn infants on." For one thing, young infants are attracted to patterns that have a large amount of light–dark transition, or **contour;** they are responsive to sharp boundaries between light and dark areas (Banks & Shannon, 1993). Since faces and scrambled faces have an equal amount of contour, they are equally interesting.

Second, young infants are attracted to movement. Newborns can and do track a moving target with their eyes, although their tracking at first is imprecise and likely to falter unless the target is moving very slowly (Easterbrook et al., 1999; Muir et al., 1994). They also look longer at moving objects and perceive their forms better than those of stationary ones (S. P. Johnson & Aslin, 1995; Slater et al., 1990).

Finally, young infants seem to be attracted to *moderately complex* patterns. They prefer a clear pattern of some kind (for example, a bold checkerboard pattern) to either a blank stimulus or a very elaborate one like a page from the *New York Times* (Fantz & Fagan, 1975). As infants mature, they come to prefer more and more complex stimuli.

In sum, we know that infants under 2 months of age have visual preferences, and we also know something about the physical properties of stimuli that attract their attention. They seek out contour, movement, and moderate complexity. As it happens, human faces have all of these physical properties. Martin Banks and his colleagues have offered a very simple explanation for these early visual preferences: *Young infants prefer to look at whatever they can see well* (Banks & Ginsburg, 1985). Based on a complex mathematical model, Banks has been able to predict what different patterns might look like to the eye of a young infant. Figure 6.2 gives an example. Because the young infant's eye is small and its neural receptors immature, it has poor visual acuity and sees a highly complex checkerboard as a big dark blob. The pattern in a moderately complex checkerboard can be seen. Less-than-perfect vision would therefore explain why young infants prefer moderate complexity to high complexity. Indeed, limited vision can account for a number of the infant's visual preferences. Young infants seem to actively seek out exactly the visual input that they can see well— input that will stimulate the development of the visual centers of their brains (Banks & Shannon, 1993; Hainline & Abramov, 1992).

At 2 months of age, Jordan is attracted to the mobile's well-defined contours (or light–dark contrasts) and bold patterns (which are neither too simple nor too complex).

To this point we have established that, from birth, infants discriminate patterns and prefer some over others. But do they really perceive forms or patterns? For example, do they just see an angle or two when they view a triangle, or do they see a whole triangular form that stands out from its background as a distinct shape? Some research suggests that even newborns and 1-month-olds are sensitive to information about whole shapes or forms (Slater et al., 1991; Treiber & Wilcox, 1980). But most studies point to an important breakthrough in the perception of forms starting at about 2 or 3 months of age.

Part of the story is told in Figure 6.3. One-month-olds focus on the outer contours of forms such as faces (M. H. Johnson, 1997; Salapatek, 1975). Even babies a few days old can recognize their mothers' faces—but only when they can see the shape of the mother's head, not when they have only her facial features to work with (Pascalis et al., 1995). Starting at about 2 months of age, infants no longer focus on some external boundary or contour; instead, they explore the interiors of figures thoroughly (for example, looking at a person's facial features rather than just at the chin, hairline, and top of the head). It is as though they are no longer content to locate

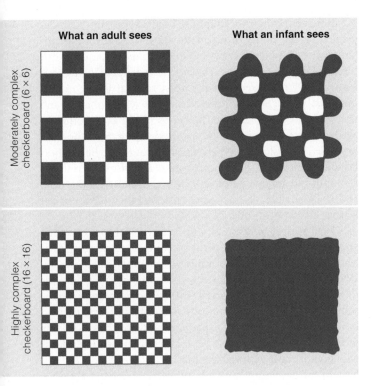

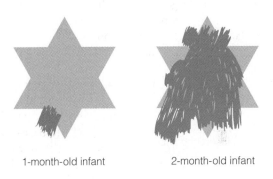

the infant's growing familiarity with faces (Hainline & Abramov, 1992; Johnson, 1997). Infants now smile when they see faces, as though they recognize them as familiar and appreciate their significance.

Much remains to be learned about early perception of faces. An intense nature–nurture debate still rages about whether infants have an innate ability to perceive face forms or can do so only after they have had some experience looking at faces. Still, we can conclude that infants truly perceive a meaningful face form, not merely an appealing pattern of light and dark, by 2 to 3 months of age. So it goes with pattern perception more generally: As infants gain experience with different objects, their attention is drawn to certain objects not only because they have certain physical properties but because their forms are recognized as familiar (Kagan, 1971).

Figure 6.2 What the young eye sees. By the time these two checkerboards are processed by eyes with undeveloped vision, only the checkerboard at top left may have any pattern remaining. Blurry vision in early infancy helps to explain a preference for moderately complex rather than highly complex stimuli.

SOURCE: Adapted from Banks & Salapatek (1983)

(a) Visual scanning of a geometric figure by 1- and 2-month-old infants

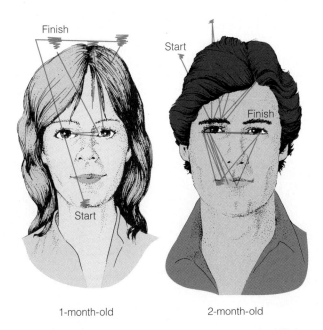

(b) Visual scanning of the human face by 1- and 2-month-old infants

Figure 6.3 Visual scanning in early infancy. The 1-month-old seems to be trying to locate where an object begins and ends, whereas the 2-month-old seems to be on the way to figuring out what an object is by exploring it inside and out.

SOURCE: Adapted from Salapatek (1975)

where an object starts and where it ends, as 1-month-olds tend to do; they seem to want to know what it is. During this time, infants also get better at shifting their gaze from one object to another (Butcher, Kalverboer, & Geuze, 2000). Initially, their gaze seems to get "stuck" on the fixated object, and they have difficulty shifting it to another object. As you might imagine, this difficulty with shifting gaze limits what a young infant can take in from the environment.

Some researchers find that even newborns prefer well-formed human faces to scrambled face forms that have the same features in some random array (Valenza et al., 1996). Most studies, however, find that a clear preference for a normal face over a scrambled face emerges only at 2 or 3 months of age (Dannemiller & Stephens, 1988; M. H. Johnson & Gilmore, 1996). James Dannemiller and Benjamin Stephens (1988) demonstrated that at 3 months of age, but not at 6 weeks, infants even prefer a normal face drawing to an otherwise identical pattern in which areas that are normally dark on a face (facial features, hair) were made light and areas that are normally light (the cheeks, for example) were made dark. Some researchers think that the preference for well-formed faces sometimes observed in newborns is an innate response controlled by a subcortical area of the brain; they note that it disappears in a matter of weeks (Johnson, 1997). By contrast, the preference for face forms evident at 2 to 3 months of age most likely reflects the maturing of the cortex of the brain and

DEPTH PERCEPTION

Another important aspect of visual perception involves perceiving depth and knowing when objects are near or far away. Although it can take years to learn to judge the size of objects off in the distance, very young infants have some intriguing abilities to interpret spatial cues involving nearby objects. For example, they react defensively when objects move toward their faces; blinking in response to looming objects first appears at about 1 months of age and becomes much more consistent over the next few months (Nanez & Yonas, 1994). Moreover, even newborns seem to operate by the principle of **size constancy:** They recognize that an object is the same size despite changes in its distance from the eyes. In one study (Slater, Mattock, & Brown, 1990), newborns who were habituated to a particular cube presented at different distances preferred to look at a different-sized cube when given a choice. This was the case even when the new cube took up the same amount of the visual field as the original cube. This indicates that infants recognize the actual size of an object, even when the object is presented at different distances and thus produces different images on the retina.

Does this evidence of early spatial perception mean that infants who have begun to crawl know enough about space to avoid crawling off the edges of beds or staircases? The first attempt to examine depth perception in infants was carried out by Eleanor Gibson and Richard Walk (1960) using an apparatus called the **visual cliff.** This cliff (see photo) consists of an elevated glass platform divided into two sections by a center board. On the "shallow" side a checkerboard pattern is placed directly under the glass. On the "deep" side the pattern is several feet below the glass, creating the illusion of a drop-off or "cliff." Infants are placed on the center board and coaxed by their mothers to cross both the "shallow" and the "deep" sides. Testing infants 6½ months of age and older, Gibson and Walk found that 27 of 36 infants would cross the shallow side to reach Mom, but only 3 of 36 would cross the deep side. Most infants of crawling age (typically 7 months or older) clearly perceive depth and are afraid of drop-offs.

An infant on the edge of a visual cliff, being lured to cross the "deep" side.

But the testing procedure used by Gibson and Walk depended on the ability of infants to crawl. Would younger infants who cannot yet crawl be able to perceive a drop-off? Joseph Campos and his colleagues (Campos, Langer, & Krowitz, 1970) figured that the heart rates of young infants might tell them. So they lowered babies over the shallow and deep sides of the visual cliff. Babies as young as 2 months of age had a slower heart rate on the deep side than on the shallow side. Why slower? When we are afraid, our hearts beat faster, not slower. A slow heart rate is a sign of interest. So, 2-month-old infants *perceive a difference* between the deep and shallow sides of the visual cliff, but they have not yet learned to *fear* drop-offs.

Fear of drop-offs appears to be learned through experience crawling about—and perhaps falling now and then, or at least coming close to it (Campos, Bertenthal, & Kermoian, 1992). Some beginning crawlers will shuffle right off the ends of beds or the tops of stairwells if they are not watched carefully. However, fear of drop-offs is stronger in infants who have logged a few weeks of experience crawling than in infants of the same age who do not yet crawl; also, providing infants who do not crawl with walkers that allow them to move about hastens the development of a healthy fear of heights (Campos et al., 1992). Both maturation and normal experiences moving about contribute to the perception and interpretation of depth, it seems.

In summary, perception of space develops rapidly in early infancy. The ability to see that an object is looming toward the face emerges within the first month of life. The perception of size constancy despite variations in distance emerges by 4 or 5 months of age. By about 2 months of age, infants also seem to perceive drop-offs, but it is only in the second half of the first year that maturation and experience result in a *fear* of drop-offs.

ORGANIZING A WORLD OF OBJECTS

Another challenge in perceptual development is to separate the visual field into distinct objects, even when parts of objects are hidden behind other objects. From an early age, infants show remarkable abilities to organize and impose order on visual scenes in much the same way that adults do. For example, Katherine Van Giffen and Marshall Haith (1984) reported that 3-month-olds, though not 1-month-olds, will focus their attention on a small irregularity in an otherwise well-formed circle or square pattern, as if they appreciated that it is a deviation from an otherwise well-formed and symmetrical pattern.

Infants must also determine where one object ends and another begins. Elizabeth Spelke and her colleagues (Kellman & Spelke, 1983; Spelke, 1990) have concluded that young infants are sensitive to a number of cues about the wholeness of objects, especially cues available when an object moves. For example, 4-month-olds seem to expect all the parts of an object to move in the same direction at the same time, and they therefore use *common motion* as an important cue in determining what is or is not part of the same object (Kellman & Spelke, 1983). It takes infants longer, until about 6 months of age, to determine the boundaries of objects that are stationary

(Gibson & Pick, 2000). Amy Needham (1999) has found that 4-month-old babies, like adults, use object shape to figure out that two objects side by side are separate. They also use "good form" (for example, logical continuation of a line) to perceive an object's unity or wholeness (S. P. Johnson et al., 2000). Thus, babies appear to have an unlearned ability to organize a visual scene into distinct objects, and they are better able to make sense of a world in motion—a world like the one they live in—than of a stationary world.

THE INFANT AS INTUITIVE THEORIST

That's not all. Researchers have been exploring infants' understandings of the physical laws that govern objects. For example, Elizabeth Spelke and her colleagues have been testing infants to determine what they know of Newtonian physics and the basic laws of object motion (Spelke & Hermer, 1996). Do babies know, for example, that a falling object will move downward along a continuous path until it encounters an obstruction? Spelke's studies suggest that infants only 4 months of age seem surprised when a ball that is dropped behind a screen is later revealed to have ended up below a shelf rather than resting on it. They look longer at this "impossible" event than at the comparison event in which the ball's motion stops when it reaches a barrier. By 6 months of age, infants also seem surprised when a ball drops behind a screen and then, when the screen is lifted, appears to be suspended in midair rather than lying at the bottom of the display unit (Kim & Spelke, 1992; Spelke et al., 1992). This hints that they know something about the laws of gravity.

Findings like these have led some developmentalists to conclude that young infants do much more than just sense the world—that they come equipped with organized systems of knowledge, called **intuitive theories,** that allow them to make sense of the world (Wellman & Gelman, 1992; Gelman, 1996). From an early age, children distinguish between the domains of knowledge we know as physics, biology, and psychology. They organize their knowledge in each domain around causal principles and seem to understand that different causal forces operate in different domains (for example, that desires influence the behavior of humans but not of rocks). According to this intuitive theories perspective, young infants have innate knowledge of the world, and they perceive and even reason about it in much the same ways adults do. Coming to know the physical world is then a matter of fleshing out understandings we have had all along, rather than constructing entirely new ones as we get older (Spelke, 1994).

As you'll see in the Explorations box on page 146, some researchers also believe that babies understand number concepts long before they ever step into a math class. All in all, it's becoming clearer than ever that young infants know a good deal more about the world around them than anyone imagined, though they still learn more and more as they get older.

In sum, the development of visual perception proceeds with remarkable speed during the first few months of life. Infants either come equipped with the perceptual skills we take for granted or soon acquire them. Perhaps because their nervous systems are immature and their vision poor, new-borns prefer sights with light–dark contour, movement, and moderately complex patterning. Within a couple of months, infants more clearly perceive whole forms such as faces; in a few more months, they fear drop-offs and show evidence of having intuitive theories of the physical world that allow them to recognize violations of laws of motion and perceive number, among other things. Perceptual development and cognitive development are intertwined as infants become better and better at interpreting what their senses detect.

Hearing

Hearing is at least as important to us as vision, especially as we depend on it to communicate with others through spoken language. Sound striking the ear creates vibrations of the eardrum, which are transmitted to the cochlea in the inner ear and converted to signals to the brain.

BASIC CAPACITIES

Newborns can hear quite well—better than they can see (Eliot, 1999). Evoked potentials show that even severely premature babies exhibit electrical activity in response to sounds

© Laura Dwight/CORBIS

From birth, infants will look in the direction of an interesting sound. This ability to localize sound improves and becomes more voluntary by 4 months of age.

Can Babies Count?

Although you may think it ridiculous to ask whether babies can count, some developmentalists have discovered that very young infants have some impressive understandings of the abstract quality we call number. Karen Wynn (1992) sought to determine whether 5-month-old infants could add and subtract numbers by seeing how long infants looked at different addition and subtraction "problems." Her test procedure, summarized in the figure here, involved showing the infant a display area with a single Mickey Mouse doll in it, raising a screen to hide the doll, and having the infant watch as a hand placed a second doll in the display area and came out empty. Infants were then observed to see how long they looked at each of two outcomes when the screen was dropped again: a correct outcome in which two dolls were in the display area when the screen was removed (1 + 1 = 2), or an incorrect outcome in which only one doll was present (1 + 1 = 1).

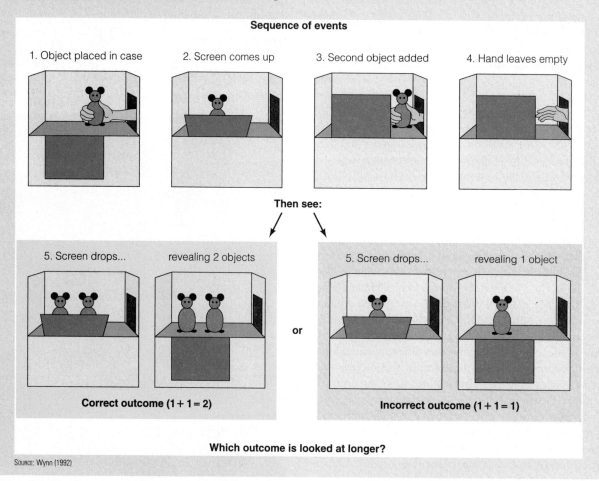

Source: Wynn (1992)

(Eliot, 1999). They can also localize sounds: They are startled by loud noises and will turn away from them, but they will turn in the direction of softer sounds (Field et al., 1980; Morrongiello et al., 1994). By 4 months of age, what was a reflexive reaction has become a voluntary one, and infants can shift their eyes and heads in the appropriate direction quickly and accurately (Morrongiello, Fenwick, & Chance, 1990; Muir, 1985).

Newborns appear to be a little less sensitive to very soft sounds than adults are (Aslin, Pisoni, & Jusczyk, 1983). As a result, a soft whisper may not be heard. However, newborns can discriminate among sounds within their range of hearing that differ in loudness, duration, direction, and frequency or pitch, and these basic capacities improve rapidly during the first months of life (Bower, 1982; Trehub et al., 1991). In general, the sounds that penetrated the womb prior to birth are

Which of these two events attracted more attention? Infants looked longer at the incorrect outcome, as though surprised by the mathematical error it represented. They also looked longer at a 1 + 1 = 3 scenario than at the correct 1 + 1 = 2 outcome. These 5-month-olds also seemed able to subtract: They were surprised when two dolls minus one doll resulted in two dolls rather than one.

But do such findings really show that babies can count and understand numerical functions? The fact that infants look more at incorrect mathematical outcomes than at correct ones is difficult to interpret (Canfield & Smith, 1996): What competencies are babies actually showing? Some research has replicated Wynn's findings (for example, Simon, Hespos, & Rochat, 1995), lending support to the idea that infants have an innate sensitivity to numerical knowledge. The picture becomes muddled, however, when we look at still other research. Tony Simon (1997, 1999) suggests that these findings show that babies come equipped with—or quickly develop—an ability to distinguish "same" from "different," but don't yet understand numbers or precise addition and subtraction. Accordingly, at steps 3 and 4

in Wynn's experiment (see the figure), babies develop some sort of mental representation of two objects. When the screen drops and two objects are revealed (the correct outcome), the image in front of the infant matches—is the same as—the mental representation he or she formed. But in the incorrect outcome, the screen drops to reveal one object, which does not match the infant's mental representation. Thus, longer looking times in the incorrect conditions may reveal only a general understanding of same versus different, not mathematical processes.

Ann Wakely and her colleagues (Wakely, Rivera, & Lanager, 2000), who found no evidence of addition and subtraction by infants using Wynn's procedures, suggest another explanation for the mixed findings. It may be that at 5 months of age, infants' numerical knowledge is "variable and fragile" (p. 1531). Overall, then, numerical competence is not so clearly innate. Early competence may be evident in some infants under some task conditions, but much remains to be learned later in life. Clearly, babies still have a lot left to learn before they will be ready to take calculus!

the ones that are easiest for the infant to hear after birth (Eliot, 1999).

Perceiving Speech

Young infants seem to be well equipped to respond to human speech, as they can discriminate basic speech sounds—called **phonemes**—very early in life. Peter Eimas (1975b, 1985) pioneered research in this area by demonstrating that infants 2 to 3 months old could distinguish consonant sounds that are very similar (for example, *ba* and *pa*). Indeed, infants seem to be able to tell the difference between the vowels *a* and *i* from the second day of life (Clarkson & Berg, 1983). Moreover, just as babies divide the spectrum of light into basic color categories, they seem to divide the continuum of speech sounds into categories corresponding to the basic sound units of language, as early as 3 months of age (Kuhl, 1991; Miller & Eimas, 1996). Among other things, this sound category system allows them to recognize a phoneme as the same phoneme even when it is spoken by different people (Marean, Werner, & Kuhl, 1992). These are impressive accomplishments.

In fact, infants can actually make some speech sound discriminations better than adults (Werker & Desjardins, 1995). We begin life biologically prepared to learn any language humans anywhere speak. As we mature, we normally become especially sensitive to the sound differences that are significant in

our own language and less sensitive to sound differences that are irrelevant to that language. For example, young infants can easily discriminate the consonants *r* and *l* (Eimas, 1975a). So can adults who speak English, French, Spanish, or German. However, Chinese and Japanese make no distinction between *r* and *l,* and adult native speakers of those languages cannot make this particular auditory discrimination as well as young infants can (Miyawaki et al., 1975). Similarly, infants raised in English-speaking homes can make discriminations that are important in Hindi but nonexistent in English, but English-speaking adults have trouble doing so (Werker et al., 1981).

By a year of age, when infants are just beginning to utter their first words, they have already become insensitive to sound contrasts that are not made in their native language (Werker & Desjardins, 1995). Their early auditory experiences have shaped the formation of neural connections, or synapses, in the auditory areas of their brains so that they are optimally sensitive to the sound contrasts they have been listening to and that are important in the language they are acquiring.

Newborns are especially attentive to female voices (Ecklund-Flores & Turkewitz, 1996), but can they recognize their mothers' voices? Using the operant conditioning technique of studying perception, Anthony DeCasper and William Fifer (1980) found that babies can indeed recognize their mothers' voices, and during the first 3 days of life. For half of

Aiding Infants and Children with Hearing Impairments

Although sensory impairments can change the course of normal life-span development, much can be done to help even individuals who are born totally deaf or blind to develop in positive directions and function effectively in everyday life. Let's briefly examine interventions for infants and children who have hearing impairments. Why tackle hearing impairments and not one of the other sensory systems? Because several estimates suggest that hearing impairments take a heavy toll on the individual and on society. Researchers at Johns Hopkins University, for example, estimate that more than $1 million will be spent over the lifetime of each infant or child who becomes deaf before acquiring language (Mohr et al., 2000).

For the 1 to 3 in 1,000 infants born deaf or hearing impaired, early identification and treatment are essential if they are to master spoken language. Unfortunately, the average hearing-impaired child is not identified until the age of 2, usually when it becomes clear that his or her language skills have not developed normally (National Institutes of Health, 1993). Because children who receive no special intervention before the age of 3 usually have lasting difficulties with speech and language, the Joint Committee on Infant Hearing (2000) recommends that all newborns in the United States be given hearing tests soon after birth. As a result, many states now require a hearing test before babies leave the hospital (Hosaka, 1999). How do you test the hearing of newborns? By using the auditory evoked potentials described at the beginning of the chapter and determining whether sounds trigger normal activity in the brain. Infants' behaviors also give us clues about their hearing. Does she turn her head when spoken to? Does he react to loud noises? Is she soothed by your voice? If the answers to these questions are no, a more thorough exam is warranted.

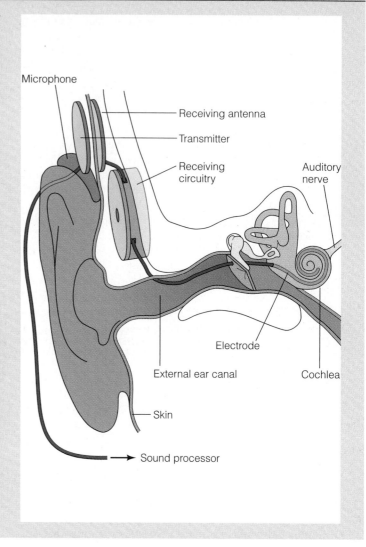

the newborns they studied, sucking faster than usual on a pacifier would activate a recording of the mother's voice, whereas sucking more slowly than usual would elicit a recording of a female stranger. Just the opposite was true for the remaining infants. These 1- to 3-day-old babies learned to suck either rapidly or slowly—whichever it took—to hear their mothers rather than strange women.

Do newborns show the same sort of recognition of their fathers' voices? Apparently not. Even by 4 months of age, infants show no preference for their father's voice over the voice of a strange man (Ward & Cooper, 1999). They can detect the difference between various male voices, however, indicating that the lack of preference for the father's voice can't be due to a failure to distinguish it.

Why would infants prefer their mother's but not their father's voice? We must look at what's happening prior to birth

to answer this. Anthony DeCasper and Melanie Spence (1986) had mothers recite a passage (for example, portions of Dr. Seuss's *The Cat in the Hat*) many times during the last six weeks of their pregnancies. At birth, the infants were tested to see if they would suck more to hear the story they had heard before birth or to hear a different story. Remarkably, they preferred the familiar story. Somehow these infants were able to recognize the distinctive sound pattern of the story they had heard in the womb. Auditory learning before birth could also explain why newborns prefer to hear their mothers' voices to those of unfamiliar women, but don't show a preference for their fathers' voices. They are literally bombarded with their mother's voice for months prior to birth, giving them ample opportunity to learn its auditory qualities.

In sum, hearing is more developed than vision at birth. Infants can distinguish between speech sounds and recognize

Once hearing-impaired infants are identified, interventions can be planned. Many programs attempt to capitalize on whatever residual hearing these children have by equipping them with hearing aids. Today, even profoundly deaf children can be helped to hear through an advanced amplification device called the **cochlear implant** (see illustration). The device is implanted in the inner ear through surgery and connected to a microphone worn outside the ear. It works by bypassing damaged hair cells and directly stimulating the auditory nerve with electrical impulses.

Deaf children who are provided with cochlear implants around age 4 recognize more spoken words and speak more intelligibly than do children who receive them later in childhood, though even children given implants later in life can benefit (O'Donoghue et al., 2000). Indeed, Mario Svirsky and colleagues (2000) report that the rate of language development among children with cochlear implants is very similar to that of children with normal hearing. Why aren't all hearing-impaired children provided with cochlear implants, then? First, they require surgery and are expensive—although the expense of cochlear implants may be offset by educational savings down the road (Cheng et al., 2000). Also, despite their benefits, cochlear implants do not have the full support of the deaf community (Tucker, 1998). Deaf children who use them, some claim, will be given the message that one should be ashamed of being deaf. They will be deprived of participation in the unique culture that has developed in communities of deaf people who share a common language and identity. Because their hearing will still be far from normal, they may end up feeling that they do not belong to either the deaf or the hearing world (Arana-Ward, 1997; Fryauf-Bertschy et al., 1997).

Another important element in early intervention programs for hearing-impaired children is parent involvement (Maxon & Brackett, 1992). In one program for hearing-impaired children, infants are fitted with hearing aids and teachers then go into the home to show parents how to make their children more aware of the world of sound (Bess & McConnell, 1981). For instance, on hearing the screech of a car's brakes outside, parents might put their hands to their ears, rush their child to the window, and talk about the noise. Similarly, parents are urged to slam doors, deliberately rattle pots and pans, and create other such opportunities for the child to become alert to sounds. All the while, parents are using words to describe everyday objects, people, and events.

This combination of the right amplification device and auditory training in the home has proven quite effective in improving the ability of hearing-impaired infants and preschoolers to hear speech and learn to speak. Yet for other deaf and severely hearing-impaired children, the most important thing may be early exposure to sign language. Early intervention programs for parents of deaf infants can teach them strategies for getting their infants' attention and involving them in conversations using sign (Chen, 1996). The earlier in life deaf children acquire some language system, whether spoken or signed, the better their command of language is likely to be later in life (Mayberry & Eichen, 1991). Deaf children whose parents are deaf and use sign language with them, as well as deaf children of hearing parents who participate in early intervention programs, generally show normal patterns of development, whereas children who are not exposed to any language system early in life suffer for it (Marschark, 1993).

familiar sound patterns such as their mothers' voices soon after birth. Within the first year, they lose sensitivity to sound contrasts that are not significant in the language they are starting to learn, and they further refine their auditory perception skills. Unfortunately, some infants experience hearing problems, placing them at risk for language and communication problems. The Applications box above examines the importance of early identification and treatment of hearing problems.

Taste and Smell

Can newborns detect different tastes and smells? Both of these senses rely on detection of chemical molecules. The sensory receptors for taste—taste buds—are located mainly on the tongue. In ways not fully understood, taste buds respond to chemical molecules and give rise to perceptions of sweet, salty, bitter, or sour tastes. At birth, babies can clearly distinguish sweet, bitter, and sour tastes, and show a clear preference for sweets. Indeed, sugar water—though not plain water—seems to have a marvelous ability to calm even premature babies and can help them cope with painful events such as needle pricks (Barr et al., 1999; B. Smith & Blass,1996).

Different taste sensations also produce distinct facial expressions in the newborn. Jacob Steiner and his colleagues (Ganchrow, Steiner, & Daher, 1983; Steiner, 1979) have found that newborns lick their lips and sometimes smile when they are tasting a sugar solution but purse their lips and even drool to get rid of the foul taste when they are given bitter quinine. Their facial expressions become increasingly pronounced as a solution becomes sweeter or more bitter, suggesting that newborns can discriminate different concentrations of a substance.

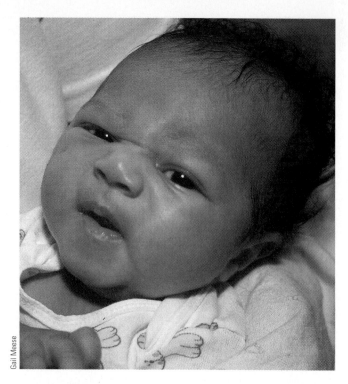

From birth, infants respond to tastes. In response to a sugar solution, newborns part their lips, lick their upper lips, make sucking movements, and sometimes smile. In response to bitter tastes, they purse their lips or open their mouths with the corners down and drool.

The sensory receptors for smell, or **olfaction,** are located in the nasal passage. Like taste, the sense of smell is working well at birth. Newborns react vigorously to unpleasant smells such as vinegar or ammonia and turn their heads away (Rieser, Yonas, & Wilkner, 1976). Even babies born at 28 weeks' gestation are capable of detecting various odors. Newborns also reliably prefer the scent of their own amniotic fluid over other amniotic fluid, suggesting that olfactory cues are detectable prenatally (Schaal, Barlier, & Soussignan, 1998). Exposure to familiar amniotic fluid can also calm newborns, resulting in less crying when their mothers are absent (Varendi et al., 1998). Further, babies who are breast-fed can recognize their mothers solely by the smell of their breasts or underarms within a week or two of birth (Cernoch & Porter, 1985; Porter et al., 1992). Babies who are bottle-fed cannot, probably because they have less contact with their mothers' skin. On the flip side, mothers can identify their newborns by smell (Porter, 1999). Thus, the sense of smell we often take for granted may help babies and their parents get to know each other right from the start.

In sum, both the sense of taste and the sense of smell are working well even before birth. Later development is mainly a matter of learning to recognize what is being tasted or smelled. As wine tasters illustrate, these senses can become highly educated indeed.

Touch, Temperature, and Pain

Receptors in the skin detect touch or pressure, heat or cold, and painful stimuli. The sense of touch seems to be operating quite nicely well before birth and, along with the body senses that detect motion, may be one of the first senses to develop (Eliot, 1999; T. Field, 1990). We saw in Chapter 5 that newborns respond with reflexes if they are touched in appropriate areas. For example, when touched on the cheek, a newborn will turn its head and open its mouth. Even in their sleep, newborns will habituate to strokes of the same spot on the skin but respond again if the tactile stimulation is shifted to a new spot—from the ear to the lips, for example (Kisilevsky & Muir, 1984). And like the motor responses discussed in Chapter 5, sensitivity to tactile stimulation develops in a cephalocaudal direction, so the face and mouth are more sensitive than lower parts of the body. No wonder babies like to put everything in their mouths—the tactile sensors in and around the mouth allow babies to collect a great deal of information about the world (Mennella & Beauchamp, 1998). Most parents realize the power of touch for soothing a fussy baby. Touch has even greater benefits, though. Premature babies who are systematically stroked over their entire body gain weight and settle into a regular sleep–wake pattern faster than premature babies who are not massaged (Field, 1995; Scafidi, Field, & Schanberg, 1993).

Newborns are also sensitive to warmth and cold; they can tell the difference between something cold and something warm placed on their cheek (Eliot, 1999). Finally, young babies clearly respond to painful stimuli such as needle pricks (Guinsburg et al., 2000). For obvious ethical reasons, researchers have not exposed infants to severely painful stimuli. However, analyses of babies' cries and facial movements as they receive injections and have blood drawn leave no doubt that these procedures are painful (Delevati & Bergamasco, 1999). Such research challenges the medical wisdom of giving babies who must undergo major surgery little or no anesthesia. It turns out that infants are more likely to survive heart surgery if they receive deep anesthesia that keeps them unconscious during the operation and for a day afterward than if they receive light anesthesia that does not entirely protect them from the stressful experience of pain (Anand & Hickey, 1992). And the American Academy of Pediatrics (2000) recommends that local anesthesia be given to newborn males undergoing circumcision.

We have now seen that each of the major senses is operating in some form at birth and that perceptual abilities improve dramatically during infancy. Let's ask one final question about infant perception: Can infants meaningfully integrate information from the different senses?

Integrating Sensory Information

It would obviously be useful for the infant who is attempting to understand the world to be able to put together information gained from viewing, fingering, sniffing, and otherwise exploring objects. It now seems clear that the senses do indeed function in an integrated way at birth. For instance, the fact that newborns will look in the direction of a sound they hear suggests that vision and hearing are linked. Moreover, infants 8 to 31 days old expect to feel objects that they can see and are frustrated by a visual illusion that looks like a graspable object but proves to be nothing but air when they reach for it (Bower, Broughton, & Moore, 1970). Thus, vision and touch, as well as vision and hearing, seem to be interrelated early in life. This integration of the senses helps babies perceive and respond appropriately to the objects and people they encounter (Hainline & Abramov, 1992; Walker-Andrews, 1997).

A somewhat more difficult task is to recognize through one sense an object that is familiar through another; this is called **cross-modal perception.** This capacity is required in children's games that involve feeling objects hidden in a bag and identifying what they are by touch alone. Some research (for example, Meltzoff & Borton, 1979) reports that infants as young as 1 month can recognize an object by sight that they had learned about through touch (by sucking on it). But other research has had trouble replicating cross-modal perception with such young infants (Maurer, Stager, & Mondloch, 1999). Consistent oral-to-visual cross-modal transfer is shown by 3 months of age, and other forms of cross-modal perception are reliably displayed at 4 to 7 months of age (Streri & Pecheux, 1986; Walker-Andrews, 1997). By that age, for example, infants integrate vision and hearing to judge distance; they actually prefer to look at an approaching train that gets louder and a departing one that gets quieter rather than at videos in which sound and sight are mismatched (Pickens, 1994). Performance on more complex cross-modal perception tasks that require matching patterns of sounds with patterns of visual stimuli continues to improve throughout childhood and even adolescence, however (Botuck & Turkewitz, 1990; Bushnell & Baxt, 1999).

Intersensory perception. The ability to recognize through one sense (here, touch) what has been learned through another (vision) increases with age during infancy and childhood. Here, the birthday girl must identify prizes in the bag by touch alone.

In sum, impressions from the different senses are "fused" early in life, much as William James believed, but not so as to create the "blooming, buzzing confusion" he described. Rather, this early sensory integration may make it easier for babies to perceive and use information that comes to them through multiple channels simultaneously (Walker-Andrews, 1997). Then, as the separate senses continue to develop and each becomes a more effective means of exploring objects, babies become more skilled at cross-modal perception and are able to coordinate information gained through one sense with information gained through another.

Influences on Early Perceptual Development

The perceptual competencies of even very young infants are remarkable, as is the progress that is made within the first few months of life. All of the major senses begin working before birth and are clearly functioning at birth; parents would be making a huge mistake to assume that their newborn is not taking in the sensory world. Many perceptual abilities—for example, the ability to perceive depth or to distinguish melodies—emerge within just a few months after birth. Gradually, basic perceptual capacities are fine-tuned, and infants become more and more able to interpret their sensory experiences—to recognize a pattern of light as a face, for example. By the time infancy ends, the most important aspects of perceptual development are complete (Bornstein, 1992). The senses and the mind are working to create a meaningful world of recognized objects, sounds, tastes, smells, and bodily sensations.

The fact that perceptual development takes place so quickly can be viewed as support for the "nature" side of the nature–nurture debate. Many basic perceptual capacities appear to be innate or to develop rapidly in all normal infants. What, then, is the role of early sensory experience in perceptual development?

EARLY EXPERIENCE AND THE BRAIN

As we saw in Chapter 5, sensory experience is critically important in determining the organization of the developing brain. To expand a bit on this theme, imagine what visual perception would be like in an infant who was blind at birth but later had surgery to permit vision. This is indeed the scenario for perhaps 3 out of every 5,000 infants with congenital cataracts, a clouding of the lens that leaves these infants nearly blind from birth if not corrected (Lambert & Drack, 1996). In the past, surgery to remove cataracts was often delayed until infants were older. But such delays meant that infants had weeks, months, even years with little or no visual input. Consequently, some never did develop normal vision, even after the lens was removed.

It turns out that the visual system requires stimulation early in life, including patterned stimulation, to develop normally. Indeed, although the visual system has some plasticity throughout childhood, the first 3–4 months after birth are considered critical (Lambert & Drack, 1996). During this time, the brain must receive clear visual information from both eyes. Unfortunately, not all infants with cataracts are identified early enough to benefit from surgery. In the United Kingdom, for example, only 57% of infants with cataracts are diagnosed by 3 months of age (Rahi & Dezateux, 1999). Even after surgery restores their sight, these infants have difficulty, at least initially, perceiving their visual world clearly (Maurer, Lewis, et al., 1999). Acuity after surgery is what you might find in a newborn without cataracts—in other words, rather poor. But it improves significantly during the month following surgery (Maurer, Lewis, et al., 1999).

The same message about the importance of early experience applies to the sense of hearing: Exposure to auditory stimulation early in life affects the architecture of the developing brain, which in turn influences auditory perception skills (Finitzo, Gunnarson, & Clark, 1990). Children who undergo cochlear implant, which bypasses damaged nerve cells in their inner ear, may struggle for many months to understand the meaning of signals reaching their brain through the implant (Allum et al., 2000; see also the Applications box on page 148). Although the brain is being fed information, it must learn how to interpret these signals. Otherwise, the signals are a crashing jumble of nonsense that can be worse than not hearing at all (Colburn, 2000). The conclusion is clear: *Maturation alone is not enough; normal perceptual development also requires normal perceptual experience.* The practical implication is also clear: Visual and hearing problems in children should be detected and corrected as early in life as possible (Joint Committee on Infant Hearing, 2000).

THE INFANT'S ACTIVE ROLE

Parents need not worry about arranging just the right sensory environment for their children because young humans actively seek just the stimulation they need in order to develop properly. Infants are active explorers and stimulus seekers from the start; they orchestrate their own perceptual, motor, and cognitive development by exploring their environment and learning what it will allow them to do (Gibson, 1988; Gibson & Pick, 2000).

According to Eleanor Gibson (1988), infants proceed through three phases of exploratory behavior:

- From birth to 4 months they explore their immediate surroundings, especially their caregivers, by looking and listening, and they learn a bit about objects by mouthing them and watching them move.
- From 5 to 7 months, once the ability to voluntarily grasp objects has developed, babies pay far closer attention to objects, exploring objects with their eyes as well as with their hands.
- By 8 or 9 months of age, after they have begun to crawl, infants extend their explorations out into the larger environment and carefully examine the objects they encounter on their journeys, learning all about their properties. Whereas a young infant may merely mouth a new toy and look at it now and then, a 12-month-old will give it a thorough examination—turning it, fingering it, poking it, and watching it intently all the while (Ruff et al., 1992).

By combining perception and action in their exploratory behavior, infants actively create sensory environments that meet their needs and contribute to their own development (Eppler, 1995). As children become more able to attend selectively to the world around them, they become even more able to choose the forms and levels of stimulation that suit them best.

CULTURAL VARIATION

Do infants who grow up in different cultural environments encounter different sensory stimulation and ultimately perceive the world in different ways? Perceptual preferences obviously differ from culture to culture. In some cultures, people think hefty women are more beautiful than slim ones or relish eating sheep's eyeballs or chicken heads. Are more basic perceptual competencies also affected by socialization?

People from different cultures differ very little in basic sensory capacities such as the ability to discriminate degrees of brightness or loudness (Berry et al., 1992). However, their perceptions and interpretations of sensory input can vary considerably. For example, we have already seen that children become insensitive, starting at the end of the first year of life, to speech sound contrasts that they do not hear because they are not important in their primary language. Michael Lynch and his associates (1990) have shown that the same is true with respect to perceptions of music. Infants from the United States, they found, noticed equally well notes that violated either Western musical scales or the Javanese pelog scale. This suggests that humans are born with the potential to perceive music from a variety of cultures. However, American adults were less sensitive to bad notes in the unfamiliar Javanese musical system than to mistuned notes in their native Western scale, suggesting that their years of experience with Western music had shaped their perceptual skills.

Another example of cultural influence concerns the ability to translate one's perceptions of the human form into a drawing. In Papua New Guinea, where there is no cultural tradition of drawing and painting, children ages 10 to 15 who have had no schooling do not have much luck drawing the human body; they draw scribbles or tadpole-like forms far more often than children in the same society who have attended school and have been exposed many times to drawings of people (Martlew & Connolly, 1996; and see Figure 6.4). We all have the capacity to create two-dimensional representations, but we apparently develop that capacity more rapidly if our culture provides us with relevant experiences. Many other examples of the effects of cultural learning experiences on visual and auditory perception can be cited (Berry et al., 1992).

In sum, a common biological heritage and common sensory experiences combine to ensure that all normal humans develop the same basic perceptual abilities. However, perceptual development is also shaped by specific sensory experiences that only some children have, as influenced by their own explorations of the world and by the cultural context in which they develop.

Figure 6.4 Children ages 10 to 15 in Papua New Guinea, unless they have attended school, lack experience with drawings of the human form and produce drawings much like those done by far younger children (such as 4-year-olds) in our society. Cultural experience influences the ability to translate visual perceptions into representations on the page.

SOURCE: Martlew & Connolly (1996)

The Child

If most sensory and perceptual development is complete by the end of infancy, what is left to accomplish during childhood? Mostly, it is a matter of learning to use the senses more intelligently. For example, children rapidly build knowledge of the world so that they can recognize and label what they sense, giving it greater meaning. As a result, it becomes even harder to separate perceptual development from cognitive development.

The Development of Attention

Much of perceptual development in childhood is really the development of **attention**—the focusing of perception and cognition on something in particular. Youngsters become better able to use their senses deliberately and strategically to gather the information most relevant to a task at hand.

From the start, infants actively use their senses to explore their environment, and they prefer some sensory stimuli to others. Still, there is some truth to the idea that the attention of the infant or very young child is "captured by" something and that of the older child is "directed toward" something. Selective as they are, 1-month-old infants do not really deliberately choose to attend to faces and other engaging stimuli. Instead, a novel stimulus attracts their attention and, once their attention is "caught," they sometimes seem unable to

turn away (Butcher et al., 2000; Ruff & Rothbart, 1996). As children get older, three things change: (1) their attention spans become longer, (2) they become more selective in what they attend to, and (3) they are better able to plan and carry out systematic strategies for using their senses to achieve goals.

LONGER ATTENTION SPAN

Young children do have short attention spans. Researchers know that they should limit their experimental sessions with young children to a few minutes, and nursery school teachers often switch classroom activities every 15 to 20 minutes. Even when they are doing things they like, such as watching a television program or playing with a toy, 2- and 3-year-olds spend far less time actually concentrating on the program or the toy than older children do (Anderson et al., 1986; Ruff & Lawson, 1990). In one study of sustained attention, children were asked to put strips of colored paper in appropriately colored boxes (Yendovitskaya, 1971). Children ages 2 to 3 worked for an average of 18 minutes and were easily distracted; children ages 5 to 6 often persisted for an hour or more. Further improvements in attention span occur later in childhood as those parts of the brain involved with attention become further myelinated (see Chapter 5).

MORE SELECTIVE ATTENTION

Although infants clearly deploy their senses in a selective manner, they are not very good at controlling their attention—deliberately concentrating on one thing while ignoring something else. With age, attention becomes more selective, starting in infancy. As infants approach 2 years of age, they also become able to form plans of action, which then guide what they focus on and what they ignore (Ruff & Rothbart, 1996). As school-age children get older, they become more and more able to selectively focus their attention, enabling them to find a target visual stimulus while disregarding distractor stimuli (Strutt, Anderson, & Well, 1975). Similarly, children become more able to tune in one speaker while ignoring another who is talking at the same time—or to monitor two conversations at the same time and recall what was said (Maccoby, 1967). These findings should suggest to teachers of young children that performance will be better if distractions in task materials and in the room are kept to a minimum.

MORE SYSTEMATIC ATTENTION

Finally, as they get older, children become more able to plan and carry out systematic perceptual searches. We have already seen that older infants are more likely than younger ones to thoroughly explore a pattern. Research with children in the former Soviet Union reveals that visual scanning becomes considerably more detailed or exhaustive over the first six years of life (Zaporozhets, 1965). But the most revealing findings come from studies of how children go about a *visual search*. Elaine Vurpillot (1968) recorded the eye movements of 4- to 10-year-olds who were trying to decide whether two houses, each with several windows containing various objects,

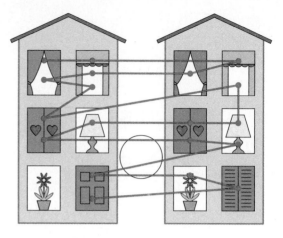

Five-year-old: "The same"   Eight-year-old: "Not the same"

Figure 6.5 Are the houses in each pair exactly the same or different? As indicated by the lines, 8-year-olds are more likely than 5-year-olds to answer correctly because they systematically scan the visual features of the two pictures.
Source: Adapted from Vurpillot (1968)

were identical or different. As Figure 6.5 illustrates, children ages 4 and 5 were not at all systematic. They often looked at only a few windows and, as a result, came to wrong conclusions. In contrast, most children older than 6 were very systematic; they typically checked each window in one house with the corresponding window in the other house, pair by pair. Still, improvements in visual search occur throughout childhood and into young adulthood (Burack et al., 2000).

In summary, learning to control attention is an important part of perceptual development during childhood. Infants and young children are without question selectively attentive to the world around them, but they haven't fully taken charge of their attentional processes. With age, children become more able to concentrate on a task for a long period, to focus on relevant information and ignore distractions, and to use their senses in purposeful and systematic ways to achieve goals. As you might expect, infants and children who can control and sustain their attention are more successful at problem solving (Choudhury & Gorman, 2000). Some children experience serious difficulties with directing or maintaining attention; we'll consider attention disorders in Chapter 16.

The Adolescent

There is little to report about perception during adolescence, except that some of the developments of childhood are not quite completed until then. For example, portions of the brain that help regulate attention are not fully myelinated until adolescence (Tanner, 1990). Perhaps this helps explain why adolescents and young adults have incredibly long attention spans on occasion, as when they spend hours cramming for tests or typing term papers into the wee hours of the morning. The ability to sustain attention improves considerably between childhood and adulthood (McKay et al., 1994).

In addition, adolescents become still more efficient at ignoring irrelevant information so that they can concentrate on the task at hand. Not only do they learn more than children do about material they are supposed to master, but they learn *less* about distracting information that could potentially interfere with their performance (Miller & Weiss, 1981). Similarly, adolescents can divide their attention more systematically between two tasks. For instance, Andrew Schiff and Irwin Knopf (1985) watched the eye movements of 9-year-olds and 13-year-olds during a two-part visual search task. Children were to push a response key when particular symbols appeared at the center of a screen and also remember letters flashed at the corners of the screen. The adolescents developed efficient strategies for switching their eyes back and forth from the center to the corners at the right times. The 9-year-olds had an unfortunate tendency to look at blank areas of the screen or to focus too much attention on the letters in the corners of the screen, thereby failing to detect the symbols in the center.

Adolescents are skilled at dividing their attention among several tasks.

In short, adolescence appears to be a time when basic perceptual and attentional skills are perfected. Adolescents are better than children at sustaining their attention and using it selectively and strategically to solve the problem at hand.

The Adult

What becomes of sensory and perceptual capacities during adulthood? There is good news and bad news, and we might as well dispense with the bad news first: Sensory and perceptual capacities decline gradually with age in the normal person. Whispers become harder to hear, seeing in the dark becomes difficult, food may not taste as good, and so on. Often these declines begin in early adulthood and become noticeable in one's 40s, sometimes giving middle-aged people a feeling that they are getting old. Further declines take place in later life, to the point that one would have a hard time finding a person aged 65 or older who does not have at least a mild sensory or perceptual impairment. The good news is that these changes are gradual and usually minor. As a result, we can usually compensate for them, making small adjustments such as turning up the volume on the TV set or adding a little extra seasoning to food. Because the losses are usually not severe, and because of the process of compensation, only a minority of old people develop serious problems such as blindness and deafness.

The losses we are talking about take two general forms. First, sensation is affected, as indicated by raised **sensory thresholds.** The threshold for a sense is the point at which low levels of stimulation can be detected—a dim light can be seen, a faint tone can be heard, a slight odor can be detected, and so on. Stimulation that is below the threshold cannot be detected, so a raising of the threshold with age means that sensitivity to very low levels of stimulation is lost. (We saw that the very young infant is also insensitive to some very low levels of stimulation.)

Second, perceptual abilities also decline in some aging adults. Even when stimulation is intense enough to be well above the detection threshold, older people sometimes have difficulty processing or interpreting sensory information. As we'll see, they may have trouble searching a visual scene, understanding rapid speech in a noisy room, or recognizing the foods they are tasting.

So, sensory and perceptual declines are typical during adulthood, although they are far steeper in some individuals than in others and can often be compensated for. These declines involve both a raising of thresholds for detecting stimulation and a loss of some perceptual abilities.

Vision

Let's begin with the question that is probably on many of your minds: Will you lose your eyesight as you get older? For the vast majority of us, the answer is no. Fewer than 2% of adults over the age of 70 are blind in both eyes, and only 4.4% are blind in one eye (Campbell et al., 1999). Still, that doesn't mean that we will go through old age with no vision problems. As Table 6.1 shows, 9 out of 10 of us will wear corrective lenses; 1 in 4 will have **cataracts,** or cloudiness of the normally clear lens; and some of us will need to use a magnifying glass to help us see. Why do these changes in our visual system occur, and is there anything we can do to prevent losses? Before we answer these questions, let's briefly review the basic workings of the visual system.

As Figure 6.6 shows, light enters the eye through the cornea and passes through the pupil and lens before being projected (upside down) on the retina. From here, images are relayed to the brain by the optic nerve at the back of each eye. The pupil of the eye automatically becomes larger or smaller depending on the lighting conditions, and the lens changes shape, or accommodates, to keep images focused on the retina. In adolescents and young adults, the visual system is normally at peak performance. Aging brings changes to all components of the visual system.

CHANGES IN THE PUPIL

As we age, our pupils become somewhat smaller and do not change as much when lighting conditions change. As a result, older adults experience greater difficulty when lighting is dim, when it is bright, and when it suddenly changes. Approximately one-third of adults over the age of 85 exhibit a tenfold loss of the ability to read low-contrast words in dim lighting (Brabyn, 2000). Put another way, an 82-year-old can see with 20/30 acuity (20/20 is considered optimal) when lighting and contrast are good, but this same adult's acuity drops to 20/120 when lighting and contrast are poor (Enoch et al., 1999). This is the adult who often has difficulty reading menus in restaurants with "mood" lighting. To compensate, she or he might use a small flashlight. And restaurants could help by providing menus that are printed with sharp contrast (black print on a pure white background).

When walking out into the sunlight after watching a movie in a darkened theater, older adults' pupils are slower than younger adults' to change from large to small, a process that helps reduce the glare of bright lights. In one study, adults over 85 years of age took more than 2 minutes to recover from

Table 6.1	Percentage of Adults 70 Years and Older Who Experience Vision Problems

Vision Condition	Percentage of Adults 70 and Older
Blind in one eye	4.4
Blind in both eyes	1.7
Any other trouble seeing	14.4
Glaucoma	7.9
Cataract(s)	24.5
Use a magnifier	17
Wear glasses	91.5

SOURCE: Adapted from Campbell et al. (1999)

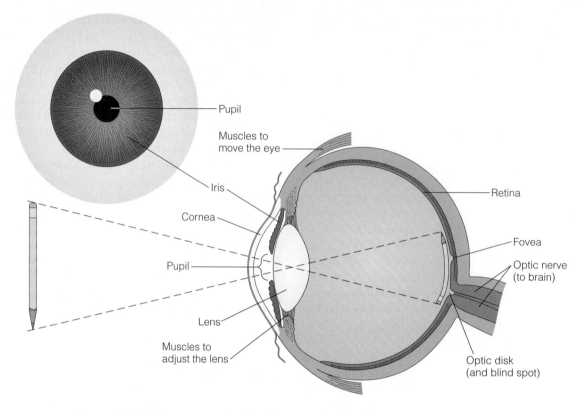

Figure 6.6 The human eye and retina. Light passes through the cornea, pupil, and lens and falls on the light-sensitive surface of the retina, where images of objects are projected upside down. The information is relayed to the brain by the optic nerve.

glare, whereas adults under 65 needed less than 15 seconds (Brabyn, 2000).

Similarly, **dark adaptation**—the process in which the eyes adapt to darkness and become more sensitive to the low level of light available—occurs more slowly in older individuals than in younger ones (Jackson, Owsley, & McGwin, 1999). As a result, the older person driving at night may have special problems when turning onto a dark road from a lighted highway.

CHANGES IN THE LENS

The lens of the eye also undergoes change as we get older. It has been gaining new cells from childhood on, making it denser and less flexible later in life. It cannot change shape, or accommodate, as well to bring objects at different distances into focus. The lens is also yellowing, and both it and the gelatinous liquid behind it are becoming less transparent. The thickening of the lens with age leads to **presbyopia,** or the decreased ability of the lens to accommodate to objects that are close to the eye (Koretz, Cook, & Kaufman, 1997). Over the years, an adult may, without even being aware of it, gradually move newspapers and books farther from the eye to make them clearer—a form of compensation for decline. Eventually, however, the arms may simply be too short to do the trick any longer. So middle-aged adults cope with problems of near vision by getting reading glasses (or, if they also have problems with distance vision, bifocals); reading fine print may still be a problem, however (Kosnik et al., 1988).

Gail Meese

As adults get older, they typically find they are more bothered by glare and need corrective lenses.

As for distance vision, visual acuity as measured by standard eye charts increases in childhood, peaks in the 20s, remains quite steady through middle age, and steadily declines in old age (Pitts, 1982). The implications for the average adult are fairly minor. For example, in one major study, 69% of 75- to 85-year-olds had corrected vision between 20/10 and 20/25 (Kahn et al., 1977). At worst, then, most of them could see at

20 feet what a person with standard acuity can see at 25 feet. As noted earlier, only a small minority of older adults have corrected vision of 20/200 or worse—a cutoff commonly used to define legal blindness. So even though most of us will need to wear corrective lenses, we won't be blind.

The minority of elderly people who experience serious declines in visual acuity typically suffer from pathological conditions of the eye. These conditions become more prevalent in old age, but are not part of aging itself (Pitts, 1982). For example, cataracts are the leading cause of visual impairment in old age. Most older adults have some degree of lens clouding, and significant clouding is present in roughly half of adults over 75 years (Suro, 1997). Fortunately, cataracts can be removed through surgery, improving vision and preventing blindness. A contributing factor to cataracts is lifelong heavy exposure to sunlight and its damaging ultraviolet rays (Kline & Schieber, 1985).

RETINAL CHANGES

We also know that in later life the web of sensory receptor cells in the retina may die or not function as efficiently as they once did. The serious retinal problem **age-related macular degeneration** results from damage to cells in the retina that are responsible for central vision. Thus, vision becomes blurry; it also begins to fade from the center of the visual field, making reading and many other activities impossible. With the success of corrective surgery for cataracts, age-related macular degeneration is now a leading cause of blindness in older adults. The causes of macular degeneration are largely unknown, but some research points to a genetic role; other research shows a connection with cigarette smoking (Evans, 2001). Currently, there is no treatment for macular degeneration, but several researchers are working to develop retinal implants that would stimulate the remaining cells and restore some useful vision to the person (see "Retinal Implant Project," 1999).

Changes in the retina also lead to decreased visual field, or a loss of peripheral (side) vision (Owsley et al., 1991). Looking straight ahead, an older adult may see only half of what a young adult sees off to the left and right of center. Can you think of what activities might be hindered by a decreased visual field? Driving a car comes to mind. For example, when approaching an intersection, you need to be able to see what is coming toward you as well as what is coming from the side roads. The Explorations box on page 158 discusses some other sensory changes that might make driving more hazardous for older drivers.

Significant loss of peripheral vision can lead to tunnel vision, a condition often caused by **retinitis pigmentosa (RP)** or by **glaucoma**. RP is actually not a single disease, but a group of hereditary disorders that all involve gradual deterioration of the light-sensitive cells of the retina. Symptoms of RP can show up as early as childhood, but it is more likely to be diagnosed in adulthood, when the symptoms have become more apparent. Individuals with RP often have a history of visual problems at night and a gradual loss of peripheral vision. There is no treatment that will cure retinal deterioration, but some promising research suggests that treatment with vitamin

A can slow (not eliminate) the progress of the disease (Berson, 2000; Sibulesky et al., 1999).

In glaucoma, increased fluid pressure in the eye can damage the optic nerve and cause a progressive loss of peripheral vision and, ultimately, blindness. It becomes more common over the age of 50. The key is to prevent the damage before it occurs through eyedrops or surgery to lower eye fluid pressure. In many cases, the damage is done before people experience any visual problems, though; only regular eye tests can reveal the buildup of eye pressure that spells trouble (Suro, 1997).

In sum, we can expect some changes in vision as we get older. Sensory thresholds increase with age so that we need higher levels of stimulation than when we were young. Acuity, or sharpness of vision, decreases, and it takes longer for our eyes to adapt to changes. Fortunately, we can correct or compensate for most of these "normal" changes. Some older adults will experience more serious visual problems, such as those due to changes in the retina, but early detection and treatment can preserve vision in most adults.

ATTENTION AND VISUAL SEARCH

As we saw when we examined perceptual development during infancy and childhood, perception is more than just seeing. It is using the senses intelligently and allocating attention efficiently. Young children have more difficulty performing complex visual search tasks and ignoring irrelevant information than older children do. Do older adults also have more difficulty than younger adults?

Older adults do worse than younger ones on a number of tests that require dividing one's attention between two tasks or selectively attending to certain stimuli while ignoring others (Juola et al., 2000). The more distractors a task involves, the more the performance of elderly adults falls short of the performance of young adults. In everyday life, this may translate into difficulty carrying on a conversation while driving or problems locating the asparagus amid all the frozen vegetables at the supermarket.

In one test of visual search skills, Charles Scialfa and colleagues (Scialfa, Esau, & Joffe, 1998) asked young adults and elderly adults to locate a target (for example, a blue horizontal line) in a display where the distractor items were clearly different (for example, red vertical lines) or on a more difficult task where the distractors shared a common feature with the target (for example, blue vertical and red horizontal lines). Older adults were slower and less accurate on the more challenging search task. They were also more distracted by irrelevant information; they were especially slow compared to young adults when the number of distractor items in the display was high. In some situations, elderly people appear to have difficulty inhibiting responses to irrelevant stimuli so that they can focus their attention more squarely on relevant stimuli (Dywan & Murphy, 1996; Hasher et al., 1991). Older adults can improve their visual search performance with practice (Plude & Hoyer, 1981), and they are more successful when they strategically use a feature of the display (for example, color) to help guide their search (Madden, Gottlob, & Allen, 1999).

Aging Drivers

Older drivers are perceived by many as more accident prone and slower than other drivers. Perhaps you have had the experience of zipping down the interstate when a slow-moving car driven by an elderly adult pulls into your path, forcing you to brake quickly. Is this experience representative, and is the stereotype of older drivers accurate? This is an important question; one estimate projects that one-fourth of all drivers (more than 50 million) will be over 65 years of age by the year 2024 (Owsley, 2000).

Unfortunately, perceiving moving objects is a problem for older adults, even those who have good visual acuity (Sivak, Olson, & Pastalan, 1981). And simultaneously processing multiple pieces of information is also difficult for older adults. Thus, older drivers have trouble reading street signs while they are driving (Dewar, Kline, & Swanson, 1994), and they are less able than younger adults to quickly change their focus from the dashboard to the rear-view mirror to the road ahead of them.

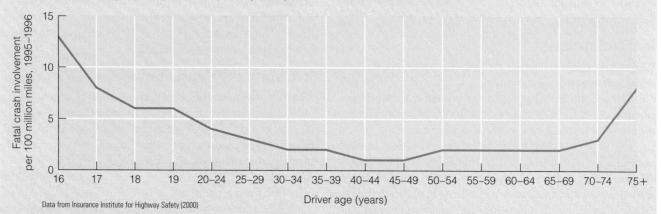

Data from Insurance Institute for Highway Safety (2000)

It's true that older adults (70 years and older) are involved in more automobile fatalities than middle-aged adults (see graph). But the most accident-prone group is actually young drivers between 16 and 24 years (U.S. Department of Transportation, 1997). When we take into account the fact that young people do more driving than elderly people do, it turns out that both elderly drivers and young drivers have more accidents *per mile driven* than middle-aged drivers do (Williams & Carsten, 1989).

Why is driving hazardous for elderly adults? Clearly, vision is essential to driving; indeed, vision accounts for approximately 90% of the information necessary to operate and navigate a car (Fishbaugh, 1995). Visual acuity or clarity is one component of problematic driving, but as noted in the text, poor acuity is fairly easy to correct, so it cannot account for all the problems that older drivers have (Owsley & McGwin, 1999).

Diminished peripheral vision also makes driving hazardous (Owsley et al., 1998). Good drivers must be able to see vehicles and pedestrians approaching from the side. Half of the fatal automobile accidents involving older drivers occur at intersections, and older drivers are more than twice as likely as young drivers to have problems making left-hand turns (Uchida, Fujita, & Katayama, 1999). Not only must drivers see obstacles moving toward them, they must evaluate the speed and trajectory of these objects and integrate this information with their own speed and trajectory to determine a course of action. For example, is the car approaching from the left going to hit my car, or will I be through the intersection before it reaches me?

After understanding the dynamics of a potentially dangerous situation, the driver must be able to react quickly to threats (for example, a child chasing a ball into the street). As we learned in the last chapter, older adults typically have slower response times than younger adults; thus, they need more time to react to the same stimulus. Finally, older adults are slower to recover from glare and adapt to the dark, which makes night driving problematic.

But the driving records of older adults are not as bad as might be expected, because many of them compensate for visual and other perceptual difficulties and slower reactions by driving less frequently, especially in conditions believed to be more hazardous—at night, during rush hour, and when the weather is poor (Ball et al., 1998). Older adults with cataracts are more likely to limit their driving than older adults without cataracts (Owsley et al., 1999). Some states have responded to concerns about elderly drivers with mandatory road retesting at the time of license renewal (Cobb & Coughlin, 1998). But most states have no distinct policies about license renewal for older adults. It's not that states don't care; rather, they face strong opposition from groups such as the American Association of Retired Persons (AARP) and individual older adults (Cobb & Coughlin, 1998). To give up driving is to give up a big chunk of independence, something any of us would be loathe to do. Most of us want to find ways to drive safely as long as possible. By understanding the strengths and limitations of our sensory–perceptual abilities, we will be in a good position to keep driving safely.

An older adult is likely to find the ice cream as efficiently as a younger adult in a familiar supermarket, but may have difficulty with this visual search task if the supermarket is unfamiliar.

In short, older adults have their greatest difficulties in processing visual information (1) when the situation is *novel*—when they're not sure exactly what to look for or where to look; and (2) when it is *complex*—when there's a great deal of distracting information to search through, or two tasks must be performed at once (Plude & Hoyer, 1985). By contrast, they have fewer problems when they have clear expectations about what they are to do and when the task is not overly complex. Thus, an older factory worker who has inspected radios for years may be just as speedy and accurate as a younger worker at this well-practiced, familiar task; but he or she might perform relatively poorly if suddenly asked to inspect pocket calculators and look for a much larger number of possible defects—a novel and complex task.

In summary, it is normal for adults to experience a gradual loss of near vision as they age and to encounter special problems when they are in either darkness or bright light. Performance on novel and complex visual perception tasks may also suffer in old age, partly because older adults are less able than younger people to filter out distracting information.

Hearing

There is some truth to the stereotype of the hard-of-hearing older person. The older the age group, the greater is the percentage of people who have at least a mild hearing loss: about 30% in the 65–75 age group and as many as 50% in the over-75 age group (National Institute on Deafness and Other Communication Disorders, 1997). Most older people experience only mild hearing impairments, though; few are deaf.

BASIC CAPACITIES

Sources of hearing problems range from excess wax buildup in the ears to infections to a sluggish nervous system. Most

age-related hearing problems seem to originate in the inner ear, however (Kline & Scialfa, 1996). The cochlear hair cells that serve as auditory receptors, their surrounding structures, and the neurons leading from them to the brain degenerate gradually over the adult years. The most noticeable result is a loss of sensitivity to high-frequency or high-pitched sounds, the most common form of **presbycusis,** or problems of the aging ear (Northern, 1996). Thus the older person may have difficulty hearing a child's high voice, the flutes in an orchestra, and high-frequency consonant sounds such as *s, z,* and *ch* (Whitbourne, 2001), but may have less trouble with deep voices, tubas, and sounds like *b.* After age 50, lower-frequency sounds also become increasingly difficult to hear (Kline & Scialfa, 1996). Thus, to be heard by the average older adult, a sound—especially a high-pitched sound but, ultimately, any sound—must be louder than it needs to be to exceed the hearing threshold of a younger adult.

Is this loss of hearing with age the inevitable result of basic aging processes, or is it caused by other factors? We know that the loss is more noticeable among men than among women, that men are more likely to work in noisy industrial jobs, and that those who do hold such jobs experience more hearing loss than other men (Martin, 1994; Reuben et al., 1998). But even when adults who have held relatively quiet jobs are studied, men show detectable hearing losses earlier in life (in their 30s) and lose hearing sensitivity at a faster rate than women (Pearson et al., 1995). It seems, then, that most people, men more than women, will experience some loss of sensitivity to high-frequency sounds as part of the basic aging process, but that certain people will experience more severe losses owing to their experiences. As Table 6.2 shows, some loud sounds—those above 75 decibels—may leave you with a loss of hearing. Fans of loud music, beware: The noise at rock concerts and discos is often in the 120- to 130-decibel range; this is loud enough to cause a temporary raising of hearing thresholds (Hetu & Fortin, 1995) and possibly even permanent hearing loss in individuals who are regularly exposed to it (Hartman,

Table 6.2 Noise Levels. The Healthy Ear Can Detect Sounds Starting at 0 Decibel. Damage to Hearing Can Start at 75–80 Decibels and Is More Likely with Long-Term Exposure to Loud Sounds.

	Decibels
Whisper	30
Quiet room	40
Normal speech	60
City traffic	80
Lawnmower	90
Rock music	110
Jet plane takeoff	120
Jackhammer	130
Firearms	140

1982). And if you can hear the music coming from your friend's personal stereo ("Walkman"), your friend may very well be damaging his hearing (H. R. Schiffman, 2000).

SPEECH PERCEPTION

Perhaps the most important thing we do with our ears in everyday life is listen to other people during conversations. The ability to hear is one requisite for understanding speech, but this complex auditory perception task also depends on cognitive processes such as attention and memory. How well do aging adults do?

Older adults typically have more difficulty understanding speech than younger adults do, even under ideal listening conditions. However, this age difference becomes small when age differences in hearing are controlled (Schneider et al., 2000). Thus, older adults' difficulties with speech perception are largely due to hearing problems rather than cognitive declines. However, under poor listening conditions—for example, when there is loud background noise—differences between older and young adults are larger, even when individual differences in hearing are accounted for (Schneider et al., 2000). Thus, older adults recall fewer details of a conversation that takes place in a crowded, noisy restaurant.

In addition, auditory perception tasks, like visual perception tasks, are more difficult for older people when they are novel and complex. In familiar, everyday situations, older adults are able to make good use of contextual cues to interpret what they hear (Fozard, 1990). In one study, for example, elderly adults were about as able as young adults to recall meaningful sentences they had just heard (Wingfield et al., 1985). However, they had serious difficulty repeating back grammatical sentences that made no sense or random strings of words, especially when these meaningless stimuli were spoken rapidly. So, an older person may be able to follow an ordinary conversation but not a technical presentation on an unfamiliar topic—especially if the speaker makes the task even harder by talking too fast.

Overall, then, most older adults have only mild hearing losses, especially for high-frequency sounds, and only minor problems understanding everyday speech, and they can compensate for their difficulties quite successfully—for example, by reading lips and relying on contextual cues. Novel and complex speech heard under poor listening conditions is likely to cause more trouble. Fortunately, there is much we can do to improve hearing or compensate for its loss, as the Applications box on page 161 discusses.

Taste and Smell

Does the aging of sensory systems also mean that older people become less able to appreciate tastes and aromas? Studies designed to measure taste thresholds suggest that with increasing age, many of us have more difficulty detecting weak taste stimulation—for example, a small amount of salt on food or a few drops of lemon juice in a glass of water (S. S. Schiffman, 1997). Thus, older adults may report that food tastes bland to them and end up using larger amounts of salt

and seasonings than when they were younger. In addition, both middle-aged and older adults sometimes have difficulty discriminating among tastes that differ in intensity. In one study, for example, adults over 70 were less able than young adults to reliably judge one solution to be saltier, or more bitter, or more acidic, than another (Weiffenbach, Cowart, & Baum, 1986). Interestingly, older adults did not have difficulty distinguishing degrees of sweetness; we don't seem to ever lose the sweet tooth that we are born with.

The ability to perceive odors also typically declines with age. Sensitivity to odors increases from childhood to early adulthood and then declines during adulthood, more so with increasing age (Finkelstein & Schiffman, 1999; Ship et al., 1996). All things considered, age takes a greater toll on the sense of smell than on the sense of taste (Rolls, 1999). However, differences between age groups are usually small, and many older people retain their sensitivity to odors quite well. Women are more likely than men to maintain their ability to label odors in scratch-and-sniff tests (Ship & Weiffenbach, 1993), partly because they are less likely than men to have worked in factories and been exposed to chemicals (Corwin, Loury, & Gilbert, 1995). Also, healthy adults of both sexes retain their sense of smell somewhat better than those who have diseases and take medications (Ship & Weiffenbach, 1993). Once again, then, we see that perceptual losses in later life are part of the basic aging process, but vary from person to person depending on environmental factors.

How do declines in the senses of taste and smell affect the older person's enjoyment of food? Susan Schiffman (1977) blindfolded young adults and elderly adults and asked them to identify blended foods by taste and smell alone. As Table 6.3 on page 162 reveals, the older people were less often correct than the college students. But was this due to a loss of taste sensitivity or smell sensitivity? Or was it a cognitive problem—difficulty coming up with the name of a food that was in fact sensed?

Claire Murphy (1985) attempted to shed light on these questions by presenting young and elderly adults with 12 of the blended foods used by Schiffman. She observed that older people often came up with the wrong specific label but the right idea (identifying sugar as fruit or salt as peanuts, for example). Thus, at least some of their difficulty may have been cognitive in nature. Murphy also tested women whose nostrils were blocked and found that both young and elderly women did miserably when they could not smell and had to rely on taste alone. This finding suggests that a reduced ability to identify foods in old age is due less to losses in the sense of taste than to losses in the sense of smell, and to declines in the cognitive skills required to remember and name what one has tasted. Other research confirms that age-related changes in odor recognition involve declines in odor detection combined with declines in memory (Murphy, Nordin, & Acosta, 1997).

If foods do not have much taste, the older person may lose interest in eating and not get proper nourishment (Rolls, 1999). Or the older person may overuse seasonings such as salt or eat spoiled food, which can threaten health in other ways. Yet these problems can be remedied. For example, when flavor enhancers were added to the food in one nursing home,

Aiding Adults with Hearing Impairments

In the Applications box on page 148, we examined ways to help infants and children who have hearing impairments, often from birth. Here, we consider the other end of the life span. What can we do to assist hearing-impaired adults, most of whom were born with normal hearing? Many are reluctant at first to admit that they have a hearing problem, so few older adults with hearing loss actually use hearing aids (Popelka et al., 1998). Those who do not have their hearing corrected may end up suffering from depression, decreased independence, and strained relationships (Appollonio et al., 1996). Imagine how hard social interaction can become when one cannot understand what is being said, misinterprets what is said, or has to keep asking people to repeat what they said. One 89-year-old woman became extremely depressed and isolated: "There is an *awfulness* about silence . . . I am days without speaking a word. It is affecting my voice. I fear for my mind. I can't hear the alarm clock, telephone ring, door bell, radio, television— or the human voice" (Meadows-Orlans & Orlans, 1990, pp. 424–425). We tend to think of vision as our most important sense, but hearing impairments may be more disruptive than visual impairments to cognitive and social functioning. Still, many individuals cope very well with their hearing impairments and maintain active, satisfying lifestyles.

Hearing aids, though beneficial, cannot really restore normal hearing; they tend to distort sounds and to magnify background noise as well as what one is trying to hear. In addition, many older people are ill served by hearing aids that are of poor quality or that are poorly matched to their spe-

cific hearing problems. Because cochlear implants work best for individuals who were exposed to spoken language before they lost their hearing, elderly people are ideal candidates for them. They tolerate the surgical procedure required for implantation well, and their hearing test scores increase significantly (Kelsall et al., 1995). In addition, adults who receive cochlear implants report that their quality of life has improved significantly (Faber & Grontved, 2000). Cochlear implants, though, cannot work overnight miracles; it can take months, even years, to learn how to interpret the messages relayed by the implant to the brain (Colburn, 2000).

Finally, the physical and social environment can be modified to help people of all ages with hearing losses (see National Institute on Aging and National Institute on Deafness and Other Communication Disorders, 1996). For example, furniture can be arranged to permit face-to-face contact; lights can be turned on to permit use of visual cues such as gestures and lip movements. Then there are the simple guidelines we can follow to make ourselves understood by hearing-impaired persons. One of the most important is to avoid shouting. Shouting not only distorts speech but raises the pitch of the voice (therefore making it more difficult for elderly people to hear) and makes it harder for the individual to lip-read. It is best to speak at a normal rate, clearly but without overarticulating, with one's face fully visible, at a distance of about 3 to 6 feet.

With modern technology, appropriate education, effective coping strategies, and help from those of us who hear, hearing-impaired and deaf individuals of all ages can thrive.

---

elders ate more, gained muscle strength, and had healthier immune system functioning than they did when they ate the usual institutional fare (Schiffman & Warwick, 1993).

Touch, Temperature, and Pain

By now, we've seen numerous indications that older adults are often less able than younger adults to detect weak sensory stimulation. This holds true for the sense of touch as well. The detection threshold for touch increases and sensitivity is gradually lost from middle childhood on (Kenshalo, 1977; Verrillo & Verrillo, 1985). It is not clear that minor losses in touch sensitivity have many implications for daily life, however.

Similarly, older people may be less sensitive to changes in temperature than younger adults are (Frank et al., 2000). Some keep their homes too cool because they are unaware of being cold; others may fail to notice that it is too hot. Since

older bodies are also less able than younger ones to maintain an even temperature, elderly people face an increased risk of death in heat waves or cold snaps (Worfolk, 2000).

It seems only fair that older people should also be less sensitive to painful stimulation, but are they? They are indeed less likely than younger adults to report *weak* levels of stimulation as painful, although the age differences in pain thresholds are not large or totally consistent (Verrillo & Verrillo, 1985). Yet older people seem to be no less sensitive to stronger pain stimuli. Unfortunately, older adults are more likely to experience chronic pain than younger adults but are less likely to obtain adequate pain relief (Gloth, 2000). Adults with arthritis, osteoporosis, cancer, and other diseases who also experience depression and anxiety are especially likely to perceive pain. Treating these secondary conditions and administering effective pain relief can improve the daily functioning and psychological well-being of older adults.

Table 6.3 Age Differences in Recognition of Foods

Pureed Food Substance	Percentage Recognizing Food	
	College Students (ages 18–22)	Elderly People (ages 67–93)
Apple	93	79
Banana	93	59
Pear	93	86
Pineapple	93	86
Strawberry	100	79
Walnut	33	28
Broccoli	81	62
Cabbage	74	69
Carrot	79	55
Celery	89	55
Corn	96	76
Cucumber	44	28
Green bean	85	62
Green pepper	78	59
Potato	52	59
Tomato	93	93
Beef	100	79
Fish	89	90
Pork	93	72
Rice	81	55

Elderly adults have more difficulty than young college students identifying most blended foods by taste and smell alone. Percentages of those recognizing food include reasonable guesses such as "orange" in response to "apple." Notice that some foods (for example, cucumber) are very difficult for people of any age to identify by taste and smell alone. Appearance and texture are important to our recognition of such foods.

SOURCE: S. Schiffman (1977)

The Adult in Perspective

Of all the changes in sensation and perception during adulthood that we have considered, those involving vision and hearing appear to be the most important and the most nearly universal. Not only are these senses less keen, but they are used less effectively in such complex perceptual tasks as searching a cluttered room for a missing book or following rapid conversation in a noisy room. Declines in the other senses are less serious and do not affect as many people.

Although people compensate for many sensory declines, their effects cannot be entirely eliminated. At some point, aging adults find that changes in sensory abilities affect their activities. As Table 6.4 shows, older adults with one or two sensory impairments are more likely to experience difficulty with basic tasks of living—walking, getting outside, getting in or out of bed or a chair, taking medicines, or preparing meals. Notice, however, that even older adults without sensory impairments report some difficulty with these tasks. People who are limited by sensory impairments usually have physical or intellectual impairments as well, most likely due to general declines in neural functioning that affect both perception and cognition (Baltes & Lindenberger, 1997; Salthouse et al., 1996). A *majority* of older adults, even those with sensory impairments, are engaged in a wide range of activities and are living full lives. Thus, although most adults will experience some declines in sensory abilities with age, these changes do not need to detract from their quality of life.

As we've seen throughout this chapter, perception is our primary means of knowing the world. How would infants gain knowledge of teddy bears, spoons, or videocassettes without being able to see them, hear them, finger them, or pop them into their mouths? How would we know anything at all without the input that our senses provide? Perception is truly at the heart of human cognitive development, the topic to which we turn in Chapter 7.

Table 6.4 Percentage of Older Adults with Visual Impairments, Hearing Impairments, Both Visual and Hearing Impairments, or No Impairments Who Report That Their Activities Are Limited

Activity Limitation	With Visual Impairments	With Hearing Impairments	With Both Visual and Hearing Impairments	Without Visual or Hearing Impairments
Difficulty walking	43.3	30.7	48.3	22.2
Difficulty getting outside	28.6	17.3	32.8	11.9
Difficulty getting in/out of bed or chair	22.1	15.1	25.0	10.4
Difficulty taking medicines	11.8	7.7	13.4	5.0
Difficulty preparing meals	18.7	11.6	20.7	7.8

SOURCE: Adapted from Campbell et al. (1999)

Summary Points

1. *Sensation* is the detection of sensory stimulation; *perception* is the interpretation of what is sensed. Developmentalists and philosophers differ about whether basic knowledge of the world is innate (the nativist position) or must be acquired through the senses (the empiricist position).

2. Methods of studying infant perception include habituation, evoked potentials, preferential looking, and operant conditioning techniques.

3. From birth, the visual system is working reasonably well. Infants under 2 months of age discriminate brightness and colors and are attracted to contour, moderate complexity, and movement. Starting at 2 or 3 months of age, they more clearly perceive whole patterns such as faces and seem to understand a good deal about objects and their properties, possibly because they already have intuitive theories of the physical world. Spatial perception also develops rapidly, and by about 7 months infants not only perceive drop-offs but also fear them.

4. Young infants can recognize their mothers' voices and distinguish speech sounds that adults cannot discriminate.

5. The senses of taste and smell are also well developed at birth. Newborns avoid unpleasant tastes and enjoy sweet tastes, and they soon recognize their mothers by odor alone. Newborns are also sensitive to touch, temperature, and pain.

6. The senses are interrelated at birth, but as they develop, performance on cross-modal perception tasks improves.

7. Although many basic perceptual abilities unfold early in life and may be innate, early perceptual development also requires normal sensory stimulation and can take somewhat different forms depending on the sensory experiences available in one's culture. Hearing-impaired children can benefit from early detection and exposure to sign or oral language (with the help of cochlear implants).

8. During childhood we learn to sustain attention for longer periods of time, to direct it more selectively (filtering out distracting information), and to plan and carry out more systematic perceptual searches.

9. During adolescence, the ability to sustain and control attention improves still more, and sensation and perception are at their peaks.

10. During adulthood, sensory and perceptual capacities gradually decline in most individuals, though many changes are minor and can be compensated for. Changes in the lens, pupil, cornea, and retina of the eye contribute to decreased vision as we get older.

11. Hearing difficulty associated with aging most commonly involves loss of sensitivity to high-frequency (high-pitched) sounds. Hearing aids can significantly improve older adults' abilities to detect sounds. Even elderly people without significant hearing losses may experience difficulty understanding novel and complex speech spoken rapidly under poor listening conditions.

12. Many older people have difficulty recognizing or enjoying foods, largely because of declines in the sense of smell; touch, temperature, and pain sensitivity also decrease slightly, but intense pain stimuli still hurt.

Critical Thinking

1. Drawing on your knowledge of the sensory and perceptual capacities of newborns, put yourself in the place of a newborn just emerging from the womb and describe your perceptual experiences.

2. You have been hired to teach a cooking course to elderly adults. First, analyze the perceptual strengths and weaknesses of your students: What perceptual tasks might be easy for them, and what tasks might be difficult? Second, considering at least three senses, think of 10 strategies you can use to help your students compensate for the declines in perceptual capacities that some of them may be experiencing.

3. You are the coordinator for social and educational activities at your community center, which means you work with people of all ages, ranging from the youngest infants to the oldest adults. In planning activities, what is important to know about capturing and holding the attention of different age groups?

4. You have an unlimited budget for redesigning a local child care center that serves children 6 week olds to 6 year olds. Given what you know about sensory and perceptual capabilities of infants and young children, what equipment and toys will you purchase, and how will you remodel and decorate the rooms?

Key Terms

sensation	cochlear implant
perception	olfaction
empiricist	cross-modal perception
nativist	attention
habituation	sensory threshold
visual acuity	cataracts
visual accommodation	dark adaptation
contour	presbyopia
size constancy	age-related macular degeneration
visual cliff	retinitis pigmentosa (RP)
intuitive theories	glaucoma
phoneme	presbycusis

On the Web

Web Sites to Explore

Census Data

From the Howard Hughes Medical Institute, the site "Seeing, Hearing, and Smelling the World" provides a great deal of scholarly, yet easy to understand, material on the senses. http://www.hhmi.org/senses

Infant Perception

Links to research articles on infant perception from the Infant Cognition Laboratory at the University of Texas–Austin. http://homepage.psy.utexas.edu/homepage/Group/CohenLab/publications.html

Hearing Impairments

From the Center for Assessment and Demographic Studies at Gallaudet University, a scholarly paper on the demographics of hearing impairments in the United States. http://gri.gallaudet.edu/Demography/factsheet.html

Search Online with InfoTrac College Edition

For additional information, explore InfoTrac College Edition, your online library. Go to

http://www.infotrac-college.com

and use the passcode that came on the card with your book. For example, search for "cochlear implants" and find several articles that supplement the discussion of this topic in the text. For another search, try combining the key word "elderly" with the key word for any of the senses (such as "hearing" or "vision"). What new findings have emerged in the past year or two about older adults' sensory capabilities?

Visit Our Web Site
Go to http://www.wadsworth.com/psychology, where you will find online resources directly linked to your book.

Life-Span CD-ROM

Go to the Wadsworth Life-Span CD-ROM for further study of the concepts in this chapter. The CD-ROM also includes quizzes and additional activities to expand your learning experience.

Cognition

Jim Corwin/Stock, Boston

LAURA (3 YEARS), removing opened can of soda from refrigerator, to mother: "Whose is this? It's not yours 'cause it doesn't have lipstick."

Michael (4 years), explaining to his mother why the moon changes shape: "Because there's a piece of blue, a piece of sky over it."

Matt (11 years) wanted to go to a hobby store on Memorial Day. Mother, doubting it was open, told him to call. Matt went off to the phone, returned, and said, "Let's go." They arrived to find the store closed. The frustrated mother inquired: "I thought you called." Matt: "I did, but they didn't answer, so I figured they were too busy to come to the phone." (DeLoache, Miller, & Pierroutsakos, 1998, p. 801)

From an early age, humans think and reason about the world around them—sometimes coming to more or less logical conclusions. At age 3, Laura shows remarkable logic when she concludes that a soda can is not her mother's because it does not have lipstick on it. By contrast, Matt, age 11, does not use the rational powers we assume 11-year-olds possess because his wishes get in the way.

In this chapter, we begin to examine the development of **cognition**—the activity of knowing and the processes through which knowledge is acquired and problems are solved. Human beings are cognitive beings throughout the life span, but as the examples above suggest, their minds change in important ways. In this chapter, we concentrate on the very influential theory of cognitive development proposed by Jean Piaget, who traced growth in cognitive capacities during infancy, childhood, and adolescence, and then ask what becomes of these capacities during adulthood. We also consider an alternative view: Vygotsky's sociocultural perspective on cognitive development. Both theorists have changed how we think about cognitive functioning and education. We explore Piaget and Vygotsky's ideas for improving cognitive skills at the end of this chapter, and we will revisit these ideas in Chapter 10 when we discuss language and education.

Piaget's Constructivist Approach

Jean Piaget was an exceptional person. As we learned in Chapter 2, Piaget became intrigued by children's *mistakes,* for he noticed that children of the same age often made similar kinds of mental mistakes—errors that were typically quite different from those made by younger or older children. Could these age-related differences in error patterns reflect developmental steps, or stages, in intellectual growth? Piaget thought so, and he devoted his life to studying *how* children think, not just what they know (Flavell, 1963). Although many of Piaget's ideas were initially formulated in the 1920s, there was little interest in or knowledge of his work in North America until the 1960s, when John Flavell's (1963) summary of Piaget's theory appeared in English.

Interested in basic questions of philosophy, Piaget defined his field of interest as **genetic epistemology**—the study of how we come to know reality and basic dimensions of it such as space, time, and causality. Epistemology is the branch of philosophy that studies knowledge of reality, and "genetic" can be translated as "emergence" or "development." In other words, Piaget sought to shed new light on the nature of human knowledge by studying how children come to know the world.

His studies began with close observation of his own three children as infants: how they explored new toys, solved simple problems that he arranged for them, and generally came to understand themselves and their world. Later, Piaget studied larger samples of children through what has become known as his **clinical method,** a flexible question-and-answer technique used to discover how children think about problems. Consider the following exchange between Piaget and 6-year-old Van (Piaget, 1929, p. 293):

> *Piaget:* Why is it dark at night?
> *Van:* Because we sleep better, and so that it shall be dark in the rooms.
> *Piaget:* Where does the darkness come from?
> *Van:* Because the sky becomes grey.
> *Piaget:* What makes the sky become grey?
> *Van:* The clouds become dark.
> *Piaget:* How is that?
> *Van:* God makes the clouds become dark.

Many contemporary researchers consider the method imprecise because it does not involve asking standardized questions of all children tested, but Piaget (1929) believed that the investigator should have the flexibility to pursue an individual child's line of reasoning so as to fully understand that child's mind. From his naturalistic observations of his own children and by using the clinical method to explore how children understand everything from the rules of games to the concepts of space and time, Piaget formulated his view of the development of intelligence.

What Is Intelligence?

Piaget's definition of intelligence reflects his background in biology: Intelligence is a basic life function that helps an organism adapt to its environment. We observe adaptation as we watch the toddler figuring out how to work a jack-in-the-box, the school-age child figuring out how to divide treats among friends, or the adult figuring out how to program a video recorder. The newborn enters an unfamiliar world with few means of adapting to it other than working senses and reflexes. But Piaget viewed infants as active agents in their own development, learning about the world of people and things by observing, investigating, and experimenting.

Knowledge gained through active exploration takes the form of one or another **scheme** (sometimes called a *schema* in the singular, *schemata* in the plural). Schemes are cognitive structures—organized patterns of action or thought that we construct to interpret our experience (Piaget, 1952, 1977). For example, the infant's grasping actions and sucking responses are early behavioral schemes, patterns of action used to adapt to different objects. During their second year, children develop symbolic schemes, or concepts. They use internal mental symbols such as images and words to represent or stand for aspects of experience, as when a young child sees a funny dance and carries away a mental model of how it was done. Older children become able to manipulate symbols in their heads to help them solve problems.

As children develop more sophisticated schemes, or cognitive structures, they become increasingly able to adapt to their environments. Because they gain new schemes as they develop, children of different ages will respond to the same stimuli differently. The infant may get to know a shoe mainly as something to chew, the preschooler may decide to let the shoe symbolize or represent a telephone and put it to her ear, and the school-age child may mentally count its shoelace eyelets.

How Does Intelligence Develop?

Piaget believed that all schemes—all forms of understanding—are created through the operation of two inborn intellectual functions, which he called organization and adaptation. These complementary processes operate throughout the entire life span. Through **organization,** children systematically combine existing schemes into new and more complex ones. Thus, our mind is not cluttered with an endless number of independent facts; it consists instead of logically ordered and interrelated actions and ideas. For example, the infant who gazes, reaches, and grasps will organize these simple schemes into a complex structure, *visually directed reaching.* Complex cognitive structures in older children grow out of reorganizations of more primitive structures.

Adaptation is the process of adjusting to the demands of the environment. It occurs through two corresponding processes, assimilation and accommodation. Imagine that you are a 2-year-old, that the world is still new, and that you see your first horse. What will you make of it? In all likelihood, you will try to relate it to something familiar. **Assimilation** is the process by which we interpret new experiences in terms of existing schemes or cognitive structures. Thus, if you already have a scheme that mentally represents your knowledge of dogs, you may label this new beast "doggie." Through assimilation, we deal with the environment in our own terms, sometimes bending the world to squeeze it into our existing categories. Throughout the life span, we rely on our existing cognitive structures to understand new events.

But if you notice that this "doggie" is bigger than most dogs and has a mane and an awfully strange "bark," you may then be prompted to change your understanding of the world of four-legged animals. **Accommodation** is the process of modifying existing schemes to better fit new experiences. Perhaps you will need to invent a new name for this animal or ask what it is and revise your concept of four-legged animals accordingly.

Don Smetzer/PhotoEdit

The grasping scheme. Infants have a range of behavioral schemes that allow them to explore new objects. Each scheme is a general pattern of behavior that can be adjusted to fit specific objects.

If we always assimilated new experiences, our understandings would never advance. Piaget believed that all new experiences are greeted with a mix of assimilation and accommodation. Once we have schemes, we apply them to make sense of the world, but we also encounter puzzles that force us to modify our understandings through accommodation. According to Piaget, when new events seriously challenge old schemes, or prove our existing understandings to be inadequate, we experience cognitive conflict. This *cognitive disequilibrium* then stimulates cognitive growth and the formation of more adequate understandings (Piaget, 1985; see Figure 7.1).

Intelligence, then, develops through the *interaction of the individual with the environment.* Piaget took an interactionist position on the nature–nurture issue: Children are neither born with innate ideas nor programmed with knowledge by adults. Instead, Piaget viewed human beings as active creators of their own intellectual development. As we noted in Chapter 2, Piaget took a position called *constructivism,* maintaining that children "construct reality," or actively create knowledge of the world, from their experiences (Siegler & Ellis, 1996). Their knowledge of the world, which takes the form of cognitive structures or schemes, changes as they organize and reorganize their existing knowledge and adapt to new experiences through the complementary processes of assimilation and accommodation. As a result of the interaction of biological maturation and experience, humans progress through four distinct stages of cognitive development:

1. The *sensorimotor* stage (birth to roughly 2 years)
2. The *preoperational* stage (roughly 2 to 7 years)
3. The stage of *concrete operations* (roughly 7 to 11 years)
4. The stage of *formal operations* (roughly 11 years or later and beyond)

These stages represent qualitatively different ways of thinking and occur in an *invariant sequence*—that is, in the same order in all children. However, depending on their experiences, children may progress through the stages at different rates, with some moving more rapidly or slowly than others.

State of Equilibrium

Current understanding of the world (internal data) is consistent with external data.

Small furry animals with fluffy tails are called cats. They meow and smell nice.

Disequilibrium

Along comes a new piece of information that doesn't fit with current understanding of the world, leading to disequilibrium—an uncomfortable state of mind that the child seeks to resolve.

That's strange—this small furry creature has a fluffy tail but it doesn't meow and it certainly doesn't smell nice!

Assimilation and Accommodation

This unbalanced (confused) state can be resolved through the processes of organization and adaptation (assimilation and accommodation).

This can't be a cat. Mommy called it a skunk, which must be a different kind of animal.

Equilibrium

These lead to a new way of understanding the world—a new state of equilibrium.

I'll have to remember that skunks and cats are different types of animals.

Figure 7.1 Process of change in Piaget's theory

Thus, the age ranges associated with the stages are only averages. What really determines the child's stage of development is his or her reasoning processes, not age.

The Infant

Piaget's **sensorimotor stage,** spanning the two years of infancy, involves coming to know the world through one's senses and actions. The dominant cognitive structures are *behavioral schemes*—patterns of action that evolve as infants begin to coordinate sensory input (seeing and mouthing an object) and motor responses (grasping it). Because infants solve problems through their actions rather than with their minds, their mode of thought is qualitatively different from that of older children.

Substages of the Sensorimotor Stage

The six substages of the sensorimotor stage are outlined in Table 7.1. At the start of the sensorimotor period, infants may not seem highly intelligent, but they are already active explorers of the world around them. We see increasing signs of intelligent behavior as infants pass through the substages, for they are gradually learning about the world and about cause and effect by observing the effects of their actions. They are transformed from *reflexive* creatures who adapt to their environment using their innate reflexes, to *reflective* ones who can solve simple problems in their heads.

The advances in problem-solving ability captured in the six substages of the sensorimotor period bring with them many important changes. Consider changes in the quality of infants' play activities. They are more interested in their own bodies than in manipulating toys in the *primary circular* reactions substage (0–3 months). In the substage of *secondary circular reactions* (4–8 months), they repeat an action, such as sucking or banging a toy, over and over. When they reach the substage of *tertiary circular reactions* (12–18 months), they experiment in varied ways with toys, exploring them thoroughly and learning all about their properties. With the final substage, the *beginning of thought,* at about 18 months, comes the possibility of letting one object represent another, so that a cooking pot becomes a hat, or a shoe becomes a telephone—a simple form of pretend play made possible by the capacity

Table 7.1   The Substages and Intellectual Accomplishments of the Sensorimotor Period

Substage	Description
1. Reflex activity (birth to 1 month)	Active exercise and refinement of inborn reflexes (e.g., accommodate sucking to fit the shapes of different objects)
2. Primary circular reactions (1–4 months)	Repetition of interesting acts centered on one's own body (e.g., repeatedly suck thumb, kick legs, or blow bubbles)
3. Secondary circular reactions (4–8 months)	Repetition of interesting acts on objects (e.g., repeatedly shake a rattle to make an interesting noise, or bat a mobile to make it wiggle)
4. Coordination of secondary schemes (8–12 months)	Combining of actions to solve simple problems (e.g., bat aside a barrier in order to grasp an object, using the scheme as a means to an end); first evidence of intentionality
5. Tertiary circular reactions (12–18 months)	Experimentation to find *new* ways to solve problems or produce interesting outcomes (e.g., explore bathwater by gently patting it, then hitting it vigorously and watching the results; stroking, pinching, squeezing, and patting a cat to see how it responds to varied actions)
6. Beginning of thought (18-24 months)	First evidence of insight; can solve problems mentally, using symbols to stand for objects and actions (e.g., visualize how a stick could be used to move an out-of-reach toy closer); is no longer limited to thinking by doing

© Laura Dwight/CORBIS

At 5 months, almost everything ends up in Eleanor's mouth. According to Piaget, infants in the sensorimotor stage of development learn a great deal about their world by investigating it with their senses and acting motorically on this information.

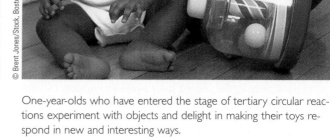

© Brent Jones/Stock, Boston Inc./PictureQuest

One-year-olds who have entered the stage of tertiary circular reactions experiment with objects and delight in making their toys respond in new and interesting ways.

for symbolic thought. It is also in this stage, according to Piaget, that infants can imitate models who are no longer present, because they can now create and later recall mental representations of what they have seen.

The Development of Object Permanence

Another important change during the sensorimotor period concerns the infant's understanding of the existence of objects. According to Piaget, newborns lack the concept of **object permanence.** This is the very fundamental understanding that objects continue to exist—they are permanent—when they are no longer visible or otherwise detectable to the senses. It probably doesn't occur to you to wonder whether your coat is still in the closet after you shut the closet door (unless perhaps you have taken a philosophy course). But very young infants, because they rely so heavily on their senses, seem to operate as though objects exist only when they are perceived or acted on. According to Piaget, the infant must construct the notion that reality exists apart from one's experience of it.

Piaget believed that the concept of object permanence develops gradually over the entire sensorimotor period. Up through roughly 4–8 months, it's "out of sight, out of mind"; infants will not search for a toy if you cover it with a cloth or screen. By Substage 4 (8–12 months), they master that trick but still rely very much on their perceptions and actions to "know" an object (Piaget, 1954). After his 10-month-old daughter, Jacqueline, had repeatedly retrieved a toy parrot from one hiding place, Piaget put it in a new spot while she watched him. Amazingly, she looked in the original hiding place. She seemed to assume that her behavior determined where the object would appear; she did not treat the object as if it existed apart from her own actions or from its initial location. The surprising tendency of 8- to 12-month-olds to search for an object in the place where they last found it (A) rather than in its new hiding place (B) is called the **A, not B, error.** The likelihood of infants making the A, not B, error increases with lengthier delays between hiding and searching and with the number of trials in which the object is found in spot A (Marcovitch & Zelazo, 1999).

In Substage 5, the 1-year-old overcomes the A, not B, error but continues to have trouble with invisible displacements—as when you hide a toy in your hand, move your hand under a pillow, and remove the hand, leaving the toy under the pillow. The infant will search where the object was last seen, seeming confused when it is not in your hand and failing to look under the pillow, where it was deposited. Finally, by 18 months or so, the infant is capable of *mentally representing* such invisible moves and conceiving of the object in its final location. According to Piaget, the concept of object permanence is fully mastered at this point.

Does research support Piaget? Recent studies suggest that infants may develop at least some understanding of object permanence far earlier than Piaget claimed (Fischer & Hencke, 1996). For example, Renee Baillargeon and Marcia Graber (1988) devised a test of the A, not B, error that did not require reaching for a hidden object, only looking toward where it should be. The 8-month-old infants they studied seemed surprised (as demonstrated by looking longer) when a toy that had disappeared behind one screen was snatched from behind a second screen 15 seconds later; the infants seemed to remember very well where the toy had been hidden. Evidence like this suggests that infants who make the A, not B, error and search in the site of their previous success can remember, at least for several seconds, where the object was actually hidden. However, they may not yet be able to act appropriately on this knowledge by searching in location B, possibly because they cannot inhibit a tendency to reach toward A, the spot they last searched (Baillargeon & Graber, 1988; Diamond, Cruttenden & Neiderman, 1994).

More generally, it seems that babies sometimes know a good deal more about object permanence than they reveal through their actions when they are given the kinds of search tasks Piaget devised (Baillargeon & DeVos, 1991). Such findings, though, are not necessarily inconsistent with Piaget's findings (Haith & Benson, 1998). Indeed, Piaget himself contended that looking behaviors were developmental precursors to the reaching behaviors that he assessed. He did not believe, though, that looking represented complete understanding of object permanence (see Fischer & Bidell, 1991; Haith & Benson, 1998). A recent analysis of infants' looking behaviors

by Carolyn Rovee-Collier (2001) suggests that Piaget was wise to distinguish between infants' looking and reaching. In some situations, looking may developmentally precede reaching for an object, as Piaget suggested. In other situations, though, infants' *actions* may actually reveal a more sophisticated understanding of the world than their looking. Regardless of the specific measure we use, infants gradually become more skilled at acting on their knowledge by searching in the right spot. They improve their looking *and* reaching skills between 8 and 12 months, and by the end of the sensorimotor period, they are masters of even very complex hide-and-seek games (Moore & Meltzoff, 1999; Newman, Atkinson, & Braddick, 2001).

The Emergence of Symbols

The crowning achievement of the sensorimotor stage is internalizing behavioral schemes to construct mental symbols that can then guide future behavior. Now the toddler can experiment *mentally* and can therefore show a kind of insight into how to solve a problem. This new **symbolic capacity**—the ability to use images, words, or gestures to represent or stand for objects and experiences—enables more sophisticated problem solving. To illustrate, consider young Lucienne's actions after she watches her father—Piaget—place an interesting chain inside a matchbox:

> [To open the box], she only possesses two preceding schemes: turning the box over in order to empty it of its contents, and sliding her fingers into the slit to make the chain come out. It is of course this last procedure that she tries first: she puts her finger inside and gropes to reach the chain, but fails completely. A pause follows during which Lucienne manifests a very curious reaction. . . . She looks at the slit with great attention; then several times in succession, she opens and shuts her mouth, at first slightly, then wider and wider! [Then] . . . Lucienne unhesitatingly puts her finger in the slit, and instead of trying as before to reach the chain, she pulls so as to enlarge the opening. She succeeds and grasps the chain. (Piaget, 1952, pp. 337–338)

Lucienne uses the symbol of opening and closing her mouth to "think" through the problem. In addition to permitting mental problem solving, the symbolic capacity will also show itself in the language explosion and pretend play that are so evident in the preschool years.

All in all, children's intellectual achievements during the six substages of sensorimotor period are truly remarkable. By its end, they have become deliberate thinkers with a symbolic capacity that allows them to solve some problems in their heads, with a grasp of object permanence and of many other concepts as well.

The Child

No one has done more to make us aware of the surprising turns that children's minds can take than Jean Piaget, who described how children enter the preoperational stage of cognitive development in their preschool years and progress to the stage of concrete operations as they enter their elementary school years.

The Preoperational Stage

The **preoperational stage** of cognitive development extends from roughly 2 to 7 years of age. The symbolic capacity that emerged at the end of the sensorimotor stage runs wild in the preschool years and is the greatest cognitive strength of the preschooler. Imagine the possibilities: The child can now use words to refer to things, people, and events that are not physically present. Instead of being trapped in the immediate present, the child can refer to both past and future. Pretend or fantasy play flourishes at this age: blocks can stand for telephones, cardboard boxes for trains. Some children—especially firstborns and only children who do not have ready access to play companions—even invent **imaginary companions** (Bouldin & Pratt, 1999; Gleason, Sebanc, & Hartup, 2000). Some are humans, some are animals, and they come with names like Ariel, Nutsy, Little Chop, and Bazooie (Taylor, Cartwright, & Carlson, 1993). Their inventors know full well that their companions are not real. Although parents may worry about such flights of fancy, they are perfectly normal. In fact, imaginative uses of the symbolic capacity are associated with advanced cognitive and social development (Singer & Singer, 1990; Taylor, 1999).

Yet the young child's mind is limited compared to that of an older child, and it was the limitations of preoperational thinking that Piaget explored most thoroughly. Although less so than infants, preschoolers are still highly influenced by their immediate perceptions, focus on the most perceptually salient aspects of a situation, and therefore can be fooled by appearances. They have difficulty with tasks that require them to use logic to arrive at the right answer. We can best illustrate this reliance on perceptions and lack of logical thought by considering Piaget's classic tests of conservation.

LACK OF CONSERVATION

One of the many lessons about the physical world that children must master is the concept of **conservation**—the idea that certain properties of an object or substance do not change when its appearance is altered in some superficial way (see Figure 7.2). So, find yourself a 4- or 5-year-old and try Piaget's conservation-of-liquid-quantity task. Pour equal amounts of water into two identical glasses, and get the child to agree that they have the same amount of water to drink. Then, *as the child watches,* pour the water from one glass into a shorter, wider glass. Now ask whether the two containers—the tall, narrow glass or the shorter, broader one—have the same amount of water to drink or whether one has more water. Children younger than 6 or 7 will usually say that the taller glass has more water than the shorter one. They lack the understanding that the volume of liquid is *conserved* despite the change in the shape it takes in different containers.

How can young children be so easily fooled by their perceptions? According to Piaget, the preschooler is unable to engage in **decentration**—the ability to focus on two or more dimensions of a problem at one time. Consider the conservation task: The child must focus on height and width simultaneously and recognize that the increased width of the short, broad container compensates for its lesser height. Preoperational thinkers engage in **centration**—the tendency to center attention on a single aspect of the problem. They focus on height alone and conclude that the taller glass has more liquid; or, alternatively, they focus on width and conclude that the short, wide glass has more. In other ways as well, preschoolers seem to have one-track minds.

A second contributor to success on conservation tasks is **reversibility**—the process of mentally undoing or reversing an action. Older children often display mastery of reversibility by suggesting that the water be poured back into its original container to prove that it is still the same amount. The young child shows *irreversibility* of thinking and may insist that the water would overflow the glass if it were poured back. Indeed, one young child tested by a college student shrieked, "Do it again!" as though pouring the water back without causing the glass to overflow were some unparalleled feat of magic.

Finally, preoperational thinkers fail to demonstrate conservation because of limitations in **transformational thought**—the ability to conceptualize *transformations,* or processes of change from one state to another, as when water is poured from one glass to another (see Figure 7.2). Preoperational thinking is *static,* or fixed.

Preoperational children do not understand the concept of conservation, then, because they engage in centration, irreversible thought, and static thought. The older child, in the stage of concrete operations, has mastered decentration, reversibility, and transformational thought. The correct answer to the conservation task is now a matter of logic; there is no longer a need to rely on perception as a guide. Indeed, a 9-year-old tested by another of our students grasped the logic so well and thought the question of which glass had more water so stupid that she asked, "Is *this* what you do in college?!"

EGOCENTRISM

Piaget believed that preoperational thought also involves **egocentrism**—a tendency to view the world solely from one's own perspective and to have difficulty recognizing other points of view. For example, he asked children to choose the drawing that shows what a display of three mountains would look like from a particular vantage point. Young children often chose the view that corresponded to their own position (Piaget & Inhelder, 1956). Similarly, young children often assume that if they know something, other people do too (Ruffman & Olson, 1989). The same holds for desires: The 4-year-old who wants to go to McDonald's for dinner may say that Mom and Dad want to go to McDonald's too, despite the fact that Mom's on a diet and Dad prefers Pizza Hut.

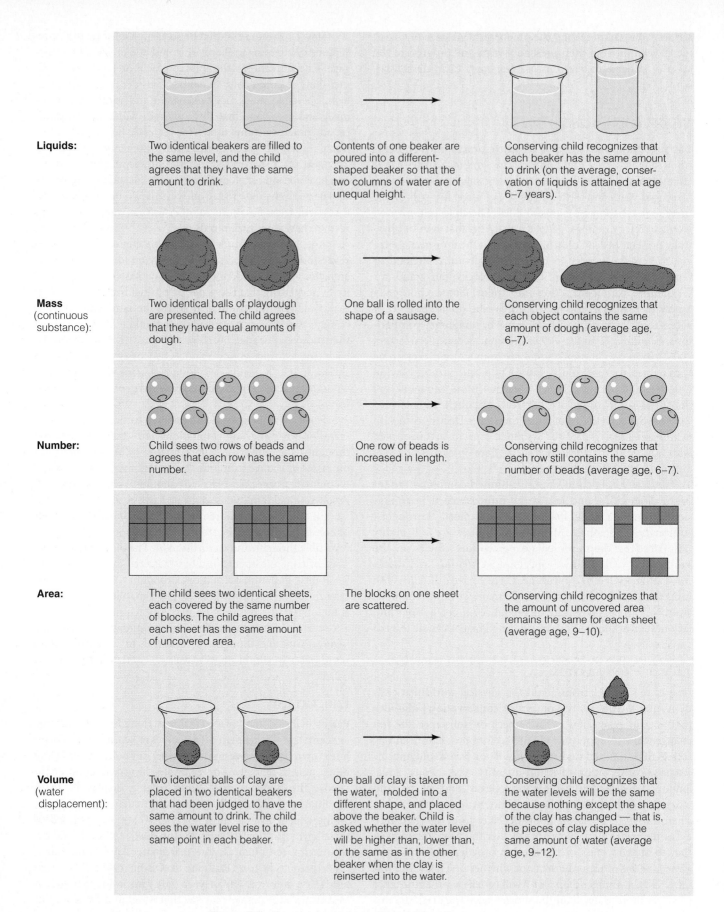

Liquids:

Two identical beakers are filled to the same level, and the child agrees that they have the same amount to drink.

Contents of one beaker are poured into a different-shaped beaker so that the two columns of water are of unequal height.

Conserving child recognizes that each beaker has the same amount to drink (on the average, conservation of liquids is attained at age 6–7 years).

Mass (continuous substance):

Two identical balls of playdough are presented. The child agrees that they have equal amounts of dough.

One ball is rolled into the shape of a sausage.

Conserving child recognizes that each object contains the same amount of dough (average age, 6–7).

Number:

Child sees two rows of beads and agrees that each row has the same number.

One row of beads is increased in length.

Conserving child recognizes that each row still contains the same number of beads (average age, 6–7).

Area:

The child sees two identical sheets, each covered by the same number of blocks. The child agrees that each sheet has the same amount of uncovered area.

The blocks on one sheet are scattered.

Conserving child recognizes that the amount of uncovered area remains the same for each sheet (average age, 9–10).

Volume (water displacement):

Two identical balls of clay are placed in two identical beakers that had been judged to have the same amount to drink. The child sees the water level rise to the same point in each beaker.

One ball of clay is taken from the water, molded into a different shape, and placed above the beaker. Child is asked whether the water level will be higher than, lower than, or the same as in the other beaker when the clay is reinserted into the water.

Conserving child recognizes that the water levels will be the same because nothing except the shape of the clay has changed — that is, the pieces of clay displace the same amount of water (average age, 9–12).

Figure 7.2 Some common tests of the child's ability to conserve

DIFFICULTY WITH CLASSIFICATION

The limitations of relying on perceptions and intuitions are also apparent when preoperational children are asked to classify objects and think about classification systems. When 2- or 3-year-old children are asked to sort objects on the basis of similarities, they make interesting designs or change their sorting criteria from moment to moment. Older preoperational children can group objects systematically on the basis of shape, color, function, or some other dimension of similarity (Inhelder & Piaget, 1964). However, even children ages 4 to 7 have trouble thinking about relations between classes and subclasses, or wholes and parts. Given a set of wooden beads, most of which are brown but a few of which are white, preoperational children do fine when they are asked whether all the beads are wooden and whether there are more brown beads than white beads. That is, they can conceive of the whole class (wooden beads) or of the two subclasses (brown and white beads). However, when the question is "Which would make the longer necklace, the brown beads or the wooden beads?" they usually say "The brown beads." They cannot *simultaneously* relate the whole class to its parts; they lack what Piaget termed the concept of **class inclusion**—the logical understanding that the parts are included within the whole. Notice that the child centers on the most striking perceptual feature of the problem—the fact that brown beads are more numerous than white ones—again being fooled by appearances.

DID PIAGET UNDERESTIMATE THE PRESCHOOL CHILD?

Are preschool children really as perception-bound and egocentric as Piaget believed? Many developmentalists believe that Piaget seriously underestimated the competencies of preschool children by giving them very complex tasks to perform (Bjorklund, 1995). Consider a few examples of the strengths uncovered by researchers using simpler tasks.

Rochel Gelman (1972) simplified Piaget's conservation-of-number task (shown in Figure 7.2) and discovered that children as young as 3 have some grasp of the concept that number remains the same even when items are rearranged spatially. She first got children to focus their attention on number by playing a game in which two plates, one holding two toy mice and one with three toy mice, were presented; and the plate with the larger number was always declared the winner. Then Gelman started introducing changes, sometimes adding or subtracting mice but sometimes just bunching up or spreading out the mice. Young children were not fooled by spatial rearrangements; they seemed to understand that number remained the same. However, they showed their limitations when they were given larger sets of numbers that they could not count.

Similarly, by reducing tasks to the bare essentials, several researchers have demonstrated that preschool children are not as egocentric as Piaget claimed. In one study, 3-year-olds were shown a card with a dog on one side and a cat on the other (Flavell et al., 1981). The card was held vertically between the child (who could see the dog) and the experimenter (who could see the cat). When children were asked what the experimenter could see, these 3-year-olds performed flawlessly.

Finally, preschool children seem to have a good deal more understanding of classification systems than Piaget believed (Markman, 1989; Taylor & Gelman, 1989; Waxman & Hatch, 1992). Sandra Waxman and Thomas Hatch (1992) asked 3- and 4-year-olds to teach a puppet all the different names they could think of for certain animals, plants, articles of clothing, and pieces of furniture. The goal was to see whether children knew terms associated with familiar classification hierarchies—for example, if they knew that a rose is a type of flower and is also a member of the larger category of plants. Children performed quite well, largely because a clever method of prompting responses was used. Depending on which term(s) the child forgot to mention (rose, flower, or plant), he or she was asked about the rose: "Is this a dandelion?" " Is this a tree?" " Is this an animal?" Very often children came up with the correct terms in response (for example, "No, silly, [it's not an animal] it's a plant!)." Even though young children typically fail the tests of class inclusion that Piaget devised, then, they appear to have a fairly good grasp of familiar classification hierarchies.

Studies like these have raised important questions about the adequacy of Piaget's theory and have led to a more careful consideration of the demands placed on children by cognitive assessment tasks. Simplified tasks that focus youngsters' attention on relevant aspects of the task and do not place heavy demands on their memories or verbal skills tend to reveal that young children develop sound understandings of the physical world earlier than Piaget thought. Yet Piaget was right in arguing that preschool children, although they have a number of sound intuitions about the world, are more perception-bound and egocentric thinkers than elementary school children are. Preschool children still depend on their perceptions to guide their thinking and fail to grasp the logic behind concepts such as conservation. They also have difficulty applying their emerging understanding to complex tasks that involve coordinating two or more dimensions.

The Concrete Operations Stage

About the time children start elementary school, their minds undergo another transformation. Piaget's third stage of cognitive development extends from roughly 7 to 11 or more years of age. The **concrete operations stage** involves mastering the logical operations that were missing in the preoperational stage—becoming able to perform *mental* actions on objects, such as adding and subtracting Halloween candies, classifying dinosaurs, or arranging objects from largest to smallest. This allows school-age children to think very effectively about the objects and events they experience in everyday life. For every limitation of the preoperational child, we can see a corresponding strength of the concrete operational child. These contrasts are summarized in Table 7.2.

CONSERVATION

Given the conservation-of-liquid task (Figure 7.2), the preoperational child centers on either the height or the width of the glasses, ignoring the other dimension. The concrete operational child can *decenter* and juggle two dimensions at

Table 7.2 **Comparison of Preoperational and Concrete Operational Thinking**

Preoperational Thinkers	Concrete Operational Thinkers
Fail conservation tasks because they have: • *Irreversible thought*—can't mentally undo an action • *Centration*—center on a single aspect of a problem, rather than two or more dimensions at one time • *Static thought*—fail to understand transformations or processes of change from one state to another	*Solve conservation tasks* because they have: • *Reversibility of thought*—can mentally reverse or undo an action • *Decentration*—can focus on two or more dimensions of a problem at the same time • *Transformational thought*—can understand the process of change from one state to another
Perceptual salience: Understanding is driven by how things look rather than derived from logical reasoning.	*Logical reasoning:* Children acquire a set of internal operations that can be applied to a variety of problems.
Transductive reasoning: Children combine unrelated facts, often leading them to draw faulty cause–effect conclusions simply because two events occur close together in time or space.	*Deductive reasoning:* Children draw cause–effect conclusions logically, based on factual information presented to them.
Egocentrism: Children have difficulty seeing things from other perspectives; assume that what is in their mind is also what others are thinking.	*Less egocentrism:* Children understand that other people may have thoughts different from their own.
Single classification: Children classify objects by a single dimension at one time.	*Multiple classification:* Children can classify objects by multiple dimensions and grasp class inclusion.

In this conservation-of-area task, Rachel first determines that the yellow boards have the same amount of space covered by blocks. But after the blocks are rearranged on one of the boards, she fails to conserve area, indicating that one board now has more open space.

once. *Reversibility* now allows the child to mentally reverse the pouring process and imagine the water in its original container. *Transformational thought* allows the child to better understand the process of change involved in pouring the water. Overall, armed with logical operations, the child now knows that there must be the same amount of water after it is poured into a different container; the child has logic, not just appearance, as a guide.

Looking back at the conservation tasks in Figure 7.2, you will notice that some forms of conservation (for example, mass and number) are understood years earlier than others (area or volume). Piaget maintained that operational abilities evolve in a predictable order as simple skills that appear early are reorganized into increasingly complex skills. He used the term **horizontal décalage** for the idea that different cognitive

skills related to the same stage of cognitive development emerge at different times.

SERIATION AND TRANSITIVITY

To appreciate the nature and power of logical operations, consider the child's ability to think about relative size. A preoperational child given a set of sticks of different lengths and asked to arrange them in order from biggest to smallest is likely to struggle along, awkwardly comparing one pair of sticks at a time. Concrete operational children are capable of the logical operation of **seriation**, which enables them to arrange items mentally along a quantifiable dimension such as length or weight. Thus they perform this seriating task quickly and correctly.

Concrete operational thinkers also master the related concept of **transitivity,** which describes the necessary relations among elements in a series. If, for example, John is taller than Mark, and Mark is taller than Sam, who is taller—John or Sam? It follows *logically* that John must be taller than Sam, and the concrete operator grasps the transitivity of these size relationships. Lacking the concept of transitivity, the preoperational child will need to rely on perceptions to answer the question; he or she may insist that John and Sam stand next to each other in order to determine who is taller. Preoperational children probably have a better understanding of such transitive relations than Piaget gave them credit for (Gelman, 1978; Trabasso, 1975), but they still have difficulty grasping the logical necessity of transitivity (Chapman & Lindenberger, 1988).

OTHER ADVANCES

The school-age child overcomes much of the egocentrism of the preoperational period, becoming better and better at recognizing other people's perspectives. Classification abilities improve as the child comes to grasp the concept of *class inclusion* and can bear in mind that subclasses (brown beads + white beads) are included in a whole class (wooden beads). Mastery of mathematical operations improves the child's ability to solve arithmetic problems and results in an interest in measuring and counting things precisely (and sometimes fury if companions don't keep accurate score in games). Overall, school-age children appear more logical than preschoolers because they now possess a powerful arsenal of "actions in the head."

But surely, if Piaget proposed a fourth stage of cognitive development, there must be some limitations to concrete operations. Indeed there are. This mode of thought is applied to objects, situations, and events that are real or readily imaginable (thus the term *concrete* operations). As we'll see in the next section, concrete operators have difficulty thinking about abstract ideas and hypothetical propositions that have no basis in reality.

The Adolescent

Although tremendous advances in cognition occur from infancy to the end of childhood, still other transformations of the mind are in store for the adolescent. If teenagers become introspective, question their parents' authority, dream of perfect worlds, and contemplate their futures, cognitive development may help explain why.

The Formal Operations Stage

Piaget set the beginning of the **formal operations stage** of cognitive development at age 11 or 12, or possibly later. If concrete operations are mental actions on *objects* (tangible things and events), formal operations are mental actions on *ideas*. Thus the adolescent who acquires formal operations can mentally juggle and think logically about ideas, which cannot be seen, heard, tasted, smelled, or touched. In other words, formal operational thought is more hypothetical and abstract

than concrete operational thought; it also involves adopting a more systematic and scientific approach to problem solving (Inhelder & Piaget, 1964).

HYPOTHETICAL AND ABSTRACT THINKING

If you could have a third eye and put it anywhere on your body, where would you put it, and why? That question was posed to 9-year-old fourth-graders (concrete operators) and to 11- to 12-year-old sixth-graders (the age when the first signs of formal operations often appear). In their drawings, all the 9-year-olds placed the third eye on their foreheads between their existing eyes; many thought the exercise was stupid. The 11- and 12-year-olds were not as bound by the realities of eye location. They could invent ideas that were contrary to fact (for example, the idea of an eye in one's palm) and think logically about the implications of such ideas (see Figure 7.3). Thus, concrete operators deal with realities, whereas formal operators can deal with possibilities, including those that contradict known reality. This may be one reason why adolescents come to appreciate absurd humor, as we see in the Explorations box on page 176.

Formal operational thought is also more abstract than concrete operational thought. The school-age child may define the justice system in terms of police and judges; the adolescent may define it more abstractly as a branch of government concerned with balancing the rights of different interests in society. Also, the school-age child may be able to think logically about concrete and factually true statements, as in this syllogism: If you drink poison, you will die. Fred drank poison. Therefore, Fred will die. The adolescent can engage in such if–then thinking about contrary-to-fact statements ("If you drink milk, you will die") or symbols (If *P*, then *Q*. *P*, therefore, *Q*).

PROBLEM SOLVING

Formal operations also permit systematic and scientific thinking about problems. One of Piaget's famous tests for formal operational thinking is the pendulum task (see Figure 7.4). The child is given a number of weights that can be tied to a string to make a pendulum and is told that he or she may vary the length of the string, the amount of weight attached to it, and the height from which the weight is released in order to find out which of these factors, alone or in combination, determines how quickly the pendulum makes its arc. How would you go about solving this problem?

The concrete operator is likely to jump right in without much advanced planning, using a *trial-and-error* approach. That is, the child may try a variety of things but fail to test out different hypotheses systematically—for example, the hypothesis that the shorter the string is, the faster the pendulum swings, all other factors remaining constant. Concrete operators are therefore unlikely to solve the problem. What they can do is draw proper conclusions from their observations—for example, from watching as someone else demonstrates what happens if a pendulum with a short string is compared to a pendulum with a long string.

Children's Humor and Cognitive Development

At age 4, John repeatedly tells his mother the following joke: Why did the football coach go to the bank? Answer: To get his quarter back. When his mom asks him why this is funny, he replies that the coach lost his quarter and needed to get it back. He misses the whole idea that the humor of the joke depends on the double meaning of "quarter back." He repeats it only because of the chuckles it elicits from his listeners who are amused, not by the joke itself, but because he is so earnest in his attempt to tell a joke. What really tickles John's funny bone is anything that looks or sounds silly—calling a "shoe" a "floo" or a "poo," for example. Once children realize that everything has a correct name, playing with language by mislabeling things and using taboo words such as "poo-poo" becomes wonderfully amusing (Ely, 1997; McGhee, 1979).

With the onset of concrete operational thought and advances in awareness of the nature of language, children come to appreciate jokes and riddles that involve linguistic ambiguities. The "quarter back" joke boils down to a classification task. School-age children who have mastered the concept of class inclusion can keep the class and subclasses in mind at once and move back and forth mentally between the two meanings of "quarter back." Appreciation of such puns is high among second-graders (7- to 8-year-olds) and continues to grow until fourth or fifth grade (McGhee & Chapman, 1980; Yalisove, 1978). And the better children are at solving riddles, the better they tend to be at reading and other language tasks (Ely, 1997).

© Jeffry W. Myers/CORBIS

Tanya's response   Ken's response   John's response

Figure 7.3 Where would you put a third eye? Tanya (age 9) did not show much inventiveness in drawing her "third eye." But Ken (age 11) said of his eye on top of a tuft of hair: "I could revolve the eye to look in all directions." John (also 11) wanted a third eye in his palm. "I could see around corners and see what kind of cookie I'll get out of the cookie jar." Ken and John show early signs of formal operational thought.

As their command of language strengthens, children also become more able to understand sarcasm, irony, and other discrepancies between what is said and what is meant, as when a teacher says to a noisy 8-year-old, "My, but you're quiet today" (Capelli, Nakagawa, & Madden, 1990; Creusere, 1999). The more they understand ironic statements, the more they appreciate the humor in them (Dews et al., 1996). Irony not only conveys humor; it may also allow speakers to convey serious points with less offense to their listeners (Creusere, 1999). We are more likely to hear an adolescent than a younger child "soften" a criticism with an ironic comment ("Well, aren't you in a pleasant mood today" to a grumpy sibling).

Children's tastes in humor change again when they enter the stage of formal operations at about age 11 or 12 (Yalisove, 1978). Simple riddles and puns are no longer cognitively challenging enough, it seems, and are likely to elicit loud groans (McGhee, 1979). Adolescents do, however, appreciate jokes that involve an absurd or contrary-to-fact premise and a punch line that is quite logical if the absurd premise is accepted. The humor in "How do you fit six elephants into a Volkswagen?" depends on appreciating that "Three in the front and three in the back" is a perfectly logical answer only if one accepts the hypothetical premise that multiple elephants could fit into a small car (Yalisove, 1978). Reality-oriented school-age children may simply consider this joke stupid; after all, elephants *can't* fit into cars. Clearly, then, children cannot appreciate certain forms of humor until they have the required cognitive abilities. Research on children's humor suggests that children and adolescents are most attracted to jokes that challenge them intellectually by requiring them to use the cognitive skills they are just beginning to master (McGhee, 1979).

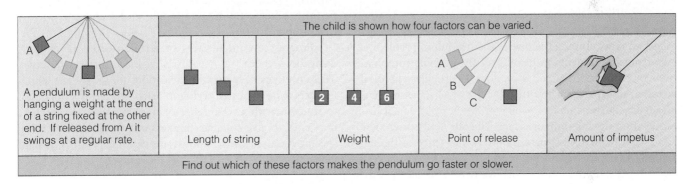

Figure 7.4 The pendulum problem
Source: Labinowicz (1980)

What will the formal operational individual do? In all likelihood, he or she will first sit and think, planning an overall strategy for solving the problem. To begin with, *all* the possible hypotheses should be generated; after all, the one that is overlooked may be the right one. Then it must be determined how each hypothesis can be tested. This is a matter of **hypothetical-deductive reasoning,** or reasoning from general ideas to their specific implications. In the pendulum problem, it means starting with a hypothesis and tracing the specific implications of this idea in an if–then fashion: "If the length of the string matters, then I should see a difference when I compare a long string to a short string while holding other factors constant." The trick in hypothesis testing is to vary each factor (for example, the length of the string) while holding all the others constant (the weight, the height from which the weight is dropped, and so on). (It is, by the way, the length of the string that matters; the shorter the string, the faster the swing.)

In summary, formal operational thought involves being able to think systematically about hypothetical ideas and abstract concepts. It also involves mastering the hypothetical-deductive approach that scientists use—forming many hypotheses and systematically testing them through an experimental method.

PROGRESS TOWARD MASTERY

Are 11- and 12-year-olds really capable of all these sophisticated mental activities? In most cases, no. Piaget (1970) himself described the transition from concrete operations to formal operations as taking place gradually over several years. Many researchers have found it useful to distinguish between early and late formal operations. For example, 11- to 13-year-olds just entering the formal operations stage are able to consider simple hypothetical propositions such as the three-eye problem. But most are not yet able to devise an overall game

Adolescents are more likely than children to benefit from some types of science instruction because formal operational thought opens the door for reasoning about abstract and hypothetical material.

plan for solving a problem or to systematically generate and test hypotheses. These achievements are more likely later in adolescence.

Consider the findings of Suzanne Martorano (1977), who gave 80 girls in grades 6, 8, 10, and 12 a battery of ten Piagetian tasks. Among them were the pendulum problem; a task requiring students to identify all the possible combinations of chemicals that could produce a particular chemical reaction; and analyzing how the behavior of a balance beam is affected by the heaviness of weights on the beam and their distances from the fulcrum, or center. The 6th- and 8th-graders (ages 11–12 and 13–14) passed only two or three of the ten tasks on the average; the 10th- and 12th-graders (ages 15–16 and 17–18) passed an average of five or six. Similarly, 10th- and 11th-graders (ages 16–17) demonstrate more advanced scientific reasoning than 7th- and 8th-graders (ages 13–14) when asked to consider evidence and evaluate theories regarding religion and social class (Klaczynski, 2000). Still, the responses of older adolescents contain biases similar to those shown by younger adolescents. Both age groups more readily accept evidence that is consistent with their preexisting beliefs than evidence that is inconsistent with these beliefs (Kuhn, 1993; Klaczynski & Gordon, 1996a, 1996b). Thus, although reasoning skills improve over the adolescent years, adolescents do not consistently show formal operations and logical scientific reasoning skills on all tasks (Klaczynski & Narasimham, 1998).

Contrary to Piaget's claim that intuitive reasoning is replaced by scientific reasoning as children get older, the two forms of reasoning seem to coexist in older thinkers (Klaczynski, 2000, 2001). Being able to shift between intuitive and scientific reasoning provides flexibility in problem-solving situations as long as one can effectively select the appropriate strategy. However, like children (and like adults as well), adolescents often seem to adopt a "seeing is believing"

strategy, leading them to conclusions that are "against their better judgment" (Klaczysnki, 2001, p. 854). This tendency, though, decreases across adolescence, perhaps because adolescents are increasingly able to **decontextualize,** or separate prior knowledge and beliefs from the demands of the task at hand (Klaczynski, 2000; Stanovich & West, 1997). For example, given the *belief* that males are better at math than females, the *evidence* that girls attain higher classroom math grades than boys may be rejected because it does not fit with the prior belief; interpretation of the evidence has been influenced by its context. Decontextualizing increases the likelihood of using reasoning to analyze a problem logically rather than relying on intuition or possibly faulty existing knowledge.

There is some evidence that today's teens (ages 13 to 15) are better able than earlier cohorts to solve formal operational tasks. For example, 66% of teens tested in 1996 showed formal operational thought on a probability test, compared to 49% of teens tested in 1967 (Flieller, 1999). Why might formal operational skills improve over time? Changes in school curricula are the likely explanation. The achievement of formal operational thinking depends on specific experiences, such as exposure to math and science education (Laurendeau-Bendavid, 1977). Research with Western and African populations shows that both age and education level influence performance on formal operational tasks; college and university students outperform adults with no advanced education, who in turn outperform adolescents (Mwamwenda & Mwamwenda, 1989; Mwamwenda, 1999).

Progress toward mastery of formal operations is obviously slow, at least as measured by Piaget's scientific tasks. These findings have major implications for secondary school teachers, who are often trying to teach very abstract material to students with a wide range of thinking patterns. Teachers may need to give concrete thinkers extra assistance by using specific examples and demonstrations to help clarify general principles.

Implications of Formal Thought

Formal operational thought contributes to other changes in adolescence—some good, some not so good. First, the good news: As we'll see in upcoming chapters, formal operational thought may prepare the individual to gain a sense of identity, think in more complex ways about moral issues, and understand other people. Advances in cognitive development help to lay the groundwork for advances in many other areas of development.

Now, the bad news: Formal operations may also be related to some of the more painful aspects of the adolescent experience. Children tend to accept the world as it is and to heed the words of authority figures. The adolescent armed with formal operations can think more independently, imagine alternatives to present realities, and raise questions about everything from why parents set down the rules they do to why there is injustice in the world. Questioning can lead to confusion and sometimes to rebellion against ideas that do not seem logical enough. Some adolescents become idealists, inventing perfect worlds and envisioning logical solutions to problems they detect in the imperfect world around them, sometimes losing sight of practical considerations and real barriers to social change. Just as infants flaunt the new schemes they develop, adolescents may go overboard with their new cognitive skills, irritate their parents, and become frustrated when the world does not respond to their flawless logic.

Some years ago, David Elkind (1967) proposed that formal operational thought also leads to **adolescent egocentrism**—difficulty differentiating one's own thoughts and feelings from those of other people. The young child's egocentrism is rooted in ignorance that different people have different perspectives, but the adolescent's reflects an enhanced ability to reflect about one's own and others' thoughts. Elkind identified two types of adolescent egocentrism: the imaginary audience and the personal fable.

The **imaginary audience** phenomenon involves confusing your own thoughts with those of a hypothesized audience for your behavior. Thus, the teenage girl who spills soda on her dress at a party may feel extremely self-conscious: "They're all thinking what a slob I am! I wish I could crawl into a hole." She assumes that everyone else in the room is as preoccupied with the blunder as she is. Or a teenage boy may spend hours in front of the mirror getting ready for a date and then be so concerned with how he imagines his date is reacting to him that he hardly notices her: "Why did I say that? She looks bored. Did she notice my pimple?" (She, of course, is equally preoccupied with how she is playing to her audience. No wonder teenagers are often awkward and painfully aware of their every slip on first dates!)

The second form of adolescent egocentrism is the **personal fable**—a tendency to think that you and your thoughts and feelings are unique (Elkind, 1967). If the imaginary audi-

ence is a product of the inability to differentiate between self and other, the personal fable is a product of differentiating too much. Thus, the adolescent who is in love for the first time imagines that no one in the history of the human race has ever felt such heights of emotion. When the relationship breaks up, of course, no one—least of all a parent—could possibly understand the crushing agony. The personal fable may also lead adolescents to feel that rules that apply to others do not apply to them. Thus, *they* won't be hurt if they speed down the highway without wearing a seat belt or drive under the influence of alcohol. And *they* won't become pregnant if they engage in sex without contraception, so they don't need to bother with contraception! As it turns out, high scores on measures of adolescent egocentrism are associated with behaving in risky ways (Greene et al., 1996; Holmbeck et al., 1994).

Elkind hypothesized that the imaginary audience and personal fable phenomena should increase when formal operations are first being acquired and then decrease as adolescents get older, gain fuller control of formal operations, and assume adult roles that require fuller consideration of others' perspectives. Indeed, both the self-consciousness associated with the imaginary audience and the sense of specialness associated with the personal fable are most evident in early adolescence and decline by late high school (Elkind & Bowen, 1979; Enright, Lapsley, & Shukla, 1979). Adolescent egocentrism may persist, though, when adolescents have insecure relationships with their parents that may make them self-conscious and lacking in self-confidence even as older adolescents (Ryan & Kuczkowski, 1994).

Contrary to what Piaget and Elkind hypothesized, however, researchers have been unable to link the onset of formal operations to the rise of adolescent egocentrism (Gray & Hudson, 1984; O'Connor & Nikolic, 1990). It now seems that

Michael Newman/PhotoEdit

A teenage girl may feel that everyone is as preoccupied with her appearance as she is, a form of adolescent egocentrism known as the imaginary audience phenomenon.

adolescent egocentrism may arise when adolescents acquire advanced social perspective-taking abilities and contemplate how other people might perceive them and react to their behavior (Lapsley et al., 1986; Vartanian & Powlishta, 1996). The truth is that researchers have not yet figured out precisely why young adolescents often feel that the whole world is watching them or that not one person in the world can truly understand them. We can conclude, though, that the acquisition of formal operations brings with it both new competencies and new challenges.

The Adult

Do adults think differently than adolescents do? Does cognition change over the adult years? Until recently, developmentalists have not asked such questions. After all, Piaget indicated that the highest stage of cognitive development, formal operations, was fully mastered by most people by age 15 to 18. Why bother studying cognitive development in adulthood? As it turns out, it has been well worth the effort. Research has revealed limitations in adult performance that must be explained, and it also suggests that at least some adults progress beyond formal operations to more advanced forms of thought.

Limitations in Adult Cognitive Performance

If many high school students are shaky in their command of formal operations, do most of us gain fuller mastery after the high school years? Gains are indeed made between adolescence and adulthood (Blackburn & Papalia, 1992). However, only about half of all college students show firm and consistent mastery of formal operations on Piaget's scientific reasoning tasks (Neimark, 1975). Similarly, sizable percentages of American adults do not solve scientific problems at the formal level, and there are some societies in which *no* adults solve formal operational problems (Neimark, 1975).

Why don't more adults do well on Piagetian tasks? An average level of performance on standardized intelligence tests seems to be necessary for a person to achieve formal operational thought (Inhelder, 1966). What seems more important than basic intelligence, though, is formal education (Neimark, 1979). In cultures in which virtually no one solves Piaget's problems, people do not receive advanced schooling. If achieving formal operational thought requires education, Piaget's theory may be culturally biased, and his stages may not be universal as he believed.

But neither lack of intelligence nor lack of formal education is a problem for most college students. Instead, they have difficulty with tests of formal operations when they lack *expertise in a domain of knowledge.* Piaget (1972) himself suggested that adults are likely to use formal operations in a field of expertise but to use concrete operations in less familiar areas. This is precisely what seems to happen. For example, Richard De Lisi and Joanne Staudt (1980) gave three kinds of formal opera-

tional tasks—the pendulum problem, a political problem, and a literary criticism problem—to college students majoring in physics, political science, and English. As Figure 7.5 illustrates, each group of students did very well on the problem relevant to that group's major field of expertise. On problems outside their fields, however, about half the students failed. Very possibly, then, many adolescents and adults fail to use formal reasoning on Piaget's scientific problems simply because these problems are unfamiliar to them and they lack expertise.

As Kurt Fischer (1980; Fischer, Kenny, & Pipp, 1990) maintains, each person may have an optimal level of cognitive performance that will show itself in familiar and well-trained content domains. However, performance is likely to be highly inconsistent across content areas unless the person has had a chance to build knowledge and skills in all these domains. More often, adults may use and strengthen formal modes of thinking *only in their areas of expertise.* By adopting a contextual perspective on cognitive development, we can appreciate that the individual's experience and the nature of the tasks he or she is asked to perform influence cognitive performance across the life span (Salthouse, 1990).

Growth beyond Formal Operations?

While some researchers have been asking why adults sometimes perform so poorly on cognitive tasks, others have been asking why they sometimes perform so well. Take Piaget himself. Was his ability to generate a complex theory of development no more than the application of formal operational thought? Or are there advances in cognitive development during adulthood that would better explain the remarkable cognitive achievements of some adults?

Several intriguing ideas have been proposed about stages of cognitive development that may lie beyond formal operations—that is, about **postformal thought** (see Commons, Richards, & Armon, 1984; Labouvie-Vief, 1992; Sinnott, 1996; Yan & Arlin, 1995). As noted earlier, adolescents who have attained formal operations sometimes get carried away with their new powers of logical thinking. They insist that there is a logically correct answer for every question—that if you simply apply logic, you'll arrive at the right answer, at some absolute truth. Perhaps formal operational adolescents need a more complex way of thinking in order to adapt to the kinds of problems adults face every day—problems in which there are many ways to look at an issue, no one right answer, and yet a need to make a decision (Sinnott, 1996).

How might thought be qualitatively different in adulthood than it is in adolescence? What might a truly adult stage of cognitive development be like? Several researchers have suggested that adults are more likely than adolescents to see knowledge as relative rather than absolute (Kitchener et al., 1989; Labouvie-Vief, 1992). **Relativistic thinking,** in this sense, means understanding that knowledge depends on the subjective perspective of the knower. An *absolutist* assumes that truth lies in the nature of reality and that there is only one truth; a *relativist* assumes that one's own starting assumptions influence the "truth" that is discovered and that a problem can be viewed in multiple ways.

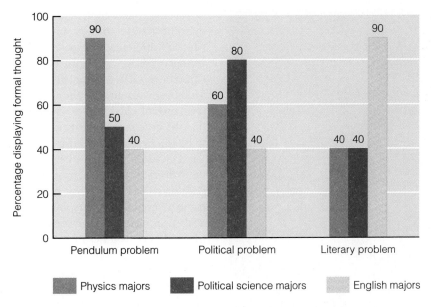

Figure 7.5 Expertise and formal operations. College students show the greatest command of formal operational thought in the subject area most related to their major.
SOURCE: Data from De Lisi & Staudt (1980)

Consider this logic problem: "'A' grows 1 cm per month. 'B' grows 2 cm per month. Who is taller?" (Yan & Arlin, 1995, p. 230). An absolutist might say "B," based on the information given, but a relativist would be more likely to say "It depends." It *does* depend, on how tall A and B were to begin with and on how much time passes before their heights are measured. A relativistic thinker will recognize that the problem is ill defined and that further information is needed, and he or she will be able to think flexibly about what the answer would be if we made certain assumptions rather than others.

Or consider this problem, given to preadolescents, adolescents, and adults by Gisela Labouvie-Vief and her colleagues (Labouvie-Vief et al., 1983, p. 5):

John is known to be a heavy drinker, especially when he goes to parties. Mary, John's wife, warns him that if he gets drunk one more time she will leave him and take the children. Tonight John is out late at an office party. John comes home drunk.

Does Mary leave John? Most preadolescents and many adolescents quickly and confidently said "yes." They did not question the assumption that Mary would stand by her word; they simply applied logic to the information they were given. Adults were more likely to realize that different starting assumptions were possible and that the answer depended on which assumptions were chosen. One woman, for example, noted that if Mary had stayed with John for years, she would be unlikely to leave him now. This same woman said, "There was no right or wrong answer. You could get logically to both answers" (p. 12). Postformal thinkers seem able to devise more than one logical solution to a problem (Sinnott, 1996).

In a fascinating study of cognitive growth over the college years, William Perry (1970) found that beginning college students often assumed that there were absolute, objective truths to be found if only they applied their minds or sought answers from their textbooks or their professors. As their college careers progressed, they often became frustrated in their search for absolute truths. They saw that many questions seemed to have a number of alternative answers, depending on the perspective of the answerer. Taking the extremely relativistic view that any opinion was as good as any other, several of these students said they weren't sure how they could ever decide what to believe. Eventually, many of them understood that some opinions can be better supported than others; they were then able to commit themselves to specific positions while being fully aware that they were choosing among relative perspectives. Between adolescence and adulthood, then, many people start out as absolutists, then become relativists, and finally are able to make commitments to positions despite their more sophisticated awareness of the nature and limits of knowledge (Sinnott, 1996).

It has also been suggested that advanced thinkers thrive on detecting paradoxes and inconsistencies among ideas and trying to reconcile them—only to repeat the process of challenging and changing their understandings again and again (Basseches, 1984; Riegel, 1973). Advanced thinkers also seem to be able to think systematically and logically about abstract systems of knowledge (Fischer et al., 1990; Richards & Commons, 1990). If the concrete operational thinker performs mental actions such as addition on concrete *objects,* and the formal operational thinker performs mental actions on *ideas,* the postformal thinker seems able to manipulate whole *systems* of ideas—for example, by comparing and contrasting psychological theories or analyzing abstract similarities and differences between mathematical operations such as addition and division.

It is not yet entirely clear whether relativistic thinking or other forms of advanced thinking might really qualify as a new, postformal stage of cognitive development. It is clear, though, that these types of thinking are shown by only a minority of adults, particularly those who have received advanced education, who are open to rethinking issues, and who

Charles Thatcher/Getty Images

Adults think very efficiently once they gain expertise on the job.

live in a culture that nourishes their efforts to entertain new ideas (Irwin, 1991; Sinnott, 1996). It is also clear that cognitive growth does not end in adolescence. Yet age itself does not tell us much about how an adult thinks; life circumstances and the demands placed on people to think at work, in the home, and in the community often tell us more.

Aging and Cognitive Skills

What becomes of cognitive capacities in later adulthood? Some mental abilities decline as the average person ages, and it appears that older adults often have trouble solving Piagetian tests of formal operational thinking (Blackburn & Papalia, 1992). Indeed, elderly adults sometimes perform poorly relative to young and middle-aged adults even on *concrete* operational tasks assessing conservation and classification skills (Blackburn & Papalia, 1992; Denney, 1982).

This does not mean that elderly adults regress to immature modes of thought, however (Blackburn & Papalia, 1992). For one thing, these studies have involved cross-sectional comparisons of different age groups. The poorer performance of older groups does not necessarily mean that cognitive abilities are lost as one ages. It could be due to a cohort effect, for

the average older adult today has had less formal schooling than the average younger adult has had. In fact, older adults who are attending college tend to perform just as well as younger college students on tests of formal operations (Blackburn, 1984; Hooper, Hooper, & Colbert, 1985). Moreover, very brief training can quickly improve the performance of older adults long out of school, which suggests that the necessary cognitive abilities are there but merely need to be reactivated (Blackburn & Papalia, 1992).

Questions have also been raised about the relevance of the skills assessed in Piagetian tasks to the lives of older adults (Labouvie-Vief, 1985). Not only are these problems unfamiliar to many older adults, but they resemble the intellectual challenges that children confront in school, not those that most adults encounter in everyday contexts. Thus, older people may not be very motivated to solve them. Also, older adults may rely on modes of cognition that have proved useful to them in daily life but that make them look cognitively deficient in the laboratory (Salthouse, 1990).

Consider this example: Kathy Pearce and Nancy Denney (1984) found that elderly adults, like young children but unlike other age groups, often group two objects on the basis of some functional relationship between them (for example, putting a pipe and matches together because matches are used to light pipes) rather than on the basis of similarity (for example, putting a pipe and a cigar together because they are both ways of smoking tobacco). In school and in some job situations, Pearce and Denney suggest, people are asked to group objects on the basis of similarity, but in everyday life it may make more sense to associate objects that are commonly used together.

Such findings suggest that what appear to be deficits in older people may merely be differences in style. Similar stylistic differences in classification skills have been observed cross-culturally and can, if researchers are not careful, lead to the incorrect conclusion that uneducated adults from non-Western cultures lack basic cognitive skills. A case in point: Kpelle adults in Africa, when asked to sort foods, clothing, tools, and cooking utensils into groups, sorted them into pairs based on functional relationships. "When an exasperated experimenter finally asked, 'How would a fool do it?' he was given sorts of the type that were initially expected—four neat piles with foods in one, tools in another, and so on" (Glick, 1975, p. 636)!

In sum, today's older adults appear not to perform concrete and formal operational tasks as well as their younger contemporaries do. Planners of adult education for senior citizens might bear in mind that some of their students (though by no means all) may benefit from more concrete forms of instruction. However, these differences may be related to factors other than age, such as education and motivation; an actual age-related decline in operational abilities has not been firmly established. Most important, older adults who perform poorly on unfamiliar problems in laboratory situations often perform far more capably on the sorts of problems that they encounter in everyday contexts (Cornelius & Caspi, 1987; Salthouse, 1990).

Piaget in Perspective

Now that we have examined Jean Piaget's theory of cognitive development, it is time to evaluate it. Let's start by giving credit where credit is due and then consider challenges to Piaget's version of things.

Piaget's Contributions

Piaget is a giant in the field of human development. As one scholar quoted by Harry Beilin (1992) put it, "assessing the impact of Piaget on developmental psychology is like assessing the impact of Shakespeare on English literature or Aristotle on philosophy—impossible" (p. 191). It is hard to imagine that we would know even a fraction of what we know about intellectual development without his groundbreaking work.

One sign of a good theory is that it stimulates research. Piaget asked fundamentally important questions about how humans come to know the world and showed that we can answer them "by paying attention to the small details of the daily lives of our children" (Gopnik, 1996, p. 225). His cognitive developmental perspective has now been applied to almost every aspect of human development, and the important questions he raised continue to guide the study of cognitive development.

We can credit Piaget with some lasting insights (Flavell, 1996). He showed us that infants are active in their own development—that from the start they seek to master problems and to understand the incomprehensible by using the processes of assimilation and accommodation to deal with cognitive disequilibrium. He taught us that young humans do indeed think differently than older humans do—and often in ways we never would have suspected. The reasoning of preschoolers, for example, often defies adult logic, but it makes perfect sense in light of Piaget's insights about their egocentrism and reliance on the perceptual salience of situations. School-age children have the logical thought processes that allow them to excel at many tasks, but still draw a blank when presented with hypothetical or abstract problems. And adolescents are impressive with their scientific reasoning skills and their ability to wrestle with abstract problems, but they may think *so much* about events that they get tangled up with whole new forms of egocentrism.

Finally, Piaget was largely right in his basic description of cognitive development. The *sequence* he proposed—sensorimotor to preoperational to concrete operations to formal operations—seems to describe quite well the course and content of intellectual development for children and adolescents from the hundreds of cultures and subcultures that have now been studied (Flavell, Miller, & Miller, 1993). Although cultural factors do influence the *rate* of cognitive growth, the direction of development is always from sensorimotor thinking to preoperational thinking to concrete operations and, for many, to formal operations (or even postformal operations).

Challenges to Piaget

Partly because Piaget's theory has been so enormously influential, it has had more than its share of criticism (see Lourenco & Machado, 1996). We will focus on five major criticisms here.

1. Underestimating young minds. Piaget seems to have underestimated the cognitive abilities of infants and young children, though he emphasized that he was more interested in understanding sequences of changes than in the specific ages at which they occur (Lourenco & Machado, 1996). When researchers use more familiar problems than Piaget's and reduce tasks to their essentials, hidden competencies of young children—and of adolescents and adults too—are sometimes revealed.

2. Failing to distinguish between competence and performance. Piaget sought to identify underlying cognitive competencies that guide performance on cognitive tasks. But there is an important difference between understanding a concept and passing a test designed to measure it. The age ranges Piaget proposed for some stages may have been off target in part because he tended to ignore the many factors besides competence that can influence task performance—everything from the individual's motivation, verbal abilities, and memory capacity to the nature, complexity, and familiarity of the specific task used to assess mastery. Piaget may have been too quick to assume that children who failed one of his tests lacked competence; they may only have failed to demonstrate their competence in a particular situation.

Perhaps more important, Piaget may have overemphasized the idea that knowledge is an all-or-nothing concept (Schwitzgebel, 1999). Instead of having or not having a particular competence, children probably gain competence gradually and experience long periods "in between" understanding and not understanding. Many of the seemingly contradictory results of studies using Piagetian tasks can be accounted for with this idea of gradual change in understanding. For instance, Piaget argued that infants do not show understanding of object permanence until 9 months, but other research indicates that at least some understanding of object permanence is present at 4 months (see Schwitzgebel, 1999). If we accept that conceptual change is gradual, then we can stop debating whether competence is present or not present at a particular age.

3. Claiming that broad stages of development exist. According to Piaget, each new stage of cognitive development is a coherent mode of thinking that is applied across a wide range of specific problems. Yet individuals are often inconsistent in their performance on different tasks that presumably measure the abilities defining a given stage. More and more researchers are arguing that cognitive development is *domain specific*—that is, it is a matter of building skills in particular content areas—and that growth in one domain may proceed much faster than growth in another (Fischer et al., 1990).

4. Failing to adequately explain development. Several critics suggest that Piaget did a better job of describing development than of explaining how it comes about (Bruner,

1997). To be sure, Piaget wrote extensively about his interactionist position on the nature–nurture issue and did as much as any developmental theorist to tackle the question of how development comes about. Presumably, humans are always assimilating new experiences in ways that their level of maturation allows, accommodating their thinking to those experiences, and reorganizing their cognitive structures into increasingly complex modes of thought. Yet this explanation is rather vague. We need to know far more about how specific maturational changes in the brain and specific kinds of experiences contribute to important cognitive advances.

5. Giving limited attention to social influences on cognitive development. Some critics claim that Piaget paid too little attention to how children's minds develop through their social interactions with more competent individuals and how they develop differently in different cultures. Piaget's child often resembles an isolated scientist exploring the world alone, when in fact children develop their minds through interactions with parents, teachers, and more competent peers and siblings. True, Piaget had interesting ideas about the role of peers in helping children overcome their egocentrism and take other perspectives (see Chapter 12 on moral development). And some scholars believe that this criticism is an unfair simplification of Piaget's true position on the social nature of development (Matusov & Hayes, 2000). Still, as we will see shortly, the significance of social interaction and culture for cognitive development is the basis of the perspective on cognitive development offered by one of Piaget's early critics, Lev Vygotsky.

So, Piaget's theory of cognitive development might have been stronger if he had designed tasks that could better reveal the competencies of infants and young children; if he had explored the many factors besides underlying competence that influence actual performance; if he had been able to provide more convincing evidence that his stages are indeed coherent; if he had been more specific about *why* development proceeds as it does; and if he had more fully considered social and cultural influences on the development of thought. It may be unfair, however, to demand of an innovator who accomplished so much that he achieve everything.

Vygotsky's Sociocultural Perspective

We can gain additional insight into Piaget's view of cognitive development by considering the quite different sociocultural perspective of Lev Vygotsky (1934/1962, 1930–1935/1978; see Bodrova & Leong, 1996; Glassman, 1994; Wertsch & Tulviste, 1992). This Russian psychologist was born in 1896, the same year as Piaget, and was an active scholar in the 1920s and 1930s when Piaget was formulating his theory. For many years, Vygotsky's work was banned for political reasons in Soviet Russia, and North American scholars lacked English translations of his work, which seriously limited considera-

tion of Vygotsky's ideas until recent decades. In addition, Vygotsky died of tuberculosis at the age of 38, before his theory was fully developed. However, his main theme is clear: *Cognitive growth occurs in a sociocultural context and evolves out of the child's social interactions.*

Culture and Thought

Culture and society play a pivotal role in Vygotsky's theory. As one scholar notes, "*society precedes the individual* and provides the conditions that allow individual thinking to emerge" (Frawley, 1997, p. 89; emphasis original). Indeed, intelligence in the Vygotskian model is held by the group, not the individual, and is closely tied to the language system and tools that the group has developed over time (Case, 1998). Our culture and social experiences affect *how* we think, not just *what* we think. Consider some research by Vygotsky's colleague, Alexander Luria, who tested groups of 9- to 12-year-old children growing up in different social environments. Children were given target words and asked to name the first thing that came to mind when they heard each word. Luria found that children growing up in a remote rural village with limited social experiences gave remarkably similar responses, whereas children growing up in a large city gave more distinctly individual answers. Vygotsky and Luria believed that this difference reflected the city children's broader exposure to various aspects of culture. On their own, the rural children were unable to develop certain types of knowledge. Knowledge, then, depends on one's social experiences.

Vygotsky would not be surprised to learn that formal operational thought is rarely used in some cultures, for he expected cognitive development to vary from society to society depending on what mental tools the culture values and makes available. How do children acquire their society's mental tools? By interacting with parents and other more experienced members of the culture and by adopting their language and knowledge (Frawley, 1997).

According to Vygotsky's theory, cognitive development is shaped by the culture in which children live and the kinds of problem-solving strategies that adults and other knowledgeable guides pass on to them.

Social Interaction and Thought

Consider this scenario: Annie, a 4-year-old, receives a jigsaw puzzle, her first, for her birthday. She attempts to work the puzzle but gets nowhere until her father comes along, sits down beside her, and gives her some tips. He suggests that it would be a good idea to put the corners together first. He points to the pink area at the edge of one corner piece and says "Let's look for another pink piece." When Annie seems frustrated, he places two interlocking pieces near each other so that she will notice them. And when she succeeds, he offers words of encouragement. As Annie gets the hang of it, he steps back and lets her work more and more independently. This kind of social interaction, claimed Vygotsky, fosters cognitive growth.

How? First, Annie and her father are operating in what Vygotsky called the **zone of proximal development**—the gap between what a learner can accomplish independently and what he or she can accomplish with the guidance and encouragement of a more skilled partner. Skills within the zone are ripe for development and are the skills at which instruction should be aimed. Skills outside the zone are either well mastered already or still too difficult. In our example, Annie obviously becomes a more competent puzzle-solver with her father's help than without it. More important, she will internalize the problem-solving techniques that she discovered in collaboration with her father, working together in her zone of proximal development, and will ultimately use them on her own, rising to a new level of independent mastery. What began as a social process involving two people becomes a cognitive process within one.

An important implication of the zone of proximal development is that knowledge is not a fixed state and no single test or score can adequately reflect the range of a person's knowledge. The mind has potential for unlimited growth. Development consists of moving toward the upper range of the zone using the tools of society. The upper limit itself continues to move upward in response to cultural changes (Smagorinsky, 1995). Support for Vygotsky's idea of the zone of proximal development comes from research showing that children's performance on assisted learning tasks is a good predictor of their future achievement (Meijer & Elshout, 2001).

In many cultures, children do not go to school with other children to learn; nor do their parents explicitly teach them tasks such as weaving and hunting. Instead, they learn through what is called **guided participation**—by actively participating in culturally relevant activities with the aid and support of their parents and other knowledgeable guides (Rogoff, 1997; Rogoff et al., 1993). Jerome Bruner (1983) had a similar concept in mind when he wrote of the many ways in which parents provide "scaffolding" for their children's development, structuring learning situations so that learning becomes easier. By calling attention to guided participation processes, in the zone of proximal development, Vygotsky was rejecting Piaget's view of children as independent explorers in favor of the view that they learn more sophisticated cognitive strategies through their interactions with more mature thinkers. To Piaget, the child's level of cognitive development determines what he or she can learn; to Vygotsky, learning in collaboration with more knowledgeable companions drives cognitive development.

The Tools of Thought

In Vygotsky's view, adults use a variety of tools to pass culturally valued modes of thinking and problem solving on to their children. Spoken language is clearly the most important tool, but writing, using numbers, and applying problem-solving and memory strategies also serve to convey information and enable thinking (Bodrova & Leong, 1996; Crain, 2000; Vygotsky, 1930–1935/1978). The type of tool used to perform a task influences performance on the task. Consider a study by Dorothy Faulkner and her colleagues (2000) with 9- and 10-year-old children. Children worked in pairs on a science project (Inhelder and Piaget's chemical combination task), using either a computer simulation of the task or the actual physical materials. The children who worked with the computerized version talked more, tested more possible chemical combinations, and completed the task more quickly than children who worked with the physical materials. The computer, then, was a tool that changed the nature of the problem-solving activity and influenced performance, as Vygotsky would have predicted.

Let's look more closely at Vygotsky's notion of how tools—especially language—influence thought. Whereas Piaget maintained that cognitive development influences language development, Vygotsky argued that language shapes thought in important ways and that thought changes fundamentally once we begin to think in words (Bodrova & Leong,

By working with a more knowledgeable partner, this child is able to accomplish more than would be possible on his own. According to Vygotsky, the difference between what a child can accomplish alone and with a partner is the zone of proximal development.

What do the theories of Piaget and Vygotsky have to contribute to the goal of optimizing mental functioning? As Piaget's views first became popular in the United States and Canada, psychologists and educators designed studies to determine whether they could speed cognitive development and help children and adults solve problems more effectively. Some researchers had a different motive: to challenge Piaget's view that concepts like conservation cannot be mastered until the child is intellectually ready.

What has been learned from these training studies? Generally, they suggest that many Piagetian concepts can be taught to children who are slightly younger than the age at which the concepts would naturally emerge. Training is sometimes difficult, and it does not always generalize well to new problems, but progress can be achieved. Dorothy Field (1981), for example, demonstrated that 4-year-olds could be trained to recognize the identity of a substance like a ball of clay before and after its appearance is altered—that is, to understand that although the clay looks different, it is still the *same* clay and has to be the same amount of clay. Field found that nearly 75% of the children given this identity training could solve at least three out of five conservation problems 2 to 5 months after training.

Similar training studies have demonstrated that children who function at the late concrete operations stage can be taught formal operations (Adey & Shayer, 1992). Researchers have had even more luck improving the cognitive performance of older adults, sometimes with very simple interventions (Blackburn & Papalia, 1992). Such studies suggest that many elderly individuals who perform poorly on Piagetian problem-solving tasks simply need a quick refresher course to demonstrate their underlying competence. Make no mistake: *No one* has demonstrated that 2-year-olds can be taught formal operations. But at least these studies establish that specific training experiences can somewhat speed a child's progress through Piaget's stages or bring out more advanced capacities in an adult who is performing at a less advanced level.

Piaget himself disapproved of attempts by Americans to speed children's progress through his stages (Piaget, 1970). He believed that parents should simply provide young children with opportunities to explore their world and that teachers should use a discovery approach in the classroom that allows children to learn by doing. Given their natural curiosity and normal opportunities to try their hand at solving problems, children would construct ever more complex understandings on their own. Many educators began building Piaget's ideas about discovery-based education into school curricula, especially in science classes (see Gallagher & Easley, 1978). Teachers have also taken seriously Piaget's notion that children understand material best if they can assimilate it into their existing understandings. So, for example, they have designed curricula to guide severely mentally retarded adults through the substages of the sensorimotor period (Williams, 1996). Finding out what the learner already knows or can do and providing instruction matched to the child's level of development are in the spirit of Piaget.

1996). Piaget and Vygotsky both noticed that preschool children often talk to themselves as they go about their daily activities, almost as if they were play-by-play sports announcers. ("I'm putting the big piece in the corner. I need a pink one. Not that one—this one.") Two preschool children playing next to each other sometimes carry on their own separate monologues rather than truly conversing. Piaget (1926) regarded such speech as egocentric—as further evidence that preoperational thinkers cannot yet take the perspectives of other people (in this case, their conversation partners) and therefore have not mastered the art of social speech. He did not believe that egocentric speech played any useful role in cognitive development.

In contrast, Vygotsky called children's recitations **private speech**—speech to oneself that guides one's thought and behavior. Rather than viewing it as a sign of cognitive immaturity, he saw it as a critical step in the development of mature thought and as the forerunner of the silent thinking-in-words that we adults engage in every day. Adults guide children's behavior with speech, a tool that children appropriate and initially use externally, just as adults did with them. Gradually, this regulatory speech is internalized.

Studies conducted by Vygotsky and other researchers support his claim (see Berk, 1992). For example, in one set of studies, Vygotsky (1934/1962) measured children's private speech first as they worked unimpeded on a task, and second as they worked to overcome an obstacle placed in their path. Their use of private speech increased dramatically when they confronted an interruption of their work—a problem to solve. Thus, young children rely most heavily on private speech when they are struggling to solve difficult problems (Berk, 1992). Even adults sometimes revert to thinking aloud when they are stumped by a problem (John-Steiner, 1992).

The incidence of private speech varies with age and task demands. Both 3- and 4-year-olds use private speech, but 4-year-olds are more likely to use it systematically when engaged in a sustained activity. Four-year-olds are presumably more goal oriented than 3-year-olds and use private speech to regu-

What would Lev Vygotsky recommend to teachers who want to stimulate cognitive growth? As you might guess, Vygotsky's theoretical orientation leads to a very different approach to education than Piaget's does—a more social one. Whereas students in Piaget's classroom would most likely be engaged in independent exploration, students in Vygotsky's classroom would be involved in guided participation, "co-constructing" knowledge during interactions with teachers and more knowledgeable peers. The roles of teachers and other more skillful collaborators would be to organize the learning activity, break it into steps, provide hints and suggestions carefully tailored to the child's current abilities, and gradually turn over more and more of the mental work to the student. According to Vygotsky's sociocultural perspective, the guidance provided by a skilled partner will then be internalized by the learner, first as private speech and eventually as silent inner speech. Education ends up being a matter of providing children with tools of the mind important in their culture, whether hunting strategies or computer skills (Bodrova & Leong, 1996; Berk & Winsler, 1995).

Is there any evidence that Vygotsky's guided participation approach might be superior to Piaget's discovery approach? Consider what Lisa Freund (1990) found when she had 3- to 5-year-old children help a puppet with a sorting task: deciding which furnishings (sofas, beds, bathtubs, stoves, and so on) should be placed in each of six rooms of a dollhouse that the puppet was moving into. First, the children were tested to determine what they already knew about proper furniture placement. Then, each child worked at a similar task, either alone (as might be the case in Piaget's discovery-based education, though here children were provided with corrective feedback by the experimenter) or with his or her mother (Vygotsky's guided learning). Finally, to assess what they had learned, Freund asked the children to perform a final, rather complex, furniture-sorting task. The results were clear: Children who had sorted furniture with help from their mothers showed dramatic improvements in sorting ability, whereas those who had practiced on their own showed little improvement. Moreover, the children who gained the most from guided participation with their mothers were those whose mothers talked the most about how to tackle the task. Collaborating with a competent peer can also produce cognitive gains that a child might not achieve working alone (Azmitia, 1992; Gauvain & Rogoff, 1989).

So, children do not always learn the most when they function as solitary scientists, seeking discoveries on their own; often, conceptual growth springs more readily from children's interactions with other people—particularly with competent people who provide an optimal amount of guidance. Yet it would seem that many children might benefit most from the best of both worlds: opportunities to explore on their own and supportive companions to offer help when needed.

late their behavior and achieve their goals (Winsler, Carlton, & Barry, 2000). As the task becomes familiar and children gain competence, use of private speech decreases (Duncan & Pratt, 1997). Private speech is also more frequent during open-ended activities (such as pretend play) that have several possible outcomes than during closed-ended tasks that have a single outcome (Krafft & Berk, 1998). Open-ended activities tend to be more child directed; they allow children to alter the difficulty level of the task so that it is appropriately challenging. In contrast, adult-directed activities provide fewer opportunities for children to regulate their own behavior.

Intellectually capable children rely more heavily on private speech in the preschool years and make the transition to inner speech earlier in the elementary school years than their less academically capable peers do (Berk & Landau, 1993; Kohlberg, Yaeger, & Hjertholm, 1968). This suggests that the preschool child's self-talk is indeed a sign of cognitive maturity, as Vygotsky claimed, rather than a sign of immature egocentrism, as Piaget claimed.

In addition, heavy use of private speech contributes to effective problem-solving performance—if not immediately, then when children encounter similar problems in the future (Behrend, Rosengren, & Perlmutter, 1989; Bivens & Berk, 1990). Not only is the amount of private speech important; the nature of what the child says is also related to performance (Chiu & Alexander, 2000). In particular, children who use metacognitive private speech ("No, I need to change this. Try it over here. Yes, that's good.") show greater motivation toward mastery; that is, they are more likely to persist on a task without adult intervention (Chiu & Alexander, 2000). Thus, private speech not only helps children think their way through challenging problems but also allows them to incorporate into their own thinking the problem-solving strategies that they learned initially during their collaborations with adults. Notice that, as in guided participation, what is at first a social process becomes an individual psychological process. In other words, *social speech* (for example, the conversation between Annie and her father as they jointly worked a puzzle) gives rise to *private speech* (Annie's talking aloud, much as her father talked to her, as she then tries to work the puzzle on her own), which in turn goes "underground" to become first mutterings and lip movements and then *inner speech* (Annie's silent verbal thought).

In sum, Vygotsky's sociocultural perspective stresses social influences on cognitive development that Piaget largely ignored. Children's minds develop (1) in response to cultural influences; (2) in collaborative interactions with skilled partners, or guided participation, on tasks that are within their zone of proximal development; and (3) as they incorporate what skilled partners say to them into what they say to themselves. As social speech is transformed into private speech and then inner speech, the culture's preferred tools of problem solving work their way from the language of competent guides into the thinking of the individual.

Evaluation of Vygotsky

Although many scholars find Vygotsky's ideas a refreshing addition to Piaget's, some concerns should be noted. While Piaget has been criticized for placing too much emphasis on the individual and not enough on the social, Vygotsky has been criticized for placing *too much* emphasis on social interaction (Feldman & Fowler, 1997). Vygotsky seemed to assume that all

knowledge and understanding of the world is transmitted through social interaction. But at least some understanding is individually constructed, as Piaget proposed. Vygotsky and Piaget are often presented as opposites on a continuum representing the extent to which cognitive development derives from social experience. In fact, a careful reading of the two theorists reveals that they are not as dissimilar as they are often presented (DeVries, 2000; Matusov & Hayes, 2000). Both Piaget and Vygotsky acknowledge the importance of the social context of development. Still, there are differences in their emphasis. Table 7.3 summarizes some of the differences between Vygotsky's sociocultural perspective and Piaget's cognitive developmental view. The Applications box on page 186 discusses their views on improving cognitive functioning.

Pause for a moment and consider the remarkable developmental accomplishments we have described in this chapter. The capacity of the human mind for thought is truly awesome. Because the human mind is so complex, we should not be surprised that it is not yet understood. Piaget attacked only part of the puzzle, and he only partially succeeded. Vygotsky alerted us to sociocultural influences on cognitive development but died before he could formalize his theory. As we will see in Chapters 8 and 9, other ways to think about mental development are needed.

Table 7.3 A Comparison of Vygotsky and Piaget

Vygotsky's Sociocultural View	Piaget's Cognitive Developmental View
1. Cognitive development is different in different social and historical contexts.	Cognitive development is mostly the same universally.
2. Appropriate unit of analysis is the social, cultural, and historical context in which the individual develops.	Appropriate unit of analysis is the individual.
3. Cognitive growth results from social interactions (guided participation in the zone of proximal development).	Cognitive growth results from the child's independent explorations of the world.
4. Children and their partners "co-construct" knowledge.	Each child constructs knowledge on his/her own.
5. Social processes become individual psychological ones (for example, social speech becomes inner speech).	Individual, egocentric processes become more social (for example, egocentric speech becomes social speech).
6. Adults are especially important (because they know the culture's tools of thinking).	Peers are especially important (because children must learn to take peers' perspectives into account).
7. Learning precedes development (tools learned with adult help become internalized).	Development precedes learning (children cannot master certain things until they have the requisite cognitive structures).

Summary Points

1. Jean Piaget, through his clinical method, formulated four stages of cognitive development, in which children construct increasingly complex schemes through an interaction of maturation and experience. Children adapt to the world through the processes of organization and adaptation (assimilating new experience to existing understandings and accommodating existing understandings to new experience).

2. According to Piaget, infants progress through six substages of the sensorimotor stage by perceiving and acting on the world; they progress from using their reflexes to adapt to the environment to using symbolic or representational thought to solve problems in their heads. Their symbolic capacity permits full mastery of object permanence.

3. In Piaget's preoperational stage (ages 2–7), children make many uses of their symbolic capacity but are limited by their dependence on appearances, lack of logical mental operations, and egocentrism. They fail to grasp the concept of conservation because they engage in centration, irreversible thinking, and static thought, though recent research suggests that preschool children's capacities are greater than Piaget supposed.

4. School-age children enter the stage of concrete operations (ages 7–11) and begin to master conservation tasks through decentration, reversibility, and transformational thought. They can think about relations, grasping seriation and transitivity, and they understand the concept of class inclusion.

5. Adolescents often show the first signs of formal operations at 11 or 12 and later master the hypothetical-deductive reasoning skills required to solve scientific problems. Cognitive changes result in other developmental advances and may also contribute to confusion, rebellion, idealism, and adolescent egocentrism (the imaginary audience and the personal fable).

6. Adults are most likely to display formal operational skills in their areas of expertise. Some adults, especially well-educated ones, may advance to postformal modes of thought such as relativistic thinking. Although aging adults often perform less well than younger adults on Piagetian tasks, factors other than biological aging may explain this.

7. Piaget has made huge contributions to the field of human development but has been criticized for underestimating the capacities of infants and young children, not considering factors besides competence that influence performance, failing to demonstrate that his stages have coherence, offering vague explanations of development, and underestimating the role of language and social interaction in cognitive development.

8. Vygotsky's sociocultural perspective emphasizes cultural and social influences on cognitive development more than Piaget's theory does. Through guided participation in culturally important activities, children learn problem-solving techniques from knowledgeable partners sensitive to their zone of proximal development.

9. Language is the most important tool that adults use to pass culturally valued thinking and problem solving to their children. Language shapes their thought and moves from social speech to private speech and later inner speech.

Critical Thinking

1. Considering the differences between preoperational thought, concrete operational thought, and formal operational thought, what should parents keep in mind as they interact with their 4-year-old, 8-year-old, and 17-year-old children?

2. Create descriptions of a Piagetian preschool and a Vygotskian preschool. What are the main differences in terms of how children will be assessed, what they will be taught, and how they will be taught?

3. How might Piaget's theory be updated to accommodate the research findings that have emerged since he originally constructed his theory?

Key Terms

cognition	transformational thought
genetic epistemology	egocentrism
clinical method	class inclusion
scheme (schema)	concrete operations stage
organization	horizontal décalage
adaptation	seriation
assimilation	transitivity
accommodation	formal operations stage
sensorimotor stage	hypothetical-deductive reasoning
object permanence	decontextualize
A, not B, error	adolescent egocentrism
symbolic capacity	imaginary audience
preoperational stage	personal fable
imaginary companions	postformal thought
conservation	relativistic thinking
decentration	zone of proximal development
centration	guided participation
reversibility	private speech

On the Web

Web Sites to Explore

Piaget

Home of the Jean Piaget Society: Society for the Study of Knowledge and Development. **http://www.piaget.org**

Reflections on Piaget's Theory

A paper written by Ernst von Glasersfeld of the Scientific Reasoning Research Institute at the University of Massachusetts that summarizes Piaget's work and puts the theory in historical perspective. **http://www.oikos.org/Piagethom.htm**

Vygotsky

This site carries links to scholarly articles about Vygotsky's theory. **http://arts.uwaterloo.ca/~acheyne/chp.html**

Review of Vygotsky

A review and analysis of Vygotsky's "Thought and Language." **http://129.7.160.115/INST5931/Vygotsky.html**

Search Online with InfoTrac College Edition

For additional information, explore InfoTrac College Edition, your online library. Go to **http://www.infotrac-college.com** and use the passcode that came on the card with your book.

InfoTrac College Edition has many articles related to Piaget and Vygotsky. Try any of the terms in this chapter as key words for your search. For example, search for "class inclusion" or "adolescent egocentrism." Also try "Vygotsky and social interaction." Try to find something that provides greater depth on a topic covered in the chapter and write a brief summary of this material.

Visit Our Web Site
Go to http://www.wadsworth.com/psychology, where you will find online resources directly linked to your book.

Life-Span CD-ROM

 Go to the Wadsworth Life-Span CD-ROM for further study of the concepts in this chapter. The CD-ROM also includes quizzes and additional activities to expand your learning experience.

CHAPTER **e i g h t**

Memory and Information Processing

"I CAN'T BELIEVE I remembered that."

"Do you remember the name of that restaurant we enjoyed so much?"

"It's on the tip of my tongue."

"Sorry, I completely forgot."

Lines like these appear often in our conversations; learning and remembering, failing to learn and forgetting, are all important parts of our daily lives. Moreover, individuals develop as they do partly because of what they have learned and remembered from their experiences.

Both Piaget and Vygotsky were centrally interested in the question of how children come to know the world around them. In this chapter, our examination of cognitive development continues, but we consider another approach to answering this key question. Cognitive psychologists, influenced by the rise of computer technology, began to think of the brain as a computer that processes input and converts it to output (correct answers on tests, for example). This information-processing perspective has revealed much about how the capacities to acquire, remember, and use information change over the life span.

The Information-Processing Approach

According to Howard Gardner (1985), the "cognitive revolution" in psychology that generated the information-processing approach could not have occurred without (1) a demonstration of the inadequacies of the behaviorist approach and (2) the rise of computer technology.

Showing deficiencies in the behaviorist approach was easiest in relation to complex learning and memory tasks. Consider learning from this textbook. Obviously, some very complex processes occur between your registering of the pattern of print on this page and your writing of an essay about it. To account for these processes, behaviorists like Watson and Skinner (see Chapter 2) would have to talk about chains of mental stimuli and responses between an external stimulus (for instance, the printed page) and an overt response. This approach proved cumbersome at best, as more cognitively oriented learning theorists such as Albert Bandura recognized.

Then came computers with their capacity for systematically converting input to output. The computer seemed to provide a good analogy to the human mind, and efforts to program computers to play chess and solve other problems as well as human experts do have revealed a great deal about the strengths and limitations of human cognition (Newell & Simon, 1961; Simon, 1995).

Any computer has a limited capacity, associated with its hardware and software, for processing information. The com-

puter's *hardware* is the machine itself—its keyboard (or input system), its storage capacity, and so on. The mind's "hardware" is the nervous system, including the brain, the sensory receptors, and their neural connections. The computer's *software* consists of the programs used to manipulate stored and received information: word processing, statistics programs, and the like. The mind, too, has its software—rules, strategies, and other mental "programs" that specify how information is to be registered, interpreted, stored, retrieved, and analyzed.

The computer, then, was the model for the **information-processing approach** to human cognition, which emphasizes the basic mental processes involved in attention, perception, memory, and decision making. When the information-processing approach began to guide studies of development, the challenge became one of determining how the hardware and software of the mind change over the life span. Just as today's more highly developed computers have greater capacity than those of the past, maturation of the nervous system plus experience presumably enable adults to remember more than young children can and to perform more complex cognitive feats with greater accuracy (Kail & Bisanz, 1992).

The Memory Systems

Figure 8.1 presents an early and very influential conception of the human information-processing system offered by Richard Atkinson and Richard Shiffrin (1968). If your history professor says that the U.S. Constitution was ratified in 1789, this statement is an environmental stimulus. Assuming that you are not lost in a daydream, your **sensory register** will log it, holding it for a fraction of a second as a kind of afterimage (or, in this example, a kind of echo). Much that strikes the sensory register quickly disappears without further processing. Attentional processes (see Chapter 6) have a good deal to do with which sensory stimuli enter the sensory register in the first place and which are processed even further. If you think you may need to remember 1789, it will be moved into **short-term memory,** which can hold a limited amount of information (perhaps only about seven items or chunks of information) for several seconds. For example, short-term memory can hold onto a telephone number while you dial it. Today, cognitive researchers distinguish between passive and active forms of short-term memory and use the term **working memory** to refer to a mental "scratch pad" that temporarily stores information while actively operating on it (Baddeley, 1986, 1992). It is what is "on one's mind," or in one's consciousness, at any moment. As you know, people can juggle only so much information at once without having some of it slipping away.

To illustrate working memory, look at the following seven numbers. Then look away, and add the numbers in your head while trying to remember them (Byrnes, 1996, p. 55):

7   2   5   6   1   4   7

Most likely, having to actively manipulate the numbers in working memory in order to add them disrupted your ability to rehearse them in order to remember them. People who are fast adders would have better luck than most people, because

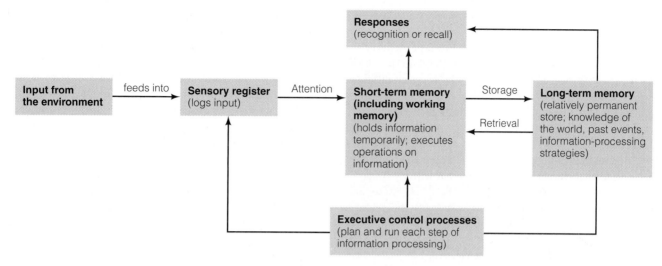

Figure 8.1 A model of information processing
Source: Adapted from Atkinson & Shiffrin (1968)

they would have more working memory space left for remembering the items (Byrnes, 1996).

To be remembered for any length of time, information must be moved from short-term memory into **long-term memory,** a relatively permanent store of information that represents what most people mean by memory. More than likely, you will hold the professor's statement in short-term memory just long enough to record it in your notes. Later, as you study your notes, you will rehearse the information in working memory to move it into long-term memory so that you can retrieve it the next day or week when you are taking the test.

This simplified model shows what you must do to learn and remember something. The first step is **encoding** the information: getting it into the system, learning it, moving it from the sensory register to short-term memory and then to long-term memory while organizing it in a form suitable for storage. If it never gets in, it cannot be remembered. Then there is **storage**—holding information in the long-term memory store. Memories fade over time unless they are appropriately stored in long-term memory. And finally, there is **retrieval**—the process of getting information out again when it is needed. We say we have successfully remembered something when we can retrieve it from long-term memory.

Retrieval can be accomplished in several ways. If you are asked a multiple-choice question about when the Constitution was ratified, you need not actively retrieve the correct date; you merely need to recognize it among the options. This is an example of **recognition memory.** If, instead, you are asked "When was the Constitution ratified?" this is a test of **recall memory;** it requires active retrieval without the aid of cues. In between recognition and recall memory is **cued recall memory,** in which one is given a hint or cue to facilitate retrieval (for example, "When was the Constitution ratified? It's the year the French Revolution began and rhymes with *wine.*"). Most people find questions requiring recognition memory easier to answer than those requiring cued recall, and those requiring cued recall easier than those requiring

pure recall. This holds true across the life span, which suggests that many things we have apparently encoded or learned are "in there someplace," although we have trouble retrieving them without cues. Breakdowns in remembering may involve difficulties in initial encoding, storage, or retrieval.

Implicit and Explicit Memory

Memory researchers have concluded that the long-term memory store responds differently depending on the nature of the task (Parkin, 1993). They distinguish between **implicit memory,** which occurs unintentionally, automatically, and without awareness, and **explicit memory,** which involves deliberate, effortful recollection of events (Howard, 1996; Roediger, 1990; Schacter, 1996). Explicit memory is tested through traditional recognition and recall tests. When implicit memory is tested, learners do not even know that their memory is being assessed. For example, individuals might be exposed to a list of words (orange, tablet, forest, and so on) to be rated for likability, not memorized. In a second task, they are given word stems such as TAB___ and asked to complete them with the first word that comes to mind. People who are exposed to the word *tablet* in the initial task are more likely than people who are not to come up with the word *tablet* rather than *table* or *tabby* to complete the word stem, demonstrating that they learned something from their earlier exposure to the words, even though they were not trying to learn. Adults with amnesia do poorly on tests of explicit memory in which they study words and then are asked to finish word stems like TAB___ with a word they studied earlier. Amazingly, though, if they are merely exposed to a list of words and then given an implicit memory test that asks them to write the first word that comes to mind, they do fine (Graf, Squire, & Mandler, 1984)! Many forms of amnesia destroy explicit memory but leave implicit memory intact (Schacter, 1996). In other words, these are two distinct components of long-term memory that operate independently.

Some scholars believe that implicit memory develops earlier in infancy than explicit memory (C. A. Nelson, 1995; Schacter, 1996). Others believe that both forms of memory are evident very early in infancy (Rovee-Collier, 1997). All agree, though, that the two types of memory follow very different developmental paths. Explicit memory capacity increases from infancy to adulthood and then declines in later adulthood. By contrast, implicit memory capacity does not change much at all; young children often do no worse than older children, and elderly adults often do no worse than younger adults on tests of implicit memory (Howard, 1996; Russo et al., 1995; Schneider & Bjorklund, 1998). Research on implicit memory tells us that young and old alike learn and retain a tremendous amount of information from their everyday experiences without any effort at all.

Problem Solving

Now imagine that you are asked how many years passed between the signing of the Declaration of Independence (1776, remember?) and the ratification of the Constitution. Here we have a simple example of **problem solving,** or use of the information-processing system to achieve a goal or arrive at a decision (in this case, to answer the question). Here, too, the information-processing model describes what happens between stimulus and response. The question will move through the memory system. You will need to draw on your long-term memory to understand the question, and then you will have to search long-term memory for the two relevant dates. Moreover, you will need to locate your stored knowledge of the mathematical operation of subtraction. You will then transfer this stored information to working memory so that you can use your subtraction "program" (1789 minus 1776) to derive the correct answer.

Notice that processing information successfully requires both knowing what you are doing and making decisions. This is why the information-processing model (see Figure 8.1) includes **executive control processes** involved in planning and monitoring what is done. These control processes run the show, guiding the selection, organization, manipulation, and interpretation of information all the way along. Stored knowledge about the world and about information processing guides what is done with new information.

Cognitive psychologists now recognize that information processing is more complex than this model or similar models suggest (Bjorklund, 1997). For example, they now appreciate that people, like computers, engage in "parallel processing," carrying out many cognitive activities simultaneously rather than performing operations one step at a time in a sequence. They also appreciate that different processing approaches are used in different domains of knowledge. Still, the information-processing approach to cognition has the advantage of focusing attention on *how* people remember things or solve problems, not just on what they recall or what answer they give. A young child's performance on a problem could break down in any number of ways: The child might not be paying attention to the relevant aspects of the problem, might be unable to hold

all the relevant pieces of information in working memory long enough to do anything with them, might lack the strategies for transferring new information into long-term memory or retrieving information from long-term memory as needed, might simply not have enough stored knowledge to understand the problem, or might not have the executive control processes needed to manage the steps in problem solving. If we can identify how information processes in the younger individual differ from those in the older person, we will have gained much insight into cognitive development.

Many processes involved in memory and problem solving improve between infancy and adulthood and then decline somewhat in old age, although this pattern is not uniform for all processes or all people. Our task in this chapter is to describe these age trends and, of even greater interest, to try to determine why they occur.

The Infant

We have already seen that infants explore the world thoroughly through their senses. But are they remembering anything of their experiences? First, we look at what research on information processing has helped us learn about early memory; then, we consider whether infants demonstrate problem-solving skills.

Memory

Assessing infant memory requires some ingenuity, since infants cannot just tell us what they recall (see Howe, 2000). Several methods have been used to uncover infants' memory capabilities. Here we consider imitation, habituation, and operant conditioning techniques before examining infants' abilities to recall previously presented information.

IMITATION

We may be able to learn something about memory by noting whether or not infants can imitate an action performed by a model. Some studies suggest that newborns can imitate certain actions, such as sticking out the tongue or opening the mouth (Meltzoff & Moore, 1983, 1989; see also photo on page 195). These findings are exciting because they challenge Piaget's claim that infants cannot imitate actions until about a year of age, when they have some ability to represent mentally what they have seen. However, a careful review of the research suggests that very young babies stick out their tongues in response to a model's doing so far more reliably than they display other imitative responses such as mouth opening (Anisfeld, 1996). Moreover, even the ability to imitate tongue protrusions fades with age after the first month or two of life (Abravanel & Sigafoos, 1984). Imitation in the newborn, then, is largely restricted to tongue thrusting and is a temporary phenomenon.

Does imitative tongue protrusion really provide evidence of memory? Some researchers now doubt it (Bjorklund, 1995; Vinter, 1986). They maintain that early "imitation" is actually a

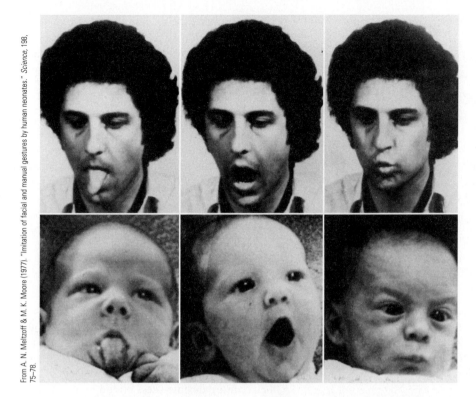

From A. N. Meltzoff & M. K. Moore (1977). "Imitation of facial and manual gestures by human neonates." *Science, 198,* 75–78.

Andrew Meltzoff is one of the researchers who has demonstrated imitation of facial expressions in newborns. These sample photographs are from videotaped recordings of 2- to 3-week-old infants imitating tongue protrusion, mouth opening, and lip protrusion. Of the three responses shown here, tongue protrusion is the most reliably observed.

reflex-like, automatic response to a specific stimulus that disappears with age (just as many of the newborn's reflexes do). Another possibility, suggested by Susan Jones (1996), is that tongue protrusion is not imitation at all but just a young infant's way of trying to explore interesting sights with their mouths before they have mastered the art of reaching. Jones demonstrated that young infants (1) stick out their tongues in reaction to many interesting sights, (2) find an adult who sticks out her tongue more interesting than one who merely opens and closes her mouth, and (3) more often stick out their tongues to snag interesting toys before they are capable of reaching for objects than afterwards. So, newborns who match the behavior of adults who stick out their tongues may be showing an automatic, biologically programmed response or attempting to explore interesting sights rather than engaging in imitation (Jones, 1996). True observational learning—storing representations of what a model did and repeating it—emerges later in infancy, after the cortex of the brain is further developed.

HABITUATION

Another method to assess memory uses *habituation,* a very simple and often overlooked form of learning introduced in Chapter 6. Habituation—learning *not* to respond to a stimulus that is repeated over and over—might be thought of as learning to be bored by the familiar (for example, the continual ticking of a clock) and is evidence that a stimulus is recognized as familiar. From birth, humans habituate to repeatedly presented lights, sounds, and smells; such stimuli are recognized as "old hat" (Friedman, 1972; Slater et al., 1991). In

other words, newborns are capable of recognition memory (Slater, 1995). They prefer a new sight to something they have seen many times (Fagan, 1984), and they show reduced interest in a word they heard spoken repeatedly 24 hours earlier (Swain, Zelazo, & Clifton, 1993). As they get older, infants need less "study time" before a stimulus becomes old hat, and they can *retain* what they have learned for days or even weeks (Fagan, 1984; Richards, 1997).

OPERANT CONDITIONING

To test long-term memory of young infants, Carolyn Rovee-Collier and her colleagues devised a clever task that relies on the operant conditioning techniques introduced in Chapter 2 (Rovee-Collier, 1997; Rovee-Collier & Boller, 1995). When a ribbon is tied to a baby's ankle and connected to an attractive mobile (see the photo on page 196), the infant will shake a leg now and then and learn in a matter of minutes that leg kicking brings about a positively reinforcing consequence: the jiggling of the mobile.

In order to test infant memory, the mobile is presented at a later time to see whether the infant will kick again. To succeed at this task, the infant must not only recognize the mobile but *recall* that the thing to do is to kick. When given two 9-minute training sessions, 2-month-olds remember how to make the mobile move for up to two days, 3-month-olds for about a week, and 6-month-olds for more than two weeks (Rovee-Collier & Boller, 1995). If, instead of two 9-minute training sessions, they receive three 6-minute sessions, 2-month-olds can remember for as long as 6-month-olds

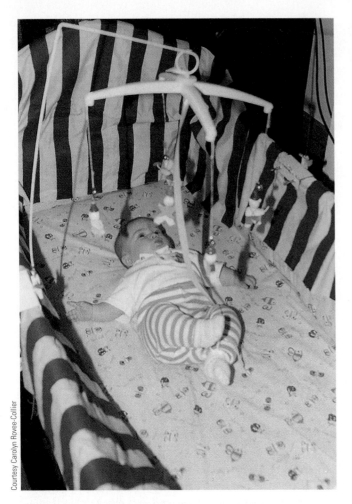

Courtesy Carolyn Rovee-Collier

When ribbons are tied to their ankles, young infants soon learn to make a mobile move by kicking their legs. Carolyn Rovee-Collier has made use of this operant conditioning paradigm to find out how long infants will remember the trick for making the mobile move.

example, the specific animals hanging from it) or the context in which they encountered it (for example, the design on the playpen liner) is even slightly different from the context in which they learned. In short, early memories are very *cue-dependent* and *context-specific*.

RECALL

When are infants capable of pure recall—of actively retrieving information from memory when no cues are available? A big breakthrough is made toward the end of the first year of life (Nelson, 1995). At about 8 to 9 months of age, infants will search for and find a hidden toy in tasks like those used to test for Piaget's concept of object permanence (Sophian, 1980). This is evidence of recall. So is deferred imitation, the ability to imitate a novel act after a delay. As early as 9 months of age, and possibly earlier if they have had repeated exposure to what a model did, infants can imitate novel actions (for example, pushing a button on a box to produce a beep) after a 24-hour delay (Barr, Dowden, & Hayne, 1996; Meltzoff, 1988). As infants get older, they demonstrate recall or deferred imitation over longer periods of time. For instance, 14- to 16-month-olds show deferred imitation after delays of 4 months (Meltzoff, 1995). And by 24 months of age, recall is more flexible—less bound by the specific cues present at the time of learning (Herbert & Hayne, 2000; Klein & Meltzoff, 1999).

Patricia Bauer (1996, 2000) and her colleagues have shown infants of different ages sequences of actions and then asked them to imitate what they saw—for example, putting a teddy bear in bed, covering him with a blanket, and reading him a story. Infants as young as 13 months of age can reconstruct a sequence of actions for as long as 6 months afterward. Older infants (16 and 20 months) can store and retrieve events for 12 months after exposure (Bauer et al., 2000). Much like children and adults, they remember best when they have repeated exposures to what they are to remember, when they are given plenty of cues to help them remember, and when the events they must remember occur in a meaningful or logical order.

By age 2, infants have become verbal and can use words to reconstruct events that happened months earlier (Howe & Courage, 1993). Katherine Nelson (1984), for example, relates how Emily, at only 24 months of age, reconstructed a trip to the library with her grandmother that had taken place 4 months earlier: "Go library. I sat in Mormor's lap. I went to the library. Probably that's what we did. Probably we did in the *bus!*" (p. 122).

In sum, developmentalists have gone from believing that infants have no memory at all beyond a few seconds to appreciating that even young 1-year-olds can recall experiences for weeks and even months under certain conditions. Infants clearly show recognition memory for familiar stimuli at birth and cued recall memory by about 2 months of age. As they get older, they can retain information longer and longer. More explicit memory, which requires actively retrieving an image of an object or event that is no longer present, appears to emerge toward the end of the first year. And by age 2 it is even clearer

(Rovee-Collier, 1999). Although the total training time is the same in the two conditions, the distributed training is more effective.

What if stronger cues to aid recall are provided? Two to four weeks after their original learning experience, infants who are "reminded" of their previous learning by seeing the mobile move kick up a storm as soon as the ribbon is attached to their ankles, whereas infants who are not reminded show no sign of remembering to kick (Rovee-Collier & Boller, 1995). It seems, then, that *cued recall* (in this case, memory cued by the mere presence of the mobile or, better yet, its rotation by the experimenter) emerges during the first couple of months of life and that infants remember best when they are reminded of what they have learned. Other research shows that verbal reminders are also effective with 15-month-olds, helping them remember an event after a month as well as they did after a week (Bauer et al., 1995, 2000).

However, this research also suggests that young infants have difficulty recalling what they have learned if cues are insufficient. They have trouble remembering if the mobile (for

Infants begin to learn problem-solving strategies around six months of age.

that infants can consciously and deliberately recall events that happened long ago, for they, like us, use language to represent and describe what happened.

Problem Solving

Infants, like children and adults, face problem-solving tasks every day. For example, they may want to obtain an object that is beyond their reach, or make a toy repeat the interesting sound it produced earlier. Can infants overcome obstacles to achieve desired goals? It appears they can. In one study, infants were presented with an object that was out of their reach; however, by pulling on a cloth, they could drag the object to within reach (Willats, 1990). Although 6-month-olds did not retrieve the object, 9-month-olds did solve this problem. And even the younger infants were successful when given hints about how they might retrieve the object (Kolstad & Aguiar, 1995). Simple problem-solving behaviors like this improve considerably over the first 2 years of life and then, as we'll see shortly, really flourish during childhood.

The Child

The 2-year-old is already a highly capable information processor, as evidenced by the rapid language learning that takes place at this age. But dramatic improvements in learning, memory, and problem solving occur throughout the childhood years, as children learn everything from how to flush toilets to how to work advanced math problems.

Explaining Memory Development

In countless situations, older children learn faster and remember more than younger children do (Kail, 1990). For example, 2-year-olds can repeat back about two digits immediately after hearing them, 10-year-olds about six digits. And

second-graders are not only faster learners than kindergartners but retain information longer (Howe, 2000). Why is this? Here are four major hypotheses about why learning and memory improve, patterned after those formulated by John Flavell and Henry Wellman (1977):

1. **Changes in basic capacities.** Older children have higher-powered "hardware" than younger children do; their brains have more working memory space for manipulating information and can process information faster.
2. **Changes in memory strategies.** Older children have better "software"; they have learned and consistently use effective methods for getting information into long-term memory and retrieving it when they need it.
3. **Increased knowledge about memory.** Older children know more about memory (for example, how long they must study to learn things thoroughly, which kinds of memory tasks take more effort, which strategies best fit each task, and so on).
4. **Increased knowledge about the world.** Older children know more than younger children about the world in general. This knowledge, or expertise, makes material to be learned more familiar, and familiar material is easier to learn and remember than unfamiliar material.

Do Basic Capacities Change?

Since the nervous system continues to develop in the early years of life, it seems plausible that older children remember more than younger children do because they have a better "computer"—a larger or more efficient information-processing system. However, we can quickly rule out the idea that the storage capacity of long-term memory enlarges. There is no consistent evidence that it changes after the first month of life (Perlmutter, 1986). In fact, both young and old alike have more room for storage than they could ever possibly use. Nor does the capacity of the sensory register to take in stimuli seem to change much (Schneider & Bjorklund, 1998). It does seem, however, that the speed of mental processes improves with age and that this allows older children and adults to perform more mental operations at once in working memory than young children can (Kail & Salthouse, 1994; LeBlanc et al., 1992).

This idea has been featured in revisions of Piaget's theory of cognitive development proposed by neo-Piagetian theorists such as Robbie Case (1985; Marini & Case, 1994). Case seeks to build on Piaget's insights into cognitive development, but has also been strongly influenced by the information-processing approach. He proposes that more advanced stages of cognitive development are made possible by increases in the capacity of working memory. For example, Piaget stressed the preschooler's tendency to *center* on one aspect of a problem and lose sight of another (for example, to attend to the height of a glass but ignore its width, or vice versa). Perhaps, say the neo-Piagetians, this is not a matter of lacking certain cognitive structures; perhaps young children simply do not have enough working memory capacity to keep both pieces of information in mind at once and coordinate them. Similarly, young children may do poorly on memory tasks because they cannot keep the first items on a list in mind while processing later ones. And they may fail to solve mathematical problems correctly because they cannot keep the facts of the problem in mind while they are performing calculations.

To test the capacity of short-term memory, researchers quickly present a list of items (such as numbers) and then count the number of items that a person can recall in order. Measured this way, short-term memory capacity seems to improve from age 2 to adulthood from just over two items to close to seven items (Dempster, 1981; Rose et al., 1997). In addition, older children are able to manipulate more information at once in working memory (Case, 1985; Kail, 1990). Partly, this is because they have become faster and more efficient at executing basic mental processes, such as identifying numbers or words to be learned (Kail, 1991); these processes become *automatized* so that they can be done with little mental effort. This, in turn, frees space in working memory for other purposes, such as storing the information needed to solve a problem.

Some research suggests that the degree of improvement in short-term memory capacity evident as children get older depends on what is being tested. That is, short-term memory capacity is *domain-specific*—it varies with background knowledge (Dempster, 1985; Schneider & Bjorklund, 1998). Very simply, greater knowledge in a domain or area of study increases the speed with which new, related information can be processed. Other research, however, indicates that developmental changes in capacity are *general*, not domain-specific (Swanson, 1999). So which is it?

Improvements with age in operating speed and working memory efficiency could be due to maturational changes in the brain, the older child's greater familiarity with numbers, letters, and other stimuli, or both (Bjorklund, 1995). There is general agreement, though, that speed of processing affects short-term memory capacity; older children process information faster than younger children can, and this is one reason why memory improves over childhood.

DO MEMORY STRATEGIES CHANGE?

If 4-year-olds were shown the 12 items in Figure 8.2 and were then asked to select the objects they had seen from a larger set of pictures, they would *recognize* nearly all of them (Brown, 1975). But if asked to *recall* the objects, they might remember only 2 to 4 of them—a far cry from the 7 to 9 items that an 8-year-old would recall or the 10 to 11 an adult would recall several minutes later. Are there specific memory strategies that evolve during childhood to permit this dramatic improvement in performance?

Children as young as 2 can deliberately remember to do "important" things, such as reminding Mom to buy candy at the grocery store (Somerville, Wellman, & Cultice, 1983). They are more likely to use external memory aids (for example, pointing at or holding a toy pig when asked to remember where it is hidden) if they are instructed to remember than if they are not (Fletcher & Bray, 1996). Yet preschoolers have not mastered many effective strategies for moving information into long-term memory. For example, when instructed to re-

Figure 8.2 A memory task. Imagine that you have 120 seconds to learn the 12 objects pictured here. What tricks or strategies might you devise to make your task easier?

member toys they have been shown, 3- and 4-year-olds will look very carefully at the objects and will often label them once, but only rarely do they use the memory strategy called **rehearsal**—the repeating of items one is trying to learn and remember (Baker-Ward, Ornstein, & Holden, 1984). To rehearse the objects in Figure 8.2, you might simply say over and over "Apple, truck, grapes, ..." John Flavell and his associates (Flavell, Beach, & Chinsky, 1966) found that only 10% of 5-year-olds repeated the names of pictures they were asked to recall, but more than half of 7-year-olds and 85% of 10-year-olds used this strategy.

Another important memory strategy is **organization,** or classifying items into meaningful groups. You might lump the apple, the grapes, and the hamburger in Figure 8.2 into a category of "foods" and form other categories for "animals," "vehicles," and "baseball equipment." You would then rehearse each category and recall it as a cluster. Another organizational strategy, *chunking,* is used when we break a long number (6065551843) into manageable subunits (606-555-1843, a phone number). Organization is mastered a bit later in childhood than rehearsal. Until about age 9 or 10, children are not much better at recalling lists of items that lend themselves readily to grouping than they are at recalling lists of unrelated words (Flavell & Wellman, 1977).

Finally, the strategy of **elaboration** involves actively creating meaningful links between items to be remembered. Elaboration is achieved by adding something to the items, in the form of either words or images. Creating and using a sentence like "The apple fell on the horse's nose" would help you remember two of the items in Figure 8.2. Elaboration is especially helpful in learning foreign languages. For example, one might link the Spanish word *pato* (pronounced pot-o) to the English word *duck* by imagining a duck in a pot of boiling water.

Memory or encoding strategies develop in a fairly predictable order, with rehearsal emerging first, followed by organization, and then elaboration (Pressley, 1982). Children don't suddenly start using strategies, though. According to Patricia Miller and her colleagues (1990, 1994; Miller & Seier, 1994), they typically progress through four phases on their way to successful strategy use. Initially, children do not produce strategies at all. This gives way to partial production of strategies, or what we might think of as precursors of mature strategy use. The third phase is what Miller calls **utilization deficiency,** in which children spontaneously produce a strategy but their task performance does not yet benefit from using the strategy. Finally, children exhibit effective strategy use by both producing and benefiting from a memory strategy.

There is ample evidence of utilization deficiencies across various age groups and for different types of strategies (see, for example, Coyle & Bjorklund, 1996; Miller & Seier, 1994; also see Bjorklund et al., 1997). Why would children who use a strategy fail to benefit from it? One possibility is that using a new strategy is mentally taxing and leaves no free cognitive resources for other aspects of the task (Bjorklund et al., 1997). Once using the strategy becomes more routinized, then other components of the task can be addressed simultaneously. Whatever the reason for utilization deficiencies, they reflect a child–task interaction; that is, they depend on how difficult a task is for a particular child rather than on task difficulty per se (Bjorklund et al., 1997).

Using effective storage strategies to learn material is only half the battle; *retrieval strategies* can also influence how much is ultimately recalled. Indeed, retrieving something from memory can often be a complex adventure in problem solving, as when you try to remember when you went on a trip by searching for cues that might trigger your memory ("Well, I still had long hair then, but it was after Muffy's wedding, and . . ."). Strange as it may seem, even when young schoolchildren are shown how to use the memory strategy of elaboration, they still may do less well than older children on memory tests because it does not occur to them to use the images they worked so hard to create to help them *retrieve* what they have learned (Pressley & Levin, 1980). In general, young children rely more on external cues for both encoding and retrieval of information than do older children (Schneider & Pressley, 1997). Thus, young children may need to put their toothbrushes next to their pajamas so that they have a physical reminder to brush their teeth before they go to bed. Older children are less likely to need the external cue. In many ways, then, command of memory strategies increases over the childhood years.

Does Knowledge about Memory Change?

The term **metamemory** refers to knowledge of memory as well as to monitoring and regulation of memory processes. It is knowing, for example, what one's memory limits are, which memory strategies are more or less effective, and which memory tasks are more or less difficult (Flavell, Miller, & Miller, 1993). It's also noting that your efforts to remember something are not working and you need to try something different (Schneider, 1998). Metamemory is one aspect of **metacognition,** or knowledge of the human mind and of the whole range of cognitive processes. Your store of metacognitive knowledge might include an understanding that you are better at language learning than at algebra, that it is harder to pay attention to a task when there is distracting noise in the background than

when it is quiet, and that it is wise to check out a proposed solution to a problem before concluding that it is correct.

When do children first show evidence of metacognition? If instructed to remember where the *Sesame Street* character Big Bird has been hidden so that they can later wake him up, even 2- and 3-year-olds will go stand near the hiding spot, or at least look or point at that spot; they do not do these things as often if Big Bird is visible and they don't need to remember where he is (DeLoache, Cassidy, & Brown, 1985). By age 2, then, children understand that to remember something, you have to work at it! Three-year-olds understand the difference between *thinking* about an object and actually perceiving it, and 4-year-olds realize that behavior is guided by beliefs (Flavell, 1999). These findings indicate that metacognitive awareness is present at least in a rudimentary form at a young age (Kuhn, 2000).

Children learn a good deal more about their memory capacities once they enter school (Schneider & Bjorklund, 1998). In one study (Yussen & Levy, 1975), preschoolers, third-graders, and adults were asked to estimate whether they would be able to recall sets of pictures of varying sizes. Preschoolers' estimates were highly unrealistic—as if they believed they could perform any memory feat imaginable—and they were unfazed by information about how another child had done on the task. If we give children a little more time before asking them to estimate how much they will be able to recall of what they just studied, accuracy is good among children as young as age 6 (Schneider et al., 2000). When asked immediately after the learning task, children (and adults) overestimate their future ability to remember, presumably based on what is still in their short-term memory. After a few minutes, this information is typically lost from short-term memory and children base their estimates on what has made it into long-term memory.

Are increases in metamemory a major contributor to improved memory performance over the childhood years? Children with greater metamemory awareness demonstrate better memory ability, but several factors influence the strength of this relationship (Bjork & Bjork, 1998). We are most likely to see a connection between metamemory and memory performance among older children and among children who have been in situations where they must remember something (Schneider & Bjorklund, 1998). Not only is task experience important, but the nature of the task is relevant. Awareness of memory processes benefits even young children on tasks that are simple and familiar, and where connections between metamemory knowledge and memory performance are fairly obvious (Schneider & Sodian, 1988). Finally, children who know what to do may not always do it, so good metamemory is no guarantee of good recall (Salatas & Flavell, 1976). It seems that children must not only know that a strategy is useful but *why* it is useful in order to be motivated to use it and to actually benefit from its use (Justice et al., 1997). The links between metamemory and memory performance, though not perfect, are strong enough to suggest the merits of teaching children more about how memory works and how they can make it work more effectively for them.

Does Knowledge of the World Change?

Ten-year-olds obviously know considerably more about the world in general than 2-year-olds do. The individual's knowledge of a content area to be learned, or **knowledge base,** as it has come to be called, clearly affects learning and memory performance. Think about the difference between reading about a topic that you already know well and reading about a new topic. In the first case, you can read quickly because you are able to link the information to the knowledge you have already stored. All you really need to do is check for any new information or information that contradicts what you already know. Learning about a highly unfamiliar topic is more difficult ("It's Greek to me").

Perhaps the most dramatic illustration of the powerful influence of knowledge base on memory was provided by Michelene Chi (1978). She demonstrated that even though adults typically outperform children on tests of memory, this age difference could be reversed if children have more expertise than adults. Chi recruited children who were expert chess players and compared their memory skills to those of adults who were familiar with the game but lacked expertise. On a test of memory for sequences of digits, the children recalled fewer than the adults did, demonstrating their usual "deficiencies." But on a test of memory for the locations of *chess pieces,* the children clearly beat the adults (Figure 8.3). Because they were experts, these children were able to form more and larger mental "chunks," or meaningful groups of chess pieces, which allowed them to remember more. When child experts were compared to adult experts, there were no differences in performance (Schneider et al., 1993).

Pause to consider the implications: On most tasks, young children are the novices and older children or adults are the experts. Perhaps older children and adults recall longer strings of digits because they are more familiar with numbers than young children are, not because they have better basic learning capacities. Perhaps they recall more words in word lists simply because they have more familiarity with language.

Perhaps memory improves over childhood simply because older children know more about all kinds of things than younger children do (Bjorklund, 1995).

In their areas of expertise—whether baseball, dinosaurs, soccer, or *Star Wars*—children appear to develop highly specialized and effective strategies of information processing, just as the young chess players studied by Chi apparently had (see Schneider & Bjorklund, 1998, for review). Indeed, children with low general intellectual ability but high expertise sometimes understand and remember more about stories in their area of expertise than children with higher intellectual ability but less expertise (Schneider, Bjorklund, & Maier-Bruckner, 1996). It seems that the more one knows, the more one *can* know. It also seems that how well a child does on a memory task depends not only on age but also on familiarity with the specific task at hand.

A Summing Up

We can now draw four conclusions about the development of learning and memory:

1. Older children have a greater information-processing *capacity* than younger children do, particularly in the sense that they are faster information processors and can juggle more information in working memory.
2. Older children use more effective *memory strategies* in encoding and retrieving information.
3. Older children know more about memory, and good *metamemory* may help children choose more appropriate strategies and control and monitor their learning more effectively.
4. Older children know more in general, and their larger *knowledge base* improves their ability to learn and remember.

Can we choose a best hypothesis? Probably not at this point. All these phenomena may contribute something to the

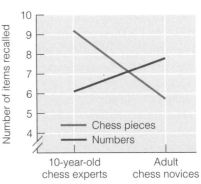

Figure 8.3 Effects of expertise on memory. Michelene Chi found that child chess experts outperformed adult chess novices on a test of recall for the location of chess pieces (though, in keeping with the usual developmental trend, these children could not recall strings of numbers as well as adults could).

Source: Adapted from Chi in Siegler (1978)

dramatic improvements in learning and memory that occur over the childhood years. They may also interact. For example, the automatization of certain information processes may leave the child with enough working memory space to use effective memory strategies that were just too mentally demanding earlier in childhood (Bjorklund, 1995). Similarly, increased knowledge may permit faster information processing. We will return to these same four hypotheses when we consider changes in learning and memory in adulthood.

Autobiographical Memory

Much of what children remember and talk about consists of everyday events that have happened to them personally. Children effortlessly remember all sorts of things: a birthday party last week, where they left their favorite toy, what to do when they go to a fast-food restaurant. Such **autobiographical memories** are essential ingredients of our present and future experiences. Let's look at how autobiographical memories are stored and organized and at factors that influence their accuracy.

WHEN DO AUTOBIOGRAPHICAL MEMORIES BEGIN?

We learned earlier in this chapter that infants and toddlers are able to store memories. We also know that children and adults have many specific autobiographical events stored in long-term memory. Yet research shows that older children and adults exhibit **childhood** (or **infantile**) **amnesia;** that is, they have very few autobiographical memories of events that occurred before the age of about 2 (Lie & Newcombe, 1999; Schneider & Bjorklund, 1998).

To determine how old we have to be at the time of significant life events in order to remember them, JoNell Usher and Ulric Neisser (1993) asked college students who had experienced (1) the birth of a younger sibling, (2) hospitalization, (3) the death of a family member, or (4) a family move early in life to answer questions about those experiences (for example, who told them their mothers were going to the hospital to give birth, what they were doing when she left, and where they were when they first saw the new baby). As Figure 8.4 shows, the proportion of memory questions students were able to answer increased dramatically as age at the time of the experience increased. Overall, children had to be at least 2 to recall the birth of a sibling or hospitalization and age 3 to recall the death of a family member or a move.

Eunhui Lie and Nora Newcombe (1999) tested 8-year-olds' explicit and implicit memory for their preschool classmates whom they had not seen for 3 years. Although the children retained some explicit memory of former classmates, their recognition was far below that of adults, who were quite good. Children demonstrated better implicit memory for their former classmates, but even this declined over the 3-year interval since the children had been together. Thus, children do have trouble remembering events from early childhood; however, it may not be fair to call this "amnesia" because they do retain some memories.

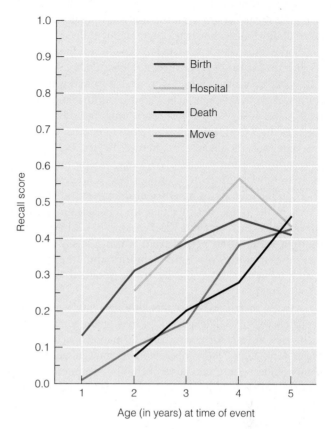

Figure 8.4 College students' recall of early life events increases as a function of how old they were at the time of the event.
Source: Usher & Neisser (1993)

Why can't we remember much about our early years? As we have seen, infants and toddlers are certainly capable of encoding their experiences (Howe, 2000; Howe & Courage, 1993; Rovee-Collier, 1997). Also, young preschool children seem to be able to remember a good deal about events that occurred when they were infants, even though older children and adults cannot (Bauer, 1996; Fivush, Gray, & Fromhoff, 1987). One explanation of childhood amnesia is that infants and toddlers may not have enough space in working memory to hold the multiple pieces of information about actor, action, and setting that are needed to encode a coherent memory of an event (White & Pillemer, 1979). As we learned earlier in this chapter, functional working memory capacity increases with age. Also, infants do not use language, and adults do. Because autobiographical memory relies heavily on language skills, we would expect such memories to increase with increased language skills (see Marian & Neisser, 2000). However, this language explanation does not account for why children can't remember nonverbal information such as the faces of preschool classmates (Lie & Newcombe, 1999).

Alternatively, perhaps memories that are no longer useful once we reach new developmental levels and face new developmental tasks are no longer retrieved and are therefore lost (Rovee-Collier & Boller, 1995). Or maybe what is lacking is a sense of self around which memories of personally experienced events can be organized as "events that happened to *me*" (Howe & Courage, 1993, 1997). Indeed, young children's ability to recognize themselves in a mirror is a good predictor of children's ability to talk about their past (Harley & Reese, 1999).

Some researchers have tried to explain childhood amnesia in terms of **fuzzy-trace theory** (Howe, 2000). According to this explanation, children store verbatim and general accounts of an event separately. Verbatim information is unstable and likely to be lost over long periods of time (Leichtman & Ceci, 1993); it is easier to remember the gist of an event than the details (Brainerd & Reyna, 1993; Koriat, Goldsmith, & Pansky, 2000). With age, we are increasingly likely to rely on gist memory traces, which are less likely to be forgotten and are more efficient than verbatim memory traces, in the sense that they take up less space in memory (Brainerd & Gordon, 1994; Klaczynski, 2001). Children pass through a transition period from storing largely verbatim memories to storing more gist memories, and the earlier verbatim memories are unlikely to be retained over time (Howe, 2000).

Finally, there is evidence that although children may lose explicit recall of early experiences, they retain some implicit memories, at least for nonverbal information (such as classmates' faces; Lie & Newcombe, 1999). As you can see, there are plenty of ideas about the causes of childhood amnesia but still no firm explanation of why a period of life that is highly important to later development is a blank for most of us (Perlmutter, 1986).

SCRIPTS

As children engage in routine daily activities such as getting ready for bed or eating at a fast-food restaurant, they construct **scripts** of these activities (K. Nelson, 1986). Scripts represent the typical sequence of actions related to an event and guide future behaviors in similar settings (Schank & Abelson, 1977). For instance, children who have been to a fast-food restaurant might have a script something like this: Wait in line, tell the person behind the counter what you want, pay for the food, carry the tray of food to a table, open packages and eat food, gather up trash and throw it away before leaving. With this script in mind, children can act effectively in similar settings. Children as young as 3 years use scripts when reporting familiar events (Nelson, 1997). When asked about their visit to a fast-food restaurant the day before, children report *generally* what happens when they go to the restaurant rather than what specifically happened during yesterday's visit (Kuebli & Fivush, 1994). As children get older, their scripts become more detailed (Farrar & Goodman, 1990). Perhaps more important than age, though, is experience: Children with greater experience of an event develop richer scripts than children with less experience (DeMarie, Norman, & Abshier, 2000).

EYEWITNESS MEMORY

Children's scripts affect their memory. For example, when presented with information that is inconsistent with their scripts, preschoolers may misremember the information so that it better fits their script (Nelson & Hudson, 1988). This indicates that memory is a reconstruction, not an exact replication (Koriat, Goldsmith, & Pansky, 2000). This, in turn, has significant implications for **eyewitness memory** (or testimony), or reporting events that one has witnessed or experienced—for example, reporting that you saw your little brother snitch some candy right before dinner. Children are

Children develop scripts in memory for routine activities, in this case, shelling seafood, that guide their behavior in these situations.

increasingly asked to report events that have happened in the context of abuse cases or custody hearings (Bruck & Ceci, 1999; Ceci & Bruck, 1998). To what extent can we "trust" a child's memory in these situations? What factors influence the accuracy of children's eyewitness memory?

When asked generally about events ("Tell me what happened at Uncle Joe's house"), preschoolers recall less information than older children, but the recall of both groups is quite accurate (Fivush & Hammond, 1989; Howe, Courage, & Peterson, 1994). Specific questions ("Was Uncle Joe wearing a red shirt?") elicit more information, but accuracy of recall begins to slip (Hilgard & Loftus, 1979). This is especially true as the questions become more directed or leading ("Uncle Joe touched you here, didn't he?"). Preschool-age children, more so than older children and adults, are suggestible and can be influenced by information implied in direct questioning as well as by relevant information that is introduced after the event (Bruck & Ceci, 1999; Goodman & Schaaf, 1997).

Perhaps it is unfortunate, then, that preschoolers, because they initially offer less information in response to open-ended questions, end up being asked a larger number of directed questions (Baker-Ward et al., 1993; Price & Goodman, 1990). They are also frequently subjected to repeated questioning, which also increases errors in reporting among children (Cassel, Roebers, & Bjorklund, 1996; Poole & White, 1993). Although repeated questioning with general, open-ended questions can increase accuracy, repeated questioning with directed or closed questions can decrease it (Memon & Vartoukian, 1996). Thus, the timing, type, and frequency of questions affect the quantity and quality of what is remembered.

In sum, most of us do not recall events that happened to us before the age of 2 or 3. Such childhood amnesia may occur because of space limitations in working memory or because early events are stored in ways that make later retrieval difficult. By age 3, children store routine daily events as scripts that they can draw on in similar situations. Our scripts influence what we remember about an event, which is also influenced by postevent information related to the event. Finally, memories are vital to problem-solving skills, which we examine in the next section.

Problem Solving

To solve any problem, one must process information about the task, as well as use stored information, to achieve a goal. How do problem-solving capacities change during childhood? Piaget provided one answer to this question by proposing that children progress through broad stages of cognitive growth, but information-processing theorists were not satisfied with this explanation. They sought to pinpoint more specific reasons why problem-solving prowess improves so dramatically as children get older.

Consider the problem of predicting what will happen to the balance beam in Figure 8.5 when weights are put on each side of the fulcrum, or balancing point. The goal is to decide which way the balance beam will tip when it is released. To judge correctly, one must take into account both the number of weights and their distances from the fulcrum. Piaget believed that concrete operational thinkers can appreciate the significance of either the amount of weight or its distance from the center but will not grasp the inverse relationship between the two factors. Only when they reach the stage of formal operations will new cognitive structures allow them to understand that balance can be maintained by decreasing a weight but moving it farther away from the fulcrum or by increasing a weight but moving it closer to the fulcrum (Piaget & Inhelder, 1966/1969).

Robert Siegler (1981, 2000) proposed that the information-processing perspective could provide a fuller analysis. His **rule assessment approach** determines what information about a problem children take in and what rules they then formulate to account for this information. This approach assumes that children's problem-solving attempts are not hit-or-miss but are governed by rules, and that children fail to solve problems because they fail to encode all the critical aspects of the problem and are guided by faulty rules.

Siegler (1981) administered balance beam problems to individuals ages 3 to 20. He detected clear age differences in the extent to which both weight and distance from the fulcrum were taken into account in the rules that guided decisions about which end of the balance beam would drop. Few 3-year-olds used any kind of rule; they guessed. By contrast, 4- and 5-year-olds were rule governed. More than 80% of these children used a rule that said that the side of the balance beam with more weight would drop; they totally ignored distance from the fulcrum. By age 8, most children had begun to consider distance from the fulcrum as well as weight; at least when the weights were equal, they appreciated that the side of the balance beam with the weights farthest from the fulcrum would drop. By age 12, the vast majority of children considered both weight and distance on a range of problems, although they still became confused on complex problems in which one side had more weights but the other had its weights farther from the fulcrum. Finally, 30% of 20-year-olds had discovered the correct rule—that the pull on each arm is a function of weight times distance. For example, if there are three weights on the second peg to the left and two weights on the fourth peg to the right, the left torque is 3 x 2 = 6 and the right torque is 2 x 4 = 8, so the right arm will go down.

In most important areas of problem solving, Siegler (1996) has now concluded, children do not simply progress from one way of thinking to another as they get older, as his balance beam research suggested. Instead, in working problems in arithmetic, spelling, science, and other school subjects,

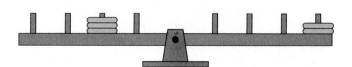

Figure 8.5 The balance beam apparatus used by Siegler to study children's problem-solving abilities. Which way will the balance beam tip?

most children in any age group use *multiple* rules or problem-solving strategies rather than just one. In working a subtraction problem such as 12 − 3 = 9, for example, children sometimes count down from 12 until they have counted off 3 and arrive at 9, but other times count up from 3 until they reach 12. In one study of second- and fourth-graders (Siegler, 1989), more than 90% of the children used three or more different strategies in working subtraction problems.

Similarly, Michael Cohen (1996) found that most preschoolers used all possible strategies when attempting to solve a practical mathematical problem in the context of playing store. He also found that children's selection and use of strategies became more efficient over multiple task trials; that is, they increasingly selected strategies that would allow them to solve the task in fewer steps.

Such results suggest that cognitive development works much as evolution does, through a process of *natural selection* in which many ways of thinking are available and the most adaptive survive (Siegler, 1996, 2000; DeLoache, Miller, & Pierroutsakos, 1998). Rather than picturing development as a series of stages resembling stair steps, Siegler argues, we should picture it as overlapping waves, as shown in Figure 8.6. At each age, children have multiple problem-solving strategies available to them; it's not "one child (or age), one rule." As children gain more experience, which typically occurs as they get older, they use less adaptive strategies less, and more adaptive strategies more, and now and then, whole new strategies may appear. Strategies evolve from their initial acquisition in a particular context to their generalization to other contexts, which helps strengthen the fledgling strategies (Chen & Siegler, 2000). Gradually, children not only learn to choose the most useful strategy for a problem but become increasingly effective at executing new strategies. Familiarity with a task and with strategies frees up processing space, allowing children to engage in more metacognitive analysis of the strategies at their disposal (Whitebread, 1999).

Notice the difference between this information-processing explanation and Piaget's explanation of cognitive change.

Piaget argued that change is qualitative, with new, more effective strategies replacing older, less effective strategies all at once as children move from one stage to another. Siegler argues that strategies emerge gradually and become more effective over time, with multiple strategies available at any given time.

Imagine how effective teachers might be if they, like Siegler, could accurately diagnose the information-processing strategies of their learners to know exactly what each child is noticing (or failing to notice) about a problem and exactly what rules or strategies each child is using when. Like a good car mechanic, the teacher would be able to pinpoint the problem and encourage less use of faulty strategies and rules and more use of adaptive ones. Much remains to be learned about how problem-solving strategies evolve as children get older, and why. However, the rule assessment approach and overlapping waves model give us a fairly specific idea of what children are doing (or doing wrong) as they attack problems and illustrate how the information-processing approach to cognitive development provides a different view of development than Piaget's account does.

The Adolescent

Although parents who are in the midst of reminding their adolescent sons and daughters to do household chores may wonder whether teenagers process any information at all, learning, memory, and problem solving continue to improve considerably during the adolescent years. How, exactly, does this improvement occur?

First, new learning and memory strategies emerge. It is during adolescence that the memory strategy of elaboration is mastered (Schneider & Pressley, 1997). Adolescents also develop and refine advanced learning and memory strategies that are highly relevant to school learning—for example, note taking and underlining skills. Ann Brown and Sandra Smiley (1978) asked students from 5th grade (age 11) to 12th grade to read and recall a story. Some learners were asked to recall the story immediately; others were given an additional 5 minutes to study it before they were tested. Amazingly, 5th-graders gained almost nothing from the extra study period, except for those few who used the time to underline or take notes. Junior high school students benefited to an extent, but only in senior high school did most students use underlining and note taking effectively to improve their recall. When some groups of students were told that they could underline or take notes if they wished, 5th-graders still did not improve, largely because they tended to underline everything rather than highlighting the most important points.

Second, adolescents make more deliberate use of strategies that younger children use more or less unconsciously (Bjorklund, 1985). For example, they may deliberately organize a list of words instead of simply using any natural organization or grouping that happens to be there already. And they use existing strategies more selectively. For example, they are

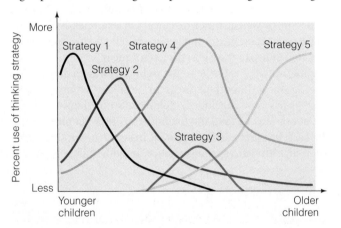

Figure 8.6 Cognitive development may resemble overlapping waves more than a staircase leading from one stage to another. Children of a particular age typically use multiple thinking strategies rather than just one.

Source: Siegler (1996)

adept at using their strategies to memorize the material on which they know they will be tested and deliberately forgetting anything else (Bray, Hersh, & Turner, 1985; Lorsbach & Reimer, 1997). To illustrate, Patricia Miller and Michael Weiss (1981) asked children to remember the locations of animals that had been hidden behind small doors, ignoring the household objects hidden behind other doors. As Figure 8.7 shows, 13-year-olds recalled more than 7- and 10-year-olds about where the animals had been hidden, but they remembered *less* about task-irrelevant information (the locations of the household objects). Apparently, they are better able to push irrelevant information out of working memory so that it does not interfere with task performance (Lorsbach & Reimer, 1997). So, during elementary school, children get better at distinguishing between what is relevant and what is irrelevant, but during adolescence they advance even further by selectively using their memory strategies only on the relevant material. If it's not going to be on the test, forget it!

Adolescents make other strides besides these changes in *memory strategies. Basic capacities* continue to increase; for example, adolescents perform any number of cognitive operations more speedily than children do (Kail, 1991). Of course, adolescents also continue to expand their *knowledge base,* so they may do better than children on some tasks simply because they know more about the topic. *Metamemory* and *metacognition* also improve. For example, adolescents become better able to tailor their reading strategies to different purposes (studying versus skimming) and better able to realize when they don't understand something (Baker & Brown, 1984). They can monitor their strategy choice, selecting elaboration over rote repetition when they realize that the former is more effective (Pressley, Levin, & Ghatala, 1984). They are also fairly accurate at monitoring whether or not they have allocated adequate study time to learn new material (Kelemen, 2000). Teens typically allocate more study time to information judged to be difficult, indicating they understand that this material needs additional processing in order to be retained (Thiede & Dunlosky, 1999). Interestingly, when pressed for time, college students devote more study time to *easy* items

(Son & Metcalfe, 2000). Apparently, they decide it is futile to work on the difficult material when they don't have adequate time, so they spend their time on what seems most likely to pay off. Hopefully, you can see the implication of this for your own studying: Set aside enough time to study *all* the material; otherwise, you may end up in a time crunch reviewing only the easy material.

Growth in strategies, basic capacities, knowledge base, and metacognition probably also helps explain the growth in everyday problem-solving ability that occurs during the adolescent years (Berg, 1989). Teenagers perfect a number of information-processing skills and become able to apply them *deliberately and spontaneously* across a wide variety of tasks (Brown et al., 1983).

The Adult

If you are about age 20, you will be pleased to know that the young adult college student has served as the standard of effective information processing against which all other age groups are compared. Although information processes are thought to be most efficient in young adults, improvements in cognitive performance do occur during the adult years before aging begins to take its toll on some memory and problem-solving capacities.

Developing Expertise

Comparisons of people who are new to their chosen fields of study with those who are more experienced tell us that experience pays off in more effective memory and problem solving. In Chapter 7, we saw that people in Piaget's highest stage of cognitive development, formal operations, often perform better in their areas of specialization than in unfamiliar areas. Similarly, information-processing research tells us that adults often function best cognitively in domains in which they have achieved expertise (Byrnes, 1996; Ericsson, 1996; Glaser & Chi, 1988). It seems to take about 10 years of training and experience to become a true expert in a field and to build a rich and well-organized knowledge base (Ericsson, 1996). But once this base is achieved, the expert not only knows and remembers more but thinks more effectively than individuals who lack expertise.

Consider first the effects of knowledge base on memory. How might adults who are baseball experts and adults who care little for baseball perceive and remember the same game? George Spilich and his associates (1979) had baseball experts and novices listen to a tape of a half inning of play. Experts recalled more of the information that was central to the game—the important plays and the fate of each batter, in proper order—whereas novices were caught up by less central facts such as the threatening weather conditions and the number of people attending the game. Experts also recalled more details—for example, noting that a double was a line drive down the left-field line rather than just a double. At any age, experts in

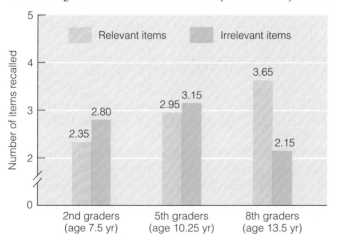

Figure 8.7 Adolescents are better able than children to concentrate on learning relevant material and to ignore irrelevant material.
SOURCE: Miller & Weiss (1981)

a field are likely to remember new information in that content domain more fully than novices do (Morrow et al., 1994).

In addition, experts are able to use their elaborately organized and complete knowledge bases to solve problems effectively and efficiently (Proffitt, Coley, & Medin, 2000). They are able to size up a situation quickly, see what the problem really is, and recognize how the new problem is similar to and different from problems encountered in the past (Glaser & Chi, 1988). They can quickly, surely, and almost automatically call up just the right information from their extensive knowledge base to devise effective solutions to problems and to carry them out efficiently.

Are the benefits of expertise content-specific, or does gaining expertise in one domain carry over into other domains and make one a more generally effective learner or problem solver? This is an interesting and important question. One research team (Ericsson, Chase, & Faloon, 1980) put an average college student to work improving the number of digits he could recall. He practiced for about an hour a day, three to five days a week, for more than a year and a half—more than 200 hours in all. His improvement? He went from a memory span of 7 digits to one of 79 digits! His method involved forming meaningful associations between strings of digits and running times—for example, seeing 3492 as "3 minutes and 49 point 2 seconds, near world-record mile time" (p. 1181). It also involved chunking numbers into groups of three or four and then organizing the chunks into large units.

Did all this work pay off in a better memory for information other than numbers? Not really. When he was given letters of the alphabet to recall, this young man's memory span was unexceptional (about six letters). Clearly the memory ability he developed was based on strategies of use only in the subject matter he was trying to remember. Similarly, Rajan Mahadevan, a man with an exceptional memory for arrays of

numbers, turns out to possess no special ability at all for remembering the positions and orientations of objects (Biederman et al., 1992), and Shakuntala Devi, a woman who can solve complex mathematical problems in her head at amazing speeds, is apparently no faster than average at performing other cognitive operations (Jensen, 1990). Each of these experts apparently relies on *domain-specific* knowledge and *domain-specific* information-processing strategies to achieve his or her cognitive feats (Ericsson & Kintsch, 1995; Schunn & Anderson, 1999).

Sometimes, domain expertise can actually be a hindrance. Tax experts typically outperform tax novices on hypothetical tax cases that don't fit a general tax principle (Marchant et al., 1991). But when primed to think about a general tax principle, experts had more trouble than novices on a tax case that violated this principle, presumably because they had trouble "overriding" the rich source of information that was activated in their memory (see also Lewandowsky & Kirsner, 2000). And although older adults *know more* about the world than younger adults, they don't always perform better on this material when given an explicit memory task (Foos & Sarno, 1998). In one study, for example, older adults first demonstrated that they had greater knowledge of U.S. presidents than younger adults. Both groups were then given a set of 20 presidents' names to study for as long as they wanted before being tested for recall and recognition of the list (Foos & Sarno, 1998). The younger adults now outperformed the older ones. The older adults spent less time studying the list than the younger adults, possibly because they were confident that they already knew the familiar material.

In sum, experts know more than novices do, their knowledge base is more organized, and they are able to use their knowledge and specialized strategies they have devised to learn, remember, and solve problems very efficiently in their areas of expertise—but not in other domains. In effect, experts do not need to think much; they are like experienced drivers who can put themselves on "autopilot" and carry out well-learned routines very quickly and accurately. By gaining expertise over the years, adults can often compensate for losses in information-processing capacities, our next topic.

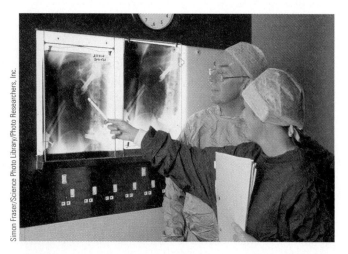

Adults who have gained proficiency in their chosen fields can draw from their well-organized knowledge bases to find just the right information to fit the problem at hand. Solving problems is automatic and effortless for experts.

Learning, Memory, and Aging

No less an expert on learning than B. F. Skinner complained about memory problems: "One of the more disheartening experiences of old age is discovering that a point you have just made—so significant, so beautifully expressed—was made by you in something you published a long time ago" (Skinner, 1983, p. 242). In fact, most elderly adults report that they have at least minor difficulties remembering things (G. E. Smith et al., 1996). They are especially likely to have trouble remembering names, routines like filling the car with gas, and items they will need later; they are also more upset than young adults by memory lapses, perhaps because they view them as signs of aging (Cavanaugh, Grady, & Perlmutter, 1983).

Forgetting: What's Normal and What's Not?

As we get older, or watch parents and grandparents get older, how can we distinguish between normal forgetfulness and abnormal memory changes? Many older adults worry that forgetting an appointment or where they put their reading glasses is a precursor to the pathological memory loss associated with Alzheimer's disease (see Chapter 16). Fortunately, most of us will *not* develop Alzheimer's disease (AD) and the atypical memory changes that accompany it. We will, though, exhibit some changes in memory and information-processing skills. So how can we discriminate between normal memory changes and those associated with disease?

Giovanni Carlesimo and his colleagues (1998) compared the memory performance of healthy younger, elderly, and very old adults with that of adults suspected of having Alzheimer's disease (AD can only be diagnosed for certain

In practical terms, it's normal to forget where you put something, but abnormal to forget how to use it (Cherry & Smith, 1998). Thus, don't worry when grandpa can't find his car keys, but be alert if he can't remember how to use them when they are in his hand. Similarly, it's normal to forget a new phone number that you recently looked up in the phone book, but abnormal to forget phone numbers that you have known and used for years.

Researchers who study memory now believe there is a third type of memory loss that is somewhere between normal loss with age and pathological loss from disease (Petersen et al., 1997, 2001). Some individuals may develop **mild cognitive impairment (MCI).** They experience significant memory problems—trouble learning new names, forgetting important appointments, and repeating themselves to the same person—but otherwise do not appear

Age, Memory Performance, and Clustering Scores of Healthy Adults and Adults with Alzheimer's Disease					
	Average Age (years)	Digit Span	Immediate Recall	Delayed Recall	Clustering Index
Young Adults	29	6.4	51	12	+.25
Elderly Adults	67	5.5	39	9	+.24
Very Old Adults	83	4.6	34	7	+.30
Alzheimer's Patients	67	4.3	18	2	−.13

by means of an autopsy after death). The table shows how the four groups compared on a digit-span test assessing how many pieces of information can be held in short-term memory and on immediate and delayed recall of semantically related items. The digit span of AD patients was worse than that of their healthy age-mates, although it was not markedly different from that of very old adults. However, recall was clearly deficient in AD patients compared not only to their age-mates but also to very old healthy adults. Even more striking was the difference in the extent to which the groups took advantage of the semantic relatedness of items to help their memory. The last column shows that the three healthy groups of adults performed at above chance levels in categorizing items, whereas the AD patients were below chance and sharply different from all the healthy groups. Clearly, normal aging does not take nearly the toll on memory skills that Alzheimer's disease does.

How, then, can we help family members and professionals recognize the difference between normal and unhealthy memory deficits? Cynthia Green (2001) suggests three criteria that can be used to alert us to atypical memory problems:

• Has memory gotten noticeably worse over the past 6 months?

• Do memory problems interfere with everyday activities at home or work?

• Are family and friends concerned about an individual's memory problems?

Answering "yes" to these questions may indicate unusual memory loss that should be evaluated by a professional.

to be suffering from dementia. At least not yet. Some research suggests that as many as 80% of those with MCI will eventually develop Alzheimer's disease (Morris et al., 2001).

The good news is that age-related memory loss may be preventable, and some losses that do occur may be reversible. Reducing stress, for example, is one way to improve memory performance (Bremner & Narayan, 1998). Chronic stress elevates levels of cortisol in the brain, which impedes memory. A study by the MacArthur Foundation found that three things predicted good memory over time: physical fitness and activity, mental activity, and a sense of control over life events (Rowe & Kahn, 1998). Mental activity—working crossword puzzles, reading, playing musical instruments—increases connections among neurons. And physical activity seems to release chemicals that protect neurons involved in cognitive function. Thus, remaining physically and mentally active can help protect against memory loss associated with aging. Having a sense of control over memory can boost both confidence and memory performance.

In sum, significant memory loss is *not* likely among healthy older adults. It's true that, relative to young adults, older adults exhibit poorer memory performance in some situations. But these changes are minor and can often be avoided by remaining physically and mentally active. We should be on the lookout for older adults who show marked declines in their memory performance. They may be experiencing mild cognitive impairment and may eventually develop Alzheimer's disease and impaired memory.

AREAS OF STRENGTH AND WEAKNESS

Much research indicates that, on average, older adults learn new material more slowly and sometimes learn it less well than young and middle-aged adults do and that they remember what they have learned less well. However, the following qualifications are important:

- Most of the research is based on cross-sectional studies comparing age groups, which suggests that the age differences detected could be related to factors other than age.
- Declines, when observed, typically do not become noticeable until the late 60s and 70s. Indeed, the memory of "young-old" adults (60–70 years) is more similar to that of young adults (18–34 years) than to that of older adults (71–82 years; Cregger & Rogers, 1998).
- Difficulties in remembering affect elderly people more noticeably as they continue to age and are most severe among the oldest-old.
- Not all older people experience these difficulties.
- Not all kinds of memory tasks cause older people difficulty.

Studies of memory skills in adulthood suggest that the aspects of learning and memory in which older adults look most deficient in comparison with young and middle-aged adults are some of the same areas in which young children compare unfavorably to older children (for reviews, see Guttentag, 1985; A. D. Smith & Earles, 1996). Here are some of the major weaknesses—and, by implication, strengths—of the older adult:

Timed Tasks   On the average, older adults are slower than younger adults to learn and retrieve information; they may need to go through the material more times to learn it equally well and may need more time to respond when their memory is tested. Thus, they are hurt by time limits (Botwinick, 1984).

Unfamiliar Tasks   Older adults fare especially poorly compared to younger adults when the material to be learned is unfamiliar or meaningless—when they cannot tie it to their existing knowledge. In a convincing demonstration of how familiarity influences memory, Barrett and Wright (1981) had young and elderly adults examine then-current words likely to be more familiar to young adults (for example, *dude*, *disco*, and *bummer*) and words from the past likely to be more familiar to older adults (for example, *pompadour*, *gramophone*, and *vamp*). Sure enough, young adults outperformed older adults on the "new" words, but older adults outperformed young adults on the "old" words. Many laboratory tasks involve learning material that is unfamiliar and thus do not allow older adults to make use of their knowledge base.

Unexercised Skills   Older adults are also likely to be at a disadvantage when they are required to use learning and memory skills that they rarely use in daily life; they hold their own when they can rely on well-practiced skills that have become effortless and automatic with practice. For example,

Lynne Reder, Cynthia Wible, and John Martin (1986) found that elderly adults were just as good as young adults at judging whether sentences presented to them were plausible based on a story they had read. Judging whether something makes sense in the context of what one has read is a well-exercised ability. However, older adults were deficient when it came to judging whether specific sentences had or had not appeared in the story—a skill that is seldom used outside school. It seems that older adults read to get the gist or significance of a story and do not bother with the details, a strategy that may be very adaptive if they have no need to memorize details and if their ability to do so has fallen off with age (Adams, 1991; Stine-Morrow, Loveless, & Soederberg, 1996). In other ways as well, age differences are smaller when well-practiced skills are assessed than when less-practiced skills are assessed (Denney, 1982).

Recall versus Recognition   Older adults are likely to be more deficient on tasks requiring recall memory than on tasks requiring only recognition of what was learned. In one study of memory for high school classmates (Bahrick, Bahrick, & Wittlinger, 1975), even adults who were almost 35 years past graduation could still recognize which of five names matched a picture in their yearbook about 90% of the time. However, the ability to actively recall names of classmates when given only their photos as cues dropped considerably as the age of the rememberer increased. A large gap between recognition and recall tells us that older people have encoded and stored the information but cannot retrieve it without the help of cues. Sometimes older adults fail to retrieve information because they never thoroughly encoded or learned it in the first place, but at other times they simply cannot retrieve information that is "in there."

Explicit Memory Tasks   Finally, older adults seem to have more trouble with explicit memory tasks that require mental effort than with implicit memory tasks that involve more automatic mental processes (Joyce et al., 1998; Light & LaVoie, 1993; Schmitter-Edgecombe, 1999). Some researchers report a small decline with age even in implicit memory, but the larger loss is in explicit memory (Maki, Zonderman, & Weingartner, 1999).

Overall, these findings suggest that older adults, like young children, have difficulty with tasks that are *cognitively demanding*—that require speed, the learning of unfamiliar material, the use of unexercised abilities, recall rather than recognition, or explicit and effortful rather than implicit and automatic memory. Yet older adults and young children have difficulty for different reasons, as we will now see.

EXPLAINING DECLINES IN OLD AGE

In asking *why* some older adults struggle with some learning and memory tasks, we can first return to the same hypotheses we used to explain childhood improvements in performance: basic processing capacities, strategy use, metamemory, and knowledge base. Then we will consider some additional possibilities.

Knowledge Base Let's start with the hypothesis that differences in *knowledge base* explain differences between older and younger adults. We immediately encounter a problem: Young children may lack knowledge, but elderly adults do not. Indeed, older adults are generally at least as knowledgeable as young adults (Camp, 1989; Hess & Pullen, 1996). They often equal or surpass younger adults on measures of vocabulary and knowledge of word meanings (Light, 1991; West, Crook, & Barron, 1992). Moreover, they know a lot about the world. For example, they know *more* than younger adults about real-world categories of information such as U.S. presidents, countries, international cities, and bodies of water (Foos & Sarno, 1998). They also still know a surprising amount of information they learned in high school Spanish, algebra, and geometry courses taken as many as 50 years earlier (Bahrick, 1984; Bahrick & Hall, 1991). So, deficiencies in knowledge base are probably not the source of most of the memory problems that many older adults display. On the contrary, gains in knowledge probably help older adults compensate for losses in information-processing efficiency (Salthouse, 1993). Thus, older pilots are as adept as younger pilots and better than nonpilots at repeating back flight commands, but they show the usual effects of aging if they are given tasks less relevant to their work (Morrow et al., 1994). Older adults perform better than younger adults on memory tasks where they can spontaneously use analogies, another indication that a rich knowledge base can aid memory (Caplan & Schooler, 2001). Knowledge enhances learning (Kaplan & Murphy, 2000). Indeed, as Paul Baltes has put it, "Knowledge is power!" (Baltes, Smith, & Staudinger, 1992, p. 143).

Metamemory Could elderly adults, like young children, be deficient in the specific knowledge called metamemory? Is their knowledge of some of the strategies that prove useful in school learning—and in laboratory memory tasks—a bit rusty? This theory sounds plausible, but research shows that older adults seem to know as much as younger adults about such things as which memory strategies are best and which memory tasks are hardest (Light, 1991). Yet there's a difference between knowing about memory and believing that you can remember things. Older adults *do* express more negative beliefs about their memory skills than younger adults do (Cavanaugh, 1996). Although actual memory loss may contribute to a drop in confidence in one's memory skills, negative beliefs about one's memory skills also appear to hurt memory performance (Cavanaugh, 1996; McDonald-Miszczak, Hultsch, & Hertzog, 1995).

Becca Levy and Ellen Langer (1994) suggest that part of the problem lies in U.S. society's negative stereotypes of aging—specifically, the stereotype of old people as forgetful. These researchers tested the memory of young and elderly adults (ages 59–91) in three groups: Hearing Americans, Deaf Americans, and Hearing Chinese. In both the American deaf and Chinese cultures, elders are respected and negative stereotypes of intellectual aging are not as prevalent as they are among hearing Americans. As Figure 8.8 shows, young adults in the three groups performed about equally well on a set of recall tasks, but Chinese elders clearly outperformed both deaf American elders (who were second best) and hearing American elders. In fact, elderly Chinese adults scored only a little lower than young Chinese adults, despite having less education. In addition, those older people in the study who believed that aging brings about memory loss performed more poorly than those who did not hold this belief. Levy (1996) has also shown that activating negative stereotypes in the minds of elderly adults (through rapid, subliminal presentation of words like "Alzheimer's" and "senile" on a computer screen) causes them to perform worse on memory tests and to express less confidence in their memory skills than when positive stereotypes of old age are planted in their minds (through words like "wise" and "sage"). Findings like these clearly call into question the idea of a universal decline in memory skills in later life and point to the influence of culture and its views of aging on performance.

Memory Strategies What about the hypothesis that failure to use effective *memory strategies* accounts for deficits in old age? Many older adults do not spontaneously use strategies such as organization and elaboration, even though they know them and are capable of using them (Light, 1991; Smith & Earles, 1996). This may indeed be an important part of the

Many adults continue to expand their knowledge bases well into old age.

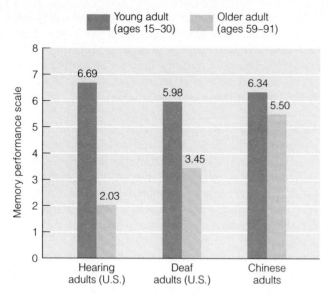

Young adult (ages 15–30)

Older adult (ages 59–91)

Figure 8.8 Declines in memory skills in old age are not universal. In deaf culture and in Chinese culture, elderly people are not stereotyped as forgetful or senile. Perhaps as a result, Chinese elders perform almost as well as young Chinese adults on memory tasks, whereas in the United States, elders, especially in the hearing population, perform poorly.

SOURCE: Adapted from Levy & Langer (1994)

problem when older adults are asked to deliberately memorize something. But *why* do many older adults fail to use effective strategies?

Basic Processing Capacities The answer may lie in our fourth hypothesis—the notion that *basic processing capacities* change with age. Which capacities? Much attention has focused on declines in the capacity to use working memory to operate actively on a lot of information simultaneously. Working memory capacity increases during childhood and adolescence, peaks at around age 45, and then begins to decline (Swanson, 1999). Moreover, an adult's working memory capacity predicts how well she or he will perform on a wide range of cognitive tasks (Engle et al., 1999; Salthouse, 1992).

Both young children and older adults, it seems, need to devote more space in working memory than older children or young adults do to carrying out basic mental operations such as recognizing stimuli (Guttentag, 1985; Kail & Salthouse, 1994). This leaves less space for other purposes, such as thinking about or rehearsing material. We have seen that both young children and older adults do relatively well when learning and remembering can take place automatically—when mental effort is *not* required—but struggle when they must exert a great deal of mental effort or carry out several activities at once. For example, research shows that trying to memorize a list of words while walking is more problematic for older adults than for middle-aged or younger adults (Li et al., 2001; Lindenberger, Marsiske, & Baltes, 2000).

Limitations in working memory capacity are most likely rooted in slower functioning of the nervous system both early and late in life (Earles & Kersten, 1999; Salthouse, 1992; also see Chapter 5). Much research tells us that speed of processing

increases during childhood and adolescence, peaks in early adulthood, and then declines slowly over the adult years (Frieske & Park, 1999; Kail & Salthouse, 1994). Much research also tells us that age differences in performance on cognitive tasks often shrink when age differences in speed of information processing are taken into account and controlled. Experience in a domain of learning can certainly enhance performance, but if children and older adults generally have sluggish "computers," they simply may not be able to keep up with the processing demands of complex learning and memory tasks (Kail & Salthouse, 1994). Slow neural transmission, then, may be behind limitations in working memory in both childhood and old age. Limitations in working memory, in turn, may contribute not only to limitations in long-term memory but also to difficulties performing a wide range of cognitive tasks, including problem-solving tasks and tests of intelligence, even those that have no time limits (Fry & Hale, 1996; Kail & Salthouse, 1994).

To this point, then, we might conclude that many older adults, although they have a vast knowledge base and a good deal of knowledge about learning and memory, experience declines in basic processing capacity that make it difficult for them to carry out memory strategies that will drain their limited working-memory capacity. But the basic processing capacity hypothesis cannot explain everything about age differences in memory (Light, 1991). We must consider some additional hypotheses, including sensory changes and a variety of contextual factors.

Sensory Changes As we learned in Chapter 6, older adults experience declines in sensory abilities. Might these affect memory performance? Yes indeed. In one study, visual and auditory skills were better predictors than processing speed of cognitive performance among older adults (Lindenberger & Baltes, 1994). We learned in Chapter 6 that many older adults experience some hearing loss. When young adults are tested under moderately noisy conditions, a situation that mimics the hearing loss experienced by many older adults, their short-term memory performance decreases (Murphy et al., 2000). Sensory loss at any age may tax available processing resources, leading to memory deficits.

Contextual Contributors Impressed by the influence of such factors as cohort differences, motivation, and task characteristics on the performance of elderly adults, many researchers are adopting a *contextual perspective* on learning and memory (Blanchard-Fields, Chen, & Norris, 1997; Dixon, 1992). They emphasize that performance on learning and memory tasks is the product of an interaction among (1) characteristics of the learner, such as goals, motivations, abilities, and health; (2) characteristics of the particular task at hand; and (3) characteristics of the broader context, including the cultural context, in which a task is performed. They are not convinced that there is a universal biological decline in basic learning and memory capacities, for older individuals often perform very capably in certain contexts.

First, *cohort differences in education and IQ* can explain age differences in some learning and memory skills in old age. Elderly people today are less educated, on average, than younger adults are, and they are further removed from their school days. In some cultures, *only* those individuals who have had formal schooling use memory strategies such as verbal rehearsal (Kuhn, 1992; Wagner, 1978). Moreover, education can compensate for aging. Older adults who are highly educated or who have high levels of intellectual ability often perform just as well as younger adults do (Cherry & LeCompte, 1999; Haught et al., 2000).

Similarly, *health and lifestyle* differences between cohorts may contribute to age differences in learning and memory. Older adults are more likely than younger adults to have chronic or degenerative diseases, and even mild diseases can impair memory performance (Houx, Vreeling, & Jolles, 1991; Hultsch, Hammer, & Small, 1993). Older adults also lead less active lifestyles and perform fewer cognitively demanding activities than younger adults do, on average. These age group differences in lifestyle also contribute to age differences in cognitive performance (Finkel & McGue, 1998; Luszcz, Bryan, & Kent, 1997). Older college professors, perhaps because they remain mentally active, outperform other older adults and equal young professors on some tests of recall (Shimamura et al., 1995).

The implications of such research are clear: Declines in information-processing skills are not inevitable or universal. Older adults may be able to maintain their memory skills quite well if they are relatively well educated, manage to stay healthy, and exercise their minds. Simply reviewing material after its presentation can help them improve their memory performance (Koutstaal et al., 1998; see the Applications box on page 212 for more ways to improve memory across the life span). At the same time, factors such as education and health cannot account completely for age differences in cognitive performance (Smith & Earles, 1996).

Older adults may also perform poorly on some cognitive tasks not because of deficient abilities but because of *motivational factors*. Motivation is important at all ages, but older adults seem to be especially likely to ask whether information is potentially useful to them before they invest energy in learning it (Schaie, 1977/1978). In one study in which adults were to learn nonsense syllables, fully 80% of the elderly subjects simply dropped out of the study; they saw no point in learning such nonsense (Hulicka, 1967)! Having a goal in mind can increase memory activities among younger adults, but it is not always motivating for older adults (West & Thorn, 2001). Older adults often get discouraged because they do not achieve the goals they set, which decreases their subsequent motivation. Overall, research suggests that older adults sometimes do poorly on cognitive tasks because of underarousal (insufficient motivation), overarousal (anxiety, especially when faced with challenging tasks), and a cautious style of responding (giving answers only when they are sure of them) (Schaie & Willis, 1996).

Finally, we must consider the hypothesis that older adults display learning and memory deficits mainly because the *kinds of tasks* that have typically been presented to them are so far removed from the everyday contexts in which they normally learn and remember (Hess & Pullen, 1996). Think about the difference between remembering a list of food terms in the laboratory and remembering what to buy at the grocery store. In learning a list, the person may have no choice but to use mental memory strategies such as organization and elaboration. But in everyday life both young and old adults rely far less on such internal strategies than on *external memory aids*—notes, lists, and the like (Cavanaugh et al., 1983). After all, why conjure up images to help you remember what to buy at the supermarket when you can simply write out a shopping list? You can even use other people as an aid to memory (Dixon, 1992); for example, you can ask your spouse to remind you to get soy sauce and have a grocery clerk help you find it!

In the everyday task of grocery shopping, the job of remembering where to find the brown sugar or the cream cheese is simplified immensely because we can draw on our previous experience in the store (our knowledge base; Blanchard-Fields et al., 1997). Moreover, items are embedded in a meaningful context (such as the baking section or the dairy section), so cues are available in the store to help us remember. In one demonstration of the importance of such contextual cues, Kathryn Waddell and Barbara Rogoff (1981) showed that elderly adults did just as well as middle-aged adults at remembering the locations of objects (toy cars, pieces of furniture, and so on) that had been placed in a meaningful landscape consisting of a parking lot, houses, a church, and other landmarks. They had difficulty only when these items were stripped of a meaningful context and placed in cubicles (see Figure 8.9 on page 214). In everyday situations, elderly adults can place new information in the context of what they already know and can make use of situational cues to help them remember. Thus, although older adults do sometimes have difficulty with everyday tasks like remembering people's names and remembering whether they locked the door or turned off the oven, they are generally able to perform much better in real life than in the lab (Hess & Pullen, 1996).

Summing Up Perhaps the truth lies somewhere between (1) the basic processing capacity view, which points to a universal decline in cognitive resources such as speed and working memory that affect performance on many cognitive tasks, and (2) the contextual view, which stresses variability from person to person and situation to situation based on cohort differences, motivational factors, and task demands. Most adults, at least if they live to an advanced old age, may well experience some loss of basic processing resources. However, they may also have developed specialized knowledge and strategies that allow them to compensate for these losses as they carry out the everyday cognitive activities most important to them (Baltes et al., 1992).

Problem Solving and Aging

We know that problem-solving skills improve steadily from early childhood through adolescence, but what becomes of

Improving Memory and Study Skills

Have you noticed that the material in this chapter has great potential value to teachers? The information-processing perspective has indeed yielded better methods for diagnosing learning problems and improving instruction. Here we'll focus on interventions aimed at boosting the memory skills of young children and older adults. Just how much can be achieved through training?

Garrett Lange and Sarah Pierce (1992) took on the challenge of teaching the memory strategy of organization (grouping) to 4- and 5-year-olds. Using pictures of objects and animals as the stimuli, they taught these preschoolers a "group-and-name trick" that involved sorting items to be learned into groups based on similarity, naming the group, naming the items within the group, and, at recall, naming the group before calling out the items within that group. Because such memory-training programs have not always been successful, these researchers also attempted to increase motivation through encouragement and praise. They even included training in metamemory: They made sure children understood the rationale for the sorting strategy, knew when it could be used, and could see firsthand that it could improve their performance.

How successful was the training? These children did virtually no sorting of items to be learned before they were trained, but they did a good deal of it after training, even seven days later. They clearly learned to use the organization strategy they were taught. They also outperformed untrained control children on measures of recall. However, the gains in recall were fairly small compared to the much larger gains in strategy use. These young children demonstrated utilization deficiencies: They could not derive full benefit from the memory strategy they were taught, possibly because they did not have the working memory capacity to carry out the strategy. Programs that teach memory strategies and metacognitive skills to elementary school children often work much better, especially with children who are underachievers and who may be capable of executing strategies but fail to do so on their own (Hattie, Biggs, & Purdie, 1996). Still, the benefits of training are often domain-specific; they do not generalize to learning tasks different from those that were the focus of training. Perhaps this makes sense if we realize that the strategies that work best in learning math skills may be quite different from the

strategies that work best in learning historical facts or basketball skills.

How well do older adults respond to attempts to teach them more effective memory strategies? Although a number of studies have shown that such training can be very effective (Verhaeghen, Marcoen, & Goossens, 1992), there are limits. Consider the interesting work of Paul Baltes and his colleagues (Baltes et al., 1992). In one study (Kliegl, Smith, & Baltes, 1989), these researchers trained young adults (ages 19–29) and elderly adults (ages 65–83) in a mnemonic technique called the **method of loci.** It involves devising a mental map of a route through a familiar place (such as one's home) and then creating images that link items to be learned to landmarks along the route. For example, the German adults in the study were taught to associate words on word lists with 40 well-known landmarks in West Berlin; they continued to practice for many sessions so that their maximal level of performance could be assessed.

The accomplishments of these adults were quite remarkable, as Figure A shows. Older adults improved from

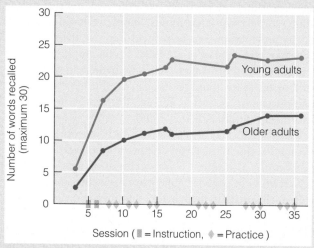

Figure A Trained to use the method of loci and then given many practice sessions, young adults improved their ability to recall word lists more than older adults did, suggesting that aging places limits on maximal performance. Still, elderly adults benefited considerably from training in this memory strategy.

Source: Baltes & Kliegl (1992)

them in adulthood? On the one hand, we might expect to see a decline in problem-solving prowess paralleling declines in learning and memory performance. On the other hand, if adults increase their knowledge bases and develop expertise as

they get older, might not older adults outwit younger novices on many problem-solving tasks?

When given traditional problem-solving tasks to perform in the laboratory, young adults typically perform better than

recalling fewer than 3 words in correct order after hearing a 30-word list only once to recalling 10 words, and young adults upped their performance even more, from 6 to 20 words. These findings tell us that there is a great deal of cognitive plasticity and potential throughout the life span. As Baltes and his colleagues put it, older adults have considerable "reserve capacity" that can be tapped through intensive training. Indeed, despite limitations in basic processing capacity, older adults can master powerful memory techniques that enable them to outperform young adults who have not learned and practiced these techniques. Memory training programs can also improve aspects of metamemory, particularly elders' negative beliefs about their memory capacities (Floyd & Scogin, 1997).

At the same time, this study and others show that older adults, especially those who have experienced steep cognitive declines, profit less from memory training than young adults do (Verhaeghen & Marcoen, 1996). And both children and elderly adults coached to use memory strategies often fail to use them in new learning situations, perhaps because these strategies simply require too much mental effort (Pressley et al., 1985; Storandt, 1992).

What, then, is the solution? If some memory strategies are too mentally taxing for many young children and elderly adults, it may make more sense to capitalize on their memory strengths. Knowing that implicit memory holds up better than explicit memory, for example, Cameron Camp and his colleagues (Camp et al., 1996; Camp & McKitrick, 1992) have tried to help patients with dementia caused by Alzheimer's disease make use of the implicit memory capacities that they, like people with amnesia, retain even though they have serious deficits in explicit memory. For example, they have taught patients with Alzheimer's disease to remember the names of staff members by having the patients name photos of staff members repeatedly and at ever longer intervals between trials. People who could not retain names for more than a minute were able to recall them weeks later after training. The technique appears to work because it makes use of implicit memory processes; adults learn quite effortlessly when they repeatedly encounter the material to be learned.

Finally, it sometimes makes more sense to change the learning environment than to change the learner (Pressley, 1983). If, for example, young children and some older adults do not spontaneously organize the material they are learning to make it more meaningful, one can organize it for them. Indeed, giving children practice at learning highly organized material can help them master the grouping strategy on their own (Best, 1993). Similarly, if the material to be learned is unfamiliar, one can use examples or analogies that will help learners relate it to something that *is* familiar (for example, teaching a senior citizens' group about the federal budget by likening it to their personal budgets). If young children and older adults need more time, let them set their own pace.

To use a real-world example, it turns out that older adults have more trouble understanding and remembering information about their drug prescriptions than young adults do (Morrell, Park, & Poon, 1989). Yet by writing clear, organized instructions and spending time explaining to older patients what they are to do, health-care professionals can simplify the learning task (Morrell et al., 1989). Alternatively, older adults can be given external memory aids. Denise Park and her colleagues (1992) explored the benefits of two such aids: an organization chart (a poster or pocket-sized table giving an hour-by-hour account of when drugs should be taken) and a medication organizer (a dispenser with columns for different days of the week and pill compartments for times of the day). Adults over 70 more often took their pills correctly when they were given both the chart and the organizer than when they were given one or the other or neither. Because we know that poor health is one contributor to poor memory functioning, it makes especially good sense to reduce the cognitive demands on old and ailing patients by letting external memory aids do the mental work for them. Surely the best of all possible worlds for the learner would be one in which materials and teaching techniques are tailored to the learner's information-processing capacities *and* training is offered in how to stretch those capacities.

middle-aged adults, who in turn outperform older adults (Denney, 1989). However, consider research using the Twenty Questions task. Subjects are given an array of items and asked to find out, using as few yes–no questions as possible, which item the experimenter has in mind (see Figure 8.10). The soundest problem-solving strategy is to ask **constraint-seeking questions**—ones that rule out more than one item (for example, "Is it an animal?"). Young children and older

Figure 8.9 Older adults are even more likely than younger adults to remember the locations of items better when they are placed in the context of a meaningful landscape (left) than when they are placed in cubicles (right). The contextual perspective on information processing reminds us that older adults can perform well or poorly depending on the nature of the task they confront.

SOURCE: Waddell & Rogoff (1981)

Figure 8.10 A Twenty Questions game. You can try it on a young child or a friend by thinking of one item in the group and asking your testee to find out which it is by asking you yes–no questions. Look for the constraint-seeking questions (for example, "Is it animate?"), and note the total number of questions required to identify the correct item.

adults tend to pursue specific hypotheses instead ("Is it a pig?" "Is it a pencil?"). Consequently, they must ask more questions to identify the right object. However, older adults do far better if the task is altered to make it more familiar; they then draw on their knowledge base to solve the problem. For example, when Denney (1980) used an array of playing cards, older adults asked plenty of constraint-seeking questions ("Is it a heart?" "Is it a face card?"). Thus, older adults are capable of using effective problem-solving strategies but do not use them in some contexts, especially when given unfamiliar tasks in a laboratory.

What if adults are asked to deal with real-life problems like grease fires in the kitchen, warm refrigerators, or family squabbles? Nancy Denney and Kathy Pearce (1989) asked elderly adults to help them devise everyday problems that would be meaningful and familiar to older individuals. One problem was to generate ideas about how a 65-year-old recently widowed woman could improve her social life; another was to advise an elderly couple living on Social Security what to do when they were unable to pay their heating bill one winter. On these everyday problems, performance increased from early adulthood to middle age and declined in old age.

Other findings echo this one: When given everyday problems to which they can apply the expertise they have gained through experience, middle-aged adults often outperform young adults. Elderly adults sometimes equal and sometimes do worse than young and middle-aged adults; either way, they show smaller deficits than they do on unfamiliar problems in the laboratory (Berg & Klaczynski, 1996; Marsiske & Willis, 1995). Ultimately, declines in basic capacities may limit the problem-solving skills of many elderly adults, not only in the laboratory but in real life as well (Denney, 1989; Kasworm & Medina, 1990). We should bear in mind, though, that cognitive competence among older adults varies widely because of differences in health, education, experience, and so on.

In sum, we get much the same message about problem-solving skills that we got about memory capacities. Although performance on unfamiliar, meaningless laboratory tasks often appears to decline after early adulthood, the ability to perform more familiar, everyday information-processing tasks often improves through middle age and is maintained until quite late in life. Once again, this supports a contextual view of cognition: The gap between age groups can be wide or nonexistent, depending on what a problem-solving task demands and whether it allows the problem solver to make use of his or her expertise.

Some cognitive researchers believe that what appear to be cognitive deficits in old age may actually be signs of cognitive adaptation and growth (Dixon, 1992; Perlmutter, 1986). Older adults may let little-needed cognitive skills grow rusty in order to maintain and strengthen those skills that are most useful to them in everyday life. They may use their expertise in important domains to compensate for losses in basic processing capacities (Baltes et al., 1992). Children improve their ability to do all kinds of things; older adults may improve their ability to perform critical learning, memory, and problem-solving tasks and forget the rest!

Summary Points

1. The information-processing approach uses a computer analogy to illustrate how the mind processes information. The human "computer" takes in information into a sensory register, short-term and working memory, and long-term memory during encoding; stores it; retrieves it (demonstrating recognition, cued recall, or recall memory); and uses it to solve problems.

2. Infants are capable of remembering from the start. They show recognition memory at birth, simple recall in the presence of cues at 2 or 3 months, recall in the absence of cues toward the end of the first year, and deliberate, conscious attempts to retrieve memories by age 2.

3. Learning and memory continue to improve during childhood: (a) Basic information-processing capacity increases as the brain matures and fundamental processes are automatized to free working-memory space; (b) memory strategies such as rehearsal, organization, and elaboration improve; (c) metamemory improves; and (d) general knowledge base grows, improving the processing of new information in areas of expertise.

4. Much of what we remember is autobiographical. Even though infants and toddlers show evidence of memory, older children and adults often experience childhood amnesia, or lack of memory for events that happened during infancy and early childhood. Possible explanations for this include lack of working memory space, lack of language, lack of a sense of self, and the storing of events as verbatim rather than gist accounts in early life.

5. Scripts of daily routines facilitate retrieval of memory and provide guidelines for how to behave in similar settings. Eyewitness memory is influenced by scripts as well as by method of questioning.

6. According to Siegler, even young children use systematic rules to solve problems, but their problem-solving skills improve as they replace faulty rules with ones that incorporate all the relevant aspects of the problem. Multiple strategies are used at any age, so that development proceeds through a natural selection process and resembles overlapping waves more than a set of stair steps leading from one way of thinking to the next.

7. Adolescents master advanced learning strategies such as elaboration, note taking, and underlining; use their strategies more deliberately and selectively; and use their increased metacognitive abilities to guide learning and remembering.

8. As adults gain expertise in a domain, they develop large and organized knowledge bases as well as highly effective, specialized, and automatized ways of retrieving and using their knowledge.

9. Many older adults, though not all, perform less well than young adults on learning and memory tasks that require speed, the learning of unfamiliar or meaningless material, the use of unexercised abilities, recall rather than recognition memory, and implicit rather than explicit memory.

10. Older adults retain their knowledge base well and have only limited deficiencies in metamemory, though their performance can be hurt by negative beliefs about memory and aging. Late-life decreases in processing speed and working memory capacity may limit the use of memory strategies and hurt performance. According to the contextual perspective, factors such as cohort differences, low motivation, and the irrelevance of many laboratory tasks to everyday life also contribute to age differences in learning and memory.

11. On average, older adults also perform less well than younger adults on laboratory problem-solving tasks, but everyday problem-solving skills are likely to improve from early adulthood to middle adulthood and to be maintained fairly well in old age.

12. The information-processing approach can be applied to improve education. Memory-skills training can benefit both young children and elderly adults. However, since transfer to new situations does not always occur, altering instruction to better match the capacities of the learner is also appropriate.

Critical Thinking

1. You are a first-grade teacher, and one of the first things you notice is that some of your students remember a good deal more than others about the stories you read to them. Based on what you have read in this chapter, what are your main hypotheses about why some children have better memories than other children the same age?

2. As a teacher in an ElderHostel program, you want to base your teaching methods on knowledge of the information-processing capacities of elderly adults. What practical recommendations would you derive from (1) the view that there is a universal decline with age in basic processing capacities and (2) the contextual perspective on cognitive aging?

Key Terms

information-processing approach	organization (as memory strategy)
sensory register	elaboration
short-term memory	utilization deficiency
working memory	metamemory
long-term memory	metacognition
encoding	knowledge base
storage	autobiographical memories
retrieval	childhood (infantile) amnesia
recognition memory	fuzzy-trace theory
recall memory	scripts
cued recall memory	eyewitness memory
implicit memory	rule assessment approach
explicit memory	mild cognitive impairment (MCI)
problem solving	method of loci
executive control processes	constraint-seeking questions
rehearsal	

On the Web

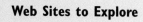

Web Sites to Explore

Memory and Aging

Site of UCLA's Memory and Aging Research Center, with links to scholarly information.
http://www.memory.ucla.edu/

Formation of Memories

From the American Psychological Association's Monitor, a nice summary of how children form memories.
http://www.snc.edu/psychkorshavn/child01.htm

Implicit and Explicit Memory

For those seeking greater depth, here is a scholarly article outlining a new theoretical framework for explicit and implicit memory.
http://psyche.cs.monash.edu.au/v3/psyche-3-02-mayes.html

Memory Loss and the Brain

The Newsletter of the Memory Disorders Project at Rutgers–Newark provides information about many of the issues covered in the chapter, including mild cognitive impairment. http://www.memory.rutgers.edu/newsletter/glossary/mci.html

Search Online with InfoTrac College Edition

For additional information, explore InfoTrac College Edition, your online library. Go to http://www.infotrac-college.com and use the passcode that came on the card with your book. Try searching for "metacognition" to locate John Flavell's 1999 *Annual Review* article, "Cognitive Development: Children's Knowledge about the Mind." Summarize what is known about children's knowledge about the mind, and indicate how researchers have studied children's "metaknowledge." In another search, use the phrase "problem solving in children" to locate several articles on teaching problem-solving skills to children. What methods work best?

Visit Our Web Site

Go to http://www.wadsworth.com/psychology, where you will find online resources directly linked to your book.

Life-Span CD-ROM

Go to the Wadsworth Life-Span CD-ROM for further study of the concepts in this chapter. The CD-ROM also includes quizzes and additional activities to expand your learning experience.

Intelligence and Creativity

GREG SMITH WAS MEMORIZING BOOKS at 14 months of age and adding numbers at 18 months (Lenhart, 1999). He sped from second to eighth grade in one year and completed high school in just under two years. He started college full-time when he was 10 years old and hopes to eventually earn three doctoral degrees.

At the age of 35, Michael lives in an institution for the mentally retarded. He has been labeled profoundly retarded and has an IQ score of 17, as nearly as it can be estimated. Michael responds to people with grins and is able to walk haltingly, but he cannot feed or dress himself and does not use language.

Some gifted children thrive as college students. Some minds develop faster and farther than others.

As these examples indicate, the range of human cognitive abilities is immense. So far, our exploration of cognitive development has focused mainly on what human minds have in common, not on how they differ. Piaget, after all, was interested in identifying *universal* stages of cognitive development. And the information-processing approach has been used mainly to understand the basic cognitive processes *all* people rely on to learn, remember, and solve problems.

This chapter continues our exploration of how the human mind normally changes over the life span. Here we introduce still another approach to the study of the mind: the *psychometric*, or testing, approach to intelligence, which led to the creation of intelligence tests. Many people find it hard to say anything nice about IQ tests. These measures do indeed have their limitations, and they have been misused. Yet they

---

Table 9.1   What Do You Know about Intelligence and Creativity?

Answer each question true or false.

1. On the leading tests of intelligence, a score of 100 is average.
2. Most scholars now conclude that there is no such thing as general intelligence; there are only separate mental abilities.
3. Individuals who are intellectually gifted are typically gifted in all mental abilities.
4. Intellectually gifted children do well in school but are more likely than most children to have social and emotional problems.
5. IQ predicts both a person's occupational status and his or her success compared to others in the same occupation.
6. On average, performance on IQ tests declines for people in their 70s and 80s.
7. Qualities we associate with "wisdom" are as common among young and middle-aged adults as among elderly adults.
8. It has been established that children's IQs are far more influenced by their environments than by their genes.
9. How well a child does on a test of creativity cannot be predicted very well from his or her IQ score.
10. Creative achievers (great musicians, mathematicians, writers, and so on) typically do all their great works before about age 40 or 45 and produce only lesser works from then on.

Answers: 1-T, 2-F, 3-F, 4-F, 5-T, 6-T, 7-T, 8-F, 9-T, 10-F

have also told us a good deal about intellectual development and about variations in intellectual performance. This chapter examines how performance on intelligence tests typically changes and stays the same over the life span, what IQ tests tell us about a person, and why people's IQ scores differ. It also looks at both gifted and mentally retarded individuals from a life-span perspective. Finally, it considers creativity, a type of intellectual ability not measured by intelligence tests. Before going further, take the quiz in Table 9.1 to see if you may have some misconceptions about intelligence and intelligence tests; this chapter will clarify why the correct answers are correct.

What Is Intelligence?

There is no clear consensus about what intelligence is. Piaget defined intelligence as "adaptive thinking or action" (Piaget, 1950). Other experts have offered different definitions, many of them centering in some way on the ability to think abstractly or to solve problems effectively (Sternberg, 2000). Early definitions of intelligence tended to reflect the assumption that intelligence is innate intellectual ability, genetically determined and thus fixed at conception. But it has now become clear that intelligence is *not* fixed, that it is changeable and subject to environmental influence (Perkins, 1996). As a result, an individual's intelligence test scores sometimes vary considerably over a lifetime. Bear in mind that our understanding of this complex human quality has changed since the first intelligence tests were created at the turn of the century—and that there is still no single, universally accepted definition of intelligence.

The Psychometric Approach

The research tradition that spawned the development of standardized tests of intelligence is the **psychometric approach** (Thorndike, 1997). According to psychometric theorists, intelligence is a trait or a set of traits that characterizes some people to a greater extent than others. The goals, then, are to identify these traits precisely and to measure them so that differences among individuals can be described. But, from the start, experts could not agree on whether intelligence is one general cognitive ability or many specific abilities.

A SINGLE ATTRIBUTE OR MANY ATTRIBUTES?

One way of trying to determine whether intelligence is a single ability or many abilities is to ask people to perform a large number of mental tasks and then to analyze their performance using a statistical procedure called **factor analysis.** This technique identifies clusters of tasks or test items (called *factors*) that are highly correlated with one another but unrelated to other clusters of items. Suppose, for example, that the items given to a group of people include many that require verbal skills (for example, defining words) and many that require mathematical skills (solving arithmetic puzzles). Now suppose that people who do well on any verbal item also do well on other verbal items, and those who do well on any math problem also do well on other math problems. Further suppose that people who do well on verbal problems may or may not perform well on math problems, and vice versa. In this case, math performance does not correlate highly with verbal performance, and factor analysis would reveal a "verbal ability factor" that is distinct from a "math ability factor." If, by contrast, correlations among the items revealed that those people who do well on any item in the test tend to do well on others as well, it would seem that one general ability factor underlies performance on both verbal and math problems.

Charles Spearman (1927) was among the first to use factor analysis to try to determine whether intelligence is one or many abilities. He concluded that a general mental ability (called *g*) exists and contributes to performance on many different kinds of tasks. However, he also noticed that a student who excelled at most tasks might also score very low on a particular measure (for example, memory for words). So he proposed that intelligence has two aspects: *g*, or general ability, and *s*, or special abilities, each of which is specific to a particular kind of task.

When Louis Thurstone (1938; Thurstone & Thurstone, 1941) factor-analyzed test scores obtained by eighth-graders and college students, he identified seven fairly distinct factors that he called *primary mental abilities:* spatial ability, perceptual speed (the quick noting of visual detail), numerical reasoning (arithmetic skills), verbal meaning (defining of words), word fluency (speed in recognizing words), memory,

and inductive reasoning (formation of a rule to describe a set of observations). Thus, Thurstone concluded that Spearman's general ability factor should be broken into several distinct mental abilities.

The controversy was not over. J. P. Guilford (1967, 1988) proposed that there are at least 120 distinct mental abilities! According to his **structure-of-intellect model,** there are four kinds of intellectual *contents* (things that people can think about, such as sights, ideas, or the behaviors of other people); five types of mental *operations* or actions that can be performed on these contents (such as recognizing, remembering, or evaluating); and six kinds of intellectual *products* or outcomes of thinking (such as a concept or an inference). Simple multiplication tells us that there are $4 \times 5 \times 6 = 120$ possible combinations of the contents, operations, and products. Guilford's model, perhaps because of its complexity, has never really been put to the test (N. Brody, 2000).

FLUID VERSUS CRYSTALLIZED INTELLIGENCE

Raymond Cattell and John Horn have greatly influenced current thinking concerning intelligence by focusing attention on two broad dimensions of intellect: fluid intelligence and crystallized intelligence (Cattell, 1963; Horn & Cattell, 1967; Horn & Noll, 1997). **Fluid intelligence** is the ability to use one's mind actively to solve novel problems—for example, to solve verbal analogies, remember unrelated pairs of words, or recognize relationships among geometric figures. The skills involved—reasoning, seeing relationships among stimuli, drawing inferences—are usually not taught and are believed to be relatively free of cultural influences (see Figure 9.1). **Crystallized intelligence,** in contrast, is the use of knowledge

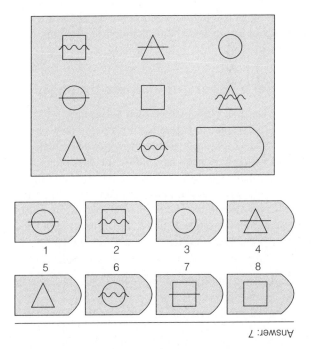

Answer: 7

Figure 9.1 An item assessing fluid intelligence (similar to those in a test called the Raven Progressive Matrices Test). Which of the numbered pieces completes the design?

acquired through schooling and other life experiences. Tests of general information ("At what temperature does water boil?"), word comprehension ("What is the meaning of *duplicate*?"), and numerical abilities are all measures of crystallized intelligence. Thus, fluid intelligence involves using one's mind in new and flexible ways, whereas crystallized intelligence involves using what one has already learned through experience.

Obviously, the use of factor analysis has not exactly settled the question of what intelligence is. Much depends on what tasks are given to test takers and how the resulting patterns of correlations are interpreted. Nonetheless, some consensus is emerging today. Intelligence is most often viewed as a hierarchy that includes (1) a general ability factor at the top that influences how well people do on a wide range of cognitive tasks, (2) a few broad dimensions of ability that are distinguishable from one another in factor analyses (for example, fluid intelligence, crystallized intelligence, memory capacity, perceptual skills, and processing speed), and (3) at the bottom, a large number of specific abilities such as numerical reasoning, spatial discrimination, and word comprehension that also influence just how well a person performs specific cognitive tasks that tap these specific abilities (Carroll, 1993; Horn & Noll, 1997).

The concepts of general ability, fluid and crystallized intelligence, and a hierarchy of abilities have proved useful, but in the end, the intelligence tests guided by psychometric theories have emphasized general intellectual ability by summarizing performance in a single IQ score, and they have assessed only some of the specialized abilities that humans possess. Critics believe these tests have not fully described what it means to be an intelligent person. Let's examine two ways of thinking about intelligence that represent challenges to the traditional view that guided the development of intelligence tests. Doing so will help us capture the nature of intelligence and help us appreciate the limitations of the tests used to measure it.

Gardner's Theory of Multiple Intelligences

Howard Gardner (1983, 1999; Chen & Gardner, 1997) rejects the idea that a single IQ score is a meaningful measure of human intelligence. He argues that there are many intelligences, most of which have been ignored by the developers of standardized intelligence tests. Instead of asking "How smart are you?" we should be asking "How are you smart?" and identifying people's strengths and weaknesses across the full range of human mental faculties (Chen & Gardner, 1997). Gardner (1983, 1999) argues that there are at least eight distinct intellectual abilities:

1. **Linguistic intelligence**—language skills, as seen in the poet's facility with words
2. **Logical-mathematical intelligence**—the abstract thinking and problem solving shown by mathematicians and computer scientists and emphasized by Piaget
3. **Musical intelligence**—based on an acute sensitivity to sound patterns

Pam Driscol Gallery, CO

Alonzo Clemons has trouble with some of the basic tasks of living, but he can quickly sculpt incredibly detailed and accurate replicas of animals that he has seen only briefly.

4. **Spatial intelligence**—most obvious in great artists who can perceive things accurately and transform what they see
5. **Bodily-kinesthetic intelligence**—the skillful use of the body to create crafts, perform, or fix things; shown, for example, by dancers, athletes, and surgeons
6. **Interpersonal intelligence**—social intelligence, social skill, exceptional sensitivity to other people's motivations and moods; demonstrated by salespersons and psychologists
7. **Intrapersonal intelligence**—understanding of one's own feelings and inner life
8. **Naturalist intelligence**—expertise in the natural world of plants and animals

Gardner has considered additional intelligences such as spiritual, existential, and moral, but so far has concluded that these do not meet all the criteria for being distinct intelligences.

Traditional IQ tests emphasize linguistic and logical-mathematical intelligence, and to some extent spatial intelligence, perhaps because those are the forms of intelligence Western societies value most highly and work the hardest to nurture in school. But IQ tests can be faulted for ignoring most of the other forms of intelligence. Although Gardner does not claim that his is *the* definitive list of intelligences, he does present evidence suggesting that each of these eight abilities is distinct. For example, it is clear that a person can be exceptional in one ability but poor in others—witness **savant syndrome,** the phenomenon in which extraordinary talent in a particular area is displayed by a person who is otherwise mentally retarded (Treffert, 2000). Leslie Lemke, one such individual, is blind, has cerebral palsy, is mentally retarded, and could not talk until he was an adult (Treffert, 2000). Yet he can hear a musical piece once and play it flawlessly on the piano or imitate songs in perfect German or Italian even though his own speech is still primitive. Other savants, despite IQs below 70, can draw well enough to gain admittance to art school or calculate on the spot what day of the week it was January 16, 1909 (O'Connor & Hermelin, 1991). Some scholars think that the skills shown by savants are so specific and depend so much on memory that they do not really qualify as separate "intelligences" (Nettelbeck & Young, 1996). However, Gardner insists that savant syndrome simply cannot be explained by theories that emphasize a general intelligence factor, g.

Gardner also marshals evidence to show that each intelligence has its own distinctive developmental course. Many of the great musical composers and athletes, for example, revealed their genius in childhood, whereas exceptional logical-mathematical intelligence typically shows up later, after the individual has gained the capacity for abstract thought and has mastered an area of science. Finally, Gardner links his distinct intelligences to distinct structures in the brain, arguing that the eight intelligences are neurologically distinct as well.

Sternberg's Triarchic Theory

Agreeing with Gardner that traditional IQ tests do not capture all that it means to be an intelligent person, Robert Sternberg (1985, 1988) has proposed a **triarchic theory of intelligence** that emphasizes three aspects of intelligent behavior: contextual, experiential, and information-processing components (see Figure 9.2).

CONTEXTUAL COMPONENT

First, Sternberg argues that what is defined as intelligent behavior depends on the sociocultural *context* in which it is displayed. Sternberg (1999) reports a study in which he and a colleague tested the analogical reasoning skills of second-graders who were in a school where instruction was conducted in English in the morning and in Hebrew in the afternoon. Some children got all of the problems wrong, suggesting that they were not very bright. However, the children had been tested with English problems in the afternoon when they normally would have received problems in Hebrew; consequently, the children read the problems from right to left. In their normal classroom context, this would have been a very smart thing to do. Thus, Sternberg argues that what is defined as intelligent behavior depends on the sociocultural context in which it is displayed. Intelligent people adapt to the environment they are in (for example, a job setting), shape that environment to make it suit them better, or find a better environment. Such people have "street smarts." Psychologists, according to Sternberg, must begin to understand intelligence as behavior in the real world, not as behavior in taking tests (Sternberg et al., 1995).

This perspective views intelligent behavior as varying from one culture or subculture to another, from one period in

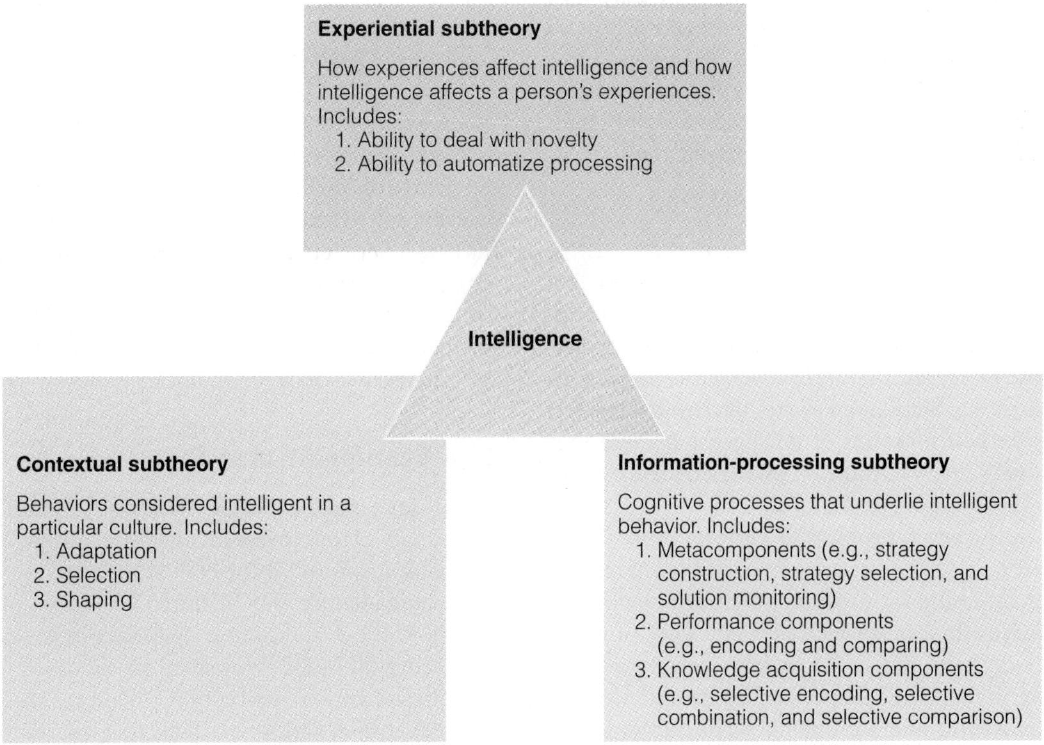

Experiential subtheory

How experiences affect intelligence and how intelligence affects a person's experiences. Includes:
1. Ability to deal with novelty
2. Ability to automatize processing

Intelligence

Contextual subtheory

Behaviors considered intelligent in a particular culture. Includes:
1. Adaptation
2. Selection
3. Shaping

Information-processing subtheory

Cognitive processes that underlie intelligent behavior. Includes:
1. Metacomponents (e.g., strategy construction, strategy selection, and solution monitoring)
2. Performance components (e.g., encoding and comparing)
3. Knowledge acquisition components (e.g., selective encoding, selective combination, and selective comparison)

Figure 9.2 Sternberg's triarchic theory of intelligence

How would you define an intelligent child? Mexican American parents, like Cambodian, Filipino, and Vietnamese parents, say that the intelligent child is motivated, socially skilled, and able to manage his or her own behavior. European American parents place less emphasis on these noncognitive aspects of intelligence (Okagaki & Sternberg, 1993). Each cultural group defines intelligence in its own way.

history to another, and from one period of the life span to another. Each culture or subculture defines the ingredients of intelligent behavior in its own way (J. G. Miller, 1997). The challenge, then, is to devise ways of measuring intelligence that are appropriate across cultures.

Sternberg also notes that what is intelligent can change over time. Numerical abilities may not play as important a role in intelligent behavior now that calculators and computers are widely used, for example, whereas analytical skills may be more important than ever in a complex, urban world. And certainly the infant learning how to master new toys shows a different kind of intelligence than the adult mastering a college curriculum. Thus, our definition of the intelligent infant must differ from our definition of the intelligent adult.

EXPERIENTIAL COMPONENT

The second aspect of the triarchic theory focuses on the role of *experience* in intelligence. What is intelligent when one first encounters a new task is not the same as what is intelligent after extensive experience with that task. The first kind of intelligence, *response to novelty*, requires active and conscious information processing. Sternberg believes that relatively novel tasks provide the best measures of intelligence because they tap the individual's ability to come up with good ideas or fresh insights.

In daily life, however, people also perform more or less intelligently on tasks they have done over and over (reading the newspaper, for example). This second kind of intelligence reflects **automatization,** or an increased efficiency of information processing with practice. It is intelligent to develop little "programs in the mind" for performing common, everyday activities efficiently and unthinkingly. Thus, according to Sternberg, it is crucial to know how familiar a task is to a person in order to assess that person's behavior. For example,

giving people of two different cultural groups an intelligence test whose items are familiar to one group and novel to the other introduces **culture bias** into the testing process, making it difficult to obtain a fair assessment of the groups' relative abilities.

INFORMATION-PROCESSING COMPONENT

The third aspect of the triarchic theory focuses on *information-processing components.* As an information-processing theorist, Sternberg believes that the theories of intelligence underlying the development of IQ tests ignore *how* people produce intelligent answers. He argues that the components of intelligent behavior range from identifying the problem to carrying out strategies to solve it; a full picture of intelligence includes not only the number of answers people get right but also the processes they use to arrive at their answers and the efficiency with which they use those processes.

So, to fully assess how intelligent people are, we must consider the *context* in which they perform (their age, culture, and historical period); their previous *experience* with a task (whether their behavior reflects response to novelty or automatized processes); and their *information-processing* strategies. Individuals who are intelligent, according to this triarchic model, are able to carry out logical thought processes efficiently and effectively in order to solve both novel and familiar problems and adapt to their environment. Unfortunately, today's widely used tests of intelligence do not reflect this sophisticated view of intelligence.

How Is Intelligence Measured?

When psychologists first began to devise intelligence tests at the turn of the century, their concern was not with defining the nature of intelligence but with the more practical task of determining which schoolchildren were likely to be slow learners—and doing so in a way that would be less biased than letting teachers judge the matter (Thorndike, 1997). Consequently, many tests had no precisely defined theory of intelligence behind them and were originally intended to assess intelligence in children, not in adults.

The Stanford-Binet Test

Alfred Binet and a colleague, Theodore Simon, produced the forerunner of our modern intelligence tests. In 1904, they were commissioned by the French government to devise a test that would identify "dull" children who might need special instruction. Binet and Simon devised a large battery of tasks measuring the skills believed to be necessary for classroom learning: attention, perception, memory, reasoning, verbal comprehension, and so on. Items that discriminated between normal children and those described by their teachers as slow were kept in the final test.

The test was soon revised to make the items *age graded.* For example, a set of "6-year-old" items could be passed by most 6-year-olds but few 5-year-olds; "12-year-old" items could be handled by most 12-year-olds but not by younger children. This approach permitted the testers to describe a child's **mental age (MA)**—the level of age-graded problems that the child is able to solve. Thus, a child who passes all items at the 5-year-old level but does poorly on more advanced items—regardless of the child's actual age—is said to have an MA of 5.

Binet's influence is still with us in the form of the modern Stanford-Binet Intelligence Scale. In 1916, Lewis Terman of Stanford University translated and published a revised version of Binet's test for use with American children. It contained age-graded items for ages 3 to 13. Moreover, Terman made use of a procedure that had been developed for comparing mental age to chronological age. It is one thing to have a mental age of 10 when one is chronologically only 8, but another thing entirely to have that same mental age when one is 15. The **intelligence quotient,** or **IQ,** was originally calculated by dividing mental age by chronological age and then multiplying by 100: $IQ = MA/CA \times 100$. An IQ score of 100 indicates average intelligence, regardless of a child's age: The normal child passes just the items that age-mates typically pass; mental age increases each year, but so does chronological age. The child of 8 with a mental age of 10 has experienced rapid intellectual growth and has a high IQ (specifically, 125); the child of 15 with a mental age of 10 has an IQ of only 67 and is clearly below average compared to children of the same age.

The Stanford-Binet, now in its 4th edition, is still in use (Thorndike, Hagen, & Sattler, 1986). Its **test norms**—standards of normal performance expressed as average scores and the range of scores around the average—are based on the performance of a large, representative sample of people (2-year-olds through adults) from many socioeconomic and racial backgrounds. The concept of mental age is no longer used to calculate IQ; instead, individuals receive scores that reflect how well or how poorly they do as compared with others of the same age. An IQ of 100 is still average, and the higher the IQ score an individual attains, the better the performance is in comparison to age-mates.

The Wechsler Scales

David Wechsler constructed a set of intelligence tests that is also in wide use. The Wechsler Preschool and Primary Scale of Intelligence (WPPSI) is for children between the ages of 3 and 8 (Wechsler, 1989). The Wechsler Intelligence Scale for Children (WISC-III) is appropriate for schoolchildren ages 6 to 16 (Wechsler, 1991), and the Wechsler Adult Intelligence Scale-Revised (WAIS-R) is used with adults (Wechsler, 1981). The Wechsler tests yield a *verbal IQ* score based on items measuring vocabulary, general knowledge, arithmetic reasoning, and the like, as well as a *performance IQ* based on such nonverbal skills as the ability to assemble puzzles, solve mazes, reproduce geometric designs with colored blocks, and rearrange pictures to tell a meaningful story (see Figure 9.3). As

with the Stanford-Binet, a score of 100 is defined as average performance for one's age. A person's *full-scale IQ* is a combination of the verbal and performance scores.

The Distribution of IQ Scores

To more fully interpret an IQ score of 130 or 85, it helps to know how IQ scores are distributed in the population at large. Scores for large groups of people form a **normal distribution,** or a symmetrical, bell-shaped spread around the average score of 100 (see Figure 9.4). Scores around the average are common; very high and very low scores are rare. About two-thirds of us have IQs between 85 and 115. Fewer than 3% have scores of 130 or above, a score that has often been used as one criterion of giftedness. Similarly, fewer than 3% have IQs below 70, a cutoff that is commonly used today to define mental retardation.

Intelligence Testing Today

Traditional IQ tests continue to be used, and new ones are continually being developed. However, some scholars, disenchanted with the way in which intelligence has traditionally been defined and measured, have sought to develop entirely new approaches to intellectual assessment.

Dismayed by the lack of theory guiding traditional intelligence tests, Alan Kaufman, for example, designed the Kaufman Assessment Battery for Children (K-ABC; Kaufman & Kaufman, 1983). This test, based on information-processing theory, focuses on *how* children solve problems rather than on what problems they solve (Kaufman, 2001; Sparrow & Davis, 2000). The K-ABC, which is appropriate for children ages 2 through 12, has two subscales. One measures a child's ability to process information sequentially; the other measures the ability to integrate several pieces of information. The test also has a separate section of questions to assess children's achievement, or acquired knowledge.

Another promising approach, called **dynamic assessment,** attempts to evaluate how well children learn new material when an examiner provides them with competent instruction (Campione et al., 1984; Lidz, 1997). Reuven Feuerstein and his colleagues, for example, have argued that, even though intelligence is often defined as the *potential* to learn from experience, IQ tests typically assess *what has been learned,* not what can be learned (Feuerstein, Feuerstein, & Gross, 1997). This approach may be biased against children from culturally different or disadvantaged backgrounds who lack opportunities to learn what the tests measure.

Feuerstein developed the Learning Potential Assessment Device to assess children's ability to learn new things with the guidance of an adult who provides increasingly helpful cues. This test interprets intelligence as the ability to learn quickly with minimal guidance. Feuerstein believes that learners first need a "mediator," a guide who structures and interprets the environment for them, and are then able to learn more from their experiences on their own. This approach should remind you of Lev Vygotsky's theory, described in Chapter 7, that

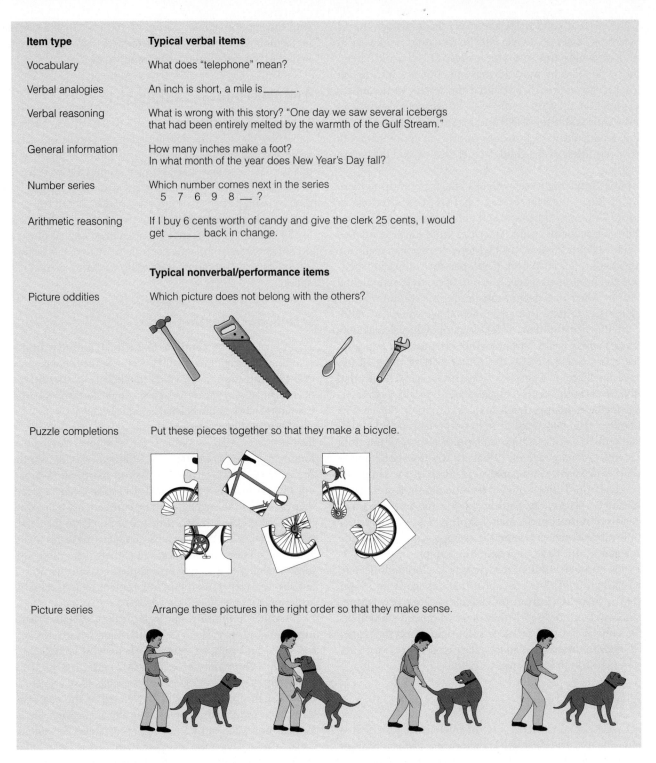

Item type	Typical verbal items
Vocabulary	What does "telephone" mean?
Verbal analogies	An inch is short, a mile is _____.
Verbal reasoning	What is wrong with this story? "One day we saw several icebergs that had been entirely melted by the warmth of the Gulf Stream."
General information	How many inches make a foot? In what month of the year does New Year's Day fall?
Number series	Which number comes next in the series 5 7 6 9 8 __ ?
Arithmetic reasoning	If I buy 6 cents worth of candy and give the clerk 25 cents, I would get _____ back in change.

Typical nonverbal/performance items

Picture oddities	Which picture does not belong with the others?
Puzzle completions	Put these pieces together so that they make a bicycle.
Picture series	Arrange these pictures in the right order so that they make sense.

Figure 9.3 Items similar to those appearing on the Wechsler intelligence test for children

Source: Shaffer (1996)

children acquire new ways of thinking through their social interactions with more experienced problem solvers; it is based in part on Vygotsky's work. The dynamic assessment of learning capacity provides information over and above what traditional IQ tests provide about a child's intellectual competence and likely achievement (J. D. Day et al., 1997; Lidz, 1997).

Still another recent approach to intelligence testing is the Cognitive Assessment System (CAS), which is based on the Planning, Attention, Simultaneous, and Successive (PASS) theory of intelligence (Kaufman, 2001; Naglieri, 2001; Naglieri & Das, 1997). According to this model, intelligence reflects four basic cognitive processes: planning a solution to a problem, at-

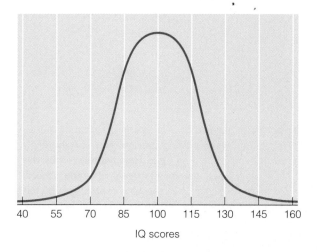

Figure 9.4 The approximate distribution of IQ scores

tending to relevant stimuli and ignoring irrelevant ones, simultaneously processing separate elements, and successively processing stimuli in a specific order. The CAS, designed to assess these four cognitive processes, provides a global score of intelligence as defined by the PASS theory. The CAS seems to do a good job predicting academic success, but it is still too new for us to know whether it is more or less successful than other IQ tests at measuring what we call intelligence.

Despite their vast influence, IQ tests have been roundly criticized. A single IQ score derived from a test that assesses only some of the many intelligences that humans can display certainly does not do justice to the complexity of human mental functioning. Moreover, it is a measure of the individual's *performance* at one point in time—an estimate that is not always a good indicator of the person's underlying intellectual *competence.* And, as Sternberg (1992) notes, it is high time to bring modern information-processing theory to bear on the testing of intelligence in order to understand *how* highly intelligent individuals succeed where others fail. In sum, the nature of intelligence is still poorly understood. We do, however, have a vast store of information about how IQ scores change over the life span and about the implications for development and achievement of having a low or high IQ.

The Infant

As we saw in Chapters 7 and 8, the mind develops very rapidly in infancy. But how can an infant's intellectual growth be measured? Is it possible to identify infants who are more or less intelligent than their age-mates? And how well does high (or low) intelligence in infancy predict high (or low) intelligence in childhood and adulthood?

Developmental Quotients

None of the standard intelligence tests can be used with children much younger than 3, because the test items require verbal skills and attention spans that infants do not have. Some

developmentalists have tried to measure infant intelligence by assessing the rate at which infants achieve important developmental milestones. Perhaps the best known and most widely used of the infant tests is the Bayley Scales of Infant Development (BSID; Bayley, 1993). This test, designed for infants ages 2 to 30 months, has three parts:

1. The *motor scale,* which measures the infant's ability to do such things as grasp a cube and throw a ball
2. The *mental scale,* which includes adaptive behaviors such as reaching for a desirable object, searching for a hidden toy, and following directions
3. The *infant behavioral record,* a rating of the child's behavior on dimensions such as goal-directedness, fearfulness, and social responsivity

On the basis of the first two scores, the infant is given a **DQ,** or **developmental quotient,** rather than an IQ. The DQ summarizes how well or how poorly the infant performs in comparison to a large norm group of infants the same age.

Infant Intelligence and Later Intelligence

As they grow older, infants do progress through many developmental milestones of the kind assessed by the Bayley Scales, so such scales are useful in charting infants' developmental progress. They are also useful in diagnosing neurological problems and mental retardation—even when these conditions are fairly mild and difficult to detect through standard pediatric or neurological examinations (Escalona, 1968; Honzik, 1983). But developmentalists have also been interested in the larger issue of continuity versus discontinuity in intellectual development: Can we predict which infants are likely to be gifted, average, or mentally retarded during the school years?

Apparently not, based on their DQs. Correlations between infant DQ and child IQ are very low, sometimes close to zero. The infant who does well on the Bayley Scales or other infant tests may or may not obtain a high IQ score later in life (Honzik, 1983; Rose et al., 1989). True, the infant who scores very low on an infant test often turns out to be mentally retarded, but otherwise there seems to be a good deal of discontinuity between early and later scores—at least until a child is 4 or older.

Why don't infant development scales do a better job of predicting children's later IQs? Perhaps the main reason is that infant tests and IQ tests tap qualitatively different kinds of abilities (Columbo, 1993). Piaget would undoubtedly approve of this argument. Infant scales focus heavily on the sensory and motor skills that Piaget believed are so important in infancy; IQ tests such as the Stanford-Binet and WISC emphasize more abstract abilities, such as verbal reasoning, concept formation, and problem solving.

Robert McCall (1981, 1983) offers a second explanation, arguing that the growth of intelligence during infancy is highly influenced by powerful and universal maturational processes. Maturational forces pull infants back on course if environmental influences cause them to stray. For this reason, higher

Early Intervention for Preschool Children

During the 1960s, a number of programs were launched to enrich the early learning experiences of disadvantaged preschoolers. Project Head Start is perhaps the best known of these interventions. The idea was to provide a variety of social and intellectual experiences that might better prepare these children for school. At first, Head Start and similar programs seemed to be a smashing success; children in the programs were posting average gains of about 10 points on IQ tests. But then discouragement set in: By the time children reached the middle years of grade school, their IQs were no higher than those of control-group children (Gray, Ramsey, & Klaus, 1982). Such findings led Arthur

High-quality Head Start programs provide the nutrition, health care, parent training, and intellectual stimulation than can get disadvantaged children off to a good start.

or lower infant test scores are likely to be nothing more than temporary deviations from a universal developmental path. As the child nears age 2, McCall argues, maturational forces become less strong, so individual differences become larger and more stable over time. Consistent differences related to both individual genetic makeup and environment now begin to emerge (see Yeates et al., 1983, for relevant evidence).

Should we give up on trying to predict later IQ on the basis of development in infancy? Perhaps not yet. The information-processing approach has given new life to the idea that there is continuity in intelligence from infancy to childhood. Several researchers have found that certain measures of infant attention predict later IQ better than infant intelligence tests do. For example, *speed of habituation* (the speed with which an infant loses interest in a repeatedly presented stimulus) and *preference for novelty* (the infant's tendency to prefer a novel stimulus to a familiar one), assessed in the first year of life,

have an average correlation of about +.45 with IQ in childhood, particularly with verbal IQ and memory skills (Bornstein & Sigman, 1986; McCall & Carriger, 1993; and see Rose & Feldman, 1997). Fast reaction time in infancy (time taken to look in the direction of a visual stimulus as soon as it appears) predicts later IQ about as well (Dougherty & Haith, 1997).

Perhaps, then, we can characterize the "smart" infant as the speedy information processor—the infant who quickly gets bored by the same old thing, seeks out novel experiences, and soaks up information rapidly. There seems to be some continuity between infant intelligence and childhood intelligence after all. Such Bayley Scale accomplishments as throwing a ball are unlikely to carry over into vocabulary learning or problem-solving skills in childhood. However, the extent to which the young infant processes information quickly can predict the extent to which he or she will learn quickly and solve problems efficiently later in childhood.

Jensen (1969, p. 2) to conclude that "compensatory education has been tried and it apparently has failed."

But that was not the end of the story. Children in some of these programs have now been followed into their teens and even 20s. Irving Lazar and Richard Darlington (1982) reported on the long-term effects of 11 early intervention programs in several areas of the United States. Other follow-up studies of Head Start and similar early education programs for disadvantaged children have been conducted since then (see Campbell & Ramey, 1995; Guralnick, 1997). These long-term studies indicate the following:

- Children who participate in early intervention programs show immediate gains on IQ and school achievement tests, whereas nonparticipants do not. However, the gains rarely last for more than three or four years after the program has ended. Impacts on measures other than IQ are more encouraging.
- Compensatory education improves both children's and mothers' attitudes about achievement. When asked to describe something that has made them feel proud of themselves, program participants are more likely than nonparticipants to mention scholastic achievements or (in the case of 15- to 18-year-olds) job-related successes. Mothers of program participants tend to be more satisfied with their children's school performance and to hold higher occupational aspirations for their children.
- Program participants are more likely to meet their school's basic requirements than nonparticipants are. They are less likely to be assigned to special education classes, to be retained in a grade, or to drop out of high school.

- There is even some evidence (though not in all studies) that teenagers who have participated in early compensatory education are less likely than nonparticipants to become pregnant, to require welfare assistance, and to be involved in delinquent behavior.

In sum, longitudinal evaluations suggest that compensatory education has been tried and it works. Programs seem most effective if they start early, last long, and involve several components. For example, Craig Ramey and his colleagues (see Campbell et al., 2001; Campbell & Ramey, 1995) have reported outstanding success with the Abecedarian Project, an early intervention for extremely disadvantaged, primarily African American, children that involved an intellectually stimulating day care program, home visits and efforts to involve parents in their children's development, and medical and nutritional care from early infancy to kindergarten entry. Program participants outperformed nonparticipants throughout childhood and into adolescence. By age 15, the impressive IQ advantage they had shown as young children had narrowed to less than 5 points, but they continued to perform better on math and reading achievement tests, were less likely to have been held back a grade, and were less in need of special education services. Some children in the study were randomly assigned to a group whose intervention did not begin until school age, when a teacher worked with their regular teachers and their parents over a 3-year period. These children did not show as many gains as those who received the preschool intervention, suggesting that it is best to intervene early in children's lives (Campbell & Ramey, 1995).

The Child

Over the childhood years, children generally become able to answer more questions, and more difficult questions, on IQ tests. That is, their mental ages increase. But what happens to the IQ scores of individual children, which reflect how they compare with peers?

How Stable Are IQ Scores during Childhood?

It was once assumed that a person's IQ reflected his or her genetically determined intellectual capacity and therefore would remain quite stable over time. In other words, a child with an IQ of 120 at age 5 was expected to obtain a similar IQ at age 10, 15, or 20. Is this idea supported by research? As we have seen,

infant DQs do not predict later IQs well at all. However, starting at about age 4 there is a fairly strong relationship between early and later IQ, and the relationship grows even stronger by middle childhood. Table 9.2 summarizes the results of a longitudinal study of more than 250 children (Honzik, Macfarlane, & Allen, 1948; also see Sternberg, Grigorenko, & Bundy, 2001). The shorter the interval between two testings, the higher the correlation between children's IQ scores. Even when a number of years have passed, however, IQ seems to be a very stable attribute: The scores that children obtain at age 6 are clearly related to those they obtain 12 years later, at age 18.

There is something these correlations are not telling us, however. They are based on a large *group* of children, and they do not necessarily mean that the IQs of *individual children* will remain stable over the years. As it turns out, many children show sizable ups and downs in their IQ scores over the course of childhood. Patterns of change over time differ con-

Table 9.2 Correlations of IQs Measured during the Preschool Years and Middle Childhood with IQs Measured at Ages 10 and 18

Age of Child	Correlation with IQ at Age 10	Correlation with IQ at Age 18
4	.66	.42
6	.76	.61
8	.88	.70
10	—	.76
12	.87	.76

SOURCE: Honzik, Macfarlane, & Allen (1948)

siderably from child to child, as though each were on his or her own developmental trajectory (Gottfried et al., 1994). One team of researchers looked at the IQ scores of 140 children who had taken intelligence tests at regular intervals from age 2 to age 17 (McCall, Appelbaum, & Hogarty, 1973). The average difference between a child's highest and lowest scores was a whopping 28.5 points. About one-third showed changes of more than 30 points, and one child changed by 74 IQ points!

How do we reconcile the conclusion that IQ is relatively stable with this clear evidence of instability? We can still conclude that, within a group, children's standings (high or low) in comparison with peers stay quite stable from one point to another during the childhood years (Sternberg et al., 2001). But, at the same time, many individual children experience drops or gains in IQ scores over the years. Remember, though, that we are talking about performance on IQ tests rather than underlying intellectual competence. IQ scores are influenced not only by a person's intelligence but by his or her motivation, testing procedures and conditions, and many other factors. As a result, IQ may be more changeable over the years than intellectual ability.

Causes of Gain and Loss

Some wandering of IQ scores upward or downward over time is just random fluctuation—a good day at one testing, a bad day at the next. Yet there are patterns, too. Children whose scores fluctuate the most tend to live in unstable home environments; their life experiences have fluctuated between periods of happiness and turmoil.

In addition, some children gain IQ points over childhood and others lose them. Who are the gainers, and who are the losers? Gainers seem to have parents who foster achievement and who are neither too strict nor too lax in child rearing (McCall et al., 1973). Noticeable drops in IQ with age often occur among children who live in poverty. Otto Klineberg (1963) proposed a **cumulative-deficit hypothesis** to explain this: Impoverished environments inhibit intellectual growth, and these negative effects accumulate over time. There is some support for the cumulative-deficit hypothesis, especially when a child's parents are not only poor but low in intellectual functioning themselves (Jensen, 1977; Ramey & Ramey, 1992). The

Explorations box on page 226 examines the success of early intervention programs designed to raise the IQ scores and academic success of children living in poverty. Overall, we can conclude that there is both continuity and change in IQ scores during childhood; IQ scores remain quite stable for many children, while mental ages rise.

The Adolescent

Intellectual growth is very rapid during infancy and childhood. What happens during adolescence, and how well does IQ predict school performance?

Continuity between Childhood and Adulthood

Intellectual growth continues its rapid pace in early adolescence and then slows down and levels off in later adolescence (Thorndike, 1997). A spurt in brain development, some studies suggest, occurs at roughly the age of 11 or 12, when children are believed to enter Piaget's formal operational stage (Case, 1992; Andrich & Styles, 1994). Brain development may give children the information-processing speed and working memory capacity they need to perform at adultlike levels on IQ tests as well (Kail & Salthouse, 1994). Thus, basic changes in the brain in early adolescence may underlie a variety of cognitive advances—the achievement of formal operations, improved memory and information-processing skills, and better performance on tests of intelligence.

Although adolescence is a time of impressive mental growth, it is also a time of increased stability of individual differences in intellectual performance. During the teen years, IQ scores become even more stable than they were in childhood and predict IQ in middle age very well (Eichorn, Hunt, & Honzik, 1981). Even while adolescents as a group are experiencing cognitive growth, then, each adolescent is establishing a characteristic level of intellectual performance that will most likely be carried into adult life unless the individual's environment changes dramatically.

IQ and School Achievement

If the original purpose of IQ tests was to estimate how well children would do in school, have these tests achieved their purpose? Yes, fairly well. The correlation between children's and adolescents' IQ scores and their grades is about +.50, making general intellectual ability one of the best predictors of school achievement available (Neisser et al., 1996). Adolescents with high IQs are also less likely to drop out of high school and more likely to go on to college than their peers with lower IQs; the correlation between IQ and years of education obtained averages +.55 (Neisser et al., 1996). However, IQ scores do not predict college grades as well as they predict high school grades (Brody & Brody, 1976). Most college students probably have at least the average intellectual ability needed to succeed in college; actual success is therefore more influenced by personal qualities such as motivation. Overall, an IQ score is a good predictor of academic achievement, but it does not tell us everything about a student. Factors such as work habits, interests, and motivation to succeed also affect academic achievement.

The Adult

Do IQ scores predict achievement after people have left school? Does performance on IQ tests change during the adult years? And do IQ scores decline in old age, as performance on Piagetian cognitive tasks and some memory tasks does?

IQ and Occupational Success

There is indeed a relationship between IQ and occupational status. Professional and technical workers perform higher on IQ tests than white-collar workers, who in turn score higher than blue-collar, or manual, workers (Reynolds et al., 1987; Weakliem, McQuillan, & Schaer, 1995). As shown in Figure 9.5, the average IQ score of workers increases as the prestige of the occupation increases (Nyborg & Jensen, 2001). This is true for both African American and European American workers, although the relationship is a little stronger among African American samples. The reason for this relationship is clear: It undoubtedly takes more intellectual ability to complete law school and become a lawyer (a high-status occupation) than it does to be a farmhand (a low-status occupation). Still, IQs vary considerably in every occupational group, so many people in low-status jobs have high IQs.

Now a second question: Are bright lawyers, electricians, or farmhands more successful or productive than their less intelligent colleagues? The answer here is also yes. The correlation between scores on tests of intellectual ability and such measures of job performance as supervisor ratings averages +.30 to +.50 (Neisser et al., 1996). General intellectual ability seems to predict job performance in a wide range of occupations better than any other indicator yet devised, and it predicts likelihood of success as accurately for members of racial and ethnic minority groups as for whites (Schmidt & Hunter, 1998). More intellectually capable adults are better able to learn what they need to know about their occupations and to solve the problems that arise day by day. This literally pays off, as shown in Figure 9.6: Individuals with greater cognitive ability earn more money that those with lower cognitive ability (Ceci & Williams, 1997).

In sum, IQ does have some bearing on occupational success, predicting both what kind of occupation an individual chooses and how well he or she performs in it. At the same time, an IQ score does not tell the whole story; personal qualities such as motivation and environmental factors such as amount of education also affect vocational outcomes (Ceci & Williams, 1997).

Change in IQ with Age

Perhaps no question about adult development has been studied as thoroughly as that of how intellectual abilities change with age. Alan Kaufman (2001) examined cross sections of adults ranging in age from 16 to 89 who were tested with the Wechsler Adult Intelligence Scale. As Figure 9.7 shows, IQs rise ever so slightly up to age 44 and then decline, with the steepest declines starting around age 80. But recall our

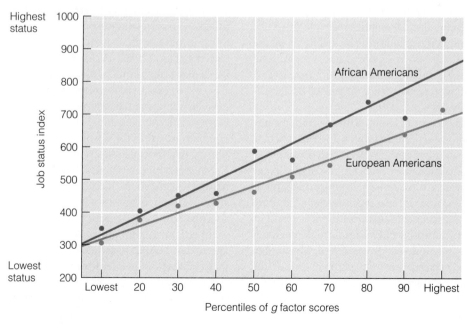

Figure 9.5 Job status in relation to intelligence test performance for African Americans and European Americans

Source: Nyborg & Jensen (2001)

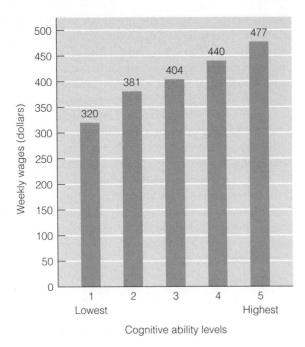

Figure 9.6 Weekly wages by level of cognitive ability

Source: Ceci & Williams (1997)

horts, including longitudinal data on some of the same people over a 28-year period.

Several findings have emerged from this important study. First, it seems that when a person was born has at least as much influence on intellectual functioning as age does. In other words, cohort or generational effects on performance do exist. This evidence confirms the suspicion that cross-sectional comparisons of different age groups yield too grim a picture of declines in intellectual abilities during adulthood. Specifically, recently born cohorts (the youngest people in the study were born in 1959) have tended to outperform earlier generations (the oldest were born in 1889) on most tests. Yet on the test of numerical ability, people born between 1903 and 1924 actually performed better than both earlier and later generations. So different generations may have a special edge in different areas of intellectual performance, showing that when one is born *does* affect one's intellectual abilities. Judging from Schaie's findings, young and middle-aged adults today can look forward to better intellectual functioning in old age than their grandparents have experienced.

Another important message of Schaie's study, and of other research as well, is that patterns of aging differ for different abilities. *Fluid intelligence* (those abilities requiring active thinking and reasoning applied to novel problems, as measured by tests like the primary mental abilities tests of reasoning and space) usually declines earlier and more steeply than *crystallized intelligence* (those abilities involving the use of knowledge acquired through experience, as in answering the verbal meaning test used by Schaie). Consistently, adults lose some of their ability to grapple with new problems starting in middle age, but their "crystallized" general knowledge and vocabulary stay steady or even improve through the 60s and then decline somewhat (Horn & Noll, 1997; Kaufman & Kaufman, 1997).

Why is this? Tests of performance and fluid IQ are often timed, and performance on timed or speeded tests declines more in old age than performance on unspeeded tests does (Jarvik & Bank, 1983). Performance, fluid, and speeded IQ test items may be less familiar to older adults who have been out of school for years than to younger adults; in this sense, the tests may be subtly biased against older adults (see Berg, 2000). However, declines in these fluid aspects of intelligence have also been linked to the slowing of central nervous system functioning that most people experience as they age (Schaie, 1996).

A clear message here is that speed of information processing is related to intellectual functioning across the life span. Not only is rapid information processing in infancy associated with high IQ scores in childhood, but young adults with quick reaction times outperform their more sluggish age-mates on IQ tests, and adults who lose information-processing speed in later life lose some of their ability to think through complex and novel problems (Jensen, 1993). And it is not just that older adults can't finish tests that have time limits; declines in performance intelligence occur in later life even on untimed tests (Kaufman & Kaufman, 1997). The problem is that the slower information processor cannot keep in mind

discussion of cross-sectional designs in Chapter 1. Cross-sectional studies compare people of different cohorts who have had different levels of education and life experiences because they were born at different times. Could the apparent declines in IQ with age reflect cohort differences?

Kaufman (2001) also studied the longitudinal performance of seven cohorts of adults over a 17-year period. The results of this longitudinal study were very similar to those obtained cross-sectionally. There was a loss of about 5 IQ points from age 40 to 57; losses of 7–8 points from age 50 to 67 and from 60 to 77; and losses of about 10 points from age 67 to 84 and from 72 to 89. Do intellectual abilities really decline with age, as these data suggest? It depends on which abilities we are talking about. In both the cross-sectional and longitudinal studies, verbal IQ was essentially unchanged with age, at least until one's 80s. In contrast, performance IQ peaked by ages 20 to 24 and then steadily declined.

We also have data on changes in IQ with age from a comprehensive *sequential study* directed by K. Warner Schaie (1983, 1996). Schaie's study began in 1956 with a sample of members of a health maintenance organization ranging in age from 22 to 70. They were given a revised test of primary mental abilities that yielded scores for five separate mental abilities (see Table 9.3). Seven years later, as many of them as could be found were retested. In addition, a new sample of adults ranging in age from their 20s to their 70s was tested. This design made it possible to determine how the performance of the same individuals changed over a period of 7 years *and* to compare the performance of people who were 20 years old in 1956 with that of a different cohort of people who were 20 in 1963. This same strategy was repeated in 1970, 1977, and 1984, giving the researchers a wealth of information about different co-

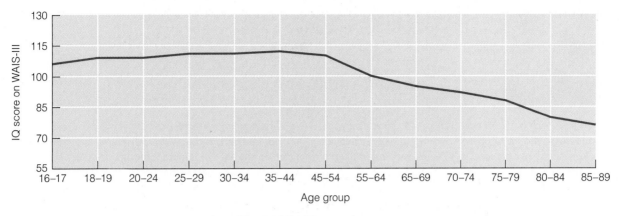

Figure 9.7 IQ scores by age

SOURCE: Based on data from Kaufman (2001)

and process simultaneously all relevant aspects of a complex problem.

We now have an overall picture of intellectual functioning in adulthood. Age group differences in performance suggest that older adults today are at a disadvantage on many tests compared to younger adults, partly because of deficiencies in the amount and quality of education they received early in life. But actual declines in intellectual abilities associated with aging are generally minor until people reach their late 60s or 70s. Even in old age, declines in fluid intelligence, performance intelligence, and performance on speeded tests are more apparent than declines in crystallized intelligence, verbal intelligence, and performance on untimed tests.

One last message of this research is worth special emphasis: *Declines in intellectual abilities are not universal.* Even among the 81-year-olds in Schaie's study, only about 30–40% had experienced a significant decline in intellectual ability in the previous 7 years (Schaie, 1990). Moreover, although few 81-year-olds maintained all five mental abilities, almost all retained at least one ability from testing to testing, and about half retained four out of five (Schaie, 1989). The range of differences in intellectual functioning in a group of older adults is extremely large (Morse, 1993). Anyone who stereotypes all elderly adults as intellectually limited is likely to be wrong most of the time.

Predictors of Decline

What is most likely to affect whether or not a person experiences declines in intellectual performance in old age? *Poor health,* not surprisingly, is one risk factor. People who have cardiovascular diseases or other chronic illnesses show steeper declines in mental abilities than their healthier peers (Schaie, 1996). Diseases (and most likely the drugs used to treat them as well) also contribute to a rapid decline in intellectual abilities within a few years of death (Johansson, Zarit, & Berg, 1992; Kleemeier, 1962). This phenomenon has been given the depressing label **terminal drop.** Perhaps there really is something, then, to the saying "Sound body, sound mind."

A second factor in decline is an *unstimulating lifestyle.* Schaie and his colleagues found that the biggest intellectual declines were shown by elderly widows who had low social status, engaged in few activities, and were dissatisfied with

Table 9.3 **The Primary Mental Abilities Measured in Schaie's Seattle Study**

Verbal meaning	Recognizing the meaning of a word by identifying the best synonym for it from a list of four words. This ability comes in handy in reading and understanding speech.
Space	Imagining how an object would look if it were rotated in space. Given one figure (an *F,* for example), quickly determine whether six other figures are or are not the *F* at another angle (for example, upside down). Spatial ability would aid in reading maps or assembling pieces of equipment.
Reasoning	Foreseeing the pattern in a series of letters. Given the pattern *b c r c d r d e r,* for example, figure out what the next letter should be *(e).* Reasoning enters into solving problems in real life, as when one analyzes a situation on the basis of past experience and plans an appropriate future course.
Number	The ability to deal with basic arithmetic problems quickly. Given an addition problem that has been worked to yield a sum, for example, decide whether it has been worked correctly. Although mathematics abilities may be less useful now that we have calculators, they still play a role in daily life.
Word fluency	Quick recall of words. During a 5-minute period, for example, write down as many words as possible that begin with the letter *s.* Presumably this ability enters into talking and reading easily.

SOURCE: Descriptions based on those provided by Schaie (1983, pp. 73-74) for the *SRA Primary Mental Abilities, Ages 11–17, Form AM* (Thurstone & Thurstone, 1948)

IQ Training for Aging Adults

Can you teach old dogs new tricks? And can you reteach old dogs who have suffered declines in mental abilities the old tricks they have lost? K. Warner Schaie and Sherry Willis (1986) sought to find out by training elderly adults in spatial ability and reasoning, two of the fluid mental abilities that are most likely to decline in old age. Within a group of older people ranging in age from 64 to 95 who participated in Schaie's longitudinal study of intelligence, they first identified individuals whose scores on one of the two abilities had declined over a 14-year period, as well as individuals who had remained stable over the same period. The goal with the decliners would be to restore lost ability; the goal with those who had maintained their ability would be to improve it. Participants took pretests measuring both abilities, received 5 hours of training in either spatial ability or reasoning, and then were given posttests on both abilities. The spatial training involved learning how to rotate objects in space, at first physically and then mentally. Training in reasoning involved learning how to detect a recurring pattern in a series of stimuli (for example, musical notes) and to identify what the next stimulus in the sequence should be.

The training worked. Both those who had suffered ability declines and those who had maintained their abilities prior to the study improved, though decliners showed significantly more improvement in spatial ability than nondecliners did. Schaie and Willis estimated that 40% of the decliners gained enough through training to bring them back up to the level of performance they had achieved 14 years earlier, before decline set in. What's more, effects of the training among those who had experienced declines in performance were still evident 7 years later (Schaie, 1996).

The larger messages? You *can* teach old dogs new tricks—and reteach them old tricks—in very little time. This research does not mean that cognitive abilities can be restored in elderly people who have Alzheimer's disease or other brain disorders and have experienced significant neural loss. Instead, it suggests that many intellectual skills decline in later life because they are not used—and that these skills can be revived with a little coaching and practice. This research, combined with research on children, provides convincing evidence of the plasticity of cognitive abilities over the entire life span.

their lives (Schaie, 1996). These women lived alone and seemed disengaged from life. Individuals who maintain their performance or even show gains tend to have above-average socioeconomic status, advanced education, intact marriages, intellectually capable spouses, and physically and mentally active lifestyles. Interestingly, married adults are affected by the intellectual environment they provide for each other. Their IQ test scores become more similar over the years, largely because the lower-functioning partner's scores rise closer to those of the higher-functioning partner (Gruber-Baldini, Schaie, & Willis, 1995).

The moral is "Use it or lose it!" This rule, applicable to muscular strength and sexual functioning, also pertains to intellectual functioning in later life (Schaie, 1983). The plasticity of the nervous system throughout the life span enables elderly individuals to benefit from intellectual stimulation and training, to maintain the intellectual skills most relevant to their activities, and to compensate for the loss of less-exercised abilities (Dixon, Kramer, & Baltes, 1985; see Applications box above). There is still much to learn about how health, lifestyle, and other factors shape the individual's intellectual growth and decline. What is certain is that most of us can look forward to many years of optimal intellectual functioning before *some* of us experience losses of *some* mental abilities in later life.

Potential for Wisdom

Many people believe, incorrectly as we have seen, that intellectual decline is an inevitable part of aging—and yet many people also believe that old people are wise. Indeed, this belief has been expressed in many cultures throughout history (Clayton & Birren, 1980; Holliday & Chandler, 1986). It is also featured in Erik Erikson's influential theory of life-span development. Erikson claims that older adults often gain wisdom as they face the prospect of death and attempt to find meaning in their lives (Erikson, 1982; see also Chapter 11). Notice, too, that the word *wise* is rarely used to describe children, adolescents, or even young adults (unless perhaps it is to call one of them a "wise guy"). Is the association between wisdom and old age just a stereotype, or is there some truth to it?

But first, what is wisdom, and how can one assess it? There is no consensus on these questions, and very little research (see Sternberg, 1990). Paul Baltes and his colleagues offer this definition of **wisdom:** "expert knowledge in the fundamental pragmatics of life that permits exceptional insight, judgment, and advice about complex and uncertain matters" (Pasupathi, Staudinger, & Baltes, 2001, p. 351). In addition, the wise person has:

- Rich factual knowledge about life (a knowledge base regarding such areas as human nature, interpersonal relations, and critical events in life)

- Rich procedural knowledge (such as strategies for giving advice and handling conflicts)
- A life-span contextual perspective (consideration of the contexts of life—family, education, work, and others)
- Relativism of values and life priorities (acknowledgment and tolerance of different values)
- Recognition and management of uncertainty (understanding that our knowledge of the world is limited and the future unknown) (Baltes & Staudinger, 2000; Pasupathi et al., 2001)

Does wisdom typically increase with age, or are life experiences more important than age in determining whether or not a person is wise? Ursula Staudinger, Jacqui Smith, and Paul Baltes (1992) attempted to find out by interviewing young (ages 25–35) and elderly (ages 65–82) women who were either clinical psychologists or similarly well-educated professionals in other fields. The goal was to assess the relative contributions of age and specialized experience to wisdom, based on the assumption that clinical psychologists stand to gain special sensitivity to human problems from their professional training and practice.

We tend to believe that age brings wisdom. It can—but wisdom is rare even in later life.

These women were interviewed about a person named Martha, who had chosen to have a family but no career and who met up with an old friend who had chosen to have a career but no family. The women were asked to talk about how Martha might review and evaluate her life after this encounter. Answers were scored for the five qualities bulleted above that were judged to be indicators of wisdom.

What was found? First, wisdom proved to be rare; it seems that only about 5% of the answers given by adults to problems like these qualify as "wise" (Smith & Baltes, 1990). Second, expertise proved to be more relevant than age to the development of wisdom. That is, clinical psychologists, whether they were young or old, displayed more signs of wisdom than other women did. Older women were generally no wiser—or less wise—than younger women.

Age, then, does not predict wisdom, at least among adults (there is some evidence that age is related to wisdom-related performance among adolescents; see Pasupathi et al., 2001). Yet the knowledge base that contributes to wisdom, like other crystallized intellectual abilities, holds up very well later in life (Baltes et al., 1995). Older adults, like younger adults, are more likely to display wisdom if they have life experiences (such as work as a clinical psychologist) that sharpen their insights into the human condition. The immediate social context also influences the degree to which wisdom is expressed; wiser problem solutions are generated when adults have an opportunity to discuss problems with someone whose judgment they value and when they are encouraged to reflect after such discussions (Staudinger & Baltes, 1996). Thus, consulting with your fellow students and work colleagues and thinking about their advice may well be the beginning of wisdom.

Finally, wisdom seems to reflect a particular combination of intelligence, personality, and cognitive style (Baltes & Staudinger, 2000). For example, individuals who have a cognitive style of comparing and evaluating relevant issues and who show tolerance of ambiguity are more likely to demonstrate wisdom than individuals without these characteristics. In addition, external factors influence the development of wisdom. Monika Ardelt (2000) found that a supportive social environment during early adulthood was positively associated with wisdom 40 years later.

At this early stage in the study of wisdom, there is much disagreement about what it is, how it develops, and how it is related to other mental abilities. However, research on wisdom provides still more evidence that different mental faculties develop and age differently over the adult years. Paul Baltes has offered a life-span perspective on intellectual development that highlights this pattern (see Baltes & Graf, 1996). Performance on the sorts of problem-solving tests that measure fluid intelligence, especially those that require speedy information processing, does indeed decline in later life as biological aging takes its toll. However, older adults are often able to compensate for this decline by making good use of their crystallized abilities—the knowledge they have accumulated over a lifetime and, for a few people, the wisdom that comes only with experience.

Factors That Influence IQ Scores

Now that we have surveyed changes in intellectual functioning over the life span, let's address a quite different question: Why do children or adults who are *the same age* differ in IQ? Part of the answer is that they differ in the kinds of motivational and situational factors that can affect performance on a given day. Yet there are real differences in underlying intellectual ability that need to be explained. And, as usual, our best explanation is that genetic and environmental factors interact to make us what we are.

Genes

The pioneers of the IQ testing movement believed that individual differences in IQ exist simply because some people inherit better genes at conception than others do. Even though IQ scores are now known *not* to be determined entirely by genes, heredity does help explain individual differences in intellectual performance. As we saw in Chapter 3, identical twins obtain more similar IQ scores than fraternal twins do, even when they have been raised apart all their lives (you might want to look again at Table 3.3). Moreover, the IQs of adopted children, once they reach adolescence anyway, are more strongly correlated with those of their biological parents than with those of their adoptive parents. Overall, most researchers find that about half of the variation in IQ scores within a group of individuals is associated with genetic differences among them (Neisser et al., 1996). Some researchers report that genetic influence on IQ differences is somewhat greater than environmental influences (Rowe, Vesterdal, & Rodgers, 1999). In either case, as much as half of the variation in scores is attributable to differences in the environments in which people develop. Children growing up in the same home show

family resemblance in IQ scores (an effect of shared environment) while they are children but not by the time they reach adolescence and adulthood (Loehlin, Horn, & Willerman, 1997; McGue et al., 1993). Most effects of environment on IQ are unique to the individual and are not shared by siblings (see Maccoby, 2000).

The fact that differences in IQ are linked to differences in genetic makeup says nothing about the extent to which IQ can be increased. Height is even more strongly associated with genetic endowment than IQ. Yet it can clearly be decreased by poor nutrition or increased by good nutrition and has, in fact, increased over several generations as nutrition has improved (Sternberg, 1997). So let's look further at aspects of the environment in infancy and early childhood that can stimulate or inhibit intellectual growth. Then we will see how far this information can take us in explaining differences in IQ scores associated with socioeconomic status and race or ethnicity.

Home Environment

Research by Arnold Sameroff and his colleagues (1993) provides a broad overview of some of the environmental factors that put children at risk for having low IQ scores—and, by implication, some of the factors associated with higher IQs. These researchers assessed the 10 risk factors shown in Table 9.4 at age 4 and again at age 13. Every one of these factors was related to IQ at age 4, and most also predicted IQ at age 13. In addition, the greater the number of these risk factors affecting a child, the lower his or her IQ. Which particular risk factors a child experienced was less important than how many he or she experienced. Clearly, it is not good for intellectual development to grow up in a disadvantaged home with an adult who is unable to provide much intellectual nurturance.

In what specific ways do parents influence their children's intellectual development? Bettye Caldwell and Robert Bradley have developed a widely used instrument for determining

---

Table 9.4 Ten Environmental Risk Factors Associated with Low IQ, with Mean IQs at Age 4 of Children Who Did or Did Not Experience Each Risk Factor

Risk Factor	Mean IQ at Age 4 if	
	Child Experienced Risk Factor	Child Did NOT Experience Risk Factor
Child is member of minority group	90	110
Head of household is unemployed or low-skilled worker	90	108
Mother did not complete high school	92	109
Family has four or more children	94	105
Father is absent from family	95	106
Family experienced many stressful life events	97	105
Parents have rigid child-rearing values	92	107
Mother is highly anxious/distressed	97	105
Mother has poor mental health/diagnosed disorder	99	107
Mother shows little positive affect toward child	88	107

SOURCE: Based on Sameroff et al. (1993)

how intellectually stimulating or impoverished a home environment is (Caldwell & Bradley, 1984; Bradley & Caldwell, 1984). Sample items from the preschool version of their **HOME inventory** (Home Observation for Measurement of the Environment) are shown in Table 9.5 (Caldwell & Bradley, 1984). Bradley and his colleagues (1989) have found that scores on the HOME predict the IQs of African American and European American children at age 3 quite well, with correlations of about .50 (see also Cleveland et al., 2000). HOME scores continue to predict IQ scores between ages 3 and 6 (Espy, Molfese, & DiLalla, 2001). Gains in IQ from age 1 to age 3 are likely to occur among children from stimulating homes, whereas children from families with low HOME scores often experience drops in IQ over the same period. The early IQ scores of Mexican American children are not very closely related to their families' HOME scores, however, so we know less about how the home environments that Hispanic parents provide influence their children's intellectual development.

What particular aspects of the home environment best predict high IQs? Studies using the HOME inventory indicate that the most important factors are parental involvement with the child and opportunities for stimulation (Gottfried et al., 1994). Other researchers (for example, Crockenberg, 1983) would add that the sheer amount of stimulation parents provide to their young children may not be as important as whether that stimulation is responsive to the child's behavior (a smile in return for a smile) and matched to the child's competencies so that it is neither too simple nor too challenging (S. A. Miller, 1986; Smith, Landry, & Swank, 2000). In short, an intellectually stimulating home is one in which parents are eager to be involved with their children and are responsive to their developmental needs and behavior (MacPhee, Ramey, & Yeates, 1984).

Do differences in stimulation in the home really *create* individual differences in IQ? We know that more intelligent parents are more likely than less intelligent parents to provide intellectually stimulating home environments for their children *and* to pass on to their children genes that contribute to high intelligence; that is, we have evidence of the *gene/environment correlations* discussed in Chapter 3. Maternal IQ, for example, is correlated with child's IQ at 3 years and also with family income and quality of home environment (Bacharach & Baumeister, 1998). So, are bright children bright because of the genes they inherited or because of the home environment their bright parents provided? Keith Yeates and his colleagues (Yeates et al., 1983) evaluated these alternative hypotheses in a longitudinal study of 112 mothers and their children ages 2 to 4. They measured the mothers' IQs, the children's IQs from age 2 to age 4, and the families' HOME environments. The best predictor of a child's IQ at age 2 was the mother's IQ, just as a genetic hypothesis would suggest; home environment had little effect. But the picture changed by the time children were 4 years old, when mother's IQ and the quality of the home environment were about equally important predictors of child's IQ. Moreover, the researchers established statistically that differences in the quality of the home environment influenced children's IQs over and above the effects of their mothers' IQs, and that much of the effect of mothers' IQs could be attributed to the fact that high-IQ mothers provided more stimulating home environments than low-IQ mothers (see also Bacharach & Baumeister, 1998). We also know that adopted children's IQ scores rise considerably when they are moved from less stimulating to more stimulating homes (Turkheimer, 1991), and we know that the quality of day care children receive predicts their verbal IQ scores (Broberg et al., 1997).

In sum, the argument that genetic influences can fully explain the apparent effects of home environment on IQ does not hold up. Yet we cannot ignore genetic influences, either, for gifted children are more likely than their less gifted peers to seek intellectual stimulation (Gottfried et al., 1994). Overall, intellectual development seems to go best when a motivated, intellectually capable child begging for intellectual

---

Table 9.5 Subscales and Sample Items from the HOME Inventory

Subscale 1: Emotional and Verbal Responsivity of Parent (11 items)

Sample items:	Parent responds verbally to child's vocalization or verbalizations.
	Parent's speech is distinct, clear, and audible.
	Parent caresses or kisses child at least once.

Subscale 2: Avoidance of Restriction and Punishment (8 items)

Sample items:	Parent neither slaps nor spanks child during visit.
	Parent does not scold or criticize child during visit.
	Parent does not interfere with or restrict child more than three times during visit.

Subscale 3: Organization of Physical and Temporal Environment (6 items)

| Sample items: | Child gets out of house at least four times a week. |
| | Child's play environment is safe. |

Subscale 4: Provision of Appropriate Play Materials (9 items)

Sample items:	Child has a push or pull toy.
	Parent provides learning facilitators appropriate to age—mobile, table and chairs, highchair, playpen, and so on.
	Parent provides toys for child to play with during visit.

Subscale 5: Parental Involvement with Child (6 items)

| Sample items: | Parent talks to child while doing household work. |
| | Parent structures child's play periods. |

Subscale 6: Opportunities for Variety in Daily Stimulation (5 items)

| Sample items: | Father provides some care daily. |
| | Child has three or more books of his or her own. |

SOURCE: Adapted from Caldwell & Bradley (1984)

nourishment is fortunate enough to get it from involved and responsive parents.

Family Size and Birth Order

Years ago, the case was made that birth order influenced intellectual and academic performance, with firstborn children scoring the highest on intellectual tests and later-born children scoring progressively worse (Zajonc, 1976). After falling out of favor for a time, this possible link between birth order and intelligence has recently been reexamined (Downey, 2001; Rodgers, 2001; Zajonc, 2001). How might birth order affect intelligence? According to Zajonc (2001), firstborn children benefit from having their parents' undivided attention and are exposed primarily to adult language. Subsequent children are also exposed to their parents' attention and language, but they are also exposed to their older sibling's language and they must share their parents' attention. According to the "resource dilution" model, parents have only so many resources (time, energy, money, and so on) and once these resources are used up, there are no more to go around (Downey, 2001). For a time, firstborns get all the resources; later-borns get fewer resources because the finite resources must be shared among more children. Firstborns are further advantaged because they are in a position to teach their younger siblings, and teaching others seems to promote intellectual development. Later-born children may or may not have opportunities to teach younger siblings.

Not all the research shows a clear connection between birth order and intelligence (see Rodgers, 2001; Rodgers et al., 2000). And in those studies that do, the actual difference in test scores between firstborns and later-borns is only a few points. Thus, a firstborn might score 118 on an intelligence test and a younger sibling 114; this 4-point difference is unlikely to have any practical significance for what the two siblings are able to accomplish in life.

Finally, birth order is connected to family size. When we compare fifth-born children, for example, with firstborns, some of the firstborns may have four or more siblings (as would be the case for the fifth-born child), but many may have only one or two siblings. Thus, the children come from families of different sizes. Research suggests that, in general, children from larger families have lower IQ scores than children from smaller families. What this research does *not* tell us is whether having a large family leads to lower IQs or whether lower-IQ parents tend to have more children and pass their lower IQ genes on to them (Rodgers et al., 2000).

Social Class Differences

Children from lower-class homes average some 10 to 20 points below their middle-class age-mates on IQ tests. This is true in all racial and ethnic groups (Helms, 1997). Socioeconomic status affects IQ scores as well as children's *rate* of intellectual growth (Espy et al., 2001). What if socioeconomic conditions were to improve?

Over the 20th century, average IQ scores have increased in all countries studied, a phenomenon called the **Flynn effect**

after its discoverer, James Flynn (1987, 1998, 1999). In the United States, the increase has amounted to 3–4 IQ points per decade. Increases of this size cannot be due to genetic evolution and therefore must have environmental causes (Flynn, 1996). Interestingly, the Flynn effect is clearer for measures of fluid intelligence than for measures of crystallized intelligence, even though one might expect crystallized intelligence to benefit more from improved educational opportunities. Flynn believes that a good portion of the trend reflects increases not in true intellectual capacity but in performance on IQ tests, because today's test takers are probably more testwise than test takers of the past. Yet he also concludes that improved nutrition, education, and living conditions over the course of the 20th century have contributed to real improvements in intellectual functioning.

Similarly, improving the economic conditions of children's homes can improve their IQs. For example, Sandra Scarr and Richard Weinberg have charted the intellectual growth of African American and European American children adopted before their first birthday (Scarr & Weinberg, 1983; Weinberg, Scarr, & Waldman, 1992). Many of these children came from disadvantaged family backgrounds and had biological parents who were poorly educated and somewhat below average in IQ. They were placed in middle-class homes with adoptive parents who were highly educated and above average in intelligence. Throughout childhood and adolescence, these adoptees have posted average or above average scores on standardized IQ tests—higher scores than they would have obtained if they had stayed in the disadvantaged environments offered by their natural parents. Research with French children who were adopted later—around age 5—indicates that increases in IQ are much larger among children adopted into affluent homes with highly educated parents than among those adopted into disadvantaged homes (Duyme, Dumaret, & Tomkiewicz, 1999).

Could social class differences in IQ be due to differences in the quality of the home environment that parents of different socioeconomic levels provide? Yes, at least partially. Scores on the HOME inventory are higher in middle-class homes than in lower-class homes, indicating that middle-class homes are more intellectually stimulating on average (Bradley et al., 1989; Gottfried, 1984). Poor nutrition, drug abuse, disruptive family experiences, and other factors associated with poverty may also contribute to the social class gap in IQ (Gottfried & Gottfried, 1984).

Racial and Ethnic Differences

Controversy regarding racial and ethnic differences in IQ has raged for many years, but the publication in 1994 of *The Bell Curve* by Richard Herrnstein and Charles Murray caused a major stir. The main theme of the book is that IQ scores have become more and more important in determining people's occupational success and socioeconomic standing and that we are becoming a society with a high-IQ, educated, and wealthy elite and a lower-IQ, less educated class of poor people. The authors also argue that racial differences in average IQ scores exist, that they cannot be explained entirely by socioeconomic differences between racial groups, and that these IQ differences are probably rooted, at least in part, in genetic differences between the races.

What do we know about this controversial topic? Racial and ethnic differences in IQ scores do exist; everyone acknowledges that. In the United States, for example, Asian American and European American children tend to score higher on IQ tests than African American, Native American, and Hispanic American children, on average (Neisser et al., 1996). Different subcultural groups sometimes also show distinctive profiles of mental abilities; for example, black children often do particularly well on verbal tasks, whereas Hispanic children, perhaps because of language differences, tend to excel on nonverbal items (Neisser et al., 1996; Taylor & Richards, 1991). Of course, it is essential to keep in mind that we are talking about *group averages*. Like the IQ scores of white children, those of minority children run the whole range, from the mentally retarded to the gifted. We certainly cannot predict an individual's IQ merely on the basis of racial or ethnic identity.

Having said that, we must ask why these average group differences exist. Let's consider the following hypotheses: (1) bias in the tests, (2) motivational factors, (3) genetic differences between groups, and (4) environmental differences between groups.

Differences in intellectual functioning within any racial or ethnic group are far greater than differences among groups.

CULTURE BIAS

There may be *culture bias* in testing; that is, IQ tests may be more appropriate for children from white middle-class backgrounds than for those from other subcultural groups (Helms, 1992; Lopez, 1997). Low-income African American children who speak a different dialect of English from that spoken by middle-class Anglo children, as well as Hispanic children who hear Spanish rather than English at home, may not understand some test instructions or items. What's more, their experiences may not allow them to become familiar with some of the information that is called for on the tests (for example, "What is a 747?" "Who wrote *Hamlet*?").

It is true that minority-group children often do not have as much exposure to the culture reflected in the tests as nonminority children do. If IQ tests assess "proficiency in European American culture," minority children are bound to look deficient (Helms, 1992). Using IQ tests designed to be fair to all ethnic groups and introducing procedures to help minority children feel more comfortable and motivated can cut the usual IQ gap between African American and European American children in half (Kaufman, Kamphaus, & Kaufman, 1985). But, even though standardized IQ test items sometimes have a white middle-class flavor, group differences in IQ probably cannot be traced solely to test bias. *Culture-fair IQ tests* include items that should be equally unfamiliar (or familiar) to people from all ethnic groups and social classes—for example, items that require completing a geometric design with a piece that matches the rest of the design. Still, racial and ethnic differences emerge on such tests (Jensen, 1980). In addition, IQ tests predict future school achievement as well for African Americans and other minorities as they do for European Americans (Neisser et al., 1996).

MOTIVATIONAL FACTORS

Another possibility is that minority individuals are not motivated to do their best in testing situations because they are anxious or resist being judged by whites (Moore, 1986; Ogbu, 1994; Steele, 1997). They may be wary of strange examiners, may see little point in trying to do well, and may shake their heads as if to say they don't know the answer before the question is ever completed. Disadvantaged children do indeed score some 7 to 10 points better when they are given time to warm up to a friendly examiner or are given a mix of easy and hard items so that they do not become discouraged by a long string of difficult items (Zigler et al., 1982). Even though most children do better with a friendly examiner (Sacks, 1952), it seems that African American children, even those from middle-class homes, are often less comfortable in testing situations than white middle-class children are (Moore, 1986).

Claude Steele and his colleagues have argued that the performance of African Americans is especially likely to suffer whenever negative stereotypes of their group come into play (Steele, 1997, 1999; Steele & Aronson, 1995). In one study, female students at Stanford University were given very difficult test items. Some students were told that they were taking a test of verbal abilities and would get feedback about their

© Barbara Stitzer/PhotoEdit, Inc.

strengths and weaknesses; others were told that they were going to do some verbal problems but that their ability would not be evaluated. As Figure 9.8 shows, African American students performed poorly when they were led to believe that the test would reveal their level of intellectual ability, but performed more like European American students when they did not think their ability would be judged. Even being asked to identify their race in a personal information section at the start of a test of intellectual ability can undermine the performance of African American college students (Steele & Aronson, 1995).

Why? Steele concluded that African Americans perform poorly on IQ tests partly because of "stereotype threat"—fear that they will be judged to have the qualities associated with negative stereotypes of African Americans (see also Aronson et al., 1999). It is not that African Americans have internalized stereotypes and believe that they are intellectually inferior, according to Steele. Instead, they become anxious and unable to perform well in testing situations that arouse concerns about being negatively stereotyped.

Other research has demonstrated that positive stereotypes about a group can *increase* the performance of members of that group. Margaret Shih and colleagues (Shih, Pittinsky, & Ambady, 1999) gave Asian American women a math test under one of three conditions. In one, their identity as women was made salient; in another, their Asian American identity was made salient; and in a third condition, no identity was emphasized. Consistent with stereotypes, these women performed worse when their gender was emphasized and better when their ethnic background was emphasized, relative to the group that was not primed to think about either identity. So, stereotypes can either hinder or enhance performance, depending on whether a person identifies with a group that is viewed negatively or positively.

GENETIC INFLUENCES

Perhaps no idea in psychology has sparked more heated debate than the suggestion that racial and ethnic differences in IQ scores could be due to group differences in genetic makeup. We know that differences in genetic makeup contribute, along with differences in environment, to IQ differences *within* either the European American or the African American population. Scholars such as Arthur Jensen (1969) and Herrnstein and Murray (1994) have gone a step further to suggest that IQ differences *between* European Americans and African Americans may be due to genetic differences between the races.

However, most psychologists do not think the evidence that heredity contributes to within-group differences says much at all about the reasons for between-group differences. Richard Lewontin (1976) makes this point with an analogy. Suppose that corn seeds with different genetic makeups are randomly drawn from a bag and planted in two fields—one that is barren and one that has fertile soil. Since all the plants within each field were grown in the same soil, their differences in height would have to be due to differences in genetic makeup. A genetic explanation of differences would fit. But, if

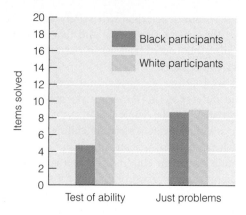

Figure 9.8 African American students perform poorly on tests of mental abilities when they think they are taking a test that may result in their being stereotyped as unintelligent.

SOURCE: Adapted from Steele & Aronson (1995)

the plants in the fertile field are generally taller than those in the barren field, this *between-field* variation must be entirely due to environment. Similarly, even though genes partially explain individual differences in IQ *within* African American and European American groups, the average difference *between* the racial groups may still reflect nothing more than differences in the environments they typically experience. There is currently no direct evidence that differences in genetic makeup between the races account for average group differences in IQ (Neisser et al., 1996).

ENVIRONMENTAL INFLUENCES

It is time to return to an environmental hypothesis about racial and ethnic differences in IQ. Many of the intellectual and academic differences that have been attributed to race or ethnicity probably reflect racial and ethnic differences in socioeconomic status instead (Patterson, Kupersmidt, & Vaden, 1990). Research on adopted children is very relevant here. Placement in more advantaged homes has allowed lower-income African American children to equal or exceed the average IQ in the general population and to exceed the IQs of comparable African American children raised in more disadvantaged environments by 20 points (Moore, 1986; Scarr & Weinberg, 1983; Weinberg et al., 1992). This could not have happened if African American children were genetically deficient.

The major message of this research is that children, whatever their racial background, perform better on IQ tests when they grow up in intellectually stimulating environments with involved, responsive parents and are exposed to the "culture of the tests and the schools" (Scarr & Weinberg, 1983, p. 261). How much of the racial gap in IQ can be explained by racial differences in neighborhood and family socioeconomic conditions, mother's education, and qualities of the home environment? Jeanne Brooks-Gunn, Pamela Klebanov, and Greg Duncan (1996) used statistical procedures to correct for these environmental differences between African American and European American children so that they could estimate what the IQ difference would be if the two racial groups had been raised in similar environments. Without any controls for environmental differences, there was an IQ gap of 18 points. The gap narrowed to only 8 points when family and neighborhood income levels were controlled and was reduced to only 3 points, a trivial difference, when racial differences in the provision of a stimulating home environment (HOME scores) were also controlled. In short, the fact that more African American than European American children live in poverty and have limited learning opportunities at home has a lot to do with the racial difference in average IQ scores.

There are signs that the IQ gap between black and white children has been decreasing in recent years as educational and economic opportunities for African Americans have improved (Vincent, 1991). Perhaps the issue of racial and ethnic differences in IQ will largely disappear as life conditions for minority-group families improve further. Culture bias, motivational factors such as stereotype threat, and socioeconomic differences between groups may all contribute to the differences we see today.

The Extremes of Intelligence

Although we have identified some of the factors that contribute to individual differences in intellectual performance, we cannot fully appreciate the magnitude of these differences without considering people at the extremes of the IQ continuum. Just how different are mentally retarded and gifted individuals? And how different are their lives?

Mental Retardation

Mental retardation is currently defined by the American Association on Mental Retardation (Luckasson et al., 1992) as significantly below-average intellectual functioning associated with limitations in areas of adaptive behavior such as self-care and social skills and originating before age 18 (see Schalock, 1999). To be diagnosed as mentally retarded, an individual must obtain an IQ score of 70 to 75 or lower *and* have difficulties meeting age-appropriate expectations in important areas of everyday functioning. According to this definition,

mental retardation is not merely a deficiency within the person; rather, it is the product of the interaction between person and environment, strongly influenced by the type and level of supportive help the individual receives (Reiss, 1994).

Individuals with mental retardation differ greatly in their levels of functioning (see Table 9.6). An adult with an IQ in the range of about 55 to 70 is likely to have a mental age comparable to that of an 8- to 12-year-old child. Individuals with mild mental retardation can learn both academic and practical skills in school, and they can potentially work and live independently or with occasional help as adults. Many of these individuals are integrated into regular classrooms where they excel academically and socially relative to comparable individuals who are segregated into special classrooms (Freeman, 2000). At the other end of the continuum, individuals with IQs below 20 to 25 and mental ages below 3 years ("profoundly retarded"), show major delays in all areas of development and require basic care, sometimes in institutional settings. They, too, can benefit considerably from training, though.

Mental retardation has many causes. Severely and profoundly retarded persons are often affected by **organic retardation,** meaning that their retardation is due to some identifiable biological cause associated with hereditary factors, diseases, or injuries. *Down syndrome,* the condition associated with an extra 21st chromosome, and *phenylketonuria (PKU)* are familiar examples of organic retardation associated with genetic factors (Simonoff, Bolton, & Rutter, 1996; and see Chapter 3). Other forms of organic retardation are associated with prenatal risk factors—an alcoholic mother, exposure to rubella, and so on (see Chapter 4). Organically retarded children, because many of them are seriously delayed or have physical defects, can often be identified at birth or during infancy. However, the most common form of mental retardation, **cultural-familial retardation,** is typically milder and appears to be due to a combination of low genetic potential and a poor, unstimulating environment (Simonoff et al., 1996). Whereas children with organic retardation come from all socioeconomic levels, children with cultural-familial retardation often come from poverty areas and have a parent or sibling who is also retarded (Zigler, 1995). From one-half to

Table 9.6   Levels and Characteristics of Mental Retardation

	Level			
	Mild	Moderate	Severe	Profound
Range of IQ scores	Approximately 52 to 70–75	35 to 51	20 to 35	Below 19
Degree of independence	Usually independent	Some independence; need some supervision	May be semi-independent with close supervision	Dependent; need constant supervision
Educational achievement	Can do some academic work—usually to sixth-grade level; focus on career education	Focus is on daily living skills rather than academics; some career training	Focus on self-care (toileting, dressing, eating) and communication skills	Focus on self-care, mobility, and basic communication

SOURCE: Based on Barack, Hodapp, & Zigler (1998)

three-quarters of mental retardation is of the cultural-familial type: exact cause unknown (Zigler & Hodapp, 1991).

Historically, about 3% of school-age children have been classified as mentally retarded, although this rate is decreasing because fewer children are diagnosed as mildly retarded today (Patton, 2000). What becomes of these children as they grow up? As a general rule, they proceed along the same paths and through the same sequences of developmental milestones as other children do (Zigler & Hodapp, 1991). Their IQs remain low, of course, because they do not achieve the same level of growth that others do. They, like nonretarded people, show signs of intellectual aging in later life, especially on tests that require speed (Devenny et al., 1996). Individuals with Down syndrome may experience even greater intellectual deterioration, as they are at risk for premature Alzheimer's disease (Day & Jancar, 1994).

As for their outcomes in life, consider a follow-up study of individuals with mild and borderline mental retardation who had been placed in segregated special education classes during the 1920s and 1930s (Ross et al., 1985). The individuals studied had a mean IQ of 67. They were compared with their siblings and with nonretarded peers about 35 years later. Generally, these mentally retarded adults had poor life outcomes in middle age in comparison with nonretarded groups (see also Schalock et al., 1992). About 80% of the men with retardation were employed, but they usually held semiskilled or unskilled jobs that required little education or intellectual ability. Women often married and became homemakers. Compared with nonretarded peers, men and women with retardation fared worse on other counts as well. For example, they had lower incomes, less adequate housing, poorer adjustment in social relationships, and a greater dependency on others.

Yet the authors of the study still found grounds for optimism. These individuals had done much better during adulthood than stereotyped expectations of persons with mental retardation would predict. After all, most of them worked and had married, and about 80% reported having had no need for public assistance in the 10 years before they were interviewed. This study, like others before it, suggests that many children who are labeled mentally retarded by the schools—and who do indeed have difficulty with the tasks demanded of them in school—"vanish" into the general population after they leave school. Apparently they can adapt to the demands of adult life. As the authors put it, "It does not take as many IQ points as most people believe to be productive, to get along with others, and to be self-fulfilled" (Ross et al., 1985, p. 149).

Giftedness

The gifted child used to be identified solely by an IQ score—one that was at least 130 or 140. Programs for gifted children still focus mainly on those with very high IQs, but there is increased recognition that some children are gifted because they have special abilities rather than because they have high general intelligence. Even high-IQ children are usually not equally talented in all areas; contrary to myth, they cannot just become anything they choose (Winner, 1996). More often, high-

IQ children have exceptional talent in an area or two and otherwise are good, but not exceptional, performers (Achter, Benbow, & Lubinski, 1997). So, today's definitions emphasize that **giftedness** involves having a high IQ *or* showing special abilities in areas valued in our society, such as mathematics, the performing and visual arts, or even leadership (Coleman, 1985).

Joseph Renzulli (1998) has long argued that giftedness emerges from a combination of above-average ability, creativity, and task commitment. According to this view, someone might have a high IQ and even creative ability, but Renzulli questions whether they are truly gifted if they are not motivated to use this intelligence. Here we focus on individuals with exceptional IQs.

How early can intellectually gifted children be identified? By toddlerhood, according to a longitudinal study by Allen Gottfried and his colleagues (1994). They tracked a large sample of children from age 1 to age 8, determined which children had IQs of 130 or above at age 8, and then looked for differences between these gifted children and other children earlier in life. The gifted children turned out to be identifiable as early as 18 months of age, primarily by their advanced language skills. They were also highly curious and motivated to learn; they even enjoyed the challenge of taking IQ tests more than most children. Linda Silverman and her colleagues at the Gifted Development Center have used the Characteristics of Giftedness Scale to identify gifted children. In particular, they (see Rogers, 1986; Silverman, Chitwood, & Waters, 1986) have found that gifted children can be distinguished from average children in terms of: rapid learning, extensive vocabulary, good memory, long attention span, perfectionism, preference for older companions, excellent sense of humor, early interest in reading, strong ability with puzzles and mazes, maturity, and perseverance.

The rest of the story of the development of high-IQ children is told by a major longitudinal study launched in 1921 by

Gifted children have either high IQ scores or special abilities. This young girl is performing with the Pacific Symphony of Orange County, California.

William Sidis: A Case of Unrealized Potential

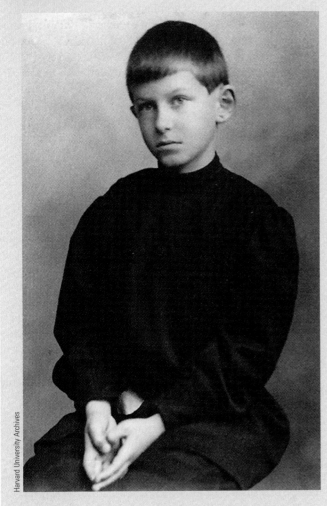

Harvard University Archives

No failed genius is more notorious than William Sidis. According to Amy Wallace's (1986) biography *The Prodigy*, Sidis was the son of a brilliant Harvard psychologist and the godson of the pioneering psychologist William James. From infancy, "Billy" was the subject of an experiment designed by his father to prove that magnificent talents can be developed in any child. Given the most enriched early environments (and probably some good genes as well), Billy could read the newspaper at 18 months of age and had learned eight languages by the time he reached school age. His school years were brief, however, for he entered Harvard at age 11 and was teaching mathematics at Rice University by age 17.

Unfortunately, his parents invested so much energy in developing his mind that they apparently neglected his social and emotional development. His social incompetence and odd habits were as widely publicized as his intellectual feats, and finally William Sidis had apparently had enough of it all. He quit the academic life, took a series of menial jobs, and lived as a hermit, writing about obscure topics and jumping at every opportunity to show children his prodigious collection of streetcar and subway tickets. Sidis seemed content with his life of obscurity, but he certainly did not achieve the greatness that might have been predicted. He died of a stroke at age 46.

William Sidis was clearly the exception to all we know about gifted children and their outcomes. Nonetheless, his story reminds us that early blooming is no guarantee of later flowering. And it works the other way, too: Late blooming does not rule out eminence in adulthood. We need only cite the case of Albert Einstein, whose name is synonymous with genius. Einstein didn't speak until age 4, could not read until age 7, and was judged by his teachers to have little future at all (Feldman, 1982)!

none other than Lewis Terman, developer of the Stanford-Binet test (Fincher, 1973; Terman, 1954; Oden, 1968). The participants were more than 1,500 California schoolchildren who were nominated by their teachers as gifted and who had IQs of 140 or higher. It soon became apparent that these high-IQ children (who came to be called Termites) were exceptional in many other ways as well. For example, they had weighed more at birth and had learned to walk and talk sooner than most toddlers. They reached puberty somewhat earlier than average and had better-than-average health. Their teachers rated them as better adjusted and more morally mature than their less intelligent peers. And, although they were no more popular than their classmates, they were quick to take on leadership responsibilities. Taken together, these findings destroy the stereotype that most gifted children are frail,

sickly youngsters who are socially inadequate and emotionally immature.

Another demonstration of the personal and social maturity of most gifted children comes from a study of high-IQ children who skipped high school entirely and entered the University of Washington as part of a special program to accelerate their education (Robinson & Janos, 1986). Contrary to the common wisdom that gifted children will suffer socially and emotionally if they skip grades and are forced to fit in with much older students, these youngsters showed no signs at all of maladjustment. Indeed, on several measures of psychological and social maturity and adjustment, they equaled their much older college classmates, as well as similarly gifted students who attended high school. Many of them thrived in college, for the first time finding friends like themselves—

friends who "got their jokes" (Noble, Robinson, & Gunderson, 1993, p. 125).

Most of Terman's gifted children remained as remarkable in adulthood as they had been in childhood. Fewer than 5% were rated as seriously maladjusted. Their rates of such problems as ill health, mental illness, alcoholism, and delinquent behavior were but a fraction of those observed in the general population (Terman, 1954), although they were no less likely to divorce (Holahan & Sears, 1995).

The occupational achievements of the men in the sample were impressive. In middle age, 88% were employed in professional or high-level business jobs, compared to 20% of men in the general population (Oden, 1968). As a group, they had taken out more than 200 patents and written some 2,000 scientific reports, 100 books, 375 plays or short stories, and more than 300 essays, sketches, magazine articles, and critiques. And gifted women? Because of the influence of gender-role expectations during the period covered by the study, gifted women achieved less than gifted men vocationally, often interrupting their careers or sacrificing their career goals entirely to raise families. Still, they were more likely to have careers, and distinguished ones, than most women of their generation.

Finally, the Termites aged well. In their 60s and 70s, most of the men and women in the Terman study were highly active, involved, healthy, and happy people (Holahan & Sears, 1995). The men kept working longer than most men do and stayed involved in work even after they retired. The women too led exceptionally active lives. Contrary to the stereotype that gifted individuals burn out early, the Termites continued to burn bright throughout their lives. Recent reports even indicate that having a high IQ is associated with living longer (Whalley & Deary, 2001).

Yet, just as it is wrong to view intellectually gifted children as emotionally disturbed misfits, it is inaccurate to conclude that intellectually gifted children are models of good adjustment, perfect in every way. Some research suggests that children with IQs closer to 180 than 130 are quite often unhappy and socially isolated, perhaps because they are so out of step with their peers, and sometimes even have serious problems (Winner, 1996). In *Terman's Kids,* Joel Shurkin (1992) describes several less-than-happy life stories of some of Terman's Termites. A woman who graduated from Stanford at age 17 and was headed for success as a writer became a landlady instead; an emotionally disturbed boy took cyanide at age 18 after being rejected in love. The Explorations box on page 241 describes a particularly tragic case of failed genius.

These are exceptions, however. Overall, most of Terman's gifted children moved through adulthood as healthy, happy, and highly productive individuals. Yet some fared better than others. Even within this elite group, for example, the quality of the individual's home environment was important. The most well-adjusted and successful adults had highly educated parents who offered them both love and intellectual stimulation (Tomlinson-Keasey & Little, 1990).

Creativity and Special Talents

Despite their many positive outcomes in life, not one of Terman's high-IQ gifted children became truly eminent. Recall that Terman had teachers nominate bright children for inclusion in the study. Is it possible that teachers overlooked some children who would be considered gifted by today's criteria because of their special talents rather than their high IQs? Might they have missed children capable of outstanding work in a particular area such as music, art, or writing? The word *creativity* comes to mind. Perhaps creativity is more important than IQ in allowing a Michelangelo or a Mozart to break new ground. But what is creativity, and what do we know about its development?

What Is Creativity?

Creativity is most often defined as the ability to produce *novel* responses that are appropriate in context and valued by others—products that are both original and meaningful (Csikszentmihalyi, 1996; Simonton, 1999; Sternberg, 1999). In his structure-of-intellect model, J. P. Guilford (1967, 1988) captured the idea of creativity by proposing that it involves divergent rather than convergent thinking. **Divergent thinking** requires coming up with a variety of ideas or solutions to a problem when there is no one right answer. **Convergent thinking** involves "converging" on the one best answer to a problem and is precisely what IQ tests measure. The most common measure of creativity, at least in children, is what is called **ideational fluency,** or the sheer number of different (including novel) ideas that a person can generate. Quick—list all the uses you can think of for a pencil. An uncreative person might say you could write letters, notes, postcards, and so forth; by contrast, one creative person envisioned a pencil as "a backscratcher, a potting stake, kindling for a fire, a rolling pin for baking, a toy for a woodpecker, or a small boat for a cricket" (Richards, 1996, p. 73).

Creativity and divergent thinking truly are distinct from general intelligence and convergent thinking. Indeed, correlations between scores on creativity measures and scores on IQ tests are only about .20 (Torrance, 1969). Creativity and general intelligence are related in the sense that highly creative people rarely have below-average IQs. Thus, a *minimum* of intelligence is probably required for creativity (Barron & Harrington, 1981; Runco, 1992; Simonton, 1999). However, among people who have average or above-average IQs, an individual's IQ score is essentially unrelated to his or her level of creativity. In all likelihood, then, the IQs of you and your classmates will not necessarily predict which of you will give the most creative answers to the problems in Figure 9.9.

Creativity in Childhood and Adolescence

What is the child who scores high on tests of creativity like? Getzels and Jackson (1962) compared children who had high

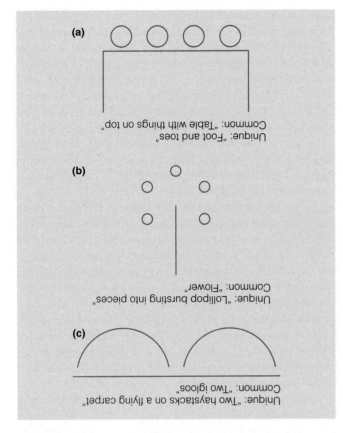

Figure 9.9 Are you creative? Indicate what you see in each of the three drawings. Below each drawing you will find examples of unique and common responses, drawn from a study of creativity in children.

Source: Wallach & Kogan (1965)

creativity scores but normal-range IQ scores with children who scored high in IQ but not in creativity. Personality measures suggested that the creative children showed more freedom, originality, humor, violence, and playfulness than the high-IQ children. Perhaps as a result, the high-IQ children were more success oriented and received more approval from teachers. Compared with their less creative peers, creative children also engaged in more fantasy or pretend play, often inventing new uses for familiar objects and new roles for themselves (Kogan, 1983). Finally, these children are more open to new experiences and ideas (Simonton, 1999).

Although average IQ scores differ across racial and socioeconomic groups, scores on creativity tests often do not (Kogan, 1983). Moreover, genetic influences (a source of individual differences in IQ) have little to do with performance on tests of creativity; twins are similar in the degree of creativity they display, but identical twins are no more similar than fraternal twins (Plomin, 1990; Reznikoff et al., 1973). This suggests that certain qualities of the home environment tend to make brothers and sisters alike in their degree of creativity. What qualities? Although we have little research to go on, parents of creative children and adolescents tend to value nonconformity and independence, accept their children as they are, encourage their curiosity and playfulness, and grant them

a good deal of freedom to explore new possibilities on their own (Getzels & Jackson, 1962; Harrington, Block, & Block, 1987; Runco, 1992). In some cases, the parent–child relationship is even distant; a surprising number of eminent creators seem to have experienced rather lonely, insecure, and unhappy childhoods (Ochse, 1990; Simonton, 1999). Out of their adversity may have come an active imagination and a strong desire to develop their talents. Overall, then, creative abilities are influenced by factors quite distinct from those that influence the cognitive abilities measured on IQ tests.

How does the capacity to be creative change with age? We really are not sure. Performance on tests of creativity generally increase over the childhood and adolescent years, but there appear to be certain ages along the way when it drops off (Kogan, 1983). Howard Gardner (Gardner, Phelps, & Wolf, 1990) suggests that preschool children are highly original, playful, and uninhibited but that school-age children become restricted in their creative expression as they attempt to master their culture's rules for art, music, dance, and other creative endeavors so that they can do things the "right" way. During adolescence, Gardner believes, some individuals give up the desire to express themselves creatively, but others regain the innovativeness and freedom of expression they had as preschoolers and put it to use, along with the technical skills they gained as children, to produce highly creative works. The ages at which creativity flourishes or is stifled seem to vary from culture to culture, depending on when children are pressured to conform (Torrance, 1975). Overall, the developmental course of creativity is not so predictable or steady as the increase in mental age seen on measures of IQ. Instead, creativity seems to wax and wane with age in response to developmental needs and cultural demands.

How well does performance on tests of creativity predict actual creative accomplishments, such as original artwork or outstanding science projects? Some researchers have found that scores on creativity tests administered in either elementary or secondary school do predict creative achievements, such as inventions and novels, in adulthood (Howieson, 1981; Runco, 1992; Torrance, 1988). However, just as it is a mistake to expect IQ to predict accomplishments, it may also be a mistake to expect tests of creativity to do so with any great accuracy (Albert, 1996). Why? First, creativity is expressed in different ways at different points in the life span; engaging in imaginative play as a child is correlated with high scores on tests of creativity (Russ, 1996), but may have little to do with being a creative scientist or musician as an adult. Also, creativity tests, like IQ tests, attempt to measure *general* cognitive abilities when, in fact, many *specific talents* exist, and each of them (artistic, mathematical, musical, and so on) requires distinct skills and experiences, as suggested by Gardner's theory of multiple intelligences.

Researchers are now looking at individuals who do indeed show exceptional talent in a particular field and are trying to identify the factors that contribute to their accomplishments (Sternberg & Lubart, 1996). David Feldman (1982, 1986), for example, has studied children who are "prodigies" in such areas as chess, music, and mathematics. These individuals were generally similar to other children in areas outside their fields of expertise. What contributed to their special achievements? They had *talent,* of course, but they also seemed to have a powerful *motivation* to develop their special talents—a real passion for what they were doing. Olympic gymnast Olga Korbutt put it well: "If gymnastics did not exist, I would have invented it" (Feldman, 1982, p. 35). Moreover, these achievers were blessed with an *environment* that recognized, valued, and nurtured their talent and motivation (see also Winner, 1996). They were strongly encouraged and supported by their families and intensively tutored or coached by experts. According to Feldman, the child with creative potential in a specific field must become intimately familiar with the current state of the field if he or she is to advance or transform it, as the groundbreaking artist or musician does. But parents and trainers must not be too pushy. For example, David Helfgott, the Australian pianist who was the subject of the movie *Shine,* was nearly destroyed by an abusive father who pushed him unmercifully to master difficult pieces (Page, 1996). Cellist Yo-Yo Ma, a prodigy himself, says this about nurturing young musicians:

> If you lead them toward music, teach them that it is beautiful, and help them learn—say, "Oh, you love music, well, let's work on this piece together, and I'll show you something . . ." That's a *creative* nurturing. But if you just push them to be stars, and tell them they'll become rich and famous—or, worse, if you try to live through them—that is damaging. (Page, 1996, p. G10)

K. Anders Ericsson and Neil Charness (1994) go even farther than Feldman in emphasizing the importance of environment in the development of creative talent. Indeed, they maintain that it is practice rather than innate talent that makes great creators great—that nature is overrated and nurture is underrated when it comes to creative achievement. Their research shows that prolonged training in a set of skills can alter cognitive and physiological processes and permit levels of performance that would have been unimaginable without training. Motivation also enters in, however, because only some individuals are willing to do what Ericsson and Charness believe is necessary to become outstanding in a field—work hard every day over a period of more than 10 years.

In summary, there are many forms of giftedness, many "intelligences." Studies of creativity have revealed that performance on creativity tests is distinct from performance on IQ tests. Yet neither tests of general intelligence nor tests of general creativity are very good at predicting which children will show exceptional talent in a *specific* field. Instead, that kind of creative achievement seems to be related to characteristics of the individual, including exceptional talent and motivation, *and* characteristics of the environment, especially support and the extensive training required to master a field.

Creative Achievement in Adulthood

Studies of creativity during the adult years have focused on a very small number of so-called eminent creators in such fields as art, music, science, and philosophy. The big question has been this: *When* in adulthood are such individuals most productive and most likely to create their best works? Is it early in adulthood, when they can benefit from youth's enthusiasm and freshness of approach? Or is it later in adulthood, when they have fully mastered their field and have the experience and knowledge necessary to make a breakthrough in it? And what becomes of the careers of eminent creators in old age?

Early studies by Harvey Lehman (1953) and Wayne Dennis (1966) provided a fairly clear picture of how creative careers unfold (see also Simonton, 1990). In most fields, creative production increases steeply from the 20s to the late 30s and early 40s and then gradually declines thereafter, though not to the same low levels that characterized very early adulthood. Peak times of creative achievement also vary from field to field. As Figure 9.10 shows, the productivity of scholars in the humanities (for example, historians and philosophers) continues well into old age and actually peaks in the 60s, possibly because creative work in these fields often involves integrating knowledge that has "crystallized" over many years. By contrast, productivity in the arts (for example, music or drama) peaks in the 30s and 40s and declines quite steeply thereafter, perhaps because artistic creativity depends on a more "fluid" or innovative kind of thinking. Scientists seem to be intermediate, peaking in their 40s and declining only in their 70s. Even within the same general field, differences in peak times have been noted. For example, poets reach their peak before novelists do, and mathematicians peak before other scientists do (Dennis, 1966; Lehman, 1953).

Still, in many fields (including psychology, by the way), creative production rises to a peak in the late 30s or early 40s, and both total number of works and number of high-quality works decline somewhat thereafter (Simonton, 1990). This same pattern can be detected across different cultures and historical periods. Even so, the percentage of a creator's works that are major, significant ones does not change much at all

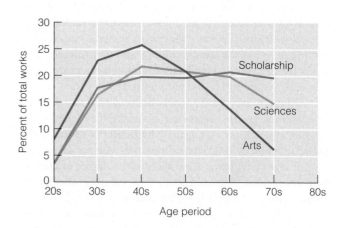

Figure 9.10 Percentage of total works produced in each decade of the lives of eminent creators. The "scholarship" group includes historians and philosophers; the "sciences" category includes natural and physical scientists, inventors, and mathematicians; the "arts" creators include architects, musicians, dramatists, poets, and the like.

Source: Based on data from Dennis (1966)

over the years (Simonton, 1990). This means that many creators are still producing outstanding works in old age—sometimes their greatest works—not just rehashes of earlier triumphs. Michelangelo, for instance, was in his 70s and 80s when he worked on St. Peter's Cathedral, and Goethe was polishing *Faust* at 83. Indeed, the most eminent among the eminent seem to start early and finish late (Simonton, 1990).

How can we account for changes in creative production over the adult years? One explanation, proposed long ago (Beard, 1874, cited in Simonton, 1984), is that creative achievement requires both enthusiasm and experience. In early adulthood, the enthusiasm is there, but the experience is not; in later adulthood, the experience is there, but the enthusiasm or vigor has fallen off. People in their 30s and 40s have it all.

Dean Simonton (1984, 1990, 1991) has offered another theory: Each creator may have a certain potential to create that is realized over the adult years; as the potential is realized, less is left to express. According to Simonton, creative activity involves two processes: *ideation* (generating creative ideas) and *elaboration* (executing ideas to produce actual poems, paintings, or scientific publications). After a career is launched, some time elapses before any ideas are generated or any works actually completed. This would explain the rise in creative achievement between the 20s and 30s. Also, some kinds of work take longer to formulate or complete than others, which helps explain why a poet (who can generate and carry out ideas quickly) might reach a creative peak earlier in life than, say, a historian (who may need to devote years to the research and writing necessary to complete a book once the idea for it is hatched).

Why does creative production eventually begin to taper off? Simonton (1990, 1991) suggests that older creators may simply have used up much of their total stock of potential ideas. They never totally exhaust their creative potential, but they have less of it left to realize. Simonton argues, then, that changes in creative production over the adult years have more to do with the nature of the creative process than with a loss of mental ability in later life. Creators who start their careers late are likely to experience the very same rise and fall of creative output that others do, only later in life. And those lucky creators with immense creative potential to realize will not burn out; they will keep right on producing great works until they die.

What about mere mortals like us? Here, researchers have fallen back on tests designed to measure creativity. In one study, scores on a test of divergent thinking abilities decreased at least modestly after about age 40 and decreased even more steeply starting at about 70 (McCrae, Arenberg, & Costa, 1987). It seems that elderly adults do not differ much from younger adults in the originality of their ideas; the main difference is that they generate fewer of them (Jaquish & Ripple, 1981). Generally, then, these studies agree with the studies of eminent achievers: Creative behavior becomes less frequent in later life, but it remains possible throughout the adult years.

Our account of cognitive development over the life span is now complete. We hope you appreciate that each of the four major approaches to the mind that we have considered—the Piagetian cognitive developmental approach and Vygotsky's theory discussed in Chapter 7, the information-processing approach discussed in Chapter 8, and the psychometric or testing approach discussed here—offers something of value. Table 9.7 lists how these four approaches compare on their views of intelligence. Perhaps we can summarize it this way: Piaget has shown us that comparing the thought of a preschooler to the thought of an adult is like comparing a tadpole to a frog. Modes of thought change qualitatively with age. Vygotsky has highlighted the importance of culturally transmitted modes of thinking and interactions with others. The information-processing approach has helped us understand thinking processes and explain why the young child cannot remember as much information or solve problems as effectively as the adult can. Finally, the psychometric approach has told us that, if we look at the wide range of tasks to which the mind can be applied, we can recognize distinct mental abilities that each person consistently displays in greater or lesser amounts. We need not choose one approach and reject the others. Our understanding of the mind is likely to be richer if all three approaches continue to thrive. There are truly many "intelligences," and it is foolish to think that a single IQ score can possibly describe the complexities of human cognitive development.

Table 9.7 Comparison of Piagetian, Vygotskian, Information-Processing, and Psychometric Approaches to Intelligence

	Piagetian Theory	Vygotskian Theory	Information-Processing Approach	Psychometric Approach
What is intelligence?	Cognitive structures that help us adapt	Tools of culture	Attention, memory, and other mental processes	Mental abilities; scores on IQ tests
What changes with age?	Stage of cognitive development	Ability to solve problems without assistance of others, and use of inner speech	Hardware (speed) and software (strategies) of the mind	Mental age (difficulty of problems solved)
What is of most interest?	Universal changes	Culturally influenced changes and processes	Universal processes	Individual differences

Summary Points

1. The psychometric or testing approach to cognition defines intelligence as a set of traits that allows some people to think and solve problems more effectively than others. It can be viewed as a hierarchy consisting of a general factor *g*, broad abilities such as fluid and crystallized intelligence, and many specific abilities. Gardner's theory of multiple intelligences, with its focus on eight distinct forms of intelligence, offers an alternative view. Sternberg's triarchic theory of intelligence, with its contextual, experiential, and information-processing components, offers another.

2. Intelligence tests such as the Stanford-Binet and the Wechsler scales compare an individual's performance on a variety of cognitive tasks with the average performance of age-mates. Scores on these tests in a large population form a normal or bell-shaped distribution, with an average score of 100. Some testers are experimenting with dynamic assessment methods that determine how well individuals learn new material with guidance. Other new tests include the Kaufman Assessment Battery for Children and the Cognitive Assessment System, which both take a theoretical approach to test construction.

3. In infancy, mental growth is rapid and is measured by developmental quotients derived from tests such as the Bayley Scales. However, infant scores do not predict later IQ as well as measures of speed of information processing such as rapid habituation and preference for novelty do.

4. During childhood, mental growth continues, and IQs at one age predict IQs at later ages quite well. However, many individuals show wide variations in their IQ scores over time. Those who gain IQ points often have favorable home environments, whereas disadvantaged children often show a cumulative deficit.

5. In adolescence, further mental growth occurs; IQs continue to be relatively stable over time and predict school achievement and years of education obtained.

6. IQ is related to the status or prestige of an adult's occupation, as well as to his or her success within that occupation. Both cross-sectional studies and longitudinal studies tend to show age-related decreases in IQ. Schaie's sequential study suggests that (a) date of birth (cohort) influences test performance, (b) no major declines in mental abilities occur until the late 60s or 70s, (c) some abilities (especially fluid ones) decline more than others (especially crystallized ones), and (d) not all people's abilities decline. Decline is most likely in those who have poor health and unstimulating lifestyles.

7. Wisdom, or exceptional insight into the human condition, is no more common, but also no less common, in later adulthood than in earlier adulthood and depends less on age than on life experiences.

8. Individual differences in IQ at a given age are linked to genetic factors and to intellectually stimulating qualities of the home environment. The low average scores of some minority groups on IQ tests may be explained better by culture bias in testing, low motivation (including anxiety caused by negative group stereotypes), and low socioeconomic status than by genetic differences. Minority children perform much better when they grow up in intellectually stimulating homes.

9. Mentally retarded individuals show varied levels of functioning, depending on their IQs and the causes (organic or cultural-familial) of their retardation. Mildly retarded individuals appear to meet the demands of adult life better than the demands of school. Children identified as gifted on the basis of high IQ scores have been found to be above average in virtually all ways.

10. Creativity—the ability to produce novel and socially valued works—is a distinct mental ability that demands divergent rather than convergent thinking; it is largely independent of IQ (above a certain minimum level), increases with age during childhood, and is fostered in homes where independence is valued. Eminent creators are typically more productive during their 30s and 40s than before or after but continue to produce great works in later life. Performance on creativity tests declines in later life, but creative capacities clearly survive into old age.

Critical Thinking

1. All things considered, do you think it was a good idea or a bad idea for psychologists such as Binet and Terman to devise IQ tests? What value do these tests have? What problems do they create?

2. Imagine that you are chosen to head a Presidential Commission on Intelligence Testing whose task it is to devise a better IQ test for use in the schools than any that currently exists. Drawing on material in this chapter, sketch out the features of your model IQ test. What would be included and excluded from your definition of intelligence? How would you go about measuring intelligence, as you define it? In what ways would your test improve upon the Stanford-Binet or WISC?

3. Putting together material from Chapters 7, 8, and 9, how would you describe the cognitive functioning of a typical 70-year-old person? What are the greatest cognitive strengths of older adults, what are their greatest limitations, and how much can an individual do to optimize his or her functioning?

4. The Maori are a socioeconomically disadvantaged group in New Zealand, a country colonized by the British long ago. Maori children typically score lower on IQ tests than children of British background. Knowing what you know about minorities in the United States, what are your top two hypotheses about why Maori children perform relatively poorly, and how might you test these hypotheses?

Key Terms

psychometric approach	developmental quotient (DQ)
factor analysis	cumulative-deficit hypothesis
structure-of-intellect model	terminal drop
fluid intelligence	wisdom
crystallized intelligence	HOME inventory
savant syndrome	Flynn effect
triarchic theory of intelligence	mental retardation
automatization	organic retardation
culture bias	cultural-familial retardation
mental age (MA)	giftedness
intelligence quotient (IQ)	creativity
test norms	divergent thinking
normal distribution	convergent thinking
dynamic assessment	ideational fluency

On the Web

Web Sites to Explore

The Role of Intelligence in Modern Society

An article by Earl Hunt, published in 1995 in *The American Scientist*, addresses the controversy raised by Herrnstein and Murray 's book, *The Bell Curve*.
http://www.sigmaxi.org/amsci/articles/95articles/Hunt-full.html

Intelligence Test

If you enjoy mental challenges and want to get an estimate of your IQ, try one of the intelligence tests at this site. Reliability and validity data for the tests are provided; you should evaluate these carefully before taking your score too seriously.
http://www.queendom.com/tests/iq/index.html

Gardner's Muliple Intelligences

Follow up on the material in the chapter regarding Gardner's eight intelligences by pursuing one of the links on this site.
http://www.edwebproject.org/edref.mi.intro.html

Mental Retardation

The first link is the home of the American Association on Mental Retardation; the second links to the Association for Retarded Citizens. Both offer a wealth of resources on mental retardation.
http://www.aamr.org/index.shtml
http://www.thearc.org

Search Online with InfoTrac College Edition

For additional information, explore InfoTrac College Edition, your online library. Go to http://infotrac-college.com and use the passcode that came on the card with your book. Search for "age and intelligence," and select two scholarly articles to explore further. How does the material reported in these articles relate to what is in the text? Is it consistent? Does it extend an idea introduced in the chapter? Also try searching for "intellect," then narrow your search by going to the subdivision "genetic aspects." Find two or three scholarly articles on genetic contributions to intelligence, summarize this material, and compare it to what is reported in this chapter.

Visit Our Web Site

Go to http://www.wadsworth.com/psychology, where you will find online resources directly linked to your book.

Life-Span CD-ROM

Go to the Wadsworth Life-Span CD-ROM for further study of the concepts in this chapter. The CD-ROM also includes quizzes and additional activities to expand your learning experience.

Language and Education

AS THE COOL STREAM GUSHED over one hand, she [Annie] spelled into the other the word *water*, first slowly, then rapidly. I stood still, my whole attention fixed upon the motions of her fingers. Suddenly I felt a misty consciousness as of something forgotten—a thrill of returning thought; and somehow the mystery of language was revealed to me. I knew then that W-A-T-E-R meant the wonderful cool something that was flowing over my hand. . . . I left the well-house eager to learn. Everything had a name, and each name gave birth to a new thought. As we returned to the house every object which I touched seemed to quiver with life. (Helen Keller, *The Story of My Life*, 1954)

T here is possibly no more important skill than mastering some type of language system. Consider how the world changed for Helen Keller, deaf and blind from a young age, when she finally realized that every object, every person, every concept could be represented with a symbol. From this point on, she was able to communicate with the people around her and participate in the world in ways that were not available without a tool such as sign or spoken language. As we learned in Chapter 7, psychologist Lev Vygotsky argued that language is the primary vehicle through which adults pass culturally valued modes of thinking and problem solving on to their children. He also believed that language is our most important tool of thinking.

In this chapter, we begin by examining how and when language is acquired. Basic language skills become established largely through an informal education system consisting of parents, other grown-ups, peers, and even the media. We then consider formal education, which uses basic language skills to cultivate the reading, writing, thinking, and problem-solving skills that allow individuals to become fully functioning members of society. Getting the most out of education requires more than acquiring language and literacy skills, though. As Terrel Bell, former Secretary of Education asserted, "there are three things to remember about education. The first one is motivation. The second one is motivation. The third one is motivation" (quoted in Maehr & Meyer, 1997, p. 372). Thus, we also examine achievement motivation and its relationship to education and educational outcomes.

Mastering Language

Although language is one of the most intricate forms of knowledge we will ever acquire, all normal children master a language very early in life. Indeed, many infants are talking before they can walk. Can language be all that complex, then? It certainly can be. Linguists (scholars who study language) have yet to fully describe the rules of English (or of any other language), and so far computers cannot understand speech as well as most 5-year-olds can. What exactly is the task facing young language learners?

What Must Be Mastered

Linguists define **language** as a communication system in which a limited number of signals—sounds or letters (or gestures, in the case of the sign language used by deaf people)—can be combined according to agreed-upon rules to produce an infinite number of messages. To master a spoken language such as English, a child must know learn basic sounds, how sounds are combined to form words, how words are combined to form meaningful statements, what words and sentences mean, and how to use language effectively in their social interactions. That is, the child must master five aspects of language: phonology, morphology, syntax, semantics, and pragmatics.

Phonology is the sound system of a language, and the basic units of sound in any given language are its phonemes. The child in an English-speaking country must come to know the 45 phonemes used in English (which correspond roughly to the familiar vowel and consonant sounds) and must also learn which ones can be combined in English and which ones cannot (for example, *st-*, but not *sb-*). Other languages have other basic sounds (or, in a sign language, basic hand shapes and motions). Children must learn to hear and to pronounce the phonemes of their language in order to make sense of the speech they hear and to be understood when they speak.

Rules of **morphology** are rules for forming words from sounds. Rules of morphology in English include the rule for forming past tenses of verbs by adding *-ed* and the rule for forming plurals by adding *-s*, as well as rules for using other prefixes and suffixes. Exceptions to these rules must be learned as well.

Rules of **syntax** are rules for forming sentences from words. Consider these three sentences: (1) Fang Fred bit. (2) Fang bit Fred. (3) Fred bit Fang. The first, as even very young children recognize, violates the rules of English sentence structure or syntax, although this word order would be perfectly acceptable in German. The second and third are both grammatical English sentences, but their different word orders convey very different meanings. Children must master rules of syntax to understand or use language, from simple declarative sentences like these to complex sentences with many clauses and phrases.

Semantics is the aspect of language that concerns meanings. Words stand for things, and the child must map the relationships between words and things. Knowledge of semantics is also required to interpret whole sentences or speeches or paragraphs. Grasping semantics obviously depends on understanding the world and thus on cognitive development.

Finally, language learners must also master **pragmatics**—rules specifying how language is used appropriately in different social contexts. That is, children have to learn when to say what to whom. They must learn to communicate effectively by taking into account who the listener is, what the listener already knows, and what the listener needs or wants to hear.

"Give me that cookie" may be grammatical English, but the child is far more likely to win Grandma's heart (not to mention a cookie) with a polite "May I please try one of your yummy cookies, Grandma?"

In short, mastering language is an incredible challenge that requires learning phonology, semantics, morphology, syntax, and pragmatics. What's more, human communication involves not only language but also forms of *nonverbal communication* (facial expressions, tone of voice, gestures, and so on). For example, **intonation**—the variations in pitch, loudness, and timing used when saying words or sentences—can be very important. Using intonation, speakers emphasize grammatically important words, signal that they are asking questions rather than making statements, and so on. Children must also learn these nonverbal signals, which often clarify the meaning of a verbal message and are important means of communicating in their own right. Let's look at the course of language development and then ask how nature and nurture contribute to the child's remarkable accomplishment.

A mother draws her 3-month-old infant into a "conversation."

The Course of Language Development

For the first 10 to 13 months of life, infants are not yet capable of speaking meaningful words, but they are building up to that achievement.

BEFORE THE FIRST WORDS

As we learned in Chapter 6, newborns seem to tune in to human speech immediately. Very young infants can distinguish between phonemes such as *b* and *p* or *d* and *t* (Eimas, 1975). Before they ever speak a word, infants are also becoming sensitive to the fact that pauses in speech fall *between* clauses, phrases, and words rather than in the middle of these important language units (Fisher & Tokura, 1996; Myers et al., 1996). Indeed, infants as young as 7½ months can segment speech into meaningful words, a skill that improves over the next several months (Houston et al., 2000; Jusczyk, 1999; Jusczyk, Houston, & Newsome, 1999). This shows sensitivity to phonology and may help infants learn the rules of grammar.

What about producing sounds? From birth, infants produce sounds—cries, burps, grunts, and sneezes. These sounds help exercise the vocal cords and give infants an opportunity to learn how airflow and different mouth and tongue positions affect sounds. Further, parents typically respond to these prelinguistic sounds as if they were genuine efforts to communicate (McCune et al., 1996). For instance, in response to her 3-month-old's hiccup sound, a mother replies, "My goodness! What's going on in there? Huh? Tell Mommy." The mother draws her infant into a sort of dialogue. Such prelinguistic sounds, and the feedback infants receive, will eventually be incorporated into meaningful speech sounds (Hoff, 2001). Perhaps most impressive about this early verbal and nonverbal "dance" between infants and their caregivers is that it relates positively to later attachment between them and to the cognitive development of the infant (Jaffe et al., 2001).

The next milestone in vocalization, at about 6 to 8 weeks of age, is **cooing**—repeating vowel-like sounds such as "ooooh" and "aaaaah." Babies coo when they are contented and often in response to being spoken to in a happy voice. Do infants this age understand the words spoken to them? Not likely—they primarily respond to the "melody" of speech. Parents can say some rather nasty things to their young infants ("You're driving me nuts today!") as long as they say them with a happy voice (Hirsh-Pasek, Golinkoff, & Hollich, 1999).

At about 3 to 4 months of age, infants expand their vocal range considerably as they begin to produce consonant sounds. They enter a period of **babbling** between about 4 and 6 months of age, repeating consonant–vowel combinations such as "baba" or "dadadada" over and over, which may be what Piaget would call a primary circular reaction—the repeating of an interesting noise for the sheer pleasure of making it.

Up to about 6 months of age, infants all over the world, even deaf ones, sound pretty much alike, but the effects of experience soon become apparent. At roughly this age, deaf infants fall behind hearing infants in their ability to produce well-formed syllables (Oller & Eilers, 1988). By the time infants are about 8 months old, they babble with something of an accent; adults can often tell from their babbling whether babies have been listening to French, Chinese, or Arabic (de Boysson-Bardies, Sagart, & Durand, 1984). These advanced babblers increasingly restrict their sounds to those that are phonemes in the language they are hearing, and they pick up the intonation patterns of that language as well (Hoff, 2001). Once these intonation patterns are added to infants' babbles, their utterances sound very much like real speech until, as Erika Hoff (2001) puts it, "you listen closely and realize that the infant is producing the melody of language without the words" (p. 103).

As they attempt to master the semantics of language, infants come to understand many words before they can produce them. That is, *comprehension (or reception) is ahead of production (or expression) in language development.* Before they really understand the specific words in a command (such as "Get the ball"), they will obey it in familiar contexts, probably by interpreting tone of voice and context cues (Benedict, 1979). Shortly before speaking their first true words, however, as they approach a year of age, they really seem to understand familiar words. How do they figure out what words mean? When Mom points to a small, four-legged furry animal and says "Furrball," how do infants come to know that this refers to the cat and not to its movement or to its tail or to the animal next door? Several researchers note the importance of **joint attention** in early word learning (Carpenter, Nagell, & Tomasello, 1998; Woodward & Markman, 1998). Infants listen to parents repeatedly labeling and pointing at objects, directing their gaze, and otherwise making salient the connection between words and their referents (Hollich, Hirsh-Pasek, & Golinkoff, 2000). If Mom says "cat" while both she and her child are looking at the furry animal, then the chances are good that this is the referent for the label. Infants also tend to assume that a word refers to a whole object rather than to some part of the object (Pan & Gleason, 2001; Woodward & Markman, 1998). Thus, infants come to realize that Furrball refers to the family's whole cat and not to individual properties of the cat.

THE FIRST WORDS

An infant's first meaningful word, spoken at about a year of age, is a special event for parents. First words have been called **holophrases** because a single word sometimes conveys an entire sentence's worth of meaning. These single-word "sentences" can serve different communication functions depending on the way they are said and the context in which they are said (Barrett, 1995). For example, 17-month-old Shelley used the word *ghetti* (spaghetti) in three different ways over a 5-minute period. First, she pointed to the pan on the stove and seemed to be asking "Is that spaghetti?" Later, the function of her holophrase was to name the spaghetti when shown the contents of the pan, as in "It's spaghetti." Finally, there was little question that she was requesting spaghetti when she tugged at her companion's sleeve as he was eating and used the word in a whining tone.

Although there are limits to the meaning that can be packed into a single word and its accompanying tone of voice and gestures, 1-year-olds in the holophrastic stage of language development do seem to have mastered such basic language functions as naming, questioning, requesting, and demanding. And at the same time they begin to use words as symbols, they also begin to use nonverbal symbols—gestures such as pointing, raising their arms to signal "up," or panting heavily to say "dog" (Acredolo & Goodwyn, 1988; Bates, O'Connell, & Shore, 1987).

What do 1-year-olds talk about? They talk mainly about familiar objects and actions (Nelson, Hampson, & Shaw, 1993; Pan & Gleason, 2001; and see Table 10.1). Katherine Nelson (1973) studied 18 infants as they learned their first 50 English words and found that nearly two-thirds of these early words were common nouns representing objects and people that the children interacted with daily. These objects were nearly all things that the child could manipulate (bottles, shoes) or that were capable of moving on their own (animals, trucks).

Initial language acquisition proceeds literally one word at a time. Three or four months may pass before the child has a vocabulary of 10 words (Nelson, 1973). Then, in what is called the **vocabulary spurt,** at around 18 months of age, when the child has mastered about 30 to 50 words, the pace of word learning quickens dramatically (Goldfield & Reznick, 1996; Nelson, 1973). By 24 months of age, children are producing an average of 186 words (Nelson, 1973). What changes? During the vocabulary spurt, toddlers seem to arrive at the critical realization, as Helen Keller did, that everything has a name; they then want to learn all the names they possibly can (Reznick & Goldfield, 1992).

With such a rapidly increasing vocabulary, it should come as no surprise that children sometimes make mistakes. While they rarely get the meaning entirely wrong, they fairly often use a word too broadly or too narrowly (Pan & Gleason, 2001). One error is **overextension,** or using a word to refer to too wide a range of objects or events, as when a 2-year-old calls all furry, four-legged animals *doggie*. The second, and opposite, error is **underextension,** as when a child initially uses the word *doggie* to refer only to basset hounds like the family pet. Notice that both overextension and underextension are examples of Piaget's concept of assimilation, using existing concepts to interpret new experiences. Getting semantics right seems to be mainly a matter of discriminating similarities and differences—for example, categorizing animals on the basis of size, shape, the sounds they make, and other perceptual features (Clark & Clark, 1977).

But might children know more about the world than their semantic errors suggest? Yes. Two-year-olds who say "doggie" when they see a cow will point to the cow rather than the dog when asked to find the cow (Thompson & Chapman, 1977). In fact, children who overextend the word *doggie* in their speech are no less able than children who do not to look

Table 10.1	Examples of Words Used by Children Younger than 20 Months
Sound effects	*baa baa, meow, moo, ouch, uh-oh, woof, yum-yum*
Food and drink	*apple, banana, cookie, cheese, cracker, juice, milk, water*
Animals	*bear, bird, bunny, dog, cat, cow, duck, fish, kitty, horse, pig, puppy*
Body parts and clothing	*diaper, ear, eye, foot, hair, hand, hat, mouth, nose, toe, tooth, shoe*
House and outdoors	*blanket, chair, cup, door, flower, keys, outside, spoon, tree, TV*
People	*baby, daddy, gramma, grampa, mommy, [child's own name]*
Toys and vehicles	*ball, balloon, bike, boat, book, bubbles, plane, truck, toy*
Actions	*down, eat, go, sit, up*
Games and routines	*bath, bye, hi, night-night, no, peekaboo, please, shhh, thank you, yes*
Adjectives/descriptives	*all gone, cold, dirty, hot*

SOURCE: Pan & Gleason (2001)

toward the cow rather than the dog when asked, "Where's the cow?" (Naigles & Gelman, 1995). Children may overextend the meaning of certain words like *doggie* not because they misunderstand word meanings but because they want to communicate, have only a small vocabulary with which to do so, and haven't yet learned to call something a "whatchamacallit" when they cannot come up with the word for it (Naigles & Gelman, 1995).

We must be careful about applying these generalizations about early language acquisition to all children because they mask some rather large individual differences in speaking style (Goldfield & Snow, 2001). As Figure 10.1 shows, one 24-month-old may have a vocabulary of approximately 50 words while another can produce more than 500 words (Fenson et al., 1994). Some children use a *referential style*—lots of nouns referring to objects. Others seem to treat language as a social tool; they use an *expressive style* of speaking, with more personal pronouns and memorized social routines such as "Bye-bye" and "I want it" (Bates et al., 1994; Nelson, 1973). Culture exerts some influence: Infants learning English use many nouns and few verbs in their early speech, whereas infants learning Korean use more verbs (Gopnik & Choi, 1995). More important, differences in the language children are exposed to daily contribute to the variability of their speech. Both quantity of speech (how many words the child hears in the home) and quality of speech (how sophisticated the speech is) affect young children's vocabularies (Huttenlocher et al., 1991; Weizman & Snow, 2001). So, individual differences in language acquisition are the norm rather than the exception.

TELEGRAPHIC SPEECH

The next step in language development, normally taken at about 18 to 24 months of age, is combining two words into a simple sentence. Toddlers all over the world use two-word sentences to express the same basic ideas (see Table 10.2). Early combinations of two, three, or more words are sometimes called **telegraphic speech** because, like telegrams, these sentences contain critical content words and omit frills such as articles, prepositions, and auxiliary verbs.

Now, it is ungrammatical in adult English to say "No want" or "Where ball." However, these two-word sentences are not just random word combinations or mistakes; they reflect children's own systematic rules for forming sentences. Psycholinguists such as Lois Bloom (1970) believe it is appropriate to describe children's early sentences in terms of a **functional grammar**—one that emphasizes the semantic relations between words, the meanings being expressed, and the functions served by sentences (such as naming, questioning, or commanding). For example, young children often use the same word order to convey different meanings. "Mommy nose" might mean "That's Mommy's nose" in one context, but for one 22-month-old girl one afternoon it meant "Mommy, I've just wiped my runny nose the length of the living room couch." Word order sometimes does matter: "Billy hit" and "Hit Billy" may mean different things. Body language and tone of voice also communicate meanings, as when a child points and whines to request ice cream, not merely note its existence.

Between the ages of 2 and 5, children come to speak sentences that are remarkably complex and adultlike. Table 10.3 gives an inkling of how fast things move in the particularly important period from age 2 to age 3. From the two-word stage of language acquisition, children progress to three-word telegraphic sentences and then to still longer sentences, beginning to add the little function words like articles and prepositions that were often missing in their early telegraphic sen-

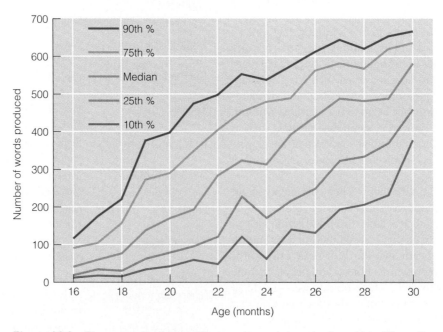

Figure 10.1 The range of individual differences in vocabulary size from 16 to 30 months
Source: Fenson et al. (1994)

Table 10.2 Two-Word Sentences Serve Similar Functions in Different Languages

Function of Sentence	Language	
	English	German
To locate or name	There book	Buch da (book there)
To demand	More milk	Mehr milch (more milk)
	Give candy	
To negate	No wet	Nicht blasen (not blow)
	Not hungry	
To indicate possession	My shoe	Mein ball (my ball)
	Mama dress	Mamas hut (Mama's hat)
To modify or qualify	Pretty dress	Armer wauwau (poor doggie)
	Big boat	
To question	Where ball	Wo ball (where ball)

SOURCE: Adapted from Slobin (1979)

tences (Hoff, 2001). They infer more and more of the rules of adult language.

How do we know when children are mastering new rules? Oddly enough, their progress sometimes reveals itself in new "mistakes." Consider the task of learning rules of morphology for forming plurals and past tenses (R. Brown, 1973; Mervis & Johnson, 1991). Typically this happens sometime during the third year. A child who has been saying "feet" and "went" may suddenly start to say "foots" and "goed." Does this represent a step backward? Not at all. The child was probably using the correct irregular forms at first by imitating adult speech, without really understanding the meaning of plurality or verb tense. The use of "foots" and "goed" is a breakthrough: He or she has now inferred the morphological rules of adding -s to pluralize nouns and adding -ed to signal past tense. At first, however, the youngster engages in **overregularization,** overapplying the rules to cases in which the proper form is irregular. When the child masters exceptions to the rules, he or she will say "feet" and "went" once more.

Children must also master rules for creating variations of the basic declarative sentence; that is, they must learn the rules for converting a basic idea such as "I am eating pizza" into such forms as questions ("Am I eating pizza?"), negative sentences ("I am not eating pizza"), and imperatives ("Eat the pizza!"). The prominent linguist Noam Chomsky (1968, 1975) drew attention to the child's learning of these rules by proposing that language be described in terms of a **transformational grammar,** or rules of syntax for transforming basic underlying thoughts into a variety of sentence forms.

How do young children learn to phrase the questions that they so frequently ask to fuel their cognitive growth? The earliest questions often consist of nothing more than two- or three-word sentences with rising intonation ("See kitty?"). Sometimes "wh" words like *what* or *where* appear ("Where kitty?"). During the second stage of question asking, children begin to use auxiliary, or helping, verbs, but their questions are of this form: "What Daddy is eating?" "Where the kitty is going?" Their understanding of transformation rules is still incomplete (Dale, 1976). Finally, they learn the transformation rule that calls for moving the auxiliary verb ahead of the subject (as in the adultlike sentence "What is Daddy eating?").

By the end of the preschool period (age 5–6), children's sentences are very much like those of adults, even though they

Table 10.3 Samples of Kyle's Speech at 24 Months and 35 Months. At 24 months, Kyle speaks in telegraphic sentences no more than three words long; by 35 months, his sentences are much longer and grammatically complex, though not error-free, and he is far more able to participate in the give-and-take of conversation (if not to heed his mother and respect the dignity of potato bugs).

Age 24 Months (His second birthday party)	Age 35 Months (Playing with a potato bug)
Want cake now.	*Mother:* Kyle, why don't you take the bug back to his friends?
Boons! Boons! [pointing to balloons]	*Kyle:* After I hold him, then I'll take the bug back to his friends. Mommy, where did the bug go?
They mine! [referring to colors]	Mommy, I didn't know where the bug go. Find it. Maybe Winston's on it [the family dog]. Winston, get off the bug! [Kyle spots the bug and picks it up.]
I wan' see.	*Mother:* Kyle, *please* let the bug go back to his friends.
See sky now.	*Kyle:* He does not want to go to his friends. [He drops the bug and squashes it, much to his mother's horror.] I stepped on it and it will not go to his friends.
Ow-ee [pointing to knee].	

have never had a formal lesson in grammar. It's an amazing accomplishment. Yet there is still more to accomplish.

LATER LANGUAGE DEVELOPMENT

School-age children improve their pronunciation skills, produce longer and more complex sentences, and continue to expand their vocabularies. The average first-grader starts school with a vocabulary of about 10,000 words and adds somewhere between 5 and 13 new words a day throughout the school years (Anglin, 1993; Bloom, 1998). During adolescence, with the help of formal operational thought, children become better able to understand and define abstract terms (McGhee-Bidlack, 1991). They also become better able to infer meanings that are not explicitly stated (Beal, 1990).

School-age children also begin to think about and manipulate language in ways that were previously impossible (Ely, 2001; Klein, 1996). They can, for example, interpret passive sentences like "Goofy was liked by Donald" and conditional sentences like "If Goofy had come, Donald would have been delighted" (Boloh & Champaud, 1993; Sudhalter & Braine, 1985). Command of grammar actually continues to improve through adolescence; teenagers' spoken and written sentences become increasingly long and complex (Clark & Clark, 1977; K. W. Hunt, 1970).

Children are also mastering the pragmatics of language, becoming increasingly able to communicate effectively in different situations (Oliver, 1995). They increasingly use **decontextualized language** as they move from talking about the immediate conversational context ("I see a dog over there") to talking about past or remote events ("I saw a dog while on vacation last week") (Ely, 2001). They can tell stories about events that happened in the past or are not part of the current context. By adolescence, these narratives are often detailed and quite lengthy.

Throughout childhood and adolescence, advances in cognitive development are accompanied by advances in language and communication skills. For example, as children become less cognitively egocentric, they are more able to take the perspective of their listeners (Hoff, 2001). Middle childhood and adolescence also bring increased **metalinguistic awareness,** or knowledge of language itself as a system (Ely, 2001). Children with metalinguistic awareness understand the concept of words and can define words (*semantics*). Adolescents are increasingly able to define abstract words (such as *courage* or *pride*), but are still outperformed by adults on difficult words (such as *idleness* or *goodness*) (Nippold et al., 1999). Development of metalinguistic awareness also means that children and adolescents can distinguish between grammatically correct and incorrect sentences (*syntax*), and understand how language can be altered to fit the needs of the specific social context in which it is used (*pragmatics*).

What happens to language skills during adulthood? Adults simply hold onto the knowledge of the phonology they gained as children, though elders can have difficulty distinguishing speech sounds if they have hearing impairments or deficits in the cognitive abilities required to make out what they hear (Sommers, 1997). They also retain their knowledge of grammar or syntax very well. Older adults do tend to use less complex sentences than younger adults do, however. Also, those with memory difficulties may have trouble understanding sentences that are highly complex syntactically (for example, "The children warned about road hazards refused to fix the bicycle of the boy who crashed"); they may not be able to remember the beginning of the sentence by the time they get to the end (Kemtes & Kemper, 1997; Stine, Soederberg, & Morrow, 1996).

Meanwhile, knowledge of the semantics of language, of word meanings, often *expands* during adulthood, at least until people are in their 70s or 80s (Obler & Albert, 1985; Schaie, 1996). After all, adults gain experience with the world from year to year, so it is not surprising that their vocabularies continue to grow and they enrich their understandings of the meanings of words. However, older adults do more often have the "tip-of-the-tongue" experience of not being able to come up with the name of an object (or especially a person's name) when they need it (Au et al., 1995; MacKay & Abrams, 1996). This problem is a matter of not being able to retrieve information stored in memory rather than a matter of no longer knowing the words.

Adults also refine their pragmatic use of language—adjusting it to different social and professional contexts (Obler, 2001). Physicians, for example, must develop a communication style that is effective with their patients. Partners who have been together for many years often develop a unique way of communicating with one another that is distinctly different from how they communicate with others. Overall, command of language holds up very well in later life unless the individual experiences major declines in cognitive functioning (Light, 1990; Stine et al., 1996).

In sum, we cannot help but be awed by the pace at which children master the fundamentals of language during their first five years of life, but we must also appreciate the continued growth that occurs in childhood and adolescence and the maintenance of language skills throughout the life span. It is time to ask how these remarkable skills are acquired.

How Language Develops

What abilities must young children bring to the language-learning task, and what help must their companions provide? Theorists attempting to explain language acquisition have differed considerably in their positions on the nature–nurture issue, as illustrated by the learning, nativist, and interactionist perspectives on language development (see Bohannon & Bonvillian, 2001).

THE LEARNING PERSPECTIVE

How do children learn language? Most adults would say that children imitate what they hear, receiving praise when they get it right and being corrected when they get it wrong. Different learning theorists emphasize different aspects of this broad process. Social learning theorist Albert Bandura (1971) and others emphasize observational learning—learning by listening to and then imitating older companions. Behaviorist

B. F. Skinner (1957) and others have emphasized the role of reinforcement. As children achieve better and better approximations of adult language, parents and other adults praise meaningful speech and correct errors. Children are also reinforced by getting what they want when they speak correctly. In general, learning theorists consider the child's social environment to be critical to what and how much he or she learns.

How well does the learning perspective account for language development? Certainly, it is no accident that children end up speaking the same language that their parents speak, down to the regional accent. Children do learn the words that they hear spoken by others—even when the words are not spoken directly to them (Akhtar, Jipson, & Callanan, 2001). For example, 2-year-olds can learn object labels and verbs by "eavesdropping" on a conversation between two adults (so be careful what you say within earshot of toddlers). In addition, young children are more likely to start using new words if they are reinforced for doing so than if they are not (Whitehurst & Valdez-Menchaca, 1988). And, finally, children whose caregivers frequently encourage them to converse by asking questions, making requests, and the like are more advanced in early language development than those whose parents are less conversational (Bohannon & Bonvillian, 2001; Pine, 1994).

However, learning theorists have had an easier time explaining the development of phonology and semantics than accounting for how syntactical rules are acquired. For example, after analyzing conversations between mothers and young children, Roger Brown, Courtney Cazden, and Ursula Bellugi (1969) discovered that a mother's approval or disapproval depended on the truth value or semantics of what was said, *not* on the grammatical correctness of the statement. Thus, when a child looking at a cow says "Her cow" (accurate but grammatically incorrect), Mom is likely to provide reinforcement ("That's right, darling"), whereas if the child were to say "There's a dog, Mommy" (grammatically correct but untruthful), Mom would probably correct the child ("No, silly—that's a cow"). Similarly, parents seem just as likely to reward a

grammatically primitive request ("Want milk") as a well-formed version of the same idea (Brown & Hanlon, 1970). Such evidence casts doubt on the idea that the major mechanism behind syntactic development is reinforcement.

Could imitation of adults account for the acquisition of syntax? We have already seen that young children produce many sentences that they are unlikely to have heard adults using ("All gone cookie," overregularizations such as "It swimmed," and so on). These kinds of sentences are not imitations. Also, an adult is likely to get nowhere in teaching syntax by saying "Repeat after me" unless the child already has at least some knowledge of the grammatical form to be learned (Baron, 1992; McNeill, 1970). Young children *do* frequently imitate other people's speech, and this may help them get to the point of producing new structures themselves. But it is hard to see how imitation and reinforcement alone can account for the learning of grammatical rules.

THE NATIVIST PERSPECTIVE

Nativists have made little of the role of the language environment and much of the role of the child's biologically programmed capacities in explaining language development (for example, Chomsky, 1995; Pinker, 1994; see also Maratsos, 1998). Noted linguist Noam Chomsky (1968, 1975, 1995) proposed that humans have an inborn mechanism for mastering language called the **language acquisition device (LAD)**. The LAD was conceived as an area in the brain equipped to identify certain universal features of language and to figure out the specific rules of any particular language. To learn to speak, children need only hear other humans speak; using the LAD, they quickly grasp the rules of whatever language they hear (see Figure 10.2).

What evidence supports a nativist perspective on language development? First, there are indeed areas of the brain that specialize in language functions; Broca's area in the frontal lobe controls speaking, for example, whereas Wernicke's area controls speech recognition (Bear, Connors, & Paradiso, 2001). Second, children do acquire an incredibly complex communication system very rapidly. For example, 7-month-olds are able to extract grammatical rules of language and generalize these rules to novel items (Marcus & Vijayan, 1999). Third, children all progress through the same sequences at roughly similar ages, and they even make the same kinds of errors, which suggests that language development is guided by a specieswide maturational plan. Fourth, these universal aspects of early language development occur despite cultural differences in the styles of speech that adults use in talking to young children. In some cultures, for example, parents believe that babies are incapable of understanding speech and do not even talk directly to them (Crago, Allen, & Hough-Eyamir, 1997).

Last but not least, we have evidence that the capacity for acquiring language has a genetic basis. The fact that some of our linguistic competencies, including the ability to combine symbols to form short sentences, are shared with chimpanzees and other primates suggests that they arose during the course of evolution and are part of our genetic endowment as

"A" is for "apple." The learning perspective helps explain how young children learn the meaning of words.

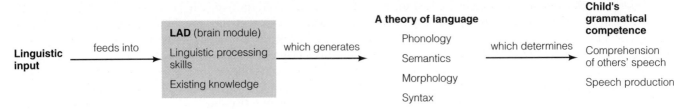

Figure 10.2 The language acquisition device (LAD)

humans (Greenfield & Savage-Rumbaugh, 1993; Pinker, 1994). Identical twins score more similarly than fraternal twins on measures of verbal skills, and certain speech, language, and reading disorders run in families, indicating that individual heredity also influences the course of language development (Lewis & Thompson, 1992; Plomin, 1990).

Although nativists are correct to emphasize the importance of biologically based capacities in language acquisition, the nativist perspective has two major limitations. First, attributing language development to a built-in language acquisition device does not really explain it. Explanations would require knowing *how* such an inborn language processor sifts through language input and infers the rules of language (Moerk, 1989). Second, nativists, in focusing on the defects of learning theories of language development, tend to underestimate the contributions of the child's language environment. The nativists base much of their argument on three assumptions: (1) that the only thing children need to develop language is exposure to speech, (2) that the speech children hear is so incredibly complex that only a highly powerful brain could possibly detect regularities in it, and (3) that adults give children little useful feedback about whether their sentences are grammatically correct. These assumptions now seem to be largely inaccurate, and most researchers currently believe that language development depends on both nature and nurture.

The Interactionist Perspective

Interactionists believe that *both* learning theorists and nativists are correct: Children's biologically based competencies *and* their language environment interact to shape the course of language development (Bohannon & Bonvillian, 2001; see also Bloom, 1998). They emphasize that acquisition of language skills depends on and is related to the acquisition of many other capacities: perceptual, cognitive, motor, social, and emotional. They point out that the capacity for acquiring language is not unique (as nativists who speak of the LAD claim); milestones in language development often occur at the same time as milestones in other aspects of cognitive development and involve the same underlying mental processes (Bates et al., 1987). For example, young children first begin to use words as meaningful symbols at the time they begin to display nonliguistic symbolic capacities, such as the ability to use gestures (waving bye-bye), and to engage in pretend play (treating a bowl as if it were a hat).

The interactionists' position is not unlike that taken by Piaget (1970). He too believed that milestones in cognitive development pave the way for progress in language development

and that maturation and environment interact to guide both cognitive development and language development. Like Piaget (but unlike learning theorists), many interactionists argue that language development depends on the maturation of cognitive abilities such as the capacity for symbolic thought. However, the interactionist position also emphasizes—as Vygotsky did but Piaget did not—ways in which social interactions with adults contribute to cognitive and linguistic development. Language is primarily a means of communicating—one that develops in the context of social interactions as children and their companions strive to get their messages across, one way or another (Tomasello, 1999).

Long before infants use words, Jerome Bruner (1983) claims, their caregivers show them how to take turns in conversations—even if the most these young infants can contribute when their turn comes is a laugh or a bit of babbling. As adults converse with young children, they create a supportive learning environment—a "scaffold" in Bruner's terms, a zone of proximal development in Vygotsky's—that helps the children grasp the regularities of language (Bruner, 1983; Harris, 1992). For example, parents may go through their children's favorite picture books at bedtime asking "What's this?" and "What's that?" This gives their children repeated opportunities to learn that conversing involves taking turns, that things have names, and that there are proper ways to pose questions and give answers. Soon the children are asking "What's this?" and "What's that?" themselves.

As children gain new language skills, adults adjust their styles of communication accordingly. Language researchers use the term **child-directed speech** to describe the speech adults use with young children: short, simple sentences, spoken slowly and in a high-pitched voice, often with much repetition, and with exaggerated emphasis on key words (usually words for objects and activities). For example, the mother trying to get her son to eat his peas might say "Eat your peas now. Not the cracker. See those *peas?* Yeah, eat the *peas.*" Child-directed speech seems to be used by adults speaking to young children in a large majority of the language communities that have been studied (Fernald et al., 1989). And infants, from the earliest days of life, seem to pay more attention to the high-pitched sounds and varied intonational patterns of child-directed speech than to the "flatter" speech adults use when communicating with one another (Cooper & Aslin, 1990; Cooper et al., 1997; Pegg, Werker, & McLeod, 1992).

Would children learn language just as well if adults talked to them in an adultlike style? Perhaps not. The nativists seem to have underestimated the contributions of environment to language development. Mere exposure to speech is not enough; children must be actively involved in using language (Locke, 1997). Catherine Snow and her associates, for example, found that a group of Dutch-speaking children, despite the fact that they watched a great deal of German television, did not acquire any German words or grammar (Snow et al., 1976). True, there are cultural groups (the Kaluli of New Guinea, the natives of American Samoa, and the Trackton people of the Piedmont Carolinas) in which child-directed speech does not seem to be used. Children in these societies still seem to acquire language without noticeable delays (Gordon, 1990; Ochs, 1982; Schieffelin, 1986). Yet even these children overhear speech and participate in social interactions in which language is used, and that is what seems to be required in order to master a human language (Lieven, 1994). Those parents who do use child-directed speech further simplify the child's task of figuring out the rules of language (Harris, 1992; Kemler Nelson et al., 1989). They converse with children daily in attention-getting and understandable ways about the very objects and events that have captured the youngsters' attention.

Adults speaking to young children also use specific communication strategies that foster language development. For example, if a child says "Kitty goed," an adult may respond with an **expansion**—a more grammatically complete expression of the same thought ("Yes, the cat went in the car").

Adults are not the only ones who use child-directed speech. Children also adjust their speech to their listener.

© Nancy Sheehan/PhotoEdit, Inc.

Adults use conversational techniques like expansions mainly to improve communication, not to teach grammar (Penner, 1987). However, these techniques also serve as a subtle form of correction after children produce grammatically incorrect sentences and show children more grammatical ways to express the same ideas (Bohannon & Stanowicz, 1988; Saxton, 1997). It's not quite true, then, that adults provide no corrective feedback concerning children's grammatical errors, as nativists claim. True, they rarely say, "No, that's wrong; say it this way." They do, however, provide a good deal of subtle corrective feedback through their responses to children, and this feedback helps children grow linguistically (Bohannon & Bonvillian, 2001).

How can adults best facilitate young children's language learning? What cognitive capacities enable children to learn how language works? Much remains to be learned about language development, but it does seem to require the interaction of a biologically prepared child with at least one conversational partner, ideally one who tailors his or her own speech to the child's level of understanding.

A CRITICAL PERIOD FOR LANGUAGE?

Young children are so adept at learning languages that some scholars have wondered whether a critical (or at least sensitive) period for language acquisition may exist. Some years ago, Eric Lenneberg (1967) claimed that there is such a critical period and that it lasts until puberty, when the development of lateralization of language functions in the left hemisphere of the brain is completed. Although we now know that lateralization of the brain occurs more rapidly than Lenneberg thought (Locke, 1997; and see Chapter 5), researchers continue to be very interested in determining whether young children are uniquely capable of language learning.

What evidence supports the critical period hypothesis of language acquisition? Some comes from studies of deaf children, some of whom (especially those with hearing parents) do not have an opportunity to learn *any* language, oral or signed, in their early years. Rachel Mayberry (1994) has studied language mastery in deaf college students who were exposed to American Sign Language at different ages and has found that the rule "the earlier, the better" applies. Mastery of the morphology, syntax, and semantics of sign language was greatest among students exposed to it in infancy or early childhood. Those who learned sign later in their development (ages 9–16) mastered it better if they had had some exposure to English early in life than if they had not been exposed to any language system at all before they encountered sign language. The Explorations box on page 258 provides more details on how the language development of deaf children compares to that of hearing children.

Elissa Newport and her colleagues (Newport, 1991) have uncovered similar evidence of a critical period for second language learning. In one study (Johnson & Newport, 1989), native speakers of Korean or Chinese who had come to the United States between the ages of 3 and 39 were tested for mastery of English grammar. Among those who began learning English before puberty, those who learned it earliest

Language Acquisition among Deaf Children

Many deaf children gain their first exposure to language by learning American Sign Language (ASL). This is a true language. For example, signs are arbitrary symbols, not attempts to mimic objects and events, and they are used according to a system of grammatical rules that determines their ordering. We ought to be able to learn something about language acquisition in general, then, by studying language acquisition among deaf children.

On average, deaf children acquire sign language in much the same sequence and at much the same rate as hearing

© Stephen McBrady/PhotoEdit, Inc.

learned it best. Among those who arrived in the United States after puberty, performance was generally poor, regardless of age of arrival or number of years using English. Such findings have been used to argue that there is a critical period for language acquisition that ends around puberty. But other research shows that, even beyond puberty, age of arrival in the United States is related to proficiency in English as a second language (Birdsong, 1999). Thus, adults relocating at age 25 develop greater proficiency than adults relocating at age 30, an advantage that is related more to age than to length of residence in the United States (G. Stevens, 1999). And although adults are less likely than children to ever attain native-like proficiency in a second language—suggesting a critical period (Mayberry, 1994)— *some* adults *do* achieve native-like proficiency (Birdsong, 1999).

Young children may indeed have advantages over adults when learning a second language. This does not necessarily mean that there is a critical period for language acquisition, however. Children are generally immersed in their second language through school and peer group activities. This greater exposure may facilitate second language acquisition in part by making the new language dominant in their lives. Adults, by contrast, may be more likely to continue using their native language as their dominant mode of communication, making second language acquisition more difficult (Jia & Aaronson, 1999).

It's possible that the language processing areas of the brain are shaped for a lifetime by early experience with language in ways that limit later learning of other languages. But it seems unlikely that there is a hard-and-fast critical period for language acquisition. It might be more accurate to say there is a "sensitive" period when languages are most easily and flawlessly acquired. Perhaps the main message is that young children are supremely capable of learning languages and advancing their cognitive development in the process. Meanwhile, college students learning a foreign language for the first time have to appreciate that they may never reach the point when they will speak it as well as someone who learned it as a young child.

children acquire spoken language, and they make many of the same kinds of errors along the way (Bellugi, 1988; Meier, 1991; Locke, 1997). Interestingly, deaf infants whose parents are deaf use sign "babble" in sign language. They experiment with gestures in much the same way that hearing infants experiment with sounds in preparation for their first meaningful communications (Petitto & Marentette, 1991). They then sign their first meaningful single words at about 12 months of age, use their first syntax (combinations of two signs) at 18–24 months, and master many rules of morphology such as past tense formation between 2 and 3 years of age (Meier, 1991). Just as hearing children have difficulty with the pronunciation of certain words and overgeneralize certain rules, deaf children make predictable errors in their signing (Meier, 1991). Moreover, for both deaf and hearing children, advances in language development are linked closely to advances in cognitive development; for example, putting signs or words together in sentences happens at about the same age that children put sequences of actions together in their play (Spencer, 1996).

The language environment experienced by deaf infants is also far more similar to that of hearing infants than you would imagine. For example, deaf mothers sign in child-directed speech; they present signs at a slower pace, repeat signs more, and exaggerate their signing motions more when they talk to their infants than when they talk to their deaf friends (Masataka, 1996). Moreover, just as hearing babies prefer the exaggerated intonations of child-directed speech, deaf infants pay more attention and show more emotional response when they are shown videos of infant-directed signing than tapes of adult-directed signing.

Finally, it turns out that language areas of the brain develop much the same in deaf children exposed to sign as in hearing children exposed to speech. For example, Helen Neville and her colleagues (1997) examined brain activity during the processing of sentences by deaf and hearing ASL users, hearing individuals (interpreters) who acquired sign late in life, and hearing individuals who did not know ASL. For the most part, reliance on areas of the left hemisphere of the cortex to process sentences was just as evident among those who acquired ASL early in life as among hearing individuals who acquired English early in life. Reliance on the left hemisphere to process syntax was not as clear among individuals who acquired a language later in life. Early learners of ASL did use their right hemispheres more in responding to sentences, perhaps because spatial skills based in the right hemisphere come into play in interpreting the gestures of someone who is signing.

As we have seen, language development is sometimes delayed among deaf children of hearing parents if they cannot hear well enough to understand spoken language but are not exposed to sign language either (Mayberry, 1994). Overall, then, studies of language acquisition among deaf children suggest that young humans are biologically prepared to master language and will do so if they are given the opportunity, whether that language is signed or spoken, whether it involves visual-spatial skills or auditory ones (Meier, 1991).

Developing language competence may be our earliest and greatest learning challenge, but it is only the beginning. There is much more to be mastered during the school years and beyond. Language lays the foundation for acquiring reading, writing, and countless other skills required for productive citizenship. But unlike language, which seems to develop effortlessly in the absence of formal education, these other skills typically require directed education. In the following sections, we look at education across the life span, examining changes in motivation for learning and changes in educational environments as learners get older.

The Infant

Before children ever begin their formal education, they are learning a great deal from the informal curriculum of their lives. Above all, they are learning to master their environments.

Mastery Motivation

Infants seem to be intrinsically motivated to master their environment (Morgan, MacTurk, & Hrncir, 1995). This **mastery motivation** can be seen clearly when infants struggle to open kitchen cabinets, take their first steps, or figure out how new toys work—and derive great pleasure from their efforts (Busch-Rossnagel, 1997; MacTurk et al., 1987; Mayes & Zigler, 1992).

Much evidence supports the claim that infants are curious, active explorers who are constantly striving to understand and to exert control over the world around them. This, you'll recall, was one of Jean Piaget's major themes. A striving for mastery or competence appears to be inborn and universal, then, and will display itself in the behavior of all normal infants without any prompting from parents. Even so, some infants appear to be more mastery oriented than others. Given a new push toy, one baby may simply look at it, while another may mouth it, bang it, and push it back and forth across the floor (Yarrow et al., 1984). Why might some infants have a stronger mastery motive than others?

Mastery motivation seems higher when parents frequently provide *sensory stimulation* designed to arouse and amuse their babies—tickling them, bouncing them, playing games of pat-a-cake, giving them stimulating toys, and so on (Busch-Rossnagel, 1997; Yarrow et al., 1984). Some experts believe that infancy is a critical period for stimulating growing minds.

Mastery motivation also flourishes when infants grow up in a *responsive environment* that provides plenty of opportunities to see for themselves that they can control their environments (Ford & Thompson, 1985). Parents who return smiles and coos or respond promptly to cries show infants that they can affect people around them. By contrast, the children of parents who are depressed show less interest in and persistence on challenging tasks, perhaps because their parents are not very responsive to them (Redding, Harmon, & Morgan, 1990).

An infant's level of mastery motivation affects his or her later achievement behavior. Babies who actively attempt to master challenges at 6 and 12 months of age score higher on tests of mental development at age 2 and 3 than their less mastery-oriented peers (Messer et al., 1986; Yarrow et al., 1975). In short, infants are intrinsically motivated to master challenges, but parents may help strengthen this inborn motive by stimulating their infants appropriately and responding to their actions. What about infants and toddlers who spend considerable amounts of time away from their parents? Is their motivation influenced by time spent in preschool?

Early Education

As we've seen in previous chapters, babies are learning a great deal in the first few years of life. But do infants and toddlers need specific educational experiences? Some reports suggest that it is never too early to start a child's education. In *U.S. News & World Report,* Linda Kulman (1997) states that "reading to children soon after they are born is being encouraged as it is now known that 80% of brain development occurs in the first year of life" (p. 10). Given statements such as this, it's not surprising that "Baby Einstein" and "Baby Mozart" videos are popular among parents who buy into the idea that early stimulation is critical to infants' intellectual development (McCormick, 1998). Formal programs such as *Bookstart,* which promotes literacy early by providing 6- to 9-month-old infants and their parents with books and literacy information, have even been developed (Hall, 2001; Wade & Moore, 1998).

Despite its popular appeal, most experts dispute the idea that children need special educational experiences during the first three years (Bruer, 1999; Kagan, 1998). And some, like David Elkind (1987), author of *Miseducation: Preschoolers at Risk,* fear that the push for earlier and earlier education may be going too far and that young children today are not given enough time simply to be children—to play and socialize as they choose. Elkind even worries that children may lose their self-initiative and intrinsic motivation to learn when their lives are orchestrated by parents who pressure them to achieve at early ages. Is there anything to these concerns?

Some research seems to confirm Elkind's fears. In one study (Hyson, Hirsch-Pasek, & Rescorla, 1989), 4-year-olds in preschools with a very strong academic thrust gained an initial advantage in basic academic skills such as knowledge of letters and numbers but lost it by the end of kindergarten. What's more, they proved to be *less* creative, *more* anxious in testing situations, and *more* negative toward school than children who attended preschool programs with a social rather than academic emphasis. Similarly, Deborah Stipek and her colleagues (1995) have found that highly academic preschool programs raise children's academic achievement test scores but decrease their expectancies of success and pride in accomplishment. So, it may well be possible to undermine achievement motivation by overemphasizing academics in the preschool years (see Gardner, 1999).

However, preschool programs that offer a healthy mix of play and academic skill-building activities can be very beneficial to young children, especially disadvantaged ones (Clarke-Stewart, 1998; Gorey, 2001). Although many children who attend preschool programs are no more or less intellectually advanced than those who remain at home, *disadvantaged* children who attend programs specially designed to prepare them for school *do* experience more cognitive growth and achieve more success in school than disadvantaged children who do not attend such programs (Campbell & Ramey, 1995; Peisner-Feinberg & Burchinal, 1997). Consider again the Abecedarian

Every day, infants and young children display their innate mastery motive.

Preschools that offer a healthy combination of preacademic and social activities can help children prepare for school.

Project, a full-time educational program from infancy (starting around 4–5 months) to age 5 for children from low-income families (Campbell et al., 2001; and see Chapter 9). Compared to children who did not participate, Abecedarian children showed impressive cognitive gains during and immediately after the program (see Figure 10.3). And although their performance level compared to test norms decreased over the subsequent years, these children continued to show an advantage over children who did not receive this intensive early educational experience.

Thus, early education can provide disadvantaged children with a boost that has lasting consequences, lending support to the basic idea of Head Start. Positive effects on later school achievement are especially likely if the preschool experience not only stimulates children's cognitive growth but also gets their parents more involved with the schools (Reynolds et al., 1996). More generally, preschool programs that build school readiness skills but also allow plenty of time for play and social interaction can do a lot to help all children make a smooth transition to kindergarten and elementary school (Parker et al., 1999; Zigler & Finn-Stevenson, 1993).

The Child

With infancy behind them, children begin to show true achievement motivation. Even by age 2, they seem capable of

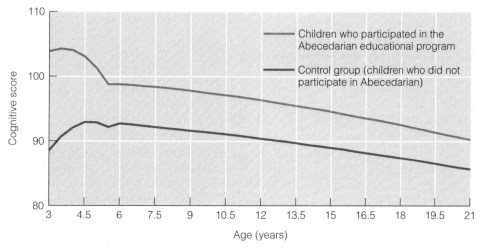

Figure 10.3 Cognitive growth curves as a function of preschool treatment
Source: Campbell et al. (2001)

appraising their performances as successes or failures and look to others for approval when they succeed and disapproval when they fail (Stipek, Recchia, & McClintic, 1992). By age 3, children have clearly internalized standards of performance and experience true pride or shame, depending on how successfully they meet those standards (Stipek et al., 1992). Some children are clearly more achievement-oriented and high-achieving than others, though, and it is these differences we now seek to explain.

Achievement Motivation

All children experience failure on occasion in their efforts to master challenges and meet achievement standards. Carol Dweck and her colleagues have attempted to understand differences between children who persist and ultimately triumph in the face of failure and those who give up (Dweck & Elliott, 1983; Dweck & Leggett, 1988). Dweck finds that high achievers tend to attribute their successes to internal and stable causes such as high ability. However, they blame their failures either on external factors beyond their control ("That test was impossibly hard," "That professor's grading is biased") or—and this is even more adaptive—on internal causes that they can overcome (particularly insufficient effort). They do *not* blame the internal but stable factor of low ability ("I'm terrible at this and will never do any better"). Students with this healthy attributional style are said to have a **mastery orientation;** they thrive on challenges and persist in the face of failure, believing that their increased effort will pay off.

By contrast, children who tend to be low achievers often attribute their successes either to the internal cause of hard work or to external causes such as luck or the easiness of the task. Thus, they do not experience the pride and self-esteem that come from viewing oneself as highly capable. Yet they often attribute their failures to an internal and stable cause—namely, lack of ability. As a result, they have low expectancies of success and tend to give up. Dweck describes children with this attributional style as having a **learned helplessness orientation**—a tendency to avoid challenges and to cease trying when one experiences failure, based on the belief that one can do little to improve.

AGE DIFFERENCES

Are children really capable of analyzing the causes of success and failure in this way? Perhaps not when they are young. Before the age of 7 or so, children tend to be unrealistic optimists who think they can succeed on almost any task (Stipek & Mac Iver, 1989). With age, children's perceptions of their academic abilities become more and more accurate (Wigfield et al., 1997). Even after repeated poor performances, young children often continue to think that they have high ability and will do well in the future, whereas older children tend to become helpless (Miller, 1985; Ruble, Eisenberg, & Higgins, 1994). Young children *can* be made to feel helpless if their failures are very clear-cut and they conclude that they have been bad (Burhans & Dweck, 1995), but they are clearly less susceptible than older children to learned helplessness.

Why is this? Young children are protected from damaging self-perceptions partly because they do not yet fully understand the concept of ability as a stable capacity (Nicholls & Miller, 1984; Pomerantz & Ruble, 1997). They believe that ability is a changeable quality and that they can get smarter if they work hard. This view of ability encourages them to adopt **learning goals** in achievement situations, aiming to learn new things so that they can improve their abilities (Covington, 2000; Dweck & Leggett, 1988).

As children get older, they begin to see ability as a fixed trait that is not altered much by effort. As a result, more and more of them adopt **performance goals** in school; they aim to *prove* their ability rather than to *improve* it and seek to be judged smart rather than dumb (Dweck & Leggett, 1988; Erdley et al., 1997; and see Table 10.4). These changes in the understanding of ability are probably due both to cognitive development—especially an increased ability to analyze the causes of successes and failures and to infer enduring traits from behavior—and to an accumulation of feedback in school (Stipek, 1984).

Table 10.4 Comparison of Learning and Performance Goals

Learning Goals	Performance Goals
Ability as a changeable trait	Ability as a fixed trait
Focus on increasing one's competence or knowledge ("I understand this material better than I did before")	Focus on increasing one's status relative to others ("I did better on this than the other students")
Self-regulated learning; monitor understanding of material and adjust behavior (e.g., effort) accordingly	Other-regulated learning; monitor performance relative to peers and increase effort (approach) to outperform them, or decrease effort (avoidance) to save face (so you can claim that failures are due to lack of effort, not incompetence)
Deep-level processing of material (e.g., learning to understand)	Superficial-level processing of material (e.g., memorizing for the test)
Feelings of pride and satisfaction associated with success; failures indicate a need for more effort or different learning strategies	Feelings of anxiety and shame associated with failure; boastful feelings associated with success

SOURCES: Based on Covington (2000); Elliot & Church (1997)

Those children who continue to focus on learning goals tend to do better in school than those who switch to performance goals (Butler, 1999; Stipek & Gralinski, 1996; see also Covington, 2000). As Table 10.4 illustrates, when students believe that ability is a fixed entity that one either has or lacks and conclude that they lack it, they set performance goals rather than learning goals; figuring that hard work will not pay off, they run the risk of becoming helpless in the classroom (Dweck & Leggett, 1988). Even gifted students can fall into this trap (Ablard & Mills, 1996). What can parents and schools do to foster healthy patterns of achievement motivation?

PARENT CONTRIBUTIONS

As we saw earlier, parents can foster mastery motivation in infancy by providing their babies with appropriate sensory stimulation, being responsive, and as we'll see in Chapter 14, building a secure attachment relationship. Parents can then strengthen their children's achievement motivation by stressing and reinforcing independence and self-reliance at an early age, encouraging children to do things on their own (Grolnick & Ryan, 1989; Deci & Ryan, 1992). They can also emphasize the importance of doing things *well*, or meeting high standards of performance (Deci & Ryan, 1992). As children begin formal schooling, parents can help foster high levels of achievement motivation by getting involved with their child's education (Stevenson & Stigler, 1994).

Finally, parents can provide a cognitively stimulating home environment (Gottfried, Fleming, & Gottried, 1998). This includes having reading material in the home, engaging in intellectual discussions, attending lectures or cultural events, visiting museums, and holding high expectations for children's education. By doing these things, parents stimulate intellectual curiosity and a desire to learn. Children who are encouraged and supported in a positive manner are likely to enjoy new challenges and feel confident about mastering them. They are also unlikely to make the kinds of counterproductive attributions ("I'm dumb") that can cause them to lose interest in schoolwork (Glasgow et al., 1997). Children typically feel competent when their parents are satisfied with their performance (McGrath & Repetti, 2000). By contrast, parents can undermine a child's school performance and intrinsic motivation to learn if they are uninvolved and offer little in the way of guidance *or* if they are highly controlling, nag continually about homework, offer bribes for good grades, and criticize bad grades (Ginsburg & Bronstein, 1993).

SCHOOL CONTRIBUTIONS

How do schools affect achievement? Nearly every school asserts that the major goal of classroom instruction is improvement of children's learning. Many of these same schools, however, are structured in ways that focus on the external rewards that students can earn (such as grades or stickers). As a result, they may encourage the setting of performance goals rather than learning goals (Covington, 2000). Many classrooms are competitive places where students try to outdo each other to earn the best grades and teacher recognition. Schools may

serve their students better by de-emphasizing grades as endpoints and focusing more on the process of learning. In many classes, students receive a grade (good or bad) indicating their performance on a test or project and that's the end of it. If they didn't fully learn the material, they are given no opportunity to do so: They learn that the grade, not learning itself, is the goal.

Martin Covington (2000; see also 1998) believes that schools can foster children's academic motivation by downplaying the competitive race for the best grades in class. How might this work? Consider some research by Elaine Elliott and Carol Dweck (1988). They asked fifth-graders to perform a novel task. The students were led to believe that they had either low or high ability and were warned that they would soon be performing similar tasks that would prove quite difficult. Half the children worked under a *performance goal* (not unlike the goals emphasized in many classrooms): They were told that their performance would be compared to that of other children and evaluated by an expert. The remaining children were induced to adopt a *learning goal:* Although they would make some mistakes, they were told, working at the tasks would "sharpen the mind" and help them at school.

As expected, the only children who displayed the telltale signs of helplessness (that is, deteriorating performance and attribution of failure to low ability) were those who believed they had low ability and were pursuing a performance goal. For them, continuing to work on the difficult task meant demonstrating again and again that they were stupid! By contrast, even "low ability" students who pursued a learning goal persisted despite their failures and showed remarkably little frustration, probably because they were convinced that they could grow from their experience. Perhaps, then, teachers undermine achievement motivation by distributing gold stars and grades and frequently calling attention to how students stand in comparison to one another (Deci, Koestner, & Ryan, 1999). Children might be better off if teachers nurtured their intrinsic motivation to master challenges (see Boggiano & Katz, 1991; Butler, 1990). Then, slow learners could view their mistakes as a sign that they should change strategies to improve their competencies rather than as further proof that they lack ability.

Finally, the school climate can influence achievement. Academic achievement is greater when schools encourage family involvement and regular parent–teacher communication and develop a system that makes family involvement possible (Rimm-Kaufman & Pianta, 1999). Schools can also try to capture students' enthusiasm for learning right from the start of schooling. Students who start out liking school are typically the same ones who like school later on; they also participate more in the classroom, which leads to higher levels of achievement (Ladd, Buhs, & Seid, 2000).

In sum, children approach achievement tasks with either a mastery orientation or a learned helplessness orientation, based on how they view their academic triumphs and disasters. As they get older, children come to understand the concept of ability as a stable trait and shift from focusing on learning goals to focusing on performance goals. These changes, brought about by both cognitive development and feedback in school, give them a more realistic picture of their own strengths and weaknesses but also make them more vulnerable to learned helplessness. Yet some children remain far more motivated to succeed in school than others, and parents as well as schools have a lot to do with that.

Learning to Read

Perhaps the most important achievement in school is acquiring the ability to read. Mastery of reading paves the way for mastering other academic skills. Skilled readers consume more printed material than unskilled or nonreaders, giving them an advantage in other academic areas that increasingly rely on reading skills over the school years (Stanovich, 1986). Unlike language acquisition, which is a natural learning task that typically requires no formal education, reading acquisition is really an "unnatural" task (Stanovich & Stanovich, 1999). Learning to read almost always requires direct instruction. How do children master this complex and important skill?

MASTERING THE ALPHABETIC PRINCIPLE

Before children can read, they must come to understand the **alphabetic principle**—the idea that the letters in printed words represent the sounds in spoken words in a systematic way (Byrne, 1998; Treiman, 2000). According to Linnea Ehri (1999), this is a four-step process. First, children in the *pre-alphabetic phase* memorize selected visual cues to remember words. They can "read" text that they have memorized during previous readings. For instance, seeing a picture of a dinosaur on a page in a favorite book cues a child to recall the words he has often heard his mother read when he and she turned to this page. Or, a child in the pre-alphabetic phase might recognize a word by its shape (physically, the printed word *bed* looks different than the word *egg*).

In the *partial alphabetic phase,* children learn the shapes and sounds of letters. For example, they recognize the curved shape of the letter *C* and begin to associate this with a particular sound. These children begin to connect at least one letter in a word—usually the first—to its corresponding sound. Not surprisingly, children typically recognize the initial letter of their first name before other letters (Treiman & Broderick, 1998).

Complete connections between written letters and their corresponding sounds are acquired during the *full alphabetic phase.* Children now acquire **phonological awareness**—the sensitivity to the sound system of language that enables them to segment spoken words into sounds or phonemes. Children who have phonological awareness can recognize that *cat* and *trouble* both have the phoneme /t/ in them, can tell you how many distinct sounds there are in the word *bunch,* and can tell you what will be left if you take the *f* sound out of *fat.* Children can decode words never before seen by applying their knowledge of phonetics. They can decipher the new word *mat* from their previous understanding of the word *cat* and the letter *m.*

In addition to decoding unfamiliar words, children in the full alphabetic phase also use *sight reading* for familiar words. Sight reading is fast and works well for words that are hard to decode (such as those with unusual spellings) as well as those that are frequently encountered. If you regularly run across the word *alligator* in your readings, you may initially read this by decoding it, or "unpacking" each sound and then putting the sounds together. But after many encounters with this word, you can sight-read it, or recall it from memory, without having to decode every sound.

Finally, in the *consolidated alphabetic phase,* letters that regularly occur together are grouped as a unit. For instance, the letter sequence *ing*, which frequently appears at the end of verbs, is perceived as a single unit rather than as three separate letters. This grouping speeds the processing of the multisyllabic words that older children are increasingly exposed to in their books.

Thus, the basic components of literacy include mastering a language system, understanding connections between sounds and their printed symbols (the alphabetic principle), and discriminating phonemes that make up words (phonological awareness). How does the child manage to pull all this together into reading?

EMERGENT LITERACY

A number of activities help to promote **emergent literacy**—the developmental precursors of actual reading skills in young children (Whitehurst & Lonigan, 1998). Emergent literacy includes knowledge, skills, and attitudes that will facilitate the acquisition of reading ability. For instance, reading storybooks to preschoolers positively influences their later literacy (Bus, van Ijzendoorn, & Pellegrini, 1995). Repetitious storybook reading enhances children's vocabulary and allows them to see the connection between printed and spoken words (Whitehurst & Lonigan, 1998). With each successive reading, parents ask increasingly complex questions about the text, moving the child from a superficial to a deeper understanding (van Kleeck et al., 1997). Even older children benefit from reading the same book on multiple occasions (Faust & Glenzer, 2000) and from shared reading with a parent (Clarke-Stewart, 1998). Parents, with their greater mastery of reading, can help their fledgling readers develop an understanding of printed words. If you think of this in Vygotsky's framework, it is an example of parent and child operating in the zone of proximal development.

Rhyming stories and games can help foster phonological awareness. For this reason, listening to books with a rhyming structure (for example, Dr. Seuss's *Cat in the Hat*) can benefit children. Young children's sensitivity to rhyme (for example, *cat–sat*) helps predict their later reading success (Bryant, 1998; Goswami, 1999).

By assessing preschool children's emergent literacy skills, we can get a fairly accurate idea of what their later reading skills will be (Lonigan, Burgess, & Anthony, 2000). In particular, differences among children in knowledge of letters (for example, knowing the alphabet) and phonological awareness predict later differences in their reading ability. This suggests

Repeatedly reading the same story fosters vocabulary and deepens children's understanding of the story content.

that parents can help children get a head start on reading by encouraging activities such as rhyming and repeating the ABCs.

SKILLED AND UNSKILLED READERS

After children have received reading instruction, why are some children quick, advanced readers while others struggle to master the most basic reading material? For starters, skilled readers have a solid understanding of the alphabetic principle—the notion that letters must be associated with phonemes. Thus, when they see the letter *b,* they know the sound that it represents. A large body of research also confirms that reading ability is influenced by a child's level of phonological awareness (Adams, Treiman, & Pressley, 1998; Bus & van Ijzendoorn, 1999). Children with higher levels of phonological awareness usually become better readers than children with lower levels of phonological awareness (Schneider, Roth, & Ennemoser, 2000).

But there is more to being a skilled reader than connecting letters with sounds. Analyses of eye movement patterns show that unskilled readers skip words or parts of words, whereas skilled readers' eyes hit all the words (Perfetti, 1999). Skilled readers do *not* use context to help them identify words, although they may use context to help with comprehension. As noted previously, they rely on phonology to identify words, something most unskilled readers have trouble with.

Some children have serious difficulties learning to read, even though they have normal intellectual ability and no sensory impairments or emotional difficulties that could account for their problems. These children have **dyslexia,** the term for reading disabilities. A minority have the kind of visual perception problem that used to be seen as the heart of dyslexia;

they cannot distinguish between letters with similar appearances, or they read words backward (*top* might become *pot*). However, it is now clear that the difficulties of the large majority of dyslexic children involve auditory perception more than visual perception (for example, Temple et al., 2000).

Specifically, children who become dyslexic readers often show deficiencies in phonological awareness well before they enter school (Bruck, 1992; Vellutino et al., 1996). There is even evidence that the brains of dyslexic children respond differently to speech sounds soon after birth (Molfese, 2000). This suggests that a perceptual deficit may develop during the prenatal period of brain development. Because dyslexic children have difficulty analyzing the sounds in speech, they also have trouble detecting sound–letter correspondences, which in turn impairs their ability to recognize printed words automatically and effortlessly (Bruck, 1990; Vellutino, 1991). They must then devote so much effort to decoding the words on the page that they have little attention to spare for interpreting and remembering what they have read. Dyslexic children continue to perform very poorly on tests of phonological awareness and tests of word recognition as adolescents and adults, even if they have managed to become decent readers (Bruck, 1990, 1992; Shaywitz et al., 1999). It is now clear that dyslexia is a lifelong disability, not just a developmental delay that is eventually overcome (Shaywitz et al., 1999).

HOW SHOULD READING BE TAUGHT?

What does all this suggest about teaching children to read? For years a so-called Great Debate has raged over the merits of two broad approaches to reading instruction: the phonics approach and the whole language approach (for example, Chall, 1967; Lemann, 1997). The phonics (or code-oriented) approach teaches children to analyze words into their component sounds; that is, it systematically teaches them letter–sound correspondence rules (Vellutino, 1991). By contrast, the whole language (or look–say) approach emphasizes reading for meaning and teaches children to recognize specific words by sight or to figure out what they mean using clues in the surrounding context. It assumes that the parts of printed words (the letters) are not as meaningful as the whole words and that by focusing on whole words children can learn to read as effortlessly and naturally as they learn to understand speech.

Research strongly supports the phonics approach. To read well, children must somehow learn that spoken words are made up of sounds and that the letters of the alphabet correspond to these sounds (Foorman, 1995). Teaching phonological awareness skills can pay off in better reading skills (National Reading Panel, 1999). Table 10.5 shows what happened when a third-grade boy with poor phonological awareness tried to read by the "look–say" method. He ended up with an interpretation that was incorrect and lost the intended meaning of the sentence. Better decoding skills (phonics) might have enabled him to read the sentence accurately.

With this in mind, several programs have been developed for at-risk and dyslexic children who have special difficulty discriminating speech sounds that are made rapidly such as *b,*

Table 10.5 One Boy's Misreading of the Sentence "A Boy Said, 'Run, Little Girl.'"

Words in Target Sentence	Strategies Employed by the Reader	Words "Read"
A	Sight word known to reader	A
boy	Unknown, uses beginning letter *b* to guess *baby*	baby
said, "Run	*Said* unknown; reader jumps ahead to the next word (*run*), which he recognizes; uses the *s* in *said* and knowledge of syntax to generate *is running*	is running
little	Sight word known to reader	little
girl."	Unknown, uses beginning letter *g* to guess *go*	go

SOURCE: Ely (2001)

d, and *t*. By playing an entertaining computer game, children are able to practice discriminating pairs of these hard-to-distinguish sounds, which are altered so that they are stretched out in time and thereby made easier to perceive (Merzenich et al., 1996; Tallal et al., 1996). After only a month of such game playing, children's ability to recognize fast sequences of speech sounds and understand language improves dramatically. These gains eventually pay off in improved reading performance as children become more able to sound out words on the page (Foorman et al., 1998). Despite the importance of phonological awareness, though, children must also make sense of what they are reading—they must be able to read for meaning. Thus, reading programs should make use of both phonics and whole language instruction, teaching letter–sound correspondences but also helping children find meaning and enjoyment in what they read (Adams, 1990).

The debate over reading instruction and its effectiveness raises a broader question about just how well schools are doing at educating our children. Let's now look at what factors contribute—or don't contribute—to effective schools.

Effective Schools

Some schools are clearly better than others at accomplishing their objectives. We regularly read news reports of schools that are above or below the national average in the percentage of students they graduate or the achievement scores of their students—two common measures of school effectiveness. As you read the next sections, you may be surprised by some of the factors that do and do not have a bearing on how effective a school is (Fraser et al., 1987; Mac Iver, Reuman, & Main, 1995; D. Reynolds, 1992; Rutter, 1983; Wang, Haertel, & Walberg, 1993).

LESS IMPORTANT FACTORS

Many people assume that pouring financial resources into schools will automatically increase school effectiveness. But the relationship between funding and student outcome is more complex than this. Some research shows that as long as schools have reasonable resources, the precise amount of money spent per pupil plays only a minor role in determining student outcomes (Hanushek, 1997; Rutter, 1983). Other research suggests that increased resources, if applied directly to classroom instruction, can increase student achievement in the earlier grades (Wenglinsky, 1998b). Thus, simply adding more money to school budgets is unlikely to improve school effectiveness unless schools invest this money wisely.

Another factor that has relatively little to do with a school's effectiveness is *average class size* (Rutter, 1983; Toch & Streisand, 1997). Within a range of from 15 to 40 students per class, reducing class sizes (from, say, 36 to 24 students) is unlikely to increase student achievement (Hanushek, 1997, 1998). Tutoring students in the early grades, especially disadvantaged and low-ability ones, one-on-one or in small groups *does* make a big difference in their learning of reading and math (Odden, 1990; Slavin, 1989; Toch & Streisand, 1997). However, more modest reductions in the student/teacher ratio do not seem to be worth the large amount of money they cost.

Finally, it does not matter much whether or not a school uses **ability grouping,** in which students are grouped according to ability and then taught in classes or work groups with others of similar academic or intellectual standing. Grouping by ability has no clear advantage over mixed-ability grouping for most students (Betts & Shkolnik, 2000; Rutter, 1983). It *can* be beneficial, especially to higher-ability students, if it means a curriculum more appropriate to students' learning needs (Kulik & Kulik, 1992). However, low-ability students are unlikely to benefit and may well suffer if they are denied access to the most effective teachers, taught less material than other children, and stigmatized as "dummies" (Mac Iver et al., 1995; Mehan et al., 1996). Too often, this is just what happens. As Hugh Mehan and his colleagues (1996) put it, "It is not that dumb kids are placed in slow groups or low tracks; it is that kids are made dumb by being placed in slow groups or low tracks" (p. 230). The Explorations box on page 268 takes a closer look at mixing students with different abilities and backgrounds.

These, then, are examples of school characteristics that do *not* seem to contribute a great deal to effective education. A school that has quite limited financial support (assuming it exceeds a basic minimum), places most students (except perhaps for beginning readers) in relatively large classes, and combines students in mixed-ability learning groups or classes is often just as effective as another school that has ample financial resources, small classes, and ability grouping.

FACTORS THAT MATTER

So what does influence how well children perform? To understand why some schools are more effective than others, we must consider characteristics of the students, characteristics of the learning environment, and the interaction between student and environment.

First, a school's effectiveness is a function of what it has to work with—the aptitudes of its students (Wang et al., 1993). On average, academic achievement tends to be higher in schools with a preponderance of economically advantaged students; any child is likely to make more academic progress in a school with a high concentration of intellectually capable peers (Brookover et al., 1979; Portes & MacLeod, 1996). However, this does *not* mean that schools are only as good as the students they serve. Many schools that serve disadvantaged populations are highly effective at motivating students and preparing them for jobs or further education (Reynolds, 1992).

So what is it about the learning environment of some schools that allows them to accomplish so much? Basically, the effective school environment is a comfortable but businesslike setting in which teachers are involved with students, students are motivated to learn, and serious teaching takes place (Mac Iver et al., 1995; Phillips, 1997; Rutter, 1983). More specifically, effective schools and classrooms teachers

- **Strongly emphasize academics.** They demand a lot from their students and expect them to succeed, regularly assign homework, and work hard to achieve their objectives in the classroom.
- **Create a task-oriented but comfortable atmosphere.** For example, they waste little time on getting activities started or dealing with distracting discipline problems, provide clear instructions and feedback, and encourage and reward good work.
- **Manage discipline problems effectively.** For example, they enforce the rules on the spot rather than sending offenders to the principal's office, and they avoid the use of physical punishment.

Effective schools also have supportive parents and supportive communities behind them (Comer, 1997). Students achieve more when their parents are interested in and value school and school achievement; participate in parent–teacher conferences, PTA meetings, and other school events; and participate in homework and other school-related activities at home (Bogenschneider, 1997; Sui-Chu & Willms, 1996). Parents with less education themselves are typically less involved in their children's education than highly educated parents are; yet they can have even more impact on their children's grades if they *do* become involved (Bogenschneider, 1997).

Finally, characteristics of the student and characteristics of the school environment often interact to affect student outcome. Lee Cronbach and Richard Snow (1977) called this phenomenon **aptitude–treatment interaction (ATI);** it is an example of the broader concept of *goodness of fit* between person and environment that we emphasize throughout this book. Much educational research has been based on the assumption that *one* teaching method, organizational system, or philosophy of education will prove superior for all students, regardless of their ability levels, learning styles, personalities, and cultural backgrounds. This assumption is often wrong. Instead, many educational practices are highly effective with *some* kinds of students but quite ineffective with other students. The secret is to find an appropriate match between learner and teaching method.

To illustrate the ATI concept, highly achievement-oriented students adapt well to unstructured classrooms in which they have a good deal of choice, whereas less achievement-oriented students often do better with more structure (Peterson, 1977). Sometimes alternative teaching methods work equally well with highly capable students, but only one of them suits less capable students. In one study, for example, highly distractible students got more from computer-assisted instruction than from a teacher's presentation of the same material, whereas more attentive students benefited from both methods (Orth & Martin, 1994). Finally, students tend to have more positive outcomes when they and their teacher share similar backgrounds (Goldwater & Nutt, 1999). Evidence of the importance of the fit between student and classroom environment implies that educational programs are likely to be most effective when they are highly individualized—tailored to suit each student's developmental competencies and needs.

In sum, some students (for example, those from advantaged homes) typically outperform others, and some learning environments (especially those in which teachers create a motivating, comfortable, and task-oriented setting and involve parents in their children's schooling) are generally more conducive to learning than others. Still, what works best for one kind of student may not work as well for another kind of student. In aptitude–treatment interactions, we have another

In a comfortable and task-oriented classroom, children are motivated to learn.

Making Integration and Inclusion Work

For many minority students of the past, especially African Americans, additional barriers to school success were created by school segregation. Black children in many states were forced to attend "black schools" that were clearly inferior to "white schools." In its landmark decision in the case of *Brown v. Board of Education of Topeka* in 1954, the Supreme Court ruled that segregated schools were "inherently unequal" and declared that they must be desegregated. What have we learned since this ruling?

Generally, the effects of school integration on children's racial attitudes, self-esteem, and school achievement have been mixed (Gray-Little & Carels, 1997; Stephan, 1978). Some studies do suggest that both African American and European American children tend to have higher self-esteem and higher achievement when they attend racially mixed schools, but the effects are often small (Gray-Little & Carels, 1997). White prejudice toward black students often does not decrease much at all. The self-esteem of black children in integrated schools is only sometimes higher than that of black children in segregated schools (Gray-Little & Carels, 1997). And although minority students sometimes achieve more in integrated schools, especially if they begin to attend them early in their academic careers (St. John, 1975; Entwisle & Alexander, 1992), school integration often does not have much effect on achievement.

Children with developmental disabilities (mental retardation, learning disabilities, physical and sensory handicaps, and other special learning needs) have had a somewhat similar history. They used to be placed in separate schools or classrooms—or, in some cases, rejected as unteachable by the public schools. But the Individuals with Disabilities Education Act (IDEA; an extension of the 1975 Education for All Handicapped Children Act) requires schools to pro-

Richard Hutchings/PhotoEdit, Inc.

vide them with a free and appropriate education that occurs "to the maximum extent appropriate . . . with children who are not disabled."

What has been achieved since? Studies of developmentally disabled children integrated into regular classrooms through a practice called **inclusion** (formerly called mainstreaming)—to emphasize the philosophy that children with special learning needs should spend the entire school day rather than only parts of it in a regular classroom and

---

nice example of the importance of the fit between individuals and their environments. In a similar vein, the Explorations box on page 270 illustrates how computers can help or hinder school achievement, depending on how they are used.

The Adolescent

Adolescents make critical decisions about such matters as how much time to devote to studying, whether to work part-time after school, whether to go to college, and what to be when they grow up. They become more capable of making these educational and vocational choices as their cognitive and social skills expand; in turn, the choices they make shape their future

development. But many of them lose interest in school when they leave elementary school.

Declining Levels of Achievement

You might think that adolescents would become more dedicated to academic success once they begin to realize that they need a good education to succeed in life. But consider what Deborah Stipek (1984) concluded after reviewing studies on the development of achievement motivation from early childhood to adolescence:

> On the average, children value academic achievement more as they progress through school, but their expectations for success and self-perceptions of competence de-

truly be included in the normal educational process—have found mixed results. Compared with similar students who attend segregated special education classes, these main-streamed youngsters sometimes fare better in terms of academic performance, self-esteem, and social adjustment but sometimes do not (Buysse & Bailey, 1993; Hunt & Goetz, 1997; Manset & Semmel, 1997). The outcome depends in part on the severity of the child's disability. The performance of higher-functioning disabled children often benefits from inclusion in the regular classroom, whereas the performance of lower-functioning children is similar in integrated and segregated classrooms (Holahan & Costenbader, 2000). In terms of peer acceptance, children with severe disabilities are better accepted by their normally developing peers than are children with mild disabilities in homogeneous regular classrooms, where those with more severe disabilities presumably stand out as different, prompting other students to adjust their expectations (Cook & Semmel, 1999). Children with mild disabilities do not markedly stand out in homogeneous classrooms and therefore do not achieve "special" status; these children are better accepted in heterogeneous classrooms (Cook & Semmel, 1999).

What we seem to be learning about both racial integration and inclusion is that simply putting diverse students into the same schools and classrooms accomplishes little. Instead, something special must be done to ensure that students of different ethnic backgrounds and ability levels interact in positive ways and learn what they are supposed to be learning.

One promising model uses **cooperative learning,** in which diverse students are assigned to work teams and are reinforced for performing well *as a team* (Salend, 1999;

Slavin, 1986; R. J. Stevens & Slavin, 1995). Consider research conducted by Uri Treisman at the University of California at Berkeley in the 1970s (Fullilove & Treisman, 1990). Treisman studied African Americans and Asian Americans enrolled in first-year calculus. The Asian Americans did quite well in the class, whereas the African Americans performed poorly. But this was not the only difference between the two groups of students. The African American students worked independently on work related to the class; the Asian Americans worked together in small study groups and often combined studying with socializing, something the African American students rarely did. Treisman decided to see whether working together and receiving support from peers could boost the African American students' performance—and indeed, it did (see also Duncan & Dick, 2000).

In cooperative learning classrooms, children of different races and ability levels interact in a context where the efforts of even the least capable team members are important to the group's success. Elementary school students come to like school better and learn more when they participate in cooperative learning groups than when they receive traditional instruction (Johnson, Johnson, & Maruyama, 1983; O'Donnell & O'Kelly, 1994; Stevens & Slavin, 1995). Moreover, team members gain self-esteem from their successes, and minority students and students with developmental disabilities are more fully accepted by their peers. In short, racial integration and inclusion *can* succeed if educators deliberately design learning experiences that encourage students from different backgrounds to pool their efforts in order to achieve common goals. Interventions like this are important if children are to be ready for the challenges of secondary school.

cline, and their affect toward school becomes more negative. Children also become increasingly concerned about achievement outcomes and reinforcement (e.g., high grades) associated with positive outcomes and less concerned about intrinsic satisfaction in achieving greater competence. (p. 153)

Many of the negative trends Stipek describes become especially apparent as young adolescents make the transition from elementary school to a middle school (typically grades 6 to 8) or a junior high school (grades 7 to 9). At this critical juncture, achievement motivation, self-esteem, and grades may all decline (Eccles et al., 1993; Seidman et al., 1994). More and more students become alienated from school; many others continue to work hard at their studies but become extrinsically rather

than intrinsically motivated (Harter, 1981): They work to obtain good grades, parent or teacher approval, and other external rewards rather than because they find learning and mastering challenges gratifying in themselves. How can we explain these discouraging trends? We'll consider five contributors: cognitive growth, negative feedback, peer pressures, pubertal changes, and a poor fit between adolescents and the schools they attend.

COGNITIVE GROWTH

As we saw earlier, children become increasingly capable with age of analyzing the causes of events, interpreting feedback from teachers, and inferring enduring traits such as high or low ability from their behavior (Stipek & Mac Iver, 1989). The result is that they come to view their strengths and weaknesses more realistically—and lose some of their high academic

Computers in the Classroom: Useful Tool or Wasteful Game?

Computers are found in most modern classrooms, and many educators and parents assume that computers are useful learning tools. But are they? To what extent do computers improve academic achievement and motivation to learn? An evaluation of computer use and math achievement conducted by the Educational Testing Service sheds some light on this issue (Wenglinsky, 1998a). Data on computer use and mathematics achievement were collected from more than 13,000 fourth- and eighth-grade students. Computer use was divided into lower-order activities such as repetitive drills and higher-order activities such as application of concepts or development of simulations.

According to the ETS study, between one-fourth and one-third of American children use computers at school at least once a week, and more than half have access to computers at home. How much time students spend on the computer is not as important as the type of work they do. Indeed, for fourth-graders, more time on the computer was associated with lower achievement. Computers can have a positive influence on math achievement when they are used for higher-order activities and when teachers are trained to incorporate them effectively into the classroom. For fourth-graders, teachers with greater computer training are more likely to use computers appropriately to engage students in math learning games. This leads to higher math achievement and a more positive school climate.

Among eighth-graders, math achievement is enhanced when computers are used primarily for applications and simulations, but is negatively influenced when the primary use of computers is for drills (Wenglinsky, 1998a). Thus, using the computer to practice basic skills can actually detract from achievement, at least in math classes for adolescents. Teacher training is key to appropriate computer use and also has direct positive effects on math achievement and school climate in the eighth grade. Apparently, schools need to ensure that when they spend money for computers, they also invest in training teachers.

© A. Ramey/PhotoEdit, Inc.

Computers are a useful tool that can enhance academic achievement, but only when used properly. And some computer use actually detracts from academic achievement. Clearly, teacher training is essential and must be expanded if we are to optimize the educational potential of computers.

---

self-esteem and high expectancies of success in the process (Stipek & Mac Iver, 1989; Wigfield et al., 1997).

NEGATIVE FEEDBACK

Declines in achievement motivation may also be caused by changes in the kinds of feedback students receive as they get older (Eccles, Lord, & Midgley, 1991; Stipek & Mac Iver, 1989). Preschool teachers often praise their young charges merely for trying and do not hand out much criticism. As Deborah Stipek (1984) notes, it would be unthinkable for an adult to say to a 5-year-old exhibiting a drawing, "What an ugly pic-

ture. You sure can't draw very well" (p. 156). The positive feedback young children receive for their efforts may contribute to their tendency to set learning rather than performance goals and sense that hard work can overcome any barrier (Rosenholtz & Simpson, 1984). By contrast, elementary and secondary school teachers increasingly reserve praise, high grades, and other forms of approval for students who turn in high-quality products. Effort alone is not enough. As they progress through school, then, children receive more and more feedback telling them precisely what capabilities they have and what capabilities they lack.

PEER PRESSURES

The adolescent's environment also changes in the sense that peers become increasingly important and sometimes can undermine parents' and teachers' efforts to encourage school achievement. Many years ago, when James Coleman (1961) asked high school students how they would like to be remembered, only 31% of the boys and 28% of the girls wanted to be remembered as bright students. They were more concerned with having the athletic and social skills that lead to popularity. Not much has changed (Suitor & Reavis, 1995).

Peer pressures that undermine achievement motivation tend to be especially strong for many lower-income minority students. Lawrence Steinberg and his colleagues (Steinberg, Dornbusch, & Brown, 1992) note that the African American and Hispanic peer cultures in many low-income areas actively discourage academic achievement, whereas European American and especially Asian American peer groups tend to value and encourage it. High-achieving African American students in some inner-city schools actually run the risk of being rejected by their African American peers if their academic accomplishments cause them to be perceived as "acting white" (Fordham & Ogbu, 1986). They may feel that they have to abandon their cultural group and racial identity in order to succeed in school, and this takes a psychological toll (Arroyo & Zigler, 1995; Phelan, Yu, & Davidson, 1994). Although African American parents are as likely as European American parents to value education and to provide the kind of authoritative parenting that encourages school achievement, their positive influences are sometimes canceled out by negative peer influences (Steinberg et al., 1992).

PUBERTAL CHANGES

It is also been suggested that the transition to middle school or junior high school is difficult because young adolescents are often experiencing major physical and psychological changes at the same time they are being asked to switch schools. Roberta Simmons and Dale Blyth (1987) found that

girls who were reaching puberty at the same time they were moving from sixth grade in an elementary school to seventh grade in a junior high school were more likely to experience drops in self-esteem and other negative changes than girls who remained in a K–8 school during this vulnerable period.

Could it be that more adolescents would remain interested in school if they didn't have to change schools at the very time they are experiencing pubertal changes? This idea became an important part of the rationale for middle schools (grades 6 to 8), which were developed in order to make the transition from elementary school to high school easier for early adolescents (Braddock & McPartland, 1993). Yet Jacquelynne Eccles and her colleagues (Eccles, Lord, & Midgley, 1991; Eccles et al., 1993) have shown that students do not necessarily find the transition to middle school any easier than the transition to junior high school. These researchers suspect that *when* adolescents make a school change is less important than what their new school is like.

POOR PERSON–ENVIRONMENT FIT

Eccles and her colleagues offer a goodness-of-fit explanation for declining achievement motivation in adolescence, arguing that the transition to a new school is likely to be especially difficult when the new school, whether a junior high or a middle school, is ill matched to the developmental needs of early adolescents. These researchers have found that the transition to middle school or junior high school often involves going from a small school with close student–teacher relationships, a good deal of choice regarding learning activities, and reasonable discipline to a larger, more bureaucratized environment in which student–teacher relationships are impersonal, good grades are more emphasized but harder to come by, opportunities for choice are limited, assignments are not very intellectually stimulating, and discipline is rigid—all at a time when adolescents are seeking more rather than less autonomy and are becoming more rather than less intellectually capable! Students who had what Carol Dweck calls *learning goals* in elementary school perceive an increased emphasis on *performance goals* when they move to middle school (Anderman & Midgley, 1997).

Eccles and her colleagues have demonstrated that the fit between developmental needs and school environment is indeed an important influence on adolescent adjustment to school. In one study (Mac Iver & Reuman, 1988), the transition to junior high school brought about a decline in intrinsic motivation to learn mainly among students who wanted more involvement in classroom decisions but ended up with fewer such opportunities than they had in elementary school. In another study (Midgley, Feldlaufer, & Eccles, 1989), students experienced negative changes in their attitudes toward mathematics only when their move from elementary school to junior high resulted in less personal and supportive relationships with math teachers. For those few students whose junior high teachers were more supportive than those they had in elementary school, interest in academics actually *increased*.

The message? Declines in academic motivation and performance are not inevitable during early adolescence.

By adolescence, some students have little motivation to achieve in the classroom.

Students may indeed form more realistic expectancies of success as their growing cognitive abilities allow them to make use of the increasingly informative feedback they receive from teachers. Experiencing pubertal changes at the same time as other stressful changes and needing to downplay academics in order to gain popularity may also hurt school achievement. However, educators can help to keep adolescents engaged in school by creating school environments that provide a better fit to the developmental needs and interests of adolescents. Whether they are called middle schools or junior high schools, such schools should provide warm, supportive relationships with teachers along with intellectual challenges and increased opportunities for self-direction (Eccles et al., 1993). Specially designed school transition programs can help students adjust to high school and reduce the risk that they will drop out (Smith, 1997).

Science and Math Education

Elementary schools necessarily spend much time on reading and writing skills. But secondary school teachers take these skills largely for granted and focus their energies on other academic areas. More advanced skills of concrete and then formal operational thought enable children to tackle more challenging academic tasks. A great deal of attention has been focused on math and science, skills that are important for success in many industrialized nations. How well do secondary school students perform in science and math? And how might achievement in these areas be optimized?

Table 10.6 shows average mathematics and science achievement test scores of eighth-grade students in various countries. Students in the United States score above the international average, but significantly below achievement levels in

Table 10.6   Average Math and Science Achievement of Eighth-Grade Students in Various Nations (1999 scores)

Mathematics		Science	
Singapore	604	Chinese Taipei	569
Republic of Korea	587	Singapore	568
Chinese Taipei	585	Hungary	552
Hong Kong SAR	582	Japan	550
Japan	579	Republic of Korea	549
Netherlands	540	Netherlands	545
Hungary	532	Australia	540
Canada	531	Czech Republic	539
Slovenia	530	England	538
Russian Federation	526	Slovenia	533
Australia	525	Canada	533
Czech Republic	520	Hong Kong SAR	530
Malaysia	519	Russian Federation	529
United States	502	United States	515
England	496	New Zealand	510
New Zealand	491	Italy	493
INTERNATIONAL AVERAGE	487	Malaysia	492
Italy	479	INTERNATIONAL AVERAGE	488
Cyprus	476	Thailand	482
Romania	472	Romania	472
Thailand	467	Cyprus	460
Turkey	429	Iran	448
Iran	422	Turkey	433
Chile	392	Chile	420
Philippines	345	Philippines	345
Morocco	337	Morocco	323
South Africa	275	South Africa	243

☐ Average is significantly higher than the U.S. average

☐ Average does not differ significantly from the U.S. average

☐ Average is significantly lower than the U.S. average

SOURCE: Martin et al. (2000)

nations such as Singapore, Japan, and Korea. When we look at the best students—those in the top 10% of all eighth-graders surveyed in the 38 nations—only 9% of U.S. students meet the criteria in math and only 15% meet it in science. In comparison, the nation with the largest percentage of students in the top 10% was Singapore, with 46% in math and 32% in science. What might account for these international differences in math and science achievement? Are students in some nations simply more intelligent than students in other nations?

Cross-cultural research conducted by Harold Stevenson and his colleagues (Chen & Stevenson, 1995; Stevenson & Lee, 1990; Stevenson, Chen, & Lee, 1993) shows that American schoolchildren perform just about as well on IQ tests as their Asian counterparts when they enter school (Stevenson et al., 1985). And they score at least as well as Japanese and Chinese students on tests of general information *not* typically covered in school (Stevenson et al., 1993). Instead, the achievement gap between American and Asian students seems to be rooted in cultural differences in attitudes concerning education and educational practices. Here is what some of this cross-cultural research on education and achievement shows:

- Asian students spend more time being educated. Elementary school teachers in Asian countries devote more class time to academics. The classroom is also a businesslike place where little time is wasted; Asian students spend about 95% of their time "on task" (in activities such as listening to the teacher and completing assignments), whereas American students spend only about 80% of their time "on task" (Stigler, Lee, & Stevenson, 1987). Asian students also attend school for more hours per day and more days per year (Stevenson, Lee, & Stigler, 1986).
- Asian students, especially Japanese students, are assigned and complete considerably more homework than American students (Larson & Verma, 1999; Stevenson & Lee, 1990). While American students are working or socializing with friends, Asian students are hitting the books (Fuligni & Stevenson, 1995).
- Asian parents are strongly committed to the educational process. About 40% think their children should have 3 hours or more of homework each day (Ebbeck, 1996). Asian parents are never quite satisfied with how their children are doing in school or with the quality of education their children are receiving; American parents seem to settle for less (Stevenson et al., 1993). Asian parents also receive frequent communications from their children's teachers in notebooks children carry to and from school each day. They find out how their children are progressing and follow teachers' suggestions for encouraging and assisting their children at home (Stevenson & Lee, 1990).
- Asian peers also value school achievement and have high standards; time spent with peers often involves doing homework rather than engaging in activities that interfere with homework (Chen & Stevenson, 1995).
- Asian parents, teachers, and students all share a strong belief that hard work or effort will pay off in better academic performance (that is, they set what Dweck calls learning goals), whereas Americans tend to put more emphasis on ability as a cause of good or poor performance. The result may be that Americans give up too quickly on a child who appears to have low intellectual ability. In doing so, they may help create a case of learned helplessness.

This cross-cultural research carries an important message: The secret of effective education is to get teachers, students, and parents working together to make education the top priority for youth, to set high achievement goals, and to invest the day-by-day effort required to attain those goals. Many states and local school districts have begun to respond to evidence that American schools are being outclassed by schools in other countries by strengthening curricula, tightening standards for teacher certification, raising standards for graduation and promotion from grade to grade, and even lengthening the school year.

Integrating Work and School

Unlike teens in many other industrialized nations, a sizable number (between one-third and one-half) of teens in the United States and Canada work part-time during their high school careers (Steinberg & Dornbusch, 1991). How do these early work experiences affect their development and, in particular, their school achievement?

Laurence Steinberg and his associates have compared working and nonworking high school students in terms of such outcomes as autonomy from parents, self-reliance, self-esteem, sense of investment in school, academic performance, delinquency, and drug and alcohol use (Greenberger & Steinberg, 1986; Steinberg & Dornbusch, 1991; Steinberg, Fegley, & Dornbusch, 1993). Overall, this research offers more bad news than good. The good news is that working students seem to gain knowledge about the world of work, consumer issues, and financial management, and sometimes greater self-reliance. However, high school students who worked 20 or more hours a week had grade-point averages about a third of a letter grade lower than those of students who did not work or who worked only 10 or fewer hours per week (Steinberg & Dornbusch, 1991). Working students were also more likely than nonworkers to be disengaged from school—bored and uninvolved in class and prone to cut class and spend little time on homework.

In addition, the more adolescents worked, the more independent they were of parental control, the more likely they were to be experiencing psychological distress (anxiety, depression, and physical symptoms such as headaches), and the more frequently they used alcohol and drugs and engaged in delinquent acts. These negative effects of work generally increased as the number of hours a student worked increased.

In a longitudinal study, Steinberg and his colleagues (1993) established that students who worked long hours were more disenchanted with school and independent of their parents even before they began working. However, working led to *further* alienation from school and *greater* distance from parents and contributed to problems that had not been apparent before. Moreover, students who worked but quit during the course of the study improved their school performance after they stopped working (see also Bachman & Schulenberg, 1993).

Kusum Singh and Mehmet Ozturk (2000) reached a similar conclusion with their research on employment during high school and performance in mathematics and science courses. They found that students with low achievement in science and math were more likely to work part-time than students with high achievement in these courses. Working reduced the number of math and science courses that students enrolled in. Ultimately, students who work during high school may limit their future educational and vocational prospects by limiting their exposure to potentially important coursework.

Not all research findings are this discouraging. Jeylen Mortimer and his colleagues (1996) also conducted a longitudinal study of high school students, but controlled for differences between working and nonworking students on factors such as family background and prior academic performance. In their study, working 20 hours or more a week did not hurt academic achievement, self-esteem, or psychological adjustment once other factors were controlled. Students who worked 1 to 20 hours a week actually earned better grades than either nonworkers or students who worked more than 20 hours a week. As in Steinberg's study, though, students who worked more than 20 hours used alcohol more frequently than students who were not employed.

These findings suggest that working while attending high school, although often more damaging than beneficial, is not always bad for adolescents. Much depends on the nature of the work adolescents do. Many teenagers work in food service jobs (pouring soft drinks behind the counter at McDonald's, scooping ice cream, and the like) or perform manual labor (especially cleaning or janitorial work). These routine and repetitive jobs offer few opportunities for self-direction or decision making and only rarely call on academic skills such as reading and math (Steinberg, 1984). They are not the kinds of jobs that "build character" or teach new skills. Adolescents experience increases in mastery motivation and become less depressed over time when the work they do provides opportunities for advancement and teaches useful skills, but lose mastery motivation and become more depressed when they hold menial jobs that interfere with their schooling (Shanahan et al., 1991; Call, Mortimer, & Shanahan, 1995). And working long hours has negative effects on adolescents when their jobs are menial but not when their jobs are of high quality (Barling, Rogers, & Kelloway, 1995).

Judging from this research, many adolescents who are flipping hamburgers might be better off postponing work or working only a limited number of hours so that they can concentrate on obtaining a solid education and exploring their career options (Steinberg, 1984). However, those adolescents lucky enough to land intellectually challenging jobs, especially jobs that tie in with their emerging vocational interests and teach them useful skills, can benefit from their work experiences.

Pathways to Adulthood

The educational paths and attainments of adolescents are already partially set long before they enter adolescence. Because many individuals' intelligence test scores remain quite stable from childhood on, some children enter adolescence with more aptitude for schoolwork than others do (see Chapter 9). Moreover, some students have more achievement motivation than others. Quite clearly, a bright and achievement-oriented student is more likely to obtain good grades and go on to college and is less likely to drop out of school than a student with less ability and less need to achieve. By early elementary school, and sometimes even before they enter school, future dropouts are often identifiable by such warning signs as low IQ and achievement test scores, poor grades, aggressive behavior, low socioeconomic status, and troubled homes (Ensminger & Slusarcick, 1992; Gamoran et al., 1997).

This does *not* mean that adolescents' fates are sealed in childhood, however; experiences during adolescence clearly make a difference. Some teenagers make the most of their intellectual abilities, whereas others who have the ability to do well in school drop out or get poor grades. The quality of an adolescent's school, the extent to which his or her parents are authoritative and encourage school achievement, and the extent to which his or her peers value school can make a big difference (B. B. Brown et al., 1993; Rutter et al., 1979; Steinberg et al., 1992).

The stakes are high. Students who achieve good grades are more likely to complete high school; currently, 91% of European American students, 84% of African American students, and an alarmingly low 63% of Hispanic students achieve this milestone (National Center for Education Statistics, 2001) They then stand a chance of being among the 24% of whites, 14% of blacks, and 9% of Hispanics who com-

Working in fast-food restaurants is not the kind of intellectually challenging work that can contribute positively to adolescent development.

plete 4 years of college or more (U.S. Bureau of the Census, 1997). These youth, in turn, are likely to have higher career aspirations and end up in higher-status occupations than their peers who do not attend college or do not even finish high school (Featherman, 1980; McCaul et al., 1992). And, if their grades are good, they are likely to perform well in those jobs and advance far in their careers (Roth et al., 1996). In a very real sense, then, individuals are steered along "high success" or "low success" routes starting in childhood. Depending on their own decisions and family, peer, and school influences, adolescents are even more distinctly "sorted out" in ways that will affect their adult lifestyles, income levels, and adjustment. Meanwhile, high school dropouts not only have less successful careers, but miss out on the beneficial effects that every year of schooling has on intellectual functioning (Ceci & Williams, 1997). They also experience more psychological problems than those who stay in school (Kaplan, Damphousse, & Kaplan, 1994).

© Janet Wishnetsky/CORBIS

Many older adults remain motivated to learn and seek challenging experiences.

The Adult

The lives of adults are dominated by work—paid or unpaid, outside the home or within the home. What becomes of achievement motivation and literacy during the adult years? What educational options are available to adults, and what are the benefits of lifelong education?

Achievement Motivation

The level of achievement motivation that we acquire in childhood and adolescence carries into adulthood to influence our decisions and life outcomes (Kagan & Moss, 1962; Spence, 1985). For instance, women who have a strong need to achieve are more likely than less achievement-oriented women to work outside the home (Krogh, 1985). Adults with strong achievement needs are also likely to be more competent workers than adults who have little concern with mastering challenges (Helmreich, Sawin, & Carsrud, 1986; Spence, 1985).

What happens to achievement motivation in later life? Is there any support for the common belief that older adults lose some of their drive to excel? Joseph Veroff, David Reuman, and Sheila Feld (1984) explored this question by analyzing motivational themes in stories that American adults told in response to pictures. Older men displayed only slightly lower levels of achievement motivation than young or middle-aged men did. Here, then, we find no support for the stereotyped idea that older adults are "unmotivated" or have ceased to pursue goals (see also Filipp, 1996; McAdams, de St. Aubin, & Logan, 1993).

Veroff and his associates (1984) did find that achievement motivation declined fairly steeply from age group to age group among women (see also Mellinger & Erdwins, 1985). However, this age trend pertained mainly to *career-related* motivation and an interest in striving for success in competitive situations. When this study was done, many women set aside career-achievement goals after they had children and made nurturing those children their top priority (Krogh, 1985). However, highly educated women often regained a strong motive to achieve outside the home once the children were older and they could invest more energy in outside work (Baruch, 1967; Malatesta & Culver, 1984). Apparently, then, women are especially likely to be motivated to achieve career success when they have the educational background that would allow them to pursue attractive career goals and when they are not pursuing family-related goals.

Overall, adults' achievement-related motives are far more affected by their changing work and family contexts than by the aging process (Filipp, 1996). Adults of different ages are often more alike than they are different, and different people tend to retain their characteristic levels of achievement motivation over the years, much as they retain many personality traits (D. P. Stevens & Truss, 1985). There is certainly little evidence that elderly adults inevitably lose their motivation to pursue important goals. Moreover, those elders who do have a strong sense of purpose and direction and feel they are achieving their goals enjoy greater physical and psychological well-being than those who do not (Hooker & Siegler, 1993; Rapkin & Fischer, 1992; Reker, Peacock, & Wong, 1987). Throughout the life span, then, setting and achieving goals are important.

Literacy

Literacy is the ability to use printed information to function in society, achieve goals, and develop one's potential (Kirsch et al., 1993). Very few adults are completely illiterate, but many adults do not have functional literacy skills despite years of formal education. The National Adult Literacy Survey (NALS), which uses a 5-point scale to estimate literacy, finds that about 22% of adults in the United States demonstrate the lowest level of literacy skills (Kirsch et al., 1993). This is roughly equivalent to a third-grade or lower reading ability; such an adult could probably find an expiration date on a driver's license or locate a specific word or phrase in a short body of text, but would have trouble filling out an application or reading a simple book to a child. Although one-quarter of this group consists of immigrants learning English as a second language, most of the individuals in this group are U.S.-born citizens. Nearly two-thirds did not finish high school. When the U.S. literacy rate is compared to rates in other countries, we find that the United States has one of the largest pockets of illiterate adults, but also has some of the most highly literate adults (U.S. Department of Education, 1997). Thus, literacy in the United States is unevenly distributed.

Literacy contributes to economic security through occupational advancement. Nearly half of the adults with the lowest literacy scores live in poverty, whereas very few adults with the highest literacy scores do (Bowen, 1999). Improving the literacy skills of impoverished adults, however, does not automatically raise them out of poverty. For many low-income and functionally illiterate adults, other obstacles must be overcome as well, including addiction, discrimination, and disabilities (Bowen, 1999).

Programs to raise the literacy level of adults have not been very successful. A number of factors limit the success of such programs. For one thing, despite having limited literacy skills, many of these adults (75%) reported that they could read or write "well" or "very well"—attitudes that must certainly make it difficult to motivate them to improve their literacy skills. Second, adults don't stay in the programs long enough to make improvements (Amstutz & Sheared, 2000). The dropout rate is as high as 70–80%, and many leave in the first weeks of the program (Quigley & Uhland, 2000). Adults who don't persist report that the programs are boring and don't meet their needs (Imel, 1996; Kerka, 1995; Quigley, 1997). Materials, for example, are often geared toward children, not adults who often have families, jobs, and very different interests than children do.

In sum, many adults are functionally illiterate despite years of formal education. Adults with lower literacy skills are more often employed in low-level and low-paying jobs than adults who are more literate. Programs to improve literacy have not been very successful, largely because so many other factors are associated with poor literacy and these factors are not addressed in most literacy programs.

Continuing Education

Increasingly, adults are seeking education beyond basic literacy skills. Nearly 40% of college students are 25 years of age or older, representing 15 million adults enrolled in college (National Center for Education Statistics, 1998). The number of "older" adults attending college is expected to increase as the overall population ages. Whether we call them adult learners, nontraditionals, returning students, mature students, or lifelong learners, these adults represent a diverse group. They bring different work and life experiences to the classroom, and they report a variety of reasons for enrolling in postsecondary education (Kopka & Peng, 1993).

Many "traditional" students (17- to 24-year-olds) are motivated to attend college by external expectations, but older students are often motivated by internal factors (Dinmore, 1997). Women are more likely to return to the classroom for personal enrichment or interest, whereas men are more likely to take classes that are required or recommended for their work (Sargant, et al., 1997). The internal motivation of adult students often leads to deeper levels of processing information (Harper & Kember, 1986). In other words, returning students may put forth greater effort to truly understand material because they want to learn and want (or need) to use the material. Traditional students who don't have the benefit of experience may learn the material necessary to do well on an exam but may not process the material in ways that will lead to long-term retention.

Continued or lifelong education has its drawbacks. Mainly, it is often difficult for adults who are already busy with jobs and family to find the time to take classes. Successful continuing education programs must devise ways to schedule classes at convenient times and must be responsive to the lifestyles of their adult learners (Parnham, 2001). Yet the benefits of lifelong education typically outweigh any drawbacks. For instance, continued education allows adults to remain knowledgeable and competitive in fields that change rapidly. Adults who return to school for bachelor's or master's degrees can also advance their careers, particularly if their education and work are closely related (Senter & Senter, 1997). Finally, higher education is associated with maintaining or improving physical and mental health (Fischer, Blazey, & Lipman, 1992).

Conclusions

In this and previous chapters, we have examined a great deal of material on thinking and learning across the life span. How can we use principles of cognitive development to improve education for all ages? Before closing this chapter, we summarize, in the Applications box on page 277, what theorists Piaget and Vygotsky have to contribute to education, and what research on information processing, intelligence, and perception suggests about optimal learning environments.

What Can Theory and Research Contribute to Education?

To help you appreciate the practical implications for school reform and school achievement of the material in Chapters 6 through 9, we provide the following recommendations.

Piaget

- Provide opportunities for independent, hands-on interaction with the physical environment, especially for younger children. Children need to "see" for themselves how things work and from this construct their own understanding of the world.
- Be aware of children's cognitive strengths and limitations (their stage of development). For example, teachers and parents should recognize that a pre-operational child is cognitively unable to master multidimensional or abstract tasks.
- With the child's current level of understanding in mind, create some disequilibrium by presenting new information that is slightly above the child's current level. Children who experience disequilibrium—cognitive discomfort with their understanding (or lack of understanding)—will work to resolve it, achieving a higher level of mastery of the material.
- Interaction with peers will expose children to other perspectives, giving them an opportunity to reevaluate and revise their own view.
- Connect abstract ideas to concrete information as much as possible.

Vygotsky

- Provide opportunities for children to interact with others who have greater mastery of the material—an older peer, teacher, or parent. These more advanced thinkers can help "pull" children to a level of understanding they would be unable to achieve on their own.
- Encourage students, especially young ones, to talk to themselves as they work on difficult tasks. Such private speech can guide behavior and facilitate thought.
- Present challenging tasks, but don't expect students to complete such tasks successfully without guidance. With support, students can accomplish tasks more difficult than they would be able to achieve independently.
- Help children master the cognitive tools of their culture—writing, computers, and so on—so that they can function successfully in the culture.

Research on Information Processing

- Provide opportunities for rehearsal and other memory strategies to move information into long-term memory. Realize that young children do not spontaneously use memory strategies but can use them when prompted.
- Structure assignments so that retrieval cues are consistent with cues present at acquisition to facilitate retrieval of information from long-term memory.
- Enable learners to develop some knowledge base and expertise in domains of study. This means presenting "facts and figures" through readings, lectures, observations, and other appropriate methods. When beginning a new lesson, start with and build on what students already know.
- Assess the knowledge and strategies required to solve assigned problems; then determine which aspects of a task pose difficulties for learners and target these for further instruction.
- Well-learned and frequently repeated tasks become automatized over time, freeing up information-processing capacity for other tasks. For example, reading is very labor intensive for those new to the task, but with practice, the process of reading becomes "invisible" and learners focus their processing resources on other aspects of the task.

Research on Intelligence

- Individual differences in intelligence have implications for the classroom. Students at both ends of the continuum may need special educational services to optimize their learning.
- Recognize that although IQ scores do a reasonably good job of predicting achievement in the classroom, such tests have weaknesses that limit their usefulness, especially in assessing members of minority groups.

Research on Sensory and Perceptual Abilities

- All children should be tested early and regularly for sensory and perceptual problems that might limit their ability to benefit from regular classroom instruction.
- Be aware of developmental differences in attention span. Clearly, a young child will not be able to attend to a task for as long as a teenager. Determine what "captures" students' attention at different ages.
- Minimize distractions in the learning environment. Younger students have trouble "tuning out" background noise and focusing on the task at hand.

Summary Points

1. To acquire language, children must master phonology (sound), semantics (meaning), morphology (word structure), and syntax (sentence structure), as well as learn how to use language appropriately (pragmatics) and to understand nonverbal communication.

2. Infants begin to discriminate speech sounds and progress from crying, cooing, and babbling to one-word holophrases (at 1 year of age) and then to telegraphic speech (at 18 months), guided by a functional grammar that allows them to name things, make requests, and achieve other communication goals.

3. Language abilities improve dramatically in the preschool years, as illustrated by overregularizations and new transformation rules. School-age children and adolescents refine their language skills and become less egocentric communicators. Knowledge of semantics continues to expand during adulthood, and language abilities hold up well in old age, despite some difficulties with speech sound perception, the tip-of-the-tongue phenomenon, and the processing of complex syntax.

4. Theories of language development include learning theories, nativist theories, and interactionist theories that emphasize both the child's biologically based capacities and experience conversing with adults who use child-directed speech and strategies such as expansion that simplify the language-learning task. A critical or at least sensitive period for language acquisition appears to exist in early childhood.

5. Mastery motivation, the forerunner of achievement motivation, is an urge for mastery evident in infancy and is nurtured by sensory stimulation, a responsive environment, and a secure attachment. Early education can help prepare disadvantaged children for formal schooling, but an overemphasis on academics at the expense of other activities may actually hinder young children's development.

6. During childhood, some children develop higher levels of achievement motivation than others do. As children come to understand the concept of ability, their expectancies of success often decrease and they become more prone to learned helplessness after failure. High academic achievers tend to have mastery-oriented rather than helpless attribution styles, and they set learning rather than performance goals in the classroom. Attempts to combat learned helplessness by emphasizing learning goals and retraining attributions to emphasize the need for greater effort have been successful. Parents can help by being authoritative and encouraging independent mastery and achievement. Schools may be able to help by focusing less on competition, encouraging more family involvement, and fostering enthusiasm for learning.

7. In order to read, children must master the alphabetic principle and develop phonological awareness so that they can grasp letter–sound correspondence rules. Emergent literacy activities such as listening to storybooks facilitate later reading. Compared to unskilled readers, skilled readers have better understanding of the alphabetic principle and greater phonological awareness; they read more of the words in a passage and rely less on context to identify words. Dyslexia refers to serious trouble with reading and often involves problems with phonological awareness. Successful reading instruction requires an emphasis on phonics as well as comprehension.

8. A school's effectiveness is not influenced much by financial support, class size, or use of ability grouping. Instead, elementary and secondary school children perform best when (a) they are intellectually capable and motivated; (b) their teachers create a learning environment that is comfortable, task-oriented, motivating, and involves parents; and (c) there is, as aptitude–treatment interaction research

suggests, a good "fit" between children's characteristics and the kind of instruction they receive.

9. Neither racial integration nor mainstreaming or inclusion for students with developmental disabilities has been very effective overall in increasing students' achievement and social acceptance, but these outcomes can be enhanced through cooperative learning methods.

10. Cognitive development, more negative teacher feedback, peer pressures, puberty, and poor person–environment fit may all contribute to declines in achievement motivation as children become adolescents and make the transition to middle school or junior high school. However, adolescents are likely to retain their achievement motivation if they attend schools that provide a good fit to their developmental need for autonomy.

11. Middle school and high school include a greater focus on science and math education. U.S. students score at about the international average but below a number of other countries in math and science. Cross-cultural research suggests that the success of Asian schools is rooted in more class time spent on academics, more homework, more parent involvement, more peer support, and a strong belief that hard work pays off.

12. Adults of different ages are quite similar in their levels of achievement motivation, although women who turn their attention to child rearing may lose some of their career-oriented achievement motivation.

13. Some adults, despite years of education, have not acquired the skills of functional literacy. Others experience literacy problems when acquiring a second language. Literacy programs have had minimal success in improving literacy rates. A growing number of adults seek continued educational opportunities for both personal and work-related reasons.

Critical Thinking

1. Imagine that you are a computer scientist and are given the task of writing a computer program that can comprehend spoken English as well as the average 3-year-old does. What information should your computer program contain, and what does it have to do with incoming speech samples? Why do you think writing such a computer program is a hugely complex task?

2. Based on everything you know about memory, thinking, problem solving, and language skills, how would you teach science to groups of elementary, middle, and high school students?

3. Using the material on effective schools, evaluate your own school and indicate ways it could improve to become a highly effective school.

4. What are the advantages and disadvantages of grouping children by ability versus grouping them by age in the classroom? When your child goes to school, which approach will you advocate?

Key Terms

language	cooing
phonology	babbling
morphology	joint attention
syntax	holophrases
semantics	vocabulary spurt
pragmatics	overextension
intonation	underextension

telegraphic speech

functional grammar

overregularization

transformational grammar

decontextualized language

metalinguistic awareness

language acquisition device
(LAD)

child-directed speech

expansion

mastery motivation

mastery orientation

learned helplessness orientation

learning goals

performance goals

alphabetic principle

phonological awareness

emergent literacy

dyslexia

ability grouping

aptitude–treatment interaction
(ATI)

inclusion

cooperative learning

literacy

On the Web

Web Sites to Explore

Reading Instruction

From the Center for Academic and Reading Skills (CARS), Barbara Foorman and her colleagues discuss their "Scientific Approach to Reading Instruction."
http://www.ldonline.org/ld_indepth/reading/cars.html

National Network for Childcare

This site provides information about all aspects of child development. Look for the links that relate to language development, reading, and education.
http://www.nncc.org/Child.Dev/child.dev.page.html

Search Online with InfoTrac College Edition

For additional information, explore InfoTrac College Edition, your online library. Go to **http://www.infotrac-college.com** and use the passcode that came on the card with your book. For example, the key words "language acquisition" will yield a large number of articles. From these articles, select ones that address genetic/biological contributions and environmental contributions to language. Does the weight of evidence support a Chomskian, Skinnerian, or interactionist position? Now search for "reading," then choose the subdivision "whole language approach." Take a look at the research on this topic and see if the findings agree with what is in the chapter.

Visit Our Web Site

Go to **http://www.wadsworth.com/psychology**, where you will find online resources directly linked to your book.

Life-Span CD-ROM

Go to the Wadsworth Life-Span CD-ROM for further study of the concepts in this chapter. The CD-ROM also includes quizzes and additional activities to expand your learning experience.

Self and Personality

The college student who wrote this is describing how she changed in the process of finding her identity. In what ways have you changed as a person over the years? In what ways have you remained the same? If you've changed considerably, why do you think that is? If you feel like "the same old person," what might account for that? Finally, project ahead: What do you think you will be like as a person when you are 70, and what makes you think so?

Do humans remain "the same people" in most significant respects, or do they undergo dramatic transformations in personality over the years from infancy to old age? The issue of continuity (stability) and discontinuity (change) in development is central in the study of human development (see Chapter 2). This chapter is about the ways in which our personalities, and our perceptions of those personalities, change—and remain the same—over the life span, as well as about the implications of personality for adjustment. Let's begin by clarifying some terms and laying out key theoretical perspectives on personality. Then we will see how self-perceptions and aspects of temperament and personality change from infancy to old age.

Conceptualizing the Self

Personality is often defined as an organized combination of attributes, motives, values, and behaviors that is unique to each individual. Most people describe personalities in terms of *personality traits*—dispositions such as sociability, independence, dominance, anxiety, and so on. Traits are assumed to be relatively consistent across different situations and over time; if you peg a classmate as insecure, you expect this person to behave insecurely at school and at work, now and next year.

When you describe yourself, you may not be describing your actual personality so much as you are revealing your **self-concept**—your *perceptions*, positive or negative, of your unique attributes and traits. We all know people who seem to have unrealistic self-conceptions—the fellow who thinks he is "God's gift to women" (who don't agree) or the woman who believes she is a dull plodder (but is actually quite brilliant). A closely related aspect of self-perception is **self-esteem**—your overall evaluation of your worth as a person, high or low, based on all the positive and negative self-perceptions that make up your self-concept. Self-concept is about "what I am,"

whereas self-esteem concerns "how good I am" (Harter, 1999). This chapter also examines how self-concept and self-esteem change and remain the same over the life span. And it takes up the question of how adolescents pull together their various self-perceptions to form an **identity**—an overall sense of who they are, where they are heading, and where they fit in society.

Theories of Personality Development

How does the personality develop? Is it formed in childhood and stable from then on, or does it continue to evolve and change throughout our lives? To get some feel for current debates about the nature of personality development, let's look at the striking differences among three major theoretical perspectives on the nature of personality and personality development: psychoanalytic theory, psychometric (trait) theory, and social learning theory.

Psychoanalytic Theory

As you recall from Chapter 2, Sigmund Freud was concerned with the development and inner dynamics of three parts of the personality: the selfish id, the rational ego, and the moralistic superego. He strongly believed that biological urges residing within the id push all children through universal stages of psychosexual development, starting with the oral stage of infancy and ending with the genital stage of adolescence when sexual maturity is attained. Freud did not see psychosexual growth continuing during adulthood. Rather, he believed that the personality was formed in infancy and early childhood—during the first five years of life, essentially—and showed considerable continuity thereafter. Anxieties arising from harsh parenting, overindulgence, or other unfavorable early experiences, he claimed, would leave a permanent mark on the personality and reveal themselves in adult personality traits.

The psychosocial theory of personality development formulated by Erik Erikson, a neo-Freudian theorist, was also introduced in Chapter 2. Like Freud, Erikson concerned himself with the inner dynamics of personality and proposed that the personality evolves through systematic stages that confront people with different challenges (Erikson 1963, 1968, 1982). Compared to Freud, however, Erikson placed more emphasis on social influences such as peers, teachers, schools, and churches; the rational ego and its adaptive powers; possibilities for overcoming the effects of harmful early experiences; and the potential for growth throughout the life span.

Erikson's eight stages of psychosocial development, listed in Table 11.1, will be highlighted in this chapter. Both maturational forces and social demands, Erikson believed, push human beings everywhere through these eight psychosocial crises. Later conflicts may prove difficult to resolve if early conflicts were not resolved successfully. For development to proceed optimally, a healthy balance between the terms of the conflict must be struck.

Table 11.1 The Eight Stages of Erikson's Psychosocial Theory

Stage	Age Range	Central Issue
1. Trust versus mistrust	Birth to 1 year	Can I trust others?
2. Autonomy versus shame and doubt	1 to 3 years	Can I act on my own?
3. Initiative versus guilt	3 to 6 years	Can I carry out my plans successfully?
4. Industry versus inferiority	6 to 12 years	Am I competent compared to others?
5. Identity versus role confusion	12 to 20 years	Who am I, really?
6. Intimacy versus isolation	20 to 40 years	Am I ready for a relationship?
7. Generativity versus stagnation	40 to 65 years	Have I left my mark?
8. Integrity versus despair	65 and older	In the end, has my life been meaningful?

In infancy, for example, trust of caregivers should outweigh mistrust, but an element of skepticism is needed as well.

Erikson clearly did not agree with Freud that the personality is largely formed by the end of early childhood; discontinuity was possible, he thought. Erikson also appreciated that development continues throughout the life span. Yet Freud and Erikson agreed on this: *People everywhere progress through the same stages of personality development, undergoing similar personality changes at similar ages.*

Psychometric (Trait) Theory

The approach to personality that has most strongly influenced efforts to study it is the *psychometric approach*—the same testing approach that guided the development of intelligence tests (see Chapter 9). According to this approach, *personality is a set of trait dimensions along which people can differ* (for example, sociable–unsociable, responsible–irresponsible). Personality scales are administered to people, and statistical procedures such as *factor analysis* are used to identify groupings of personality test items that appear to be distinct trait dimensions. Trait theorists assume that personality traits are relatively enduring; like psychoanalytic theorists, they expect to see carryover in personality over the years. Unlike psychoanalytic theorists, however, they do not believe that the personality unfolds in a series of stages.

How many personality trait dimensions are there? Just as scholars have disagreed about how many distinct mental abilities exist, they have disagreed about how many personality dimensions exist. However, a consensus is now forming around the idea that human personalities can be described in terms of five major dimensions, called the **Big Five,** believed by many theorists to capture the essential ways in which personalities differ (Digman, 1990; Costa & McCrae, 1994). These five personality dimensions—openness to experience, conscientiousness, extraversion, agreeableness, and neuroticism—have emerged from studies involving factor analysis of personality test items and are described in Table 11.2. We have evidence that all five are genetically influenced and biologically based, and that they are related to aspects of temperament that are evident starting in infancy. The Big Five also seem to be universal; they capture personality differences in cultures with very different parenting styles, value systems, and languages (McCrae & Costa, 1997; McCrae et al., 2000). We will soon see what happens to these trait dimensions as we get older.

Social Learning Theory

Finally, social learning (or social cognitive) theorists such as Albert Bandura (1986) and Walter Mischel (1973; Mischel & Shoda, 1995; Shoda & Mischel, 2000) not only reject the notion of universal stages of personality development but have

Table 11.2 The Big Five Personality Dimensions (as a mnemonic device, notice that their first letters spell "ocean")

Dimension	Basic Definition	Key Characteristics
Openness to experience	Curiosity and interest in variety vs. preference for sameness	Openness to fantasy, esthetics, feelings, actions, ideas, values
Conscientiousness	Discipline and organization vs. lack of seriousness	Competence, order, dutifulness, achievement striving, self-discipline, deliberation
Extraversion	Sociability and outgoingness vs. introversion	Warmth, gregariousness, assertiveness, activity, excitement seeking, positive emotions
Agreeableness	Compliance and cooperativeness vs. suspiciousness	Trust, straightforwardness, altruism, compliance, modesty, tender-mindedness
Neuroticism	Emotional instability vs. stability	Anxiety, hostility, depression, self-consciousness, impulsiveness, vulnerability

SOURCE: Adapted from Costa & McCrae (1992)

questioned the existence of enduring personality traits that show themselves in a wide variety of situations and over long stretches of the life span. Instead, they emphasize that *people change if their environments change.* An aggressive boy can become a warm and caring man if his aggression is no longer reinforced; a woman who has been socially withdrawn can become more outgoing if she begins to interact closely with friends who serve as models of outgoing, sociable behavior. From this perspective, personality is a set of behavior tendencies shaped by our interactions with other people in specific social situations.

Social learning theorists believe strongly in situational influences on behavior. If there is consistency in personality, they claim, it is that we consistently behave one way in one situation and another way in another situation. Luis may be shy in a crowd but friendly and animated in a twosome, whereas Robert may be the life of the party but be quite unsure of himself in one-on-one situations. They may not differ overall in their degree of extraversion, but each person may show characteristic reactions in particular situations (Shoda & Mischel, 2000). From a social learning theory perspective, consistency over time in personality is most likely if the social environment remains the same. If Rick the rancher continues to run the same ranch in the same small town for a lifetime, he might well stay the "same old Rick."

However, most of us experience major changes in our social environments as we become older. Just as we behave differently when we are in a library than when we are at a party, we become "different people" as we take on new roles in life, develop new relationships, or move to new locations. An excellent example of this principle comes from research on the relationship between birth order and personality. How would you characterize firstborns? Second-borns? Last-borns? Many of us have strong beliefs about the differences; we think of firstborns as bossy, dominant, and achievement oriented, and last-borns as rebellious and spoiled. Yet most research reveals few differences between the personalities of firstborns and later-borns (Harris, 2000).

Why might we be misled into thinking such differences exist? Judith Rich Harris (2000) notes that we see members of our families in a family context and observe real differences in personality *in that context.* However, the differences are created by the family context and don't necessarily carry over into other situations. Thus, for example, the firstborn, who is older than his or her sibs and who is responsible for babysitting them, may well be dominant and "bossy" in that context—yet not in interactions with peers who are similar in age and competence and can't be pushed around as easily. Different context, different personality.

To the social learning theorist, then, personality development is a very individual process whose direction depends on each person's social experiences and social environments. Theorists who adopt a contextual/systems perspective on development (see Chapter 2) make similar assumptions. Indeed, contextual theorists are likely to say that personality traits, considered apart from the social contexts that shape and give meaning to a person's actions, are meaningless abstractions.

Obviously, Freud, Erikson, and other psychoanalytic theorists, psychometric trait theorists, and social learning theorists do not see eye to eye about what personality is and how it develops. Psychoanalytic theorists propose universal, age-related personality changes, although Freud believed that the personality emerges early in life and remains largely stable thereafter, whereas Erikson saw more discontinuity than Freud and believed that stagelike personality changes occur throughout the life span. Trait theorists emphasize the continuity of major dimensions of personality such as the Big Five, whereas social learning theorists call attention to the potential for discontinuity in personality across different situations and over time.

This chapter explores continuity and discontinuity in personality traits and in conceptions and evaluations of self across the life span. When do infants become aware of themselves as unique individuals, and when do they begin to display their unique personalities? What influences how children perceive and evaluate themselves, and to what extent are the personalities they will have as adults already evident? How do adolescents go about finding their identities as individuals? Finally, do people's personalities and self-perceptions change systematically over the adult years, or do they remain essentially the same, and what does it all mean for their adjustment?

The Infant

When do infants display an awareness that they exist and a sense of themselves as distinct individuals? Let's explore this issue and then see whether there is evidence that infants have unique "personalities."

The Emerging Self

Most developmental scientists believe that infants are born without a sense of self. The first glimmers of the capacity to differentiate oneself from the world can be detected in the first two or three months of life as infants discover that they can cause things to happen (Thompson, 1998). For example, 2-month-old infants whose arms are connected by strings to audiovisual equipment delight in producing the sight of a smiling infant's face and the theme from *Sesame Street* by pulling the strings (Lewis, Alessandri, & Sullivan, 1990). When the strings are disconnected and they can no longer produce such effects, they pull all the harder and become frustrated and angry. By 3 months of age, babies also seem to be able to put together information from their eyes and their sense of bodily movement to recognize videotapes of their leg kicking as their own rather than another baby's (Rochat & Morgan, 1995). These studies suggests that, over the first six months of life, infants discover properties of their physical selves, distinguish between the self and the rest of the world, and appreciate that they can act upon other people and objects (Thompson, 1998).

In the second six months of life, infants come to realize that they and their companions are separate beings with different perspectives, perspectives that can be shared

(Thompson, 1998). This is illustrated by the phenomenon of **joint attention,** in which infants about 9 months of age or older and their caregivers share perceptual experiences by looking at the same object at the same time (Mitchell, 1997). When infants point at objects and look toward their companions in an effort to get their attention focused on the object, they show an awareness that self and other do not always share the same perceptions.

During the middle of their second year of life, infants recognize themselves visually as distinct individuals and become able to tell themselves apart from other infants. To establish this, Michael Lewis and Jeanne Brooks-Gunn (1979) used an ingenious technique first used with chimpanzees to study **self-recognition**—the ability to recognize oneself in a mirror or photograph. Mother daubs a spot of rouge on an infant's nose and then places the infant in front of a mirror. If infants have some mental image of their own faces and recognize their mirror images as themselves, they should soon notice the red spot and reach for or wipe their own noses rather than the nose of the mirror image. When infants 9 to 24 months old were given this rouge test, the youngest infants showed no self-recognition: They seemed to treat the image in the mirror as if it were "some other kid." Some 15-month-olds recognized themselves, but only among 18- to 24-month-olds did a large majority of infants show clear evidence of self-recognition (see also Asendorpf, Warkentin, & Baudonnière, 1996). They touched their noses rather than the mirror, apparently realizing that they had a strange mark on their faces that warranted investigation. They knew exactly who that kid in the mirror was!

As babies learn to recognize themselves, they also form a **categorical self;** that is, they classify themselves into social categories based on age, sex, and other visible characteristics, figuring out what is "like me" and what is "not like me." Before they are 18 months old, toddlers can tell themselves apart from toddlers of the other sex or from older individuals but are less able to distinguish between photos of themselves and photos of other infants of the same sex. As they approach age 2, they also master this task (Brooks-Gunn & Lewis, 1981; Lewis & Brooks-Gunn, 1979). By 18 to 24 months of age, then, most infants definitely have an awareness of who they are—at least as a physical self with a unique appearance and as a categorical self belonging to specific age and gender categories. They will then use their emerging language skills to talk about themselves and to construct stories about events in their lives, past and present (Thompson, 1998).

To what can we attribute this emerging self-awareness? First, the ability to recognize the self depends on *cognitive development* (Bertenthal & Fischer, 1978). Children who are mentally retarded are slow to recognize themselves in a mirror but can do so once they have attained a mental age of at least 18 to 20 months (Hill & Tomlin, 1981). Second, self-awareness depends on *social experiences.* Chimpanzees who have been raised in complete isolation, unlike those who have had contact with other chimps, do not recognize themselves in a mirror (Gallup, 1979). As it turns out, human toddlers who have formed secure attachments to their parents are better able to

Joseph Pobereskin/Getty Images

Does this boy really know that the fascinating tot in the mirror is him? Probably not if he is younger than 18 months of age, which is about when self-recognition is mastered by most toddlers.

recognize themselves in a mirror and know more about their names and genders than do toddlers whose relationships are less secure (Pipp, Easterbrooks, & Harmon, 1992).

The critical role of social interaction in the development of the self was appreciated long ago by Charles Cooley (1902) and George Herbert Mead (1934). Cooley used the term **looking-glass self** to emphasize that our understanding of self is a reflection of how other people respond to us; that is, our self-concepts are the images cast by a social mirror. Through their actions and words, parents and other companions communicate to infants that they are babies and are also either girls or boys. Later, social feedback helps children determine what they are like and what they can and cannot do well. Throughout life, we forge new self-concepts through our social interactions—from the social feedback we receive, good or bad (Harter, 1999). Thus the development of the self is closely related to both cognitive development and social interaction, beginning in infancy.

Awareness of the self paves the way for many important emotional and social developments (DesRosiers et al., 1999; Pipp-Siegel & Foltz, 1997). Toddlers who recognize themselves in the mirror are more able than those who do not to talk about themselves and to assert their wills (DesRosiers et al.,

1999). They are more likely to experience self-conscious emotions such as embarrassment—for example, if asked to show off by dancing in front of strangers (Lewis et al., 1989). Also, toddlers who have gained self-awareness are more aware of other people. They are more able than other toddlers to communicate with their playmates by imitating their actions (Asendorpf et al., 1996), and they can cooperate in simple ways with peers to achieve common goals such as retrieving toys from containers (Brownell & Carriger, 1990). Once infants are aware of themselves, then, they become more able to coordinate their own perspectives with those of other individuals.

Temperament

Even though it takes infants some time to become aware of themselves as individuals, they *are* individuals with their own distinctive personalities from the very first weeks of life. The study of infant personality has centered on dimensions of **temperament**—early, genetically based tendencies to respond in predictable ways to events that serve as the building blocks of personality by influencing the kinds of interactions the individual has with his or her environment. Learning theorists have tended to view babies as "blank slates" who can be shaped in any number of directions by their experiences. However, it is now clear that babies differ from the start in such characteristics as how they react to stimuli (for example, whether they smile or fuss, and how strongly) and how they regulate these reactions (for example, whether they attend to arousing stimuli or avoid them; Rothbart, Ahadi, & Evans, 2000). Temperament has been defined and measured in a number of different ways, as we will now see.

EMOTIONALITY, ACTIVITY, AND SOCIABILITY

Arnold Buss and Robert Plomin (1984) have called attention to three dimensions of temperament: **emotionality, activity,** and **sociability.** Some babies are more emotionally reactive, or easily and intensely irritated by events, than others are. Some are highly active; others are relatively sluggish. Some are very sociable, or interested in and responsive to people; others are more standoffish. Behavioral genetics research using twins and adopted children tell us that these three aspects of temperament are partly influenced by genetic endowment and partly influenced by the individual's unique experiences. Identical twins have quite similar temperaments, whereas fraternal twins hardly resemble each other at all (Buss & Plomin, 1984; Rowe, 1994). Growing up in the same home does little to make adoptive brothers and sisters alike in these aspects of temperament (Schmitz et al., 1996).

BEHAVIORAL INHIBITION

Jerome Kagan and his colleagues identified another aspect of early temperament that they believe is highly significant—**behavioral inhibition,** or the tendency to be extremely shy, restrained, and distressed in response to unfamiliar people and situations (Kagan, 1994; Reznick et al., 1986). In the language of Buss and Plomin, inhibited children could be considered extremely high in emotionality and low in sociability.

Kagan (1989) estimates that about 15% of toddlers have this inhibited temperament, whereas 10% are extremely uninhibited, eager to jump into new situations.

At 4 months of age, infants who will later be recognized as inhibited children wriggle and fuss and fret more than most infants in response to new sights and sounds such as a moving mobile (Fox et al., 2001). At 21 months, they take a long time to warm up to a strange examiner, retreat from unfamiliar objects such as a large robot, and fret and cling to their mothers. By contrast, uninhibited toddlers readily and enthusiastically interact with strangers, robots, and all manner of new experiences. In follow-up tests at 5½ and 7½ years of age, children who were highly inhibited as toddlers were more likely than children who had been uninhibited to be shy in a group of strange peers and to be afraid to try a balance beam. Even at age 13, differences between inhibited and uninhibited children were still evident (Kagan, 1994). The inhibited adolescents talked and smiled less than the uninhibited ones. After failing a difficult task, the inhibited adolescents just looked glum, whereas the uninhibited ones smiled, as though laughing at themselves. Overall, of the children who had maintained the same temperament from age 2 to age 7, about half still had the same temperament by adolescence, suggesting a fair amount of continuity.

Kagan and his colleagues have also found that inhibited youngsters show distinctive physiological reactions to novel events; they become highly aroused (as indicated by high heart rates) in situations that barely faze other children. And there is evidence that behavioral inhibition is genetically influenced (Kagan, 1994). In one study (DiLalla, Kagan, & Reznick, 1994), the correlation between the inhibition scores of identical twins was +.82, that for fraternal twins .47. Very possibly, then, genes affect temperament by influencing the development of the nervous system and the way it responds to stimuli.

Children with an inhibited temperament are not sure they want to try new experiences.

EASINESS/DIFFICULTNESS

Finally, we have learned much about infant temperament from Alexander Thomas, Stella Chess, and their colleagues (Chess & Thomas, 1999; Thomas & Chess, 1986). These researchers gathered information about several dimensions of infant behavior, including typical mood, regularity or predictability of biological functions such as feeding and sleeping habits, tendency to approach or withdraw from new stimuli, intensity of emotional reactions, and adaptability to new experiences and changes in routine. Based on the overall patterning of these temperamental qualities, most infants could be placed into one of three categories:

- **Easy temperament.** Easy infants are even tempered, typically content or happy, and quite open and adaptable to new experiences such as the approach of a stranger or their first taste of strained plums. They have regular feeding and sleeping habits, and they tolerate frustrations and discomforts well.
- **Difficult temperament.** Difficult infants are active, irritable, and irregular in their habits. They often react very negatively (and vigorously) to changes in routine and are slow to adapt to new people or situations. They cry frequently and loudly and often have tantrums when they are frustrated by such events as being restrained or having to live with a dirty diaper.
- **Slow-to-warm-up temperament.** Slow-to-warm-up infants are relatively inactive, somewhat moody, and only moderately regular in their daily schedules. Like difficult infants, they are slow to adapt to new people and situations, but they typically respond in mildly, rather than intensely, negative ways. For example, they may resist cuddling by looking away from the cuddler rather than by kicking or screaming. They do eventually adjust, showing a quiet interest in new foods, people, or places.

Of the infants in Thomas and Chess's longitudinal study of temperament, 40% were easy infants, 10% were difficult infants, and 15% were slow-to-warm-up infants, The remaining third could not be clearly placed in one category or another because they shared qualities of two or more categories. Thomas and Chess went on to study the extent of continuity and discontinuity in temperament from infancy to early adulthood (Chess & Thomas, 1984; Thomas & Chess, 1986). Difficult infants who had fussed when they could not have more milk often became children who fell apart if they could not work math problems correctly. By adulthood, though, an individual's adjustment had little to do with his or her temperament during infancy, suggesting a good deal of discontinuity over this long time span. Apparently, many easy infants turn into maladjusted adults, and many difficult infants outgrow their behavior problems. Both continuity and discontinuity in temperament are evident.

GOODNESS OF FIT

What determines whether or not temperamental qualities persist? Much may depend on what Thomas and Chess call the **goodness of fit** between child and environment—the extent to which the child's temperament is compatible with the demands and expectations of the social world to which he or she must adapt. A good example comes from observations of the Masai of East Africa (DeVries, 1984). In most settings, an easy temperament is likely to be more adaptive than a difficult one, but among the Masai during famine, babies with *difficult* temperaments outlived easy babies. Why? Perhaps because Masai parents believe that difficult babies are future warriors or perhaps because babies who cry loud and long get noticed and fed. As this example suggests, a particular temperament may be a good fit to the demands of one environment but maladaptive under other circumstances. The goodness-of-fit concept is another example of how individual predispositions and the environment interact to influence developmental outcomes.

Similarly, the difficult children studied by Chess and Thomas (1999) often continued to display difficult temperaments later in life if the person/environment fit was bad—if their parents were impatient, inconsistent, and demanding with them. However, difficult infants whose parents adapted to their temperaments and gave them more time to adjust to new experiences enjoyed a good fit to the environment and became able to master new situations effectively and energetically (see the Explorations box on page 287). Similarly, if the parents of inhibited children overprotect their sensitive children from stress, these children do not learn to control their inhibition; parents also err if they become angry and impatient. Instead, it is best for parents to prepare inhibited youngsters for potentially upsetting experiences and then make reasonable demands that they cope (Kagan, 1994).

Interestingly, parents' own personalities may help determine whether an infant's home environment is a good or poor fit to his or her personality. Mothers who are low in empathy tend to use power assertion (threats and physical force) with infants who show a lot of negative emotion, perhaps because they cannot understand why these babies are so irritable (Clark, Kochanska, & Ready, 2000). By contrast, mothers who are high in empathy are able to refrain from strong-arm tactics even when they are faced with an irritable child. They are therefore able to provide care that is a better fit to the child's difficult temperament.

In sum, by the end of the first two years of life, infants have become aware of themselves as individuals. Toddlers recognize themselves in a mirror, refer to themselves by name, and understand that they are physically distinct from other

Table 11.3 Summary of Temperament Categories

Researchers	Dimension
Buss and Plomin	Emotionality Activity Sociability
Kagan	Behaviorally inhibited temperament Uninhibited temperament
Thomas and Chess	Easy temperament Difficult temperament Slow-to warm up temperament

Goodness of Fit and the Case of Carl

The case of Carl illustrates the significance for later personality development of the match between a child's temperament and his or her social environment. Early in life, Carl was one of the most difficult children Stella Chess and Alexander Thomas had ever encountered: "Whether it was the first bath or the first solid foods in infancy, the beginning of nursery and elementary school, or the first birthday parties or shopping trips, each experience evoked stormy responses, with loud crying and struggling to get away" (1984, p. 188). Carl's mother became convinced that she was a bad parent, but his father accepted and even delighted in Carl's "lusty" behavior and patiently and supportively waited for him to adapt to new situations. As a result, Carl did not develop serious behavior problems as a child.

Carl's difficult temperament did come out in force when he entered college and had to adapt to a whole new environment. He became extremely frustrated and thought about dropping out but eventually reduced his course load and got through this difficult period successfully. By age 23, he was no longer considered by the researchers to have a difficult temperament. How different his later personality and adjustment might have been had the fit between his difficult temperament and his parents' demands and expectations been poor! When children have difficult temperaments and grow up with parents who cannot control their behavior effectively, they are likely to have serious behavior problems as adolescents (Maziade et al., 1990). Clearly, then, healthy personality development depends on the goodness of fit between child and home environment. The moral for parents is clear: Get to know your baby as an individual, and allow for his or her personality quirks.

---

human beings. Cognitive development and experiences with the social looking glass make this new self-awareness possible. Moreover, each toddler has his or her own distinct temperamental qualities that are sketched in the genetic code and expressed from the first days of life—qualities such as emotionality, activity, and sociability; behavioral inhibition; and an easy, difficult, or slow-to-warm-up temperament. However, the personality is by no means set in infancy; there is both continuity and discontinuity. Early temperamental qualities *may or may not* be elaborated into later personality, depending on the goodness of fit between the individual's predispositions and his or her social environment and the kinds of transactions that take place between child and caregiver (Caspi, 1998).

The Child

Children's personalities continue to take form, and children acquire much richer understandings of themselves as individuals, as they continue to experience cognitive growth and interact with other people. Ask children of different ages to tell you about themselves. You'll find their responses amusing, and you'll learn something about how children come to know themselves as individuals.

Elaborating on a Sense of Self

Once toddlers begin to talk, they can and do tell us about their emerging self-concepts. By age 2, some toddlers are already using the personal pronouns *I, me, my,* and *mine* (or their names) when referring to the self and *you* when addressing a companion (Lewis & Brooks-Gunn, 1979; Stipek, Gralinski, & Kopp, 1990). This linguistic distinction suggests that 2-year-olds have formed a concept of "self" and can distinguish self from other. Toddlers also show us that they are developing a categorical self when they describe themselves in terms of age and sex ("Katie big girl").

The preschool child's self-concept is very concrete and physical (Damon & Hart, 1982, 1988). When asked to describe themselves, preschoolers dwell on observables—their physical characteristics ("I look like a kid. I have skin. I have clothes."), their possessions ("I have a bike"), their physical activities and accomplishments ("I can jump"), and their preferences ("I like cake"). One exuberant 3-year-old said this (Harter, 1999, p. 37):

> I'm 3 years old and I live in a big house with my mother and father and my brother, Jason, and my sister, Lisa. I have blue eyes and a kitty that is orange and a television in my own room. I know all of my ABC's, listen: A, B, C, D, E, F, G, H, J, L, K,O, M, P, Q, X, Z. I can run real fast. I like pizza and I have a nice teacher at preschool. I can count up to 100, want to hear me? I love my dog Skipper.

Very few young children mention their psychological traits or inner qualities when describing themselves. At most, young children use global terms such as "nice" or "mean," "good" or "bad," to describe themselves and others (Livesley & Bromley, 1973). However, their descriptions of their characteristic behavior patterns and preferences ("I like to play by myself at school") may provide the foundation for their later personality trait descriptions ("I'm shy") (Eder, 1989).

Preschool children emphasize the "active self" in their self-descriptions, noting things they can do but saying little about their psychological traits.

By the age of 8 or so, children begin to define themselves as part of social units ("I'm a Kimball, a second-grader at Brookside School, a Brownie Scout"); that is, they begin to form a social identity (Damon & Hart, 1988). They are also more able to infer and describe their enduring inner qualities (Harter, 1999; Livesley & Bromley, 1973). As a result, their self-descriptions are filled with personality-trait terms ("I'm friendly," "I'm funny," "I'm curious," and so on). Moreover, they now describe not just what they typically do or what they can do but how their abilities compare with those of their companions (Secord & Peevers, 1974). The preschooler who claimed to be able to hit a baseball now becomes the elementary school child who claims to be a better batter than her teammates. What has changed? For one thing, 8-year-olds have gained the cognitive skills needed to infer from regularities in their behavior that they have certain consistent traits. For another, they are more capable of evaluating themselves through **social comparison**—of using information about how they stack up compared to other individuals to judge themselves (Pomerantz et al., 1995). They then define and evaluate themselves in terms of whether they are more or less competent than other children.

Young children often seem oblivious to information about how they compare to others and seem to have difficulty interpreting and acting on such information when they receive it (Butler, 1990; Ruble, 1983). They tend to believe that they are the greatest, even in the face of compelling evidence that they have been outclassed by their peers. By age 5 or so, children do watch their classmates and make social comparisons (Frey & Ruble, 1985). However, they usually do this to be sociable ("Same lunchbox—we're twinsies!") or to find out how to do their work ("Where did you write your name?") rather than to evaluate themselves. By contrast, first-grade children begin to seek information that will tell them whether they are more or less competent than their peers; they glance at each other's papers, ask "How many did you miss?" and say things like "I got more right than you did." Older elementary school children are more politically astute and avoid making potentially embarrassing social comparisons out loud, but they still sneak looks at classmates' papers and pay close attention to where they stand in the classroom pecking order (Frey & Ruble, 1985; Pomerantz et al., 1995).

So, social comparison becomes more common and also more subtle with age. Yet the extent to which children engage in social comparison is very much influenced by the sociocultural context. It is common in the United States because parents, teachers, and others emphasize individual achievement. However, Israeli children living in communal kibbutzim do less of it than children raised in Israeli cities, perhaps because cooperation and teamwork are so strongly emphasized in the kibbutzim (Butler & Ruzany, 1993).

Self-Esteem

As children amass a wide range of perceptions of themselves and engage in social comparisons, they begin to evaluate their worth. Susan Harter (1999) has developed self-perception scales for use across the life span and has found that preschool children distinguish only two broad aspects of self-esteem: their competence (both physical and cognitive) and their personal and social adequacy (for example, their social acceptance). By mid-elementary school, children differentiate among five aspects of self-worth, all measured by Harter's self-perception scale: *scholastic competence* (feeling smart, doing well in school); *social acceptance* (being popular, feeling liked); *behavioral conduct* (not getting in trouble); *athletic competence* (being good at sports); and *physical appearance* (feeling good-looking). When Harter's scale was given to third- through ninth-graders, even third-graders showed that they had well-defined positive or negative feelings about themselves. Moreover, children made clear distinctions between their competency in one area and their competency in another. They did not just have generally high or generally low self-esteem.

This suggests that self-esteem is *multidimensional* rather than unidimensional. Differentiation among different aspects of the self-concept becomes sharper over the elementary school years (Marsh, Craven, & Debus, 1999), and adolescents distinguish even more aspects of self-esteem (Harter, 1999). However, self-esteem is also *hierarchical* in nature; children come to integrate their self-perceptions in distinct domains to form an overall, abstract sense of self-worth (Harter, 1999). Figure 11.1 shows the self-esteem hierarchy that results, with global self-worth at the top and specific dimensions of self-concept below it.

The accuracy of children's self-evaluations increases steadily over the elementary school years (Marsh, Craven, & Debus, 1999; Harter, 1999). Children as young as 5 do have a good sense of whether they are worthy and lovable, and it predicts how they will feel about themselves later in childhood (Verschueren, Buyck, & Marcoen, 2001). However, the self-esteem scores of young children (4- to 7-year-olds) often reflect their *desires* to be liked or to be "good" at various activities as much as their actual competencies (Eccles et al., 1993; Harter & Pike, 1984). They cannot always respond meaningfully to self-esteem scales (Davis-Kean & Sandler, 2001). Starting at about age 8, children's self-evaluations become more realistic and accurate. For example, those with high scholastic self-esteem are rated as intellectually competent by their teachers, and those with high athletic self-esteem are frequently chosen by peers in sporting events (Harter, 1999). At the same time, children are increasingly realizing what they "should" be like and are forming an ever-grander **ideal self.** As a result, the gap between the real self and the ideal self increases with age, and older children run a greater risk than younger children do of thinking that they fall short of what they could or should be (Glick & Zigler, 1985; Oosterwegel & Oppenheimer, 1993).

Influences on Self-Esteem

Why do some children have higher self-esteem than others? Basically, because some children (1) are more competent than others and (2) receive more positive social feedback (Harter, 1999). Some children are in fact more competent and socially attractive than others; they experience more success in areas important to them and come out better in social comparisons (Luster & McAdoo, 1995). Genes may be part of the reason: Genetically similar siblings have more similar levels of self-esteem than genetically dissimilar ones (McGuire et al., 1999). Apart from actual competence, though, social feedback from parents, teachers, peers, and other important people plays a critical role in shaping self-perceptions. Most notably, children with high self-esteem tend to have parents who are warm and democratic (Coopersmith, 1967; Lamborn et al., 1991).

Parents who are loving, form secure attachments with their children, and frequently communicate approval and acceptance are likely to help their children think positively about themselves (Doyle et al., 2000; Verschueren, Marcoen, & Schoefs, 1996). Saying, whether through words, looks, or actions, "You're not important" or "Why can't you be more like your older brother?" is likely to have the opposite effect on self-esteem. This is the concept of the looking-glass self in action: Children will form self-concepts that reflect the evaluations of significant people in their lives.

Tim Pannell//corbisstockmarket.com

The looking-glass self takes shape as children receive social feedback from the people around them.

Parents whose children have high self-esteem also enforce clearly stated rules of behavior while allowing their children to express their opinions and participate in decision making. This democratic parenting style most likely gives children a firm basis for evaluating their behavior and sends them the message that their opinions are respected. The relationship between high self-esteem and a warm, democratic parenting style has been observed in most ethnic groups in the United States, as well as in other countries (Scott, Scott, & McCabe, 1991; Steinberg, Dornbusch, & Brown, 1992).

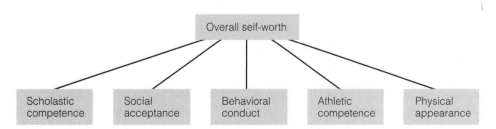

Figure 11.1 The multidimensional and hierarchical nature of self-esteem
SOURCE: Harter (1996)

Boosting Self-Esteem

As Susan Harter's (1999) research has shown, some children suffer from low self-esteem because they think they fall short in domains they consider important or because they look into the social looking glass and feel unaccepted by significant people in their lives. What can psychologists and other helping professionals do for such children?

When low self-esteem is rooted in negative self-evaluations, children can be helped either to gain the skills they wish they had (for example, through social skills training) or to establish more realistic standards of judging themselves (Shirk & Harter, 1996). When low self-esteem is rooted in parental neglect or rejection, the therapist may help by providing the unconditional acceptance that the child lacks or by using family therapy to help parents communicate love to their children. When children feel rejected by their peers, the solution may be to teach them more effective social skills or to convince them that their peers are not as rejecting as they may seem.

Consider the case of Chris, a 16-year-old high school junior who wanted to kill himself, despite the fact that he was an A student, a starter on the basketball team, a popular student, and a model son (Shirk & Harter, 1996). A perfectionist, he was highly self-critical when he fell short of his own demanding standards (for example, when he did not get the highest grade on a physics exam). He had supportive parents and caring friends, so negative social feedback was not the source of his low self-esteem. Instead, he had come to link lack of perfection in schoolwork with social rejection, figuring that no one would accept him if he were a "loser." An adopted child, he had concluded that his birth mother gave him away because he was imperfect: "If I had been flawless (perfect), she would have kept me" (p. 192). Therapy focused on helping Chris understand the distortions in his thinking about himself, revise his standards of self-evaluation, and see that there was nothing wrong with him.

Clearly, self-esteem can be increased through systematic interventions (Harter, 1999). But should we as a society put so much emphasis on boosting self-esteem? In one private school, for example, students are taught to recite again and again, "I am okay. I am capable. There is no one exactly like me" (Fletcher, 2000, p. A3). In his book, *Greater Expectations,* William Damon (1994) argues that we err by trying to make all children feel good about themselves, regardless of their talents and behavior. Self-esteem, he maintains, means nothing unless it grows out of one's accomplishments. Besides, children need opportunities to learn not only about their successes and strengths but about their failures and limitations. And, he argues, by emphasizing the importance of loving oneself, we underemphasize the importance of caring about others. Perhaps, then, there is merit in being more selective about when we intervene to make youth feel better about who they are.

Teachers, peers, and other significant individuals contribute to self-esteem in much the same way that parents do. As children get older, peer influences on self-esteem become more and more evident, although feedback from parents remains as important as ever (Harter, 1999; Thorne & Michaelieu, 1996). The judgments of other people, along with all the information that children gain by observing their own behavior and comparing it with that of their peers, shape their overall self-evaluations. Once a child's level of self-esteem has been established, it tends to remain quite stable over the elementary school years. Moreover, high self-esteem is positively correlated with a variety of measures of good adjustment (Coopersmith, 1967; Harter, 1999).

In sum, a major change in self-conception occurs at about age 8, as children shift from describing their physical and active selves to talking about their psychological and social qualities. Other changes include increased social comparison, formation of an overall sense of self-worth, more accurate self-evaluation, and widening of the ideal self–real self gap. Competence and positive social feedback from warm, democratic parents contribute to high self-esteem. As the Applications box above illustrates, psychotherapy can help boost low self-esteem. However, some observers think our society is obsessed with boosting esteem.

The Personality Gels

The biologically based response tendencies that we call temperament are shaped by the individual's social experiences into a full-blown personality during childhood. Certain aspects of early temperament clearly carry over into later personality. For example, in a longitudinal study of children in New Zealand, Avshalom Caspi (2000) and his colleagues have found that inhibited 3-year-olds who are shy and fearful tend to become teenagers who are cautious and unassertive and young adults who have little social support and tend to be depressed. By contrast, 3-year-olds who are difficult to control, irritable, and highly emotional tend to be difficult to manage later in childhood and end up as impulsive adolescents and adults who do not get along well with other people at home and on the job, get into scrapes with the law, and abuse alcohol. Finally, well-adjusted ("easy") 3-year-olds tend to remain well-adjusted. Interestingly, the assessments of personality at age 3 that proved predictive of later personality and adjustment were made on the basis of only 90 minutes of observation by an adult examiner who did not know the child.

Yet we cannot always be confident that the difficult or inhibited young child will remain that way. Many important dimensions of personality do not fully "gel" and become stable until the elementary school years (Hartup & van Lieshout, 1995; Shiner, 2000). They then begin to be even better predictors of later personality and adjustment. This is probably because some behavior patterns are reinforced and strengthened as the years go by because they set in motion certain kinds of interactions with the social environment and evoke certain reactions from other people (Caspi, Elder, & Bem, 1987, 1988). For example, a child who has an explosive personality and is irritable and prone to temper tantrums may lose friends and alienate teachers as a child, lose jobs or experience marital problems as an adult, and so experience a snowballing of the negative consequences of her early personality. She may also evoke hostile reactions from other people that further reinforce her tendency to be ill-tempered.

The goodness of fit between person and environment helps determine which traits carry over into later life and which do not. Personality traits are likely to be stable over time when they are valued by society—when there is goodness of fit between the trait and social expectations (Kagan & Moss, 1962; Kerr et al., 1994). Traits that conflict with cultural norms—for example, aggressiveness in a girl or passivity in a boy in a society in which those traits clash with traditional gender roles—may be discouraged and may fail to endure.

The Adolescent

Perhaps no period of the life span is more important to the development of the self than adolescence. Adolescence is truly a time for "finding oneself," as research on adolescent self-conceptions, self-esteem, identity formation, and vocational choice illustrates.

Self-Conceptions

Raymond Montemayor and Marvin Eisen (1977) learned a great deal about the self-concepts of children and adolescents from grades 4 to 12 by asking students to write 20 different answers to the question "Who am I?" What age differences can you detect in these answers given by a 9-year-old, an 11½-year-old, and a 17-year-old (pp. 317–318)?

9-year-old: My name is Bruce C. I have brown eyes. I have brown hair. I love! sports. I have seven people in my family. I have great! eye sight. I have lots! of friends. I live at . . . . I have an uncle who is almost 7 feet tall. My teacher is Mrs. V. I play hockey! I'm almost the smartest boy in the class. I love! food. . . . I love! school.

11½-year-old: My name is A. I'm a human being . . . a girl . . . a truthful person. I'm not pretty. I do so-so in my studies. I'm a very good cellist. I'm a little tall for my age. I like several boys. . . . I'm old fashioned. I am a very good swimmer. . . . I try to be helpful. . . . Mostly I'm good, but I lose my temper. I'm not well liked by some girls and boys. I don't know if boys like me . . . .

17-year-old: I am a human being . . . a girl . . . an individual . . . . I am a Pisces. I am a moody person . . . an indecisive person . . . an ambitious person. I am a big curious person. . . . I am lonely. I am an American (God help me). I am a Democrat. I am a liberal person. I am a radical. I am conservative. I am a pseudoliberal. I am an Atheist. I am not a classifiable person (i.e., I don't want to be).

There are several notable differences between the self-descriptions of children and adolescents (see also Damon & Hart, 1988; Harter, 1999; Livesley & Bromley, 1973). First, self-descriptions become *less physical and more psychological* as children get older. Second, these self-portraits become *less concrete and more abstract.* Recall Piaget's theory that children begin to shift from concrete operational to formal operational thinking at about age 11 or 12. Children entering adolescence (11- to 12-year-olds) get beyond describing their traits in largely concrete terms ("I love! food") and more often generalize about their broader personality traits ("I am a truthful person"). High school students' self-descriptions are even more abstract, focusing not only on personality traits but also on important values and ideologies or beliefs ("I am a pseudoliberal").

Third, adolescents reflect more about what they are like; they are *more self-aware* than children are (Selman, 1980). Their new ability to think about their own and other people's thoughts and feelings can make them painfully self-conscious. Fourth, adolescents have a *more differentiated* self-concept than children. For example, the child's "social self," which reflects perceived acceptance by peers, splits into distinct aspects such as acceptance by the larger peer group, acceptance by close friends, and acceptance by romantic partners (Harter, 1999). Finally, older adolescents gain the ability to combine their differentiated self-perceptions into a *more integrated, coherent self-portrait.* Instead of merely listing traits, they organize their self-perceptions, including those that seem contradictory, into a coherent picture—a theory of what makes them tick.

To illustrate the phases adolescents go through in coming to know and accept themselves, consider an interesting study by Susan Harter and Ann Monsour (1992). Adolescents 13, 15, and 17 years old were asked to describe themselves when they are with their parents, with friends, in romantic relationships, and in the classroom. The adolescents were then asked to sort through their self-descriptions, identify any opposites or inconsistencies, and indicate which opposites confused or upset them.

The 13-year-olds were quite unaware of inconsistencies within themselves—and when they did detect any, they were not especially bothered by them. By age 15, students identified many more inconsistencies and were clearly confused by them (see Figure 11.2). One ninth-grade girl, for example, noted that she was both attentive and lazy in school, talkative and nervous in romantic relationships, smart at school and fun-loving with friends, and so on. In discussing her tendency to be happy with friends but depressed at home, she said, "I really think of myself as a happy person, and I want to be that way with everyone because I think that's my true self, but I get depressed with my family and it bugs me because that's not what I want to be like" (Harter & Monsour, 1992, p. 253). These 15-year-olds, especially the girls, seemed painfully aware that they had several different selves and were concerned about figuring out which was the "real me."

The oldest adolescents studied by Harter and Monsour, the 17-year-olds, overcame many of the uncomfortable feelings the 15-year-olds had. They were able to integrate their conflicting self-perceptions into a more coherent view of themselves. Thus a 17- or 18-year-old boy might conclude that it is perfectly understandable to be relaxed and confident in most situations but nervous on dates if one has not yet had much dating experience or that "moodiness" can explain being cheerful with friends on some occasions but irritable on others. Harter and Monsour believe that cognitive development—specifically the ability to compare abstract trait concepts and to integrate them through higher-order concepts like "moodiness"—is behind this change in self-perceptions.

In sum, self-understandings become more psychological, abstract, differentiated, and integrated, and self-awareness increases, from childhood to adolescence and over the course of adolescence. At first oblivious to contradictions within the self, teenagers become painfully aware that they express different selves in different situations. Eventually, they can integrate their various selves. Many adolescents even become sophisticated personality theorists who reflect upon and understand the workings of their personalities and those of their companions.

Self-Esteem

The founder of developmental psychology, G. Stanley Hall, characterized adolescence as a time of emotional turmoil and psychological *storm and stress*. By this account, adolescents might be expected to experience low, or at least very unstable, levels of self-esteem. Does research support this view?

For about 20% of teenagers, adolescence is indeed a time of storm and stress characterized by significant mental health problems (Harter, 1999; Offer & Schonert-Reichl, 1992). And for some young adolescents, leaving elementary school as the oldest and most revered of students and entering the larger world of middle school or junior high school as the youngest and least competent damages self-esteem temporarily (Harter, 1999). However, this dip in self-esteem does not affect all teens. It tends to be greatest among white females facing multiple stressors—for example, making the transition to junior high school and also coping with pubertal changes, beginning to date, and perhaps dealing with a family move all at the same time (Gray-Little & Hafdahl, 2000; Simmons et al., 1987).

Overall, though, adolescence is not hazardous to the self, and most adolescents do not experience significant drops in self-esteem. Instead, most emerge from this developmental period with somewhat higher self-esteem than they had at the onset (Trzesniewski, Donnellan, & Robins, 2001). Apparently, they revise their self-concepts in fairly minor ways as they experience the physical, cognitive, and social changes of adolescence. Assuming that they have opportunities to feel competent in areas important to them and have the approval and support of parents, peers, and other important people in their

What I am like with different people

Figure 11.2 The multiple selves experienced by a 15-year-old girl. Can you identify any inconsistencies in her self-perceptions?

Source: Harter (1999)

The start of junior high school or middle school can temporarily damage the self-esteem of adolescents, especially girls facing multiple stressors and developmental challenges.

lives, they are likely to feel good about themselves (Harter, 1999). Overall, then, Hall's characterization of adolescence as a stormy time for the self is inaccurate for most adolescents.

Forming a Sense of Identity

Like G. Stanley Hall, Erik Erikson believed that adolescence is a time of dramatic changes in the self. It was Erikson (1968) who characterized adolescence as a critical period in the lifelong process of forming one's identity as a person and who proposed that adolescents experience the psychosocial conflict of **identity versus role confusion.** The concept of identity, introduced at the start of the chapter, is slippery. It refers to a firm and coherent definition of who you are, where you are going, and where you fit into society. To achieve a sense of identity, the adolescent must somehow integrate the many separate perceptions that are part of the self-concept into a coherent sense of self and must feel that he or she is, deep down, the same person yesterday, today, and tomorrow—at home, at school, or at work (van Hoof, 1999). The search for identity involves grappling with many important questions: What kind of career do I want? What religious, moral, and political values can I really call my own? Who am I as a man or woman and as a sexual being? Where do I fit in the world? What do I really want out of my life?

Can you recall struggling with identity issues yourself? Are you currently struggling with some of them? If so, you can appreciate the uncomfortable feelings that adolescents may experience when they can't seem to work out a clear sense of who they are. Erikson believed that many young people in complex societies like the United States experience a full-blown and painful "identity crisis"; indeed, he coined the term. There are many reasons why they might do so. First, their bodies change, and therefore they must revise their body images (a part of their self-concepts) and adjust to being sexual beings. Second, cognitive growth allows adolescents to think systematically about hypothetical possibilities, includ-

ing possible future selves. Third, social demands are placed on them to "grow up"—to decide what they want to do in life and to get on with it. According to Erikson (1968), our society supports youths by allowing them a **moratorium period**—a period of time in high school and college when they are relatively free of responsibilities and can experiment with different roles in order to find themselves (see Arnett, 2000). But our society also makes establishing an identity harder than it may be in many other cultures by giving youths a huge number of options and encouraging them to believe that they can be anything they want to be.

DEVELOPMENTAL TRENDS

James Marcia (1966) expanded on Erikson's theory and stimulated much research on identity formation by developing an interview that allows investigators to assess where an adolescent is in the process of identity formation. Adolescents are classified into one of four *identity statuses* based on their progress toward an identity in each of several domains (for example, occupational, religious, and political/ideological). The key questions are whether or not an individual has experienced a *crisis* (or has seriously grappled with identity issues and explored alternatives) and whether or not he or she has achieved a *commitment* (that is, a resolution of the questions raised). On the basis of crisis and commitment, the individual is classified into one of the four identity statuses shown in Table 11.4.

How long does it take to achieve a sense of identity? Philip Meilman's (1979) study of college-bound boys between 12 and 18, 21-year-old college males, and 24-year-old young men provides an answer (see Figure 11.3). Most of the 12- and 15-year-olds were in either the identity diffusion or the foreclosure status. At these ages, many adolescents simply have not yet thought about who they are—either they have no idea or they know that any ideas they do have are very likely to change (the **diffusion status,** with no crisis and no commitment). Other adolescents may say things like "I'm going to be a doctor like my dad" and appear to have their acts together. However, it becomes apparent that they have never really thought through *on their own* what suits them best and have simply accepted identities suggested to them by their parents or other people (the **foreclosure status,** involving a commitment without a crisis—the status illustrated by the young woman quoted at the start of the chapter).

As Figure 11.3 indicates, progress toward identity achievement becomes more evident starting at age 18. Notice that diffusion drops off steeply and more and more individuals begin to fall into the **moratorium status,** in which the individual is currently experiencing a crisis or is actively exploring identity issues. Presumably, entering the moratorium status is a good sign; if the individual can find answers to the questions raised, he or she will move on to the identity achievement status. Yet notice that only 20% of the 18-year-olds, 40% of the college students, and slightly more than half of the 24-year-olds in Meilman's study had achieved a firm identity based on a careful weighing of alternatives (the **identity achievement status**).

Table 11.4 The Four Identity Statuses as They Apply to Religious Identity

	No Commitment Made	Commitment Made
No Crisis Experienced	**Diffusion Status** The person has not yet thought about or resolved identity issues and has failed to chart directions in life. Example: "I haven't really thought much about religion, and I guess I don't know what I believe exactly."	**Foreclosure Status** The individual seems to know who he or she is but has latched onto an identity prematurely, without much thought (for example, by uncritically becoming what parents or other authority figures suggest he or she should). Example: "My parents are Baptists, and I'm a Baptist; it's just the way I grew up."
Crisis Experienced	**Moratorium Status** The individual is currently experiencing an identity crisis and is actively raising questions and seeking answers. Example: "I'm in the middle of evaluating my beliefs and hope that I'll be able to figure out what's right for me. I like many of the answers provided by my Catholic upbringing, but I've also become skeptical about some teachings and have been looking into Unitarianism to see if it might help me answer my questions."	**Identity Achievement Status** The individual has resolved his or her identity crisis and made commitments to particular goals, beliefs, and values. Example: "I really did some soul-searching about my religion and other religions too and finally know what I believe and what I don't."

Is the identity formation process different for females than it is for males? In most respects, no (Meeus et al., 1999; Kroger, 1997). Females progress toward achieving a clear sense of identity at about the same rate that males do. However, one reliable sex difference has been observed: Although today's college women are just as concerned about establishing a career identity as men are, they attach greater importance to and think more about the aspects of identity that center on sexuality, interpersonal relations, and how to balance career and family goals (Archer, 1992; Kroger, 1997; Meeus et al., 1999). These concerns probably reflect the continuing influence of traditional gender roles.

Judging from such research, identity formation *takes quite a bit of time.* Not until the late teens and early 20s do

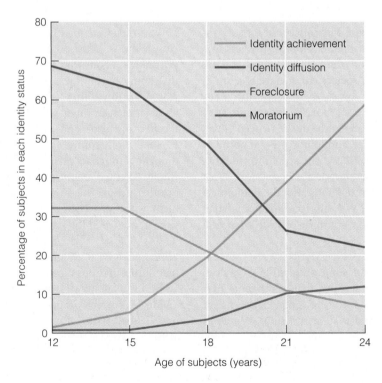

Figure 11.3 Percentage of subjects in each of Marcia's four identity statuses as a function of age. Note that only 4% of the 15-year-olds and 20% of the 18-year-olds had achieved a stable identity.
SOURCE: Based on Meilman (1979)

Forging a Positive Ethnic Identity

The process of identity development includes forging an **ethnic identity**—a sense of personal identification with an ethnic group and its values and cultural traditions (Phinney, 1996). Everyone has an ethnic and racial background, of course, but members of minority groups tend to put more emphasis than white adolescents on defining who they are ethnically or racially.

The process begins during the preschool years, when children learn that different racial and ethnic categories exist and gradually become able to classify themselves correctly into one group or another (Spencer & Markstrom-Adams, 1990). For example, Mexican American preschool children learn behaviors associated with their culture such as how to give a Chicano handshake, but they often do not know until about age 8 what ethnic labels apply to them, what they mean, or that they will last a lifetime (Bernal & Knight, 1997).

Forming a positive ethnic identity during adolescence seems to proceed through the same identity statuses as forming a vocational or religious identity, even though we don't choose our racial or ethnic heritage in the way we choose our occupations (Phinney, 1993). School-age children and young adolescents say either that they identify with their racial or ethnic group because their parents and others in their ethnic group influenced them to do so (foreclosure status) or that have not given the issue much thought (diffusion status). Between the ages of 16 and 19, many minority youths move into the moratorium and achievement statuses with respect to ethnic identity. One Mexican American female described her moratorium period this way:"I want to know what we do and how our culture is different from others. Going to festivals and cultural events helps me to learn more about my own culture and about myself" (Phinney, 1993, p. 70). When ethnic identity is achieved, youth feel comfortable being what they are.

Virtually all North American minorities have a term for community members who identify too closely with the mainstream European American culture, be it the "apple" (red on the outside, white on the inside) for Native Americans, the "coconut" for Hispanics, the "banana" for Asians, or the "Oreo" for African Americans. Minority adolescents must decide what *they* are inside. Biracial adolescents who are able to identify clearly as either African American or European American tend to be better adjusted than those who cannot decide what they are (DeBerry, Scarr, & Weinberg, 1996). For other minority youths, identifying with two groups can be healthy. For example, Native American youth have the highest sense of well-being when they identify with both the Anglo and Native American ways of life and the lowest when they identify with neither (Moran et al., 1999).

Achieving a positive ethnic identity contributes to high self-esteem and a sense of well-being (R. E. Roberts et al., 1999). It is most likely to happen when parents teach their children about their group's cultural traditions, try to prepare them to live in a culturally diverse society and deal with prejudice, and provide the warm and democratic parenting that seems to foster self-esteem and healthy identity development (Bernal & Knight, 1997; Marshall, 1995). Most minority adolescents cope well with the special challenges in identity formation they face. They settle questions of ethnic identity and resolve other identity issues at about the same ages as European American youth (Markstrom-Adams & Adams, 1995), and they wind up with equal or even higher self-esteem (Gray-Little & Hafdahl, 2000; Harter, 1999).

David Young-Wolff/PhotoEdit

many young men and women move from the diffusion or the foreclosure status into the moratorium status and then achieve a sense of identity (Waterman, 1982). But this is by no means the end of the identity formation process. Some adults continue in a moratorium status for years; others reopen the question of who they are after thinking they had all the answers earlier in life (Kroger, 1996). A divorce, for example, may cause a woman to rethink what it means to be a woman and reraise questions about other aspects of her identity as well. The result may be new psychosocial growth.

Not only does identity formation take a long time but it *occurs at different rates in different domains of identity* (Kroger, 1996). For example, Sally Archer (1982) assessed the identity statuses of 6th- to 12th-graders in four domains: occupational choice, gender-role attitudes, religious beliefs, and political ideologies. Only 5% of the adolescents were in the same identity status in all four areas, and more than 90% were in two or three categories across the four areas. Apparently, then, some aspects of identity take shape earlier than others. The process of identity formation may be even more complex for members of racial and ethnic minority groups. As the Explorations box on page 295 shows, they face the challenge of forming a positive *ethnic identity*.

Finally, the patterns of identity development discovered in longitudinal studies are *not always consistent with theory* (Meeus et al., 1999; van Hoof, 1999). For example, there is a good deal of evidence that identify diffusion decreases with age and identity achievement increases with age, but it is not as clear how one gets from diffusion to identity achievement (Meeus et al., 1999). Contrary to theory, some individuals appear to get there via foreclosure rather than through the period of moratorium that Erikson and others theorize is critical to identity development (Meeus et al., 1999). These youth may settle on an identity early and only later reflect on their choice. In short, identity development is complex. It takes a long time, occurs at different rates in different domains, and does not always unfold in the theoretically expected way.

INFLUENCES ON IDENTITY FORMATION

The adolescent's progress toward achieving identity is a product of at least four factors: (1) cognitive growth, (2) relationships with parents, (3) experiences outside the home, and (4) the broader cultural context. *Cognitive development* enables adolescents to imagine and contemplate possible future identities. Adolescents who have achieved solid mastery of formal operational thought and who think in complex and abstract ways are more likely to raise and resolve identity issues than adolescents who are less cognitively mature (Waterman, 1992). In addition, adolescents in the moratorium and achievement statuses have an information-processing style that involves actively seeking out relevant information rather than relying on others for guidance, as foreclosed adolescents tend to do, or putting off decisions and making impulsive choices at the last minute, as diffused adolescents tend to do (Berzonsky & Neimeyer, 1994). College freshmen in the achievement and moratorium statuses are in an excellent position to cope with the challenges of college life because they

are self-directed and autonomous and do not need to look to others so much for reassurance (Berzonsky & Kuk, 2000).

Second, adolescents' *relationships with parents* affect their progress in forging an identity (Markstrom-Adams, 1992; Waterman, 1982). Youths in the diffusion status of identity formation are more likely than those in the other categories to be neglected or rejected by their parents and to be distant from them. It can be difficult to forge one's own identity without first having the opportunity to identify with respected parental figures and to take on some of their desirable qualities. At the other extreme, adolescents categorized as being in the foreclosure status appear to be extremely close—sometimes too close—to parents who are loving but overly protective and controlling. Because foreclosed adolescents love their parents and have little opportunity to make decisions on their own, they may never question parental authority or feel any need to forge a separate identity.

By comparison, students who are classified in the moratorium and identity achievement statuses appear to have a solid base of affection at home combined with freedom to be individuals in their own right. In family discussions, for example, these adolescents experience a sense of closeness and mutual respect while feeling free to disagree with their parents (Grotevant & Cooper, 1986). Notice that this is the same warm and democratic parenting style that seems to help younger children gain a strong sense of self-esteem.

Experiences outside the home are a third influence on identity formation. For example, adolescents who go to college are exposed to diverse ideas and encouraged to think issues through independently. Although college students may be more confused for a time about their identities than peers who begin working after high school (Munro & Adams, 1977), going to college provides the kind of "moratorium period" that Erikson felt was essential to identity formation.

Finally, identity formation is influenced by *the broader cultural context* in which it occurs—a point that Erikson himself strongly emphasized. The very notion that adolescents should choose a personal identity after carefully exploring many options may well be peculiar to modern industrialized Western societies (Cote & Levine, 1988; Flum & Blustein, 2000). As was true of adolescents in earlier eras, adolescents in many traditional societies today simply adopt the adult roles they are expected to adopt, without any soul-searching or experimentation. For many of these adolescents, what Marcia calls identity foreclosure is probably the most adaptive route to adulthood (Cote & Levine, 1988). Indeed, some researchers are concluding that identity foreclosure can be an adaptive outcome in our society as well; it tends to be associated with well-being as high as that associated with the identity achievement status (Meeus et al., 1999). Lowest in well-being are those in the moratorium status—those in the middle of agonizing about who they are.

In Western society at least, the adolescent who is able to raise serious questions about the self and answer them—that is, the individual who achieves identity—is likely to be better off. Identity achievement is associated with psychological well-being and high self-esteem, complex thinking about

Yellow Dog Productions/Getty Images

Adolescents sometimes experiment with a variety of looks in their search for a sense of identity.

stars, or whatever else strikes them as glamorous and exciting. As Linda Gottfredson (1996) emphasizes, however, children are already beginning to narrow their ideas about future careers to those that are consistent with their emerging self-concepts—as human beings rather than bunnies or ninja turtles, as males rather than females, and so on. As early as kindergarten, for instance, almost all boys choose traditionally masculine occupations, and most girls name traditionally female occupations such as nurse or teacher (Etaugh & Liss, 1992; Phipps, 1995). Still, most children make pretty unrealistic choices of careers, and most have little clue what it takes to achieve their dream careers (Phipps, 1995).

During Ginzberg's second stage of vocational choice, the *tentative stage,* adolescents aged 11 to 18 begin to weigh factors other than their wishes and to make preliminary decisions. After considering their *interests* (Would I enjoy counseling people?), they take into account their *capacities* (Am I skilled at relating to people, or am I too shy and insecure for this kind of work?) and then also think about their *values* (Is it really important to me to help people, or do I value power, money, or intellectual challenge more?).

As adolescents leave this tentative stage, they begin to take into account the realities of the job market and the physical and intellectual requirements for different occupations (Ginzberg, 1972, 1984). During Ginzberg's third stage of vocational choice, the *realistic stage,* from about age 18 to age 22, they narrow things down to specific choices based on interests, capacities, values, and available opportunities and begin serious preparation for their chosen occupations. Over their childhood and adolescent years, individuals steadily accumulate knowledge about the characteristics of different occupations and what it takes to enter them (Walls, 2000). By late adolescence, they are in a good position to consider the availability of job openings in a field such as school counseling, the years of education required, the work conditions, and other relevant factors.

The main developmental trend evident in Ginzberg's stages is increasing realism about what one can be. As adolescents narrow down career choices in terms of both personal factors (their own interests, capacities, and values) and environmental factors (the opportunities available and the realities of the job market), they seek the vocation that best suits them. According to vocational theorists, vocational choice is just this: *an effort to find an optimal fit between one's self-concept or personality and an occupation* (Holland, 1985; Super, Savickas, & Super, 1996).

As they get older, adolescents from lower-income families, especially those from minority backgrounds, often make compromises in their career plans (Gottfredson, 1996). They lower their career aspirations and aim toward the jobs they think they are likely to get rather than the jobs they most want (Armstrong & Crombie, 2000; Rojewski & Yang, 1997). Similarly, the vocational choices of females have been and continue to be constrained by traditional gender norms. Although young women are increasingly aspiring toward high-status jobs, many do not seriously consider traditionally male-dominated jobs, doubt their ability to attain such jobs,

moral issues and other matters, a willingness to accept and cooperate with other people, and a variety of other psychological strengths (Waterman, 1992). By contrast, those individuals who fail to achieve a sense of identity may find themselves lacking self-esteem and drifting aimlessly, trapped in the identity diffusion status. Erikson recognized that identity issues can and do crop up later in life even for those people who form a positive sense of identity during adolescence. Nonetheless, he quite rightly marked the adolescent period as a key time in life for defining who we are.

Vocational Identity and Choice

Vocational identity is a central aspect of identity with major implications for adult development. How do adolescents go about choosing careers that express their sense of self as they prepare for adult life? According to an early theory of vocational choice proposed by Eli Ginzberg (1972, 1984), vocational choice unfolds in three stages: (1) the fantasy stage, (2) the tentative stage, and (3) the realistic stage. In the *fantasy stage* of vocational development, children up to about age 10 years base their choices primarily on wishes and whims, wanting to be zookeepers, pro basketball players, firefighters, rock

and aim instead toward feminine-stereotyped, and often lower-status, occupations (Armstrong & Crombie, 2000; Morinaga, Frieze, & Ferligoj, 1993). Those who have adopted traditional gender-role attitudes and expect to marry and start families early in adulthood are especially likely to set their vocational sights low (Morinaga et al., 1993). They may feel that they cannot achieve important family goals without scaling down their career ambitions. Many other teenagers simply do not do what Erik Erikson and vocational theorists would advise them to do—explore a wide range of possible occupations and then make a choice.

In short, as adolescents progress through fantasy, tentative, and realistic stages of vocational development, societal influences discourage many low-income youths of both sexes and young women of all backgrounds from seriously considering many options that might well fit their interests, capacities, and values. Many other teenagers do not explore a range of possible occupations. Those who *do* consider a wide range of options are more likely than those who do not to choose careers that fit their personalities well (Grotevant & Cooper, 1986). A good fit between vocation and personality is associated, in turn, with greater job satisfaction and success (Spokane, Meir, & Catalano, 2000; Tinsley, 2000). The saving grace is that those who do not explore very thoroughly as adolescents still have opportunities as adults to change their minds and chart new life courses.

The Adult

As we enter adulthood, having gained a great deal of understanding of what we are like as individuals, our personalities and self-conceptions are generally well formed. To what extent are our self-perceptions and personality traits shaped by the culture in which we develop? How do they change over the adult years, and how are they related to the changes adults experience as their careers unfold?

Self-Conceptions and Culture

By adulthood, self-conceptions show the effects not only of individual experiences such as the receipt of positive or negative feedback from parents but also of broader cultural influences. In an **individualistic culture,** individuals define themselves as individuals and put their own goals ahead of their social group's goals, whereas in a **collectivist culture,** people define themselves in terms of group memberships and give group goals higher priority than personal goals (Triandis, 1989, 1995). Individualistic cultures emphasize socializing children to be independent and self-reliant, whereas collectivistic ones emphasize interdependence with others, social harmony, and the importance of sacrificing self-interest for the good of the group. North American and Western European societies typically have an individualistic orientation, whereas many societies in Latin America, Africa, and Asia are collectivist. Note, however, that all cultures include a mix of individualism and collectivism and that the differences we are talking about are matters of degree.

How do self-conceptions actually differ in these two types of cultures? Hazel Markus and her colleagues have been studying cultural differences in the meaning of self in the United States and Japan (Cross, 2000; Markus, Mullally, & Kitayama, 1997). They have found, in a series of studies, that being a person in the United States (an individualistic culture) means being one's own person, independent and unique, whereas being a person in Japan (a collectivist culture) means being interdependent, connected to others in one's social groups. Thus, when asked to describe themselves, American adults talk about their unique personal qualities, whereas Japanese adults more often refer to their social roles and identities and mention other people (for example, "I try to make my parents happy").

In addition, Americans describe their generalizable personality traits—traits they believe they display in most situations and relationships. By contrast, Japanese adults describe their behavior in specific contexts such as home, school, or work and may describe themselves quite differently depending on the social situation or context they are talking about. Indeed, the Japanese language has no word to refer to "I" apart from social context (Cross, 2000).

Finally, Americans are obsessed with maintaining high self-esteem; most believe that they are above average in many respects (like the children of Garrison Keillor's "Lake Wobegon"). Japanese adults are more modest and self-critical; their self-descriptions contain more negative and fewer positive statements (Cross, 2000). They readily note their inadequacies and seem reluctant to "stand out from the crowd" by calling attention to their positive qualities. In Japan, making a point of one's strengths would mean slighting the importance of one's group (Shweder et al., 1998, p. 907; and see Table 11.5).

Culture influences not only how people define and describe themselves but whether they feel a need to do so. For example, in Iceland, another collectivist culture, the population is highly homogenous, differences among people are minimized, and people have great difficulty describing themselves. Asked "What are you like?" one Icelander spoke for many by replying, "I can't describe that at all" (Hart & Fegley, 1997, p. 141).

Cross-cultural studies of individualistic and collectivist cultures challenge our Western assumption that one cannot develop normally without coming to know oneself as an individual. They also suggest that our methods for studying the self—asking people who they are, having them respond to personality scale items about how they *generally* behave across social contexts—may be culturally biased. Many of the world's people seem to get on quite nicely by being part of a collective and not thinking much about how they differ from other group members. It is wise to bear in mind, then, that both self-conceptions and personality are culturally defined.

Self-Conceptions and Aging

In our society, it is commonly believed that adults gain self-esteem as they cope successfully with the challenges of adult

Table 11.5 Views of the Self in Individualistic and Collectivist Cultures

Individualistic (United States)	Collectivist (Japan)
Separate	Connected
Independent	Interdependent
Traitlike—personal qualities transcend specific situations and relationships	Flexible—different in different social contexts
Need for self-esteem results in seeing self as above average	Self-critical, aware of inadequacies
Emphasis on uniqueness	Emphasis on group memberships, similarities to others

SOURCE: Based on Markus, Mullally, & Kitayama (1997)

life but then lose it as aging, disease, and losses of roles and re- lationships take their toll in later life. As it turns out, adults in our society often do gain self-esteem during the transition from adolescence to adulthood (Trzesniewski et al., 2001). Young, middle-aged, and elderly adults, however, seem to have similar levels of self-esteem and well-being, and they describe themselves in similar ways (Helgeson & Mickelson, 2000; Ruth & Coleman, 1996). There is little truth, then, to the stereo- typed view that older adults suffer from a poor self-image. Even elderly women living in poverty are more likely to view themselves as fortunate and blessed than as old, poor, and pitiful (Barusch, 1997). The interesting question becomes this: How do elderly people manage to maintain positive self- images even as they experience some of the losses that come with aging?

First, *older people adjust their ideal selves to be more in line with their real selves.* Adults of different ages do not differ much in how they evaluate their present selves, but they *do* differ in their views of what they could or should be in the fu- ture. Carol Ryff (1991) asked young, middle-aged, and elderly adults to assess their (1) ideal, (2) likely future, (3) present, and (4) past selves with respect to six dimensions of self- perceived well-being: self-acceptance, relationships with oth- ers, autonomy, mastery of the environment, purpose in life, and personal growth. Figure 11.4 shows the average scores on the self-acceptance scale only. Ratings of the present self changed little from age group to age group. However, older adults scaled down their visions of what they could ideally be and what they will be in the future. They also judged more positively what they had been in the past, so that their ideal, future, present, and past selves all converged. Notice, then, that the gap between the ideal self and real self that grows larger during childhood and adolescence, and that gives us a sense of falling short, apparently closes again in later life, helping us to maintain self-esteem (see also Heidrich, 1999).

Second, many "losses" experienced in later life are not in- terpreted as losses because *people's goals and standards change with age* (Helgeson & Mickelson, 2000; Carstensen & Freund, 1994). The 45-year-old may be devastated at being passed over for a promotion, whereas the 60-year-old nearing retirement may not be any more bothered than 45-year-olds are by "not being able to jump on their beds, and draw pictures with crayons" (Carstensen & Freund, 1994, p. 87). Perhaps, then, as our goals change over the life span, we apply different meas-

uring sticks in evaluating ourselves and do not mind failing to achieve goals that are no longer important.

Third, older adults maintain self-esteem because *the peo- ple with whom they compare themselves change* (Helgeson & Mickelson, 2000; Brandtstädter & Greve, 1994). Older adults do not compare themselves to young adults but to people who have the same kinds of chronic diseases and impairments they have—or even worse ones. Indeed, stereotypes of aging in our society are so bleak that older adults can feel good about their own aging simply by conjuring up an image of the typical "old person" (Brandtstädter & Greve, 1994)!

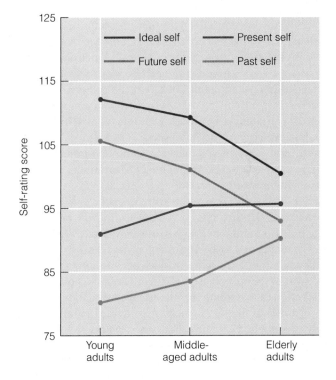

Figure 11.4 Favorability of ratings of their ideal, likely future, present (real), and past selves by young, middle-aged, and elderly adults. The gap between ideal and real self that widens during childhood and adolescence shrinks during adulthood, as indicated by the converging lines in the graph. As they age, adults become more comfortable with the idea of remaining as they are and as they have been in the past.
SOURCE: Adapted from Ryff (1991)

In sum, adults of different ages generally feel equally good about themselves and describe themselves in similar ways. This may be true in part because older adults perceive a smaller gap between their real and ideal selves, evaluate their self-worth by different standards, and make social comparisons to other older people. Each adult also maintains much the same level of self-esteem over the years, although life events can and do bring about temporary changes in self-perception (Giarrusso et al., 2000; Mortimer, Finch, & Kumka, 1982).

Continuity and Discontinuity in Personality

Could continuity in self-perceptions be a reflection of continuity in personality traits? To address the issue of continuity versus discontinuity in adult personality, we must ask two questions: Do *individual* adults retain their rankings compared to others in a group on trait dimensions over the years? Do *average* scores on personality trait measures increase, decrease, or remain the same as age increases?

DO PEOPLE RETAIN THEIR RANKINGS?

Paul Costa, Robert McCrae, and their colleagues have closely studied personality change and continuity by giving adults from their 20s to their 90s personality tests and administering these tests repeatedly over the years (Costa & McCrae, 1994; McCrae & Costa, 1990). Focusing on the Big Five dimensions of personality listed in Table 11.2, they have found a good deal of stability in individual differences, as indicated by high correlations between scores on the same trait dimensions at different ages. In other words, the person who tends to be extraverted as a young adult is likely to be extraverted as an elderly adult, and the introvert is likely to remain introverted over the years. Similarly, the adult who shows high or low levels of neuroticism, conscientiousness, agreeableness, or openness to new experiences is likely to retain that ranking compared to peers years from now. Correlations between personality trait scores on two occasions 20 to 30 years apart average about .60 across the five personality dimensions. Correlations this size suggest consistency in personality over time but also room for change (Costa & McCrae, 1994).

The tendency to be consistent increases with age. In a meta-analysis of 152 studies in which personality was assessed on two or more occasions, Brent Roberts and Wendy DelVecchio (2000) found that the average correlation between scores at two testings 6 to 7 years apart was .31 in infancy and early childhood, .54 in the college years, .64 at age 30, and .74 from age 50 on. Because they are still forming, personalities are unsettled in childhood and even in the teens and 20s. They appear to become more firmly established by the time adults are in their 30s and beyond.

In sum, research has confirmed the argument of trait theorists that relatively enduring personality traits exist, and yet it also tells us that people change over the years. Evidence of continuity in rankings on personality scales may explain why we often perceive ourselves as being the same basic people we used to be and why people we have not seen for years often

seem not to have changed much at all. If this is bad news for people who are dissatisfied with their current personalities, it is good news for those who want to predict what they and other people will be like in the future or how they will respond to life events. For example, individuals who score high on measures of neuroticism and low on measures of extraversion are likely to experience more negative and fewer positive life events than other people (Magnus et al., 1993) and to have more difficulty coping with stressful events as well (Hoffman, Levy-Shiff, & Malinski, 1996).

DO PERSONALITIES CHANGE SYSTEMATICALLY?

Do most people change systematically in certain common directions over the years? You may be consistently more extraverted than I over the years, and yet both of us, along with our peers, could become less extraverted at age 70 than we were at age 20. Let's examine a second major meaning of continuity in personality: stability in the average level of a trait displayed over the years.

Early cross-sectional studies suggested that younger and older adults have quite different personalities on average. However, some age-group differences have turned out to be generational, or cohort, differences rather than true maturational changes. People's personalities are clearly affected by when they were born and by what sorts of experiences they had in their formative years (Schaie & Parham, 1976). For example, Jean Twenge (2000) has shown that recent cohorts of children and adults have scored higher on measures of anxiety and neuroticism than earlier generations did. Indeed, the average child living in the United States in the 1980s reported levels of anxiety higher than those reported by children receiving psychiatric treatment in the 1950s. High crime and divorce rates and other social problems may make it harder for today's children to feel connected to others and safe (Twenge, 2000).

Only longitudinal studies can tell us whether people's personalities actually change in systematic ways *as they age.* Some longitudinal studies point to personality growth from adolescence to middle age. For example, one longitudinal study revealed that people become more intellectually engaged and achievement oriented, as well as more self-confident, during this period (Haan, 1981; Jones & Meredith, 1996). Robert McCrae, Paul Costa, and their colleagues (2000) have assembled evidence of similar age-group differences in scores on the Big Five personality dimensions across cultures. Specifically, neuroticism, extraversion (especially excitement seeking), and openness to experience all decline modestly from adolescence to middle age, whereas agreeableness and conscientiousness increase modestly over this same age range (McCrae et al., 1999). That is, during the years from adolescence to middle adulthood, we become less anxious and emotionally unstable, less outgoing and more introverted, less open to new experiences, more cooperative and easy to get along with, and more disciplined and responsible.

This same pattern of age difference has been observed among both men and women in cross-sectional studies conducted in countries as diverse as Turkey, the Czech Republic,

Japan, and Estonia. Since these societies have undergone different social changes at different times, it is hard to see how cohort effects could explain this universal pattern of age differences. This evidence, along with evidence that the Big Five personality trait dimensions are genetically influenced, has led McCrae and Costa to conclude that the Big Five are biologically based temperaments that are relatively resistant to environmental influences and undergo a universal process of maturational change. They even go on to suggest that evolution may be behind this maturation process: For our ancestors, a good deal of extraversion and openness to new experiences might have proven useful in finding mates during adolescence, whereas for adults raising children, conscientiousness and agreeableness may have proven more adaptive. Although convinced that some aspects of personality development are universal, McCrae and Costa acknowledge that the specific ways in which people adapt to their environments and learn habits and attitudes are very much influenced by their specific social environments.

What personality changes can we expect from middle age to old age? There are only a few signs that most people change in similar ways during this period. Adults' activity levels (their tendencies to be energetic and action oriented) begin to decline in the 50s and continue declining through the 80s and 90s (Costa & McCrae, 1994). And people may continue to become less extraverted and more introverted and introspective in old age (Field & Millsap, 1991; Leon et al., 1979). Still, most of us will not undergo similar personality changes as part of the aging experience. Either we will remain much the same, or we will change in response to life experiences but in our own individual ways, depending our personalities (Wink, 1996).

Where do we stand, then? Most evidence points to (1) a good deal of cross-age consistency in people's rankings compared to others on Big Five personality trait dimensions such as extraversion and neuroticism, but some change as well; (2) cohort effects suggesting that the historical context in which people grow up affects their personality development; (3) modest personality growth from adolescence to middle adulthood—a strengthening of qualities such as achievement orientation and self-confidence and universal changes in the Big Five; and (4) little personality change from middle adulthood to later adulthood except for modest decreases in activity level and increases in introversion. In short, there is both continuity and discontinuity in personality during adulthood.

WHY DO PEOPLE CHANGE OR REMAIN THE SAME?

Having figured out that personality exhibits both stability and change in over the life span, developmentalists are asking why people stay the same and why they change. What makes a personality stable? First, the influence of *heredity* is at work. Genes, along with experience, contribute to individual differences in adult personality, including all five of the Big Five personality factors (Borkenau et al., 2001; Loehlin et al., 1998). Second, *lasting effects of childhood experiences* may contribute; we have seen, for example, that parents can either help a child overcome a difficult temperament or contribute to its becoming an enduring pattern of response. Third, traits re-

main stable because people's *environments remain stable*. Here the argument is that both early and later experiences promote personality stability because individuals consistently seek out and have experiences that suit and reinforce their personalities (Caspi, 1998).

The mechanism at work in promoting continuity may be *gene/environment correlations:* Genetic endowment influences the kinds of experiences we have, and those experiences, in turn, strengthen genetically based predispositions (see Chapter 3). Thus, an extravert's early sociability will elicit friendly responses from others, and she will seek out and create environments to her liking—places where she can socialize and where her initial tendency to be extraverted will be strengthened. The individual genetically predisposed to be an introvert, by contrast, may avoid crowds, keep to herself, and therefore remain an introverted individual, comfortable with herself and her lifestyle. In a kind of snowball effect, the consequences of having one early temperament rather than another will cumulate over the years (Caspi, 1998).

What, then, might cause the significant changes in personality that some adults experience? *Biological factors* such as disease could contribute. The nervous system deterioration associated with *Huntington's disease,* for example, causes victims to become moody and irritable. Adults also change in response to *changes in the social environment,* including major life events (Caspi, 1998). For example, young adults who land good jobs after college tend to gain confidence, whereas those who face job insecurity and unemployment in their early careers lose confidence (Mortimer et al., 1982). In this way, life events help determine whether traits evident in early adulthood will persist or change, much as social learning theorists claim.

Finally, change is more likely when *there is a poor fit between person and environment.* For example, Florine Livson (1976) discovered that independent women who did not have traditionally feminine traits experienced more personality change during midlife than traditional women who fit the stereotypically feminine roles of wife and mother better. Bothered by the mismatch between their personalities and their traditionally feminine roles, the nontraditional women redirected their lives in their 40s and experienced improvements in psychological health by their 50s. Similarly, men who fit the traditional male role well changed less over the years than nontraditional men who felt cramped by this role and who, after a crisis in their 40s, began to express their more feminine, emotional sides (Livson, 1981). For men and women both, then, a mismatch between personality and environment (or lifestyle) prompted personality change. This message about the importance of person–environment fit is the same one that has emerged from research on children with easy, difficult, and slow-to-warm-up temperaments.

In conclusion, personalities are both stable and changeable during adulthood. Genes, early childhood experiences, and the tendency to seek out or end up in environments that match and reinforce earlier predispositions all contribute to stability. Change in personality becomes more likely if people's biologies or environments change considerably or if there is a poor fit between their personalities and their lifestyles.

Eriksonian Psychosocial Growth

Researchers who conclude that adults hardly change at all over the years typically study personality by administering standardized personality scales. These tests were designed to assess enduring traits and may well tell us about the most stable aspects of personality. However, researchers who interview people in depth about their lives often detect considerably more change and growth (Wrightsman, 1994). This is quite clear in research on Erikson's theory of psychosocial development through the life span. To provide background, we will briefly review the psychosocial changes through adolescence highlighted in this chapter. Then we will ask whether Erikson was right to call attention to the potential for further psychological growth during adulthood.

THE PATH TO ADULTHOOD

During Erikson's first psychosocial conflict, **trust versus mistrust,** infants learn to trust other people if their caregivers are responsive to their needs; otherwise, the balance of trust versus mistrust will tip in the direction of mistrust. Erikson believed that infants, in resolving the psychosocial conflict of basic trust versus mistrust, begin to recognize that they are separate from the caregivers who respond to their needs. And indeed, as we saw earlier in this chapter, infants begin to distinguish self from other (typically the mother) during the first two or three months of life.

Toddlers acquire an even clearer sense of themselves as individuals as they struggle with the psychosocial conflict of **autonomy versus shame and doubt.** According to Erikson, they develop a sense of themselves and assert that they have wills of their own. Consistent with this view, toddlers recognize themselves in a mirror and lace their speech with "me" and "no" at about 18 months of age. Four- and 5-year-olds who have achieved a sense of autonomy then enter Erikson's stage of **initiative versus guilt.** They develop a sense of purpose by devising bold plans and taking great pride in accomplishing the goals they set. As we have seen, preschoolers define themselves primarily in terms of their physical activities and accomplishments.

A sense of initiative, Erikson believed, paves the way for success when elementary school children face the conflict of **industry versus inferiority** and focus on mastering important cognitive and social skills. As we have seen, elementary school children seem intent on evaluating their competencies; they engage in more social comparison than younger children and are likely to acquire a sense of industry rather than inferiority only if those comparisons turn out favorably.

According to Erikson, children who successfully master each of these childhood psychosocial conflicts gain new ego strengths. Moreover, they learn a good deal about themselves and position themselves to resolve the adolescent crisis of *identity versus role confusion.* As we have seen in some detail, adolescence is indeed a time for raising and answering identity questions. But what happens to adolescents with newfound identities during the adult years? Erikson claimed that stagelike changes in personality continue during adulthood.

EARLY ADULT INTIMACY

As Erikson saw it, young adulthood is a time for dealing with the psychosocial conflict of **intimacy versus isolation.** He theorized that one must achieve a sense of individual identity before becoming able to commit oneself to a *shared identity* with another person—that is, you must know yourself before you can love someone else. The young adult who has no clear sense of self may be threatened by the idea of entering a committed, long-term relationship and being "tied down," or he or she may become overdependent on a romantic partner (or possibly a close friend) as a source of identity.

Does identity indeed pave the way for genuine intimacy? To find out, Susan Whitbourne and Stephanie Tesch (1985) measured both identity status and intimacy status among college seniors and 24- to 27-year-old alumni from the same university. The researchers interviewed people about their closest relationships and placed each person in one of six intimacy statuses. These included being a social isolate with no close relationships, being in a shallow relationship with little communication or involvement, being in a deep relationship but not

Early adulthood is the time, according to Erik Erikson, for deciding whether to commit to a shared identity with another person.

yet being ready to make a long-term commitment to one's partner, and being in a genuinely intimate relationship that has it all—involvement, open communication, and a long-term commitment.

More alumni than college students fell into either the moratorium (active questioning) or the achievement status of identity formation. Thus, progress toward achieving identity continues to be made *after* college graduation. College graduates had also progressed further than college seniors in resolving intimacy issues; more of them were in long-term, committed relationships. Finally, and most important, the college graduates who had well-formed identities were more likely than those who did not to be capable of genuine and lasting intimacy—precisely what Erikson had theorized (see also Stein & Newcomb, 1999).

So far, so good, then. As Erikson claimed, we apparently must know ourselves before we can truly love another person. Yet there are interesting differences between women and men in this process (Adams & Archer, 1994; Hodgson & Fischer, 1979). Erikson believed that women cannot fully resolve identity questions until they choose a mate and fashion an identity around their roles as wife and mother-to-be. Is this rather sexist view correct? Not quite. Most men follow the identity-then-intimacy route, becoming psychologically ready for a serious relationship only after they have settled on a career and perhaps even launched it. Influenced by traditional sex-role expectations, some women resolve intimacy issues before identity issues: They marry, raise children, and only after the children are more self-sufficient ask who they really are as individuals (Hodgson & Fischer, 1979). Today, women with feminine gender-role orientations are likely to tackle identity and intimacy issues simultaneously, perhaps forging a personal identity that centers on caring for other people or defining themselves in the context of a love relationship (Dyk & Adams, 1990). For feminine women, then, Erikson may have been right in saying that women fuse the tasks of achieving identity and intimacy. However, women with masculine gender-role orientations and many masculine-stereotyped traits such as assertiveness tend to follow the identity-before-intimacy route that characterizes men (Dyk & Adams, 1990). Overall, then, Erikson's theory seems to fit men better than it fits women because fewer women follow the identity-then-intimacy path. Sex differences in routes to identity and intimacy are likely to diminish, however, as more women postpone marriage to pursue careers.

Middle Age Generativity

Does psychosocial growth continue in middle age? George Vaillant (1977), a psychoanalytic theorist, conducted an in-depth longitudinal study of mentally healthy Harvard men from college to middle age, as well as a longitudinal study of blue-collar workers (Vaillant, 1983; Vaillant & Milofsky, 1980). Vaillant found support for Erikson's view that the 20s are a time to raise intimacy issues. He found that in their 30s, men shifted their energies to advancing their careers and were not very reflective or concerned about others. Finally, in their 40s, many men became concerned with Erikson's issue of **genera-**

tivity versus stagnation, which involves gaining the capacity to generate or produce something that outlives you and to genuinely care about the welfare of future generations. These men expressed more interest than ever before in passing on something of value, either to their own children or to younger people at work. They reflected on their lives and experienced the kind of intellectual vitality that adolescents sometimes experience as they struggle with identity issues. Few of these men experienced a full-blown and turbulent midlife crisis, just as few had experienced a severe identity crisis as college students. Nonetheless, they were growing as individuals, often becoming more caring and self-aware as they entered their 50s. One of these men expressed the developmental progression Vaillant detected perfectly: "At 20 to 30, I think I learned how to get along with my wife. From 30 to 40, I learned how to be a success in my job. And at 40 to 50, I worried less about myself and more about the children" (1977, p. 195).

Research tells us that middle-aged men and women are more likely than young adults to have achieved a sense of generativity (McAdams, Hart, & Maruna, 1998). Moreover, those adults who have achieved a sense of identity and intimacy are more likely than other adults to achieve generativity as well, as Erikson predicted (Christiansen & Palkovitz, 1998). Generative adults are caring people, committed parents, productive workers and mentors, and community leaders. They tend to be agreeable and open to new experiences while being low in neuroticism (McAdams et al., 1998). They think in more sophisticated ways about moral issues than less generative adults (Pratt et al., 1999), and they are more satisfied with their lives and work (Ackerman, Zuroff, & Moskowitz, 2000).

Erikson believed that nurturing one's children as they prepare to leave the nest is central to acquiring a sense of generativity. Among men, though not among women, the experience of having children and being actively involved in caring for them fosters a sense of generativity (Christiansen & Palkovitz, 1998; McKeering & Pakenham, 2000). Women apparently achieve generativity earlier in adulthood, and do so even if they do not become parents, possibly because they often adopt nurturing and mentoring roles at work. Overall, we find support for Erikson's view that both women and men are capable of impressive psychosocial growth during middle adulthood.

Old Age Integrity

Elderly adults, according to Erikson, confront the psychosocial issue of **integrity versus despair.** They try to find a sense of meaning in their lives that will help them face the inevitability of death. Most older adults, when asked what they would do differently if they had their lives to live over again, say there is little, if anything, they would change (Erikson, Erikson, & Kivnick, 1986). This suggests that most older adults do attain a sense of integrity. But how?

Some years ago, gerontologist Robert Butler (1963, 1975) proposed that elderly adults engage in a process called **life review,** in which they reflect on unresolved conflicts of the past in order to come to terms with themselves, find new meaning and coherence in their lives, and prepare for death. Do older adults in fact engage in life review, and does it help them achieve a healthy sense of integrity? Contrary to the stereotype, elderly people do not really spend more time thinking about the old days or dwelling in the past than younger people do (Webster & McCall, 1999). However, whereas younger adults often reminisce to relieve boredom or to work on identity issues, older adults use their reminiscences to evaluate and integrate the pieces of their lives and to prepare for death—exactly what life review is all about (Molinari & Reichlin, 1984-1985; Webster & McCall, 1999).

More important, those elders who do use the life review process to confront and come to terms with their failures display a stronger sense of ego integrity and better overall adjustment than those who do not reminisce or those who stew about how poorly life has treated them (Taft & Nehrke, 1990; Wong & Watt, 1991). Believing that life review can be beneficial in later life, Butler and others have used it as a form of therapy, asking elderly adults to reconstruct and reflect on their lives with the help of photo albums and other memorabilia. Participation in life review therapy can indeed help elderly adults (Molinari, 1999).

On balance, Erikson's theory of psychosocial development has gained a good deal of support from research. Although few studies have directly tested Erikson's ideas about psychosocial development during childhood, his theorizing about the adolescent stage of identity versus role confusion has been tested extensively and is quite well supported. In addition, achieving a sense of identity in adolescence does pave the way for forming a truly intimate relationship with another person as a young adult; many middle-aged adults do attain a sense of generativity; and many older adults work toward a sense of integrity through the process of life review. As Erikson proposed, then, humans experience personal growth and change throughout the life span.

Midlife Crisis?

We have now established that personality traits such as extraversion and neuroticism remain quite consistent over the years, but that people do confront new psychological conflicts as they age. Where in all of this is the midlife crisis that many people believe is a standard feature of personality development in middle age? Erikson saw few signs of a midlife crisis, but another psychoanalytic theorist, Daniel Levinson (1986, 1996; Levinson et al., 1978), did. He proposed an influential stage theory of adult development based on intensive interviews with men. Just before his death in 1994, Levinson and his wife Judy completed a book reporting that the same stages emerged in interviews with women (Levinson, 1996).

Levinson's stages describe the unfolding of what he calls an individual's **life structure**—an overall pattern of life that reflects the person's priorities and relationships with other people and the larger society. Levinson proposes that adults go through a repeated process of first building a life structure and then questioning and altering it. Structure-building periods, during which the person goes about pursuing career, family, and personal goals, alternate with transitional periods, when

the person questions his or her life decisions. Levinson believed that his stages are both maturational in nature and universal. Environmental factors will influence the specifics of an adult's life, but the basic pattern of building, questioning, and rebuilding will still be evident under the surface. Levinson's stages are outlined in Table 11.6.

According to Levinson, the transition period from age 40 to 45 is an especially significant time developmentally, a time of **midlife crisis**—of questioning one's entire life structure and raising unsettling issues about where one has been and where one is heading. Most of the middle-aged men Levinson studied did not seek divorces, quit their jobs, buy red sports cars, or behave like lovesick adolescents, as popular images of the midlife crisis would have it. However, Levinson characterized 80% of the men in his study as having experienced a bona fide crisis—a period of intense inner struggles and disturbing realizations—in their early 40s. And, in his in-depth study of 45 women between the ages 35 and 45, Levinson (1996) concluded that women too faced major issues during both the Age 30 Transition (28 to 33) and the Midlife Transition (40 to 45).

Many researchers agree that middle age is a time when many important issues arise and when some men and women perceive themselves to be engaged in a painful self-evaluation process (Hermans & Oles, 1999; Rosenberg, Rosenberg, & Farrell, 1999). Still, most researchers doubt that most adults experience a genuine "crisis" at midlife or that this crisis occurs in the narrowly defined age range of 40 to 45, as Levinson claimed. Although many middle-aged adults evaluate their lives, only a minority experience a painful upheaval that could be called a crisis (Hedlund & Ebersole, 1983; Vaillant, 1977). What's more, people question their lives at a variety of ages rather than only in their early 40s, and often do so in response to specific life events such as getting married, changing jobs, or experiencing marital problems.

If a stage of midlife crisis in the early 40s were widespread, we might expect men and women to experience significant personality changes at midlife or to show signs of emotional disturbance or decreasing well-being. This does not seem to be the case (Charles, Reynolds, & Gatz, 2001; McCrae & Costa, 1990). Finally, if midlife crises were widespread, we might expect middle-aged adults to be dissatisfied with their work. Instead, middle-aged men and women are generally *more* satisfied with their jobs than younger adults are (Warr, 1992). In sum, Levinson may have overestimated the extent to which midlife crisis occurs. It would seem more appropriate to call the phenomenon midlife *questioning*, to recognize that it can occur in response to life events at a variety of ages, and to appreciate that it is usually not a true psychological crisis.

Vocational Development and Adjustment

Although Levinson's concept of midlife crisis is not well supported, he was quite right to emphasize that adults revise important life decisions as they develop. We can illustrate this by looking at research on vocational development during adulthood. After engaging in much experimentation as young adults, people settle into a chosen occupation, ideally one that

Table 11.6 Daniel Levinson's Stages of Adult Development

Stage	Age	Characteristics
Early adult transition	17–21	Young people make the transition from adolescence to early adulthood, try to establish independence from parents, and explore possibilities for an adult identity. They form *the dream,* a vision of their life goals.
Entering the adult world	22–28	Adults build their first life structure, often by making and testing out a career choice and getting married. They work to succeed, find a supportive spouse and/or mentor if possible, and do not question their lives much.
Age 30 transition	28–33	In this period of questioning, adults ask whether their career choices and marriages are really what they want. If any uncomfortable feelings arise from their questioning, they either ignore them and plug away, make small adjustments in their life structure, or plan a more major life changes (for example, a job change, a divorce, or a decision to return to school).
Settling down	33–40	This is a time for building and living out a new, and often somewhat different, life structure and "making it," or realizing one's dream. An adult may outgrow his or her need for a mentor and become his or her own person. As in the structure-building period of Entering the Adult World, adults tend to be ambitious, task oriented, and unreflective.
Midlife transition	40–45	In this major period of questioning, Levinson believes adults ask, if they have been successful, whether the dreams they formulated as young adults were worth achieving. If they have not achieved their dreams, they face the fact that they may never achieve them. They may make major changes in their life structures.
Entering middle adulthood	45–50	Middle-aged adults create a new life structure appropriate to middle age. If they successfully confronted and resolved midlife issues during the Midlife Transition, they may gain self-understanding, a capacity for mentoring younger adults at work, and a deeper concern for their families, much like the middle-aged adult whom Erik Erikson describes as having acquired a sense of generativity.

suits their personality, in their 30s, and strive for success. Ultimately, they prepare for the end of their careers, make the transition into retirement, and attempt to establish a satisfying lifestyle during their "golden years."

ESTABLISHING A CAREER

Early adulthood is a time for exploring vocational possibilities, launching careers, making tentative commitments, revising them if necessary, seeking advancement, and establishing oneself firmly in what one hopes is a suitable occupation. Using data from a longitudinal study of males tracked from adolescence to age 36 (see Super et al., 1996), Susan Phillips (1982) examined whether men's decisions about jobs at different ages were tentative and exploratory (for example, "to see if I really liked that kind of work") or more final (for example, "to get started in a field I wanted"). The proportions of decisions that were predominantly exploratory were 80% at age 21, 50% at age 25, and 37% at age 36. From age 21 to 36, young adults progressed from wide-open exploration of different career possibilities, to tentative or trial commitments, to a stabilization of their choices. Even in their mid-30s, though, about a third of adults were still exploring what they wanted to be when they grew up! The average man held *seven* full-time jobs or training positions between the ages of 18 and 36 (Phillips, 1982). The picture for women is similar (Jenkins, 1989). After their relatively unsettled 20s and decision-making 30s, adults often reach the peaks of their careers in their 40s (Simonton, 1990). They often have major responsibilities and define themselves in terms of their work.

Personality is an important influence on vocational development in adulthood. For example, boys who are aggressive at age 8 and are poorly adjusted at home and in school at age 14 tend to become young men with unstable careers (Roenkae & Pulkkinen, 1995). Adults who are high in extraversion and low in neuroticism tend to achieve more vocational success and are more satisfied with their jobs than other workers (Seibert & Kraimer, 2001). Person–environment fit can be critical, too: People tend to become dissatisfied and open to changing jobs when the fit between their personality and aptitudes and the demands of their job is poor (Bretz & Judge, 1994.

Gender is another significant influence on vocational development. Although women are entering a much wider range of fields today than they were a few decades ago, it is still the case that most secretaries, teachers, and nurses are women. Partly because they are clustered in traditionally feminine-stereotyped occupations, U.S. women earned 76 cents for every dollar men earned on average in 1998—an improvement over the 62 cents to every dollar ratio in 1979, but still less than men (Grimsley, 2000). Why the gap? It is probably due to a combination of discrimination in the workplace and the choices women make in their careers.

The first factor, discrimination, is evident when traditionally "female" jobs pay less than "male" jobs even when the intellectual demands of the work are similar (England, Reid, & Kilbourne, 1996). It is also evident when women who enter jobs with the same management degrees and salaries as men, and receive equal performance ratings, still do not rise as far

in the organization or earn as much as men (Cox & Harquail, 1991).

The second factor is that gender-role expectations have prompted many women to choose to subordinate career goals to family goals. Steady movement up the career ladder is most likely when an employee works full-time and continuously in the same organization (Sorensen, 1991; Van Velsor & O'Rand, 1984). However, women often interrupt their careers, drop down to part-time work, or take less demanding jobs in order to bear and raise children (Moen, 1992). In the process, they hurt their chances of rising to high-paid, responsible positions. Meanwhile, the women who *do* make it to the top of the career ladder, especially in male-dominated fields, sometimes achieve this success by remaining single, divorcing, or limiting their childbearing (Jenkins, 1989). Women without children achieve more in their careers on average than women with children do (Carr et al., 1998).

The vocational choices we make and the jobs we hold influence our subsequent personality development and adjustment. For example, compared to young adults who remain in school, those who make the transition from school to work—and therefore to a new environment—experience more personality change. The changes are typically positive ones, such as decreased neuroticism and depression and greater self-esteem (van der Velde, Feij, & Taris, 1995). In addition, workers whose work is complex and intellectually challenging, especially older workers, grow as a result of the intellectual stimulation they receive on the job, becoming more able to handle intellectual problems adeptly, more self-confident, and even more tolerant of other people (Kohn & Schooler, 1982; Schooler, Mulatu, & Oates, 1999).

In sum, although we make vocational choices as adolescents, we remain open to making new choices as young adults and take some time to settle on a career. Both personality and gender affect the process of vocational development, and vocational experiences in turn affect personality development and adjustment.

THE AGING WORKER

Many people believe that adults become less able or less motivated to perform well on the job as they approach retirement,

but it turns out that the job performance of workers in their 50s and 60s is not very different overall from that of younger workers (Avolio & Sosik, 1999; Hansson et al., 1997). Age is simply not a very good predictor of how well a person will perform his or her job. Not only are older workers generally as competent as younger workers, but they often have more positive attitudes toward their work (Rhodes, 1983). They tend to be *more* satisfied with their jobs, *more* involved in their work, and *less* interested in finding a new job than younger workers are.

Why isn't the performance of older workers hurt by some of the age-related physical and cognitive declines we have discussed in this book? Partly because these declines typically do not become significant until people are in their 70s and 80s, long after they have retired. Many older workers have also accumulated a good deal of on-the-job expertise that can help them perform well (Hansson et al., 1997). Finally, the answer may also lie in the strategies that aging adults use to cope with aging. Gerontologists Paul and Margaret Baltes (1990) theorize that older people can best cope with aging through a strategy they call **selective optimization with compensation.** Three processes are involved: *selection* (focus on the skills one most needs and wants to keep sharp), *optimization* (practice those skills to keep them sharp), and *compensation* (develop ways to get around the need for other skills). Using selective optimization with compensation, an overworked 60-year-old lawyer might, for example, avoid spreading herself too thin by delegating lower-priority tasks to younger workers (selection), put a lot of time into staying up-to-date in her main area of specialization (optimization), and hide her weaknesses from the head of the law firm (compensation).

In a study testing this model (Abraham & Hansson, 1995), workers aged 40 to 69 completed scales measuring their reliance on selection, optimization, and compensation strategies. Among older but not younger adults in the sample, especially those with highly stressful jobs, heavy reliance on these strategies did indeed help workers to maintain a high level of performance and attain their goals at work. There are limits, of course, but many older workers seem able to draw on their expertise and on tactics like selective optimization with compensation to maintain a high level of achievement at work, despite age-related declines in some competencies. They are able to maintain a good person–environment fit between their abilities and the demands of their jobs (Hansson et al., 1997). The federal government seems to have recognized that older workers are typically effective workers. It has raised or eliminated mandatory retirement ages, increased the age of eligibility for receiving Social Security, and, through the Age Discrimination in Employment Act, protected older workers from age discrimination in hiring and retention (Hansson et al., 1997).

RETIREMENT

A century ago, most working adults continued working as long as they were able. As late as 1930, more than half of all men aged 65 or older were still working (Palmore et al., 1985). The introduction of Social Security in 1934 and the increased availability of private pension plans has changed all that, making it financially possible for more men and women to retire. As a result, only about 22% of U.S. adults aged 65–74 and 4% of those aged 75 and older hold regular jobs (Herzog et al., 1989). The average age of retirement, for white and black men and women alike, is about 63, younger than it used to be (Gendell & Siegel, 1996).

How do people adjust to the final chapter of the work life cycle? Robert Atchley (1976) proposed that adults progress through a series of phases as they make the transition from worker to retiree. The process of adjustment begins with a *preretirement phase* in which workers nearing retirement gather information and plan for the future. The closer workers feel they are to retiring, the more they think and talk about it (Ekerdt, Kosloski, & DeViney, 2000). Deciding when to retire is an important part of the process. Some workers are forced to retire early because of poor health or because they are pushed out of their jobs, but others choose to retire early because they have enough money to do so, do not feel very attached to their jobs, or simply like the idea of retiring (Beehr et al., 2000; Hansson et al., 1997).

Just after they retire, workers often experience a *honeymoon phase* in which they relish their newfound freedom and perhaps head for the beach, golf course, or camping grounds and do all the projects they never had time to do while they worked. Then, according to Atchley, many enter a *disenchantment phase* as the novelty wears off; they feel aimless and sometimes unhappy. Finally, they move on to a *reorientation phase* in which they begin to put together a realistic and satisfying lifestyle. Research supports this view. For example, David Ekerdt and his colleagues (Ekerdt, Bossé, & Levkoff, 1985) found that (1) men who had been retired only a few months were indeed in a honeymoon period in which they were highly satisfied with life and optimistic about the future, (2) men who had been retired 13 to 18 months were rather disenchanted with life, and (3) men who had been retired for longer periods were relatively satisfied once again (see also Gall, Evans, & Howard, 1997).

So, retirement takes getting used to. After retirees have adjusted, though, are they worse off than they were before they retired? Negative images of the retired person abound in our society; the retiree supposedly ends up feeling useless, old, bored, sickly, and generally dissatisfied with life. Yet the bulk of research indicates that retirement has few effects at all on adults (Gall et al., 1997; Hansson et al., 1997; Palmore et al., 1985). Retirement's most consistent effect is to reduce the individual's income—on average, to about three-fourths of what it was before retirement (Palmore et al., 1985). Retired people generally do *not* experience a decline in health simply because they retire. Poor health more often causes retirement than retirement causes poor health. Retirees' activity patterns and social lives don't change much either (Palmore et al., 1985). Indeed, retirement typically has no noticeable effect on the size of people's social networks, the frequency of their social contacts, or their satisfaction with the social support they receive. Finally, retirement does not seem to disrupt marriages or reduce life satisfaction or mental health.

Overall, then, retirees are likely to experience an adjustment process involving preretirement and then honeymoon, disenchantment, and reorientation phases. They end up adapting quite successfully to retirement and to the drop in income that it typically involves. Yet there are huge individual differences in adjustment. What makes for a favorable adjustment? Adults who (1) retire voluntarily rather than involuntarily, (2) enjoy good health, (3) have the financial resources to live comfortably, and (4) are married or otherwise have strong social support typically fare better than those who are forced to retire because of poor health and find themselves with inadequate incomes and few social ties (Gall et al., 1997; Palmore et al., 1985; Szinovacz & Ekerdt, 1995).

Personality and Successful Aging

Gerontologists have long been interested in the question of what makes not only for a successful transition to retirement but, more generally, for a happy and fulfilling old age. One theory of successful aging, **activity theory,** holds that aging adults will find their lives satisfying to the extent that they can maintain their previous lifestyles and activity levels, either by continuing old activities or by finding substitutes—for example, by replacing work with hobbies, volunteer work, or other stimulating pursuits (Havighurst, Neugarten, & Tobin, 1968; and see Fry, 1992). According to this theory, psychological needs do not really change as people enter old age, and most aging individuals continue to want an active lifestyle.

Other theorists have taken almost precisely the opposite stand on the keys to successful aging. **Disengagement theory** claims that successful aging involves a mutual withdrawal of the aging individual and society (Cumming & Henry, 1961; and see Achenbaum & Bengtson, 1994). The aging individual is said to have needs different from those she or he once had and seeks to leave old roles behind and *reduce* activity. Meanwhile, society both encourages and benefits from the older person's disengagement.

Which is it? Throughout this text, we have seen evidence that individuals who remain active in old age benefit from their activity. Those who are physically active maintain their health longer (see Chapter 5), those who are intellectually

Many older adults subscribe to the activity theory of aging, attempting to find substitutes for lost roles and activities. Others find happiness through disengagement and would just as soon sit and watch.

active maintain their cognitive functions longer (see Chapter 9), and those who remain involved in meaningful social relationships are likely to be more satisfied with their lives (see Chapter 14). In other words, there is more support for activity theory than for disengagement theory.

But before we conclude that activity theory tells us all we need to know about successful aging, let's add three qualifications. First, the relationship between sheer level of activity and life satisfaction or well-being is surprisingly weak (Fry, 1992). Apparently many individuals who are quite inactive are nonetheless satisfied with their lives, and many who are very busy are nonetheless miserable. This suggests that the *quality* of one's activity is probably more important than its quantity (Pinquart & Sorensen, 2000).

Second, some messages of disengagement theory have merit (Achenbaum & Bengtson, 1994). As we saw earlier in this chapter, for example, older adults sometimes become more introspective than they were earlier in life. This sort of

psychological withdrawal could be viewed as a form of disengagement. Moreover, most older people today do withdraw voluntarily from certain roles and activities. Most notably, both older and younger members of society are very supportive of the concept of retirement, suggesting that disengagement from work roles is mutually satisfying.

But third, neither activity theory *nor* disengagement theory adequately allows for the fact that the personality traits that people carry with them from childhood influence their well-being in old age. Generally, for example, people who are highly extraverted and conscientious, but not very neurotic, have a higher sense of well-being than other adults (Siegler & Brummett, 2000). Even more important, people are most satisfied in old age when they can achieve *a good fit between their lifestyle and their individual needs, preferences, and personality* (Fry, 1992; Seleen, 1982). Activity theorists assume that most people will benefit from maintaining an active lifestyle; disengagement theorists assume that most people will be best off if they disengage. In fact, an energetic and outgoing person may well want to maintain his or her active lifestyle in old age, whereas a person who always found work to be a hassle may like nothing better than to take it easy and might be miserable if forced to continue working or to participate in a retirement community's sing-alongs and other planned recreational activities.

Still other older adults may find satisfaction in maintaining a few highly important roles, relationships, and activities but selectively withdrawing from others (Turk-Charles & Carstensen, 1999; Rapkin & Fischer, 1992). The coping strategy of selective optimization with compensation that helps aging workers maintain good job performance also appears to work well as a strategy for maintaining a sense of well-being in old age (Freund & Baltes, 1998). By selecting a few priority areas, optimizing one's performance in those areas, and compensating for declines in other areas, older adults can continue to feel very good about themselves and their lives. In short, we cannot assume, as both activity theory and disengagement theory do, that what suits one suits all. Rather, we should once again adopt an interactional model of development that emphasizes the goodness of fit between person and environment.

Summary Points

1. Personality is an organized combination of attributes unique to the individual; self-concept (perceptions of one's attributes) and self-esteem (overall evaluations of one's worth) do not always accurately reflect one's actual personality traits.

2. Psychoanalytic theorists maintain that we all experience stagelike personality changes at similar ages and that early personality affects later personality, but Erikson saw more potential for growth during adulthood than Freud did. Psychometric (trait) theorists, such as those who conceptualize personality in terms of the Big Five trait dimensions, also believe that aspects of personality are enduring but do not propose stages of personality development. By

contrast, social learning theorists and contextual theorists maintain that people can change in any number of directions at any time in life if their social environments change.

3. Early in their first year, infants acquire some sense that they exist separately from the world around them; by 18 to 24 months of age, they display self-recognition and form a categorical self based on age and sex.

4. Infants differ in temperament: emotionality, activity, and sociability; behavioral inhibition; and easy, difficult, and slow-to-warm-up temperaments. Early temperament is partially influenced by genetic endowment but also shaped by the goodness of fit between child and environment and is only moderately related to later personality.

5. The self-concepts of preschool children are concrete and physical. By about age 8, children begin to describe their inner psychological traits and evaluate their competencies through social comparison processes. Children are most likely to develop high self-esteem when they are competent, fare well in social comparisons, and have warm, democratic parents.

6. During middle childhood, the personality "gels"; traits become more consistent and enduring than they were earlier in life, especially if they are culturally valued and therefore represent a good fit to the environment.

7. During adolescence, self-concepts become more psychological, abstract, and integrated, and self-awareness increases. Most adolescents experience only temporary disturbances in self-esteem at the onset of adolescence and gain self-esteem thereafter.

8. The most difficult challenge of adolescence is resolving Erikson's conflict of identity versus role confusion. From the diffusion and foreclosure identity statuses, many college-age youths progress to the moratorium and identity achievement statuses. Identity formation is uneven across domains of identity, often continues into adulthood, and is influenced by cognitive development and social experiences such as interactions with loving parents who encourage individuality.

9. According to Eli Ginzberg, adolescents' vocational choices become increasingly realistic as they progress through the fantasy, tentative, and realistic stages. Social factors sometimes constrain the choices made by females and by low-income youth of both sexes, and many adolescents do not engage in enough systematic career exploration.

10. Self-conceptions differ in individualistic and collectivist cultures, but self-conceptions and self-esteem change relatively little over the adult years. Older adults maintain self-esteem by bringing their ideal selves closer to their real selves, changing their goals and standards of self-evaluation, and comparing themselves to other older adults.

11. Individuals' rankings on Big Five dimensions of personality become more stable with age, but there is both continuity and discontinuity in personality during adulthood. From adolescence to middle adulthood, many people appear to gain personal strengths such as confidence; across cultures, Big Five profiles shift with age toward less neuroticism, extraversion, and openness to experience, and more agreeableness and conscientiousness. From middle age to old age, only a few systematic changes occur, notably a decrease in activity level and an increase in introspectiveness or introversion.

12. Stability of personality may be due to genetic makeup, lasting effects of early experience, and people's tendencies to seek out and encounter experiences that reinforce their earlier personalities. Personality change may be associated with changes in the social environment and a poor fit between person and environment.

13. Erikson's theory of psychosocial development is supported by evidence that resolution of conflicts centering on trust, autonomy, initiative, and industry paves the way for achieving a positive sense of identity in adolescence, and that identity then lays a foundation for achieving intimacy in early adulthood, generativity in middle age, and a sense of integrity through life review in old age.

14. Daniel Levinson's theory that adults experience a recurring process of building and questioning life structures—highlighted by a midlife crisis—is only partly supported. Midlife crisis in one's early 40s does not seem to be universal, although adults do reevaluate their lives at various times.

15. Young adults engage in much career exploration and questioning before they settle down in their 30s and achieve peak success in their 40s. Personality influences vocational success, and work activities in turn influence personality, but women face gender discrimination and often subordinate career to family, limiting their vocational success. Older workers are as productive as and often more satisfied than younger workers, possibly because they use selective optimization with compensation to cope with aging.

16. Retiring workers go through an adjustment process with preretirement, honeymoon, disenchantment, and reorientation phases; they typically experience a drop in income but little change in health or psychological well-being.

17. In attempting to identify paths to successful adjustment in old age, neither activity theory nor disengagement theory places enough emphasis on person–environment fit—on the fact that older adults are likely to be most satisfied when their retirement lifestyles suit their individual personalities and preferences.

Critical Thinking

1. Write four brief descriptions of yourself to show how you might have answered the question "Who am I?" at (1) age 4, (2) age 9, (3) age 14, and (4) age 21. What developmental changes in self-conceptions do your self-descriptions illustrate?

2. Teddie the Toddler tends to get very stressed when his routines are changed, a stranger comes to the door, or he is asked to try something he has never tried before. Help his parents understand his temperament and what it may mean for his personality as a 70-year-old.

3. What might parents and society do to make the process of achieving a positive identity during adolescence particularly difficult, and what might they do to help adolescents find themselves?

4. Interview 10 adults and ask them how well-adjusted, on a scale of 1 to 10, they felt they were in first grade, seventh grade, and now. You might also ask respondents to explain the basis for their ratings. Does your survey point to continuity or discontinuity of adjustment? Show how you could analyze your data to find out.

5. Aunt Rosalia is about to retire and wants to establish a satisfying lifestyle for her old age. What would an activity theorist, a disengagement theorist, and a selective-optimization-with-compensation theorist recommend that she do?

Key Terms

personality	slow-to-warm-up temperament
self-concept	goodness of fit
self-esteem	social comparison
identity	ideal self
Big Five	identity versus role confusion
joint attention	moratorium period
self-recognition	diffusion status
categorical self	foreclosure status
looking-glass self	moratorium status
temperament	identity achievement status
emotionality	ethnic identity
activity	individualistic culture
sociability	collectivist culture
behavioral inhibition	trust versus mistrust
easy temperament	autonomy versus shame and doubt
difficult temperament	

initiative versus guilt

industry versus inferiority

intimacy versus isolation

generativity versus stagnation

integrity versus despair

life review

life structure

midlife crisis

selective optimization with compensation

activity theory

disengagement theory

On the Web

Web Sites to Explore

The Big Five Personality Dimensions

This site will acquaint you with the Big Five and the specific traits that belong under each of the five major dimensions. You'll find background information, a comparison of this model of personality to others, and information about tests available for assessing the Big Five.
http://www.centacs.com/

Erikson's Theory

This site provides a closer look at Erikson's eight stages of psychosocial development; it includes a summary chart, descriptions of the stages, Erikson's biography, and critiques of his theory.
http://snycorva.cortland.edu/~ANDERSMD/ERIK

Midlife

This site, intended to be "inspirational," is dedicated to middle age and its characteristics and challenges.
http://www.middleage.org

Retirement

The Administration on Aging's Web site has resources for people planning their retirements. Look at what's there, and then talk to one of your grandparents or another elder about what they did to plan for retirement and how well they think they anticipated their needs in retirement. See especially "Life Course Planning."
www.aoa.gov/retirement/rpg.html

Search Online with InfoTrac College Edition

For additional information, explore InfoTrac College Edition, your online library. Go to http://www.infotrac-college.com and use the pass code that came on the card with your book. For example, using the key word "temperament," find three research articles on temperament. See how each study defines temperament and what dimensions of temperament are measured. You may run into one of the approaches to temperament discussed in the chapter, or you may not, as researchers today use many different approaches.

Visit Our Web Site

Go to http://www.wadsworth.com/psychology, where you will find online resources directly linked to your book.

Life-Span CD-ROM

Go to the Wadsworth Life-Span CD-ROM for further study of the concepts in this chapter. The CD-ROM also includes quizzes and additional activities to expand your learning experience.

Gender Roles and Sexuality

DEVELOPMENTAL PSYCHOLOGIST CAROLE BEAL (1994) learned an interesting lesson about the significance of being a girl or a boy when she was interviewing 9-year-olds:

> I had just finished one interview and was making some quick notes when the next child came into the office. I looked up, and an odd thing happened: I could not tell whether the child was a boy or a girl. The usual cues were not there: The child's hair was trimmed in a sort of pudding-bowl style, not really long but not definitively short either. The child was dressed in a gender-neutral outfit of jeans, sneakers, and a loose T-shirt, like most of the children at the school. The name on the interview permission slip was "Cory," which did not clarify matters much as it could be either a boy's or a girl's name. Still puzzled, I began the interview and found myself becoming increasingly frustrated at not knowing Cory's sex. I quickly realized how many unconscious assumptions I usually made about boys and girls; for example, that a girl would probably like a particular story about a horse and be willing to answer a few extra questions about it, or that a boy would probably start to get restless after a certain point and I would have to work a bit harder to keep his attention. (p. 3)

Unlike Cory, most children are readily identified as girls or boys and treated accordingly. How much does it really matter, in terms of development, whether a child is perceived and treated as a girl or perceived and treated as a boy? How much does it matter whether a child actually *is* a girl or a boy biologically? These are the kinds of questions we tackle in this chapter.

In our society, gender clearly matters. When proud new parents telephone to announce a birth, the first question friends and family tend to ask is "Is it a boy or a girl?" (Intons-Peterson & Reddel, 1984). Before long, girls discover that they are girls, and many acquire a taste for frilly dresses and dollhouses, while boys discover that they are boys and often wrestle each other on the lawn. As adults, we never lose our awareness of being either men or women. We define ourselves partly in terms of our "feminine" or "masculine" qualities, and we play roles that conform to society's view of what a woman or a man should be. In short, being female or male is a highly important aspect of the self throughout the life span.

In this chapter, we'll be looking at how the characteristics and life experiences of male and female humans are similar and different—and why. We'll see how girls and boys learn to play their parts as girls or boys and how they are groomed for their roles as women or men. We'll also consider some of the ways in which adult men and women are steered along different developmental paths. In addition, we'll examine the development of sexuality and its implications for relationships between the sexes. Before going any

Table 12.1   Which of These Sex Differences Is Real?

Which of the following do you think are consistent sex differences that have been demonstrated in studies comparing males and females? Mark each statement T (true) or F (false). Answers are printed upside down; they will be clarified in the discussion that follows.

____ 1. Males are more aggressive than females.

____ 2. Males are more active than females.

____ 3. Females are more social than males.

____ 4. Females have stronger verbal abilities than males.

____ 5. Males have greater achievement motivation than females.

____ 6. Males are more analytical than females.

____ 7. Females are more suggestible and prone to conform than males.

____ 8. Females are more emotionally unstable than males.

____ 9. Males are more rational and logical than females.

____ 10. Males have greater spatial and mathematical abilities than females.

Answers: 1-T, 2-T, 3-F, 4-T, 5-F, 6-F, 7-F, 8-F, 9-F, 10-T

further, try the quiz in Table 12.1 to see if you know which of our many ideas about male–female differences have some truth to them.

Male and Female

What difference does it make whether one is a male or a female? It matters in terms of physical differences, psychological differences, and differences in roles played in society. The physical differences are undeniable. A zygote that receives an X chromosome from each parent is a genetic (XX) female, whereas a zygote that receives a Y chromosome from the father is a genetic (XY) male. In rare cases of gender chromosome abnormalities (see Chapter 3), this is not the case; a girl may have only one X chromosome or a boy three chromosomes (XYY or XXY). Chromosomal differences result in different prenatal hormone balances in males and females, and hormone balances before and after birth are responsible for the facts that the genitals of males and females differ and that only females can bear children. Moreover, males typically grow to be taller, heavier, and more muscular than females, although females may be the hardier sex in that they live longer and are less susceptible to many physical disorders (for example, Giampaoli, 2000). As we'll see later in the chapter, some theorists argue that biological differences between males and females are ultimately responsible for psychological and social differences as well.

However, there is much more to being male or female than biology. Virtually all societies expect the two sexes to adopt different **gender roles**—the parts or patterns of behavior that females and males should adopt in a particular society (for example, the parts of wife, mother, and woman or of husband, father, and man).[1] Characteristics and behaviors viewed as desirable for males or females are specified in **gender-role norms**—society's expectations or standards concerning what males and females *should* be like. Each society's norms generate **gender-role stereotypes,** which are overgeneralized and largely inaccurate beliefs about what males and females *are* like.

Through the process of **gender typing,** children not only become aware that they are biological males or females but also acquire the motives, values, and patterns of behavior that their culture considers appropriate for members of their biological sex. Through the gender-typing process, for example, Susie may learn a gender-role norm stating that women should strive to be good mothers and gender-role stereotypes indicating that women are more skilled at nurturing children than men are. As an adult, Susan may then adopt the traditional feminine role by switching from full- to part-time work when her first child is born and devoting herself to the task of mothering.

It would be a mistake, then, to attribute any differences that we observe between girls and boys (or women and men) solely to biological causes. They could just as easily be due to differences in the ways males and females are perceived and raised. But before we try to explain sex differences, perhaps we should find out what these differences are believed to be and what they actually are.

Gender Norms and Stereotypes

Which sex is more likely to express emotions? To be neat and organized? To be competitive? To use harsh language? If you are like most people, you undoubtedly have ideas about how men and women differ psychologically and can offer some ready answers to these questions.

The female's role as childbearer has shaped the gender-role norms that prevail in many societies, including our own. At the heart of the feminine gender role is **communality,** an orientation that emphasizes connectedness to others and includes traits of emotionality and sensitivity to others (Best & Williams, 1993; Conway & Vartanian, 2000). Girls who adopt communal traits will presumably be prepared to play the roles of wife and mother—to keep the family functioning and to raise children successfully. By contrast, the central aspect of the masculine gender role is **agency,** an orientation toward individual action and achievement that emphasizes traits of dominance, independence, assertiveness, and competitiveness. Boys have been encouraged to adopt agentic traits in order to fulfill the traditionally defined roles of husband and father, which involve providing for the family and protecting it from harm. Similar norms for males and females apply in many, though certainly not all, societies (Whiting & Edwards, 1988; Williams & Best, 1990).

Because cultural norms demand that females play a communal role and males play an agentic role, we tend to form stereotypes saying that females possess communal traits and males possess agentic traits (Williams & Best, 1990). Unfortunately, feminine traits are stereotyped as more childlike and less adultlike than masculine traits, placing adults who are perceived as having feminine traits at a disadvantage (Powlishta, 2000). If you're thinking that these stereotypes have disappeared as attention to women's rights has increased and as more women have entered the labor force, think again. Although some change has occurred, adolescents and young adults still endorse many traditional stereotypes about men and women (Bergen & Williams, 1991; Botkin, Weeks, & Morris, 2000; Lueptow, Garovich-Szabo, & Lueptow, 2001). Moreover, males and females continue to describe themselves differently. When Jean Twenge (1997) analyzed studies conducted from 1970 to 1995 in which standard scales assessing gender-relevant traits had been administered, she found that men and women in the mid-1990s described themselves more similarly than did men and women 20 years previously, largely because modern women saw themselves as having more masculine traits. However, male and female personality profiles continued to differ in ways consistent with gender stereotypes. Might beliefs about sex differences, then, have a basis in fact? Let's see.

Are There Actual Gender Differences?

A great deal of research has attempted to answer the question of whether there are actual sex or gender differences in behavior. Although differences in some areas have been identified, other areas show no gender differences whatsoever. Let's review the areas where there are some differences, keeping in mind that these are often small, group differences. That is, even when research shows that women, on average, score higher (or lower) than men, on average, there will still be individual women who score lower (or higher) than individual men. With this in mind, here's what the research shows:

- *Females sometimes display greater verbal abilities than males, but the difference is small.* According to Eleanor Maccoby and Carol Jacklin's (1974) classic review of more than 1,500 studies, girls tend to develop verbal skills at an earlier age than boys and show a small but consistent advantage on tests of vocabulary, reading comprehension, and speech fluency. Sex differences in verbal ability have all but disappeared in more recent studies, but girls continue to achieve higher classroom grades in English (Cahan & Ganor, 1995; Feingold, 1988; Hyde & Linn, 1988; Nowell & Hedges, 1998; Wentzell, 1988).
- *Males outperform females on tests of spatial ability* (for example, arranging blocks in patterns, identifying the same figure from different angles; see Figure 12.1). Although Maccoby and Jacklin concluded in their 1974 review that these differences emerge only in adolescence, differences on some tests—especially mental rotations—can be detected in childhood and then persist across the life span

---

[1] We use the term *sex* when referring to the distinction between biological males and biological females and the term *gender* when discussing masculine and feminine traits and behavior patterns that develop as social influences interact with biology. Although many developmentalists speak of *sex roles* or *sex-role stereotypes* where we speak of *gender roles* or *gender-role stereotypes,* we believe that it is useful to emphasize through our use of terms that most differences between the sexes are not purely biological but are related as well to socialization experiences.

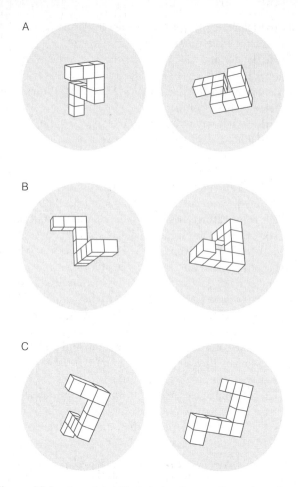

Figure 12.1 A spatial ability task. Are the two figures in each pair alike or different? The task assesses the ability to mentally rotate visual information and is a task on which average differences between males and females are quite large.

SOURCE: Shepard & Metzler (1971)

(Kerns & Berenbaum, 1991; Nordvik & Amponsah, 1998; Voyer, Voyer, & Bryden, 1995).

- Maccoby and Jacklin also concluded that males outperform females, on average, on tests of mathematical ability, starting in adolescence. However, a more recent review of the evidence by Janet Hyde and her associates (Hyde, Fennema, & Lamon, 1990) suggests that *girls actually have a slight edge in computational skills; the sexes do not differ in their understanding of math concepts; and males outperform females primarily on mathematical word problems, starting in adolescence.* The male advantage in mathematical problem-solving skills is especially clear in samples of high math performers; that is, more males than females are mathematically talented (Stumpf & Stanley, 1996). Some research shows that this male advantage is evident in the earliest grades (Mills, Ablard, & Stumpf, 1993; Nowell & Hedges, 1998; N. M. Robinson et al., 1996). As it turns out, more males than females are also *low* math achievers; on a number of cognitive ability tests, more males than females show up at both the top and the bottom of the scale (Feingold, 1992).

- *Males engage in more physical and verbal aggression than females, starting as early as age 2* (Buss & Perry, 1992; Eagly & Steffen, 1986). Males clearly commit more serious crimes (Knight, Fabes, & Higgins, 1996), but sex differences are clearer for physical aggression than for other forms of aggression. For example, females tend to specialize in subtle, indirect, and relational forms of aggression such as gossiping about and excluding others (Bjorkqvist, 1994; Crick & Bigbee, 1998).
- Even before birth and continuing throughout childhood, *boys are more physically active* than girls (Almli, Ball, & Wheeler, 2001; Eaton & Enns, 1986); they fidget and squirm more as infants and run around more as children.
- *Boys are more developmentally vulnerable,* not only to prenatal and perinatal stress (for example, they die more often before birth) but to a number of diseases and to disorders such as reading disabilities, speech defects, hyperactivity, emotional problems, and mental retardation (Henker & Whalen, 1989; Jacklin, 1989; Raz et al., 1994).
- *Girls are more compliant with the requests of adults,* though they are no more likely than boys to give in to peers (Maccoby, 1998).
- *Girls are more tactful and cooperative,* as opposed to forceful and demanding, when attempting to persuade others to comply with them (Cowan & Avants, 1988; Maccoby, 1998).
- *Both males and females report that females are more nurturant and empathic; sex differences in actual behaviors, though, are nearly nonexistent* (Deutsch, 1999; Fabes, Eisenberg, & Miller, 1990; Feingold, 1994b). Females do take more interest in and are more responsive to infants (Reid & Trotter, 1993).
- *Females are somewhat more anxious, cautious, and fearful,* though not in social situations (Feingold, 1994b). They are also more prone to develop anxiety disorders and phobias (Eichler & Parron, 1987; Myers et al., 1984).
- *Males show a small edge over females in self-esteem* (Kling et al., 1999). Overall, the largest gender difference in self-esteem is found during late adolescence.
- *Males are more likely to engage in risky behaviors,* although this varies with age and has decreased somewhat over the years (Byrnes, Miller, & Schafer, 1999).

Despite this evidence from some researchers, others take the contrasting view that even the largest of the "real" psychological differences between the sexes are trivial. For example, if you imagine all the differences in aggressiveness among individuals, from the most aggressive to the least aggressive person in a group, it turns out that only 5% of that variation can be traced to whether a person is a male or a female (Hyde, 1984); apparently, the remaining 95% of the variation is due to other differences among people. It is worth reiterating the point we made at the beginning of this section: *Average* levels of a behavior such as aggression for males and females may be noticeably different, but within each sex there are both extremely aggressive and extremely nonaggressive individuals. Thus, it is impossible to predict accurately how aggressive a person is simply by knowing his or her gender. Sex differences in most other abilities and personality traits are similarly small. Moreover, some sex differences are smaller today than they used to be (Hyde et al., 1990; Stumpf & Stanley, 1996).

Where is all the evidence that males possess agentic traits and females possess communal ones? Where is the evidence that females are more suggestible, or lack achievement motivation, or are less capable of logical thought? Most of our stereotypes of males and females are just that—overgeneralizations unsupported by fact (Maccoby & Jacklin, 1974). Females and males are far more psychologically similar than different.

Why do unfounded stereotypes persist? Partly because we, as the holders of male/female stereotypes, are biased in our perceptions. We are more likely to notice and remember behaviors that confirm our beliefs than to notice and remember exceptions, such as independent behavior in a woman or emotional sensitivity in a man (Martin & Halverson, 1981). Alice Eagly's (1987) **social-role hypothesis** suggests that differences in the roles that women and men play in society also do a lot to create and maintain gender-role stereotypes (see also Eagly & Steffen, 2000). For example, men have traditionally occupied powerful roles in business and industry that require them to be dominant and forceful. Women have more often filled the role of homemaker and therefore have been called upon to be nurturant and sensitive to their children's needs. As a result, we begin to see men as by nature "dominant" and women as by nature "nurturant." We lose sight of the fact that it is differences in the social roles they play that cause men and women to behave differently. It could be that sex differences in behavior might actually be reversed if women ran companies and men raised children.

As Eagly's social-role hypothesis suggests, we must adopt a contextual perspective on psychological differences between males and females. Sex differences that are evident in one culture or social context often are not evident in another (Deaux & Major, 1990; Feingold, 1994a). For example, women do better on tests of mathematical ability—and sometimes even outperform men—in countries like Israel, where women have excellent occupational opportunities in technical fields (Baker & Jones, 1992). This suggests that sex differences in abilities are not biologically inevitable. From a contextual perspective, it is really quite silly to speak about the "nature of women" or the "nature of men." Differences between males and females can be large or small depending on the social contexts in which they find themselves.

Although psychological sex differences are often small, however, it still makes a very real difference in our society whether one is a male or a female. First, gender norms and stereotypes, even when they are unfounded, affect how we perceive ourselves and other people. As long as people *expect* females to be less competent in math than males, for example, females may well lack confidence in their abilities and perform less competently (Eccles, Jacobs, & Harold, 1990). The fact that many stereotypes are unfounded does not make them any less potent.

In addition, even though males and females are not very different psychologically, they are still steered toward different *roles in society*. In childhood, girls and boys conform to their gender roles by segregating themselves by sex and developing different interests and play activities (Maccoby, 1998). As adolescents and adults, males and females pursue different vocations and lifestyles. Although more women are entering male-dominated fields today than in the past, they are underrepresented in many traditionally male-dominated fields, and men are not often entering female-dominated fields (U.S. Department of Labor, 2001). If you go to a college graduation ceremony today, you will still see relatively few women among the engineers and few men among the nursing graduates. More men are sharing child-rearing and household responsibilities with their partners today, but most couples still divide the labor along traditional lines, so that she is primarily responsible for child care and housework and he is primarily responsible for income and money management (Zick & McCullough, 1991). When we think about who asks whom out on a date, who stays home from work when a child has the chicken pox, or who sews the buttons back on shirts, we must conclude that, despite significant social change, traditional gender roles are alive and well!

In short, we continue to live in a society where, for better or worse, being male or female *matters*. The psychological differences between the sexes may be few and small, but the physical differences are always visible, and the roles that most men and women play in society continue to differ. Now, let's trace how girls and boys master their "gender-role curriculum" and how they apply what they learn throughout their lives.

The Infant

At birth there are very few differences, other than the obvious anatomical ones, between males and females (Maccoby & Jacklin, 1974), and even these few differences tend to be small and inconsistent. Nonetheless, it does not take long after newborns are labeled as girls or boys for gender stereotypes to affect how they are perceived and treated—and for infants themselves to notice that males and females are different.

According to Eagly's social-role theory, this man would be perceived as nurturant, warm, and caring because he has assumed the role of caregiver.

Differential Treatment

While the baby is still in the hospital delivery room or nursery, parents tend to call an infant son "big guy" or "tiger" and to comment on the vigor of his cries, kicks, and grasps. Girl infants are more likely to be labeled "sugar" or "sweetie" and to be described as soft, cuddly, and adorable (Maccoby, 1980). Even when objective examinations reveal no such differences between boys and girls at birth, adults perceive boys as strong, large featured, and coordinated while viewing girls as weaker, finer featured, and more awkward (Rubin, Provenzano, & Luria, 1974; see also Burnham & Harris, 1992; Stern & Karraker, 1989). Soon boys and girls are decked out in either blue or pink and provided with "sex-appropriate" hairstyles, toys, and room furnishings (Pomerleau et al., 1990).

In one study (Condry & Condry, 1976), college students watched a videotape of a 9-month-old infant who was introduced as either a girl ("Dana") or a boy ("David"). Students who saw "David" interpreted his strong reaction to a jack-in-the-box as "anger," whereas students who watched "Dana" concluded that the very same behavior was "fear." Although stereotyping of boys and girls from birth could be partly the effect of actual differences between the sexes (Burnham & Harris, 1992), it may also be a *cause* of such differences.

Early Learning

Yet infants are not merely the passive targets of other people's reactions to them; they are actively trying to get to know the social world around them, as well as themselves. By the end of the first year, babies can already distinguish women from men in photographs (women are the long-haired ones) and look longer when male or female voices match up properly with male or female faces than when a male voice is paired with a female face or vice versa (Fagot & Leinbach, 1993; Poulin-Dubois et al., 1994). As they begin to categorize other people as males and females, they also figure out which of these two significant social categories they themselves belong to. By 18 months of age, most toddlers seem to have an emerging understanding that they are either like other males or like other females, even if they cannot verbalize it (Lewis & Weinraub, 1979). Almost all children give verbal proof that they have acquired a basic sense of **gender identity,** or an awareness that they are either a boy or a girl, by the age of 2½ to 3 (Thompson, 1975).

As they acquire their gender identities, boys and girls are also beginning to behave differently. Boys aged 14 to 22 months usually prefer trucks and cars to other playthings, whereas girls of this age would rather play with dolls and soft toys (P. K. Smith & Daglish, 1977). Many 18- to 24-month-old toddlers will actually refuse to play with toys regarded as appropriate for the other sex—even when there are no other toys to play with (Caldera, Huston, & O'Brien, 1989). As they approach the age of 2, then, infants are already beginning to behave in ways that are considered gender appropriate in our society.

In sum, the two years of infancy lay the groundwork for later gender-role development. Because their sex is important to those around them, and because they see for themselves that males and females differ, infants begin to form categories of "male" and "female," establish a basic gender identity, and pursue "gender-appropriate" pastimes (Lewis & Weinraub, 1979).

The Child

Much of the "action" in gender-role development takes place during the toddler and preschool years. Having already come to understand their basic gender identity, young children rapidly acquire (1) gender stereotypes, or ideas about what males and females are supposedly like; and (2) gender-typed behavior patterns, or tendencies to favor "gender-appropriate" activities and behaviors over those typically associated with the other sex.

Acquiring Gender Stereotypes

Remarkable as it may seem, young children begin to learn society's gender stereotypes at about the same time they become aware of their basic gender identities. Deanna Kuhn and her associates (Kuhn, Nash, & Brucken, 1978) showed a male doll ("Michael") and a female doll ("Lisa") to children aged 2½ to 3½ and asked each child which of the two dolls would engage in various sex-stereotyped activities. Even among the 2½-year-olds, many boys and girls agreed that girls talk a lot, never hit, often need help, like to play with dolls, and like to help their mothers with chores such as cooking and cleaning. Boys, of course, like to play with cars, help their fathers, build things, and utter comments like "I can hit you." Apparently 2- and 3-year-olds know a lot already about gender stereotypes.

Over the next several years, children's heads become filled with considerably more "knowledge" about the toys and activities considered appropriate for girls or boys (Serbin, Powlishta, & Gulko, 1993; Welch-Ross & Schmidt, 1996). Gary Levy and his associates (Levy, Sadovsky, & Troseth, 2000) asked 4- and 6-year-olds whether men or women would be better in two masculine-stereotyped occupations (car mechanic and airplane pilot) and two feminine-stereotyped occupations (clothes designer and secretary). Children believed that men would be more competent than women as mechanics and pilots whereas women would make better designers and secretaries. Boys and girls also expressed positive emotions at the thought of growing up and holding gender-stereotypic occupations. They reported negative reactions, though, when asked to consider holding gender-counterstereotypic occupations.

How seriously do children take the gender-role norms and stereotypes that they are rapidly learning? It depends on how old they are. Robin Banerjee and Vicki Lintern (2000) tested the rigidity of 4- to 9-year-olds' gender-stereotypic beliefs with four brief stories in which characters had either gender-stereotypic interests (for example, a boy named Tom who was best friends with another boy and liked playing with airplanes) or gender-counterstereotypic interests (for example, a boy named John who was best friends with a girl and liked playing with doll carriages). Children were then asked whether the target child would like to play with dolls, play football, skip, or play with toy guns. Younger children (4- and 6-year-olds) were considerably more rigid in their beliefs than older children; they did not believe that boys would want to play with dolls or skip (stereotypic girl activities) or that girls would want to play with footballs or toy guns (stereotypic boy activities). Consistent with earlier research (Damon, 1977), rigidity about gender stereotypes actually increased from 4 to 6 years of age, then decreased significantly from age 6 to age 8–9. Why? Between ages 4 and 6, most children acquire a clear understanding that their sex will remain constant, making them intolerant of anyone who violates traditional gender-role standards. These norms now have the force of absolute moral laws and must be obeyed. For instance, when William Damon (1977) asked children whether a boy named George could play with dolls if he wanted to, 6-year-old Michael replied, "No sir! . . . He should stop playing with girls' dolls and start playing with G.I. Joe" (p. 255).

Why do 6- or 7-year-olds interpret gender stereotypes as though they were absolute moral rules rather than social conventions? Perhaps it is because they view any rule or custom as a natural law, like the law of gravity, that must always be correct (Carter & Patterson, 1982). Or perhaps young children must exaggerate gender roles in order to cognitively clarify these roles (Maccoby, 1998). Once their gender identities are more firmly established, children can afford to be more flexible in their thinking about what is "for boys" and what is "for girls." They still know the stereotypes, but they no longer believe as many of them (Signorella, Bigler, & Liben, 1993).

Gender-Typed Behavior

Finally, children rapidly come to behave in "gender-appropriate" ways. As we have seen, preferences for gender-appropriate toys are already detectable in infancy. Apparently, babies establish preferences for "boy" toys or "girl" toys even before they have established clear identities as males or females or can correctly label toys as "boy things" or "girl things" (Blakemore, LaRue, & Olejnik, 1979; Fagot, Leinbach, & Hagan, 1986). In childhood, preference for same-sex toys is still evident, although there are occasions when both boys and girls would like to play with "boys' toys" more than "girls' toys" (Klinger, Hamilton, & Cantrell, 2001). Moreover, children quickly come to favor same-sex playmates. Several studies show that by 30 to 36 months of age, children form new friendships primarily with same-sex partners (for example, Howes, 1988; Martin & Fabes, 2001).

During the elementary school years, boys and girls develop even stronger preferences for peers of their own sex and show increased **gender segregation,** separating themselves into boys' and girls' peer groups and interacting far more often with their own sex than with the other sex (Maccoby, 1998). Gender segregation occurs in a variety of cultures, from Kenya to India to the Philippines, and it increases with age (Leaper, 1994; Whiting & Edwards, 1988). At age 4½, children in the United States spend 3 times more time with same-sex peers than with peers of the other sex; by age 6½, they spend 11 times more time (see Figure 12.2; Maccoby & Jacklin,

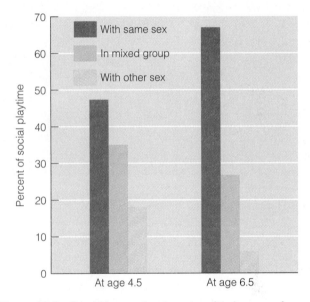

Figure 12.2 Do children prefer playmates of their own sex? Apparently so. Both boys and girls spend more time playing with same-sex peers, especially at age 6.
SOURCE: Macccoby & Jacklin (1987)

Calvin and Hobbes © 1995 Watterson. Distributed by Universal Press Syndicate. Reprinted with permission. All rights reserved.

Do boys and girls segregate themselves into same-sex play groups because they have different play styles?

ridiculed and rejected if they do not conform to it (Martin, 1990).

In sum, gender-role development proceeds with remarkable speed. By the time they enter school, children have long been aware of their basic gender identities, have acquired many stereotypes about how the sexes differ, and have come to prefer gender-appropriate activities and same-sex playmates. During middle childhood, their knowledge continues to expand as they learn more about gender-stereotyped psychological traits, but they also become more flexible in their thinking about gender roles. Their *behavior*, especially if they are boys, becomes even more gender-typed, and they segregate themselves even more from the other sex.

The Adolescent

After going their separate ways in childhood, boys and girls come together in the most intimate ways during adolescence. How do they prepare for the masculine or feminine gender roles that they will be asked to play in adulthood?

Adhering to Gender Roles

As we have just seen, young elementary school children are highly rigid in their thinking about gender roles, whereas older children think more flexibly, recognizing that gender norms are not absolute, inviolable laws. Curiously, children once again seem to become highly intolerant of certain role violations and stereotyped in their thinking about the proper roles of males and females in adolescence. They are more likely than somewhat younger children to make negative judgments about peers who violate expectations by engaging in cross-sex behavior or expressing cross-sex interests (Alfieri, Ruble, & Higgins, 1996; Sigelman, Carr, & Begley, 1986).

Consider what Trish Stoddart and Elliot Turiel (1985) found when they asked children ages 5 to 13 questions about boys who wear a barrette or put on nail polish and about girls who sport a crew cut or wear a boy's suit. Both the kindergartners and the adolescents judged these behaviors to be very wrong, whereas third- and fifth-graders viewed them far more tolerantly. Like the elementary school children, eighth-graders clearly understood that gender-role expectations are just social conventions that can easily be changed and do not necessarily apply in all societies. However, these adolescents had also begun to conceptualize gender-role violations as a sign of psychological abnormality and could not tolerate them.

Increased intolerance of deviance from gender-role expectations is tied to a larger process of **gender intensification,** in which sex differences may be magnified by hormonal changes associated with puberty and increased pressure to conform to gender roles (Boldizar, 1991; Galambos, Almeida, & Petersen, 1990; Hill & Lynch, 1983). Boys begin to see themselves as more masculine; girls emphasize their feminine side.

1987). This is due in part to incompatibilities between boys' and girls' play styles. Boys are too rowdy, domineering, and unresponsive to suit the tastes of many girls, so girls gravitate toward other girls and develop a style of interacting among themselves that is quite different from the rather timid style they adopt in the company of boys (Maccoby, 1998; Moller & Serbin, 1996).

As it turns out, children who insist most strongly on clear boundaries between the sexes and avoid consorting with "the enemy" tend to be socially competent and popular, whereas children who violate gender segregation rules tend to be less well adjusted and run the risk of being rejected by their peers (Kovacs, Parker, & Hoffman, 1996; Sroufe et al., 1993). Boys face stronger pressures to adhere to gender-role expectations than girls do. This may be why they develop stronger gender-typed preferences at earlier ages (Banerjee & Lintern, 2000; O'Brien et al., 2000). Just ask your female classmates if they were "tomboys" when they were young, and you're likely to find that about half were (Burn, O'Neil, & Nederend, 1996). But we defy you to find many male classmates who are willing to admit that they were "sissies" in their youth! The masculine role is very clearly defined in our society, and boys are

Girls often become more involved with their mothers, boys with their fathers (Crouter, Manke, & McHale, 1995). Why might this gender intensification occur? Hormonal influences may be at work, or adolescents may emphasize gender more once they mature physically and begin to look like either a man or a woman. Parents may also contribute: As children enter adolescence, mothers do more with their daughters and fathers do more with their sons (Crouter, Manke, & McHale, 1995).

Peers may be even more important. Adolescents increasingly find that they must conform to traditional gender norms in order to appeal to the other sex. A girl who was a tomboy and thought nothing of it may find, around age 12 to 13, that she must dress and behave in more "feminine" ways to attract boys and must give up her tomboyish ways (Burn et al., 1996). A boy may find that he is more popular if he projects a more sharply "masculine" image. Social pressures on adolescents to conform to traditional roles may even help explain why sex differences in cognitive abilities sometimes become more noticeable as children enter adolescence (Hill & Lynch, 1983; Roberts et al., 1990). Later in adolescence, teenagers become more comfortable with their identities as men and women and more flexible in their thinking once again (Urberg, 1979).

We have now surveyed some major milestones in gender-role development from infancy to adolescence—the development of basic gender identity in toddlerhood, gender segregation in childhood, and a return to quite rigid thinking about gender as part of gender intensification during adolescence. Now comes the most intriguing question about gender-role development in childhood and adolescence: How can it be explained?

Theories of Gender-Role Development

"Once there was a baby named Chris . . . [who] went to live on a beautiful island . . . [where] there were only boys and men; Chris was the only girl. Chris lived a very happy life on this island, but she never saw another girl or woman" (Taylor, 1996, p. 1559). Do you think Chris developed traditionally masculine or traditionally feminine characteristics? When Marianne Taylor (1996) asked children about Chris's toy preferences, occupational aspirations, and personality traits, she found that 4- to 8-year-olds took the nature side of the nature–nurture controversy: They expected Chris's biological status as a girl to determine her development. The 9- and 10-year-olds in the study emphasized the role of nurture in Chris's development, expecting her to be influenced by the masculinizing environment in which she was raised. Where do you come down in this debate, and why?

Several theories of the development of gender roles have been proposed. Some theories emphasize the role of biological differences between the sexes, whereas others emphasize social influences on children. Some emphasize what society does to children, others what children do to themselves as they try to understand gender and all its implications. Let's briefly examine a biologically oriented theory and then consider the more "social" approaches offered by psychoanalytic theory, social learning theory, cognitive developmental theory, and gender schema theory.

BIOSOCIAL THEORY

The biosocial theory of gender-role development proposed by John Money and Anke Ehrhardt (1972) calls attention to the ways in which biological events influence the development of boys and girls. But it also focuses on ways in which early biological developments influence how people *react* to a child and suggests that these social reactions then have much to do with children's assuming gender roles.

Chromosomes, Hormones, and Social Labeling.
Money and Ehrhardt stress that the male (XY) or female (XX) chromosomes most of us receive at conception are merely a starting point in biological differentiation of the sexes. A number of critical events affect a person's eventual preference for the masculine or feminine role (see also Breedlove, 1994):

1. If certain genes on the Y chromosome are present, a previously undifferentiated tissue develops into testes as the embryo develops; otherwise, it develops into ovaries.
2. The testes of a male embryo normally secrete more of the male hormone *testosterone,* which stimulates the development of a male internal reproductive system, and another hormone that inhibits the development of female organs. Without these hormones, the internal reproductive system of a female will develop from the same tissues.
3. Three to four months after conception, secretion of additional testosterone by the testes normally leads to the growth of a penis and scrotum. If testosterone is absent (as in normal females), or if a male fetus's cells are insensitive to the male sex hormones he produces, female external genitalia (labia and clitoris) will form.
4. The relative amount of testosterone alters the development of the brain and nervous system. For example, it signals the male brain to stop secreting hormones in a cyclical pattern so that males do not experience menstrual cycles at puberty.

Thus, fertilized eggs have the potential to acquire the anatomical and physiological features of either sex. Events at each critical step in the sexual differentiation process determine the outcome.

Once a biological male or female is born, social labeling and differential treatment of girls and boys interact with biological factors to steer development. Parents and other people label and begin to react to the child on the basis of the appearance of his or her genitalia. If a child's genitals are abnormal and he or she is mislabeled as a member of the other sex, this incorrect label will have an impact of its own on the child's future development. For example, if a biological male were consistently labeled and treated as a girl, he would, by about age 3, acquire the gender identity of a girl. Finally, biological factors enter the scene again at puberty when large quantities of hormones are released, stimulating the growth of the reproductive system and the appearance of secondary sex characteristics. These events, in combination with one's earlier self-concept as a male or female, provide the basis for adult gender identity and role behavior. The complex series of critical points in biological maturation and social reactions to biological changes that Money and Ehrhardt (1972) propose is diagrammed in Figure 12.3. But how much is nature, and how much is nurture?

Evidence of Biological Influences. A good deal of evidence suggests that biological factors influence the development of males and females in many species of animals (Breedlove, 1994). Evolutionary psychologists notice that most societies socialize males to have agentic traits and females to have communal ones and conclude that traditional gender roles may be a reflection of our species heredity (Archer, 1996; Buss, 1995). In addition, individual differences in masculinity and femininity may be partly genetic. Twin studies suggest that individual heredity accounts for 20–50% of the variation in the extent to which people describe themselves as having masculine and feminine psychological traits (Loehlin, 1992; Mitchell, Baker, & Jacklin, 1989). In other words, experience does not explain everything.

Biological influences on development are also evident in studies of children who are exposed to the "wrong" hormones prenatally (Ehrhardt & Baker, 1974; Money & Ehrhardt, 1972; see also Gandelman, 1992). Before the consequences were known, some mothers who had previously had problems carrying pregnancies to term were given drugs containing progestins, which are converted by the body into the male hormone testosterone. These drugs had the effect of masculinizing female fetuses so that, despite their XX genetic endowment and female internal organs, they were born with external organs that resembled those of a boy (for example, a large clitoris that

looked like a penis and fused labia that resembled a scrotum). Several of these **androgenized females** (girls exposed to excess androgens) were recognized as genetic females, underwent surgery to alter their genitals, and were then raised as girls. When Money and Ehrhardt compared them with their sisters and other girls, it became apparent that many more androgenized girls were tomboys and preferred boys' toys and vigorous activities to traditionally feminine pursuits (see also Berenbaum & Hines, 1992). As adolescents, they began dating somewhat later than other girls and felt that marriage should be delayed until they had established their careers. A high proportion (37%) described themselves as homosexual or bisexual (Money, 1985; see also Dittman, Kappes, & Kappes, 1992). Androgenized females also perform better than most other females on tests of spatial ability, further evidence that early exposure to male hormones has "masculinizing" effects on a female fetus (Kimura, 1992; Resnick et al., 1986).

In addition, male exposure to testosterone and other male hormones may be part of the reason why males are more likely than females to commit violent acts (Rubinow & Schmidt, 1996). Evidence from experiments conducted with animals is quite convincing. For example, female rhesus monkeys exposed prenatally to the male hormone testosterone often threaten other monkeys, engage in rough-and-tumble play, and try to "mount" a partner as males do at the beginning of a sexual encounter (Young, Goy, & Phoenix, 1964; Wallen, 1996). Men with high testosterone levels tend to have high rates of delinquency, drug abuse, abusiveness, and violence, although nature interacts with nurture so that these links between testosterone and antisocial behavior are not nearly as evident among men high in socioeconomic status as among men low in socioeconomic status (Dabbs & Morris, 1990).

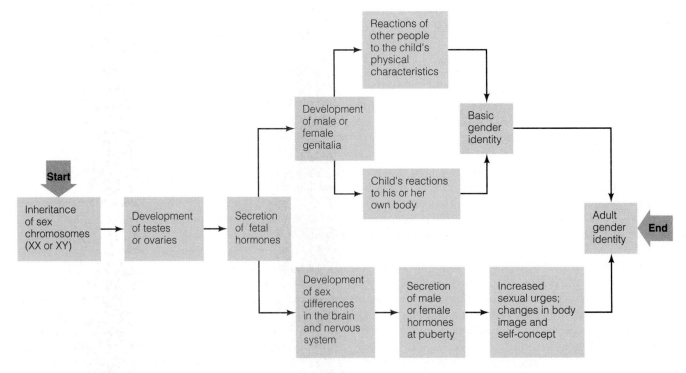

Figure 12.3   Critical events in Money and Ehrhardt's biosocial theory of gender typing
Source: Money & Ehrhardt (1972)

320   **Chapter 12**   Gender Roles and Sexuality

Is the Social Label Everything, or Is Biology Destiny?

When biological sex and social labeling conflict, which wins out? Consider the fascinating case of a male identical twin whose penis was damaged beyond repair during a botched circumcision (Money & Tucker, 1975). On the advice of John Money, the parents agreed to a surgical procedure that made their 21-month-old boy anatomically a girl. From then on, they treated him like a girl. By age 5, this boy-turned-girl was reportedly quite different from her genetically identical brother. According to John Money and the team in charge of her treatment, she most certainly knew that she was a girl; had developed strong preferences for feminine toys, activities, and apparel; and was far neater and daintier than her brother. This, then, is a vivid demonstration that the most decisive influence on gender-role development is how a child is labeled and treated during the critical period for such development. Or is it?

Milton Diamond and Keith Sigmundson (1997) followed up on this "John" turned "Joan" and found that the story had a twist ending (see also Colapinto, 1997). Joan was never really comfortable with doll play and other traditionally feminine pursuits; she preferred to dress up in men's clothing, play with her twin brother's toys, and take things apart to see how they worked. She used the jumping rope she was given to whip people and tie them up; she was miserable when she was forced to become a Girl Scout rather than a Boy Scout and make daisy chains (Colapinto, 1997). Somewhere around the age of 10, she had the distinct feeling that she was not a girl: "I began to see how different I felt and was . . . I thought I was a freak or something . . . but I didn't want to admit it. I figured I didn't want to wind up opening a can of worms" (pp. 299–300). Being rejected by other children because of her masculine looks and feminine dress and being called "cavewoman" and "gorilla" also took their toll, as did continued pressure from psychiatrists to behave in a more feminine manner. Finally, at age 14 and after years of inner turmoil and suicidal thinking, Joan had had it and simply refused to take the female hormones prescribed for her and pretend to be a girl any longer. When finally told that she was a chromosomal male, she/he was relieved: "Suddenly it all made sense why I felt the way I did. I *wasn't* some sort of weirdo" (Colapinto, 1997, p. 92). She then received male hormone shots, a double mastectomy, and surgery to construct a penis and emerged as a nice

young man who eventually dated girls, married at age 25, and appears to be comfortable with his hard-won identity as John. He now speaks out against the sex reassignment treatment that has long been applied to infants with injured or ambiguous genitals (Colapinto, 1997). This case study shows that we should back off from the conclusion that social learning is all that matters. Apparently, biology matters too.

A second source of evidence that biology matters is a study of 18 biological males in the Dominican Republic who had a genetic condition that made their cells insensitive to the effects of male hormones (Imperato-McGinley et al., 1979; see also Herdt & Davidson, 1988). They had begun life with ambiguous genitals, were mistaken for girls, and so were labeled and raised as girls. However, under the influence of male hormones produced at puberty, they sprouted beards and became entirely masculine in appearance. How, in light of Money and Ehrhardt's critical-period hypothesis, could a person possibly adjust to becoming a man after leading an entire childhood as a girl?

Amazingly, 16 of these 18 individuals seemed able to accept their late conversion from female to male and to adopt masculine lifestyles, including the establishment of heterosexual relationships. One retained a female identity and gender role, and the remaining individual switched to a male gender identity but still dressed as a female. This study also casts doubt on the notion that socialization during the first three years is critical to later gender-role development. Instead, it suggests that hormonal influences may be more important than social influences. It is possible, though, that Dominican adults, knowing that this genetic disorder was common in their society, treated these girls-turned-boys differently from other girls when they were young or that these youngsters recognized on their own that their genitals were not normal (Ehrhardt, 1985). As a result, these "girls" may never have fully committed themselves to being girls.

What studies like these of individuals with genital abnormalities appear to teach us is this: We are predisposed by our biology to develop as males or females; the first three years of life are a sensitive period perhaps, but not a critical period, for gender-role development; and *both* biology *and* social labeling contribute to gender-role development.

Because testosterone levels rise as a result of aggressive and competitive activities, it has been difficult to establish unambiguously that high concentrations of male hormones *cause* aggressive behavior in humans (Archer, 1991). Still, animal studies tell us that early experiences can alter the developing nervous systems of males and females and, in turn, their behavior (Breedlove, 1994). Much evidence now suggests that

prenatal exposure to male or female hormones has lasting effects on the organization of the brain and, in turn, on sexual behavior, aggression, cognitive abilities, and other aspects of development (Rubinow & Schmidt, 1996). Yet biology does not dictate gender-role development. Instead, *gender-role development evolves from the complex interaction of biology, social experience, and the individual's behavior.*

Evidence of Social-Labeling Influences. We must also take seriously the *social* aspect of Money and Ehrhardt's biosocial theory. How a child is labeled and treated can also have a considerable impact on gender development. For instance, some androgenized females were labeled as boys at birth and raised as such until their abnormalities were detected. Money and Ehrhardt (1972) report that the discovery and correction of this condition (by surgery and relabeling as a girl) caused few if any adjustment problems if the sex change took place *before the age of 18 months*. After age 3, sexual reassignment was exceedingly difficult because these genetic females had experienced prolonged masculine gender typing and had already labeled themselves as boys. These findings led Money and Ehrhardt to conclude that there is a *critical period* (between 18 months and 3 years) for the establishment of gender identity when the label society attaches to the child is likely to "stick." Yet some studies in which infants are presented to some people as boys but to others as girls indicate that labeling itself has little impact on how people perceive and treat these infants (Stern & Karraker, 1989). And, as the Explorations box on page 321 shows, biological males who are labeled as girls during the so-called critical period sometimes adopt a male gender identity later in life despite their early labeling and socialization, suggesting that we should speak of a *sensitive* rather than a critical period.

In sum, Money and Ehrhardt's biosocial theory stresses the importance of early biological developments that influence how parents and other social agents label a child at birth and that possibly also affect behavior more directly. Whether children are labeled and socialized as boys or girls also influences their gender-role development. In short, biological and social factors interact.

PSYCHOANALYTIC THEORY

As is true of thinking about most areas of development, thinking about gender-role development was shaped early on by Freud's psychosexual theory. The 3- to 6-year-old child in Freud's phallic stage is said to harbor a strong, biologically based love for the parent of the other sex, experience internal conflict and anxiety as a result of this incestuous desire, and resolve the conflict through a process of **identification** with the same-sex parent. According to Freud, a boy experiencing his **Oedipus complex** loves his mother, fears that his father will retaliate by castrating him, and ultimately is forced to identify with his father, thereby emulating his father and adopting his father's attitudes and behaviors. Freud believed that a boy would show weak masculinity later in life if his father was inadequate as a masculine model, was often absent from the home, or was not dominant or threatening enough to foster a strong identification based on fear.

Meanwhile, a preschool-age girl is said to experience an **Electra complex** involving a desire for her father (and envy of him for the penis she lacks) and a rivalry with her mother. To resolve her unconscious conflict, she identifies with her mother. Her father also contributes to gender-role development by reinforcing her for "feminine" behavior resembling that of her mother. Thus, Freud emphasized the role of emo-

tions (love, fear, and so on) in motivating gender-role development and argued that children adopt their roles by patterning themselves after their same-sex parents.

We can applaud Freud for identifying the preschool years as a critical time for gender-role development. In addition, his view that boys, because of fear of castration, have a more powerful motivation than girls to adopt their gender role is consistent with the finding that boys seem to learn gender stereotypes and gender-typed behaviors faster and more completely than girls do. It is also true that boys whose fathers are absent from the home tend to be less traditionally sex-typed than other boys (Stevenson & Black, 1988). Finally, Freud's notion that fathers play an important role in the gender typing of their daughters as well as their sons has been confirmed (Parke, 1996).

On other counts, however, psychoanalytic theory has not fared well. Many preschool children are so ignorant of male and female anatomy that it is hard to see how most boys could fear castration or most girls could experience penis envy (Bem, 1989). Moreover, Freud assumed that a boy's identification with his father is based on fear, but most researchers find that boys identify most strongly with fathers who are warm

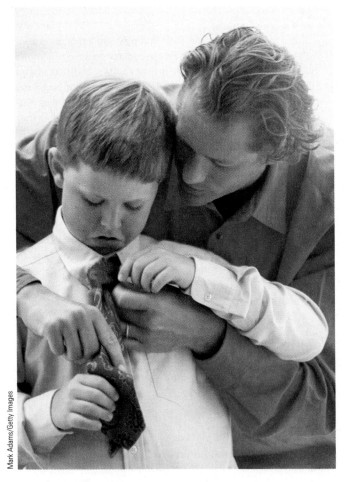

Mark Adams/Getty Images

According to psychoanalytic theory, children become appropriately "masculine" or "feminine" through identification with the same-sex parent. Social learning theorists call this same process observational learning.

and nurturant rather than overly punitive and threatening (Hetherington & Frankie, 1967; Mussen & Rutherford, 1963). Finally, children are not especially similar psychologically to their same-sex parents (Maccoby & Jacklin, 1974). Apparently, other individuals besides parents influence a child's gender-related characteristics. It seems we must look elsewhere for more complete explanations of gender-role development.

SOCIAL LEARNING THEORY

According to social learning theorists such as Albert Bandura (1986) and Walter Mischel (1970), children learn masculine or feminine identities, preferences, and behaviors in two ways. First, through *differential reinforcement*, children are rewarded for sex-appropriate behaviors and punished for behaviors considered more appropriate for members of the other sex. Second, through *observational learning*, children adopt the attitudes and behaviors of same-sex models. In this view, a child's gender-role development depends on which of his or her behaviors people reinforce or punish and on what sorts of social models are available. Change the social environment, and you change the course of gender-role development.

Differential Reinforcement. Parents do use differential reinforcement to teach boys how to be boys and girls how to be girls (Lytton & Romney, 1991). Beverly Fagot and Mary Leinbach (1989), for example, have found that parents are already encouraging sex-appropriate play and discouraging cross-sex play during the second year of life, before children have acquired their basic gender identities or display clear preferences for male or female activities. By the tender age of 20 to 24 months, daughters are reinforced for dancing, dressing up (as women), following their parents around, asking for help, and playing with dolls; they are discouraged from manipulating objects, running, jumping, and climbing. By contrast, sons are often reprimanded for such "feminine" behavior as playing with dolls or seeking help and are often actively encouraged to play with "masculine" toys such as blocks, trucks, and push-and-pull toys (Fagot, 1978). Mothers and fathers may also discipline their sons and daughters differently, with fathers more likely to use physical forms of discipline (such as spanking) than mothers and mothers more likely to use reasoning to explain rules and consequences (Conrade & Ho, 2001; Russell et al., 1998). In addition, boys end up on the receiving end of a spanking more often than girls do (Day & Peterson, 1998).

Does this "gender curriculum" in the home influence children? It certainly does. Parents who show the clearest patterns of differential reinforcement have children who are relatively quick to label themselves as girls or boys and to develop strongly sex-typed toy and activity preferences (Fagot & Leinbach, 1989; Fagot, Leinbach, & O'Boyle, 1992). It turns out that fathers play a central role in gender socialization; they are more likely than mothers to reward children's gender-appropriate behavior and to discourage behavior considered more appropriate for the other sex (Leve & Fagot, 1997; Lytton & Romney, 1991). Women who choose nontraditional professions are more likely than women in traditionally female fields to have had fathers who encouraged them to be as-

sertive and competitive (Coats & Overman, 1992). Fathers, then, seem to be an especially important influence on the gender-role development of both sons and daughters.

Could differential treatment of boys and girls by parents also contribute to sex differences in ability? Possibly so. Jacquelynne Eccles and her colleagues (1990) have conducted a number of studies to determine why girls tend to shy away from math and science courses and are underrepresented in occupations that involve math and science (see also Benbow & Arjmand, 1990). They suggest that parental expectations about sex differences in mathematical ability become self-fulfilling prophecies. The plot goes something like this:

1. Parents, influenced by societal stereotypes about sex differences in ability, expect their sons to outperform their daughters in math.
2. Parents attribute their sons' successes in math to ability but credit their daughters' successes to hard work. These attributions for performance further reinforce the belief that girls lack mathematical talent and turn in respectable performances only through plodding effort.
3. Children begin to internalize their parents' views, so that girls come to believe that they are "no good" in math.
4. Thinking that they lack ability, girls become less interested in math, less likely to take math courses, and less likely than boys to pursue career possibilities that involve math after high school.

In short, parents who expect their daughters to have trouble with numbers get what they expect. The negative effects of low parental expectancies on girls' self-perceptions are evident even when boys and girls perform equally well on tests of math aptitude and attain similar grades in math (Eccles et al., 1990). Girls whose parents are nontraditional in their gender-role attitudes and behaviors do not show the declines in math and science achievement in early adolescence that girls from more traditional families display, so apparently the chain of events Eccles describes can be broken (Updegraff, McHale, & Crouter, 1996).

Peers, like parents, reinforce boys and girls differentially (Beal, 1994). As Beverly Fagot (1985) discovered, boys only 21 to 25 months of age belittle and disrupt each other for playing with "feminine" toys or with girls, and girls express their disapproval of other girls who choose to play with boys. Some scholars believe peers contribute at least as much to gender typing as parents do (Beal, 1994). And, as we see in the Explorations box on page 324, teachers may contribute too by paying more attention to boys than to girls.

Observational Learning. Not only do social learning theorists call attention to differential treatment of girls and boys by parents, peers, and teachers, but they emphasize that observational learning also contributes in important ways to gender typing. Children see which toys and activities are "for girls" and which are "for boys" and imitate individuals of their own sex. At about the age of 6 or 7, children begin to pay much closer attention to same-sex models than to other-sex models; for example, they will choose toys that members of

Are Single-Sex Schools Good for Girls?

Cassy Cohen/PhotoEdit

To what extent do teachers treat girls and boys differently in the classroom? We can probably all think of instances in which teachers subtly communicate that boys and girls are different—for example, when teachers ask the boys in the room to help move furniture for the class party but the girls to pour punch. Some scholars feel that sexist treatment in the classroom undermines the confidence and achievement of girls (Beal, 1994). What does research tell us?

A number of studies suggest that teachers pay more attention to boys than to girls (Beal, 1994; Jussim & Eccles, 1992; Sadker & Sadker, 1994). Teachers call on boys more often and give them more feedback. It's not that boys are praised more than girls; instead, they tend to receive both more positive and more negative feedback (Brody, 1985; Hamilton et al., 1991). A good part of the attention they receive is occasioned by their troublemaking, but attention, positive or negative, may signal to girls that boys matter more than they do.

Concerned that girls are being held back academically by this differential treatment, some scholars and educators argue forcefully that girls would be better off in all-girl schools or classrooms than in co-ed ones, and some school systems are experimenting with same-sex education (Sadker & Sadker, 1994). What does the evidence tell us here? Some early studies suggested that all-girl schooling was indeed advantageous to girls (Lee & Bryk, 1986). However, these studies often did not control properly for differences between the students and educational programs in same-sex and co-ed schools. More recent and more carefully designed studies of students attending Catholic schools find few differences in school-related attitudes and levels of achievement (LePore & Warren, 1997; Marsh, 1989; Signorella, Frieze, & Hershey, 1996). In a 1997 study of all-girl, all-boy, and co-ed Catholic high schools, for example, students in single-sex schools generally did no better than students in co-ed schools. The few differences that were observed suggested that boys benefit more academically from same-sex schooling than girls do (LePore & Warren, 1997). It seems, then, that all-girl schooling is not as beneficial as some educators believe; perhaps the reason is that sexist treatment of girls (and boys too) can occur in any type of school (Lee, Marks, & Byrd, 1994).

their own sex prefer even if it means passing up more attractive toys (Frey & Ruble, 1992). Children who see their mothers perform so-called masculine tasks and their fathers perform household and child care tasks tend to be less aware of gender stereotypes and less gender typed than children who are exposed to traditional gender-role models at home (Turner & Gervai, 1995). Similarly, boys with sisters and girls with brothers have less gender-typed activity preferences than children who grow up with same-sex siblings (Colley et al., 1996; Rust et al., 2000).

Not only do children learn by watching the children and adults with whom they interact, but they also learn from the media—radio, television, movies, magazines—and even from their picture books and elementary school readers. Although sexism in children's picture books has decreased over the past 50 years, it is still the case that male characters are more likely than female characters to engage in active, independent activities such as climbing, riding bikes, and making things, whereas female characters are more often depicted as passive, dependent, and helpless, spending their time picking flowers, playing quietly indoors, and "creating problems that require masculine solutions" (Kortenhaus & Demarest, 1993; and see Turner-Bowker, 1996).

It is similar in the world of television: Male characters dominate in children's programs, prime-time programs, and advertisements (Barner, 1999; Furnham & Mak, 1999). Typically, men are influential individuals who work at a profession, whereas many women—especially those portrayed as married—are passive, emotional creatures who manage a home or work at "feminine" occupations such as nursing (Signorielli & Kahlenberg, 2001). Women portrayed as single are often cast in traditionally male occupations. The message children receive is that men work regardless of their marital status and they do important business, but women only work at important jobs if they are single (Signorielli & Kahlenberg, 2001). Children who watch a large amount of television are more likely to choose gender-appropriate toys and to hold stereotyped views of males and females than their classmates who watch little television (McGhee & Frueh, 1980; Signorielli & Lears, 1992). As more women play detectives and more men raise families on television, children's notions of female and male roles are likely to change. Indeed, watching nonsexist programs is associated with holding less stereotyped views of the sexes (Rosenwasser, Lingenfelter, & Harrington, 1989; Signorielli, 1990).

In sum, there is much evidence that both differential reinforcement and observational learning contribute to gender-role development. However, social learning theorists have often portrayed children as the passive recipients of external influences: Parents, peers, television characters, and others show them what to do and reinforce them for doing it. Perhaps this perspective does not put enough emphasis on what children *themselves* contribute to their own gender socialization. Youngsters do not receive gender-stereotyped birthday presents simply because their parents foist those toys upon them. In fact, parents tend to select gender-neutral and often educational toys for their children, but their boys beg for trucks and their girls for tea sets (C. C. Robinson & Morris, 1986)!

COGNITIVE THEORY

Some theorists have emphasized cognitive aspects of gender-role development, noting that as children acquire understanding of gender, they actively teach themselves to be girls or boys. Lawrence Kohlberg based his cognitive theory on Piaget's cognitive developmental theory, whereas Martin and Halverson based their theory on an information-processing approach to cognitive development.

Cognitive Developmental Theory. Lawrence Kohlberg (1966) proposed a cognitive theory of gender typing that is quite different from the other theories we have considered and helps explain why boys and girls adopt traditional gender roles even when their parents do not want them to do so. Among Kohlberg's major themes are these:

1. Gender-role development depends on stagelike changes in cognitive development; children must acquire certain understandings about gender before they will be influenced by their social experiences.
2. Children engage in *self-socialization;* instead of being the passive targets of social influence, they actively socialize themselves.

According to both psychoanalytic theory and social learning theory, children are influenced by their companions to adopt "male" or "female" roles and *then* come to view themselves as girls or boys and to identify with (or habitually imitate) same-sex models. Kohlberg suggests that children *first* come to understand that they are girls or boys and then actively seek out same-sex models and a wide range of information about how to act like a girl or a boy. To Kohlberg, it's not "I'm treated like a boy; therefore, I must be a boy." It's more like "I'm a boy, and so now I'll do everything I can to find out how to behave like one."

What understandings are necessary before children will teach themselves to behave like boys or girls? Kohlberg believes that children everywhere progress through the following three stages as they acquire an understanding of what it means to be a female or male:

1. Basic gender identity is established by age 2 or 3, when the child recognizes that he or she is a male or a female.
2. Somewhat later, the child also acquires **gender stability**—that is, comes to understand that this gender identity is stable *over time*. Boys invariably become men, and girls grow up to be women.
3. The gender concept is complete, somewhere between the ages of 5 and 7, when the child achieves **gender consistency** and realizes that one's sex is also stable *across situations*. Now, children know that one's sex cannot be altered by superficial changes such as dressing up as a member of the other sex or engaging in cross-sex activities.

Children 3 to 5 years of age often do lack the concepts of gender stability and gender consistency; they often claim that a boy could become a mommy if he really wanted to or that a girl could become a boy if she cut her hair and wore a hockey uniform (Warin, 2000). As children enter Piaget's concrete operational stage of cognitive development and come to grasp concepts like conservation of liquids, they also realize that gender is conserved despite changes in appearance. In support of Kohlberg's theory, Warin (2000) found that children who have achieved the third level of understanding display more gender-stereotypic play preferences than children without gender consistency. In addition, children have been shown to progress through Kohlberg's three stages in a variety of cultures, which suggests that cognitive maturation is an important influence on the child's emerging understanding of gender (Munroe, Shimmin, & Munroe, 1984).

Criticisms? Sandra Bem (1989) has shown that children need not reach the concrete operations stage to understand gender stability and consistency if they have sufficient knowledge of male and female anatomy to realize that it is one's genitals that make one a male or a female. The most controversial aspect of Kohlberg's cognitive developmental theory, though, has been his claim that only when children fully grasp that their biological sex is unchangeable, at the age of 5 to 7, do they actively seek out same-sex models and attempt to acquire values, interests, and behaviors that are consistent with their cognitive judgments about themselves. Although some evidence supports Kohlberg, this chapter shows that children learn many gender-role stereotypes and develop clear preferences for same-sex activities and playmates long before they master the concepts of gender stability and gender consistency and then attend more selectively to same-sex models (Ruble & Martin, 1998). It seems that only a rudimentary understanding of gender is required before children learn gender stereotypes and preferences.

Gender Schema Theory. Carol Martin and Charles Halverson (1981, 1987) have proposed a somewhat different cognitive theory, an information-processing one, that overcomes the key weakness of Kohlberg's theory. Like Kohlberg, they believe that children are intrinsically motivated to acquire values, interests, and behaviors that are consistent with their cognitive judgments about the self. However, Martin and Halverson argue that self-socialization begins as soon as children acquire a *basic* gender identity, at the age of 2 or 3. According to their *schematic-processing model*, children acquire **gender schemata**—organized sets of beliefs and expec-

tations about males and females that influence the kinds of information they will attend to and remember.

First, children acquire a simple *in-group/out-group schema* that allows them to classify some objects, behaviors, and roles as appropriate for males and others as appropriate for females (for example, cars are for boys, girls can cry but boys should not, and so on). Then, they seek out more elaborate information about the role of their own sex, constructing an *own-sex schema*. Thus, a young girl who knows her basic gender identity might first learn that sewing is for girls and building model airplanes is for boys. Then, because she is a girl and wants to act consistently with her own self-concept, she gathers a great deal of information about sewing to add to her own-sex schema, largely ignoring any information that comes her way about how to build model airplanes (see Figure 12.4).

Consistent with this schematic-processing theory, children do appear to be especially interested in learning about objects or activities that fit their own-sex schemata. In one study, 4- to 9-year-olds were given boxes of gender-neutral objects (hole punches, burglar alarms, and so on) and were told that some objects were "girl" items and some were "boy" items (Bradbard et al., 1986). Boys explored "boy" items more than girls did, and girls explored "girl" items more than boys did. A week later, the children easily recalled which items were for boys and which were for girls; they had apparently sorted the objects according to their "in-group/out-group" schemata. In addition, boys recalled more in-depth information about "boy" items than did girls, whereas girls recalled more than boys about these very same objects if they had been labeled "girl" items. If children's information-gathering efforts are indeed guided by their own-sex schemata in this way, we can easily see how boys and girls might acquire very different stores of knowledge as they develop.

Once gender schemata are in place, children will actually distort new information in memory so that it is consistent with

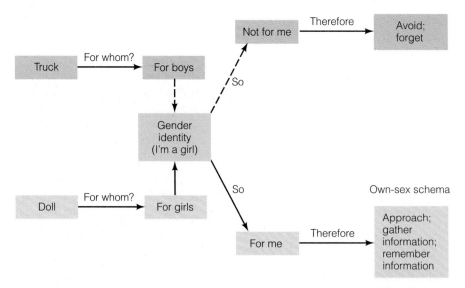

Figure 12.4 Gender schema theory in action. A young girl classifies new information according to an "in-group/out-group schema" as either "for boys" or "for girls." Information about boys' toys and activities is ignored, but information about toys and activities for girls is relevant to the self and so is added to an ever-larger "own-sex schema."

SOURCE: Adapted from Martin & Halverson in Carter (1987)

Table 12.2   An Integrative Overview of the Gender-Typing Process

Developmental Period	Events and Outcomes	Pertinent Theory(ies)
Prenatal period	The fetus develops male or female genitalia, which others will react to once the child is born.	Bisocial
Birth to 3 years	Parents and other companions label the child as a boy or a girl and begin to encourage gender-consistent behavior while discouraging cross-sex activities. As a result of these social experiences and the development of very basic classification skills, the young child acquires some gender-typed behavioral preferences and the knowledge that he or she is a boy or a girl (basic gender identity).	Social learning
3 to 6 years	Once children acquire a basic gender identity, they begin to seek information about sex differences, form gender schemata, and actively try to behave in ways viewed as "appropriate" for their own sex.	Gender schema
7 to puberty	Children finally acquire the concepts of gender stability and consistency, recognizing that they will be males or females all their lives and in all situations. At this point, they begin to look closely at the behavior of same-sex models in order to acquire attributes consistent with their firm categorization of themselves as male or female.	Cognitive developmental
Puberty and beyond	The biological changes of adolescence, along with social pressures, cause an intensification of gender differences and stimulate formation of an adult gender identity.	Biosocial Social learning Gender schema Cognitive developmental

their schemata (Liben & Signorella, 1993; Martin & Halverson, 1983). For example, Martin and Halverson (1983) showed 5- and 6-year-olds pictures of children performing gender-consistent activities (for example, a boy playing with a truck) and pictures of children performing gender-inconsistent activities (for example, a girl sawing wood). A week later, the children easily recalled the sex of the actor when activities were gender-consistent; when an actor's behavior was gender-inconsistent, though, children often distorted the scene to make it gender-consistent (for example, by saying that it was a boy, not a girl, who had sawed wood). This research gives us some insight into why inaccurate gender stereotypes persist. The child who believes that women cannot be doctors may be introduced to a female doctor but is likely to remember meeting a nurse and still insist that women cannot be doctors!

AN ATTEMPT AT INTEGRATION

The biosocial, social learning, and cognitive perspectives all contribute to our understanding of sex differences and gender-role development. The biosocial model offered by Money and Ehrhardt notes the importance of biological developments that influence how people label and treat a child. Yet socialization agents—not only parents, as noted by Freud, but also siblings, peers, and teachers, as noted by social learning theorists—are teaching children how to be girls or boys well before they even understand that they *are* girls or boys. Differences in social learning experiences may also help explain why, even though virtually all children form gender concepts and schemata, some children are far more gender-typed than others in their preferences and activities (Serbin et al., 1993).

Kohlberg's cognitive developmental theory and Martin and Halverson's gender schema approach convince us that cognitive growth and self-socialization processes also contribute to gender-role development. Once children acquire a basic gender identity as a boy or a girl and form gender schemata, they become highly motivated to learn their appropriate roles. When they finally grasp, at age 5 to 7, that their sex will never change, they become even more determined to learn their gender roles and pay special attention to same-sex models. Parents who want to avoid socializing their children into traditional gender roles are often amazed to see their children turn into traditional girls and boys all on their own.

In short, children have a male or female biological endowment that helps guide their development, are influenced by other people from birth on to become "real boys" or "real girls," and actively socialize themselves to behave in ways that seem consistent with their understandings that they are either boys or girls (see Table 12.2). Most developmentalists today would agree that what children learn regarding how to be males or females depends on an interaction between biological factors and social influences. Thus, we must respect the role of genes and hormones in gender-role development but also view this process from a contextual perspective and appreciate that the patterns of male and female development that we observe in our society today are not inevitable. In another era, in another culture, the process of gender-role socialization could produce quite different kinds of boys and girls.

The Adult

You might think that once children and adolescents have learned their gender roles, they simply play them out during adulthood. Instead, as people face the challenges of adult life and enter new social contexts, their gender roles and their concepts of themselves as men and women change.

Gender Roles

Although males and females fill their masculine or feminine roles throughout their lives, the specific content of those roles changes considerably over the life span. The young boy may act out his masculine role by playing with trucks or wrestling with his buddies; the grown man may play his role by holding down a job. Moreover, the degree of difference between male and female roles also changes. Children and adolescents do adopt behaviors consistent with their "boy" or "girl" roles, but the two sexes otherwise adopt quite similar roles in society—namely, those of children and students. Even as they enter adulthood, males' and females' roles do not differ much, because members of both sexes are often single and in school or working.

However, the roles of men and women become more distinct when they marry and, especially, when they have children. In most couples, for example, the wife typically does more housework than her husband, whether or not she is employed—about 17 to 18 hours per week for her compared to 10 hours for him (Bianchi et al., 2000). If this doesn't seem like a large discrepancy on a weekly basis, consider that over the course of one year, wives contribute more than 400 hours more to housework than their husbands do. By their silver wedding anniversary, she will have logged about 10,000 more hours than he has! Further, specific tasks tend to be parceled out along traditional lines—she doing the cooking, he taking out the garbage (Bianchi et al., 2000). The birth of a child tends to make even quite egalitarian couples divide their labors in more traditional ways than they did before the birth (Cowan & Cowan, 2000). It is she who becomes primarily responsible for child care and household tasks; he tends to emphasize his role as "breadwinner" and center his energies on providing for the family. Even as men today increase their participation in child care and housework, they still tend to play a "helper" role and spend only two-thirds as much time with their children as women do (Bianchi, 2000).

What happens after the children are grown? The roles played by men and women become more similar again starting in middle age, when the nest empties and child care responsibilities end. The similarity between gender roles continues to increase as adults enter old age; as retirees and grandparents, men and women lead similar lives. It would seem, then, that the roles of men and women are fairly similar before marriage, maximally different during the child-rearing years, and more similar again later on (Gutmann, 1997).

Do these sorts of shifts in the roles played by men and women during adulthood affect them psychologically? Let's see.

Masculinity, Femininity, and Androgyny

For many years, psychologists assumed that masculinity and femininity were at opposite ends of a continuum. If one possessed highly masculine traits, one must be very unfeminine; being highly feminine implied being unmasculine. Sandra Bem (1974) challenged this assumption by arguing that individuals of either sex can be characterized by psychological **androgyny**—that is, by a balancing or blending of *both* desirable masculine-stereotyped traits (being assertive, analytical, forceful, independent) and desirable feminine-stereotyped traits (being affectionate, compassionate, gentle, understanding). In Bem's model, then, masculinity and femininity are *two separate dimensions* of personality. A male or female who has many desirable masculine-stereotyped traits and few feminine ones is defined as a *masculine sex-typed* person. One who has many feminine- and few masculine-stereotyped traits is said to be *feminine sex-typed*. The *androgynous* person possesses both masculine and feminine traits, whereas the *undifferentiated* individual lacks both these kinds of attributes (see Figure 12.5).

How many of us are androgynous? Bem (1974, 1979) and other investigators (Spence & Helmreich, 1978) have developed self-perception inventories that contain both a masculinity (or instrumentality) scale and a femininity (or expressivity) scale. In one large sample of college students (Spence & Helmreich, 1978), roughly 33% of the test takers were "masculine" men or "feminine" women; about 30% were androgynous, and the remaining individuals were either undifferentiated (low on both scales) or "sex-reversed" (masculine sex-typed females or feminine sex-typed males). Around 30% of children can also be classified as androgynous (Boldizar, 1991; Hall & Halberstadt, 1980). Although constructed in the 1970s, these inventories remain valid measures of gender roles today (Holt & Ellis, 1998). Androgynous individuals do indeed exist, and in sizable numbers. But do perceived masculinity, femininity, and androgyny change over the adult years?

CHANGES WITH AGE

David Gutmann (1987, 1997) has offered the intriguing hypothesis that gender roles and gender-related traits in adulthood are shaped by what he calls the **parental imperative**—the requirement that mothers and fathers adopt different roles in order to raise children successfully. Drawing on his own cross-cultural research and that of others, he suggests that in many cultures, young and middle-aged men must emphasize their "masculine" qualities in order to feed and protect their families, whereas young and middle-aged women must express their "feminine" qualities in order to nurture the young and meet the emotional needs of their families.

According to Gutmann, all this changes dramatically starting in midlife, when men and women are freed from the demands of the parental imperative. Men become less active and more passive, take less interest in community affairs, and focus more on religious contemplation and family relationships. They also become more sensitive and emotionally expressive. Women, meanwhile, are changing in precisely the opposite direction. After being passive, submissive, and nurturing in their younger years, they become more active, domineering, and assertive in later life. In many cultures, they take charge of the household after being the underlings of their mothers-in-law and become stronger forces in their communities. In short, Gutmann's parental imperative hypothesis

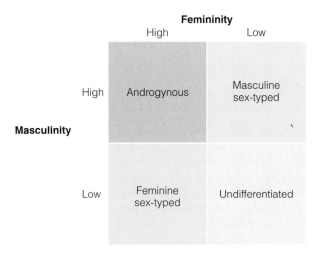

Femininity

	High	Low
Masculinity High	Androgynous	Masculine sex-typed
Masculinity Low	Feminine sex-typed	Undifferentiated

Figure 12.5 Categories of gender-role orientation based on viewing masculinity and feminity as separate dimensions of personality.

states that, over the course of adulthood, psychologically "masculine" men become "feminine" men and "feminine" women become "masculine" women—that the psychological traits of the two sexes flip-flop.

A similar but somewhat different hypothesis is that adults experience a midlife **androgyny shift.** Instead of giving up traits they had as young adults, men and women retain their gender-typed qualities but add to them qualities traditionally associated with the other sex; that is, they become more androgynous. Ideas along this line were proposed some time ago by the psychoanalytic theorist Carl Jung (1933), who believed that we have masculine and feminine sides all along but learn to integrate them and express both facets of our human nature only in middle age. Let's see how these ideas have fared.

What age differences do researchers find when they administer masculinity and femininity scales to men and women of different ages? In one study, Shirley Feldman and her asso-

ciates (Feldman, Biringen, & Nash, 1981) gave Bem's androgyny inventory to individuals at eight different stages of the family life cycle. Consistent with Gutmann's notion of a parental imperative, taking on the role of parent seemed to lead men to perceive themselves as more masculine in personality and women to perceive themselves as having predominantly feminine strengths (see also Abrahams, Feldman, & Nash, 1978). Among adults who were beyond their parenting years, especially among grandparents, sex differences in self-perceptions were smaller. Contrary to Gutmann's hypothesis, however, grandfathers did not replace their masculine traits with feminine traits, and grandmothers did not become less feminine and more masculine. Instead, both sexes appeared to experience an androgyny shift: Grandfathers retained their masculine traits while gaining feminine attributes, and grandmothers retained their feminine traits while taking on masculine attributes as well (see also Wink & Helson, 1993). This finding is particularly interesting in view of the fact that today's older people should, if anything, be *more* traditionally gender-typed than younger adults who have grown up in an era of more flexible gender norms.

In sum, young adults who are not parents are relatively androgynous, the parenting role brings out traditionally sex-typed traits in both men and women, and androgyny once again emerges when the parenting years are over. These changes in gender-role orientations during adulthood appear to be related more to the roles men and women play than to how old they are, as Alice Eagly's social-role hypothesis would predict. For example, young mothers are more psychologically feminine than nonmothers of the same age (Feldman et al., 1981), and working women are more assertive and independent than nonworking women (Wink & Helson, 1993). Again, we must adopt a contextual perspective on gender-role development and appreciate that males and females can develop in any number of different directions depending on their social, cultural, and historical context and on the social roles they play.

After the androgyny shift, women may feel freer to express their "masculine" side, and men may express "feminine" qualities that they suppressed during the parenting years.

Changing Gender-Role Attitudes and Behavior

Some people believe that the world would be a better place if boys and girls were no longer socialized to adopt traditional masculine or feminine roles, interests, and behaviors. Children of both sexes would then have the freedom to be androgynous; women would no longer suffer from a lack of assertiveness in the world of work, and men would no longer be forced to suppress their emotions. Just how successful are efforts to encourage more flexible gender roles?

In a number of projects designed to change gender-role behavior, children have been exposed to nonsexist films, encouraged to imitate models of cross-sex behavior, reinforced by teachers for trying out cross-sex activities, and provided with nonsexist educational materials (Katz, 1986; Katz & Walsh, 1991). For example, Rebecca Bigler and Lynn Liben (1990) reasoned that if they could alter children's gender stereotypes, they could head off the biased information processing that stereotypes promote. They exposed 6- to 11-year-olds to a series of problem-solving discussions emphasizing that (1) the most important considerations in deciding who could perform well in such traditionally masculine or feminine occupations as construction worker and beautician are the person's interests and willingness to learn and (2) the person's gender is irrelevant. Compared to children who received no such training, program participants showed a clear decline in occupational stereotyping, especially if they had entered the study with firm ideas about which jobs are for women and which are for men. Moreover, this reduction in stereotyping brought about the predicted decrease in biased information processing: Participants were more likely than nonparticipants to remember counterstereotypic information presented to them in stories (for example, recalling that the "garbage man" in a story was actually a woman).

Yet many efforts at change that work in the short run fail to have lasting effects. Children encouraged to interact in mixed-sex groups revert to their preference for same-sex friends as soon as the program ends (Lockheed, 1986; Serbin, Tonick, & Sternglanz, 1977). Why is it so difficult to change children's thinking? Perhaps because children are groomed for their traditional gender roles from birth and are bombarded with traditional gender-role messages every day. A short-term intervention project may have little chance of succeeding in this larger context. If, on the other hand, the broad social changes of the 20th century continue, children may all react as one 13-year-old did when asked whether a new mother of her acquaintance had delivered a boy or a girl: "Why do you want to know?" (Lorber, 1986, p. 567).

IS ANDROGYNY ADVANTAGEOUS?

If a person can be both assertive and sensitive, both independent and understanding, being androgynous sounds psychologically healthy. Is it? College students—both males and females—believe that the ideal person is androgynous (Slavkin & Stright, 2000). Bem (1975, 1978) demonstrated that androgynous men and women behave more flexibly than more sex-typed individuals. For example, androgynous people, like masculine sex-typed people, can display the "masculine" agentic trait of independence by resisting social pressure to conform to undesirable group activities. Yet they are as likely as feminine sex-typed individuals to display the "feminine" communal trait of nurturance by interacting positively with a baby. Androgynous people seem to be highly adaptable, able to adjust their behavior to the demands of the situation at hand (Shaffer, Pegalis, & Cornell, 1992). Perhaps this is why androgynous parents are viewed as warmer and more supportive than nonandrogynous parents (Witt, 1997). In addition, androgynous individuals appear to enjoy higher self-esteem and are perceived as better adjusted than their traditionally sex-typed peers, though this is largely because of the masculine qualities they possess (Boldizar, 1991; Spence & Hall, 1996).

Before we jump to the conclusion that androgyny is a thoroughly desirable attribute, can you imagine any disadvantages of androgyny? During *childhood*, expressing too many of the traits considered more appropriate in the other sex can result in rejection by peers and low self-esteem (Lobel, Slone, & Winch, 1997). It may be premature, then, to conclude that it is better in all respects to be androgynous rather than either masculine or feminine in orientation. Still, we can at least conclude that it is unlikely to be damaging for men to become a little more "feminine" or for women to become a little more "masculine" than they have traditionally been. The Applications box above looks at whether researchers have had any success in changing gender-role attitudes and behavior.

Sexuality over the Life Span

A central part of the process of becoming a woman or a man is the process of becoming a sexual being, so it is appropriate that we examine sexual development here. It is a lifelong process that starts in infancy.

Are Infants Sexual Beings?

Sigmund Freud made the seemingly outrageous claim that humans are sexual beings from birth onward. We are born, he said, with a reserve of sexual energy that is redirected toward different parts of the body as we develop. Freud may have been wrong about some things, but he was quite right that infants are sexual beings.

Babies are, of course, biologically equipped at birth with male or female chromosomes, hormones, and genitals. Moreover, young infants in Freud's oral stage of development *do* appear to derive pleasure from sucking, mouthing, biting, and other oral activities. But the clincher is this: Both male babies and female babies have been observed to touch and manipulate their genital areas, to experience physical arousal, and to undergo what appear to be orgasms (Deda et al., 2001; Leung & Robson, 1993). Parents in some cultures, well aware of the pleasure infants derive from their genitals, occasionally use genital stimulation as a means of soothing fussy babies (Ford & Beach, 1951).

What should we make of this infant sexuality? Infants feel bodily sensations, but they are hardly aware that their behavior is "sexual" (Crooks & Baur, 1999). Infants are sexual beings primarily in the sense that their genitals are sensitive and their nervous systems allow sexual responses. They are also as curious about their bodies as they are about the rest of the world. They enjoy touching all parts of their body, especially those that produce pleasurable sensations, and are likely to continue touching themselves unless reprimands from parents or other grown-ups discourage this behavior (at least in front of adults). From these early experiences, children begin to learn what human sexuality is about and how the members of their society regard it.

Childhood Sexuality

Although boys and girls spend much of their time in gender-segregated groups, they are nonetheless preparing for the day when they will participate in sexual relationships with the other sex. They learn a great deal about sexuality and reproduction, continue to be curious about their bodies, and begin to interact with the other sex in ways that will prepare them for dating in adolescence.

KNOWLEDGE OF SEX AND REPRODUCTION

As children get older, they learn that sexual anatomy is the key differentiator between males and females and acquire a more correct and explicit vocabulary for discussing sexual organs (Brilleslijper & Baartman, 2000; Goldman & Goldman, 1982; Gordon, Schroeder, & Abrams, 1990). As Anne Bernstein and Philip Cowan (1975) have shown, their understandings of "where babies come from" also change as they develop cognitively. Young children often seem to assume either that babies are just there all along or that they are somehow manufactured, much as toys might be. According to Jane, age 3½, "You find [the baby] at a store that makes it. . . . Well, they get it and then they put it in the tummy and then it goes quickly out"

(p. 81). Another preschooler, making what he could of an explanation about reproduction from his mom, created this scenario:

> The woman has a seed in her tummy that is fertilized by something in the man's penis. (*How does this happen?*) The fertilizer has to travel down through the man's body into the ground. Then it goes underground to get to the woman's body. It's like in our garden. (*Does the fertilizer come out of his penis?*). Oh no. Only pee-pee comes out of the penis. It's not big enough for fertilizer. (Author's files)

As these examples illustrate, young children construct their own understandings of reproduction well before they are told the "facts of life." Consistent with Piaget's theory of cognitive development, children construct their understanding of sex by assimilating and accommodating information into their existing cognitive structures. Between the ages of 9 and 11, most children come to understand that sexual intercourse plays a role in the making of babies (Goldman & Goldman, 1982). By 11 or 12, most children have integrated information about sexual intercourse with information about the biological union of egg and sperm (Bernstein & Cowan, 1975). Thus, as children mature cognitively and as they gain access to information, they are able to construct ever more accurate understandings of sexuality and reproduction.

SEXUAL BEHAVIOR

According to Freudian theory, preschoolers in the *phallic stage* of psychosexual development are actively interested in their genitals and seek bodily pleasure through masturbation, but school-age children enter a *latency period* during which they repress their sexuality and turn their attention instead to schoolwork and friendships with same-sex peers. It turns out that Freud was half right and half wrong.

Freud was correct that preschoolers are highly curious about their bodies, masturbate, and engage in both same-sex and cross-sex sexual play. He was wrong to believe that such activities occur infrequently among school-age children. By the age of 6, about half of children have engaged in "sex play" (playing doctor or house), and about 30% have masturbated (Okami, Olmstead, & Abramson, 1997). Children are curious about their own genitals as well as those of other children. Games that involve examining and touching genitals are fairly common among young children and should not be cause for alarm by parents (Daniluk, 1998; Simon & Gagnon, 1998). Children in Freud's latency period may be more discreet about their sexual experimentation than preschoolers, but they have by no means lost their sexual curiosity. Surveys show, for example, that about 50% of boys and 30% of girls have masturbated prior to reaching puberty (Elias & Gebhard, 1969).

Indeed, Gilbert Herdt and Martha McClintock (2000) have gathered evidence that age 10 is an important landmark in sexual development, a time when many boys as well as girls experience their first sexual attraction (often for a member of the other sex if they later become heterosexual, or for a member of their own sex if they later become gay or lesbian). This

Preschoolers are naturally curious about the human body.

milestone in development appears to be influenced by the maturation of the adrenal glands (which produce male androgens). It comes well before the maturation of the sex organs during puberty and therefore challenges the view of Freud (and many of the rest of us) that puberty is the critical milestone in sexual development. As Herdt and McClintock note, our society does little to encourage fourth-graders to have sexual thoughts, especially about members of their own sex, so perhaps a hormonal explanation of early sexual attraction makes more sense than an environmental one. Indeed, the adrenal glands mature around age 6–8 and produce low, but increasing, amounts of androgens (McClintock & Herdt, 1996).

Yet sexual development is also shaped by the sociocultural context in which children develop (Miller & Fox, 1987). Eric Widmer and colleagues (Widmer, Treas, & Newcomb, 1998) compared attitudes toward sex in 24 countries and found wide variations in sexual beliefs. Still, the researchers were able to discern four sets of beliefs that characterized most of the countries. The "teen permissive" countries, which included Germany, Austria, and Sweden, reported the highest levels of acceptance of both early teenage sex and premarital sex. The United States, along with Ireland, Northern Ireland, and Poland, were categorized as "sexual conservatives." People in these countries were most disapproving of all types of nonmarital sex. For example, they were more likely than people in other countries to report that teenage sex, extramarital sex, and homosexual sex were "always wrong." Several countries— the Netherlands, Norway, Czech Republic, Canada, and Spain—were classified as "homosexual permissives" because of their relatively high acceptance of homosexual sex. Otherwise, these countries were similar in attitudes to the sexual conservatives. Most of the remaining countries were classified as "moderate," and were actually rather heterogeneous in their sexual attitudes.

In the United States, children learn from their peers how to relate to the other sex. As Barrie Thorne's (1993) observations in elementary schools demonstrate, boys and girls may

be segregated by gender, but they are hardly oblivious to each other. They talk constantly about who "likes" whom and who is "cute"; they play kiss-and-chase games in which girls attempt to catch boys and infect them with "cooties"; and they have steady boyfriends and girlfriends (if only for a few days). At times, boys and girls seem like mortal enemies. But by loving and hating each other, kissing and running away, they are grooming themselves for more explicitly sexual—but still often ambivalent—heterosexual relationships later in life (Thorne, 1993).

CHILD SEXUAL ABUSE

Every day in this country, children, adolescents, and even infants are sexually abused by the adults closest to them. A typical scenario would be this: A girl aged 7 or 8—though it happens to boys too—is abused repeatedly by her father, stepfather, or another male relative or family friend (Trickett & Putnam, 1993). Estimates of the percentages of girls and boys who are sexually abused vary wildly, perhaps because so many cases go unreported. In one representative sample of U.S. adults, though, 27% of the women and 16% of the men reported having experienced some form of childhood sexual abuse, ranging from being touched in ways they considered abusive to being raped (Finkelhor et al., 1989). This study suggests it is a serious and widespread social problem.

What is the impact of sexual abuse on the victim? Kathleen Kendall-Tackett, Linda Williams, and David Finkelhor (1993) offer a useful account, based on their review of 45 studies. No one distinctive "syndrome" of psychological problems characterizes abuse victims. Instead, they may experience any number of problems commonly seen in emotionally disturbed individuals, including anxiety, depression, low self-esteem, aggression, acting out, withdrawal, and school learning problems. Roughly 20–30% experience each of these problems, and boys seem to experience much the same types and degrees of disturbance as girls do.

Many of these aftereffects boil down to lack of self-worth and difficulty trusting others (Cole & Putnam, 1992). A college student who had been abused repeatedly by her father and by other relatives as well wrote this about her experience:

> It was very painful, emotionally, physically, and psychologically. I wanted to die to escape it. I wanted to escape from my body. . . . I developed a "good" self and a "bad" self. This was the only way I could cope with the experiences. . . . I discovered people I trusted caused me harm. . . . It is difficult for me to accept the fact that people can care for me and expect nothing in return. . . . I dislike closeness and despise people touching me. (Author's files)

Two problems seem to be especially linked to being sexually abused. First, about a third of victims engage in "sexualized behavior," acting out sexually by putting objects in vaginas, masturbating in public, behaving seductively, or if they are older, behaving promiscuously (Kendall-Tackett et al., 1993). One theory is that this sexualized behavior helps victims master or control the traumatic events they experienced (Tharinger, 1990). Second, about a third of victims display the symptoms of **posttraumatic stress disorder.** This clinical disorder, involving nightmares, flashbacks to the traumatizing events, and feelings of helplessness and anxiety in the face of danger, affects some soldiers in combat and other victims of extreme trauma (Kendall-Tackett et al., 1993).

In a minority of children, sexual abuse may contribute to severe psychological disorders, including multiple-personality disorder, the splitting of the psyche into distinct personalities (Cole & Putnam, 1992; Ross et al., 1991). Yet about a third of children seem to experience no psychological symptoms at all (Kendall-Tackett et al., 1993). Some of these symptomless children may experience problems in later years. But it is also true that some children are less severely damaged and more able to cope than others are.

Which children have the most difficulty? We know that the effects of abuse are likely to be most severe when the abuse involved penetration and force and occurred frequently over a long period of time; when the perpetrator was a close relative such as the father; and when the child's mother did not serve as a reliable source of emotional support (Beitchman et al., 1991; Kendall-Tackett et al., 1993; Trickett & Putnam, 1993). Children are likely to recover much better if their mothers believe their stories and can offer them a stable and loving home environment (Kendall-Tackett et al., 1993). Psychotherapy aimed at treating the anxiety and depression many victims experience and teaching them coping and problem-solving skills so that they will not be revictimized can also contribute to the healing process (Finkelhor & Berliner, 1995). Recovery takes time, but it does take place.

Adolescent Sexuality

Although infants and children are sexual beings, sexuality assumes far greater importance once sexual maturity is achieved. Adolescents must now incorporate into their identities as males or females concepts of themselves as *sexual* males or females. Moreover, they must figure out how to express their sexuality in relationships. As part of their search for identity, teenagers raise questions about their sexual attractiveness, their sexual values, and their goals in close relationships. They also experiment with sexual behavior— sometimes with good outcomes, sometimes with bad ones.

SEXUAL ORIENTATION

Part of establishing a sexual identity, part of the larger task of resolving Erikson's conflict of identity versus role confusion, is becoming aware of one's **sexual orientation**—that is, one's preference for sexual partners of the same or other sex. Sexual orientation exists on a continuum; not all cultures categorize sexual preferences as ours does (Paul, 1993), but we commonly describe people as having primarily heterosexual, homosexual, or bisexual orientations. Most adolescents establish a heterosexual sexual orientation without much soul-searching. For youths who are attracted to members of their own sex, however, the process of accepting that they have a homosexual orientation and establishing a positive identity in the face of negative societal attitudes can be a long and tor-

turous one. Many have an initial awareness of their sexual preference before reaching puberty but do not accept being gay or lesbian, or gather the courage to "come out," until their mid-20s (Garnets & Kimmel, 1991; Savin-Williams, 1995).

Experimentation with homosexual activity is fairly common during adolescence, but few adolescents become part of the estimated 5–6% of adults who establish an enduring homosexual or bisexual sexual orientation (T. W. Smith, 1991). Contrary to societal stereotypes of gay men as effeminate and lesbian women as masculine, gay and lesbian individuals have the same wide range of psychological and social attributes that heterosexual adults do. Knowing that someone prefers same-sex romantic partners tells us no more about his or her personality than knowing that someone is heterosexual.

What influences the development of one's sexual orientation? Part of the answer lies in the genetic code. Twin studies have established that identical twins are more alike in sexual orientation than fraternal twins (Bailey & Pillard, 1991; Bailey et al., 1993). As Table 12.3 reveals, though, in about half the identical twin pairs, one twin is homosexual or bisexual but the other is heterosexual. This means that environment contributes at least as much as genes to the development of sexual orientation (Bailey, Dunne, & Martin, 2000).

Research also tells us that many gay men and lesbian women expressed strong cross-sex interests when they were young, despite being subjected to the usual pressures to adopt a traditional gender role (Bailey et al., 2000; LeVay, 1996). Richard Green (1987), for example, studied a group of highly feminine boys who didn't just engage in cross-sex play now and then but who strongly and consistently preferred female roles, toys, and friends. He found that 75% of these boys (compared with 2% of a control group of gender-typical boys) were exclusively homosexual or bisexual 15 years later. Yet the genetic research by Bailey and Pillard suggests that sexual orientation is every bit as heritable among gay men who were typically masculine boys and lesbian women who were typically feminine girls as among those who showed early cross-sex interests (Bailey & Pillard, 1991; Bailey et al., 1993). All that is clear, then, is that many gay and lesbian adults know from an early age that traditional gender-role expectations do not suit them.

What environmental factors may help to determine whether or not a genetic predisposition toward homosexuality is actualized? We really do not know as yet. The old psychoanalytic view that male homosexuality stems from having a domineering mother and a weak father has received little support (LeVay, 1996). Growing up with a gay or lesbian parent also seems to have little impact on later sexual orientation (Golombok & Tasker, 1996; Patterson, 1992). Nor is there support for the idea that homosexuals were seduced into a homosexual lifestyle by older individuals.

A more promising hypothesis is that hormonal influences during the prenatal period influence sexual orientation (Ellis et al., 1988; Meyer-Bahlburg et al., 1995). For example, the fact that androgenized females are more likely than most other women to adopt a lesbian or bisexual orientation suggests that high prenatal doses of male hormones may predispose at least some females to homosexuality (Dittman et al., 1992; Money,

Table 12.3 If one twin is gay (or lesbian), in what percentage of twin pairs does the other twin also have a homosexual or bisexual sexual orientation? Higher rates of concordance (similarity) for identical twin pairs than for fraternal twin pairs provide evidence of genetic influence on homosexuality. Less-than-perfect concordance points to the operation of environmental influences as well.

	Identical Twins	Fraternal Twins
Both male twins are gay/bisexual if one is:	52%	22%
Both female twins are lesbian/bisexual if one is:	48%	16%

SOURCES: Male figures from Bailey & Pillard (1991); female figures from Bailey et al. (1993)

1988). Another possibility is that nature and nurture interact. Biological factors may predispose an individual to have certain psychological traits, which in turn influence the kinds of social experiences the person has, which in turn shape his or her ultimate sexual orientation (Byne, 1994). However, the fact is that no one yet knows exactly which factors in the prenatal or postnatal environment contribute, along with genes, to a homosexual orientation (Byne, 1994; LeVay, 1996).

SEXUAL MORALITY

Whatever their sexual orientation, adolescents establish attitudes regarding what is and is not appropriate sexual behavior. The sexual attitudes of adolescents changed dramatically during the 20th century, especially during the 1960s and 1970s; yet many of the "old" values have endured. Three generalizations emerge from the research on sexual attitudes.

First, most adolescents have come to believe that *sex with affection is acceptable.* They no longer buy the traditional view that premarital intercourse is always morally wrong. They also don't go so far as to view casual sex as acceptable, though males have more permissive attitudes about this than females (Oliver & Hyde, 1993). Most adolescents insist that the partners be "in love" or feel a close emotional involvement with each other.

A second finding is that the **double standard** *has declined over the years.* According to the double standard, sexual behavior that is viewed as appropriate for males is considered inappropriate for females; there is one standard for males, another for females. In the "old days," a young man was expected to "sow some wild oats," whereas a young woman was expected to remain a virgin until she married. Although the double standard has declined, it has by no means disappeared (for example, Simon & Gagnon, 1998). Fathers still look more favorably on the sexual exploits of their sons than on those of their daughters (Brooks-Gunn & Furstenberg, 1989), and college students still tend to believe that a woman who has many sexual partners is more immoral than an equally promiscuous man (I. Robinson et al., 1991). Adolescent girls generally hold less permissive attitudes about sex than adolescent boys do (de Gaston, Weed, & Jensen, 1996). However, Western societies have been moving for some time toward a single standard of sexual behavior used to judge both males and females.

A third generalization that emerges from research on sexual attitudes is that adolescents are *confused about sexual norms.* Adolescents continually receive mixed messages about

sexuality (Ponton, 2001). They are encouraged to be popular and attractive to the other sex, and they watch countless television programs and movies that glamorize sexual behavior. Yet they are also told to value virginity and to fear and avoid pregnancy, bad reputations, and AIDS and other sexually transmitted diseases. Adults often tell teens that they are too young to engage in sexual activity with a peer, yet they make teens feel shameful about masturbating (Halpern et al., 2000; Ponton, 2001). The standards for males and females are now more similar, and adolescents tend to agree that sexual intercourse in the context of emotional involvement is acceptable; but teenagers still must forge their own codes of behavior, and they differ widely in what they decide.

SEXUAL BEHAVIOR

If attitudes about sexual behavior have changed over the years, has sexual behavior itself changed? Yes, it has. Today's teenagers are involved in more intimate forms of sexual behavior at earlier ages than adolescents of the past were. Several themes emerge from the research on teens' sexual behavior:

1. Rates of sexual activity climbed in the 1960s and continued to climb through the 1980s (Dreyer, 1982; Forrest & Singh, 1990). This upward trend showed its first signs of dropping off in the 1990s (Althaus, 2001).
2. The percentages of both males and females who have had intercourse increased steadily throughout the 20th century.
3. Perhaps reflecting the decline of the double standard, the sexual behavior of females has changed much more than that of males, and the difference between the sexes has narrowed (Althaus, 2001).

The percentage of adolescents with sexual experience increases steadily over the adolescent years. About 20% of white teens report having sexual intercourse by age 15, and 50% have had intercourse sometime between ages 15 and 19 (Althaus, 2001). The rate is somewhat higher among black teens, with 30% of 14-year-olds reporting they have engaged in sex (DiIorio et al., 2001). Among college students, the rate is around 70–80% (Reinisch et al., 1992; Siegel, Klein, & Roghmann, 1999). Early sexual involvement is most likely among adolescents whose mothers were teenage parents; indeed, twin studies indicate that age of first intercourse is genetically influenced (Dunne et al., 1997). In addition, adolescents who become sexually active early are not very invested in school; instead, they are involved in problem behaviors such as substance abuse and delinquency (Crockett et al., 1996).

Males and females feel differently about their sexual encounters. For example, females are more insistent than males that sex and love—physical intimacy and emotional intimacy—go together. In one survey, 61% of college women, but only 29% of college men, agreed with the idea "No intercourse without love" (Darling, Davidson, & Passarello, 1992; see also DeGaston et al., 1996). Females are also more likely than males to have been in a steady relationship with their first sexual partner (Darling et al., 1992). This continuing gap between the sexes can sometimes create misunderstandings and hurt feelings, and it may partly explain why females are more likely than males to wish they had waited to have sex (de Gaston, Jensen, & Weed, 1995).

In sum, both the sexual attitudes and the sexual behaviors of adolescents have changed considerably in the past century. Sexual involvement is now part of the average adolescent's experience. This is true of all major ethnic groups, rich and poor. In fact, the differences in sexual activity among social groups have been shrinking (Forrest & Singh, 1990). Although most adolescents seem to adjust successfully to becoming sexually active, there have also been some casualties among those who are psychologically unready for sex or who end up with an unintended pregnancy or a sexually transmitted disease.

Sexually active adolescent couples often fail to use contraception, partly because they are cognitively immature and do not take seriously the possibility that their behavior could have unfortunate long-term consequences (Loewenstein & Furstenberg, 1991; Morrison, 1985). Although condom use has increased over the past decade, it is still low (Kaplan et al., 2001). In one study, for example, only 45% of adolescent males said they always used a condom during intercourse (Kaplan et al., 2001). Adolescent females report less frequent condom use than males, possibly because their sexual partners are often several years older and condom use among males actually declines from mid to late adolescence (Kaplan et al., 2001; Sneed et al., 2001). This may reflect the fact that adolescent couples who are in long-term, monogamous relationships stop using condoms because they no longer fear transmission of HIV or STDs.

For the adolescent who gives birth, the consequences of teenage sexuality are likely to include an interrupted education, low income, and a difficult start for both her and her child (Furstenberg, Brooks-Gunn, & Chase-Lansdale, 1989). This young mother's life situation and her child's developmental status are likely to improve later on, especially if she goes back to school and limits her family size, but she is likely to remain economically disadvantaged compared with her peers who postpone parenthood until their 20s (Furstenberg, Brooks-Gunn, & Morgan, 1987).

What effect has the threat of AIDS had on adolescent sexual behavior? Most studies find change, but perhaps not enough. As noted, teens are more likely to use condoms (at least some of the time) than they used to be, and rates of teenage pregnancy have actually begun to decline recently as a result (Vobejda & Havemann, 1997). However, few adolescents are doing what they would need to do to protect themselves from HIV infection: abstaining from sex or using a condom (latex, with a spermicide) *every* time. In a national survey of college students, for example, only 30% of students who had had sexual intercourse in the past 3 months used a condom in their last sexual encounter (Centers for Disease Control, 1997). No wonder many educators are now calling for stronger programs of sex education and distribution of free condoms at school. There is little chance of preventing the unwanted consequences of teenage sexuality unless more adolescents either postpone sex or practice safer sex. One encouraging finding is that warmth and connectedness between mothers and their children can delay the age of first intercourse (Sieving, McNeely, & Blum, 2000), as can parent–child communication about sexuality (Blake et al., 2001).

Adult Sexuality

Just as adults' sexual orientations are varied, so are their sexual lifestyles. Some adults remain single—some of them actively seeking a wide range of partners, others having one partner at a time, and still others leading celibate lives. More than 9 of 10 Americans marry at some point, and most adults are married at any given time. Men have more sexual partners than women during their adult lives, but most members of both sexes have just one sexual partner at a time (Laumann et al., 1994).

What becomes of people's sex lives as they get older? Many young people can barely conceive of their parents or—heaven forbid—their grandparents as sexual beings. We tend to stereotype elderly people as sexless or asexual. But we are wrong: People continue to be sexual beings throughout the life span. Perhaps the most amazing discoveries about sex in late adulthood are those of Bernard Starr and Marcella Weiner

Michael Newman/PhotoEdit

Many of today's adolescents become involved in sexual activity very early and give little thought to the long-term consequences of their behavior.

(1981), who surveyed 800 elderly volunteers ages 60 to 91. In this group, more than 90% claimed to like sex, almost 80% were still sexually active, and 75% said that their sex lives were the same as or better than when they were younger. One 70-year-old widow, asked how often she would like to have sex, was not bashful at all about replying "Morning, noon, and night" (p. 47).

Obviously, people can remain highly interested in sex and sexually active in old age. Yet Starr and Weiner's findings are likely to be exaggerated, since only the most sexually active people may have agreed to complete such a survey. More reliable findings are reported by Tom Smith (1991) based on a survey of a representative sample of American adults that asked about many things, including sexual behavior. As Figure 12.6 shows, the percentage of adults who reported at least some sexual contact in the past year declined steadily from age group to age group, although almost a third of adults in their 70s and older were still sexually active. Men were more likely to be sexually active than women, and, as you might expect, adults were more likely to be sexually active if they were married (91%) than if they were separated or divorced (74–80%) or widowed (only 14%).

In sum, sexual activity declines with age, especially among older women. Yet most people do not end their sex lives when they turn 65. Many older adults continue having sexual intercourse, and many of those who cease having it or have it less frequently continue to be sexually motivated (Clements, 1996).

How can we explain declines with age in sexual interest and activity? Consider first the physiological changes in sexual capacity that occur with age, as revealed by the pioneering research of William Masters and Virginia Johnson (1966, 1970). Males are at their peak of sexual responsive-

ness in their late teens and early 20s and gradually become less responsive thereafter. A young man is easily and quickly aroused; his orgasm is intense; and he may have a refractory, or recovery, period of only minutes before he is capable of sexual activity again. The older man is likely to be slower—slower to arouse, slower to ejaculate after being aroused, and slower to recover afterward. In addition, levels of male sex hormones decline gradually with age in many men. This may contribute to diminished sexual functioning among older men (Schiavi et al., 1991), although most researchers do not believe that hormonal factors fully explain the changes in sexual behavior that most men experience (Kaye, 1993).

Physiological changes in women are far less dramatic. Females reach their peak of sexual responsiveness later than men do, often not until their late 30s. Women are capable of more orgasms in a given time span than men are because they have little or no refractory period after orgasm, and this capacity is retained into old age. As noted in Chapter 5, menopause does not seem to reduce sexual activity or interest for most women. However, like older men, older women typically are slower to become sexually excited. Moreover, some experience discomfort associated with decreased lubrication.

All things considered, the physiological changes that men and women experience don't really explain why many of them become less sexually active in middle and old age. Masters and Johnson concluded that both men and women are physiologically capable of sexual behavior well into old age. Women retain this physiological capacity even longer than men, yet they are the ones who are less sexually active in old age.

Apparently, we must turn to factors other than biological aging to explain changes in sexual behavior. In summarizing these factors, Pauline Robinson (1983) quotes Alex Comfort (1974): "In our experience, old folks stop having sex for the same reason they stop riding a bicycle—general infirmity, thinking it looks ridiculous, and no bicycle" (p. 440).

Under the category of infirmity, diseases and disabilities, as well as the drugs prescribed for them, can limit sexual functioning (Clements, 1996; Marsiglio & Donnelly, 1991). This is a particular problem for men, who may become impotent if they have high blood pressure, coronary disease, diabetes, or other health problems. *Mental* health problems are also very important: Many cases of impotence among middle-aged and elderly men are attributable to psychological causes such as stress at work and depression rather than to physiological causes (Felstein, 1983; Persson & Svanborg, 1992).

The second source of problems is social attitudes that view sexual activity in old age as "ridiculous," or at least inappropriate. Old people are stereotyped as sexually unappealing and sexless (or as "dirty old men") and are discouraged from expressing sexual interests. These negative attitudes may be internalized by elderly people, causing them to suppress their sexual desires (Kaye, 1993; Purifoy, Grodsky, & Giambra, 1992). Older females may be even further inhibited by the "double standard of aging," which regards aging in

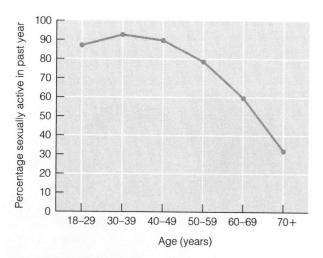

Figure 12.6 Percentage of U.S. adults of different ages who reported having at least one sexual partner in the past year. Cross-sectional data like these can be misleading about the degree to which sexual activity declines with age, but longitudinal studies also point to decreased involvement.

SOURCE: Adapted from T. W. Smith (1991)

Most older adults continue to be sexual beings who seek love and affection.

women more negatively than aging in men (Arber & Ginn, 1991).

Third, there is the "no bicycle" part of Comfort's analogy—the lack of a partner, or at least of a willing and desirable partner (Clements, 1996). Most older women are widowed, divorced, or single and face the reality that, for every 100 women, there are only 69 men. Moreover, most of these men are married, and those who are single are very often looking for a younger partner (Robinson, 1983). Lack of a partner, then, is *the* major problem for elderly women, many of whom continue to be interested in sex, physiologically capable of sexual behavior, and desirous of love and affection.

Perhaps we should add one more element to Comfort's bicycle analogy: lack of cycling experience. Masters and Johnson (1966, 1970) proposed a "use it or lose it" principle of sexual behavior to reflect two findings. First, an individual's level of sexual activity early in adulthood predicts his or her level of sexual activity in later life. The relationship is not necessarily causal, by the way; it could simply be that some people are more sexually motivated than others throughout adulthood. A second aspect of the "use it or lose it" rule may well be causal, however: Middle-aged and elderly adults who experience a long period of sexual abstinence often have difficulty regaining their sexual capacity afterward.

In summary, elderly people can continue to enjoy an active sex life if they retain their physical and mental health, do not allow negative attitudes surrounding sexuality in later life to stand in their way, have a willing and able partner, and can avoid long periods of abstinence. It seems likely that elderly people of the future, influenced by trends toward increased sexual permissiveness, will be freer than the elderly people of today to express their sexual selves.

Summary Points

1. Differences between males and females can be detected in the physical, psychological, and social realms; gender differences arise from an interaction of biological influences and socialization into gender roles (including the learning of gender-role norms and stereotypes).

2. Research comparing males and females indicates that the two sexes are far more similar than different psychologically. The average male is more aggressive and better at spatial and mathematical problem-solving tasks, but less adept at verbal tasks, than the average female. Males also tend to be more active, assertive, and developmentally vulnerable than females, who tend to be more compliant with adults' requests, tactful, nurturant, and anxious. Most sex differences are small, however, and some are becoming even smaller.

3. During infancy, boys and girls are very similar, but adults treat them differently. By age 2, infants have often gained knowledge of their basic gender identity and display "gender-appropriate" play preferences.

4. Gender typing progresses most rapidly during the toddler and preschool years, with 2- and 3-year-olds already learning gender stereotypes; school-age children are at first quite rigid and then more flexible in their thinking about gender norms and segregate themselves by sex.

5. Adolescents become intolerant in their thinking about gender-role deviations and, through gender intensification, show increased concern with conforming to gender norms.

6. Theories of gender-role development include the biosocial theory proposed by Money and Ehrhardt, which emphasizes prenatal biological developments but also stresses the importance of how a child is labeled and treated during a critical period for gender identity information. From Freud's psychoanalytic perspective, gender-role development results from the child's identification with the same-sex parent. Social learning theorists focus on differential reinforcement and observational learning. Cognitive perspectives emphasize understanding of gender and active self-socialization: Kohlberg's cognitive developmental theory emphasizes that children master gender roles once they master the concepts of gender identity,

Will & Deni McIntyre/Photo Researchers, Inc.

gender stability, and gender consistency; gender schema theory holds that children socialize themselves as soon as they have a basic gender identity and can construct gender schemata. Each theory has some support, but none is completely right.

7. Adults are influenced by the changing demands of gender roles. Marriage and parenthood appear to cause men and women to adopt more traditionally sex-typed roles. Freed from the parental imperative, middle-aged and elderly adults tend to experience a shift toward androgyny, blending desirable masculine-stereotyped and feminine-stereotyped qualities (though not switching personalities). Androgyny tends to be associated with good adjustment and adaptability.

8. We are sexual beings from infancy onward. Contrary to Freud's theory, sexual curiosity continues into the latency period; school-age children engage in sex play and appear to experience their first sexual attractions at about age 10.

9. In adolescence, forming a positive sexual identity is an important task, one that can be difficult for those with a gay or lesbian sexual orientation. During the past century, we have witnessed increased endorsement of the view that sex with affection is acceptable, a weakening of the double standard, and increased confusion about sexual norms. Although the trend reversed in the 1990s, more adolescents have been engaging in sexual behavior at earlier ages than in the past.

10. Most adults marry and become less sexually active as they get older. Declines in the physiological capacity for sex cannot fully explain declines in sexual activity; poor physical or mental health, lack of a partner, negative societal attitudes, and periods of sexual abstinence also contribute.

Critical Thinking

1. Jen and Ben are fraternal twins whose parents are determined that they should grow up to be androgynous. Nonetheless, when the twins are only 4, Jen wants frilly dresses and loves to play with her Barbie doll, and Ben wants a machine gun and loves to pretend he's a football player and tackle people. Each seems headed for a traditional gender role. Which of the theories in this chapter do you think explains this best, and which has the most difficulty explaining it, and why?

2. Not as many women as men become architects. Drawing on the material in this chapter, discuss the extent to which nature and nurture may be responsible for this, citing evidence.

3. The extent to which males and females differ changes from infancy to old age. When are gender differences in psychological characteristics and roles played in society greatest, and when are they least evident? How would you account for this pattern?

Key Terms

gender role

gender role norms

gender-role stereotypes

gender typing

communality

agency

social-role hypothesis

gender identity

gender segregation

gender intensification

androgenized females

identification

Oedipus complex

Electra complex

gender stability

gender consistency

gender schema (*plural:* schemata)

androgyny

parental imperative

androgyny shift

posttraumatic stress disorder

sexual orientation

double standard

On the Web

Web Sites to Explore

Sexuality

The site of Planned Parenthood Federation has a wealth of information about sexual and reproductive health, birth control, sexually transmitted diseases, and sex education.
http://www.plannedparenthood.org

Gender Equity

This site is focused on the Women's Educational Equity Act and issues surrounding gender equity in education, including the issue of whether single-sex education is a good idea. It links to many other organizations that have some stake in the issues and will give you a sense of what is being done at a national level to ensure equal opportunity for girls and women.
http://www.edc.org/WomensEquity/

Search Online with InfoTrac College Edition

For additional information, explore InfoTrac College Edition, your online library. Go to **http://www.infotrac-college.com** and use the passcode that came on the card with your book. One of the journals available through InfoTrac College Edition is *Sex Roles,* which contains scholarly work related to many of the issues in this chapter. Using PowerTrac, type in "Sex Roles" as the journal source and then select one or more articles to pursue a topic from the chapter that has piqued your interest.

Visit Our Web Site

Go to **http://www.wadsworth.com/psychology**, where you will find online resources directly linked to your book.

Life-Span CD-ROM

Go to the Wadsworth Life-Span CD-ROM for further study of the concepts in this chapter. The CD-ROM also includes quizzes and additional activities to expand your learning experience.

Social Cognition and Moral Development

Richard Hutchings/PhotoEdit

ON MARCH 5, 2001, Charles "Andy" Williams, age 15, took a .22-caliber revolver from his father's locked gun collection and went on a shooting spree at Santana High School in suburban San Diego (Fletcher & Waxman, 2001). Another in a long line of youthful murderers, the most notorious of which were the Columbine High School duo of Eric Harris and Dylan Klebold, Williams injured 13 and killed 2. And a nation wondered why.

Andy was always talking big, his friends said, so they just ignored him when he bragged that he was going to steal a car or, shortly before the shooting, that he was going to take a gun to school and shoot the place up. A short, skinny loner who had long been the target of name-calling and bullying, he had moved to California with his father within a year of the incident and immediately became the target of even worse taunting, to the point that he talked of killing himself. Not able to fit in with the high school crowd, he hung out with skateboarders who experimented with drugs. He was known as a latchkey child who spent a lot of time at friends' houses. He showed no remorse when interviewed by the police. His friends said Andy was mad at something (Booth & Snyder, 2001). Yet they also could not believe that he did what he did: "He didn't seem like that kind of person" (Fletcher & Waxman, 2001, p. A4). When asked about her son, his mother, who lives in South Carolina and had been divorced from Andy's father for a decade, could only say tearfully, "He's lost" (Booth & Snyder, 2001).

Charles Andrew Williams, age 15, in court, accused of murder in a school shooting in Santee, California. The obvious question: Why?

What might have been going through Andy Williams's head as he played out his drama? Did he think about the consequences of his act, for himself and others? Did he have any empathy for his victims? Did he know that what he was doing was wrong? Should this 15-year-old be tried as an adult? Did he have the same capacity to judge right and wrong that an adult has?

In this chapter, we continue our examination of the development of the self by exploring how we come to understand the world of people and think through social issues, including issues of right and wrong, and how our thinking about self and others is related to our behavior. We will begin by exploring **social cognition**—thinking about the perceptions, thoughts, emotions, motives, and behaviors of self and others (Flavell, 1985). We will then take a close look at thinking about moral issues, asking how children acquire a set of moral standards, how they go about deciding what is right and wrong, how cognition and emotion influence their actual behavior, and how their moral decision making changes over the life span. In the process, we stand to gain some insights into why Andy Williams shot his classmates.

Social Cognition

Infants come to know parents, siblings, and other companions by appearance and form expectations about how these companions will behave. However, infants cannot analyze the personalities of other people or recognize that their companions have their own distinct motives, feelings, and thoughts. These skills are examples of social cognition, which includes thinking not only about individuals, including the self, but about groups and whole social systems. We have already touched on some important aspects of social cognitive development in this book, seeing, for example, that older children think differently than younger children about what they are like as individuals and about how males and females differ. Here we'll focus on developmental changes in the ability to understand human psychology, describe other people, and adopt other people's perspectives.

Developing a Theory of Mind

Imagine that you are a young child and are brought to the laboratory and led through the research scenario portrayed in Figure 13.1. A doll named Sally puts her marble in her basket and leaves the room. While she is gone, Anne moves the marble to her box. Sally returns to the room. Now you are asked the critical question: Where will Sally look for her marble?

This task, called a **false belief task,** assesses the understanding that people can hold beliefs that are incorrect and that these beliefs, even though incorrect, can influence their behavior. The task was used in a pioneering study by Simon Baron-Cohen, Alan Leslie, and Uta Frith (1985) to determine whether young children, children with Down syndrome, and children with *autism* (see Chapter 16) have a **theory of mind.** A theory of mind is the understanding that people have mental states such as desires, beliefs, and intentions and that these mental states guide (or "cause," if you like) their behavior. The fact that we all rely on a theory of mind to theorize about human behavior is evident in the way we refer to mental states

© Reuters NewsMedia Inc./CORBIS

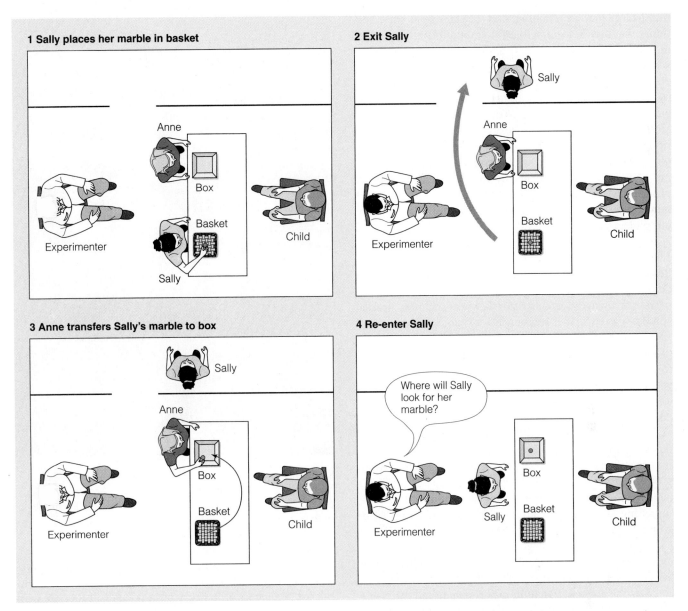

1 Sally places her marble in basket

Anne

Box

Basket

Child

Experimenter

Sally

2 Exit Sally

Sally

Anne

Box

Basket

Child

Experimenter

3 Anne transfers Sally's marble to box

Sally

Anne

Box

Basket

Child

Experimenter

4 Re-enter Sally

Where will Sally look for her marble?

Box

Basket

Child

Experimenter

Sally

Figure 13.1 The experimental arrangement in the false belief task involving Sally and Anne. As Sally does not know that Anne transferred Sally's marble from Sally's basket to Anne's box, she falsely believes it is in her basket, and the child who has a theory of mind should say that she will look for it there.

SOURCE: Adapted from Baron-Cohen et al. (1985)

every day; for example, we say that people did what they did because they *wanted* to, or *intended* to, or *believed* that doing so would have a desired effect.

Children pass the false belief task in Figure 13.1, and therefore show evidence of having a theory of mind, when they say that Sally will look for her marble in the basket (where she falsely *believes* it to be) rather than in the box (where it actually is). Children who have a theory of mind believe that Sally's behavior will be guided by her false belief about the marble's location; they are able to set aside their own knowledge of where the marble ended up after Anne moved it. They have formulated what Chapter 6 described as an *intuitive theory*—here, a theory of human psychology that helps them (and the rest of us) explain why people do what

they do. In Baron-Cohen's study, about 85% of 4-year-olds of normal intelligence and children with Down syndrome passed the false belief task. Yet despite mental ages greater than those of the children with Down syndrome, 80% of the autistic children *failed*. They incorrectly claimed that Sally would look where they knew the marble to be (in the box) rather than where Sally had every reason to believe it was (in the basket).

This study served as the basis for hypothesizing that autistic children display the severe social deficits that they do because they lack a theory of mind and suffer from a kind of "mind blindness" (Baron-Cohen, 1995; and see Chapter 16 on autism). Imagine trying to understand and interact with people if you are unable to appreciate such fundamentals of human psychology as the fact that people look for things where they believe they are, choose things that they want and reject things that they hate, sometimes attempt to plant false beliefs in others, and so on. Temple Grandin, a woman with autism who is intelligent enough to be a professor of animal sciences, describes having to compensate for lack of a theory of mind by creating a memory bank of how people behave and what emotions they express in various situations and then having to "compute" how people might be expected to behave in similar situations (Sacks, 1993). Just as we cannot understand falling objects without the employing the concept of gravity, we cannot understand human beings without invoking the concept of mental states. In all likelihood, the ability to read people's minds proved adaptive to our ancestors and became part of our biological endowment (Mitchell, 1997).

FIRST STEPS

Research on theory of mind has not only stimulated a great deal of thinking about the nature and causes of autism; it has prompted many researchers to ask when and how normal children develop the components of a theory of mind. Although children normally do not pass false belief tasks until the age of 4 or at the earliest 3, researchers have detected forerunners of a theory of mind as early as the end of the first year of life and now believe that a theory of mind takes form long before children pass false belief tasks (Bloom & German, 2000; Gopnik, Capps, & Meltzoff, 2000).

Consider these early milestones in the development of a theory of mind (and see Flavell, 1999). By 6 months, if not sooner, infants know that people behave differently toward people than toward inanimate objects—that people talk to a person but reach for an object behind a screen, and that it is surprising if they talk to what turns out to be an object or swipe at what turns out to be a person (Legerstee, Barna, & DiAdamo, 2000). This suggests that infants distinguish between people and objects and understand that other people, like them, treat people and objects differently.

Starting at about 9 months of age, infants and their caregivers also engage in a good deal of **joint attention,** both looking at the same object at the same time. At this age, infants sometimes point to toys and then look toward their companions, encouraging others to look at what they are looking at. By doing so, infants show an awareness that other people have different perceptual experiences than they do, but that two people can share perceptual experiences.

Similarly, when infants engage in their first simple *pretend play,* between 1 and 2 years of age, they show at least a primitive understanding of the difference between pretense (a kind of false belief) and reality (see Chapter 14). They know the difference between a pretend tea party and a real one, for example. Yet if you pretend to spill pretend tea on the table and hand a 2-year-old a paper towel, he or she will quickly wipe it up, no questions asked (Harris, 1989)! Imitating other people in the first year of life reveals an ability to mentally represent their actions. Finally, comforting a playmate who is crying (see later section) or teasing a sibling in the second year of life reflect an understanding that other people have emotions and that these emotions can be influenced (Flavell, 1999). The

Even 1-year-olds show an awareness that other people can have mental states (perceptions) different from their own when they point at objects so that their companions and they can jointly attend to the same object.

four abilities we have been discussing—joint attention, pretend play, imitation, and emotional understanding—are considered precursors of a theory of mind, and all four are deficient in autistic children (Charman, 2000).

We have even more evidence that children are developing theories of mind when they begin to refer to mental states in their speech starting at around age 2 (Bretherton & Beeghly, 1982). For example, Ross (at 2 years, 7 months) was asked why he keeps asking why and replied, "I want to say 'why,'" explaining his behavior in terms of his desire; Adam (at 3 years, 3 months) commented about a bus, "I thought it was a taxi," showing an awareness that he held a false belief about the bus (Wellman & Barsch, 1994, p. 345).

Finally, some research suggests that children as young as 2½ years old will attempt to deceive an adult about which of several containers holds a bag of gold coins and jewels (Chandler, Fritz, & Hala, 1989). That is, they seem capable of trying to plant a false belief in another person if they are shown how to erase telltale footprints leading toward the hiding place and to lay new footprints heading in the wrong direction. Other studies suggest that 3-year-olds may be too young to deceive other people deliberately, as they lay false tracks even when they are supposed to help someone find a prize rather than keep someone from finding it (Sodian, 1994). Interestingly, 77% of the mothers polled in one study claimed that 4-year-olds are capable of deliberately lying, but only 29% thought 3-year-olds have this capacity to plant false beliefs (Stouthamer-Loeber, 1991). Still, many children are quite capable of deception before they ever pass false belief tasks (Newton, Reddy, & Bull, 2000). Overall, children clearly understand perceptions, desires, pretense, and hide-and-seek deception games before they pass false belief tasks, suggesting that a theory of mind takes form gradually, starting in infancy (Custer, 1996; Szarkowicz, 1999; Wellman, Phillips, & Rodriguez, 2000).

DESIRE AND BELIEF-DESIRE PSYCHOLOGIES

Henry Wellman (1990) has theorized that children first develop a **desire psychology** at about age 2. They talk about what they want and even explain their own behavior and that of others in terms of wants or desires. This early desire psychology could be seen even among 18-month-olds in a clever study by Betty Repacholi and Alison Gopnik (1997). An experimenter tried two foods—Goldfish crackers and broccoli florets—and expressed happiness in response to one but disgust in response to the other. Since the toddlers almost universally preferred the crackers themselves, the acid test was a scenario in which toddlers saw the experimenter express liking for broccoli but disgust at the crackers ("Eww! Crackers! I tasted crackers! Eww!"). When confronted with the two bowls of food and asked to give the experimenter some, would these toddlers give her broccoli or crackers? The 14-month-olds in the study either did not comply with the request or gave the experimenter crackers, despite her distaste for them. However, the 18-month-olds gave her broccoli (undoubtedly against their better judgment!), showing that they were able to infer her desire from her previous emotional reactions to the two foods.

By age 4, and possibly as early as age 3, children normally progress to a **belief-desire psychology.** Not only do they understand that people's desires guide their behavior, but they begin to pass false belief tasks like the one about Sally and her marble and demonstrate an understanding that beliefs are not always an accurate reflection of reality. They appreciate that people do what they do because they *desire* certain things and *believe* that certain actions will help them fulfill their desires.

Based on a meta-analysis of 178 studies of theory of mind, Wellman, Cross, and Watson (2001) concluded that research strongly supports this shift from a desire psychology at 2 to a belief-desire psychology at around 4. Although simplifying the tasks children are given sometimes helps both younger and older children perform better, it does not enable young children to perform as well as older children, suggesting that there is a real conceptual change during the preschool years. Apparently, children discover that their desire theory of human psychology cannot explain everything people do and go on to build into their theory a concept of true and false beliefs.

However, it is better to think of theory of mind as a set of understandings that children begin to develop well before age

4, and continue to refine and learn how to use long afterwards, than to view it as something children "have" at 3 or 4 (Mitchell, 1997). For example, it is only after the preschool period that children can use information about others' beliefs to select or devise persuasive arguments specifically tailored to alter those beliefs (Bartsch & London, 2000). And in late elementary school, children are still mastering the complexities of thinking about other people's beliefs (Bosacki, 2000)—for example, making sense of statements such as "Mary thinks that Jeff thinks that she hates him." Moreover, it is not until middle childhood or later that children really understand that different human minds construct different views of reality and that their interpretations of events are influenced by their biases (Flavell, 1999).

CONTRIBUTORS

What factors contribute to the development of a theory of mind? Developing a theory of mind is partly just a matter of getting older and maturing neurologically and cognitively. Abnormal brain development in children with autism may be the reason for their great difficulty with tasks assessing theory-of-mind mastery. Some researchers have proposed that the brain contains a specialized module or modules devoted to understanding mental states that is the product of evolution (Leslie, 1994; Scholl & Leslie, 2001). Others view developing a theory of mind as the outgrowth of broader cognitive changes (Gopnik et al., 2000). For example, children who do well on false belief tasks also use many terms for mental states in their speech and engage in sophisticated pretend play in which they assign one another roles and pretend that objects are something else entirely (Nielsen & Dissanayake, 2000). And children seem to need to attain a certain level of language development before they can master false belief tasks, probably because both language development and theory of mind require representational or symbolic thinking skills and because language provides a means for describing and sharing one's experience of reality (K. Nelson, 2000).

Finally, acquiring a theory of mind, like acquiring language, requires experience interacting with other humans. As it turns out, children with siblings seem to grasp the elements of a theory of mind earlier than children without siblings (Jenkins & Astington, 1996; Perner, Ruffman, & Leekam, 1994). Engaging in pretend play with siblings may be especially helpful, as this provides practice understanding that belief and reality are not necessarily the same (Taylor & Carlson, 1997; Youngblade & Dunn, 1995). In multichild families, there may also be more talk about mental states ("She thought you were done with your ice cream," "He didn't mean to step on your head"), and this kind of discussion may contribute to early mastery of a theory of mind (Dunn et al., 1991).

Preschoolers who interact frequently with adults also do well on theory-of-mind tasks, however (Lewis et al., 1996). Parents can contribute positively to the development of theory-of-mind skills in their preschool children by forming secure attachments with their children, being sensitive to their needs and perspectives, and expressing their own emotions freely, even their feelings of depression and anxiety (Symons &

Clark, 2000). As they discuss everyday experiences with their companions, children begin to see that they and other people do not always have the same perspectives, thoughts, or feelings.

What would happen if children did not have many opportunities to "talk psychology" every day? Among the Junin Quechua people of Peru, adults rarely talk about beliefs and thoughts and have few words in their language for them. The result is that children as old as 8 have trouble understanding that beliefs can be false (Vinden & Astington, 2000). Similarly, in a part of Papua, New Guinea, children as old as 15 could not answer questions about other people's thoughts that 5-year-olds in our society handle easily (Vinden & Astington, 2000). It appears that children everywhere develop a theory of mind and progress from a desire psychology to a belief-desire psychology (Tardif & Wellman, 2000). However, there are striking cultural differences in the extent to which people focus on overt behavior versus mental states in talking about and explaining other people's behavior and in the number of terms they have for mental states, as well as in the rate at which children master theory-of-mind tasks, suggesting that cultural experiences also shape theory of mind (Lillard, 1998; Vinden & Astington, 2000).

Finally, although they eventually catch up to their seeing peers, blind children are slow to master false belief tasks, probably because they do not get as much social input as other children (Peterson, Peterson, & Webb, 2000). Deaf children of hearing parents sometimes also take longer than usual to master false belief tasks, whereas deaf children of deaf parents develop theory-of-mind skills on schedule because they are able to communicate easily and frequently with their companions using sign language (Courtin, 2000; Peterson & Siegal, 1999). The fact that deaf children with limited language experience show deficits in theory-of-mind performance rivaling those of autistic children casts doubt on the "brain module" view of theory of mind, for there is no evidence that deaf children's brains function improperly (Wellman & Lagattuta, 2000). Instead, it is possible that autistic children, partly because of their language deficits, simply lack the social input they need in order to learn to read minds.

In sum, acquiring a theory of mind—the foundation for all later social-cognitive development—begins with first steps such as joint attention and pretend play and advances from a desire psychology to a belief-desire psychology universally. It requires normal neurological, cognitive, and linguistic development, plus social experiences that involve talking about mental states with parents, siblings, and other companions. Children who have mastered theory-of-mind tasks generally tend to have better social skills than those who have not (Watson et al., 1999). As we will see later, they are also more attuned to others' feelings and welfare when they think through the morality of such acts as snatching a friend's toy (Dunn, Cutting, & Demetriou, 2000).

Person Perception

Although research on theory of mind tells us that even preschool children are budding psychologists, they still have a way to go to understand other people in terms of their enduring personality traits and to use their knowledge of other people's personalities to predict how they will react and what they will do. In studies of *person perception,* children are asked to describe people they know—parents, friends, disliked classmates, and so on. The descriptions offered by young children and older children are very different.

As we discovered in Chapter 11, children younger than 7 or 8 describe themselves primarily in physical rather than psychological terms. They describe other people that way too (Livesley & Bromley, 1973; Yuill, 1993). Thus, 4-year-old Evan says of his father, "He has one nose, one Mom, two eyes, brown hair." And 5-year-old Keisha says, "My daddy is big. He has hairy legs and eats mustard. Yuck! My daddy likes dogs—do you?" Not much of a personality profile there!

Young children perceive others in terms of their physical appearance, possessions, and activities. When they do use psychological terms, the terms are often global, evaluative ones such as "nice" or "mean," "good" or "bad," rather than specific personality trait labels (Livesley & Bromley, 1973; Ruble & Dweck, 1995). Moreover, they do not yet view traits as enduring qualities that can predict how a person will behave in the future or explain why a person behaves as he or she does. The 5-year-old who describes a friend as "dumb" is often using this trait label only to describe that friend's recent "dumb" behavior; he or she may well expect "smart" behavior tomorrow. Some researchers find that young children are able to use information about classmates' previous behavior to predict their future behavior if the task is made simple enough (Droege & Stipek, 1993). Still, young children typically use trait terms more to describe or evaluate behavior than to explain it (Ruble & Dweck, 1995).

Around age 7 or 8, children become more able to "get below the surface" of human beings and infer their enduring psychological traits. Thus, 10-year-old Kim describes her friend Tonya: "She's funny and friendly to everyone, and she's in the gifted program because she's smart, but sometimes she's too bossy." Over the elementary school years, children increasingly believe that traits such as being smart or getting along with others characterize other children across situations and over time, while also becoming more aware that people can change their traits if they work at it (Pomerantz & Saxon, 2001). As children reach the age of 11 or 12, they also make more use of psychological traits to explain why people behave as they do, claiming, for instance, that Mike pulled the dog's tail *because* he's cruel (Gnepp & Chilamkurti, 1988). Clearly, then, children become more and more psychologically minded as their emerging social-cognitive abilities permit them to make inferences about enduring inner qualities from the concrete behavior they observe in the people around them.

When asked to describe people they know, adolescents offer personality profiles that are even more psychological than those provided by children (Livesley & Bromley, 1973). They see people as unique individuals with distinctive personality traits, interests, values, and feelings. Moreover, they are able to create more integrated, or organized, person descriptions, analyzing how an individual's diverse and often inconsistent traits fit together and make sense as a whole personality. Dan, for example, may notice that Noriko brags about her abilities at times but seems very unsure of herself at other times, and he may integrate these seemingly discrepant impressions by concluding that Noriko is basically insecure and boasts only to hide her insecurity. Some adolescents spend hours psychoanalyzing their friends and acquaintances, trying to figure out what really makes them tick.

Just as was the case with children's descriptions of themselves, then, we can detect a progression in person perception from physical descriptions and global evaluations of other people as good or bad during the preschool years, to more differentiated descriptions that refer to specific personality traits starting at age 7 or 8, and finally, to more integrated personality profiles that show how even seemingly inconsistent traits fit together during adolescence.

Role-Taking Skills

Another important aspect of social-cognitive development involves outgrowing the egocentrism that Piaget believed characterizes young children and developing **role-taking skills**—the ability to adopt another person's perspective and understand his or her thoughts and feelings in relation to one's own. Role-taking skills are obviously essential in thinking about moral issues, predicting the consequences of one's actions for others, and empathizing with them. Robert Selman (1976, 1980; Yeates & Selman, 1989) contributed greatly to our understanding of role-taking abilities by asking children questions about interpersonal dilemmas:

> Holly is an 8-year-old girl who likes to climb trees. She is the best tree climber in the neighborhood. One day while climbing down from a tall tree, she falls . . . but does not hurt herself. Her father sees her fall. He is upset and asks her to promise not to climb trees anymore. Holly promises.
>
> Later that day, Holly and her friends meet Shawn. Shawn's kitten is caught in a tree and can't get down. Something has to be done right away or the kitten may fall. Holly is the only one who climbs trees well enough to reach the kitten and get it down but she remembers her promise to her father. (Selman, 1976, p. 302)

To assess how well a child understands the perspectives of Holly, her father, and Shawn, Selman asks: "Does Holly know how Shawn feels about the kitten? How will Holly's father feel if he finds out she climbed the tree? What does Holly think her father will do if he finds out she climbed the tree? What would you do in this situation?" Children's responses to these questions led Selman (1976) to conclude that role-taking abilities develop in a stagelike manner.

According to Selman, children aged 3 to 6 years are largely egocentric. Unaware of perspectives other than their own, they assume that they and other people see eye to eye. If young children like kittens, for example, they assume that Holly's father does too and therefore will be delighted if Holly saves the kitten.

However, as concrete operational cognitive abilities emerge, children become better able to consider another person's point of view. By age 8 to 10, for example, they appreciate that two people can have different points of view even if they have access to the same information. They are able to think about their own thoughts *and* the thoughts of another person, and they realize that their companions can do the same. Thus, they can appreciate that Holly may think about her father's concern for her safety but conclude that he will understand her reasons for climbing the tree.

Finally, adolescents who have reached the formal operational stage of cognitive development, at roughly age 12, become capable of mentally juggling multiple perspectives, including the perspective of the "generalized other," or the broader social group. The adolescent might consider how fathers *in general* react when children disobey them, while also considering whether Holly's father is similar to or different from the typical father (Selman, 1980; Yeates & Selman, 1989). Adolescents thus become mental jugglers, keeping in the air their own perspective, that of another person, *and* that of an abstract "generalized other" representing a larger social group.

These advances in social cognition have important implications for children's and adolescents' relationships. Experience interacting with peers seems to sharpen role-taking skills, and sophisticated role-taking skills, in turn, help make the child a more sensitive and desirable companion. As it turns out, children whose role-taking skills are advanced are more likely than age-mates who perform poorly on tests of role taking to be sociable and popular and to have established close peer relationships (Kurdek & Krile, 1982; LeMare & Rubin, 1987). What's more, children who are disruptive can be helped to improve their behavior through social skills training that includes coaching in perspective taking (Grizenko et al., 2000).

Adolescents who have advanced role-taking, or social perspective-taking, skills are better able than those who do not to resolve conflicts with their parents (Selman et al., 1986). They are better able to adopt the perspectives of their parents (and parents in general) and to identify a mutually beneficial agreement.

Social Cognition in Adulthood

As we have seen in earlier chapters, nonsocial cognitive abilities, such as those used in remembering material and testing scientific hypotheses, often improve during early and middle adulthood. Compared with adolescents, who seem to want to force facts into one neat and logical system, some adults become better able to accept contradictions and ambiguities and are more aware that problems can be viewed from a number of different perspectives (see Chapter 7). However, some elderly people experience declines in performance on tasks that assess nonsocial cognition. Do important social-cognitive skills, such as the ability to adopt other people's perspectives, also increase early in adulthood but decline in later life?

Social-cognitive development during adulthood does appear to involve both gains and losses (Blanchard-Fields, 1996; Hess, 1999). Fredda Blanchard-Fields (1986) presented adolescents, young adults, and middle-aged adults with three dilemmas requiring them to engage in role taking and to integrate discrepant perspectives: (1) two conflicting historical accounts, (2) a conflict between a teenage boy and his parents over whether he must visit his grandparents with the family, and (3) a disagreement between a man and a woman about an unintended pregnancy. Adults, especially middle-aged ones, were better able than adolescents to see both sides of the issues and to integrate the perspectives of *both* parties into a workable solution. Here, then, is evidence that the social-cognitive skills of adults may continue to expand after adolescence. Indeed, through a combination of social experience and cognitive growth, middle-aged adults have the potential to become quite sophisticated students of human psychology. As we saw in Chapter 9, a few even gain a kind of wisdom that gives them exceptional insight into the complexities of human existence.

Do elderly people continue to display the sophisticated social-cognitive skills that middle-aged adults display? For the most part, yes. They perform as well as young and middle-aged adults on many social-cognitive tasks (Hess, 1994; Pratt & Norris, 1999). For example, they do at least as well as college students on theory-of-mind tasks that require inferring the thoughts, feelings, and intentions of story characters who engage in bluffing or tell white lies (Happe, Winner, & Brownell, 1998). Yet other studies suggest that, on average, older adults are not always as adept as middle-aged adults at taking others' point of view, integrating different perspectives, and thinking in complex ways about the causes of people's behavior (Blanchard-Fields, 1996; Pratt et al., 1996). The declines in working memory and processing speed that limit the performance of older adults on nonsocial cognitive tasks also have some impact on their ability to take in and manipulate social information (Hess, 1999).

The most important message on adult social cognition, though, is that some older adults maintain their social-cognitive abilities and others do not. Whether they do or do not depends far more on the extent and nature of their social experiences than on their age. Those elderly adults who have the sharpest social-cognitive skills tend to be socially active; they are deeply involved in meaningful social roles such as

those of spouse, grandparent, church member, and worker (Dolen & Bearison, 1982). They have opportunities to talk to other people about problems they are experiencing, and they tend to be well-educated and in good health (Pratt et al., 1996). It is mainly when elderly people become socially isolated or inactive that their reasoning about personal and interpersonal issues becomes less complex.

Having now examined some important and dramatic changes in social cognition over the life span, let's focus in on an important area of development in which social-cognitive skills play a critical role: moral development.

Perspectives on Moral Development

Although we could debate endlessly what **morality** really is, most of us might agree that the term implies an ability (1) to distinguish right from wrong, (2) to act on this distinction, and (3) to experience pride when one does the right thing and guilt or shame when one does not. Accordingly, three basic components of morality have been of interest to developmental scientists:

1. An *affective,* or emotional, component, consisting of the feelings (guilt, concern for others' feelings, and so on) that surround right or wrong actions and that motivate moral thoughts and actions.
2. A *cognitive* component, centering on the way we conceptualize right and wrong and make decisions about how to behave; this component involves social-cognitive skills such as role taking.
3. A *behavioral* component that reflecting how we actually behave when, for example, we experience the temptation to cheat or are called upon to help a needy person.

As it turns out, each of the three major theoretical perspectives on moral development has focused on a different component of morality. So, let's briefly see what psychoanalytic theory has to say about moral affect, what cognitive developmental theory has to say about moral cognition or reasoning, and what social learning theory can tell us about moral behavior.

Moral Affect: Psychoanalytic Theory

What kinds of **moral affects,** or emotions, do you feel if you contemplate cheating or lying? Chances are you experience such negative feelings as shame, guilt, anxiety, and fear of being detected—feelings that keep you from doing things you know are wrong. **Empathy**—the vicarious experiencing of another person's feelings (for example, smiling at the good fortune of another or experiencing another person's distress)—is another important moral affect (Hoffman, 2000). Empathizing with individuals who are suffering can motivate **prosocial behavior**—positive social acts, such as helping or sharing, that reflect a concern for the welfare of others.

Mary Kate Denny/PhotoEdit

Learning to resist the temptation to break moral rules (here, one about taking turns) is an important part of moral development.

Positive emotions, such as pride and self-satisfaction when one has done the right thing, are also an important part of morality. We are generally motivated to avoid negative moral emotions and to experience positive ones by acting in moral ways.

Assuming that young infants are unlikely to feel these sorts of moral emotions, when do they arise? Freud's (1935/1960) psychoanalytic theory offered an early answer (see Chapter 2). As you'll recall, Freud believed that the mature personality has three components: the selfish and irrational id, the rational ego, and the moralistic superego. The *superego,* or conscience, has the important task of ensuring that any plans formed by the ego to gratify the id's urges are morally acceptable. Infants and toddlers, Freud claimed, lack a superego and are essentially "all id." They will therefore act on their selfish motives unless their parents control them.

The superego is formed during the phallic stage (ages 3–6), when children are presumed to experience an emotional conflict over their love for the other-sex parent. To resolve his *Oedipus complex,* Freud claimed, a boy identifies with and patterns himself after his father, particularly if the father is a threatening figure who arouses fear. Not only does he learn his masculine role in this manner, but through the process of *identification,* he takes on his father's moral standards as his

own. Similarly, a girl resolves her *Electra complex* by identifying with her mother and internalizing her mother's moral standards. However, Freud believed that, because they do not experience the intense fear of castration that boys experience, females develop weaker superegos than males do.

Having a superego, then, is like having a parent inside your head—always there, even when your parent isn't, to tell you what is right or wrong and to arouse emotions such as shame and guilt if you so much as think about doing wrong. We can applaud Freud for pointing out that emotion is a very important part of morality, that parents contribute in important ways to moral development, and that children must somehow internalize moral standards if they are to behave morally even when no authority figure is present to detect and punish them.

However, the specifics of Freud's theory are largely unsupported:

1. Cold, threatening, and punitive parents who make their children anxious about losing their parents' love do *not* raise morally mature youngsters; instead, as modern psychoanalytic thinkers appreciate, children form strong consciences when they are securely attached to warm and responsive parents (Hoffman, 2000).
2. Males do *not* appear to have stronger superegos than females.
3. Moral development begins well before the phallic stage, as we will see shortly.
4. Children who are 6 or 7 years old, and who have presumably achieved moral maturity by resolving their Oedipal conflicts, are actually far from completing their moral growth.

Freud's broad themes have merit, but the particulars of his theory of moral development lack support. Most researchers have therefore set Freud's theory aside, but they are more interested than ever in understanding the role of emotions in moral development (Eisenberg, 2000).

Moral Reasoning: Cognitive Developmental Theory

Cognitive developmentalists study morality by looking at the development of **moral reasoning**—the thinking process that occurs when we decide whether an act is right or wrong. These theorists assume that moral development depends on social-cognitive development. Moral reasoning is said to progress through an *invariant sequence*—a fixed and universal order of stages, each of which represents a consistent way of thinking about moral issues that is different from the stage preceding or following it. To cognitive developmental theorists, what is really of interest is *how we decide* what to do, not what we decide or what we actually do. A young child and an adult may both decide not to steal a pen that is there for the taking, but the reasons they give for their decision may be entirely different.

Inspired by Piaget's pioneering work on moral development, which we will mention later, Lawrence Kohlberg (1963, 1981, 1984; Colby & Kohlberg, 1987) formulated the cognitive developmental theory that has dominated the study of moral development (Lapsley, 1996). Born in 1927, Kohlberg put his own moral principles into action as a youth by helping to transport Jewish refugees from Europe to Israel after World War II, spent most of his career at Harvard, and died in 1987 when, suffering from a painful physical condition, he committed suicide by walking into the Atlantic Ocean (Walsh, 2000).

Kohlberg began his work by asking 10-, 13-, and 16-year-old boys questions about various moral dilemmas to assess how they thought about these issues. Careful analysis of the responses led Kohlberg to conclude that moral growth progresses through a universal and invariant sequence of three broad moral levels, each of which is composed of two distinct stages. Each stage grows out of the preceding stage and represents a more complex way of thinking about moral issues. According to Kohlberg, a person cannot skip stages, and a person who has reached a higher stage will not regress to earlier stages.

Think about how you would respond to the following moral dilemma posed by Kohlberg and his colleagues (Colby et al., 1983, p. 79):

> There was a woman who had very bad cancer, and there was no treatment known to medicine that would save her. Her doctor, Dr. Jefferson, knew that she had only about 6 months to live. She was in terrible pain, but she was so weak that a good dose of a pain killer like ether or morphine would make her die sooner. She was delirious and almost crazy with pain, and in her calm periods she would ask Dr. Jefferson to give her enough ether to kill her. She said she couldn't stand the pain and she was going to die in a few months anyway. Although he knows that mercy killing is against the law, the doctor thinks about granting her request.

Should Dr. Jefferson give her the drug that would make her die? Why or why not? Should the woman have the right to make the final decision? Why or why not? These are among the questions that people are asked after hearing the dilemma. Remember, Kohlberg's goal is to understand *how* an individual thinks, not whether he or she is for or against providing the woman with the drug. Individuals at each stage of moral reasoning might well endorse *either* of the alternative courses of action, but for different reasons. Following are Kohlberg's three levels of moral reasoning, and the two stages within each level.

LEVEL 1: PRECONVENTIONAL MORALITY

At the level of **preconventional morality,** rules are external to the self rather than internalized. The child conforms to rules imposed by authority figures in order to avoid punishment or to obtain personal rewards. The perspective of the self dominates: What is right is what one can get away with or what is personally satisfying.

Stage 1: Punishment-and-obedience orientation. The goodness or badness of an act depends on its consequences. The child will obey authorities to avoid punishment but may not consider an act wrong if it will not be punished. The greater the harm done or the more severe the punishment, the more "bad" the act is.

Stage 2: Instrumental hedonism. A person at the second stage of moral development conforms to rules in order to gain rewards or satisfy personal needs. There is some concern for the perspectives of others, but it is ultimately motivated by the hope of benefit in return. "You scratch my back and I'll scratch yours" is the guiding philosophy.

LEVEL 2: CONVENTIONAL MORALITY

At the level of **conventional morality,** the individual has internalized many moral values. He or she strives to obey the rules set forth by others (parents, peers, the government) in order to win their approval and recognition for good behavior or to maintain social order. The perspectives of other people are clearly recognized and given serious consideration.

Stage 3: "Good boy" or "good girl" morality. What is right is now that which pleases, helps, or is approved by others. People are often judged by their intentions; "meaning well" is valued, and being "nice" is important.

Stage 4: Authority and social-order-maintaining morality. Now what is right is what conforms to the rules of legitimate authorities. The reason for conforming is not so much a fear of punishment as a belief that rules and laws maintain a social order that is worth preserving. Doing one's duty and respecting law and order are valued.

LEVEL 3: POSTCONVENTIONAL MORALITY

At the third and final level of moral reasoning, **postconventional morality,** the individual defines what is right in terms of broad principles of justice that have validity apart from the views of particular authority figures. The individual may distinguish between what is morally right and what is legal, recognizing that some laws—for example, the racial segregation laws that Dr. Martin Luther King, Jr., challenged—violate basic moral principles. Thus, the person transcends the perspectives of particular social groups or authorities and begins to take the perspective of *all* individuals.

Stage 5: Morality of contract, individual rights, and democratically accepted law. At this "social contract" stage, there is an increased understanding of the underlying purposes served by laws and a concern that rules be arrived at through a democratic consensus so that they express the will of the majority and maximize social welfare. Whereas the person at Stage 4 is unlikely to challenge an established law, the Stage 5 moral reasoner might call for democratic change in a law that compromises basic rights. The principles embodied in the U.S. Constitution illustrate Stage 5 morality.

Stage 6: Morality of individual principles of conscience. At this "highest" stage of moral reasoning, the individual defines right and wrong on the basis of self-generated principles that are broad and universal in application. The Stage 6 thinker does *not* just make up whatever principles he or she happens to favor, but discovers abstract principles of respect for all individuals and their rights that *all* religions or moral authorities would view as moral. Kohlberg (1981) described

Sample Responses to the Mercy-Killing Dilemma at Kohlberg's Three Levels of Moral Reasoning

Preconventional Morality

Give the Drug

Stage 1: Dr. Jefferson should give the terminally ill woman a drug that will kill her because there is little chance that he will be found out and punished and he would not have to live with her agony anymore.

Stage 2: Dr. Jefferson should give her the drug because he might benefit from the gratitude of her family in the long run if he does what she wants. He should think of it as the right thing to do if it serves his purposes.

Do Not Give the Drug

Stage 1: The doctor runs a big risk of losing his license and being thrown in prison if he gives her the drug.

Stage 2: Besides, he really has little to gain personally by taking such a big chance. If the woman wants to kill herself, that's her business, but why should he help her if he stands to gain little in return?

Conventional Morality

Give the Drug

Stage 3: Most people would understand that the doctor was motivated by concern for the woman rather than by self-interest. They would be able to forgive him for what was essentially an act of kindness. (*Note:* Many Stage 3 thinkers would be likely to disapprove of mercy killing, however.)

Stage 4: The doctor should give the woman the drug because of the Hippocratic oath, which spells out a doctor's duty to relieve suffering. This oath should be taken seriously by all doctors.

Do Not Give the Drug

Stage 3: Most people are likely to disapprove of mercy killing. Dr. Jefferson would clearly lose the respect of his colleagues and friends if he administered the drug. A good person simply would not do this.

Stage 4: Mercy killing is against the laws that we as citizens are obligated to uphold. The Bible is another com-pelling authority, and it too says "Thou shalt not kill." Dr. Jefferson simply can't take the law into his own hands; rather, he has a duty to uphold the law.

Postconventional Morality

Give the Drug

Stage 5: Although most of our laws have a sound basis in moral principle, laws against mercy killing do not. The doctor's act is morally justified in that it relieves the suffering of an agonized human being without harming others. Yet, if Dr. Jefferson breaks the law in the service of a greater good, he should still be willing to be held legally accountable because society would be damaged if everyone simply ignored laws they do not like.

Stage 6: One must consider the effects of this act on everyone concerned—the doctor, the dying woman, other terminally ill people, all people everywhere. Basic moral principle dictates that all people have a right to dignity and self-determination, as long as others are not harmed by their decisions. Assuming that no one else will be hurt, then, the dying woman has a right to live and die as she chooses. The doctor is doing right by respecting her integrity as a person and saving her, her family, and all of society from needless suffering.

Do Not Give the Drug

Stage 5: The laws against mercy killing protect citizens from harm at the hands of unscrupulous doctors and should be upheld. If the laws were to be changed through the democratic process, that might be another thing. But right now the doctor can best serve society by adhering to them.

Stage 6: If we truly adhere to the principle that human life should be valued above all else and all lives should be valued equally, it is morally wrong to "play God" and decide that some lives are worth living and others are not. Before long, we would have a world in which no life has value.

Stage 6 thinking as a kind of "moral musical chairs" in which the person facing a moral dilemma is able to take the perspective or "chair" of each and every person or group that could potentially be affected by a decision and arrive at a solution that would be regarded as just from every "chair." Stage 6 is Kohlberg's vision of ideal moral reasoning, but it is so rarely observed that Kohlberg stopped attempting to measure its existence.

In the Explorations box above, we present examples of how people at the preconventional, conventional, and postconventional levels might reason about the mercy-killing dilemma. Progress through Kohlberg's stages of moral reasoning depends in part on the development of perspective-taking abilities (Selman, 1980). Specifically, as individuals become more able to consider perspectives other than their own, moral reasoning progresses from an egocentric focus on personal welfare at the preconventional level, to a concern with the perspectives of other people (parents, friends, and other members of one's own society) at the conventional level, and ultimately, to an ability to coordinate multiple perspectives and determine what is right from the perspective of *all* people at the postconventional level (Carpendale, 2000).

Moral Behavior: Social Learning Theory

Social learning theorists such as Albert Bandura (1986, 1991; Bandura et al., 2001), whose social cognitive theory was introduced in Chapter 2, have been primarily interested in the behavioral component of morality—in what we actually *do* when faced with temptation. These theorists claim that moral behavior is learned in the same way that other social behaviors are learned: through observational learning and reinforcement and punishment principles. They also consider moral behavior to be strongly influenced by the nature of the specific situations in which people find themselves. Finally, they emphasize the importance of cognitions that help people adhere to moral standards, gain control over their emotions, and feel capable of regulating their moral behavior (Bandura et al., 2001).

To highlight the difference between Bandura's social cognitive theory and other perspectives, let's see how different theorists might try to predict whether a teenager (we'll call him Waldo) will cheat on his upcoming math test.

Freud would want to know whether Waldo identified strongly with his father in early childhood. If he did, presumably he has developed a strong superego as part of his personality; as a result, he will be less likely to cheat, lie, or steal than a child with a weak superego (unless, of course, his father had a weak superego). Kohlberg would be more interested in Waldo's cognitive development and, specifically, in the stage at which he reasons about moral dilemmas. Although one's level of moral reasoning does not necessarily predict which decision one will make, Kohlberg would at least expect Waldo's mode of decision making to be consistent across many situations. Moreover, since Kohlberg be-

lieves that each higher stage permits a more adequate way of making moral decisions, he might expect the child whose moral reasoning is advanced to be less likely to cheat than the child who still thinks at the preconventional level and is "looking out for number one." Notice that both the psychoanalytic perspective and the cognitive developmental perspective view morality as a kind of personality trait—a quality that each of us possesses and that consistently influences our judgments and actions.

What might a social-cognitive theorist say about Waldo? This theorist would be most interested in the moral habits Waldo has learned, the expectations he has formed about the probable consequences of his actions, and his ability to resist temptation. If Waldo's parents, for example, have consistently reinforced him when he has behaved morally and punished him when he has misbehaved, he will be more likely to behave in morally acceptable ways than a child who has not had adequate moral training. Waldo will also be better off if he has been exposed to models of morally acceptable behavior rather than brought up in the company of liars, cheaters, and thieves.

But social learning theorists are skeptical of the notion that morality is a single, highly consistent trait or mode of thinking that will show itself in all situations. Even if Waldo's parents have taught him to be honest, that learning may not generalize well to math class when Waldo faces an opportunity to cheat. *Situational influences* will also shape his behavior. What if he observes his classmates cheating on the test and sees that they are getting away with it? What if he needs a B in this course in order to keep his scholarship?

In sum, the social learning perspective on moral development holds that morality is *situation-specific behavior* rather than a generalized trait such as a strong superego or a postconventional mode of moral reasoning. Influenced by specific learning experiences, we do acquire moral (or immoral) habits that express themselves in situations in which it is possible to cheat, lie, steal, help a person in need, and so on. However, each specific moral situation we encounter also affects our behavior.

We are now ready to trace the development of morality from infancy to old age. Our coverage charts the development of the self as a moral being, examining moral affect, cognition, and behavior as they have been conceptualized by psychoanalytic, cognitive developmental, and social learning theorists.

How many students in your class would admit to having cheated in high school? Fifty years ago, only about 1 in 5 college students admitted to it, but in recent surveys at least 3 in 5, and often more than 90%, admit to having cheated in high school (Kleiner & Lord, 1999). Techniques have changed too; use of preprogrammed calculators, cell phones to relay information about the test, hidden miniature cameras, and online term paper mills suggest that cheating has gone "high-tech." Why do you think cheating is so rampant in schools today?

The Infant

Do infants have any sense of right or wrong? If a baby takes a toy that belongs to another child, would you label the act stealing? If an infant bashes another child in the head with a toy, would you insist that the infant be put on trial for assault? Of course not. Adults in our society, including psychologists, view infants as **amoral**—that is, lacking any sense of morality. Since we do not believe that infants are capable of evaluating

Felicia Martinez/PhotoEdit

Children learn very early that some acts have distressing consequences.

their behavior in the light of moral standards, we do not hold them morally responsible for any wrongs they commit (although we certainly attempt to prevent them from harming others). Nor do we expect them to be "good" when we are not around to watch them. Yet it is now clear that these initially amoral creatures begin to learn fundamental moral lessons during their first two years of life (Emde et al., 1991; Kochanska, 1993).

Early Moral Training

Moral socialization begins early. Roger Burton (1984) relates how his daughter Ursula, age 1½, was so taken by the candy that she and her sisters had gathered on Halloween that she snatched some from her sisters' bags. The sisters immediately said "No, that's mine," and conveyed their outrage in the strongest terms. A week later, the sisters again found some of their candy in Ursula's bag and raised a fuss, and it was their mother's turn to explain the rules to Ursula. The problem continued until finally Burton himself came upon Ursula looking at some forbidden candy. Ursula looked up and said, "No, this is Maria's, not Ursula's" (p. 199).

It is through such social learning experiences, accumulated over the years, that children come to understand moral rules and standards. Children must learn two lessons, really: (1) to experience negative emotions when they violate rules, and (2) to control their impulses to engage in prohibited behaviors (Kochanska, 1993). Ursula and other young children learn from being reprimanded to associate the act of stealing with negative emotional responses. As they near the age of 2, children are already beginning to show visible signs of distress when they break things or otherwise violate standards of behavior (Cole, Barrett, & Zahn-Waxler, 1992; Kagan, 1981). Made to think that they have caused a doll's head to fall off, some toddlers even show signs of guilt, as opposed to mere distress, and try frantically to make amends (Kochanska, Casey, & Fukumoto, 1995). This means 18- to 24-month-old

children are beginning to internalize rules and to anticipate disapproval when they fail to comply with them. They are also able, at least to a limited degree, to exert the self-control it takes to resist the temptation to engage in forbidden behaviors (Kochanska, Murray, & Coy, 1997). By temperament, some toddlers have more capacity than others do to control their behavior (for example, to lower their voices, or slow or stop their activity). This capacity for self-control is critical if they are to resist temptation (Kochanska, Murray, & Harlan, 2000).

Parents contribute to early moral socialization in several ways. It is important, first of all, for parents to form a secure attachment with their children and express a lot of positive emotion. It is also important for parents to discuss their children's behavior in an open way, expressing their feelings and evaluating acts as good or bad (Laible & Thompson, 2000). This kind of emotion-centered discussion contributes more to the development of conscience than talk about the physical damage done by the child or about family rules of conduct. By establishing rules, reacting to children's rule-breaking behavior, and working toward mutual understandings of what is acceptable and what is not, parents give children a rule system to internalize (Emde et al., 1991; Gralinski & Kopp, 1993). If parents are firm but not harsh as they attempt to get toddlers to comply with their demands, these young children are likely to become cooperative rather than defiant and will become more and more able to control their own behavior even when parents are not around to catch them (Crockenberg & Litman, 1990).

The approach to socialization adopted by parents is not the only important influence on early moral development, however. A child's temperament may interact with his or her parents' approach to influence outcomes. Grazyna Kochanska (1995, 1997) has discovered that the children who are easiest to socialize are temperamentally *fearful,* or inhibited (see Chapter 11); they are hesitant to try activities such as jumping on a trampoline or putting on an ape mask, and they become highly anxious when reprimanded. These children can be effectively socialized to refuse to touch certain toys and to comply cheerfully with requests through a gentle approach to discipline that capitalizes on their anxiety but does not terrorize them so much that they cannot pay attention to the lesson they are to learn (Fowles & Kochanska, 2000).

Other toddlers, though, are *fearless,* or uninhibited. They are not very emotionally reactive to the gentle reprimands that work with inhibited tots, but will not internalize their parents' rules if they are treated harshly, either. Fearless children are most likely to learn to comply with rules and requests when their parents are warm and responsive and create a secure attachment bond that makes them want to cooperate with and please their parents (Fowles & Kochanska, 2000). Most children, of course, are more eager to comply with adults with whom they have secure, loving relationships than with adults who are insensitive to their needs. However, a secure attachment seems to be especially critical in motivating fearless children, as fear tactics do not work on them.

Here, then, is another example of the importance of the *goodness of fit* between a child's temperament and his or her social environment. Children with a fearful temperament respond best to gentle persuasion and mild discipline that makes them anxious (but not too anxious), whereas fearless children, not bothered much by reprimands, respond to a warm, responsive parenting style that makes them want to cooperate. Given appropriate socialization, most toddlers will internalize many rules of conduct and acquire the beginnings of a moral sense.

Prosocial Behavior

Not only are infants capable of internalizing rules of behavior, but they are not quite so selfish, egocentric, and unconcerned about other people as Freud, Piaget, Kohlberg, and many other theorists have assumed. Perhaps the strongest evidence of this comes from studies of empathy and prosocial behavior. Even newborns display a very primitive form of empathy: They become distressed by the cries of other newborns, suggesting that empathy may be part of our evolutionary heritage (Hoffman, 2000; Martin & Clark, 1982). It is unlikely that young infants really distinguish between another infant's distress and their own, though.

During their second year of life, infants become capable of a truer form of empathy. They understand that someone else's distress is different from their own, and they begin to respond in ways that are likely to comfort the person in distress (Hoffman, 2000). Carolyn Zahn-Waxler and her colleagues (1992) report that more than half of the 13- to 15-month-old infants they observed engaged in at least one act of prosocial behavior—helping, sharing, expressing concern, comforting, and so on. These behaviors became increasingly common from age 1 to age 2, when all but one child in the study acted prosocially.

Consider some concrete examples described by Hoffman (2000). One 10-month-old, watching a peer cry, looked sad and buried her head in her mother's lap, as she often did when *she* was distressed. A 12-month-old looked sad and brought her own mother to comfort a friend, even though the friend's mother was also present and would have been more comforting. A 2-year-old brought his own teddy to comfort a distressed friend, but when it failed to do the trick, offered the *friend's* teddy instead, beginning to show an ability to take the perspective of the friend. Finally, consider the reaction of 21-month-old John to his distressed playmate, Jerry:

> Today Jerry was kind of cranky; he just started . . . bawling and he wouldn't stop. John kept coming over and handing Jerry toys, trying to cheer him up . . . . He'd say things like "Here, Jerry," and I said to John "Jerry's sad; he doesn't feel good; he had a shot today." John would look at me with his eyebrows wrinkled together like he really understood that Jerry was crying because he was unhappy. (Zahn-Waxler, Radke-Yarrow, & King, 1979, pp. 321–322)

Overall, then, infants are amoral in some senses, particularly when it comes to making judgments of right and wrong. Yet their "moral socialization" has begun. They internalize

rules of conduct and become distressed when they violate the rules, and they show the rudiments of empathy, an important motivator of moral behavior that may well be part of our species heredity as human beings (Hoffman, 2000).

The Child

During the years from age 2 to age 12, children's standards of morality and their motivation to live up to these standards grow out of their social experiences in the family, peer group, and wider society. Research on moral development during childhood has explored how children of different ages think about moral issues. It has also told us a good deal about how children actually behave when their moral values are tested.

Kohlberg's View

The hypothetical moral dilemmas that Lawrence Kohlberg devised to assess stages of moral reasoning (for example, the mercy-killing dilemma presented earlier) are too complex for preschool children to understand. How do school-age children do? They generally reason at the preconventional level, taking an egocentric perspective on morality and defining as right those acts that are rewarded and as wrong those acts that are punished (Colby et al., 1983). At best, they are beginning to make the transition to conventional moral reasoning by displaying a Stage 3 concern with being a "good boy" or a "good girl" who gains the approval of others.

In short, from Kohlberg's perspective, most children, and especially young children, are not really moral beings yet; they have not yet adopted conventional societal values as their own. Kohlberg's stages are more useful in describing the moral reasoning of adolescents and adults than in describing that of young children. Other researchers, however, have looked more closely at the moral reasoning of young children and have found that they engage in some fairly sophisticated thinking about right and wrong.

Piaget's View

Cognitive developmental theorist Jean Piaget (1932/1965) was interested in moral thinking and stimulated a good deal of research on it, including Kohlberg's (see Lapsley, 1996). He studied children's concepts of rules by asking Swiss children about their games of marbles, and he explored children's concepts of justice by presenting them with moral dilemmas to ponder. For example, he told children about two boys, John, who accidentally knocked over a tray of 15 cups while coming to dinner as requested, and Henry, who broke only one cup while sneaking jam from the cupboard. The key question he posed was which child was naughtier, and why.

Based on children's responses to such questions, Piaget formulated a theory of moral development that claimed the following:

1. Preschool children are "premoral"; they have little awareness or understanding of rules.
2. Children 6 to 10 take rules dead seriously, believing that they are handed down by parents and other authority figures and are sacred and unalterable. They also judge rule violations as wrong to the extent that they have damaging consequences, even if the violator had good intentions (as the boy who broke 15 cups did).
3. At the age of 10 or 11, most children enter a final stage of moral development in which they begin to appreciate that rules are agreements between individuals—agreements that can be changed through a consensus of those individuals. In judging actions, they pay more attention to whether an actor's intentions were good or bad; they see Henry, the misbehaving boy who broke one cup, as naughtier than John, the well-intentioned boy who broke 15.

According to Piaget, progress through these stages depends on both cognitive maturation and social experience, especially with peers. He believed that peers contribute more to moral development than parents do. Because peers are equals, they must learn to take one another's perspectives and resolve disagreements among themselves through negotiation, which sharpens their role-taking skills and help them discover principles of fairness. By contrast, parents can just impose their rules on children through brute force and therefore contribute less to moral development. According to Piaget, then, moral growth requires developing, through interactions with peers, an ability to recognize and coordinate multiple perspectives on a moral issue (Carpendale, 2000).

Consistent with Piaget's theory, children gain a deeper understanding of rules as they get older, and their levels of moral reasoning depend on their levels of cognitive development and on their interactions with peers (Lapsley, 1996). At the same time, however, it has become clear that Piaget, like Kohlberg, badly underestimated the moral sophistication of preschool and young grade-school children.

IGNORING INTENTIONS?

Consider Piaget's claim that young children judge acts as right or wrong on the basis of their consequences rather than on the basis of the intentions that guided them. His moral-decision story about the two boys and the cups—asking whether a child who causes a small amount of damage in the service of bad intentions is naughtier than a child who causes a large amount of damage despite good intentions—was flawed in that it confounded the two issues, goodness of intentions with amount of damage done. Sharon Nelson (1980) overcame this flaw in an interesting experiment. Three-year-olds listened to stories in which a character threw a ball to a playmate. The actor's motive was described as *good* (his friend had nothing to play with) or *bad* (the actor was mad at his friend), and the consequences of his act were either *positive* (the friend caught the ball and was happy to play with it) or *negative* (the ball hit the friend in the head and made him cry). To make the task simpler, Nelson showed children drawings of what happened (see Figure 13.2 for an example).

Figure 13.2 Examples of drawings used by Nelson to convey an actor's intentions to preschool children. Here we see negative intent and a negative consequence.
SOURCE: Nelson (1980)

Not surprisingly, the 3-year-olds in the study judged acts that had positive consequences more favorably than acts that caused harm. However, they also judged the well-intentioned child who had wanted to play more favorably than the child who intended to hurt his friend, *regardless of the consequences of his actions.* Apparently, then, even very young children can base their moral judgments on *both* an actor's intentions *and* the consequences of his or her act (see also Bussey, 1992).

Theory-of-mind research has also given us many new insights into the moral sensibilities of young children. As we saw earlier, 4-year-old children who have a theory of mind know enough about intentions to cry, "I didn't mean it! I didn't mean it!" when they stand to be punished. Moreover, their understandings of an actor's beliefs at the time he or she committed a harmful act ("Donnie didn't know Marie was in the box when he pushed it down the stairs!") influences their judgments of whether the act was intentional and therefore how bad it was (Chandler, Sokol, & Wainryb, 2000). A theory of mind also gives children a basis for understanding people's emotional reactions to others' acts, an important consideration in judging right and wrong. At the age of only 3, for example, children can use their emerging theory-of-mind skills to figure out that Lewis, who likes tarantulas but fears puppies, will be upset if his friend gives him a puppy—and that it is therefore "bad" to give Lewis a puppy even though it may be "nice" to give almost any other child a puppy (Helwig, Zelazo, & Wilson, 2001). Preschool children who have mastered theory-of-mind tasks are also able to think through the emotional consequences of calling a friend a bad name or taking his or her toys (Dunn et al., 2000). Overall, Piaget was correct to conclude that young children assign more weight to consequences and less weight to intentions than older children do, but he was wrong to conclude that young children are incapable of considering both intentions and consequences when they evaluate others' conduct. He also did not appreciate their ability to apply their theory-of-mind skills in judging right and wrong.

VIEWING RULES AS SACRED?

Piaget also claimed that 6- to 10-year-old children view rules as sacred prescriptions laid down by respected authority figures. These moral absolutes cannot be questioned or changed.

However, Elliot Turiel (1978, 1983) has observed that children actually distinguish between two kinds of rules in daily life: (1) **moral rules,** or standards that focus on the welfare and basic rights of individuals, and (2) **social-conventional rules,** standards determined by social consensus that tell us what is appropriate in a particular social setting. Moral rules include rules against hitting, stealing, lying, and otherwise harming others or violating their rights. Social-conventional rules are more like rules of social etiquette; they include the rules of games as well as school rules that forbid eating snacks in class or using the restroom without permission.

Even preschool children in our society understand that moral and social-conventional rules are different and that moral rules are more compelling and unalterable (Nucci & Nucci, 1982; Smetana, Schlagman, & Adams, 1993). Judith Smetana (1981), for example, discovered that children as young as age 2 regard moral transgressions such as hitting, stealing, or refusing to share as much more serious and deserving of punishment than social-conventional violations such as not staying in one's seat in nursery school or not saying grace before eating. Even more remarkable is what these youngsters said when asked if a violation would be okay if there were no rule against it: They claimed that it was *always* wrong to hit people or commit other moral transgressions, rule or no rule, but they felt that it would be perfectly okay for children to get out of their seats at nursery school or violate other social conventions if there were not rules against it.

Meanwhile, 6- to 10-year-old children, who according to Piaget view any law laid down by adults as "sacred," are very capable of questioning adult authority (Tisak & Tisak, 1990). These children claim that it is perfectly fine for parents to enforce rules against stealing and other moral violations, but they believe that it can be inappropriate and unjustifiable for parents to arbitrarily restrict their children's friendships. And they maintain that not even God can proclaim that stealing is morally right and make it so (Nucci & Turiel, 1993). In other words, school-age children will not blindly accept any dictate offered by an authority figure as legitimate.

Overall, then, it seems that both Piaget and Kohlberg failed to appreciate how much moral growth takes place in early childhood. Both regarded young children as selfish and amoral creatures who have not yet internalized rules of moral conduct and cannot be expected to behave morally. Yet we now know that even toddlers learn rules of conduct, experience moral emotions such as guilt and empathy, and behave in prosocial ways. And we know that even preschool children are quite capable of judging acts as right or wrong according to whether the actor's intentions were good or bad (although they weight the consequences of an act more heavily than older children do) and that they use their theories of mind to analyze people's motives and the emotional consequences of their acts. In addition, children do not view *all* rules as absolute, sacred, and unchangeable. They realize that social-conventional rules are more arbitrary and less binding than moral rules, and they challenge adult authority when they believe it is illegitimate. Young children have by no means completed their moral growth, but they are well on their way to becoming moral beings long before late childhood and early adolescence, the periods that Piaget and Kohlberg mark as times of substantial moral growth.

Moral Behavior

To many people, the ultimate goal of moral socialization is to produce a child who not only has internalized moral rules but will abide by them. Can children be trusted to do so? Consider a classic study of moral behavior reported by Hugh Hartshorne and Mark May (1928–1930). Their purpose was to investigate the moral character of 10,000 children (ages 8–16) by tempting them to lie, cheat, or steal in a variety of situations. It readily became apparent that almost all children espoused "sound" moral values, claiming that honesty was good, that cheating and stealing were wrong, and so on. Yet most children cheated or otherwise broke one of their moral rules in at least one of the situations the researchers created to test their moral behavior. In other words, Hartshorne and May had a tough time finding children who not only espoused the right values but consistently acted according to those values. Most children's moral behavior was, in fact, quite inconsistent from situation to situation.

Reanalyses of these data and new studies suggest that children are somewhat more consistent in their behavior than Hartshorne and May concluded (Burton, 1963; Hoffman, 2000). Across a set of situations, some children tend to be more honest, more likely to resist temptation, or more helpful than other children. Still, moral thought, affect, and behavior are not as closely interrelated in childhood as they will be by adolescence or adulthood (Blasi, 1980).

Why are children relatively inconsistent in their moral behavior? One explanation may be that they are reasoning at Kohlberg's preconventional level. When punishment and re-

Although it is often difficult to tell whether children are working together or using each other's work, most youngsters can be tempted to cheat if the situational factors are right. Children's moral conduct is fairly inconsistent from situation to situation.

ward are the primary considerations in defining acts as right or wrong, perhaps it is not surprising that a child may see nothing much wrong with cheating when the chances of detection and punishment are slim. In addition, as social learning theorists would emphasize, moral inconsistency results from *situational* influences on behavior—such factors as the importance of the goal that can be achieved by transgressing, the probability of being detected, and the amount of encouragement provided by peers (Burton, 1976).

How, then, can parents best raise a child who can be counted on to behave morally in most situations? Social learning theorists would advise parents to (1) reinforce moral behavior, (2) punish immoral behavior, and (3) serve as models of moral behavior. Reinforcement such as praise can be used to strengthen prosocial behaviors such as sharing or to teach children acceptable alternatives to acts that one wants to discourage (Fischer, 1963; Perry & Parke, 1975). Punishment of misdeeds can also contribute to moral growth if it is not overly harsh, if it teaches children to associate negative emotions with their wrongdoing, if it is accompanied by an explanation of why the forbidden act is wrong and should be avoided, and if it is supplemented by efforts to encourage and reinforce more acceptable behavior (Perry & Parke, 1975). The problem with punishment, especially severe physical punishment, is that it may have undesirable side effects (such as making children resentful or overly anxious or teaching them that aggression is an appropriate means of solving problems). Finally, social learning theorists emphasize that parents should serve as models of moral behavior. Children will follow the examples of adults who resist temptation (Toner, Parke, & Yussen, 1978). They are especially likely to do so if those models state the rule they are following and a rationale for not committing the prohibited act (Grusec et al., 1979).

The important work of Martin Hoffman (2000) has provided additional insights into how to foster not only moral behavior but moral thought and affect as well. Many years ago, Hoffman (1970) reviewed the child-rearing literature to determine which parental approaches were associated with high levels of moral development. Three major approaches were compared:

1. **Love withdrawal:** withholding attention, affection, or approval after a child misbehaves—or, in other words, creating anxiety by threatening a loss of reinforcement from parents
2. **Power assertion:** using power to administer spankings, take away privileges, and so on—in other words, using punishment
3. **Induction:** explaining to a child why the behavior is wrong and should be changed by emphasizing how it affects other people

Suppose that little Ronnie has just put the beloved family cat through a cycle in the clothes dryer. Using love withdrawal, a parent might say "How could you do something like that? I can't even bear to look at you!" Using power assertion, a parent might say "Get to your room this minute; you're going to get it." Using induction, a parent might say "Ronnie, look how

scared Fluffball is. You could have killed her, and you know how sad we'd be if she died." Induction, then, is a matter of providing rationales or explanations that focus special attention on the consequences of wrongdoing for other people (or cats, as the case may be).

Which approach best fosters moral development? Induction is more often positively associated with children's moral maturity than either love withdrawal or power assertion, probably because it helps children understand why an act is bad and empathize with those affected by it (Brody & Shaffer, 1982). Love withdrawal has been found to have positive effects in some studies but negative effects in others. The use of power assertion is actually more often associated with moral *immaturity* than with moral maturity. However, Hoffman (2000) now concludes that power assertion is useful now and then, as long as it does not arouse too much fear, because it can motivate a child to pay close attention to an induction. Like other techniques, it works best in the context of a loving parent–child relationship.

Hoffman's work provides a fairly clear picture of how parents can best contribute to the moral growth of their children. As he puts it, the winning formula is "a blend of frequent inductions, occasional power assertions, and a lot of affection" (Hoffman, 2000, p. 23). Yet we must also appreciate that a particular moral socialization technique can have different effects depending on the particular misdeed, child, parent, and context. More important than the particular socialization strategies parents use may be the quality of the parent–child relationship and the parent's understanding of the particular child and of the situation at hand (Grusec, Goodnow, & Kuczynski, 2000).

To illustrate, the history of the parent–child relationship can have an impact on the effectiveness of a parent's efforts to control a child's behavior: Abused children tend to be most compliant with requests to clean up a play room if their mothers do not show much negative emotion, whereas nonabused children are more compliant if their mothers *do* show negative emotion (Koenig, Cicchetti, & Rogosch, 2000). A child's temperament also helps to determine how morally trainable he or she is, and the approach to moral training that parents use. As we saw earlier, Grazyna Kochanska (1993) has found that some children are, by temperament, more fearful than others and therefore are more likely to become appropriately anxious and distressed when they are disciplined. In addition, some children are less impulsive than others and therefore are more able to inhibit their urges to engage in wrongdoing (Kochanska, Murray, & Coy, 1997).

Children who are high in emotionality but low in impulsivity are relatively easy to socialize using positive disciplinary techniques such as induction; as a result, their parents are likely to use induction frequently and may not have much need to resort to power assertion (Keller & Bell, 1979). However, children who are not easily led to associate guilt and other negative emotions with their wrongdoings or who have difficulty controlling their impulses tend to drive parents to use more power-assertive (and ineffective) discipline (Anderson, Lytton, & Romney, 1986; Lytton, 1990). In other words, parents affect children, but children also affect their parents as moral socialization proceeds.

The Adolescent

As adolescents gain the capacity to think about abstract and hypothetical ideas, and as they begin to chart their future identities, many of them reflect a great deal on their values and moral standards. Others do not reflect enough, it seems, and end up engaging in serious antisocial behavior.

Changes in Moral Reasoning

Although most teenagers break the law now and then, adolescence is actually a period of considerable growth in moral reasoning and a time when many individuals become increasingly motivated to behave morally. Consider first the results of a 20-year longitudinal study that involved repeatedly asking the 10-, 13-, and 16-year-old boys originally studied by Kohlberg to respond to moral dilemmas (Colby et al., 1983). Figure 13.3 shows the percentage of judgments offered at each age that reflected each of Kohlberg's six stages.

A number of interesting developmental trends can be seen here. Notice that the preconventional reasoning (Stage 1 and 2 thinking) that dominates among 10-year-olds decreases considerably during the teen years. During the adolescent years, conventional reasoning (Stages 3 and 4) becomes the dominant mode of moral thinking. So, among 13- to 14-year-olds, most moral judgments reflect either a Stage 2 (instrumental hedonism) approach—"You scratch my back and I'll scratch yours"—or a Stage 3 ("good boy"/"good girl") concern with being nice and earning approval. More than half of the judgments offered by 16- to 18-year-olds embody Stage 3

reasoning, but about a fifth were scored as Stage 4 (authority and social-order-maintaining morality) arguments. These older adolescents were beginning to take a broad societal perspective on justice and were concerned about acting in ways that would help maintain the social system.

In short, the main developmental trend in moral reasoning during adolescence is a shift from preconventional thinking to more conventional reasoning. During this period, most individuals seem to rise above a concern with external rewards and punishments and begin to express a genuine concern with living up to the moral standards that parents and other authorities have taught them and ensuring that laws designed to make human relations orderly and fair are taken seriously and maintained. Many teens also begin to view morality as an important part of their identity and want to be able to think of themselves as honest, fair, and caring individuals (Damon & Hart, 1992). Postconventional reasoning does not emerge until adulthood (if at all).

Antisocial Behavior

Although most adolescents internalize society's moral standards, a minority of youths, like Andy Williams described at the beginning of the chapter, are involved in serious antisocial conduct—muggings, rapes, armed robberies, knifings, drive-by shootings. Might adolescents who engage repeatedly in aggressive, antisocial acts simply be cases of arrested moral development who have not internalized conventional values? Studies do suggest that juvenile offenders are more likely than nondelinquents to use preconventional, egocentric, moral reasoning (Gregg, Gibbs, & Basinger, 1994; Trevethan & Walker, 1989). Aggressive youths were also less likely as children to show empathy or concern for others (Hastings et al., 2000). Some offenders clearly lack a sense of right and wrong and feel little remorse about their criminal acts. Yet the relationship between moral reasoning and antisocial behavior is weak. A sizable number of delinquents are capable of conventional moral reasoning but commit illegal acts anyway (Blasi, 1980). This suggests that to understand the origins of antisocial conduct, we must consider a wider range of factors (see Moeller, 2001).

DODGE'S SOCIAL INFORMATION-PROCESSING MODEL

Kenneth Dodge has advanced our understanding by offering a social information-processing model of social behavior that has been used to analyze contributors to aggressive behavior (Crick & Dodge, 1994; Dodge, 1986; also see Pettit, Polaha, & Mize, 2001). Imagine that you are walking down the aisle in a classroom and trip over a classmate's leg. As you fall to the floor, you are not quite sure what happened. Dodge and other social information-processing theorists believe that the individual's reactions to frustration, anger, or provocation depend not so much on the social cues present in the situation as on the ways in which the person processes and interprets this information.

An individual who is provoked (as by being tripped) progresses through six steps in information processing, according to Dodge:

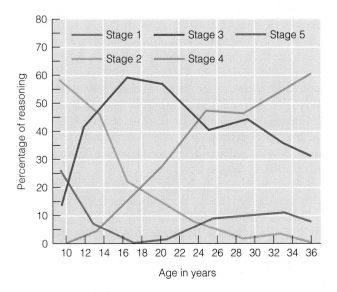

Figure 13.3 Average percentage of moral reasoning at each of Kohlberg's stages for males from age 10 to age 36
SOURCE: Colby et al. (1983)

1. *Encoding*—taking in information
2. *Interpretation*—making sense of this information and deciding what caused the other person's behavior
3. *Clarification of goals*—deciding what one wants to achieve in the situation
4. *Response search*—thinking of possible actions to achieve the goal
5. *Response decision*—weighing the pros and cons of these alternative actions
6. *Behavioral enactment*—doing something

We do not necessarily go through these steps in precise order; we can cycle back and forth among them or work on two or more simultaneously (Crick & Dodge, 1994). And at any step, we may draw not only on information available in the immediate situation but on a stored database that includes memories of previous social experiences and information about the social world.

As you might imagine, the skills involved in carrying out these six steps in social information processing increase with age (Dodge & Price, 1994). Older children are more able than younger ones to do such things as encode all the relevant cues in a situation, accurately interpret cues to determine what caused another person to behave as he or she did, generate a range of responses, and carry off intended behaviors skillfully. Why, then, are some children of a given age more aggressive than others?

Highly aggressive youths, including adolescents incarcerated for violent crimes, show deficient or biased information processing at every step of the way (Dodge, 1993; Slaby & Guerra, 1988). For example, a highly aggressive adolescent who is tripped by a classmate is likely to (1) process relatively few of the available cues in the situation and show a bias toward information suggesting that the tripping was deliberate rather than accidental (for example, noticing a fleeting smirk on the classmate's face); (2) make an *attribution of hostile intent,* inferring, based on the information gathered, that the classmate meant to cause harm; (3) set a goal of getting even (rather than, for example, a goal of smoothing relations), (4)

think of only a few possible ways to react, mostly aggressive ones; (5) conclude, after evaluating alternative actions, that an aggressive response will have favorable outcomes (or perhaps not think through the possible negative consequences of an aggressive response); and (6) carry out the particular aggressive response selected (see Table 13.1).

Many aggressive youths also skip steps of the model and act impulsively, "without thinking"; they respond automatically based on their database of past experiences. These youths tend to see the world as a hostile place and are easily angered. If a situation is ambiguous (as a tripping or bumping incident is likely to be), they are more likely than nonaggressive youths to quickly attribute hostile intent to whoever harms them (Crick & Dodge, 1994; Slaby & Guerra, 1988). Interestingly, 4- to 6-year-olds who are rejected by peers because of their aggressive and otherwise irritating behavior do as well as their more popular peers on theory-of-mind tasks, but appear to have developed a "theory of 'nasty minds,'" attributing hostile intentions and motives to other people even at this early age (Badenes, Estevan, & Garcia Bacete, 2000). Severely violent youths have often experienced abandonment, neglect, abuse, and other traumas that may have given them cause to view the world as a hostile place and to feel morally justified in going after anyone who threatens or wrongs them (Garbarino, 1999; Margolin & Gordis, 2000).

Aggressive youths also tend to evaluate the consequences of aggression far more positively than other adolescents do. They expect their aggressive acts to achieve the desired results, view being "tough" and controlling others as important to their self-esteem, and feel morally justified in acting because they believe they are only retaliating against individuals who are "out to get them" (Coie et al., 1991; Smithmyer, Hubbard, & Simons, 2000). They often belong to peer groups whose members value toughness and reinforce one another for bullying classmates or otherwise misbehaving (Poulin & Boivin, 2000).

Dodge's social information-processing model is helpful in understanding why children and adolescents might behave aggressively in particular situations. However, it leaves somewhat

Table 13.1 The Six Steps in Dodge's Social Information-Processing Model, with Likely Responses of a Highly Aggressive Youth to Provocation

Step	Behaviors	Likely Response of Aggressive Youth
1. Encoding of cues	Search for, attend to, and register cues in the situation	Focus on cues suggesting hostile intent; ignore other relevant information
2. Interpretation of cues	Interpret situation; infer other's motive	Infer that provoker had hostile intent
3. Clarification of goals	Formulate goal in situation	Make goal to retaliate
4. Response search	Generate possible responses	Generate few options, most of them aggressive
5. Response evaluation	Assess likely consequences of responses generated; choose the best	See advantages in responding aggressively rather than nonaggressively (or fail to evaluate consequences at all, act impulsively)
6. Behavioral enactment	Produce chosen response; act	Behave aggressively

NOTE: Social information processors make use of a database of information about past social experiences, social rules, and social behavior at each step of the process and skip around from step to step. See Crick & Dodge (1994) for further details and relevant research.

unclear the extent to which the underlying problem is *how one thinks* (how skilled one is at processing social information), *what one thinks* (for example, whether one believes that other people are hostile or that aggression pays), or *whether one thinks* (how impulsive one is). It has also been criticized for focusing too little attention on the powerful emotions that often interact with cognition to give rise to aggressive behavior. For example, children who are by temperament high in emotionality but have difficulty regulating and controlling their emotions are especially likely to show deficiencies in social information processing and to engage in problem behavior (Eisenberg et al., 1996; Lemerise & Arsenio, 2000). Finally, we need other research to tell us why some children and not others develop the social information-processing styles that are associated with aggressive behavior.

Patterson's Coercive Family Environments

Family influences on aggression may be part of the answer. Gerald Patterson and his colleagues have found that highly antisocial children and adolescents often experience **coercive family environments** in which family members are locked in power struggles, each trying to control the others through coercive tactics such as threatening, yelling, and hitting (Patterson, DeBaryshe & Ramsey, 1989; Kiesner, Dishion, & Poulin, 2001). In some cases, parents use harsh discipline or are even abusive (Margolin & Gordis, 2000). Coercive family processes were first identified in families with boys who were out of control, but they also surface in the families of girls with behavior problems (Eddy, Leve, & Fagot, 2001). Parents learn (through negative reinforcement) that they can stop their children's misbehavior, temporarily at least, by threatening, yelling, and hitting. Meanwhile, children learn (also through negative reinforcement) that they can get their parents to lay off them by ignoring requests, whining, throwing full-blown temper tantrums, and otherwise being as difficult as possible. As both parents and children learn to rely more and more on coercive tactics, parents increasingly lose control over their children's behavior until even the loudest lectures and hardest spankings have little effect and the child's conduct problems spiral out of control.

Growing up in a coercive family environment sets in motion the next steps in the making of an antisocial adolescent (see Figure 13.4): The child, already aggressive and unpleasant to be around, ends up performing poorly in school and being rejected by other children. By default, he or she becomes involved in a peer group made up of other low-achieving, antisocial, and unpopular youths and is then steered even further in the direction of a delinquent career by these colleagues in crime, who positively reinforce one another's talk about rule breaking and delinquent acts (Dishion, Andrews, & Crosby, 1995; Kiesner et al., 2001). Overall, there is a good deal of support for the view that ineffective parenting in childhood results in behavior problems, involvement with antisocial peers, and, in turn, antisocial behavior in adolescence.

Nature and Nurture

Ultimately, severe antisocial behavior is the product of a complex interplay between genetic predisposition and social learning experiences (Moeller, 2001). We can start by putting aggression in an evolutionary context. For example, it has been argued that male aggression evolved because it serves adaptive functions such as enabling males to compete with other males for mates and to control their mates so that they remain faithful (Buss, 1999; Hilton, Harris, & Rice, 2000). In addition, some individuals are more genetically predisposed than others to have hostile, irritable temperaments and to engage in aggressive, delinquent, and criminal behavior (Miles & Carey, 1997; Simonoff, 2001). Some of these individuals may be predisposed to violence by neurological deficits or low levels of certain neurotransmitters (Teichner & Golden, 2000). Through the mechanism of *gene/environment correlation*, children who inherit a genetic predisposition to become aggressive evoke the kind of coercive parenting that breeds aggression, even when they grow up with adoptive parents rather than with their biological parents. Coercive parenting, in turn, further reinforces their aggressive tendencies (Lytton, 2000; O'Connor et al., 1998).

Many social influences can also help determine whether a child genetically predisposed to be aggressive ends up on a healthy or unhealthy developmental trajectory. Some cultural contexts are more likely to breed aggression than others. In Japan, a *collectivist culture* in which children are taught very early to value social harmony, children are less angered by in-

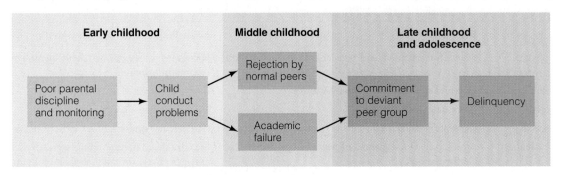

Figure 13.4 Patterson's model of the development of antisocial behavior starts with poor discipline and coercive cycles of family influence.

Source: Adapted from Patterson et al. (1989)

terpersonal conflicts and less likely to react to them aggressively than American children are (Zahn-Waxler et al., 1996). By contrast, children in the United States see violence glorified on television every day, and at least some of them become more aggressive as a result of their viewing (D. R. Anderson et al., 2001; Bushman & Huesmann, 2001). They live in an especially violent country that leads all industrialized countries in rapes and murders (Wolff, Rutten, & Bayer, 1992). And they live in a society in which guns are all too accessible to children and adolescents. Geoffrey Jackman and his colleagues (2001) brought 8- to 12-year-old boys into a clinic examining room in pairs or trios. They were told they could play with toys on the counter but were not to open any cabinets. The researchers had planted two water pistols in one cabinet drawer and a real handgun in another. Sure enough, within the 15 minutes available to them, 72% of the groups studied found the handgun. Only one group left to inform an adult about it. Rather, 76% of the groups handled the gun, and one or more of the boys in 48% of the groups pulled the trigger! If boys cannot be trusted around guns, an obvious way to reduce youth violence is to make guns less accessible by not keeping them in the home or locking them up at all times.

Subcultural and neighborhood factors can also contribute to youth violence. Rates of aggression and violent crime are 2 to 3 times higher in lower socioeconomic neighborhoods and communities, especially transient ones, than in middle-class ones (Elliott & Ageton, 1980; Maughan, 2001). Community norms that support the use of violence to resolve conflicts and social stressors that make it difficult for parents to monitor and manage their children both contribute (Jagers, Bingham, & Hans, 1996). Certain schools also have higher rates of delinquency and aggression than others, even when socioeconomic factors are controlled (Maughan, 2001). This may be because negative peer influences prevail in these schools. In school environments that breed aggression, peer influences can turn even an adolescent without a genetic predisposition to be aggressive into an aggressive youth (Rowe, Almeida, & Jacobson, 1999). Since both bullies and victims of bullies (like Andy Williams) are more likely than others youths to commit violent acts later in life, many schools are now taking active steps to combat bullying instead of writing it off as normal child behavior (Strauss, 2001).

In sum, the severe antisocial behavior that some adolescents display is much more than a matter of immature moral reasoning, although many delinquent youths do reason at Kohlberg's preconventional level. Antisocial behavior can also be traced to deficiencies in social information-processing skills that make youngsters quick to attribute hostile intentions to other people and convinced of the value of aggression. This information-processing style, in turn, may be rooted in genetically influenced temperamental traits that make for strong negative emotions and little emotional control. Social learning experiences in the family (coercive family environments), peer group, and wider social environment also contribute.

Gangs in inner city areas are only part of the larger problem of youth violence.

All these factors interact to help to determine whether youths enter adulthood as model citizens or menaces to society. Although most severely antisocial adults started their antisocial careers in childhood, most children and adolescents who engage in aggressive behavior and other antisocial acts do not grow up to be antisocial adults (Maughan & Rutter, 2001). There seem to be two subgroups of antisocial youths: one group that is persistently antisocial across the life span, and another that is antisocial mainly in adolescence (Moffitt & Caspi, 2001). About one-third to two-thirds of young children who engage repeatedly in antisocial behavior—who fight, are cruel to animals, lie, and fail to get along with peers—become delinquent adolescents and go on to engage in serious violent and criminal behavior as adults (Loeber & Farrington, 2000). Persistently aggressive children tend to have distinctive personalities and receive inadequate parenting (Moffitt & Caspi, 2001). The consequences of their early misbehavior cumulate, and they find themselves leaving school early, participating in troubled relationships, and having difficulty keeping jobs (Loeber & Stouthamer-Loeber, 1998; Maughan & Rutter, 2001). Genetic factors probably play a more significant role for these early-onset, persistent delinquents than for adolescent-onset delinquents. Adolescent-onset delinquents do not begin their antisocial careers until their teens, probably in response to a combination of stress and peer group influences, and often do not persist in their antisocial behavior as adults (Loeber & Stouthhamer-Loeber, 1998; Moffitt & Caspi, 2001). In sum, there seem to be multiple pathways to a career as an antisocial adult and many factors that can deflect a person off one pathway and onto another. Perhaps as a result, violence prevention and treatment programs can take many forms, as the Applications box on page 360 suggests.

Combating Youth Violence

In recent years, U.S. society has been struggling with the problem of how to prevent and treat serious aggression and violence on the part of children and adolescents like Andy Williams, the troubled teenager described at the start of this chapter. Many believe that violence prevention needs to start in infancy or toddlerhood—perhaps even at conception—with a strong emphasis on positive parenting, followed by programs to improve the social skills and impulse control of young children at risk (Tremblay, 2000). School-based violence prevention programs can also be effective if they teach children appropriate social-cognitive skills and more prosocial behavior (Henrich, Brown, & Aber, 1999). Here, though, we focus on how three perspectives described in this chapter—Kohlberg's theory of moral development, Dodge's social information-processing model, and Patterson's coercive family environment model—have been applied to the challenge of treating youths who have already become antisocial.

Improving Moral Reasoning

How can we foster strong moral values and advanced moral thinking among children and adolescents? If, as both Piaget and Kohlberg claim, peers are at least as important as parents in stimulating moral growth, one sensible approach is to harness "peer power." This is precisely what many psychologists and educators have tried to do, putting children or adolescents together in pairs or small groups to discuss hypothetical moral dilemmas. The rationale is simple: Opportunities to take other people's perspectives and exposure to forms of moral reasoning more mature than their own will create cognitive disequilibrium, which will motivate children to devise more mature modes of thinking.

Does participation in group discussions of moral issues produce more mature moral reasoning? It appears so (Rest et al., 1999). Average changes that are the equivalent of

about 4 to 5 years of natural development can be achieved in programs lasting only 3 to 12 weeks. Moreover, researchers have learned what kinds of discussion are most helpful. For example, it is indeed important that students be exposed to reasoning that is slightly more mature than their own (Lapsley, 1996). Also, moral growth is most likely to occur when students actively transform, analyze, or otherwise act upon what their conversation partners have said—when they say things like "You're missing an important difference here" or "Here's something I think we can agree on" (Berkowitz & Gibbs, 1983). Participation in Kohlbergian moral discussion groups can even raise the level of moral thinking of institutionalized delinquents (Niles, 1986). However, it does not appear to decrease their delinquent behavior, so the search for ways to bring about lasting behavior change continues (Gibbs et al., 1996; Niles, 1986).

Building Social Information-Processing Skills

As we saw earlier, Kenneth Dodge's social information-processing model identifies six steps at which a highly aggressive youth may display deficient or biased information processing. Nancy Guerra and Ronald Slaby (1990) coached small groups of incarcerated and violent juveniles of both sexes (1) to look for situational cues other than those suggesting hostile intentions, (2) to control their impulses so that they do not lash out without considering the consequences, and (3) to generate more nonaggressive solutions to conflicts. After a 12-week intervention, these adolescents showed dramatic improvements in social information-processing skills, believed less strongly in the value of aggression, and behaved less aggressively in their interactions with authority figures and other inmates.

Trained offenders were only somewhat less likely than untrained offenders (34% versus 46%) to violate their paroles after release, however, suggesting that they may have

The Adult

As adults assume responsibilities as parents, work supervisors, and community leaders, their moral decisions affect more and more people. How does moral thinking change during adulthood, and what role do religious beliefs play in the moral thinking of adults?

Moral Development

As we have discovered (see Figure 13.3 on page 356), Kohlberg's postconventional moral reasoning appears to

emerge *only* during the adult years (if it emerges at all). In Kohlberg's 20-year longitudinal study (Colby et al., 1983), the large majority of adults in their 30s still reasoned at the conventional level, although many of them had shifted from Stage 3 to Stage 4. A minority of individuals—one-sixth to one-eighth of the sample—had begun to use Stage 5 postconventional reasoning, showing a deeper understanding of the basis for laws and distinguishing between just and unjust laws. Clearly, there is opportunity for moral growth in early adulthood. College provides an excellent social context for that growth (Rest et al., 1999).

Do these growth trends continue into later adulthood, or do older adults instead revert to less mature forms of moral

reverted to their antisocial ways once back in the environment in which their aggressive tendencies originated. Indeed, for many young African American and Hispanic males in gang-dominated inner-city neighborhoods, being quick to detect others' hostile intentions and defend oneself against assault may well be an important survival skill (Hudley & Graham, 1993).

Breaking Coercive Cycles

Gerald Patterson and his colleagues maintain that the secret to working with violent youths is to change the dynamics of interactions in their families so that aggressive tactics of controlling other family members are no longer reinforced and the cycle of coercive behavior is broken. In one study, Patterson and his team (Bank et al., 1991) randomly assigned adolescent boys who were repeat offenders to either a special parent training intervention or the service usually provided by the juvenile court. In the parent training program, therapy sessions held with each family (usually including the boy) taught parents how to observe both prosocial and antisocial behaviors in their son; to communicate closely with their son's school and gather teachers' reports on his performance and behavior at school; and, using methods derived from social learning theory, to establish behavior contracts that detail what the youth can expect in the way of reinforcers for prosocial behavior and penalties for antisocial behavior.

Overall, the parent training intervention was judged at least a partial success. It improved family processes, although it did not fully resolve the problems these dysfunctional families had. Rates of serious crime among this group dropped and remained lower even 3 years after the intervention ended. The alternative family intervention also reduced crime rates but took longer to work its effects. The research team concluded that a program involving a 6-month placement with foster parents trained in behavioral techniques, combined with parenting skills training for the youth's natural parents, might be more effective (Bank et al., 1991).

Other research tells us that such foster care programs for adolescent offenders can indeed be very effective, but only when they (1) improve parents' parenting skills and (2) limit involvement with antisocial peers (Eddy & Chamberlain, 2000). As Patterson and others have observed, peers can reinforce patterns of aggression that took form in coercive family environments. They can also undermine the effectiveness of treatment programs. Indeed, programs that put antisocial youths together in treatment groups or facilities can actually *increase* problem behavior and negative outcomes, such as drug use and delinquency, if they mainly provide antisocial youths with opportunities to reinforce one another's deviance (Dishion, McCord, & Poulin, 1999). A better strategy is to form groups with a mix of well-adjusted and aggressive youths (and hope that the well-adjusted ones prevail!).

In sum, efforts to treat aggressive youths have included attempts to apply the work of Kohlberg (by using discussion of moral issues to raise levels of moral reasoning), Dodge (by teaching effective social information-processing skills), and Patterson (by replacing coercive cycles in the family environment with positive behavior management techniques and taming negative peer influences). Many interventions have achieved short-term gains in skills but have failed to reduce rates of antisocial behavior in the long run. The most promising approaches to preventing and treating aggressive youths appear to recognize that changing patterns of antisocial behavior requires an ecological perspective, seeking to change not only the individual but his or her family and the broader social environment (Elliott, Williams, & Hamburg, 1998).

reasoning? Most studies find no major age differences in stage of moral reasoning, at least when relatively educated adults are studied and when the age groups compared have similar levels of education (Pratt & Norris, 1999). Older adults sometimes do less well than younger adults at gathering and coordinating information about the different perspectives that can be taken on a moral issue, perhaps because of declines in working memory or perhaps because they rely more on general rules in judging what is right and wrong and are not as interested in the details of different people's points of view (Pratt & Norris, 1999). However, even up to age 75, they seem to reason about moral issues as complexly as younger adults do, whether they are given Kohlberg's hypothetical dilemmas to ponder or asked to discuss real-life situations in which they were "unsure about the right thing to do" (Pratt et al., 1991, 1996). In addition, older adults have a greater sense of having learned important lessons from moral dilemmas they have faced during their lives (Pratt et al., 1999). Here, then, is an aspect of social-cognitive development that holds up very well in later life.

Religious Faith

How is religious development related to moral development? James Fowler (1981, 1991) has argued that we progress through stages of religious development that closely parallel

It's a myth that people become more religious as they near death; most religious elders were religious earlier in adulthood as well.

the stages of moral development described by Kohlberg. Fowler's interviews with individuals ranging in age from 3 to 84 indicate that children think very concretely about the religious images to which they are exposed; that adolescents and adults formulate more abstract belief systems that they can call their own; and that a few middle-aged and elderly adults progress to a kind of universalizing faith in which they transcend specific belief systems and achieve a sense of oneness with all beings.

Many people believe that religion plays an increasingly central role in people's lives and moral thinking as they get older. Although many older individuals are indeed highly religious, there is actually little change from middle age to late old age in the tendency to view religion as important and as greatly comforting (Blazer & Palmore, 1976; McFadden, 1996; Palmore, 1981). In other words, research offers no support for the idea that people "get religion" or cling to it more strongly as they approach death. Most people remain as religious later in life as they were earlier. Poor health forces some elderly people to cut back on their participation in organized religious activities, but many of them compensate with increased involvement in private religious activities such as prayer and Bible study (Ainlay & Smith, 1984; Young & Dowling, 1987).

In short, adults have the potential for both moral and religious growth during early and middle adulthood and are then likely to maintain the levels of moral reasoning and religious commitment in old age that they established earlier. Kohlberg (1973) himself argued that experience confronting moral issues and taking responsibility for one's decisions during a lifetime may help adults form more coherent philosophies of life and continue their growth as moral beings.

Kohlberg's Theory of Moral Development in Perspective

We have now seen that children think about hypothetical moral dilemmas primarily in a preconventional manner, that adolescents adopt a conventional mode of moral reasoning, and that a minority of adults progress to the postconventional level. Kohlberg appears to have discovered an important developmental progression in moral thought. Now let's complete our discussion of moral development by evaluating Kohlberg's influential theory, examining both its supporting evidence and its limitations.

Support for Kohlberg

As you'll recall, Kohlberg claims that his stages form an invariant and universal sequence of moral growth. Do all people progress through the stages in precisely the order Kohlberg specified? It appears that they do, to a point. Longitudinal studies of moral growth in several countries demonstrate this (see Colby & Kohlberg, 1987; Rest et al., 1999). Regardless of their culture, individuals do not skip stages. Moreover, only about 5% of them regress from a higher stage to a lower stage from one testing to the next; these instances of regression are so rare that they probably reflect scoring errors.

However, the idea that everyone progresses through Stages 1 to 4 in order is better supported than the idea that people continue to progress from Stage 4 to Stages 5 and 6 (Boom, Brugman, & van der Heijden, 2001). Stage 3 or 4 is the end of the developmental journey for most individuals worldwide (Snarey, 1985). And, contrary to Kohlberg's view that each person is guided by one coherent approach to moral issues, most people continue to draw on the thinking of lower stages of moral reasoning even after they have advanced to higher stages; what changes with age—and gradually at that—is the person's degree of reliance on different types of thinking (Rest et al., 1999).

Factors That Promote Moral Growth

How much support is there for Kohlberg's thinking about the factors that contribute to moral growth? Basically, he argued (as did Piaget), two influences are most important: cognitive growth and relevant social experiences.

COGNITIVE GROWTH

As Kohlberg predicted, reaching the conventional level of moral reasoning and becoming concerned about living up to the moral standards of one's parents or society requires the ability to take other people's perspectives (L. J. Walker, 1980). Gaining the capacity for postconventional or "principled" moral reasoning requires still more cognitive growth—namely, a solid command of formal operational thinking (Tomlinson-Keasey & Keasey, 1974; Walker, 1980). The person who bases moral judgments on abstract principles must be able to reason abstractly and take all possible perspectives on a moral issue. Not all proficient role takers reach the conventional level of moral reasoning, and not all formal operators progress to the postconventional level. It is just that these milestones in moral development cannot be achieved without the requisite cognitive skills.

RELEVANT SOCIAL EXPERIENCE

Kohlberg also stressed the need for social experiences that require children and adolescents to take the perspectives of others so that they can appreciate that they are part of a larger social order and that moral rules are a consensus of individuals in society. Interacting with people who hold views different from one's own also creates *cognitive disequilibrium*—a conflict between existing cognitive structures and new ideas—which in turn stimulates new ways of thinking.

Like Piaget, Kohlberg maintained that interactions with peers or equals, in which children experience and discuss differences between their own and others' perspectives, probably contribute more to moral growth than one-sided interactions with adult authority figures in which children are expected to defer to the adult's power. As it turns out, though, parents play a very significant role in moral development, and not just by using inductive discipline and being warm, supportive parents.

For example, Lawrence Walker and his colleagues (Walker, Hennig, & Krettenauer, 2000) directly compared parent and peer influences on moral development. Both 11- and 15-year-olds discussed moral dilemmas with a parent and then separately with a friend. Four years later, they were asked to respond to moral dilemmas. Interactions with both parents and friends influenced these individuals' moral development, but

in somewhat different ways. Friends were more likely than parents to challenge and disagree with a child or adolescent's ideas, and they were most likely to contribute positively to moral growth when they *did* confront and challenge. Parents, because they functioned at more advanced stages of moral development than their children, engaged them in more intellectually stimulating discussions. Parents contributed most to development when they used a positive, supportive style in which they checked to make sure they understood what their children were trying to say and probed their thinking in a gentle, Socratic manner. They did more damage than good when they took an authoritarian approach and lectured about right and wrong (see also Walker & Taylor, 1991).

Other research suggests that children may think more actively and deeply about their own and their partners' moral ideas in discussions with peers than in talks with their mothers or other adults and that discussions with peers are more likely to stimulate moral growth (Kruger, 1992; Kruger & Tomasello, 1986). There does it seem to be something special, then, about hashing out disagreements with one's peers and having to take their perspectives. But although Piaget and Kohlberg were right to call attention to the role of peers in moral development, they failed to appreciate that parents also have much to contribute.

Another important kind of social experience is advanced schooling. Consistently, adults who go on to college and receive many years of education think more complexly about moral issues than do those who are less educated (Pratt et al., 1991). Advanced educational experiences not only contribute to cognitive growth but also provide exposure to the diverse ideas and perspectives that produce cognitive conflict and soul-searching.

Adults in many rural societies seem to have no need for postconventional moral reasoning because they share the same moral perspective.

Finally, participating in a complex, diverse, and democratic society can stimulate moral development. Just as we learn the give-and-take of mutual perspective taking by discussing issues with our friends, we learn in a diverse democracy that the opinions of many groups must be weighed and that laws reflect a consensus of the citizens rather than the arbitrary rulings of a dictator. Indeed, cross-cultural studies suggest that postconventional moral reasoning emerges primarily in Western democracies; people in rural villages in underdeveloped countries show no signs of it (Snarey, 1985). Individuals in these homogeneous communities may have less experience with the kinds of political conflicts and compromises that take place in a more complex society and so may never have any need to question conventional moral standards.

In sum, Kohlberg not only devised a stage sequence that appears to have universal applicability, but he also correctly identified some of the major factors that determine how far an individual progresses in the sequence. Advanced moral reasoning is most likely if the individual has acquired the necessary cognitive skills (particularly perspective-taking skills and, later, the ability to reason abstractly). Moreover, an individual's moral development is highly influenced by social learning experiences, including interactions with parents, discussions with peers, exposure to higher education, and participation in democracy.

But when a theory arouses the enormous interest that Kohlberg's has aroused, you can bet that it will also provoke criticism. Many of the criticisms have centered on two themes: the possibility that Kohlberg's theory is biased against certain groups of people, and the fact that it says much about moral reasoning but little about moral affect and behavior.

Is the Theory Biased?

Some critics have charged that Kohlberg's theory reflects a cultural bias, a liberal bias, and/or a sexist bias. That is, it has been said that the stage theory unfairly makes people from non-Western cultures, people with conservative values, or the half of the human race that is female appear to be less morally mature.

Culture Bias?

Although research indicates that children and adolescents in all cultures proceed through the first three or four of Kohlberg's stages in order, we have seen that postconventional reasoning, as Kohlberg defines it, simply does not exist in some societies. Critics charge that Kohlberg's highest stages reflect a Western ideal of justice centered on individual rights, making the stage theory biased against people who live in non-Western societies (Shweder, Mahapatra, & Miller, 1990). People in collectivist societies, which emphasize social harmony and place the good of the group ahead of the good of the individual, may be viewed as conventional moral thinkers in Kohlberg's system but may actually have sophisticated concepts of justice (Snarey, 1985; Tietjen & Walker, 1985). The theme that moral development can vary considerably from society to society is explored further in the Explorations box on page 365.

Liberal Bias?

Similarly, critics charge that a person must hold liberal values—for example, opposing capital punishment or supporting civil disobedience in the name of human rights—in order to be classified as a postconventional moral reasoner. In one study (de Vries & Walker, 1986), 100% of the college students who showed signs of postconventional thought opposed capital punishment, whereas none of the men and only a third of the women who were transitional between Stage 2 and Stage 3 moral reasoning opposed capital punishment. As de Vries and Walker (1986) note, it could be that opposition to capital punishment is a more valid moral position than support of capital punishment in that it involves valuing life highly. However, it could also be that the theory is unfair to conservatives who emphasize law-and-order principles (Lapsley et al., 1984).

Gender Bias?

Criticisms of culture bias and liberal bias may have some merit, but no criticism of Kohlberg has stirred more heat than the charge that his theory is biased against women. Carol Gilligan (1977, 1982, 1993) was disturbed by the fact that Kohlberg's stages were developed based on interviews with males and that, in some studies, women seemed to be the moral inferiors of men, reasoning at Stage 3 when men usu-

Carol Gilligan maintains that girls are socialized into a morality of care rather than the morality of justice that interested Kohlberg.

Cultural Differences in Moral Thinking

Is each of the following acts wrong? If so, how serious a violation is it?

1. A young married woman is beaten black and blue by her husband after going to a movie without his permission despite having been warned not to do so again.
2. A brother and sister decide to get married and have children.
3. The day after his father died, the oldest son in a family gets a haircut and eats chicken.

These are 3 of 39 acts presented by Richard Shweder, Manamohan Mahapatra, and Joan Miller (1990, pp. 165–166) to children ages 5 to 13 and adults in India and the United States. You may be surprised to learn that Hindu children and adults rated the son's having a haircut and eating chicken after his father's death as among the most morally offensive of the 39 acts they rated. The husband's beating of his disobedient wife was not considered wrong at all! American children and adults, of course, viewed beating one's wife as far more serious than breaking seemingly arbitrary rules about appropriate mourning behavior. Although Indians and Americans could agree that a few acts, such as brother–sister incest, were serious moral violations, they did not agree on much else.

Moreover, Indian children and adults viewed the Hindu ban against behavior disrespectful of one's dead father as a universal moral rule; they thought it would be best if everyone in the world followed it, and they strongly disagreed that it would be acceptable to change the rule if most people in their society wanted to change it. For similar reasons, they believed that it is a serious moral offense for a widow to eat fish or for a woman to cook food for her family during her menstrual period. To orthodox Hindus, rules against such behaviors are required by natural law; they are not just arbitrary social conventions created by members of society. Similarly, Hindus regard it as morally necessary for a man to beat his disobedient wife in order to uphold his obligations as head of the family.

Shweder also observed very different developmental trends in moral thinking in India and the United States, as the figure shows. With age, Indian children saw more and more issues as matters of universal moral principle, whereas American children saw fewer and fewer issues this way. Moreover, even the youngest children in both societies expressed moral outlooks very similar to those expressed by adults in their own society and very different from those expressed by either children or adults in the other society.

Based on these cross-cultural findings, Shweder calls into question Kohlberg's claims that all children everywhere construct similar moral codes at similar ages and that certain universal moral principles exist. In addition, Shweder questions Turiel's claim that children everywhere distinguish from an early age between moral rules and more arbitrary social-conventional rules. Overall, then, these fascinating findings challenge the cognitive developmental position that important aspects of moral development are universal. Instead, they support a social learning or contextual perspective on moral development and suggest that children's moral judgments are shaped by the social context in which they develop. Possibly children all over the world think in more and more complex ways about moral issues as they get older, as Kohlberg claimed, but at the same time adopt quite different notions about what is right and what is wrong, as Shweder claims.

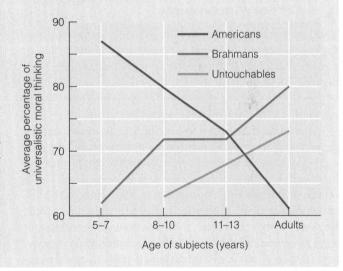

ally reasoned at stage 4. She hypothesized that females develop a distinctly *feminine* orientation to moral issues, one that is no less mature than the orientation adopted by most men and incorporated into Kohlberg's theory.

Gilligan suggests that boys, who are traditionally raised to be independent, assertive, and achievement oriented, come to view moral dilemmas as conflicts between the rights of two or more parties and to view laws and other social conventions as necessary for resolving these inevitable conflicts (a perspective reflected in Kohlberg's Stage 4 reasoning). Girls, Gilligan argues, are brought up to be nurturant, empathic, and concerned with the needs of others and to define their sense of "goodness" in terms of their concern for other people (a perspective that approximates Stage 3 in Kohlberg's scheme). What this differences boils down to is the difference between a "masculine" **morality of justice** (focused on laws defining individual rights) and a "feminine" **morality of care** (focused on one's responsibility for the welfare of other people).

Despite the appeal of Gilligan's ideas, there is little support for her claim that Kohlberg's theory is systematically biased against females. In most studies, women reason just as complexly about moral issues as men do when their answers are scored by Kohlberg's criteria (Jaffee & Hyde, 2000). Moreover, most studies do not support Gilligan's view that males and females think differently about moral dilemmas, and those that do find differences find only small ones indicating that females sometimes use more care reasoning than males and males sometimes use more justice reasoning than females (Jaffee & Hyde, 2000). It seems that both men and women use both types of reasoning—for example, a lot of care-based reasoning when they ponder dilemmas involving relationships, and a lot of justice-based reasoning when issues of rights arise. The nature of the moral dilemma is far more important than the gender of the moral reasoner (Wark & Krebs, 1996). And there is surprisingly little support for Gilligan's view that boys and girls are socialized differently in the area of morality (Lollis, Ross, & Leroux, 1996).

Although her hypothesis about sex differences in moral reasoning and their origin has not received much support, Gilligan's work *has* increased our awareness that both men and women often think about moral issues in terms of their responsibilities for the welfare of other people. Kohlberg emphasized only one way—a very legalistic and abstract way—of thinking about right and wrong. Gilligan has called attention to the value of tracing the development of *both* a morality of justice and a morality of care in *both* males and females (Brabeck, 1983; Moshman, 1999).

Is the Theory Incomplete?

Another major criticism of Kohlberg's theory is that it focuses too much attention on moral reasoning or cognition. It fails to recognize that people often make moral decisions quite automatically, based on habit, with little reflection at all (J. S. Walker, 2000). And the theory slights moral affect and moral behavior (Hoffman, 2000; Moshman, 1999).

As Martin Hoffman (2000) emphasizes, emotional responses such as empathy provide the motivation to take others' perspectives and needs seriously and to act to improve their welfare rather than our own. Emotions clearly play a central role in morality, and any theory that overlooks the role of emotions and motivations is therefore incomplete. Recognizing this, researchers today are looking more closely at what emotions children and adults experience when they engage in both immoral and moral behavior, and how they regulate these emotions (Eisenberg, 2000).

Kohlberg also did not pay much attention to how people actually behave. As already noted, a person may decide to uphold or to break a law at any of the stages of moral reasoning. What distinguishes one stage from the next is the complexity or structure of a person's reasoning, not the specific decisions he or she reaches. Nonetheless, Kohlberg has argued that more advanced moral reasoners are more likely to behave in accordance with widely accepted moral standards than less advanced moral reasoners are. He would predict, for example,

that the preconventional thinker might readily decide to cheat on a test if the chances of being detected were small and the potential rewards high. The postconventional thinker would be more likely to appreciate that cheating is wrong in principle, regardless of the chances of detection, because it infringes on the rights of others and undermines social order.

How well *does* a person's stage of moral reasoning predict his or her behavior? Individuals at higher stages of moral reasoning, especially when their empathy is aroused, are indeed more likely than individuals at lower stages to behave prosocially (Miller et al., 1996). For instance, Elizabeth Midlarsky and her colleagues (1999) gave elderly adults moral dilemmas focused on prosocial behavior (for example, about whether to donate blood to a very sick person at considerable cost to oneself). Adults whose responses to these moral dilemmas were based on abstract moral principles were more helpful in everyday life than those who reasoned at less advanced levels.

Advanced moral reasoners are also less likely to cheat or engage in delinquent and criminal activity (Judy & Nelson, 2000; Rest et al., 1999). For instance, Kohlberg (1975) found that only 15% of students who reasoned at the postconventional level cheated when given an opportunity to do so, compared with 55% of students at the conventional level reasoning and 70% of those at the preconventional level. Still, relationships between stage of moral reasoning and moral behavior are typically weak (Bruggeman & Hart, 1996). Many personal qualities besides level of moral reasoning, and many situational or contextual factors as well, also influence whether a person will behave morally or immorally in daily life.

In sum, Kohlberg's theory of moral development describes a universal sequence of changes in moral reasoning extending from childhood through adulthood. Moreover, the evidence supports Kohlberg's view that both cognitive growth and experiences taking others' perspectives contribute to moral growth. However, the theory may not be entirely fair to people who live in non-Western societies, who hold values other than liberal, democratic ones, or who emphasize a morality of care rather than a morality of justice. Furthermore, because Kohlberg's theory focuses entirely on moral reasoning, we must rely on other perspectives to understand how moral affect and moral behavior develop and how thought, emotion, and behavior interact to make us the moral beings we ultimately become.

We have now completed our series of chapters on the development of the self, or the person as an individual, looking at the development of self-conceptions and distinctive personality traits (Chapter 11), identities as males or females (Chapter 12), and now social-cognitive skills and morality. But individual development does not occur in a vacuum. Repeatedly, we have seen that the individual's development may take different paths depending on the social context in which it occurs. Our task in upcoming chapters will be to put the individual even more squarely into a social context. It should become clear that throughout our lives we are both independent and interdependent—separate from and connected to other developing persons.

Summary Points

1. Social cognition (thinking about self and others) is involved in all social behavior, including moral behavior. Starting in infancy with milestones such as joint attention and pretend play, children develop a theory of mind—an understanding that mental states exist and guide behavior. At 2, they show evidence of a desire psychology; by age 4, they master a belief-desire psychology and pass false belief tasks. Developing a theory of mind requires normal neurological, cognitive, and language development as well as appropriate social experience (for example, discussing mental states with parents and siblings).

2. In characterizing other people, preschool children focus on their physical features and activities, whereas children 8 and older describe people's inner psychological traits. With age, children also overcome their egocentrism and become more adept at adopting others' perspectives. Both person perception and role-taking abilities become more abstract during adolescence. Social-cognitive skills often improve during adulthood, but may decline late in life if a person is socially isolated.

3. Morality has cognitive, affective, and behavioral components; it is the ability to distinguish between right and wrong, to act on that distinction, and to experience appropriate moral emotions.

4. Freud's psychoanalytic theory describes moral development in terms of the formation of the superego and moral *emotions* such as guilt. Cognitive developmental theorist Lawrence Kohlberg proposed three levels of moral *reasoning*—preconventional, conventional, and postconventional—each with two stages. Social learning theorists have focused on how moral *behavior* is influenced by past learning and situational pressures.

5. Although infants are amoral in some respects, they begin learning about right and wrong through their early disciplinary encounters, internalization of rules, and displays of empathy and prosocial behavior by age 2. Their moral growth depends on the goodness of fit between their temperament and the approach to moral training their parents adopt.

6. According to Kohlberg, most children operate at the preconventional level of moral reasoning. Piaget proposed that children's moral thinking progresses through stages, but both Kohlberg and Piaget underestimated the moral sophistication of young children (for example, their ability to consider both intentions and consequences in judging acts, to distinguish between moral and social-conventional rules, and to question adult authority). Situational influences contribute to moral inconsistency. Reinforcement, modeling, and the disciplinary approach of induction can foster moral growth, but a child's temperament also influences his or her response to moral training.

7. During adolescence, a shift from preconventional to conventional moral reasoning is evident, and many adolescents incorporate moral values into their sense of identity as an individual.

8. Antisocial behavior can be understood in terms of Dodge's steps in social information processing; Patterson's coercive family environments and the negative peer group influences they set in motion; and more generally, the interaction of genetic predisposition with social-environmental influences ranging from culture to neighborhood, school, and family. Attempts to prevent and reduce youth violence have applied the work of Kohlberg (through moral discussion groups designed to raise levels of moral reasoning), Dodge (by teaching effective social information-processing skills), and Patterson (by teaching parents positive child management strategies in hopes of changing coercive family environments).

9. *Some* adults progress from the conventional to the postconventional level of moral reasoning and advance in their religious thinking as well; elderly adults typically do not "regress" in their moral thinking and usually maintain the level of commitment to religion they had earlier in adulthood.

10. Kohlberg's stages of moral reasoning form an invariant sequence, with progress through them influenced by cognitive growth and social experiences that involve taking others' perspectives. It has been charged that Kohlberg's theory is biased against people from non-Western cultures, people who do not share his liberal values, and women who express Gilligan's morality of care rather than a morality of justice. Critics also claim that the theory says too little about moral affect and behavior and cannot predict behavior well.

Critical Thinking

1. Listen closely to a conversation in which your friends talk about people, and write down any statements in which they refer to people's beliefs, desires, intentions, and the like in attempting to explain their behavior. Do you see evidence that your friends have a theory of mind? How could we explain each other's behavior without one?

2. A preconventional thinker, a conventional thinker, and a postconventional thinker all face a moral dilemma on final exam day: There's a very smart student in the row ahead of them whose exam answers are in plain sight. Should they cheat or not? Provide examples of the reasoning you might expect at each of the three main levels of moral development—one argument in favor of cheating and one against it at each level. (Are any of these arguments especially difficult to make?)

3. Look back at the chapter-opening description of Andy Williams, the youth who murdered two people in a shooting rampage at his school. Drawing on material in this chapter, why might he have done what he did? Profile him in terms of (a) his likely temperament, (b) his stage of moral reasoning, (c) his social information-processing style, (d) the discipline approaches his parents used, and (e) any other factors you think may have been significant contributors to his actions.

Key Terms

social cognition	preconventional morality
false belief task	conventional morality
theory of mind	postconventional morality
joint attention	amoral
desire psychology	moral rules
belief-desire psychology	social-conventional rules
role-taking skills	love withdrawal
morality	power assertion
moral affects	induction
empathy	coercive family environment
prosocial behavior	morality of justice
moral reasoning	morality of care

On the Web

Web Sites to Explore

Kohlberg

This site details Kohlberg's stages of moral development (though it uses different names for them) and provides some interesting values clarifications surveys that can help you think about your own moral development.
http://mentalhelp.net/psyhelp/chap3/chap3h.htm

Gilligan

If you would like to read a little more about Gilligan's ideas on gender differences, this site provides a good summary of her thinking, along with critiques.
http://afirstlook.com/archive/diffvoice.cfm?source=archther

Youth Violence

For a major analysis of youth violence and how to combat it, see *Youth Violence: A Report of the Surgeon General.* It provides statistics, summarizes research findings, confronts myths, and outlines strategies for preventing this major social problem.
http://www.surgeongeneral.gov/library/youthviolence/

More on Youth Violence

Another useful reference is *Best Practices of Youth Violence Prevention: A Sourcebook for Community Action,* available at the Centers for Disease Control and Prevention "Safe USA" site. This book, available online, draws on intervention research in areas such as parenting and conflict resolution skills. The "Safe USA" site is also searchable.
http://www.cdc.gov/safeusa/publications/bestpractices.htm

Search Online with InfoTrac College Edition

For additional information, explore InfoTrac College Edition, your online library. Go to
http://www.infotrac-college.com and use the passcode that came on the card with your book. Because adolescence is a time of considerable moral growth, you might try searching for "morality and adolescence." Find a recent research study and see what it tells you about morality during this period of the life span.

Visit Our Web Site

Go to http://www.wadsworth.com/psychology, where you will find online resources directly linked to your book.

Life-Span CD-ROM

Go to the Wadsworth Life-Span CD-ROM for further study of the concepts in this chapter. The CD-ROM also includes quizzes and additional activities to expand your learning experience.

Attachment and Social Relationships

THE LITTLE GIRL IN the photo below is Baby Jessica, and she is about to be whisked away from the only parents she has ever known (Ingrassia & Springen, 1994). In August 1993, a nation watched in horror as this 2-year-old was taken from the DeBoers (the parents who thought they had adopted her, though the adoption was contested from the start and never finalized) and awarded by the court to the Schmidts (her biological parents).

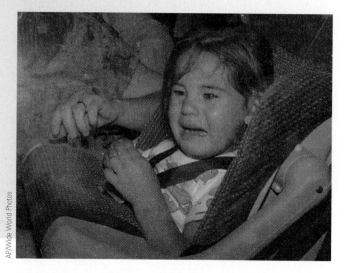

Baby Jessica leaves the only parents she knows.

How do you think this experience affected Jessica's later development? Will she be able to form close attachments to her biological parents? Will she be ever fearful of abandonment, whether by parents, friends, or lovers? Think about Jessica, and think about her more as you read this chapter. It concerns our closest relationships across the life span and their implications for our development (and ends with a "Critical Thinking" item that will update you on Baby Jessica). Whatever you predict about Baby Jessica's future, you would probably agree that close interpersonal relationships play a critical role in our lives and in development. The poet John Donne wrote, "No man is an island, entire of itself"; it seems equally true that no human being can *become* entire without the help of other human beings.

This chapter addresses questions such as these: What sorts of social relationships are especially important during different phases of the life span, and what is the character of these relationships? When and how do we develop the social competence it takes to interact smoothly with other people and to enter into intimate relationships with them? What are some of the developmental implications of being deprived of close relationships? We begin with some broad perspectives concerning the significance of social relationships for human development.

Perspectives on Relationships

What is it, really, that close social relationships contribute to our development? We can provide a reasonable answer by saying that they provide (1) learning experiences and (2) social support. The *learning experiences* provided by social interactions affect virtually all aspects of development. We acquire language as young children, for example, because people converse with us, serving as models of how to communicate and reinforcing our communication attempts. And, of course, it is other people who teach us social skills and patterns of social behavior. The infant learns from face-to-face interactions with a parent how to take turns with a social partner; the child learns from other children that expressing interest in someone is a better way to make friends than snatching toys; and the adult continues to look to other people for guidance about how to behave as a lover, parent, worker, or group leader.

A second major function of close relationships is to provide **social support**—the emotional and practical help from others that bolsters us as individuals and protects us from stress. Many researchers use the term *social network* to describe the array of significant individuals who serve as sources of social support. However, Robert Kahn and Tony Antonucci (1980) prefer to describe these significant people as a **social convoy** to emphasize the idea of a social support system that changes in size and composition over the life span.

An infant's convoy may consist only of parents. The social convoy enlarges over the years as others (relatives, friends, supportive teachers, romantic partners, colleagues) join it, and then it shrinks in old age (Levitt, Guacci-Franco, & Levitt, 1993; Levitt, Weber, & Guacci, 1993). As new members are added, some members drift away. Others remain in the convoy, but our relationships with them change, as when the infant son who is thoroughly dependent on his mother becomes the adolescent son clamoring for his independence—and later the middle-aged son who helps his mother manage her money and care for her house.

In sum, other people are important to us for an endless range of reasons, but their most critical roles in the developmental process are as sources of learning and social support. We could not learn our culture's patterns of social behavior without them, and we could not meet life's challenges nearly so well without the social support provided by our social convoys. Yet developmental theorists have disagreed about which relationships are most critical to development. Many noted theorists have argued that no social relationship is more important than the very first: the bond between parent and infant. Sigmund Freud (1905/1930) left no doubt about his opinion: A stable mother–child relationship is essential for normal personality development. His follower Erik Erikson tended to agree, emphasizing the importance of trust in the parent–infant relationship. These theorists, in turn, influenced John Bowlby, the developer of attachment theory, to believe that the parent–infant relationship has lasting effects on later relationships and developments. Yet, as we will see later, other theorists believe that peers are at least as significant as parents in the developmental process.

Attachment Theory

Attachment theory, today's most influential theory of parent–child and other close relationships, was formulated by John Bowlby (1969, 1973, 1980, 1988), a British psychiatrist who died in 1990, and elaborated on by his colleague Mary Ainsworth, an American developmental psychologist who died in 1999 (1989; Ainsworth et al., 1978). It was based on ethological theory (see Chapter 3), along with concepts from psychoanalytic theory and cognitive theory.

According to Bowlby (1969), an **attachment** is a strong affectional tie that binds a person to an intimate companion. For most of us, the first attachment we form, at about 6 or 7 months of age, is to a parent. How do we know when baby Michael becomes attached to his mother? He will try to maintain proximity to her—crying, clinging, approaching, following, doing whatever it takes to maintain closeness. He will prefer her to other individuals, reserving his biggest smiles for her and seeking her out when he is upset, discomforted, or afraid; she is irreplaceable in his eyes. He will also be confident about exploring his environment so long as he knows that his mother is there to provide the security he needs.

Notice that an infant attached to a parent is rather like an adult "in love." True, close emotional ties are expressed in different ways, and serve different functions, at different points in the life span. Adults, for example, do not usually feel compelled to follow their mates around the house, and they look to their loved ones for more than comforting hugs and smiles. Nonetheless, there are basic similarities among the infant attached to a caregiver, the child attached to a best friend, and the adult attached to a mate or lover. Throughout the life span, the objects of our attachments are special, irreplaceable people with whom we are motivated to maintain proximity and from whom we derive a sense of security (Ainsworth, 1989).

NATURE, NURTURE, AND ATTACHMENT

One of Bowlby's messages to his fellow psychiatrists was that it is normal rather than pathological to need other people throughout the life span. Making use of ethological theory and research, Bowlby argued that infants (and parents too) are biologically predisposed to form attachments. As we saw in Chapter 3, ethologists assume that all species, including human beings, are born with a number of innate behavioral tendencies that have in some way contributed to the survival of the species over the course of evolution. It makes sense to think, for example, that young birds tended to survive if they stayed close to their mothers so that they could be fed and protected from predators—but starved and were gobbled up, and therefore failed to pass on their genes to future generations, if they strayed away. Thus, chicks, ducks, and goslings may have gradually evolved so that they engage in **imprinting,** an innate form of learning in which the young will follow and become attached to a moving object (usually the mother) during a critical period early in life.

Groundbreaking ethologist Konrad Lorenz (1937) observed imprinting in young goslings and noted that (1) it is automatic—young fowl do not have to be taught to follow; (2) it occurs only within a *critical period* shortly after the bird has hatched; and (3) it is irreversible—once the gosling begins to follow a particular object, whether that object is its mother or Konrad Lorenz, it will remain attached to it. The imprinting response Lorenz observed is a prime example of a species-specific and largely innate behavior that has evolved over time because it has survival value.

What about human infants? Babies may not become imprinted to their mothers in the same way that young fowl do, but they most certainly follow their love objects around. Bowlby argued that they come equipped with a number of other behaviors besides following that help ensure that adults will love them, stay with them, and meet their needs. Among these behaviors are sucking, clinging, smiling, and vocalizing (crying, cooing, and babbling). Moreover, just as infants are programmed to respond to the sight, sound, and touch of their caregivers, Bowlby argued that adults are biologically programmed to respond to an infant's signals. It is difficult indeed for an adult to ignore a baby's cry or fail to warm up to a baby's big grin. In short, both human infants and human caregivers have evolved in ways that predispose them to form close attachments, and this ensures that infants will receive the care, protection, and stimulation they need to survive and thrive.

Just as the imprinting of goslings occurs during a critical period, human attachments form during what Bowlby viewed as a *sensitive period* for attachment, the first three years of life. But attachments do not just form automatically. According to Bowlby, whether an attachment forms and how secure it is will be influenced by the ongoing interaction between infant

Ethologist Konrad Lorenz demonstrated that goslings would become imprinted to him rather than to their mother if he was the first moving object they encountered during their critical period for imprinting. Human attachment is a bit more complex.

and caregiver and by the ability of each partner to respond to the other's signals. The infant's preprogrammed signals to other people may eventually wane if a caregiver is unresponsive to them. And infants themselves must learn to react sensitively to their caregiver's signals so that they can adjust their own behavior to mesh well with that of their love object. So, although Bowlby believed that humans are biologically prepared to form attachments, he also stressed that mutual learning processes contribute to the unfolding of a secure relationship.

IMPLICATIONS OF ATTACHMENT

Bowlby maintained that the quality of the early parent–infant attachment has important effects on later development, including the kinds of relationships people have with friends, romantic partners, and their own children. He proposed that, based on their interactions with caregivers, infants construct **internal working models**—cognitive representations of themselves and other people that shape their expectations about relationships and their processing of social information (Bowlby, 1973; see also Bretherton, 1996). Securely attached infants who have received responsive care will form internal working models suggesting that they are lovable individuals and that other people can be trusted to care for them. By contrast, insecurely attached infants subjected to insensitive, neglectful, or abusive care may conclude that they are difficult to love and that other people are unreliable. These insecure infants would be expected to have difficulties in later interpersonal relationships. They may, for example, be wary of forming close relationships or jealous and overly dependent if they do form one.

In sum, attachment theory, as developed by Bowlby and elaborated by Ainsworth, claims that (1) the capacity to form attachments is part of our evolutionary heritage; (2) attachments unfold through an interaction of biological and environmental forces during a sensitive period early in life; (3) the first attachment relationship, that between infant and caregiver, shapes later development and the quality of later relationships; and (4) internal working models of self and other serve as the mechanism through which early experience affects later development.

Peers and the Two Worlds of Childhood

Although the parent–infant relationship is indeed important, some theorists—among them, Jean Piaget—argue that relationships with peers are at least as significant. In effect, they argue, there are "two social worlds of childhood"—one involving adult–child relationships and the other involving peer relationships and a whole peer culture—and these two worlds contribute differently to development (J. R. Harris, 1998; Youniss, 1980).

A **peer** is someone who is one's social equal, someone who functions at a similar level of behavioral complexity—often, though not always, someone of similar age (Lewis & Rosenblum, 1975). As Piaget (1932/1965) observed, rela-

tionships with peers are quite different from relationships with parents. Because parents have more power than children do, children are in a subordinate position and must defer to adult authority. By contrast, two children have equal power and influence and must learn to appreciate each other's perspectives, to negotiate and compromise, and to cooperate with each other if they hope to get along. For this reason, Piaget believed that peers can make a unique contribution to social development that adult authority figures cannot make.

Another theorist who believed that peer relationships contribute significantly to development was neo-Freudian theorist Harry Stack Sullivan (1953; see also Buhrmester & Furman, 1986). He believed that interpersonal needs are important throughout life, but that these needs change as we get older and are gratified through different kinds of social relationships at different ages. The parent–child relationship is central up to about age 6; infants need tender care and nurturance from their parents, and preschool children need their parents to serve as playmates and companions. From about age 6 on, however, peers become increasingly important in children's lives. At first, children need peers as companions or playmates. Then, in grade school, they need acceptance by the peer group so that they will have opportunities to learn social skills within the group.

Around age 9 to 12, children begin to need intimacy in the form of a close friendship. Sullivan placed special emphasis on the developmental significance of **chumships,** or close friendships with peers of the same sex that emerge at about this age. It is with their close chums, he believed, that children become capable of truly caring about another person and learn the importance of trust, loyalty, and honesty in relationships. In fact, Sullivan believed that a close chumship could do much to make up for any insecurities caused by a poor parent–child relationship or by rejection by the peer group. Moreover, the lessons about intimacy learned in the context of same-sex chumships would then carry over into the intimate romantic relationships formed during adolescence and adulthood. Sullivan believed that a child who never had a chum would be poorly adjusted later in life.

Finally, in the Explorations box on page 373, we look at the thinking of Judith Rich Harris, a disabled grandmother and textbook writer who was kicked out of Harvard's doctoral program many years ago but who has now written a very controversial and influential book arguing that peers are far more important than parents in shaping development. Debates about the relative significance of parents and peers for later development continue to rage, with some developmentalists agreeing with Freud and Bowlby that the quality of an infant's attachment to an adult is the most significant influence on later personality and social development and others sharing the belief of Piaget, Sullivan, and now Harris that relationships with peers are at least as significant. We hope this chapter will convince you that close relationships with *both* caregivers and peers are essential to healthy development across the life span.

Are Peers More Important Than Parents?

Judith Harris (1995,1998, 2000) has created quite a stir among developmental scientists by arguing that the impact of parents on development is overrated and that peers are far more important: "Children would develop into the same sort of adults if we left their lives outside the home unchanged and left them in their schools and their neighborhoods—but switched all the parents around" (Harris, 1998, p. 359). She cites the example of immigrant children, who readily learn the local culture and language from peers, even though their parents come from a different culture and speak a different language.

Specifically, Harris makes the following claims:

1. Developmental scientists have long assumed that correlations between parenting behaviors and child development outcomes are due to socialization processes in the family, when in fact they are largely due to genes shared by parents and children.
2. Even when parenting behaviors affect children, they do so mainly in the home environment; learning rarely generalizes outside the home and beyond childhood.
3. Because much learning is context-specific, peers are more important than parents in socializing children for the world outside the home.

Harris reviews behavioral genetics research (see Chapter 3) showing that genes make a contribution to virtually all aspects of human development, that they influence the kinds of experiences children have, and that, whatever parents do to children, it does little to make different children growing up in the same house more alike in the long run. Even identical twins are no more alike when they grow up in the same family than when they are raised apart from an early age. Harris correctly notes that countless studies that claim to demonstrate the importance of variations in parenting do not take into account genetic influences and therefore cannot separate the effects of parental genes from the effects of parental behavior. Moreover, recent studies that include siblings with different degrees of genetic relatedness increasingly show that genes and environment are correlated, suggesting that parents react to genetic differences among their children rather than create these differences (Reiss et al., 2000).

Harris argues that most important socialization takes place in peer groups and makes children from different families alike. Children figure out what social category they belong to based on age, sex, and other characteristics and then want to be like members of their social group. They adopt the norms of behavior that prevail in their peer group, learn by observing other children, and take on their attitudes, speech, dress styles, and behavior. When children later gravitate toward peers who are similar to themselves, their genetically based tendencies are magnified; the budding delinquent becomes more delinquent, the studious child becomes more studious. Moreover, Harris believes that the ways in which children are typecast by peers (for example, as the "athletic one" or the "dumb one") can leave lasting imprints on their personalities.

Many developmental scientists have reacted strongly to Harris's message, charging that she overstates her case (Collins et al., 2000; Vandell, 2000). They claim that she lacks solid evidence that peers are the primary influence on adult personality and adjustment. Moreover, she overlooks solid evidence that, even when genetic influences are taken into account, what parents do *does* matter and that intervening to change how parents treat children can change the course of development (Begley, 1998; Vandell, 2000; and see, for example, the research on coercive family environments in Chapter 13). Harris also overlooks the fact that the impact of parents is not limited to making all their children alike (to what behavioral geneticists call *shared environmental effects*). Rather, because parents notice differences among their children and treat them differently, part of their influence is registered in behavioral genetics studies as effects of the *nonshared environment*, which is typically as important as or more important than genes in accounting for individual differences (Vandell, 2000).

Despite challenges to her interpretation of the research evidence, Harris deserves credit for stimulating greater attention to peer group influences. She has also challenged developmentalists to demonstrate more convincingly, though better research designs that take genetic influences into account, that parents truly influence their children's development. She also offers reassurance to parents who have been led to believe that they are entirely to blame for their wayward children. As this chapter will demonstrate, *both* parents and peers—and siblings, teachers, and other socialization agents as well—contribute to human development (Vandell, 2000).

The Infant

Human infants are social beings from the start, but their social relationships change dramatically once they form close attachments to parents or other companions and develop the social skills that allow them to coordinate their own activities with those of other infants. Because attachments are emotional ties that have many implications for emotional development, let us begin by setting the development of parent–infant attachment in the context of early emotional development.

Early Emotional Development

Until fairly recently, most researchers believed that infants did not really have emotional lives—or at least that their emotional expressions were only globally positive or negative in nature. Parents, by contrast, have long felt that their babies' faces reveal a wide range of specific emotions (W. Johnson et al., 1982). Parents are right.

DEVELOPMENT OF SPECIFIC EMOTIONS

Carroll Izard (1982; Izard & Ackerman, 2000) and his colleagues maintain that basic emotions play distinct roles in motivating and organizing behavior and that many of them are evident very early in life. Izard videotaped infants' responses to such events as grasping an ice cube, having a toy taken away, or seeing their mothers return after a separation. By analyzing specific facial movements (such as the raising of the brows and the wrinkling of the nose) and by asking raters to judge what emotion a baby's face reveals, Izard has established that infants do indeed express distinct emotions in response to different experiences and that adults can readily interpret which emotions they are expressing (see the photos).

From Izard's work and that of others, we can piece together this account of the development of basic emotions (Lewis, 2000; and see Figure 14.1). At birth, babies show con-

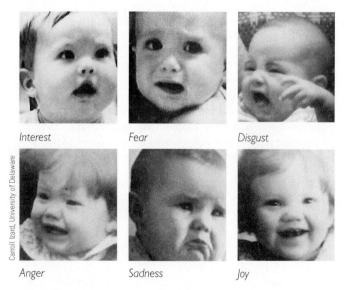

Interest   Fear   Disgust

Anger   Sadness   Joy

Carroll Izard, University of Delaware

Infants express a wide range of emotions.

tentment, interest (by staring intently at objects), and distress (in response to pain or discomfort). Within the first six months, more specific emotions evolve from these three. By 3 months of age or so, contentment becomes joy, or excitement at the sight of something familiar like Mom's face, and interest becomes surprise, as when expectations are violated in games of peekaboo. Distress very soon evolves into disgust (in response to foul-tasting foods) and sadness. Angry expressions appear as early as about 4 months—about the same time that infants acquire enough control of their limbs to push unpleasant stimuli away. Fear makes its appearance as early as 5 to 7 months. These "primary" emotions seem to be biologically programmed. They emerge in all normal infants at roughly the same ages and are displayed and interpreted similarly in all cultures (Izard, 1982; Malatesta et al., 1989). Cognitive advances play a role in their emergence. For example, babies cannot fear strangers until they are able to represent mentally what *familiar* companions look like (Lewis, 2000).

Next, as Figure 14.1 shows, come the so-called "secondary" or **self-conscious emotions.** These emotions, such as embarrassment, require an awareness of self and emerge at about 18 months of age. Once infants become able to recognize themselves in the mirror, they begin to show embarrassment when they are asked to perform for guests and empathy when a playmate breaks into tears (Lewis, 2000). Finally, when toddlers become able to judge their behavior against standards of performance, at around the age of 2, they become capable of the self-conscious emotions of pride, shame, and guilt (Lewis, 2000).

SOCIALIZATION OF EMOTIONS

Although the earliest emotional expressions seem to be biologically programmed, the sociocultural environment and the relationships in which infants participate soon begin to influence the meanings that emotions have for them (Sroufe, 1996; Saarni, 1999). Observational studies of face-to-face interactions between mothers and infants suggest that young infants display a wide range of positive and negative emotions, changing their expressions with lightning speed (once every 7 seconds) while their mothers do the same (Malatesta et al., 1986, 1989). Mothers mainly display interest, surprise, and joy, thus serving as models of positive emotions. What's more, mothers respond selectively to their babies' expressions; over the early months they become increasingly responsive to their babies' expressions of interest and surprise and less responsive to their negative emotions (Malatesta et al., 1986, 1989). Through basic learning processes, then, infants are trained to show a pleasant face more frequently and an unpleasant face less frequently—and they do just that over time. They are beginning to learn which emotional expressions are socially acceptable in their culture. Toward the end of the first year, infants also begin to monitor others' emotional reactions in ambiguous situations and use this information to decide how they should feel and behave (Feinman, 1992; Sroufe, 1996). If their mothers are wary, so are they.

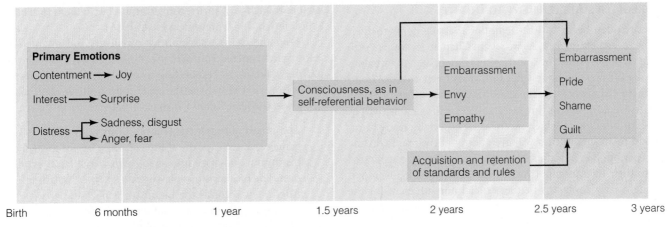

Figure 14.1 The emergence of different emotions. Primary emotions emerge in the first six months of life, secondary or self-conscious emotions emerge starting about 18 months to 2 years of age.
Source: Lewis (2000)

Gradually, in the context of a secure parent–child relationship, infants and young children learn to understand emotions quite well (P. L. Harris, 2000). As parents talk about their own feelings and encourage their growing children to share theirs, children become more sensitive to the world of emotions. As it turns out, 1-year-olds who enjoy secure attachments turn into 6-year-olds who are able to understand complex emotions better than children whose early relationships were insecure (Steele et al., 1999). Their good understanding of emotions, in turn, helps them become popular with their peers (P. L. Harris, 2000).

EMOTION REGULATION

In order to conform to their culture's rules about when and how different emotions should be expressed, and to keep themselves from being overwhelmed by their emotions, infants must develop strategies for **emotion regulation**—the processes involved in initiating, maintaining, and altering emotional responses (Bridges & Grolnick, 1995; Grolnick, McMenamy, & Kurowski, 1999). Young infants have only a few, simple emotion regulation strategies, but they are active from the start in regulating their emotions (Sroufe, 1996). For example, they are able to reduce their negative arousal by turning away from unpleasant stimuli or by sucking vigorously on a pacifier (Mangelsdorf, Shapiro, & Marzolf, 1995). More often, they rely on their caregivers to help them regulate their emotions—for example, by soothing them when they are distressed (Cole, Michel, & Teti, 1994; Kopp, 1989).

By the end of the first year, infants acquire other strategies, such as rocking themselves and moving away from upsetting events. They also actively seek out attachment figures when they are distressed; the very presence of these individuals has a calming effect. By 18 to 24 months of age, toddlers will try to control the actions of people and objects, such as mechanical toys, that upset them (Mangelsdorf et al., 1995); they are able to cope with the frustration of waiting for snacks and gifts by playing with toys and otherwise distracting themselves (Grolnick, Bridges, & Connell, 1996). They will even

knit their brows or compress their lips in an attempt to suppress their anger or sadness (Malatesta et al., 1989). As children gain the capacity for symbolic thought and language, they also become able to regulate their distress symbolically—for example, by saying "Mommy coming soon, Mommy coming soon" after mother goes out the door (Thompson, 1994).

The development of emotions and of strategies for regulating emotions is closely intertwined with the development of attachment relationships (Bell & Calkins, 2000). Attachment figures play critical roles in helping infants regulate their emotions and in teaching them how to do so on their own. Attachment figures also arouse powerful emotions, positive and negative, that need to be controlled; infants can become uncomfortably overstimulated during joyful bouts of play with parents, and they can become highly distressed when their parents leave them. Finally, infants develop distinct styles of emotional expression designed to keep attachment figures close (Bridges & Grolnick, 1995). One infant may learn to suppress negative emotions such as fear and anger so as not to anger an irritable caregiver, whereas another may learn to scream loud and long in order to keep an unreliable caregiver close. Clearly, emotions and emotion regulation develop in the context of attachment relationships and affect the quality of these and other relationships (Bell & Calkins, 2000).

In sum, biologically based primary emotions appear in a universal sequence over the first year of life. Self-conscious emotions follow in the second and third years, and emotions increasingly become socialized through learning processes such as reinforcement and observational learning. As infants get older, they rely less on caregivers and more on their own emotion regulation strategies to manage the emotions aroused by their social interactions.

The First Relationship

Like any relationship, the parent–infant attachment is reciprocal. Parents become attached to their infants, and infants become attached to their parents as the relationship unfolds.

CAREGIVER'S ATTACHMENT TO INFANT

Parents often begin to form emotional attachments to their babies even before birth. As we saw in Chapter 4, mothers who have an opportunity for skin-to-skin contact with their babies during the first few hours after birth may form a special bond to them (Klaus & Kennell, 1976). Studies of other primates suggest that the two or three weeks after birth is a sensitive period for bonding in which mothers are especially ready to respond to an infant; they will even adopt alien infants during this period, but not after it has passed, if they are separated from their own infants (Maestripieri, 2001). As it turns out, though, early contact is neither crucial nor sufficient for the development of strong parent-to-infant attachments among humans.

Not only are babies cute, but their early reflexive behaviors such as sucking, rooting, and grasping help endear them to their parents (Bowlby, 1969). Smiling may be an especially important signal. Although it is initially a reflexive response to almost any stimulus, it is triggered by voices at 3 weeks of age and by faces at 5 or 6 weeks of age (Bowlby, 1969; Wolff, 1963). Finally, when infants begin to coo and babble, their parents

Smiling is one of the behaviors that helps to ensure that adults will fall in love with babies.

can enjoy back-and-forth "conversations" with them (Keller & Scholmerich, 1987; Stevenson et al., 1986).

Over the weeks and months, caregivers and infants develop **synchronized routines** much like dances, in which the partners take turns responding to each other's leads (Stern, 1977; Tronick, 1989). Note the synchrony as this mother plays peekaboo with her infant (Tronick, 1989, p. 112):

> The infant abruptly turns away from his mother as the game reaches its "peak" of intensity and begins to suck on his thumb and stare into space with a dull facial expression. The mother stops playing and sits back watching. . . . After a few seconds the infant turns back to her with an inviting expression. The mother moves closer, smiles, and says in a high-pitched, exaggerated voice, "Oh, now you're back!" He smiles in response and vocalizes. As they finish crowing together, the infant reinserts his thumb and looks away. The mother again waits. [Soon] the infant turns . . . to her and they greet each other with big smiles.

Smooth interactions like this are most likely to develop if caregivers limit their social stimulation to those periods when a baby is alert and receptive and avoid pushing things when the infant's message is "Cool it—I need a break from all this stimulation." A moderate rather than an extremely high or low degree of synchrony in the back-and-forth vocalizations between parent and infant appears to predict a secure attachment relationship later in infancy (Jaffe et al., 2001).

In sum, infants play an active role in persuading adults to love them. Babies are physically appealing, come equipped with a number of reflexes that promote the formation of an attachment, and are highly responsive to people and capable of synchronizing their behavior with that of their "dance partners." As caregiver and infant perfect their interaction routines, the parent–infant relationship normally blossoms into a strong reciprocal attachment. Yet not all parents become closely attached to their infants. First, some babies are hard to love. Parents may have a difficult time establishing stable and synchronized routines with irritable or unresponsive infants (Field, 1987). Second, some adults—for example, mothers suffering from depression—have difficulty responding sensitively to their babies' signals (Dawson & Ashman, 2000; Hipwell et al., 2000). It takes two to tango, after all.

INFANT'S ATTACHMENT TO CAREGIVER

Infants take some time before they are developmentally ready to form attachments. They progress through the following phases (Ainsworth, 1973; Bowlby, 1969):

1. **Undiscriminating social responsiveness (birth to 2 or 3 months).** Very young infants are responsive to voices, faces, and other social stimuli, but any human is of interest to them. They do not yet show a clear preference for one person over another.

2. **Discriminating social responsiveness (2 or 3 months to 6 or 7 months).** Now infants begin to express preferences for familiar companions. They are likely to direct their biggest grins and most enthusiastic babbles toward those companions, though they are still quite friendly toward strangers.

How Babysitters Can Combat Stranger Anxiety

It is not unusual for 1- or 2-year-olds meeting a new babysitter or being approached by a nurse or doctor at the doctor's office to break into tears and cling to their parents. Stranger-wary infants often stare at the stranger for a moment and then turn away, whimper, and seek the comfort of their parents. Occasionally, infants become terrified and highly upset. Obviously, it is in the interests of babysitters and other "strangers" to be able to prevent such negative reactions. What might we suggest?

• **Keep familiar companions available.** Stranger anxiety is less likely to occur if an attachment figure is nearby to serve as a "secure base." In one study, fewer than one-third of 6- to 12-month-olds were wary of an approaching stranger when they were seated on their mothers' laps (Morgan & Ricciuti, 1969). Yet about two-thirds of these infants frowned, turned away, whimpered, or cried if they were seated only 4 feet from their mothers. Babysitters would do well to insist that parents be present when they first meet the children they will tend. If parents must leave, a security blanket or beloved stuffed animal can have much the same calming effect as a parent's presence for some infants (Passman, 1977).

• **Arrange for the infant's companions to respond positively to you.** As we have seen, infants use other people's emotional reactions to guide their own responses to a situation. The implication is that infants are likely to respond much more favorably to a stranger's approach if their mothers or fathers greet the stranger warmly than if the parents react neutrally or negatively toward this person. It may help, then, for babysitters to initiate a pleasant exchange with Mom or Dad before directing their attention to the infant.

• **Make the setting more "familiar."** Stranger anxiety is less likely to occur in familiar settings than in unfamiliar ones (Sroufe, Waters, & Matas, 1974). Stranger anxiety should be less severe if the babysitter comes to the child's home than if the child is taken to the babysitter's home or some other unfamiliar place. Yet an unfamiliar environment can become a familiar one if infants are given the time to get used to it. Alan Sroufe and his colleagues (1974) found that more than 90% of 10-month-olds became upset if a stranger approached within a minute after they had been placed in an unfamiliar room; only 50% did so when they were given 10 minutes to become accustomed to the room.

• **Be a sensitive, unobtrusive stranger.** Not surprisingly, an infant's response to a stranger depends on the stranger's behavior (Sroufe, 1996). The meeting is likely to go best if the stranger initially keeps his or her distance and then approaches slowly while smiling, talking, and offering a familiar toy or suggesting a familiar activity (Bretherton, Stolberg, & Kreye, 1981; Sroufe, 1977). It also helps if the stranger, like any sensitive caregiver, takes his or her cues from the infant (Mangelsdorf, 1992). Babies prefer strangers they can control! Intrusive strangers who approach quickly and force themselves on infants (for example, by trying to pick them up before they have time to adjust) probably get what they deserve.

• **Try not to look any stranger than you must.** Finally, infants are most likely to be afraid of people who violate their schemas or expectations (Kagan, 1972). Babysitters who have unusual physical features such as beards or Mohawks or who dress in unusual outfits elicit more wariness than those who resemble the people infants encounter every day. Babysitters who favor the latest faddish dress might try to make themselves more readily recognizable as members of the human race!

3. Active proximity seeking/true attachment (6 or 7 months to about 3 years). At about 6 or 7 months of age, infants form their first clear attachments, most often to their mothers. Now able to crawl, an infant will follow along behind her mother to stay close, protest when her mother leaves, and greet her mother warmly when she returns. Within weeks after forming their first attachments, most infants become attached to other people as well—fathers, siblings, grandparents, regular babysitters (Schaffer & Emerson, 1964). By 18 months of age, very few infants are attached to only one person, and some are attached to several.

4. Goal-corrected partnership (3 years and older). By about the age of 3, partly because they have more advanced social-cognitive abilities, children can take a parent's goals and plans into consideration and adjust their behavior accordingly to achieve the goal of maintaining optimal proximity to the attachment figure. Thus, a 1-year-old cries and tries to follow when Dad leaves the house to talk to a neighbor, whereas a 4-year-old probably understands where Dad is going and can control her need for his attention until he returns. This final, more partner-like, give-and-take phase of attachment lasts a lifetime.

ATTACHMENT-RELATED FEARS

Infants no sooner experience the pleasures of love than they discover the agonies of fear. One form of fear, **separation anxiety,** is actually an important sign that an attachment has formed. Once attached to a parent, babies often become wary or fretful when separated from that parent and will follow behind the parent to try to avoid separation. Separation anxiety normally appears at the time infants are forming their first genuine attachments, peaks at 14 to 18 months, and gradually becomes less frequent and less intense throughout infancy and the preschool period (Weinraub & Lewis, 1977). Still, even children and adolescents may become homesick and distressed when separated from their parents for a long time (Thurber, 1995).

A second fearful response that often emerges shortly after an infant becomes attached to someone is **stranger anxiety**—a wary or fretful reaction to the approach of an unfamiliar person (Schaffer & Emerson, 1964). Anxious reactions to strangers—often mixed with signs of interest—become common at 8 to 10 months of age, continue through the first year, and gradually decline in intensity over the second year (Sroufe, 1996). The Explorations box on page 377 describes the circumstances under which stranger anxiety is most and least likely to occur and suggests how babysitters and health-care professionals can head off outbreaks of fear and trembling.

EXPLORATORY BEHAVIOR

The formation of a strong attachment to a caregiver has another important consequence: It facilitates exploratory behavior. Mary Ainsworth (Ainsworth et al., 1978) emphasized that an attachment figure serves as a **secure base** for exploration—a point of safety from which an infant can feel free to venture away. Thus Wendy, a securely attached infant visiting a neighbor's home with Mom, may be comfortable exploring the living room as long as she can check back occasionally to see that Mom is still there but may be reluctant to explore if Mom disappears into the bathroom. Paradoxical as it may seem, infants apparently need to rely on another person in order to feel confident about acting independently.

So, though social from the start, infants form their first attachments at about 6 or 7 months of age, and this milestone often brings with it both fearful emotions (separation and stranger anxiety) and confidence (willingness to use the attachment figure as a secure base for exploration). However, not all parent–infant attachments are equal.

Quality of Attachment

Mary Ainsworth made her most notable contribution to attachment theory by devising a way to assess differences in the quality of parent–infant attachments (see Weinfield et al., 1999). She and her associates created the **Strange Situation,** a procedure for measuring the quality of an attachment (Ainsworth et al., 1978). It consists of a series of eight episodes that gradually escalate the amount of stress infants experience as they react to the approach of an adult stranger and the departure and return of their caregiver (see Table 14.1). On the basis of an infant's pattern of behavior across the episodes, the quality of his or her attachment to a parent can be characterized as one of four types: secure, resistant, avoidant, or disorganized/disoriented.

1. Secure attachment. About 65–70% of 1-year-olds in our society are securely attached to their mothers (Ainsworth et al., 1978). The securely attached infant actively explores the room when alone with the mother because she serves as a secure base. The infant may be upset by separation but greets the mother when she returns and welcomes physical contact with her. The child is outgoing with a stranger while the mother is present.

2. Resistant attachment. About 10% of 1-year-olds show a resistant attachment, or an insecure attachment characterized by ambivalent reactions. The resistant infant is quite anxious and often does not venture off to play even though the mother is present, which suggests that she does not serve as a secure base for exploration. Yet this infant becomes very distressed when the mother departs, often showing more separation anxiety than the securely attached infant—perhaps because it's not quite clear whether mother will return. Then, when mother does return, the infant is ambivalent: He or she may try to remain near the mother but seems to resent her for having left, may resist if she tries to make physical contact, and may even hit and kick her in anger (Ainsworth et al., 1978). Resistant infants are also quite wary of strangers, even when their mothers are present. It seems, then, that the resistant or ambivalent infant very much wants affection and works very hard to get the attention of his or her caregiver, but is never sure it will be forthcoming.

3. Avoidant attachment. Avoidant infants (about 15% of 1-year-olds) seem uninterested in exploring, show little distress when separated from their mothers, and avoid contact when their mothers return. These insecurely attached infants are not particularly wary of strangers but sometimes avoid or

Table 14.1   The Episodes of the Strange Situation

Episode	Events	Attachment Behavior Observed
1	Experimenter leaves parent and baby to play	
2	Parent sits while baby plays	Use of parent as secure base
3	Stranger enters and talks to parent	Stranger anxiety
4	Parent leaves; stranger lets baby play, offers comfort if needed	Separation anxiety
5	Parent returns, greets baby, offers comfort if needed; stranger leaves	Reactions to reunion
6	Parent leaves	Separation anxiety
7	Stranger enters and offers comfort	Stranger anxiety; ability to be soothed by stranger
8	Parent returns, greets baby, offers comfort, lets baby return to play	Reactions to reunion

SOURCE: Based on Ainsworth et al. (1978)

Table 14.2 Behaviors Associated with the Secure, Resistant, Avoidant, and Disorganized/Disoriented Attachment Styles in the Strange Situation Test

	Type of Attachment			
Behavior	**Secure**	**Resistant**	**Avoidant**	**Disorganized/ Disoriented**
Explores when caregiver is present to provide a "secure base" for exploration?	Yes, actively	No—clings	Yes, but play is not as constructive as that of secure infant	No
Responds positively to stranger?	Yes, comfortable if caregiver is present	No, fearful even with caregiver present	No, often indifferent, as he/she is to caregiver	No, confused responses
Protests when separated from caregiver?	Yes, at least mildly distressed	Yes—extremely upset	No—seemingly unfazed	Sometimes; unpredictable
Responds positively to caregiver at reunion?	Yes, happy to be reunited	Yes and no— seeks contact, but resents being left; ambivalent	No, ignores or avoids caregiver	Confused; may approach or avoid caregiver or do both

ignore them in much the same way that they avoid or ignore their mothers. Avoidant infants, then, seem to have distanced themselves from their parents, almost as if they were denying their need for affection.

4. Disorganized/disoriented attachment. About 15% of infants—more in high-risk families—display what is now recognized as a fourth pattern of attachment, one that may reflect even more insecurity than the resistant and avoidant styles (van IJzendoorn, Schuengel, & Bakermans-Kranenburg, 1999). Disorganized/disoriented attachment combines features of the resistant and avoidant styles and reflects confusion about whether to approach or avoid the parent (Main & Solomon, 1990). Reunited with their mothers after a separation, these infants may act dazed and freeze; or they may seek contact but then abruptly move away as their mothers approach them; or they may show both patterns in different reunion episodes. Unlike secure, resistant, or avoidant infants, infants with a disorganized/disoriented attachment have not been able to devise any coherent strategy for regulating negative emotions such as separation anxiety; they seem frightened of the parent and stuck between approaching and avoiding this frightening figure (Hesse & Main, 2000).

Table 14.2 summarizes the features of these four patterns of attachment, which have been the subject of considerable research. As we will see later, styles of relating to other people much like these infant attachment styles can be detected when adults are interviewed about their romantic relationships. Indeed, the concepts of attachment theory have now been applied successfully across the life span.

What determines which of these attachment patterns will characterize a parent–infant relationship? Early studies of the quality of attachments focused almost entirely on the qualities of caregivers that make infants form secure attachments to them, but we now know that infants make their own contributions to the attachment bond as well.

THE CAREGIVER'S CONTRIBUTIONS

According to Freud, infants in the oral stage of psychosexual development become attached to the individual who provides them with oral pleasure. The attachment will be most secure if a mother is relaxed and generous in her feeding practices. In a classic study conducted by Harry Harlow and Robert Zimmerman (1959), Freud's hypothesis was put to the test. Monkeys were reared with two surrogate mothers: a wire "mother" and a cloth "mother" wrapped in foam rubber and covered with terrycloth (see photo). Half the infants were fed by the cloth mother, and the remaining half by the wire mother. To which mother did these infants become attached? There was no contest, really: Infants strongly preferred the cuddly cloth mother, *regardless of which mother had fed them.* Even if their food came from the wire mother, they spent more time clinging to the cloth mother, ran to "her" when they were upset or afraid, and showed every sign of being attached to her. Harlow's research demonstrated that what he called **contact comfort,** or the pleasurable tactile sensations provided by a soft and cuddly "parent," is a more powerful contributor to attachment in monkeys than feeding or the reduction of hunger. Research with humans also contradicts Freud's view. Many infants become attached to someone other than the adult who feeds them, and variations in feeding schedules and the age at which infants are weaned have little impact on the quality of infants' attachments (Schaffer & Emerson, 1964).

Meanwhile, research confirms that contact comfort plays a role in promoting human attachments (Anisfeld et al., 1990). Mainly, it tells us that infants develop secure attachments to mothers and fathers who are sensitive and responsive to their needs and emotional signals (Ainsworth et al., 1978; De Wolff & van IJzendoorn, 1997). These parents are good at reading and empathizing with their children's feelings (Oppenheim, Koren-Karie, & Sagi, 2001).

The wire and cloth surrogate "mothers" used in Harlow's research. This infant monkey has formed an attachment to the cloth mother that provides "contact comfort," even though it must stretch to the wire mother in order to feed.

What parenting styles contribute to insecure attachments? Babies who show a resistant pattern of attachment often have parents who are inconsistent in their caregiving; they react enthusiastically or indifferently, depending on their moods, and are unresponsive a good deal of the time (Isabella, 1993; Isabella & Belsky, 1991). Mothers who are depressed, for example, often have difficulty responding sensitively to their babies' signals and do not provide the comforting that helps babies regulate their negative emotions (Dawson & Ashman, 2000). The infant copes with inconsistent caregiving by trying desperately—through clinging, crying, and other attachment behaviors—to obtain emotional support and comfort and then becomes both saddened and resentful when these efforts fail.

The parents of infants with an avoidant attachment tend to provide either too little or too much stimulation. Some tend to be rejecting; they are impatient, unresponsive to the infant's signals, and resentful when the infant interferes with their own plans (Ainsworth, 1979; Isabella, 1993). Interestingly, other parents of infants with avoidant attachments are "intrusive"; they are overzealous and provide high levels of stimulation even when their babies become uncomfortably aroused and need a break so that they can regulate their emotions (Isabella & Belsky, 1991; Swanson, Beckwith, & Howard, 2000). Infants with an avoidant attachment style may be responding adaptively by learning to avoid adults who seem to dislike their company or who bombard them with stimulation they do not want and cannot handle. Whereas re-

sistant infants make vigorous attempts to gain emotional support, avoidant infants seem to have learned not to express their emotional needs (Bridges & Grolnick, 1995).

Finally, a disorganized/disoriented style of attachment is evident in as many as 80% of infants who have been physically abused or maltreated (Carlson et al., 1989), and in many infants whose mothers are severely depressed and may, as a result, mistreat or neglect them (Murray et al., 1996). Infants might naturally be confused about whether to approach or avoid a parent who is loving one minute but angry or indifferent the next.

THE INFANT'S CONTRIBUTIONS

Clearly, the ways in which parents interact with their babies relate in predictable ways to the quality of the attachments that form. However, the infant's characteristics also have a bearing. Cognitive developmental theorists emphasize that the ability to form attachments depends in part on the infant's level of cognitive development and knowledge of the surrounding world. For example, the infant must recognize that close companions continue to exist even when they are absent in order to experience separation anxiety when a caregiver leaves the room (Kohlberg, 1969; Lester et al., 1974). That is, infants will not form attachments until they have acquired some concept of *person permanence* (a form of the object permanence concept studied by Jean Piaget and discussed in Chapter 7). Partly as a result, neurological problems in an infant can interfere with the formation of a secure attachment (Cox, Hopkins, & Hans, 2000).

The infant's temperament is an even more important influence: An attachment is less likely to be secure if the infant is by temperament fearful, irritable, or unresponsive (Colin, 1996). Because of temperamental differences between siblings, it is not uncommon for a parent to develop a secure relationship with one child but an insecure relationship with another child in the family (Deater-Deckard & O'Connor, 2000).

Which has a stronger bearing on the quality of the attachment, then—the caregiver's style of parenting or the infant's temperament? Both are significant, and the two sometimes interact. To illustrate, Figure 14.2 shows the percentages of 12-month-olds who tested as securely attached as a function of whether they were at-risk infants (premature) and whether their mothers were depressed (Poehlmann & Fiese, 2001). Only when a depressed mother was coupled with a hard-to-read, premature infant did the odds of a secure attachment become low. This suggests the value of identifying and intervening to help parent–infant pairs in which both parent and child have characteristics associated with insecure attachments.

Although both parent and child contribute to the quality of the attachment, it is also clear that the caregiver's behavior has more to do with whether or not a secure attachment ultimately forms than do characteristics of the infant (Goldberg et al., 1986; Vaughn et al., 1989). If the infant's temperament were the main influence on security of attachment, it would be difficult to explain why so many infants are securely attached to one parent but insecurely attached to the other (van IJzendoorn & De Wolff, 1997). Finally, even temperamentally difficult babies are likely to establish secure relationships with caregivers who are patient and adjust their caregiving to the baby's temperamental quirks (Mangelsdorf et al., 1990; van IJzendoorn et al., 1992). These findings are consistent with the *goodness of fit* model introduced in Chapter 11: Secure bonds evolve when parents can respond sensitively to whatever temperamental characteristics their babies display, whereas insecure bonds are more likely when there is a mismatch between caregiving style and infant's temperament (Sroufe, 1985).

CONTEXTUAL CONTRIBUTORS

In addition, the broader social context surrounding caregiver and infant can affect how they react to each other. For example, the stresses associated with living in poverty or experiencing marital difficulties may make it difficult for parents to be responsive to their babies and may therefore result in insecure attachments (P. Howes & Markman, 1989; Murray et al., 1996). The cultural context in which caregiver and baby interact can also color their relationship. For instance, German parents strongly encourage independence and discourage clingy behavior, which may explain why German infants are more likely than infants in many other societies to ignore or avoid their parents when they are reunited after a separation and why many of them are therefore classified as avoidantly attached when given the Strange Situation test (Grossmann et al., 1985). The Strange Situation may similarly underestimate the security of attachment of U.S. babies who regularly receive nonmaternal care and who therefore are not very bothered by separations (Clarke-Stewart, Goossens, & Allhusen, 2001). By contrast, Japanese babies, who are rarely separated from their mothers early in life, become very distressed by separations

such as those they must endure in the Strange Situation and are more likely than American babies to be classified as resistant as a result (Takahashi, 1990; van IJzendoorn & Sagi, 1999).

Could this mean that research on infant attachment is culturally biased? Fred Rothbaum and his colleagues (2000) think so. They observe that in Western, *individualistic cultures*, optimal development means becoming an autonomous being, whereas in Eastern, *collectivist cultures* such as Japan, the goal is to become integrated into the group. Instead of encouraging exploration, Japanese parents keep their infants in close contact and encourage them to be dependent. No wonder these infants become upset when separated from their mothers in the Strange Situation. Moreover, Japanese parents *anticipate* their children's needs and desires. As a result, they may be judged from a Western perspective to be unresponsive to their children's actual expressions of their needs and desires when in fact they are very loving and competent parents (Rothbaum et al., 2000). Most Japanese infants are probably securely attached *when judged by their own culture's standards.*

In short, although most new parents quickly fall in love with their infants, characteristics of the baby, the caregiver, and the surrounding social environment can clearly affect the quality of the emerging attachment.

Implications of Early Attachment

From Freud on, almost everyone has assumed that the parent–child relationship is critical in shaping human development. Just how important *is* it? Three lines of research offer some answers: (1) studies of socially deprived infants; (2) studies of children who attend day care facilities; and (3) studies of the later development of securely and insecurely attached infants.

EFFECTS OF SOCIAL DEPRIVATION

What becomes of babies (like Baby Jessica, at the start of the chapter) who are separated from their caregivers as a result of illness, death, or other unforeseen circumstances? Worse yet, what happens to infants who never have an opportunity to form *any* attachment bond? Drawing on research with families in which infant or parent was hospitalized or a parent died, John Bowlby (1960, 1980) described three phases of grief that infants who are old enough to have formed attachments could be expected to display (see also Colin, 1996): a *protest* phase of searching desperately for the lost caregiver; a *despair* phase, in which infants seem sad and listless as they lose hope of a reunion; and a *detachment* phase, in which they take renewed interest in toys and companions and may ignore or avoid the missing caregiver if she or he returns, as if the infant were defending against being hurt again. If their caregivers return, infants who have displayed these reactions may then become very needy of the lost caregiver's affection and may not let him or her out of sight. Infants who experience a series of separations from caregivers or are moved around from foster home to foster home may be permanently marred by their experiences of loving and losing; they may enter a fourth phase of grieving that involves *withdrawal* from human

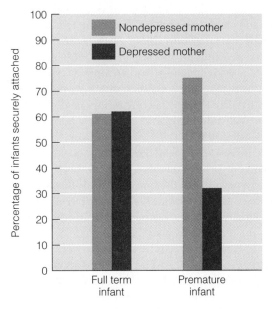

Figure 14.2 The combination of a depressed mother and a premature infant means low odds that that a secure attachment will form.

SOURCE: Data from Poehlmann & Fiese (2001)

relationships (Bowlby, 1980; Colin, 1996). Whether early separation does lasting damage depends on many factors, including the characteristics of the child, the security of the parent–infant attachment, and the quality of care the infant receives after the separation (Rutter, 1981).

So much for having loved and lost. Studies of infants who grow up in deprived institutional settings and never form attachments indicate that it may be better to have loved and lost than never to have loved at all (Goldfarb, 1943, 1947; Provence & Lipton, 1962). Recently, researchers have studied children from deprived institutions in Romania who were adopted into homes in the United States and Canada after the fall of the Romanian government in 1990 (Gunnar, Bruce, & Grotevant, 2000; Holden, 1996). Note that *most* infants adopted from other countries are no more or less likely than other infants to form secure attachments (Juffer & Rosenboom, 1997). However, the Romanian adoptees reportedly spent their infancies in orphanages with 20 to 30 children in a room and only one caregiver for every 10 to 20 children; they spent most of their time rocking back and forth in their cribs with little human contact, much less hugs, bouts of play, and synchronous routines (L. Fisher et al., 1997). Infants who spent 8 months or more in such orphanages displayed eating problems as well as medical problems; many were withdrawn and seemingly overwhelmed in interactions with siblings and peers (Fisher et al., 1997).

These children have also proved to be more likely than most infants to display insecure patterns of attachment. Although rarely avoidantly attached, they often display resistant or disorganized patterns of attachment. Many are indiscriminately friendly and have superficial and anxious relationships (Zeanah, 2000). These abnormal attachment

behaviors often persist after they are adopted (T. G. O'Connor & Rutter, 2000).

In addition, these children show unusually high levels of the stress-related hormone cortisol even under nonstressful conditions; they seem to have an overly reactive stress response system and experience difficulty coping with stressful events later in life (Gunnar, 2000). Along with their social and emotional problems, such children also show delays in physical growth and cognitive development (Gunnar et al., 2000). Some children overcome these developmental problems if they were not institutionalized too long and if they are adopted into stimulating and loving homes. Other children experience continuing problems, especially in the area of interpersonal relationships (Gunnar et al., 2000).

Why does institutional deprivation have such damaging effects on development? Lack of proper nutrition, hygiene, and medical care, lack of stimulation, and lack of stable attachment relationships may all contribute (Gunnar et al., 2000). The deficits are probably not due entirely to lack of sensory and intellectual stimulation; institutionalized children who are provided with such stimulation but lack a stable team of caregivers are still developmentally delayed and have emotional difficulties even as adolescents (Hodges & Tizard, 1989). Nor is it the lack of a single "mother figure." In adequately staffed institutions in the People's Republic of China and in Israel, infants cared for by a few responsive caregivers turn out quite normal (Kessen, 1975; Oppenheim, Sagi, & Lamb, 1988). Apparently, then, normal development requires *sustained interactions with responsive caregivers*—whether one or several.

DAY CARE

With more than 60% of mothers in the United States now working outside the home at least part-time, questions have naturally arisen about the effects of care outside the home on infant and child development. According to U.S. Department of Labor statistics, only about 30% of infants of working mothers are cared for by their parents, 30% are tended by a relative, 20% are in family day care homes (typically run by a woman who takes a few children into her own home for payment), 10% are in large day care centers, and a small percentage are with nonrelatives in the child's home (Pungello & Kurtz-Costes, 1999).

Do infants who attend day care homes or centers suffer in any way compared to infants who stay at home with a parent? Research suggests that they are not usually damaged by the experience (Clarke-Stewart, 1993; Scarr & Eisenberg, 1993). In a major longitudinal study conducted in 10 cities in the United States, infants were assessed at 1, 6, and 15 months of age (NICHD Early Child Care Research Network, 1997). Infants in alternative forms of care were no less securely attached to their mothers than infants tended by parents. A mother's sensitivity to her infant had a lot more to do with attachment security than whether or not an infant was in alternative care. Moreover, under some circumstances, high-quality day care counteracted the negative effects of insensitive parenting. In another study, it turned out that infants who received day care

Infants do not develop normally if they lack continuing relationships with responsive caregivers—whether one or several.

© Bettmann/CORBIS

did not even differ from home-reared infants in the total amount of care they received from their mothers; mothers who worked engaged in more social interactions during their nonwork hours to compensate for being gone all day (Ahnert, Rickert, & Lamb, 2000).

In most studies, infants and young children who receive day care are not much different physically, cognitively, or socially and emotionally from infants and young children cared for at home (Broberg et al., 1997; Scarr, 1997). Recent findings from the NICHD study are mixed: Although children who spent a good deal of time in day care did better than home-reared children on some measures of cognitive and language skills, they tended to demand a lot of attention and show other signs of behavior problems (Gardner, 2001). Still, the differences between home-reared and day care infants detected in some studies may be due to differences between the families that place their children in day care and those that do not, or to relationships between parents' adequacy as parents and the quality of the day care arrangements they choose. Parents supply children with genes, a home environment, and a day care environment, and this can make it difficult to determine the effects of day care itself (Scarr, 1997). The real message may be that some children do better in day care than others. Consider a few factors that influence how well infants adjust:

1. **Quality of the day care.** The effects of day care depend on the quality of care provided in the particular day care setting (Burchinal et al., 2000; Clarke-Stewart, 1993). Just as some parents are highly nurturant while others are neglecting or abusive, some day care experiences are actually more beneficial than at-home care and others are dreadful. An infant's development clearly will suffer if he or she ends up with an alcoholic babysitter or must compete for adult attention as one of many infants in a large, understaffed center. Better developmental outcomes are likely in high-quality day care that has (1) a reasonable child-to-caregiver ratio (up to 3 infants, 4 toddlers, or 8 preschoolers per adult), (2) caregivers who have been educated for their roles and who are warm, emotionally expressive, and responsive to children, (3) little staff turnover, so that children can feel comfortable with and become attached to their caregivers, and (4) planned activities that are age appropriate (see Burchinal et al., 2000; Clarke-Stewart, 1993; Howes, Phillips, & Whitebrook, 1992). Unfortunately, day care centers often lose more than half of their staff each year because most other jobs pay a good deal more (Russakoff, 2000).

2. **Characteristics of the child.** Some infants fare better in alternative care than others do. First, infants from disadvantaged homes that place them at risk actually experience *faster* intellectual growth if they attend a high-quality day care program specially designed to meet their needs than if they stay at home and receive little intellectual stimulation (Campbell & Ramey, 1994; Scarr, 1997). Second, girls tend to adapt better to day care than boys (Baydar & Brooks-Gunn, 1991; Belsky & Rovine, 1988). Third, infants and toddlers with "easy" temperaments are likely to adjust better than children who have "difficult" or "slow-to-warm-up" temperaments (Belsky & Rovine, 1988). Fourth, babies who are tended primarily by their parents during their first year tend to be more securely attached than infants who spend many hours in alternative care before the age of 1 (Belsky & Rovine, 1988; Lamb, Sternberg, & Prodromidis, 1992).

3. **Parents' attitudes and behaviors.** The outcomes of day care placement are likely to be better if a mother has positive attitudes about working and about being a mother and if she has the personal qualities it takes to provide warm and sensitive care (Belsky & Rovine, 1988; Crockenberg & Litman, 1991). Ultimately, the quality of parenting that infants receive at home has far more to do with their development than the kind of alternative care they receive when they are not at home (Broberg et al., 1997; Fuller, Holloway, & Liang, 1996).

Most important of all may be interactions between some of these factors that suggest that day care is fine for some but not for others. In the NICHD (1997) study, for example, infants fared poorly if their mothers were not very responsive to them *and* they were subjected to poor-quality day care; under these circumstances, about half of the infants were insecurely attached to their mothers. By contrast, infants who received high-quality care somewhere, either at home or at day care, were usually securely attached.

In sum, we cannot draw simple conclusions about the effects of alternative care on infant development; these effects range from beneficial to damaging. It does seem, however, that alternative care is least likely to disrupt development if infants are old enough to have already formed attachments to their parents and if they interact with *both* responsive substitute caregivers and responsive parents. Infants under age 1, especially boys with difficult temperaments, sometimes do not thrive, especially if they receive low-quality day care and do not have warm, responsive parents. Unfortunately, many parents who work must struggle to find and keep competent sitters or high-quality day care placements, and to pay for them (Russakoff, 2000).

LATER DEVELOPMENT OF SECURELY AND INSECURELY ATTACHED INFANTS

Now consider infants raised at home. How much difference does having secure or insecure attachment make later in life? According to Bowlby and Ainsworth's attachment theory, a secure attachment allows "exploration from a secure base." This implies that securely attached children should be more cognitively competent (because they will be curious, explore the environment freely, and not shy away from challenges) and more socially competent (because they will also explore the world of people freely, will expect positive reactions from others because of the positive internal working models they form, and will have learned in the parent–child relationship how to interact smoothly with others). Does research support these predictions?

Indeed it does. In an early longitudinal study, Everett Waters and his associates (Waters, Wippman, & Sroufe, 1979) measured the quality of infants' attachments to their mothers at 15 months of age and then observed these children in nursery school at age 3. Children who had been securely attached as infants were social leaders in the nursery school setting:

They often initiated play activities, were sensitive to the needs and feelings of other children, and were popular with their peers. A close give-and-take relationship with a parent apparently helps children develop positive patterns of social behavior that in turn allow them to form close relationships with their peers (Clark & Ladd, 2000; Schneider, Atkinson, & Tardif, 2001).

Securely attached infants also became children whose teachers described them as curious, self-directed, and eager to learn. By contrast, children who had been insecurely attached at age 15 months, displaying either resistant or avoidant attachment patterns, became 3-year-olds who were socially and emotionally withdrawn and were hesitant to engage other children in play activities. These children were also less curious, less interested in learning, and less forceful in pursuing their goals than securely attached children. Lacking a secure base for exploration, they seemed to be less independent than other children.

Quality of attachment in infancy is also related to later emotional development. For example, Grazyna Kochanska (2001) assessed children at 9, 14, 22, and 33 months in laboratory situations designed to provoke fear (for example, the approach of an unpredictable toy dog), anger (confinement to a car seat), and joy (a hand puppet show). Infants with resistant attachments at 14 months were the most fearful and the least joyful of the children tested; they showed fear even in tests designed to provoke joy and displayed less positive emotion as they got older. Infants with avoidant attachments were at first not very emotionally expressive but became quite fearful by 33 months of age. Infants with disorganized attachments became more and more angry over time. Whereas these insecurely attached groups expressed more negative emotions as they got older, securely attached infants became less angry with age and were not overly fearful.

Recent research by Stephen Suomi, Megan Gunnar, and others suggests that a secure attachment also helps shape the capacity to cope with stress and regulate emotions later in life. In experimental studies, infant monkeys who experienced traumatic separations from their mothers have been compared to monkeys who enjoyed secure attachment relationships with their mothers. Securely attached monkeys show more adaptive physiological responses to stress later in life and other positive outcomes, including good parenting skills that result in their own infants' becoming securely attached (Suomi, 1997, 1999; Suomi & Levine, 1998). Research also demonstrates that young rhesus monkeys who are genetically prone to be highly emotionally reactive develop in healthy ways and are able to cope with stress if they are reared by calm mothers for the first 6 months of their lives (Suomi, 1997). These same infants turn out socially incompetent if they are reared by emotionally reactive mothers. Similarly, human infants who are temperamentally prone to be anxious show a lower rise in cortisol (stress hormone) levels and are better able to cope physiologically with stressful experiences if they have enjoyed secure attachments than if they have not (Gunnar, 1998, 2000).

Do these early effects of secure attachment last? In late childhood and adolescence, children who have enjoyed secure relationships with their parents continue to be well-adjusted—intellectually, socially, and emotionally. They are self-confident and do well in school (Jacobsen & Hofmann, 1997), and they are accepted by the peer group and have close friends (Elicker, Englund, & Sroufe, 1992; Kerns, Klepac, & Cole, 1996). As we will see later, lasting effects of early attachments can be detected even in adulthood. Meanwhile, infants who are abused and who develop disorganized attachments are at risk to turn into children who are suspicious of others, aggressive, and prone to other mental health problems (van IJzendoorn et al., 1999), while neglected children tend to develop resistant attachments and to be withdrawn and lacking in self-esteem (Finzi et al., 2000).

In sum, children are unlikely to develop normally if their first relationships in life are repeatedly disrupted by separation or if they never have the opportunity to form an attachment. Meanwhile, a secure attachment during infancy has positive implications for social, emotional, and intellectual development. Yet we must avoid concluding that infants who are insecurely attached to their mothers are doomed. First, infants are part of an attachment network involving many family members (Cowan, 1997). Affectionate ties to *fathers* (or perhaps siblings or grandparents) can compensate for insecure mother–infant relationships. Although most infants have the same kind of attachment with their mothers that they have with their fathers, many infants who are insecurely attached to one parent are securely attached to the other (Cook, 2000; van IJzendoorn & De Wolff, 1997). Although infants who have a secure relationship with *both* parents are likely to be more socially competent than those who are attached to only one parent, the infant who has one secure relationship is better off than the infant who is not securely attached to either parent (Biller, 1993; Main & Weston, 1981).

In addition, early attachments may have no long-term consequences if they change later on, and the quality of attachments often does change with age. For example, Everett Waters and his colleagues (2000) studied 12-month-old infants in the Strange Situation and 20 years later interviewed them using the Adult Attachment Interview to determine how they viewed their childhood attachment relationships and how securely attached they were as adults. In this middle-class sample, 64% of the adults fell into the same secure, resistant, or avoidant category as the one in which they had been classified as infants. Where changes had occurred, they tended to be associated with negative life events such as loss of a parent, parental divorce, or illness in the family. Stressful life changes may explain why only about 39% of the infants in a sample of low-income families retained their attachment classification as adults (Weinfeld, Sroufe, & Egeland, 2000).

Apparently, then, attachment security is stable across long stretches of the life span when lives are relatively stable but can also change if life circumstances and important relationships change. Infancy is not the only period of the life span that shapes development (Schaffer, 2000). As Arlene Skolnick

(1986) puts it, "Secure attachment to the mother does not make one invulnerable to later problems and socioemotional difficulties, and poor early relations with the mother do not doom a person to a life of loneliness, poor relationships, or psychopathology" (p. 193).

All things considered, the Bowlby-Ainsworth ethological attachment theory is quite well supported by research evidence. Many evolved behaviors such as smiling and clinging do seem to contribute to the formation of attachments. Moreover, the experiences of caregivers and infants as they interact strongly influence whether a secure, resistant, avoidant, or disorganized/disoriented attachment will form. Studies of the later consequences of early attachment support Bowlby's claim that "internal working models" of self and others formed early in life shape later relationships and development. Despite the significance of the infant–parent bond, however, many of us learn new social skills and different attitudes toward relationships in our later interactions not only with parents, but with peers, close friends, lovers, and spouses. It is time, then, to supplement our discussion of parent–child relations with a look at the "second world of childhood"—the world of peer relations.

First Peer Relations

Although babies show an interest in other babies from the first months of life, they do not really interact until about the middle of the first year. By then, infants will often smile or babble at their tiny companions, vocalize, offer toys, and gesture to one another (Hay, Nash, & Pedersen, 1983; Vandell, Wilson, & Buchanan, 1980). At first many of these friendly gestures go unnoticed and unreciprocated. Infants then pass through three stages of early sociability from age 1 to age 2 (Mueller & Lucas, 1975; Mueller & Vandell, 1979). At first, in the *object-centered* stage, two infants may jointly focus on a toy but will pay more attention to the toy than to each other. During the second, or *simple interactive* stage, infants more obviously influence one another and respond appropriately to one another's behavior. They treat peers as if they were interesting "toys" that are responsive and can be controlled (Brownell, 1986).

By about 18 months of age, infants progress to the third, or *complementary interactive* stage, in which their interactions are even more clearly social and reciprocal. They now delight in imitating each other and turn these rounds of imitation into social games (Eckerman & Stein, 1990; Howes & Matheson, 1992). Indeed, they seem highly attuned to peers: They are more likely to imitate peers who carry out simple actions than to imitate adult models who perform the same actions (Ryalls, Gul, & Ryalls, 2000). Eighteen-month-olds also adopt roles in their play and can reverse roles. Thus, the toddler who receives a toy may immediately offer a toy in return, or the one who has been the "chaser" will become the "chasee." Toward the end of the second year, infants have become quite proficient at this kind of turn taking and reciprocal exchange, especially if they are securely attached to their parents (Fagot, 1997).

Surprising as it may seem, some infants also form special relationships with preferred playmates—friendships (Howes, 1996). On Israeli kibbutzim, where children are cared for in groups, Martha Zaslow (1980) discovered that many pairs of infants as young as 1 year of age became truly attached to each other. Hadara and Rivka, for instance, consistently sought each other out as playmates, mourned each other's absence, and disturbed everyone with their loud babbling "conversations" when they were confined to their cribs. Clearly the caregiver–infant relationship is not the only important social relationship that develops during infancy.

The Child

How do relationships with parents and peers change from infancy to later childhood? And just how important are children's social relationships to their development?

Parent–Child Attachments

The parent–child attachment changes qualitatively during childhood. According to John Bowlby (1969), it becomes a "goal-corrected partnership" in which parent and child accommodate to each other's needs; the child becomes a more sensitive partner and also becomes more independent of the parent. Older preschoolers still seek attention and approval from their parents, and they most certainly rush to their parents for comfort when they are frightened or hurt. But they also become increasingly dependent on *peers* for social and emotional support (Furman & Buhrmester, 1992).

Peer Networks

Over the years from age 2 to age 12, children spend more and more time with peers and considerably less time with adults. This trend emerged clearly in a study by Sharri Ellis and her colleagues (Ellis, Rogoff, & Cromer, 1981), who observed 436 children playing in their homes and around the neighborhood. Interestingly, this study revealed that youngsters of all ages spent less time with age-mates (defined as children whose ages were within a year of their own) than with children who were more than a year older or younger than they were.

Another finding of this study is a familiar one: Even 1- to 2-year-olds played more often with same-sex companions than with other-sex companions, and this *gender segregation* became increasingly strong with age (see Chapter 12). Once in their sex-segregated worlds, boys and girls experience different kinds of social relationships. You may have heard, for example, that boys travel in "packs," whereas girls travel in "pairs." It's true: By age 6, boys spend about three-fourths of their time in group activities, whereas girls spend only about one-sixth of their time in groups, preferring to play with one other girl at a time (Benenson, Apostoleris, & Parnass, 1997).

Overall, then, children spend an increasing amount of time with peers rather than parents. These peers are typically same-sex children, roughly similar in age, who enjoy the same sex-typed activities.

Play

It is in the context of play that children develop social relationships with their peers and acquire social skills. So important is play in the life of the child from age 2 to age 5 that these years are sometimes called "the play years." This is when children hop about the room shrieking with delight, don capes and go off on dragon hunts, and whip up cakes and cookies made of clay, sand, or thin air. We can detect two major changes in play between infancy and age 5: It becomes more social, and it becomes more imaginative. After age 5 or so, the exuberant and fanciful play of the preschool years gives way to somewhat more serious play.

PLAY BECOMES MORE SOCIAL

Many years ago, Mildred Parten (1932) devised a useful method for classifying the types of play engaged in by nursery school children of different ages. Her six categories of activity, arranged from least to most social, are as follows:

1. **Unoccupied play.** Children stand idly, look around, or engage in apparently aimless activities such as pacing.
2. **Solitary play.** Children play alone, typically with objects, and appear to be highly involved in what they are doing.
3. **Onlooker play.** Children watch others play, taking an active interest and perhaps even talking to the players, but not directly participating.
4. **Parallel play.** Children play next to one another, doing much the same thing, but they interact very little (for ex-

ample, two girls might sit near each other, both drawing pictures, without talking to each other to any extent).
5. **Associative play.** Children interact by swapping materials, conversing, or following each other's lead, but they are not really united by the same goal (for example, our two girls may swap crayons and comment on each other's drawings as they draw).
6. **Cooperative play.** Children truly join forces to achieve a common goal; they act as a pair or group, dividing their labor and coordinating their activities in a meaningful way (for example, our two girls collaborate to draw a mural for their teacher).

The major message of Parten's study (and of others like it) is that play becomes increasingly social and socially skilled from age 2 to age 5 (Barnes, 1971; Smith, 1978; see also Howes & Matheson, 1992). Unoccupied and onlooker activities are quite rare at all ages. Solitary and parallel play become less frequent with age, although solitary play has its place throughout childhood. Meanwhile, associative and cooperative play, the most social and complex of the types of play, become more frequent with age (see Figure 14.3).

PLAY BECOMES MORE IMAGINATIVE

The first **pretend play**—play in which one actor, object, or action symbolizes or stands for another—occurs at about the age of 1, when an infant may raise an empty cup, or perhaps a forbidden treat, to her lips, smile, give a parent a knowing glance, and make loud lip-smacking sounds (Nicolich, 1977). The earliest pretend play is just like this: The infant performs actions that symbolize familiar activities such as eating, sleeping, and washing.

By age 2, toddlers readily join in pretense if you hand them a towel and suggest that they wipe up the imaginary tea

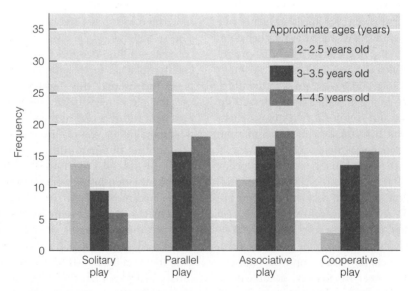

Figure 14.3 Frequency of activities engaged in by preschool children of different ages. With age, solitary and parallel play occur less frequently, whereas associative and cooperative play occur more frequently.

SOURCE: Adapted from Barnes (1971)

you just spilled (P. L. Harris & Kavanaugh, 1993). Since there is no "tea" in sight, this willingness to clean it up is really quite remarkable. It means that toddlers are capable of using their new symbolic capacity to construct a mental representation of a pretend event and of acting according to this representation. Pretend play fully blossoms from age 2 to age 5, increasing in both frequency and sophistication (Howes & Matheson, 1992). As children get older, they can depict heroes and heroines very different from themselves and can enact elaborate dramas using very few props.

Most important, children combine their capacity for increasingly social play and their capacity for pretense into **social pretend play** (Howes & Matheson, 1992). Starting at age 2 or 3, children less often enact scenes on their own using dolls and other toys and more often cooperate with playmates to enact their dramas. These pretend play episodes can become quite elaborate and require a good deal of social competence. Consider the following example, in which a 5-year-old (M) wants her partner (E), playing the role of a mother, to leave her babies and come to her house and the two negotiate what will happen next, managing to stay in role while they do so (Garvey, 1990, p. 137).

> M: You come here. The babies are sleeping now and . . . (interrupted).
> E: No, they'll cry when I leave 'cause they'll hear the car.
> M: Nooo. The car's broken. I have the car.
> E: All right, but one baby will have to take care of these little babies.

Although social pretend play is universal and becomes more frequent with age in all cultures, the quality of preschoolers' play is shaped by the culture in which they live (Haight et al., 1999). For example, in the United States and Turkey, children engage in a good deal of one-on-one play with their caregivers, but in India and Guatemala, where children are more integrated into adult life, they spend more time in group activities with other adults and children (Goencue, Mistry, & Mosier, 2000). And, in a comparison of the social pretend play of Korean and American preschoolers, Jo Ann Farver and Yoolim Shin (1997) found that U.S. children liked to play superheroes and act out themes of danger and fantasy, whereas Korean children took on family roles and enacted everyday activities. American children also talked a lot about their own actions, rejected other children's ideas, and bossed others around, whereas Korean children were more focused on their partners' activities and were more prone to make polite requests and agree with one another. Through their play, then, children in the United States (an *individualistic culture*) were learning to assert their identities as individuals, whereas children in Korea (a *collectivist culture*) were learning how to keep their egos and emotions under control to achieve group harmony.

PLAY BECOMES MORE RULE-GOVERNED

After they enter school, children engage less frequently in symbolic play. Now they spend more of their time playing organized games with rules—board games, games of tag or hide-and-seek, organized sports, and so on (Athey, 1984). They also develop individual hobbies, such as building model cars or making scrapbooks, that allow them to develop skills and gain knowledge.

According to Jean Piaget (1932/1965), it is not until children enter the stage of concrete operations, at about age 6 or 7, that they become capable of joining with other children to follow the rules of games. Older children—11- and 12-year-olds who are entering the stage of formal operations—gain a more flexible concept of rules, recognizing that they are arbitrary agreements that can be changed as long as the players agree. Partly because of cognitive gains, then, the play of the school-age child is more organized and rule-governed—and less fanciful—than that of the preschool child.

WHAT GOOD IS PLAY?

In 19th-century America, child's play was discouraged because it was viewed as a frivolous waste of time (Athey, 1984). Now we know better. Play contributes to virtually all areas of children's development. Indeed, the fact that playful activity occurs among the young of so many species strongly suggests that play is an evolved behavior that helps prepare the young for adult life (Gandelman, 1992).

Children who engage in a great deal of pretend play (or are trained to do so) perform better on tests of cognitive development, language skills, and creativity than children who rarely pretend (E. P. Fisher, 1992; Farver, Kim, & Lee-Shin, 2000). As Piaget maintained, play provides opportunities to practice emerging cognitive skills and to strengthen them in the process. And perhaps because of the social experience they gain, preschoolers who engage in a great deal of social pretend play tend to be more popular and socially skilled than children who do not (Connolly & Doyle, 1984; Farver et al., 2000).

Finally, play contributes to healthy emotional development; it provides opportunities to express bothersome feelings, resolve emotional conflicts, and master challenges (Landreth & Homeyer, 1998). If Danny, for example, has recently been scolded by his mother for drawing on the wall, he may gain control of the situation by scolding his "child" for doing the same thing. And Jackie, an abused 5-year-old, apparently coped with his abuse by having an alligator puppet swallow a small child doll and then smashing the alligator with a mallet and burying it in the sandbox (Landreth & Homeyer, 1998).

Children who are suffering from emotional disturbances not only reveal their concerns through their play but have difficulty playing in mature and creative ways (Gordon, 1993). For example, Mavis Hetherington and her colleagues (Hetherington, Cox, & Cox, 1979) found that, compared to children from intact families, children from divorcing families acted out fewer themes in their play, had difficulty using props in multiple ways or getting by without realistic props, and adopted fewer roles. Moreover, the many aggressive themes in their play reflected their anger and anxiety about divorce. Other research suggests that children who have a strong interest in violent fantasy may be headed for trouble: They tend to display a lot of anger and aggressive behavior and not much prosocial behavior (Dunn & Hughes, 2001).

Social pretend play during the preschool years contributes to intellectual, social, and emotional development.

Let it never be said, then, that play is useless; it is truly the child's work. Although children play because it is fun, not because it sharpens their skills, they indirectly contribute to their own development—physical, intellectual, social, and emotional—by doing so. Parents can help their children's development along by getting involved in the give-and-take that play episodes require (Lindsey & Mize, 2000).

Peer Acceptance and Popularity

As children play and interact, they typically discover that they like some peers more than others. Researchers study peer-group acceptance through **sociometric techniques**—methods for determining who is liked and disliked in a group. In a sociometric survey, children in a classroom may be asked to nominate several classmates whom they like and several whom they dislike, or they may be asked to rate all of their classmates in terms of their desirability as companions (see Cillessen & Bukowski, 2000; Terry & Coie, 1991). It is very important to find out who is liked *and* who is disliked, for this allows children to be classified into four quite distinct categories of social status (Coie, Dodge, & Coppotelli, 1982):

1. Popular—well liked by most, rarely disliked
2. Rejected—rarely liked, often disliked
3. Neglected—neither liked nor disliked; isolated children who seem to be invisible to their classmates
4. Controversial—liked by many but also disliked by many; for example, the fun-loving child with leadership skills who also has a nasty habit of starting fights

Why are some children more popular than others, and why are some children rejected by their peers? Popularity is affected by some personal characteristics that a child can do little about. For instance, physically attractive children are usually more popular than physically unattractive children, and children who are relatively intelligent tend to be more socially

accepted than those who are not, probably because cognitive ability contributes to social competence (Bellanti et al., 2000). Social competence—the ability to apply social-cognitive skills successfully in initiating social interactions, responding positively to peers, resolving interpersonal conflicts smoothly, and so on—clearly predicts popularity (Coie, Dodge, & Kupersmidt, 1990; Ladd, 1999). Children who are socially awkward, argumentative, and disruptive are unlikely to be popular. Interestingly, though, some highly aggressive boys make it into the ranks of popular children, probably because their toughness is perceived as cool by peers (Rodkin et al., 2000).

"Rejected" children are usually highly aggressive, although some are socially isolated, submissive children who are overly sensitive to teasing and are seen by others as "easy to push around" (Parkhurst & Asher, 1992; Rabiner, Keane, & MacKinnon-Lewis, 1993). Rejected children are less aware than other children are of who likes them and who doesn't, one of many signs that they are not very socially astute (MacDonald & Cohen, 1995). By contrast, children who fall into the "neglected" category of sociometric status often have reasonably good social skills; they are usually nonaggressive and tend to be shy, withdrawn, and unassertive (Coie et al., 1990; Harrist et al., 1997). As a result, no one really notices them.

To appreciate how social skills contribute to popularity, consider what happens when children try to enter and gain acceptance in play groups (Dodge et al., 1990; Putallaz & Wasserman, 1989). When children who ultimately become popular want to join a group's activity, they first hold back and assess what is going on and then smoothly blend into the group, commenting pleasantly about whatever the other children are discussing. By contrast, children who are eventually rejected by their peers tend to be pushy and disruptive. Jimmy, for example, may sit beside two boys who are playing a computer game and distract them by talking about a TV program he saw the night before. Even worse, he may criticize the way the boys are playing, start pecking computer keys, or threaten to turn off the computer if he is not allowed to play. By contrast, children who end up being neglected by their peers often hover around a group without taking any positive steps to initiate contact, and they shy away from peers who attempt to make contact with them.

As we've seen, children who experienced secure attachments to their parents as infants tend to be popular with their peers; they have learned social skills and styles of interacting in the parent–child relationship that shape the quality of their relationships with peers (Black & Logan, 1995; Kerns, 1996). Parents of popular children also make explicit attempts to teach their children how to relate to peers, and these attempts pay off (Mize & Pettit, 1997). By contrast, as we saw in Chapter 13, harsh discipline at home tends to breed the aggressive behavior that prompts peers to reject a child (Pettit et al., 1996). And parents who are not very sensitive to their children during conversations tend to have children who are not very skilled conversation partners and who end up being rejected because of it (Black & Logan, 1995).

In sum, popularity is affected by many factors. It helps to have an attractive face and cognitive skills, but it is probably more important to behave in socially competent ways. Definitions of social competence vary from culture to culture, of course. Thus, for example, children who are shy are likely to be unpopular in Canada but popular in China, where being quiet and reserved is more socially desirable (Chen, Rubin, & Sun, 1992). The ingredients of popularity also change with age: Establishing close relationships with members of the other sex enhances popularity during adolescence, but consorting with "the enemy," and thereby violating norms of gender segregation, can *detract* from popularity during childhood (Sroufe et al., 1993). Many such contextual factors influence who is popular and who is not.

Do the outcomes of these popularity polls really matter? Yes—especially for the 10–15% of children who are rejected by their peers (Malik & Furman, 1993). Children who are neglected by peers often gain greater acceptance later, but those who are rejected, especially because of aggressive behavior, are likely to maintain their rejected status from grade to grade (Cillessen et al., 1992). More significantly, rejected children may end up with worse behavior problems by virtue of having been rejected (Coie et al., 1992; DeRosier, Kupersmidt, & Patterson, 1994).

Friendships

Being accepted by the wider peer group and having close friends are distinct and serve different functions for children. Popular children are more likely than unpopular children to have friends, but many unpopular children manage to enter into at least one reciprocated friendship, and many popular children do not. In one study of 7- and 8-year-olds, for example, 39% of children rejected by peers had at least one mutual friendship, whereas 31% of popular children lacked a friendship (Gest, Graham-Bermann, & Hartup, 2001).

Children are better off if they do have one reciprocated friendship than if they do not. Not only are they likely to be less lonely (Parker & Asher, 1993), but they are likely to be happier and more socially competent, especially if their friendships are with peers who are well adjusted and supportive (Vaughn et al., 2000; Hartup & Stevens, 1997). Moreover, just as Harry Stack Sullivan theorized, a true chum can sometimes compensate for a poor relationship with parents and provide children with a sense of self-worth they might otherwise lack (Gauze et al., 1996).

Contributions of Peers to Development

We now appreciate that peers, and especially friends, may be every bit as important as parents to child development. Parents excel at caregiving and typically provide their children with a sense of emotional security that enables them to explore their environment and participate in social relationships (Kerns, 1996). However, acceptance by and interactions with peers may be critical in the learning of social skills and normal patterns of social behavior (Ladd, 1999). As Piaget pointed out, interactions with peers involve more give-and-take and accommodation and less power assertion and coercion than do interactions with parents (Adams & Laursen, 2001). Peer relationships, therefore, provide a splendid training ground for social relations.

The influence of peers extends far beyond the realm of social development (Newcomb & Bagwell, 1995; Hartup, 1996). Peers, especially close friends, contribute to emotional development by teaching children how to participate in emotionally intimate relationships and by offering social support and comfort that can help children feel better about themselves, weather stressful events such as a divorce, avoid loneliness, and feel bolder when faced with new challenges such the first day of kindergarten (Hartup, 1996; Ladd, 1999). Moreover, social interactions with peers stimulate not only social skill learning but cognitive growth; children acquire new knowledge and problem-solving skills from other children (Gauvain & Rogoff, 1989; Ladd, 1999). In short, optimal child development seems to require both attachments to adults and close relationships with peers, especially friends (Sroufe, Egeland, & Carlson, 1999).

Children in the neglected category of sociometric status are shy and tend to hover on the fringes of a group without daring to enter it.

The Adolescent

Although children are already highly involved in peer activities, adolescents spend even more time with peers and less time with parents (Buhrmester & Furman, 1986; Fallon & Bowles, 1997). The quality of the individual's attachment to parents continues to be highly important throughout adolescence, but peers, including romantic partners, begin to rival or surpass parents as sources of intimacy and support (Furman & Buhrmester, 1992; Lempers & Clark-Lempers, 1992). Moreover, the *quality* of peer relations changes. Not only do adolescents begin to form boy–girl friendships and go on dates, but they become more capable of participating in truly deep and intimate attachments.

Attachments to Parents

Just as infants must have a secure base if they are to explore, adolescents seem to need the security provided by supportive parents in order to become more independent and autonomous individuals (Kobak et al., 1993; Kenny & Rice, 1995). If they have experienced separation from parents through divorce, death, or other reasons, their attachments to their parents are likely to be less secure and they may feel less equipped to cope with the challenges of adolescence (Woodward, Fergusson, & Belsky, 2000).

For many youths in our society, going off to college qualifies as a "naturally occurring strange situation" (Kenny, 1987)—a potentially stressful test of one's ability to cope with the unfamiliar. Students who go home on weekends or call or email home frequently during their first semester are engaging in "attachment behavior" just as surely as the infant who whimpers for his mommy. From an attachment theory perspective, experiencing separation anxiety in this situation is perfectly normal and adaptive. Preoccupation with parents typically decreases over the first semester and predicts adjustment problems only when it is extreme (Berman & Sperling, 1991).

Students who are securely attached to their parents display better psychological and social adjustment during the potentially difficult transition to college than students who are insecurely attached (Lapsley, Rice, & FitzGerald, 1990). Ofra Mayseless and her colleagues (Mayseless, Danieli, & Sharabany, 1996) found that securely attached students cope well with the task of separating from their parents, forming close romantic relationships while maintaining close communication with their parents. Resistantly attached students have more difficulty forming romantic relationships and find even minor separations from parents very upsetting. Avoidant youths claim not to be bothered much by separation, as if denying that they could need their parents for anything.

Going to college is a "Strange Situation" that activates attachment behaviors, such as hugging and emailing, designed to maintain contact with attachment figures.

More generally, adolescents who enjoy secure attachments with their parents seem to have a stronger sense of identity, higher self-esteem, greater social competence, and better emotional adjustment than their less securely attached peers (Kenny & Rice, 1995). They also report fewer symptoms of depression and anxiety than insecurely attached college students (Vivona, 2000). When parents provide emotional support and a secure base for exploration but also encourage autonomy, their adolescents seem to thrive.

Friendships

Friendships in early childhood are based on enjoying common activities; friendships in late childhood center on mutual loyalty and caring (Aboud & Mendelson, 1996; Hartup & Stevens, 1997). Adolescent friendships increasingly hinge on *intimacy and self-disclosure* (Berndt & Perry, 1990; Buhrmester, 1996). Like children, teenagers form friendships with peers who are similar to themselves in observable ways. For example, most high school students, particularly African Americans, tend to choose friends of the same ethnic background (Hamm, 2000). However, they increasingly choose friends whose *psychological qualities*—interests, attitudes, values, and personalities—match their own. Now friends are like-minded individuals who can confide in each another.

Although same-sex friendships remain important throughout adolescence, teenagers increasingly enter into close cross-sex friendships. How do these other-sex friendships compare with same-sex friendships? Ruth Sharabany and her colleagues (Sharabany, Gershoni, & Hofman, 1981) asked 5th to 11th graders to assess their same- and cross-sex friendships in terms of such aspects of emotional intimacy as spontaneity, trust and loyalty, sensitivity to the other's feelings, and attachment. As you can see in Figure 14.4, same-sex friendships were highly intimate in most respects throughout this age range, but cross-sex friendships did not attain a high level of intimacy until 11th grade. These findings offer some support for Harry Stack Sullivan's view that children learn lessons about intimate attachments in their same-sex chumships that they only later apply in their heterosexual relationships.

We can also see that girls tended to report higher degrees of intimacy in their friendships than boys did, and that they achieve emotional intimacy in their cross-sex relationships at earlier ages. This may help to explain why girls are later more likely than boys to describe their romantic relationships in terms of friendship-like qualities, such as disclosing feelings and providing emotional support (Feiring, 1999).

Changing Social Networks

Elementary school children take interest in members of the other sex, talk at length about who likes whom, and in the process prepare themselves for heterosexual relationships

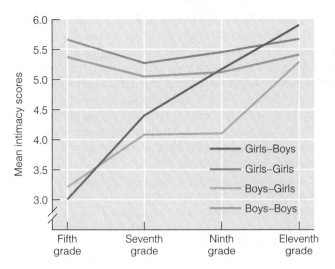

Figure 14.4 Changes during adolescence in the intimacy of same-sex and cross-sex friendships. The "Girls–Boys" scores reflect how girls rated the intimacy of their relationships with boys; "Boys–Girls" scores reflect how boys rated their relationships with girls. Cross-sex friendships clearly become more and more intimate during the adolescent years, ultimately achieving the levels of intimacy that characterize same-sex friendships throughout this developmental period.

Source: Sharabany, Gershoni, & Hofman (1981)

(Thorne, 1993). Still, one has to wonder how boys and girls who live in their own, gender-segregated worlds arrive at the point of dating "the enemy." Some time ago, Dexter Dunphy (1963) offered a plausible account of how peer-group structures change during adolescence to pave the way for dating relationships. His five stages, outlined in Figure 14.5, are still helpful today in understanding how peer relations lay the foundation for later romantic attachments (see, for example, Connolly, Furman, & Konarski, 2000).

CLIQUES AND CROWDS

The process begins in late childhood, when boys and girls become members of same-sex **cliques,** or small friendship groups, and have little to do with the other sex. Second, members of boy cliques and girl cliques begin to interact with each other more frequently. Same-sex cliques provide what amounts to a secure base for exploring ways to behave with members of the other sex: Talking to a girl at the mall with your friends there is far less threatening than doing so on your own. In the third stage, the most popular boys and girls form a *heterosexual* clique. Popular children are quicker than unpopular children to form cross-sex friendships, so they lead the way (George & Hartmann, 1996).

As less popular peers also enter into heterosexual cliques, a new peer group structure, the **crowd,** completes its evolution. The crowd, a collection of several heterosexual cliques, is involved in arranging organized social activities on the weekend—parties, outings to the lake or mall, and so on. Those adolescents who become members of a mixed-sex

clique and a crowd (not all do) have many opportunities to get to know members of the other sex. Eventually, however, interacting with the other sex in group settings is not enough. Couples form and the crowd disintegrates in late high school after having served its purpose of bringing boys and girls together.

Not all high school crowds are the same. The names may vary, but every school has its crowds of, for example, "populars," "jocks," "druggies," and "losers," each consisting of adolescents who are similar to one another in some way and different from the adolescents in other crowds (Brown, Mory, & Kinney, 1994; Stone & Brown, 1999). Everyone in high school seems to recognize these differences: "[The brains] all wear glasses and 'kiss up' to teachers and after school they all tromp uptown to the library" (Brown et al., 1994, p. 128). "The partyers goof off a lot more than the jocks do, but they don't come to school stoned like the burnouts do" (p. 133). Which crowd or crowds an adolescent belongs to has important implications for his or her social identity and self-esteem; it's easier to feel good about oneself if one is a "popular" or a "jock" than if one is a "dweeb," a "druggie," or a social isolate who does not belong to any crowd (Brown & Lohr, 1987).

Crowd membership also has a good deal to do with whether peer pressures pull in the direction of deviant behavior or conventional behavior. "Druggies" encourage drug use, whereas "brains" discourage it, so which crowd one travels with can make a big difference in one's experience of adolescence

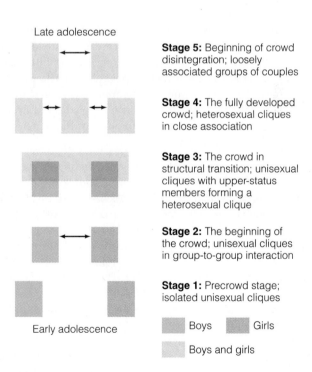

Figure 14.5 Stages in the evolution of the peer group during adolescence, from same-sex cliques (*bottom*) to dating couples (*top*).

Source: Dunphy (1963)

and development. Adolescents are least likely to engage in delinquent behavior, become depressed, or feel lonely if they have friends who do not engage in deviant behavior. By comparison, both adolescents with deviant friends and adolescents without any friends are more prone to delinquency and depression, although those with deviant friends are at least less lonely than those without friends (Brendgen, Vitaro, & Bukowski, 2000).

As the structure of peer groups changes from childhood to adolescence, bases for popularity may also change. William Bukowski and his colleagues (Bukowski, Sippola, & Newcomb, 2000) found that young adolescents tend to devalue things they associate with childhood (such obeying teachers and achieving in school) and to value peers who stand out and seem independent and adultlike. As a result, boys who are aggressive troublemakers and who may therefore seem mature may become more popular for a time than they were in childhood.

Overall, adolescence is a time of transition from same-sex to cross-sex peer relationships. Peer influences can be healthy or destructive, depending on which cliques and crowds an adolescent belongs to.

DATING

As Dunphy's model suggests, the transition to dating takes place in the context of the peer group. These days, it involves heavy use of phones, as illustrated by this snippet from the life of a seventh-grade boy, Chris, who was being pressured by his friends to have sex with Kim—and, of course, to report back (Hersch, 1998, p. 130):

> The phone rings, and it is Kim, the first of what will be many long calls between them each day. Before long her friends start calling too and have long conversations with Chris about how the relationship is going. His friends call to see what's happening. The permutations seem endless. There are conference calls. Several people backed up on call waiting. Chris's bedroom phone is at the center of a huge communication network.

Candice Feiring (1996) has provided an interesting picture of typical dating experiences in a sample of 15-year-olds. Almost 90% of these adolescents had dated by the age of 15, though only 21% were currently dating. Most couples did not go out alone on dates as much as they dated within the context of the peer group or crowd. While dating, couples saw each other or talked on the phone (for an average of 60 minutes per call!) every day. These dating relationships were usually casual and lasted an average of only 4 months. Although partners were fascinated with one another, dating relationships were in most respects more like same-sex friendships than like adult romantic attachments; they were mainly sources of companionship rather than of love and security (Feiring, 1996). Perhaps this is why increased involvement in dating relationships often means less time spent with same-sex friends (Zimmer-Gembeck, 1999).

Dating relationships in early adolescence are more superficial and short-lived than later dating relationships (Brown, Feiring, & Furman, 1999). Teens are at first concerned about having a relationship and the status it brings; only in later adolescence will most form a true attachment to a special partner (Brown, 1999). It takes adolescents some time to integrate their needs for security (satisfied during childhood by parents), intimacy (obtained from same-sex friends, or chums), and sexual gratification (a new need) in a love relationship (Furman & Wehner, 1994).

How does dating affect adolescent adjustment and development? It clearly serves important functions—helping adolescents to achieve autonomy from both parents and peers, gain status as grown-ups, and, from an evolutionary perspective, distance themselves from their parents to avoid incestuous relationships as they reach puberty (Gray & Steinberg, 1999). A longitudinal study of 10th- and 11th-graders by Patrick Davies and Michael Windle (2000) indicates that entering a steady relationship has its pros and cons: It is associated with a decrease in problem behaviors such as drinking and minor delinquency, but it also entails withdrawing somewhat from the wider peer culture and getting into more conflicts with friends. Being in a steady relationship is good for self-esteem, whereas teens whose steady relationships end tend to feel less attractive and report symptoms of depression. Increased involvement in casual dating, by contrast, is associated with closer ties with friends and higher rates of problem behavior. Overall, though, adolescents who date tend to be better adjusted emotionally than those who do not (Davies & Windle, 2000).

Parent and Peer Influence

Should parents worry about the fact that adolescents become more and more involved in both same-sex and cross-sex relationships with peers as they get older? Will they lose influence over their children? One approach to answering these questions has been to study **conformity**—the tendency to yield to the opinions and wishes of others. Conformity to parents' wishes tends to decrease gradually and steadily during adolescence; conformity to peers, including peers who advocate law-breaking, increases until about age 14 or 15 and then declines (Berndt, 1979; Steinberg & Silverberg, 1986). Thus, parents do have some grounds for worrying that their adolescents may get into trouble by "going along with the crowd," especially around age 14 or 15. Those adolescents who are willing to break their parents' rules and let their school performance slide in order to be popular do indeed get into more trouble and do less well in school than other adolescents (Fuligni et al., 2001).

Why does conformity to peers' misconduct *decrease* by the end of high school? Increased dependence on peers in early adolescence may represent a first step toward the development of autonomy (Steinberg & Silverberg, 1986). Although parents whose teenagers end up at the police sta-

It is no accident that teenagers wear the same hairstyles and dress alike. Peers exert more influence than parents in these matters.

tion may not be totally comforted by this thought, teenagers may need the "secure base" that peer acceptance provides before they are ready to become truly autonomous in later adolescence. As adolescents progress in their quest for autonomy, they become less dependent on *both* parents and peers for guidance and more able to make their own choices.

Parents retain a good deal more influence over their adolescents than is commonly believed, though. Peers do influence adolescents' social activities and tastes, but parents continue to be the major shapers of their educational and vocational plans and important values (Sebald, 1986; Wilks, 1986). More important, teenagers who have close attachments to warm and authoritative parents who establish and enforce clear standards of behavior are likely to be academically and socially competent and to associate with conventional rather than antisocial peer groups; they are thus less likely to be exposed to negative peer pressures, and are less susceptible to such pressures when they do encounter them, than are adolescents whose family relationships are poor (Brown et al., 1993; Fuligni & Eccles, 1993; Santor, Messervey, & Kusumakar, 2000).

In fact, problems for youths who "get in with the wrong crowd" and engage in antisocial behavior usually begin at home. One way parents can go wrong is by being too strict, failing to adjust to adolescents' needs for greater autonomy. This may cause teenagers to become alienated from their parents and overly susceptible to negative peer influences (Fuligni & Eccles, 1993). Parents can also go wrong by failing to provide enough discipline and by not monitoring their children's activities sufficiently (Brown et al., 1993; Dishion et al., 1991).

When parents are warm and accepting, and neither too controlling nor too lax in their discipline, adolescents have little need to rebel or to seek acceptance in the peer group that they cannot obtain at home; they tend to have the academic and social competencies it takes to enter crowds that reinforce rather than undermine parental values (Brown et al., 1993; Dishion et al., 1991). Finally, if parents do it in moderation, they can help the cause by encouraging some peer relationships and discouraging or even prohibiting others (Mounts, 2001).

In summary, adolescent socialization is not a continual war of parents versus peers; instead, these two important sources of influence combine to affect development. Adolescents are most likely to be well adjusted when they have close attachments to *both* parents *and* peers (Laible, Carlo, & Raffaelli, 2000). As their teenage children become more involved in activities with peers and more susceptible for a while to peer pressures, parents continue to be important forces in their children's lives, influencing life choices and values as well as the kinds of friends their children have. As a result, most adolescents enjoy healthy peer relationships and acquire social competencies that allow them to form and maintain good relationships as adults.

The Adult

Relationships with family and friends are no less important during adulthood than they are earlier in life, but they take on different qualities over the adult years. Let's examine how people's social networks change over the adult years and then look more closely at their romantic relationships and friendships.

Social Networks

With whom do adults of different ages interact, and how socially active are they? Young adults are busily forming romantic relationships and friendships, typically choosing to associate with people who are similar to themselves in important ways, just as children and adolescents do. Harry Reis and his colleagues (1993), in a 10-year study of college students, found that young adults do more socializing with members of the other sex and less with members of the same sex after college graduation than they did while in college; this was true of both sexes and of unmarried as well as married people. In other words, trends toward greater intimacy with the other sex that began in adolescence continue during early adulthood.

Young adults, especially single ones, seem to have more friends than middle-aged and older adults do. As adults marry, have children, take on increasing job responsibilities, and age, their social networks shrink (C. S. Fischer & Phillips, 1982; J. L. Fischer et al., 1989). The trend toward smaller social networks with age is evident in many ethnic groups, but subcultural groups differ too. For example, from early adulthood on, African American adults' networks tend to be smaller, to be more dominated by kin, and to involve more frequent contact than those of European Americans (Ajrouch, Antonucci, & Janevic, 2001).

Laura Carstensen's (1992) **socioemotional selectivity theory** explains shrinking networks as a choice aging adults make to better meet their emotional needs (also see Turk-Charles & Carstensen, 1999). As we get older and see less time left ahead of us, Carstensen argues, we put less emphasis on the goal of acquiring knowledge for use in the future and more emphasis on the goal of meeting immediate emotional needs. As a result, we actively choose to narrow our range of social partners to those who can best meet our emotional needs, usually family members and close friends whose company we enjoy, and let other social relationships fall by the wayside. Whereas younger adults need the social stimulation and new information that contacts with strangers and acquaintances often provide, and are even willing to sacrifice some emotional well-being to have many social contracts, older adults put their emotional well-being first. From this perspective, the shrinking of the social network in later life is not about loss and social isolation; it is an adaptive change that involves sacrificing the quantity of our relationships to strengthen their quality.

Does the evidence support socioemotional selectivity theory? Despite the fact that middle-aged adults interact less frequently with acquaintances and friends than young adults do, they interact often with their spouses and siblings and actually feel closer emotionally to the most significant people in their lives than younger adults do (Carstensen, 1992). Elderly adults drop even more friends and acquaintances over the years, but they continue to maintain a core of "very close" relationships.

If they do not have living spouses or children, they strengthen relationships with other relatives or friends so that they can maintain this inner circle of intimates (Lang & Carstensen, 1994). Consistent with socioemotional selectivity theory, then, older adults apparently choose to restrict their interactions to the people who really count and can meet their emotional needs. They end up just as satisfied, if not more satisfied, with their relationships and are less likely than young adults to want more friends (Lansford, Sherman, & Antonucci, 1998).

Socioemotional selectivity theory also gives us insight into the emotional lives of adults. In one study, Carstensen and her colleagues (2000) sampled the emotional experiences of African American and European American adults between the ages of 18 and 94 by paging them over a one-week period as they went about their lives. Contrary to ageist stereotypes, younger and older adults did not differ in the frequency with which they experienced positive emotions; negative emotions actually became less common from early adulthood to about age 60, after which they leveled out. Older adults also experienced longer-lasting positive emotions and more fleeting periods of negative emotion, suggesting that they were better able than younger adults to regulate their emotions. Finally, older adults seemed to have more complex emotional experiences, possibly because they "realize not only what they have but also that what they have cannot last forever" (p. 653). According to socioemotional selectivity theory, then, the realization that little time is left causes older adults to seek emotionally meaningful interactions with fewer people and to experience richer, more complex emotional lives than ever before (Turk-Charles & Carstensen, 1999).

Attachment Styles

Several researchers, intrigued by the parallels between an infant's attachment to a parent figure and a young adult's love for a romantic partner, have begun to study romantic relationships from the perspective of attachment theory (Crowell et al., 1999; Feeney & Noller, 1996). Obviously, parent–infant attachments and adult romantic attachments are not identical. Yet the adult who is in love, like the infant who is attached to a parent, experiences strong affection for his or her partner, wants to be close, takes comfort from the bond, and is upset by separations. Indeed, married adults who are separated from their spouses because of war or the demands of work experience the same kinds of distress and despair that infants experience when separated from their mothers and fathers (Vormbrock, 1993). Like parent–child attachment, attachment between romantic partners is also biologically adaptive; it increases the odds of children, as well as the odds that these children will have two parents to nurture them (Colin, 1996). Perhaps it is not surprising, then, that the concept of romantic love is not just a Western phenomenon, as many people believe. Instead, the phenomenon of romantic love has been documented in at least 88% of the world's cultures, including many in which marriages are arranged by family elders (Jankowiak & Fischer, 1992). Adult love bonds aren't all about passionate love, though; like the love of parent for infant, they also involve deep attachment, commitment, and emotional intimacy (Hatfield & Rapson, 2000).

Table 14.3 shows one scheme for thinking about how the internal working models that we construct from our experiences in early relationships may affect our romantic relationships (Bartholomew & Horowitz, 1991; see also Crowell, Fraley, & Shaver, 1999). Interviewed about their memories of attachment experiences during childhood and their current feelings about relationships, adults with a *secure* working model feel good about both themselves and others; they are not afraid of entering into intimate relationships or of being abandoned once they do. People with a *preoccupied* working model have a positive view of other people but feel unlovable. Like resistantly attached infants, they crave closeness to others as a means of validating their self-worth, are highly fearful of abandonment, and tend to become overly dependent on their partners.

Adults with a *dismissing* style of attachment have a positive view of self but do not trust other people, possibly because their caregivers were unreliable (Beckwith, Cohen, & Hamilton, 1999). Like avoidantly attached infants, they defend themselves against hurt by not expressing their need for love or their fear of abandonment. They deny that they need people or that relationships really matter to them, find it hard to trust partners, and feel that others want them to be more intimate than they wish to be. Bowlby (1973) described dismissing or avoidant individuals as "compulsively self-reliant."

Finally, adults with a *fearful* working model resemble infants with a disorganized/disoriented attachment; they take a dim view of both themselves and other people and display a confusing mix of neediness and fear of closeness.

In a pioneering study conceptualizing romantic love as attachment, Cindy Hazan and Phillip Shaver (1987) classified 56% of the adults they studied as having a secure attachment style, 19% as resistant, and 25% as avoidant (they did not attempt to measure the fearful or disorganized/disoriented attachment style). Adults' styles of attachment were related to the quality of their romantic relationships. For example, adults with a *secure* attachment style experience a good deal of trust and many positive emotions in their current love relationships. Their relationships also tend to last longer than those of adults with insecure attachment styles. Avoidant lovers fear intimacy, whereas resistant individuals tend to be obsessed with their partners. Both *avoidant* and *resistant* adults report a lot of jealousy and emotional extremes of love and pain in love relationships. They also feel unable to regulate their negative moods and to manage conflicts with their partners (Creasey, Kershaw, & Boston, 1999). Adults with different attachment styles even express their jealousy differently, it seems: Secure individuals express their anger directly to their partners, resistant individuals hold it in, and avoidant individuals turn their anger on the person who threatened the relationship (Sharpsteen & Kirkpatrick, 1997).

Table 14.3 **Four Types of Internal Working Models Associated with Having Positive or Negative Views of Self and Other People, Based on One's Experiences in Relationships**

		Model of Self	
		Positive	**Negative**
Model of Others	**Positive**	SECURE *Secure attachment history* Healthy balance of attachment and autonomy (freedom to explore)	PREOCCUPIED *Resistant attachment history* Desperate for love to feel worthy as a person; worry about abandonment; express anxiety and anger openly
	Negative	DISMISSING *Avoidant attachment history* Shut out emotions; defend against hurt by avoiding intimacy, dismissing the importance of relationships, being "compulsively self-reliant"	FEARFUL *Disorganized/disoriented attachment history* Need relationships but doubt own worth and fear intimacy; lack a coherent strategy for meeting attachment needs

SOURCE: Adapted from Bartholomew & Horowitz (1991)

NOTE: To check your understanding of internal working models, indicate which one—secure, dismissing, preoccupied, or fearful—is expressed in each of the following statements (Bartholomew & Horowitz, 1991, p. 244, adapted from Hazan & Shaver, 1987). Also see if you can identify the internal working model that best describes you.

1. "I want to be completely emotionally intimate with others, but I often find that others are reluctant to get as close as I would like. I am uncomfortable being without close relationships, but I sometimes worry that others don't value me as much as I value them."

2. "I am somewhat uncomfortable getting close to others. I want emotionally close relationships, but I find it difficult to trust others completely, or to depend on them. I sometimes worry that I will be hurt if I allow myself to become too close to others."

3. "It is relatively easy for me to become emotionally close to others. I am comfortable depending on others and having others depend on me. I don't worry about being alone or having others not accept me."

4. "I am comfortable without close emotional relationships. It is very important to me to feel independent and self-sufficient, and I prefer not to depend on others or have others depend on me."

ANSWER KEY: 1. Preoccupied, 2. Fearful, 3. Secure, 4. Dismissing

Hazan and Shaver also discovered that adults with a secure attachment style recalled warm relationships with their parents during childhood, but adults with insecure attachment styles tended to remember their parents as unfair, critical, or cold. They also tend to have experienced traumas such as abuse, neglect, and divorce in their early relationships or to have parents whose problems with substance abuse, depression, and so on made them unreliable caregivers (Mickelson, Kessler, & Shaver, 1997). Here, then, is more support for Bowlby's (1973) hypothesis that internal working models of self and other formed on the basis of our earliest attachments affect the quality of our later relationships (see also Feeney & Noller, 1996). It seems that receiving warm and supportive parenting as a child is associated with engaging in warm, supportive behavior in one's romantic relationships as a young adult—and, as a result, enjoying high-quality relationships (Conger et al., 2000).

As Bowlby theorized, internal working models also predict the extent to which adults have the confidence to take on and master challenges. Close relationships with spouses or romantic partners provide the "secure base" that allows adults to explore the environment, work productively, and enjoy life (Hazan & Shaver, 1990). Securely attached adults enjoy work and are good at it; preoccupied, or resistantly attached, adults want approval and grumble about not being valued enough by their bosses and coworkers; and dismissing, or avoidantly attached, adults bury themselves in their work and do little socializing.

The internal working models of self and other that grow out of early experiences in the family also appear to affect an adult's capacity to be a loving parent: Mothers and fathers who had secure relations with their parents tend to interact in more sensitive ways with their children and form more secure attachments with them than parents whose early attachments were resistant, avoidant, or disorganized (Steele, Steele, & Fonagy, 1996; van IJzendoorn, 1995); indeed, in up to 75% of cases, mother and infant have the same attachment style. What's more, grandmothers, mothers, and children all tend to fall in the same attachment category (Benoit & Parker, 1994). Although genes may contribute to these family resemblances, it is also possible that internal working models of relationships are passed down from one generation to the next through observational learning.

Finally, attachment styles continue to be relevant to adjustment in later life. Whereas majorities of young and middle-aged adults appear to have secure attachment styles, Carol Magai and her colleagues (2001) have found that most European American and African American elderly adults fall in the dismissing/avoidant category based on their responses to attachment measures; they express some discomfort with closeness and tend to be compulsively self-reliant. Elderly people with either a secure or a dismissive (avoidant) attachment style tend to be happier than those whose styles are preoccupied or fearful, suggesting that the independent dismissive style may be adaptive in old age (Webster, 1998).

Overall, internal working models of self and other have many implications for adult development and adjustment.

But they are termed "working" models because they are subject to revision if later experiences in relationships suggest that change is warranted. Although research on secure, preoccupied, dismissing, and fearful styles of attachment in adulthood is intriguing, we must remember that early attachment experiences may predict the future but do not determine it.

Adult Friendships

Close friendships serve important functions across the entire life span (Sherman, de Vries, & Lansford, 2000). Although young adults typically have more friends than older adults do, even adults aged 85 and older usually have at least one close friend and are in frequent contact with friends (C. L. Johnson & Troll, 1994). Elderly adults especially value friendships that have lasted a lifetime (Adams, 1985–1986) Almost three-fourths of the women Rebecca Adams interviewed claimed that "old friends are the best friends." However, most elderly people also continue to make new friends late in life.

What happens to friendships as older adults begin to develop significant health problems and disabilities? When one friend needs more aid than the other and is able to give less aid in return, this imbalance can cause difficulties (Silverstein & Waite, 1993). Social psychologists have long emphasized the importance of **equity,** or a balance of contributions and gains, to satisfaction with close relationships (Walster, Walster, & Berscheid, 1978). A person who receives more from a relationship than he or she gives is likely to feel guilty; a person who gives a great deal and receives little in return may feel angry or resentful (Walster et al., 1978).

Consistent with this equity view, Karen Roberto and Jean Scott (1986) found that elderly adults experience less distress in friendships they perceive as equitable than in those they perceive as inequitable. Interestingly, *overbenefited,* or dependent, friends experience more distress than underbenefited, or support-giving, friends. Apparently being able to help others boosts the self-esteem of elderly adults (Krause & Shaw, 2000). By contrast, elderly adults who are unable to contribute equally to a friendship may feel uncomfortable being dependent. Perhaps because inequity threatens friendships, older adults usually call on family rather than friends when they need substantial help or emotional support, unless they have no kin nearby (Felton & Berry, 1992; Kendig et al., 1988). By not overburdening their friends, they stand to keep them longer. Friends do become a major source of care for some elderly adults, but typically when the friend is not married, does not work, and therefore does not have other roles and responsibilities (Himes & Reidy, 2000).

In sum, adults of all ages seem to enjoy close friendships, new and old, and often are able to carry with them through life—as part of their social convoy—old friends with whom they share a lifetime of experiences and with whom they maintain an equitable relationship. Just how much do friendships and other close relationships contribute to well-being, especially in later life?

Cleo Freelance Photography

Close friendships that have lasted for years are particularly important to adults.

Adult Relationships and Adult Development

We have emphasized throughout this chapter that close attachments to other people are essential to normal cognitive, social, and emotional development. It should not surprise you to learn, then, that adults are better off in many ways if they enjoy meaningful social relationships. Much attention has been centered on the significance of social networks and social support to elderly people—possibly because researchers, like members of the general public, have incorrectly assumed that most elderly adults are socially isolated. The major generalization that has emerged from research is this: *It is the quality rather than the quantity of an individual's social relationships that is most closely related to that person's sense of well-being or life satisfaction* (B. P. O'Connor, 1995; Pinquart & Sorensen, 2000). Just as people can feel lonely despite being surrounded by other people, adults apparently can feel deprived of social support even though they receive a lot of it—or they can have quite restricted social networks and yet feel satisfied with their relationships.

The size of an adult's social network is not nearly so important as whether it includes at least one **confidant**—a spouse, relative, or friend to whom the individual feels especially attached and with whom thoughts and feelings can be shared (de Jong-Gierveld, 1986; Levitt, 1991). For most married adults, spouses are the most important confidants; for older adults whose spouses have died, children or friends often step in to fill these needs; for single adults, siblings sometimes become especially important (Connidis & Davies, 1992). Whoever an older adult's key sources of support are, it is less important how much assistance they provide than that interactions with them are rewarding rather than stressful (Krause, 1995). For example, although high-quality relationships with adult children are often more important to well-being than close friendships (Pinquart & Sorensen, 2000), interactions with adult children can *undermine* rather than increase well-being if the parent–child attachment is insecure (Barnas, Pollina, & Cummings, 1991).

In sum, a small number of close and harmonious relationships can do much to make negative life events more bearable and improve the overall quality of an adult's life. It's more than that, though: Social support, especially from family members, actually has positive effects on the cardiovascular, endocrine, and immune systems, keeps blood pressure in the normal range, improves the body's ability to cope with stress, and can contribute to a longer life, especially in old age (Tucker et al., 1999; Uchino, Cacioppo, & Keicolt-Glaser, 1996). It can help prevent declines in everyday functioning in old age and can help elders recover from disabilities (Mendes de Leon et al., 1999). Whatever our age, our well-being and developmental outcomes hinge considerably on the quality of our ties to fellow humans—and particularly on our having a close bond with at least one person. It is fitting, then, that we conclude this chapter by illustrating, in the Applications box on page 398, approaches to improving social relationships across the life span.

Building Stronger Social Relationships

Developmentalists naturally have become interested in applying what they have learned about social development to help individuals develop richer social relationships. They have been quite successful.

As we have seen, parents who are likely to be insensitive to their infants and infants who have difficult temperaments are at risk for forming insecure attachments (see van IJzendoorn, Juffer, & Duyvesteyn, 1995). In one study, low-income mothers in Holland with irritable babies received a series of three 2-hour training sessions designed to make them more sensitive and responsive caregivers (van den Boom, 1995). Home visitors worked with the mothers during everyday interactions to help them respond appropriately to their infants' positive and negative cues. Not only did the mothers who received training become more sensitive caregivers, but their infants were more likely than those of mothers who received no training to be securely attached to their mothers at 12 months of age and to remain securely attached at 3. What's more, these children apparently transferred positive skills they learned in the parent–infant relationship to their relationships with peers.

Children who are neglected or, worse, rejected by their peers are another group at risk. They can be helped through interventions designed to teach them the social and social-cognitive skills they lack (Ladd, 1999; Malik & Furman, 1993). In social skills coaching programs, an adult therapist models or displays social skills, explains why they are useful, allows children to practice them, and then offers feedback to help children improve on their performances. Sherrie Oden and Steven Asher (1977) coached third- and fourth-grade social isolates in four important social skills: how to participate in play activities, how to take turns and share, how to communicate effectively, and how to give attention and help to peers. Not only did the children who were coached become more outgoing and positive in their social behavior,

but a follow-up assessment a year later revealed that they had achieved gains in sociometric status within the classroom. Similar coaching programs have been found effective with lonely college students who have trouble relating to members of the other sex (Christopher, Nangle, & Hansen, 1993; Jones, Hobbs, & Hockenbury, 1982).

However, not all individuals who are lonely and isolated are socially incompetent. For some individuals, the real problem is a restricted social environment—a lack of opportunities for forming close relationships (Rook, 1984, 1991). Such was the case for the socially isolated elderly people described by Marc Pilisuk and Meredith Minkler (1980). Living in inner-city hotels in San Francisco, these individuals were often prisoners in their rooms because of disability, poverty, and fear of crime. To change this situation, public health nurses began to offer free blood pressure checkups in the lobby of one hotel. As the nurses got to know the residents, they were able to draw them into conversations and to link individuals who had common interests. After about a year, the residents formed their own activities club; organized discussions, film showings, and parties; and were well on their way out of their social isolation. The trick was to change their social environment rather than their social skills.

Because development is influenced by both individual and environmental factors, it makes sense to think that children and adults who lack healthy social relationships can be helped most through efforts to improve their social skills *and* to change their social environments to increase opportunities for meaningful interaction. The ultimate goal might be to ensure that every human being enjoys the many developmental benefits that come from a social convoy that includes a secure bond with at least one caregiver during infancy, a close friendship in childhood or adolescence, and an intimate romantic relationship or friendship in adulthood.

Summary Points

1. Social relationships contribute immensely to human development, primarily by providing critical learning opportunities and social support (through our changing social convoys). The developmental significance of early parent–child relationships was emphasized by Freud and continues to be emphasized in the Bowlby-Ainsworth attachment theory, which draws on ethological theory to

argue that attachments are built into the human species, develop through an interaction of nature and nurture during a sensitive period early in life, and affect later development by shaping internal working models of self and other. Peer relationships are believed to be especially important by Piaget, who emphasized their reciprocal nature; Sullivan, who held that childhood chumships can compensate for poor parent–child relationships or peer rejection and prepare children for romantic relationships; and more recently Harris, who argues that children are socialized more by peer groups than by parents.

2. Biologically based emotions such as anger and fear appear in the first year of life, and self-conscious emotions emerge in the second year; emotions quickly become socialized through modeling and reinforcement. As infants get older, they rely less on caregivers and more on their own emotion regulation strategies to manage their emotions in interactions with their attachment objects.

3. Because infants have endearing qualities, parents typically become attached to them before or shortly after birth. Parent and child normally establish synchronized routines, although some pairs have difficulty doing so. In forming attachments to their parents, infants progress through phases of undiscriminating social responsiveness, discriminating social responsiveness, active proximity seeking, and goal-corrected partnership. The formation of attachments at about 6 or 7 months of age is accompanied by separation anxiety and stranger anxiety, as well as exploration from a secure base.

4. Research using Ainsworth's Strange Situation indicates that quality of attachment can be classified as secure, resistant, avoidant, or disorganized/disoriented. Although the Freudian view that infants become attached to those who feed them lacks support, Erik Erikson was correct to emphasize the caregiver's responsiveness as the key influence on attachment quality. Secure attachments are associated with sensitive, responsive parenting; resistant attachments with inconsistent, unresponsive care; avoidant attachments with either rejection or overstimulation; and disorganized/disoriented attachments with abusive treatment. Infant characteristics (temperament and achievement of cognitive developmental milestones such as person permanence) also contribute.

5. Long-term separation from attachment figures can trigger protest, despair, and detachment. Worse is social deprivation that makes it impossible for an infant to attach to anyone, which can result in numerous developmental problems. By contrast, attending day care normally does not disrupt development, assuming the quality of care at home and in the day care facility is reasonably good. Secure attachments contribute to later social competence and independence, but attachment quality often changes over time, and insecurely attached and socially deprived infants are not inevitably doomed to a lifetime of poor relationships.

6. Infants are interested in peers and become increasingly able to coordinate their own activity with that of their small companions. By 18 months of age, they participate in complementary interactive exchanges and form friendships.

7. During the years from 2 to 12, children participate in goal-corrected partnerships with their parents and spend increasing amounts of time with peers, especially same-sex ones, engaging in increasingly social and imaginative play such as social pretend play and then in organized games. Physical attractiveness, cognitive ability, and social competence contribute to popular, as opposed to rejected, neglected, or controversial sociometric status. Children who are rejected by their peers are especially at risk for future problems, for peer interactions affect all aspects of development.

8. During adolescence, same- and cross-sex friendships increasingly involve emotional intimacy and self-disclosure, and heterosexual cliques and crowds facilitate the transition from same-sex peer groups, to mixed-sex cliques and larger crowds, and finally to dating relationships. Although susceptibility to negative peer pressures peaks at about age 14 or 15, peers are more often a positive than a negative force unless poor family relationships result in the adolescent's becoming involved with an antisocial crowd.

9. Most adults of all ages have high-quality relationships, though social networks shrink with age because of increased socioemotional selectivity—a greater emphasis on meeting emotional needs in a few very close relationships.

10. Adults have secure, preoccupied, dismissing, and fearful internal working models of self and others that appear to be rooted in their early attachment experiences and that affect their romantic relationships, approaches to work, and ability to form secure attachments with their own children.

11. Although adults are highly involved with their spouses or romantic partners, they continue to value friendships, especially long-lasting and equitable ones. Well-being is influenced more by the quality than by the quantity of relationships; it is especially important to have at least one confidant.

Critical Thinking

1. Let's return to Baby Jessica, the little girl introduced at the start of the chapter who was snatched at age 2 from the only parents she had ever known. Now that you have read the chapter, see if you can develop a set of hypotheses, based on attachment theory and research on attachment, about her later development. Do not read further until you do.

Now it's time to fill you in. By age 3, Jessica had been renamed Anna Jacqueline Schmidt and was reportedly a happy, well-adjusted preschooler (Ingrassia & Springen, 1994). As her mother, Cara Schmidt, reported it, the traumatic effects of loss of attachment figures that theorists like Freud and Bowlby would expect never occurred: "Everyone guaranteed—*guaranteed*—that she would have short-term trauma, that she wouldn't eat, she wouldn't sleep, she'd cry. It didn't happen. She progressed, rapidly" (Ingrassia & Springen, 1994, p. 60). Jessica did remember the day of the van ride ("I got in the van and was crying and crying," p. 66), and she remembered her first parents, the DeBoers, but she did not pine for them. As it turned out, they were far more devastated than Jessica by the severing of the relationship. They adopted another child, divorced in 1999, and later made plans to remarry ("Nation in Brief," 2001). Meanwhile, the Schmidts also divorced in 1999; Jessica-now-Anna lives with her father and a sister and was doing well at last report, despite all the changes in her life ("Nation in Brief," 2001; Ingrassia, 2000).

The moral? We should not make too much of one case. Jessica had eight visits with her biological parents before being sent to live with them and therefore had an opportunity to begin to form an attachment to them (Ingrassia & Springen, 1994). We also do not know how she will fare later in life. Yet her story, combined with the studies of institutionalized children discussed earlier, tell us once more that children have a good deal of resilience provided that they are given reasonable opportunities to socialize and to love someone.

2. Ethological theory, psychoanalytic theory, and cognitive psychology all influenced John Bowlby as he formulated attachment theory. Which elements of attachment theory do you think most reflect each of these three theoretical perspectives, and why?

3. Billy, age 10, does not have a best friend and has never really had one. Why do you think this is, and what implications do you think lack of a friend might have for Billy's later development?

4. Carstensen's socioemotional selectivity theory suggests that adults narrow their social networks with age in order to better meet their emotional needs. Can you develop alternative hypotheses about why young adults might have larger social networks than elderly adults?

Key Terms

social support	secure attachment
social convoy	resistant attachment
attachment theory	avoidant attachment
attachment	disorganized/disoriented attachment
imprinting	contact comfort
internal working models	pretend play
peer	social pretend play
chumships	sociometric techniques
self-conscious emotions	clique
emotion regulation	crowd
synchronized routines	conformity
separation anxiety	socioemotional selectivity theory
stranger anxiety	equity
secure base	confidant
Strange Situation	

On the Web

Web Sites to Explore

Attachment

This site by developmental psychologist Everett Waters gives you an opportunity to read a number of papers on attachment theory and attachment research, including papers by attachment theorist Mary Ainsworth.

http://www.psy.sunysb.edu/ewaters/gal-menu.htm

Pretend Play

This visually engaging and creative site focuses on pretend play, covering Piaget's views on play, types of play, and much more. A fun experience.

http://wwwed.sturt.flinders.edu.au/DLT/2000/play/Final/

Day Care Quality

The site of the Child Welfare League of America offers guidance on judging the quality of day care centers.

http://www.cwla.org/programs/daycare

Adult Attachment

This is the Web site of Phillip Shaver's Adult Attachment Lab. Along with papers on adult attachment and descriptions of measures of adult attachment styles, it offers a self-scoring "Close Relationships Questionnaire" that will allow you to see what your attachment style might be.

http://psychology.ucdavis.edu/Shaver/lab.html

Search Online with InfoTrac College Edition

For additional information, explore InfoTrac College Edition, your online library. Go to http://www.infotrac-college.com and use the passcode that came on the card with your book. You may find it interesting to search for "attachment and college" and see what research has been conducted recently on the implications of attachment styles for adjustment during the college years.

Visit Our Web Site

Go to http://www.wadsworth.com/psychology, where you will find online resources directly linked to your book.

Life-Span CD-ROM

Go to the Wadsworth Life-Span CD-ROM for further study of the concepts in this chapter. The CD-ROM also includes quizzes and additional activities to expand your learning experience.

The Family

"FROM A YOUNG AGE, I have had to grow up fast. I see families that are loving and fathers who care for their children, and I find myself hating them. . . . I have nightmares pertaining to my father. I get angry and frustrated when family is around" (St. George, 2001, p. A20).

These sobering words were written by Sonyé Herrera, an abused adolescent who for years had been hit, threatened with guns, choked, and otherwise victimized—and had witnessed her mother abused as well—by an alcoholic father. The abuse continued even after the couple divorced. At age 15, unable to stand any more, she finally had her father charged with assault, almost but not quite relenting when her father promised he would pay child support and leave them alone. Then he returned one afternoon when she was 15; he hit her. She locked herself in the bathroom and dialed 911 but the police came too slowly. He shot and killed both Sonyé and her mother, and before her father turned his gun on himself, he screamed at Sonyé, "See what you made me do!" (St. George, 2001, p. A21).

Possibly only individuals who have had destructive experiences in the family can fully appreciate what most of us take for granted—the many ways in which our families positively support and nurture our development. For good or bad, we are all bound to our families. We are born into them, work our way toward adulthood in them, start our own as adults, and remain connected to them in old age. We are part of our families, and they are part of us. James Garbarino (1992) has gone so far as to characterize the family as the "basic unit of human experience" (p. 7).

This chapter examines the family and its central roles in human development throughout the life span. What is a family, and how has the family changed in recent years? How do infants, children, and adolescents experience family life, and how are they affected by their relationships with parents and siblings? How is adult development affected by such family transitions as marrying, becoming a parent, watching children leave the nest, and becoming a grandparent? Finally, what are the implications of the diversity that characterizes today's family lifestyles—and of such decisions as remaining childless or divorcing?

Understanding the Family

The family is a system, a system within other systems, a changing system, and a changing system in a changing world.

The Family as a System

It may not be possible to define family in a way that applies across all cultures and eras; many forms of family life have worked and continue to work for humans (Coontz, 2000). By one recent definition, a family is "two or more persons related by birth, marriage, adoption, or choice" who have emotional ties and responsibilities to each other (Allen, Fine, & Demo, 2000, p. 1). However we define what a family is, proponents of **family systems theory** conceptualize it as a *system*. This means that the family, like the human body, is truly a whole consisting of interrelated parts, each of which affects and is affected by every other part, and each of which contributes to the functioning of the whole (Fingerman & Bermann, 2000; Klein & White, 1996). In the past, developmentalists did not adopt this family systems perspective. They typically focused almost entirely on the mother–child relationship, assuming that the only process of interest within the family was the mother's influence on the child's development (Ambert, 1992).

The **nuclear family** consists of husband/father, wife/ mother, and at least one child. Even a simple man, woman, and infant "system" can be very complex. An infant interacting with her mother is already involved in a process of *reciprocal* influence: The baby's smile is likely to be greeted by a smile from Mom, and Mom's smile is likely to be reciprocated by the infant's grin. However, the presence of *both* parents "transforms the mother–infant dyad into a *family system* [comprising] a husband–wife as well as mother–infant and father–infant relationships" (Belsky, 1981, p. 17). Every individual and every relationship within the family affects every other individual and relationship through reciprocal influence (see Figure 15.1). You can see why it was rather naive to think

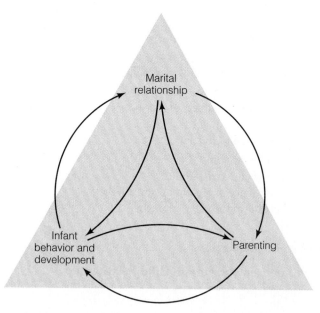

Figure 15.1 A model of the family as a social system. Parents affect infants, who affect each parent and the marital relationship. Of course, the marital relationship may affect the parenting the infant receives, the infant's behavior, and so on. Clearly, families are complex social systems. As an exercise, you may wish to rediagram the patterns of influence within a family after adding a sibling or two.
SOURCE: Belsky (1981)

that the family could be understood by studying only the ways in which mothers mold their children.

Now think about how complex the family system becomes if we add another child (or two or six) to it; we must then understand the unique relationships between each parent and each of these children, as well as relationships between siblings. Or consider the complexity of an **extended family household,** in which parents and their children live with other kin—some combination of grandparents, siblings, aunts, uncles, nieces, and nephews. Extended family households are very common in many cultures of the world (Ruggles, 1994). Among African Americans in the United States, being part of an extended family household can be especially adaptive for economically disadvantaged single mothers, who can obtain needed help with child care and social support by living with their mothers (Burton, 1990; R. L. Taylor, 2000). African Americans, Hispanic Americans, and other ethnic minorities tend to place more emphasis on extended family bonds than European Americans do (Gadsden, 1999; Leyendecker & Lamb, 1999). Even though relatives often live in their own nuclear family households, members of the extended family share responsibility for raising children (Gadsden, 1999). As a result, many single-parent mothers have more help in raising their children than it appears.

The Family as a System within Other Systems

Whether a family is of the nuclear or the extended type, it does not exist in a vacuum. Adopting Urie Bronfenbrenner's *ecological approach* to studying the family (see Chapter 2) helps us to view the family as a system embedded in larger social systems such as a neighborhood, a community, a subculture, and a broader culture. For example, parents who are facing financial problems experience less stress and are better able to maintain effective parenting practices if they have strong social support than if they do not (Burchinal, Follmer, & Bryant, 1996). The larger culture is important too; the family experience in our culture is quite different from that in cultures where new brides become underlings in the households of their mothers-in-law, or where men can have several wives. There is an almost infinite variety of family forms and family contexts in the world, and a correspondingly wide range of developmental experiences within the family.

The Family as a Changing System

It would be difficult enough to study the family as a system if it kept the same members and continued to perform the same activities over and over again for as long as it existed. However, this is obviously not the case. Family membership changes as new children are born and as grown children leave the nest. Moreover, each family member is a developing individual, and the *relationships* between husband and wife, parent and child, and sibling and sibling also develop in systematic ways over time. Since the family is truly a system, changes in family membership and changes in any individual or relationship within the family are bound to affect the dynamics of the whole.

Thus, the family must be viewed as a developing organism (Klein & White, 1996). The earliest theories of family development featured the concept of a **family life cycle**—a sequence of changes in family composition, roles, and relationships from the time people marry until they die (Hill & Rodgers, 1964). Family theorist Evelyn Duvall (1977) outlined eight stages of the family life cycle (see Table 15.1). In each stage, family members play distinctive roles and carry out distinctive developmental tasks—for example, establishing a satisfying relationship in the newlywed phase, adjusting to the demands of new parenthood in the childbearing phase, and adapting to the departure of children in the "launching" phase.

In this chapter, we'll look at the impact of these family transitions on adults, and we'll examine how the child's experience of the family changes as he or she develops. We'll also see, however, that an increasing number of people do not experience this traditional family life cycle. They remain single or childless, or they marry multiple times, or they otherwise deviate from a scenario in which a man and woman form a nuclear family, raise children, and grow old together. As a result, many family researchers now reject the simple concept of the family life cycle and its set stages (Dilworth-Anderson & Burton, 1996; Klein & White, 1996). However, they have not rejected the concept that families, like the individuals in them, are developing organisms.

In sum, family systems theorists encourage us to view the family as a system in which all members affect all others; Bronfenbrenner and other ecological theorists encourage us to see the family as a system embedded in other systems such as communities and cultures; and family development theorists insist that we understand the family life cycle and the processes of change that each family undergoes.

A Changing System in a Changing World

Not only is the family a system embedded within systems, and not only is it a developing system, but the world in which it is embedded is ever changing. During the second half of the 20th century, several dramatic social changes altered the makeup of the typical family and the quality of family experience. Drawing on several analyses of U.S. Census data and other surveys, we'll highlight the following trends, many of which were rapid in the 1970s and 1980s but slowed or stopped in the 1990s (see Amato, 1999; Fox, 2001a; Hernandez, 1997; Teachman, 2000; U.S. Census Bureau, 2000):

1. More single adults. More adults are living as singles today than in the past. However, don't be deceived into thinking that marriage is out of style: About 95% of adults can still be expected to marry at some time in their lives (U.S. Census Bureau, 2000).

2. Postponed marriage. Many adults are not rejecting marriage but are simply delaying it while they pursue educational and career goals. The average age of first marriage decreased during the first half of the 20th century, but it has since risen again, to about 24 for women and 26 for men (U.S.

Table 15.1 Stages of the Family Life Cycle

Stage	Available Roles
1. **Married couple without children**	Wife Husband
2. **Childbearing family:** oldest child birth to 30 months	Wife/mother Husband/father Infant daughter or son
3. **Family with preschool children:** oldest child 30 months to 6 years	Wife/mother Husband/father Daughter/sister Son/brother
4. **Family with school-age children:** oldest child up to 12 years	Wife/mother Husband/father Daughter/sister Son/brother
5. **Family with teenagers:** oldest child 13 to 20 years	Wife/mother Husband/father Daughter/sister Son/brother
6. **Family launching young adults:** first child gone to last child gone	Wife/mother/grandmother Husband/father/grandfather Daughter/sister/aunt Son/brother/uncle
7. **Family without children:** empty nest to retirement	Wife/mother/grandmother Husband/father/grandfather
8. **Aging family:** retirement to death	Wife/mother/grandmother Husband/father/grandfather Widow or widower

SOURCE: Adapted from Duvall (1977)

Census Bureau, 2000), despite increased rates of teenage pregnancy among lower-income groups.

3. Fewer children. Today's adults are not only waiting longer after they marry to have children, but they are having fewer of them—about 1.8 on average, compared to 3.0 in 1950—and therefore spend fewer years of their lives raising children (El-Khorazaty, 1996). Increasing numbers of young women are also remaining childless, although most want children at some time; many are childless because of infertility, health problems, and other reasons besides a decision not to have children (Heaton, Jacobson, & Holland, 1999). Among 40- to 44-year-old women who have married at some time in their lives, 13.7% have had no children (U.S. Census Bureau, 2000).

4. More women working. In 1950, 12% of married women with children under age 6 worked outside the home; now the figure is about 62%, a truly dramatic social change (U.S. Census Bureau, 2000). Fewer and fewer children have a mother whose full-time job is that of homemaker.

5. More divorce. It is well known that the divorce rate has been increasing over the past several decades, though it leveled off in about 1980. About 4 in 10 newly married couples can expect to divorce (Vobejda, 1998).

6. More single-parent families. Partly because of a rising rate of out-of-wedlock births, but mostly because of the rise in divorce rates, more children live in single-parent families. In 1960, only 9% of children lived with one parent, usually a widowed one; in 1998, 23% of children under 18 lived with their mothers only, and 4% with their fathers only (U.S. Census Bureau, 2000).

7. More children living in poverty. The higher number of single-parent families has meant an increase in the proportion of children living below the poverty line. Almost 1 in 5 children in the United States lives in poverty today (U.S. Census Bureau, 2000). Minority children are more likely than European American children to be poor; 36% of African American children and almost 34% of Hispanic American children are poor. Overall, more than one-third of children living in female-headed homes live in poverty.

8. More remarriages. As more married couples divorce, more adults are remarrying. Often they are forming new, **reconstituted families** that include at least a parent, a stepparent, and a child and sometimes blend multiple children from two families into a new family (Glick, 1989). About 25% of American children will spend some time in a reconstituted family (Hetherington & Jodl, 1994).

9. More years without children. Because modern couples are compressing their childbearing into a shorter time span, because some divorced individuals do not remarry, and mainly because people are living longer, adults today spend more of their later years as couples—or, especially if they are women, as single adults—without children in their homes (C. L. Johnson & Troll, 1996). Of adults age 65 and older, 30% live alone, 55% live with a spouse, and 15% live with someone else, such as a sibling or adult child (U.S. Census Bureau, 2000).

10. More multigeneration families. As a result of these same trends, more children today than in the past know their grandparents and even their great-grandparents, parent–child and grandparent–child relationships are lasting longer, and multigenerational bonds are becoming more important (Bengtson, 2001). As three- and even four-generation families have become more common, the result has been a **beanpole family** characterized by more generations, but smaller ones, than in the past (Bengtson, Rosenthal, & Burton, 1990; Johnson & Troll, 1996).

We'll be looking at the impact of some of these trends on development later in this chapter. Some observers view these trends as evidence of a "decline of the family," noting the negative effects on human development of increased poverty, divorce, and single-parent families. Other scholars find good news along with the bad in these trends; they see the family today as different than it used to be, but not necessarily worse (Teachman, 2000; L. White & Rogers, 2000). For example, men's and women's roles in the family are more equal than they used to be, more children have relationships with their grandparents and great-grandparents, and families are better off financially with two wage earners rather than only one. Also, some of the trends suggesting a weakening of the family—for example, the rise in single-parent families and in numbers of children living in poverty—began to reverse in the 1990s.

Perhaps the most important message is this: The American family is more *diverse* than ever before (see Demo, Allen, & Fine, 2000). Our stereotyped image of the family—the traditional *Leave It to Beaver* nuclear family with a breadwinner/father, a full-time housewife/mother, and children—has become just that: a stereotype. By one estimate, about 45% of families in 1960, but only 12% of families in 1995, conformed to this pattern (Hernandez, 1997). Although the family is by no means dying, we must broaden our image of it to include the many dual-career, single-parent, reconstituted, childless, and other nontraditional families that exist today. We must also avoid assuming that any family that does not fit the *Leave It to Beaver* model is somehow deficient. Bear that in mind as we begin our excursion into family life at the beginning—with the birth of an infant.

The Infant

We begin our look at family development by adopting a child's perspective and following a child's development in the family context from infancy to adolescence. Later, we'll adopt

the perspective of this child's parents and see how the events of the family life cycle look to them.

Mother–Infant and Father–Infant Relationships

Once developmentalists took seriously the idea that the family is a system, they discovered that fathers are part of the family. Therefore, they began to look more carefully at how both mothers and fathers interact with their children and at what each parent contributes to a child's development. They have also asked how mothers' and fathers' roles have changed as more and more mothers have gone to work and as divorce rates have climbed.

Gender stereotypes would suggest that fathers are not cut out to care for infants and young children; however, the evidence suggests that they are (Biller, 1993; Parke, 1996; Phares, 1999). Again and again, researchers find that fathers and mothers are more similar than different in the ways they interact with infants and young children. In one study, for example, mothers and fathers were observed while they fed their babies (Parke & Sawin, 1976). Fathers were no less able than mothers to perform this caregiving task effectively and to ensure that the milk was consumed; nor were they any less sensitive to the infant's cues during the feeding session. Similarly, fathers, just like mothers, become objects of their infants' love and serve as secure bases for their explorations (Cox et al., 1992). We really have no basis for thinking that mothers are uniquely qualified to parent or that men are hopelessly inept around babies. However, the fact that fathers are *capable* of sensitive parenting does not necessarily mean they play the same roles in their children's lives that mothers do. Fathers and mothers *do* differ in both the quantity and quality of the parenting they provide (Marsiglio et al., 2000; Parke, 1996; Phares, 1999).

Consider first the matter of quantity. Mothers simply spend more time with children than fathers do (Bianchi, 2000; Phares, 1999). True, fathers in our society are more involved with their children today than they were in the past (Marsiglio et al., 2000), and some are truly sharing responsibility for child care equally with their spouses rather than just "helping" (Deutsch, 2001). Yet there is still a gap. According to data analyzed by Suzanne Bianchi (2000), fathers in 1965 spent about half as much time with their children as mothers did; in 1998, they spent about two-thirds as much time. Because mothers today spend less time on housework, because families are smaller, and because fathers are more involved, children in two-parent families may actually enjoy more time with their parents today than they used to (Bianchi, 2000). Yet increases in separation and divorce have meant that growing numbers of children see very little of their fathers at all (Cabrera et al., 2000).

Now consider the issue of quality. Mothers and fathers also differ in their typical styles of interacting with young children. When mothers interact with their babies, a large proportion of their time is devoted to *caregiving*: offering food, changing diapers, wiping noses, and so on. Although fathers in some societies play an active role in teaching their children, especially their sons, how to perform work activities (Hewlett, 1992), fathers in our society spend much of their time with children in *playful interaction*. Fathers often specialize in tickling, poking, bouncing, and surprising infants, whereas mothers hold, talk to, and play quietly with infants (Neville & Parke, 1997). Yet fathers are quite able to adopt a "motherlike" caregiver role if they have primary responsibility for their children, so their playful parenting is more about being in the role of the "backup" parent than about being a male rather than a female (Phares, 1999).

In view of the roles that fathers play in their children's lives, what are their contributions to child development? Fathers contribute to healthy development by supporting their children financially, whether they live with their children or not (Marsiglio et al., 2000). They also contribute by being warm and effective parents. The quality of the father–child relationship is more important than the time father and child spend together (Marsiglio et al., 2000). Babies are likely to be more socially competent if they are securely attached to *both* parents than if they are securely attached to just one (Biller, 1993; Main & Weston, 1981). In addition, children whose fathers are warm and involved with them tend to become high achievers in school (Cabrera et al., 2000). Finally, it turns out that a father's acceptance or rejection of his children may have as much or more influence than a mother's on whether a child develops certain psychological problems such as substance abuse, aggression, and depression (Rohner, 1998). Children generally have fewer psychological disorders and problems if their fathers are caring, involved, and effective parents than if they are not (Cabrera et al., 2000; Marsiglio et al., 2000).

In short, mothers remain tremendously important forces in human development, but fathers also richly deserve the increased respect they have been getting from developmentalists. Although they spend less time than mothers with their children, and often adopt a playful rather than caregiving role, they are not only capable of sensitive and responsive parenting, but they can contribute in many positive ways to their children's development.

Mothers, Fathers, and Infants: The System at Work

We now need to view the new family as a *three-person* system. The mother–child relationship cannot be understood without considering the father; nor can father–child interactions be understood without examining how the mother influences that relationship. This is because parents have **indirect effects** on their children through their ability to influence the behavior of their spouses. More generally, indirect effects within the family are instances in which the relationship between two individuals is modified by the behavior or attitudes of a third family member.

Fathers indirectly influence the mother–infant relationship in many ways. For example, mothers who have close, supportive relationships with their husbands tend to interact

Fathers are just as capable as mothers of sensitive, responsive parenting.

more patiently and sensitively with their babies than do mothers who are experiencing marital tension and feel that they are raising their children largely without help (Cox et al., 1992). Their infants are therefore more likely to be securely attached (Doyle et al., 2000). Meanwhile, mothers indirectly affect the father–infant relationship. For example, fathers who have just had arguments with their wives are less supportive and engaged when they interact with their sons than fathers who have just had pleasant conversations with their wives (Kitzmann, 2000). In sum, both mothers and fathers can affect their children indirectly through their interactions with their spouses. Overall, children appear to be best off when the marital relationship is solid and couples provide *mutual* support and encouragement that allow *both* to be more sensitive and responsive parents.

Now perhaps you can better appreciate the family systems theory view that even the simplest of families is a true social system that is bigger than the sum of its parts. Because mothers, fathers, and children all affect one another, both directly and indirectly, socialization within the family is obviously not a one-way street in which influence flows only from parent to child. Indeed, family socialization is not even just a two-way street—it is more like the busy intersection of many avenues of influence.

The Child

As children reach the age of 2 or 3, parents continue to be caregivers and playmates, but they also become more concerned with teaching their offspring how (and how not) to behave, and they use some approach to child rearing and discipline to achieve this end. Siblings also serve as socialization agents and become an important part of the child's experience of the family.

Parenting Styles

How can I be a good parent? Certainly this question is uppermost in most parents' minds. We can go far in understanding which parenting styles are effective by considering just two dimensions of parenting: *acceptance/responsiveness* and *demandingness/control* (Darling & Steinberg, 1993; Maccoby & Martin, 1983; Schaefer, 1959).

DIMENSIONS OF CHILD REARING

Parental **acceptance/responsiveness** refers to the extent to which parents are supportive, sensitive to their children's needs, and willing to provide affection and praise when their children meet their expectations. Accepting, responsive parents are affectionate and often smile at, praise, and encourage their children, though they also let children know when they misbehave. Less accepting and responsive parents are often quick to criticize, belittle, punish, or ignore their children and rarely communicate to children that they are loved and valued.

Demandingness/control (sometimes called permissiveness–restrictiveness) refers to how much control over decisions lies with the parent as opposed to the child. Controlling/demanding parents set rules, expect their children to follow them, and monitor their children closely to ensure that the rules are followed. Less controlling and demanding parents (often called permissive parents) make fewer demands and allow their children a great deal of autonomy in exploring the environment, expressing their opinions and emotions, and making decisions about their own activities.

By crossing these two dimensions, we have four basic patterns of child rearing to consider, as shown in Figure 15.2.

1. **Authoritarian parenting.** This is a restrictive parenting style combining high demandingness/control and low acceptance/responsiveness. Parents impose many rules, expect strict obedience, rarely explain why the child should comply with rules, and often rely on power tactics such as physical punishment to gain compliance.

2. **Authoritative parenting.** Authoritative parents are more flexible; they are demanding and exert control, but they are also accepting and responsive. They set clear rules and consistently enforce them, but they also explain the

rationales for their rules and restrictions, are responsive to their children's needs and points of view, and involve their children in family decision making. They are reasonable and democratic in their approach; although it is clear that they are in charge, they communicate respect for their children.

3. **Permissive parenting.** This style is high in acceptance/responsiveness but low in demandingness/control. Permissive parents are indulgent; they make relatively few demands on children to behave maturely, encourage children to express their feelings and impulses, and rarely exert control over their behavior.

4. **Neglectful parenting.** Finally, parents who combine low demandingness/control and low acceptance/responsiveness are relatively uninvolved in their children's upbringing. They seem not to care much about their children and may even reject them—or else they are so overwhelmed by their own problems that they cannot devote sufficient energy to setting and enforcing rules (Maccoby & Martin, 1983).

We assume that you have no difficulty deciding that parental acceptance and responsiveness are preferable to parental rejection and insensitivity. As we have seen in this book, warm, responsive parenting is associated with secure attachments to parents, academic competence, high self-esteem, positive social skills, peer acceptance, a strong sense of morality, and many other virtues. Children want to please loving parents and so are motivated to do what is expected of them and to learn what their parents would like them to learn. By contrast, lack of parental acceptance and affection contributes to depression and other psychological problems (Ge et al., 1996).

Degree of demandingness/control is also important. The authoritarian, authoritative, and permissive parenting styles were originally identified and defined by Diana Baumrind

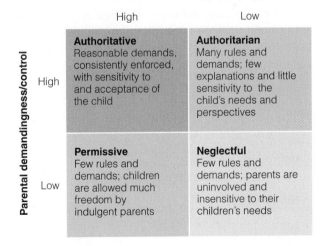

Figure 15.2 The acceptance/responsiveness and demandingness/control dimensions of parenting. Which combination best describes your parents' approach?

SOURCE: Based on Maccoby & Martin (1983)

(1967, 1977, 1991). In a pioneering longitudinal study, Baumrind found that children raised by authoritative parents were the most well-adjusted: They were cheerful, socially responsible, self-reliant, achievement oriented, and cooperative with adults and peers. Children of authoritarian parents tended to be moody and seemingly unhappy, easily annoyed, relatively aimless, and not very pleasant to be around. Finally, children of permissive parents were often impulsive, aggressive, self-centered, rebellious, lacking in self-control, aimless, and low in independence and achievement. The advantages of being raised authoritatively were still evident in adolescence (Baumrind, 1991).

Subsequent research has shown that the worst developmental outcomes are associated with a neglectful, uninvolved style of parenting. Children of neglectful parents display behavior problems such as aggression and frequent temper tantrums as early as age 3 (Miller et al., 1993). They tend to become hostile and antisocial adolescents who abuse alcohol and drugs and get in trouble (Lamborn et al., 1991; Weiss & Schwarz, 1996). Parents who provide little guidance and communicate that they don't care breed children who are resentful and prone to strike back at their uncaring parents and other authority figures.

In short, children develop best when they have love *and* limits. If they are indulged or neglected and given little guidance, they won't learn self-control and may become selfish, unruly, and lacking in direction. If they receive too much guidance, as the children of authoritarian parents do, they will have few opportunities to learn self-reliance and may lack confidence in their own decision-making abilities.

SOCIAL CLASS, ECONOMIC HARDSHIP, AND PARENTING

It is important to recognize that parenting styles are not trait-like characteristics that parents display consistently regardless of the child, the child's age, or the context. Although parents do differ in their broad approaches to parenting, they also respond flexibly to the specific child-rearing situations that face them (Holden & Miller, 1999). With that as warning, we can note that middle-class and lower-class parents often pursue different goals, emphasize different values, and rely on different parenting styles in raising children. Compared to middle-

and upper-class parents, lower- and working-class parents tend to (1) stress obedience and respect for authority, (2) be more restrictive and authoritarian, (3) reason with their children less frequently, and (4) show less warmth and affection (Maccoby, 1980; McLoyd, 1990). Although we will find a wide range of parenting styles in any social group, these *average* social-class differences in parenting have been observed in many cultures and across racial and ethnic groups in the United States.

Why might these social class differences exist? One explanation focuses on the skills needed by workers in white-collar and blue-collar jobs (Arnett, 1995; Kohn, 1969). Parents from lower socioeconomic groups may emphasize obedience to authority figures because that is what is required in blue-collar jobs like their own. Middle- and upper-class parents may reason with their children and stress individual initiative, curiosity, and creativity because these are the attributes that count for business executives, professionals, and other white-collar workers. It could be, then, that both middle- and lower-income parents have devised styles of parenting that are well adapted to the distinctive demands of their sociocultural setting.

Most explanations, though, center on the stresses associated with low-income living and their effects on parenting (McLoyd, 1990; Seccombe, 2000). Rand Conger and his associates (1992, 1995), for example, have shown that parents who are experiencing financial problems tend to become depressed, which increases conflict between them. Marital conflict, in turn, disrupts each partner's ability to be a supportive, involved, and effective parent—another example of indirect effects within the family system. This breakdown in parenting then contributes to negative child outcomes such as low self-esteem, poor school performance, poor peer relations, and adjustment problems such as depression and aggression (see Figure 15.3).

Stresses are magnified for families living below the poverty line or moving in and out of poverty as a result of economic crises. Research tells us that parents living in poverty tend to be restrictive, punitive, and inconsistent, sometimes to the point of being abusive and neglectful (Seccombe, 2000; Brooks-Gunn, Britto, & Brady, 1999). In high-crime poverty

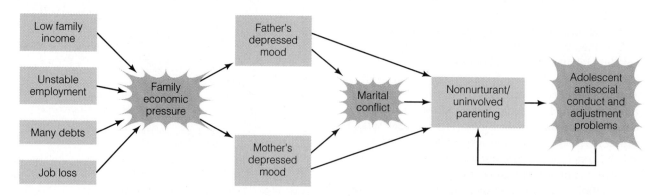

Figure 15.3 A model of the relationship among family economic stress, patterns of parenting, and adolescent adjustment.
SOURCE: Adapted from Conger et al. (1992)

areas, parents may also feel the need to be more authoritarian and controlling to protect their children from danger (R. D. Taylor et al., 2000).

Although parenting practices do not account for all of the negative effects of poverty on child development, these effects are serious and far-reaching. They include health problems, behavior problems, and school failure (Brooks-Gunn et al., 1999; R. M. Lerner, Sparks, & McCubbin, 2000; Rank, 2000). Federal and state welfare reform policies that require welfare mothers to work are not necessarily alleviating these problems. A single working mother with two children who earns a minimum wage is unlikely to earn enough to rise above the poverty line (Seccombe, 2000). She probably does not receive health coverage through her job, and she still has to worry about finding affordable child care and a myriad of other problems.

In sum, the more authoritarian parenting style used by many lower-income parents may reflect both (1) an adaptive attempt to prepare children for jobs in which they will be expected to obey a boss and (2) the damaging effects of economic stress, particularly of living in poverty, on the ability to parent effectively. Parenting styles also differ in interesting ways across cultural and subcultural groups, as the Explorations box on page 410 illustrates.

Models of Influence in the Family

In thinking about influences within the family, we'll bet that you, like most developmental scientists, think first about parents affecting children. But children also affect their parents, and the best way to think of influences within the family is to view them as reciprocal (Sameroff, 1975). Three different models—parent effects, child effects, and transactional models—represent different ways of thinking about directions of influence in the family.

PARENT EFFECTS MODEL

The study of human development has been guided through most of its history by a simple **parent effects model** of family influence. This model assumes that influences run one way, from parent (particularly mother) to child. We have just reviewed research demonstrating effects of parenting styles on child development. But what if we think a bit differently: Could it be that a child's behavior influences the style of parenting his or her parents adopt, and that what appear to be parent effects are instead child effects?

CHILD EFFECTS MODEL

A **child effects model** of family influence highlights instances in which children influence their parents rather than vice versa (Ambert, 1992). One clear example of a child effect is the influence of a child's age and competence on the style of parenting used with that child. For example, infants in their first year of life require and elicit sensitive care, whereas older infants who are asserting their wills and toddling here and there force parents to provide more instruction and discipline (Fagot & Kavanaugh, 1993). Normally, parents then become

less restrictive as their children mature and gradually, with parental guidance, become capable of making their own decisions (Steinberg, 2002).

Now consider the possibility that a child's personality influences the parenting he or she receives. Isn't it possible that easygoing, manageable children *cause* their parents to be warm and authoritative? Couldn't difficult, stubborn, and aggressive children help mold parents who are rejecting and who either rule with an authoritarian iron hand or throw up their hands in defeat and become neglectful? Barbara Keller and Richard Bell (1979) set out to challenge the finding (reported in Chapter 13) that a parent's use of the disciplinary technique of *induction* (explanations emphasizing the consequences of a child's behavior for other people) fosters moral maturity in a child. Isn't it possible instead, they reasoned, that children who are already "good" are more likely than less responsive children to elicit inductive explanations from adults? Keller and Bell had female college students attempt to convince 9-year-old girls to behave altruistically (for example, to spend more time sewing a pillow for a handicapped child than sewing a pillow for themselves). The girls had been taught to respond either very attentively or very inattentively. As expected, students who were confronted with an attentive child used a great deal of induction, pointing out how other children might feel if the child behaved selfishly. By contrast, college students who interacted with an inattentive child relied on power-assertion techniques such as promising rewards for altruism and threatening penalties for selfishness.

In another demonstration of child effects in the family, Kathleen Anderson, Hugh Lytton, and David Romney (1986; also see Lytton, 2000) studied mothers of boys who were clinically diagnosed as having conduct disorders—boys who were highly aggressive and had histories of arson, truancy, temper outbursts, and other serious problems. The researchers had each of these mothers interact with her own conduct-disordered son, another mother's conduct-disordered son, and a non-conduct-disordered boy. Meanwhile, mothers of non-conduct-disordered boys also interacted with their own sons and with both another non-conduct-disordered boy and a conduct-disordered boy.

The findings were clear: Boys with conduct disorders were so noncompliant and difficult that they brought out a negative, coercive behavior parenting style in every mother with whom they interacted. In this study, at least, there was little evidence that the mothers of conduct-disordered boys were any worse disciplinarians than other mothers or that their parenting was the main cause of their sons' aggressive, destructive behavior. Child effects proved stronger than parent effects.

TRANSACTIONAL MODEL

Research now tells us that severe antisocial behavior probably results when a child who is genetically predisposed to be aggressive behaves in ways that elicit negative parenting and this negative parenting, in turn, causes a child to become even more aggressive (Ge et al., 1996; O'Connor et al., 1998; and see Chapter 13). When such a destructive family process

Cultural and Ethnic Variation in Parenting

The link between authoritative parenting and positive developmental outcomes is evident in most ethnic groups and socioeconomic groups studied to date in the United States (Glasgow et al., 1997; Steinberg et al., 1995) and in a variety of other cultures as well (Pinto, Folkers, & Sines, 1991; Scott, Scott, & McCabe, 1991). At the same time, even when differences in socioeconomic status are taken into account, parents of different ethnic backgrounds sometimes hold different beliefs and values about child rearing that shape their parenting practices and, in turn, affect their children's development (MacPhee, Fritz, & Miller-Heyl, 1996; McLoyd et al., 2000).

To illustrate, Native American and Hispanic parents—perhaps because their cultures are *collectivist,* emphasizing the goals of the group rather than of the individual—place more emphasis than European American parents on teaching children to be polite and respectful of authority figures (particularly their fathers), rather than independent and competitive (MacPhee et al., 1996). In addition, the impact of a particular parenting style sometimes differs depending on the cultural context in which it is used. For example, use of physical, coercive discipline (short of abuse) is not as strongly linked to aggression and antisocial behavior among African American youths as it is among European Americans, possibly because it is viewed by African American children as a sign that their parents care (Deater-Deckard et al., 1996). Similarly, parents' efforts to restrict their adolescents as they seek greater autonomy is associated with a poor parent–child relationship and poor adolescent functioning among middle-class European American youth, but is linked to a *strong* parent–child relationship and *good* adolescent functioning among low-income, predominantly African American adolescents who are struggling in school (Boykin-McElhaney & Allen, 2001). Apparently in that social context, adolescents interpreted positively their parents' expressions of concern about their comings and goings and attempts to rein them in.

Authoritarian parenting may also mean something quite different to Chinese children than to American ones. Ruth Chao (1994, 2000) was puzzled by the fact that Chinese children do no better in school when their parents use an authoritative style of parenting than when their parents use what appears to Westerners to be an authoritarian style. She observed that Chinese parents seem strict and controlling to us because they offer clear and specific guidelines for behavior, believing that this is the best way to express their love and train their children properly. Chinese children do not view this style as authoritarian and overly controlling; rather, they sense that their parents care about them. As a result, this style works very effectively and is associated with good developmental outcomes in the Chinese cultural context.

So, authoritative parenting stands out as an effective parenting approach in most cultural contexts, but other parenting styles can be effective in certain cultural contexts. We should be careful not to judge parenting in other cultures and subcultures as deficient just because it is not the style favored by middle-class European American parents (Ogbu, 1981, 1994).

Charles Gupton/Stock, Boston

develops—the child elicits coercive and ineffective parenting from parents at the same time that parents elicit antisocial behavior from the child—it becomes hard to say who is more influential. This scenario is best described by a **transactional model** of family influence, in which parent and child are seen as influencing one another reciprocally (Sameroff, 1975; also see Cook, 2001). According to this model, child problems can evolve if the relationship between parent and child goes bad as the two interact over time. Similarly, optimal child development is likely to result when parent–child transactions evolve in a more positive way.

Genes have a role of in all this; as Chapter 3 showed, genetic endowment influences not only a child's behavior but the parenting style and home environment he or she experiences (Collins et al., 2000; Reiss et al., 2000). Through the process of gene/environment correlation (Scarr & McCartney, 1983; see Chapter 3), the genes children inherit (and share with their parents) influence how their parents and other people react to them and what experiences they seek out. The antisocial child is likely to elicit a harsh, controlling style of parenting even from adoptive parents; the child's hostile behavior and the parent's ineffective parenting then feed on each other through a transactional process (Ge et al., 1996).

Demonstrations of child effects and transactional effects within the family are certainly important. Yet parent effects remain significant. Thanks to more sophisticated research designs, we have more solid evidence than ever that parents really do influence their children's development, even when genetic influences are controlled (Collins et al., 2000), and that parents most likely influence children more strongly than children influence them (Baumrind, 1991; Simons, Robertson, & Downs, 1989). For example, longitudinal studies demonstrate that parents who adopt an authoritative parenting style and who firmly demand that their children follow their rules have children who become more compliant and well-behaved over time than other children (Collins et al., 2000). Meanwhile, experimental studies show that parent training programs can have a positive impact on child development by changing parenting practices (Forgatch & DeGarmo, 1999). Still, we should not assume, as early child development researchers did, that parents are solely responsible for whether their children turn out "good" or "bad." We must remind ourselves again and again that the family is a system in which family members are influenced in reciprocal ways by both their genetic endowments and the environments they create for one another.

Sibling Relationships

A family system consisting of mother, father, and child is perturbed by the arrival of a new baby and becomes a new—and considerably more complex—family system. How do children adapt to a new baby in the house, and how does the sibling relationship change as children get older?

A NEW BABY ARRIVES

When Judy Dunn and Carol Kendrick (1982; see also Dunn, 1993) carefully studied young children's reactions to a new sibling, they found that mothers typically pay less attention to their firstborns after the new baby arrives than before. Partly for this reason, firstborns often find being "dethroned" a stressful experience. They become more difficult and demanding, or more dependent and "clingy," and they often develop problems with their sleeping, eating, and toileting routines. Most of their battles are with their mothers, but a minority of them are not above hitting, poking, and pinching their younger brothers or sisters. Security of attachment to mother decreases significantly, especially if firstborns are 2 years old or older and can fully appreciate how much they have lost (Teti et al., 1996). Although positive effects such as an increased insistence on doing things independently are also common, it is clear that firstborns are not entirely thrilled to have an attention-grabbing new baby in the house. They resent losing their parents' attention, and their own difficult behavior may alienate their parents even further.

Nazli Baydar, Patricia Hyle, and Jeanne Brooks-Gunn (1997) have found that firstborns coping with a new sibling's presence not only display temporary behavior problems but, if they are economically disadvantaged, score lower than similarly disadvantaged children on reading readiness tests and have less positive self-perceptions. These researchers were able to identify specific ways in which the birth of a younger sibling altered the family environment and, in turn, child development. When mothers cut back on work outside the home, for example, they became more available to their children but family income dropped. This meant fewer material resources and learning materials in the home and fewer opportunities for firstborns to develop skills. As a result of economic stresses, mothers also tended to become more controlling and punitive, especially with their daughters.

How can problems be minimized? Adjustment to a new sibling is easier if the marital relationship is good and if the firstborn had secure relationships with both parents before the younger sibling arrived—and continues to enjoy close relationships afterward (Dunn & Kendrick, 1982; Teti et al., 1996; Volling & Belsky, 1992). Parents are advised to guard against ignoring their firstborn, to continue providing love and attention, and to maintain the child's routines as much as possible. They can also encourage older children to become aware of the new baby's needs and feelings and to assist in his or her care (Dunn & Kendrick, 1982; Howe & Ross, 1990).

AMBIVALENCE IN SIBLING RELATIONSHIPS

Fortunately, most older siblings adjust fairly quickly to having a new brother or sister (Dunn & Kendrick, 1982). Yet even in the best of sibling relationships, **sibling rivalry**—the spirit of competition, jealousy, and resentment between brothers and sisters—is normal. The number of skirmishes between very young siblings can range as high as 56 per hour (Dunn, 1993)! Jealousies, bouts of teasing, shouting matches, and occasional kicks and punches continue to be part of the sibling relationship throughout childhood; squabbles are most often about possessions (McGuire et al., 2000). Levels of conflict decrease after early adolescence as teenagers spend more time away from the family (Furman & Buhrmester, 1992; Larson et al.,

1996). The sibling relationship then becomes more equal but less intense (Steinberg & Morris, 2000).

Some sibling relationships are consistently closer than others over the years (Dunn, Slomkowski, & Beardsall, 1994). The personalities of the siblings is one influence, but the quality of parents' relationships with their children also has a lot to do with just how smooth or stormy the sibling relationship is (G. H. Brody & Stoneman, 1996). For example, brothers and sisters are most likely to be able to work out their disagreements if their parents show good conflict resolution skills with each other and in their relationships with each of their children individually (Reese-Weber, 2000). Sibling relationships are also friendlier and less conflictual if mothers and fathers respond warmly and sensitively to *all* their children and do not consistently favor one over another (Dunn, 1993; McHale et al., 2000).

But we should not overemphasize sibling rivalry. The most important thing to know about sibling relationships is that they are *ambivalent*—they involve *both* closeness and conflict. Interestingly, school-age siblings who are similar in age report more warmth and closeness than other sibling pairs and yet are also the most likely to experience rivalry and conflict (Furman & Buhrmester, 1985a, 1985b).

CONTRIBUTIONS TO DEVELOPMENT

For most children, interactions with siblings are mostly positive, and siblings play mostly positive roles in one another's development. Even the battles may contribute positively to social development by teaching children how to assert themselves, manage conflict, and tolerate negative emotions (Bedford, Volling, & Avioli, 2000). Only when sibling relationships are extremely hateful and destructive, and children experience harsh parenting as well, should we worry that siblings may contribute negatively to development (Garcia et al., 2000).

One of the important positive functions of siblings is to provide *emotional support*. Brothers and sisters confide in one another, often more than they confide in their parents (Howe et al., 2000). They protect and comfort one another in rough times. Even preschoolers jump in to comfort their infant siblings when their mothers leave them or when strangers approach (Stewart & Marvin, 1984).

Second, older siblings often provide *caretaking* services for younger siblings. Indeed, in a study of 186 societies, older children were the *principal* caregivers for infants and toddlers in 57% of the cultures studied (Weisner & Gallimore, 1977; and see Ambert, 1994). In U.S. society as well, older siblings, especially girls, frequently babysit or tend their younger siblings.

Finally, older siblings serve as *teachers*. One 5-year-old was quite aware of how much her 2-year-old sister acquired from her through observational learning: "See. I said, 'Bye, I'm going on the slide,' and she said, 'Bye.' She says whatever I say." Older siblings may actually have more influence on their younger siblings' gender-role development than parents do (McHale et al., 2001). Older brothers and sisters are not always as skilled teachers as parents are (Perez-Granados & Callanan, 1997), but they clearly feel a special responsibility to teach, and younger siblings actively seek their guidance.

In many societies, older siblings are major caregivers for young children.

In sum, there is a good deal of reciprocal influence in families that contain preschool or school-age children. Parents, by adopting a particular style of child rearing with each of their children, influence their youngsters' development. Children, meanwhile, through child effects and transactional effects, help to influence the extent to which their parents are accepting/responsive and demanding/controlling. Once a couple has a second child, the family system changes profoundly. Although rivalry and conflict seem to be a normal part of sibling relationships, these ambivalent relationships also offer emotional support, caretaking, and teaching.

The Adolescent

When you picture the typical relationship between a teenager and his or her parents, do you envision a teenager who is out all the time with friends, resents every rule and restriction, and talks back at every opportunity? Do you imagine parents wringing their hands in despair and wondering if they'll ever survive their children's adolescent years? Many people believe that the period of the family life cycle during which parents have adolescents in the house is a particularly stressful time, with close parent–child relationships deteriorating into bitter tugs of war. How much truth is there to these characterizations?

Continuity in the Parent–Child Relationship

Although many people believe that adolescents lose respect for their parents and feel less close to them than they did as children, these beliefs simply do not hold up. A temporary and modest increase in parent–child conflict *is* common at the onset of puberty (Steinberg, 2002). However, most adolescents still respect their parents and describe their family relationships in positive ways (Fuligni, 1998; Offer, Ostrov, & Howard, 1981). They also continue to respect the legitimacy of their parents' authority to set and enforce rules (Smetana, 2000). Mainly, adolescents and their parents squabble a bit more about relatively minor matters such as disobedience, homework, household chores, and access to privileges such as use of the car.

Andrew Fuligni (1998) has found that adolescents from different ethnic groups in the United States differ in their beliefs about how much authority parents should have and how much autonomy adolescents should have. For example, Filipino and Mexican American adolescents are more likely than European American adolescents to believe that one should not disagree with one's parents, and Chinese Americans are less likely to expect to be given the freedom to go to parties and to date at a young age. Adolescents in Japan are even more strongly socialized to expect limited autonomy. They remain closer to their parents than American adolescents throughout the adolescent years, do not feel as much need to distance themselves from their parents, and spend less time with peers (Rothbaum et al., 2000). In collectivist cultures such as Japan, then, the parent–child relationship does not change much at all from childhood to adolescence. And even in our individualistic culture, there is much continuity from childhood to adolescence, and certainly much parent–child closeness.

Renegotiating the Relationship

However, the parent–child relationship *does* change during adolescence—not so much in its degree of closeness as in the balance of power between parents and adolescents.

Most theorists agree that a critical developmental task of adolescence is to achieve **autonomy**—the capacity to make decisions independently and manage life tasks without being overly dependent on other people. If adolescents are to "make it" as adults, they can't be rushing home for reassuring hugs after every little setback or depending on parents to get them to work on time or manage their checkbooks.

As children reach puberty and become more physically and cognitively mature and more capable of acting autonomously, they assert themselves more. As they do so, parents turn over more power to them, and the parent–child relationship changes from one in which parents are dominant to one in which parents and their sons and daughters are on a more equal footing (Steinberg, 2002). It is usually best for their development if adolescents maintain a close attachment

with their families even as they are gaining autonomy and preparing to leave the nest (Beyers & Goossens, 1999; Kobak et al., 1993; Lamborn & Steinberg, 1993). Gaining too much emotional autonomy from parents is unhealthy, except when it serves to protect an adolescent from rejecting parents (Fuhrman & Holmbeck, 1995). Autonomy *and* attachment, or independence *and* interdependence, are most desirable.

As it turns out, adolescents are most likely to become autonomous, achievement oriented, and well adjusted if their parents consistently enforce a reasonable set of rules, involve their teenagers in decision making and recognize their need for greater autonomy, monitor their comings and goings, gradually loosen the reins, *and* continue to be warm, supportive, and involved throughout adolescence (Beyers & Goossens, 1999; Lamborn et al., 1991). In other words, the winning approach is an authoritative style of parenting—the same style that appears to foster healthy child development. Although we must again remind ourselves that children also affect their parents, an authoritative parenting style gives adolescents opportunities to strengthen their independent decision-making skills while still having the benefit of their parents' guidance and advice. It creates a climate in which teenagers confide in their parents—and parents, therefore, do not have to spy to know where their children are and who they are with (Kerr & Stattin, 2000). It is when parents are rejecting and extremely strict, or rejecting and extremely lax, that teenagers are most likely to be psychologically distressed and to get into trouble (Koestner, Zuroff, & Powers, 1991; Lamborn et al., 1991).

The parent–adolescent relationship is truly a partnership, and its quality depends on what both parents and adolescents do to renegotiate their relationship. Apparently, most parents and their teenagers maintain positive feelings for each other while reworking their relationship to allow the adolescent more freedom. As a result, most adolescents are able to achieve autonomy and at the same time shift toward a more mutual relationship with their parents.

The Adult

So far we have concentrated on the child's experience of family life. How do *adults* develop and change as they progress through the family life cycle?

Establishing the Marriage

In U.S. society, 95% of adults choose to marry at some point in their lives (U.S. Census Bureau, 2000), and most choose to marry individuals they love. Marriages in many other cultures are not formed on the basis of love but are arranged by leaders of kin groups who are concerned with acquiring property, allies, and the rights to any children the marriage produces (Ingoldsby & Smith, 1995). As Corinne Nydegger (1986) puts it, "These matters are too important to be left to youngsters" (p. 111). So, in reading what follows, remember that our way of establishing families is not the only way.

Marriage is a significant life transition for most adults: It involves taking on a new role (as husband or wife) and adjusting to life as a couple. We rejoice at weddings and view newlyweds as supremely happy beings. Indeed, they feel on top of the world, and their self-esteem rises (Giarrusso et al., 2000). Yet individuals who have just been struggling to achieve autonomy and assume adult roles soon find that they must compromise with their partners and adapt to each other's personalities and preferences.

Ted Huston and his colleagues have found that the honeymoon is short (Huston, McHale, & Crouter, 1986; Huston et al., 2001; also see Kurdek, 1999). In a longitudinal study of newlywed couples, these researchers discovered that perceptions of the marital relationship became less favorable during the first year after the wedding. For example, couples became less satisfied with their marriages and with their sex lives; they less frequently said "I love you," complimented each other, or disclosed their feelings to each other. Although they spent only somewhat less time together, more of that time was devoted to getting tasks done and less to having fun or just talking. The couples whose relationships deteriorated the most were those who had engaged in a great deal of mutual criticism and other negative behavior from the start.

Although most couples are far more satisfied than dissatisfied with their relationships after the "honeymoon" is over, adapting to marriage clearly involves strains. Blissfully happy relationships evolve into still happy but more ambivalent ones as couples become somewhat disillusioned with each other and their relationship (Huston et al., 2001). Whether this happens because couples begin to see "warts" that they didn't notice before marriage, stop trying to be on their best behavior, or simply start to take each other for granted, it is quite normal. This "honeymoon is over" drop in marital satisfaction early in the marriage is followed by another dip in satisfaction around the time of the so-called "seven-year itch" (Kurdek, 1999).

Does the quality of a couple's relationship early in their marriage have any implications for their later marital adjustment? Apparently it does. Huston and his colleagues (2001) have now assessed couples 2 months, 1 year, and 2 years into their marriages, and again 13 to 14 years after the wedding. It is commonly believed that marriages crumble when negative feelings build up and conflicts escalate, but Huston's findings provide little support for this "escalating conflict" view. Compared to couples who were happily married after 13 years, couples who remained married but were unhappy had had relatively poor relationships all along. Even as newlyweds, and probably even before they married, these couples were less blissfully in love and more negative toward each other than were couples who stayed married and remained happy in their marriages. Apparently, it is not the case that all marriages start out blissfully happy and then some turn sour. Some actually start out sour.

Even couples who ended up divorcing did not experience a buildup of conflict over time; it was often more a matter of losing their positive feelings for each other than building up resentments. Couples who divorced within the first seven years of marriage were already ambivalent early in the marriage and engaged in a lot of negative behavior toward one another from the start. Those who divorced later seemed to have had overly romantic views of their marriage initially; they started out even more affectionate than couples who would remain happily married for many years, but they became seriously disillusioned. All in all, the establishment phase of the family life cycle involves a loss of enthusiasm for most couples. Some couples are already on the path to long-term marital satisfaction, whereas others are headed for divorce or for staying in a marriage that will continue to be less than optimal.

New Parenthood

How does the arrival of a new baby affect wife, husband, and the marital relationship? One popular view holds that having children draws a couple closer together; other people believe that children introduce additional strains into a relationship. Which is it?

On average, new parenthood is best described as a stressful life transition that involves both positive and negative changes (Cowan & Cowan, 2000; Monk et al., 1996). Most parents claim that having a child improves their lives and brings them a good deal of joy and fulfillment (Emery & Tuer, 1993). But let's analyze the situation more closely. Couples have added new roles (as mothers and fathers) to their existing roles (as spouses, workers, and so on). New parents often find juggling work and family responsibilities stressful. They not only have an incredible amount of new work to do as caregivers, but they lose sleep, worry about their baby, find that they have less time to themselves, and often face financial difficulties as well. In addition, even egalitarian couples who previously shared household tasks begin to divide their labors along more traditional lines. She specializes in the "feminine" role by becoming the primary caregiver and housekeeper, often reducing her involvement in work outside the home, while he concentrates on his "masculine" role as provider (Cowan & Cowan, 2000; Sanchez & Thomson, 1997).

What are the effects of increased stress and of the tendency of husband and wife to establish somewhat separate lifestyles? Marital satisfaction typically declines in the first year after a baby is born (Belsky, Lang, & Rovine, 1985; Gottman & Notarius, 2000). This decline is usually steeper for women than for men, primarily because the burden of child care responsibilities typically falls more heavily on mothers and they may resent what they regard as an unfair division of labor (Levy-Shiff, 1994). New mothers often feel trapped, isolated, and overwhelmed by their responsibility; new fathers worry about money (Fox, 2001b).

However, individuals vary widely in their adjustment to new parenthood. Some new parents experience the transition as a bowl of cherries, others as the pits—as a full-blown crisis in their lives. Some get through the typical strains and conflicts of the first year and regain a high level of marital satisfaction; others do not (Cox et al., 1999). What might make this life event easier or harder to manage? We can answer that question by focusing on the nature of the *event* with which a parent must cope, the *person* who must cope with it, and the *resources* the individual has available.

The *event*, of course, is the baby. Clearly, infants who are difficult for some reason (for example, because of an illness that causes endless crying or an irritable temperament) create more stresses and anxieties for parents than infants who are quiet, sociable, responsive, and otherwise easy to love (Levy-Shiff, 1994; Sirignano & Lachman, 1985).

As for the *person*, some adults are better equipped than others to cope with stress; they have good problem-solving and communication skills and find adaptive ways to restructure and organize their lives to accommodate a new baby (Cox et al., 1999; Levy-Shiff, 1994). Similarly, parents who have realistic expectations about how parenthood will change their lives and about children tend to adjust more easily than those who expect the experience to be more positive than it turns out to be (Kalmuss, Davidson, & Cushman, 1992; Mylod, Whitman, & Borkowski, 1997). Also, couples who both recall their own parents as warm and accepting are likely to experience a smoother transition to new parenthood than couples in which either spouse was raised in an aloof or rejecting manner—one of many signs that approaches to parenting are passed from one generation to the next (Belsky & Isabella, 1985; van IJzendoorn, 1992). Similarly, mentally healthy parents fare better than parents who are experiencing mental health problems such as depression going into new parenthood (Cox et al., 1999).

Finally, *resources* can make a great deal of difference to the new parent. Most important of all is spouse support: Things go considerably better for a new mother when she has a good relationship with her husband, and when he shares the burden of child care and housework, than when she has no partner or an unsupportive one (Levy-Shiff, 1994; Demo & Cox, 2000). Social support from friends and relatives can also help new parents cope (Stemp, Turner, & Noh, 1986), as can interventions designed to help expecting parents prepare realistically for the challenges ahead and support one another as they deal with these challenges (Cowan & Cowan, 2000).

In sum, parents who have an easy baby to contend with, who possess positive personal qualities and coping skills, and who receive reliable support from their spouses and others are in the best position to cope adaptively with new parenthood, a transition that is normally both satisfying and stressful, and become effective parents.

The Child-Rearing Family

The child-rearing family is the family with children in it. What can parents look forward to as they have additional children and as their children grow older? A heavier workload! The stresses and strains of caring for a toddler are greater than those of caring for an infant (Crnic & Booth, 1991), and the arrival of a second child means additional stress on top of that (O'Brien, 1996). Parents must not only devote time to the new baby but deal with their firstborn child's normal anxieties about this change in lifestyle. They complain of the hassles of cleaning up food and toys, constantly keeping an eye on their

children, and dealing with their perfectly normal but irritating demands for attention, failures to comply with requests, and bouts of whining (O'Brien, 1996). Because the workload increases, fathers often become more involved in child care after a second child is born (Phares, 1999). However, the mother who is raising children as a single parent or whose husband is not highly involved in family life may find herself without a moment's rest as she tries to keep up with two or more active, curious, mobile, and needy youngsters.

Additional challenges sometimes arise for parents when their children enter adolescence. As we saw earlier, parent–child conflicts become more frequent for a while as children reach puberty. In addition, there is intriguing evidence that living with adolescents who are becoming physically and sexually mature and beginning to date may cause parents to engage in more than the usual amount of midlife questioning about what they have done with their lives and what they can expect next (Silverberg & Steinberg,1990). Here, then, may be another example of child effects within the family system. Or is it? It is also possible that parents who are psychologically distressed and preoccupied with their own midlife problems cannot provide the emotional support their children need and cause them to seek it elsewhere, in the peer group. Parents who are insecure about attachment relationships sometimes have trouble letting go of their adolescents and serving as a secure base as their children seek to become more autonomous (Hock et al., 2001).

Although most parents are far more satisfied than dissatisfied with their marriages and with their relationships with their children, children clearly complicate their parents' lives by demanding everything from fresh diapers and close monitoring to college tuition. By claiming time and energy that might otherwise go into nourishing the marital relationship and by adding stresses to their parents' lives, children do seem to have a negative—though typically only slightly negative—effect on the marital relationship (Kurdek, 1999; Rollins & Feldman 1970).

The Empty Nest

As children reach maturity, the family becomes a "launching pad" that fires adolescents and young adults off into the world to work and start their own families. The term **empty nest** describes the family after the departure of the last child—a phase of the family life cycle that became common only in the 20th century (Fox, 2001a). Clearly, the emptying of the nest involves changes in roles and lifestyle for parents, particularly for mothers who have centered their lives on child rearing. There can be moments of deep sadness:

> Pamela automatically started to toss Doritos and yucky dip into her cart—and then remembered. "I almost burst into tears," she recalls. "I wanted to stop some complete stranger and say, 'My son's gone away to college.' I had such a sense of loss." (Span, 2000, p. 15)

Overall, though, parents react quite positively to the emptying of the nest. Whereas the entry of children into the

"Your attitude is sucking all the fulfillment out of motherhood."

family causes modest decreases in marital satisfaction, the departure of the last child causes modest *increases* in marital satisfaction (Gagnon et al., 1999; L. White & Edwards, 1990). After the nest empties, women often feel that their marriages are more equitable and that their spouses are more accommodating to their needs (Mackey & O'Brien, 1995; Suitor, 1991). Only a minority of parents find this transition very disturbing.

Why do parents generally react positively to the empty nest? Possibly it is because they have fewer roles and responsibilities and, therefore, experience less stress and strain. Empty nest couples also have more time to focus on their marital relationship and to enjoy activities together, as well as more money to spend on themselves. Moreover, parents are likely to view the emptying of the nest as evidence that they have done their job of raising children well and have earned what Erik Erikson called a sense of generativity. One 44-year-old mother put it well: "I have five terrific daughters who didn't just happen. It took lots of time to mold, correct, love, and challenge them. It's nice to see such rewarding results." Of course, most parents continue to enjoy a good deal of contact with their children after the nest empties, so it is not as if they are really losing this important relationship (White & Edwards, 1990).

In recent years, an increasing number of adult children have been remaining in the nest or leaving and then "refilling" it, often because of unemployment, limited finances, divorce, or other difficulties in getting their adult lives on track (Ward & Spitze, 1992; White & Rogers, 1997). Some parents find having adult children in the house distressing (Aquilino, 1991; Umberson, 1992). However, most empty nesters adapt to having adult children in the house, especially if their children are responsible young adults who are in school or employed rather than irresponsible freeloaders (White & Rogers, 1997).

In the end, parenthood is a source of both stress and satisfaction. We have seen how the demands of parenting can detract from the marital relationship, but there is a positive side too: Being a parent can breed personal strengths such as a sense of competence, emotional maturity, and a capacity to care (Palkovitz, 1996; McKeering & Pakenham, 2000). In other words, by nurturing their children, parents may well nurture their own development.

Grandparenthood

Although we tend to picture grandparents as white-haired, jovial elders who knit mittens and bake cookies, most adults become grandparents when they are middle-aged, not elderly, and when they are likely to be highly involved in work and community activities. The average age of first-time grandparenthood is 47 (Conner, 2000). Grandparenting styles are diverse, as illustrated by the results of a national survey of grandparents of teenagers conducted by Andrew Cherlin and Frank Furstenberg (1986). These researchers determined the prevalence of three major styles of grandparenting:

1. **Remote:** Remote grandparents (29% of the sample) were symbolic figures seen only occasionally by their grandchildren. Primarily because they were geographically distant, they were emotionally distant as well.
2. **Companionate:** This was the most common style of grandparenting (55% of the sample). Companionate grandparents saw their grandchildren frequently and enjoyed sharing activities with them. They only rarely played a parental role; they served as companions rather than as caregivers. Like most grandparents, they were reluctant to

meddle in the way their adult children were raising their children and were quite happy not to have child care responsibilities. As one put it, "You can love them and then say, 'Here, take them now, go on home'" (p. 55).

3. **Involved:** Finally, 16% of the grandparents assumed a parentlike role. Like companionate grandparents, they saw their grandchildren frequently and were playful with them, but unlike companionate grandparents, they often helped with child care, gave advice, and played other practical roles in their grandchildren's lives. Some involved grandparents were truly substitute parents who lived with and tended their grandchildren because their daughters were unmarried or recently divorced and worked outside the home.

We see, then, that grandparenting takes many forms but that most grandparents see at least some of their grandchildren frequently and prefer a role that is high in enjoyment and affection but low in responsibility. The vast majority of grandparents find the role very gratifying, especially if they do indeed see their grandchildren frequently (Cherlin & Furstenberg, 1986; Peterson, 1999). Remote grandparents are the least satisfied, largely because they wish they lived closer to their grandchildren. Like grandparents, grandchildren report a good deal of closeness in the grandparent–grandchild relationship and only wish they could see their grandparents more (Block, 2000).

There can also be too much of a good thing, however: Grandmothers experience an increase in symptoms of depression when grandchildren move in with them and they must become substitute parents (Szinovacz, DeViney, & Atkinson, 1999). This has been happening more and more; in 1997, 5.5% of children under 18 lived in homes maintained by their grandparents (Bryson & Casper, 1999). Single women, African Americans, and low-income adults are especially likely to be drawn into this kind of highly involved caregiving role (Fuller-Thomson, Minkler, & Driver, 1997). Although grandparents may also benefit from the intellectual challenge that parenting represents (Ehrle, 2001), their development and well-being can suffer if they become overwhelmed by their responsibilities.

Grandparents, it seems, serve as "the family national guard," always ready to come to the rescue when there is a crisis in the family, never knowing when they will be called (Hagestad, 1985). So, when a teenage daughter becomes pregnant, grandmother and grandfather may find themselves serving as primary caregivers for the baby (Oyserman, Radin, & Benn, 1993). Some women become grandparents and primary caregivers for their grandchildren in their 30s or even late 20s because their teenage daughters have children. These women are less enthusiastic about the role than those who become grandmothers "on time" (Burton, 1996). Similarly, grandparents may step in to help raise their grandchildren after a divorce; if their child does not obtain custody, however, their access to their grandchildren may be reduced or even cut off, causing them much anguish (Cooney & Smith, 1996).

The nature and quality of the grandparent–grandchild relationship often hinges on the quality of the grandparent–parent relationship (King & Elder, 1995). In our society, relationships between grandchildren and their maternal grandmothers are typically the closest (Chan & Elder, 2000). Traditional gender roles may help explain this, for women often serve as "kin-keepers" in the family, keeping up contacts and ensuring that close, affectionate relationships are maintained (Hagestad, 1985; Lye, 1996).

In short, grandparenthood is an important role in the lives of middle-aged and elderly adults. It can take a remote, companionate, or involved form, depending on such factors as the geographical distance between grandparents and grandchildren and changes in the lives of grandchildren and their parents. It is most likely to be gratifying when grandparents can enjoy plenty of companionship with their grandchildren but need not assume major caregiving duties. All three generations typically benefit when relationships between the generations are close (Giarrusso et al., 2000).

Changing Family Relationships

Family relationships develop and change with time. Let's see what becomes of relationships between spouses, siblings, and parents and their children during the adult years.

THE MARITAL RELATIONSHIP

As we've seen, marital satisfaction, although generally high for most couples throughout their lives together, dips somewhat after the honeymoon period is over, dips still lower in the

Most grandparents prefer and adopt a companionate style of grandparenting.

new-parenthood phase, continues to drop as new children are added to the family, and recovers only when the children leave the nest. Women, because they have traditionally been more involved than men in rearing children, tend to be more strongly affected by family life transitions—for good or for bad—than men are.

The nature and quality of marital relationships also changes over the years. Women often perceive inequity in their marriages during the parenting years, when they are doing the lion's share of the family's work. As we have seen, their marriages feel fairer, more equal, and less conflictual after the nest empties. And, although frequency of sexual intercourse decreases over the years, psychological intimacy often increases. Elderly couples are more affectionate than middle-aged couples when they interact, have fewer conflicts, and are able to resolve their conflicts without venting as many negative emotions (Carstensen, Levenson, & Gottman, 1995; Gagnon et al., 1999).

Overall, though, knowing what stage of the family life cycle an adult is in does not allow us to predict very accurately how satisfied that person is with his or her marriage. To do that, we have to consider other factors. For example, couples who are happy early in their marriage tend to be happy later; young couples who are miserable tend to remain miserable. Marital satisfaction, like many personality traits, tends to be quite stable over the years (Dickson, 1995; T. L. Huston et al., 2001). In fact, happily married people have more pleasant personality traits than unhappily married people; for example, they score low on neuroticism scales and rarely vent negative feelings (Robins, Caspi, & Moffitt, 2000). Moreover, their personalities are similar, and are likely to remain similar over the years, as each partner reinforces in the other the traits that brought them together in the first place (Caspi, Herbener, & Ozer, 1992). It is when "opposites attract" and find their personalities clashing day after day that marital problems tend to arise (Kurdek, 1991a; Russell & Wells, 1991).

The family life cycle ends with widowhood. Marriages face new challenges if one of the partners becomes seriously ill or impaired and needs care. Wives suffer more ill effects than daughters when they must care for a dying husband/father, but they generally cope reasonably well with their spouse's death, often feeling afterward that they have grown (M. M. Seltzer & Li, 2000; and see Chapter 17). By the time they reach age 75 or older, about 70% of men are still married and living with their wives, but about 70% of women are widowed or otherwise living alone (U.S. Census Bureau, 2000).

Without question, the marital relationship is centrally important in the lives and development of most adults. Older adults who are divorced or widowed, especially if they have seen more than one relationship end, are lonelier than those who have partners (Peters & Liefbroer, 1997). Men in particular enjoy a boost in life satisfaction when they gain a spouse and a drop in life satisfaction when they lose one (Chipperfield & Havens, 2001). More generally, married adults are "happier, healthier, and better off financially" than other adults and are likely to remain so if they can manage to weather bad times in their marriages (Waite & Gallagher, 2000).

SIBLING RELATIONSHIPS

Relationships between brothers and sisters change once siblings no longer live together in the same home. Starting in adolescence, both closeness and conflict between siblings diminish as brothers and sisters forge their own lives. Sibling relationships also become more equal (Buhrmester & Furman, 1990; Cicirelli, 1995). Victor Cicirelli (1982, 1995) finds that adult siblings typically see each other several times a year and communicate through phone calls or letters. Few discuss intimate problems or help one another, but siblings typically feel that they can count on each other in a crisis (see also Connidis, 1994).

The same ambivalence that characterizes sibling relationships during childhood seems to carry over into adulthood. A great deal of emotional closeness persists, despite decreased contact; indeed, siblings often grow even closer in old age (Cicirelli, 1995). The potential for sibling rivalry persists too, however. Conflict is far less frequent than during childhood, but old rivalries can and do flare up again during adulthood (Cicirelli, 1995). Siblings who enjoyed a close relationship during childhood are likely to be drawn even closer after significant life events such as a parent's illness or death, whereas siblings who had poor relationships during childhood are likely to clash in response to the same life events (M. J. Lerner et al., 1991; Ross & Milgram, 1982). Still, most adults seem to accept sibling rivalry as part of the bargain and can cite ways in which they have benefited over the years from rivalries with their siblings (Bedford et al., 2000).

In the end, the sibling relationship is typically the longest-lasting relationship we have, linking us to individuals who share many of our genes and experiences (Cicirelli, 1991). It is a relationship that can be very close, very tense and conflictual, or, for most of us, some of both.

PARENT–CHILD RELATIONSHIPS

Parent and child generations in most families are in close contact and enjoy affectionate give-and-take relationships throughout the adult years. And when aging parents eventually need support, children are there to help.

Forming More Mutual Relationships.   As young adults leave the nest, they don't sever ties with their parents; instead, they and their parents jointly negotiate a new relationship, often a more intimate one in which they move beyond playing out their roles as "child" and "parent" and become more like friends (Aquilino, 1997; Greene & Boxer, 1986). This more mutual relationship is especially likely develop after children marry, begin their careers, and assume other adult roles (Aquilino, 1997; Fingerman, 2000), especially between married daughters and their mothers. Parents often perceive the relationship more positively than their children do, possibly because middle-aged parents want a sense of continuity with the younger generation whereas young adults are still trying to define themselves as unique individuals who are different from their parents (Aquilino, 1999). Still, children also appreciate more equal relationships with their parents:

I am understanding her now more than I ever did before. I have started to understand that I had to stop blaming her for everything in my life. I felt she had been a lousy parent. Now, I'm more understanding that my mother is a person and that she has her own problems and her own life. . . . I accepted her as a mother—but she actually is a human being. (K. White, Speisman, & Costos, 1983, p. 73)

What happens to the parent–child relationship when children become middle-aged and their parents become elderly? The two generations typically continue to care about, socialize with, and help one another throughout the adult years (Bengtson, Rosenthal, & Burton, 1996; Umberson & Slaten, 2000). According to national surveys, 80% of people over 65 have living children; about half either live with a child (18%) or live within 10 minutes of at least one child (34%); and about three-fourths see at least one child at least once a week (Shanas, 1980; see also Taeuber, 1990). Aging mothers enjoy closer relations and more contact with their children, especially their daughters, than aging fathers do (Umberson & Slaten, 2000). And African American, Hispanic American, and other minority elders often enjoy even more supportive relationships with their families than European Americans do (Bengtson et al., 1996). Finally, both adult children and their parents gain in self-esteem when the parent–child relationship is affectionate (Giarrusso et al., 2000).

We see little support here for the view that today's families have abandoned their elders. Instead, these findings suggest that the predominant family form in the United States is neither the isolated nuclear family nor the extended family household but what has been called the **modified extended family**—an arrangement in which nuclear families live in their own separate households but have close ties and frequent communication and interaction with other kin (Litwak, 1960). Most elderly people in our society prefer just this pattern. They do not want to have to live with and burden their children when their health fails (E. Brody, Johnsen, & Fulcomer, 1984; Conner, 2000).

Young adults and their parents often negotiate a more mutual, friendlike relationship.

Relationships between the generations are not only close and affectionate, but they are generally quite equitable as well: Each generation gives something, and each generation gets something in return (Conner, 2000; Markides, Boldt, & Ray, 1986). This reciprocity is healthy; aging parents can become demoralized when their children help them too much, for then equity is lost and they feel like a burden (Lee, Netzer, & Coward, 1995; Silverstein, Chen, & Heller, 1996). Contrary to myth, then, most aging families do not experience what has been called **role reversal**—a switching of roles late in life such that the parent becomes the needy, dependent one and the child becomes the caregiver (E. Brody, 1990). Parent–child relationships remain close and reciprocal throughout most of the life span. Only when parents reach advanced ages and begin to develop serious physical or mental problems does the parent–child relationship finally become less reciprocal.

Caring for Aging Parents. Elaine Brody (1985, 1990) uses the term **middle generation squeeze** (others call it the "sandwich generation" phenomenon) to describe the situation of middle-aged adults pressured by demands from both the younger and the older generations simultaneously. Put yourself in the shoes of Julia, a 52-year-old African American working woman:

My girl and grand girl had babies young. Now, they keep on rushin' me, expectin' me to do this and that, tryin' to make me old 'fore my time. I ain't got no time for myself. I takes care of babies, grown children, and the old peoples. I work too. I get so tired. I don't know if I'll ever get to do somethin' for myself. (Burton, 1996, p. 155)

Julia's situation may not be typical, but it is certainly middle generation squeeze! More and more adults with children find themselves caring for their aging parents; indeed, middle-aged adults who have children are more likely than those who do not to be drawn into caring for parents or other relatives, possibly because they are more closely tied in to kin networks (Gallagher & Gerstel, 2001). Spouses are actually the first in line to care for frail elders, assuming they are alive and up to the challenge, but most caregivers of ailing elders are daughters or daughters-in law in their 40s and 50s. Daughters are about three times more likely than sons to provide assistance to aging parents (Dwyer & Coward, 1991). When there is no daughter available, daughters-in-law often step in (Allen, Blieszner, & Roberto, 2000).

In many Asian societies, daughters-in-law are the first choice. Aging parents are often taken in by a son, usually the oldest, and cared for by his wife (Youn et al., 1999). In our society, where most aging parents do not want to have to live with their children (Burr & Mutchler, 1999), much elder care is provided from a distance (Bengtson et al., 1996). Nonetheless, families are the major providers of care for the frail elderly today; again, we see no signs that younger generations are dodging their responsibilities to their elders (Conner, 2000). African American, Hispanic, and Asian American families feel even more strongly than European American ones that they have a responsibility to help

(Conner, 2000). Some ethnic groups have more potential helpers available to them, too. Whereas European American elders look primarily to their children or, if they live long enough, their grandchildren to look after them in old age, for example, African American elders can more often call on siblings and members of the extended family such as cousins and nieces and nephews for help (C. L. Johnson, 2000). As a result, they are less likely to find themselves without family support when they reach advanced ages.

Middle-aged adults who must foster their children's (and possibly grandchildren's) development while tending to their own development *and* caring for aging parents sometimes find their situation quite overwhelming. They may experience what has come to be called **caregiver burden**—the psychological distress associated with providing care for someone with physical and/or cognitive impairments. We should not overlook the fact that caring for an aging parent can be very rewarding. Nonetheless, many adult children providing such care experience emotional, physical, and financial strains (Aneshensel et al., 1995; E. Brody, 1990). A woman who is almost wholly responsible for a dependent elder often feels angry and resentful because she has no time for herself and little freedom to pursue her own goals. If her parent has Alzheimer's disease or another cognitive impairment, she is likely to care for the parent for about seven years at home, make the difficult decision to put the parent in a nursing home, and then have to grieve the parent's decline and death (Aneshensel et al., 1995). She may experience conflict between her caregiver role and her roles as wife, mother, and employee, and this role conflict, in turn, may undermine her sense of well-being (Stephens et al., 2001).

Not all caregivers feel that providing care is a burden or suffer negative mental health effects. Much depends on their perceptions of the situation (Stephens et al., 2001; Yates, Tennstedt, & Chang, 1999). The burden of care is likely to be perceived as especially weighty if the elderly parent has cognitive impairments rather than just physical ones, especially if he or she engages in many of the disruptive and socially inappropriate behaviors often shown by people with dementia (Clyburn et al., 2000; Gaugler et al., 2000). The caregiver's personality also makes a difference; caregivers who lack a sense of mastery or control may have difficulty coping and may become more and more depressed over time (Li, Seltzer, & Greenberg, 1999).

The strain is also likely to be worse if a caregiving daughter is unmarried and, therefore, does not have a husband to lean on for practical and emotional support (E. Brody et al., 1992); if her marriage is an unsupportive one (Stephens & Franks, 1995); or if for other reasons she lacks social support (Clyburn et al., 2000). In the end, the caregiver–parent relationship and the marital relationship affect one another. A solid marriage can provide social support that lightens the burden of care; a troubled marriage can get in the way. Similarly, caring for an ailing parent can detract from the marital relationship, or it can improve it by making a daughter feel better about herself (Stephens & Franks, 1995).

What really motivates adult children to help? In an interesting attempt to find out, Victor Cicirelli (1993) assessed whether daughters helped their aging mothers out of love ("I feel lonely when I don't see my mother often") or out of a sense of duty ("I feel that I should do my part in helping"). Both daughters who were highly motivated to help based on a strong attachment to their mothers and daughters who were motivated by a sense of obligation spent more time helping than women whose motivations to help were weaker. However, those who helped out of love experienced helping as far less stressful and burdensome than those who helped mainly out of a sense of duty. Least motivated to help were adult children who had felt rejected by their parents earlier in life and did not have either a strong attachment or a sense of obligation (Whitbeck, Hoyt, & Huck, 1994).

So, the caregivers most likely to experience psychological distress are those who have highly impaired parents, who are not very close to them, and who help mainly because they feel they must rather than because they love and cherish their parents. These individuals need support and relief from their burden. Interventions can help them sharpen their caregiving skills and learn to react less negatively to the difficult behavior often shown by elderly adults with Alzheimer's disease and other forms of dementia, reducing their sense of burden in the process (Ostwald et al., 1999).

In sum, generations within a family maintain close relationships throughout adulthood by living as modified extended families and mutually supporting one another. Yet the quality of parent–child relationships often changes over the

Caring for an ailing parent can result in middle generation squeeze and caregiver burden.

life span. The child who is dependent on parents becomes the adult who can truly be interdependent with them—and may ultimately become the person on whom aging parents must depend.

Diversity in Family Life

Useful as it is, the concept of a family life cycle simply does not capture the diversity of adult lifestyles and family experiences. Many of today's adults do not progress in a neat and orderly way through the stages of the traditional family life cycle—marrying, having children, watching them leave the nest, and so on. A small number never marry; a larger number never have children. Some continue working while their children are young; others stop or cut down. And many adults move in and out of wedded life by marrying, divorcing, and remarrying. Let's examine some of these variations in family life.

Singles

It is nearly impossible to describe the "typical" single adult. This category includes not only young adults who have not yet married but middle-aged and elderly people who have experienced divorce or the death of a spouse or who have never married. It is typical to start adulthood as a single person. A majority of adults in the 18 to 29 age range are not married (U.S. Census Bureau, 2000). Because adults have been postponing marriage, the number of young, single adults has been growing.

Many singles live with a romantic partner without being married (J. A. Seltzer, 2000; Sweet & Bumpass, 1987). Adults who engage in **cohabitation** are diverse; for example, some live together as a step toward a first marriage, whereas others have seen their marriages end and are looking for an alternative to marriage (Seltzer, 2000). Quite a number have children; by one estimate, 1 in 4 children will live in a family headed by a cohabiting couple sometime during childhood (Graefe & Lichter, 1999).

It makes sense to think that couples who live together before marrying would have more opportunity than those who do not to determine whether they are truly compatible. Yet couples who live together and then marry seem to be *more* dissatisfied with their marriages (Thomson & Colella, 1992) and *more* likely to divorce (Seltzer, 2000) than couples who do not live together before marrying. Why is this? It is unlikely that the experience of cohabitation itself is responsible (Booth & Johnson, 1988). Instead, it seems that the kinds of people who choose to live together may be somewhat more susceptible to marital problems and less committed to marriage than the kinds of people who do not. They tend, for example, to be less religious, less conventional in their family attitudes, less committed to the idea of marriage as a permanent arrangement, and more open to the idea of divorcing (Axinn & Barber, 1997; DeMaris & MacDonald, 1993). All in all, there is

no support for the notion that cohabitation enables people to select their mates more wisely.

What of the 5% of adults who never marry? Stereotypes suggest that they are miserably lonely and maladjusted, but they often make up for their lack of spouse and children by forming close bonds with siblings, friends, or younger adults who become like sons or daughters to them (Rubinstein et al., 1991). As "old-old" people in their 80s and 90s, never-marrieds sometimes do lack relatives who can assist or care for them (C. L. Johnson & Troll, 1996). Yet it is divorced rather than never-married single adults who tend to be the loneliest and least happy adults (Kurdek, 1991b; Peters & Liefbroer, 1997).

Childless Married Couples

Like single adults who never marry, married couples who remain childless do not experience all the phases of the traditional family life cycle. Many childless couples want children but cannot have them, but a growing number of adults, especially highly educated adults with high-status occupations, voluntarily decide to delay having children or not to have them at all, though many change their minds later (Heaton et al., 1999).

How are childless couples faring while their peers are having, raising, and launching children? Generally, quite well. Their marital satisfaction is higher than that of couples with children during the child-rearing years (Kurdek, 1999). And middle-aged and elderly childless couples seem to be no less satisfied with their lives than parents whose children have left the nest (Allen, Blieszner, & Roberto, 2000; Rempel, 1985). However, elderly women who are childless *and* widowed may find themselves without anyone to help them if they develop health problems (C. L. Johnson & Troll, 1996). It seems, then, that childless couples derive a good deal of satisfaction from their marriages and are happier than single adults, but may suffer from a lack of social support very late in life after their marriages end.

Dual-Career Families

As more and more mothers of infants and young children have gone to work outside the home (U.S. Census Bureau, 2000), developmental scientists have naturally asked what impact maternal employment has on families. Some have focused on the concept of **spillover effects**—ways in which events at work affect home life and events at home carry over into the workplace. Most of their research has focused on negative spillover effects, in which problems at work adversely affect family life or in which family problems undermine an individual's effectiveness at work (Barnett et al., 1995; Perry-Jenkins, Repetti, & Crouter, 2000). One child showed a good understanding of negative spillover from work to home when he said this about his working parents: "If they have had a bad day, I just leave them alone. I just give them time to cool down" (Galinsky, 1999, p. xvii). However, *positive* spillover effects can also occur. A good marriage and rewarding interactions with children can protect a woman from the negative psychological effects of stresses at work (Barnett, 1994), and a rewarding, stimulating job can have positive effects on her interactions within the family (Greenberger, O'Neil, & Nagel, 1994).

Overall, dual-career families are faring well. Women are giving up personal leisure time (not to mention sleep!) and cutting back on housework time to give themselves more time with their children; meanwhile, their husbands are slowly but steadily increasing their participation in household and child care activities (Cabrera et al., 2000; Coltrane, 2000). There is no indication that a mother's working, in and of itself, has damaging effects on child development; it can have positive or negative effects depending on the circumstances. It is likely to be best for children when it means an increase in family income, when mothers are satisfied with the choice they have made (that is, when they would rather be working than at home), when fathers become more involved, and when children are adequately supervised after school (Hoffman, 2000; J. V. Lerner & Noh, 2000). Girls may also benefit from the role model a working mother provides and tend to adopt less stereotyped views of men's and women's roles than children whose mothers do not work (Hoffman, 2000).

Some scholars have been concerned that more and more children of working parents are becoming **latchkey children,** caring for themselves after school without their parents there to supervise them. Although some research suggests that being a latchkey child may be harmful to the academic and social development of young elementary school children (Pettit et al., 1997), most latchkey children suffer no ill effects. Even when working parents are not around to supervise their children in person, many establish clear ground rules and monitor their children quite effectively through phone calls and other means (Jacobson & Crockett, 2000).

Having a working mother *can* be a negative experience, however (Goldberg, Greenberger, & Nagel, 1996). Latchkey children and adolescents can get into trouble when their parents do not monitor them and they lack adult supervision after school (Perry-Jenkins et al., 2000). They can also suffer if a working mother is unable to remain a warm and involved parent who shares "quality time" with them (Beyer, 1995). Martha Moorehouse (1991) found that 6-year-olds whose mothers began working full-time were actually *more* cognitively and socially competent (according to their teachers) than children whose mothers were homemakers if these youngsters frequently shared activities such as reading, telling stories, and talking with their mothers. However, they fared worse than children with stay-at-home mothers if they lost out on such opportunities. Fortunately, most working mothers manage to spend almost as much time with their children as nonworking mothers do (Bryant & Zick, 1996; Nock & Kingston, 1988), and their husbands are more involved than ever in child care (Bianchi, 2000). As a result, most dual-career couples are able to enjoy the personal and financial benefits of working without compromising their children's development.

Gay and Lesbian Families

The family experiences of gay men and lesbian women are most notable for their diversity (Savin-Williams & Esterberg, 2000). In the United States, several million gay men and lesbian women are parents, most through previous heterosexual marriages but others through adoption or artificial insemination (Flaks et al., 1995). Some no longer live with their children, but others raise them as single parents, and still others raise them in families that have two mothers or two fathers. Other gay men and lesbian women remain single and childless or live as couples without children throughout their lives. All in all, the diverse families of gay and lesbian adults are not very well described by traditional family concepts such as the family life cycle, which were developed with heterosexual nuclear families in mind. Gay and lesbian families also face challenges because they are often not recognized as families by society (Demo & Allen, 1996).

Those gay and lesbian adults who live as couples are likely to have more egalitarian relationships than heterosexual couples do; rather than following traditional gender stereotypes, partners tend to work out a division of labor, through trial and error, based on who is especially talented at what or who hates doing what (M. Huston & Schwartz, 1995). Otherwise, their relationships evolve through the same stages of development, are satisfying or dissatisfying for the same reasons, and are typically as rewarding as those of married or cohabiting heterosexuals (Kurdek, 1995). Moreover, those gay and lesbian adults who raise children are as likely as heterosexual parents to produce competent and well-adjusted children (Savin-Williams & Esterberg, 2000; Patterson, 1995). And, contrary to what many people believe, their children are no more likely than the children of heterosexual parents to develop a homosexual or bisexual sexual orientation; more than 90% of the children of gay fathers and lesbian mothers are heterosexual (Bailey et al., 1995; Golombok & Tasker, 1996). There is certainly no evidence that it is in the best interests of children to deny gay and lesbian parents custody of their children or the right to adopt children (Patterson, 2000).

Children raised by lesbian couples develop much like other children do, on average.

Table 15.2 Top 10 reasons checked by divorcing men and women in California for their divorce. Respondents were given a checklist with 27 items. Notice that incompatibility and lack of emotional fulfillment are strong themes and that more women than men voiced several of these complaints.

Reasons for Divorce: Checklist Responses	Percentage of Males (N = 189)	Percentage of Females (N = 212)
1. Gradual growing apart, losing sense of closeness	79	78
2. Not feeling loved and appreciated by spouse	60	73
3. Sexual intimacy problems	65	64
4. Serious differences in lifestyle or values	57	63
5. Spouse not able/willing to meet my major needs	48	64
6. Frequently feel put down or belittled by spouse	37	59
7. Emotional problems of spouse	44	52
8. Conflict regarding spending and handling of money	44	50
9. Severe and intense conflict; frequent fighting	35	44
10. Problems and conflicts with roles (i.e., divisions of responsibility for household jobs or other chores outside the house)	33	47

SOURCE: Adapted from Gigy & Kelly (1992)

Families Experiencing Divorce

Orderly progress through the family life cycle is disrupted when a couple divorces. Divorce is *not* just one life event; rather, it is a series of stressful experiences for the entire family that begins with marital conflict before the divorce and includes a whole complex of life changes as the marriage unravels and its members reorganize their lives (Amato, 2000; Emery, 1999). Why do people divorce? What effects does divorce typically have on family members? And how can we explain the fact that some adults and children eventually thrive after a divorce whereas others experience persisting problems?

BEFORE THE DIVORCE

Gay Kitson and her colleagues (Kitson, Babri, & Roach, 1985; Kitson, 1992) have pieced together a profile of the couples at highest risk for divorce. Generally, they are young adults, in their 20s and 30s, who have been married for an average of about seven years and often have young children. They are especially likely to divorce if they married as teenagers, had a short courtship, or conceived a child before marrying—all factors that might suggest an unreadiness for marriage and unusually high financial and psychological stress accompanying new parenthood. Finally, they are more likely to be low in socioeconomic status than high. Not surprisingly, divorcers also express low satisfaction with their marriages, think about breaking up, and express few positive emotions and/or many negative ones in their interactions with one another (Gottman & Levenson, 2000).

Contrary to the notion that today's couples don't really give their marriages a chance to work, research suggests that most divorcing couples experience a few years of marital distress and conflict and often try out separations before they make the final decision to divorce (Gottman & Levenson, 1992; Kitson, 1992). Reasons for divorcing are no longer restricted to traditionally important precipitators such as nonsupport, alcoholism, or abuse (Gigy & Kelly, 1992). Instead, couples today typically divorce because they feel their marriages are lacking in communication, emotional fulfillment, or compatibility (see Table 15.2). Wives tend to have longer lists of complaints than their husbands do and often have more to do with initiating the breakup (Thompson & Amato, 1999).

AFTER THE DIVORCE: CRISIS AND REORGANIZATION

Most families going through a divorce experience it as a genuine *crisis*—a period of considerable disruption that often lasts for at least one to two years (Amato, 2000; Hetherington, Bridges, & Insabella, 1998). The wife, who usually obtains custody of any children, is likely to be angry, depressed, and otherwise distressed, although often relieved as well. The husband is also likely to be distressed, particularly if he did not want the divorce and feels shut off from his children. Both individuals must revise their identities (as single rather than married people) and revise their relationship as well. Both may feel isolated from former friends and unsure of themselves as they become involved in new romantic relationships. Divorced women with children are likely to face the added problem of getting by with considerably less money (Amato, 2000).

Because of all these stressors, divorced adults are at higher risk than married adults for depression and other forms of psychological distress, physical health problems, and even death (Amato, 2000; Lillard & Panis, 1996). Their adjustment is especially likely to be poor if they have little income, do not find a new relationship, take a dim view of divorce, and were not the one who initiated the divorce (Wang & Amato, 2000). Some do feel better about themselves and more in control of their lives after extracting themselves from a miserable marriage. Thus, divorce is at least temporarily stressful for most adults, but it can have negative or positive effects in the long run depending on the individual and the circumstances (Amato, 2000).

As you might suspect, psychologically distressed adults do not make the best of parents. Moreover, children going through a divorce do not make the best of children, for they too are suffering. They are often angry, fearful, depressed, and guilty, especially if they fear that they were somehow responsible for what happened (Hetherington, 1981). They are also likely to be whiny and dependent, disobedient, and downright disrespectful. A vicious circle of the sort described by the transactional model of family influence results: Children's behavior problems and parents' ineffective parenting styles feed on each other.

Mavis Hetherington and her associates (Hetherington, Cox, & Cox, 1982; Hetherington & Kelly, 2002) have found that custodial mothers, preoccupied with their own problems, often become impatient and insensitive to their children's needs. In terms of the dimensions of child rearing we have discussed, they become less accepting and responsive, less authoritative, and less consistent in their discipline, now and then trying to seize control of their children with a heavy-handed, authoritarian style of parenting but more often failing to carry through in enforcing rules and making few demands that their children behave maturely. Noncustodial fathers, meanwhile, are likely to be overly permissive, indulging their children during visits as if they were Santa Claus. This is not the formula for producing well-adjusted, competent children! The behavior problems that children display undoubtedly make effective parenting difficult, but a deterioration in parenting style aggravates those behavior problems.

When this breakdown in family functioning occurs, children are likely to display not only behavior problems at home but also strained relations with peers and academic problems and adjustment difficulties at school (Amato, 2000; Hetherington et al., 1982). Relationships between siblings may also become strained; in some families, siblings are even separated after the divorce and live with different parents (Beaudry et al., 2000). It does not seem to matter much whether children live with their mother or live with their father in a single-parent home; the negative effects of divorce are often still evident (Downey, Ainsworth-Darnell, & Dufur, 1998).

Families typically begin to pull themselves back together about two years after the divorce; by then, many of the differences between children of divorce and children of intact families have disappeared (Hetherington et al., 1998). Yet even after the crisis phase has passed and most children have adapted, divorce can leave a residue of negative effects on some individuals that lasts for years (Amato, 2000). Girls and boys who have experienced divorce are likely to have lower school achievement at age 16 than their peers (Jonsson & Gahler, 1997). As adolescents, children of divorce are also less likely than other children to perceive their relationships with their parents, especially their fathers, as close and caring (Emery, 1999; Woodward, Fergusson, & Belsky, 2000). Even years after the divorce, many adolescents are still negative about what it has done to their lives and unhappy that it happened (Emery, 1999).

The negative aftereffects of the divorce experience may even carry into adulthood (Amato, 2000). For example, a study of middle-aged adults revealed that 24% of those whose parents had divorced when they were younger had never married, compared to 14% of adults from intact families (Maier & Lachman, 2000). Adults whose parents divorced are also more likely than adults from intact families to experience marital conflict and divorce themselves (Amato, 1996). And they are more likely to experience psychological problems (Chase-Lansdale, Cherlin, & Kiernan, 1995; Maier & Lachman, 2000).

In sum, divorce is a difficult experience for all involved. A transactional model of family influence is required to understand all the interacting factors involved and to predict whether the outcomes for adults and children will be positive or negative (Hetherington et al., 1998). Problems reach crisis proportions about a year after the divorce. Although most negative effects disappear over the next couple of years, some children, negatively affected by their own distress and by a breakdown in parenting, have more persistent problems, problems they sometimes carry into adulthood.

But now let's offset this gloomy picture of the typical divorce with more encouraging messages. The majority of parents and children rebound and adapt well in the long run (Hetherington & Kelly, 2002). A conflict-ridden two-parent family is more detrimental to a child's development than a cohesive single-parent family. Children from families experiencing marital conflict do display more behavior problems after a divorce than before, but they show even larger increases in behavior problems if they remain with their warring parents (Morrison & Coiro, 1999). Indeed, many of the behavior problems that children display after a divorce are actually evident well *before* the divorce. They may be caused not by divorce but by long-standing family conflict or even by genes that predispose certain parents and their children to experience psychological problems (Cherlin et al., 1991; O'Connor et al., 2000).

Interestingly, Alan Booth and Paul Amato (2001) have found that children whose parents did *not* fight a lot before the divorce often suffer more after it than those whose parents did fight. Why might this be? For children from low-conflict homes, divorce is probably a shock; children may blame themselves and be unprepared to cope. For children from high-conflict homes, however, divorce may represent a welcome escape from parental warfare. By allowing one or both warring parents to become more effective parents, divorce may even benefit these children (Booth, 1999).

As Booth and Amato (2001) conclude, "divorce may be beneficial or harmful to children, depending on whether it reduces or increases the amount of stress to which children are exposed" (p. 210). As we see in the Explorations box on page 425, a number of factors can help facilitate a positive adjustment to divorce and prevent lasting damage—among them, adequate finances, effective parenting by the custodial parent, effective parenting by the noncustodial parent, other sources of social support, and a minimum of additional stressors.

"Good" and "Bad" Divorces: Factors Influencing Adjustment

Some adults and children thrive after a divorce, whereas others suffer many negative and long-lasting effects. Why is this? Here are some factors can make a big difference.

1. Adequate financial support. Families fare better after a divorce if the father pays child support and the family therefore has adequate finances (Marsiglio et al., 2000). The Family Support Act of 1988 was passed to clamp down on so-called "deadbeat Dads" and make them meet their obligations (Thompson & Amato, 1999). However, only about half of noncustodial fathers do pay child support (Sorensen, 1997). Adjustment is likely to be more difficult for mother-headed families that fall into poverty and must struggle to survive.

2. Good parenting by the custodial parent. The custodial parent plays a critical role in what happens to the family. If she or he can continue to be warm, authoritative, and consistent, children are far less likely to experience problems (Hetherington et al., 1992; Simons et al., 1994). It is difficult to be an effective parent when one is depressed and under stress, but parents who understand the stakes may be more able to give their children the love and guidance they need. Moreover, interventions can help them. Marion Forgatch and David DeGarmo (1999) randomly assigned divorced mothers of boys to either a parenting skills program designed to prevent them from becoming less positive and more coercive toward their children or to a control group. Compared to control group mothers, trained mothers relied less on coercive methods and remained more positive toward their sons over a 12-month period. Better yet, these positive changes in their parenting behaviors were tied to improvements in their children's adjustment at school and at home (see also Wolchik et al., 2000).

3. Good parenting by the noncustodial parent. If parents continue to squabble after the divorce and are hostile toward each other, both will likely be upset, the custodial parent's parenting is likely to suffer, and children will feel torn in their loyalties and experience behavior problems (Amato, 1993). Children may also suffer when they lose contact with their noncustodial parent. A quarter or more of children living with their mothers do lose contact with their fathers, and many others see their fathers only rarely (Demo & Cox, 2000). More important than amount of contact, though, is the quality of contact. Noncustodial fathers who are authoritative parents and who are emotionally close to their children help children make a positive adjustment to life in a single-parent home (Marsiglio et al., 2000).

Ideally, then, children should be able to maintain affectionate ties with both parents and should be protected from any continuing conflict between parents. It may not be as important that parents obtain joint custody as that they both maintain high-quality relationships with their children (Emery & Tuer, 1993; Kline et al., 1989). Couples can often choose between mediation and litigation in solving disputes over child custody. A recent experiment in which parents were randomly assigned to one or the other suggests that working together with the help of a mediator to resolve issues, rather than battling each other with the help of lawyers, helps to keep noncustodial parents cooperating with their spouses and involved in their children's lives up to 12 years after the divorce (Emery et al., 2001). For example, 30% of noncustodial parents who had a mediator saw their children weekly or more, whereas only 9% of those who were assigned to the normal litigation approach did.

4. Additional social support. Divorcing adults are less depressed if they have close confidants (Menaghan & Lieberman, 1986). Children also benefit from having close friends to give them social support (Lustig, Wolchik, & Braver, 1992), as well as from participating in peer-support programs in which they and other children of divorce can share their feelings, correct their misconceptions, and learn positive coping skills (Grych & Fincham, 1992). Friends, relatives, school personnel, and other sources of social support outside the family can all do much to help families adjust to divorce.

5. A minimum of additional stressors. Generally, families respond most positively to divorce if additional disruptions are kept to a minimum—for example, if parents do not have to move, go through court hearings, get new jobs, cope with the loss of their children, and so on (Buehler et al., 1985–1986). Obviously, it is easier to deal with a couple of changes than a mountain of stressors. Although families cannot always control events, they can strive to keep their lives as simple as possible.

Here, then, we have the first steps in the path toward a positive divorce experience—as well as a better understanding of why divorce is more disruptive for some families than others. As Paul Amato (1993) concludes, adjustment to divorce will depend on the "total configuration" of stressors the individual faces and resources he or she has available to aid in coping, including both personal strengths (such as good coping skills) and social supports.

Explorations

Remarriage and Reconstituted Families

Within three to five years of a divorce, about 75% of single-parent families experience yet another major transition when a parent remarries and the children acquire a stepparent—and sometimes new siblings as well (Hetherington, 1989; Hetherington & Stanley-Hagan, 2000). Since about 60% of remarried couples divorce, some adults and children today find themselves in a recurring cycle of marriage, marital conflict, divorce, single status, and remarriage.

How do children fare when their custodial parent remarries? The first few years are a time of conflict and disruption as new family roles and relationships are ironed out (Hetherington & Stanley-Hagan, 2000). The difficulties are likely to be aggravated if both parents bring children to the family (Mekos, Hetherington, & Reiss, 1996). Girls are often so closely allied with their mothers that they may resent either a stepfather competing for their mother's attention or a stepmother attempting to play a substitute-mother role. Perhaps as a result, they tend to benefit less than boys do from remarriage, although most children adapt and fare well in time (Hetherington et al., 1998).

Even this quick examination of the diverse experiences of single adults, married but childless adults, dual-career families, gay and lesbian families, and divorced and remarried families should convince us that it is difficult indeed to generalize about the family. We can gain many insights by tracing the progression of developing human beings through the stages of the traditional family life cycle, but we must also recognize that an increasing number of individuals live and develop in families quite different from the traditional nuclear one. We must also appreciate that different individuals are affected differently by their experiences of any particular form of family life.

The Problem of Family Violence

As this chapter has illustrated, humans develop within a family context, and family relationships contribute positively to human development at every point in the life span. At the same time, families can be the cause of much anguish and of development gone astray. Nowhere is this more obvious than in cases of family violence.

Child abuse is perhaps the most visible form of family violence. Every day, infants, children, and adolescents are burned, bruised, beaten, starved, suffocated, sexually abused, or otherwise mistreated by their caretakers. About 3 million reports of child maltreatment are filed with social service agencies in the United States every year, and about one-third of them are substantiated as true (Emery & Laumann-Billings, 1998). Surveys reveal even higher rates, as much child abuse goes unreported. According to a national survey of U.S. families, for example, 11% of children had reportedly been kicked, bitten, hit, hit with an object, beaten up, burned, or threatened or attacked with a knife or gun by a parent in the past year (Wolfner & Gelles,

1993). Close to half a million youths are sexually abused each year (see Finkelhor & Dziuba-Leatherman, 1994; and see Chapter 11). Others are victims of psychological maltreatment—rejected, verbally abused, or terrorized by their parents (Wiehe, 1996). The largest proportion are neglected, deprived of the basic care and stimulation they need to develop normally.

Abuse of children by their caregivers is only one form of family violence, however. In all possible relationships within the family, the potential for violence exists. Multiple forms of abuse often occur within the same troubled families (Emery & Laumann-Billings, 1998). Children and adolescents batter, and in rare cases kill, their parents (Agnew & Huguley, 1989); siblings abuse one another in numerous ways (Cicirelli, 1995). And spouse abuse, rampant in our society, appears to be the most common form of family violence worldwide. An analysis of family violence in 90 nonindustrial societies by David Levinson (1989) revealed that wife beating occurs in 85% of them; in almost half of these societies, it occurs in most or all households, suggesting that it is an accepted part of family life. Although spouse abuse is viewed as intolerable in most segments of U.S. society, Murray Straus and Richard Gelles (1986, 1990) nonetheless estimate, based on surveys they have conducted, that 16 of 100 married couples in the United States experience some form of marital violence in a year's time—often "only" a shove or a slap, but violence nonetheless—and that almost 6% experience at least one instance of severe violence (such as kicking or beating). Much "mild" spouse abuse is mutual; in more serious cases, one spouse, usually the woman, is repeatedly terrorized and injured by a partner whose goal is control (M. P. Johnson & Ferraro, 2000).

Elderly adults are also targets of family violence. Frail or impaired older people are physically or psychologically mistreated, neglected, financially exploited, and stripped of their rights—most often by adult children or spouses serving as their caregivers (Conner, 2000; Lachs et al., 1997; Wolf, 2000). No one knows how many cases of elder abuse there are, but all agree that many go unreported. Cognitive impairment is an important risk factor (Lachs et al., 1997); in one sample of elderly adults with Alzheimer's disease, 5% had been physically abused by their caregivers in the year since they had been diagnosed (Paveza et al., 1992).

This is not a pretty picture. Here we have a social problem of major dimensions that causes untold suffering and harms the development of family members of all ages. What can be done to prevent it, or to stop it once it occurs? To answer this question, we must first try to gain some insight into why family violence occurs in the first place.

Why Does Family Violence Occur?

The various forms of family violence have many similarities. Because child abuse has been studied the longest, let's see what has been learned about the causes of child abuse.

The Abuser

Hard as it may be to believe, only about 1 child abuser in 10 appears to have a severe psychological disorder (Kempe &

Child abuse occurs in all ethnic and racial groups.

Kempe, 1978). Rather, the abusive parent most often is a young mother with many children who lives in poverty, is unemployed, and often has no spouse to share her load (Wiehe, 1996; Wolfner & Gelles, 1993). Yet child abusers come from all races, ethnic groups, and social classes. Many of them appear to be fairly typical, loving parents—except for their tendency to become extremely irritated with their children and to do things they will later regret.

A few reliable differences between parents who abuse their children and those who do not have been identified. First, abusive parenting, like effective parenting, tends to be passed from generation to generation; child abusers tend to have been abused as children (van IJzendoorn, 1992). Although most maltreated children do not abuse their own children when they become parents, roughly 30% do (Kaufman & Zigler, 1989). We do not know whether genes or environmental factors are primarily responsible for this intergenerational transmission. The "cycle of abuse" is not inevitable, however; it can be broken if abused individuals receive emotional support from parent substitutes, therapists, or spouses and are spared from severe stress as adults (Egeland, Jacobvitz, & Sroufe, 1988; Vondra & Belsky, 1993).

Second, abusive mothers are often battered women—victims of abuse in their romantic relationships (Coohey & Braun, 1997; McCloskey, Figueredo, & Koss,1995). As it turns out, adults are more likely to be in an abusive romantic relationship or marriage if they were abused or witnessed abuse as a child (Stith et al., 2000). It seems, then, that abusive mothers may have learned through their experiences as children and as wives that violence is the way to solve problems, or they may take out some of their frustrations on their children.

Third, abusers are often insecure individuals with low self-esteem. Their unhappy experiences in insecure attach-

ment relationships with their parents, reinforced by their negative experiences in romantic relationships, may lead them to formulate negative internal working models of themselves and others (Pianta, Egeland, & Erickson, 1989; and see Chapter 13). These adults may feel like victims but have also learned to be victimizers (Pianta et al., 1989).

Fourth, abusive parents seem to have unrealistic expectations about what children can be expected to do at different ages and have difficulty tolerating the normal behavior of young children (Haskett, Johnson, & Miller, 1994). For example, Byron Egeland and his colleagues (Egeland, 1979; Egeland, Sroufe, & Erickson, 1983) found that when infants cry to communicate needs such as hunger, nonabusive mothers correctly interpret these cries as signs of discomfort, but abusive mothers often infer that the baby is somehow criticizing or rejecting them.

In short, abusive parents tend to have been exposed to harsh parenting and abusive relationships themselves, have low self-esteem, and find caregiving more stressful, unpleasant, and ego-threatening than other parents do. Still, it has been difficult to identify a particular kind of person who is highly likely to turn into a child abuser. Could some children bring out the worst in parents?

THE ABUSED

An abusive parent often singles out only one child in the family as a target; this offers us a hint that child characteristics might matter (Gil, 1970). No one is suggesting that children are to *blame* for being abused, but some children do appear to be somewhat more at risk than others. For example, children who are hyperactive or difficult in some way are more likely to be abused than quiet, healthy, and responsive infants who are easier to care for (Ammerman & Patz, 1996; Sherrod et al.,

1984). Yet many difficult children are not mistreated, and many seemingly cheerful and easygoing children are.

Just as characteristics of the caregiver cannot fully explain why abuse occurs, then, neither can characteristics of children. There's now intriguing evidence that the *combination* of a high-risk parent and a high-risk child spells trouble. Specifically, the combination of a child who has a disability or illness or is otherwise difficult and a mother who feels powerless to deal with her child and overreacts emotionally when the child cannot be controlled increases the likelihood of abuse (Bugental, 2001). Parents who lack a sense of control as parents tend to feel threatened by children who are not responsive to them, become emotionally aroused, and may use force in a desperate attempt to establish that they have power after all (Bugental et al., 1999). However, even the match between child and caregiver may not be enough to explain abuse. We should, as always, consider the ecological context surrounding the family system.

THE CONTEXT

Quite consistently, abuse is most likely to occur when a parent is under great stress and has little social support (Egeland et al., 1983; Haskett et al., 1994). Life changes such as the loss of a job or a move to a new residence can disrupt family functioning and contribute to abuse or neglect (McLoyd et al., 1994; Wolfner & Gelles, 1993). Abuse rates are highest in deteriorating neighborhoods where families are poor, transient, socially isolated, and lacking in community services and informal social support. These high-risk neighborhoods are areas in which adults do not feel a sense of community and do not look after each other's children, neighborhoods in which the motto "It takes a village to raise a child" has little meaning (Korbin, 2001).

Finally, the larger *macroenvironment* is important. Ours is a violent society in which the use of physical punishment is common and the line between physical punishment and child abuse difficult to define (Whipple & Richey, 1997). Parents who believe strongly in the value of physical punishment are more at risk than those who do not to become abusive if they are under stress (Crouch & Behl, 2001). By contrast, child abuse is less common in societies that discourage physical punishment and advocate nonviolent ways of resolving interpersonal conflicts (Gilbert, 1997; Levinson, 1989). Child abuse is particularly rare in Scandinavian countries, where steps have been taken to outlaw corporal (physical) punishment of children, not only in the schools but at home (Finkelhor & Dziuba-Leatherman, 1994).

As you can see, child abuse is a complex phenomenon with a multitude of causes and contributing factors. It is not easy to predict who will become a child abuser and who will not, but abuse seems most likely to result when a vulnerable individual faces overwhelming stress with insufficient social support. Much the same is true of spouse abuse, elder abuse, and other forms of family violence.

What Are the Effects of Family Violence?

As you might imagine, child abuse is not good for child development. Physically abused and otherwise maltreated children tend to have many problems, ranging from physical injuries and cognitive and social deficits to behavior problems and psychological disorders (Margolin & Gordis, 2000). Shaking and other physically abusive behaviors can cause brain damage in infants and young children, and child neglect means receiving little of the intellectual stimulation from nurturing adults that contributes so much to intellectual growth (Eckenrode, Laird, & Doris, 1993). Not surprisingly, then, intellectual deficits and academic difficulties are common among mistreated children (Malinosky-Rummell & Hansen, 1993; Shonk & Cicchetti, 2001).

Behavior problems are also common among physically abused children. They tend to be explosively aggressive youngsters, rejected by their peers for that reason (Bolger & Patterson, 2001). Both physically abused and neglected children also tend to have emotional problems (Cicchetti & Barnett, 1991; McCloskey et al., 1995). Moreover, their behavior problems and emotional difficulties are likely to be long lasting: Adults who were abused as children tend to be violent, both inside and outside the family, and they have higher-than-average rates of depression, anxiety, and other psychological problems (Margolin & Gordis, 2000).

The social skills of many abused children are also deficient (Darwish et al., 2001). One of the most disturbing consequences of physical abuse is a lack of normal empathy in response to the distress of others. When Mary Main and Carol George (1985) observed the responses of abused and nonabused toddlers to the fussing and crying of peers, they found that nonabused children typically attended carefully to the distressed child, showed concern, and even attempted to provide comfort. As shown in Figure 15.4, not one abused child showed appropriate concern in this situation. Instead, abused toddlers were likely to become

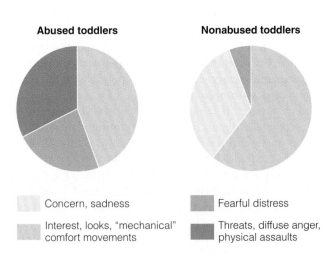

Figure 15.4 Responses to distressed peers observed in abused and nonabused toddlers in day care. Abused children distinguish themselves by a lack of concern and a tendency to become upset, angry, and aggressive when other children cry.

SOURCE: Adapted from Main & George (1985)

Battling Family Violence

The fact that family violence has many causes is discouraging. Where do we begin to intervene, and just how many problems must we correct before we can prevent or stop the violence and its damaging effects on development? Despite the complexity of the problem, progress has been made.

Consider first the task of preventing violence before it starts. This requires identifying high-risk families—a task that is greatly aided by the kinds of studies we have reviewed. For example, once we know that an infant is at risk for abuse because he or she is particularly irritable or unresponsive, it makes sense to help the child's parents appreciate the baby's positive qualities. Learning how to elicit smiles, reflexes, and other positive responses from premature infants makes parents more responsive to their babies, which in turn helps these at-risk babies develop more normally (Widmayer & Field, 1980).

Efforts to prevent abuse can also be directed at high-risk parents. Steven Schinke and his associates (1986), for example, decided to improve the coping techniques of one high-risk group of mothers—unwed and highly stressed teenagers. These mothers were taught problem-solving strategies, self-praise for handling difficult situations, communication skills (such as refusing unreasonable demands and requesting help), relaxation techniques, and even techniques for building stronger social support networks. Three months later, the mothers who had received the training outperformed the control group on several measures. They had improved their problem-solving skills, had established stronger social support networks, enjoyed higher self-esteem, and were more confident about their parenting skills.

Home visitation programs aimed at poor, young, single mothers at risk to become abusers are the approach of choice in the United States. A national home visitor program called Healthy Families America, launched in 1992, is now available in hundreds of communities (Emery & Laumann-Billings, 1998). The home visitors are trained paraprofessionals supervised by a social worker and health personnel; their goals are to help new parents become effective parents and to link them with appropriate community services. Such prevention programs have been shown to be effective, although they by no means eradicate abuse (Leventhal, 2001).

What about the parents who are already abusive? Here the problem is more complex. A couple of visits from a so-

cial worker are unlikely to solve the problem. A more promising approach is Parents Anonymous, a self-help program based on Alcoholics Anonymous that helps caregivers understand their problems and gives them the emotional support they often lack. However, Robert Emery and Lisa Laumann-Billings (1998) argue that the social service system needs to distinguish more sharply between milder forms of abuse, for which supportive interventions such as Parents Anonymous are appropriate, and severe forms, where it may be necessary to prosecute the abuser and protect children from injury and death by removing them from the home. Courts traditionally have been hesitant to break up families, but too often children known to have been abused are abused again.

Ultimately, a comprehensive approach is likely to be most effective. Abusive parents need emotional support and the opportunity to learn more effective parenting and coping skills, and the victims of abuse need day care programs and developmental training to help them overcome cognitive, social, and emotional problems caused by abuse (Oates & Bross, 1995; Wiehe, 1996). The ultimate goal in combating child abuse and other forms of family violence must be to convert a pathological family system into a healthy one.

Tony Freeman/PhotoEdit

angry and attack the crying child, reacting to the distress of peers much as their abusive parents react to their distress (see also Klimes-Dougan & Kistner, 1990).

> Martin (an abused boy of 32 months) tried to take the hand of the crying other child, and when she resisted, he slapped her on the arm with his open hand. He then turned away from her to look at the ground and began vocalizing very strongly, "Cut it out! CUT IT OUT!," each time saying it a little faster and louder. He patted her, but when she became disturbed by his patting, he retreated, hissing at her and baring his teeth. He then began patting her on the back again, his patting became beating, and he continued beating her despite her screams. (Main & George, 1985, p. 410)

Remarkable as it may seem, many other neglected and abused children turn out fine, especially if they have a close relationship with at least one nonabusive adult (Egeland et al., 1988). Without question, though, child abuse often has damaging long-term consequences for cognitive, social, and emotional development. The important question then becomes this: Knowing what we know about the causes and effects of abuse, what can be done to prevent it, stop it, and undo the damage? What would you propose? The Applications box on page 429 offers some solutions.

Summary Points

1. The family, whether it is nuclear or extended in form, is best viewed as a changing social system embedded in larger social systems that are also changing. The family systems, family development (family life cycle), and ecological perspectives must all be brought to bear to understand family processes. Social trends affecting family life today include greater numbers of single adults; the postponement of marriage; a decline in childbearing; more female participation in the labor force; more divorces, single-parent families, child poverty, and remarriages; more years with an empty nest; and more multigenerational families.

2. Infants affect and are affected by their parents. Compared to mothers, fathers are less involved in caregiving and more involved in rowdy play. Developmental outcomes are likely to be positive when *both* parents are involved with their children and have positive *indirect* effects on their children by virtue of their influence on each other.

3. Child rearing can be described in terms of the dimensions of acceptance/responsiveness and demandingness/control; generally, children are most socially and cognitively competent when their parents adopt an authoritative style of parenting, combining acceptance and demandingness, and less competent when their parents are authoritarian, permissive, or neglectful.

4. Lower-income parents tend to be more punitive and authoritarian than middle-class parents, due both to the demands of blue-collar jobs and to the negative effects of economic hardship on parenting. Ethnic differences in parenting also exist, and parenting styles can have different effects in different cultural contexts. However, authoritative parenting is generally effective across contexts.

5. Research related to the parent effects, child effects, and transactional models of family influence reminds us that children's problem behaviors are not always caused by ineffective parenting—that children's genes influence their behavior, which in turn influences the parenting they receive, which in turn influences their behavior.

6. When a second child enters the family system, mothers typically become less attentive to their firstborns, and firstborns find the experience stressful. Sibling relationships are characterized by rivalry *and* affection and provide emotional support, caregiving, and teaching.

7. Parent–child relationships typically remain close in adolescence but are renegotiated. Adolescents are most likely to gain autonomy and thrive when parents remain authoritative—that is, both supportive and appropriately demanding.

8. Marital satisfaction declines somewhat as newlyweds adjust to each other and declines still further as couples face the challenges of new parenthood. This phase is less stressful if the baby is easy, parents have relevant knowledge and coping skills, and resources such as spouse support are available. Marital satisfaction continues to decline during the child-rearing years and then often increases again after the empty nest transition, which most adults view more positively than negatively. Empty nest adults take pleasure in becoming grandparents, most often playing a companionate role rather than a remote or involved role.

9. Although marital satisfaction declines during the parenting years, especially among women, it is affected by many additional factors, including previous satisfaction, personality, and degree of similarity in personality.

10. In adulthood, siblings have less contact but normally continue to feel both emotionally close and rivalrous. Young adults often establish more mutual and intimate relationships with their parents. Middle-aged adults continue to experience mutually supportive relationships with their elderly parents rather than role reversal, though some, particularly daughters, do experience the stresses of middle generation squeeze and caregiver burden.

11. Among the adults whose lives are inadequately described by the traditional family life cycle concept are single adults (some of whom cohabitate), childless married couples (who usually enjoy high marital and life satisfaction), dual-career families (whose children typically are not damaged by a mother's working), and gay and lesbian adults (whose family patterns are diverse and whose children are generally no different from other children).

12. Divorce creates a crisis in the family for a year or two. Some children experience long-lasting social and academic problems, but factors such as financial support, quality of parenting, and social support influence adjustment. Most single-parent families adapt well to becoming part of a reconstituted family, but the transition is often hard, especially for girls.

13. Family violence occurs in all possible relationships within the family. Extensive research on child abuse indicates that parent characteristics such as a history of abuse and hypersensitivity to child behavior, child characteristics such as a difficult temperament, and contextual factors such as low social support and a deteriorating

neighborhood all contribute to the problem and must be considered in formulating solutions such as home visitor programs.

Critical Thinking

1. Your 16-year-old daughter's best friend has just called you from the police station to inform you that your daughter, drunk and high on marijuana, just plowed your car into a tree and is being cited for driving under the influence. You need to go to the police station. How will you respond to this situation, and what parenting style does your planned response reflect?

2. Martha, three months after her divorce, has become depressed and increasingly withdrawn. Her son Matt, age 7, has become a terror around the house and a discipline problem at school. From the perspective of (a) the parent effects model, (b) the child effects model, and (c) the transactional model of family influence, and referring to relevant research, how would you explain what is going on in this single-parent family?

3. Moose is a traditional man, Muffy a traditional woman. How are their experiences of the family life cycle, including new parenthood, the empty nest, middle generation squeeze, and grandparenthood, likely to differ?

Key Terms

family systems theory	parent effects model
nuclear family	child effects model
extended family household	transactional model
family life cycle	sibling rivalry
reconstituted family	autonomy
beanpole family	empty nest
indirect effects	modified extended family
acceptance/responsiveness	role reversal
demandingness/control	middle generation squeeze
authoritarian parenting	caregiver burden
authoritative parenting	cohabitation
permissive parenting	spillover effects
neglectful parenting	latchkey children

On the Web

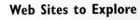

Web Sites to Explore

Divorce

This site contains selected materials from a college course on divorce, on topics such as the effects of divorce on children, co-parenting after a divorce, and interventions to help families cope.
http://www.hec.ohio-state.edu/famlife/divorce/desc.htm#readings

Child Abuse

For a wealth of information about child abuse, sexual abuse, and other forms of domestic violence, including statistics on the prevalence of abuse, try the site of the National Committee to Prevent Child Abuse.
http://www.childabuse.org/

Child Abuse and Neglect

The site of the National Clearinghouse on Child Abuse and Neglect Information is a rich source of information about the topic. It provides statistics, prevention approaches, and a searchable database.
http://www.calib.com/nccanch

Parents Anonymous

Parents Anonymous has chapters throughout the United States that offer support to parents in an effort to prevent child abuse and neglect. Here at the national Web site is a Network List that will help you find the Parents Anonymous organization in your state.
http://www.parentsanonymous-natl.org/

Grandparenthood

This site is designed to help grandparents get the most out of grandparenthood. It includes ideas on the roles grandparents play and how they can relate to their grandchildren, research on grandparenthood, and updates on legislation affecting grandparents (for example, regarding visitation rights).
http://www.grandparenting.org

Search Online with InfoTrac College Edition

For additional information, explore InfoTrac College Edition, your online library. Go to
http://www.infotrac-college.com
and use the passcode that came on the card with your book. You might search for "grandparents" to see what issues face grandparents today as more and more assume responsibility for the care of grandchildren. Alternatively, if you are interested in how parents can be optimally effective in raising adolescents, search for "parents and adolescents." Look in particular for research correlating parenting styles with adolescent outcomes such as school achievement and good adjustment.

Visit Our Web Site

Go to http://www.wadsworth.com/psychology, where you will find online resources directly linked to your book.

Life-Span CD-ROM

Go to the Wadsworth Life-Span CD-ROM for further study of the concepts in this chapter. The CD-ROM also includes quizzes and additional activities to expand your learning experience.

Developmental Psychopathology

PEGGY, A 17-YEAR-OLD FEMALE, was referred by her pediatrician to a child psychiatry clinic for evaluation of an eating disorder. She had lost 10 pounds in 2 months and her mother was concerned. . . . At the clinic she stated that she was not trying to lose weight, had begun to sleep poorly about 2 months ago unless she had several beers, and that she and friends "got trashed" on weekends. Her relationship with her parents was poor; she had attempted suicide a year previously with aspirin and was briefly hospitalized. The day before this evaluation she had taken a razor to school to try to cut her wrists, but it was taken away by a friend. She admitted being depressed and wanting to commit suicide and finally told of discovering that she was pregnant 4 months earlier. Her boyfriend wanted her to abort, she was ambivalent, and then she miscarried spontaneously about 2 months after her discovery. After that, "It didn't really matter how I felt about anything." (Committee on Adolescence, 1996, pp. 71–72)

We do not all have as many problems as Peggy, but it is the rare human being who makes it through the life span without having at least some difficulty adapting to the challenges of living. Each phase of life has its own unique challenges, and some of us inevitably run into trouble mastering them. This chapter is about some of the ways in which human development can go awry. It is about how development influences psychopathology and how psychopathology alters development. By applying knowledge of human development to the study of psychological disorders, we can understand them better. And by learning more about abnormal patterns of development, we can gain new perspectives on the forces that guide and channel—or block and distort—human development more generally.

What Makes Development Abnormal?

It is the job of clinical psychologists, psychiatrists, and other mental health professionals to decide who has a psychological disorder and who does not. They often apply three broad criteria in defining the line between normal and abnormal behavior and diagnosing psychological disorders:

1. **Statistical deviance.** Does the person's behavior fall outside the normal range of behavior? By this criterion, a mild case of the "blahs" or "blues" would not be diagnosed as clinical depression because it is so statistically common, but a more enduring, severe, and persistent case might be.
2. **Maladaptiveness.** Does the person's behavior interfere with personal and social adaptation or pose a danger to self or others? Psychological disorders disrupt functioning and create problems for the individual and/or other people.
3. **Personal distress.** Does the behavior cause personal anguish or discomfort? Many psychological disorders involve a good deal of personal suffering and are of concern for that reason alone.

Although these guidelines provide a start at defining abnormal behavior, they are not very specific. We must ask *which* forms of statistical deviation, *which* failures of adaptation, or *which* kinds of personal distress are significant.

DSM-IV Diagnostic Criteria

Professionals who diagnose and treat psychological disorders find more specific diagnostic criteria in the *Diagnostic and Statistical Manual of Mental Disorders,* published in 1994 by the American Psychiatric Association. The fourth edition of this manual, known as **DSM-IV,** spells out defining features and symptoms for the whole range of psychological disorders.

Because we will be looking closely at depression in this chapter, we will use it here as an example of how DSM-IV defines disorders. Depression is actually a family of several affective or mood disorders, some relatively mild and some severe. One of the most important is **major depressive disorder,** defined in DSM-IV as at least one episode of feeling profoundly depressed, sad, and hopeless, and/or losing interest in and the ability to derive pleasure from almost all activities, for at least two weeks (American Psychiatric Association, 1994). More specifically, a major depressive episode cannot be diagnosed unless the individual experiences at least five of the following symptoms, including one or the other of the first two, persistently during a two-week period:

1. Depressed mood (or irritable mood in children and adolescents) nearly every day
2. Greatly decreased interest or pleasure in usual activities
3. Significant weight loss or weight gain (or in children, failure to make expected weight gains)
4. Insomnia or too much sleeping
5. Psychomotor agitation or sluggishness/slowing of behavior
6. Fatigue and loss of energy
7. Feelings of worthlessness or extreme guilt
8. Decreased ability to concentrate or indecisiveness
9. Recurring thoughts of death, suicidal ideas, or a suicide attempt

By these criteria, a man suffering from major depression might, for example, feel extremely discouraged; no longer seem to care about his job or even about sexual relations with his wife; lose weight or have difficulty sleeping; speak and move very slowly, as though lacking the energy to perform even the simplest actions; have trouble getting his work done; dwell on how guilty he feels about his many failings; and even begin to think he would be better off dead. Major depressive disorder would *not* be diagnosed if this young man were merely a little "down," if his symptoms were directly due to drug abuse or a medical condition, or if he were going through the normal grieving process after the death of a loved one. Many more people experience depressive *symptoms* than qualify as having a clinically defined depressive *disorder*.

Although it does not say a great deal about them, DSM-IV notes that cultural and developmental considerations should be taken into account in making a diagnosis of major depressive disorder. For example, it indicates that Asians who are depressed tend to complain of bodily ailments such as tiredness rather than talking about their psychological symptoms (American Psychiatric Association, 1994). And although DSM-IV takes the position that depression in a child is fundamentally similar to depression in an adult, it notes that depressed children often express their depression by being irritable rather than sad.

In sum, the clinical approach to diagnosing a psychological disorder such as major depressive disorder involves consideration of the broad criteria of statistical deviance, maladaptiveness, and personal distress and also requires the application of specific diagnostic criteria such as those in DSM-IV. However, developmental scientists have felt the need for a far more developmental approach to psychological disorder—and have created one.

Developmental Psychopathology

Psychologists and psychiatrists have long brought major theories of human development to bear in attempting to understand and treat psychological disorders. Freudian psychoanalytic theory once guided most thinking about psychopathology and clinical practice; behavioral theorists have applied learning principles to the understanding and treatment of behavior problems; and cognitive psychologists have called attention to how individuals interpret their experiences and perceive themselves. More recently, evolutionary psychologists have begun asking interesting questions about the adaptive functions psychological disorders may serve in helping individuals to cope with abuse and other stressors (K. W. Fischer et al., 1997; Nesse, 2000).

In the past two decades, though, psychologists have become convinced of the need for a whole new field devoted to the study of abnormal behavior from a developmental perspective—**developmental psychopathology** (Cummings, Davies, & Campbell, 2000; Rutter & Sroufe, 2000). As defined by Alan Sroufe and Michael Rutter (1984), developmental psychopathology is the study of the origins and course of maladaptive behavior. Developmental psychopathologists are well aware of the need to evaluate abnormal behavior in relation to normal development; they seek to understand how the individual's level of development influences what disorders he or she is likely to display and how those problems are likely to be manifested as he or she develops. They are most interested in studying how psychological disorders originate and evolve over time and identifying causal pathways and mechanisms that lead to normal or abnormal adjustment later in life (Rutter & Sroufe, 2000).

PSYCHOPATHOLOGY AS DEVELOPMENT, NOT DISEASE

Some developmental psychopathologists fault DSM-IV and similar diagnostic systems for being rooted in a medical or disease model of psychopathology that views psychological problems as disease-like entities that people either "have" or do not have. Alan Sroufe (1997) argues that psychopathology is better seen as development than as disease; it is a pattern of adaptation that unfolds over time. Developmental psychopathologists also view psychological disorders not as defects that lie within the person but as the products of complex transactions between person and environment over time (Sameroff, 2000). They do not think one can understand psychological disorder without understanding not only the person's characteristics, developmental status, and history of adaptation but also those processes within his or her family and wider social context that either support or undermine healthy development (Cummings et al., 2000).

Figure 16.1 illustrates the concept of psychopathology as development. It portrays progressive branchings that lead development on either an optimal or a less-than-optimal course. Some individuals stay on a route to competence and good adjustment all along; some start out poorly but get back on a more adaptive course later; others start off well but deviate later; and still others start on a maladaptive course and deviate further and further from developmental norms as they get older because their early problems make them less able to master later developmental tasks and challenges. Different pathways can lead to the same outcome; any particular pathway can lead in multiple directions. Change is possible at many points, and the lines between normal and abnormal development are blurred. A developmental pathways model of this sort may seem complex, but it fits the facts of development.

CONSIDERING SOCIAL NORMS AND AGE NORMS

Developmental psychopathologists appreciate that behaviors are abnormal or normal only within particular social and developmental contexts (Cummings et al., 2000; Lopez & Guarnaccia, 2000). **Social norms** are the expectations about how to behave that prevail in a particular social context—whether a culture, subculture, or everyday setting. What is normal in one social context may be abnormal in another. For example, John Weisz and his colleagues (1997) have discovered that Thai children are more likely than American children to have (or to be reported to have) symptoms of inner distress such as anxiety and depression and are less likely to engage in aggression and other forms of "acting out." One reason for the difference may be that the Thai culture places high value on emotional control and socializes children to internalize rather than vent their negative emotions. Cases of refusal to go to school (school phobia) are climbing in Japan, where mothers place strong pressure on their children to succeed academically (Kameguchi & Murphy-Shigematsu, 2001). Both definitions and rates of abnormal behavior vary from culture to culture, from subculture to subculture, and from historical period to historical period. In a very real sense, abnormality is in the eye of a particular group of beholders.

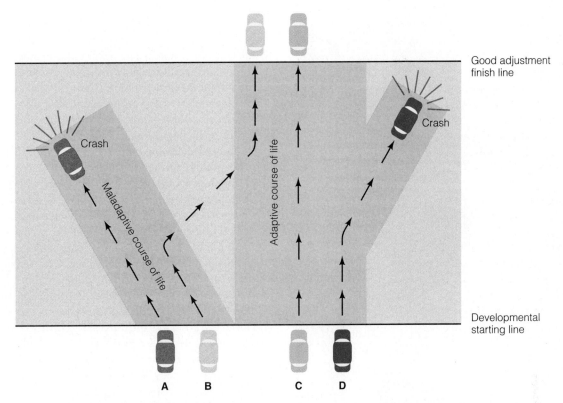

Figure 16.1 Developmental pathways leading to normal and abnormal outcomes. Some individuals start out on a maladaptive course and deviate even further from developmental norms as they get older (route A); some start out poorly but get back on a more adaptive course later (B); others stay on a route to competence and good adjustment all along (C); and still others start off well but deviate later in life (D).

SOURCE: Adapted from Sroufe (1997)

In addition, developmental psychopathologists recognize that abnormal behavior must be defined in relation to **age norms**—societal expectations about what behavior is appropriate or normal at various ages. This point is particularly important from a life-span developmental perspective. Is it abnormal for a 4-year-old girl to fear the dark? Not really; more than 90% of children report at least one specific fear like this (Kendall, 2000). Similarly, the 4-year-old boy who frequently cries, acts impulsively, wets his bed, is afraid of the dark, and talks to his imaginary friend may be perceived as—and may be—perfectly normal. Yet the 40-year-old who does the same things needs serious help! We simply cannot define abnormal behavior and development without having a solid grasp of *normal* behavior and development.

DEVELOPMENTAL ISSUES

As they attempt to understand developmental pathways associated with adaptive or maladaptive functioning, developmental psychopathologists grapple with the same developmental issues that have concerned us throughout this book—most notably, the nature–nurture issue and the issue of continuity and discontinuity in development. Addressing these issues involves asking important questions such as these:

- How do biological, psychological, and social factors interact over time to give rise to psychological disorders?
- What are the important risk factors for psychological disorders, and what are the protective factors that keep some individuals who are at risk from developing disorders?
- Are most childhood problems passing phases that have no bearing on adult adjustment, or does poor functioning in childhood predict poor functioning later in life?
- How do expressions of psychopathology change as the developmental status of the individual changes?

THE DIATHESIS/STRESS MODEL

In their efforts to understand how nature and nurture contribute to psychopathology, developmental psychopathologists have found a **diathesis/stress model** of psychopathology useful (see Coyne & Whiffen, 1995; R. E. Ingram & Price, 2001). This model proposes that psychopathology results from the interaction over time of a predisposition or vulnerability to psychological disorder (a diathesis that can involve a particular genetic makeup, physiology, cognitions, and/or personality) and the experience of stressful events. This model helps to explain why "'bad' things have 'bad' effects among

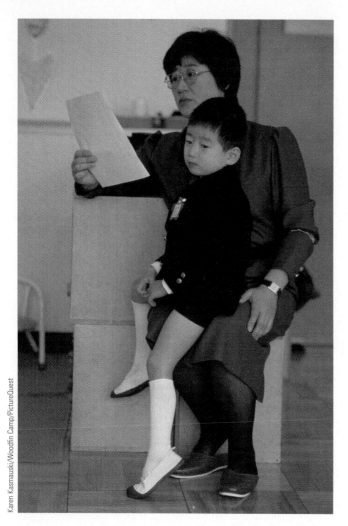

As Japanese mothers have increased pressure on their children to succeed in school, cases of children refusing to attend school have become more prevalent.

some—but not all—people, some—but not all—of the time" (Steinberg & Avenevoli, 2000).

Consider depression. We know that certain people are genetically predisposed to become depressed (Sullivan, Neale, & Kendler, 2000). Even in late adulthood, identical twins are more similar than fraternal twins in the extent to which they report symptoms of depression (Carmelli et al., 2000). A genetic vulnerability to depression manifests itself as imbalances in a number of key neurotransmitters that affect mood, as well as in such characteristics as high emotional reactivity to stress and self-defeating patterns of cognition in the face of negative events (Garber & Flynn, 2001). According to the diathesis/stress model, though, individuals who are predisposed to become depressed are not likely to do so unless they also experience significant losses or other stressful events, as illustrated in Figure 16.2. One stressful life event (such as the death of a loved one or a divorce) is usually not enough to trigger major depression, but when negative events pile up or everyday strains become overwhelming, a vulnerable person may succumb (Lieberman, 1983). Experiencing stressful or traumatic events in childhood can sensitize people to stress and lower the point at which stress triggers depression later in life (Hammen, Henry, & Daley, 2000). Meanwhile, individuals who do not have a diathesis—the genetic makeup or personality that makes them vulnerable to depression—may withstand high levels of stress and yet not become depressed. In short, depressive disorders—and many other psychological disorders as well—evolve from the ongoing interaction of person and environment, nature and nurture.

As Laurence Steinberg and Shelli Avenevoli (2000) note, we are unlikely to find specific relationships between particular environmental contexts and stressors and particular disorders. The same stressful events might make a person who is vulnerable to depression depressed, make a person who is vulnerable to aggression aggressive, and have no effect on a third

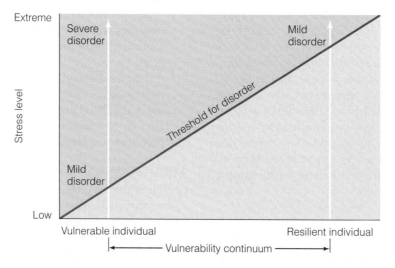

Figure 16.2 The diathesis/stress model. For a vulnerable individual, even mild stress can result in disorder, whereas for an individual who is resilient and does not have a vulnerability or diathesis to disorder, it would take extremely high levels of stress to cause disorder, and even then the disorder might be only mild and temporary.

Source: Adapted from Ingram & Price (2001)

person who does not have susceptibilities to psychological disorder. For some disorders we will examine in this chapter, the diathesis is strong and may be more important than environmental influences in causing a disorder. Environment may still play an important role, however, by shaping the course of the disorder and its ultimate impact on development (Steinberg & Avenevoli, 2000). The depressed adolescent growing up in a hostile, disturbed family context, for example, is likely to fare worse than the depressed adolescent who receives a good deal of parental support and appropriate professional treatment.

Questions about nature and nurture and about continuity and discontinuity must be answered, and diathesis/stress factors must be identified, if we want to understand the development of psychological disorders. This chapter highlights a sampling of developmental problems associated with each phase of the life span (for example, autism to illustrate disorders arising in infancy, anorexia nervosa to illustrate disorders associated with adolescence, and Alzheimer's disease to illustrate disorders of old age). In addition, we examine research on depression in *every* developmental period in order to see whether this widespread disorder is indeed the same phenomenon at any age or whether its symptoms and significance change over the life span.

The Infant

Adults worry about infants who do not eat properly, who cry endlessly, or who seem overly withdrawn and timid. Because infant development is strongly channeled by biological maturation, very few infants develop severe psychological problems. Yet psychopathology does exist in infancy, and its effects can be tragic.

Autism

Jeremy, three and a half years old, has big brown eyes and a sturdy body. His mother carries him down the corridor toward the examiner, who greets them. Jeremy glances at the examiner's face but does not smile or say hello. They walk together into a playroom. Jeremy's mother puts him down, and he sits on the carpet in front of some toys. He picks up two blocks, bangs them together, and begins to stack the blocks, one on top of the other, not stopping until he has used the entire set. Jeremy does not look at the examiner or his mother while he works, nor when he finishes. And he does not make a sound. The examiner asks him to give her a red block. He does not respond. On their way out, Jeremy and his mother stop to look at a poster of a waterfall surrounded by redwood trees. "Yosemite Valley," Jeremy reads out—the name beneath the picture. His voice sounds automated, almost robotic (Sigman & Capps, 1997, p. 1).

Autism, first identified and described by Leo Kanner in 1943, is a disorder that begins in infancy and is characterized by three core symptoms: impaired social interaction, deviant communication development, and repetitive, stereotyped behavior. It is part of a larger group of related disorders called *pervasive developmental disorders*—severe disorders that appear early in life and are associated with gross abnormalities in several areas of development (American Psychiatric Association, 1994). Autistic children are autistic before the age of 3. However, because at first they often seem to be exceptionally good babies, or because physicians are slow to make the diagnosis even when parents express concerns about their child's development, many autistic children are not diagnosed until age 6 or even later (Filipek et al., 2000). Efforts are now being made to improve early screening and detection so that children can receive early treatment. Autism affects at least 2–5 children per 10,000; it affects 4 times as many boys as girls (American Psychiatric Association, 1994).

To appreciate how very different the autistic child is from the normally developing one, picture the typical infant that we have described in this book: a very social being who responds to others and forms close attachments starting at 6 or 7 months of age, a linguistic being who babbles and later uses one- and two-word sentences to converse, and a curious being who is fascinated by new objects and experiences. Now consider the three defining features of autism highlighted in DSM-IV (American Psychiatric Association, 1994; also see Volkmar et al., 1999):

1. Deviant social development. Autistic children have difficulty forming normal social relationships, responding appropriately to social cues, and sharing social experiences with other people; like Jeremy, they live in a world of their own. They are far less likely than other infants to make eye contact, jointly attend to something with a social partner, seek other people for comfort, snuggle when held, and make friends. In stark contrast to normal children, autistic children seem to find social contact aversive rather than pleasurable. They also have difficulty reading others' emotions or responding with empathy when others are distressed. Although they can form attachments to their parents, and sometimes even secure ones, they often display what we referred to in Chapter 14 as a disorganized/disoriented pattern of attachment (Sigman & Capps, 1997).

2. Deviant language and communicative skills. Many autistic children are mute; others acquire limited language skills but cannot really carry on a conversation. As infants, autistic children often do not babble, gesture, or speak single words at the normal ages (Filipek et al., 2000). When they do speak, they may use a flat, robot-like tone; reverse pronouns (for example, use "you" to refer to the self); and engage in **echolalia** (a parroting back of what someone else says). Even those autistic children who have mastered basic sentence structure or grammar have difficulty using language in true give-and-take social exchanges (Tager-Flusberg, 2000).

3. Repetitive, stereotyped behavior. Autistic children have an obsessive need for sameness and can become terribly upset by novelty or change. They engage in stereotyped behaviors such as rocking, flapping their hands in front of their faces, or spinning toys, as though they were seeking sensory stimulation. They also become strongly attached to particular objects and highly distressed when their physical environment is altered (for example, when a chair in the living room is moved a few feet).

The autistic child's development is clearly *deviant,* or distorted, rather than merely delayed (Rutter & Schopler, 1987). Many people believe that autistic individuals are exceptionally intelligent. In fact, some have normal IQs, and some show special talents such as the ability to quickly calculate days of the week corresponding to dates on the calendar (see the discussion of *savant syndrome* in Chapter 9). However, about 80% of autistic children show some degree of mental retardation and display both the deviant behaviors associated with autism and the developmental delays associated with mental retardation (Volkmar et al., 1999). Individuals with autism vary greatly in the degree and nature of their deficits, and mild cases characterized by social and language deficits are increasingly being identified. It is now clear that there is a spectrum of autistic disorders (Brown, 2000). The condition is indeed pervasive; it impairs many aspects of development—cognitive, social, and emotional—sometimes severely. Yet some researchers now believe that many of the problems autistic children display may be rooted in a cognitive deficit.

SUSPECTED CAUSES

Most autistic children display a lack of understanding of mental states such as feelings, desires, beliefs, and intentions and of their role in human behavior—a lack of what was characterized in Chapter 13 as a *theory of mind* (see Baron-Cohen, 2000). As infants, they do not show some of the early precursors of theory of mind such as empathy for others, pointing and joint attention to objects and events with a social partner, pretend play, and imitation (Charman, 2000). As children, most do not appreciate that someone who believes that she left her running shoes in the hall closet will look for them

Many individuals with autism continue to function poorly as adolescents and adults, but some improve with age. One "improver," Jerry, described his childhood as a reign of "confusion and terror" in which "nothing seemed constant; everything was unpredictable and strange" (Bemporad, 1979, p. 192).

there and will be surprised if they are not there. Lacking a theory of mind, autistic children simply cannot conceive of someone's having a false belief that contradicts the facts of a situation. Indeed, they may not understand that people have beliefs, false or otherwise.

For a time, many researchers believed that lack of a theory of mind was *the* source of the social, emotional, and communicative problems autistic children display. Now researchers are not so sure: They note that autistic children are not so deficient on theory-of-mind tasks if they have good verbal ability (Yirmiya et al., 1996), and they have identified other cognitive deficits that may help explain autism (Baron-Cohen, 2000; Happé, 1994). Some believe that these children have a broader deficiency in their ability to engage in symbolic, or representational, thought—that the inability to represent people's mental states is only part of a larger problem. Other researchers think that autism is rooted in a deficit in **executive functions** (planning and organizational functions that reside in the prefrontal cortex of the brain), particularly the ability to integrate pieces of information into meaningful wholes (Perner & Lang, 2000). Whether lack of a theory of mind, a deficiency in symbolic thinking, poor executive or integrative abilities, or some other cognitive impairment will prove to be at the heart of the problems autistic children display, this disorder clearly involves a number of severe cognitive impairments.

What causes these impairments? We are not yet sure (A. Bailey, Phillips, & Rutter, 1996). Early theorists suggested that rigid and cold parenting by "refrigerator moms" caused autism, but this harmful myth has long been put to rest (Achenbach, 1982; Donenberg & Baker, 1993). It is now understood that parents and children influence each other reciprocally and that interacting with an autistic child can easily cause parents to be tense and frustrated.

The fact that autism is such a severe disorder present so early in life strongly suggests that it has a biological basis. Indeed, many autistic children, though not all, display neurological abnormalities, and up to a third of them develop epilepsy (Bailey et al., 1996; Hooper & Tramontana, 1997). However, the neurological abnormalities are varied, and it is not clear which are most central to autism or how they arise. Some attention has centered on disruption of the development of the cerebellum and limbic system during prenatal development and on high levels of the neurotransmitters serotonin and norepinephrine (Scott, Clark, & Brady, 2000). Ever since it became known that the mothers of some autistic infants took the drug thalidomide as a tranquilizer early in their pregnancies, Patricia Rodier (2000) has been pursuing the hypothesis that autism is caused by a disruption of the development of the brain stem during the prenatal period. The brain stem controls basic functions such as disengaging from one stimulus to attend to a new stimulus; autistic children, as it happens, have abnormalities of the brain stem and tend to fixate on particular stimuli for long periods of time. Some autistic children also have slight physical abnormalities of the ear, abnormal eye movements, and other problems that would be consistent with abnormal development of the brain stem, whether caused by an external agent such as thalidomide or malfunctioning genes.

Genes clearly contribute to autism (J. L. Ingram et al., 2000; Rodier, 2000). One research team found that, if one identical twin was autistic, the other was autistic in 60% of the twin pairs studied; the concordance rate for fraternal twin pairs was 0% (A. Bailey et al., 1995). Moreover, when the broader spectrum of autism-related cognitive, linguistic, and social deficits was considered, 92% of the identical twins but only 10% of the fraternal twins were concordant. One gene—a variant of a gene called HOXA1—is capturing much attention because many, though not all, individuals with autism have it. What's more, HOXA1 is known to be involved in the development of the brain stem, supporting Rodier's hypothesis about the role of abnormal brain stem development in autism (Ingram et al., 2000).

The fact that not all autistic individuals have the HOXA1 gene (and that individuals who are not autistic have it) and the fact that one identical twin can be autistic though the other is not suggest that early environmental influences also contribute to at least some cases of the disorder, although it is not clear how. It seems very unlikely that one, clear-cut biological defect will be found that can explain all cases of autism. Instead, autism is a complex spectrum of disorders associated with many neurological and behavioral problems.

DEVELOPMENTAL OUTCOMES

What becomes of autistic children as they get older? The long-term outcome has usually been poor, undoubtedly because autism is such a pervasive and severe disorder and because it is so often accompanied by mental retardation. Many autistic individuals improve over the years, but most are autistic for life, showing limited social skills even as adults and continuing to depend on their parents or others for help (Bristol et al., 1996; Howlin, Mawhood, & Rutter, 2000). Positive outcomes are most likely among those who have normal IQ scores and who can communicate using speech before they are 6 years old (Gillberg & Steffenburg, 1987).

Can treatment help autistic children overcome their problems? Researchers continue to search for drugs that will correct the suspected brain dysfunctions of these children, but they are a long way from discovering a "magic pill." Some autistic children are given drugs to control behavior problems such as hyperactivity or obsessive-compulsive behavior. These medications can help such individuals benefit from educational programs, but they do nothing to cure autism (Volkmar, 2001).

At present, the most effective approach to treating autism is intensive and highly structured behavioral and educational programming, beginning as early as possible, continuing throughout childhood, and involving the family (Connor, 1998; Koegel, Koegel, & McNerney, 2001; Volkmar et al., 1999). O. Ivar Lovaas and his colleagues pioneered the use of reinforcement principles to shape social and language skills in autistic children and have had startling success. In one study, Lovaas (1987) compared two groups of autistic children treated at UCLA. Nineteen children received intensive treatment—more than 40 hours a week of one-on-one treatment for two or more years during their preschool years. Trained student therapists worked with these children using reinforce-

ment principles to reduce their aggressive and self-stimulatory behavior and to teach them developmentally appropriate skills such as how to imitate others, play with toys and with peers, use language, and master academic concepts. The training procedures involve many repetitions of simple learning tasks and the delivery of reinforcers such as bits of cereal for successful performance. Parents were taught to use the same behavioral techniques at home, and these children were mainstreamed into preschools that served normal children. The children who received this intensive treatment were compared with similarly disturbed children who, because of staff shortages or transportation problems, received a similar treatment program but were exposed to it for only 10 or fewer hours a week.

In the intensively trained group, all but two children scored in the mentally retarded range on tests of intellectual functioning at the start. Yet by age 6 or 7, their IQ scores averaged 83—about 30 points higher than the average in the control group. Moreover, 9 of the 19—47 percent—not only had average or above-average IQ scores at follow-up but had been mainstreamed into regular first-grade classes and were adapting well. At age 13, 8 of the 19 treated students were still within the normal range of both IQ and school adjustment (Lovaas, Smith, & McEachin, 1989). In contrast, children in the comparison group displayed the usual intellectual deficits of autism, and most attended special classes for autistic and retarded children.

Some researchers have criticized this study's design (notice that it was not a true experiment with random assignment to treatment groups) and are not convinced that early behavioral interventions can achieve such stunning results (Gresham & MacMillan, 1998). However, other evidence reinforces the conclusion that some autistic children, especially those who are young and not severely retarded, have a good deal of potential if they receive intensive cognitive and behavioral training and comprehensive family services starting early in life (Connor, 1998). It may be especially important to motivate autistic children to initiate social interactions so that they do not miss out on important social learning experiences (Koegel et al., 2001).

In sum, autism is one of the most vivid examples we have of human development gone awry. The profound problems that autistic children display in their social interactions, language development, and responses to the physical environment make it clear that their development is deviant and not merely delayed. Moreover, most of them remain disordered, at least to some extent, throughout their lives. Yet we can be encouraged by recent reports of the long-term benefits of early behavioral intervention, and we can also hope that researchers will better pinpoint the brain dysfunctions and cognitive impairments responsible for this disorder and develop effective treatments to correct them.

Depression

Does it seem possible to you that an infant could experience major depressive disorder as defined by clinicians? Infants are surely not capable of the negative cognitions that are common

Failure to Thrive

Infants diagnosed as having *failure to thrive* have, by definition, failed to grow normally. They also show many of the symptoms of depression, as well as delays in their cognitive and social development and bizarre behaviors such as drinking from toilets (Bauchner, 1996; Green, 1986). In some

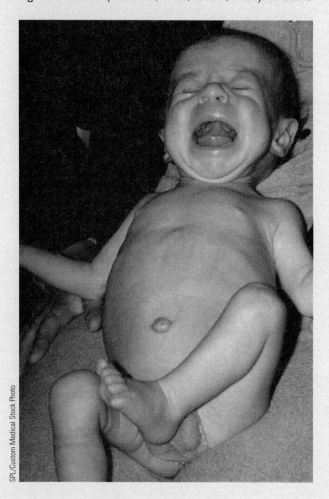

SPL/Custom Medical Stock Photo

cases, an organic or biological cause, such as an illness, a heart defect, or difficulties in the sensory and motor skills involved in feeding and swallowing, can be identified (Wright & Birks, 2000; Creskoff & Haas, 1999). In other cases, labeled nonorganic failure to thrive, the causes seem to be emotional rather than physical. To illustrate, a normally developing boy whose mother was coping with marital problems and an unwanted pregnancy became the target of his mother's resentment when the father walked out on her. Soon this infant was a 13-month-old who was about the size of the average 7-month-old, whereas his fraternal twin sister grew at a normal rate (L. J. Gardner, 1972).

Other infants with nonorganic failure to thrive have mothers who are stressed, depressed, and socially isolated, mothers whose own mothers were emotionally unresponsive or even abusive to them (Gorman, Leifer, & Grossman, 1993). These women tend to neglect their babies, interact in insensitive ways with them, and express tension and anger rather than affection in their interactions (Black et al., 1994; Hutcheson, Black, & Starr, 1993). They have had unresolved losses and are insecure in their relationships; their babies are similarly insecure, often displaying a disorganized pattern of attachment in which they seems confused about how to relate to attachment figures (Ward, Lee, & Lipper, 2000).

Babies with nonorganic failure to thrive gain weight and overcome their depression-like emotional symptoms almost immediately when they are removed from their homes (Bauchner, 1996). They tend to relapse if they are returned to parents who have not been helped to become more emotionally responsive. Some of these children then remain smaller than normal and display long-term social and intellectual deficits (Bauchner, 1996; Heffer & Kelley, 1994). Their outcomes are especially poor if they have a history of both failure to thrive and maltreatment (Kerr, Black, & Krishnakumar, 2000).

among depressed adults—the low self-esteem, guilt, worthlessness, hopelessness, and so on (Garber, 1984). After all, they have not yet acquired the capacity for symbolic thought that would allow them to reflect on their experience. Yet infants *can* exhibit some of the behavioral symptoms (loss of interest in activities, psychomotor slowing) and **somatic symptoms** (bodily symptoms such as loss of appetite and disruption of normal sleep patterns) of depression. Researchers are still debating whether true depressive disorders can occur in infancy, but it is clear that babies can and do experience *depression-like* states and symptoms (Cytryn & McKnew, 1996).

Depressive symptoms are most likely to be observed in infants who lack a secure attachment relationship or who experience a disruption of an all-important emotional bond (Boris & Zeanah, 1999; Cytryn & McKnew, 1996). Infants who are permanently separated from their mothers between 6 and 12 months of age tend to become sad, weepy, listless, unresponsive, and withdrawn and to show delays in virtually all aspects of their development (Spitz, 1946). Abused and neglected infants sometimes show similar symptoms (Zeanah, Boris, & Scheeringa, 1997). Infants who show a disorganized pattern of attachment, in which they do not seem to know whether to approach or avoid the attachment figure (see Chapter 14)—an attachment style common among abused children—are especially at risk (Boris & Zeanah, 1999).

Infants whose mothers are depressed are also at risk. As infants, they adopt an interaction style that resembles that of their depressed caregivers; they vocalize very little and look sad, even when interacting with women other than their mothers, and they begin to show developmental delays by the age of 1 (Field, 1995). They are at increased risk of becoming clinically depressed themselves later in life and of developing other psychological disorders as well. This may be due to a combination of genetic endowment and stressful experiences with their unpredictable mothers (that is, to diathesis/stress). The outcome is that these babies are easily distressed and unable to regulate their negative emotions effectively (Dawson & Ashman, 2000; Goodman & Gotlib, 1999). Moreover, these children are likely to interact with their own children in a negative manner, increasing the chances that depression will be passed on to still another generation (Whitbeck et al., 1992). Interventions designed to help depressed mothers appreciate and interact more sensitively with their babies can help to prevent these outcomes (Gelfand et al., 1996).

Some infants who are neglected, abused, separated from attachment figures, or otherwise raised in a stressful or unaffectionate manner may develop the life-threatening disorder called **failure to thrive.** These youngsters fail to grow normally, lose weight, and become seriously underweight for their age. They are the subject of the Explorations box on page 440.

In sum, even babies can display many of the symptoms of depression. Although young infants do not have the cognitive capacity to think depressive thoughts, they can show many of the behavioral and somatic symptoms of "adult" depression. They can also experience disruptions of their psychological development or a failure to thrive if they experience long-term or permanent separation from their attachment figures or are brought up by depressed, unresponsive, or rejecting caregivers.

The Child

Many children experience developmental problems of one sort or another—fears, recurring stomachaches, temper tantrums, and so on. A much smaller proportion are officially diagnosed as having one of the psychological disorders that typically begins in infancy, childhood, or adolescence—or as having one of the psychological disorders (such as major depressive disorder) that can occur at any age. Table 16.1 lists major childhood disorders as categorized in DSM-IV.

Many developmental problems can also be placed in one or the other of two broad categories that reflect whether the child's behavior is out of control or overly inhibited (Achenbach & Edelbrock, 1978). When children have **externalizing problems,** or *undercontrolled disorders,* they "act out" in ways that disturb other people and place them in conflict with social expectations. They may be aggressive, disobedient, difficult to control, or disruptive (see Chapter 13 on aggressive behavior). If their problems are severe, they may be diagnosed as having a conduct disorder or as hyperactive. **Internalizing problems,** or *overcontrolled disorders,* involve inner distress; they are more disruptive to the child than to other people and include anxiety disorders (such as persistent worrying about separation from loved ones), phobias, severe shyness and withdrawal, and depression. Externalizing behaviors decrease with age from 6 to 17, whereas internalizing difficulties increase (Crijnen, Achenbach, & Verhulst, 1997). Externalizing problems are more common among boys, whereas internalizing problems are more prevalent among girls—across cultures (Crijnen et al., 1997). To give you a feel for these two categories of childhood disorder, we will look at one problem of externalization or undercontrol—hyperactivity—and one problem of internalization or overcontrol—depression.

Attention-Deficit Hyperactivity Disorder

Even at age 6, Zach was, according to each of his parents, "unpredictable" and "antsy." His mother, a real estate

Table 16.1 Some Psychological Disorders Usually First Diagnosed in Infancy, Childhood, or Adolescence

DSM Category	Major Examples
Mental retardation	Subaverage general intellectual functioning
Learning disorders	Reading, math, and writing disorders
Motor skill disorder	Developmental coordination disorder (extreme clumsiness, lack of coordination)
Communication disorders	Expressive language disorder; stuttering
Pervasive developmental disorders	Autism and similarly severe conditions
Attention-deficit and disruptive behavior disorders	Attention-deficit hyperactivity disorder; conduct disorders (persistent antisocial behavior); oppositional defiant disorder
Feeding and eating disorders	Pica (eating nonnutritive substances such as paint or sand)
Tic disorders	Tourette's disorder (involuntary grimaces, grunts, foul language)
Elimination disorders	Enuresis (inappropriate urination); encopresis (inappropriate defecation)

Source: Based American Psychiatric Association (1994)

agent, reported that "he's always on the go, but I'm not always sure where he is going. He's into so many things." Zach's father, an attorney for a large firm, described Zach as "rash and impetuous" and "having his engine running constantly." Both parents were distressed when Zach's school performance suffered because of his impulsivity and poor attention. (Kendall, 2000, p. 65)

When it was first identified, hyperactivity was defined principally as a problem of excess motor activity, and the term was used to describe children who could not seem to sit still and were continually on the go. Now hyperactivity is viewed as first and foremost a problem of *attention.* According to DSM-IV criteria, a child has **attention-deficit hyperactivity disorder (ADHD)** if some combination of these three symptoms is present (and see Weyandt, 2001):

1. **Inattention**—for example, the child does not seem to listen, is easily distracted, and does not stick to activities or finish tasks
2. **Impulsivity**—for example, the child acts before thinking and cannot inhibit an urge to blurt something out in class or have a turn in a group activity
3. **Hyperactivity**—perpetual fidgeting, finger tapping, chattering, and restlessness

About 3–5% of school-age children, possibly more, are diagnosable as ADHD (American Psychiatric Association, 1994). There are three boys for every girl with ADHD. Some critics believe that ADHD is overdiagnosed in the United States. It is indeed more common here than in some countries, but it is reported throughout the world, and rates are consistently higher for boys than for girls (Luk, 1996).

Some children with attention-deficit hyperactivity disorder, many of them girls, are mainly inattentive but not hyperactive and impulsive; they are not disruptive but they often have difficulty in school (Weyandt, 2001). Those children with ADHD who are predominantly hyperactive and impulsive as well as inattentive are often diagnosed as having conduct disorders or other externalizing problems as well. They are likely to irritate adults and become locked in coercive power struggles with their parents, interactions that only aggravate their problems (Barkley et al., 1991; Buhrmester et al., 1992). Because their behavior is so disruptive, they are also rejected by peers, which can have its own damaging effects on their adjustment and later development (Deater-Deckard, 2001; Whalen et al., 1989).

Not only do many children with ADHD have conduct disorders and behave aggressively, but many also have diagnosable learning disabilities, and some suffer from depression or anxiety disorders (Biederman et al., 1996; Silver, 1992). This co-occurrence of two or more conditions in the same individual is called **comorbidity** and is extremely common. Many troubled individuals of all ages have multiple psychiatric diagnoses rather than just one (L. A. Clark, Watson, & Reynolds, 1995). Comorbidity complicates the task of understanding the causes and consequences of any particular psychological disorder.

DEVELOPMENTAL COURSE

ADHD expresses itself in somewhat different ways at different ages. The condition often reveals itself first in infancy. As infants, children with ADHD are often very active, have difficult temperaments, or show irregular feeding and sleeping patterns (Teeter, 1998). As preschool children, they are in perpetual motion, quickly moving from one activity to another. Since most young children are energetic and have short attention spans, behavior must be evaluated in terms of developmental norms; otherwise, we might well mistake most average 3- and 4-year-olds for hyperactive children! Finally, by the grade school years, overactive behavior is less of a problem, but children with ADHD are fidgety, restless, and inattentive to schoolwork (American Psychiatric Association, 1994).

What becomes of hyperactive children later in life? It used to be thought that hyperactive children outgrew their problems, so parents sometimes delayed getting help, expecting their children's difficulties to go away by adolescence (Kendall, 2000). Most children with ADHD do outgrow their overactive behavior, but most continue to have difficulty concentrating, and many display adjustment difficulties throughout the life span (Wender, 1995; Weyandt, 2001). Adolescents with ADHD tend to be restless, may have difficulty attending to their academic work, and may continue to behave impulsively; they often perform poorly in school or drop out altogether, and they are prone to commit reckless delinquent acts without thinking about the consequences (M. Fischer et al., 1990; Wallander & Hubert, 1985). The picture is more positive by early adulthood; most individuals with ADHD seem to adjust better to the workplace than they did to school (Wallander & Hubert, 1985). Yet many get in trouble because they have lapses of concentration, make impulsive decisions, and procrastinate (Wender, 1995). And, especially if they had conduct disorders along with ADHD as children, they are also likely to have more than their share of car accidents and law breaking, to abuse alcohol and drugs, and to have emotional problems as adults (Greene et al., 1997; Weiss & Hechtman, 1993).

SUSPECTED CAUSES

What causes this disorder? Researchers agree that ADHD has a neurological basis, but they have had difficulty pinpointing it (Hooper & Tramontana, 1997; Weyandt, 2001). No consistent evidence of brain damage or structural defects in the brain is found in most children with ADHD. Many cannot even be distinguished cleanly from non-ADHD children on the basis of neuropsychological tests because they do not all show clear deficits in neuropsychological functions or show them in the same areas (Doyle et al., 2000). Still, it is widely agreed that the brains of children with ADHD process stimulation differently than the brains of other children do, and that the cause is most likely subtle differences in brain chemistry rather than physical brain damage.

Russell Barkley has put forth the view that the frontal lobes of individuals with ADHD do not function properly, resulting in deficiencies in the *executive functions* that allow us to plan and control our behavior and to inhibit unwise responses (Barkley, 1997, 2000; Weyandt, 2001). Abnormal functioning in area of the brain involved in regulating motor behavior has also been detected. Underactivity in this brain area seems to predict well the problems that children with ADHD have sitting still and performing well on attention tasks; moreover, these problems can be corrected if the child is given stimulant medication (Teicher et al., 2000). Several different abnormalities in neurotransmitters may be involved, and very possibly different individuals have different biochemical abnormalities (Weyandt, 2001).

Similarly, nature and nurture may contribute differently to the origins of neurological abnormalities in different cases (Cantwell, 1996). We know that some individuals are genetically predisposed to develop ADHD; one identical twin is highly likely to have it if the other does, and adoptive relatives of a child with ADHD are less likely to have ADHD than biological relatives are (Levy et al., 1997; Sprich et al., 2000). There is not one ADHD gene, however; instead, there appear to be different forms of ADHD and different genetic makeups associated with each (Todd, 2000).

Environmental factors also enter in, often not so much as the main cause of ADHD but as forces that help determine whether the individual adapts well or poorly as he or she develops. Low birth weight and prenatal exposure to nicotine, both of which are associated with a shortage of oxygen prenatally, appear to contribute to some cases of ADHD (Bradley & Golden, 2001). An intrusive, highly controlling parenting style may also contribute to, or at least aggravate, the problem in some cases; when parents are highly intrusive, infants and young children may not learn to regulate their own emotions and behavior effectively (Jacobvitz & Sroufe, 1987; Sroufe, 1997). Family risk factors such as marital conflict and socioeconomic disadvantage may worsen the outcomes of children with ADHD (Biederman et al., 1995), whereas providing them with structured learning opportunities and appropriate reinforcement at home and at school can greatly improve their outcomes (Teeter, 1998; Weyandt, 2001).

Are you one of the many people who believe that hyperactivity is caused by food additives such as red food coloring? High sugar intake? If so, your beliefs are largely incorrect. Although a minority of children with ADHD have allergic reactions to food additives, carefully controlled studies in which children and their families do not know whether they are getting a diet with food additives or a diet without them show that food additives have little effect on most children with ADHD (Bradley & Golden, 2001; Harley et al., 1978). Similarly, having hyperactive boys drink sugary drinks, as compared to drinks containing the sugar substitute aspartame, has no effect on their behavior or learning performance (Milich & Pelham, 1986). All in all, ADHD is still not well understood, but it most likely has a number of both genetic and environmental causes and contributors, and its developmental course can take many forms.

TREATMENT

What can be done to help individuals with ADHD? Many are given stimulant drugs such as methylphenidate (Ritalin), and

CLOSE TO HOME   JOHN McPHERSON

"He does not have a discipline problem! He's just had a little too much sugar, that's all."

Consuming too much sugar does *not* cause ADHD.

70% or so are helped by these drugs (Cantwell, 1996). Although it may seem odd to give overactive children drugs that increase their heart rates and activity levels, stimulants make children with ADHD—and non-ADHD children and adults as well, something that physicians do not always understand—better able to focus their attention (Kendall, 2000).

Why, then, does controversy surround the use of stimulants with ADHD children? Some critics feel that these drugs are prescribed to too many children, including some who do not really have ADHD. Other skeptics are concerned that stimulants are now being prescribed to preschool children, despite little research on their effects on development. One team of researchers identified 223 children age 3 or younger in Michigan who had been diagnosed with ADHD and found that more than half of them received medication—not just stimulants but a variety of other medications as well (Rappley et al., 1999). While it is probably true that Ritalin and other stimulants are overprescribed in some communities, other evidence suggests that many ADHD children who could benefit from drug treatment go untreated (Jensen, 2000). Other opponents of stimulant drug treatment are concerned that these drugs have undesirable side effects such as loss of appetite and headaches and do not really correct the central problems that individuals with ADHD face or improve their academic and social functioning in the long run (Riddle, Kastelic, & Frosch, 2001). It is true that stimulants improve functioning only temporarily until their effects wear off at the end of the day

(Schachar et al., 1997). And so far, there is not much evidence that individuals with ADHD who took stimulants as children are better off as adolescents or adults than those who did not (Hart et al., 1995). Many experts have concluded that drugs should be prescribed with caution and that drugs alone cannot resolve all the difficulties faced by individuals with ADHD and their families.

What, then, is the best approach to treatment? The recently completed Multimodal Treatment of Attention-Deficit Hyperactivity Disorder Study, a national study of 579 children with ADHD ranging in age from 7 to 9, is our best source of information about the pros and cons of medication and behavioral treatment for ADHD (Jensen et al., 2001). This study compared children who received optimally delivered medication, state-of-the-art behavioral treatment (a combination of parent training, child training through a summer program, and a school intervention), a combination of the two approaches, or routine care in the community. The findings were quite clear: Medication alone is more effective than behavioral treatment alone or routine care in reducing ADHD symptoms. However, a combination of medication and behavioral treatment was superior to medication alone when the goal was defined as not only reducing ADHD symptoms but improving academic performance, social adjustment, and parent–child relations. So, medication is indeed effective, but it can be even more so if supplemented by behavioral programs designed to teach children with ADHD to stay focused on tasks and to control their impulsiveness, and by parent training designed to help parents understand and manage the behavior of these often-difficult youngsters. It is also essential that psychiatrists monitor doses closely and bear in mind that "children are not small adults" when it comes to drug dosages (Riddle et al., 2001).

In sum, attention-deficit hyperactivity disorder interferes with cognitive, social, and emotional development from the early years of life into the adult years. A difficult infant may become an uncontrollable and overactive preschooler, an inattentive grade school student, a low-achieving and delinquent adolescent, and even an impulsive and restless adult. Many children with ADHD do adapt well later in life, but perhaps even more will do so as we learn more about the causes of this disorder and develop pharmacological and psychological treatments that achieve longer-lasting effects.

Depression

As we saw earlier, the depression-like symptoms displayed by deprived or traumatized infants probably do not qualify as major depressive disorder. When *can* children experience true clinical depression, then? For years many psychologists and psychiatrists, especially those influenced by psychoanalytic theory, argued that young children simply could not be depressed. Feelings of worthlessness, hopelessness, and self-blame were not believed to be possible until the child formed a strong superego, or internalized moral standards (Garber, 1984). When it was finally appreciated that even very young children *could* become depressed, some researchers argued

that childhood depression is qualitatively different from adult depression (Cytryn & McKnew, 1996). Children, it was said, display **masked depression,** or depression in the guise of symptoms such as aggression or anxiety, problems other than those we associate directly with depression (Quay, Routh, & Shapiro, 1987).

We now know that young children—as early as age 3—can meet the same criteria for major depressive disorder that are used in diagnosing adults (Garber & Flynn, 2001). Depression in children is rarer than depression in adolescents and adults, but an estimated 2% of children have diagnosable depressive disorders (Gotlib & Hammen, 1992). Many youngsters who show the key symptoms of depression *do* have comorbid problems such as conduct disorder, ADHD, and anxiety disorder. These disorders are distinct problems, though, not just veiled symptoms of depression (Kaslow et al., 2000). Anxiety and depression are particularly likely to co-occur. Often, the anxiety precedes the depression developmentally and may contribute to it, not only in children but in adolescents and adults (Zahn-Waxler, Klimes-Dougan, & Slattery, 2000).

Although the concept of masked depression in childhood is faulty, there is some truth to the idea that depression expresses itself somewhat differently in a young child than in an adult (Garber & Flynn, 2001). Depressed preschool children are more likely to display the behavioral and somatic symptoms of depression (losing interest in activities, eating poorly, and so on) than to display cognitive symptoms (hopelessness, excessive guilt) or to talk about being depressed (American Psychiatric Association, 1994; Kaslow et al., 2000). Some become irritable, but others withdraw quietly to their rooms and cry and may not even be noticed. Even school-age children often show their depression more clearly in what they do than in what they say. But in late elementary school, depressed children begin to express more cognitive symptoms of depression such as low self-esteem, hopelessness, and self-blame. One 11-year-old child said "The devil is in me"; another claimed "I'm a burden on the family" (Kosky, 1983, p. 459).

The message is clear: Parents and other adults need to become more aware that childhood is not always a happy, care-free time and that children *can* develop serious depressive disorders. Indeed, children as young as age 2 or 3 are capable of attempting suicide (Rosenthal & Rosenthal, 1984; Shaffer & Pfeffer, 2001). At age 3, Jeffrey repeatedly hurled himself down a flight of stairs and banged his head on the floor; upset by the arrival of a new brother, he was heard to say "Jeff is bad, and bad boys have to die" (Cytryn & McKnew, 1996, p. 72). An 8-year-old, after writing out her will, approached her father with a large rock and asked in all seriousness, "Daddy, would you crush my head, please?" (Cytryn & McKnew, 1996, pp. 69–70). Other children have jumped from high places, run into traffic, and stabbed themselves, often in response to abuse, rejection, or neglect. Suicide attempts in childhood are very rare, but the rates are climbing, and they may not tell the whole story because some apparent accidents may actually be suicide attempts (Cytryn & McKnew, 1996). Moreover, children who attempt suicide once often try again (Shaffer & Pfeffer, 2001).

Again, the moral is clear: Children's claims that they want to die should be taken seriously.

Do depressed children tend to have recurring bouts of depression, becoming depressed adolescents and adults? Most children do get through mild episodes of sadness. However, 5- and 6-year-olds who report many depression symptoms are more likely than their peers to be depressed, to think suicidal thoughts, to struggle academically, and to be perceived as in need of mental health services when they are adolescents (Ialongo, Edelsohn, & Kellam, 2001). Moreover, it is estimated that half of children and adolescents diagnosed as having major depressive disorder have recurrences in adulthood (Kessler, Avenevoli, & Merikangas, 2001). Even if they do not have further episodes, the depression these children experience can disrupt their intellectual development and school achievement as well as their social adjustment for years to come (Kovacs & Goldston, 1991).

Fortunately, most depressed children respond well to psychotherapy; cognitive-behavioral therapies that focus on changing distorted thinking have proven especially effective (Asarnow, Jaycox, & Tompson, 2001). Because children are not adults, though, treating children with depression and other psychological disorders poses a number of challenges for psychotherapists, as the Applications box on page 446 reveals. Many children are also being treated effectively with Prozac and similar antidepressant drugs (called selective serotonin reuptake inhibitors) that correct for low levels of the neurotransmitter serotonin in the brains of depressed individuals (Jensen et al., 1999; K. D. Wagner & Ambrosini, 2001). Earlier antidepressant drugs had not proven to be as effective with children as they were with adults.

In sum, children, even young ones, can become clinically depressed and even suicidal (though rarely). Moreover, depression in childhood is very similar to depression in adulthood, although it manifests itself somewhat differently as the developing person gains new cognitive capacities. If adults become more sensitive to signs of depression in children, they will be better able to offer appropriate treatment and reduce the likelihood of recurrences later in life.

Nature, Nurture, and Childhood Disorders

Most of us have a strong belief in the power of the social environment, particularly the family, to shape child development. This belief often leads us to blame parents—especially mothers (Phares, 1999)—if their children are sad and withdrawn, uncontrollable and "bratty," or otherwise different from *most* children. Parents whose children develop problems often draw the very same conclusion, feeling guilty because they assume they are somehow at fault.

It is essential to view developmental disorders from a family systems perspective and to appreciate how emerging problems affect and are affected by family interactions. This perspective tells us that the power of parents to influence their children's adjustment may not be quite as great as many people believe. True, youngsters with depression and many other psychological disorders often come from problem-ridden families and have insecure attachments to their parents (Graham & Easterbrooks, 2000; van IJzendoorn & Bakermans-Kranenburg, 1996). They are also more likely than other children to have mothers and/or fathers who have histories of psychological disorder themselves. Surely this means that children develop problems because they live in disturbed family environments with adults whose own psychological problems and marital conflicts make it difficult for them to parent effectively.

Or are there other interpretations? We cannot always be sure that unfavorable home environments *cause* childhood disorders. One alternative explanation is a genetic one. We know, for example, that some individuals are predisposed by their genetic makeup—in interaction, as always, with their experiences—to become clinically depressed (Sullivan et al., 2000). Genes account for at least half of the variation among individuals in mood disorders, presumably by affecting balances of neurotransmitters (Zahn-Waxler et al., 2000). The risk is there even if the child is adopted into another home early in life. Perhaps the son of a depressed mother becomes depressed not so much because his mother was unresponsive or rejecting as because he inherited her genetic predisposition to become depressed.

In addition, "poor parenting" could be partly the *effect* of a child's disorder rather than its cause (Reiss et al., 2000; Sines, 1987). As we have seen many times in this book, and as we clearly saw in the discussion of *child effects* in the family in Chapter 15, children contribute to their own development by shaping their social environment. Parental rejection may be a factor in the development of behavior problems, but we cannot ignore the possibility that children's problem behaviors negatively affect their parents' moods, marital relationships, and parenting behaviors. Problem-prone children are known to precipitate stressful events that, in turn, aggravate their problems (Rudolph et al., 2000).

Unquestionably, though, family disruption and conflict and ineffective parenting *do* contribute to and aggravate many childhood problems. Indeed, one study demonstrated that although parents with psychological disorders typically use less effective parenting approaches than parents without psychological disorders, their children were not likely to develop disorders themselves *unless* the parenting they received was in fact maladaptive (J. G. Johnson et al., 2001). Apparently, it was not sufficient to inherit a genetic predisposition to a disorder; as the diathesis/stress model suggests, a stressful environment was also necessary.

Overall, it is high time to move beyond the simple view that parents are to blame for all their children's problems. It is also a mistake to view genes as the only important factor. Abnormal development, like normal development, is the product of both nature and nurture and of a history of complex transactions between person and environment in which each influences the other (Rutter, 2000).

Do Childhood Problems Persist?

The parents of children who develop psychological problems very much want to know this: Will my child outgrow these

Challenges in Treating Children and Adolescents

According to Surgeon General David Satcher, fewer than 1 in 5 U.S. children with psychological disorders receives treatment (Shute, 2001). When children and adolescents do enter treatment, their therapists must recognize that they are not adults and cannot be treated as such (Kazdin, 2000). First, children rarely seek treatment on their own; they are referred for treatment by adults, usually parents, who are disturbed by their behavior. This means that therapists must view the child *and* his or her parents as the "client." Sometimes the child does not think he or she has a problem; sometimes parents do in fact misperceive normal behavior, such as having toileting accidents at the age of 2 or 3, as abnormal (Kazdin, 2000).

Second, children's therapeutic outcomes often depend greatly on the cooperation of their parents. Whether or not a disturbed family environment has contributed to a child's problem, the participation of parents in treatment is often critical in resolving the problem (C. E. Bailey, 2000). Sometimes all members of the family must be treated for any enduring change in the child's behavior to occur—a principle derived from family systems theory that serves as a basis for the use of family therapy as a treatment approach. However, not all parents agree to participate in treatment.

Third—a point that is very familiar to students of human development—children function at very different levels of cognitive and emotional development than adults do, and this must be taken into consideration in both diagnosing and treating their problems (R. A. Gardner, 1993; Kazdin,

2000). For example, young children cannot easily participate in therapies that require them to verbalize their problems and gain insight into the causes of their behavior. More developmentally appropriate techniques include play therapy, in which disturbed children are encouraged to act out concerns that they cannot easily express in words, and behavioral approaches that do not require insight and verbal skills.

Is psychotherapy for children and adolescents effective? John Weisz and Bahr Weiss (1993) pulled together analyses of more that 200 studies. Two major categories of psychotherapy were compared: (1) behavioral therapies (those using reinforcement principles and modeling techniques to alter maladaptive behaviors and to teach more adaptive ones), and (2) nonbehavioral therapies (primarily psychoanalytic therapies based on Freudian theory and other "talking cures" in which therapists help clients to express, understand, and solve their problems). These studies examined a wide range of problems (both externalizing and internalizing) and measured a wide range of outcomes (anxiety, cognitive skills and school achievement, personality and self-concept, social adjustment, and so on).

So, does psychotherapy work with children and adolescents? Indeed it does—at least as well as it works with adults—and the benefits appear to be lasting. Moreover, undercontrolled, or externalizing, problems such as hyperactivity and aggression are just as responsive to treatment as internalizing problems such as phobias, suggesting that externalizing problems need not persist if they are effectively treated. Behavioral therapies appeared to be more effective with children than nonbehavioral therapies, although these alternative forms of therapy have often proved equally effective in treating adults. Very possibly, this is because children do indeed lack the cognitive and verbal skills to participate in "talk therapies."

Today, psychiatrists are increasingly turning to medications to treat children—Ritalin for children with ADHD, Prozac and other antidepressants for depressed children as young as preschool age, and so on (Shute, Locy, & Pasternak, 2000). Both psychological and pharmacological treatments for children and adolescents with psychological disorders clearly can achieve positive results (Asarnow et al., 2001). Yet they do not always work; for example, about 40–50% of clinically depressed children and adolescents do not respond to psychotherapy, and about the same percentage do not respond to antidepressant medications (Asarnow et al., 2001). Apparently, we have much left to learn about how best to meet the needs of children and adolescents with psychological problems—and their families.

SIU BioMed/Custom Medical Stock Photo

Play therapy can help young children who lack verbal skills to express their feelings.

problems, or will they persist? Parents are understandably concerned with the issue of continuity versus discontinuity in development. We have already seen that autism, ADHD, and major depression *do* tend to persist beyond childhood, in many individuals at least. To answer the continuity/discontinuity question more fully, let's consider the entire spectrum of childhood problems. Recall the distinction between externalizing (or undercontrolled) problems and internalizing (or overcontrolled) problems.

Avshalom Caspi and his colleagues (1996) used data from a longitudinal study in New Zealand to determine whether children's behavioral styles, or temperamental characteristics, at age 3 predicted their susceptibility to psychological disorders at age 21—a span of 18 years. As part (a) of Figure 16.3 shows, children who had externalizing problems as young children and were described as irritable, impulsive, and rough were more likely than either inhibited, overcontrolled children or well-adjusted children to be diagnosed as having antisocial personality disorder and to have records of criminal behavior as young adults.

Meanwhile, as part (b) of Figure 16.3 shows, inhibited, overcontrolled children who were shy, anxious, and easily up-

set were more likely than other children to be diagnosed as depressed later in life; contrary to prediction, however, they were not at significantly higher risk for anxiety disorders. Finally, children in both the externalizing (undercontrolled) and internalizing (overcontrolled) groups were more likely to attempt suicide, and boys in both groups were more likely to become dependent on alcohol. This study and others point to *continuity* in susceptibility to problems over the years and suggest that early problems tend to have significance for later development (Mesman, Bongers, & Koot, 2001).

Relationships between early behavior problems and later psychopathology in this study and others tend to be weak, though, so there is also *discontinuity* in development. Notice that most children with temperaments that put them at risk did *not* have diagnosable problems as adults. Similarly, in a 14-year follow-up of children and adolescents with behavioral and emotional problems, about 40% still had significant problems in adulthood, but the majority did not (Hofstra, Van der Ende, & Verhulst, 2000). In other words, having serious psychological problems as a child does not doom most individuals to a life of maladjustment.

Why might we see continuity of problem behavior in some children but discontinuity in others? If children have severe rather than mild psychological problems and receive little help, their difficulties are likely to persist. Autistic children usually remain autistic, children with major depression often have recurrences, and severely antisocial children tend to become antisocial adults. However, as Norman Garmezy (1994) and Michael Rutter (1996) emphasize, other children show remarkable resilience, functioning well despite exposure to risk factors for disorder or overcoming early problems to become well adjusted (see also Cummings et al., 2000). Such children appear to have **protective factors** working for them—processes that keep them from becoming maladjusted in the face of risk. These protection factors include their own competencies (especially intellectual ability and social skills) and strong social support (especially a stable family situation with at least one caring parent figure).

What we need to understand is that there is *both* continuity and change in children with psychological disorders. Many children, especially those with mild problems and many protective factors, outgrow their difficulties. At the same time, many adolescents and adults with severe problems are continuing to act out a pattern of maladaptive behavior that took form much earlier in life.

The Adolescent

If any age group has a reputation for having problems and causing trouble, it is adolescents. This is supposedly the time when angelic children are transformed into emotionally unstable, unruly, problem-ridden monsters. The view that adolescence is a time of emotional **storm and stress** was set forth by the founder of developmental psychology, G. Stanley Hall (1904). It has been with us ever since.

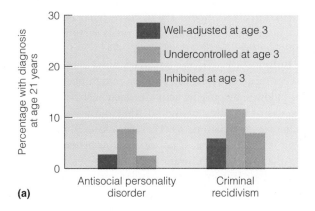

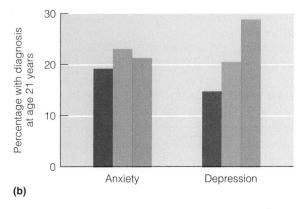

Figure 16.3 Relationships between behavior at age 3 and psychological disorders at age 21. Part (a) shows that children with undercontrolled, externalizing behavioral styles are more likely than other children to show antisocial behavior and repeated criminal behavior at age 21. Part (b) shows that inhibited, overcontrolled children are at high risk of depression, but not anxiety disorders, at 21.
SOURCE: Adapted from Caspi et al. (1996)

Is Adolescence Really a Period of Storm and Stress?

Are adolescents really more likely than either children or adults to experience psychological problems? In truth, adolescents have a far worse reputation than they deserve. It simply is not the case that *most* adolescents are emotionally disturbed or that *most* develop serious problem behaviors such as drug abuse and chronic delinquency. Instead, significant mental health problems—real signs of storm and stress—characterize about 20% of adolescents (Kazdin, 2000; Offer & Schonert-Reichl, 1992). Moreover, many of these adolescents were maladjusted before they reached puberty and continue to be maladjusted during adulthood (Reinherz et al., 1999; Strober, 1986). Overall rates of diagnosed psychological disorder are not much different in adolescence than they are in adulthood (Kazdin, 2000).

Yet adolescence *is* a period of heightened vulnerability to *some* forms of psychological disorder. Teenagers face greater stress than children; they must cope with physical maturation, the emergence of new cognitive abilities, dating, changes in family dynamics, moves to new and more complex school settings, societal demands to become more responsible and to assume adult roles, and much more (Hill, 1993). Most adolescents cope with these challenges remarkably well and undergo impressive psychological growth, although it is not unusual for them to feel depressed, anxious, and irritable now and then. For a minority, a buildup of stressors during adolescence can precipitate serious psychopathology.

In sum, it can be a mistake to either overestimate or underestimate levels of psychopathology among adolescents. If we cling too strongly to the storm-and-stress view of adolescence and expect most teens to be half crazy, we may dismiss serious and potentially long-lasting problems as simply a normal "phase kids go through," a phase they will "outgrow." Yet, if we think adolescents are too young to have serious psychological problems, we can also fail to provide emotionally troubled youths with the help they need.

What special mental health risks *do* adolescents face? Many adolescents of both sexes get themselves into trouble by overusing alcohol and drugs, engaging in delinquent behavior, and displaying other so-called adolescent problem behaviors. These problem behaviors, though common, usually do not reach the level of seriousness to qualify as psychological disorders and typically wane as adolescents become adults (Jessor, 1998). Here we'll focus on two types of disorder that become more prevalent in adolescence. Among females, diagnosable eating disorders such as anorexia nervosa and bulimia can make the adolescent period treacherous indeed. In addition, rates of depression increase dramatically from childhood to adolescence, especially among females, and suicide rates climb accordingly. These problems interfere with normal adolescent development; yet they become far more understandable when we view them in the context of this development.

Eating Disorders

Perhaps no psychological disorders are more associated with adolescence than the eating disorders that disproportionately strike adolescent girls, either during the transition from childhood to adolescence or during the transition from adolescence to adulthood (Keel & Fulkerson, 2001). Both anorexia nervosa and bulimia have become more common in recent years in a number of industrialized countries (Gordon, 2000). And both are serious—indeed, potentially fatal—conditions that are difficult to cure.

Anorexia nervosa, which literally means "nervous loss of appetite," has been defined as a refusal to maintain a weight that is at least 85% of the expected weight for one's height and age (American Psychiatric Association, 1994). Anorexic individuals are also characterized by a strong fear of becoming overweight, a distorted body image (a tendency to view themselves as fat even when they are emaciated), and, if they are females, an absence of regular menstrual cycles. Anorexia and other eating disorders typically emerge in adolescence, although they can begin earlier or later. The typical individual with anorexia may begin dieting soon after reaching puberty and simply continue, insisting, even when she weighs only 60 or 70 pounds and resembles a cadaver, that she is well nourished and could stand to lose a few more pounds (Hsu, 1990). Praised at first for losing weight, she becomes increasingly obsessed with dieting and exercising and gains a sense of power by resisting the urging of parents and friends to eat more (Levenkron, 2000). About 1% of adolescent girls suffer from this condition, and 95 out of 100 of its victims are females (American Psychiatric Association, 1994).

Bulimia nervosa, the so-called binge/purge syndrome, involves recurrent episodes of consuming huge quantities of food followed by purging activities such as self-induced vomiting, use of laxatives, or rigid dieting and fasting (American Psychiatric Association, 1994). Like anorexia nervosa, it is rooted in a strong "fear of fat"; its victims believe they are far fatter than they are and want to be far thinner. Bulimia is especially prevalent in college populations, affecting few men but as many as 5% of college women (Hsu, 1990). Like anorexia, it is life threatening: Laxatives and diuretics used as purging agents can deplete the body of potassium and cause cardiac arrhythmia and heart attacks, and regular vomiting can cause hernias.

A bulimic girl or woman typically binges on the very foods that are taboo to dieters, eating entire half gallons of ice cream, multiple bags of cookies and potato chips, or whole pies and cakes—as much as *55,000 calories* in a single binge session (C. L. Johnson et al., 1982). Not surprisingly, bulimic individuals experience a good deal of anxiety and depression in connection with their binge eating. They may learn to engage in purging activities to relieve these negative feelings (Hinz & Williamson, 1987).

Individuals with bulimia can be found in all weight ranges, whereas individuals with anorexia are by definition underweight (American Psychiatric Association, 1994). It is a myth that these eating disorders are restricted to European American females from upper middle-class backgrounds. They are evident at all socioeconomic levels (Gard & Freeman, 1996) and in all racial and ethnic groups, although African American females are less concerned with being thin and di-

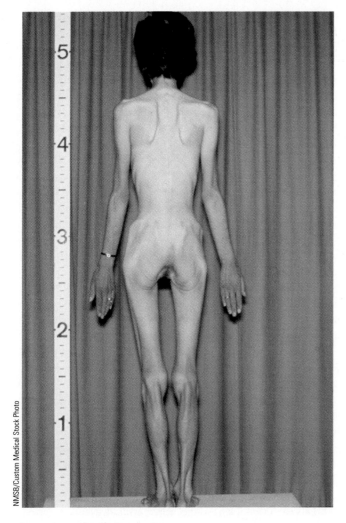

Anorexia can be life threatening.

standards of beauty: To match the proportions of those Barbie dolls girls love so much, the average woman would have to gain 5 inches in the chest and lose 6 inches in the waist (Brownell & Napolitano, 1995)! As girls experience normal pubertal changes, they naturally gain fat and become, in their minds anyway, less attractive. They have more reason than ever to be obsessed with controlling their weight (Murnen & Smolak, 1997; Rodin, Striegel-Moore, & Silberstein, 1990). This may be why adolescence is a prime time for the emergence of eating disorders.

Still, why do relatively few adolescent females become anorexic or bulimic, even though almost all of them experience social pressure to be thin? To begin with, genes predispose some individuals to develop eating disorders (Bulik et al., 2000; Strober et al., 2000). At least one gene involved in the control of appetite has been implicated (Vink et al., 2001). Genes may also be responsible for the low levels of the neurotransmitter serotonin associated with both eating disorders and mood disorders (Keel & Fulkerson, 2001).

Genes may also put certain individuals at risk by influencing their personalities. Anorexic females tend to be introverted young women who worry a good deal and are perfectionists, whereas bulimic females tend to be extraverted and impulsive (Hsu, 1990). Both groups have low self-esteem, a good deal of self-directed anger, and little sense that they can control their lives (G. J. Williams et al., 1993).

Yet an eating disorder may not emerge unless a susceptible girl experiences disturbed family relationships and stressful events—that is, unless there is both diathesis and stress, unless heredity and environment interact in an unfavorable way (Keel & Fulkerson, 2001). Girls who are overly concerned about their weight tend to grow up in families that are preoccupied with weight (Gordon, 2000; Strober et al., 2000). They are often insecurely attached to their parents and have often constructed *internal working models* of self and other that lead them to think poorly of themselves and to expect others to think poorly of them too (Sharpe et al., 1998). Much emphasis has been placed on disturbed mother–daughter relationships, but poor father–daughter relationships also contribute (Dominy, Johnson, & Koch, 2000).

The family experiences of anorexic and bulimic women differ somewhat, however. Salvador Minuchin and his colleagues (Minuchin, Rosman, & Baker, 1978) discovered that anorexic females have difficulty with the adolescent task of forming an identity separate from their parents because their families tend to be "enmeshed," or overly interdependent. Their parents are overprotective and do not allow their daughters to argue or to express negative emotions. The result may be a young woman who has not been able to separate herself from her parents and who desperately wants to establish some sense of control over her life, which she can do by dieting (Levenkron, 2000). Sufferers of bulimia, by contrast, often perceive their parents as hostile and distant (Wonderlich, Klein, & Council, 1996).

Ultimately, it may take a pileup of stressors to push a young woman over the edge. For example, vulnerable adolescents who are experiencing pubertal changes and weight

eting than European and Asian American females and have lower rates of eating disorders (Wildes, Emery, & Simons, 2001).

SUSPECTED CAUSES

Eating disorders stem partly from the sociocultural context in which we live—a society obsessed with thinness as the standard of physical attractiveness that makes it hard for young women to form positive identities (Gordon, 2000). As European American values emphasizing the desirability of a slim figure have spread to other countries, rates of eating disorders in those countries have risen (Gordon, 2000). Interestingly, the coming of television to the island of Fiji converted a nation of girls who viewed plump bodies as a status symbol associated with the generous sharing of food into girls who feel too fat and try to control their weight (Becker & Burwell, cited in "Eating Disorders Rise," 1999).

Well before they reach puberty, large proportions of girls in our society associate being thin with being attractive, fear becoming fat, and wish they were thinner (Ricciardelli & McCabe, 2001). About 25% of second-grade girls diet (Thelen et al., 1992). Girls are pressured to work toward impossible

gains, becoming involved in mixed-sex relationships, and changing schools, all at the same time, may have more than they can handle and may then develop an eating disorder (Smolak & Levine, 1996). Emotional, sexual, or physical abuse sometimes precipitates the disorder (Kent & Waller, 2000). In eating disorders, then, we have a prime example of how characteristics of the person, family, and wider social environment can interact to produce developmental problems. The young woman who is at risk for eating disorders may be predisposed, partly owing to her genetic makeup, to have difficulty coping with the developmental tasks of adolescence. However, she may not actually develop an eating disorder unless she also grows up in a culture that overvalues thinness and in a family that makes it hard to form a secure attachment and to forge an identity as an individual—and then faces an accumulation of stressful events.

TREATMENT

Fortunately, most anorexic and bulimic individuals can be successfully treated (Gordon, 2000). Effective therapies for eating-disordered individuals include behavior modification programs designed to bring their eating behavior under control, individual psychotherapy designed to help them understand and gain control over their problem, family therapy designed to help build healthier parent–child relationships, and, for some, antidepressant medication (Bowers, Evans, & Van Cleve, 1996). About half of women with bulimia have recovered 5 to 10 years after they were diagnosed (Keel & Mitchell, 1997), although may continue to show poor social adjustment years later. Women with anorexia are more difficult to treat because they so strongly resist admitting that they have a problem. They often relapse and may require intensive treatment over a long period of time before they recover (Levenkron, 2000). Progress is being made, however, with the help of Prozac and similar antidepressants.

Depression and Suicidal Behavior

Children become quite a bit more vulnerable to depression as they enter adolescence, especially if they are girls. Depression rates for males and females are quite similar in childhood, but females become twice as likely as males to be depressed starting in adolescence (Frank & Young, 2000). Up to 35% of adolescents experience depressed moods at some time, and as many as 7% have diagnosable depressive disorders (Petersen et al., 1993).

Because they are more intellectually mature than children and have typically become capable of formal operational thought, depressed adolescents display the same cognitive symptoms of depression that adults display. Hopelessness, feelings of worthlessness, suicidal thinking, and other negative cognitions are common (Garber, Weiss, & Shanley, 1993). Yet depressed adolescents, like depressed children, typically display other comorbid problems along with their depression— substance abuse, eating disorders, anxiety, antisocial behavior, and more (Compas, Connor, & Hinden, 1998). Some depressed teenagers look more like budding juvenile delinquents on the surface than like victims of depression. Thus, diagnos-

ing depression during adolescence can still be tricky, for adolescents share some of the qualities of both depressed adults and depressed children.

As depression becomes more common from childhood to adolescence, so do suicidal thoughts, suicide attempts, and actual suicides. Suicide is the third leading cause of death for this age group, far behind accidents and just behind homicides; the yearly rate is 11 per 100,000 15- to 24-year-olds (U.S. Bureau of the Census, 2000). For every adolescent suicide, there are many unsuccessful attempts—as many as 50 to 200 by some estimates (Garland & Zigler, 1993). Also, suicidal thoughts that may or may not lead to action are shockingly common, to the point of being normal during this period (Shaffer & Pfeffer, 2001). In one survey of adolescents whose average age was 15, for instance, 56% reported at least one instance of suicidal thinking in their lives, and 15% had actually attempted suicide (Windle & Windle, 1997).

Before we conclude that adolescence is the peak time for suicidal behavior, however, let's consider the suicide rates for different age groups, as shown in Figure 16.4. It is clear that *adults* are more likely to commit suicide than adolescents are. The suicide rate for females peaks in middle age, and the suicide rate for white males climbs throughout adulthood. As a result, elderly white men are actually the group most likely to commit suicide. Increased attention is now being focused on the problem of late life suicide. Lives could be saved if suicide-prone individuals received treatment for the depression that typically prompts them to commit suicide (Pearson, 2000).

Overall, males are more likely to commit suicide than females, by a ratio of at least 3 to 1—a difference that holds up across most cultures studied (Girard, 1993; Shaffer & Pfeffer, 2001). When we look at suicide *attempts*, however, this ratio is reversed, with females leading males by a ratio of about 3 to 1. Apparently, then, females attempt suicide more often than males do, but males more often commit suicide when they try, probably because they use more lethal techniques (especially guns). Interestingly, the tendency of females to attempt suicide more often than males disappears by the end of the teen years, as shown in Figure 16.5, even though females continue to have higher rates of major depression than males during the adult years (Lewinsohn et al., 2001).

If suicide rates are actually higher in adulthood than in adolescence, why do we hear so much about teenage suicide? Probably because adolescents attempt suicide more frequently than adults do. The typical adolescent suicide attempt has been characterized as a "cry for help"—a desperate effort to get others to notice and help resolve problems that have become unbearable (Berman & Jobes, 1991). The adolescent who attempts suicide often wants a better life; the elderly adult who attempts suicide is more often determined to end his or her life (Lester, 1994). This by no means suggests that adolescent suicide attempts should be taken lightly, though. Their message is clear: "I've got serious problems; wake up and help me!"

Suicidal behavior in adolescence is most likely the product of diathesis/stress. More than 90% of adolescent suicide victims, partly because of their genetic endowment, suffered from depression, substance use disorder, or another psycho-

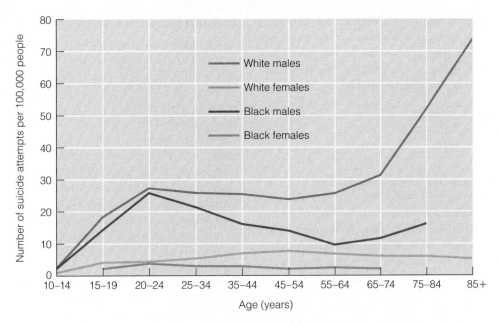

Figure 16.4 Number of suicides per 100,000 people by age and sex among European and African Americans in the United States. Data from the oldest African Americans are not shown because too few cases were studied.

SOURCE: Data from U.S. Bureau of the Census (1996)

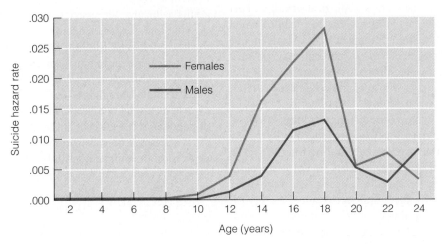

Figure 16.5 Rates of attempted suicide climb from childhood to adolescence among both males and females. A gender difference also emerges: Rates are higher for female adolescents than for male adolescents. This sex difference in suicide attempts disappears as adolescents become adults, even though females continue to have higher rates of depression than males as adults.

SOURCE: Adapted from Lewinsohn et al. (2001)

logical disorder at the time of their death, so screening teenagers for depression and other psychological disorders make good sense as an approach to prevention (Shaffer & Pfeffer, 2001). Many have histories of troubled family relationships: They have run away from home, or they do not live with both their parents; in some cases, they have been physically or sexually abused (Vannatta, 1996; B. M. Wagner, 1997). In the period leading up to a suicide attempt, the adolescent has often experienced a buildup of stressful life events—deteriorating relationships with parents and peers, academic and social failures, run-ins with the law—and begun to feel

incapable of coping (Berman & Jobes, 1991). The adolescent who attempts suicide once may try again if he or she receives little help and continues to feel incapable of coping with problems. As a result, professional help is definitely called for after an unsuccessful suicide attempt (Rotheram-Borus et al., 2000).

All in all, adolescence does appear to be a potentially treacherous period of the life span—but only for a minority of individuals. Moreover, problems tend to come in bundles when they come, suggesting that many of the same root causes underlie a wide range of adolescent problem behaviors (Windle & Windle, 1997). However, let's remind ourselves that the large majority of adolescents, even though they may drink too many beers or think a depressive or even suicidal thought now and then, emerge from this period as well-adjusted and competent young adults. They will face new challenges in adapting to the demands of adult life.

The Adult

At any age, psychological problems may result when a vulnerable individual faces overwhelming stress. As it turns out, adults typically experience the greatest number of life changes and strains in early adulthood (McLanahan & Sorensen, 1985; Pearlin, 1980). Life strains decrease from early adulthood to middle adulthood, perhaps as adults settle into more stable lifestyles. And, despite increased stress related to health, elderly adults report even fewer hassles and strains overall than middle-aged adults do (Aldwin, 1994; Folkman et al., 1987; Martin, Grunendahl, & Martin, 2001). This may be because they have fewer roles and responsibilities to juggle or because they no longer perceive problems they have encountered before as stressful.

Age differences in stressful experiences may help to explain age differences in rates of psychological disorder. The National Institute of Mental Health conducted a major survey of community mental health: Adults aged 18 or older were interviewed in their homes about the psychological symptoms they were experiencing, and estimates were then made of the percentages of respondents who met the criteria for several psychological disorders (Myers et al., 1984; Robins & Regier, 1991). Overall, a fairly large proportion of adults—15% to 22% of those surveyed in each city—were judged to have suffered from a diagnosable psychological disorder in the previous 6 months. Rates of affective disorders (major depression and related mood disorders), alcohol abuse and dependence, schizophrenia, anxiety disorders, and antisocial personality all decreased from young adulthood to later adulthood. (As you appreciate, this could be either a true age effect or a cohort effect suggesting that recent generations are more vulnerable than previous generations to psychological disorder.) The only type of impairment that increased with age was cognitive impairment, undoubtedly because some older individuals were developing Alzheimer's disease and other forms of dementia (to be discussed later in this chapter).

Mainly, it appears that young adults, because they experience more stress than older adults, are a group at high risk for mental health problems. With that as background, let's look more closely at one of the disorders to which young adults are especially susceptible, depression, and then turn to an examination of Azheimer's disease and related cognitive impairments.

Depression

Major depression and other affective disorders are among the most common psychological problems experienced by adults. Who gets depressed, and what does this tell us?

AGE AND SEX DIFFERENCES

As just noted, and contrary to stereotypes, young adults are actually more vulnerable to major depression and other severe affective disorders than elderly adults are (Wolfe, Morrow, & Fredrickson, 1996). This is especially true if elderly adults can avoid the physical illnesses that can contribute to depression at any age—and that can also be caused or aggravated by long-standing problems with depression (Meeks, Murrell, & Mehl, 2000). Still, there are good reasons to be concerned about depression in old age, especially when we know that depressed elders are more likely than depressed adolescents to take their own lives. Also, although only about 1–3% of elderly adults have major depressive disorder, about 15% report symptoms of depression (Mulsant & Ganguli, 1999). Might some of the individuals who report symptoms actually qualify as having major depression or a related disorder?

Depression can be difficult to diagnose in later adulthood (Blazer & Koenig, 1996). Think about it: Symptoms of depression include fatigue, sleeping difficulties, cognitive deficits, and somatic complaints. What if a clinician notes these symptoms in an elderly person but interprets them as nothing more than normal aging, or as the result of the chronic illnesses that are so common in old age, or as signs of dementia? A case of depression can easily be missed. Elderly adults who are depressed may also hide their depression, denying that they are sad and claiming instead that they have medical problems (Mulsant & Ganguli, 1999). This, too, can lead to underdiagnosis of depression in the elderly population. Yet *over*diagnosis of depression in older adults can also occur if bodily complaints that are actually caused by physical disease or disability are uncritically interpreted as symptoms of depression (Grayson et al., 2000).

Depression in elderly individuals is not so different from depression in young and middle-aged adults that entirely different criteria must be developed to detect it (La Rue, Dessonville, & Jarvik, 1985). Still, clinicians working with elderly adults need to be very sensitive to the differences between normal aging processes and psychopathology. Moreover, they

Mark Richards/PhotoEdit

Although few elderly adults have diagnosed depression, a sizable minority experience at least some symptoms of depression.

Why Are Females More Depressed Than Males?

How can we explain the fact that females have about twice the rate of depression as males starting in adolescence and continuing through at least middle age? Adolescent females may be especially at risk because they are more likely than males to experience a cumulation of stressful events, such as starting middle school or junior high school, undergoing pubertal changes, and dating in early adolescence (Ge et al., 1994; Nolen-Hoeksema & Girgus, 1994). Most likely, pubertal hormone changes and social forces interact to place adolescent females at risk. Jill Cyranowski and her colleagues (2000) have proposed the following explanation for the steep rise in depression among females at puberty: (1) Increases in levels of the hormone oxytocin (a hormone that contributes to the development of bonding with a romantic partner as well as to maternal caregiving behaviors), coupled with gender-role expectations and social pressures, predispose pubertal girls to place a high priority on close social relationships. (2) Especially if they have poor relationships with their parents, anxious or inhibited temperaments, and limited coping skills, girls may have difficulty with the transition from close attachments to parents to close attachments to romantic partners during adolescence and find themselves in insecure, unstable romantic relationships. (3) Because females value relationships so highly, they may be more likely than males to become depressive when their romantic relationships become stormy or end, or when they face other stressful life events with interpersonal consequences. In short, biological changes associated with puberty, coupled with social influences, may sensitize certain young women to the depression-provoking effects of negative life events, especially disruptions of relationships.

Intriguing as this hypothesis is, there are others, especially when it comes to explaining why females *continue* to have higher rates of depression than men as adults (see

Kessler, 2000). First, young and middle-aged women playing out traditional adult gender roles may have more to cope with—and therefore more to be depressed about—than men. Women do experience more chronic strain than men, possibly because they bear the lion's share of family responsibilities (Nolen-Hoeksema et al., 1999). Second, even if men and women are similarly distressed, differences in gender-role socialization may lead them to express their distress differently. Specifically, men may externalize their distress by behaving antisocially or abusing alcohol and drugs, whereas women may internalize theirs and express it as depression, anxiety, and related disorders (Horwitz & White, 1987; Stapley & Haviland, 1989).

Finally, as Susan Nolen-Hoeksema and her colleagues have hypothesized, women and men may cope with their bad moods differently. Men tend to respond to depression with *distraction* strategies: They engage in enjoyable activities such as sports to get their minds off their problems. Women more often engage in *rumination:* They think repeatedly about their problems and try to analyze why they feel the way they do (Nolen-Hoeksema, 1990; Strauss et al., 1997). By responding as they do, men may sidestep or minimize their depression, whereas women may actually aggravate theirs.

It now seems clear that there may be some truth to all of these views. In one study, women not only experienced more chronic stress and strain than men, but had a lower sense of mastery and engaged in more rumination when they face problems; moreover, all of these sex differences helped to explain the difference in the percentage of males and females who were depressed (Nolen-Hoeksema, Larson, & Grayson, 1999). In sum, gender differences in biology, levels of stress, ways of expressing distress, and styles of coping with distress may all contribute to higher rates of depression in females than in males.

should evaluate elderly patients carefully to better distinguish between clinical depression and psychological distress stemming from poor health, the side effects of drugs, or poor nutrition (Zarit, Eiler, & Hassinger, 1985). Finally, the fact that relatively few elderly people suffer from severe clinical depression should not blind us to the fact that a much larger number feel depressed or demoralized and could benefit from treatment, even though they may not meet DSM-IV diagnostic criteria (Blazer & Koenig, 1996). The elderly adults most at risk tend to be female, very old, physically ill, psychologically disturbed, poor, and/or socially isolated (Blazer, 1993; Falcon & Tucker, 2000).

Women are more likely than men to be diagnosed as depressed—by a margin of about 2 to 1 (American Psychiatric

Association, 1994). This gender gap first emerges during adolescence (Frank & Young, 2000). It then reaches its widest point in the 30-to-60 age range and becomes less pronounced or even disappears in old age (Wolfe et al., 1996; Nolen-Hoeksema, 1990). How would you explain this? Hint: It is not just because women are more likely than men to admit they are depressed or to seek help when they are depressed (Kessler, 2000). The Explorations box above looks at some other hypotheses.

TREATMENT

One of the biggest challenges in treating adults with major depression and other psychological disorders is getting them to seek treatment. Many young and middle-aged adults with psychological disorders receive no professional treatment (Kessler et al., 1994). Elderly adults are especially likely to go undiagnosed and untreated (Baldwin, 2000). Possibly this is because today's elderly generation grew up in a time when it was considered shameful to have psychological problems (Gatz et al., 1985). Older adults and members of their families may also believe, wrongly, that problems such as depression and anxiety are just a normal part of getting older or becoming ill (Meador & Davis, 1996). Still another barrier to treatment may be negative attitudes among mental health professionals that cause them to prefer working with younger people, to perceive elderly individuals as untreatable, and to misdiagnose their problems.

Despite these barriers, when depressed elderly adults do seek psychotherapy, they benefit every bit as much as younger adults (Karel & Hinrichsen, 2000; Scogin & McElreath, 1994). Moreover, those who are treated with antidepressant drugs not only overcome their depression but show improved cognitive functioning (Butters et al., 2000). As with many psychological problems, the most effective approach is often a combination of drug treatment and psychotherapy (Baldwin, 2000). Just as human beings can fall prey to psychological problems at any point in the life span, they have an impressive capacity throughout the life span to overcome problems and to experience new psychological growth.

Aging and Dementia

Perhaps nothing scares us more about aging than the thought that we will become "senile." **Dementia,** the technical term for senility, is a progressive deterioration of neural functioning associated with memory impairment, declines in tested intellectual ability, poor judgment, difficulty thinking abstractly, and often personality changes. Becoming "senile" is *not* a normal part of the aging process. Yet rates of dementia increase steadily with age. Overall, dementia and other moderate and severe cognitive impairments affect about 5% of the 65-and-older population (Blazer, 1996; Regier et al., 1988).

Dementia is not a single disorder. Indeed, much damage can be done by labeling any older person with cognitive impairments as senile—or even as having Alzheimer's disease—and then assuming that he or she is a lost cause. Many different conditions can produce the symptoms we associate with senility, and some of them are curable or reversible (Heston & White, 1991; Gillick, 1998). It is also a mistake to assume that any elderly person who becomes somewhat forgetful or absentminded—who occasionally misplaces keys or cannot remember someone's name—is becoming senile. As we saw in Chapter 8, small declines in memory capacities in later life are common and usually do not have much effect on daily functioning. If this were all it took to warrant a diagnosis of dementia, many young and middle-aged adults, not to mention textbook writers, would qualify too! So let's look at some of the specific forms of dementia.

ALZHEIMER'S DISEASE

With Alzheimer's disease, you just know you're going to forget things, and it's impossible to put things where you can't forget them because people like me can always find a place to lose things and we have to flurry all over the house to figure where in the heck I left whatever it was. . . . It's usually my glasses. . . . You've got to have a sense of humor in this kind of business, and I think it's interesting how many places I can find to lose things. . . . [People with Alzheimer's] want things like they used to be. And we just hate the fact that we cannot be what we used to be. It hurts like hell. (Cary Henderson, age 64, former history professor diagnosed with Alzheimer's disease at age 55; Rovner, 1994, pp. 12–13)

Alzheimer's disease, or Dementia of the Alzheimer's Type (DAT) as it is termed in DSM-IV, is the most common cause of dementia, accounting for about 70% of all cases, including Ronald Reagan's (Tanzi & Parson, 2000). Dementia can strike in middle age but becomes increasingly likely with advancing age. The rate of Alzheimer's disease doubles every 5 years beyond age 65; because more and more people are living into advanced old age, more and more will end up with the disease unless ways of preventing it or slowing its progress are found (National Institute on Aging, 2000).

Alzheimer's disease leaves two telltale signs in the brain (Selkoe, 1997; M. E. Williams, 1995): *senile plaques* (masses of dying neural material with a toxic protein called **beta-amyloid** at their core that injures neurons), and *neurofibrillary tangles* (twisted strands of neural fibers within the bodies of neural cells). Elderly adults without Alzheimer's have senile plaques and neurofibrillary tangles too; it is not only the

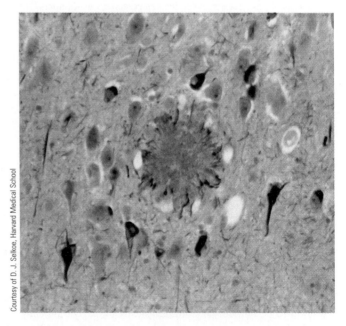

Courtesy of D. J. Selkoe, Harvard Medical School

Beta-amyloid plaques (the mass in the center) and neurofibrillary tangles make the brain of a person with advanced Alzheimer's disease look quite different from the brain of a normally aging adult.

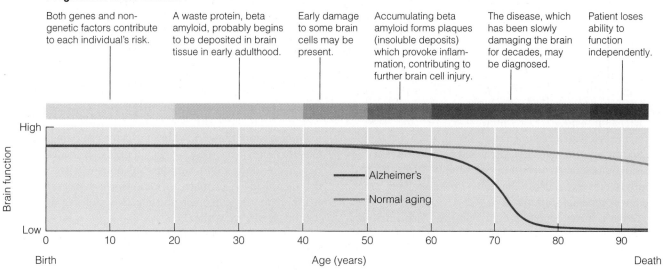

Progression of the disease:

Both genes and non-genetic factors contribute to each individual's risk.

A waste protein, beta amyloid, probably begins to be deposited in brain tissue in early adulthood.

Early damage to some brain cells may be present.

Accumulating beta amyloid forms plaques (insoluble deposits) which provoke inflammation, contributing to further brain cell injury.

The disease, which has been slowly damaging the brain for decades, may be diagnosed.

Patient loses ability to function independently.

Figure 16.6 Alzheimer's disease emerges gradually over the adult years; brain cells are damaged long before noticeable cognitive impairment results in old age. Changes in brain functioning are significantly different from those associated with normal aging.

SOURCE Adapted from Okie (2000)

number but their exact type and location that mark the difference between Alzheimer's disease and normal aging (Snowdon, 1997). The result of Alzheimer's is a progressive—and irreversible or incurable—deterioration of neurons and increasingly impaired mental functioning, along with personality changes.

The first sign of Alzheimer's disease, detectable 2 to 3 years before dementia can be diagnosed, is usually difficulty learning and remembering verbal material (Howieson et al., 1997). As we saw in Chapter 8, *mild cognitive impairment* in some older adults may be an early warning that dementia will follow (Morris et al., 2001). In the early stages, free recall tasks are difficult but memory is good if cues to recall are provided; over time, individuals cannot recall even with the aid of cues and become increasingly frustrated (Grober & Kawas, 1997; Williams, 1995). As the disorder progresses, Alzheimer's patients have more and more trouble coming up with the words they want during conversations and may forget what to do next midway through making a sandwich or getting ready for bed. If tested, they may be unable to answer simple questions about where they are, what the date is, and who the president of the United States is. Eventually, they become incapable of caring for themselves, lose all verbal abilities, and die, some earlier and some later, but on average about 8 to 10 years after onset (National Institute on Aging, 2000; and see Figure 16.6). Not only do patients with Alzheimer's disease become increasingly unable to function, but they often test the patience of caregivers by forgetting they have left something cooking on the stove, wandering away and getting lost, accusing people of stealing the items they have misplaced, seeing wild animals in their room, or taking off their clothes in public. Many become highly agitated and uncontrollable; large numbers

suffer from depression; and some experience psychotic symptoms such as hallucinations (Gillick, 1998).

What causes Alzheimer's disease? Many cases appear to have a hereditary basis, but there is no single "Alzheimer's gene" (Tanzi & Parson, 2000). Alzheimer's disease does strike repeatedly and early in some families. By analyzing blood samples from families with many Alzheimer's victims, genetic researchers made a big breakthrough when they located a gene for the disease on the 21st pair of chromosomes. Anyone who inherits just one of these apparently dominant genes will eventually develop the disease. Genes on Chromosomes 1 and 14 have also been implicated in early-developing Alzheimer's disease, and other genes are being discovered as we write (Hendrie, 2001; Tanzi & Parson, 2000). However, only about 5% of cases of Alzheimer's disease begin before age 60; 95% are late-onset cases and are not the inevitable result of a particular gene (W. R. Clark, 1999).

The genetic contributors to late-onset Alzheimer's disease are different. Rather than making Alzheimer's disease inevitable, they only increase a person's risk (Tanzi & Parson, 2000). One variant of a gene on Chromosome 19 that is responsible for the production of apolipoprotein (ApoE), a protein involved in processing cholesterol, may be especially important. Having two of the risk-inducing ApoE4 genes means having up to 8 times the normal risk of Alzheimer's; having one of the genes means 2 to 4 times the normal risk (Hendrie, 2001). Not having the ApoE4 gene means a good chance of maintaining one's cognitive functioning into very late adulthood (Riley et al., 2000). It is believed that this gene may increase the buildup of beta-amyloid—the substance in senile plaques that appears to be so damaging to the brain—and therefore speed the progression of the disease (National

Institute on Aging, 2000). Yet not everyone with the gene, or even a pair of them, develops Alzheimer's, so as-yet unidentified environmental factors must also play a role.

Alzheimer's disease is clearly more complicated than one gene on one chromosome. Moreover, many individuals who fall prey to Alzheimer's disease, especially after age 70, have no apparent history of it in their families (Gillick, 1998). Here, environmental factors may be significant. Head injuries in earlier adulthood, for example, increase the risk of Alzheimer's disease (Plassman et al., 2000), and a diet that increases the odds of high cholesterol and vascular disease is increasingly looking like another contributor (Hendrie, 2001; Nourhashemi et al., 2000). The search for causes, both genetic and environmental, continues.

What is being done to prevent and treat Alzheimer's disease? Because victims have a deficit in the neurotransmitter acetylcholine, which is essential for normal learning and memory, some researchers have been trying to develop drugs to correct this problem. No pill to prevent or reverse Alzheimer's disease has yet been discovered, but some drugs have been tested and are now prescribed (Cognex and Aricept, for example). They modestly improve cognitive functioning and slow the progression of the disease in some patients by inhibiting the breakdown of acetylcholine (Allen, 2001; National Institute on Aging, 2000). More such drugs are likely to follow.

A second promising approach attempts to combat the buildup of beta-amyloid in the brain. Anti-inflammatory drugs such as ibuprofen, estrogen (taken by postmenopausal women), and antioxidants such as vitamins E and C may delay the onset and progression of Alzheimer's disease by inhibiting the damaging oxidating effects on neurons of beta-amyloid (National Institute on Aging, 2000; Pratico & Delanty, 2000).

Finally, much excitement has been stirred by early tests in animals of a vaccine made of beta-amyloid. The vaccine stimulates the immune system to produce antibodies that then attack beta-amyloid and either prevent or reverse its buildup (Schenk et al., 1999). This vaccine appears to have the desired effect on amyloid levels, improve brain functioning, and positively affect learning performance in mice that have been genetically engineered to develop the mouse equivalent of Alzheimer's disease (Bacskai et al., 2001; Morgan et al., 2000).

Even if Alzheimer's disease cannot be prevented entirely, researchers are hopeful that its onset and progression can be slowed. And, even though deterioration leading to death must be expected in today's Alzheimer's patients, a great deal can be done through psychological interventions such as cognitive-behavioral therapy, support groups, and memory training to help people with the disease as well as their family members understand and cope with dementia and function better (Kasl-Godley & Gatz, 2000; Miller & Morris, 1993).

Other Causes of Cognitive Impairment

The second most common type of dementia, accounting for 10–15% of all cases of dementia by itself and another 10–15% in combination with Alzheimer's disease, is **vascular dementia**

(M. E. Williams, 1995). Also called multi-infarct dementia, it is caused by a series of minor strokes that cut off the blood supply to areas of the brain. Whereas Alzheimer's disease usually progresses slowly and steadily, vascular dementia often progresses in a steplike manner as each small stroke brings about a new deterioration in functioning (American Psychiatric Association, 1994). Whereas Alzheimer's disease is strongly influenced by genes, vascular dementia is more closely associated with environmental risk factors for cerebrovascular diseases that affect blood flow in the brain, such as smoking, eating a fatty diet, and being obese (Bergem, Engedal, & Kringlen, 1997; Kaplan & Sadock, 1998). Huntington's disease (a genetic disorder described in Chapter 3), Parkinson's disease, and even AIDS are among the other possible causes of irreversible dementia (Heston & White, 1991).

A minority of cases of dementia—perhaps 10–20%—are not related to any of these causes and, more important, are *reversible* or curable (Gurland, 1991). Such problems as alcoholism, toxic reactions to medication, infections, metabolic disorders, and malnutrition can cause symptoms of dementia. If these problems are corrected—for example, if the individual is taken off a recently prescribed medicine or is placed on a proper diet—a once "senile" person can be restored to normal mental functioning. By contrast, if that same person is written off as "senile" or as a victim of Alzheimer's disease, a potentially curable condition may become a progressively worse and irreversible one.

Similarly, some elderly adults are mistakenly diagnosed as suffering from irreversible dementia when they are actually experiencing **delirium.** This reversible condition develops more rapidly than dementia, comes and goes over the course of the day, and is a disturbance of consciousness characterized by periods of disorientation, wandering attention, confusion, and hallucinations (American Psychiatric Association, 1994; Kaplan & Sadock, 1998). Roughly 25% of patients over age 70 who are admitted to hospitals for illness experience delirium (M. E. Williams, 1995). Any number of stresses to the body—illness, surgery, drug overdose, malnutrition—can trigger it. Here, too, it is essential to look carefully for such causes and treat them quickly; in most cases, the symptoms will then disappear in a week or two (Kaplan & Sadock, 1998).

Finally, elderly adults who are depressed are all too frequently misdiagnosed as suffering from dementia because they seem forgetful and mentally slow (Kaszniak, 1990). As we have seen, treatment with antidepressant drugs and psychotherapy can dramatically improve the functioning of such individuals. However, if their depression goes undetected and they are written off as "senile," they are likely to deteriorate further.

The moral is clear: *It is absolutely critical to distinguish among irreversible dementias (notably, dementia of the Alzheimer's type and vascular dementia), reversible dementias, delirium, depression, and other conditions that may be mistaken for irreversible dementias—including old age itself* (Peskind & Raskind, 1996). This requires a thorough assessment, including a medical history, physical and neurological examinations, assessments of cognitive functioning, and more (Beck et al., 2000). Only after all other causes, especially potentially treatable ones, have been ruled out should a diagnosis of Alzheimer's disease be made. Unfortunately, many primary care physicians fail to notice symptoms of dementia, or do not appreciate the importance of thorough testing to determine the underlying problem and whether it is treatable (Boise et al., 1999).

It can be discouraging to read about the countless ways in which genes and environment can conspire to make human development go awry. Yet research provides a basis for attempting to prevent developmental psychopathology through a two-pronged strategy of eliminating risk factors, such as defective genes and abusive parenting, and strengthening protective factors such as social support. If prevention proves impossible, most psychological disorders and developmental problems can be treated successfully, enabling the individual to move back onto a healthier developmental track.

Summary Points

1. To diagnose many psychological disorders, psychologists and psychiatrists consider the broad criteria of statistical deviance, maladaptiveness, and personal distress. The *Diagnostic and Statistical Manual of Mental Disorders* (DSM-IV) spells out specific diagnostic criteria for a wide range of psychological disorders, including major depressive disorder.

2. Developmental psychopathology is concerned with the origins and course of psychopathology, treats the disorder as a pathway of development rather than as a disease, and emphasizes the importance of evaluating abnormal behavior in relation to social and age norms. A diathesis/stress model has proven useful in understanding how nature and nurture contribute to psychological disorders.

3. Autism is characterized by early onset, deviant social responses, language and communication deficits, and repetitive behavior; it may be rooted in part in cognitive impairments such as lack of a theory of mind or deficiencies in symbolic thought or executive functions. Genetic mechanisms account for most cases. Many, but not all, autistic individuals remain impaired in later life, but early, intensive behavioral training can bring about great improvements in functioning.

4. Some infants who have been emotionally starved or separated from attachment figures, including infants whose parents are depressed and infants suffering from failure to thrive, display depression-like symptoms, if not true clinical depression.

5. Children with attention-deficit hyperactivity disorder, an externalizing (undercontrolled) disorder, display inattention, impulsivity, and hyperactivity. They can be helped through a combination of stimulant drugs and behavioral training, but many do not entirely outgrow their problems.

6. Diagnosable depression, an internalizing (overcontrolled) disorder, can occur during childhood. It manifests itself somewhat differently at different ages, tends to recur, and can be treated successfully with antidepressant drugs and psychotherapy.

7. It is too simple to view "bad" parenting as the cause of all childhood problems; heredity also contributes, and children's problems are partly the cause as well as the effect of disturbed parent–child relationships. Fortunately, despite some continuity, many childhood problems, especially mild ones, are only temporary.

8. Contrary to the "storm and stress" view, adolescents are no more vulnerable to psychological disorders than adults are. Anorexia nervosa and bulimia, both serious eating disorders, seem to arise when a vulnerable adolescent, typically a girl, is raised in a troubled family, lives in a society that strongly encourages dieting, and experiences stressful events.

9. Risks of depression rise during adolescence, especially among females. Adolescents, in a cry for help, are more likely to attempt but less likely to commit suicide than adults (especially older European American men).

10. Probably because young adults experience more life strains and stressors than older adults do, most psychological disorders besides cognitive impairment are more common in early adulthood than in later adulthood. Depression tends to be most common in early adulthood and among women, but elderly adults may be underdiagnosed.

11. The most common forms of dementia—a progressive loss of cognitive capacities affecting about 5% of the elderly population—are Alzheimer's disease, in which a buildup of beta-amyloid within senile plaques damages neurons, and vascular dementia. These irreversible dementias must be carefully distinguished from correctible conditions such as reversible dementias, delirium, and depression.

Critical Thinking

1. The major theories of development discussed throughout this book—for example, Freud's or Erikson's psychoanalytic theory, Bandura's social learning theory, Piaget's cognitive developmental theory, Bronfenbrenner's ecological theory—should have something to say about why a school-age child might become depressed. Try your hand at describing what two of these theorists might say. (You may want to refer back to Chapter 2.)

2. Peggy, the young woman described at the beginning of the chapter, attempted suicide. Use the material on suicide in this chapter to explain why she might have done so, showing how both diathesis and stress may have contributed.

3. Lucille, though you don't know her, has struggled with major depressive disorder on and off for her entire life. Describe how she may have expressed her depression as an infant, preschool child, school-age child, adolescent, adult, and elderly adult. To what extent is depression depression regardless of one's age, and to what extent is it manifested differently at different ages?

4. Grandpa Fred is starting to display memory problems; sometimes he asks questions that he just asked, forgets where he left his car keys, and can't come up with the names of visiting grandchildren. Fred's son Will is convinced that his father has Alzheimer's disease and can't be helped. What possibilities would you like to rule out before accepting that conclusion—and why?

Key Terms

DSM-IV

major depressive disorder

developmental psychopathology

social norm

age norm

diathesis/stress model

autism

echolalia

executive functions

somatic symptoms

failure to thrive

externalizing problems

internalizing problems

attention-deficit hyperactivity disorder (ADHD)

comorbidity

masked depression

protective factors

storm and stress

anorexia nervosa

bulimia nervosa

dementia

Alzheimer's disease

beta-amyloid

vascular dementia

delirium

On the Web

Web Sites to Explore

General Resources on Psychological Disorders

The National Institute of Mental Health Web site provides general information and research updates on most of the disorders discussed in this chapter.

http://www.nimh.nih.gov

Another good general reference, Mental Help Net, is a searchable site that includes pages on most disorders, as well as on a variety of mental health topics, references to other Web sites, and help in finding therapists. For fun, take your problems to the computer therapist, Eliza Oracle.

http://www.mentalhelp.net

Autism

This is an interesting and informative site on autism that provides access to several articles about the condition.

http://www.autism-info.com

Depression

Information about depression is available at the general sites above, but this Planet Rx Web site has helpful information on research on and treatment of depression.

http://www.depression.com

Alzheimer's Disease

The Alzheimer's Association Web site offers a good deal of useful information on the fundamentals of Alzheimer's disease; see especially Ten Warning Signs that families can use to help them distinguish between normal cognitive declines and emerging Alzheimer's.

http://www.alz.org

Another useful site is the National Institute on Aging's Alzheimer's Disease Education and Referral Center, with a searchable database and a progress report on Alzheimer's research that was cited in this chapter.

http://www.alzheimer's.org

Search Online with InfoTrac College Edition

For additional information, explore InfoTrac College Edition, your online library. Go to

http://www.infotrac-college.com

and use the passcode that came on the card with your book. You might enter the keywords "depression and children and treatment" in the Search box to get a sense of the controversies surrounding use of antidepressant medication with children. Try "Alzheimer's and treatment" to see some of the approaches used to make Alzheimer's disease more manageable, even though it cannot currently be cured. Finally, by entering "facilitated communication" (with the quotation marks) in the Search box, you can look at the fascinating story of an approach that was believed to be effective in helping nonverbal autistic children express themselves—but that proved to be more a matter of wishful thinking than scientific fact.

Visit Our Web Site

Go to http://www.wadsworth.com/psychology, where you will find online resources directly linked to your book.

Life-Span CD-ROM

Go to the Wadsworth Life-Span CD-ROM for further study of the concepts in this chapter. The CD-ROM also includes quizzes and additional activities to expand your learning experience.

The Final Challenge: Death and Dying

AP/Wide World Photos

KELLY COLASANTI'S HUSBAND CHRIS was one of the unlucky people working in the World Trade Center on September 11, 2001. The next morning, Kelly's 4-year-old daughter Cara stood outside her bedroom, and Kelly had to say something:

> Cara . . . had not wanted to accept her mother's word at first. "Maybe Daddy fainted," she said hours after she had been told. "If he did faint," Kelly answered, "he also stopped breathing and died." She could not believe her own words, but if nothing else, Cara had to know the truth. . . .
>
> When the house emptied, Kelly gave Cara a bath, dressed her in pajamas and helped her into bed. She lay down in the adjoining trundle bed and started to tell a story that Chris loved to tell about his childhood—only she couldn't tell it so well. At the end of the story, the 4-year-old ordered her to leave and suggested that she go into the other room and read Harry Potter. Kelly was crushed; she wanted to sleep right there next to her daughter. She wandered across the hall and fell into bed, then got up and went to the closet for Chris's blue and green flannel bathrobe, the one he'd had forever. She took the robe to bed, burying her face in the cloth, again trying to smell him. Her chest went cold and her ribs ached and she opened her eyes, staring at the ceiling. My husband is dead, she said. I'm alone. (Maraniss, Hull, & Schwartzman, 2001, p. A18)

Death hurts. Whether we are 4, 34, or 84 when death strikes a loved one, it still hurts. By adulthood, most of us have experienced a significant loss, even if it was "only" the death of a beloved pet. Even when death is not striking so closely, it is there, lurking somewhere in the background as we go about the tasks of living—in the newspaper, on television, or in our minds. And sooner or later we all face the ultimate developmental task: the task of dying.

This chapter explores death and its place in life-span human development. What is death, and why do we die? How have theorists characterized the experiences of dying and bereaved people? What does death mean, and how is it experienced in infancy, childhood, adolescence, and adulthood? Why do some individuals cope far more ably with death than others do? We will discover that death is part of the human experience throughout the life span, but that each person's experience of it depends on his or her level of development, personality, life circumstances, and sociocultural context. Finally, we'll see what can be done to help dying and bereaved individuals through their ordeals.

Life and Death Issues

What is death, really? When are we most vulnerable to it, and what kills us? And why is it that all of us eventually die of "old age" if we don't die earlier? These "life and death" questions serve to introduce the topic of death and dying.

What Is Death?

As you have probably noticed, there is a good deal of confusion in our society today about when life begins and when it ends. Proponents and opponents of legalized abortion argue vehemently about when life really begins. And we hear similarly heated debates about whether a person in an irreversible coma is truly alive and whether a terminally ill patient who is in agonizing pain should be kept alive with the help of life support machines or allowed to die naturally. Definitions of death as a biological phenomenon are changing; so are the social meanings attached to death.

BIOLOGICAL DEFINITIONS OF DEATH

It used to be easy enough to tell that someone was dead: There was no breathing, no heartbeat, no sign of responsiveness. However, technological breakthroughs have forced the medical community to rethink what it means to say that someone is dead. The problem is that biological death is not a single event but a *process* (Medina, 1996). Different systems of the body die at different rates, and some individuals who have stopped breathing or who lack a heartbeat or pulse can now be revived before their brains cease to function. Moreover, basic bodily processes such as respiration and blood circulation can be maintained by life support machines in patients who have fallen into a coma and whose brains have ceased to function.

In 1968 an ad hoc committee of the Harvard Medical School offered a definition of biological death that has influenced modern legal definitions of death (Berger, 1993). The Harvard group defined biological death as **total brain death:** an irreversible loss of functioning in the entire brain, both the higher centers of the cerebral cortex that are involved in thought and the lower centers of the brain that control basic life processes such as breathing. Specifically, to be judged dead a person must meet the following criteria:

1. Be totally unresponsive to stimuli, including painful ones
2. Fail to move for 1 hour and fail to breathe for 3 minutes after being removed from a ventilator
3. Have no reflexes (for example, no eye blink and no constriction of the eye's pupil in response to light)
4. Register a flat electroencephalogram (EEG), indicating an absence of electrical activity in the cortex of the brain

As an added precaution, the testing procedure is repeated 24 hours later. Moreover, since a coma is sometimes reversible if the cause is either a drug overdose or an abnormally low body temperature, these conditions must be ruled out before a coma victim is pronounced dead.

Now consider some of the life and death issues that have revolved around this definition of biological death (Stillion & McDowell, 1996; Urofsky, 1993). In 1975, a now famous young woman named Karen Ann Quinlan lapsed into a coma at a party, probably because of the combination of alcohol and drugs she had consumed (see Cantor, 2001; Urofsky, 1993). Quinlan was totally unconscious, but her bodily functioning was maintained with the aid of a ventilator and other life support systems. When a court finally granted her parents permission to turn off the respirator, on the grounds that patients are entitled to choose their own course of treatment (or to have their surrogates do so on their behalf), Quinlan continued to breathe without it, much to everyone's surprise. She lived on in a vegetative state, lacking all consciousness and being fed through a tube, for 10 years.

This famous right-to-die case highlighted the different positions one can take on the issue of when a person is dead. The position laid out in the Harvard definition of total brain death (and in most state laws) is quite conservative. By the Harvard criteria, Karen Ann Quinlan was not dead, even though she was in an irreversible coma, because the lower portions of her brain were still functioning enough to support breathing and other basic bodily functions. Shouldn't we keep such seemingly hopeless patients alive in case we discover ways to revive or cure them? A more liberal position is that a person should be declared dead when the cerebral cortex is irreversibly dead, even if bodily functioning is still maintained by the more primitive portions of the brain. After all, is a person really a person if he or she lacks any awareness and if there is no hope that conscious mental activity will be restored? Should families have to stand by helplessly for years and governments have to pick up the tab for medical care? Most states, influenced by the work of a Presidential commission in the early 1980s, have arrived at the position that death can be declared when there is either an irreversible cessation of circulatory and respiratory functions *or* an irreversible cessation of all brain functions (Capron, 1999). This allows doctors to declare a person dead if he or she meets the traditional criteria of death—no heartbeat or breathing—even when assessments of brain functions have not been performed, but it requires a brain assessment if the person is in a coma and is breathing with the help of life support systems.

Cases like Quinlan's also raise issues concerning **euthanasia**—a term meaning "happy" or "good" death that usually refers to hastening the death of someone who is suffering from an incurable illness or injury. The Explorations box on page 462 explores some of these issues. Clearly, we as a society continue to grapple with defining life and death and deciding whether euthanasia is morally and legally acceptable (see Cantor, 2001; Emanuel, 2001; Kastenbaum, 1998).

SOCIAL MEANINGS OF DEATH

Death is not only a biological process but also a psychological and social one. The social meanings attached to death vary widely from historical era to historical era and from culture to culture (Rosenblatt, 2001). Indeed, we have just discovered that *society* defines who is dead and who is alive! True, people everywhere die, and people everywhere grieve deaths in some fashion. Moreover, all societies have evolved some manner of reacting to this universal experience—of interpreting its meaning, disposing of corpses, and expressing grief. Beyond these universals, however, the similarities end.

As Phillippe Ariès (1981) has shown, the social meanings of death have changed over the course of history. In Europe during the Middle Ages, people were expected to recognize that their deaths were approaching so that they could bid their farewells and die with dignity surrounded by loved ones. Since the late 19th century, Ariès argues, Western societies have engaged in a "denial of death." We have taken death out of the home and put it in the hospital and funeral parlor; we have shifted responsibility for the care of the dying from family and friends to "experts"—physicians and funeral directors. We have made death a medical failure rather than a natural part of the life cycle. Right-to-die and death-with-dignity advocates have been arguing forcefully that we should return to some of the old ways, bringing death out into the open rather than avoiding all mention of it, allowing it to occur more naturally, and making it once again an experience to be shared within the family.

If we look at how people in other cultures interpret and cope with death, we quickly realize that there are many alternatives to our Western ways and no single, biologically mandated grieving process (Klass, 2001; Metcalf & Huntington, 1991; Rosenblatt, 2001). Depending on the society, "funerals are the occasion for avoiding people or holding parties, for fighting or having sexual orgies, for weeping or laughing, in a thousand different combinations" (Metcalf & Huntington, 1991, p. 24). Corpses are treated in a remarkable number of ways, too: They "are burned or buried, with or without animal or human sacrifice; they are preserved by smoking, embalming, or pickling; they are eaten—raw, cooked, or rotten; they are ritually exposed as carrion or simply abandoned; or they are dismembered and treated in a variety of these ways" (Metcalf & Huntington, 1991, p. 24). In most societies, there is some concept of spiritual immortality. Yet here, too, there is much variety, from concepts of heaven and hell to the idea of reincarnation to a belief in ancestral ghosts who can meddle in the lives of the living (Rosenblatt, 1993).

We need not look beyond North America to find considerable variation in the social meanings of death, as different ethnic and racial groups clearly have different rules for expressing grief (Cook & Dworkin, 1992; Irish, Lundquist, & Nelson, 1993). It is customary among Puerto Ricans, especially women, to display intense, hysterical emotions after a death (Cook & Dworkin, 1992). Japanese Americans, by contrast, are likely to have been taught to restrain their grief—to smile so as not to burden others with their pain and to avoid the shame associated with losing control of oneself (Cook & Dworkin, 1992). Japanese Americans, European Americans, and others socialized to restrain their grief might view Puerto Rican mourners as psychologically disturbed when all they are doing is following the rules for emotional display that prevail in their cultural group.

Different ethnic and racial groups also have different mourning rituals and notions of how long a death should be mourned. Irish Americans are likely to believe that the dead deserve a good send-off—a wake with food, drink, and jokes, the kind of party the deceased might have enjoyed (McGoldrick et al., 1991). African Americans share this belief

Should We Hasten Death?

Do you believe in euthanasia if a person is terminally ill and in constant pain? Before you answer, note that there are actually two very different forms of euthanasia. *Active euthanasia,* or "mercy killing," is deliberately and directly causing a person's death—for example, by administering a lethal dose of drugs to a pain-racked patient in the late stages of cancer or smothering a spouse who is in the late stages of Alzheimer's disease. *Passive euthanasia,* by contrast, means allowing a terminally ill person to die of natural causes—for example, by withholding extraordinary life-saving treatments, as happened when Karen Ann Quinlan was removed from her respirator. In-between active euthanasia and passive euthanasia is **assisted suicide**—not killing someone, as in active euthanasia, but making available to a person who wishes to die the means by which *he or she* may do so. This includes physician-assisted suicide—for example, a doctor's writing a prescription for sleeping pills or pain killers at the request of a terminally ill patient who has made known her desire to die, in full knowledge that she will probably take an overdose (Quill, 1993).

How do we as a society view these options? There is overwhelming support among medical personnel and members of the general public for passive euthanasia (Stillion & McDowell, 1996). And more than 68% of a Texas sample recently expressed support for assisted suicide, especially when the assistance is provided by a doctor rather than by a relative or friend (Worthen & Yeatts, 2000–2001). In addition, a surprising majority of Americans support a form of active euthanasia in which a doctor ends a patient's life by some painless means if the patient and his or her family request it (Caddell & Newton, 1995).

In most states, as a result of lobbying efforts by the right-to-die movement, it is now legal to withhold extraordinary life-extending treatments from terminally ill patients and to "pull the plug" on life support equipment when that is the wish of the dying person or when the immediate family can show that the individual expressed, when he or she was able to do so, a desire to reject life support measures (Cantor, 2001). By writing a **Living Will** when they are healthy, people can state that they do not want any extraordinary medical procedures applied if they become hopelessly ill, and most states will honor their wishes. By contrast, active euthanasia is still viewed as murder and is punishable as such.

In 1994, Oregon became the first state to pass a law allowing physician-assisted suicide. It allows doctors, after careful evaluation, to give terminally ill patients who request them drugs with which to take their own lives (Stillion & McDowell, 1996). Other states have not followed Oregon's example, however; indeed, several states have passed laws *against* assisted suicide (Emanuel, 2001). Similarly, euthanasia and physician-assisted suicide have been legalized in the Netherlands, but other countries have not followed suit. One reason for caution is that patients' wishes may change. When the mental states of elderly cancer patients were assessed over time in one study, the patients showed large swings in the strength of their will to live, even from day to day, suggesting that it may be difficult to establish that a patient truly wants to end his or her life (Chochinov et al., 1999). Another reason for caution is that terminally ill patients may be in no shape to make life-and-death decisions, and others speaking for them may not have their best interests at heart (Cantor, 2001; Mishara, 1999b).

On many life-and-death issues, right-to-die advocates, who maintain that people should have a say in how they die, fight head-to-head against right-to-life advocates, who claim that everything possible should be done to maintain life and that nothing should be done to cut it short. It makes sense to think through these issues now in case you must someday decide whether you or a loved one should live or die.

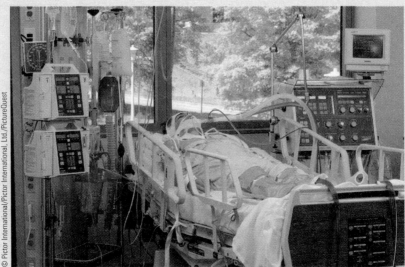

Carl D. Walsh/Aurora Photos

Mourning rituals differ considerably from culture to culture.

that it is important to go out in style; however, they tend to regard the funeral not as a time for rowdy celebration but as a forum for expressing grief, in some congregations by wailing and singing spirituals (McGoldrick et al., 1991; Perry, 1993). Jewish families are even more restrained; they quietly withdraw from normal activities for a week of mourning, called *shiva,* and then honor the dead again at the one-month and one-year marks (Cytron, 1993). The tradition among the Navajos is to try to forget the loved one as rapidly as possible and resume normal activities after only three or four days of mourning (Cook & Dworkin, 1992). By contrast, Japanese Americans may follow the Japanese tradition of preparing an altar containing a photograph of the deceased and worshipping before it each and every morning as a way of maintaining a relationship with the deceased (Klass, 2001).

In short, the experiences of dying individuals and of their survivors are very much shaped by the historical and cultural context in which death occurs. Death may be universal, and the tendency to react negatively to the loss of an attachment figure may be universal (Parkes, 2000), but our specific experiences of death and dying are not. Death is truly what we humans make of it, which means that we must not presume that there is one "right" way to die or to grieve a death. As Paul

Rosenblatt (1993) concludes, "It pays to treat everyone as though he or she were from a different culture" (p. 18).

What Kills Us and When?

How long are we likely to live, and what is likely to kill us? In the United States the **life expectancy** at birth—the *average* number of years a newborn can be expected to live—is 76.5 years (U.S. Bureau of the Census, 2000). This average life expectancy disguises important differences between males and females, among racial and ethnic groups, and between social classes. The life expectancy for white males has risen to almost 75, whereas the life expectancy for white females is almost 80. Female hormones seem to protect women from high blood pressure and heart problems, and they are also less vulnerable than men to violent deaths and accidents and to the effects of smoking, drinking, and similar health hazards (Kaplan & Erickson, 2000). No one is quite sure of all the reasons, but females live longer than men in most other countries as well. Meanwhile, life expectancies for African Americans, many of whom experience the health hazards associated with poverty, are a good deal lower than those for European Americans: 68 for males, 75 for females. Life expectancies are also higher—and have been rising faster—in affluent areas than in poor areas (Malmstrom et al., 1999).

Life expectancies have increased steadily over the centuries, from 30 years in ancient Rome to around 80 in modern affluent societies such as Japan and Sweden (Harman, 2001). Life expectancies in some countries lag far behind, however, as illustrated in Figure 17.1. In less developed countries plagued by malaria, famine, AIDS, and other such killers—in Uganda, for example—the life expectancy barely exceeds 40 (Kinsella & Gist, 1998). Worse, the AIDS epidemic in hard-hit African countries such as Botswana and Zimbabwe is now resulting in *decreases* in life expectancies; they are projected to fall to between 30 and 40 years of age by 2010 if the devastation continues and to drop in Latin American, the Caribbean, and Asia as well (U.S. Agency for International Development, 2000).

Vulnerability to death changes over the life span. Infants are relatively vulnerable; infant mortality in the United States has dropped considerably, though, and now stands at 7 out of 1,000 live births (U.S. Bureau of the Census, 2000). Assuming that we survive infancy, we have a relatively small chance of dying during childhood, adolescence, or early adulthood. Death rates then climb steadily throughout middle age and old age.

What kills us? The leading causes of death change dramatically over the life span, as shown in Table 17.1 (U.S. Bureau of the Census, 2000). Infant deaths are mainly associated with complications in the period surrounding birth and congenital abnormalities that infants bring with them to life. The leading cause of death among preschool and school-age children is accidents (especially car accidents but also poisonings, falls, fires, drownings, and so on). Adolescence and early adulthood are generally periods of good health. Accidents (especially car accidents), homicides, and suicides are the leading killers of adolescents; HIV infection, accidents, and cancers

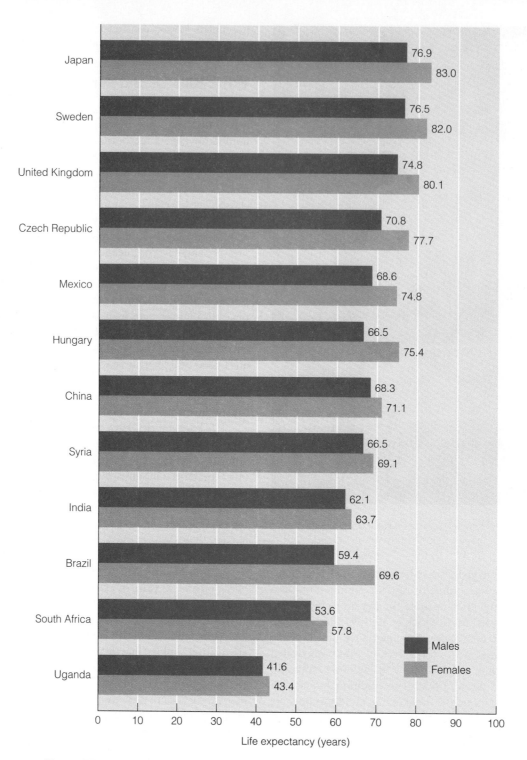

Figure 17.1 Male and female life expectancies at birth in selected countries. Life expectancies vary widely from country to country but are generally higher for females than for males.

SOURCE: Data from Kinsella & Gist (1998)

kill young adults. Starting in the 45–64 age group, chronic diseases—notably cancers and heart disease—begin to dominate the list of leading killers. The incidence of these chronic conditions climbs steadily with age, raising overall death rates considerably. Among adults 65 and older, heart disease leads the list by far, accounting for 35% of deaths, followed by cancers and cerebrovascular diseases (strokes).

In sum, life expectancies are higher than ever. After we make it through the vulnerable period of infancy, we are at low risk of death through early adulthood and are most likely

Table 17.1 Leading Causes of Death for Different Age Groups

Age Group	#1	#2	#3
1–4	Accidents	Congenital anomalies	Cancers
5–14	Accidents	Cancers	Homicide
15–24	Accidents	Homicide	Suicide
25–44	HIV infection	Accidents	Cancers
45–64	Cancers	Heart disease	Accidents
65+	Heart disease	Cancers	Cerebrovascular diseases

SOURCE: Data from U.S. Bureau of the Census (2000)

to die suddenly because of an accident if we do die. As we age, we become more and more vulnerable to death, particularly from chronic diseases. But now a more fundamental question: Why is it that all of us eventually die? Why does no one live to be 200 or 600? To understand why death is an inevitable part of human development, we need the help of theories of aging.

Theories of Aging: Why Do We Age and Die?

There is no simple answer to the question of why we ultimately age and die. However, several theories have been proposed, and each of them says something important about the aging process. These theories can be divided into two main categories: **Programmed theories of aging** emphasize the systematic genetic control of aging processes; **damage theories of aging** call attention to more haphazard processes that cause errors in cells to accumulate and organ systems to deteriorate (W. R. Clark, 1999; Medina, 1996; Wickens, 1998). The question, really, is whether aging and death are the result of a biological master plan or of random insults to the body while we live.

PROGRAMMED THEORIES

Human beings, like other species, have a characteristic **maximum life span**—a ceiling on the number of years that anyone lives. The longest documented and verified life so far is that of Jeanne Louise Calment, a French woman who died in 1997 at the age of 122 (W. R. Clark, 1999). Nearly blind and deaf and confined to a wheelchair, she maintained her sense of humor to the end, attributing her longevity to everything from having a stomach "like an ostrich's" to being forgotten by God (Trueheart, 1997). Ms. Calment and others who live almost as long are the basis for setting the maximum human life span at around 120. Interestingly, this maximum has not increased nearly as much over the centuries as average life expectancy has, although it appears to have nudged upward to some degree (Wilmoth et al., 2000).

Humans are long-lived compared to most species. The maximum life span for the mouse is $3\frac{1}{2}$ years, for the dog 20, for the chimpanzee 50, and for the long-lived Galapagos tortoise 150 (Walford, 1983). The very fact that each species has its own characteristic maximum life span should convince us that species-wide genes influence how long people generally

live. Moreover, we know that the individual's genetic makeup, in combination with environmental factors, influences how rapidly he or she ages and how long he or she lives compared to other humans (Wickens, 1998). A fairly good way to estimate how long you will live is to average the longevity of your parents and grandparents (Medvedev, 1991). It is not clear yet how genes influence aging and longevity, however. There are almost certainly several genes, rather than only one, involved—some lengthening life, others hastening death (Hodes, McCormick, & Pruzan, 1996). More is involved than just genes that increase susceptibility to the diseases that tend to kill people.

Biological researchers have long been exploring the possibility that we are programmed with an "aging clock" in every cell of our bodies. Their work has built on that of Leonard Hayflick (1976, 1994), who grew cells in cultures, allowed them to divide or double, and measured the number of doublings that occurred. He discovered that cells from human embryos could double only a certain number of times—50 times, plus or minus 10, to be exact—an estimate now referred to as the **Hayflick limit.** Hayflick also demonstrated that cells taken from human adults divide even fewer times, presumably because they have already used up some of their capacity for reproducing themselves. Moreover, the maximum life span of a species is related to the Hayflick limit for that species: The short-lived mouse's cells can go through only 14 to 28 doublings; the long-lived Galapagos tortoise's cells can manage 90 to 125.

Now many researchers believe that the cellular aging clock suggested by Hayflick's limit on cell division is timed by a shortening of **telomeres**—the stretches of DNA that form the tips of chromosomes (A. G. Bodnar et al., 1998; Klapper, Parwaresch, & Krupp, 2001). When a cell divides, each of its chromosomes replicates itself, but the chromosome's telomere does not. Instead, half of the telomere goes to one of the new chromosomes that is formed and half goes to the other. The result is shorter and shorter telomeres as we age; eventually, the theory goes, this progressive shortening of telomeres makes cells unable to replicate any more, causes them to malfunction and die, and ultimately causes the organism itself to die. Many questions remain about whether an eventual inability of cells to divide can ever explain the death of the whole organism (Wickens, 1998). Still, the idea that telomeres function as an aging clock within cells is a good example of a theory

An individual's genetic makeup, combined with environmental factors, influences how rapidly the person ages and how long he or she lives.

Children with the genetic disorder progeria experience early graying, wrinkling, and hair loss, cardiovascular problems, Alzheimer's disease, and death. They provide clues to the genetic basis for aging.

maintaining that aging and death are genetically programmed processes.

Using techniques of modern genetic analysis, researchers are now identifying specific genes that become more or less active from middle age to old age and that therefore may be implicated in the aging process (Ly et al., 2000). Many of the genes that become less active with age in normal adults are also inactive in children who have **progeria,** a genetic disorder caused by a single dominant gene that makes victims age prematurely and die early, often of heart disease and other killers that normally strike in old age (DeBusk, 1972). Many of the genes that become inactive with age also turn out to be involved in regulating cell division—for example, in stopping cells with genetic errors from dividing (Ly et al., 2000).

Other programmed theories of aging have centered on genetically guided, systematic changes in body systems, such as the neuroendocrine system and the immune system (Cristofalo, 1996; Knight, 2000). We know that the hypothalamus of the brain, guided by a genetic program, sets in motion the hormonal changes responsible for puberty and menopause (see Chapter 5). Possibly the hypothalamus also serves as an aging clock, systematically altering levels of hormones and brain chemicals in later life so that bodily functioning is no longer regulated properly and we die. Other researchers are investigating genetically governed changes in the immune system. These changes not only decrease its ability to defend against potentially life-threatening foreign agents such as infections, but also cause it to mistake normal cells for invaders (Wickens, 1998). All of these programmed theories of aging hold that aging and dying are the inevitable products of our biological endowment as human beings, and all have some support.

DAMAGE THEORIES

In contrast to programmed theories of aging, damage theories generally propose that wear and tear—an accumulation of haphazard or random damage to cells and organs over the years—ultimately causes death.

According to one of the most promising damage theories, **free radical theory,** toxic by-products of normal metabolic processes damage cells (Harman, 2001; Wickens, 1998). Free radicals are molecules that have an extra or "free" electron, are chemically unstable, and react with other molecules in the body to produce substances that damage normal cells, including their DNA. Over time, the genetic code contained in the DNA of more and more cells becomes scrambled, and the body's mechanisms for repairing such damage simply cannot keep up with the chaos. More and more cells then function improperly or cease to function, and the organism eventually dies.

"Age spots" on the skin of older people are a visible sign of the damage free radicals can cause. Free radicals have also been implicated in some of the major diseases that become more common with age—cardiovascular diseases, cancer, Alzheimer's disease, and others (Harman, 2001). However, the damage of most concern is damage to DNA. Unfortunately, we cannot live and breathe without producing free radicals, which are a by-product of the metabolism of oxygen. Some studies suggest that **antioxidants** such as vitamins E and C, at least when included in one's diet rather than taken in pill form, may increase longevity, though not for very long, by inhibiting free radical activity and in turn preventing age-related diseases such as cardiovascular disease, dementia, and cancer (W. R. Clark, 1999; Medina, 1996; Meydani, 2001).

NATURE AND NURTURE CONSPIRING

The theories just discussed are some of the most promising explanations of why we age and die. Programmed theories of aging generally claim that aging and dying are as much a part of nature's plan as sprouting teeth or uttering one's first words. The telomere explanation of the Hayflick limit on cell replication, changes in the levels of activity of various genes as we age, systematic changes in endocrine functioning, and declines in the effectiveness of the immune system all suggest that aging and dying are genetically controlled. By contrast, damage theories of aging hold that we eventually succumb to haphazard destructive processes, most notably those caused by free radicals, that result in increasingly faulty DNA and abnormal cell functioning.

Neither of these broad theories of aging has proved to be *the* explanation; instead, many interacting mechanisms are at work (Knight, 2000; Wickens, 1998). For example, genes influence the capacity of cells to repair environmentally caused damage, and the random damage caused by free radicals alters genetic material. John Medina (1996) summarizes it this way: "Toxic waste products accumulate because genes shut off. Genes shut off because toxic waste products accumulate" (p. 291). In short, nature and nurture, biological and environmental factors, interact to bring about aging and dying—just as they interact to produce development.

The Applications box on page 468 explores efforts to apply research on theories of aging to the task of extending life, or finding the so-called fountain of youth. However, none of our efforts to delay death will keep us from dying. So let's turn to the question of how humans cope with death and dying.

Psychiatrist Elisabeth Kübler-Ross has called on physicians to emphasize caring rather than curing.

Can We Delay Death?

What does research on the basic causes of aging and death say about our prospects for finding the fountain of youth, or extending the life span? Both genetic theories and damage theories of aging provide leads. Genetic researchers are making remarkable progress. It is not at all unthinkable that they might discover some of the genetic mechanisms behind aging and dying and devise ways of manipulating genes to increase the maximum life span (Medina, 1996). For example, researchers are currently looking for ways to keep telomeres from shortening and thus to keep cells replicating indefinitely. However, success is a long way off, and some point out that cancer cells replicate indefinitely and that lifting restrictions on cell replication may backfire by making cells cancerous (W. R. Clark, 1999). Researchers are also looking for ways to genetically engineer antioxidant enzymes that would slow the damage caused by free radicals; however, it is unclear whether any drug or form of gene therapy could ever offer complete protection against free radicals (Wickens, 1998).

At present, the only technique that has been demonstrated experimentally to extend the life span is **dietary restriction:** a highly nutritious but severely restricted diet representing a 30–40% or more cut in normal total caloric intake (Harman, 2001; Lane et al., 2001). Laboratory studies involving rats, and recently primates, suggest that dietary restriction extends not only the average longevity but also the maximum life span of a species, and that it delays or slows the progression of many age-related diseases as well (Lane et al., 2001). A 40% reduction in daily calories results in a 40% decrease in body weight, a 40% increase in average longevity, and a 49% increase in the maximum life span of diet-restricted rats (Harman, 2001).

How does dietary restriction achieve these results? Through mechanisms that are still unclear, it reduces the number of free radicals and other toxic products of metabolism (Wickens, 1998). By looking at the activity of genes in restricted-diet and normal-diet mice, researchers are also finding that dietary restriction prevents an age-related decrease in the activity of genes involved in repairing the random damage caused by free radicals and other agents (Lee et al., 1999). However, we do not know whether dietary restriction works as well for humans as it apparently has for rats, what calorie counts and combinations of nutrients are optimal, or whether humans who have a choice would put up with being half-starved for most of their lives. Experimenting with self-starvation at this point is not a good idea. Rather, you may want to wait for the findings of research currently underway to develop agents that would have the same benefits as dieting without the need to diet (Roth, Ingram, & Lane, 2001)!

While we wait for the breakthroughs that might extend the maximum life span of human beings, we can at least reduce our chances of dying young. As suggested in Chapter 5, for example, we can stop smoking, drink only in moderation, eat nutritious food, exercise regularly, and take other steps to ward off the diseases that make us die prematurely.

The Experience of Dying

People who die suddenly may be blessed, for those who develop life-threatening illnesses face the challenge of coping with the knowledge that they are seriously ill and are likely to die. Perhaps no one has done more to focus attention on the emotional needs of dying patients than psychiatrist Elisabeth Kübler-Ross (1969, 1974), whose "stages of dying" are widely known and whose 1969 book *On Death and Dying* revolutionized the care of dying people.

Kübler-Ross's Stages of Dying

In interviews with more than 200 terminally ill patients, Kübler-Ross (1969) detected a common set of emotional responses to the knowledge that one had a serious, and probably fatal, illness. She believed that similar reactions might occur in response to any major loss, so bear in mind that the family and friends of the dying person may experience some of these same emotional reactions during the loved one's illness and after the death. Kübler-Ross's five stages of dying are as follows:

1. Denial and isolation. A common first response to dreadful news is to say "No! It can't be!" **Denial** is a defense mechanism in which anxiety-provoking thoughts are kept out of, or "isolated" from, conscious awareness. A woman who has just been diagnosed as having lung cancer may insist that the diagnosis is wrong—or accept that she is ill but be convinced that she will beat the odds and recover. Denial can be a marvelous coping device: It can get us through a time of acute crisis until we are ready to cope more constructively. Sometimes, both doctors and patients deceive themselves about the odds of recovery (The et al., 2000). Even after dying patients face the facts and become ready to talk about dying, those around them often engage in their own denial, saying such things as "Don't be silly—you'll be well in no time."

2. Anger. As the bad news begins to register, the dying person asks "Why me?" Feelings of rage or resentment may be directed at anyone who is handy—doctors, nurses, or family members. Kübler-Ross advises those close to the dying person to be sensitive to this reaction so that they won't try to avoid this irritable person or become angry in return.

3. Bargaining. When the dying person bargains, he or she says "Okay, me, but please . . . ." The bargainer asks for some concession from God, the medical staff, or someone else. A woman with lung cancer may beg for a cure or perhaps simply for a little more time, a little less pain, or a chance to ensure that her children will be taken care of after she dies.

4. Depression. When the dying person becomes even more aware of the reality of the situation, depression, despair, and a sense of hopelessness become the predominant emotional responses. Grief focuses on the losses that have already occurred (for example, the loss of the ability to function as one once did) and the losses to come (separation from loved ones, the inability to achieve one's dreams, and so on).

5. Acceptance. Assuming that the dying person is able to work through all the complex emotional reactions of the preceding stages, he or she may come to accept the inevitability of death in a calm and peaceful manner. Kübler-Ross (1969) describes the acceptance stage this way: "It is almost void of feelings. It is as if the pain had gone, the struggle is over, and there comes a time for 'the final rest before the long journey,' as one patient phrased it" (p. 100).

In addition to these five "stages of dying," Kübler-Ross emphasizes a sixth response that runs throughout the stages: *hope.* She believes that it is essential for terminally ill patients to retain some sense of hope, even if it is only the hope that they can die with dignity.

Criticisms and Alternative Views

Kübler-Ross deserves immense credit for sensitizing our society to the emotional needs of dying persons and convincing medical professionals to emphasize *caring* rather than curing in working with such persons. At the same time, there are flaws in her account of the dying person's experience (Corr, 1993; Kastenbaum, 2000). Among the most important criticisms are these: (1) Kübler-Ross's use of the term *stage* is inappropriate; (2) she largely ignores the course of the individual's illness; and (3) she makes little of individual differences in emotional responses to dying.

The major problem with Kübler-Ross's "stages" is that they appear not to be stages at all. Research suggests that the dying process is simply not stagelike (Kastenbaum, 2000). Although dying patients usually display some of the symptoms of depression as death nears, the other emotional reactions Kübler-Ross describes seem to affect only minorities of individuals (Schulz & Aderman, 1974). Moreover, when these responses do occur, they do not unfold in a set order. Even Kübler-Ross (1974) acknowledged that her "stages" do not necessarily follow one another in a standard order, as stages should. It might have been better if Kübler-Ross had, from the start, described her "stages" simply as common

emotional reactions to dying. Unfortunately, some over-zealous medical professionals have tried to push dying patients through the "stages" in order, believing incorrectly that their patients would never come to accept death unless they experienced the "right" emotions at the "right" times (Kastenbaum, 2000).

Edwin Shneidman (1973, 1980) has argued that dying patients actually experience a complex and ever-changing interplay of emotions, alternating between denial and acceptance of death. One day a patient may seem to accept that death is near; the next day he or she may talk of getting better and going home. Along the way many reactions—disbelief, hope, terror, bewilderment, rage, apathy, calm, anxiety, and others—come and go and are even experienced simultaneously. According to Shneidman, then, dying people experience many unpredictable emotional changes rather than distinct stages of dying.

A second major problem in Kübler-Ross's theory is that it does not allow for differences in emotional responses to dying associated with the course or trajectory of an illness and the specific events that occur along the way (Glaser & Strauss, 1968). When a patient is slowly and gradually worsening over time, the patient, family members, and staff can all become accustomed to the fact that death lies ahead, whereas when the path toward death is more erratic, emotional ups or downs are likely each time the patient's condition takes a turn for better or worse. Kübler-Ross expects different patients to experience similar responses even when their diseases and pathways to death are very different.

Finally, Kübler-Ross's approach overlooks the fact that each individual's personality influences how he or she experiences dying. People cope with dying much as they have coped with life (Schulz & Schlarb, 1987–1988). For example, cancer patients who faced life's problems directly and effectively, were satisfied with their lives, and maintained good interpersonal relationships *before* they became ill display less anger and irritability and are less depressed and withdrawn during their illnesses than patients who were not so well-adjusted before their illnesses (Hinton, 1975). Similarly, nursing home residents who have high self-esteem and are not depressed tend to survive longer than those who lack these strengths (O'Connor & Vallerand, 1998). Depending on their predominant personality traits, coping styles, and social competencies, some dying persons may deny until the bitter end, some may "rage against the dying of the light," some may quickly be crushed by despair, and still others may display incredible strength. Most will display combinations of these responses, each in his or her own unique way.

In sum, the experiences of dying persons are far more complex than Kübler-Ross's five "stages" of dying suggest. As Shneidman emphasizes, there is likely to be a complex interplay of many emotions and thoughts, with swings back and forth between acceptance and denial. Moreover, to understand which emotions will predominate and how these emotions will be patterned over time, we must take into account the nature and course of the individual's condition and the individual's prior personality and coping style.

The Experience of Bereavement: An Attachment Model

Most of us know a good deal more about the process of grieving a death than about the process of dying. To describe responses to the death of a loved one, we must distinguish among three terms: **Bereavement** is a state of loss, **grief** is an emotional response to loss, and **mourning** is a culturally prescribed way of displaying one's reactions. Thus, we can speak of a bereaved person who grieves by experiencing such emotions as sadness, anger, and guilt, and who mourns by attending the funeral and laying flowers on the grave each year.

Unless a death is sudden, relatives and friends, like the dying person, will experience many painful emotions *before* the death, from the initial diagnosis through the last breath (Grbich, Parker, & Maddocks, 2001). They too may alternate between acceptance and denial. They too may experience what has been termed **anticipatory grief**—grieving before death occurs for what is happening and for what lies ahead (Rando, 1986).

Yet no amount of preparation and anticipatory grief can eliminate the need to grieve after the death actually occurs. How, then, do we grieve? Much important research on the grieving process has been conducted by Colin Murray Parkes and his colleagues in Great Britain (Parkes, 1996, 1991; Parkes & Weiss, 1983). John Bowlby (1980), whose influential ethological theory of attachment was outlined in Chapter 14, and Parkes have conceptualized grieving in the context of attachment theory as a reaction to separation from a loved one that is part of our evolutionary heritage. From this perspective, the grieving adult can be likened to the infant who experiences separation anxiety when his or her mother disappears from view.

The **Parkes/Bowlby attachment model of bereavement** describes four predominant reactions. They overlap considerably and therefore should *not* be viewed as clear-cut "stages," even though the balances among them do change over time. These reactions are numbness, yearning, disorganization and despair, and reorganization (see also Jacobs et al., 1987–1988; Shuchter & Zisook, 1993).

1. Numbness. In the first few hours or days after the death, the bereaved person is often in a daze—gripped by a sense of unreality and disbelief and almost empty of feelings. He or she may make plane reservations, call relatives, or order flowers—all as if in a dream. Underneath this state of numbness and shock is a sense of being on the verge of bursting, and occasionally painful emotions do break through. The bereaved person is struggling to defend himself or herself against the full weight of the loss. The bad news has not fully registered.

2. Yearning. As the numbing sense of shock and disbelief diminishes, the bereaved person experiences more and more agony. Grief comes in pangs or waves that typically are most severe from 5 to 14 days after the death. The grieving person

has feelings of panic, bouts of uncontrollable weeping, and physical aches and pains. He or she is likely to be extremely restless, unable to concentrate or to sleep, and preoccupied with thoughts of the loved one and of the events leading to the death.

According to Parkes and Bowlby, the reaction that most clearly makes grieving different from other kinds of emotional distress is *separation anxiety*—the distress of being parted from the object of one's attachment. The bereaved person pines and yearns for the loved one and actually searches for the deceased, as if the finality of the loss has not yet been accepted. A widow may think she heard her husband's voice or saw him in a crowd; she may sense his presence in the house and draw comfort from it; she may be drawn to his favorite chair or wear his bathrobe. Ultimately, of course, the quest to be reunited is doomed to fail.

Both anger and guilt are also common reactions during these early weeks and months of bereavement. Bereaved people often feel irritable and on edge and sometimes experience intense rage—at the loved one for dying, at the doctors for not doing a better job, at almost anyone. To make sense of the death, they seem to need to pin blame somewhere. Unfortunately, they often find reason to blame themselves—to feel guilty. A father may moan that he should have spent more time teaching his son gun safety; the friend of a young man who dies of AIDS may feel that he was not a good enough friend. One of the London widows studied by Parkes actually felt guilty because she never made her husband bread pudding.

3. Disorganization and despair. As time passes, pangs of intense grief and yearning become less frequent, though they still occur. As it sinks in that a reunion with the loved one is impossible, depression, despair, and apathy increasingly predominate. During most of the first year after the death, and longer in many cases, bereaved individuals often feel apathetic or even defeated. They may have difficulty managing and taking interest in their lives.

4. Reorganization. Eventually, bereaved persons begin to pull themselves together again as their pangs of grief and periods of apathy become less frequent. They come to invest less emotional energy in their attachment to the deceased and more in their attachments to the living. If they have lost a spouse, they begin to make the transition from being a wife or husband to being a widow or widower, revising their identities. They may also revise their internal working models of self and other and think in new ways about their relationship with the person who died (I. C. Noppe, 2000). They begin to feel ready for new activities and possibly for new relationships or attachments.

Some researchers would disagree with the specifics of this view of bereavement. However, most would agree on this: *Bereavement is a complex and multidimensional process that varies from person to person and normally takes a long time.* Many emotional reactions are involved, and their course and intensity differ from person to person. An analysis of research by George Bonanno and Stacey Kaltman (2000) suggests that modest disruptions in cognitive, emotional, physical, and in-

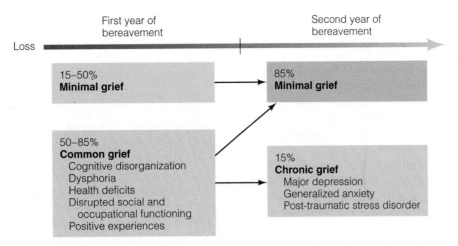

Figure 17.2 Patterns of grief differ greatly from person to person. Some people show little grief; most experience disrupted functioning for about a year and then minimal grief in the second year; and about 15% experience chronic and significant psychological problems.

Source: Adapted from Bonanno & Kaltman (2000)

terpersonal functioning are typical, that they usually last for a year, and that less severe signs of grief then continue to be evident for several years (Bonanno & Kaltman, 2000). Positive thoughts about the deceased, expressions of love, and feelings of gaining from the loss are also part of the typical picture. A surprisingly high proportion of bereaved people, from 15% to 50% depending on the study, experience minimal grief even in the early months after the death. Finally, about 15% can be characterized as chronic grievers: They continue to experience serious disruptions in functioning one to two years after their loss, they often have diagnosable major depression or anxiety disorder, and they may therefore be candidates for treatment (see Figure 17.2). Some people never fully recover from a crushing loss or give up their attachment to the loved one who died (Wortman & Silver, 2001).

Yet the rest of us expect quick recovery: We are very sympathetic toward the bereaved immediately after a death—eager to help in any way we can—but then we quickly grow weary of someone who is depressed, irritable, or preoccupied. We begin to think, sometimes after only a few weeks, that it is time for the bereaved person to cheer up and get on with life. We are wrong! To be of help to bereaved people, one must understand that their reactions of numbness and disbelief, yearning, and despair are likely to linger for a very long time.

We have now presented some of the major theories of how people experience dying and bereavement. However, these theories have been based primarily on the responses of adults. How do infants, children, and adolescents respond to death? What does death even mean to infants and young children? A life-span perspective on death and dying is needed.

The Infant

Infants surely do not comprehend death as the cessation of life, but they gain an understanding of concepts that pave the way for an understanding of death. Infants may, for example, come to grasp the concepts of being and nonbeing from such experiences as watching objects and people appear and disappear, playing peekaboo, and even going to sleep and "coming alive" again in the morning (Maurer, 1961). As infants begin to acquire the concept of object permanence during Piaget's sensorimotor stage, they search for missing or hidden objects and can become quite frustrated when those objects are "all gone." Very possibly, then, infants first form a global category of things that are "all gone" and later divide it into subcategories, one of which is "dead" (Kastenbaum, 2000).

The experience that is most directly relevant to an emerging concept of death is the disappearance of a loved one. It is here that John Bowlby's theory of attachment is helpful. After infants form their first attachments at about the age of 6 or 7 months, they begin to display signs of separation anxiety and to protest when their beloved caregivers leave them. They have begun to grasp the concept that persons, like objects, have permanent existence, and they expect a loved one who has disappeared to reappear. According to Bowlby, they are biologically programmed to protest separations by crying, searching for their loved one, and attempting to follow, because these behaviors increase the chances that they will be reunited with a caregiver and protected from harm.

Bowlby (1980) observed that infants separated from their attachment figures display many of the same reactions that bereaved adults do. Whether the cause of separation from a parent is death or a vacation trip, infants first engage in vigorous *protest*—yearning and searching for the loved one and expressing outrage when they fail. One 17-month-old girl said only, "Mum, Mum, Mum" for three days after her mother died. She was willing to sit on a nurse's lap but would turn her back, as if she did not want to see that the nurse was not "Mum" (Freud & Burlingham, cited in Bowlby, 1980).

If, after a week or so of protest, an infant has not succeeded in finding the loved one, he or she begins to *despair* and show depression-like symptoms; the baby loses hope, ends the search, and becomes apathetic and sad. Grief may be reflected in a poor appetite, a change in sleeping patterns, excessive clinginess, or regression to less mature behavior (Furman, 1984; and see the discussion in Chapter 16 of infant depression and failure to thrive). Eventually, such infants begin to seek new relationships. They will recover from their loss most completely if they can count on an existing attachment figure (for example, the surviving parent) or can attach themselves to someone new.

Clearly, then, infants who are at least 6 months of age or so and who have formed genuine attachment bonds are old enough to experience intense grief and depression-like symptoms when a parent or other loved one dies. Moreover, the responses they display—the protest and yearning, the despair and depression—are the same sorts of responses that bereaved adults display. What is the difference? It is mainly that infants lack the concept that death means permanent separation or loss. Without the cognitive capacity to interpret what has happened, an infant whose mother has died may have little idea why she is gone, where she is, or why she does not return.

The Child

As much as parents would like to shelter their children from unpleasant life experiences, children do encounter death in their early years, if only of bugs and birds. How do they come to understand and cope with their experiences of death?

Grasping the Concept of Death

Contrary to what many adults would like to believe, young children are highly curious about death, think about it with some frequency, and are quite willing to talk about it (Kastenbaum, 2000). Yet their beliefs about death often differ considerably from those of adults. In our society, a "mature" understanding of death has several components (Brent et al., 1996; Hoffman & Strauss, 1985; Mishara, 1999a; Slaughter, Jaakkola, & Carey, 1999). We see death as characterized by

1. **Finality:** It is the cessation of life and of all life processes, such as movement, sensation, and thought.
2. **Irreversibility:** It cannot be undone.
3. **Universality:** It is inevitable and happens to all living beings.

4. **Biological causality:** It is the result of natural processes internal to the organism, even if external causes set off these internal changes.

Researchers have studied children's conceptions of death by asking them the sorts of questions contained in Table 17.2 or having them draw pictures of their images of death. Children between the ages of 3 and 5 have some understanding of death, especially its universality, but they are a long way from having a mature concept of it (Brent et al., 1996). Rather than viewing death as a final cessation of life functions, they tend to think of the dead as living under altered circumstances and retaining at least some of their capacities (Slaughter et al., 1999). According to preschoolers, the dead may not be as lively and capable as the living, but they may well be able to move around a bit, hear what is going on outside their coffins, experience hunger, think, and dream (Hoffman & Strauss, 1985).

Preschool-age children also tend to view death as reversible rather than irreversible. They liken it to sleep (from which one can awaken) or to a trip (from which one can return). With the right medical care, the proper foods, or a bit of magic, a dead person might be brought back to life (Speece & Brent, 1984). As one youngster put it, one can "help [dead people], give them hot food, and keep them healthy so it won't happen again" (Koocher, 1974, p. 408). Finally, young children think death is caused by one concrete, external agent or another. One may say that people die because they eat aluminum foil; another may say the cause is eating a dirty bug or a Styrofoam cup (Koocher, 1974).

Children ages 5 to 7 make considerable progress in acquiring a mature concept of death. The majority of children this age understand that death is characterized by finality (cessation of life functions), irreversibility, and universality (Grollman, 1995; Speece & Brent, 1992). What most still lack is a mature understanding of the biological causality of death. Although early elementary school children can catalog guns, poisons, and other concrete causes of death, they fail to appreciate that all deaths ultimately involve a failure of internal biological processes (Slaughter et al., 1999). Paula, age 12, had mastered this concept: "When the heart stops, blood stops circulating, you stop breathing and that's it . . . there's lots of ways it can get started, but that's what really happens" (Koocher, 1974, pp. 407–408).

Some children have a far more sophisticated understanding of death than their age-mates. Why might this be? Chil-

Table 17.2 Western Concepts of Death and Questions Pertaining to Them

Concept	Questions
Finality	Can a dead person move? Get hungry? Speak? Think? Dream? Do dead people know that they are dead?
Irreversibility	Can a dead person become a live person again? Is there anything that could make a dead animal come back to life?
Universality	Does everyone die at some time? Will your parents die someday? Your friends? Will you die?
Biological causality	What makes a person die? Why do animals die?

SOURCES: Based on Hoffman & Strauss (1985), Florian & Kravetz (1985), and other sources

dren's concepts of death appear to be influenced by (1) their level of cognitive development and (2) their life experiences. Young children in Piaget's preoperational stage of cognitive development tend to think magically and concretely about death and may easily come to wrong conclusions about how or why someone died. Major breakthroughs in the understanding of death occur in about the 5-to-7 age range—precisely when children are making the transition from the preoperational stage of cognitive development to the concrete operational stage. Children's understanding of death, like their understanding of many other concepts, becomes more adultlike as they begin to master important logical operations (Essa & Murray, 1994).

But children's concepts of death are also influenced by the cultural context in which they live and the specific cultural and religious beliefs to which they are exposed (Stambrook & Parker, 1987). For example, Jewish and Christian children in Israel, who are taught our Western concept of death, provide more "mature" answers to questions about death than Druze children, who are taught to believe in reincarnation (Florian & Kravetz, 1985). Understandably, a child who is taught that people are reincarnated after they die may not view death as an irreversible cessation of all life processes. Indeed, as children in both the United States and China approach adolescence and are increasingly exposed to religious teachings and to information about biology and medicine, they lose some of their conviction that death is irreversible and final (Brent et al., 1996). They begin to believe that the dead might be brought back to life through medical or divine intervention or might live on in an afterlife.

Within any society, children's unique life experiences will also affect their understanding of death. Children who have life-threatening illnesses or who frequently encounter violence and death sometimes grasp death sooner than other children (Essa & Murray, 1994; O'Halloran & Altmaier, 1996). How parents and others communicate with children about death can also make a difference. How is a young child to overcome the belief that death is temporary, for example, if parents and other adults claim that relatives who have died are "asleep"? Isn't it also understandable that such a child might become afraid of going to bed at night? We must also wonder about statements that liken death to a journey, as in "Grandma has gone away." For all the young child knows, Grandma might be across town or in Chicago and surely could return if she really cared.

Experts on death insist that adults only make death more confusing and frightening to young children when they use such euphemisms (Aspinall, 1996). They point out that children often understand more than we think, as illustrated by the 3-year-old who, after her father explained that her long-ill and just deceased grandfather had "gone to live on a star in the sky," looked at him quizzically and said, "You mean he is dead?" (Silverman, 2000, pp. 2–3). Experts recommend that parents give children simple but honest answers to the many questions they naturally ask about death and capitalize on events such as the death of a pet to teach children about death and help them understand and express their emotions

In the weeks after the September 11 attack on the World Trade Center, Sesame Workshop asked school-age children to draw pictures of their fears and worries. Many drew pictures like this. As one child wrote, "My worries is that terrist [sic] will harm my family, and I will be left with no family like the kids in New York" (Stepp, 2001, p. C4). Another child was concerned about war: "I'm afraid we will be bombed again and it will be World War III. I hate technology" (Stepp, 2001, p. C1). Children's concepts of death are clearly affected by their sociocultural context.

(Silverman, 2000). Appropriate programs at school can also help familiarize children with the concept of death and accelerate the development of a mature understanding of it (Aspinall, 1996; Schonfeld & Kappelman, 1990).

In sum, young children are naturally curious about death and form ideas about it from an early age. During the preschool years, they may understand that death is universal but view it as only a lessening rather than a cessation of life processes, as reversible, and as attributable to very concrete external causes. By early elementary school, they have mastered the concepts that death is a final, irreversible, and universal cessation of life functions; later, they will come to appreciate that death is ultimately due to a failure of internal biological processes. Each child's grasp of death will depend on his or her level of cognitive development and death-related experience. Is it any different for children who are actually dying?

The Dying Child

Parents and doctors often assume that terminally ill children are unaware that they will die and are better off remaining so. Yet research shows that dying children are far more aware of what is happening to them than adults realize; their tragic experience gives them an understanding of death before their time (Essa & Murray, 1994). Consider what Myra Bluebond-Langner (1977) found when she carefully observed children ranging in age from 2 to 14 who had leukemia. Even preschool children arrived, over time, at an understanding that they were going to die and that death is irreversible. Despite the secretiveness of adults, these children were closely attuned to what was going on around them. They noticed changes in their treatments and subtle changes in the way adults interacted with them, and they noticed what happened to other children who had the same disease and were receiving the same treatments. Over time, many of these ill children stopped talking about the long-term future and wanted to celebrate holidays such as Christmas early. A doctor trying to get one boy to cooperate with a procedure said, "I thought you would understand, Sandy. You told me once you wanted to be a doctor." Sandy threw an empty syringe at the doctor and screamed, "I'm not going to be anything!" (p. 59).

How do terminally ill children cope with the knowledge that they are dying? They are not all the models of bravery that some people suppose them to be. Instead, they experience the same wide range of emotions that dying adults experience (Waechter, 1984). Preschool children may not talk about dying, but they may reveal their fears by having temper tantrums or portraying violent acts in their pretend play. School-age children understand more about their situation and can talk about their feelings if given an opportunity to do so. They very much want to participate in normal activities so that they will not feel inadequate compared with their peers, and they want to maintain a sense of control or mastery, even if the best they can do is take charge of deciding which finger should be pricked for a blood sample.

In short, children with terminal illnesses often become painfully aware of the fact that they are dying. They experience a full range of unpleasant emotions and reveal in their behavior, if not in their words, that they are anxious and upset. What, then, can be done to help them cope? Quite obviously, they need the love and support of parents, siblings, and other significant individuals in their lives. The children with cancer who adapt best emotionally have a strong sense that their parents are in control of the situation (Worchel,

Copeland, & Barker, 1987). They also have opportunities to talk with adults about their feelings (Faulkner, 1997). In other words, they are not the victims of a well-intentioned but ultimately counterproductive conspiracy of silence on the part of parents and medical care providers.

The Bereaved Child

Children's coping capacities are also tested when a parent, sibling, pet, or other loved one dies. Three major messages have emerged from studies of bereaved children: (1) Children most certainly grieve; (2) they express their grief differently than adults do; (3) they lack some of the coping resources that adults command; and (4) they are vulnerable to long-term negative effects of bereavement (Osterweis, Solomon, & Green, 1984; I. C. Noppe, 2000; Silverman, 2000).

Consider some of the reactions that have been observed in young children whose parents have died (Silverman, 2000; Silverman & Worden, 1993). These children often misbehave or strike out in rage at their surviving parent. They ask endless questions: Where is Daddy? When is he coming back? Will I get a new Daddy? Anxiety about attachment and separation are common; more than half of the bereaved children in one study reported being scared that other family members might die (Sanchez et al., 1994). Other children go about their activities as if nothing had happened, denying the loss or distracting themselves from it by immersing themselves in play. You can readily see how a parent might be disturbed by some of these behaviors—the seemingly inexplicable tantrums, the distressing questions, or, worse, the apparent lack of concern about the death. Yet all of these behaviors indicate that the loss is affecting the child greatly.

Because they lack some of the coping skills that older individuals command, it is natural that young children might attempt to deny and avoid emotions that are simply too overwhelming to face. Because of their cognitive limitations, young children may have difficulty reconciling the idea that a loved one is dead with the idea that he or she is coming back (Noppe, 2000). Older children are able to use cognitive coping strategies such as revising their interpretations of events or conjuring up cognitive representations of their lost parents (Compas et al., 2001). It is important, then, for adults to recognize that children express their grief and cope with it in ways that reflect their level of development.

What grief symptoms do children most commonly experience? Reactions differ greatly from child to child, but the preschooler's grief is likely to manifest itself in problems with sleeping, eating, toileting, and other daily routines (Osterweis et al., 1984; Oltjenbruns, 2001). Negative moods, dependency, and temper tantrums are also common. Older children express their sadness, anger, and fear more directly. Somatic symptoms such as headaches and other physical ailments are also common, though (Worden & Silverman, 1996).

Because children are highly dependent on their parents, and because they do not have the coping capacities that adults do, some take years to recover fully from the death of a parent. Even before the parent's death, children of a terminally ill par-

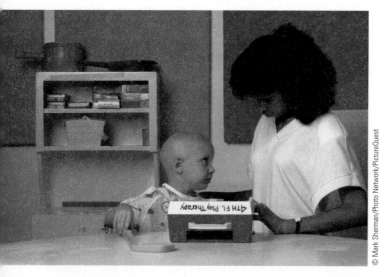

Children who are dying need to know that they are loved and to have opportunities to express their concerns and fears.

ent show higher levels of depression and anxiety symptoms than other children (Siegel, Karus, & Raveis, 1996). And well beyond the first year after the death, some bereaved children continue to display problems such as unhappiness, low self-esteem, social withdrawal, difficulty in school, and problem behavior (Worden & Silverman, 1996; Osterweis et al., 1984). In one longitudinal study of school-age children, 1 in 5 children who had lost a parent had serious adjustment problems two years after the death (Worden & Silverman, 1996; and see Downdney, 2000). Some even develop psychological problems that carry into adulthood (Harris & Bifulco, 1991). However, *most* bereaved children—especially those who have positive coping skills and a good deal of social support—adjust quite successfully. As their cognitive capacities expand, they also have opportunities to look back on earlier losses and gain new perspectives on them (Oltjenbruns, 2001).

The Adolescent

Once adolescents have attained Piaget's stage of formal operations, they typically understand death as the irreversible cessation of biological processes and are able to think in more abstract ways about it (Corr, 1995; Koocher, 1973). Adolescents do not necessarily face up to the fact that they too will die; they take risks that they might not take if they truly believed that death is final, universal, and irreversible (Noppe & Noppe, 1996). However, they do use their new cognitive capacities to ponder and discuss the meaning of death and such hypotheticals as an afterlife (Noppe & Noppe, 1997; Wass, 1991).

Just as children's reactions to death and dying reflect their developmental capacities and needs, adolescents' reactions to becoming terminally ill are likely to reflect the themes of adolescence (Adams & Deveau, 1986; Stevens & Dunsmore, 1996). Concerned about their body images as they experience physical and sexual maturation, they may be acutely disturbed if their illness brings with it hair loss, weight gain, amputation, or other such physical changes. Wanting to be accepted by peers, they may feel like "freaks" or become upset when friends who do not know what to say or do abandon them. Eager to become more autonomous, they may be distressed by having to depend on parents and medical personnel and may struggle to assert their will and maintain a sense of control. Trying to establish their own identity and chart future goals, adolescents may be angry and bitter at having their dreams snatched from them.

Similarly, the reactions of adolescents to the deaths of family members and friends are likely to reflect the themes of the adolescent period (Balk & Corr, 2001; Tyson-Rawson, 1996). For example, even as teenagers become increasingly independent of their parents, they depend quite heavily on their elders for emotional support and guidance. The adolescent whose parent dies often wants to maintain the attachment and may carry on an internal dialogue with the dead parent for years (Silverman & Worden, 1993). And, given the importance of peers in this developmental period, it is not surprising that

Compared to children, adolescents often express very abstract concepts of death that are influenced by their religious training. The 16-year-old girl who drew this picture explained: "The water represents the depth of death. The bubbles represent the releasing of the soul. The tree represents the memories we leave behind. The flame represents Hell and the halo represents Heaven."

adolescents are often devastated when a close friend dies in a car accident, commits suicide, or succumbs to a deadly disease. Unfortunately, grief over the loss of a friend is often not taken as seriously as grief over the loss of a family member (Ringler & Hayden, 2000).

For the most part, adolescents grieve much as adults do. However, they are sometimes reluctant to express their grief for fear of seeming abnormal or losing control and may express their anguish instead through delinquent behavior and somatic ailments (D. C. Clark, Pynoos, & Goebel, 1994; Osterweis et al., 1984). The adolescent who yearns for a dead parent may feel that he or she is being sucked back into the dependency of childhood and may therefore bottle up these painful feelings:

"When my mother died I thought my heart would break," recalled Geoffrey, age 14. "Yet I couldn't cry. It was locked inside. It was private and tender and sensitive like the way I loved her. They said to me, 'You're cool man, real cool, the way you've taken it,' but I wasn't cool at all. I was hot—hot and raging. All my anger, all my sadness was building up inside me. But I just didn't know any way to let it out." (Raphael, 1983, p. 176)

In sum, by the time children reach adolescence, they have acquired a mature concept of death, understanding it as a final cessation of life that is irreversible, universal, and biologically caused, and thinking more abstractly about it. Whereas young children often express their grief indirectly through their behavior (by wetting their beds, throwing tantrums, and so on), older children and adolescents more directly experience and express painful thoughts and emotions. In each period, children's reactions to bereavement or to the knowledge that they are dying reflect their developmental needs and the developmental tasks that they are facing. Thus, when a life-threatening illness strikes, the young child may most want reassurance of parental love and protection, the school-age child may most wish to keep up with peers in school, and the adolescent may most want to maintain a sense of identity and autonomy. They all need their parents and other adults to listen to them and help them cope with their very real emotional reactions.

The Adult

How do adults cope with death and dying? We have already introduced models describing adults' experiences of dying and bereavement that partially answer that question. Here we'll elaborate by examining bereavement in the context of the family life cycle and then exploring differences between normal and abnormal grief reactions.

Death and the Family Life Cycle

Given the importance of family attachments throughout the life span, it is not surprising that the deaths of family members are typically harder to bear than other deaths. We cannot fully understand bereavement unless we adopt a family systems approach and attempt to understand how a death alters relationships, roles, and patterns of interaction within the family, as well as interactions between the family and its environment (Shapiro, 2001; Silverman, 2000). So let's examine some of the special challenges associated with three kinds of death in the family: the loss of a spouse, the loss of a child, and the loss of a parent.

THE LOSS OF A SPOUSE

Most of what we know about bereavement is based on studies of widows and widowers. Experiencing the death of a spouse becomes increasingly likely as we age; it is something most women can expect to endure, as women tend both to live longer than men and to marry men who are older than they are. The marital relationship is a central one for most adults, and the loss of a marriage partner can mean the loss of a great deal indeed. Moreover, the death of a spouse often precipitates other changes—the need to move, enter the labor force or change jobs, assume responsibilities that the spouse formerly performed, parent single-handedly, and so on. Thus, widows or widowers must redefine their roles and even their identities in fundamental ways (Lopata, 1996; Parkes, 1996). If they are women, their wealth is also likely to decline substantially (Zick & Holden, 2000). Similar challenges may confront anyone, married or not, who loses a romantic attachment figure.

As we noted earlier in this chapter, Colin Murray Parkes, in his extensive research on widows and widowers, has concluded that bereaved adults progress through overlapping phases of numbness, yearning, disorganization and despair, and reorganization. What toll does this grieving process take on the individual's physical, emotional, and cognitive functioning? Table 17.3 shows some of the symptoms that widows and widowers commonly report (Parkes, 1996; also see Bonanno & Kaltman, 2000; Shuchter & Zisook, 1993).

Widows and widowers are at risk for illness and physical symptoms such as loss of appetite and sleep disruption, and they tend to overindulge not only in alcohol but also in tranquilizers and cigarettes. Cognitive functions such as memory and decision making are often impaired, and emotional problems such as loneliness and anxiety are common. Most bereaved spouses do not become clinically depressed, but most do display symptoms of depression in the first

Table 17.3   Percentage of Bereaved and Nonbereaved Adults Reporting Various Symptoms within the Past Year

Symptoms	Bereaved	Nonbereaved
Admitted to hospital	12%	4%
Awakening during the night	27	8
Changes in appetite	34	20
Increased alcohol consumption	19	2
Sought help for emotional problems	23	5
Wonder if anything is worthwhile	34	18
Worried by loneliness	44	17
Depressed or very unhappy (in past few weeks)	33	20
Restless	33	15
Memory not all right	20	6
Hard to make up mind	36	22
Feel somewhat apart or remote even among friends	23	10

NOTE: Responses were gathered in the Harvard Bereavement Study from men and women under the age of 45 who had lost their spouses 14 months before the interviews. Nonbereaved respondents were married adults matched to members of the bereaved sample so that they were similar in age, sex, family size, geographic area, nationality, and socioeconomic status.
SOURCE: Based on Parkes (1996)

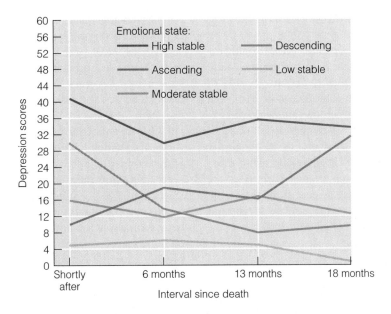

Figure 17.3 Not everyone who grieves experiences symptoms of depression. Here we see five different patterns of change in depression scores assessed over 18 months within a sample of widowed men and women. Notice that only a minority show a pattern most of us view as normal: lots of depression symptoms early, and fewer later on. Notice, too, that some mourners experience little depression at any point.

SOURCE: Adapted from Levy et al. (1994)

months after the death (Harlow, Goldberg, & Comstock, 1991).

Although losing a spouse is difficult at any age, young and middle-aged adults appear to suffer somewhat more emotionally than elderly adults, perhaps because the death of a spouse at these ages is off-time and therefore unexpected (Parkes, 1996; Zisook & Shuchter, 1991). However, elderly people who tend an ailing spouse and feel strained doing so are at risk not only for depression but also for death (Schulz & Beach, 1999). Not only may they neglect their own health while caring for their spouse but, because their immune systems have lost effectiveness over the years, they are more vulnerable to illness when they are under stress than younger adults are (Robinson-Whelen, Kiecolt-Glaser, & Glaser, 2000).

A stressful event, bereavement takes a toll on the body by increasing the production of stress hormones and reducing the effectiveness of the immune system (Goodkin et al., 2001). The result is that widows and widowers as a group have higher-than-average rates not only of illness but of death (M. Stroebe, 2001b). In an immense study of widowed adults in Finland, for example, risks of death due to accidental and violent causes, alcohol-related causes, heart disease, and lung cancer were all found to be higher than normal, especially in the first six months after a spouse's death (Martikainen & Valkonen, 1996). These extra risks of illness and mortality are higher for men than for women, for reasons that are still unclear (M. Stroebe, 2001b). We know that more men than women become significantly depressed after the loss of a spouse, and that may be part of the explanation for higher death rates among men (G. R. Lee et al., 2001).

Many widows and widowers begin to show signs of recovery in the second year after the death. Yet grieving and symptoms of distress may continue for many, many years (Parkes & Weiss, 1983; Wortman & Silver, 2001). Darrin Lehman, Camille Wortman, and Allan Williams (1987) compared adults whose spouses had died in car accidents four to seven years previously to similar nonbereaved adults. Even this long after their tragedies, bereaved adults showed more depression, hostility, and anxiety; had more worries; and felt less of a sense of psychological well-being than nonbereaved adults. Perhaps because these deaths were sudden and violent, 62% still had recurring thoughts that the death was unfair or that they had been cheated, and 68% said that they had been unable to find any meaning in the death. In other research, adults bereaved as a result of suicides, accidents, and homicides suffered at least as many post-traumatic stress symptoms, such as anxiety and terrifying memories, four years later as victims of physical assaults—even though they were not personally involved in the traumatic events that killed their loved ones (Green et al., 2001).

It is difficult to generalize about adults who lose their spouses, as their reactions are so diverse. With this diversity in mind, one team of researchers attempted to identify subgroups of widowed men and women based on their patterns of psychological distress over a period of 18 months (Levy, Martinkowski, & Derby, 1994). As Figure 17.3 shows, some adults were quite depressed throughout the 18-month period, others showed little sign of depression at any point, and still others became more and more depressed over time. Only a third showed the pattern most of us would consider typical:

high levels of depression early and then a lessening of distress in the months following the death.

In sum, the loss of a spouse is a painful and damaging experience. During the first weeks and months after the death, the psychological pain is typically most acute, and the risks of developing serious physical or mental health problems or even dying are at a peak. However, many widows and widowers experience emotional aftereffects for years afterward. If this picture seems too dismal, let us emphasize that the vast majority of bereaved adults do *not* die and do *not* develop a major physical or psychological disorder, even though their risks are higher than average. Instead, most recover from their grief and get on with their lives—and manage to do so without professional treatment (Bonanno & Kaltman, 2000).

THE LOSS OF A CHILD

My child has died! My heart is torn to shreds. My body is screaming. My mind is crazed. . . . The question is always present on my mind. Why? How could this possibly have happened? The anger is ever so deep, so strong, so frightening. (Bertman, 1991, p. 323, citing a mother's reflections on how she reacted to her 16-year-old daughter's death in a car accident after the initial numbness wore off)

No loss is more difficult for an adult than the death of a child (Cleiren, 1993; Rubin & Malkinson, 2001; W. Stroebe & Schut, 2001). Even when there is forewarning, the loss of a child is experienced as unexpected, untimely, and unjust: Parents are supposed to protect their children from harm, and children aren't supposed to die before their parents do (Sprang & McNeil, 1995). Moreover, the parent role is a central one for most adults, and their attachments to their children run deep.

Compared to adults who have lost a spouse or a parent, parents who have lost a child are exceptionally angry, guilty, and depressed, and they have a greater number of physical complaints (Sanders, 1979–1980; Sprang & McNeil, 1995). Understandably, they experience a raging anger, and they often feel that they were somehow to blame or failed in their role as parent and protector (Rando, 1991). They very often carry on a relationship with the lost child long after the death (Rubin & Malkinson, 2001).

The age of the child who dies has little impact on the severity of the grief: Parents can experience severe grief reactions even after a miscarriage, stillborn delivery, or abortion (Janssen, Cuisinier, & Hoogduin, 1996). Their difficulties can be aggravated when friends and relatives fail to appreciate that a real loss has occurred and offer no support (Osterweis et al., 1984). It goes without saying that the death of an infant, child, or adolescent can be devastating. What may be more surprising is the fact that the death of an adult child is usually no less difficult to bear than the death of a younger child (Lesher & Bergey, 1988; Rubin & Malkinson, 2001).

The death of a child alters the whole family system and affects the well-being of the marital relationship, as well as of siblings and grandparents. The odds of marital problems and divorce may increase after the death of a child, although most couples stay together and some feel closer than ever (Dijkstra & Stroebe, 1998; Najman et al., 1993). The marital relationship is likely to be strained because each partner grieves in his or her own way and is not always able to provide emotional support to the other (Bohannon, 1990–1991). Strains are likely to be especially severe if the marriage was shaky before the death.

Grieving parents may also have difficulty giving their surviving children the love and support they need to cope with *their* loss. Children are deeply affected when a brother or sister dies, but their grief is often not fully appreciated (Silverman, 2000). Siblings of children battling cancer, for example, may resent it if they are neglected by their parents, may be anxious about their own health, may feel guilty about some of the unsavory feelings of rivalry they have, and may feel pressure after the death to replace the lost child in their parents' eyes (Adams & Deveau, 1987). They have been found to experience stomachaches and headaches and have difficulty sleeping for up to three years after the death (Davies, 1995).

One 12-year-old boy whose brother died described his experience this way: "My dad can't talk about it, and my mom cries a lot. It's really hard on them. I pretend I'm O.K. I usually just stay in my room" (Wass, 1991, p. 29). If siblings are isolated from their understandably upset parents or if their grief is not taken seriously, they may have an especially hard time recovering. Bereaved siblings fare better if their parents are not overwhelmed by grief, remain warm and supportive, and encourage open discussion of feelings (Applebaum & Burns, 1991; Graham-Pole et al., 1989).

Finally, grandparents also grieve following the death of a child, both for their grandchild *and* for their child, the bereaved parent. As one grandparent said, "It's like a double whammy!" (DeFrain, Jakub, & Mendoza, 1991–1992, p. 178). Grandparents are likely to feel guilty about surviving their grandchildren and helpless to protect their adult children from pain (Fry, 1997). Clearly, then, those who are attempting to help bereaved families need to include the *whole* family in their efforts.

THE LOSS OF A PARENT

Even if we escape the death of a child or spouse, the death of a parent is a normative life transition that the vast majority of us will experience. As noted already, children sometimes experience long-lasting problems after the death of a parent. Fortunately, most of us do not have to face this event until we are middle-aged. We are typically less emotionally dependent on our parents by then, and most of us are heavily invested in our own families. Moreover, we expect that our parents will die someday and have prepared ourselves, at least to some degree. Finally, we are likely to share the widespread societal belief that the death of an elderly person is somehow less tragic than that of a young person who has not yet had a chance to live.

Perhaps for all of these reasons, adjusting to the death of a parent is usually not as difficult as adjusting to the death of a spouse or child (Bower, 1997; Cleiren, 1993; Leahy, 1992-1993). This is not to say that a parent's death is easy to bear, however. Adult children may feel vulnerable and alone in the world when their parents no longer stand between them and death (Scharlach & Fredriksen, 1993). Guilt about not doing enough for the parent who died is also common (Moss et al., 1993). These concerns take a toll: Compared to adults who are not bereaved, adults who have lost a parent in the past three years have higher rates of psychological distress, alcohol use, and health problems (Umberson & Chen, 1994).

Perhaps the soundest conclusion we can reach about deaths in the family is that *all* of them have the potential to cause a great deal of suffering, to put adults at risk for physical and psychological problems and even death, and to perturb the family system. Still, reactions to the loss of a spouse, child, or parent are also influenced by the special qualities of each of those attachments, and the death of a child often takes a greater toll than the death of a parent.

Challenges to the Grief Work Perspective

The view that has guided much of the research on bereavement we have discussed is what has come to be called the **grief work perspective**—the view that in order to cope adaptively with death, bereaved people must confront their loss, experience painful emotions, work through those emotions, and move toward a detachment from the deceased (M. Stroebe, 2001a). This view, which grew out of Freudian psychoanalytic theory, is widely held in our society, not only among therapists but among people in general, and it influences what we view as an abnormal reaction to death (Wortman & Silver, 2001). From the grief work perspective, either *chronic grief* that lasts longer and/or is more intense than usual or an *absence, inhibition, or delay of grief,* in which the bereaved denies the loss and never seems to confront and express painful feelings, is viewed as "pathological" or "complicated" grief (see, for example, Raphael,1983). This grief work perspective has now come under serious attack (see Bonanno, 2001; Wortman & Silver, 2001).

First, cross-cultural studies tell us that there are many different ways to grieve and suggest that the grief-work model of bereavement may be culturally biased. As we discovered in Chapter 16, it is not always easy to pin down the dividing line between normal and abnormal behavior, and both age norms and social norms must be considered in doing so. As we have seen, children often express their grief differently than adults do and may be more likely to use denial and acting out as coping mechanisms than to "work through" their feelings (Raphael, 1983). In addition, grieving occurs in a cultural context (Klass, 2001; Lopata, 1996). An Egyptian mother may be conforming to her culture's norms of mourning if she sits alone, withdrawn and mute, for months or even years after a child's death. Likewise, a Balinese mother is following the rules of her culture if she is calm, composed, and even seemingly cheerful soon after a child's death, even though she may be suffering inside (Wikan, 1988, 1991). We would be wrong to conclude, based on our own society's norms, that the Egyptian mother is suffering from chronic grief or the Balinese mother from absent or inhibited grief.

Second, there is surprisingly little support for the grief work perspective's assumption that bereaved individuals must confront their loss and experience painful emotions in order to cope successfully (Bonanno & Kaltman, 1999; M. Stroebe et al., 1992; Wortman & Silver, 1989, 2001). As it turns out, bereaved individuals who ruminate a lot about what they might have done differently and why they are coping so poorly and who engage in heavy self-analysis after a loss often end up more distressed months later than people who are less reflective (Nolen-Hoeksema, McBride, & Larson, 1997). In addition, bereaved individuals who fail to show much emotional distress during the early months after the loss do not seem to pay for their lack of grief with a delayed grief reaction later on—as the grief work model says they should. On the contrary, the individuals who adjust best to death in the long run are often those who express relatively few negative emotions in the months after the death, who do not invest a lot of effort in making sense of the loss and their reactions to it, and who experience *positive* emotions and thoughts during the bereavement period (Bonanno & Field, 2001; Bonanno & Kaltman, 2000). Particularly in the face of losses as traumatic as those that took place during the Holocaust (or in the World Trade Center disaster), repressing painful emotions so that one can get on with life may be more adaptive than "working through" them (Kaminer & Lavie, 1993).

Finally, the grief work view that we must break our bonds to the deceased in order to overcome our grief is being challenged. This view goes back to Freud, who believed that bereaved people had to let go in order to invest their psychic energy elsewhere. By contrast, John Bowlby (1980) noticed that many bereaved individuals revise their internal working models of self and others and continue their relationships with their deceased loved ones on new terms (Bonanno & Kaltman, 1999; I. C. Noppe, 2000). Recent research tells us that many bereaved individuals do in fact maintain their attachments to lost loved ones indefinitely rather than severing those bonds. Indeed, bereavement rituals in some cultures are designed to *ensure* a continued bond between the living and the dead (Klass, 2001). Moreover, people who continue their bonds do not necessarily show poorer adjustment than those who do not (Field et al., 1999; Lohnes & Kalter, 1994).

Nigel Field and his colleagues (1999) have discovered that some forms of continuing attachment are healthier than others, however. They investigated whether continuing attachment to a deceased spouse was positively or negatively related to levels of grief symptoms among widows and widowers at 6 months, 14 months, and 25 months after their loss. It all depended on the type of continuing attachment behavior displayed. Those who used their spouse's possessions to comfort themselves showed high levels of distress at the 6-month mark and little decrease in grief over the coming months. By contrast, those who expressed their continuing attachment by having and sharing fond memories of the deceased and by sensing that their loved one was watching over and guiding them showed relatively low levels of distress. Some bereaved individuals are clearly so obsessed with the deceased person that their grief can be viewed as pathological. However, we should be cautious about labeling as abnormal individuals who sense the presence of a lost loved one and consult with him or her about

Is it pathological to maintain a relationship with one's deceased parent for many years? Probably not. It is common practice in Japan to remember each morning during worship ancestors who have died, to leave them food and otherwise care for them, and to tell them about one's triumphs and disasters (Klass, 2001). Continuing attachment to rather than detachment from the deceased is perfectly normal in some cultural contexts.

important decisions years after a death. Continuing attachment to the deceased is not only quite normal but can also be quite adaptive (Klass, 2001; M. Stroebe, 2001a).

In sum, recent studies challenge the assumptions of the grief work perspective that there is a "normal" way to grieve that applies across cultures, that it must involve experiencing and working through painful emotions, and that it is resolved by breaking rather than continuing one's bond to the deceased. Norms for expressing grief vary widely across cultures; it is not clear that one must express negative emotions in order to adjust to a loss, or that bereaved people who do not express such emotions will pay later with a delayed grief reaction; and people need not sever their attachment to the deceased in order to adjust to a loss. More fundamentally, researchers are now questioning the whole idea, embedded in the grief work model, that grief is a pathological process—like a disease that we catch, suffer from, and eventually recover from (Bonanno, 2001). As we saw earlier, only about 15% of bereaved individuals experience complications of grief so severe that they can be described as pathological (Bonanno & Kaltman, 2000). What's more, many people experience positive emotions along with the negative ones, and many find ways to benefit from their losses and grow as individuals (Davis & Nolen-Hoeksema, 2001; Folkman & Moskowitz, 2000; Harvey, 2001). Overall, we must conclude that grief takes many forms, involves positive as well as negative emotions, and is more complex and less pathological than the grief work model implies.

Who Copes and Who Succumbs?

Even if it is difficult to find the line between normal grief and pathological grief, we can still ask what risk and protective factors distinguish people who cope well with loss from people who cope poorly. Coping with bereavement is influenced by the individual's personal resources, the nature of the loss to be coped with, and the surrounding context of support and stressors.

PERSONAL RESOURCES

Just as some individuals are better able to cope with their own dying than others are, some are better equipped than others to handle the stresses of bereavement. Bowlby's attachment theory emphasizes that *early experiences in attachment relationships* influence the internal working models of self and other we form and, in turn, how we later relate to others and handle losses of relationships (Shaver & Tancredy, 2001; I. C. Noppe, 2000). If infants and young children receive loving and responsive care, they form internal working models of self and other that tell them that they are lovable and that other people can be trusted (see Chapter 14). Having a secure attachment style is associated with coping relatively well with the death of a loved one (Field et al., 2001). By contrast, infants or young children who receive inconsistent care or who suffer the loss of an important attachment figure may have more difficulty coping with loss later in life. They may, for example, develop a resistant (or ambivalent) style of attachment that leads them to be overly dependent on others and to display extreme and chronic grief and anxiety after a loss (Bowlby, 1980; Shaver & Tancredy, 2001). Or they may develop an avoidant attachment style that causes them to be "compulsively self-reliant" and to have difficulty accepting a loss and expressing grief—or a disorganized attachment style that makes them show confused responses to loss.

Several aspects of *personality and coping style* also influence how successfully people cope with death. For example, individuals who have difficulty coping tend to have low self-esteem (Lund et al., 1985–1986) and lack a sense that they are in control of their lives (Haas-Hawkings et al., 1985). Many were experiencing psychological problems such as depression long before they were bereaved (Norris & Murrell, 1990; Zisook & Shuchter, 1991). They are more likely than other bereaved individuals to blame themselves for the death and to cling to the deceased's belongings (Field & Bonanno, 2001). They are less likely to be highly religious, and to have the social support and means of finding meaning that may come with religious involvement (W. Stroebe & Schut, 2001). So, among the bereaved, as among the dying, the enduring capacity of the individual to cope with life's problems is an important influence on outcomes.

THE NATURE OF THE LOSS

Bereavement outcomes are also influenced by characteristics of the event with which the person must cope. The closeness of one's *relationship to the deceased* is obviously very important. We grieve harder for attachment figures such as spouses and children than for people with whom we have not formed true attachment bonds (Cleiren, 1993). Moreover, children grieve especially hard for parents to whom they were closely attached (Umberson & Chen, 1994), and spouses grieve especially hard for partners with whom they shared a common identity and on whom they were highly dependent (Carr et al., 2000; DeGarmo & Kitson, 1996).

The *cause of death* can also influence bereavement outcomes. One of the reasons why the death of a child is so painful is that children's deaths are often the result of "senseless" and violent events such as car accidents and homicides. Needless to say, bereavement can also be especially difficult if the bereaved person contributed in some way, even accidentally, to the death (Osterweis et al., 1984). Surprisingly, bereavement reactions are not strongly influenced by the *suddenness or unexpectedness of the death* (Saldinger et al., 1999). In one recent study, widowed men yearned more for their wives when the death was the anticipated result of illness than when it was sudden and unexpected, but women tended to have more emotional difficulty after a sudden death (Carr et al., 2001). Levels of shock, anger, depression, and overall grief 6 and 18 months after the loss were simply not influenced by whether the death was sudden or anticipated. True, the survivors of sudden death have had no opportunity to engage in anticipatory grief and are thrown into a state of shock. However, those who have forewarning often had to care for their dying loved one, and we know that coping with a long death watch can take as great a toll on mental health as coping with the death that follows (J. C. Bodnar & Kiecolt-Glaser, 1994; Hays, Kasl, & Jacobs, 1994).

THE CONTEXT OF SUPPORTS AND STRESSORS

Finally, grief reactions are influenced positively by the presence of a strong social support system and negatively by additional life stressors (Lopata, 1996; W. Stroebe & Schut, 2001). Social support is crucial at all ages. It is especially important for the young child whose parent dies to have adequate substitute parenting. Children tend to have more problems if their surviving parent is crippled by grief and insensitive to their needs than if the surviving parent or substitute caregiver keeps the lines of communication open, helps them express their grief, and is able to maintain a loving home environment (Raveis, Siegel, & Karus, 1999; Van Eerdewegh, Clayton, & Van Eerdewegh, 1985). Too often, adults attempt to protect children from the pain of death and inadvertently isolate them from the rest of the family when they are most in need of support.

Bereaved adults also benefit from social support (Stroebe & Schut, 2001). Indeed, family members of all ages recover best when they are close to one another and can share their distress (Kissane et al., 1996). How can family members and friends be most supportive? Bereaved individuals do not appreciate people who try to cheer them up or force them out of their grief or tell them it was for the best. Instead, they are helped most by people who say they are sorry to hear of the loss, make themselves available to serve as confidants, and allow bereaved individuals to express their painful feelings freely if they choose (Herkert, 2000; Lehman, Ellard, & Wortman, 1986).

Just as social support helps the bereaved, additional stressors hurt. For example, outcomes tend to be poor for widows who must cope with financial problems after bereavement and for widowers who have difficulty managing household tasks without their wives (Lopata, 1996; Umberson, Wortman, & Kessler, 1992). Widows and widowers may have more than the usual difficulty resolving their grief if they must also take on the challenges of caring single-handedly for young children, finding a new job, or moving (Parkes, 1996; Worden & Silverman, 1993).

By taking into account the person who has experienced a death, the nature of the death, and the context surrounding it, we can put together a profile of the individuals who are most likely to develop long-term problems after bereavement. These individuals have had an unfortunate history of interpersonal relationships, perhaps suffering the death of a parent when they were young or insecurity in their early attachments. They have had previous psychological problems and generally have difficulty coping effectively with adversity. The person who died is someone on whom they depended greatly, and the death was untimely and seemingly senseless. Finally, these high-risk individuals lack the kinds of social support that can aid them in overcoming their loss, and they are burdened by stresses in addition to the stress of bereavement itself.

Bereavement and Human Development

The grief work perspective on bereavement has tended to put the focus on the negative side of bereavement—on the damaging effects of loss and the need to "recover" from "symptoms" of grief. Today, psychologists are coming to appreciate that bereavement has positive as well as negative outcomes and is the kind of life event that has the potential to foster personal growth (Davis & Nolen-Hoeksema, 2001; Folkman & Moskowitz, 2000; Lopata, 1996). Granted, it can be a painful way to grow, and we could hardly recommend it as a plan for optimizing human development. Still, the literature on death and dying is filled with testimonials about the lessons that can be learned.

Many bereaved individuals believe that they have become more confident, family-oriented, open, and religious people with a greater appreciation of life (Davis & Nolen-Hoeksema, 2001; Lehman et al., 1993). Many widows master new skills, become more independent, and emerge with new identities and higher self-esteem (Lopata, 1996). These testimonials make the point:

> A bereaved spouse: "I feel that [in] my present relationship I'm better able to be a real good friend, and I don't take things so personally." (Davis & Nolen-Hoeksema, 2001, p. 735)

> A widow, surprised by how successfully she had built a new and satisfying life: "I'm doing things I never thought I could do. I hate being alone but I have good friends and we care about each other. I'm even traveling. I enjoy my work. I never thought I'd hear myself say that I don't mind being single." (Silverman, 1981, p. 55)

> And a mother whose infant died: "Now I can survive anything." (DeFrain, Taylor, & Ernst, 1982, p. 57)

So perhaps it is by encountering tragedy that we learn to cope with tragedy, and perhaps it is by struggling to find meaning in death that we come to find meaning in life.

Taking the Sting Out of Death

A number of efforts are underway to help children and adults who are dying or who are bereaved grapple with death and their feelings about it. Here is a sampling.

For the Dying

Dramatic changes in the care of dying persons have occurred within the past few decades, thanks in part to the efforts of Elisabeth Kübler-Ross and others. Still, many signs suggest that hospital personnel continue to place much emphasis on curing terminally ill patients and keeping them alive and little on controlling their pain and allowing them to "die with dignity" (Colburn, 1995). Out of such concerns has arisen an approach to caring for the dying person that is intended to be more humane: the hospice.

A **hospice** is a program that supports dying persons and their families through a philosophy of "caring" rather than "curing" (Connor, 2000). The first such facility was St. Christopher's Hospice near London, opened in 1967 under the direction of Dr. Cicely Saunders (1977). The concept spread quickly to North America, where hospices have now been established in most communities to serve individuals with cancer, AIDS, and other life-threatening diseases (Kastenbaum, 1998; Siebold, 1992). In many hospice programs today, though, there is no care facility like St. Christopher's; instead, dying patients stay at home and are visited by hospice workers.

What makes hospice care different from hospital care? Whether hospice care is provided in a facility or at home, it entails these key features (Connor, 2000; Corr & Corr, 1992; Siebold, 1992):

1. The dying person and his or her family—not the "experts"—decide what support they need and want.
2. Attempts to cure the patient or prolong his or her life are deemphasized.
3. Pain control is emphasized.
4. The setting for care is as normal as possible (preferably the patient's own home, or at least a homelike facility that does not have the sterile atmosphere of many hospital wards).
5. Bereavement counseling is provided to the family before and after the death.

The contrasts between hospice care and traditional hospital care are striking. In the hospital, medical experts have control, efforts are directed at staving off death as long as possible, the setting is sterile and clinical, and family members are too often viewed as nuisances rather than as the most important of all caregivers. When one thinks about what individuals dying of cancer are experiencing, one can appreciate that hospice care is a better fit to their needs than traditional hospital care. As death approaches, cancer parents become less and less able to carry out activities of daily living; they are more in pain and often become more interested in being comfortable than in having their lives extended (McCarthy et al., 2000). By the time they are close to death, two-thirds of them do not want to be resuscitated if they stop breathing.

Do dying patients and their families indeed fare better when they spend their last days together receiving hospice care? An evaluation of hospice facility care, at-home hospice care, and conventional hospital care in Great Britain found that hospice patients spent more of their last days without pain, underwent fewer medical interventions and operations, and received nursing care that was more oriented to their emotional needs (Seale, 1991). Their families grieved as much as those of hospitalized patients, but were more satisfied with the care they received.

Similarly, Susan Nolen-Hoeksema and her colleagues found that 95% of the families served by hospices in the San Francisco area felt that the hospice had been helpful. Those who had complaints tended to be women who had a history of depression and were dissatisfied with the support they had received from family and friends as well (Nolen-Hoeksema, Larson, & Bishop, 2000; and see Baer & Hanson, 2000). In another study, spouses, parents, and other relatives of dying people who received hospice care participated more fully in the funeral and displayed fewer symptoms of grief and greater well-being one to two years after the death than similar relatives who had coped with a death without benefit of hospice care (Ragow-O'Brien, Hayslip, & Guarnaccia, 2000).

The hospice approach may not work for all, but for some it does mean an opportunity to die with dignity, free of pain and surrounded by loved ones. As one hospice patient put it, "it's the attitude of the staff, everybody from the cleaner on, they're all caring" (McKinlay, 2001, p. 22). The next challenge may be to extend the hospice philosophy of caring rather than curing to children. Of children who die of cancer, half die in a hospital, many suffering from pain that is not adequately controlled, possibly because neither their doctors nor their parents want to accept the fact that the child is dying and so continue to treat the cancer aggressively (Wolfe et al., 2000).

For the Bereaved

Part of the mission of hospice programs is to help family members prepare for and cope with their loss. What other help is available for bereaved individuals? Most bereaved individuals do not need psychological interventions to help them cope with death; they deal with this normal life transition on their own and with support from significant others. At the same time, there are many options for bereaved individuals, ranging from counseling intended to prevent problems before they develop to interventions designed to treat serious psychological disorders precipitated by a loss (Raphael, Minkov, & Dobson, 2001). Bereaved individuals at risk for depression—because of a history of losses, a history of depression or other psychological disorders, a lack of social support, or other factors—may benefit from therapy or counseling aimed at preventing them from becoming depressed (Murray et al., 2000; Zisook & Shuchter, 2001). And, like anyone with major depression, bereaved individuals who become seriously depressed can benefit from individual or group psychotherapy and antidepressant medication (see Chapter 16).

Because death takes place in a family context, family therapy often makes a good deal of sense, especially when children are involved (Moore & Carr, 2000). Family therapy can help bereaved parents and children communicate more openly and share their grief. It can also enable parents to maintain the kind of warm and supportive parenting style that can be so important in facilitating their children's recovery.

Another approach to helping the bereaved that has proven popular is the mutual support or self-help group (Goodkin et al., 2001; Silverman, 2000; Zisook & Shuchter, 2001). One such program is Compassionate Friends, serving parents whose children have died. Other groups are aimed at widows and widowers. Parents without Partners, THEOS (They Help Each Other Spiritually), The Widowed Person's Service, and similar groups bring widows and widowers together to offer everything from help and advice on such practical matters as settling finances or finding a job to emotional support and friendship.

Bereavement support groups have also been designed for HIV-infected individuals who have experienced the AIDS-related deaths of partners, family members, and friends. Karl Goodkin and his colleagues (2001) have found that a carefully designed support group program for HIV-infected individuals who have experienced losses (often several of them) can reduce the distress these people experience, help them adopt more effective coping strategies, and increase their use of social support. Moreover, the researchers were able to demonstrate that the intervention had significant positive effects on participants' neuroendocrine and immune system functioning and reduced the number of times they visited doctors, suggesting that it might have positive effects on their health outcomes as well. Finally, program participants were better able than nonparticipants to cope with subsequent deaths.

Hospice care helps people live even when they're dying.

Participation in mutual support groups can be beneficial for widows as well. Compared to nonparticipants, participants tend to be less depressed and anxious, use less medication, and have a greater sense of well-being and self-esteem (Lieberman & Videka-Sherman, 1986). Perhaps this is because other bereaved people are in the best position to understand what a bereaved person is going through and to offer effective social support. One widow summed it up this way: "What's helpful? Why, people who are in the 'same boat.' Unless you've been there you just can't understand" (Bankoff, 1983, p. 230).

Summary Points

1. In defining death as a biological process, the Harvard definition of total brain death has been influential, but many controversies still surround the definition, along with the issues of active and passive euthanasia and assisted suicide. The social meanings of death vary across cultures, subcultures, and individuals.

2. The average life expectancy for a newborn in the United States has risen to 76.5 years, higher than that in less developed countries. Death rates decline after infancy and rise dramatically after early adulthood. As we age, accidents give way to chronic diseases as primary causes of death.

3. Programmed theories of aging claim that aging is governed by species heredity and individual genetic endowment; such theories include the notion that the shortening of telomeres at the end of

chromosomes is responsible for the Hayflick limit on number of cell divisions. Damage theories of aging focus on an accumulation of random damage to DNA caused by destructive free radicals and other agents. In the end, many genetic and environmental factors interact to bring about aging and death.

4. Elisabeth Kübler-Ross stimulated much concern for dying patients by describing five "stages" of dying (denial/isolation, anger, bargaining, depression, and acceptance). However, dying people do not seem to progress through clear-cut stages; as Shneidman proposes, they experience ever-changing emotions, and their experiences depend on the course of their disease and on their personality.

5. Bereavement precipitates grief and mourning, which are expressed, according to Parkes and Bowlby's attachment theory perspective, in overlapping phases of numbness, yearning, disorganization and despair, and finally, after a year or two, reorganization.

6. Infants do not comprehend death but clearly grieve, protesting and despairing after separations in ways that parallel adults' responses to bereavement.

7. Children are curious about death and usually understand by age 5 to 7 that it is a final cessation of life processes that is irreversible and universal, later realizing that it is ultimately caused by internal biological changes. Terminally ill children often become very aware of their situation. Bereaved children express their grief less directly than adults do; they often experience bodily symptoms, academic difficulties, and behavior problems.

8. Adolescents use their advanced cognitive capacities to understand death more abstractly. They cope with dying and bereavement in ways that reflect the developmental themes of adolescence.

9. Widows and widowers experience many physical, emotional, and cognitive symptoms, are at increased risk of dying, and often show emotional aftereffects for years. The death of a child is often even more difficult for an adult to bear and affects siblings and grandparents as well. The death of a parent, because it is expected, is often easier.

10. The grief work perspective, which claims that people must work through their grief and detach from the deceased in order to cope effectively with loss, has been challenged recently. Definitions of normal grief vary depending on social and age norms, and many people adjust well (and do not experience delayed grief) if they express few negative and many positive emotions after the death and if they continue rather than sever their attachments.

11. Intense and prolonged grief is especially likely among individuals who had painful early attachment experiences or lack positive personality traits and coping skills; who had close and dependent relationships with individuals who died violently and senselessly; and who lack positive social support and face additional stressors.

12. Successful efforts to take the sting out of death have included hospice programs for dying patients and their families and individual therapy, family therapy, and mutual support groups for the bereaved.

Critical Thinking

1. Look carefully at the five stages of dying that Kübler-Ross believes terminally ill patients experience and at the four phases of adjustment bereaved persons experience according to Parkes and Bowlby. What common themes do you see? How do they differ?

2. Lucy (age 3), Lilly (age 9), and Lally (age 16) have all been diagnosed with cancer. They have been given chemotherapy and radiation treatments for a number of months but seem to be getting worse rather than better. Write a short monologue for each child expressing (a) whether and how she understands that she is dying, and (b) her major concerns and wishes, based what you know of normal development at her age.

3. Many people have misconceptions about what is normal and what is abnormal when it comes to grieving; this chapter has highlighted some of these misconceptions. Identify three misconceptions and, using relevant research, show why they are just that—misconceptions.

Key Terms

total brain death	life expectancy
euthanasia	programmed theories of aging
assisted suicide	damage theories of aging
Living Will	maximum life span
Hayflick limit	grief
telomere	mourning
progeria	anticipatory grief
dietary restriction	Parkes/Bowlby attachment model
free radical theory	of bereavement
antioxidants	grief work perspective
denial	hospice
bereavement	

On the Web

Web Sites to Explore

Issues in Death and Dying

This Canadian site provides updates on laws in the United States and Canada regarding euthanasia and related death and dying topics.
http://www.religioustolerance.org/euthanas.htm

Compassionate Friends

This site is for parents and others coping with the death of a child. It includes media stories on grief and the results of a survey of bereaved parents.
http://www.compassionatefriends.org

Widows and Widowers

This American Association of Retired Persons' site on Coping with Grief and Loss has useful guidance for bereaved people of all ages. The AARP's Widowed Persons Service provides support groups for widows and widowers.
http://www.aarp.org/griefandloss

Hospice

This site has good material on many death and dying topics, including articles about the hospice concept, talking to children about death, pain relief, and more.
http://www.hospicenet.org

Search Online with InfoTrac College Edition

For additional information, explore InfoTrac College Edition, your online library. Go to
http://www.infotrac-college.com
and use the passcode that came on the card with your book. If you type the term "physician-assisted suicide" (with the quotation marks) in the Search box, you will be in position to develop a list of the pros and cons of allowing doctors to give dying patients the means to end their lives. You may also want to search for the term "hospice" and look for new research on the effects of hospice care on dying people and their families.

Visit Our Web Site

Go to http://www.wadsworth.com/psychology, where you will find online resources directly linked to your book.

Life-Span CD-ROM

Go to the Wadsworth Life-Span CD-ROM for further study of the concepts in this chapter. The CD-ROM also includes quizzes and additional activities to expand your learning experience.

Fitting the Pieces Together

Major Trends in Human Development

Infants (Birth to Age 2)
Preschool Children (Ages 2 through 5)
School-Age Children (Ages 6 through 11)
Adolescents (Ages 12 through 19)
Young Adults (Ages 20 through 39)
Middle-Aged Adults (Ages 40 through 64)
Older Adults (Age 65 and Up)

Major Themes in Human Development

We Are Whole Persons throughout the Life Span
Human Development Proceeds in Multiple Directions
There Is Both Continuity and Discontinuity in Development
There Is Much Plasticity in Development
Nature and Nurture Truly Interact in Development
We Are Individuals, Becoming Even More Diverse with Age
We Develop in a Cultural and Historical Context
We Are Active in Our Own Development
Development Is a Lifelong Process
Development Is Best Viewed from Multiple Perspectives

Photos courtesy of Allen Klamik and Maryann Craver

Our survey of human development from conception to death, and of the many forces that influence it, is now complete. In this epilogue, our goal is to help you integrate what you have learned—to see the "big picture." We summarize significant trends in physical, cognitive, personal, and social aspects of development, age period by age period. We then pull together the major themes that have emerged from recent theory and research.

Major Trends in Human Development

Throughout this book, we have seen that each phase of the life span has distinct characteristics. Here, at the risk of oversimplifying, we offer portraits of the developing person in seven periods of life—sketches that show how the strands of development, intertwined, make a *whole person*.

Infants (Birth to Age 2)

What is most striking about infant development is the staggering speed with which babies acquire all the basic capacities that make us human. Thanks to orderly and rapid development before birth, the newborn starts life marvelously equipped to adapt to its environment using reflexes, to take in information through all of its senses, and to learn from and remember its experiences. The rapid growth of body and brain during the first two years of life then transforms this neonate into a toddler who is walking, talking, and asserting a newfound sense of self.

As the cortical centers of the brain mature and become organized, and as infants gain sensory and motor experience, many automatic reflexes disappear and are replaced by voluntary motor behaviors. In a predictable sequence, infants sit, creep and crawl, and then walk independently, at about 1 year of age; during their first year, they also perfect a pincer grasp and become better able to manipulate objects with their hands. As they become more able to make sense of the perceptual world, and as their motor skills advance, they explore the world around them more effectively—and actively contribute to their own cognitive development in the process.

As babies progress through the substages of Piaget's *sensorimotor period,* they develop their minds through their own active efforts to perceive and act upon the world. They come to understand that objects have permanent existence, even when they are out of sight. They also acquire *symbolic capacity*—the ability to let one thing stand for another—which is central to intellectual activity throughout the remainder of the life span. By the end of the sensorimotor period, they can use symbols such as images to mentally devise solutions to problems before trying them out. Meanwhile, their capacities to learn and remember are expanding, allowing them to recall events in the absence of cues and imitate actions after a delay toward the end of the first year, and to de-liberately reconstruct events that happened months earlier by age 2. After cooing and babbling, they will utter their first words at the age of 1 and form two-word sentences such as "Go car" by the age of 2. As Vygotsky would remind us, these cognitive and linguistic breakthroughs grow out of the child's social interactions with parents and other guides.

As their cognitive capacities expand, infants become more aware of themselves as individuals. By 18 months of age, they recognize themselves in the mirror and know that they are girls or boys. In fact, infants are individuals from birth, each with a distinctive and genetically influenced temperament that serves as a foundation for later personality.

Infants' temperaments, coupled with their parents' styles of interacting with them, influence how successfully they resolve Erikson's first psychosocial conflict, that of *trust versus mistrust,* and whether they form secure, resistant, or avoidant attachments to their caregivers starting at about 7 months of age. The parent–child attachment relationship dominates the social world of the infant and serves as a training ground for later social relationships, as theorized by John Bowlby. Cognitive changes and daily exchanges with attachment figures give rise to more sophisticated social skills that infants then apply in encounters with peers. Equipped with the ability to perceive and act upon the environment, with impressive cognitive and linguistic capacities, with an awareness of self, and with attachments to their caregivers, infants are ready to venture out into a larger social world.

Preschool Children (Ages 2 through 5)

During the preschool years, 2-year-olds who toddle and teeter along and speak in two-word sentences become young children ready for formal schooling. As their brains continue to mature and as they gain motor experience, preschool children acquire the gross motor control they need to hop and catch balls and the fine motor skills they need to trace letters and use scissors.

During Piaget's *preoperational stage* of cognitive development, young children make wonderful use of their symbolic capacity, mastering all the basic rules of language (with the help of adults willing to converse with them) and joining with other children in imaginative sessions of social pretend play. True, young children often have difficulty with problems that require logical thinking. They fail Piaget's tests of *conservation,* thinking that the juice poured from a stocky glass into a tall, narrow glass somehow becomes "more juice." They are egocentric at times, failing to appreciate differences between their own perspectives and those of other individuals and assuming that their listeners know what they know. They are distractible and lack some of the information-processing skills that allow older children to think about two or more aspects of a problem at once and to use strategies such as rehearsal and organization to learn and remember more efficiently.

Preschoolers' personalities continue to take shape as they struggle with Erikson's conflicts of *autonomy versus shame* and *initiative versus guilt.* If all goes well, they develop the confidence to assert themselves and to carry out bold plans, and

Alice at 6 months old. She was born July 9, 1906, in Holly, Michigan, to Gertrude Belle Wright and John Henry Alger.

As a 2-year-old, she was very active. One of her earlist memories is riding in a basket swing suspended from the living room ceiling.

As a teenager, Alice loved sports. She played on a softball team and started playing tennis with her father at age 10. At 18, she was the first Women's State Tennis Champion in Wisconsin, a title she would earn twice. In college, she worked hard to help support her family through the Depression. Finally, she had to drop out of medical school. She continued taking night courses and met her future husband, whom she followed to California.

Alice married in 1939 at age 33. She and her husband, George, traveled frequently and visited Catalina during the first year of their marriage. Three years later, they started a family. Alice worked as a manuscript typist for several well-known authors in Santa Barbara, California, and taught tennis to help support the family.

At 45, Alice enjoyed outings with her three young children at Monterey, California. She was involved in her children's activities at home and school. She even hosted an American Field Service exchange student from Germany for a year.

Still active at 92, Alice plays tennis 3 days a week, and is seen here flying a sailplane in the Santa Ynez Valley, California. She is also a Literacy Volunteer and knits cotton bandages for lepers through the Direct Relief Foundation. She reads voraciously and loves crossword puzzles. She sadly gave up playing bridge at age 90 because she was tired of being the "designated driver."

At 80 she poses with her grown children and husband of 47 years in Santa Barbara, California.

At 95, Alice is still active and continues to play weekly tennis matches. Here she is seen tending fruit trees in the orchard at her home.

their self-esteem is high. They learn a good deal about themselves and other people, developing a *theory of mind* that allows them to predict and explain human behavior in terms of mental states, although they still describe people largely in terms of physical characteristics and activities rather than inner qualities. Although relatively lacking in self-control, they increasingly become socialized by those around them to internalize and follow rules of moral conduct. And in no time at all, they also learn what they must know to be a boy or a girl in their society.

Preschool children's attachments to their caregivers continue to be central in their social worlds, but they hone their social skills in interactions with peers, learning to take their playmates' perspectives, engage in truly cooperative play, and enter into friendships. All in all, preschoolers are endlessly fascinating: charming and socially skilled but a bit egocentric at times, immensely curious and intellectually alive but sometimes quite illogical, here one moment but off on some new adventure the next.

School-Age Children (Ages 6 through 11)

Compared with preschool children, elementary school children seem considerably more self-controlled, serious, skilled, and logical. Their bodies grow slowly and steadily each year, and they continue to refine their motor skills and use their senses ever more intelligently by directing their attention where it most needs to be directed. As they enter Piaget's *concrete operations stage,* they become able to perform in their heads actions that previously had to be performed with their hands. They can mentally add, subtract, classify, and order objects; grasp conservation problems that fool the preschooler; and draw many logical conclusions about the workings of the physical world. They master the fine points of the rules of language, use what Vygotsky called *private speech* (speech inside the head) as a tool in problem solving, and become better able to take the perspectives of their listeners in conversations. They acquire the memory strategies and other information-processing skills it takes to do schoolwork. And, although their scores on intelligence tests can fluctuate from year to year, their IQs begin to predict fairly well their intellectual standing as adolescents or adults.

The cognitive growth that occurs during the school years, along with social experience, allows children to understand themselves and other people in terms of inner personality traits and underlying motives. School-age children work through Erikson's conflict of *industry versus inferiority* as they attempt to master new skills, compare their accomplishments with those of their classmates, and absorb feedback about where they stand in their reading groups and where they finish in races. The unrealistically high self-esteem of the preschooler drops as children gain a more accurate view of their strengths and weaknesses. Most children also develop fairly consistent personalities, at least parts of which survive into adulthood.

School-age children also continue to learn about and conform to prevailing social standards regarding how boys and girls should behave, but their thinking is more flexible than that of preschoolers. Under the guidance of parents and teachers, and through their interactions with peers, children also learn the values and moral standards of the society around them. Most are at Kohlberg's level of *preconventional morality,* in which what matters most is whether their acts will be rewarded or punished.

The social world of school-age children is more extensive than that of infants and preschool children. Family life is still very important, but more and more time is spent with peers— usually those of the same sex—playing organized games and developing caring friendships or chumships. Youngsters who are rejected by their peers and don't have friends miss out on these important social learning opportunities and tend to become maladjusted adults. Teachers, coaches, TV characters, and sports stars also help children gain the skills and values they will need to do the serious work of adulthood.

Adolescents (Ages 12 through 19)

Adolescence, the passage between childhood and adulthood, is a time of substantial physical, cognitive, and social change. Adolescents who are adjusting to their growth spurt and to the sexual maturation of their bodies at around 12 to 14 are naturally preoccupied with their physical appearance and are often more upset by their misshapen noses or gargantuan feet than by any intellectual or character flaws they may possess. Puberty brings with it not only new physical capacities and unfamiliar sexual urges but also new, more adultlike relationships with members of the other sex and with parents.

Meanwhile, as the brain undergoes a growth spurt, particularly in the prefrontal areas of the cortex that are involved in planning and sustained attention, the mind undergoes its own transformation (Kwon & Lawson, 2000). The child who could reason logically about real-world problems becomes the adolescent who can think systematically about worlds that do not even exist and ideas that contradict reality. When adolescents fully master Piaget's *formal operations stage,* they can formulate and test hypotheses to solve scientific problems and can grasp abstract theories and philosophies. These and other new cognitive capacities sometimes leave adolescents susceptible to *adolescent egocentrism,* thoroughly confused about what to believe, painfully aware of gaps between what is and what should be, and rebellious when their parents or other authority figures are not "logical" enough for their tastes.

Cognitive gains also put adolescents in a position to think about themselves and other people in more sophisticated ways. Teenagers begin to describe themselves in more abstract terms, referring to their core values and philosophies of life. They are more introspective and self-aware than they were as children and can analyze themselves and other people to determine what really makes them tick. By late adolescence, many can integrate their self-perceptions into a coherent sense of who they are, resolving Erikson's conflict of *identity versus role confusion* and charting careers and other life goals. Conventional moral reasoning is achieved as young adolescents first emphasize the importance of being a "good boy" or "good girl," as defined by parents and society, and later appreciate the need for law and order in the larger social system.

Partly because teenagers become more physically and cognitively mature, and partly because society demands that they take seriously the task of readying themselves for adult roles, social relationships change a good deal during the adolescent years. The balance of power in the family shifts so that adolescents increasingly participate in making decisions about their lives. Adolescents become more and more involved in peer activities, intimate friendships with same- and other-sex peers, and dating relationships, often showing heightened conformity to gender-role norms. Heightened conformity to peer influence gets many adolescents into a brush or two with the law, but the peer group serves the useful function of helping children who depend heavily on their parents become adults who are less reliant on either parents or peers. Although about 20% of adolescents experience emotional storm and stress during this period of the life span, most teenagers emerge with impressive physical, intellectual, and social competencies, and with at least preliminary notions of who they are and what they will be as adults.

Young Adults (Ages 20 through 39)

The years of infancy, childhood, and adolescence are all a preparation for entry into adult life. Physiologically, young adults are at their peak; strength, endurance, reaction time, perceptual abilities, and sexual responsiveness are all optimal, even though the aging process is taking slight, and usually not even noticeable, tolls on the body. Early adulthood is also a period of effective cognitive functioning. Some young adults will solidify and possibly expand upon their command of formal operational thought, especially in their areas of expertise. Most adults continue to be conventional moral reasoners, but about 1 in 6 begins to think at the level of *postconventional morality,* grasping the moral principles underlying society's rules and regulations. If they continue to use their minds, young adults will often improve somewhat on the IQ test scores they obtained as adolescents.

It is fortunate that young adults are physically and intellectually capable, for they face many challenges. They must often continue to work on the adolescent task of identity formation, exploring different options before they settle on a career direction. Meanwhile, they are likely to be working through Erikson's early-adult crisis of *intimacy versus isolation* and, if all goes well, committing themselves to a partner. Young adults are changed by marriage, new parenthood, and other normal events of the family life cycle, just as they are affected by their work experiences. Parenthood tends to lower marital satisfaction and push young husbands and wives into more divergent and traditional gender roles.

In view of the many life changes experienced by young adults, perhaps it is not surprising that this period is characterized by higher divorce rates and more stress-related mental health problems than the later adult years. However, for most young adults, this is also an exciting and productive time of life, a time for gaining expertise, independence, and confidence.

Middle-Aged Adults (Ages 40 through 64)

Middle adulthood often strikes us as a more settled period than early adulthood, but it is certainly not devoid of change. Gradual declines in the body and its physical capacities that began in the 20s and 30s may now become noticeable. Gray hairs (or no hairs!), a shortness of breath after exercise, and a need for reading glasses proclaim that one is aging. Women experience the changes of menopause around the age of 50; both men and women become more vulnerable to heart disease and other chronic illnesses. Yet most of the physical changes that middle-aged adults experience occur quite slowly and are not severe, giving people plenty of time to adjust to and compensate for them.

Meanwhile, although intellectual capacities generally remain quite stable, middle-aged adults gradually gain some intellectual capacities and lose others. They amass knowledge and often perform better than young adults on measures of crystallized intelligence (vocabulary or general information). Moreover, they build expertise that allows them to solve everyday problems very effectively and reach peaks of creative achievement in their careers. Toward the end of middle adulthood, some individuals may feel that their memories are slipping a bit or may begin to struggle with the sorts of unfamiliar problems that measure fluid intelligence, but most intellectual skills hold up well in middle age.

Personalities that took form during childhood and that solidified during adolescence and early adulthood tend to persist into later adulthood, although significant change is possible. According to Erikson, middle-aged adults successfully resolve the conflict of *generativity versus stagnation* if they can invest their energies in nurturing the younger generation or in producing something of lasting value, but they may experience a sense of stagnation if they feel they have failed their children or are preoccupied with their own needs. Midlife crisis is quite rare. Indeed, after the nest empties and middle-aged adults are freed of major parenting responsibilities, they often find their marriages more satisfying, take pride in their grown children and grandchildren, and become more androgynous, expressing both their masculine and feminine sides.

Older Adults (Age 65 and Up)

The poet Robert Browning expressed a very positive image of late adulthood when he wrote: "Grow old along with me! The best is yet to be, the last of life for which the first was made." By contrast, William Shakespeare, in *As You Like It* (Act II, Scene 7), characterized the seventh and final age of life as "second childishness and mere oblivion; sans teeth, sans eyes, sans taste, sans everything." The truth lies somewhere in between: Old age does bring with it some losses and declines in functioning, but it is also, for most, a period of continued growth and many satisfactions.

By the time adults are in their 60s and 70s, most of them have a physical impairment of some kind—a chronic disease, a disability, failing eyesight or hearing, or, at the least, a slower nervous system and slower reactions. As they enter their 80s and 90s, more and more adults take longer to learn things, experience occasional memory lapses, or have difficulty solving novel problems. Although the odds of Alzheimer's disease increase with age, only a minority of elderly people have it or other forms of dementia. Most retain well the knowledge that they have crystallized over a lifetime and the cognitive and linguistic skills that they practice every day.

Although physical and cognitive declines are part of the experience of aging for most adults, we should be equally impressed by how successfully most adults adapt to these changes. They typically continue to carry out daily activities effectively, and they enjoy just as much self-esteem and life satisfaction as younger adults do. They do not crumble in the face of life changes such as retirement or widowhood. They continue to lead active social lives, use their sophisticated social-cognitive skills to understand other people and engage in complex moral reasoning, and enjoy close ties with both family and friends. And in the end, most are able to successfully resolve Erikson's conflict of *integrity versus despair,* finding meaning in their lives and coming to terms with the inevitability of death.

These, then, are the broad themes of later life. Yet what may be most striking of all about elderly adults is their immense diversity. Many older adults are healthy, active, and highly capable; others show clear signs of physical and cognitive decline. Moreover, each adult carries into old age his or her own unique abilities, fund of knowledge, personality traits, and values and will cope with the challenges of aging and dying in his or her own way.

The following table summarizes much of this discussion of physical, cognitive, personal, and social development within each period of the life span. This table can serve as a handy description of normal human development, but we also need to understand some of the processes behind these changes.

Major Themes in Human Development

Another way in which to leave you with the "big picture" is highlighting some major generalizations about human

Summary of Physical, Cognitive, Personal, and Social Development across the Life Span

Period	Physical Development	Cognitive Development
Infant (0 to 2)	Rapid brain and body growth. Reflexes, then more voluntary motor control, walking at 1 year. Functioning senses at birth; early ability to make sense of sensory information.	Sensorimotor period: Through senses and actions, infants acquire symbolic capacity and object-permanence concept. Cooing, babbling, and then one-word and two-word sentences. Learning capacity and recognition memory from birth; improvements in recall.
Preschool child (2 to 5)	Continued rapid brain development. Improved coordination and fine motor skills. Perceptual abilities are good; attention span is short.	Preoperational stage: Thought guided by perceptions rather than logic. Blossoming of symbolic capacity (language acquisition and pretend play). Some limits in information-processing capacity, use of memory strategies, and reasoning.
School-age child (6 to 11)	Slow physical growth, gradually improved motor skills. Increased ability to control attention and use the senses intelligently.	Concrete operations stage: Logical actions in the head; mastery of conservation. Mastery of fine points of language; improved memory strategies and problem solving with concrete objects. IQs begin to stabilize.
Adolescent (12 to 19)	Dramatic growth spurt and attainment of sexual maturity. Improved physical functioning. Concern with body image.	Formal operations stage: Hypothetical and abstract thought; scientific problem solving. Continued improvement of attention and information-processing skills linked to brain growth spurt.
Young adult (20 to 39)	Time of peak functioning, but gradual declines in physical and perceptual capacities begin.	Sophisticated cognitive skills, especially in areas of expertise. Possibility of growth beyond formal thought and gains in knowledge.
Middle-aged adult (40 to 64)	Physical declines become noticeable (e.g., some loss of endurance, need for reading glasses). Increased chronic illness. Menopause and male climacteric.	Mostly stable intellectual functioning and often peak expertise and creative achievement. Fluid intelligence may begin to decline, but crystallized knowledge is maintained well.
Older adult (65 and older)	Continued physical decline; more chronic disease, disability, and sensory impairment; slower reaction time. But also continued plasticity and reorganization of the brain in response to intellectual stimulation.	Declines in cognition are common, but not inevitable. Slower learning, memory problems, declines in IQ and problem solving, especially if skills are rarely exercised, but crystallized intelligence survives longer than fluid.

development and the processes behind it. Many of these larger themes are incorporated in the life-span developmental perspective introduced in Chapter 1 (Baltes, 1987; Baltes, Lindenberger, & Staudinger, 1998); some represent stands on the developmental issues laid out in Chapter 2; and most have been echoed throughout this book. We leave you with the following thoughts.

We Are Whole Persons throughout the Life Span

As our review of major developments in each life phase should make clear, it is the intermeshing of physical, cognitive, personal, and social development that gives each period of the life span—and each individual human—a distinctive and coherent quality. Thus, the fact that 7-month-old infants become attached to their caregivers is not just a milestone in social development divorced from other aspects of development. The maturation of sensory and motor abilities permits infants to crawl after their parents to maintain the proximity they desire, and their cognitive growth makes them aware that caregivers continue to exist when they leave the room (and

therefore can be retrieved). The emergence of attachment bonds, in turn, affects development in other areas—for example, by providing toddlers with the security that allows them to explore the world around them and, in the process, develop their motor skills and cognitive capacities all the more. All the threads of development are interwoven in the whole developing person.

Human Development Proceeds in Multiple Directions

Chapter 5 introduced Heinz Werner's (1957) *orthogenetic principle*, which states that development proceeds from global states to states of increasing differentiation and integration of specific, differentiated states into coherent wholes. The orthogenetic principle is indeed a useful way of summarizing many developmental trends. The single, undifferentiated cell formed at conception becomes billions of highly specialized cells (neurons, blood cells, and so on), all organized into functioning systems (such as the brain). The young infant flails its whole body as a unit (global response); the older child moves specific parts of the body on command (differentiation) and

Personal Development	Social Development
Acquisition of sense of self, self-recognition, early signs of theory of mind such as joint attention. Awareness of gender identity. Temperament as basis for later personality. Erikson's conflict of trust versus mistrust.	A social being from birth. Attachment to caregiver at 7 months; separation and stranger anxiety follow. Increased social skills with parents and peers; capacity for simple pretend play. Family-centered lifestyle.
Concrete, physical self-concept. Rapid acquisition of gender role. Mastery of theory of mind concept that people can have false beliefs; largely egocentric notion of morality. Conflicts of autonomy versus shame and initiative versus guilt.	Parent–child relationship still central in social world. Increased social-cognitive abilities allow more cooperation with peers, and social pretend play blossoms. First exposure to schooling.
Self-concept includes psychological traits. Personality "gels." Strong gender typing. Internalization of moral standards, but mainly preconventional morality. Much social comparison as cope with conflict of industry versus inferiority.	Increased involvement with same-sex peers; formation of close chumships. Role-taking skills advance. Play centers on organized games with rules. School and television are important socialization agents.
More abstract and integrated self-concept. Adjustment to sexuality and gender role. Conventional moral reasoning reflecting internalization of society's rules. Conflict of identity versus role confusion.	Peak peer involvement and conformity. More emotionally intimate friendships; dating relationships begin. Parent–child relationship becomes more equal; autonomy increases. Involved in school and career exploration.
Continued work on identity. Some shift from conventional to postconventional moral reasoning. Increased confidence. Divergence of roles in family according to sex. Personality fairly stable. Conflict of intimacy versus isolation.	Social networks continue to expand; romantic relationships form. Most establish families and take on roles as spouses and parents. Careers are launched; job switching is common. Period of much life change; high risk of divorce and psychological problems.
Continued personality stability; for a minority, midlife questioning and androgyny shift. Conflict of generativity versus stagnation.	The nest empties and the grandparent role is often added to existing roles. High responsibility for younger and older generations. Career is more stable, and peak success is attained. Family and work roles dominate.
Most maintain their characteristic personality traits, self-esteem, and life satisfaction. Many grow as they resolve conflict of integrity versus despair.	Continued close ties to family and friends; loneliness is rare. Generally smooth adjustment to retirement, and maintenance of social activities. For women especially, loss of spouse requires adjustment.

All photos courtesy of Maryann Craver

Francis Allen Shearer was born February 8, 1904, in Southeastern Pennsylvania. He was the youngest of three sons. His father was station master for the railroad.

Francis, shown here on the right with his three brothers and two cousins, traveled to York Academy by using the rail pass available to railroad employee's family members. He completed York Academy's 4-year college preparatory program in three years and went on to Gettysburg College, graduating in 1923. During this time, Francis decided he wanted to become a clergyman, which led him to The Lutheran Theological Seminary in Philadelphia.

Francis and his wife, Emma Sipe Shearer, on their wedding day in 1927. During the economic hard times of the Depression, their community often relied on Francis and Emma for leadership and strength. The couple even opened their home to young men escaping the Nazi roundup of Jews in Germany. Later, Francis would spend time in Europe working on the relocation of war refugees.

Recognized as a national authority in his field, his expertise was sought after his retirement, leading to a series of "second careers." For example, he served as the only non-medical member of a committee that reviewed and monitored animal research protocols for Philadelphia medical institutions. This involved reading tomes of highly technical data, but it became a fascinating new project for him in his mid-90s. Francis and Emma continue to amaze friends and family with their zest for life and active lifestyle even as they near the century mark.

As a newly ordained clergyman, Francis was assigned a parish in Clark Summit, Penn. This involved not only getting the congregation started, but also constructing the sanctuary. The young pastor helped out with planning and designing his first church, as well as with its actual construction. Times were hard for these parishioners and some of his salary came in the form of eggs and produce from caring members of this small but growing congregation.

Francis and Emma celebrated their 70th wedding anniversary with friends and family, including their two daughters and 5 grandchildren. Their family now includes 6 great-grandchildren as well.

Over the years, Francis became increasingly involved in socio-political activities. He was instrumental in developing state and national legislation to regulate the operation of orphanages, nursing facilities, and retirement homes. He served on state and national commissions related to these activities and won many tributes, including an Honorary Doctorate.

coordinates separate movements to ride a bike (integration). Similarly, young children describe other people's personalities in global terms ("He's nice" "She's mean"); school-age children develop a more differentiated vocabulary of trait labels for characterizing companions; and adolescents become true personality theorists, integrating all they have learned about their companions—contradictions included—into coherent theories about what makes these people tick.

Yet not all developmental change is a matter of acquiring more complex and organized behaviors or progressing toward some "mature" endpoint. As we have seen, human development involves gains *and* losses at every age, as well as systematic changes that make us neither better nor worse than we were before but simply different. Thus, children who are gaining many academic learning skills are also losing some of their intrinsic motivation to learn as they progress through school, and older adults are losing mental speed but at the same time gaining knowledge, and sometimes even wisdom, that helps them compensate for slower information processing. Paul Baltes has suggested that every gain may have its corresponding loss, and every loss its corresponding gain. Alice James, sister of pioneering psychologist William James and author Henry James, saw this even as her vision failed: "All loss is gain. Since I have become so near-sighted I see no dust or squalor, and therefore conceive of myself as living in splendor" (cited in Baltes, Smith, & Staudinger, 1992, p. 158).

We simply must abandon the tired old view that human development consists of growth or improvement up to adulthood, stability into middle age, and decline in old age. There are gains, losses, and just plain changes during *all* phases of the life span.

There Is Both Continuity and Discontinuity in Development

As we have seen throughout this book, developmentalists have long grappled with the issue of *continuity versus discontinuity* in human development. You should now appreciate the wisdom of staking out a middle ground on the continuity/discontinuity issue.

For example, research supports Piaget's claim that children progress through qualitatively different stages of cognitive development, but we now know that these advances in cognitive development are achieved quite gradually and occur faster in familiar than in less familiar domains of cognitive functioning (Flavell, Miller, & Miller, 1993). It seems that development often proceeds in a continuous, gradual manner that ultimately leads to stagelike discontinuities—qualitatively different performances that make us appreciate just how much growth has occurred.

Similarly, we have seen that some traits, including general intelligence and Big Five personality traits such as extraversion/introversion, carry over from childhood and become even more stable and consistent during adulthood. However, this continuity or consistency is far from perfect, and there is ample room for change. A bright child may lose intellectual capacity if he or she is abused and neglected at home and at-tends inferior schools, and an introverted child may gain confidence and blossom into a more outgoing individual with the aid of supportive friends. Such discontinuity means that predicting the character of the adult from knowledge of the child remains a risky business, even in the face of much continuity in development.

There Is Much Plasticity in Development

Repeatedly we have seen that human beings of all ages are characterized by considerable *plasticity*—by a remarkable capacity to change in response to experience and to get off one developmental pathway and onto another. Thus, infants whose intellectual development is stunted by early malnutrition can catch up if they are given an adequate diet and enriching experiences. Adults not only learn new intellectual tricks but sprout new neural synapses and even new neurons in response to experience—evidence that the brain is plastic throughout the life span and that the first three years of life are not the only years during which intellectual stimulation is important (Thompson & Nelson, 2001).

Evidence of plasticity and change in later life is especially heartening to those of us who want to foster healthy development. Contrary to what Freud believed, early experiences rarely make or break us. Instead, there are opportunities throughout the life span—within limits, of course—to undo the damage done by early traumas, to teach new skills, and to redirect lives along more fruitful paths. If adverse early experiences are followed by adverse later experiences, we can expect poor outcomes. But if potentially damaging early experiences are offset by favorable later experiences, we can expect developing humans to display considerable plasticity and resilience.

Nature and Nurture Truly Interact in Development

In a very important sense, the *nature–nurture issue* has been resolved. It is now clear that multiple causal forces, representing *both* nature and nurture and ranging from changes in cell chemistry to changes in the prevailing culture, conspire and interact to shape the course of human development. Biological and environmental influences jointly explain both universal developmental trends and individual differences in development. This is precisely the perspective taken by contextual and systems theories of development.

Consider a universal accomplishment such as acquiring language. Biological maturation, guided by a species-wide genetic blueprint, clearly makes this achievement possible, for no amount of stimulation from adults can make a 1-month-old baby speak sentences. Yet, even though an infant is maturationally ready, language skills will not be acquired without the input from the environment available in all societies— namely, opportunities to converse with speakers of the language. So it goes for many other developmental milestones: Nothing much happens unless the child is maturationally ready to learn *and* has the requisite learning experiences.

Why do individuals differ from one another in, for example, their command of language skills? We could argue that it is because different people inherit different intellectual potentials, but we would also have to acknowledge that a genetic potential for high intelligence will never be realized if a child has no opportunities for intellectual stimulation. We could stress the importance of stimulation, but we would have to acknowledge that children with the genes for high intelligence are more likely to actively seek out, elicit, and profit from such stimulation than children with limited genetic potential. In short, the experiences we have influence whether our genetic potentials are realized or not (*gene/environment interactions*), and the genes we inherit influence what experiences we seek out and have and how we respond to them (*gene/environment correlations*).

To illustrate, we have seen that the *goodness of fit* between the person's genetically influenced predispositions and his or her environment can be important (Chess & Thomas, 1999). The child who is genetically predisposed to be irritable and difficult may become the rebellious, angry adolescent if parents are rigid, impatient, and punitive, but the same child may develop in more positive directions if the mesh between his or her temperament and the demands of the social environment is better. Similarly, the adolescent starving for autonomy may do poorly in a middle school with rigid rules and little room for choice but thrive in a setting that allows more self-direction (Eccles et al., 1993). When there is goodness of fit between genetic predispositions and environment, nature and nurture work together in the person's favor.

The twin and adoption studies done by behavior geneticists also testify to the importance of both nature and nurture. Genetic differences among us help explain variation in virtually every human trait that has been studied, from hair color to verbal ability to depression-proneness and social attitudes. Yet environmental factors count too, particularly the unique experiences that we do not share with siblings and that make us different from them. Depending on which aspect of human development we study, we may find that either heredity or environment is more influential, but we cannot escape the conclusion that development always reflects the ongoing and interacting contributions of *both*.

We Are Individuals, Becoming Even More Diverse with Age

In any human development textbook, there is a tendency to emphasize developmental phenomena that are shared by all or most individuals—to highlight the regularities and commonalities. We do indeed share a good deal with our fellow developing humans. But let us not lose sight of the fact that each of us is truly one of a kind. Indeed, the diversity of developing humans is so great that it often seems impossible to generalize about them.

Individuality is apparent starting at birth if we look closely at each infant's temperament, daily rhythms, and rate of development. As we get older, our individual genetic en-

dowments express themselves more fully, and we increasingly accumulate our own unique histories of life experiences. The result? We can tell a good deal about an individual knowing that he or she is 2 weeks or 2 years old, whereas we know very little at all about a person simply knowing that he or she is 25 or 65. Indeed, because diversity increases with age, elderly adults are the most diverse group of human beings of all and, therefore, the age group we should work hardest to avoid stereotyping (Harris et al., 1992; Morse, 1993).

We Develop in a Cultural and Historical Context

Repeatedly we have seen that humans are embedded in a sociocultural context that affects their development, a central theme in the sociocultural theory of Vygotsky and the bioecological theory of Bronfenbrenner (Bronfenbrenner & Morris, 1998; Vygotsky, 1978). Human development takes different forms in different cultures, social classes, and racial and ethnic groups; human development in the 12th or 17th century was different from human development in the 20th century; and each person's development is influenced by social changes and historical events occurring during his or her lifetime.

We know, for example, that children reach puberty earlier and adults live longer now than they did a century ago. Today's cohorts of adults are also healthier and are functioning better intellectually and maintaining their intellectual capacities longer than adults who were born early in the 20th century and received less education and poorer health care (Schaie, 1996). Future cohorts of adults are likely to maintain their physical and mental abilities even longer. Changes in the family and in men's and women's roles, technological and scientific breakthroughs such as the World Wide Web and the Human Genome Project, the terrorist attack on the World Trade Center and Pentagon and its aftermath, and significant historical events and social changes yet to take place may all make human development in the 21st century quite different from human development in the 20th century.

We Are Active in Our Own Development

Early developmental theorists tended to view human beings as passively shaped by forces beyond their control. Sigmund Freud saw the developing child as driven by biological urges and molded by early experiences in the family; John Watson and other early learning theorists emphasized that human behavior is controlled by environmental stimuli. Jean Piaget did much to alter this image of developing humans by emphasizing how children *actively* explore the world around them and *actively* invent their own understandings, rather than merely absorbing lessons fed to them by adults. Piaget's insights about the developing child are now firmly embedded in our assumptions about human development at all ages. Certainly we are affected by those around us and are sometimes the passive recipients of environmental influence. But just as certainly we create our own environments, influence those around us, and by doing so, contribute to our own development. It is this ongoing, dynamic transaction between an active person and a changing environment, each influencing the other in a reciprocal manner, that steers development.

Development Is a Lifelong Process

Developmentalists have never before been as aware of the importance of understanding linkages between earlier and later development as they are today, as illustrated by the emergence of the field of *developmental psychopathology* with its emphasis on the various pathways that can lead to normal or abnormal developmental outcomes. It is valuable, of course, to study infancy, adolescence, or any other developmental period in its own right. But it is more valuable still to view behavior during any one phase of life from a life-span perspective. It helps to understand that the teenage girl who bickers with her parents in an effort to forge her own identity might not have the confidence to do so unless she had enjoyed a warm, secure attachment with them as an infant and child. It is important, too, to recognize that this adolescent's quest for a separate identity and increased independence will help her achieve a readiness for intimacy and interdependence with another person. Because development *is* a process, it helps to know where it started and where it is heading.

Development Is Best Viewed from Multiple Perspectives

As the content of this book testifies, many disciplines have something to contribute to a comprehensive understanding of human development. Geneticists, developmental neuroscientists, and other representatives of the biological sciences must help us understand the genes, hormones, and neural networks that guide human development and aging and how they both affect and are affected by environmental factors. Meanwhile, psychologists must help us understand the individual and his or her social relationships, and anthropologists, sociologists,

historians, and economists must contribute their analyses of the changing sociocultural context in which that individual develops.

Multiple theories must also be brought to bear on the task of understanding human development. As we noted in Chapter 2, many developmental scientists are *eclectics:* They embrace several theories rather than feeling that they must select one and reject the rest. As we have seen throughout this book, psychoanalytic, social learning, cognitive developmental, ethological, and contextual and systems theories *all* have something important to say about how and why we change and remain the same as we get older. Indeed, we may be able to integrate some of the messages of universal stage theories such as Erikson's and Piaget's with a contextual perspective emphasizing variations in development (Lerner & Kauffman, 1985). Such an integrated theory would reflect our understanding that people all over the world develop along certain well-worn pathways but that human development can also take quite different directions depending on the day-to-day transactions between the maturing individual and the particular social world in which he or she is developing.

Often, it seems that the more one learns about a topic, the more one realizes how much more there is to learn. This is certainly true of human development. As developmental scientists increasingly incorporate contextual assumptions into their thinking, they are asking new questions that might not have occurred to them in the past about how transactions between changing persons and their changing environments actually play themselves out over the years. In the study of human development, then, there are always more questions than answers. We find this to be both a humbling and an inspiring thought. And we hope that you, too, feel both humbled and inspired as you complete your introduction to life-span human development. We hope that you are intrigued enough to observe more closely your own development and that of those around you—or even to take further course work. And we sincerely hope that you will use what you learn to steer your own and others' development in healthier directions.

Glossary

A

A, not B, error The tendency of 8- to 12-month-old infants to search for a hidden object in the place where they last found it (A) rather than in its new hiding place (B).

ability grouping The practice in education of grouping students according to ability and then educating them in classes with students of comparable academic or intellectual standing; also called ability tracking or simply tracking.

acceptance/responsiveness A dimension of parenting capturing the extent to which parents are supportive, sensitive to their children's needs, and willing to provide affection and praise when their children meet their expectations.

accommodation In Piaget's cognitive developmental theory, the process of modifying existing schemata to incorporate or adapt to new experiences; compare *assimilation*. In vision, a change in the shape of the eye's lens to bring objects at differing distances into focus.

acquired immune deficiency syndrome (AIDS) The life-threatening disease in which a virus (HIV) destroys the immune system and makes victims susceptible to rare, so-called opportunistic, infections that eventually kill them. Transmitted through sexual activity, drug needle sharing, and from mother to child before or during birth.

activity A dimension of temperament that refers to the activity or energy level of an individual.

activity/passivity issue Debate in developmental theory centering on whether humans are active contributors to their own development or are passively shaped by forces beyond their control.

activity theory A perspective holding that aging adults will find satisfaction to the extent that they maintain an active lifestyle. Compare *disengagement theory*.

adaptation In Piaget's cognitive developmental theory, one's inborn tendency to adjust to the demands of the environment, consisting of the complementary processes of assimilation and accommodation.

adolescent egocentrism A characteristic of adolescent thought that involves difficulty differentiating between one's own thoughts and feelings and those of other people; evident in the *personal fable* and *imaginary audience* phenomena.

adolescent growth spurt The rapid increase in physical growth that occurs during adolescence.

age effects In developmental research, the effects of getting older or of developing. Compare *cohort effects* and *time of measurement effects*.

age grades Socially defined age groups or strata, each with different statuses, roles, privileges, and responsibilities in society.

agency An orientation toward individual action and achievement that emphasizes traits of dominance, independence, assertiveness, and competitiveness; considered masculine.

age norm Expectations about what people should be doing or how they should behave at different points in the life span.

age of viability A point (currently at about the 24th prenatal week) when a fetus may survive outside the uterus if the brain and respiratory system are well enough developed and if excellent medical care is available.

age-related macular degeneration Damage to cells in the retina that are responsible for central vision.

aging To most developmentalists, positive, negative, and neutral changes in the mature organism; different from *biological aging*.

alphabetic principle The idea that letters in printed words represent the sounds in spoken words.

Alzheimer's disease A pathological condition of the nervous system that results in an irreversible loss of cognitive capacities; the leading cause of dementia in later life.

amniocentesis A method of extracting amniotic fluid from a pregnant woman so that fetal body cells within the fluid can be tested for chromosomal abnormalities and other genetic defects.

amnion A watertight membrane that surrounds the developing embryo, serving to regulate its temperature and to cushion it against injuries.

amoral Lacking any sense of morality; without standards of right and wrong.

androgenized female Genetic female who was exposed to male sex hormones during the prenatal period and therefore developed malelike external genitals and some masculine behaviors.

androgens Male hormones that help trigger the adolescent growth spurt, as well as the development of the male sex organs, secondary sex characteristics, and sexual motivation.

androgyny A gender-role orientation in which the person blends both positive masculine-stereotyped and positive feminine-stereotyped personality traits.

androgyny shift A psychological change that begins in midlife, when parenting responsibilities are over, in which both men and women retain their gender-typed qualities but add to them qualities traditionally associated with the other sex, thus becoming more androgynous.

anorexia nervosa A life-threatening eating disorder characterized by failure to maintain a normal weight, a strong fear of weight gain, and a distorted body image; literally, "nervous lack of appetite."

anoxia A lack of sufficient oxygen to the brain; may result in neurological damage or death.

anticipatory grief Grieving before death occurs for what is happening and for what lies ahead.

antioxidant Vitamins C, E, and similar substances that may increase longevity, though not for long, by inhibiting the free radical activity associated with oxidation and thus preventing age-related diseases.

Apgar test A test that is routinely used to assess a newborn's heart rate, respiration, color, muscle tone, and reflexes immediately after birth and then 5 minutes later; used to identify high-risk babies.

aptitude–treatment interaction (ATI) A phenomenon in which characteristics of the student and of the school environment interact to affect student outcome, such that any given educational practice may be effective only with a particular kind of student.

artificial insemination A method of conception that involves injecting sperm from a woman's partner or from a donor into the uterus.

assimilation Piaget's term for the process by which children interpret new experiences in terms of their existing schemata. Compare *accommodation*.

assisted suicide Making available to an individual who wishes to commit suicide the means by which he or she may do so, as when a physician provides a terminally ill patient who wants to die with enough medication to overdose.

attachment A strong emotional tie that binds a person to an intimate companion and is characterized by affection and a desire to maintain proximity.

attachment theory Theory of close relationships developed by Bowlby and Ainsworth and grounded in ethological theory (combined with psychoanalytic theory and cognitive theory); it claims that close emotional bonds such as parent–child attachments are biologically based and contribute to species survival.

attention The focusing of perception and cognition on something in particular.

attention-deficit hyperactivity disorder (ADHD) A disorder characterized by attentional difficulties, impulsive behavior, and overactive or fidgety behavior.

authoritarian parenting A restrictive style of parenting combining high demandingness/control and low acceptance/responsiveness in which adults impose many rules, expect strict obedience, and often rely on power tactics rather than explanations to elicit compliance.

authoritative parenting A flexible style of parenting combining high demandingness/control and high acceptance/responsiveness in which adults lay down clear rules but also grant a fair amount of autonomy to their children and explain the rationale for their restrictions.

autism A pervasive and severe developmental disorder that begins in infancy and is characterized by such problems as an aversion to social contact, deviant communication or mutism, and repetitive, stereotyped behavior.

autobiographical memory Memory of everyday events that the individual has experienced.

automatization The process by which information processing becomes effortless and highly efficient as a result of continued practice or increased expertise.

autonomy The capacity to make decisions independently, serve as one's own source of emotional strength, and otherwise manage life tasks without being overdependent on other people; an important developmental task of adolescence.

autonomy versus shame and doubt Psychosocial conflict in which toddlers attempt to demonstrate their independence from and control over other people; second of Erikson's stages.

avoidant attachment An insecure infant–caregiver bond or other intimate relationship characterized by little separation anxiety and a tendency to avoid or ignore the attachment object upon reunion.

B

babbling An early form of vocalization that appears between 4 and 6 months of age and involves repeating consonant–vowel combinations such as "baba" or "dadada."

baby biographies Carefully recorded observations of the growth and development of children by their parents over a period of time. The first scientific investigations of development.

baby boom generation The huge generation of people born between 1946 (the close of World War II) and 1964.

beanpole family A multigenerational family structure characterized by many small generations.

behavioral genetics The scientific study of the extent to which genetic and environmental differences among individuals are responsible for differences among them in traits such as intelligence and personality.

behavioral inhibition A temperamental characteristic reflecting one's tendency to withdraw from unfamiliar people and situations.

behaviorism A school of thinking in psychology that holds that conclusions about human development should be based on controlled observations of overt behavior rather than on speculation about unconscious motives or other unobservable phenomena; the philosophical underpinning for early theories of learning.

belief-desire psychology The *theory of mind* reflecting an understanding that people's desires and beliefs guide their behavior and that their beliefs are not always an accurate reflection of reality; evident by age 4. Compare *desire psychology*.

bereavement A state of loss that provides the occasion for grief and mourning.

beta-amyloid A toxic protein that injures neurons; located in the senile plaques associated with Alzheimer's disease.

Big Five The five major dimensions used to characterize people's personalities: neuroticism, extraversion, openness to experience, agreeableness, and conscientiousness.

bioecological approach Bronfenbrenner's view emphasizing that the developing person is embedded in and interacts with a series of environmental systems (*microsystem, mesosystem, exosystem,* and *macrosystem*).

biological aging The deterioration of organisms that leads inevitably to their death.

blastula A hollow sphere of about 100 to 150 cells that the zygote forms by rapid cell division as it moves through the fallopian tube.

brain growth spurt Period spanning the last three months of prenatal life and the first two years after birth in which the brain undergoes its most rapid development.

breech presentation A delivery in which the fetus emerges feet first or buttocks first rather than head first.

bulimia nervosa A life-threatening eating disorder characterized by recurrent eating binges followed by purging activities such as vomiting.

C

caregiver burden The psychological distress associated with providing care for someone with physical and/or cognitive impairments.

carrier In genetics, an individual who possesses a recessive gene associated with a disease and who, while he or she does not have the disease, can transmit the gene for it to offspring.

cataracts A pathologic condition of the eye involving opacification (clouding) of the lens that can impair vision or cause blindness.

catch-up growth A phenomenon in which children who have experienced growth deficits grow very rapidly to "catch up" to the growth trajectory that they are genetically programmed to follow.

categorical self A person's classification of the self along socially significant dimensions such as age and sex.

centenarian An individual who lives to be 100 years of age.

centration In Piaget's theory, the tendency to focus on only one aspect of a problem when two or more aspects are relevant.

cephalocaudal principle The principle that growth proceeds from the head (cephalic region) to the tail (caudal region).

cerebral cortex The convoluted outer covering of the brain that is involved in voluntary body movements, perception, and higher intellectual functions such as learning, thinking, and speaking.

cerebral palsy A neurological disability caused by anoxia that is associated with difficulty controlling muscle movements.

cesarean section A surgical procedure in which an incision is made in the mother's abdomen and uterus so that the baby can be removed through the abdomen.

child-directed speech Manner of speaking used by adults with young children; it involves short, simple sentences, spoken slowly and in a high-pitched voice, often with much repetition, and with exaggerated emphasis on key words.

child effects model A model of family influence in which children are believed to influence their parents rather than vice versa.

chorion A membrane that surrounds the amnion and becomes attached to the uterine lining to gather nourishment for the embryo.

chorionic villus sampling (CVS) An alternative to amniocentesis in which a catheter is inserted through the cervix to withdraw fetal cells from the chorion for prenatal testing to detect genetic defects.

chromosome A threadlike structure made up of genes; in humans, there are 46 chromosomes in the nucleus of each cell.

chromosome abnormalities Conditions in which a child has too few, too many, or incomplete chromosomes because of errors in the formation of sperm or ova.

chumship A close friendship with a peer of the same sex that emerges at about age 9 to 12, according to Sullivan.

class inclusion The logical understanding that parts or subclasses are included in the whole class and that the whole is therefore greater than any of its parts.

classical conditioning A type of learning in which a stimulus that initially had no effect on the individual comes to elicit a response owing to its association with a stimulus that already elicits the response.

climacteric The loss of reproductive capacity in either sex in later life.

clinical method An unstandardized interviewing procedure used by Jean Piaget in which a child's response to each successive question (or problem) determines what the investigator will ask next.

clique A small friendship group that interacts frequently. See also *crowd*.

cloning The process of converting a single cell from one animal into a new animal that is a genetic duplicate of the original animal.

cochlear implant A surgically implanted amplification device that stimulates the auditory nerve in order to provide the sensation of hearing to a deaf individual.

codominance In genetics, an instance in which two different but equally powerful genes produce a phenotype in which both genes are equally expressed.

coercive family environment A home in which family members are locked in power struggles, each trying to control the other through aggressive tactics such as threatening, yelling, and hitting.

cognition The activity of knowing and the processes through which knowledge is acquired (including attending, perceiving, remembering, and thinking).

cohabitation The living together of two single adults as an unmarried couple.

cohort A group of people born at the same time; a particular generation of people.

cohort effects In cross-sectional research, the effects on findings of the fact that the different age groups (cohorts) being compared were born at different times and had different formative experiences. Compare *age effects* and *time of measurement effects*.

collectivist culture A culture in which people define themselves in terms of group memberships, give group goals higher priority than personal goals, and socialize children to seek group harmony. Compare *individualistic culture*.

communality An orientation that emphasizes the well-being of others and includes traits of emotionality and sensitivity to others; considered feminine.

comorbidity The co-occurrence of two or more psychiatric conditions in the same individual.

conception The moment of fertilization, when a sperm penetrates an ovum, forming a zygote.

concordance rate The percentage of cases in which a particular attribute is present for both members of a pair of people (for example, twins) if it is present for one member.

concrete operations stage Piaget's third stage of cognitive development, lasting from about age 7 to age 11, when children are acquiring logical operations and can reason effectively about real objects and experiences.

conditioned response (CR) A learned response to a stimulus that was not originally capable of producing the response.

conditioned stimulus (CS) An initially neutral stimulus that comes to elicit a particular response after being paired with an unconditioned stimulus that always elicits the response.

confidant A spouse, relative, or friend to whom a person feels emotionally close and with whom he or she can share thoughts and feelings.

conformity The tendency to go along with the opinions or wishes of someone else or to yield to group pressures.

conservation The recognition that certain properties of an object or substance do not change when its appearance is altered in some superficial way.

constraint-seeking questions In the Twenty Questions Task and similar hypothesis-testing tasks, questions that rule out more than one answer to narrow the field of possible choices rather than asking about only one hypothesis at a time.

constructivism Position taken by Piaget claiming that children actively create their own understandings of the world from their experiences, as opposed to being born with innate ideas or being programmed by the environment.

contact comfort The pleasurable tactile sensations provided by a parent or a soft, terry cloth mother substitute; believed to foster attachments in infant monkeys and possibly in humans.

contextual and systems theories Theories of development holding that changes over the life span arise from the ongoing interrelationship between a changing organism and a changing world.

continuity/discontinuity issue The debate among theorists about whether human development is best characterized as gradual and continuous or abrupt and stagelike.

contour The amount of light/dark transition or boundary area in a visual stimulus.

conventional morality Kohlberg's term for the third and fourth stages of moral reasoning in which societal values are internalized and judgments are based on a desire to gain approval or uphold law and social order.

convergent thinking Type of thinking that involves "converging" on the one best answer to a problem; what IQ tests measure. Compare *divergent thinking*.

cooing An early form of vocalization that involves repeating vowel-like sounds.

cooperative learning methods Procedures that involve assigning students, usually of different races or ability levels, to work in teams that are reinforced for performing well as teams, thus encouraging cooperation among teammates.

correlation coefficient A measure, ranging from +1.00 to −1.00, of the extent to which two variables or attributes are systematically related to each other in either a positive or a negative way.

correlational method A research technique that involves determining whether two or more variables are related to one another. It cannot indicate that one thing caused another, but it can suggest that a causal relationship exists and allows us to predict one characteristic from our knowledge of another.

creativity The ability to produce novel responses or works.

critical period A defined period in the development of an organism when it is particularly sensitive to certain environmental influences; outside this period, the same influences will have far less effect.

crossing over A process in which genetic material is exchanged between pairs of chromosomes during meiosis.

cross-modal perception The ability to use one sensory modality to identify a stimulus or pattern of stimuli that is already familiar through another modality.

cross-sectional design A developmental research design in which different age groups are studied at the same point in time and compared.

crowd A network of heterosexual cliques that forms during adolescence and serves to facilitate mixed-sex social activities. See also *clique*.

crystallized intelligence Those aspects of intellectual functioning that involve making use of knowledge acquired through experience. Compare *fluid intelligence*.

cued recall memory Recollecting objects, events, or experiences in response to a hint or cue. Compare *recall memory* and *recognition memory*.

cultural-familial retardation Mental retardation that appears to be due to some combination of low genetic potential and a poor family environment rather than to a specific biological cause. Compare *organic retardation*.

culture A system of meanings shared by a population of people and transmitted from one generation to the next.

culture bias The situation that arises in testing when one cultural or subcultural group is more familiar with test items than another group and therefore has an unfair advantage.

cumulative-deficit hypothesis The notion that impoverished environments inhibit intellectual growth and that these inhibiting effects accumulate over time.

cystic fibrosis A disease caused by a *mutation* that results in the buildup of sticky mucus in the lungs, makes breathing difficult, and shortens the lives of affected children.

D

damage theories of aging Theories that emphasize a number of haphazard processes that cause cells and organ systems to deteriorate. Compare *programmed theories*.

dark adaptation The process by which the eyes become more sensitive to light over time as they remain in the dark.

decentration The ability to focus on two or more dimensions of a problem at one time.

decontextualization Separation of prior knowledge and beliefs from the demands of the task at hand.

decontextualized language Language that is not bound to the immediate conversational context but refers to past or remote events.

defense mechanisms Devices used by the ego to defend itself against anxiety caused by conflict between the id's impulses and social demands.

delirium A clouding of consciousness characterized by alternating periods of disorientation and coherence.

demandingness/control A dimension of parenting reflecting the extent to which parents as opposed to children exert control over decisions and set and enforce rules; also called permissiveness–restrictiveness.

dementia A progressive loss of cognitive capacities such as memory and judgment that affects some aging individuals and that has a variety of causes.

denial A defense mechanism in which anxiety-provoking thoughts are kept out of, or isolated from, conscious awareness.

dependent variable The aspect of behavior that is measured in an experiment and that is assumed to be under the control of, or "dependent" on, the *independent variable*.

depression See *major depressive disorder*.

desire psychology The earliest *theory of mind*: an understanding that desires guide behavior (that is, people seek out things they like and avoid things they hate). Compare *belief-desire psychology*.

development Systematic changes in the individual occurring between conception and death; such changes can be positive, negative, or neutral.

developmental norm The age at which half of a large group of infants or children master a skill or display a behavior; the average age for achieving a milestone in development.

developmental psychopathology A field of study concerned with the origins and course of maladaptive or psychopathological behavior.

developmental quotient (DQ) A numerical measure of an infant's performance on a developmental test relative to the performance of other infants the same age.

developmental stage A distinct phase within a larger sequence of development; a period characterized by a particular set of abilities, motives, behaviors, or emotions that occur together and form a coherent pattern.

diathesis/stress model The view that psychopathology results from the interaction of a person's predisposition to psychological problems and the experience of stressful events.

dietary restriction A technique involving a highly nutritious but severely calorie-restricted diet that has been demonstrated to extend the life span of laboratory animals.

difficult temperament Characteristic mode of response in which the individual is irregular in his or her habits and adapts slowly, often with vigorous protest, to changes in routine or new experiences. Compare *easy temperament* and *slow-to-warm-up temperament*.

diffusion status Identity status characterizing individuals who have not questioned who they are and have not committed themselves to an identity.

disengagement theory A perspective that holds that successful aging involves a mutually satisfying withdrawal of the aging individual and society from one another. Compare *activity theory*.

disorganized/disoriented attachment An insecure infant–caregiver bond, common among abused children, that combines features of the resistant and avoidant attachment styles and is characterized by the infant's dazed response to reunion and confusion about whether to approach or avoid the caregiver.

divergent thinking Type of thinking that requires coming up with a variety of ideas or solutions to a problem when there is no one right answer. Compare *convergent thinking*.

dominant gene A relatively powerful gene that is expressed phenotypically and masks the effect of a less powerful, *recessive gene*.

double standard The view that sexual behavior appropriate for members of one gender is inappropriate for members of the other.

Down syndrome A chromosomal abnormality in which the child has inherited an extra 21st chromosome and is, as a result, mentally retarded; also called trisomy 21.

DSM-IV The diagnostic and statistical manual of mental disorders published by the American Psychiatric Association and used by clinicians to diagnose psychological disorders.

dynamic assessment An approach to assessing intelligence that evaluates how well individuals learn new material when an examiner provides them with competent instruction.

dynamic systems approach A perspective on development applied to motor development that proposes that more and more sophisticated patterns of motor behavior emerge over time through a "self-organizing" process in which children modify their motor behavior in adaptive ways on the basis of the sensory feedback they receive when they try different movements.

dyslexia Serious difficulties learning to read in children who have normal intellectual ability and no sensory impairments or emotional difficulties that could account for their learning problems.

E

easy temperament Characteristic mode of response in which the individual is even-tempered, content, and open and adaptable to new experiences. Compare *difficult temperament* and *slow-to-warm-up temperament*.

echolalia The repetition of sounds, as when an autistic child parrots back what someone else says.

eclectic In the context of science, an individual who recognizes that no single theory can explain everything but that each has something to contribute to our understanding.

ego Psychoanalytic term for the rational component of the personality.

egocentrism The tendency to view the world from one's own perspective while failing to recognize that others may have different points of view.

elaboration A strategy for remembering that involves adding something to or creating meaningful links between the bits of information one is trying to retain.

Electra complex Female version of the Oedipus complex, in which a 4- to 6-year-old girl is said to envy her father for possessing a penis and would choose him as a sex object in the hope of sharing this valuable organ that she lacks.

embryo See *period of the embryo*.

emergent literacy The developmental precursors of reading skills in young children; includes knowledge, skills, and attributes that will facilitate the acquisition of reading competence.

emotionality A dimension of temperament that refers to the tendency to be easily or intensely irritated by events.

emotion regulation The processes involved in initiating, maintaining, and altering emotional responses.

empathy The vicarious experiencing of another person's feelings.

empiricist An individual whose approach to human development emphasizes the contribution of environmental factors; specifically, one who believes that infants enter the world as blank slates and know nothing except what they learn through their senses. Compare *nativist*.

empty nest Term used to describe the family after the last child departs the household.

encoding The first step in learning and remembering something; the process of getting information into the information-processing system, learning it, and organizing it in a form suitable for storing.

endocrine gland Type of gland that secretes chemicals called hormones directly into the bloodstream. Endocrine glands play critical roles in stimulating growth and regulating bodily functions.

environment Events or conditions outside the person that are presumed to influence and be influenced by the individual.

equity A balance of contributions and gains in a social relationship that results in neither partner's feeling over- or underbenefited.

estrogen The female hormone responsible for the development of the breasts, the female sex organs, and secondary sex characteristics, as well as the beginning of menstrual cycles.

ethnic identity A sense of personal identification with one's ethnic group and its values and cultural traditions.

ethology A discipline and theoretical perspective that focuses on the evolved behavior of different species in their natural environments.

eugenics The alteration of the genetic makeup of a population in an attempt to improve the human race.

euthanasia Literally, "good death"; specifically, hastening, either actively or passively, the death of someone who is suffering from an incurable illness or injury.

evolutionary psychology A perspective guided by Darwinian evolutionary theory that asks about the adaptive functions of behavior over the history of the species.

executive control processes Processes that direct and monitor the selection, organization, manipulation, and interpretation of information in the information-processing system; include *executive functions*.

executive functions The planning and organizational functions that reside in the prefrontal cortex of the brain.

exosystem In Bronfenbrenner's bioecological approach, settings not experienced directly by the individual that nonetheless influence his or her development (for example, the effects of events at a parent's workplace on a child's development).

expansion A conversational tactic used by adults in speaking to young children in which they respond to a child's utterance with a more grammatically complete expression of the same thought.

experiment A research strategy in which the investigator manipulates or alters some aspect of a person's environment in order to measure what effect it has on the individual's behavior or development.

experimental control In an experiment, the holding constant of all other factors besides the independent variable, so that any changes in the dependent variable can be said to be caused by the manipulation of the independent variable.

explicit memory Memory that involves consciously recollecting the past. Compare *implicit memory*.

extended family household A family unit composed of parents and children living with other kin such as grandparents, aunts and uncles, and/or cousins.

externalizing problem Childhood behavior problem that involves "undercontrolled" behavior such as aggression, or acting out difficulties in ways that disturb other people. Compare *internalizing problem*.

extinction The gradual weakening and disappearance of a learned response when it is no longer reinforced.

eyewitness memory Remembering and reporting events one has witnessed or experienced.

F

factor analysis A technique that identifies clusters of tasks or test items (called factors) that are highly correlated with one another and unrelated to other items.

failure to thrive A condition observed in infants who, due either to physical causes or to emotional deprivation, are characterized by stunted growth, weight loss, and delays in cognitive and socioemotional development.

false belief task A research paradigm used to assess an important aspect of a *theory of mind*, mainly the understanding that people can hold incorrect beliefs and be influenced by them.

family life cycle The sequence of changes in family composition, roles, and relationships that occurs from the time people marry until they die.

family systems theory The conceptualization of the family as a whole consisting of interrelated parts, each of which affects and is affected by every other part, and each of which contributes to the functioning of the whole.

fetal alcohol syndrome (FAS) A group of symptoms commonly observed in the off-spring of mothers who use alcohol heavily during pregnancy, including a small head, widely spaced eyes, and mental retardation.

fetus See *period of the fetus.*

fine motor skills Skills that involve precise movements of the hands and fingers or feet and toes. Compare *gross motor skills.*

fixation In psychoanalytic theory, a defense mechanism in which development is arrested and part of the libido remains tied to an early stage of development.

fluid intelligence Those aspects of intelligence that involve actively thinking and reasoning to solve novel problems. Compare *crystallized intelligence.*

Flynn effect The rise in average IQ scores over the 20th century.

foreclosure status Identity status characterizing individuals who appear to have committed themselves to a life direction but who have adopted an identity prematurely, without much thought.

formal operations stage Piaget's fourth and final stage of cognitive development (age 11 or 12 and beyond), when the individual begins to think more rationally and systematically about abstract concepts and hypothetical ideas.

fraternal twins Twins who are not identical and who result when a mother releases two ova at roughly the same time and each is fertilized by a different sperm.

free radical theory The theory of aging that views it as damage caused by free radicals, chemically unstable by-products of metabolism that have an extra electron and react with other molecules to produce toxic substances that damage cells.

functional grammar An analysis of the semantic relations (meanings such as naming and locating) that children express in their earliest sentences.

fuzzy-trace theory The view that verbatim and general or gistlike accounts of an event are stored separately in memory.

G

gender consistency The stage of gender typing in which children realize that one's sex is stable across situations or despite changes in activities or appearance.

gender identity One's basic awareness that one is either a male or a female.

gender intensification A magnification of differences between males and females during adolescence associated with increased pressure to conform to traditional gender roles.

gender role A pattern of behaviors and traits that defines how to act the part of a female or a male in a particular society.

gender-role norms Society's expectations or standards concerning what males and females should be like and how they should behave.

gender-role stereotypes Overgeneralized and largely inaccurate beliefs about what males and females are like.

gender schemata Organized sets of beliefs and expectations about males and females that guide information processing.

gender segregation The formation of separate boys' and girls' peer groups during childhood.

gender stability The stage of gender typing in which children realize that one's sex remains the same over time.

gender typing The process by which children become aware of their gender and acquire the motives, values, and behaviors considered appropriate for members of their biological sex.

gene A functional unit of heredity made up of DNA and transmitted from generation to generation.

gene/environment correlation A systematic interrelationship between an individual's genes and his or her environment; ways in which genes influence the kind of home environment provided by parents (passive gene/environment correlation), social reactions to the individual (evocative gene/environment correlation), and the types of experiences the individual seeks out (active gene/environment correlation).

gene/environment interaction The phenomenon in which the effects of one's genes depend on the kind of environment one experiences and in which the effects of the environment depend on one's genetic endowment.

generativity versus stagnation The psychosocial conflict in which middle-aged adults must gain the sense that they have produced something that will outlive them and genuinely care for younger generations in order to avoid self-preoccupation; seventh of Erikson's stages.

gene therapy Interventions that involve substituting normal genes for the genes associated with a disease or disorder, or otherwise altering a person's genetic makeup.

genetic counseling A service designed to inform people about genetic conditions they or their unborn children are at risk of inheriting.

genetic epistemology The study of how humans come to know reality and basic dimensions of it such as space, time, and causality; Piaget's field of interest.

genotype The genetic endowment that an individual inherits. Compare *phenotype.*

germinal period First phase of prenatal development, lasting for about two weeks from conception until the developing organism becomes attached to the wall of the uterus.

gerontology The study of aging and old age.

giftedness The possession of unusually high general intellectual potential or of special abilities in such areas as creativity, mathematics, or the arts.

glaucoma A condition in which increased fluid pressure in the eye damages the optic nerve and causes progressive loss of peripheral vision and ultimately blindness.

goodness of fit The extent to which the child's temperament and the demands of the child's social environment are compatible or mesh, according to Thomas and Chess; more generally, a good match between person and environment.

grief The emotional response to loss. Compare *mourning.*

grief work perspective The view commonly held, but now challenged, that in order to cope adaptively with death, bereaved people must confront their loss, experience painful emotions, work through these emotions, and move toward a detachment from the deceased.

gross motor skills Skills that involve large muscles and whole body or limb movements (for example, kicking the legs or drawing large circles). Compare *fine motor skills.*

growth The physical changes that occur from conception to maturity.

growth hormone Hormone produced by the pituitary gland that stimulates childhood physical growth and the adolescent growth spurt.

guided participation A process in which children learn by actively participating in culturally relevant activities with the aid and support of their parents and other knowledgeable individuals.

H

habituation A simple form of learning that involves learning *not* to respond to a stimulus that is repeated over and over; learning to be bored by the familiar.

Hayflick limit The estimate that human cells can double only 50 times, plus or minus 10, and then will die.

hemophilia A deficiency in the blood's ability to clot; it is more common among males than females because it is associated with a sex-linked gene on the X chromosome.

heritability The amount of variability in a population on some trait dimension that is attributable to genetic differences among those individuals.

holophrase A single-word utterance used by an infant that represents an entire sentence's worth of meaning.

HOME inventory A widely used instrument that allows an observer to determine how intellectually stimulating or impoverished a home environment is.

horizontal décalage A term used by Piaget to characterize the fact that different cognitive skills related to the same stage of cognitive development emerge at different times.

hormone replacement therapy (HRT) The taking of estrogen and progestin to compensate for hormone loss due to menopause in women.

hospice A program that supports dying persons and their families through a philosophy of "caring" rather than "curing," either in a facility or at home.

hot flash A sudden experience of warmth and sweating, often followed by a cold shiver, that occurs in a menopausal woman.

Human Genome Project A massive, government-sponsored effort to decipher the human genetic code.

Huntington's disease A genetic disease caused by a single, dominant gene that strikes in middle age to produce a deterioration of physical and mental abilities and premature death.

hyperactivity See *attention-deficit hyperactivity disorder (ADHD)*.

hypothesis A theoretical prediction about what will hold true if we observe a phenomenon.

hypothetical-deductive reasoning A form of problem solving in which one starts with general or abstract ideas and deduces or traces their specific implications; "if–then" thinking.

I

id Psychoanalytic term for the inborn component of the personality that is driven by the instincts or selfish urges.

ideal self Idealized expectations of what one's attributes and personality "should" be like.

ideational fluency The most common measure of creativity; the sheer number of different, including novel, ideas that one can generate.

identical twins Monozygotic twins who develop from a single zygote that later divides to form two genetically identical individuals.

identification Freud's term for the individual's tendency to emulate, or adopt the attitudes and behaviors of, another person, particularly his or her same-sex parent.

identity One's self-definition or sense of who one is, where one is going, and how one fits into society.

identity achievement status Identity status characterizing individuals who have carefully thought through identity issues and made commitments or resolved their identity issues.

identity versus role confusion The psychosocial conflict in which adolescents must form a coherent self-definition or else remain confused about their life directions; fifth of Erikson's stages.

imaginary audience A form of adolescent egocentrism that involves confusing your own thoughts with the thoughts of a hypothesized audience for your behavior and concluding that others share your preoccupations.

imaginary companion A play companion invented by a child in the preoperational stage who has developed the capacity for symbolic thought.

implicit memory Memory that occurs unintentionally and without consciousness or awareness. Compare *explicit memory*.

imprinting An innate form of learning in which the young of certain species will follow and become attached to moving objects (usually their mothers) during a critical period early in life.

inclusion The educational practice of integrating students with disabilities into regular classrooms rather than placing them in segregated special education classes; also called mainstreaming.

incomplete dominance Condition in which a stronger gene fails to mask all the effects of a weaker partner gene; a phenotype results that is similar but not identical to the effect of the stronger gene.

independent variable The aspect of the environment that a researcher deliberately changes or manipulates in an experiment in order to see what effect it has on behavior; a causal variable. Compare *dependent variable*.

indirect effect Instance in which the relationship between two individuals in a family is modified by the behavior or attitudes of a third family member.

individualistic culture A culture in which individuals define themselves as individuals and put their own goals ahead of their group's goals, and in which children are socialized to be independent and self-reliant. Compare *collectivist culture*.

induction A form of discipline that involves explaining why a child's behavior is wrong and should be changed by emphasizing its effects on other people.

industry versus inferiority Psychosocial conflict in which school-age children must master important cognitive and social skills or else feel incompetent; fourth of Erikson's stages.

infant states Coherent patterns of waking and sleeping evident in the fetus and young infant (for example, quiet sleep, active sleep, active waking).

infantile amnesia A lack of memory for the early years of one's life.

information-processing approach An approach to cognition that emphasizes the fundamental mental processes involved in attention, perception, memory, and decision making.

initiative versus guilt Psychosocial conflict in which preschool children must learn to initiate new activities and pursue bold plans or else become self-critical; third of Erikson's stages.

instinct An inborn biological force assumed to motivate a particular response or class of responses.

integrity versus despair Psychosocial conflict in which elderly adults attempt to find a sense of meaning in their lives and to accept the inevitability of death; eighth of Erikson's stages.

intelligence quotient (IQ) A numerical measure of a person's performance on an intelligence test relative to the performance of other examinees of the same age, typically with a score of 100 defined as average.

internalizing problem Childhood behavior problem that represents an "overcontrolled" pattern of coping with difficulties and is expressed in anxiety, depression, and other forms of inner distress. Compare *externalizing problem*.

internal working model In attachment theory, cognitive representation of self and other people that children construct from their interactions with caregivers and that, in turn, shapes their expectations about relationships.

intimacy versus isolation Psychosocial conflict in which young adults must commit themselves to a shared identity with another person or else remain aloof and unconnected to others; sixth of Erikson's stages.

intonation Variations in pitch, loudness, and timing when saying words or sentences.

intuitive theories Organized systems of knowledge, believed to be innate, that allow children to make sense of the world in areas such as physics and psychology.

in vitro fertilization (IVF) A method of conception in which fertilized eggs are transferred to a woman's uterus in the hopes that one will implant on the wall of the uterus.

J

joint attention The act of looking at the same object at the same time with someone else; a way in which infants share perceptual experiences with their caregivers.

K

karyotype A chromosomal portrait created by staining chromosomes, photographing them under a high-power microscope, and arranging them into a predetermined pattern.

Klinefelter syndrome A sex chromosome abnormality in which males inherit two or more X chromosomes (XXY or XXXY); these males fail to develop secondary sex characteristics and often show deficiencies on tests of verbal abilities.

knowledge base One's existing information about a content area, significant for its influence on how well one can learn and remember.

L

Lamaze method Prepared childbirth in which parents attend classes and learn mental exercises and relaxation techniques to ease delivery.

language A symbolic system in which a limited number of signals can be combined according to rules to produce an infinite number of messages.

language acquisition device (LAD) A set of linguistic processing skills that nativists believe to be innate; presumably, the LAD enables a child to infer the rules governing others' speech and then to use these rules to produce language.

latchkey children Children who care for themselves after school with little or no adult supervision.

lateralization The specialization of the two hemispheres of the cerebral cortex of the brain.

learned helplessness orientation A tendency to avoid challenges and to cease trying in the face of failure, due primarily to a tendency to attribute failure to lack of ability and therefore to believe that one can do little to improve. Compare *mastery orientation.*

learning A relatively permanent change in behavior (or behavior potential) that results from one's experiences or practice.

learning goal A goal adopted by learners in which they seek to learn new things so that they can improve their abilities. Compare *performance goal.*

libido Freud's term for the biological energy of the sex instinct.

life expectancy The average number of years a newborn baby can be expected to live; 76.5 years at present in the United States.

life review Process in which elderly adults reflect on unresolved conflicts of the past and evaluate their lives; it may contribute to a sense of integrity and readiness for death.

life-span perspective A perspective that views development as a lifelong, multidirectional process that involves gain and loss, is characterized by considerable plasticity, is shaped by its historical/cultural context, has many causes, and is best viewed from a multidisciplinary perspective.

life structure In Levinson's theory of adult development, an overall pattern of life that reflects the person's priorities and relationships.

literacy The ability to use printed information to function in society, achieve goals, and develop one's potential.

Living Will A document in which a person states in advance that he or she does not wish to have extraordinary medical procedures applied if he or she is hopelessly ill.

longitudinal design A developmental research design in which one group of subjects is studied repeatedly over a period of months or years.

long-term memory Memory store in which information that has been examined and interpreted is stored relatively permanently.

looking-glass self The idea that a person's self-concept is largely a reflection of the ways in which other people respond to him or her.

love withdrawal A form of discipline that involves withholding attention, affection, or approval after a child misbehaves.

M

macrosystem In Bronfenbrenner's bioecological approach, the larger cultural or subcultural context of development.

macular degeneration See *age-related macular degeneration.*

major depressive disorder An affective or mood disorder characterized by at least one episode of feeling profoundly sad and hopeless and/or losing interest in almost all activities.

masked depression Discredited view that depression, particularly in a child, manifests itself more in terms of problems such as aggression and restlessness than in overtly depressed behavior and that depression is therefore "disguised" as problems other than depression.

mastery motivation An intrinsic motive to master and control the environment, evident early in infancy.

mastery orientation A tendency to thrive on challenges and persist in the face of failure, due to healthy attributions that lead to the belief that increased effort will pay off. Compare *learned helplessness orientation.*

maturation Developmental changes that are biologically programmed by genes rather than being caused primarily by learning, injury, illness, or some other life experience.

maximum life span A ceiling on the number of years that any member of a species lives; 120 years for humans.

meiosis The process in which a germ cell divides, producing gametes (sperm or ova), each containing half of the parent cell's original complement of chromosomes; in humans, the products of meiosis normally contain 23 chromosomes.

menarche A female's first menstrual period.

menopause The ending of a woman's menstrual periods and reproductive capacity at around age 51.

mental age (MA) A measure of intellectual development that reflects the level of age-graded problems that a child is able to solve; the age at which a child functions intellectually.

mental retardation Significantly below average general intellectual functioning associated with impairments in adaptive behavior and manifested during the developmental period.

mesosystem In Bronfenbrenner's bioecological approach, interrelationships between microsystems or immediate environments (for example, ways in which events in the family affect a child's interactions at a day care center).

meta-analysis A research method in which the results of multiple studies addressing the same question are synthesized to produce overall conclusions.

metacognition Knowledge of the human mind and of the whole range of cognitive processes, including thinking about one's own thought processes.

metalinguistic awareness Knowledge of language itself as a system.

metamemory One's knowledge about memory as well as the monitoring and regulation of memory processes.

method of loci A mnemonic technique that involves establishing a mental map of a familiar route and then creating images linking each item to be learned to a landmark along the route.

microsystem In Bronfenbrenner's bioecological approach, the immediate settings in which the person functions (for example, the family).

middle generation squeeze The phenomenon in which middle-aged adults sometimes experience heavy responsibilities for both the younger and older generations in the family.

midlife crisis A period of major questioning, inner struggle, and reevaluation hypothesized to occur in an adult's early 40s.

mild cognitive impairment (MCI) A level of memory loss between normal loss with age and pathological loss from disease.

mitosis The process in which a cell duplicates its chromosomes and then divides into two genetically identical daughter cells.

modified extended family An arrangement in which nuclear families that are related by kinship maintain separate households but frequently interact with one another rather than functioning in isolation.

moral affect The emotional component of morality, including feelings of guilt, shame, and pride regarding one's conduct.

morality The ability to distinguish right from wrong, to act on this distinction, and to experience pride when one does something right and to experience guilt or shame when one does something wrong. Morality has affective, cognitive, and behavioral components.

morality of care Gilligan's term for what she claims is the dominant moral orientation of females, in which the individual emphasizes concern and responsibility for the welfare of other people rather than abstract rights. Compare *morality of justice*.

morality of justice Gilligan's term for what she claims is the dominant moral orientation of males, in which moral dilemmas are viewed as inevitable conflicts between the rights of two or more parties that must be settled by law. Compare *morality of care*.

moral reasoning The cognitive component of morality; the thinking that occurs when people decide whether acts are right or wrong.

moral rules Standards of conduct that focus on the basic rights and privileges of individuals. Compare *social-conventional rules*.

moratorium period A period of time in high school or college when young adults are relatively free of responsibilities and can experiment with different roles in order to find their identities.

moratorium status Identity status characterizing individuals who are currently experiencing an identity crisis or actively exploring identity issues but who have not yet achieved an identity.

morphology Rules governing the formation of words from sounds (for example, rules for forming plurals and past tenses).

mourning Culturally prescribed ways of displaying one's reactions to a loss. Compare *grief*.

mutation A change in the structure or arrangement of one or more genes that produces a new phenotype.

myelin A fatty sheath that insulates neural axons and thereby speeds the transmission of neural impulses.

N

nativist An individual whose approach to human development emphasizes the contribution of genetic factors; specifically, one who believes that infants enter the world equipped with knowledge that allows them to perceive a meaningful world from the start. Compare *empiricist*.

natural selection The evolutionary principle that individuals who have characteristics advantageous for survival in a particular environment are the ones who are most likely to survive and reproduce. Over many generations, this process of "survival of the fittest" will lead to changes in a species and the development of new species.

naturalistic observation A research method in which the scientist observes people as they engage in common everyday activities in their natural habitats. Compare *structured observation*.

nature–nurture issue The debate within developmental psychology over the relative importance of biological predispositions (nature) and environmental influences (nurture) as determinants of human development.

negative punishment The process in operant conditioning in which a response is weakened or made less probable when its consequence is the removal of a pleasant stimulus from the situation.

negative reinforcement The process in operant conditioning in which a response is strengthened or made more probable when its consequence is the removal of an unpleasant stimulus from the situation.

neglectful parenting A parenting style that is low in demandingness/control and low in acceptance/responsiveness; uninvolved parenting.

neonate The newborn; the infant from birth to approximately 1 month of age.

neuron The basic unit of the nervous system; a nerve cell.

nonshared environmental influences Experiences unique to the individual that are not shared by other members of the family and that tend to make members of the same family different from each other. Compare *shared environmental influences*.

normal distribution A symmetrical (bell-shaped) curve that describes the variability of characteristics within a population; most people fall at or near the average score, with relatively few high or low scores.

nuclear family A family unit consisting of husband/father, wife/mother, and at least one child. Compare *extended family household*.

O

object permanence The understanding that objects continue to exist when they are no longer visible or otherwise detectable to the senses; fully mastered by the end of infancy.

observational learning Learning that results from observing the behavior of other people; emphasized in Bandura's social learning theory.

Oedipus complex Freud's term for the conflict that 4- to 6-year-old boys experience when they develop an incestuous desire for their mothers and, at the same time, a jealous and hostile rivalry with their fathers.

olfaction The sense of smell, made possible by sensory receptors in the nasal passage that react to chemical molecules in the air.

operant conditioning A form of learning in which freely emitted acts (or "operants") become either more or less probable depending on the consequences they produce; also called instrumental conditioning.

organic retardation Mental retardation due to some identifiable biological cause associated with hereditary factors, diseases, or injuries. Compare *cultural-familial retardation*.

organization In Piaget's cognitive developmental theory, one's inborn tendency to combine and integrate available schemes into more coherent and complex systems or bodies of knowledge; as a memory strategy, technique that involves grouping or classifying stimuli into meaningful clusters.

organogenesis The process, occurring during the period of the embryo, in which every major organ takes shape in a primitive form.

orthogenetic principle Werner's principle that development proceeds from global and undifferentiated states toward more differentiated and integrated patterns of response.

osteoarthritis A joint problem among older adults, resulting from a gradual deterioration of the cartilage that cushions the bones and keeps them from rubbing together.

osteoporosis A disease affecting older adults in which bone tissue is lost, leaving bones fragile and easily fractured.

overextension The young child's tendency to use a word to refer to a wider set of objects, actions, or events than adults do (for example, using the word *car* to refer to all motor vehicles).

overregularization The overgeneralization of observed grammatical rules to irregular cases to which the rules do not apply (for example, saying *mouses* rather than *mice*).

P

parental imperative The notion that the demands of parenthood cause men and women to adopt distinct roles and psychological traits.

parent effects model A model of family influence in which parents (particularly mothers) are believed to influence their children rather than vice versa.

Parkes/Bowlby attachment model of bereavement Model of grieving describing four predominant reactions to loss of an attachment figure: numbness, yearning, disorganization and despair, and reorganization.

peer A social equal; one who functions at a level of behavioral complexity similar to that of the self, often someone of similar age.

perception The interpretation of sensory input.

performance goal A goal adopted by learners in which they attempt to prove their ability rather than to improve it. Compare *learning goal*.

perinatal environment The environment surrounding birth.

period of the embryo Second phase of prenatal development, lasting from the third through the eighth prenatal week, during which the major organs and anatomical structures begin to develop.

period of the fetus Third phase of prenatal development, lasting from the ninth prenatal week until birth; during this period, the major organ systems begin to function effectively and the fetus grows rapidly.

permissive parenting A lax style of parenting combining low demandingness/control and high acceptance/responsiveness in which adults love their children but make few demands on them and rarely attempt to control their behavior.

personal fable A form of adolescent egocentrism that involves thinking that oneself and one's thoughts and feelings are unique or special.

personality The organized combination of attributes, motives, values, and behaviors that is unique to each individual.

phenotype The way in which a person's genotype is actually expressed in observable or measurable characteristics.

phenylketonuria (PKU) A genetic disease in which the child is unable to metabolize phenylalanine; if left untreated, it soon causes hyperactivity and mental retardation.

phoneme One of the basic units of sound used in a particular spoken language.

phonological awareness The understanding that spoken words can be decomposed into some number of basic sound units, or *phonemes;* an important skill in learning to read.

phonology The sound system of a language and the rules for combining these sounds to produce meaningful units of speech.

pincer grasp A grasp in which the thumb is used in opposition to the fingers, enabling an infant to become more dexterous at lifting and manipulating objects.

pituitary gland The "master gland" located at the base of the brain that regulates the other endocrine glands and produces growth hormone.

placenta An organ, formed from the chorion and the lining of the uterus, that provides for the nourishment of the unborn child and the elimination of its metabolic wastes.

plasticity An openness of the brain cells (or of the organism as a whole) to positive and negative environmental influence; a capacity to change in response to experience.

polygenic trait A characteristic that is influenced by the action of many gene pairs rather than a single pair.

population A well-defined group that a researcher who studies a *sample* of individuals is ultimately interested in drawing conclusions about.

positive punishment The process in operant conditioning whereby a response is weakened when its consequence is an unpleasant event.

positive reinforcement The process in operant conditioning whereby a response is strengthened when its consequence is a pleasant event.

postconventional morality Kohlberg's term for the fifth and sixth stages of moral reasoning, in which moral judgments are based on a more abstract understanding of democratic social contracts or on universal principles of justice that have validity apart from the views of particular authority figures.

postformal thought Proposed stages of cognitive development that lie beyond formal operations.

postnatal depression An episode of severe, clinical depression lasting for months in a woman who has just given birth; to be contrasted with milder cases of the "maternity blues," in which a new mother is tearful and moody in the first days after birth.

posttraumatic stress disorder A psychological disorder involving flashbacks to traumatizing events, nightmares, and feelings of helplessness and anxiety in the face of danger experienced by victims of extreme trauma such as soldiers in combat and sexually abused children.

power assertion A form of discipline that involves the use of superior power to administer spankings, withhold privileges, and so on.

pragmatics Rules specifying how language is to be used appropriately in different social contexts to achieve goals.

preconventional morality Kohlberg's term for the first two stages of moral reasoning, in which society's rules are not yet internalized and judgments are based on the punishing or rewarding consequences of an act.

premenstrual syndrome (PMS) A number of symptoms experienced shortly before each menstrual period that include having tender breasts and a bloated feeling, as well as being irritable and moody.

prenatal environment The physical environment of the womb.

preoperational stage Piaget's second stage of cognitive development, lasting from about age 2 to age 7, when children think at a symbolic level but have not yet mastered logical operations.

presbycusis Problems of the aging ear, which commonly involve loss of sensitivity to high-frequency or high-pitched sounds.

presbyopia Problems of the aging eye, especially loss of near vision related to a decreased ability of the lens to accommodate to objects that are close to the eye.

pretend play Symbolic play in which one actor, object, or action symbolizes or stands for another.

private speech Nonsocial speech, or speech for the self, commonly used by preschoolers to guide their activities and believed by Vygotsky to be the forerunner of inner speech, or silent thinking-in-words.

problem solving The use of the information-processing system to achieve a goal or arrive at a decision.

progeria A genetic disorder caused by a single dominant gene that makes victims age prematurely and die early.

programmed theories of aging Theories that emphasize the systematic genetic control of aging processes. Compare *damage theories of aging.*

prosocial behavior Positive actions toward other people, such as helping and cooperating.

protective factors Factors, such as personal resources and a supportive postnatal environment, that work to prevent at-risk individuals from developing problems.

proximodistal principle In development, the principle that growth proceeds from the center of the body (or the proximal region) to the extremities (or distal regions).

psychoanalytic theory The theoretical perspective associated with Freud and his followers that emphasizes unconscious motivations for behavior, conflicts within the personality, and stages of psychosexual development.

psychometric approach The research tradition that spawned standardized tests of intelligence and that views intelligence as a trait or a set of traits that can be measured and that varies from person to person.

psychosexual stages Freud's five stages of development, associated with biological maturation and shifts in the libido: oral, anal, phallic, latency, and genital.

puberty The point at which a person reaches sexual maturity and is physically capable of conceiving a child.

punishment Consequences that decrease the probability that an act will recur. See *positive punishment* and *negative punishment.*

Q

quasi-experiment An experiment-like study that evaluates the effects of different treatments but does not randomly assign individuals to treatment groups.

R

random assignment A technique in which research participants are placed in experimental conditions in an unbiased or random way so that the resulting groups are not systematically different from one another.

random sample A sample that is formed by identifying all members of the larger population of interest and then selecting a portion of them in an unbiased or random way to participate in the study; a technique to ensure that the sample studied is representative or typical of the larger population of interest.

reaction time The time interval between the presentation of a stimulus and a response to it.

recall memory Recollecting or actively retrieving objects, events, and experiences when examples or cues are not provided. Compare *recognition memory.*

recessive gene A less powerful gene that is not expressed phenotypically when paired with a *dominant gene.*

reciprocal determinism The notion in social learning theory that the flow of influence between people and their environments is a two-way street; the environment may affect the person, but the person's characteristics and behavior will also influence the environment.

recognition memory Identifying an object or event as one that has been experienced before, as when one must select the correct answer from several options. Compare *recall memory.*

reconstituted family A new family that forms after the remarriage of a single parent, sometimes involving the blending of two families into a new one.

reflex An unlearned and automatic response to a stimulus.

regression A defense mechanism that involves retreating to an earlier, less traumatic stage of development.

rehearsal A strategy for remembering that involves repeating the items one is trying to retain.

reinforcement Consequences that increase the probability that an act will recur. See *positive reinforcement* and *negative reinforcement.*

relativistic thinking A form of post–formal operational thought in which it is understood that there are multiple ways of viewing a problem and that the solutions one arrives at will depend on one's starting assumptions and perspective.

REM sleep A state of active, irregular sleep associated with dreaming; named for the rapid eye movements associated with it.

research ethics Standards of conduct that investigators are ethically bound to honor in order to protect their research participants from physical or psychological harm.

reserve capacity The ability of many organ systems to respond to demands for extraordinary output, as when the heart and lungs work at maximal capacity.

resilience The self-righting or recuperative capacity that allows many children to recover from early disadvantages and get back on a normal course of development.

resistant attachment An insecure infant–caregiver bond or other intimate relationship characterized by strong separation anxiety and a tendency to show ambivalent reactions to the attachment object upon reunion, seeking and yet resisting contact.

retrieval The process of getting information out of long-term memory when it is needed.

reversibility In Piaget's theory, the ability to reverse or negate an action by mentally performing the opposite action.

rhythmic stereotypies The repetitive movement observed in infants shortly before a new motor skill emerges.

role reversal A switching of child and parent roles late in life such that the parent becomes the dependent one and the child becomes the caregiver.

role-taking skills The ability to assume another person's perspective and understand his or her thoughts, feelings, and behaviors.

rubella A disease that has little effect on a pregnant woman but may cause a number of serious birth defects such as blindness, deafness, and mental retardation in unborn children who are exposed in the first 3 to 4 months of gestation; German measles.

rule assessment approach Robert Siegler's approach to studying the development of problem solving that determines what information about a problem children take in and what rules they then formulate to account for this information.

S

sample The group of individuals chosen to be the subjects of a study.

savant syndrome The phenomenon in which extraordinary talent in a particular area is displayed by a person who is otherwise mentally retarded.

scheme (or **schema**; plural, **schemes** or **schemata**) A cognitive structure or organized pattern of action or thought that is used to deal with experiences.

schizophrenia A serious form of mental illness characterized by disturbances in logical thinking, emotional expression, and interpersonal behavior.

scientific method An attitude or value about the pursuit of knowledge that dictates that investigators must be objective and must allow their data to decide the merits of their theorizing.

script A mental representation of a typical sequence of actions related to an event that is created in memory and that then guides future behaviors in similar settings.

secular trend A trend in industrialized society toward earlier maturation and greater body size now than in the past.

secure attachment An infant–caregiver bond or intimate relationship in which the individual welcomes close contact, uses the attachment object as a source of comfort, and dislikes but can manage separations.

secure base A point of safety, represented by an infant's attachment figure, that permits exploration of the environment.

selective breeding A method of studying genetic influence that involves deliberately determining whether a trait can be bred in animals through selective mating.

selective optimization with compensation The concept that older people cope with aging through a strategy that involves focusing on the skills most needed, practicing those skills, and developing ways to get around the need for other skills.

self-concept One's perceptions of one's unique attributes or traits.

self-conscious emotions A "secondary emotion," such as embarrassment or pride, that requires an awareness of self that is unlikely to emerge until about 18 months of age.

self-esteem One's overall evaluation of one's worth as a person based on an assessment of the qualities that make up the self-concept.

self-recognition The ability to recognize oneself in a mirror or photograph, which occurs in most infants by 18 to 24 months of age.

semantics The aspect of language centering on meanings.

semenarche A boy's first ejaculation.

sensation The process by which information is detected by the sensory receptors and transmitted to the brain; starting point in *perception*.

sensorimotor stage Piaget's first stage of cognitive development, spanning the first two years of life, in which infants rely on their senses and motor behaviors in adapting to the world around them.

sensory register The first memory store in information processing, in which stimuli are noticed and are very briefly available for further processing.

sensory threshold The point at which low levels of stimulation can be detected.

separation anxiety A wary or fretful reaction that infants display when they are separated from their attachment objects.

sequential design A developmental research design that combines the cross-sectional approach and the longitudinal approach in a single study to compensate for the weaknesses of each.

seriation A logical operation that allows one to mentally order a set of stimuli along a quantifiable dimension such as height or weight.

sex-linked characteristic An attribute determined by a gene that appears on one of the two types of sex chromosomes, usually the X chromosome.

sexual orientation One's preference for sexual partners of the same or other sex, often characterized as primarily heterosexual, homosexual, or bisexual.

shared environmental influences Experiences that individuals living in the same home environment share and that work to make them similar to one another. Compare *nonshared environmental influences*.

short-term memory Memory store in which limited amounts of information are temporarily held; called *working memory* when its active quality is being emphasized.

sibling rivalry A spirit of competition, jealousy, or resentment that may arise between two or more brothers or sisters.

sickle-cell disease A genetic blood disease in which red blood cells assume an unusual sickled shape and become inefficient at distributing oxygen throughout the body.

single gene-pair inheritance Genetic mechanism through which a characteristic is influenced by only one pair of genes, one gene from the mother and its partner from the father.

size constancy The tendency to perceive an object as the same size despite changes in its distance from the eyes.

slow-to-warm-up temperament Characteristic mode of response in which the individual is relatively inactive and moody and displays mild resistance to new routines and experiences but gradually adapts. Compare *easy temperament* and *difficult temperament*.

sociability A dimension of temperament that refers to the individual's degree of interest in and responsiveness to people.

social clock A personal sense of when things should be done in one's life and when one is ahead of or behind the schedule dictated by age norms.

social cognition Thinking about the thoughts, feelings, motives, and behavior of the self and other people.

social cognitive theory Bandura's social learning theory; see *social learning theory*.

social comparison The process of defining and evaluating oneself by comparing oneself to other people.

social-conventional rules Standards of conduct determined by social consensus that indicate what is appropriate within a particular social setting. Compare *moral rules*.

social convoy The changing cadre of significant people who serve as sources of social support to the individual during his or her life.

socialization The process by which individuals acquire the beliefs, values, and behaviors judged important in their society.

social learning theory Bandura's theory that children and adults can learn novel responses merely by observing the behavior of a model, making mental notes on what they have seen, and then using these mental representations to reproduce the model's behavior at some future time; more broadly, a number of theories that emphasize the cognitive processing of social experiences.

social norm A socially defined expectation about how people should behave in particular social contexts.

social pretend play A form of play that involves both cooperation with playmates and the use of pretend or symbolic activity.

social-role hypothesis Eagly's view that gender-role stereotypes are created and maintained by differences in the roles that men and women play in society rather than being inherent in males and females.

social support The several forms of assistance from other people that bolster individuals and protect them from stress.

sociocultural perspective Vygotsky's contextual theory of development, which maintains that cognitive development is shaped by the sociocultural context in which it occurs and grows out of the child's social interactions with members of his or her culture.

socioeconomic status (SES) The position people hold in society based on such factors as income, education, occupational status, and the prestige of their neighborhoods.

socioemotional selectivity theory Carstensen's notion that our needs change as we grow older and that we actively choose to narrow our range of social partners to those who can best meet our emotional needs.

sociometric techniques Methods for determining who is well liked and popular and who is disliked or neglected in a group.

somatic symptoms Physical or bodily signs of emotional distress, such as loss of appetite or disruption of normal sleep patterns.

species heredity The genetic endowment that members of a particular species have in common; responsible for universal species traits and patterns of maturation.

spillover effects The notion that events at work affect home life, and events at home carry over into the workplace.

storage In information processing, the holding of information in the long-term memory store.

storm and stress G. Stanley Hall's term for the emotional ups and downs and rapid changes that he believed characterize adolescence.

stranger anxiety A wary or fretful reaction that infants often display when approached by an unfamiliar person.

Strange Situation A series of mildly stressful experiences involving the departure of the parent and exposure to a stranger, used to determine the quality of an infant's attachment; developed by Mary Ainsworth.

structured observation A research method in which scientists create special conditions designed to elicit the behavior of interest in order to achieve greater control over the conditions under which they gather behavioral data. Compare *naturalistic observation*.

structure-of-intellect model Guilford's factor-analytic model of intelligence, which proposes that there are as many as 180 distinct mental abilities.

sudden infant death syndrome (SIDS) The death of a sleeping baby due to a failure of the respiratory system; linked to maternal smoking.

superego Psychoanalytic term for the component of the personality that consists of one's internalized moral standards.

surfactant A substance that aids breathing by preventing the air sacs of the lungs from sticking together.

symbolic capacity The capacity to use symbols such as words, images, or actions to represent or stand for objects and experiences; representational thought.

synapse The point at which the axon or dendrite of one neuron makes a connection with another neuron.

synaptogenesis The process in early brain development that involves the formation of connections among neurons.

synchronized routine Harmonious, dance-like interaction between infant and caregiver in which each adjusts his or her behavior in response to that of the other.

syntax Rules specifying how words can be combined to form meaningful sentences in a language.

syphilis A common sexually transmitted disease that may cross the placental barrier in the middle and later stages of pregnancy, causing miscarriage or serious birth defects.

T

tabula rasa The idea that the mind of an infant is a "blank slate" and that all knowledge, abilities, behaviors, and motives are acquired through experience.

Tay-Sachs disease A genetic disease, occurring most commonly in children of Eastern European Jewish ancestry, that is caused by a pair of recessive genes and that results in a degeneration of the nervous system and death.

telegraphic speech Early sentences that consist primarily of content words and omit the less meaningful parts of speech such as articles, prepositions, pronouns, and auxiliary verbs.

telomere A stretch of DNA that forms the tip of a chromosome and that shortens after each cell division, timing the death of cells.

temperament A genetically based pattern of tendencies to respond in predictable ways; building blocks of personality such as activity level, sociability, and emotionality.

teratogen Any disease, drug, or other environmental agent that can harm a developing fetus.

terminal drop A rapid decline in intellectual abilities that people who are within a few years of dying often experience.

test norms Standards of normal performance on psychometric instruments that are based on the average scores and range of scores obtained by a large, representative sample of test takers.

testosterone The most important of the male hormones, or androgens; essential for normal sexual development during the prenatal period and at puberty.

thalidomide A mild tranquilizer that, taken early in pregnancy, can produce a variety of malformations of the limbs, eyes, ears, and heart.

theory A set of concepts and propositions designed to organize, describe, and explain a set of observations.

theory of mind The understanding that people have mental states (feelings, desires, beliefs, intentions) and that these states underlie and help to explain their behavior.

time of measurement effects In developmental research, the effects on findings of historical events occurring at the time when the data for a study are being collected (for example, psychological changes brought about by an economic depression rather than as a function of getting older). Compare *age effects* and *cohort effects*.

total brain death An irreversible loss of functioning in the entire brain, both the higher centers of the cerebral cortex that are involved in thought and the lower centers of the brain that control basic life processes such as breathing.

transactional model A model of family influence in which parent and child are believed to influence one another reciprocally.

transformational grammar Rules of syntax that allow one to transform declarative statements into questions, negatives, imperatives, and other kinds of sentences.

transformational thought In Piaget's theory, the ability to conceptualize transformations, or processes of change from one state to another, which appears in the stage of concrete operations.

transitivity The ability to recognize the necessary or logical relations among elements in a serial order (for example, that if A is taller than B, and B is taller than C, then A must be taller than C).

triarchic theory of intelligence An information-processing theory of intelligence that emphasizes three aspects of intelligent behavior: the context in which people display intelligence, the previous experience they have with cognitive tasks, and the information-processing components they use to go about solving problems.

trust versus mistrust Psychosocial conflict of infancy, in which infants must learn to trust others to meet their needs in order to trust themselves; first stage in Erikson's theory.

Turner syndrome A sex chromosome abnormality in which females inherit only one X chromosome (XO); they remain small in stature, fail to develop secondary sex characteristics, and may show some mental deficiencies.

U

ultrasound Method of examining physical organs by scanning them with sound waves—for example, scanning the womb and thereby producing a visual outline of the fetus to detect gross abnormalities.

umbilical cord A soft tube containing blood vessels that connects the embryo to the placenta and serves as a source of oxygen and nutrients and as a vehicle for the elimination of wastes.

unconditioned response (UCR) The unlearned response elicited by an unconditioned stimulus.

unconditioned stimulus (UCS) A stimulus that elicits a particular response without any prior learning.

unconscious motivation Freud's term for feelings, experiences, and conflicts that influence a person's thinking and behavior, even though they cannot be recalled.

underextension The young child's tendency to use general words to refer to a smaller set of objects, actions, or events than adults do (for example, using *candy* to refer only to mints). Compare *overextension*.

universality/context-specificity issue The debate over the extent to which developmental changes are common to everyone (*universal*, as in most stage theories) or different from person to person (particularistic or context-specific).

utilization deficiency The failure of children to benefit from a memory strategy that they are able to produce due to task performance deficits.

V

vascular dementia The deterioration of functioning and cognitive capacities caused by a series of minor strokes that cut off the blood supply to areas of the brain; also called multi-infarct dementia.

vicarious reinforcement In observational learning, the consequences experienced by a model following his or her behavior that affect the observer's likelihood of engaging in the behavior.

visual accommodation The ability of the lens of the eye to change shape in order to bring objects at different distances into focus.

visual acuity The ability to perceive detail in a visual stimulus.

visual cliff An elevated glass platform that creates an illusion of depth, used to test the depth perception of infants.

vocabulary spurt A dramatic increase in the pace of word learning that occurs at around 18 months of age.

W

wisdom Exceptional insight or judgment regarding life's problems.

working memory A memory store, often referred to as a mental "scratch pad," that temporarily holds information while it is being actively operated on; the active use of the short-term memory store.

X

X chromosome The longer of the two sex chromosomes; normal females have two X chromosomes, whereas normal males have only one.

Y

Y chromosome The shorter of the two sex chromosomes; normal males have one Y chromosome, whereas females have none.

Z

zone of proximal development Vygotsky's term for the difference between what a learner can accomplish independently and what a learner can accomplish with the guidance and encouragement of a more skilled partner.

zygote A single cell formed at conception from the union of a sperm and an ovum.

References

Chapter 1: Understanding Life-Span Human Development

American Psychological Association. (1982). *Ethical principles in the conduct of research with human participants.* Washington, DC: Author.

Anderson, D. R., Huston, A. C., Schmitt, K. L., Linebarger, D. L., & Wright, J. C. (2001). Early childhood television viewing and adolescent behavior. *Monographs of the Society for Research in Child Development, 66* (Serial No. 264, No. 1).

Ariès, P. (1962). *Centuries of childhood.* New York: Knopf.

Arnett, J. J. (1999). Adolescent storm and stress, reconsidered. *American Psychologist, 54,* 317–326.

Baltes, P. B. (1987). Theoretical propositions of life-span developmental psychology: On the dynamics between growth and decline. *Developmental Psychology, 23,* 611–626.

Baltes, P. B., Lindenberger, U., & Staudinger, U. M. (1998). Life-span theory in developmental psychology. In R. M. Lerner (Ed.), William Damon (Editor-in-Chief), *Handbook of child psychology: Vol. 1. Theoretical models of human development* (5th ed.). New York: Wiley.

Baltes, P. B., Reese, H. W., & Lipsitt, L. P. (1980). Life-span developmental psychology. *Annual Review of Psychology, 31,* 65–110.

Bengston, V. L., Cuellar, J. B., & Ragan, P. K. (1977). Stratum contrasts and similarities in attitudes toward death. *Journal of Gerontology, 32,* 76–88.

Brewster, K. L., & Padavic, I. (2000). Changes in gender-ideology, 1977–1996: The contributions of intracohort change and population turnover. *Journal of Marriage and the Family, 62,* 477–487.

Bronfenbrenner, U. (1979). *The ecology of human development: Experiments by nature and design.* Cambridge, MA: Harvard University Press.

Brown, D. (2000, June 12). New look at longevity offers disease insight. *Washington Post,* A9.

Burton, L. M. (1996). Age norms, the timing of family role transitions, and intergenerational caregiving among aging African American women. *Gerontologist, 36,* 199–208.

Bushman, B., & Huesmann, L. R. (2001). Effects of televised violence on aggression. In D. Singer & J. Singer (Eds.), *Handbook of children and the media.* Thousand Oaks, CA: Sage.

Cairns, R. B. (1998). The making of developmental psychology. In R. M. Lerner (Ed.), William Damon (Editor-in-Chief), *Handbook of child psychology: Vol. 1.*

Theoretical models of human development (5th ed.). New York: Wiley.

Charlesworth, W. R. (1992). Darwin and developmental psychology: Past and present. *Developmental Psychology, 28,* 5–16.

Cole, T. R. (1992). *The journey of life: A cultural history of aging in America.* Cambridge, England: Cambridge University Press.

Coontz, S. (2000). Historical perspectives on family studies. *Journal of Marriage and the Family, 62,* 283–297.

Cunningham, H. (1996). The history of childhood. In C. P. Hwang, M. E. Lamb, & I. E. Sigel (Eds.), *Images of childhood.* Mahwah, NJ: Erlbaum.

Darwin, C. A. (1877). A biographical sketch of an infant. *Mind, 2,* 285–294.

deMause, L. (1974). The evolution of childhood. In L. deMause (Ed.), *The history of childhood.* New York: Psychohistory Press.

Dublin, L. I., & Lotka, A. J. (1936). *Length of life: A study of the life table.* New York: Ronald Press.

Elder, G. H., Jr. (1998). The life course as developmental theory. *Child Development, 69,* 1–12.

Elder, G. H., Jr., Liker, J. K., & Cross, C. E. (1984). Parent–child behavior in the Great Depression: Life course and intergenerational influences. In P. B. Baltes & O. G. Brim, Jr. (Eds.), *Life-span development and behavior* (Vol. 6). Orlando, FL: Academic Press.

Elkind, D. (1992, May/June). The future of childhood: Waaah!! Why kids have a lot to cry about. *Psychology Today,* pp. 38–41, 80–81.

Ella Galbraith Miller: Va. woman lived to 119. (2000, November 23). *Washington Post,* B6.

Fisher, C. B. (1999). Preparing successful proposals for Institutional Review Boards: Challenges and prospects for developmental scientists. *SRCD Newsletter, 42*(2), 7–9.

Friedrich, L. K., & Stein, A. H. (1973). Aggressive and prosocial television programs and the natural behavior of preschool children. *Monographs of the Society for Research in Child Development, 38*(4, Serial No. 51).

Fry, C. L. (1985). Culture, behavior, and aging in the comparative perspective. In J. E. Birren & K. W. Schaie (Eds.), *Handbook of the psychology of aging* (2nd ed.). New York: Van Nostrand Reinhold.

Fry, C. L. (1999). Anthropological theories of age and aging. In V. L. Bengtson & K. W. Schaie (Eds.), *Handbook of theories of aging.* New York: Springer.

Furstenberg, F. F. (2000). The sociology of adolescence and youth in the 1990s: A critical commentary. *Journal of Marriage and the Family, 62,* 896–910.

Glass, G. V., McGaw, B., & Smith, M. L. (1981). *Meta-analysis in social research.* Beverly Hills, CA: Sage.

Gotlib, I. H., & Hammen, C. L. (1992). *Psychological aspects of depression: Toward a cognitive-interpersonal integration.* Chichester, England: Wiley.

Hall, G. S. (1891). The contents of children's minds on entering school. *Pedagogical Seminary, 1,* 139–173.

Hall, G. S. (1904). *Adolescence* (2 vols.). New York: Appleton.

Hall, G. S. (1922). *Senescence: The last half of life.* New York: Appleton.

Hersch, P. (1998). *A tribe apart: A journey into the heart of American adolescence.* New York: Ballantine.

Hine, T. (1999). *The rise and fall of the American teenager.* New York: Bard.

Hobbs, F. B. (2001). The elderly population. U.S. Census Bureau [On-line], http://www.census.gov/population/www/population/www/pop-profile/elderpop.html.

Hyde, J. S. (1984). How large are gender differences in aggression? A developmental meta-analysis. *Developmental Psychology, 20,* 722–736.

Jason, L. A., Kennedy Hanaway, L., & Brackshaw, E. (1999). Television violence and children: Problems and solutions. In T. P. Gullotta et al. (Eds.), *Violence in homes and communities: Prevention, intervention, and treatment. Issues in children's and families' lives.* Thousand Oaks, CA: Sage.

Kean, A. W. G. (1937). The history of the criminal liability of children. *Law Quarterly Review, 3,* 364–370.

Keith, J. (1985). Age in anthropological research. In R. H. Binstock & E. Shanas (Eds.), *Handbook of aging and the social sciences* (2nd ed.). New York: Van Nostrand Reinhold.

Keniston, K. (1970). Youth: A "new" stage of life. *American Scholar, 39,* 631–654.

Kett, J. F. (1977). *Rites of passage: Adolescence in America, 1790 to the present.* New York: Basic Books.

Knight, G. P., Fabes, R. A., & Higgins, D. A. (1996). Concerns about drawing causal inferences from meta-analyses: An example in the study of gender differences in aggression. *Psychological Bulletin, 119,* 410–421.

Koocher, G. P., & Keith-Spiegel, P. (1994). Scientific issues in psychosocial and educational research with children. In M. Grodin & L. H. Glantz (Eds.), *Children as research subjects: Science, ethics, and law.* New York: Oxford University Press.

Lipsey, M. W., & Wilson, D. B. (2001). *Practical meta-analysis.* Thousand Oaks, CA: Sage.

Longman, P. J. (1999, March 1). How global aging will challenge the world's economic well-being. *U.S. News & World Report*, pp. 30–39.

McCall, R. B. (1977). Challenges to a science of developmental psychology. *Child Development, 48*, 333–344.

McLanahan, S. S., & Sorensen, A. B. (1985). Life events and psychological well-being over the life course. In G. H. Elder, Jr. (Ed.), *Life course dynamics: Trajectories and transitions, 1968–1980.* Ithaca, NY: Cornell University Press.

Moen, P., & Wethington, E. (1999). Midlife development in a life course context. In S. L. Willis & J. D. Reid (Eds.), *Life in the middle: Psychological and social development in middle age.* San Diego, CA: Academic Press.

Munroe, R. L., Hulefeld, R., Rodgers, J. M., Tomeo, D. L., & Yamazaki, S. K. (2000). Aggression among children in four cultures. *Cross-Cultural Research, 34*, 3–25.

Neugarten, B. L. (1968). Adult personality: Toward a psychology of the life cycle. In B. L. Neugarten (Ed.), *Middle age and aging: A reader in social psychology.* Chicago: University of Chicago Press.

Neugarten, B. L., Moore, J. W., & Lowe, J. C. (1965). Age norms, age constraints, and adult socialization. *American Journal of Sociology, 70*, 710–717.

Ogbu, J. U. (1981). Origins of human competence: A cultural-ethological perspective. *Child Development, 52*, 413–429.

Parke, R. D., Ornstein, P. A., Rieser, J. J., & Zahn-Waxler, C. (1994). The past as prologue: An overview of a century of developmental psychology. In R. D. Parke, P. A. Ornstein, J. J. Rieser, & C. Zahn-Waxler (Eds.), *A century of developmental psychology.* Washington, DC: American Psychological Association.

Pellegrini, A. D. (1996). *Observing children in their natural worlds: A methodological primer.* Mahwah, NJ: Erlbaum.

Phinney, J. S. (2000). Identity formation across cultures: The interaction of personal, societal, and historical change. *Human Development, 43*, 27–31.

Reid, T. R. (1993, January 16). 2 million accept duty of being 20. *Washington Post*, pp. A14, A24.

Sales, B. D., & Folkman, S. (2000). *Ethics in research with human participants.* Washington, DC: American Psychological Association.

Schaie, K. W. (1994). Developmental designs revisited. In S. H. Cohen & H. W. Reese (Eds.), *Life-span developmental psychology: Methodological contributions.* Hillsdale, NJ: Erlbaum.

Settersten, R. A., Jr. (1998). A time to leave home and a time never to return? Age constraints on the living arrangements of young adults. *Social Forces, 76*, 1373–1400.

Shanahan, M. J. (2000). Pathways to adulthood in changing societies: Variability and mechanisms in life course perspective. *Annual Review of Sociology, 26*, 667–692.

Singer, J. L., & Singer, D. G. (1981). *Television, imagination, and aggression: A study of preschoolers.* Hillsdale, NJ: Erlbaum.

Society for Research in Child Development, Committee for Ethical Conduct in Child Development Research. (1990, Winter). SRCD ethical standards for research with children. *SRCD Newsletter*, pp. 5–7.

Squires, S. (1999, April 20). Midlife without the crisis. *Washington Post Health*, pp. 20–24.

Tousignant, M. (1995, November 17). The lesson of a lifetime: 2nd-graders thrill to 114-year-old Ella Miller's tales of growing up. *Washington Post*, p. B1.

Tousignant, M. (1996, November 9). A seasoned voter speaks her mind: At 115 years old, Vienna woman says age of candidate is not an issue. *Washington Post*, p. B5.

Trafford, A. (1996, March 26). The old gray-haired: They ain't what they used to be. *Washington Post Health*, p. 6.

U.S. Census Bureau. (2000). *Statistical abstracts of the United States: 2000.* Washington, DC: Government Printing Office.

Vinovskis, M. A. (1996). Changing perceptions and treatment of young children in the United States. In C. P. Hwang, M. E. Lamb, & I. E. Sigel (Eds.), *Images of childhood.* Mahwah, NJ: Erlbaum.

Wachs, T. D. (2000). *Necessary but not sufficient: The respective roles of single and multiple influences on individual development.* Washington, DC: American Psychological Association.

Washington, E. B., & Milloy, M. (1996). Wise souls: Listening to our elders. *Essence, 27*(3), 64–68.

Willis, S. L., & Reid, J. D. (Eds.). (1999). *Life in the middle: Psychological and social development in middle age.* San Diego, CA: Academic Press.

Willis, S. L., & Schaie, K. W. (1999). Intellectual functioning in midlife. In S. L. Willis & J. D. Reid (Eds.), *Life in the middle: Psychological and social development in middle age.* San Diego, CA: Academic Press.

Wilson, M. N. (1989). Child development in the context of the Black extended family. *American Psychologist, 44*, 380–385.

Chapter 2: Theories of Human Development

Babikian, H. M., & Goldman, A. (1971). A study of teen-age pregnancy. *American Journal of Psychiatry, 128*, 755–760.

Bandura, A. (1965). Influence of models' reinforcement contingencies on the acquisition of imitative responses. *Journal of Personality and Social Psychology, 1*, 589–595.

Bandura, A. (1977). *Social learning theory.* Englewood Cliffs, NJ: Prentice-Hall.

Bandura, A. (1986). *Social foundations of thought and action: A social cognitive theory.* Englewood Cliffs, NJ: Prentice-Hall.

Bandura, A. (1989). Social cognitive theory. In R. Vasta (Ed.), *Annals of child development: Vol. 6. Theories of child development: Revised formulations and current issues.* Greenwich, CT: JAI Press.

Bandura, A. (2000). Exercise of human agency through collective efficacy. *Current Directions in Psychological Science, 9*, 75–78.

Benda, B. B., & DiBlasio, F. A. (1994). An integration of theory: Adolescent sexual contacts. *Journal of Youth and Adolescence, 23*, 403–420.

Bronfenbrenner, U. (1979). *The ecology of human development: Experiments by nature and design.* Cambridge, MA: Harvard University Press.

Bronfenbrenner, U. (1989). Ecological systems theory. In R. Vasta (Ed.), *Annals of child development: Vol. 6. Theories of child development: Revised formulations and current issues.* Greenwich, CT: JAI Press.

Bronfenbrenner, U. (1995). Developmental ecology through space and time: A future perspective. In P. Moen, G. H. Elder, Jr., & K. Luscher (Eds.), *Examining lives in context: Perspectives on the ecology of human development.* Washington, DC: American Psychological Association.

Bronfenbrenner, U., & Evans, G. W. (2000). Developmental science in the 21st century: Emerging questions, theoretical models, research designs and empirical findings. *Social Development, 9*, 115–125.

Bronfenbrenner, U., & Morris, P. A. (1998). The ecology of developmental processes. In R. M. Lerner (Ed.), William Damon (Editor-in-Chief), *Handbook of child psychology: Vol. 1. Theoretical models of human development* (5th ed.). New York: Wiley.

Brooks-Gunn, J., & Furstenberg, F. F., Jr. (1989). Long-term implications of fertility-related behavior and family formation on adolescent mothers and their children. In K. Kreppner & R. M. Lerner (Eds.), *Family systems and life-span development.* Hillsdale, NJ: Erlbaum.

Cairns, R. B. (1998). The making of developmental psychology. In R. M. Lerner (Ed.), William Damon (Editor-in-Chief), *Handbook of child psychology: Vol. 1. Theoretical models of human development* (5th ed.). New York: Wiley.

Carrera, M., Kaye, J. W., Philliber, S., & West, E. (2000). Knowledge about reproduction, contraception, and sexually transmitted infections among young adolescents in American cities. *Social Policy, 30*, 41–50.

Cobliner, W. G. (1974). Pregnancy in the single adolescent girl: The role of cognitive functions. *Journal of Youth and Adolescence, 3*, 17–29.

Coley, R. L., & Chase-Lansdale, P. L. (1998). Adolescent pregnancy and parenthood: Recent evidence and future directions. *American Psychologist, 53*, 152–166.

Corcoran, J. (1999). Ecological factors associated with adolescent pregnancy: A review of the literature. *Adolescence, 34*, 603–619.

Cotterell, J. L. (1986). Work and community influences on the quality of child rearing. *Child Development, 57*, 362–374.

Crews, F. (1996). The verdict on Freud [Review of *Freud evaluated: The completed arc*]. *Psychological Science, 7*, 63–68.

Dent-Read, C., & Zukow-Goldring, P. (Eds.). (1997). *Evolving explanations of development.* Washington, DC: American Psychological Association.

Domjan, M. J. (1993). *Principles of learning and behavior* (3rd ed.). Pacific Grove, CA: Brooks/Cole.

Erikson, E. H. (1963). *Childhood and society* (2nd ed.). New York: Norton.

Erikson, E. H. (1968). *Identity: Youth and crisis.* New York: Norton.

Erikson, E. H. (1982). *The life cycle completed: A review.* New York: Norton.

Fisher, S., & Greenberg, R. P. (1977). *The scientific credibility of Freud's theories and therapy.* New York: Basic Books.

Flynn, C. P. (1994). Regional differences in attitudes toward corporal punishment. *Journal of Marriage and the Family, 56*, 314–324.

Fonagy, P., & Target, M. (2000). The place of psychodynamic theory in developmental psychopathology. *Development and Psychopathology, 12*, 407–425.

Franklin, C., & Corcoran, J. (2000). Preventing adolescent pregnancy: A review of programs and practices. *Social Work, 45,* 40–52.

Freud, S. (1933). *New introductory lectures in psychoanalysis.* New York: Norton.

Freud, S. (1964). An outline of psychoanalysis. In J. Strachey (Ed.), *The standard edition of the complete psychological works of Sigmund Freud* (Vol. 23). London: Hogarth Press. (Original work published 1940)

Friedman, L. J. (1999). *Identity's architect: A biography of Erik H. Erikson.* New York: Scribner.

Furstenberg, F. F., Jr., Brooks-Gunn, J., & Morgan, S. P. (1987). *Adolescent mothers in later life.* New York: Cambridge University Press.

Furstenberg, F. F., Jr., Lincoln, R., & Menken, J. (Eds.). (1981). *Teenage sexuality, pregnancy, and childbearing.* Philadelphia: University of Pennsylvania Press.

Gleaves, D. H., & Hernandez, E. (1999). Recent reformulations of Freud's development and abandonment of his seduction theory: Historical/scientific clarification or a continued assault on truth? *History of Psychology, 2,* 324–354.

Goldhaber, D. E. (2000). *Theories of human development: Integrative perspectives.* Mountain View, CA: Mayfield.

Gottlieb, G. (2000). Environmental and behavioral influences on gene activity. *Current Directions in Psychological Science, 9,* 93–97.

Gottlieb, G., Wahlsten, D., & Lickliter, R. (1998). The significance of biology for human development: A developmental psychobiological systems view. In R. M. Lerner (Ed.), William Damon (Editor-in-Chief), *Handbook of child psychology: Vol. 1. Theoretical models of human development* (5th ed.). New York: Wiley.

Hall, C. S. (1954). *A primer of Freudian psychology.* New York: New American Library.

Hart, B., & Hilton, I. (1988). Dimensions of personality organization predictors of teenage pregnancy risk. *Journal of Personality Assessment, 52,* 116–132.

Hogan, D. P., Sun, R., & Cornwell, G. T. (2000). Sexual and fertility behaviors of American females aged 15–19 years: 1985, 1990, and 1995. *American Journal of Public Health, 90,* 1421–1425.

Jones, M. C. (1924). A laboratory study of fear: The case of Peter. *Pedagogical Seminary, 31,* 308–315.

Kohlberg, L. (1966). Cognitive stages and preschool education. *Human Development, 9,* 5–17.

Kopp, C. B., & Krakow, J. B. (1982). *The child: Development in a social context.* Reading, MA: Addison-Wesley.

Lerner, R. M., & Kauffman, M. B. (1985). The concept of development in contextualism. *Developmental Review, 5,* 309–333.

Lourenco, O., & Machado, A. (1996). In defense of Piaget's theory: A reply to 10 common criticisms. *Psychological Review, 103,* 143–164.

Macmillan, M. (1991). *Freud evaluated: The completed arc.* New York: Elsevier.

Masson, J. M. (1984). *The assault on truth: Freud's suppression of the seduction theory.* New York: Farrar, Straus, and Giroux.

McDonald, M. (1998, October 19). Burying Freud and praising him. *U.S. News & World Report,* pp. 60–61.

Meschke, L. L., Bartholomae, S., & Zentall, S. R. (2000). Adolescent sexuality and parent–adolescent processes: Promoting healthy teen choices. *Family Relations, 49,* 143–154.

Miller, B. C., Benson, B., & Galbraith, K. A. (2001). Family relationships and adolescent pregnancy risk: A research synthesis. *Developmental Review, 21,* 1–38.

Miller, P. H. (2002). *Theories of developmental psychology* (4th ed.). New York: Worth.

Orlofsky, J. L. (1993). Intimacy status: Theory and research. In J. E. Marcia, A. S. Waterman, D. R. Matteson, S. L. Archer, & J. L. Orlofsky (Eds.), *Ego identity: A handbook for psychosocial research.* New York: Springer-Verlag.

Parke, R. D., Ornstein, P. A., Rieser, J. J., & Zahn-Waxler, C. (1994). The past as prologue: An overview of a century of developmental psychology. In R. D. Parke, P. A. Ornstein, J. J. Rieser, & C. Zahn-Waxler (Eds.), *A century of developmental psychology.* Washington, DC: American Psychological Association.

Pepper, S. C. (1942). *World hypotheses: A study in evidence.* Berkeley: University of California Press.

Perry, D. G., & Parke, R. D. (1975). Punishment and alternative response training as determinants of response inhibition in children. *Genetic Psychology Monographs, 91*(2), 257–279.

Piaget, J. (1950). *The psychology of intelligence.* New York: Harcourt Brace & World.

Piaget, J. (1952). *The origins of intelligence in children.* New York: International Universities Press.

Reese, H. W., & Overton, W. F. (1970). Models of development and theories of development. In L. R. Goulet & P. B. Baltes (Eds.), *Life-span developmental psychology: Research and theory.* New York: Academic.

Riegel, K. F. (1979). *Foundations of dialectical psychology.* New York: Academic.

Rilling, M. (2000). John Watson's paradoxical struggle to explain Freud. *American Psychologist, 55,* 301–312.

Singh, S., & Darroch, J. E. (2000). Adolescent pregnancy and childbearing: Levels and trends in developed countries. *Family Planning Perspectives, 32,* 14–23.

Skinner, B. F. (1953). *Science and human behavior.* New York: Macmillan.

South, S. J. (1999). Historical changes and life course variation in the determinants of premarital childrearing. *Journal of Marriage and the Family, 61,* 752–763.

Straus, M. A. (with D. A. Donnelly). (1994). *Beating the devil out of them: Corporal punishment in American families.* New York: Lexington Books.

Thompson, L., & Spanier, G. B. (1978). Influence of parents, peers, and partners on the contraceptive use of college men and women. *Journal of Marriage and the Family, 40,* 481–492.

Unger, J. B., Molina, G. B., & Teran, L. (2000). Perceived consequences of teenage childbearing among adolescent girls in an urban sample. *Journal of Adolescent Health, 26,* 205–212.

U.S. Census Bureau. (2000). *Statistical abstracts of the United States: 2000.* Washington, DC: Government Printing Office.

Ventura, S. J., Martin, J. A., Curtin, S. C., Mathews, T. J., & Park, M. M. (2000). Births: Final data for 1998. *National Vital Statistics Report, 48*(3), 1–25.

Vygotsky, L. S. (1962). *Thought and language* (E. Hanfmann & G. Vakar, Eds. & Trans.). Cambridge, MA: MIT Press. (Original work published 1934)

Vygotsky, L. S. (1978). *Mind in society: The development of higher mental processes* (M. Cole, V. John-Steiner, S. Scribner, & E. Souberman, Eds.). Cambridge, MA: Harvard University Press. (Original work published 1930, 1933, 1935)

Wachs, T. D. (2000). *Necessary but not sufficient: The respective roles of single and multiple influences on individual development.* Washington, DC: American Psychological Association.

Watson, J. B. (1913). Psychology as the behaviorist views it. *Psychological Review, 20,* 158–177.

Watson, J. B. (1925). *Behaviorism.* New York: Norton.

Watson, J. B., & Raynor, R. (1920). Conditioned emotional reactions. *Journal of Experimental Psychology, 3,* 1–14.

Weisberg, P. (1963). Social and nonsocial conditioning of infant vocalization. *Child Development, 34,* 377–388.

Whitbeck, L. B., Yoder, K. A., Hoyt, D. R., & Conger, R. D. (1999). Early adolescent sexual activity: A developmental study. *Journal of Marriage and the Family, 61,* 934–946.

Chapter 3: Genes, Environment, and Development

Aldridge, S. (1996). *The thread of life: The story of genes and genetic engineering.* Cambridge, England: Cambridge University Press.

Anastasi, A. (1958). Heredity, environment, and the question, "how?" *Psychological Review, 65,* 197–208.

Archer, J. (1992). *Ethology and human development.* Hertfordshire, England: Harvester Wheatsheaf.

Bailey, J. M., Dunne, M. P., & Martin, N. G. (2000). Genetic and environmental influences on sexual orientation and its correlates in an Australian twin sample. *Journal of Personality and Social Psychology, 78,* 524–536.

Bailey, J. M., & Pillard, R. C. (1991). A genetic study of the male sexual orientation. *Archives of General Psychiatry, 48,* 1089–1096.

Baker, L. A., & Daniels, D. (1990). Nonshared environmental influences and personality differences in adult twins. *Journal of Personality and Social Psychology, 58,* 103–110.

Beardsley, T. (1997). Fetal checkup. *Scientific American, 275,* 38.

Begley, S. (1997, March 10). Little lamb, who made thee? *Newsweek,* pp. 53–59.

Belsky, J., Steinberg, L., & Draper, P. (1991). Childhood experience, interpersonal development, and reproductive strategy: An evolutionary theory of socialization. *Child Development, 62,* 647–670.

Bishop, J. A., & Cooke, L. M. (1975). Moths, melanism and clean air. *Scientific American, 232,* 90–99.

Bishop, J. E., & Waldholz, M. (1990). *Genome: The story of the most astonishing scientific adventure of our time—The attempt to map all the genes in the human body.* New York: Simon & Schuster.

Bouchard, T. J., Jr. (1984). Twins reared together and apart: What they tell us about human diversity. In S. W. Fox (Ed.), *Individuality and determinism. Chemical and biological bases.* New York: Plenum.

Bouchard, T. J., Jr., Lykken, D. T., McGue, M., Segal, N. L., & Tellegen, A. (1990). Sources of human psychological differences: The Minnesota study of twins reared apart. *Science, 250,* 223–228.

Bouchard, T. J., Jr., & McGue, M. (1981). Family studies of intelligence: A review. *Science, 212,* 1055–1059.

Bouchard, T. J., Jr., & Pedersen, N. (1999). Twins reared apart: Nature's double experiment. In M. C. LaBuda & E. L. Grigorenko (Eds.), *On the way to individuality: Methodological issues in behavioral genetics.* Commack, NY: Nova Science Publishers.

Burns, G. W., & Bottino, P. J. (1989). *The science of genetics* (6th ed.). New York: Macmillan.

Buss, A. H., & Plomin, R. (1984). *Temperament: Early developing personality traits.* Hillsdale, NJ: Erlbaum.

Buss, D. M. (1999). *Evolutionary psychology. The new science of the mind.* Boston: Allyn & Bacon.

Campbell, F. A., Pungello, E. P., Miller-Johnson, S., Burchinal, M., & Ramey, C. T. (2001). The development of cognitive and academic abilities: Growth curves from an early childhood educational experiment. *Developmental Psychology, 37,* 231–242.

Carlson, B. M. (1994). *Human embryology and developmental biology.* St. Louis: Mosby.

Centerwall, S. A., & Centerwall, W. R. (2000). The discovery of phenylketonuria: The story of a young couple, two retarded children, and a scientist. *Pediatrics, 105,* 89–103.

Collins, W. A., Maccoby, E. E., Steinberg, L., Hetherington, E. M., & Bornstein, M. H. (2000). Contemporary research on parenting: The case for nature and nurture. *American Psychologist, 55,* 218–232.

Couzin, J. (1999a, November 1). Quandaries in the genes: As genetic testing expands, so do ethical complications. *U.S. News & World Report,* pp. 64, 66.

Couzin, J. (1999b, May 24). What's killing clones? *U.S. News & World Report,* p. 65.

Darwin, C. (1859). *The origin of species.* New York: Modern Library.

Davis, J. O., Phelps, J. A., & Bracha, H. S. (1999). Prenatal development of monozygotic twins and concordance for schizophrenia. In S. J. Ceci & W. M. Williams (Eds.), *The nature–nurture debate. The essential readings.* Malden, MA: Blackwell.

Devlin, B., Daniels, M., & Roeder, K. (1997). The heritability of IQ. *Nature, 388*(6641), 468–471.

de Waal, F. B. M. (1999, June 4). Culture and nature are inseparable. *Chronicle of Higher Education,* pp. B4–B6.

Difiglia, M. (2000). Genetics of childhood disorders: X. Huntington disease. *Journal of the American Academy of Child and Adolescent Psychiatry, 39,* 120–122.

Down syndrome prevalence at birth: United States, 1983–1990 (1994, August 26). *Mortality and Morbidity Weekly Reports, 43,* 617–622.

Downey, J., Elkin, E. J., Ehrhardt, A. A., Meyer-Bahlburg, H. F., Bell, J. J., & Morishima, A. (1991). Cognitive ability and everyday functioning in women with Turner syndrome. *Journal of Learning Disabilities, 24,* 32–39.

Dunn, J., & Plomin, R. (1990). *Separate lives: Why siblings are so different.* New York: Basic Books.

Eaves, L., Martin, N., Heath, A., Schieken, R., Meyer, J., Silberg, J., Neale, M., & Corey, L. (1997). Age changes in the causes of individ-

ual differences in conservatism. *Behavior Genetics, 27,* 121–124.

Finkel, D., Pedersen, N. L., Plomin, R., & McClearn, G. E. (1998). Longitudinal and cross-sectional twin data on cognitive abilities in adulthood: The Swedish Adoption/Twin Study of Aging. *Developmental Psychology, 34,* 1400–1413.

Fischer, J. (2000a, February 14). Best hope or broken promise? After a decade, gene therapy goes on trial. *U.S. News and World Report,* 46.

Fischer, J. (2000b, October 23). Snipping away at human disease: Into the era of individually tailored therapies. *U.S. News and World Report,* 58–59.

Francis, D., Diorio, J., Liu, D., & Meaney, M. J. (1999). Nongenomic transmission across generations of maternal behavior and stress responses in the rat. *Science, 286,* 1155–1158.

Gandelman, R. (1992). *Psychobiology of behavioral development.* New York: Oxford University Press.

Geary, D. C. (2000). Evolution and proximate expression of human paternal investment. *Psychological Bulletin, 126,* 55–77.

Gottesman, I. I. (1991). *Schizophrenia genesis: The origins of madness.* New York: W. H. Freeman.

Gottlieb, G. (1991). Experiential canalization of behavioral development: Theory. *Developmental Psychology, 27,* 4–13.

Gottlieb, G. (2000). Environmental and behavioral influences on gene activity. *Current Directions in Psychological Science, 9,* 93–97.

Gottlieb, G., Wahlsten, D., & Lickliter, R. (1998). The significance of biology for human development: A developmental psychobiological systems view. In R. M. Lerner (Ed.), William Damon (Editor-in-Chief), *Handbook of child psychology: Vol. 1. Theoretical models of human development* (5th ed.). New York: Wiley.

Grilo, C. M., & Pogue-Geile, M. F. (1991). The nature of environmental influences on weight and obesity: A behavior genetic analysis. *Psychological Bulletin, 110,* 520–537.

Gusella, J. F., Wexler, N. S., Conneally, P. M., Naylor, S. L., Anderson, M. A., Tanzi, R. E., Watkins, P. C., Ottina, K., Wallace, M. R., Sakaguchi, A. Y., Young, A. B., Shoulson, I., Bonilla, E., & Martin, J. B. (1983). A polymorphic DNA marker genetically linked to Huntington disease. *Nature, 306,* 234–238.

Harris, J. R. (1998). *The nurture assumption: Why children turn out the way they do.* New York: Free Press.

Hawley, R. S., & Mori, C. A. (1999). *The human genome: A user's guide.* San Diego, CA: Academic Press.

Henig, R. M. (2000). *The monk in the garden: The lost and found genius of Gregor Mendel, the father of genetics.* Boston: Houghton Mifflin.

Heston, L. L. (1970). The genetics of schizophrenia and schizoid disease. *Science, 167,* 249–256.

Hinde, R. A. (1983). Ethology and child development. In M. M. Haith & J. J. Campos (Vol. Eds.; P. H. Mussen, General Ed.), *Handbook of child psychology: Vol. 2. Infancy and developmental psychobiology* (4th ed.). New York: Wiley.

Humpherys, D., Eggan, K., Akutsu, H., Hochedlinger, K., Rideout, W. M., III, Biniszkiewicz, D., Yanagimachi, R., & Jaenisch, R. (2001). Epigenetic instability in ES cells and cloned mice. *Science, 293*(5527), 95–97.

Kendler, K. S., Neale, M., Kessler, R., Heath, A., & Eaves, L. (1993). A twin study of recent life events and difficulties. *Archives of General Psychiatry, 50,* 789–796.

Ketelaar, T., & Ellis, B. J. (2000). Are evolutionary explanations unfalsifiable? Evolutionary psychology and the Lakatosian philosophy of science. *Psychological Inquiry, 11,* 1–21.

Kettlewell, H. B. D. (1959). Darwin's missing evidence. *Scientific American, 200*(3), 48–53.

Lewontin, R. C., Rose, S., & Kamin, L. J. (1984). *Not in our genes.* New York: Pantheon.

Loehlin, J. C. (1985). Fitting heredity/environment models jointly to twin and adoption data from the California Psychological Inventory. *Behavior Genetics, 15,* 199–221.

Loehlin, J. C. (1992). *Genes and environment in personality development (Individual differences and development series, Vol. 2).* Newbury Park, CA: Sage.

Loehlin, J. C., McCrae, R. R., Costa, P. T., Jr., & John, O. P. (1998). Heritabilities of common and measure-specific components of the Big Five personality factors. *Journal of Research in Personality, 32,* 431–453.

Lykken, D. T., Tellegen, A., & Iacono, W. G. (1982). EEG spectra in twins: Evidence for a neglected mechanism of genetic determination. *Physiological Psychology, 10,* 60–65.

Lytton, H. (2000). Toward a model of family-environmental and child-biological influences on development. *Developmental Review, 20,* 150–179.

Maccoby, E. E. (2000). Parenting and its effects on children: On reading and misreading behavior genetics. *Annual Review of Psychology, 51,* 1–27.

Mandoki, M. W., Sumner, G. S., Hoffman, R. P., & Riconda, D. L. (1991). A review of Klinefelter's syndrome in children and adolescents. *Journal of the American Academy of Child and Adolescent Psychiatry, 30,* 167–172.

Manke, B., McGuire, S., Reiss, D., Howe, G., Hetherington, E., & Plomin, R. (1995). Genetic contributions to adolescents' extrafamilial social interactions: Teachers, best friends, and peers. *Social Development, 4,* 238–256.

Massie, R. K., & Massie, S. (1975). *Journey.* New York: Knopf.

McCall, R. B. (1981). Nature–nurture and the two realms of development: A proposed integration with respect to mental development. *Child Development, 52,* 1–12.

McCartney, K., Harris, M. J., & Bernieri, F. (1990). Growing up and growing apart: A developmental meta-analysis of twin studies. *Psychological Bulletin, 107,* 226–237.

McGue, M., Bouchard, T. J., Jr., Iacono, W. G., & Lykken, D. T. (1993). Behavioral genetics of cognitive ability: A life-span perspective. In R. Plomin & G. E. McClearn (Eds.), *Nature, nurture, and psychology.* Washington, DC: American Psychological Association.

McGue, M., Sharma, A., & Benson, P. (1996). The effect of common rearing on adolescent adjustment: Evidence from a US adoption cohort. *Developmental Psychology, 32,* 604–613.

McKusick, V. A. (1990). *Mendelian inheritance in man* (9th ed.). Baltimore: Johns Hopkins Press.

Miller, J. A. (1995). Strictest diet avoids subtle detriments of PKU. *Bioscience, 45,* 244–245.

Mortensen, P. B., Pedersen, C. B., Westergaard, T., Wohlfahrt, J., Ewald, H., Mors, O.,

Andersen, P. K., & Melbye, M. (1999). Effects of family history and place and season of birth on the risk of schizophrenia. *New England Journal of Medicine, 340,* 603–608.

Neale, M. C., & Martin, N. G. (1989). The effects of age, sex, and genotype on self-report drunkenness following a challenge dose of alcohol. *Behavior Genetics, 19,* 63–78.

Normile, D. (1998). Bid for better beef gives Japan a leg up on cattle. *Science, 282*(5396), 1975–1976.

O'Connor, T. G., Deater-Deckard, K., Fulker, D., Rutter, M., & Plomin, R. (1998). Genotype-environment correlations in late childhood and early adolescence: Antisocial behavioral problems and coercive parenting. *Developmental Psychology, 34,* 970–981.

Patrick, C. L. (2000). Genetic and environmental influences on the development of cognitive abilities: Evidence from the field of developmental behavior genetics. *Journal of School Psychology, 38,* 79–108.

Pedersen, N. L., McClearn, G. E., Plomin, R., & Friberg, L. (1985). Separated fraternal twins: Resemblance for cognitive abilities. *Behavior Genetics, 15,* 407–419.

Pennisi, E. (2000). Evolution: Nature steers a predictable course. *Science, 287*(5451), 207, 209.

Pike, A., Manke, B., Reiss, D., & Plomin, R. (2000). A genetic analysis of differential experiences of adolescent siblings across three years. *Social Development, 9,* 96–114.

Plomin, R. (1986). *Development, genetics, and psychology.* Hillsdale, NJ: Erlbaum.

Plomin, R. (1990). *Nature and nurture. An introduction to human behavioral genetics.* Pacific Grove, CA: Brooks/Cole.

Plomin, R. (2000, September). Psychology in a post-genomics world: It will be more important than ever. *Observer, 13*(7), 3, 27.

Plomin, R., & Bergeman, C. S. (1991). The nature of nurture: Genetic influence on environmental measures. *Behavioral and Brain Sciences, 14,* 373–385.

Plomin, R., Corley, R., DeFries, J. C., & Fulker, D. W. (1990). Individual differences in television viewing in early childhood: Nature as well as nurture. *Psychological Science, 1,* 371–377.

Plomin, R., DeFries, J. C., & Loehlin, J. C. (1977). Genotype-environment interaction and correlation in the analysis of human behavior. *Psychological Bulletin, 84,* 309–322.

Plomin, R., DeFries, J. C., McClearn, G. E., & McGuffin, P. (2001). *Behavioral genetics* (4th ed.). New York: Worth.

Plomin, R., Pedersen, N. L., Lichtenstein, P., & McClearn, G. E. (1994). Variability and stability in cognitive abilities are largely genetic later in life. *Behavior Genetics, 24,* 207–215.

Plomin, R., Pedersen, N. L., McClearn, G. E., Nesselroade, J. R., & Bergeman, C. S. (1988). EAS temperaments during the last half of the life span: Twins reared apart and twins reared together. *Psychology and Aging, 3,* 43–50.

Reiss, D., & Neiderhiser, J. M. (2000). The interplay of genetic influences and social processes in developmental theory: Specific mechanisms are coming into view. *Development and Psychopathology, 12,* 357–374.

Reiss, D., with J. M. Neiderhiser, E. M. Hetherington, & R. Plomin. (2000). *The relationship code: Deciphering genetic and social influences on adolescent development.* Cambridge, MA: Harvard University Press.

Reznikoff, M., Domino, G., Bridges, C., & Honeyman, M. (1973). Creative abilities in identical and fraternal twins. *Behavior Genetics, 3,* 365–377.

Roche, M. I., & Kuller, J. A. (1996). Autosomal disorders: Cystic fibrosis, Tay-Sachs disease, and Huntington disease. In J. A. Kuller, N. C. Chescheir, & R. C. Cefalo (Eds.), *Prenatal diagnosis and reproductive genetics.* St. Louis: Mosby.

Rose, R. J. (1995). Genes and human behavior. *Annual Review of Psychology, 46,* 625–654.

Rowe, D. C. (1994). *The limits of family influence: Genes, experience, and behavior.* New York: Guilford.

Rowe, D. C., & Jacobson, K. C. (1999). In the mainstream: Research in behavioral genetics. In R. A. Carson & M. A. Rothstein (Eds.), *Behavioral genetics: The clash of culture and biology.* Baltimore: Johns Hopkins University Press.

Scarr, S., & Kidd, K. K. (1983). Developmental behavior genetics. In M. M. Haith & J. J. Campos (Vol. Eds.); P. H. Mussen, General Ed.), *Handbook of child psychology: Vol. 2. Infancy and developmental psychobiology* (4th ed.). New York: Wiley.

Scarr, S., & McCartney, K. (1983). How people make their own environments: A theory of genotype→environment effects. *Child Development, 54,* 424–435.

Scarr, S., & Weinberg, R. A. (1978). The influence of family background on intellectual attainment. *American Sociological Review, 43,* 674–692.

Scarr, S., & Weinberg, R. A. (1983). The Minnesota adoption studies: Genetic differences and malleability. *Child Development, 54,* 260–267.

Segal, N. L. (2000). Virtual twins: New findings on within-family environmental influences on intelligence. *Journal of Educational Psychology, 92,* 442–448.

Shafer, J. H., & Kuller, J. A. (1996). Increased maternal age and prior aneuploid conception. In J. A. Kuller, N. C. Chescheir, & R. C. Cefalo (Eds.), *Prenatal diagnosis and reproductive genetics.* St. Louis: Mosby.

Shiloh, S. (1996). Genetic counseling: A developing area of interest for psychologists. *Professional Psychology: Research and Practice, 27,* 475–486.

State, M. W., Lombroso, P. J., Pauls, D. L., & Leckman, J. F. (2000). The genetics of childhood psychiatric disorders: A decade of progress. *Journal of the American Academy of Child and Adolescent Psychiatry, 39,* 946–962.

Stoolmiller, M. (1999). Implications of the restricted range of family environments for estimates of heritability and nonshared environment in behavior-genetic adoption studies. *Psychological Bulletin, 125,* 392–409.

Strayer, F. F. (1980). Social ecology of the preschool peer group. In W. A. Collins (Ed.), *Minnesota Symposia on Child Psychology: Vol. 13. Development of cognition, affect and social relations.* Hillsdale, NJ: Erlbaum.

Strigini, P., Sansone, R., Carobbi, S., & Pierluigi, M. (1990). Radiation and Down's syndrome. *Nature, 347,* 717.

Tang, Y., Shimizu, E., Dube, G. R., Rampon, C., Kerchner, G. A., Zhuo, M., Liu, G., Tsien, J. Z. (1999). Genetic enhancement of learning in memory and mice. *Nature, 401*(6748), 63–69.

Thompson, R. F. (1975). *Introduction to physiological psychology.* New York: Harper & Row.

Tryon, R. C. (1940). Genetic differences in maze learning in rats. *Yearbook of the National Society for Studies in Education, 39,* 111–119.

Turkheimer, E. (2000). Three laws of behavior genetics and what they mean. *Current Directions in Psychological Science, 9,* 160–164.

Turkheimer, E., & Waldron, M. C. (2000). Nonshared environment: A theoretical, methodological, and quantitative review. *Psychological Bulletin, 126,* 78–108.

Wachs, T. D. (2000). *Necessary but not sufficient: The respective roles of single and multiple influences on individual development.* Washington, DC: American Psychological Association.

Weiss, R. (2000, May 23). For DNA, a defining moment: With code revealed, challenge will be to find its meaning and uses. *Washington Post,* pp. A1, A16–A17.

Weiss, R. (2001a, July 6). Clone study casts doubt on stem cells. *Washington Post,* pp. A1, A9.

Weiss, R. (2001b, November 26). First human embryos are cloned in U.S. *Washington Post,* pp. A1, A12.

Weiss, R. (2001c, February 11). Life's blueprint in less than an inch. *Washington Post,* pp. A1, A10.

Weiss, R., & Gillis, J. (2000, June 27). DNA-mapping milestone heralded. *Washington Post,* pp. A1, A12–13.

Wheeler, D. L. (1999, January 29). Geneticists near end of quest for source of a deadly disease. *Chronicle of Higher Education,* pp. A17, A20.

Wiggins, S., Whyte, P., Huggins, M., Adam, S., Theilmann, J., Bloch, M., Sheps, S. B., Schechter, M. T., Hayden, M. R. (1992). The psychological consequences of predictive testing for Huntington's disease. *New England Journal of Medicine, 327,* 1401–1405.

Wilson, E. O. (1975). *Sociobiology: The new synthesis.* Cambridge, MA: Belknap Press of Harvard University Press.

Wilson, R. S. (1978). Synchronies in mental development: An epigenetic perspective. *Science, 202,* 939–948.

Wilson, R. S. (1983). The Louisville twin study: Developmental synchronies in behavior. *Child Development, 54,* 298–316.

Wright, L. (1995). Double mystery. *New Yorker, 71,* 44–62.

Yashin, A. I., Iachine, I. A., & Harris, J. R. (1999). Half of the variation in susceptibility to mortality is genetic: Findings from Swedish twin survival data. *Behavior Genetics, 29,* 11–19.

Chapter 4: Prenatal Development and Birth

Abel, E. L. (1989). *Behavioral teratogenesis and behavioral mutagenesis: A primer in abnormal development.* New York: Plenum

Ackermann-Liebrich, U., Voegeli, T., Gunter-Witt, K., Kunz, I., Zullig, M., Schindler, C., & Maurer, M. (1996). Home versus hospital deliveries: Follow up study of matched pairs for procedures and outcome. *British Medical Journal, 313,* 1313–1318.

Aldridge, S. (1996). *The thread of life: The story of genes and genetic engineering.* Cambridge, England: Cambridge University Press.

Allen, M. C., & Capute, A. J. (1986). Assessment of early auditory and visual abilities of extremely premature infants. *Developmental Medicine and Child Neurology, 28,* 458–466.

Ames, E. W. (1997). *The development of Romanian orphanage children adopted to Canada: Final report.* Burnaby, British Columbia: Simon Fraser University.

Amini, S. B., Catalano, P. M., Dierker, L. J., & Mann, L. I. (1996). Births to teenagers: Trends and obstetric outcomes. *Obstetrics and Gynecology, 87,* 668–674.

Anslow, P. (1998). Birth asphyxia. *European Journal of Radiology, 26,* 148–153.

Apgar, V., & Beck, J. (1974). *Is my baby all right?* New York: Pocket Books.

Apgar, V., & James, L. S. (1962). Further observations on the newborn scoring system. *American Journal of Diseases of Children, 104,* 419–428.

Arendt, R., Singer, L., Angelopoulos, J., Bass-Busdiecker, O., & Mascia, J. (1998). Sensorimotor development in cocaine-exposed infants. *Infant Behavior and Development, 21,* 627–640.

Autti-Rämö, I. (2000). Twelve-year follow-up of children exposed to alcohol in utero. *Developmental Medicine & Child Neurology, 42,* 406–411.

Baird, P. A., Anderson, T. W., Newcombe, H. B., & Lowry, R. B. (1988). Genetic disorders in children and young adults: A population study. *American Journal of Human Genetics, 42,* 677–693.

Baker, R. L., & Mednick, B. R. (1984). *Influences on human development: A longitudinal perspective.* Boston: Kluwer Nijhoff.

Barclay, L., & Lupton, D. (1999). The experiences of new fatherhood: A socio-cultural analysis. *Journal of Advanced Nursing, 29,* 1013–1020.

Barker, D. J. P. (1994). *Mothers, babies, and disease in later life.* London: BMJ.

Barr, H. M., & Streissguth, A. P. (1991). Caffeine use during pregnancy and child outcome: A 7-year prospective study. *Neurotoxicology and Teratology, 13,* 441–448.

Barr, H. M., Streissguth, A. P., Darby, B. L., & Sampson, P. D. (1990). Prenatal exposure to alcohol, caffeine, tobacco, and aspirin: Effects on fine and gross motor performance in 4-year-old children. *Developmental Psychology, 26,* 339–348.

Batshaw, M. L. (1997). *Children with disabilities* (4th ed.). Baltimore: Paul H. Brookes.

Beck, M. (1994, January 17). How far should we push mother nature? *Newsweek,* pp. 54–57.

Bellinger, D., Leviton, A., Waternaux, C., Needleman, H., & Rabinowitz, M. (1987). Longitudinal analyses of prenatal and postnatal lead exposure and early cognitive development. *New England Journal of Medicine, 316,* 1037–1043.

Billing, L., Eriksson, M., Jonsson, B., Steneroth, G., & Zetterstrom, R. (1994). The influence of environmental factors on behavioural problems in 8-year-old children exposed to amphetamine during fetal life. *Child Abuse and Neglect, 18,* 3–9.

Bradley, R. H., Whiteside, L., Mundfrom, D. J., & Casey, P. H. (1994). Impact of the Infant Health and Development Program (IHDP) on the home environments of infants born prematurely and with low birthweight. *Journal of Educational Psychology, 86,* 531–541.

Brazelton, T. B. (1979). Behavioral competence of the newborn infant. *Seminars in Perinatology, 3,* 35–44.

Britt, G. C., & Myers, B. J. (1994). The effects of the Brazelton intervention. *Infant Mental Health Journal, 15,* 278–292.

Bronfenbrenner, U., & Crouter, A. C. (1983). The evolution of environmental models in developmental research. In W. Kessen (Vol. Ed.; P. H. Mussen, General Ed.), *Handbook of child psychology: Vol. 1. History, theory, and methods* (4th ed.). New York: Wiley.

Brooks-Gunn, J., Klebanov, P. K., Liaw, F., & Spiker, D. (1993). Enhancing the development of low birthweight, premature infants: Changes in cognition and behavior over the first three years. *Child Development, 64,* 736–753.

Brown, D. (2000, July 14). Drug preventing AIDS in infants. *Washington Post,* p. A17.

Brown, H. S. (1996). Physician demand for leisure: Implications for cesarean section rates. *Journal of Health Economics, 15,* 233–42.

Caldwell, P. (1996). Child survival: Physical vulnerability and resilience in adversity in the European past and the contemporary third world. *Social Science and Medicine, 43,* 609–619.

Carter, S. L. (1998). Motor impairment associated with neurological injury in premature infants. Available online: http://www.comeunity.com/disability/cerebral_palsy/cerebralpalsy.html

Castro, A. (1999). Commentary: Increase in cesarean sections may reflect medical control not women's choice. *British Medical Journal, 319,* 1401–1402.

Chalmers, B. (1996). Cross-cultural comparisons of birthing: Psycho-social issues in Western and African birth. *Psychology and Health, 12,* 11–21.

Chandler, S., & Field, P. A. (1997). Becoming a father: First-time fathers' experience of labor and delivery. *Journal of Nurse-Midwifery, 42* 17–24.

Chapman, L. L. (2000). Expectant fathers and labor epidurals. *American Journal of Maternity and Child Nursing, 25,* 133–138.

Chiriboga, C. A., Brust, J. C. M., Bateman, D., & Hauser, W. A. (1999). Dose-response effect of fetal cocaine exposure on newborn neurologic function. *Pediatrics, 103,* 79–85.

Cicero, T. J. (1994). Effects of paternal exposure to alcohol on offspring. *Alcohol Health & Research World, 18,* 37–41.

Clarke, S. C., & Taffel, S. M. (1996). Rates of cesarean and VBAC delivery, United States, 1994. *Birth, 23,* 166–168.

Cnattingius, S., Signorell, L. B., Anneren, G., Clausson, B., Ekbom, A., Ljunger, E., Blot, W. J., McLaughlin, J. K., Petersson, G., Rane, A., & Granath, F. (2000). Caffeine intake and the risk of first-trimester spontaneous abortion. *New England Journal of Medicine, 343,* 1839–1945.

Cohen, B. B., Friedman, D. J., Zhang, A., Trudeau, E. B., Walker, D. K., Anderka, M., Fogerty, S., Franklin, S., & McKenna, P. A. (1999). Impact of multiple births on low birthweight: Massachusetts, 1989–1996. *Morbidity & Mortality Weekly Report, 48,* 289–293.

Colburn, D. (1996, September 24). Fetal alcohol babies face life of problems. *Washington Post Health,* p. 5.

Cooper, P. J., & Murray, L. (1998). Postnatal depression. *British Medial Journal, 316,* 1884–1886.

Day, N. L., Zuo, Y., Richardson, G. A., Goldschmidt, L., Larkby, C. A., & Cornelius, M. D. (1999). Prenatal alcohol use and offspring size at 10 years of age. *Alcoholism: Clinical & Experimental Research, 23,* 863–869.

Dempsey, D. A., Hajnal, B. L., Partridge, C., Jacobson, S. N., Good, W., Jones, R. T., & Ferriero, D. M. (2000). Tone abnormalities are associated with maternal cigarette smoking during pregnancy in in-utero cocaine-exposed infants. *Pediatrics, 106,* 79–85.

Dempsey, D. A., Partridge, C., Jones, R. T., & Rowbotham, M. C. (1998). Cocaine, nicotine, caffeine, and metabolite plasma concentrations in neonates. *Journal of Analytic Toxicology, 22,* 220–224.

DESAction (2000). Health risks and care for DES daughters. Available online: http://www.desaction.org/

Diaz, J. (1997). *How drugs influence behavior: A neuro-behavioral approach.* Upper Saddle River, NJ: Prentice-Hall.

DiMatteo, M. R., Morton, S. C., Lepper, H. S., & Damush, T. M. (1996). Cesarean childbirth and psychosocial outcomes: A meta-analysis. *Health Psychology, 15,* 303–314.

DiPietro, J. A., Hodgson, D. M., Costigan, K. A., Hilton, S. C., & Johnson, T. R. B. (1996a). Fetal antecedents of infant temperament. *Child Development, 67,* 2568–2583.

DiPietro, J. A., Hodgson, D. M., Costigan, K. A., Hilton, S. C., & Johnson, T. R. B. (1996b). Fetal neurobehavioral development. *Child Development, 67,* 2553–2567.

Durik, A. M., Hyde, J. S., & Clark, R. (2000). Sequelae of cesarean and vaginal deliveries: Psychosocial outcomes for mothers and infants. *Developmental Psychology, 36,* 251–260.

Elbourne, D., & Wiseman, R. A. (2000). Types of intra-muscular opioids for maternal pain relief in labour. *Cochrane Database Systems Review 2000* (CD001237).

Emory, E. K., Schlackman, L. J., & Fiano, K. (1996). Drug-hormone interactions on neurobehavioral responses in human neonates. *Infant Behavior and Development, 19,* 213–220.

Field, T. (2001). Massage therapy. *Current Directions in Psychological Science, 10,* 51–54.

Fowles, E. R. (1999). The Brazelton Neonatal Behavioral Assessment Scale and maternal identity. *American Journal of Maternity and Child Nursing, 24,* 287–293.

Fraser, M. W. (1997). The ecology of childhood: A multisystems perspective. In M. W. Fraser (Ed.), *Risk and resilience in childhood: An ecological perspective* (pp. 1–9). Washington, DC: NASW Press.

French Pediatric HIV Infection Study Group, European Collaborative Study. (1997). Morbidity and mortality in European children vertically infected by HIV-1. *Journal of Acquired Immune Deficiency Syndrome Human Retrovirology, 14,* 442–450.

Fretts, R. C., & Usher, R. H. (1997). Causes of fetal death in women of advanced maternal age. *Obstetrics and Gynecology, 89,* 40–45.

Fried, P. A., O'Connell, C. M., & Watkinson, B. (1992). 60- and 72-month follow-up of children prenatally exposed to marijuana, cigarettes, and alcohol: Cognitive and language assessment. *Developmental and Behavioral Pediatrics, 13,* 383–391.

Friedman, J. M., & Polifka, J. E. (1996). *The effects of drugs on the fetus and nursing infant:*

A handbook for health care professionals. Baltimore: Johns Hopkins University Press.

Gabriel, K., Hofmann, C., Glavas, M., & Weinberg, J. (1998). The hormonal effects of alcohol use on the mother and fetus. *Alcohol Health & Research World, 22,* 170–177.

Gatten S. L., Arceneaux, J. M., Dean, R. S., & Anderson, J. L. (1994). Perinatal risk factors as predictors of developmental functioning. *International Journal of Neuroscience, 75,* 167–174.

Genc, M., & Ledger, W. J. (2000). Syphilis in pregnancy. *Sexual Transmission Information, 76,* 73–79.

Gilbert, W. M., Nesbitt, T. S., & Danielsen, B. (1999). Childbearing beyond age 40: Pregnancy outcomes in 24,302 cases. *Obstetrics and Gynecology, 93,* 9–14.

Gleicher, N., Oleske, D. M., Tur-Kaspa, I. Vidali, A., & Karande, V. (2000). Reducing the risk of high-order multiple pregnancy after ovarian stimulation with gonadotropins. *New England Journal of Medicine, 343,* 2–7.

Global focus: Talk about Romanian orphans. (1999, June 25). The Washington Post Company. Available online: http://www.washingtonpost.com/wp-srv/inatl/zforum/99/federici062599.htm

Goldberg, G. R., & Prentice, A. M. (1994). Maternal and fetal determinants of adult diseases. *Nutrition Reviews, 52,* 191–200.

Golombok, S., Cook, R., Bish, A., & Murray, C. (1995). Families created by the new reproductive technologies: Quality of parenting and social and emotional development of the children. *Child Development, 66,* 285–298.

Golub, M., Gorman, K., Grantham-McGregor, S., Levitsky, D., Schürch, B., Strupp, B., & Wachs, T. (1996). A reconceptualization of the effects of undernutrition on children's biological, psychosocial, and behavioral development. *Social Policy Report, Society for Research in Child Development, 10,* 1–21.

Gotlib, I. H., Whiffen, V. E., Wallace, P. M., & Mount, J. (1991). Prospective investigation of postpartum depression: Factors involved in onset and recovery. *Journal of Abnormal Psychology, 100,* 122–132.

Gottlieb, G. (1996). Commentary: A systems view of psychobiological development. In D. Magnusson (Ed.), *The lifespan development of individuals: Behavioral, neurobiological, and psychosocial perspectives—A synthesis.* Cambridge, England: Cambridge University Press.

Guyer, B., Freedman, M. A., Strobino, D. M., & Sondik, E. J. (2000). Annual summary of vital statistics: Trends in the health of Americans during the 20th century. *Pediatrics, 106,* 1307–1317.

Guyer, B., Hoyert, D. L., Martin, J. A., Ventura, S. J., MacDorman, M. F., & Strobino, D. M. (1999). Annual summary of vital statistics—1998. *Pediatrics, 104,* 1229–1246.

Hack, M., & Fanaroff, A. A. (1999). Outcomes of children of extremely low birthweight and gestational age in the 1990's. *Early Human Development, 53,* 193–218.

Hack, M., Klein, N. C., & Taylor, H. G. (1995). Long-term developmental outcomes of low birth weight infants. *The Future of Children, 5,* 176–196.

Hahn, C., & DiPietro, J. A. (2001). In vitro fertilization and the family: Quality of parenting, family functioning, and child psychosocial adjustment. *Developmental Psychology, 37,* 37–48.

Hallgren, A., Kihlgren, M., Forslin, L., & Norberg, A. (1999). Swedish fathers' involvement in and experiences of childbirth preparation and childbirth. *Midwifery, 15,* 6–15.

Halpern, S. H., Leighton, B. L., Ohlsson A., Barrett, J. F., & Rice, A. (1998). Effect of epidural vs. parenteral opioid analgesia on the progress of labor: A meta-analysis. *Journal of the American Medical Association, 280,* 2105–2110.

Hansen, D., Lou, H. C., &Olsen, J. (2001). Serious life events and congenital malformations: A national study with complete followup. *Obstetrical & Gynecological Survey, 56,* 68–69.

Harrington, L. C., Miller, D. A., McClain, C. J., & Paul, R. H. (1997). Vaginal birth after cesarean in a hospital-based birth center staffed by certified nurse-midwives. *Journal of Nurse-Midwifery, 42,* 304–307.

Hart, M. A., & Foster, S. N. (1997). Couples' attitudes toward childbirth participation: Relationship to evaluation of labor and delivery. *Journal of Perinatal & Neonatal Nursing, 11,* 10–20.

Haug, K., Irgens, L. M., Skjaerven, R., Markestad, T., Baste, V., & Schreuder, P. (2000). Maternal smoking and birthweight: Effect modification of period, maternal age and paternal smoking. *Acta Obstetric Gynecology Scandinavia, 79,* 485–489.

Hodnett, E. D., & Osborn, R. W. (1989). A randomized trial of the effects of monitrice support during labor: Mothers' views two to four weeks postpartum. *Birth, 16,* 177–183.

Hogan, D. P., & Park, J. M. (2000). Family factors and social support in the developmental outcomes of very low-birth weight children. *Clinical Perinatology, 27,* 433–459.

Hughes, D., & Simpson, L. (1995). The role of social change in preventing low birth weight. *The Future of Children, 5,* 87–102.

Jacobson, J. L., & Jacobson, S. W. (1999). Drinking moderately and pregnancy: Effects on child development. *Alcohol Research and Health, 25,* 25–30.

Jacobson, J. L., Jacobson, S. W., Sokol, R. J., Martier, S. S., Ager, J. W., & Kaplan-Estrin, M. G. (1993). Teratogenic effects of alcohol on infant development. *Alcoholism: Clinical and Experimental Research, 17,* 174–183.

Jacobson, S. W., Fein, G. G., Jacobson, J. L., Schwartz, P. M., & Dowler, J. K. (1984). Neonatal correlates of exposure to smoking, caffeine, and alcohol. *Infant Behavior and Development, 7,* 253–265.

Jeffery, R., & Jeffery, P. M. (1993). Traditional birth attendants in rural north India: The social organization of childbearing. In S. Lindenbaum & M. Lock (Eds.), *Knowledge, power and practice: The anthropology of medicine and everyday life.* Berkeley: University of California Press.

Johanson, R. B., & Menon, B. K. (2000). Vacuum extraction versus forceps for assisted vaginal delivery. *Cochrane Database System Review,* 2:CD000224.

John Henry's NICU Story. (2000). Available online: http://members.aol.com/Suzanne900/index1.html

Kacew, S. (1999). Effect of over-the-counter drugs on the unborn child: What is known and how should this influence prescribing? *Paediatric Drugs, 1,* 75–80.

Källén, K. (1997). Maternal smoking during pregnancy and limb reduction malformations in Sweden. *American Journal of Public Health, 87,* 29–32.

Kaufman, R. H., Adam, E., Hatch, E. E., Noller, K., Herbst, A. L., Palmer, J. R., & Hoover, R. N. (2000). Continued follow-up of pregnancy outcomes in diethylstilbestrol-exposed offspring. *Obstetric Gynecology, 96,* 483–489.

Keller, R. & Snyder-Keller, A. (2000). Prenatal cocaine exposure. *Annals of New York Academy of Sciences,909,* 217–232.

Kelley-Buchanan, C. (1988). *Peace of mind during pregnancy: An A–Z guide to the substances that could affect your unborn baby.* New York: Facts on File.

Kennell, J., Klaus, M., McGrath, S., Robertson, S., & Hinkley, C. (1991). Continuous emotional support during labor in a US hospital: A randomized controlled trial. *Journal of the American Medical Association, 265,* 2197–2201.

Key, S. & DeNoon, D. (1998, January 12). Statistics show fewer babies born with HIV. *AIDS Weekly Plus,* p. 21.

Kochanevich-Wallace, P. M., McCluskey-Fawcett, K. A., Meck, N. E., & Simons, C. J. (1988). Method of delivery and parent–newborn interaction. *Journal of Pediatric Psychology, 13,* 213–221.

Koller, H., Lawson, K., Rose, S. A., Wallace, I., & McCarton, C. (1997). Patterns of cognitive development in very low birthweight children during the first six years of life. *Pediatrics, 99,* 383–389.

Konner, M. J. (1981). Evolution of human behavior development. In R. H. Munroe, R. L. Munroe, & B. B. Whiting (Eds.), *Handbook of cross-cultural human development.* New York: Garland STPM Press.

Kopp, C. B., & Kahler, S. R. (1989). Risk in infancy. *American Psychologist, 44,* 224–230.

Kowalski, K. A. (2000). High-tech conception in the 21st century. *Current Health (Human Sexuality Supplement), 26,* 1–4.

Lamaze, F. (1958). *Painless childbirth: Psychoprophylactic method.* London: Burke.

Lefkowitz, M. M. (1981). Smoking during pregnancy: Long-term effects on offspring. *Developmental Psychology, 17,* 192–194.

LeVine, R. A. (1974). Prenatal goals: A crosscultural view. *Teachers College Record, 76,* 226–239.

LeVine, R. A. (1988). Human parental care: Universal goals, cultural strategies, individual behavior. In R. A. LeVine, P. M. Miller, & M. M. West (Eds.), *Parental behavior in diverse societies: New directions for child development* (No. 40). San Francisco: Jossey-Bass.

Lindegren, M. L., Byers, R. H., Thomas, P., Davis, S. F., Caldwell, B., Rogers, M., Gwinn, M., Ward, J. W., & Fleming, P. L. (1999). Trends in perinatal transmission of HIV/AIDS in the United States. *Journal of the American Medical Association, 282,* 531–538.

Lobel, M. (1994). Conceptualizations, measurement, and effects of prenatal maternal stress on birth outcomes. *Journal of Behavioral Medicine, 17,* 225–272.

Lobel, M., DeVincent, C. J., Kaminer, A., & Meyer, B. A. (2000). The impact of prenatal maternal stress and optimistic disposition on birth outcomes in medically high-risk women. *Health Psychology, 19,* 544–553.

Lorenz, J. M. (2000). Survival of the extremely preterm infant in North America in the 1990s. *Clinics in Perinatology, 27,* 255–262.

Luke, B., Johnson, T., & Petrie, R. (1993). *Clinical maternal-fetal nutrition.* Boston: Little, Brown.

Lundy, B. L., Jones, N. A., Field, T., Nearing, G., Davalos, M., Pietro, P. A., Schanberg, S., & Kuhn, C. (1999). Prenatal depression effects on neonates. *Infant Behavior and Development, 22,* 119–129.

Macario, A., Scibetta, W. C., Navarro, J., & Riley, E. (2000). Analgesia for labor pain: A cost model. *Anesthesiology, 92,* 643–645.

MacFarlane, A. (1977). *The psychology of childbirth.* Cambridge, MA: Harvard University Press.

Mayes, L. C., Feldman, R., Granger, R. H., Haynes, O. M., Bornstein, M. H., & Schottenfeld, R. (1997). The effects of polydrug use with and without cocaine on mother–infant interaction at 3 and 6 months. *Infant Behavior and Development, 20,* 489–502.

McCarton, C. M., Brooks-Gunn, J., Wallace, I. F., Bauer, C. R., Bennett, F. C., Bernbaum, J. C., Broyles, S., Casey, P. H., McCormick, M. C., Scott, D. T., Tyson, J., Tonascia, J., & Meinert, C. L. (1997). Results at age 8 years of early intervention for low-birth-weight premature infants. *Journal of the American Medical Association, 277,* 126–132.

McCubbin, J. A., Lawson, E. J., Cox, S., Sherman, J. J., Norton, J. A., & Read, J. A. (1996). Prenatal maternal blood pressure response to stress predicts birth weight and gestational age: A preliminary study. *American Journal of Obstetrics and Gynecology, 175,* 706–712.

Miceli, P. J., Goeke-Morey, M. C., Whitman, T. L., Kolberg, K. S., Miller-Loncar, C., & White, R. D. (2000). Brief report: Birth status, medical complications, and social environment: Individual differences in development of preterm, very low birth weight infants. *Journal of Pediatric Psychology, 25,* 353–358.

Mishra, G. D., Dobson, A. J., & Schofield, M. J. (2000). Cigarette smoking, menstrual symptoms and miscarriage among young women. *Australian-New Zealand Journal of Public Health, 24,* 413–420.

Molnar, A. M., Oliver, L. M., & Geyman, J. P. (2000). Patient preferences for management of first-trimester incomplete spontaneous abortion. *Journal of American Board of Family Practice, 13,* 333–337.

Monk, C., Fifer, W. P., Myers, M. M., Sloan, R. P., Trien, L., & Hurtado, A. (2000). Maternal stress responses and anxiety during pregnancy: Effects on fetal heart rate. *Developmental Psychobiology, 36,* 67–77.

Moore, K. L. (1977). *The developing human.* Philadelphia: W. B. Saunders.

Morelli, G. A., Rogoff, B., Oppenheim, D., & Goldsmith, D. (1992). Cultural variation in infants' sleeping arrangements: Questions of independence. *Developmental Psychology, 28,* 604–613.

Morris, J. (1999, October 18). Assessing children's toxic risks. *U.S. News & World Report,* p. 80.

Murphy, S. L. (2000). Deaths: Final data for 1998. *National Vital Statistics Report, 48,* 1–105.

Murray, L., Sinclair, D., Cooper, P., Ducournau, P., Turner, P., & Stein, A. (1999). The socioemotional development of 5-year-old children of postnatally depressed mothers. *Journal of Child Psychology & Psychiatry, 40,* 1259–1271.

Myers, R. E., & Myers, S. E. (1979). Use of sedative, analgesic, and anesthetic drugs during labor and delivery: Bane or boon. *American Journal of Obstetrics and Gynecology, 133,* 83–104.

Najman, J. M., Williams, G. M., Nikles, J., Spence, S., Bor, W., O'Callaghan, M., Le Brocque, R., & Andersen, M. J. (2000). Mothers' mental illness and child behavior problems: Cause–effect association or observation bias? *Journal of the American Academy of Child & Adolescent Psychiatry, 39,* 592–602.

Nichols, M. (1999). Clinging to life. *Maclean's, 112,* 66.

Nordentoft, M., Lou, H. C., Hansen, D., Nim, J., Pryds, O., Rubin, P., & Hemmingsen, R. (1996). Intrauterine growth retardation and premature delivery: The influence of maternal smoking and psychosocial factors. *American Journal of Public Health, 86,* 347–354.

Nsamenang, A. B. (1992). *Human development in cultural context: A third world perspective.* Newbury Park, CA: Sage.

O'Dempsey, T. J. D. (1988). Traditional belief and practice among the Pokot people of Kenya with particular reference to mother and child health: 2. Mother and child health. *Annals of Tropical Paediatrics, 8,* 125.

O'Grady, J. P., Pøpe, C. S., & Patel, S. S. (2000). Vacuum extraction in modern obstetric practice: A review and critique. *Current Opinion in Obstetric Gynecology, 12,* 475–480.

O'Hara, M. W., Schlechte, J. A., Lewis, D. A., & Varner, M. W. (1991). Controlled prospective study of postpartum mood disorders: Psychological, environmental, and hormonal variables. *Journal of Abnormal Psychology, 100,* 63–73.

Olds, D. L., Henderson, C. R., Jr., & Tatelbaum, R. (1994). Prevention of intellectual impairment in children of women who smoke cigarettes during pregnancy. *Pediatrics, 93,* 228–233.

Orvus, H., Nyirati, I., Hajdu, J., Pal, A., & Kovacs, L. (1999). Is adolescent pregnancy associated with adverse perinatal outcome? *Journal of Perinatal Medicine, 27,* 199–203.

Paarlberg, K. M., Vingerhoets, J. J. M., Passchier, J., Dekker, G. A., & van Geijn, H. P. (1995). Psychosocial factors and pregnancy outcome: A review with emphasis on methodological issues. *Journal of Psychosomatic Research, 39,* 563–595.

Paneth, N. S. (1995). The problem of low birth weight. *The Future of Children, 5,* 19–34.

Parazzini, F., Luchini, L., La Vecchia, C., & Crosignani, P. G. (1993). Video display terminal use during pregnancy and reproductive outcomes: A meta-analysis. *Journal of Epidemiology and Community Health, 47,* 265–268.

Pollack, H., Lantz, P. M., & Fruhna, J. G. (2000). Maternal smoking and adverse birth outcomes among singletons and twins. *American Journal of Public Health, 90,* 395–400.

Post, T. (1994, November 28). Quality not quantity. *Newsweek,* pp. 36–37.

Ratcliffe, S. D., Byrd, J. E., & Sakornbut, E. L. (1996). *Handbook of pregnancy and perinatal care in family practice: Science and practice.* Philadelphia: Hanley & Belfus.

Reed, R. (1996, Spring). Birthing fathers. *Mothering,* pp. 50–55.

Reichman, N. E., & Pagnini, D. L. (1997). Maternal age and birth outcomes: Data from New Jersey. *Family Planning Perspectives, 29,* 268–273.

Reifsnider, E., & Gill, S. L. (2000). Nutrition for the childbearing years. *JOGNN, 29,* 43–55.

Richman, A. L., LeVine, R. A., New, R. S., Howrigan, G. A., Welles-Nystrom, B., & LeVine, S. E. (1988). Maternal behavior to infants in five cultures. In R. A. LeVine, P. M. Miller & M. M. West (Eds.), *Parental behavior in diverse societies: New directions for child development* (No. 40). San Francisco: Jossey-Bass.

Richman, A. L., Miller, P. M., & LeVine, R. A. (1992). Cultural and educational variations in maternal responsiveness. *Developmental Psychology, 28,* 614–621.

Rodier, P. M. (2000). The early origins of autism. *Scientific American, 282,* 56–63.

Rolater, S. (2000). One drink too many: Is there no safe level of alcohol consumption during pregnancy? *American Journal of Nursing, 100,* 64–66.

Rossner, S. (1998). Obesity and pregnancy. In G. Bray, C. Bouchard, & W. James (Eds.), *Handbook of obesity* (pp. 775–790). New York: Marcel Dekker.

Rothberg, A. D., & Lits, B. (1991). Psychosocial support for maternal stress during pregnancy: Effect on birth weight. *American Journal of Obstetrics and Gynecology, 165,* 403–407.

Russell, C. (1995, March 28). Baby study links busy days, fussy nights. *Washington Post Health,* p. 7.

Rutter, M. (1996). Romanian orphans adopted early overcome deprivation. *Brown University Children & Adolescent Behavior Letter, 12,* 1–3.

Rutter, M. (1998). Developmental catch-up, and deficit, following adoption after severe global early privation. *Journal of Child Psychology & Psychiatry & Allied Disciplines, 39,* 465–476.

Sadler, T. W. (1996). Embryology and experimental teratology. In J. A. Kuller, N. C. Chescheir, & R. C. Cefalo (Eds.), *Prenatal diagnosis and reproductive genetics.* St. Louis: Mosby.

Saigal, S., Hoult, L. A., Stoskopf, B. L., Rosenbaum, P. L., & Streiner, D. L. (2000). School difficulties at adolescence in a regional cohort of children who were extremely low birth weight. *Pediatrics, 105,* 325–331.

Sameroff, A. J., & Chandler, M. J. (1975). Reproductive risk and the continuum of caretaking casualty. In F. D. Horowitz, M. Hetherington, S. Scarr-Salapatek, & G. Siegel (Eds.), *Review of child development research* (Vol. 4). Chicago: University of Chicago Press.

Scafidi, F. A., Field, T. M., Schanberg, S. M., Bauer, C. R., Vega-Lahr, N., Garcia, R., Poirier, J., Nystrom, G., & Kuhn, C. M. (1986). Effects of tactile/kinesthetic stimulation on the clinical course and sleep/wake behavior of preterm neonates. *Infant Behavior and Development, 9,* 91–105.

Scafidi, F. A., Field, T. M., Schanberg, S. M., Bauer, C. R., Vega-Lahr, N., Garcia, R., Poirer, J., Nystrom, G., & Kuhn, C. M. (1990). Massage stimulates growth in preterm infants: A replication. *Infant Behavior and Development, 13,* 167–188.

Schaefer, M., Hatcher, R. P., & Barglow, P. D. (1980). Prematurity and infant stimulation: A review of research. *Child Psychiatry and Human Development, 10,* 199–212.

Schnoll, S. H. (1986). Pharmacologic basis of perinatal addiction. In I. J. Chasnoff (Ed.), *Drug use in pregnancy: Mother and child.* Boston: MTP Press.

Schuetze, P., & Zesking, P. S. (1997). Relation between reported maternal caffeine consumption during pregnancy and neonatal state and heart rate. *Infant Behavior and Development, 20,* 559–562.

Scott, K. D., Klaus, P. H., & Klaus, M. H. (1999). The obstetrical and postpartum benefits of continuous support during childbirth. *Journal of Women's Health and Gender Based Medicine, 8,* 1257–1264.

Sheiner, E., Shoham-Vardi, I., Sheiner, E. K., Press, F., Hackmon-Ram, R., Mazor, M., & Katz, M. (2000). A comparison between the effectiveness of epidural analgesia and parenteral pethidine during labor. *Archives of Gynecology & Obstetrics, 263,* 95–98.

Simpson, K. R., & Crechan, P. A. (1996). *Perinatal nursing.* Philadelphia: Lippincott-Raven.

Singer, L. T., Arendt, R., Fagan, J., Minnes, S., Salvator, A., Bolek, T., & Becker, M. (1999). Neonatal visual information processing in cocaine-exposed and non-exposed infants. *Infant Behavior and Development, 22,* 1–15.

Slotkin, T. A. (1998). Fetal nicotine or cocaine exposure: Which one is worse? *Journal of Pharmacology and Experimental Therapy, 285,* 931–945.

Smotherman, W. P., & Robinson, S. R. (1996). The development of behavior before birth. *Developmental Psychology, 32,* 425–434.

Somers-Smith, M. J. (1999). A place for the partner? Expectations and experiences of support during childbirth. *Midwifery, 15,* 101–108.

Sorensen, L. C., & Borch, K. (1999). Neonatal asphyxia—prognosis based on clinical findings during delivery and the first day of life: A retrospective study of 54 newborn infants with asphyxia. *Ugeskr Laeger, 161,* 3094–3098.

Spiby, H., Henderson, B., Slade, P., Escott, D., & Fraser, R. B. (1999). Strategies for coping with labour: Does antenatal education translate into practice? *Journal of Advanced Nursing, 29,* 388–394.

Spreen, O., Tupper, D., Risser, A., Tuokko, H., & Edgell, D. (1984). *Human developmental neuropsychology.* New York: Oxford University Press.

Stanner, S. A., Bulmer, K., Andres, C., Lantseva, O. E., Borodina, V., Poteen, V. V., & Yudkin, J. S. (1997). Does malnutrition in utero determine diabetes and coronary heart disease in adulthood? Results from the Leningrad siege study, a cross sectional study. *British Medical Journal, 315,* 1342–1348.

Stein, Z. A., & Susser, M. W. (1976). Prenatal nutrition and mental competence. In J. D. Lloyd-Still (Ed.), *Malnutrition and intellectual development.* Littleton, MA: Publishing Sciences Group.

Stein, Z. A., Susser, M. W., Saenger, G., & Marolla, F. (1975). *Famine and human development: The Dutch hunger winter of 1944–1945.* New York: Oxford University Press.

Steinberg, E. P., Holtz, P. M., Sullivan, E. M., & Villar, C. P. (1998). Profiling assisted reproductive technology: Outcomes and quality of infertility management. *Fertility and Sterility, 69,* 617–623.

Steinberg, S. (1996). Childbearing research: A transcultural review. *Social Science and Medicine, 43,* 1765–1784.

Stone, R. (1992). Can a father's exposure lead to illness in his children? *Science, 258,* 31.

Stratton, K., Howe, C., & Battaglia, F. (Eds.). (1996). *Fetal alcohol syndrome: Diagnosis, epidemiology, prevention, and treatment.* Washington, DC: National Academy Press.

Streissguth, A. P., Barr, H. M., Bookstein, F. L., Sampson, P. D., & Olson, H. C. (1999). The long-term neurocognitive consequences of prenatal alcohol exposure: A 14-year study. *Psychological Science, 10,* 186–190.

Streissguth, A. P., & Dehaene, P. (1993). Fetal alcohol syndrome in twins of alcoholic mothers: Concordance of diagnosis and IQ. *American Journal of Medical Genetics, 47,* 857–861.

Streissguth, A. P., Randels, S. P., & Smith, D. F. (1991). A test–retest study of intelligence in patients with fetal alcohol syndrome: Implications for care. *Journal of the American Academy of Child and Adolescent, 30,* 584–587.

Streissguth, A. P., Sampson, P. D., Barr, H. M., Bookstein, F. L., & Olson, H. C. (1994). The effects of prenatal exposure to alcohol and tobacco: Contributions from the Seattle Longitudinal Prospective Study and implications for public policy. In H. L. Needlebaum & D. Bellinger (Eds.), *Prenatal exposure to toxicants.* Baltimore: Johns Hopkins University Press.

Strigini, P., Sansone, R., Carobbi, S., & Pierluigi, M. (1990). Radiation and Down's syndrome. *Nature, 347,* 717.

Super, C. M., & Harkness, S. (1981). Figure, ground, and Gestalt: The cultural context of the active individual. In R. M. Lerner & N. A. Busch-Rossnagel (Eds.), *Individuals as producers of their development: A life-span perspective.* New York: Academic Press.

Susser, M., & Stein, Z. (1994). Timing in prenatal nutrition: A reprise of the Dutch Famine Study. *Nutrition Reviews, 52,* 84–94.

Teixeira, J. M., Fisk, N. M., & Glover, V. (1999). Association between maternal anxiety in pregnancy and increased uterine artery resistance index: Cohort based study. *British Medical Journal, 318,* 153–157.

Thorne, C., & Newell, M. (2000). Epidemiology of HIV infection in the newborn. *Early Human Development, 58,* 1–16.

Tronick, E. Z., & Beeghly, M. (1999). Prenatal cocaine exposure, child development, and the compromising effects of cumulative risk. *Clinics in Perinatology, 26,* 151–171.

Van Beveren, T. T., Little, B. B., & Spence, M. (2000). Effects of prenatal cocaine exposure and postnatal environment on child development. *American Journal of Human Biology, 12,* 417–428.

Vaughn, B. E., Bradley, C. F., Joffe, L. S., Seifer, R., & Barglow, P. (1987). Maternal characteristics measured prenatally are predictive of ratings of temperament "difficulty" on the Carey Infant Temperament Questionnaire. *Develepmental Psychology, 23,* 152–161.

Ventura, S., Martin, J., Curtin, S., Menacker, F., & Hamilton, B. E. (2001). Births: Final data for 1999. *National Vital Statistics Report, 49,* 1–100.

Vorhees, C. V., & Mollnow, E. (1987). Behavioral teratogenesis: Long-term influences on behavior from early exposure to environmental agents. In J. D. Osofsky (Ed.), *Handbook of infant development* (2nd ed.). New York: Wiley.

Wachs, T. D. (1995). Relation of mild-to-moderate malnutrition to human development: Correlational studies. *Journal of Nutrition Supplement, 125,* 2245S–2254S.

Waldenström, U., Borg, I., Olsson, B., Sköld, M., & Wall, S. (1996). The childbirth experience: A study of 295 new mothers. *Birth, 23,* 144–153.

Werner, E. E. (1989a). Children of the Garden Island. *Scientific American, 260,* 106–111.

Werner, E. E. (1989b). High-risk children in young adulthood: A longitudinal study from birth to 32 years. *American Journal of Orthopsychiatry, 59,* 72–81.

Werner, E. E., & Smith, R. S. (1982). *Vulnerable but invincible: A longitudinal study of resilient children and youth.* New York: McGraw-Hill.

Werner, E. E., & Smith, R. S. (1992). *Overcoming the odds: High risk children from birth to adulthood.* Ithaca, NY: Cornell University Press.

Widmayer, S., & Field, T. (1980). Effects of Brazelton demonstrations on early interactions of preterm infants and their teenage mothers. *Infant Behavior and Development, 3,* 79–89.

Wilcock, A., Kobayashi, L., & Murray, I. (1997). Twenty-five years of obstetric patient satisfaction in North America: A review of the literature. *Journal of Perinatal and Neonatal Nursing, 10,* 36–47.

Wilson, R. S. (1985). Risk and resilience in early mental development. *Developmental Psychology, 21,* 795–805.

Winn, H. N., & Hobbins, J. C. (Eds.). (2000). *Clinical maternal-fetal medicine.* London: Parthenon.

Wisborg, K., Kesmodel, U., Henriksen, T. B., Olsen, S. F., & Secher, N. J. (2000). A prospective study of smoking during pregnancy and SIDS. *Archives of Disease in Childhood, 83,* 203–206.

Wright, K. (2000). Thalidomide is back. *Discover, 21,* 31–33.

Zander, L., & Chamberlain, G. (1999). Place of birth. *British Medical Journal, 318,* 721.

Chapter 5: The Physical Self

Ackerman, S. (1992). *Discovering the brain.* Washington, DC: National Academy of Sciences.

Adler, S. R., Fosket, J. R., Kagawa-Singer, M., McGraw, S. A., Wong-Kim, E., Gold, E., & Sternfeld, B. (2000). Conceptualizing menopause and midlife: Chinese American and Chinese women in the U.S. *Maturitas, 35,* 11–23.

Adolph, K. E. (1997). Learning in the development of infant locomotion. *Monographs of the Society for Research in Child Development, 61*(Serial No. 251).

Adolph, K. E., & Avolio, A. M. (2000). Walking infants adapt locomotion to changing body dimensions. *Journal of Experimental Psychology: Human Perception and Performance, 26,* 1148–1166.

Ainscough, C. E. (1990). Premenstrual emotional changes: A prospective study of symptomatology in normal women. *Journal of Psychosomatic Research, 34,* 35–45.

Archer, J. (1991). The influence of testosterone on human aggression. *British Journal of Psychology, 82,* 1–28.

Arlt, W., Callies, F., van Vlijmen, J. C., Koehler, I., Reincke, M., Bidlingmaier, M., Huebler, D., Oettel, M., Ernst, M., Schulte, H. M., & Allolio, B. (1999). Dehydroepiandrosterone replacement in women with adrenal insufficiency. *New England Journal of Medicine, 341,* 1013–1020.

Aylward, G. P. (1997). *Infant and early childhood neuropsychology.* New York: Plenum.

Baird, A. A., Gruber, S. A., Fein, D. A., Maas, L. C., Steingard, R. J., Renshaw, P. F., Cohen, B. M., & Yurgelun-Todd, D. A. (1999). Functional magnetic resonance imaging of facial affect recognition in children and adolescents. *Journal of the American Academy of Child and Adolescent Psychiatry, 38,* 195–199.

Barbach, L. G. (2000). *The pause: Positive approaches to perimenopause and menopause.* New York: Plume.

Bartlett, D. (1997). Primitive reflexes and early motor development. *Journal of Developmental and Behavioral Pediatrics, 18,* 151–157.

Bayley, N. (1993). *Bayley scales of infant development* (2nd ed.). San Antonio: Psychological Corporation.

Benes, F. M. (1998). Human brain growth spans decades. *American Journal of Psychiatry, 155,* 1489.

Bertenthal, B. I., Campos, J. J., & Kermoian, R. (1994). An epigenetic perspective on the development of self-produced locomotion and its consequences. *Current Directions in Psychological Science, 3,* 140–145.

Bertenthal, B. I., & von Hofsten, C. (1998). Eye, head and trunk control: The foundation for manual development. *Neuroscience and Biobehavioral Reviews, 22,* 515–520.

Birren, J. E., Butler, R. N., Greenhouse, S. W., Sokoloff, L., & Yarrow, M. R. (Eds.). (1963). *Human aging: A biological and behavioral study.* Washington, DC: U.S. Government Printing Office.

Birren, J. E., & Fisher, L. M. (1995). Aging and speed of behavior: Possible consequences for psychological functioning. *Annual Review of Psychology, 46,* 329–353.

Black, J. E., Isaacs, K. R., & Greenough, W. T. (1991). Usual vs. successful aging: Some notes on experiential factors. *Neurobiology of Aging, 12,* 325–328.

Bondareff, W. (1985). The neural basis of aging. In J. E. Birren & K. W. Schaie (Eds.), *Handbook of the psychology of aging* (2nd ed.). New York: Van Nostrand Reinhold.

Boodman, S. G. (1995, June 13). Researchers study obesity in children. *Washington Post Health,* pp. 10–15.

Bower, T. G. R. (1982). *Development in infancy* (2nd ed.). San Francisco: Freeman.

Brody, J. A., Grant, M. D., Frateschi, L. J., Miller, S. C., & Zhang, H. (2000). Reproductive longevity and increased life expectancy. *Age and Ageing, 29,* 75–78.

Brown, J. L. (1964). States in newborn infants. *Merrill-Palmer Quarterly, 10,* 313–327.

Buchanan, C. M., Eccles, J. S., & Becker, J. B. (1992). Are adolescents the victims of raging hormones? Evidence for activational effects of hormones on moods and behavior at adolescence. *Psychological Bulletin, 111,* 62–107.

Buchner, D. M. (1997). Preserving mobility in older adults. *Western Journal of Medicine, 167,* 258–264.

Bulcroft, R. A. (1991). The value of physical change in adolescence: Consequences for the parent–adolescent exchange relationship. *Journal of Youth and Adolescence, 20,* 89–105.

Bushnell, E. M., & Boudreau, J. P. (1993). Motor development in the mind: The potential role of motor abilities as a determinant of aspects of perceptual development. *Child Development, 64,* 1005–1021.

Carskadon, M. A., Harvey, K., Duke, P., Anders, T. F., Litt, I. F., & Dement, W. C. (1980). Pubertal changes in daytime sleepiness. *Sleep, 2,* 453–460.

Carskadon, M. A., Vieira, C., & Acebo, C. (1993). Association between puberty and delayed phase preference. *Sleep, 16,* 258–262.

Casey, B. J., Giedd, J. N., & Thomas, K. M. (2000). Structural and functional brain development and its relation to cognitive development. *Biological Psychology, 54,* 241–257.

Cherry, K. E., & Morton, M. R. (1989). Drug sensitivity in older adults: The role of physiologic and pharmacokinetic factors. *International Journal of Aging and Human Development, 28,* 159–174.

Christofalo, V. J. (1988). An overview of the theories of biological aging. In J. E. Birren & V. L. Bengtson (Eds.), *Emergent theories of aging.* New York: Springer.

Clark, D. O., & Maddox, G. L. (1992). Racial and social correlates of age-related changes in functioning. *Journal of Gerontology: Social Sciences, 47,* S222–S232.

Cleckner-Smith, C. S., Doughty, A. S., & Grossman, J. A. (1998). Premenstrual symptoms: Prevalence and severity in an adolescent sample. *Journal of Adolescent Health, 22,* 403–408.

Condon, J. T. (1993). The premenstrual syndrome: A twin study. *British Journal of Psychiatry, 162,* 481–486.

Coren, S., Porac, C., & Duncan, P. (1981). Lateral preference behaviors in preschool children and young adults. *Child Development, 52,* 443–450.

Courchesne E., and others. (2000). Normal brain development and aging: Quantitative analysis at in vivo MR imaging in healthy volunteers. *Radiology, 216,* 672–682.

Cunningham, D. A., Rechnitzer, P. A., Pearce, M. E., & Donner, A. P. (1982). Determinants of self-selected walking pace across ages 19 to 66. *Journal of Gerontology, 37,* 560–564.

Cyr, M., Calon, F., Morissette, M., Grandbois, M., Di Paolo, T., & Callier, S. (2000). Drugs with estrogen-like potency and brain activity: Potential therapeutic application for the CNS. *Current Pharmaceutical Design, 6,* 1287–1312.

Dahl, R. E. (1999). The consequences of insufficient sleep for adolescents: Links between sleep and emotional regulation. *Phi Delta Kappan, 80,* 354–359.

de Bode, S., & Curtiss, S. (2000). Language after hemispherectomy. *Brain Cognition, 43,* 135–138.

Diamond, J. (1997). *Male menopause.* Naperville, IL: Sourcebooks.

Dimmock, P. W., Wyatt, K. M., Jones, P. W., & O'Brien, P. M. S. (2000). Efficacy of selective serotonin-reuptake inhibitors in premenstrual syndrome: A systematic review. *Lancet, 356,* 1131–1136.

Dosoky, M., & Amoudi, F. (1997). Menarcheal age of school girls in the city of Jeddah, Saudia Arabia. *Journal of Obstetrics & Gynaecology, 17,* 195–198.

Dubas, J. S., Graber, J. A., & Petersen, A. C. (1991). The effects of pubertal development on achievement during adolescence. *American Journal of Education, 99,* 444–460.

Dustman, R. E., Emmerson, R. Y., Steinhaus, L. A., Shearer, D. E., & Dustman, T. J. (1992). The effects of videogame playing on neuropsychological performance of elderly individuals. *Journal of Gerontology, 47,* 168–171.

Dustman, R. E., Ruhling, R. O., Russell, E. M., Shearer, D. E., Bonekat, H. W., Shigeoka, J. W., Wood, J. S., & Bradford, D. C. (1989). Neurobiology of aging. In A. C. Ostrow (Ed.), *Aging and motor behavior.* Indianapolis: Benchmark Press.

Dwyer, J. T., & Stone, E. J. (2000). Prevalence of marked overweight and obesity in a multi-ethnic pediatric population: Findings from the Child and Adolescent Trial for Cardiovascular Health (CATCH) study. *Journal of the American Dietetic Association, 100,* 1149–1155.

Earles, J. L., & Salthouse, T. A. (1995). Interrelations of age, health, and speed. *Journal of Gerontology: Psychological Sciences and Social Sciences, 50,* P33–P41.

Eaton, W. O., & Ritchot, K. F. M. (1995). Physical maturation and information-processing speed in middle childhood. *Developmental Psychology, 31,* 967–972.

Eliot, L. (1999). *What's going on in there? How the brain and mind develop in the first five years of life.* New York: Bantam.

Ellis, B. J., & Garber, J. (2000). Psychosocial antecedents of variation in girls' pubertal timing: Maternal depression, stepfather presence, and marital and family stress. *Child Development, 71,* 485–501.

Englander-Golden, P., Sonleitner, F. J., Whitmore, M. R., & Corbley, G. J. M. (1986). Social and menstrual cycles: Methodological and substantive findings. In V. L. Olesen & N. F. Woods (Eds.), *Culture, society, and menstruation.* Washington, DC: Hemisphere.

Epstein, H. T. (2001). An outline of the role of brain in human cognitive development. *Brain and Cognition, 45,* 44–51.

Eriksson, P. S., Perfilieva, E., Bjork-Eriksson, T., Alborn, A. M., Nordborg, C., Peterson, D. A., & Gage, F. H. (1998). Neurogenesis in the adult human hippocampus. *Natural Medicine, 4,* 1313–1317.

Faust, M. S. (1977). Somatic development of adolescent girls. *Monographs of the Society for Research in Child Development, 42*(Whole No. 169).

Federal Interagency Forum on Aging-Related Statistics. (2000). Older Americans 2000: Key indicators of well-being. Available online: http://www.agingstats.gov/chartbook2000/healthstatus.html

Fentress, J. C., & McLeod, P. J. (1986). Motor patterns in development. In E. M. Blass (Ed.), *Handbook of behavioral neurobiology: Vol. 8. Developmental psychobiology and developmental neurobiology.* New York: Plenum.

Flint, M. (1982). Male and female menopause: A cultural put-on. In A. M. Voda, M. Dinnerstein, & S. R. O'Donnell (Eds.), *Changing perspectives on menopause.* Austin: University of Texas Press.

Forys, K., & Rider, E. (2000, April). *Factors influencing self-esteem during the transition from elementary to middle school.* Paper presented at the Annual Meeting of the Eastern Psychological Assocation, Baltimore.

Foy, M. R., Henderson, V. W., Berger, T. W., & Thompson, R. F. (2000). Estrogen and neural plasticity. *Current Directions in Psychological Science, 9,* 148–152.

Francis, K. L., & Spirduso, W. W. (2000). Age differences in the expression of manual asymmetry. *Experimental Aging Research, 26,* 169–180.

Frankenburg, W. K., Dodds, J. B., Archer, P., Shapiro, H., & Bresnick, B. (1992). The Denver II: A major revision and restandardization of the Denver Development Screening Test. *Pediatrics, 89,* 91–97.

Franklin, M. B. (1995, April 25). New hope for osteoporosis sufferers? *Washington Post Health,* pp. 8–9.

Freedland, R. L., & Bertenthal, B. I. (1994). Developmental changes in interlimb coordination: Transition to hands-and-knees crawling. *Psychological Science, 5,* 26–32.

Gable, S., & Lutz, S. (2000). Household, parent, and child contributions to childhood obesity. *Family Relations, 49,* 293–300.

Gallant, S. J., & Derry, P. S. (1995). Menarche, menstruation, and menopause: Psychosocial research and future directions. In A. L. Stanton & S. J. Gallant (Eds.), *The Psychology of Women's Health* (pp. 199–259). Washington, DC: American Psychological Association.

Gannon, L., & Ekstrom, B. (1993). Attitudes toward menopause: The influence of sociocultural paradigms. *Psychology of Women Quarterly, 17,* 275–288.

Gazzaniga, M. S. (1998). The split brain revisited. *Scientific American, 279,* 50–55.

Gazzaniga, M. S. (2000). Regional differences in cortical organization. *Science, 289,* 1887–1888.

Geithner, C. A., Satake, T., Woynarowska, B., & Malina, R. M. (1999). Adolescent spurts in body dimensions: Average and modal sequences. *American Journal of Human Biology, 11,* 287–295.

German, P. S., Burton, L. C., Shapiro, S., Steinwachs, D. M., Tsuji, I., Paglia, M. J., & Damiano, A. M. (1995). Extended coverage for preventive services for the elderly: Response and results in a demonstration population. *American Journal of Public Health, 85,* 379–386.

Gold, E. B., Sternfeld, B., Kelsey, J. L., Brown, C., Mouton, C., Reame, N., Salamone, L., & Stellato, R. (2000). Relation of demographic and lifestyle factors to symptoms in a multiracial/ethnic population of women 40–55 years of age. *American Journal of Epidemiology, 152,* 463–473.

Goldberg, A. P., & Hagberg, J. M. (1990). Physical exercise in the elderly. In E. L. Schneider & J. W. Rowe (Eds.), *Handbook of the biology of aging* (3rd ed.). San Diego: Academic Press.

Gortmaker, S. L., Must, A., Sobol, A. M., Peterson, K., Colditz, G. A., & Dietz, W. H. (1996). Television viewing as a cause of increasing obesity among children in the United States. *Archives of Pediatric and Adolescent Medicine, 150,* 356–362.

Gould, D. C., Petty, R., & Jacobs, H. S. (2000). The male menopause—does it exist? *British Medical Journal, 320,* 858–861.

Graber, J. A., Lewinsohn, P. M., Seeley, J. R., & Brooks-Gunn, J. (1997). Is psychopathology associated with the timing of pubertal development? *Journal of the American Academy of Child and Adolescent Psychiatry, 36,* 1768–1776.

Gray, A., Berlin, J. A., McKinlay, J. B., & Longcope, C. (1991). An examination of research design effects on the association of testosterone and male aging: Results of a meta-analysis. *Journal of Clinical Epidemiology, 44,* 671–684.

Greene, J. G. (1984). *The social and psychological origins of the climacteric syndrome.* Hants, England & Brookfield, VT: Gower.

Greenough, W. T., Black, J. E., & Wallace, C. S. (1987). Experience and brain development. *Child Development, 58,* 539–559.

Grilo, C. M., & Pogue-Geile, M. F. (1991). The nature of environmental influences on weight and obesity: A behavior genetic analysis. *Psychological Bulletin, 110,* 520–537.

Grodstein, F., Manson, J. E., Colditz, G. A., Willett, W. C., Speizer, F. E., & Stampfer, M. J. (2000). A prospective, observational study of postmenopausal hormone therapy and primary prevention of cardiovascular disease. *Annals of Internal Medicine, 133,* 933–941.

Haber, D. (1994). *Health promotion and aging.* New York: Springer.

Haddow, J. F. (1999). Maternal thyroid deficiency during pregnancy and subsequent neuropsychological development of the child. *New England Journal of Medicine, 341,* 549–555.

Hales, D. (1997). *An invitation to health.* Pacific Grove, CA: Brooks/Cole.

Hall, J. G. (2000). Folic acid: The opportunity that still exists. *Canadian Medical Association Journal, 162,* 571–572.

Halverson, H. M. (1931). An experimental study of prehension in infants by means of systematic cinema records. *Genetic Psychology Monographs, 10,* 107–286.

Harman, S. M., & Talbert, G. B. (1985). Reproductive aging. In C. E. Finch & E. L. Schneider (Eds.), *Handbook of the biology of aging* (2nd ed.). New York: Van Nostrand Reinhold.

Harper, S. (1999). Building an intergenerational activity program for older adults: Implications for physical activity. *Journal of Physical Education, Recreation & Dance, 70,* 68–70.

Harris, J. R., Pedersen, N. L., McClearn, G. E., Plomin, R., & Nesselroade, J. R. (1992). Age differences in genetic and environmental influences for health from the Swedish Adoption/Twin Study of Aging. *Journal of Gerontology: Psychological Sciences, 47,* P213–P220.

Hauspie, R. C., Chrzastek-Spruch, H., Verleye, G., Kozlowska, M. A., & Susanne, C. (1996). Determinants of growth in body length from birth to 6 years of age: A longitudinal study of Lublin children. *American Journal of Human Biology, 8,* 21–29.

Hayward, C., Killen, J. D., Wilson, D. M., Hammer, L. D., Litt, I. F., Kraemer, H. C., Haydel, F., Varady, A., & Taylor, C. B. (1997). Psychiatric risk associated with puberty in adolescent girls. *Journal of the American Academy of Child and Adolescent Psychiatry, 36,* 255–262.

Hellige, J. B. (1993) *Hemispheric asymmetry: What's right and what's left.* Cambridge, MA: Harvard University Press.

Henderson, J. E., & Goltzman, D. (Eds.). (2000). *The osteoporosis primer.* Cambridge, UK: Cambridge University Press.

Herkowitz, J. (1978). Sex-role expectations and motor behavior of the young child. In M. V. Ridenour (Ed.), *Motor development: Issues and applications.* Princeton, NJ: Princeton Book Company.

Herman-Giddens, M. E., Slora, E. J., Wasserman, R. C., Bourdony, C. J., Bhapkar, M. V., Koch, G. G., & Hasemeier, C. M. (1997). Secondary sexual characteristics and menses in young girls seen in office practice: A study from the Pediatric Research in Office Settings Network. *Pediatrics, 99,* 505–512.

Hobbs, F. B. (with B. L. Damon). (1996). *65+ in the United States.* Washington, DC: U.S. Bureau of the Census.

Hopwood, N. J., Kelch, R. P., Hale, P. M., Mendes, T. M., Foster, C. M., & Beitins, I. Z. (1990). The onset of human puberty: Biological and environmental factors. In J. Bancroft & J. M. Reinisch (Eds.), *Adolescence and puberty.* New York: Oxford University Press.

Houx, P. J., Vreeling, F. W., & Jolles, J. (1991). Rigorous health screening reduces age effect on memory scanning task. *Brain and Cognition, 15,* 246–260.

Hubel, D. H., & Wiesel, T. N. (1970). The period of susceptibility to the physiological effects of unilateral eye-closure in kittens. *Journal of Physiology, 206,* 419–436.

Hurd, L. C. (1999). "We're not old!" Older women's negotiation of aging and oldness. *Journal of Aging Studies, 13,* 419–439.

Huston, A. C., Wright, J. C., Marquis, J., & Green, S. B. (1999). How young children spend their time: Television and other activities. *Developmental Psychology, 35,* 912–925.

Janowsky, J. S., & Carper, R. (1996). Is there a neural basis for cognitive transitions in school-age children? In A. J. Sameroff & M. M. Haith (Eds.), *The five to seven year shift: The age of reason and responsibility.* Chicago: University of Chicago Press.

Johnson, M. H. (1997). *Developmental cognitive neuroscience.* Cambridge, MA: Blackwell.

Johnson, M. H. (1999). Cortical plasticity in normal and abnormal cognitive development: Evidence and working hypotheses. *Development and psychopathology, 11,* 419–437.

Jones, M. C. (1965). Psychological correlates of somatic development. *Child Development, 56,* 899–911.

Jungblut, P. R., Ostorne, J. A., Quigg, R. J., McNeal, M. A., Clauser, J., Muster, A. J., & McPherson, D. D. (2000). Echocardiographic Doppler evaluation of left ventricular diastolic filling in older, highly trained male endurance athletes. *Echocardiography, 17,* 7–16.

Kail, R. (1991). Developmental change in speed of processing during childhood and adolescence. *Psychological Bulletin, 109,* 490–501.

Kalat, J. W. (1998). *Biological psychology* (6th ed.). Belmont, CA: Wadsworth.

Kandel, E. R., & Jessell, T. (1991). Early experience and the fine tuning of synaptic connections. In E. R. Kandel, J. H. Schwartz, & T. Jessell (Eds.), *Principles of neural science* (3rd ed., pp. 945–958). Norwalk, CT: Appleton & Lange.

Kart, C. S., Metress, E. K., & Metress, S. P. (1992). *Human aging and chronic disease.* Boston: Jones and Bartlett.

Kempen, G. I-J. M., Ormel, J., & Relyveld, J. (1997). Adaptive responses among Dutch elderly: The impact of eight chronic medical conditions on health-related quality of life. *American Journal of Public Health, 87,* 38–44.

Kendler, K. S., Silberg, J. L., Neale, M. C., Kessler, R. C., Heath, A. C., & Eaves, L. J. (1992). Genetic and environmental factors in the aetiology of menstrual, premenstrual and neurotic symptoms: A population-based twin study. *Psychological Medicine, 22,* 85–100.

Keough, J., & Sugden, D. (1985). *Movement skill development.* New York: Macmillan.

King, A. C., Castro, C., Wilcox, S., Eyler, A. A., Sallis, J. F., & Brownson, R. C. (2000). Personal and environmental factors associated with physical inactivity among different racial-ethnic groups of U.S. middle-aged and older-aged women. *Health Psychology, 19,* 354–364.

King, A. C., Taylor, C. B., & Haskell, W. L. (1993). Effects of differing intensities and formats of 12 months of exercise training on psychological outcomes in older adults. *Health Psychology, 12,* 292–300.

Knecht, S., Deppe, M., Drager, B., Bobe, L., Lohmann, H., Ringelstein, E., & Henningsen, H. (2000). Language lateralization in healthy right-handers. *Brain, 123,* 74–81.

Koff, E., & Rierdan, J. (1995). Early adolescent girls' understanding of menstruation. *Women and Health, 22,* 1–19.

Kolb, B., & Whishaw, I. Q. (1998). Brain plasticity and behavior. *Annual Review of Psychology, 49,* 43–63.

Krucoff, C. (May 16, 2000). Good to the bone. *Washington Post Health,* p. 8.

Kwon, Y., & Lawson, A. (2000). Linking brain growth with the development of scientific reasoning ability and conceptual change during adolescence. *Journal of Research in Science Teaching, 37,* 44–62.

Lakatta, E. G. (1990). Heart and circulation. In E. L. Schneider & J. W. Rowe (Eds.), *Handbook of the biology of aging* (3rd ed.). San Diego: Academic Press.

Lampinen, P., Heikkinen, R., & Ruoppila, I. (2000). Changes in intensity of physical exercise as predictors of depressive symptoms among older adults: An eight-year follow-up. *Preventive Medicine, 30,* 371–380.

Lampl, M., Veldhuis, J. D., & Johnson, M. L. (1992). Saltation and stasis: A model of human growth. *Science, 258,* 801–803.

Lamy, P. P. (1986). The elderly and drug interactions. *Journal of the American Geriatrics Society, 34,* 586–592.

Langlois, J. A., Keyl, P. M., Guralnik, J. M., Foley, D. J., Marottoli, R. A., & Wallace, R. B. (1997). Characteristics of older pedestrians who have difficulty crossing the street. *American Journal of Public Health, 87,* 393–397.

Laumann, E. O., Paik, A., & Rosen, R. C. (1999). Sexual dysfunction in the United States: Prevalence and predictors. *Journal of the American Medical Association, 281,* 537–544.

Lewis, D. A., Sesack, S. R., Levey, A. I., & Rosenberg, D.R. (1998). Dopamine axons in primate prefrontal cortex: Specificity of distribution, synaptic targets, and development. *Advances in Pharmacology, 42,* 703–706.

Lima, S. D., Hale, S., & Myerson, J. (1991). How general is general slowing? Evidence from the lexical domain. *Psychology and Aging, 6,* 416–425.

Lipsitt, L. P. (1990). Learning processes in the human newborn: Sensitization, habituation and classical conditioning. *Annals of the New York Academy of Sciences, 608,* 113–127.

Livson, N., & Peskin, H. (1980). Perspectives on adolescence from longitudinal research. In J. Adelson (Ed.), *Handbook of adolescent psychology.* New York: Wiley.

Lock, M. (1993). *Encounters with aging: Mythologies of menopause in Japan and North America.* Berkeley: University of California Press.

Loovis, E. M., & Butterfield, S. A. (2000). Influence of age, sex, and balance on mature skipping by children in grades K–8. *Perceptual and Motor Skills, 90,* 974–978.

Lundy-Ekman, L. (1998). *Neuroscience: Fundamentals for rehabilitation.* Philadelphia: Saunders.

Magnusson, D. (1995). Individual development: A holistic, integrated model. In P. Moen, G. H. Elder, Jr., & K. Luscher (Eds.), *Examining lives in context: Perspectives on the ecology of human development.* Washington, DC: American Psychological Association.

Malina, R. M., & Bouchard, C. (1991). Growth, maturation, and physical activity. Champaign, IL: Human Kinetics Academic.

Marshall, W. A., & Tanner, J. M. (1970). Variation in the Pattern of Pubertal Changes in Boys, *Archives of Disease in Childhood.*

Masters, W. H., & Johnson, V. E. (1966). *Human sexual response.* Boston: Little, Brown.

Matthews, K. A. (1992). Myths and realities of the menopause. *Psychosomatic Medicine, 54,* 1–9.

Matthews, K. A., Wing, R. R., Kuller, L. H., Meilahn, E. N., Kelsey, S. F., Costello, E. J., & Caggiula, A. W. (1990). Influences of natural menopause on psychological characteristics and symptoms of middle-aged healthy women. *Journal of Consulting and Clinical Psychology, 58,* 345–351.

Maurer, D., & Maurer, C. (1988). *The world of the newborn.* New York: Basic Books.

McClintock, M. K., & Herdt, G. (1996). Rethinking puberty: The development of sexual attraction. *Current Directions in Psychological Science, 5,* 178–183.

McFarlane, J. A., & Williams, T. M. (1990). The enigma of premenstrual syndrome. *Canadian Psychology, 31,* 95–108.

McKinlay, S. M., Brambilla, D. J., & Posner, J. G. (1992). The normal menopause transition. *Maturitas, 14,* 103–115.

McMaster, J., Pitts, M., & Poyah, G. (1997). The menopausal experiences of women in a developing country—"There is a time for everything—To be a teenager, a mother and a granny." *Women & Health, 26,* 1–14.

Metz, M. E., & Miner, M. H. (1998). Psychosexual and psychosocial aspects of male aging and sexual health. *Canadian Journal of Human Sexuality, 7,* 245–259.

Minard, K. L., Freudigman, K., & Thoman, E. B. (1999). Sleep rhythmicity in infants: Index of stress or maturation. *Behavioural Processes, 47,* 189–206.

Molfese, D. L. (1977). Infant cerebral asymmetry. In S. J. Segalowitz & F. A. Gruber (Eds.), *Language development and neurological theory.* Orlando, FL: Academic Press.

Molina, B. S. G., & Chassin, L. (1996). The parent–adolescent relationship at puberty: Hispanic ethnicity and parent alcoholism as moderators. *Developmental Psychology, 32,* 675–686.

Moore, S. M. (1995). Girls' understanding and social constructions of menarche. *Journal of Adolescence, 18,* 87–104.

Morgan, M., Phillips, J. G., Bradshaw, J. L., Mattingley, J. B., Iansek, R., & Bradshaw, J. A. (1994). Age-related motor slowness: Simply strategic? *Journal of Gerontology, 49,* M133–M139.

Morse, C. A., Dudley, E., Guthrie, J., & Dennerstein, L. (1998). Relationships between premenstrual complaints and perimenopausal experiences. *Journal of Psychosomatic Obstetrics and Gynaecology, 19,* 182–191.

Morse, C. K. (1993). Does variability increase with age? An archival study of cognitive measures. *Psychology and Aging, 8,* 156–164.

Murray, M. P., Kory, R. C., & Clarkson, B. H. (1969). Walking patterns in healthy old men. *Journal of Gerontology, 24,* 169–178.

Must, A., Jacques, P. F., Dallal, G. E., Bajema, C. J., & Dietz, W. H. (1992). Long-term morbidity and mortality of overweight adolescents: A follow-up of the Harvard Growth Study of 1922 to 1935. *New England Journal of Medicine, 327,* 1350–1355.

National Academy of Sciences. (2000). *Sleep needs, patterns and difficulties of adolescents: Summary of a workshop.* Available online: http://www.nap.edu/openbook/030907177/html/3.html

National Center for Health Statistics. (2000a). Centers for Disease Control and Prevention growth charts. Available online: http://www.cdc.gov/growthcharts

National Center for Health Statistics. (2000b). *Health, United States, 2000.* Hyattsville, MD: U.S. Department of Health and Human Services.

National Institutes of Health, National Center on Sleep Disorders Research and Office of Prevention, Education, and Control (1997). *Working group report on problem sleepiness.* Washington, DC: U.S. Government Printing Office.

National Sleep Foundation. (2000). *Adolescent sleep needs and patterns: Research report and resource guide.* Washington, DC: Author.

Newstead, A. H., Walden, J. G., Wood, R. C., & Gitter, A. J. (2000). A comparison of gait parameters in older adults with and without a history of falls during various gate tasks. *Physical Therapy, 80,* 49.

Nilsson, M., Perfilieva, E., Johansson, U., Orwar, O., & Eriksson, P. S. (1999). Enriched environment increases neurogenesis in the adult rat dentate gyrus and improves spatial memory. *Journal of Neurobiology, 39,* 569–578.

Nowakowski, R. S. (1987). Basic concepts of CNS development. *Child Development, 58,* 568–595.

Nowakowski, R. S., & Hayes, N. L. (1999). CNS development: An overview. *Development and Psychopathology, 11,* 395–417.

Ochs, A. L., Newberry, J., Lenhardt, M. L., & Harkins, S. W. (1985). Neural and vestibular aging associated with falls. In J. E. Birren & K. W. Schaie (Eds.), *Handbook of the psychology of aging* (2nd ed.). New York: Van Nostrand Reinhold.

Paikoff, R. L., & Brooks-Gunn, J. (1991). Do parent–child relationships change during puberty? *Psychological Bulletin, 110,* 47–66.

Prebeg, Z., & Bralic, I. (2000). Changes in menarcheal age in girls exposed to war conditions. *American Journal of Human Biology, 12,* 503–508.

Rakic, P. (1991). Plasticity of cortical development. In S. E. Brauth, W. S. Hall, & R. J. Dooling (Eds.), *Plasticity of development*. Cambridge, MA: Bradford/MIT Press.

Rees, M. (1993). Menarche when and why? *Lancet, 342,* 1375–1376.

Resnick, S. M. (2000). One-year age changes in MRI brain volumes in older adults. *Cerebral Cortex, 10,* 464–72.

Richards, M. H., Boxer, A. W., Petersen, A. C., & Albrecht, R. (1990). Relation of weight to body image in pubertal girls and boys from two communities. *Developmental Psychology, 26,* 313–321.

Robertson, N. R. C. (1993). *A manual of neonatal intensive care* (3rd ed.). London: Edward Arnold.

Robinson, G. (1996). Cross-cultural perspectives on menopause. *Journal of Nervous and Mental Disease, 184,* 453–458.

Rose, S., & Maffulli, N. (1999). Hip fractures: An epidemiological review. *Bulletin of Joint Disease, 58,* 197–201.

Rosenfeld, R. G. (1997). Is growth hormone just a tall story? *Journal of Pediatrics, 130,* 172–174.

Rosetta, L. (1993). Female reproductive dysfunction and intense physical training. *Oxford Reviews of Reproductive Biology, 15,* 113–142.

Rowe, J. W. & Kahn, R. L. (1998). *Successful aging.* New York: Pantheon.

Ruchlin, H. S., & Lachs, M. S. (1999). Prevalence and correlates of exercise among older adults. *Journal of Applied Gerontology, 18,* 341–356.

Sadeh, A., Raviv, A., & Gruber, R. (2000). Sleep patterns and sleep disruptions in school-age children. *Developmental Psychology, 36,* 291–300.

Salthouse, T. A. (1984). Effects of age and skill in typing. *Journal of Experimental Psychology: General, 113,* 345–371.

Samson, M. M., Meeuwsen, I. B. A. E., Crowe, A., Dessens, J. A. G., Duursma, S. A., & Verhaar, H. J. J. (2000). Relationships between physical performance measures, age, height and body weight in healthy adults. *Age and Ageing, 29,* 235–242.

Saul, S. (1983). *Aging: An album of people growing old* (2nd ed.). New York: Wiley.

Sayre, N. E., & Gallagher, J. D. (2001). *The young child and the environment.* Boston: Allyn & Bacon.

Schairer, C., Lubin, J., Troisi, R., Sturgeon, S., Brinton, L., Hoover, R. (2000). Menopausal estrogen and estrogen-progestin replacement therapy and breast cancer risk. *Journal of the American Medical Association, 283,* 485–491.

Schiavi, R. C., Schreiner-Engel, P., White, D., & Mandeli, J. (1991). The relationship between pituitary-gonadal function and sexual behavior in healthy aging men. *Psychosomatic Medicine, 53,* 363–374.

Schmidt, P. J., Nieman, L. K., Danaceau, M. A., Adams, L. F., & Rubinow, D. R. (1998). Differential behavioral effects of gonadal steroids in women with and in those without premenstrual syndrome. *New England Journal of Medicine, 338,* 209–216.

Segalowitz, S. J., Unsal, A., & Dywan, J. (1992). Cleverness and wisdom in 12-year-olds: Electrophysiological evidence for late maturation of the frontal lobe. *Developmental Neuropsychology, 8,* 279–298.

Seiffge-Krenke, I. (1998). *Adolescents' health: A developmental perspective.* Mahwah, NJ: Erlbaum.

Selkoe, D. J. (1992). Aging brain, aging mind. *Scientific American, 267,* 135–142.

Sharpe, P. A., Jackson, K. L., White, C., Vaca, V. L., Hickey, T., Gu, J., & Otterness, C. (1997). Effects of a one-year physical activity intervention for older adults at congregate nutrition sites. *Gerontologist, 37,* 208–215.

Shaw, C. (1997). The perimenopausal hot flash: Epidemiology, physiology, and treatment. *Nurse Practitioner, 22,* 55–66.

Shepard, R. J. (1997). Curricular physical activity and academic performance. *Pediatric Exercise Science, 9,* 113–126.

Shumway-Cook, A., Brauer, S., & Woollacott, M. (2000). Predicting the probability for falls in community-dwelling older adults using the timed up & go test. *Physical Therapy, 80,* 896–902.

Siegel, A. C., & Burton, R. V. (1999). Effects of baby walkers on motor and mental development in human infants. *Journal of Developmental and Behavioural Pediatrics, 20,* 355–361.

Simmons, R. G., & Blyth, D. A. (1987). *Moving into adolescence: The impact of pubertal change and school context.* New York: Hawthorne, Aldine de Gruyter.

Singh, B., Berman, B. M., Simpson, R. L., & Annechild, A. (1998). Incidence of premenstrual syndrome and remedy usage: A national probability sample study. *Alternative Therapeutic Health Medicines, 4,* 75–79.

Sliwinski, M., Buschke, H., Kuslansky, G., Senior, G., & Scarisbrick, D. (1994). Proportional slowing and addition speed in old and young adults. *Psychology and Aging, 9,* 72–80.

Smith, L. B., & Thelen, E. (1993). *A dynamic systems approach to development: Applications.* Cambridge, MA: MIT Press.

Smoll, F. L., & Schutz, R. W. (1990). Quantifying gender differences in physical performance: A developmental perspective. *Developmental Psychology, 26,* 360–369.

Somsen, R. J. M., van Klooster, B. J., van der Molen, M. W., van Leeuwen, H. M. P., & Licht, R. (1997). Growth spurts in brain maturation during middle childhood as indexed by EEG power spectra. *Biological Psychology, 44,* 187–209.

Sparling, P. B., O'Donnell, E. M., & Snow, T. K. (1998). The gender difference in distance running performance has plateaued: An analysis of world rankings from 1980 to 1996. *Medicine and Science in Sports and Exercise, 30,* 1725–1729.

Spear, L. P. (2000a). The adolescent brain and age-related behavioral manifestations. *Neuroscience and Biobehavioral Reviews, 24,* 417–463.

Spear, L. P. (2000b). Neurobehavioral changes in adolescence. *Current Directions in Psychological Science, 9,* 111–114.

Spirduso, W. W., & MacRae, P. G. (1990). Motor performance and aging. In J. E. Birren & K. W. Schaie (Eds.), *Handbook of the psychology of aging* (3rd ed.). San Diego: Academic Press.

Springer, S., & Deutsch, G. (1997). *Left brain, right brain: Perspectives from cognitive neuroscience* (5th ed.). New York: W. H. Freeman.

Stattin, H., & Magnusson, D. (1990). *Paths through life: Vol 2. Pubertal maturation in female development.* Hillsdale, NJ: Erlbaum.

Stein, J. H., & Reiser, L. W. (1994). A study of white middle-class adolescent boys' responses to "semenarche" (the first ejaculation). *Journal of Youth and Adolescence, 23,* 373–384.

Steinberg, L. (1989). Pubertal maturation and parent–adolescent distance: An evolutionary perspective. In G. R. Adams, R. Montemayor, & T. P. Gullotta (Eds.), *Advances in adolescent behavior and development* (pp. 71–97). Newbury Park, CA: Sage.

Stelmach, G. E., & Nahom, A. (1992). Cognitive-motor abilities of the elderly driver. *Human Factors, 34,* 53–65.

St. George, I. M., Williams, S., & Silva, P. A. (1994). Body size and the menarche: The Dunedin study. *Journal of Adolescent Health, 15,* 573–576.

St. James-Roberts, I., & Plewis, I. (1996). Individual differences, daily fluctuations, and developmental changes in amounts of waking, fussing, crying, feeding, and sleeping. *Child Development, 67,* 2527–2540.

Stones, M. J., & Kozma, A. (1985). Physical performance. In N. Charness (Ed.), *Aging and human performance.* Chichester, England & New York: Wiley.

Swarr, A. E., & Richards, M. H. (1996). Longitudinal effects of adolescent girls' pubertal development, perceptions of pubertal timing, and parental relations on eating problems. *Developmental Psychology, 32,* 636–646.

Tan, U., & Tan, M. (1999). Incidences of asymmetries for the palmar grasp reflex in neonates and hand preference in adults. *Neuroreport: For Rapid Communication of Neuroscience Research, 10,* 3253–3256.

Tanner, J. M. (1990). *Foetus into man: Physical growth from conception to maturity* (2nd ed.). Cambridge, MA: Harvard Universtiy Press.

Thelen, E. (1984). Learning to walk: Ecological demands and phylogenetic constraints. In L. P. Lipsitt & C. Rovee-Collier (Eds.), *Advances in infancy research* (Vol. 3). Norwood, NJ: Ablex.

Thelen, E. (1995). Motor development: A new synthesis. *American Psychologist, 50,* 79–95.

Thelen, E. (1996). The improvising infant: Learning about learning to move. In M. R. Merrens & G. G. Brannigan (Eds.). *The developmental psychologists: Research adventures across the life span* (pp. 21–35). McGraw-Hill.

Thelen, E., & Smith, L. B. (1994). *A dynamic systems approach to the development of cognition and action.* Cambridge, MA: MIT Press.

Thoman, E. B., & Whitney, M. P. (1990). Behavioral states in infants: Individual differences and individual analyses. In J. Columbo and J. Fagen (Eds.), *Individual differences in infancy: Reliability, stability, prediction.* Hillsdale, NJ: Erlbaum.

Thomas, J. R., & French, K. E. (1985). Gender differences across age in motor performance: A meta-analysis. *Psychological Bulletin, 98,* 260–282.

Thomas, J. R., Yan, J. H., & Stelmach, G. E. (2000). Movement substructures change as a function of practice in children and adults. *Journal of Experimental Child Psychology, 75,* 228–244.

Thompson A. M., & Smart, J. L. (1993). A prospective study of the development of laterality: Neonatal laterality in relation to perinatal factors and maternal behavior. *Cortex, 29,* 649–659.

Thompson, P. M., Giedd, J. N., Woods, R. P., MacDonald, D., Evans, A. C., & Toga, A. W. (2000). Growth patterns in the developing brain detected by using continuum mechanical tensor maps. *Nature, 404,* 190–193.

Thompson, R. F. (1993). *The brain: A neuroscience primer* (2nd ed.). New York: W. H. Freeman.

Thys-Jacobs, S. (2000). Micronutrients and the premenstrual syndrome: The case for calcium. *Journal of the American College of Nutrition, 19,* 220–227.

Tremblay, M. S., Inman, J. W., & Willms, J. D. (2000). The relationship between physical activity, self-esteem, and academic achievement in 12-year-old children. *Pediatric Exercise Science, 12,* 312–323.

Tremblay, M. S., Pella, T., & Taylor, K. (1996). The quality and quantity of school-based physical education: A growing concern. *CAHPERD Journal, 62,* 4–7.

Tschann, J. M., Adler, N. E., Irwin, C. E., & Millstein, S. G. (1994). Initiation of substance use in early adolescence: The roles of pubertal timing and emotional distress. *Health Psychology, 13,* 326–333.

Tuckman, B. W. (1999). The effects of exercise on children and adolescents. In A. J. Goreczny & M. Hersen (Eds.), *Handbook of pediatric and adolescent health psychology* (pp. 275–286). Boston: Allyn & Bacon.

Vance, M. L., Mauras, N., & Wood, A. (1999). Growth hormone therapy in children and adults. *New England Journal of Medicine, 341,* 1206–1216.

van Galen, G. P. (1993). Handwriting: A developmental perspective. In A. F. Kalverboer, B. Hopkins, & R. H. Geuze (Eds.), *Motor development in early and later childhood: Longitudinal approaches.* Cambridge, England: Cambridge University Press.

Varea, C., Bernis, C., Montero, P., Arias, S., Barroso, A., & Gonzalez, B. (2000). Secular trend and intrapopulational variation in age of menopause in Spanish women. *Journal of Biosocial Science, 32,* 383–393.

Vining, E. P. G., Freeman, J. M., Pillas, D. J., Uematsu, S., Carson, B. S., Brandt, J., Boatman, D., Pulsifer, M. B., & Zuckerberg, A., (1997). Why would you remove half a brain? The outcome of 58 children after hemispherectomy—the Johns Hopkins experience: 1968 to 1996. *Pediatrics, 100,* 163–171.

Vita, A. J., Terry, R. B., Hubert, H. B., & Fries, J. F. (1998). Aging, health risks, and cumulative disability. *New England Journal of Medicine, 338,* 1035–1041.

von Hofsten, C. (1993). Studying the development of goal-directed behaviour. In A. F. Kalverboer, B. Hopkins, & R. H. Geuze (Eds.), *Motor development in early and later childhood: Longitudinal approaches.* Cambridge, England: Cambridge University Press.

Wagner, E. H., LaCroix, A. Z., Buchner, D. M., & Larson, E. B. (1992). Effects of physical activity on health status in older adults. I. Observational studies. *Annual Review of Public Health, 13,* 451–468.

Wahlstrom, K. L. (1999). The prickly politics of school starting times. *Phi Delta Kappan, 80,* 344.

Wahlstrom, K. L., & Bemis, A. (1998). *School start time study: Report of findings.* Minneapolis: University of Minnesota, Center for Applied Research and Educational Improvement.

Werner, H. (1957). The concept of development from a comparative and organismic point of view. In D. B. Harris (Ed.), *The concept of development: An issue in the study of human behavior.* Minneapolis: University of Minnesota Press.

Whipp, B. J., & Ward, S. A. (1992). Will women soon outrun men? *Nature, 355,* 25.

Whitbourne, S. K. (2001). *Adult development and aging: Biopsychosocial perspectives.* New York: Wiley.

Wilbur, J., Miller, A., & Montgomery, A. (1995). The influence of demographic characteristics, menopausal status, and symptoms on women's attitudes toward menopause. *Women and Health, 23,* 19–39.

Williams, J. M., & Currie, C. (2000). Self-esteem and physical development in early adolescence: Pubertal timing and body image. *Journal of Early Adolescence, 20,* 129–149.

Williams, M. R. (2000, September 27). Teen recklessness linked to still-developing brains. *Charleston Gazette.*

Williams, P. T. (1997). Evidence for the incompatibility of age-neutral overweight and age-neutral physical activity standards from runners. *American Journal of Clinical Nutrition, 65,* 1391–1396.

Wilson, G. T. (1994). Behavioral treatment of childhood obesity: Theoretical and practical implications. *Health Psychology, 13,* 371–372.

Winterich, J. A., & Umberson, D. (1999). How women experience menopause: The importance of context. *Journal of Women & Aging, 11,* 57.

Wolfe, W. S., Campbell, C. C., Frongillo, E. A., Haas, J. D., & Melnik, T. A. (1994). Overweight schoolchildren in New York State: Prevalence and characteristics. *American Journal of Public Health, 84,* 807–813.

Wolfson, A. R. & Carskadon, M. A. (1998). Sleep schedules and daytime functioning in adolescents. *Child Development, 69,* 875–998.

Wyly, M. V. (1997). *Infant assessment.* Boulder, CO: Westview.

Yan, J. H., Thomas, J. R., & Stelmach, G. E. (1998). Aging and rapid aiming arm movement control. *Experimental Aging Research, 24,* 155–168.

Yan, J. H., Thomas, J. R., Stelmach, G. E., & Thomas, K. T. (2000). Developmental features of rapid aiming arm movements across the lifespan. *Journal of Motor Behavior, 32,* 121–140.

Zani, B. (1991). Male and female patterns in the discovery of sexuality during adolescence. *Journal of Adolescence, 14,* 163–178.

Zweifel, J. E., & O'Brien, W. H. (1997). A meta-analysis of the effect of hormone replacement therapy upon depressed mood. *Psychoneuroendocrinology, 22,* 189–212.

Chapter 6: Perception

Adams. R., Maurer, D., & Davis, M. (1986). Newborns' discrimination of chromatic from achromatic stimuli. *Journal of Experimental Child Psychology, 41,* 267–281.

Allum, J. H., Greisiger, R., Straubhaar, S., & Carpenter, M. G. (2000). Auditory perception and speech identification in children with cochlear implants tested with the EARS protocol. *British Journal of Audiology, 34,* 293–303.

American Academy of Pediatrics. (2000). Prevention and management of pain and stress in the neonate (RE9945). *Pediatrics, 105,* 454–461.

Anand, K. J., & Hickey, P. R. (1992). Halothane-morphine compared with high-dose sufentanil for anesthesia and postoperative analgesia in neonatal cardiac surgery. *New England Journal of Medicine, 326,* 1–9.

Anderson, D. R., Lorch, E. P., Field, D. E., Collins, P. A., & Nathan, J. G. (1986). Television viewing at home: Age trends in visual attention and time with TV. *Child Development, 57,* 1024–1033.

Appollonio, I., Carabellese, C., Frattola, L., & Trabucchi, M. (1996). Effects of sensory aids on the quality of life and mortality of elderly people: A multivariate analysis. *Age and Ageing, 25,* 89–96.

Arana-Ward, M. (1997, May 11). As technology advances, a bitter debate divides the deaf. *Washington Post,* p. A1.

Aslin, R. N. (1988). Perceptual development. *Annual Review of Psychology, 39,* 435–473.

Aslin, R. N., Pisoni, D. B., & Jusczyk, P. W. (1983). Auditory development and speech perception in infancy. In M. M. Haith & J. J. Campos (Eds.), *Handbook of child psychology: Vol. 2. Infancy and developmental psychobiology* (4th ed.). New York: Wiley.

Ball, K., Owsley, C., Stalvey, B., Roenker, D. L., Sloane, M. E., & Graves, M. (1998). Driving avoidance and functional impairment in older drivers. *Accident Analysis and Prevention, 30,* 313–322.

Baltes, P. B., & Lindenberger, U. (1997). Emergence of a powerful connection between sensory and cognitive functions across the adult life span: A new window to the study of cognitive aging? *Psychology and Aging, 12,* 12–21.

Banks, M. S., & Ginsburg, A. P. (1985). Infant visual preferences: A review and new theoretical treatment. In H. W. Reese (Ed.), *Advances in child development and behavior* (Vol. 19). Orlando, FL: Academic Press.

Banks, M. S., in collaboration with Salapatek, P. (1983). Infant visual perception. In M. M. Haith & J. J. Campos (Eds.; P. H. Mussen, Gen. Ed.), *Handbook of child psychology: Vol. 2. Infancy and developmental psychobiology* (4th ed.). New York: Wiley.

Banks, M. S., & Shannon, E. (1993). Spatial and chromatic visual efficiency in human neonates. In C. E. Granrud (Ed.), *Visual perception and cognition in infancy.* Hillsdale, NJ: Erlbaum.

Barr, R. G., Pantel, M. S., Young, S. N., Wright, J. H., Hendricks, L. A., & Gravel, R. (1999). The response of crying newborns to sucrose: Is it a "sweetness" effect? *Physiological Behavior, 66,* 409–417.

Berry, J. W., Poortinga, Y. H., Segall, M., & Dasen, P. R. (1992). *Cross-cultural psychology: Research and applications.* Cambridge, England: Cambridge University Press.

Berson, E. L. (2000). Nutrition and retinal degenerations. *International Ophthalmology Clinic, 40,* 93–111.

Bess, F. H., & McConnell, F. E. (1981). *Audiology, education, and the hearing impaired child.* St. Louis: Mosby.

Bornstein, M. H. (1992). Perception across the lifespan. In M. H. Bornstein & M. E. Lamb (Eds.), *Developmental Psychology. An ad-*

vanced textbook (3rd ed.). Hillsdale, NJ: Erlbaum.

Botuck, S., & Turkewitz, G. (1990). Intersensory functioning: Auditory-visual pattern equivalence in younger and older children. *Developmental Psychology, 26,* 115–120.

Bower, T. G. R. (1982). *Development in infancy* (2nd ed.). San Francisco: W. H. Freeman.

Bower, T. G. R., Broughton, J. M., & Moore, M. K. (1970). The coordination of vision and tactile input in infancy. *Perception and Psychophysics, 8,* 51–53.

Brabyn, J. (2000). Visual function in the oldest old. Papers from the 15th Biennial Eye Research Seminar. New York: *Research to Prevent Blindness.* [Available online: http://www.rpbusa.org/new/pdf/jbrabyn1.pdf]

Burack, J. A., Enns, J. T., Iarocci, G., & Randolph, B. (2000). Age differences in visual search for compound patterns: Long- versus short-range grouping. *Developmental Psychology, 36,* 731–740.

Bushnell, E. W., & Baxt, C. (1999). Children's haptic and cross-modal recognition with familiar and unfamiliar objects. *Journal of Experimental Psychology: Human Perception and Performance, 25,* 1867–1881.

Butcher, P. R., Kalverboer, A. F., & Geuze, R. H. (2000). Infants' shifts of gaze from a central to a peripheral stimulus: A longitudinal study of development between 6 and 26 weeks. *Infant Behavior & Development, 23,* 3–21.

Campbell, V. A., Crews, J. E., Moriarty, D. G., Zack, M. M., & Blackman, D. K. (1999). Surveillance for sensory impairment, activity limitation, and health-related quality of life among older adults: United States, 1993–1997. *CDC MMWR Surveillance Summaries, 48* (SS08), 131–156.

Campos, J. J., Bertenthal, B. I., & Kermoian, R. (1992). Early experience and emotional development: The emergence of wariness of heights. *Psychological Science, 3,* 61–64.

Campos, J. J., Langer, A., & Krowitz, A. (1970). Cardiac responses on the visual cliff in prelocomotor human infants. *Science, 170,* 196–197.

Canfield, R. L., & Smith, E. G. (1996). Number-based expectations and sequential enumeration by 5-month-old infants. *Developmental Psychology, 32,* 269–279.

Cernoch, J. M., & Porter, R. H. (1985). Recognition of maternal axillary odors by infants. *Child Development, 56,* 1593–1598.

Chen, D. (1996). Parent–infant communication: Early intervention for very young children with visual impairment or hearing loss. *Infants and Young Children, 9,* 1–12.

Cheng, A. K., Rubin, H. R., Powe, N. R., Mellon, M. K., Francis, H. W., & Niparko, J. K. (2000). Cost–utility analysis of the cochlear implant in children. *Journal of the American Medical Association, 284,* 850–856.

Choudhury, N., & Gorman, K. S. (2000). The relationship between sustained attention and cognitive performance in 17–24-month old toddlers. *Infant and Child Development, 9,* 127-146.

Clarkson, M. G., & Berg, W. K. (1983). Cardiac orienting and vowel discrimination in newborns: Crucial stimulation parameters. *Child Development, 54,* 162–171.

Cobb, R. W., & Coughlin, J. F. (1998). Are elderly drivers a road hazard? Problem definition and political impact. *Journal of Aging Studies, 12,* 411–420.

Colburn, D. (2000, October 3). Wired for sound. *Washington Post Health,* pp. 13–18.

Corwin, J., Loury, M., & Gilbert, A. N. (1995). Workplace, age, and sex as mediators of olfactory function: Data from the National Geographic Smell Survey. *Journals of Gerontology Series B: Psychological Sciences and Social Sciences, 50,* 179–186.

Dannemiller, J. L., & Stephens, B. R. (1988). A critical test of infant pattern preference models. *Child Development, 59,* 210–216.

DeCasper, A. J., & Fifer, W. P. (1980). Of human bonding: Newborns prefer their mothers' voices. *Science, 208,* 1174–1176.

DeCasper, A. J., & Spence, M. J. (1986). Prenatal maternal speech influences newborns' perception of speech sounds. *Infant Behavior and Development, 9,* 133–150.

Delevati, N. M., & Bergamasco, N. H. P. (1999). Pain in the neonate: An analysis of facial movements and crying in response to nociceptive stimuli, *Infant Behavior & Development, 22,* 137–143.

Descartes, R. (1965). La dioptrique. In R. J. Herrnstein & E. G. Boring (Eds.), *A sourcebook in the history of psychology.* Cambridge, MA: Harvard University Press. (Original work published 1638)

Dewar, R. E., Kline, D. W., & Swanson, H. A. (1995). Age differences in the comprehension of traffic sign symbols. *Transportation Research Record, 1456,* 1-10.

Dywan, J., & Murphy, W. E. (1996). Aging and inhibitory control in text comprehension. *Psychology and Aging, 11,* 199–206.

Easterbrook, M. A., Kisilevsky, B. S., Muir, D. W., & Laplante, D. P. (1999). Newborns discriminate schematic faces from scrambled faces. *Canadian Journal of Experimental Psychology, 53,* 231–241.

Ecklund-Flores, L., & Turkewitz, G. (1996). Asymmetric headturning to speech and nonspeech in human newborns. *Developmental Psychobiology, 29,* 205–217.

Eimas, P. D. (1975a). Auditory and phonetic cues for speech: Discrimination of the (r-l) distinction by young infants. *Perception and Psychophysics, 18,* 341–347.

Eimas, P. D. (1975b). Speech perception in early infancy. In L. B. Cohen & P. Salapatek (Eds.), *Infant perception: From sensation to cognition.* New York: Academic Press.

Eimas, P. D. (1985). The perception of speech in early infancy. *Scientific American, 252,* 46–52.

Eliot, L. (1999). *What's going on in there? How the brain and mind develop in the first five years of life.* New York: Bantam.

Enoch, J. M., Werner, J. S., Haegerstrm-Portnoy, G., Lakshminarayanan, V., & Rynders, M. (1999). Forever young: Visual functions not affected or minimally affected by aging: A review. *Journal of Gerontology: Biological Sciences, 54A,* B336–B351.

Eppler, M. A. (1995). Development of manipulatory skills and the deployment of attention. *Infant Behavior & Development, 18,* 391–405.

Evans, J. R. (2001). Risk factors for age-related macular degeneration. *Progress in Retinal and Eye Research, 20,* 227.

Faber, C. E., & Grontved, A. M. (2000). Cochlear implantation and change in quality of life. *Acta Otolaryngology Supplement, 543,* 151–153.

Fantz, R. L. (1961). The origin of form perception. *Scientific American, 204,* 66–72.

Fantz, R. L. (1963). Pattern vision in newborn infants. *Science, 140,* 296–297.

Fantz, R. L. (1965). Visual perception from birth as shown by pattern selectivity. *Annals of the New York Academy of Sciences, 118,* 793–814.

Fantz, R. L., & Fagan, J. F. (1975). Visual attention to size and number of pattern details by term and preterm infants during the first six months. *Child Development, 46,* 3–18.

Field, J., Muir, D., Pilon, R., Sinclair, M., & Dodwell, P. (1980). Infants' orientation to lateral sounds from birth to three months. *Child Development, 51,* 295–298.

Field, T. (1990). *Infancy.* Cambridge, MA: Harvard University Press.

Field, T. (1995). Massage therapy for infants and children. *Journal of Developmental and Behavioral Pediatrics, 16,* 105–111.

Finitzo, T., Gunnarson, A. D., & Clark, J. L. (1990). Auditory deprivation and early conductive hearing loss from otitis media. *Topics in Language Disorders, 11,* 29–42.

Finkelstein, J. A., & Schiffman, S. S. (1999). Workshop on taste and smell in the elderly: An overview. *Physiological Behavior, 66,* 173–176.

Fishbaugh, J. (1995). Look who's driving now: Visual standards for driver licensing in the United States. *Journal of the American Society of Ophthalmic Registered Nurses, 20,* 11–20.

Fozard, J. L. (1990). Vision and hearing in aging. In J. E. Birren & K. W. Schaie (Eds.), *Handbook of the psychology of aging* (3rd ed.). San Diego: Academic Press.

Frank, S. M., Raja, S. N., Bulcao, C., & Goldstein, D. S. (2000). Age-related thermoregulatory differences during core cooling in humans. *American Journal of Physiological Regulation, Integration, and Comparative Physiology, 279,* R349–354.

Fryauf-Bertschy, H., Tyler, R. S., Kelsay, D. M. R., Gantz, B. J., & Woodworth, G. G. (1997). Cochlear implant use by prelingually deafened children: The influence of age at implant and length of device use. *Journal of Speech, Language, and Hearing Research, 40,* 183– 199.

Ganchrow, J. R., Steiner, J. E., & Daher, M. (1983). Neonatal facial expressions to different qualities and intensities of gustatory stimuli. *Infant Behavior and Development, 6,* 189–200.

Gelman, S. A. (1996). Concepts and theories. In R. Gelman & T. K. Au (Eds.), *Perceptual and cognitive development.* San Diego: Academic Press.

Gibson, E. J. (1988). Exploratory behavior in the development of perceiving, acting, and the acquiring of knowledge. *Annual Review of Psychology, 39,* 1–41.

Gibson, E. J., & Pick, A. D. (2000). *An ecological approach to perceptual learning and development.* New York: Oxford University Press.

Gibson, E. J., & Walk, R. D. (1960). The "visual cliff." *Scientific American, 202,* 64–71.

Gloth, F. M. (2000). Geriatric pain: Factors that limit pain relief and increase complications. *Geriatrics, 55,* 51–54.

Greenspan, S. I. (1997). *The growth of the mind.* Reading, MA: Addison-Wesley.

Guinsburg, R., de Araujo Peres, C., Branco de Almeida, M. F., de Cassia Xavier Balda, R., Cassia Berenguel, R., Tonelotto, J., & Kopelman, B. I. (2000). Differences in pain expression between male and female newborn infants. *Pain, 85,* 127–133.

Hainline, L., & Abramov, I. (1992). Assessing visual development: Is infant vision good enough? *Advances in Infancy Research, 7,* 39–102.

Hartman, B. T. (1982). An exploratory study of the effects of disco music on the auditory and vestibular systems. *Journal of Auditory Research, 22,* 271–274.

Hasher, L., Stoltzfus, E. R., Zacks, R. T., & Rypma, B. (1991). Age and inhibition. *Journal of Experimental Psychology: Learning, Memory, and Cognition, 17,* 163–169.

Hetu, R., & Fortin, M. (1995). Potential risk of hearing damage associated with exposure to highly amplified music. *Journal of the American Academy of Audiology, 6,* 378–386.

Hosaka, T. (1999, August 10). Don't come without it: Many states are requiring hospitals to screen newborns for hearing loss. *Washington Post Health,* p. 9.

Insurance Institute for Highway Safety, Highway Loss Data Institute. (2000). Available online: http://www.hwysafety.org/safety_facts/fatality_facts/elderly_plots.htm

Jackson, G. R., Owsley, C., & McGwin, G. (1999). Aging and dark adaptation. *Vision Research, 39,* 3975–3982.

James, W. (1890). *Principles of psychology* (2 vols.). New York: Holt.

Johnson, M. H. (1997). *Developmental cognitive neuroscience.* Oxford, England: Blackwell.

Johnson, M. H., & Gilmore, R. O. (1996). Developmental cognitive neuroscience: A biological perspective on cognitive change. In R. Gelman & T. K. Au (Eds.), *Perceptual and cognitive development.* San Diego: Academic Press.

Johnson, S. P., & Aslin, R. N. (1995). Perception of object unity in 2-month-old infants. *Developmental Psychology, 31,* 739–745.

Johnson, S. P., Bremner, J. G., Slater, A. M., & Mason, U. (2000). The role of good form in young infants' perception of partly occluded objects. *Journal of Experimental Child Psychology, 76,* 1–25.

Joint Committee on Infant Hearing. (2000). Year 2000 position statement: Principles and guidelines for early hearing detection and intervention programs. *Pediatrics, 106,* 798–817.

Juola, J. F., Koshino, H., Warner, C. B., McMickell, M., & Peterson, M. (2000). Automatic and voluntary control of attention in young and older adults. *American Journal of Psychology, 113,* 159–178.

Kagan, J. (1971). *Change and continuity in infancy.* New York: Wiley.

Kahn, H. A., Leibowitz, H. M., Ganley, J. P., Kini, M. M., Colton, T., Nickerson, R. S., & Dawber, T. R. (1977). The Framingham eye study: I. Outline and major prevalence findings. *American Journal of Epidemiology, 106,* 17–32.

Kant, I. (1958). *Critique of pure reason.* New York: Modern Library. (Original work published 1781)

Kellman, P. J., & Banks, M. S. (1998). Infant visual perception. In W. Damon (Editor-in-Chief) and D. Kuhn & R. S. Siegler (Vol. Eds.), *Handbook of Child Psychology* (5th ed., pp. 103–146). New York: Wiley.

Kellman, P. J., & Spelke, E. S. (1983). Perception of partly occluded objects in infancy. *Cognitive Psychology, 15,* 483–524.

Kelsall, D. C., Shallop, J. K., & Burnelli, T. (1995). Cochlear implantation in the elderly. *American Journal of Otology, 16,* 609–615.

Kenshalo, D. R. (1977). Age changes in touch, vibration, temperature, kinesthesis and pain sensitivity. In J. E. Birren & K. W. Schaie (Eds.), *Handbook of the psychology of aging.* New York: Van Nostrand Reinhold.

Kim, K., & Spelke, E. J. (1992). Infants' sensitivity to effects of gravity on visible object motion. *Journal of Experimental Psychology: Human Perception and Performance, 18,* 385–393.

Kisilevsky, B. S., & Muir, D. W. (1984). Neonatal habituation and dishabituation to tactile stimulation during sleep. *Developmental Psychology, 20,* 367–373.

Kline, D. W., & Schieber, F. (1985). Vision and aging. In J. E. Birren & K. W. Schaie (Eds.), *Handbook of the psychology of aging* (2nd ed.) New York: Van Nostrand Reinhold.

Kline, D. W., & Scialfa, C. T. (1996). Visual and auditory aging. In J. E. Birren & K. W. Schaie (Eds.), *Handbook of the psychology of aging* (4th ed.) San Diego: Academic Press.

Koretz, J. F., Cook, C. A., & Kaufman, P. L. (1997). Accommodation and presbyopia in the human eye. *Investigations in Ophthalmology and Visual Science, 38,* 569–578.

Kosnik, W., Winslow, L., Kline, D., Rasinski, K., & Sekuler, R. (1988). Visual changes in daily life throughout adulthood. *Journal of Gerontology: Psychological Sciences, 43,* P63–P70.

Kuhl, P. K. (1991). Perception, cognition, and the ontogenetic and phylogenetic emergence of human speech. In S. E. Brauth, W. S. Hall, & R. J. Dooling (Eds.), *Plasticity of development.* Cambridge, MA: MIT Press.

Lambert, S. R., & Drack, A. V. (1996). Infantile cataracts. *Survey of Ophthalmology, 40,* 427–458.

Locke, J. (1939). An essay concerning human understanding. In E. A. Burtt (Ed.), *The English philosophers from Bacon to Mill.* New York: Modern Library. (Original work published 1690)

Lynch, M. P., Eilers, R. E., Oller, D. K., & Urbano, R. C. (1990). Innateness, experience, and music perception. *Psychological Science, 1,* 272–276.

Maccoby, E. E. (1967). Selective auditory attention in children. In L. P. Lipsitt & C. C. Spiker (Eds.), *Advances in child development and behavior.* New York: Academic Press.

Madden, D. J., Gottlob, L. R., & Allen, P. A. (1999). Adult age differences in visual search accuracy: Attentional guidance and target detectability. *Psychology and Aging, 14,* 683–694.

Marean, G. C., Werner, L. A., & Kuhl, P. K. (1992). Vowel categorization by very young infants. *Developmental Psychology, 28,* 396–405.

Marschark, M. (1993). *Psychological development of deaf children.* New York: Oxford University Press.

Martin, F. N. (1994). *Introduction to audiology* (5th ed.). Englewood Cliffs, NJ: Prentice Hall.

Martlew, M., & Connolly, K. J. (1996). Human figure drawings by schooled and unschooled children in Papua New Guinea. *Child Development, 67,* 2743–2762.

Maurer, D., Lewis, T. L., Brent, H. P., & Levin, A. V. (1999). Rapid improvement in the acuity of infants after visual input. *Science, 286,* 108–110.

Maurer, D., Stager, C. L., & Mondloch, C. J. (1999). Cross-modal transfer of shape is difficult to demonstrate in one-month-olds. *Child Development, 70,* 1047–1057.

Maxon, A. B., & Brackett, D. (1992). *The hearing-impaired child: Infancy through high school years.* Boston: Andover Medical Publishers.

Mayberry, R. I., & Eichen, E. B. (1991). The long-lasting advantage of learning sign language in childhood: Another look at the critical period for language acquisition. *Journal of Memory and Language, 30,* 486–512.

McKay, K. E., Halperin, J. M., Schwartz, S. T., & Sharma, V. (1994). Developmental analysis of three aspects of information processing: Sustained attention, selective attention, and response organization. *Developmental Neuropsychology, 10,* 121–132.

Meadows-Orlans, K. P., & Orlans, H. (1990). Responses to loss of hearing in later life. In D. F. Moores & K. P. Meadows-Orlans, (Eds.), *Educational and developmental aspects of deafness.* Washington, DC: Gallaudet University Press.

Meltzoff, A. N., & Borton, R. W. (1979). Intermodal matching by human neonates. *Nature, 282,* 403–404.

Mennella, J. A., & Beauchamp, G. K. (1998). Early flavor experiences: Research update. *Nutrition Review, 56,* 205–211.

Miller, J. L., & Eimas, P. D. (1996). Internal structure of voicing categories in early infancy. *Perception and Psychophysics, 58,* 1157–1167.

Miller, P. H., & Weiss, M. G. (1981). Children's attention allocation, understanding of attention, and performance on the incidental learning task. *Child Development, 52,* 1183–1190.

Miyawaki, K., Strange, W., Verbrugge, R., Liberman, A. M., Jenkins, J. J., & Fujimura, D. (1975). An effect of linguistic experience: The discrimination of [r] and [l] by native speakers of Japanese and English. *Perception and Psychophysics, 18,* 331–340.

Mohr, P. E., Feldman, J. J., Dunbar, J. L., McConkey-Robbins, A., Niparko, J. K., Rittenhouse, R. K., & Skinner, M. W. (2000). The societal costs of severe to profound hearing loss in the United States. *International Journal of Technology and Assessment of Health Care, 16,* 1120–1135.

Morrongiello, B. A., Fenwick, K. D., & Chance, G. (1990). Sound localization activity in very young infants: An observer-based testing procedure. *Developmental Psychology, 26,* 1003.

Morrongiello, B. A., Fenwick, K. D., Hillier, L., & Chance, G. (1994). Sound localization in newborn human infants. *Developmental Psychobiology, 27,* 519–538.

Muir, D. W. (1985). The development of infants' auditory spatial sensitivity. In S. E. Trehub & B. Schneider (Eds.), *Advances in the study of communication and affect: Vol. 10. Auditory development in infancy.* New York: Plenum.

Muir, D. W., Humphrey, D. E., & Humphrey, G. K. (1994). Pattern and space perception in young infants. *Spatial Vision, 8,* 141–165.

Murphy, C. (1985). Cognitive and chemosensory influences on age-related changes in the ability to identify blended foods. *Journal of Gerontology, 40,* 47–52.

Murphy, C., Nordin, S., & Acosta, L. (1997). Odor learning, recall, and recognition memory in young and elderly adults. *Neuropsychology, 11,* 126–137.

Nanez, J. E., & Yonas, A. (1994). Effects of luminance and texture motion on infant defensive reactions to optical collision. *Infant Behavior and Development, 17,* 165–174.

National Institute on Aging and National Institute on Deafness and Other Communication Disorders. (1996). Hearing and older people. In L. M. Ross (Ed.), *Communication Disorders Sourcebook* (Vol. 11, pp. 183–184). Detroit: Omnigraphics.

National Institute on Deafness and Other Communication Disorders. (1997). *Presbycusis.* National Institutes of Health, Publication No. 97-4233.

National Institutes of Health. (1993, March 1–3). Consensus Statement on the Early Identification of Hearing Impairment in Infants and Young Children. In L. M. Ross (Ed.), *Communication Disorders Sourcebook* (Vol. 11, pp. 51–53). Detroit: Omnigraphics.

Needham, A. (1999). The role of shape in 4-month-old infants' object segregation. *Infant Behavior & Development, 22,* 161–178.

Northern, J. L. (1996). *Hearing disorders* (3rd ed.). Boston: Allyn and Bacon.

O'Donoghue, G. M., Nikolopoulos, T. P., & Archbold, S. M. (2000). Determinants of speech perception in children after cochlear implantation. *Lancet, 356,* 466–468.

Owsley, C. (2000). The aging driver. Papers from the 15th Biennial Eye Research Seminar. New York: *Research to Prevent Blindness.* [Available online: http://www.rpbusa.org/new/pdf/cowsley1.pdf]

Owsley, C., Ball, K., McGwin, G., Sloane, M. E., Roenker, D. L., White, M. F., & Overley, E. T. (1998). Visual processing impairment and risk of motor vehicle crash among older adults. *Journal of the American Medical Association, 279,* 1083–1088.

Owsley, C., Ball, K., Sloane, M. E., & Bruni, J. R. (1991). Visual/cognitive correlates of vehicle accidents in older drivers. *Psychology and Aging, 6,* 403–415.

Owsley, C., & McGwin, G. (1999). Vision impairment and driving. *Survey of Ophthalmology, 43,* 535–550.

Owsley, C., Stalvey, B., Wells, J., & Sloane, M. E. (1999). Older drivers and cataract: Driving habits and crash risk. *Journal of Gerontology: Biological Sciences and Medical Sciences, 54,* M203–211.

Pascalis, O., Deschonen, S., Morton, J., Deruelle, C., & Fabregrenet, M. (1995). Mother's face recognition by neonates: A replication and an extension. *Infant Behavior & Development, 18,* 79–85.

Pearson, J. D., Morell, C. H., Gordon-Salant, S., Brant, L. J., Metter, E. J., Klein, L., & Fozard, J. L. (1995). Gender differences in a longitudinal study of age-associated hearing loss. *Journal of the Acoustical Society of America, 97,* 1196–1205.

Peeples, D. R., & Teller, D. Y. (1975). Color vision and brightness discrimination in two-month-old human infants. *Science, 189,* 1102–1103.

Pickens, J. (1994). Perception of auditory-visual distance relations by 5-month-old infants. *Developmental Psychology, 30,* 537–544.

Pitts, D. G. (1982). The effects of aging on selected visual functions: Dark adaptation, visual acuity, stereopsis, and brightness contrast. In R. Sekuler, D. Kline, & K. Dismukes (Eds.), *Aging and human visual function.* New York: Alan R. Liss.

Plude, D. J., & Hoyer, W. J. (1981). Adult age differences in visual search as a function of stimulus mapping and processing load. *Journal of Gerontology, 36,* 598–604.

Plude, D. J., & Hoyer, W. J. (1985). Attention and performance: Identifying and localizing age deficits. In N. Charness (Ed.), *Aging and human performance.* Chichester, England: Wiley.

Popelka, M. M., Cruickshanks, K. J., Wiley, T. L., Tweed, T. S., Klein, B. E., & Klein, R. (1998). Low prevalence of hearing aid use among older adults with hearing loss: The Epidemiology of Hearing Loss Study. *Journal of the American Geriatric Society, 46,* 1075–1078.

Porter, R. H. (1999). Olfaction and human kin recognition. *Genetica, 104,* 259–263.

Porter, R. H., Makin, J. W., Davis, L. B., & Christensen, K. M. (1992). Breast-fed infants respond to olfactory clues from their own mother and unfamiliar lactating females. *Infant Behavior and Development, 15,* 85–93.

Rahi, J. S., & Dezateux, C. (1999). National cross sectional study of detection of congenital and infantile cataract in the United Kingdom: Role of childhood screening and surveillance. *British Medical Journal, 318,* 362–365.

Retinal Implant Project. (1999). Available online: http://rleweb.mit.edu/retina/firstpage.html

Reuben, D. B., Walsh, K., Moore, A. A., Damesyn, M., & Greendale, G. A. (1998). Hearing loss in community-dwelling older persons: National prevalence data and identification using simple questions. *Journal of the American Geriatric Society, 46,* 1008–1011.

Rieser, J., Yonas, A., & Wilkner, K. (1976). Radial localization of odors by human newborns. *Child Development, 47,* 856–859.

Rolls, B. J. (1999). Do chemosensory changes influence food intake in the elderly? *Physiological Behavior, 66,* 193–197.

Rosser, R. (1994). *Cognitive development: Psychological and biological perspectives.* Boston: Allyn & Bacon.

Rovee-Collier, C. (2001). Information pick-up by infants: What is it, and how can we tell? *Journal of Experimental Child Psychology, 78,* 35–49.

Ruff, H. A., & Lawson, K. R. (1990). Development of sustained, focused attention in young children during free play. *Developmental Psychology, 26,* 85–93.

Ruff, H. A., & Rothbart, M. K. (1996). *Attention in early development: Themes and variations.* New York: Oxford University Press.

Ruff, H. A., Saltarelli, L. M., Coppozzoli, M., & Dubiner, K. (1992). The differentiation of activity in infants' exploration of objects. *Developmental Psychology, 27,* 851–861.

Salapatek, P. (1975). Pattern perception in early infancy. In L. B. Cohen & P. Salapatek (Eds.), *Infant perception: From sensation to cognition* (Vol. 1). New York: Academic Press.

Salthouse, T. A., Hancock, H. E., Meinz, E. J., & Hambrick, D. Z. (1996). Interrelations of age, visual acuity, and cognitive functioning. *Journals of Gerontology: Psychological Sciences and Social Sciences, 51,* 317–330.

Scafidi, F. A., Field, T., & Schanberg, S. M. (1993). Factors that predict which preterm infants benefit most from massage therapy. *Journal of Developmental and Behavioral Pediatrics, 14,* 176–180.

Schaal, B., Barlier, L., & Soussignan, R. (1998). Olfactory function in the human fetus: Evidence from selective neonatal responsiveness to the odor of amniotic fluid. *Behavioral Neuroscience, 112,* 1438–1449.

Schiff, A. R., & Knopf, I. J. (1985). The effect of task demands on attention allocation in children of different ages. *Child Development, 56,* 621–630.

Schiffman, H. R. (2000). *Sensation and perception* (5th ed.) New York: Wiley.

Schiffman, S. S. Food recognition by the elderly. *Journal of Gerontology, 32,* 586–592.

Schiffman, S. S. (1997). Taste and smell losses in normal aging and disease. *Journal of the American Medical Association, 278,* 1357–1362.

Schiffman, S. S., & Warwick, Z. S. (1993). Effect of flavor enhancement of foods for the elderly on nutritional status: Food intake, biochemical indices, and anthropometric measures. *Physiological Behavior, 53,* 395–402.

Schneider, B. A., Daneman, M., Murphy, D. R., & See, S. K. (2000). Listening to discourse in distracting settings: The effects of aging. *Psychological Aging, 15,* 110–125.

Scialfa, C. T., Esau, S. P., & Joffe, K. M. (1998). Age, target–distractor similarity, and visual search. *Experimental Aging Research, 24,* 337–358.

Ship, J. A., Pearson, J. D., Cruise, L. J., Brant, L. J., & Metter, E. J. (1996). Longitudinal changes in smell identification. *Journals of Gerontology: Biological Sciences and Medical Sciences, 51,* M86–M91.

Ship, J. A., & Weiffenbach, J. M. (1993). Age, gender, medical treatment, and medication effects on smell identification. *Journal of Gerontology, 48,* M26–M32.

Sibulsky, L., Hayes, K. C., Pronczuk, A., Weigel-DiFranco, C., Rosner, B., & Berson, E. L. (1999). Safety of <7500 RE (<25000 IU) vitamin A daily in adults with retinitis pigmentosa. *American Journal of Clinical Nutrition, 69,* 656–663.

Simon, T. J. (1997). Reconceptualizing the origins of number knowledge: A "non-numerical" account. *Cognitive Development, 12,* 349–372.

Simon, T. J. (1999). The foundations of numerical thinking in a brain without numbers. *Trends in Cognitive Science, 3,* 363–365.

Simon, T. J., Hespos, S. J., & Rochat, P. (1995). Do infants understand simple arithmetic? A replication of Wynn (1992). *Cognitive Development, 10,* 253–269.

Sivak, M., Olson, P. L., & Pastalan, L. A. (1981). Effect of driver's age on nighttime legibility of highway signs. *Human Factors, 23,* 59–64.

Slater, A., Mattock, A., & Brown, E. (1990). Size constancy at birth: Newborn infants' response to retinal and real size. *Journal of Experimental Child Psychology, 49,* 314–322.

Slater, A., Mattock, A., Brown, E., & Bremner, J. G. (1991). Form perception at birth: Cohen and Younger (1984) revisited. *Journal of Experimental Child Psychology, 51,* 395–406.

Slater, A., Morison, V., Somers, M., Mattock, A., Brown, E., & Taylor, D. (1990). Newborn and older infants' perception of partly occluded objects. *Infant Behavior and Development, 13,* 33–49.

Smith, B., & Blass, E. M. (1996). Taste-mediated calming in premature, preterm, and full-term human infants. *Developmental Psychology, 32,* 1084–1089.

Smith, L. B., & Katz, D. B. (1996). Activity-dependent processes in perceptual and cognitive development. In R. Gelman & T. K. Au (Eds.), *Perceptual and cognitive development.* San Diego: Academic Press.

Spelke, E. S. (1990). Principles of object perception. *Cognitive Science, 14,* 29–56.

Spelke, E. S. (1994). Initial knowledge: Six suggestions. *Cognition, 50,* 431–445.

Spelke, E. S., Breinlinger, K., Macomber, J., & Jacobson, K. (1992). Origins of knowledge. *Psychological Review, 99,* 605–632.

Spelke, E. S., & Hermer, L. (1996). Early cognitive development: Objects and space. In R. Gelman & T. K. Au (Eds.), *Perceptual and cognitive development.* San Diego: Academic Press.

Steiner, J. E. (1979). Human facial expressions in response to taste and smell stimulation. In H. W. Reese & L. P. Lipsitt (Eds.), *Advances in child development and behavior* (Vol. 13). New York: Academic Press.

Streri, A., & Pecheux, M. (1986). Vision-to-touch and touch-to-vision transfer of form in 5-month-old infants. *British Journal of Developmental Psychology, 4,* 161–167.

Strutt, G. F., Anderson, D. R., & Well, A. D. (1975). A developmental study of the effects of irrelevant information on speeded classification. *Journal of Experimental Child Psychology, 20,* 127–135.

Suro, M. D. (1997, March 11). Sight for sore eyes: New research aims at preventing vision loss. *Washington Post Health,* pp. 12–14.

Svirsky, M. A., Robbins, A. M., Iler Kirk, K., Pisoni, D. B., & Miyamoto, R. T. (2000). Language development in profoundly deaf children with cochlear implants. *Psychological Science, 11,* 153–158.

Tanner, J. M. (1990). *Foetus into man: Physical growth from conception to maturity* (2nd ed.). Cambridge, MA: Harvard University Press.

Teller, D. Y., Peeples, D. R., & Sekel, M. (1978). Discrimination of chromatic from white light by two-month-old human infants. *Vision Research, 25,* 821–831.

Trehub, S. E., Schneider, B. A., Thorpe, L. A., & Judge, P. (1991). Observational measures of auditory sensitivity in early infancy. *Developmental Psychology, 27,* 40–49.

Treiber, F., & Wilcox, S. (1980). Perception of a "subjective contour" by infants. *Child Development, 51,* 915–917.

Tucker, B. P. (1998). Deaf culture, cochlear implants, and elective disability. *Hastings Center Report, 28,* 6–14.

U.S. Department of Transportation. (1997). *Improving transportation for a maturing society.* Washington, DC: DOT-P10-97-01.

Uchida, N., Fujita, K., & Katayama, T. (1999). Detection of vehicles on the other crossing path at an intersection: Visual search performance of elderly drivers. *Japanese Society of Automotive Engineers Review, 20,* 381.

Valenza, E., Simion, F., Cassia, V. M., & Umilta, C. (1996). Face preference at birth. *Journal of Experimental Psychology: Human Perception and Performance, 22,* 892–903.

Van Giffen, K., & Haith, M. M. (1984). Infant visual response to Gestalt geometric forms. *Infant Behavior and Development, 7,* 335–346.

Varendi, H., Christensson, K., Porter, R. H., & Winberg, J. (1998). Soothing effect of amniotic fluid smell in newborn infants. *Early Human Development, 51,* 47–55.

Verrillo, R. T., & Verrillo, V. (1985). Sensory and perceptual performance. In N. Charness (Ed.), *Aging and human performance.* Chichester, England: Wiley.

Vurpillot, E. (1968). The development of scanning strategies and their relation to visual differentiation. *Journal of Experimental Child Psychology, 6,* 632–650.

Wakeley, A., Rivera, S., & Langer, J. (2000). Can young infants add and subtract? *Child Development, 71,* 1525–1534.

Walker-Andrews, A. S. (1997). Infants' perception of expressive behaviors: Differentiation of multimodal information. *Psychological Bulletin, 121,* 437–456.

Ward, C. D., & Cooper, R. P. (1999). A lack of evidence in 4-month-old human infants for paternal voice preference. *Developmental Psychobiology, 35,* 49–59.

Weiffenbach, J. M., Cowart, B. J., & Baum, B. J. (1986). Taste intensity perception in aging. *Journal of Gerontology, 41,* 460–468.

Wellman, H. M., & Gelman, S. A. (1992). Cognitive development: Foundational theories of core domains. *Annual Review of Psychology, 43,* 337–375.

Werker, J. F., & Desjardins, R. N. (1995). Listening to speech in the first year of life: Experiential influences on phoneme perception. *Current Directions in Psychological Science, 4,* 76–81.

Werker, J. F., Gilbert, J. H. V., Humphrey, K., & Tees, R. C. (1981). Developmental aspects of cross-language speech perception. *Child Development, 52,* 349–355.

Whitbourne, S. K. (2001). *Adult development and aging: Biopsychosocial perspectives.* New York: Wiley.

Williams, A. F., & Carsten, O. (1989). Driver age and crash involvement. *American Journal of Public Health, 79,* 326–327.

Wingfield, A., Poon, L. W., Lombardi, L., & Lowe, D. (1985). Speed of processing in normal aging: Effects of speech rate, linguistic structure, and processing time. *Journal of Gerontology, 40,* 579–595.

Worfolk, J. B. (2000). Heat waves: Their impact on the health of elders. *Geriatric Nursing, 21,* 70–77.

Wynn, K. (1992). Addition and subtraction by human infants. *Nature, 358,* 749–750.

Yendovitskaya, T. V. (1971). Development of attention. In A. V. Zaporozhets & D. B. Elkonin (Eds.), *The psychology of preschool children.* Cambridge, MA: MIT Press.

Zaporozhets, A. V. (1965). The development of perception in the preschool child. *Monographs of the Society for Research in Child Development, 30*(2, Serial No. 100), 82–101.

Chapter 7: Cognition

Adey, P. S., & Shayer, M. (1992). Accelerating the development of formal thinking in middle and high school students: II. Postproject effects on science achievement. *Journal of Research in Science Teaching, 29,* 81–92.

Azmitia, M. (1992). Expertise, private speech, and the development of self-regulation. In R. M. Diaz & L. E. Berk (Eds.), *Private speech: From social interaction to self-regulation.* Hillsdale, NJ: Erlbaum.

Baillargeon, R., & DeVos, J. (1991). Object permanence in young infants: Further evidence. *Child Development, 62,* 1227–1246.

Baillargeon, R., & Graber, M. (1988). Evidence of location memory in 8-month-old infants in a nonsearch AB task. *Developmental Psychology, 24,* 502–511.

Basseches, M. (1984). *Dialectical thinking and adult development.* Norwood, NJ: Ablex.

Behrend, D. A., Rosengren, K., & Perlmutter, M. (1989). A new look at children's private speech: The effects of age, task difficulty, and parent presence. *International Journal of Behavioral Development, 12,* 305–320.

Beilin, H. (1992). Piaget's enduring contribution to developmental psychology. *Developmental Psychology, 28,* 191–204.

Berk, L. E. (1992). Children's private speech: An overview of theory and the status of research. In R. M. Diaz & L. E. Berk (Eds.), *Private speech: From social interaction to self-regulation.* Hillsdale, NJ: Erlbaum.

Berk, L. E., & Landau, S. (1993). Private speech of learning disabled and normally achieving children in classroom academic and laboratory contexts. *Child Development, 64,* 556–571.

Berk, L. E., & Winsler, A. (1995). *Scaffolding children's learning: Vygotsky and early childhood education.* Washington, DC: National Association for the Education of Young Children.

Bivens, J. A., & Berk, L. E. (1990). A longitudinal study of the development of elementary school children's private speech. *Merrill-Palmer Quarterly, 36,* 443–463.

Bjorklund, D. F. (1995). *Children's thinking: Developmental function and individual differences.* Pacific Grove, CA: Brooks/Cole.

Blackburn, J. A. (1984). The influence of personality, curriculum, and memory correlates on formal reasoning in young adults and elderly persons. *Journal of Gerontology, 39,* 207–209.

Blackburn, J. A., & Papalia, D. E. (1992). The study of adult cognition from a Piagetian perspective. In R. J. Sternberg & C. A. Berg (Eds.), *Intellectual development.* New York: Cambridge University Press.

Bodrova, E., & Leong, D. J. (1996). *Tools of the mind: The Vygotskian approach to early childhood education.* Englewood Cliffs, NJ: Prentice Hall.

Bouldin, P., & Pratt, C. (1999). Characteristics of preschool and school-age children with imaginary companions. *The Journal of Genetic Psychology, 160,* 397–410.

Bruner, J. S. (1983). *Child's talk: Learning to use language.* New York: Norton.

Bruner, J. S. (1997). Celebrating divergence: Piaget and Vygotsky. *Human Development, 40,* 63–73.

Capelli, C. A., Nakagawa, N., & Madden, C. M. (1990). How children understand sarcasm: The role of context and intonation. *Child Development, 61,* 1824–1841.

Case, R. (1998). The development of conceptual structures. In W. Damon (Editor-in-chief) and D. Kuhn and R. S. Siegler (Vol. Eds.), *Handbook of Child Psychology* (5th ed., Vol. 2, pp. 745–800). New York: Wiley.

Chapman, M., & Lindenberger, U. (1988). Functions, operations, and decalage in the development of transitivity. *Developmental Psychology, 24,* 542–551.

Chiu, S., & Alexander, P. A. (2000). The motivational function of preschoolers' private speech. *Discourse Processes, 30*, 133–152.

Commons, M. L., Richards, F. A., & Armon, C. (Eds.). (1984). *Beyond formal operations. Late adolescent and adult cognitive development.* New York: Praeger.

Cornelius, S. W., & Caspi, A. (1987). Everyday problem solving in adulthood and old age. *Psychology and Aging, 2*, 144–153.

Crain, W. (2000). *Theories of development: Concepts and applications* (4th ed.). Upper Saddle River, NJ: Prentice Hall.

Creusere, M. A. (1999). Theories of adults' understanding and use of irony and sarcasm: Applications to and evidence from research with children. *Developmental Review, 19*, 213–262.

De Lisi, R., & Staudt, J. (1980). Individual differences in college students' performance on formal operations tasks. *Journal of Applied Developmental Psychology, 1*, 163–174.

DeLoache, J. S., Miller, K. F., & Pierroutsakos, S. L. (1998). Reasoning and problem solving In W. Damon (Editor-in-chief) and D. Kuhn and R. S. Siegler (Vol. Eds.), *Handbook of Child Psychology* (5th ed., Vol. 2, pp. 801–850). New York: Wiley.

Denney, N. W. (1982). Aging and cognitive changes. In B. B. Wolman (Ed.), *Handbook of developmental psychology.* Englewood Cliffs, NJ: Prentice-Hall.

DeVries, R. (2000). Vygotsky, Piaget, and education: A reciprocal assimilation of theories and educational practices. *New Ideas in Psychology, 18*, 187–213.

Dews, S., Winner, E., Kaplan, J., Rosenblatt, E., Hunt, M., Lim, K., Mcgovern, A., Qualter, A., & Smarsh, B. (1996). Children's understanding of the meaning and functions of verbal irony. *Child Development, 67*, 3071–3085.

Diamond, A., Cruttenden, L., & Neiderman, D. (1994). AB with multiple wells: 1. Why are multiple wells sometimes easier than two wells? 2. Memory or memory + inhibition? *Developmental Psychology, 30*, 192–205.

Duncan, R. M., & Pratt, M. W. (1997). Microgenetic change in the quantity and quality of preschoolers' private speech. *International Journal of Behavioral Development, 20*, 367.

Elkind, D. (1967). Egocentrism in adolescence. *Child Development, 38*, 1025–1034.

Elkind, D., & Bowen, R. (1979). Imaginary audience behavior in children and adolescents. *Developmental Psychology, 15*, 38–44.

Ely, R. (1997). Language and literacy in the school years. In J. K. Gleason (Ed.), *The development of language* (4th ed.). Boston: Allyn & Bacon.

Enright, R., Lapsley, D., & Shukla, D. (1979). Adolescent egocentrism in early and late adolescence. *Adolescence, 14*, 687–695.

Faulkner, D., Joiner, R., Littleton, K., Miell, D., & Thompson, L. (2000). The mediating effect of task presentation on collaboration and children's acquisition of scientific reasoning. *European Journal of Psychology of Education, 15*, 417–430.

Feldman, D. H., & Fowler, R. C. (1997). The nature(s) of developmental change: Piaget, Vygotsky, and the transition process. *New Ideas in Psychology, 3*, 195–210.

Field, D. (1981). Can preschool children really learn to conserve? *Child Development, 52*, 326–334.

Fischer, K. W. (1980). A theory of cognitive development: The control and construction of hierarchies of skills. *Psychological Review, 87*, 477–531.

Fischer, K. W., & Bidell, T. (1991). Constraining nativist inferences about cognitive capacities. In S. Carey & Gelman (Eds.), *The epigenesis of mind: Essays on biology and cognition.* Hillsdale, NJ: Erlbaum.

Fischer, K. W., & Hencke, R. W. (1996). Infants' construction of actions in context: Piaget's contribution to research on early development. *Psychological Science, 7*, 204–210.

Fischer, K. W., Kenny, S. L., & Pipp, S. L. (1990). How cognitive processes and environmental conditions organize discontinuities in the development of abstractions. In C. N. Alexander & E. J. Langer (Eds.), *Higher stages of human development: Perspectives on adult growth.* New York: Oxford University Press.

Flavell, J. H. (1963). *The developmental psychology of Jean Piaget.* New York: Van Nostrand Reinhold.

Flavell, J. H. (1996). Piaget's legacy. *Psychological Science, 7*, 200–203.

Flavell, J. H., Everett, B. H., Croft, K., & Flavell, E. R. (1981). Young children's knowledge about visual perception: Further evidence for the level 1–level 2 distinction. *Developmental Psychology, 17*, 99–103.

Flavell, J. H., Miller, P. H., & Miller, S. A. (1993). *Cognitive development.* Englewood Cliffs, NJ: Prentice Hall.

Flieller, A. (1999). Comparison of the development of formal thought in adolescent cohorts aged 10 to 15 years (1967–1996 and 1972–1993). *Developmental Psychology, 35*, 1048–1058.

Frankenberger, K. D. (2000). Adolescent egocentrism: A comparison among adolescents and adults. *Journal of Adolescence, 23*, 343–354.

Frawley, W. (1997). *Vygotsky and cognitive science: Language and the unification of the social and computational mind.* Cambridge, MA: Harvard University Press.

Freedle, R., & Lewis, M. (1977). Prelinguistic conversation. In M. Lewis & L. Rosenblum (Eds.), *Interaction, conversation, and the development of language.* New York: Wiley.

Freund, L. S. (1990). Maternal regulation of children's problem-solving behavior and its impact on children's performance. *Child Development, 61*, 113–126.

Gallagher, J. M., & Easley, J. A., Jr. (Eds.). (1978). *Knowledge and development: Vol. 2. Piaget and education.* New York: Plenum.

Gauvain, M., & Rogoff, B. (1989). Collaborative problem-solving and children's planning skills. *Developmental Psychology, 25*, 139–151.

Gelman, R. (1972). The nature and development of early number concepts. In H. W. Reese (Ed.), *Advances in child development and behavior* (Vol. 7). New York: Academic Press.

Gelman, R. (1978). Cognitive development. *Annual Review of Psychology, 29*, 297–332.

Glassman, M. (1994). All things being equal: The two roads of Piaget and Vygotsky. *Developmental Psychology, 14*, 186–214.

Gleason, T. R., Sebanc, A. M., & Hartup, W. W. (2000). Imaginary companions of preschool children. *Developmental Psychology, 36*, 419–428.

Glick, J. C. (1975). Cognitive development in cross-cultural perspective. In F. Horowitz (Ed.), *Review of child development research* (Vol. 1). Chicago: University of Chicago Press.

Gopnik, A. (1996). The post-Piaget era. *Psychological Science, 7*, 221–225.

Gray, W. M., & Hudson, L. M. (1984). Formal operations and the imaginary audience. *Developmental Psychology, 20*, 619–627.

Greene, K., Krcmar, M., Walters, L. H., Rubin, D. L., & Hale, J. L. (2000). Targeting adolescent risk-taking behaviors: The contributions of egocentrism and sensation-seeking. *Journal of Adolescence, 23*, 439–461.

Greene, K., Rubin, D. L., Hale, J. L., & Walters, L. H. (1996). The utility of understanding adolescent egocentrism in designing health promotion messages. *Health Communication, 8*, 131–152.

Haith, M. M., & Benson, J. B. (1998). Infant cognition. In W. Damon (Editor-in-Chief) and D. Kuhn and R. S. Siegler (Vol. Eds.), *Handbook of Child Psychology* (5th ed., Vol. 2, pp. 199–254). New York: Wiley.

Holmbeck, G. N., Crossman, R. E., Wandrei, M. L., & Gasiewski, E. (1994). Cognitive development, egocentrism, self-esteem, and adolescent contraceptive knowledge, attitudes, and behavior. *Journal of Youth and Adolescence, 23*, 169–193.

Hooper, F. H., Hooper, J. O., & Colbert, K. K. (1985). Personality and memory correlates of intellectual functioning in adulthood: Piagetian and psychometric assessments. *Human Development, 28*, 101–107.

Inhelder, B. (1966). Cognitive development and its contribution to the diagnosis of some phenomena of mental deficiency. *Merrill-Palmer Quarterly, 12*, 299–319.

Inhelder, B., & Piaget, J. (1964). *Early growth of logic in the child: Classification and seriation.* New York: Harper & Row.

Irwin, R. R. (1991). Reconceptualizing the nature of dialectical postformal operational thinking: The effects of affectively mediated social experiences. In J. D. Sinnott & J. C. Cavanaugh (Eds.), *Bridging paradigms: Positive development in adulthood and cognitive aging.* New York: Praeger.

John-Steiner, V. (1992). Private speech among adults. In R. M. Diaz & L. E. Berk (Eds.), *Private speech: From social interaction to self-regulation.* Hillsdale, NJ: Erlbaum.

Kitchener, K. S., King, P. M., Wood, P. K., & Davison, M. L. (1989). Sequentiality and consistency in the development of reflective judgment: A six-year longitudinal study. *Journal of Applied Developmental Psychology, 10*, 73–95.

Klaczynski, P. A. (2000). Motivated scientific reasoning biases, epistemological beliefs, and theory polarization: A two-process approach to adolescent cognition. *Child Development, 71*, 1347–1366.

Klaczynski, P. A. (2001). Analytic and heuristic processing influences on adolescent reasoning and decision-making. *Child Development, 72*, 844–861.

Klaczynski, P. A., & Gordon, D. H. (1996a). Everyday statistical reasoning during adolescence and young adulthood: Motivational, general ability, and developmental influences. *Child Development, 67*, 2873–2892.

Klaczynski, P. A., & Gordon, D. H. (1996b). Self-serving influences on adolescents' evaluations of belief-relevant evidence. *Journal of Experimental Child Psychology, 62*, 317–339.

Klaczynski, P. A., & Narasimham, G. (1998). Development of scientific reasoning biases: Cognitive versus ego-protective explanations. *Developmental Psychology, 34*, 175–187.

Kohlberg, L., Yaeger, J., & Hjertholm, E. (1968), Private speech: Four studies and a review of theories. *Child Development, 39*, 691–736.

Krafft, K. C., & Berk, L. E. (1998). Private speech in two preschools: Significance of open-ended activities and make-believe play for verbal self-regulation. *Early Childhood Research Quarterly, 13*, 637–658.

Kuhn, D. (1993). Connecting scientific and informal reasoning. *Merrill-Palmer Quarterly, 39*, 74–103.

Labouvie-Vief, G. (1985). Intelligence and cognition. In J. E. Birren & K. W. Schaie (Eds.), *Handbook of the psychology of aging* (2nd ed.). New York: Van Nostrand Reinhold.

Labouvie-Vief, G. (1992). A neo-Piagetian perspective on adult cognitive development. In R. J. Sternberg & C. A. Berg (Eds.), *Intellectual development.* New York: Cambridge University Press.

Labouvie-Vief, G., Adams, C., Hakim-Larson, J., & Hayden, M. (1983, April). *Contexts of logic: The growth of interpretation from pre-adolescence to mature adulthood.* Paper presented at the biennial meeting of the Society for Research in Child Development, Detroit.

Lapsley, D. K. (1993). Toward an integrated theory of adolescent ego development: The "new look" at adolescent egocentrism. *American Journal of Orthopsychiatry, 63*, 562–571.

Lapsley, D. K., Fitzgerald, D. P., Rice, K. G., & Jackson, S. (1989). Separation-individuation and the "new look" at the imaginary audience and personal fable: A test of an integrative model. *Journal of Adolescent Research, 4*, 483–505.

Lapsley, D. K., Milstead, M., Quintana, S. M., Flannery, D., & Buss, R. R. (1986). Adolescent egocentrism and formal operations: Tests of a theoretical assumption. *Developmental Psychology, 22*, 800–807.

Laurendeau-Bendavid, M. (1977). Culture, schooling, and cognitive development: A comparative study of children in French Canada and Rwanda. In P. R. Dasen (Ed.), *Piagetian psychology: Cross-cultural contributions* (pp. 123–168). New York: Gardner Press.

Lourenco, O., & Machado, A. (1996). In defense of Piaget's theory: A reply to 10 common criticisms. *Psychological Review, 103*, 143–164.

Marcovitch, S., & Zelazo, D. (1999). The A-not-B error: Results from a logistic meta-analysis. *Child Development, 70*, 1297–1313.

Markman, E. M. (1989). *Categorization and naming in children.* Cambridge, MA: MIT Press.

Martorano, S. C. (1977). A developmental analysis of performance on Piaget's formal operations tasks. *Developmental Psychology, 13*, 666–672.

Matusov, E., & Hayes, R. (2000). Sociocultural critique of Piaget and Vygotsky. *New Ideas in Psychology, 18*, 215–239.

McGhee, P. E. (1979). *Humor: Its origin and development.* San Francisco: Freeman.

McGhee, P. E., & Chapman, A. J. (1980). *Children's humour.* London: Wiley.

Meijer, J., & Elshout, J. J. (2001). The predictive and discriminant validity of the zone of proximal development. *British Journal of Educational Psychology, 71*, 93–113.

Moore, M. K., & Meltzoff, A. N. (1999). New findings on object permanence: A developmental difference between two types of occlusion. *British Journal of Developmental Psychology, 17*, 563–584.

Mwamwenda, T. S. (1999). Undergraduate and graduate students' combinatorial reasoning and formal operations. *Journal of Genetic Psychology, 160*, 503–506.

Mwamwenda, T. S., & Mwamwenda, B. A. (1989). Formal operational thought among African and Canadian college students. *Psychological Reports, 64*, 43–46.

Neimark, E. D. (1975). Longitudinal development of formal operations thought. *Genetic Psychology Monographs, 91*, 171–225.

Neimark, E. D. (1979). Current status of formal operations research. *Human Development, 22*, 60–67.

Newman, C., Atkinson, J., & Braddick, O. (2001). The development of reaching and looking preferences in infants to objects of different sizes. *Developmental Psychology, 37*, 561–572.

O'Connor, B. P., & Nikolic, J. (1990). Identity development and formal operations as sources of adolescent egocentrism. *Journal of Youth and Adolescence, 19*, 149–158.

Pearce, K. A., & Denney, N. W. (1984). A lifespan study of classification preference. *Journal of Gerontology, 39*, 458–464.

Perry, W. G., Jr. (1970). *Forms of intellectual and ethical development in the college years: A scheme.* New York: Holt, Rinehart & Winston.

Piaget, J. (1926). *Language and thought in the child.* London: Routledge & Kegan Paul.

Piaget, J. (1929). *The child's conception of the world.* New York: Harcourt, Brace & World.

Piaget, J. (1952). *The origins of intelligence in children.* New York: International Universities Press.

Piaget, J. (1954). *The construction of reality in the child.* New York: Basic Books.

Piaget, J. (1970). Piaget's theory. In P. H. Mussen (Ed.), *Carmichael's manual of child psychology* (Vol. 1). New York: Wiley.

Piaget, J. (1972). Intellectual evolution from adolescence to adulthood. *Human Development, 15*, 1–12.

Piaget, J. (1977). The role of action in the development of thinking. In W. F. Overton & J. M. Gallagher (Eds.), *Knowledge and development* (Vol. 1). New York: Plenum.

Piaget, J. (1985). *The equilibration of cognitive structures: The central problem of intellectual development* (T. Brown & K. J. Thampy, Trans.). Chicago: University of Chicago Press.

Piaget, J., & Inhelder, B. (1956). *The child's conception of space.* New York: Norton.

Richards, F. A., & Commons, M. L. (1990). Postformal cognitive-developmental theory and research: A review of its current status. In C. N. Alexander & E. J. Langer (Eds.), *Higher stages of human development: Perspectives on adult growth.* New York: Oxford University Press.

Riegel, K. F. (1973). Dialectic operations: The final period of cognitive development. *Human Development, 16*, 346–370.

Rogoff, B. (1997, April). *Development as transformation of participation in sociocultural activities.* Paper presented at the biennial meeting of the Society for Research in Child Development, Washington, DC.

Rogoff, B., Mistry, J., Goncu, A., & Mosier, C. (1993). Guided participation in cultural activity by toddlers and caregivers. *Monographs of the Society for Research in Child Development, 58*(8, Serial No. 236).

Rovee-Collier, C. (2001). Information pick-up by infants: What is it and how can we tell? *Journal of Experimental Child Psychology, 78*, 35–49.

Ruffman, T. K., & Olson, D. R. (1989). Children's ascriptions of knowledge to others. *Developmental Psychology, 25*, 601–606.

Ryan, R. M., & Kuczkowski, R. (1994). The imaginary audience, self-consciousness, and public individuation in adolescence. *Journal of Personality, 62*, 219–238.

Salthouse, T. A. (1990). Cognitive competence and expertise in aging. In J. E. Birren & K. W. Schaie (Eds.), *The handbook of the psychology of aging* (3rd ed.). San Diego: Academic Press.

Schwitzgebel, E. (1999). Gradual belief change in children. *Human Development, 42*, 283–296.

Shwe, H. K. (1999, April). *Gricean pragmatics in preschoolers: Young children's understanding of sarcasm and irony.* Paper presented at the biennial meeting of the Society for Research in Child Development, Albuquerque.

Siegler, R. S., & Ellis, S. (1996). Piaget on childhood. *Psychological Science, 7*, 211–215.

Singer, D. G., & Singer, J. L. (1990). *The house of make-believe: Children's play and the developing imagination.* Cambridge, MA: Harvard University Press.

Sinnott, J. (1996). The developmental approach: Postformal thought as adaptive intelligence. In F. Blanchard-Fields & T. M. Hess (Eds.), *Perspectives on cognitive change in adulthood and aging.* New York: McGraw-Hill.

Smagorinsky, P. (1995). The social construction of data: Methodological problems of investigating learning in the zone of proximal development. *Review of Educational Research, 65*, 191–212.

Stanovich, K. E., & West, R. F. (1997). Reasoning independently of prior belief and individual differences in actively open-minded thinking. *Journal of Educational Psychology, 89*, 342–357.

Taylor, M. (1999). *Imaginary companions and the children who create them.* New York: Oxford University Press.

Taylor, M., Cartwright, B. S., & Carlson, S. M. (1993). A developmental investigation of children's imaginary companions. *Developmental Psychology, 29*, 276–285.

Taylor, M., & Gelman, S. A. (1989). Incorporating new words into the lexicon: Preliminary evidence for language hierarchies in two-year-old children. *Child Development, 60*, 625–636.

Trabasso, T. (1995). Representation, memory, and reasoning: How do we make transitive inferences? In A. D. Pick (Ed.), *Minnesota symposia on child psychology* (Vol. 9). Minneapolis: University of Minnesota.

Vartanian, L. R. (2000). Revisiting the imaginary audience and personal fable constructs of adolescent egocentrism: A conceptual review. *Adolescence, 35*, 639–661.

Vartanian, L. R., & Powlishta, K. K. (1996). A longitudinal examination of the social-cognitive foundations of adolescent egocentrism. *Journal of Early Adolescence, 16*, 157–178.

Vygotsky, L. S. (1962). *Thought and language* (E. Hanfmann & G. Vakar, Eds. & Trans.). Cambridge, MA: MIT Press. (Original work published 1934)

Vygotsky, L. S. (1978). *Mind in society: The development of higher mental processes* (M. Cole, V. John-Steiner, S. Scribner, & E. Souberman, Eds.). Cambridge, MA: Harvard University Press. (Original work published 1930, 1933, 1935)

Waxman, S. R., & Hatch, T. (1992). Beyond the basics: Preschool children label objects flexibly at multiple hierarchical levels. *Journal of Child Language, 19,* 153–166.

Werker, J. F., & Desjardins, R. N. (1995). Listening to speech in the first year of life: Experiential influences on phoneme perception. *Current Directions in Psychological Science, 4,* 76–81.

Wertsch, J. V., & Tulviste, P. (1992). L. S. Vygotsky and contemporary developmental psychology. *Developmental Psychology, 28,* 548–557.

Williams, K. C. (1996). Piagetian principles: Simple and effective application. *Journal of Intellectual Disability Research, 40,* 110–119.

Winsler, A., Carlton, M. P., & Barry, M. J. (2000). Age-related changes in preschool children's systematic use of private speech in a natural setting. *Journal of Child Language, 27,* 665–687.

Yalisove, D. (1978). The effect of riddle structure on children's comprehension of riddles. *Developmental Psychology, 14,* 173–180.

Yan, B., & Arlin, P. K. (1995). Nonabsolute/relativistic thinking: A common factor underlying models of postformal reasoning? *Journal of Adult Development, 2,* 223–240.

Chapter 8: Memory and Information Processing

Abravanel, E., & Sigafoos, A. D. (1984). Exploring the presence of imitation during early infancy. *Child Development, 55,* 381–392.

Adams, C. (1991). Qualitative age differences in memory for text: A life-span developmental perspective. *Psychology and Aging, 6,* 323–336.

Anisfeld, M. (1996). Only tongue protrusion modeling is matched by neonates. *Developmental Review, 16,* 149–161.

Atkinson, R. C., & Shiffrin, R. M. (1968). Human memory: A proposed system and its control processes. In K. W. Spence & J. T. Spence (Eds.), *The psychology of learning and motivation: Advances in research and theory* (Vol. 2). New York: Academic Press.

Baddeley, A. (1986). *Working memory.* Oxford: Oxford University Press.

Baddeley, A. (1992). Working memory. *Science, 255,* 556–559.

Bahrick, H. P. (1984). Semantic memory content in permastore: Fifty years of memory for Spanish learned in high school. *Journal of Experimental Psychology: General, 113,* 1–29.

Bahrick, H. P., Bahrick, P. O., & Wittlinger, R. P. (1975). Fifty years of memory for names and faces: A cross-sectional approach. *Journal of Experimental Psychology: General, 104,* 54–75.

Bahrick, H. P., & Hall, L. K. (1991). Lifetime maintenance of high school mathematics content. *Journal of Experimental Psychology: General, 120,* 20–33.

Baker, L., & Brown, A. L. (1984). Metacognitive skills and reading. In P. D. Pearson (Ed.), *A handbook of reading research.* New York: Longman.

Baker-Ward, L., Gordon, B. N., Ornstein, P. A., Larus, D. M., & Clubb, P. A. (1993). Young children's long-term retention of a pediatric examination. *Child Development, 64,* 1519–1533.

Baker-Ward, L., Ornstein, P. A., & Holden, D. J. (1984). The expression of memorization in early childhood. *Journal of Experimental Child Psychology, 37,* 555–575.

Baltes, P. B., & Kliegl, R. (1992). Further testing of limits of cognitive plasticity: Negative age differences in a mnemonic skill are robust. *Developmental Psychology, 28,* 121–125.

Baltes, P. B., Smith, J., & Staudinger, U. M. (1992). Wisdom and successful aging. In T. B. Sonderegger (Ed.), *Nebraska Symposium on Motivation: Vol. 39. Psychology and aging.* Lincoln: University of Nebraska Press.

Barr, R., Dowden, A., & Hayne, H. (1996). Developmental changes in deferred imitation by 6- to 24-month-old infants. *Infant Behavior & Development, 19,* 159–170.

Barrett, T. R., & Wright, M. (1981). Age-related facilitation in recall following semantic processing. *Journal of Gerontology, 36,* 194–199.

Bauer, P. J. (1996). What do infants recall of their lives? Memory for specific events by one- to two-year-olds. *American Psychologist, 51,* 29–41.

Bauer, P. J., Hertsgaard, L. A., & Wewerka, S. S. (1995). Effects of experience and reminding on long-term recall in infancy: Remembering not to forget. *Journal of Experimental Child Psychology, 59,* 260–298.

Bauer, P. J., Wenner, J. A., Dropik, P. L., & Wewerka, S. S. (2000). Parameters of remembering and forgetting in the transition from infancy to early childhood. *Monographs of the Society for Research in Child Development, 65*(Serial No. 263).

Berg, C. A. (1989). Knowledge of strategies for dealing with everyday problems from childhood through adolescence. *Developmental Psychology, 25,* 607–618.

Berg, C. A., & Klaczynski, P. A. (1996). Practical intelligence and problem solving: Searching for perspectives. In F. Blanchard-Fields & T. M. Hess (Eds.), *Perspectives on cognitive change in adulthood and aging.* New York: McGraw-Hill.

Best, D. L. (1993). Inducing children to generate mnemonic organizational strategies: An examination of long-term retention and materials. *Developmental Psychology, 29,* 324–336.

Biederman, I., Cooper, E. E., Fox, P. W., & Mahadevan, R. S. (1992). Unexceptional spatial memory in an exceptional memorist. *Journal of Experimental Psychology: Learning, Memory, and Cognition, 18,* 654–657.

Bjork, R. A., & Bjork, E. L. (Eds.) (1998). *Memory.* New York: Academic Press.

Bjorklund, D. F. (1985). The role of conceptual knowledge in the development of organization in children's memory. In C. J. Brainerd & M. Pressley (Eds.), *Basic processes in memory development: Progress in cognitive development research.* New York: Springer-Verlag.

Bjorklund, D. F. (1995). *Children's thinking: Developmental function and individual differences.* Pacific Grove, CA: Brooks/Cole.

Bjorklund, D. F. (1997). In search of a metatheory for cognitive development (or, Piaget is dead and I don't feel so good myself). *Child Development, 68,* 144–148.

Bjorklund, D. F., Miller, P. H., Coyle, T. R., & Slawinski, J. L. (1997). Instructing children to use memory strategies: Evidence of utilization deficiencies in memory training studies. *Developmental Review, 17,* 411–441.

Blanchard-Fields, F., Chen, Y., & Norris, L. (1997). Everyday problem solving across the adult life span: Influence of domain specificity and cognitive appraisal. *Psychology and Aging, 12,* 684–693.

Botwinick, J. (1984). *Aging and behavior: A comprehensive integration of research findings* (3rd ed.). New York: Springer.

Brainerd, C. J., & Gordon, L. L. (1994). Development of verbatim and gist memory for numbers. *Developmental Psychology, 30,* 163–177.

Brainerd, C. J., & Reyna, V. F. (1993). Domains of fuzzy trace theory. In M. L. Howe & R. Pasnak (Eds.), *Emerging themes in cognitive development: Vol. 1. Foundations.* New York: Springer-Verlag.

Bray, N. W., Hersh, R. E., & Turner, L. A. (1985). Selective remembering during adolescence. *Developmental Psychology, 21,* 290–294.

Bremner, J. D., & Narayan, M. (1998). The effects of stress on memory and the hippocampus throughout the life cycle: Implications for childhood development and aging. *Development and Psychopathology, 10,* 871–886.

Brown, A. L. (1975). The development of memory: Knowing, knowing about knowing, and knowing how to know. In H. W. Reese (Ed.), *Advances in child development and behavior* (Vol. 10). New York: Academic Press.

Brown, A. L., Bransford, J. D., Ferrara, R. A., & Campione, J. C. (1983). Learning, remembering and understanding. In J. H. Flavell & E. M. Markman (Eds.), *Handbook of child psychology: Vol. 3. Cognitive development* (4th ed.). New York: Wiley.

Brown, A. L., & Smiley, S. S. (1978). The development of strategies for studying text. *Child Development, 49,* 1076–1088.

Bruck, M., & Ceci, S. J. (1999). The suggestibility of children's memory. *Annual Review of Psychology, 50,* 419–439.

Byrnes, J. P. (1996). *Cognitive development and learning in instructional contexts.* Boston: Allyn & Bacon.

Camp, C. J. (1989). World-knowledge systems. In L. W. Poon, D. C. Rubin, & B. A. Wilson (Eds.), *Everyday cognition in adulthood and late life.* Cambridge, England: Cambridge University Press.

Camp, C. J., Foss, J. W., O'Hanlon, A. M., & Stevens, A. B. (1996). Memory interventions for persons with dementia. *Applied Cognitive Psychology, 10,* 193–210.

Camp, C. J., & McKitrick, L. A. (1992). Memory interventions in Alzheimer's-type dementia populations: Methodological and theoretical issues. In R. L. West & J. D. Sinnott (Eds.), *Everyday memory and aging: Current research and methodology* (pp. 155–172). New York: Springer-Verlag.

Caplan, L. J., & Schooler, C. (2001). Age effects on analogy-based memory for text. *Experimental Aging Research, 27,* 151–165.

Carlesimo, G. A., Mauri, M., Graceffa, A. M. S., Fadda, L., Loasses, A., Lorusso, S., & Caltagirone, C. (1998). Memory performances in young, elderly, and very old healthy individuals versus patients with Alzheimer's disease: Evidence for discontinuity between normal and pathological aging. *Journal of Clinical and Experimental Neuropsychology, 20,* 14–29.

Case, R. (1985). *Intellectual development: Birth to adulthood.* Orlando, FL: Academic Press.

Cassel, W. S., Roebers, C. M., & Bjorklund, D. F. (1996). Developmental patterns of eyewitness responses to repeated and increasingly suggestive questions. *Journal of Experimental Child Psychology, 61,* 116–133.

Cavanaugh, J. C. (1996). Memory self-efficacy as a moderation of memory change. In F. Blanchard-Fields & T. M. Hess (Eds.), *Perspectives on cognitive change in adulthood and aging.* New York: McGraw-Hill.

Cavanaugh, J. C., Grady, J. G., & Perlmutter, M. (1983). Forgetting and use of memory aids in 20 to 70 year olds' everyday life. *International Journal of Aging and Human Development, 17,* 113–122.

Ceci, S. J., & Bruck , M. (1998). Children's testimony: Applied and basic issues. In W. Damon (Editor-in-Chief), I. E. Sigel & K. A. Renninger (Vol. Eds.), *Handbook of child psychology: Vol. 4. Child psychology in practice* (5th ed., pp. 713–774). New York: Wiley.

Chen, Z., & Siegler, R. S. (2000). Across the great divide: Bridging the gap between understanding of toddlers' and older children's thinking. *Monographs of the Society for Research in Child Development, 65*(Serial No. 261).

Cherry, K. E., & LeCompte, D. C. (1999). Age and individual differences influence prospective memory. *Psychology and Aging, 14,* 60–76.

Cherry, K. E., & Smith, A. D. (1998). Normal memory aging. In M. Hersen & V. B. Van Hasselt (Eds.), *Handbook of clinical geropsychology* (pp. 87–110). New York: Plenum.

Chi, M. T. H. (1978). Knowledge structures and memory development. In R. Siegler (Ed.), *Children's thinking: What develops?* Hillsdale, NJ: Erlbaum.

Cohen, M. (1996). Preschoolers' practical thinking and problem solving: The acquisition of an optimal solution strategy. *Cognitive Development, 11,* 357–373.

Coyle, T. R., & Bjorklund, D. F. (1996). The development of strategic memory: A modified microgenetic assessment of utilization deficiencies. *Cognitive Development, 11,* 295–314.

Cregger, M. E., & Rogers, W. A. (1998). Memory for activities for young, young-old, and old adults. *Experimental Aging Research, 24,* 195–201.

DeLoache, J. S., Cassidy, D. J., & Brown, A. L. (1985). Precursors of mnemonic strategies in very young children's memory. *Child Development, 56,* 125–137.

DeLoache, J. S., Miller, K. F., & Pierroutsakos, S. L. (1998). Reasoning and problem solving. In W. Damon (Editor-in-Chief), D. Kuhn & R. Siegler (Vol. Eds.), *Handbook of child psychology* (5th ed.): *Vol. 2: Cognition, perception, and language* (pp. 801–850). New York: Wiley.

DeMarie, D., Norman, A., & Abshier, D. W. (2000). Age and experience influence different verbal and nonverbal measures of children's scripts for the zoo. *Cognitive Development, 15,* 241–262.

Dempster, F. N. (1981). Memory span: Sources of individual and developmental differences. *Psychological Bulletin, 89,* 63–100.

Dempster, F. N. (1985). Short-term memory development in childhood and adolescence. In C. J. Brainerd & M. Pressley (Eds.), *Basic processes in memory development: Progress in cognitive development research.* New York: Springer-Verlag.

Denney, N. W. (1980). Task demands and problem-solving strategies in middle-aged and older adults. *Journal of Gerontology, 35,* 559–564.

Denney, N. W. (1982). Aging and cognitive changes. In B. B. Wolman (Ed.), *Handbook of developmental psychology.* Englewood Cliffs, NJ: Prentice-Hall.

Denney, N. W. (1989). Everyday problem solving: Methodological issues, research findings, and a model. In L. W. Poon, D. C. Rubin, & B. A. Wilson (Eds.), *Everyday cognition in adulthood and late life.* Cambridge, England: Cambridge University Press.

Denney, N. W., & Pearce, K. A. (1989). A developmental study of practical problem solving in adults. *Psychology and Aging, 4,* 438–442.

Dixon, R. A. (1992). Contextual approaches to adult intellectual development. In R. J. Sternberg & C. A. Berg (Eds.), *Intellectual development.* New York: Cambridge University Press.

Earles, J. L., & Kersten, A. W. (1999). Processing speed and adult age differences in activity memory. *Experimental Aging Research, 25,* 243–253.

Engle, R. W., Tuholski, S. W., Laughlin, J. E., & Conway, A. R. A. (1999). Working memory, short-term memory and general fluid intelligence: A latent variable approach. *Journal of Experimental Psychology: General, 128,* 309–331.

Ericsson, K. A. (1996). The acquisition of expert performance: An introduction to some of the issues. In K. A. Ericsson (Ed.), *The road to excellence: The acquisition of expert performance in the arts and sciences, sports, and games.* Mahwah, NJ: Erlbaum.

Ericsson, K. A., Chase, W. G., & Faloon, S. (1980). Acquisition of a memory skill. *Science, 208,* 1181–1182.

Ericsson, K. A., & Kintsch, W. (1995). Long-term working memory. *Psychological Review, 102,* 211–245.

Fagan, J. F., Jr. (1984). Infant memory: History, current trends, relations to cognitive psychology. In M. Moscovitch (Ed.), *Infant memory: Its relation to normal and pathological memory in humans and other animals.* New York: Plenum.

Farrar, M. J., & Goodman, G. S. (1990). Developmental differences in the relation between script and episodic memory: Do they exist? In R. Fivush & J. Hudson (Eds.), *Knowing and remembering in young children* (pp. 30–64). New York: Cambridge University Press.

Finkel, D., & McGue, M. (1998). Age differences in the nature and origin of individual differences in memory: A behavior genetic analysis. *International Journal of Aging and Human Development, 47,* 217–239.

Fivush, R., Gray, J. T., & Fromhoff, F. A. (1987). Two-year-olds talk about the past. *Cognitive Development, 2,* 393–409.

Fivush, R., & Hammond, N. R. (1989). Time and again: Effects of repetition and retention interval on 2-year-olds' event recall. *Journal of Experimental Child Psychology, 47,* 259–273.

Flavell, J. H. (1999). Cognitive development: Children's knowledge about the mind. *Annual Review of Psychology, 50,* 21–45.

Flavell, J. H., Beach, D. R., & Chinsky, J. M. (1966). Spontaneous verbal rehearsal in a memory task as a function of age. *Child Development, 37,* 283–299.

Flavell, J. H., Miller, P. H., & Miller, S. A. (1993). *Cognitive development.* Englewood Cliffs, NJ: Prentice Hall.

Flavell, J. H., & Wellman, H. M. (1977). Metamemory. In R. V. Kail & J. W. Hagen (Eds.), *Perspectives on the development of memory and cognition.* Hillsdale, NJ: Erlbaum.

Fletcher, K. L., & Bray, N. W. (1996). External memory strategy use in preschool children. *Merrill-Palmer Quarterly, 42,* 379–396.

Floyd, M., & Scogin, F. (1997). Effects of memory training on the subjective memory functioning and mental health of older adults: A meta-analysis. *Psychology and Aging, 12,* 150–161.

Foos, P. W., & Sarno, S. J. (1998). Adult age differences in semantic and episodic memory. *Journal of Genetic Psychology, 159,* 297–312.

Friedman, S. B. (1972). Habituation and recovery of visual response in the alert human newborn. *Journal of Experimental Child Psychology, 13,* 339–349.

Frieske, D. A., & Park, D. C. (1999). Memory for news in young and old adults. *Psychology and Aging, 14,* 90–98.

Fry, A. F., & Hale, S. (1996). Processing speed, working memory, and fluid intelligence: Evidence for a developmental cascade. *Psychological Science, 7,* 237–241.

Gardner, H. (1985). *The mind's new science: A history of the cognitive revolution.* New York: Basic Books.

Glaser, R., & Chi, M. T. H. (1988). Overview. In M. T. H. Chi, R. Glaser, & M. Farr (Eds.), *The nature of expertise.* Hillsdale, NJ: Erlbaum.

Goodman, G. S., & Schaaf, J. M. (1997). Over a decade of research on children's eyewitness testimony: What have we learned? Where do we go from here? *Applied Cognitive Psychology, 11,* 5–20.

Graf, P. (1990). Life-span changes in implicit and explicit memory. *Bulletin of the Psychonomic Society, 28,* 353–358.

Graf, P., Squire, L. R., & Mandler, G. (1984). The information that amnesic patients do not forget. *Journal of Experimental Psychology: Learning, Memory, and Cognition, 10,* 164–178.

Green, C. R. (2001). *Total memory workout: 8 easy steps to maximum memory fitness.* New York: Bantam Doubleday.

Guttentag, R. E. (1985). Memory and aging: Implications for theories of memory development during childhood. *Developmental Review, 5,* 56–77.

Harley, K., & Reese, E. (1999). Origins of autobiographical memory. *Developmental Psychology, 35,* 1338–1348.

Hattie, J., Biggs, J., & Purdie, N. (1996). Effects of learning skills interventions on student learning: A meta-analysis. *Review of Educational Research, 66,* 99–136.

Haught, P. A., Hill, L. A., Nardi, A. H., & Walls, R. T. (2000). Perceived ability and level of education as predictors of traditional and practical adult problem solving. *Experimental Aging Research, 26,* 89–101.

Herbert, J., & Hayne, H. (2000). Memory retrieval by 18–30-month-olds: Age-related changes in representational flexibility. *Developmental Psychology, 36,* 473–484.

Hess, T. M., & Pullen, S. M. (1996). Memory in context. In F. Blanchard-Fields & T. M. Hess (Eds.), *Perspectives on cognitive change in adulthood and aging.* New York: McGraw-Hill.

Hilgard, E. R., & Loftus, E. F. (1979). Effective interrogation of the eyewitness. *International Journal of Clinical and Experimental Psychology, 27,* 342–357.

Houx, P. J., Vreeling, F. W., & Jolles, J. (1991). Rigorous health screening reduces age effect on memory scanning task. *Brain and Cognition, 15,* 246–260.

Howard, D. V. (1996). The aging of implicit and explicit memory. In F. Blanchard-Fields & T. M. Hess (Eds.), *Perspectives on cognitive change in adulthood and aging.* New York: McGraw-Hill.

Howe, M. L. (2000). *The fate of early memories: Developmental science and the retention of childhood experiences.* Washington, DC: American Psychological Association.

Howe, M. L., & Courage, M. L. (1993). On resolving the enigma of infantile amnesia. *Psychological Bulletin, 113,* 305–326.

Howe, M. L., & Courage, M. L. (1997). The emergence and early development of autobiographical memory. *Psychological Review, 104,* 499–523.

Howe, M. L., Courage, M. L., & Peterson, C. (1994). How can I remember when "I" wasn't there: Long-term retention of traumatic experiences and emergence of the cognitive self. *Consciousness and Cognition, 3,* 327–355.

Hulicka, I. M. (1967). Age differences in retention as a function of interference. *Journal of Gerontology, 22,* 180–184.

Hultsch, D. F., Hammer, M., & Small, B. J. (1993). Age differences in cognitive performance in later life: Relationships to self-reported health and activity life style. *Journal of Gerontology: Psychological Sciences, 48,* P1–P11.

Jensen, A. R. (1990). Speed of information processing in a calculating prodigy. *Intelligence, 14,* 259–274.

Jones, S. S. (1996). Imitation or exploration? Young infants' matching of adults' oral gestures. *Child Development, 67,* 1952–1969.

Joyce, C. A., Paller, K. A., McIsaac, H. K., & Kutas, M. (1998). Memory changes with normal aging: Behavioral and electrophysiological measures. *Psychophysiology, 35,* 669–678.

Justice, E. M., Bakerward, L., Gupta, S., & Jannings, L. R. (1997). Means to the goal of remembering: Developmental changes in awareness of strategy use–performance relations. *Journal of Experimental Child Psychology, 65,* 293–314.

Kail, R. (1990). *The development of memory in children* (3rd ed.). New York: Freeman.

Kail, R. (1991). Developmental change in speed of processing during childhood and adolescence. *Psychological Bulletin, 109,* 490–501.

Kail, R., & Bisanz, J. (1992). The information-processing perspective on cognitive development in childhood and adolescence. In R. J. Sternberg & C. A. Berg (Eds.), *Intellectual development.* New York: Cambridge University Press.

Kail, R., & Salthouse, T. A. (1994). Processing speed as a mental capacity. *Acta Psychologica, 86,* 199–225.

Kaplan, A. S., & Murphy, G. L. (2000). Category learning with minimal prior knowledge. *Journal of Experimental Psychology: Learning, Memory, and Cognition, 26,* 829–845.

Kasworm, C. E., & Medina, R. A. (1990). Adult competence in everyday tasks: A cross-sectional secondary analysis. *Educational Gerontology, 16,* 27–48.

Kelemen, W. L. (2000). Metamemory cues and monitoring accuracy: Judging what you know and what you will know. *Journal of Educational Psychology, 92,* 800–810.

Klaczynski, P. A. (2001). Analytic and heuristic processing influences on adolescent reasoning and decision-making. *Child Development, 72,* 844–861.

Klein, P. J., & Meltzoff, A. N. (1999). Long-term memory, forgetting, and deferred imitation in 12-month-old infants. *Developmental Science, 2,* 102–113.

Kliegl, R., Smith, J., & Baltes, P. B. (1989). Testing-the-limits and the study of adult age differences in cognitive plasticity of a mnemonic skill. *Developmental Psychology, 25,* 247–256.

Kolstad, V., & Aguiar, A. (1995, March). *Means–end sequences in young infants.* Paper presented at the biennial meeting of the Society for Research in Child Development, Indianapolis.

Koriat, A., Goldsmith, M., & Pansky, A. (2000). Toward a psychology of memory accuracy. *Annual Review of Psychology, 51,* 481–538.

Koutstaal, W., Schacter, D. L., Johnson, M. K., Angell, K. E., & Gross, M. S. (1998). Post-event review in older and younger adults: Improving memory accessibility of complex everyday events. *Psychology and Aging, 13,* 277–296.

Kuebli, J., & Fivush, R. (1994). Children's representation and recall of event alternatives. *Journal of Experimental Child Psychology, 58,* 25–45.

Kuhn, D. (1992). Cognitive development. In M. H. Bornstein & M. E. Lamb (Eds.), *Developmental psychology: An advanced textbook* (3rd ed.). Hillsdale, NJ: Erlbaum.

Kuhn, D. (2000). Metacognitive development. *Current Directions in Psychological Science, 9,* 178–181.

Lange, G., & Pierce, S. H. (1992). Memory-strategy learning and maintenance in preschool children. *Developmental Psychology, 28,* 453–462.

LeBlanc, R. S., Muise, J. G., & Blanchard, L. (1992). Backward masking in children and adolescents: Sensory transmission, accrual rate and asymptotic performance. *Journal of Experimental Psychology, 53,* 105–114.

Leichtman, M. D., & Ceci, S. J. (1993). The problem of infantile amnesia: Lessons from fuzzy-trace theory. In M. L. Howe & R. Pasnak (Eds.), *Emerging themes in cognitive development: Vol. 1. Foundations.* New York: Springer-Verlag.

Levy, B. (1996). Improving memory in old age through implicit self-stereotyping. *Journal of Personality and Social Psychology, 71,* 1092–1107.

Levy, B., & Langer, E. (1994). Aging free from negative stereotypes: Successful memory in China and among the American deaf. *Journal of Personality and Social Psychology, 66,* 989–997.

Lewandowsky, S., & Kirsner, K. (2000). Knowledge partitioning: Context-dependent use of expertise. *Memory & Cognition, 28,* 295–305.

Li, K. Z. H., Lindenberger, U., Freund, A. M., & Baltes, P. B. (2001). Walking while memorizing: Age-related differences in compensatory behavior. *Psychological Science, 12,* 230–237.

Lie, E., & Newcombe, N. S. (1999). Elementary school children's explicit and implicit memory for faces of preschool classmates. *Developmental Psychology, 35,* 102–112.

Light, L. L. (1991). Memory and aging: Four hypotheses in search of data. *Annual Review of Psychology, 42,* 333–376.

Light, L. L., & LaVoie, D. (1993). Direct and indirect measures of memory in old age. In P. Graf & M. E. J. Masson (Eds.), *Implicit memory: New directions in cognition, development and neuropsychology* (pp. 207–230). Hillsdale, NJ: Erlbaum.

Lindenberger, U., & Baltes, P. B. (1994). Sensory functioning and intelligence in old age: A strong connection. *Psychology and Aging, 9,* 339–355.

Lindenberger, U., Marsiske, M., & Baltes, P. B. (2000). Memorizing while walking: Increase in dual-task costs from young adulthood to old age. *Psychology and Aging, 15,* 417–436.

Lorsbach, T. C., & Reimer, J. F. (1997). Developmental changes in the inhibition of previously relevant information. *Journal of Experimental Child Psychology, 64,* 317–342.

Luszcz, M. A., Bryan, J., & Kent, P. (1997). Predicting episodic memory performance of very old men and women: Contributions from age, depression, activity, cognitive ability, and speed. *Psychology and Aging, 12,* 340–351.

Maki, P. M., Zonderman, A. B., & Weingartner, H. (1999). Age differences in implicit memory, fragmented object identification, and category exemplar generation. *Psychology and Aging, 14,* 184–194.

Marchant, G., Robinson, J., Anderson, U., & Schadewald, M. (1991). Analogical transfer and expertise in legal reasoning. *Organizational Behavior & Human Decision Making, 48,* 272–290.

Marian, V., & Neisser, U. (2000). Language-dependent recall of autobiographical memories. *Journal of Experimental Psychology: General, 129,* 361–367.

Marini, Z., & Case, R. (1994). The development of abstract reasoning about the physical and social world. *Child Development, 65,* 147–159.

Marsiske, M., & Willis, S. L. (1995). Dimensionality of everyday problem solving in older adults. *Psychology and Aging, 10,* 269–283.

McDonald-Miszczak, L., Hertzog, C., & Hultsch, D. F. (1995). Stability and accuracy of metamemory in adulthood and aging: A longitudinal analysis. *Psychology and Aging, 10,* 553–564.

Meltzoff, A. N. (1988). Infant imitation and memory: Nine-month-olds in immediate and deferred tests. *Child Development, 59,* 217–225.

Meltzoff, A. N. (1995). What infant memory tells us about infantile amnesia: Long-term recall and deferred imitation. *Journal of Experimental Child Psychology, 59,* 497–515.

Meltzoff, A. N., & Moore, M. K. (1977). Imitation of facial and manual gestures by human neonates. *Science, 198,* 75–78.

Meltzoff, A. N., & Moore, M. K. (1983). Newborn infants imitate adult facial gestures. *Child Development, 54,* 702–709.

Meltzoff, A. N., & Moore, M. K. (1989). Imitation in newborn infants: Exploring the range of gestures initiated and the underlying mechanisms. *Developmental Psychology, 25,* 954–962.

Memon, A., & Vartoukian, R. (1996). The effects of repeated questioning on young children's eyewitness testimony. *British Journal of Psychology, 87,* 403–415.

Miller, P. H. (1990). The development of strategies of selective attention. In D. F. Bjorklund (Ed.), *Children's strategies: Contemporary views of cognitive development.* Hillsdale, NJ: Erlbaum.

Miller, P. H. (1994). Individual differences in children's strategic behavior: Utilization deficiencies. *Learning and Individual Differences, 6,* 285–307.

Miller, P. H., & Seier, W. S. (1994). Strategy utilization deficiencies in children: When, where and why. In H. W. Reese (Ed.), *Advances in child development and behavior* (Vol. 25, pp. 107–156). New York: Academic Press.

Miller, P. H., & Weiss, M. G. (1981). Children's attention allocation, understanding of attention, and performance on the incidental learning task. *Child Development, 52,* 1183–1190.

Morrell, R. W., Park, D. C., & Poon, L. W. (1989). Quality of instructions on prescription drug labels: Effects on memory and comprehension in young and old adults. *Gerontologist, 29,* 345–354.

Morris, J. C., Storandt, M., Miller, J. P., McKeel, D., Price, J. L., Rubin, E. H., & Berg, L. (2001). Mild cognitive impairment represents early-stage Alzheimer disease. *Archives of Neurology, 58,* 397–410.

Morrow, D., Leirer, V., Altieri, P., & Fitzsimmons, C. (1994). When expertise reduces age differences in performance. *Psychology and Aging, 9,* 134–148.

Murphy, D. R., Craik, F. I. M., Li, K. Z. H., & Schneider, B. A. (2000). Comparing the effects of aging and background noise on short-term memory performance. *Psychology and Aging, 15,* 323–334.

Nelson, C. A. (1995). The ontogeny of human memory: A cognitive neuroscience perspective. *Developmental Psychology, 31,* 723–738.

Nelson, K. (1986). *Event knowledge: Structure and function in development.* Hillsdale, NJ: Erlbaum.

Nelson, K. (1984). The transition from infant to child memory. In M. Moscovitch (Ed.), *Infant memory: Its relation to normal and pathological memory in humans and other animals.* New York: Plenum.

Nelson, K. (1997). Event representations then, now, and next. In P. W. van den Broek & P. J. Bauer (Eds.), *Developmental spans in event comprehension and representation: Bridging fictional and actual events* (pp. 1–26). Mahwah, NJ: Erlbaum.

Nelson, K., & Hudson, J. (1988). Scripts and memory: Functional relationship in development. In F. E. Weinert & M. Perlmutter (Eds.), *Memory development: Universal changes and individual differences.* Hillsdale, NJ: Erlbaum.

Newell, A., & Simon, H. A. (1961). Computer simulation of human thinking. *Science, 134,* 2011–2017.

Park, D. C., Morrell, R. W., Frieske, D., & Kincaid, D. (1992). Medication adherence behaviors in older adults: Effects of external cognitive supports. *Psychology and Aging, 7,* 252–256.

Parkin, A. J. (1993). *Memory: Phenomena, experiment and theory.* Oxford, England: Blackwell.

Perlmutter, M. (1986). A life-span view of memory. In P. B. Baltes, D. L. Featherman, & R. M. Lerner (Eds.), *Life-span development and behavior* (Vol. 7). Hillsdale, NJ: Erlbaum.

Petersen, R. C., Smith, G. E., Waring, S. C., & Ivnik, R. J. (1997). Aging, memory, and mild cognitive impairment. *International Psychogeriatrics, 65*(Supplement).

Petersen, R. C., Stevens, J. C., Ganguli, M., Tangalos, E. G., Cummings, J. L., & DeKosky, S. T. (2001). Early detection of dementia: Mild cognitive impairment. *Neurology, 56,* 1133–1142.

Piaget, J., & Inhelder, B. (1969). *The psychology of the child* (H. Weaver, Trans.). New York: Basic Books. (Original work published 1966)

Poole, D. A., & White, L. T. (1993). Two years later: Effects of question repetition and retention interval on eyewitness testimony of children and adults. *Developmental Psychology, 29,* 844–853.

Pressley, M. (1982). Elaboration and memory development. *Child Development, 53,* 296–309.

Pressley, M. (1983). Making meaningful materials easier to learn: Lessons from cognitive strategy research. In M. Pressley & J. R. Levin (Eds.), *Cognitive strategy research: Educational applications.* New York: Springer-Verlag.

Pressley, M., Forrest-Pressley, D. L., Elliott-Faust, D., & Miller, G. (1985). Children's use of cognitive strategies, how to teach strategies, and what to do if they can't be taught. In M. Pressley & C. J. Brainerd (Eds.), *Cognitive learning and memory in children: Progress in cognitive development research.* New York: Springer-Verlag.

Pressley, M., & Levin, J. R. (1980). The development of mental imagery retrieval. *Child Development, 51,* 558–560.

Pressley, M., Levin, J. R., & Ghatala, E. S. (1984). Memory strategy monitoring in adults and children. *Journal of Verbal Learning and Verbal Behavior, 23,* 270–288.

Price, D. W. W., & Goodman, G. S. (1990). Visiting the wizard: Children's memory for a recurring event. *Child Development, 61,* 664–680.

Proffitt, J. B., Coley, J. D., & Medin, D. L. (2000). Expertise and category-based induction. *Journal of Experimental Psychology: Learning, Memory, and Cognition, 26,* 811–828.

Reder, L. M., Wible, C., & Martin, J. (1986). Differential memory changes with age: Exact retrieval versus plausible inference. *Journal of Experimental Psychology: Learning, Memory, and Cognition, 12,* 72–81.

Richards, J. E. (1997). Effects of attention on infant's preference for briefly exposed visual stimuli in the paired-comparison recognition-memory paradigm. *Developmental Psychology, 32,* 22–31.

Roediger, H. L. (1990). Implicit memory: Retention without remembering. *American Psychologist, 45,* 1043–1056.

Rose, S. A., Feldman, J. F., Futterweit, L. R., & Jankowski, J. J. (1997). Continuity in visual cognition memory: Infancy to 11 years. *Intelligence, 24,* 381–392.

Rovee-Collier, C. (1997). Dissociations in infant memory: Rethinking the development of implicit and explicit memory. *Psychological Review, 104,* 467–498.

Rovee-Collier, C. (1999). The development of infant memory. *Current Directions in Psychological Science, 8,* 80–85.

Rovee-Collier, C., & Boller, K. (1995). Current theory and research on infant learning and memory: Application to early intervention. *Infants and Young Children, 7,* 1–12.

Rowe, J. W., & Kahn, R. L. (1998). *Successful aging.* Laguna Niguel, CA: Pantheon Press.

Russo, R., Nichelli, P., Gibertoni, M., & Cornia, C. (1995). Developmental trends in implicit and explicit memory: A picture completion study. *Journal of Experimental Child Psychology, 59,* 566–578.

Salatas, H., & Flavell, J. H. (1976). Behavioral and metamnemonic indicators of strategic behaviors under remember instructions in first grade. *Child Development, 47,* 81–89.

Salthouse, T. A. (1992). Why do adult age differences increase with task complexity? *Developmental Psychology, 28,* 905–918.

Salthouse, T. A. (1993). Speed and knowledge as determinants of adult age differences in verbal tasks. *Journal of Gerontology: Psychological Sciences, 48,* P29–P36.

Schachter, D. L. (1996). *Searching for memory: The brain, the mind, and the past.* New York: Basic Books.

Schaie, K. W. (1977/1978). Toward a stage theory of adult cognitive development. *International Journal of Aging and Human Development, 8,* 129–138.

Schaie, K. W., & Willis, S. L. (1996). *Adult development and aging* (4th ed.). New York: HarperCollins.

Schank, R. C. & Abelson, R. P. (1977). *Scripts, plans, goals, and understanding.* Hillsdale, NJ: Erlbaum.

Schmitter-Edgecombe, M. (1999). Effects of divided attention and time course on automatic and controlled components of memory in older adults. *Psychology and Aging, 14,* 331–345.

Schneider, W. (1998). The development of procedural metamemory in childhood and adolescence. In G. Mazzoni & T. O. Nelson (Eds.), *Metacognition and cognitive neuropsychology: Monitoring and control processes* (pp. 1–21). Mahwah, NJ: Erlbaum.

Schneider, W., & Bjorklund, D. F. (1998). Memory. In W. Damon (Editor-in-Chief), D. Kuhn & R. S. Siegler (Vol. Eds.), *Handbook of child psychology: Vol. 2. Cognition, perception, and language* (5th ed., pp. 467–522). New York: Wiley.

Schneider, W., Bjorklund, D. F., & Maier-Bruckner, W. (1996). The effects of expertise and IQ on children's memory: When knowledge is, and when it is not enough. *International Journal of Behavioral Development, 19,* 773–796.

Schneider, W., Gruber, H., Gold, A., & Opwis, K. (1993). Chess expertise and memory for chess positions in children and adults. *Journal of Experimental Child Psychology, 56,* 328–349.

Schneider, W., & Pressley, M. (1997). *Memory development between two and 20* (2nd ed.). Mahwah, NJ: Erlbaum.

Schneider, W., & Sodian, B. (1988). Metamemory-memory behavior relationships in young children: Evidence from a memory-for-location task. *Journal of Experimental Child Psychology, 45*, 209–233.

Schneider, W., Visé, M., Lockl, K., & Nelson, T. (2000). Developmental trends in children's memory monitoring: Evidence from a judgment-of-learning task. *Cognitive Development, 15*, 115–134.

Schunn, C. D., & Anderson, J. R. (1999). The generality/specificity of expertise in scientific reasoning. *Cognitive Science, 23*, 337–370.

Shimamura, A. P., Berry, J. M., Mangels, J. A., Rusting, C. L., & Jurica, P. J. (1995). Memory and cognitive abilities in university professors: Evidence for successful aging. *Psychological Science, 6*, 271–277.

Siegler, R. S. (1978). The origins of scientific reasoning. In R. S. Siegler (Ed.), *Children's thinking: What develops?* Hillsdale, NJ: Erlbaum.

Siegler, R. S. (1981). Developmental sequences within and between concepts. *Monographs of the Society for Research in Child Development, 46*(2, Serial No. 189).

Siegler, R. S. (1989). Hazards of mental chronometry: An example from children's subtraction. *Journal of Educational Psychology, 81*, 497–506.

Siegler, R. S. (1996). *Emerging minds: The process of change in children's thinking.* New York: Oxford University Press.

Siegler, R. S. (2000). The rebirth of children's learning. *Child Development, 71*, 26–35.

Simon, H. A. (1995). The information-processing theory of mind. *American Psychologist, 50*, 507–508.

Skinner, B. F. (1983). Intellectual self-management in old age. *American Psychologist, 38*, 239–244.

Slater, A. (1995). Visual perception and memory at birth. *Advances in Infancy Research, 9*, 107–111.

Slater, A., Mattock, A., Brown, E., & Bremner, J. G. (1991). Form perception at birth: Cohen and Younger (1984) revisited. *Journal of Experimental Child Psychology, 51*, 395–406.

Smith, A. D., & Earles, J. L. K. (1996). Memory changes in normal aging. In F. Blanchard-Fields & T. M. Hess (Eds.), *Perspectives on cognitive change in adulthood and aging.* New York: McGraw-Hill.

Smith, G. E., Petersen, R. C., Ivnik, R. J., Malec, J. F., & Tangalos, E. G. (1996). Subjective memory complaints, psychological distress, and longitudinal change in objective memory performance. *Psychology and Aging, 11*, 272–279.

Somerville, S. C., Wellman, H. M., & Cultice, J. C. (1983). Young children's deliberate reminding. *Journal of Genetic Psychology, 143*, 87–96.

Son, L. K., & Metcalfe, J. (2000). Metacognitive and control strategies in study-time allocation. *Journal of Experimental Psychology: Learning, Memory, and Cognition, 26*, 204–221.

Sophian, C. (1980). Habituation is not enough: Novelty preferences, search, and memory in infancy. *Merrill-Palmer Quarterly, 26*, 239–257.

Spilich, G. J., Vesonder, G. T., Chiesi, H. L., & Voss, J. F. (1979). Text processing of domain-related information for individuals with high and low domain knowledge. *Journal of Verbal Learning and Verbal Behavior, 18*, 275–290.

Stine-Morrow, E. A. L., Loveless, M. K., & Soederberg, L. M. (1996). Resource allocation in on-line reading by younger and older adults. *Psychology and Aging, 11*, 475–486.

Storandt, M. (1992). Memory-skills training for older adults. In T. B. Sonderegger (Ed.), *Nebraska Symposium on Motivation: Vol. 39. Psychology and aging.* Lincoln: University of Nebraska Press.

Swain, I. U., Zelazo, P. R., & Clifton, R. K. (1993). Newborn infants' memory for speech sounds retained over 24 hours. *Developmental Psychology, 29*, 312–323.

Swanson, H. L. (1999). What develops in working memory? A life span perspective. *Developmental Psychology, 35*, 986–1000.

Thiede, K. W., & Dunlosky, J. (1999). Toward a general model of self-regulated study: An analysis of selection of items for study and self-paced study time. *Journal of Experimental Psychology: Learning, Memory, and Cognition, 25*, 1024–1037.

Usher, J. A., & Neisser, U. (1993). Childhood amnesia and the beginnings of memory for four early life events. *Journal of Experimental Psychology: General, 122*, 155–165.

Verhaeghen, P., & Marcoen, A. (1996). On the mechanisms of plasticity in young and older adults after instruction in the method of loci: Evidence for an amplification model. *Psychology and Aging, 11*, 164–178.

Verhaeghen, P., Marcoen, A., & Goossens, L. (1992). Improving memory performance in the aged through mnemonic training: A meta-analytic study. *Psychology and Aging, 7*, 242–251.

Vinter, A. (1986). The role of movement in eliciting early imitations. *Child Development, 57*, 66–71.

Waddell, K. J., & Rogoff, B. (1981). Effect of contextual organization on spatial memory of middle-aged and older women. *Developmental Psychology, 17*, 878–885.

Wagner, D. A. (1978). Memories of Morocco: The influence of age, schooling, and environment on memory. *Cognitive Psychology, 10*, 1–28.

West, R. L., Crook, T. H., & Barron, K. L. (1992). Everyday memory performance across the life span: Effects of age and noncognitive individual differences. *Psychology and Aging, 7*, 72–82.

West, R. L., & Thorn, R. M. (2001). Goal-setting, self-efficacy, and memory performance in older and younger adults. *Experimental Aging Research, 27*, 41–65.

White, S. H., & Pillemer, D. B. (1979). Childhood amnesia and the development of a socially accessible memory system. In J. F. Kihlstrom & F. J. Evans (Eds.), *Functional disorders of memory.* Hillsdale, NJ: Erlbaum.

Whitebread, D. (1999). Interactions between children's metacognitive abilities, working memory capacity, strategies and performance during problem-solving. *European Journal of Psychology of Education, 14*, 489–507.

Willats, P. (1990). Development of problem solving strategies in infancy. In D. F. Bjorklund (Ed.), *Children's strategies.* Hillsdale, NJ: Erlbaum.

Yussen, S. R., & Levy, V. M. (1975). Developmental changes in predicting one's own memory span of short-term memory. *Journal of Experimental Child Psychology, 19*, 502–508.

Chapter 9: Intelligence and Creativity

Achter, J. A., Benbow, C. P., & Lubinski, D. (1997). Rethinking multipotentiality among the intellectually gifted: A critical review and recommendations. *Gifted Child Quarterly, 41*, 5–15.

Albert, R. S. (1996). Some reasons why childhood creativity often fails to make it past puberty into the real world. In M. A. Runco (Ed.), *Creativity from childhood through adulthood: The developmental issues.* San Francisco: Jossey-Bass.

Ambady, N., Shih, M., & Pittinsky, T. (2001, January). Stereotype susceptibility in children: Effects of identity activation on quantitative performance. *Psychological Science, 12*, 385–390.

Andrich, D., & Styles, I. (1994). Psychometric evidence of intellectual growth spurts in early adolescence. *Journal of Early Adolescence, 14*, 328–344.

Ardelt, M. (2000). Antecedents and effects of wisdom in old age. *Research on Aging, 22*, 360–394.

Aronson, J., Lustina, M. J., Good, C., Keough, K., Steele, C. M., & Brown, J. (1999). When white men can't do math: Necessary and sufficient factors in stereotype threat. *Journal of Experimental Social Psychology, 35*, 29–46.

Bacharach, V. R., & Baumeister, A. A. (1998). Direct and indirect effects of maternal intelligence, maternal age, income, and home environment on intelligence of preterm, low-birth-weight children. *Journal of Applied Developmental Psychology, 19*, 361–375.

Baltes, P. B., & Graf, P. (1996). Psychological aspects of aging: Factors and frontiers. In D. Magnusson (Ed.), *The lifespan development of individuals: Behavioral, neurobiological, and psychosocial perspectives. A synthesis.* Cambridge, England: Cambridge University Press.

Baltes, P. B., & Staudinger, U. M. (2000). Wisdom: A metaheuristic (pragmatic) to orchestrate mind and virtue toward excellence. *American Psychologist, 55*, 122–136.

Baltes, P. B., Staudinger, U. M., Maercker, A., & Smith, J. (1995). People nominated as wise: A comparative study of wisdom-related knowledge. *Psychology and Aging, 10*, 155–166.

Barack, J. A., Hodapp, R. M., & Zigler, E. (Eds.) (1998). *Handbook of mental retardation and development.* New York: Cambridge University Press.

Barron, F. X., & Harrington, D. M. (1981). Creativity, intelligence, and personality. *Annual Review of Psychology, 32*, 439–476.

Bayley, N. (1993). *Bayley Scales of Infant Development* (2nd ed.). San Antonio, TX: Psychological Corporation.

Berg, C. A. (2000). Intellectual development in adulthood. In R. J. Sternberg (Ed.), *The handbook of intelligence* (pp. 117–137). New York: Cambridge University Press.

Bornstein, M. H., & Sigman, M. D. (1986). Continuity in mental development from infancy. *Child Development, 57*, 251–274.

Bradley, R. H., & Caldwell, B. M. (1984). 174 children: A study of the relationship between home environment and cognitive development during the first 5 years. In A. W. Gottfried (Ed.), *Home environment and early cognitive development: Longitudinal research.* Orlando, FL: Academic Press.

Bradley, R. H., Caldwell, B. M., Rock, S. L., Ramey, C. T., Barnard, K. E., Gray, C.,

Hammond, M. A., Mitchell, S., Gottfried, A. W., Siegel, L., & Johnson, D. L. (1989). Home environment and cognitive development in the first 3 years of life: A collaborative study involving six sites and three ethnic groups in North America. *Developmental Psychology, 25,* 217–235.

Broberg, A. G., Wessels, H., Lamb, M. E., & Hwang, C. P. (1997). Effects of day care on the development of cognitive abilities in 8-year-olds: A longitudinal study. *Developmental Psychology, 33,* 62–69.

Brody, E. B., & Brody, N. (1976). *Intelligence: Nature, determinants, and consequences.* New York: Academic Press.

Brody, N. (2000). History of theories and measurements of intelligence. In R. J. Sternberg (Ed.), *The handbook of intelligence* (pp. 16–33). New York: Cambridge University Press.

Brooks-Gunn, J., Klebanov, P. K., & Duncan, G. J. (1996). Ethnic differences in children's intelligence test scores: Role of economic deprivation, home environment, and maternal characteristics. *Child Development, 67,* 396–408.

Caldwell, B. M., & Bradley, R. H. (1984). *Manual for the Home Observation for Measurement of the Environment.* Little Rock: University of Arkansas.

Campbell, F. A., Pungello, E. P., Miller-Johnson, S., Burchinal, M., & Ramey, R. (2001). The development of cognitive and academic abilities: Growth curves from an early childhood educational experiment. *Developmental Psychology, 37,* 231–242.

Campbell, F. A., & Ramey, C. T. (1995). Cognitive and school outcomes for high-risk African-American students at middle adolescence: Positive effects of early intervention. *American Educational Research Journal, 32,* 743–772.

Campione, J. C., Brown, A. L., Ferrara, R. A., & Bryant, N. R. (1984). The zone of proximal development: Implications for individual differences and learning. In B. Rogoff & J. V. Wertsch (Eds.), *Children's learning in the "zone of proximal development"* (New Directions for Child Development, No. 23). San Francisco: Jossey-Bass.

Carroll, J. B. (1993). *Human cognitive abilities: A survey of factor-analytic studies.* Cambridge, England: Cambridge University Press.

Case, R. (1992). The role of the frontal lobes in the regulation of cognitive development. *Brain and Cognition, 20,* 51–73.

Cattell, R. B. (1963). Theory of fluid and crystallized intelligence: A critical experiment. *Journal of Educational Psychology, 54,* 1–22.

Ceci, S. J., & Williams, W. M. (1997). Schooling, intelligence, and income. *American Psychologist, 52,* 1051–1058

Chen, J. Q., & Gardner, H. (1997). Alternative assessment from a multiple intelligences theoretical perspective. In D. P. Flanagan, J. Genshaft, & P. L. Harrison (Eds.), *Contemporary intellectual assessment: Theories, tests, and issues.* New York: Guilford.

Clayton, V. P., & Birren, J. E. (1980). The development of wisdom across the life span: A reexamination of an ancient topic. In P. B. Baltes & O. G. Brim, Jr. (Eds.), *Life-span development and behavior* (Vol. 3). New York: Academic Press.

Cleveland, H. H., Jacobson, K. C., Lipinski, J. J., & Rowe, D. C. (2000). Genetic and shared environmental contributions to the relationship between the home environment and child and adolescent achievement. *Intelligence, 28,* 69–86.

Coleman, L. J. (1985). *Schooling the gifted.* Menlo Park, CA: Addison-Wesley.

Columbo, J. (1993). *Infant cognition: Predicting later intellectual functioning.* Newbury Park, CA: Sage.

Crockenberg, S. (1983). Early mother and infant antecedents of Bayley Scale performance at 21 months. *Developmental Psychology, 19,* 727–730.

Csikszentmihalyi, M. (1996). *Creativity: Flow and the psychology of discovery and invention.* New York: HarperCollins.

Day, J. D., Engelhardt, J. L., Maxwell, S. E., & Bolig, E. E. (1997). Comparison of static and dynamic assessment procedures and their relation to independent performance. *Journal of Educational Psychology, 89,* 358–368.

Day, K., & Jancar, J. (1994). Mental and physical health and ageing in mental handicap: A review. *Journal of Intellectual Disability Research, 38,* 241–256.

Dennis, W. (1966). Creative productivity between the ages of 20 and 80 years. *Journal of Gerontology, 21,* 1–8.

Devenny, D. A., Silverman, W. P., Hill, A. L., Jenkins, E., Sersen, E. A., & Wisniewski, K. E. (1996). Normal ageing in adults with Down's syndrome: A longitudinal study. *Journal of Intellectual Disability Research, 40,* 208–221.

Dixon, R. A., Kramer, D. A., & Baltes, P. B. (1985). Intelligence: A life-span developmental perspective. In B. B. Wolman (Ed.), *Handbook of intelligence: Theories, measurements, and applications.* New York: Wiley.

Dougherty, T. M., & Haith, M. M. (1997). Infant expectations and reaction time as predictors of childhood speed of processing and IQ. *Developmental Psychology, 33,* 146–155.

Downey, D. B. (2001). Number of siblings and intellectual development: The resource dilution explanation. *American Psychologist, 56,* 497–504.

Duyme, M., Dumaret, A., & Tomkiewicz, S. (1999). How can we boost IQs of "dull children"? A late adoption study. *Proceedings of the National Academy of Sciences of the United States of America, 96,* 8790–8794.

Eichorn, D. H., Hunt, J. V., & Honzik, M. P. (1981). Experience, personality, and IQ: Adolescence to middle age. In D. H. Eichorn, J. A. Clausen, N. Haan, M. P. Honzik, & P. H. Mussen (Eds.), *Present and past in middle life.* New York: Academic Press.

Ericsson, K. A., & Charness, N. (1994). Expert performance: Its structure and acquisition. *American Psychologist, 49,* 725–747.

Erikson, E. H. (1982). *The life cycle completed: A review.* New York: Norton.

Escalona, S. (1968). *The roots of individuality: Normal patterns of individuality.* Chicago: Aldine.

Espy, K. A., Molfese, V. J., & DiLalla, L. F. (2001). Effects of environmental measures on intelligence in young children: Growth curve modeling of longitudinal data. *Merrill-Palmer Quarterly, 47,* 42–73.

Feldman, D. H. (1986). *Nature's gambit: Child prodigies and the development of human potential.* New York: Basic Books.

Feldman, R. D. (1982). *Whatever happened to the Quiz Kids? Perils and profits of growing up gifted.* Chicago: Chicago Review Press.

Feuerstein, R., Feuerstein, R., & Gross, S. (1997). The learning potential assessment device. In D. P. Flanagan, J. Genshaft, & P. L. Harrison (Eds.), *Contemporary intellectual assessment: Theories, tests, and issues.* New York: Guilford.

Fincher, J. (1973). The Terman study is 50 years old: Happy anniversary and pass the ammunition. *Human Behavior, 2,* 8–15.

Flynn, J. R. (1987). Massive IQ gains in 14 nations: What IQ tests really measure. *Psychological Bulletin, 101,* 171–191.

Flynn, J. R. (1996). What environmental factors affect intelligence: The relevance of IQ gains over time. In D. K. Detterman (Ed.), *Current topics in human intelligence: Vol. 5. The environment.* Norwood, NJ: Ablex.

Flynn, J. R. (1998). IQ gains over time: Toward finding the causes. In U. Neisser (Ed.), *The rising curve: Long-term gains in IQ and related measures.* Washington, DC: American Psychological Association.

Flynn, J. R. (1999). Search for justice: The discovery of IQ gains over time. *American Psychologist, 54,* 5–20.

Freeman, S. F. N. (2000). Academic and social attainments of children with mental retardation in general education and special education settings. *Remedial & Special Education, 21,* 3–19.

Gardner, H. (1983). *Frames of mind: The theory of multiple intelligences.* New York: Basic Books.

Gardner, H. (1999). *Intelligence reframed: Multiple intelligences for the 21st century.* New York: Basic Books.

Gardner, H., Phelps, E., & Wolf, D. (1990). The roots of adult creativity in children's symbolic products. In C. N. Alexander & E. J. Langer (Eds.), *Higher stages of human development. Perspectives on adult growth.* New York: Oxford University Press.

Getzels, J. W., & Jackson, P. W. (1962). *Creativity and intelligence: Explorations with gifted children.* New York: Wiley.

Gottfried, A. W. (1984). Home environment and early cognitive development: Integration, meta-analyses, and conclusions. In A. W. Gottfried (Ed.), *Home environment and early cognitive development: Longitudinal research.* Orlando, FL: Academic Press.

Gottfried, A. W., & Gottfried, A. E. (1984). Home environment and cognitive development in young children of middle-socioeconomic-status families. In A. W. Gottfried (Ed.), *Home environment and early cognitive development: Longitudinal research.* Orlando, FL: Academic Press.

Gottfried, A. W., Gottfried, A. E., Bathurst, K., & Guerin, D. W. (1994). *Gifted IQ: Early developmental aspects: The Fullerton Longitudinal Study.* New York: Plenum.

Gray, S. W., Ramsey, B. K., & Klaus, R. A. (1982). *From 3 to 20: The early training project.* Baltimore: University Park Press.

Gruber-Baldini, A. L., Schaie, K. W., & Willis, S. L. (1995). Similarity in married couples: A longitudinal study of mental abilities and rigidity–flexibility. *Journal of Personality and Social Psychology, 69,* 191–203.

Guilford, J. P. (1967). *The nature of human intelligence.* New York: McGraw-Hill.

Guilford, J. P. (1988). Some changes in the structure-of-the-intellect model. *Educational and Psychological Measurement, 40,* 1–4.

Guralnick, M. J. (Ed.). (1997). *The effectiveness of early intervention.* Baltimore: Brookes.

Harrington, D. M., Block, J. H., & Block, J. (1987). Testing aspects of Carl Rogers's theory of creative environments: Child-rearing antecedents of creative potential in young adolescents. *Journal of Personality and Social Psychology, 52,* 851–856.

Helms, J. E. (1992). Why is there no study of cultural equivalence in standardized cognitive-ability testing? *American Psychologist, 47,* 1083–1101.

Helms, J. E. (1997). The triple quandry of race, culture, and social class in standardized cognitive ability testing. In D. P. Flanagan, J. Genshaft, & P. L. Harrison (Eds.), *Contemporary intellectual assessment: Theories, tests, and issues.* New York: Guilford.

Herrnstein, R. J., & Murray, C. (1994). *The bell curve: Intelligence and class structure in American life.* New York: Free Press.

Holahan, C. K., & Sears, R. R. (1995). *The gifted group in later maturity.* Stanford, CA: Stanford University Press.

Holliday, S. G., & Chandler, M. J. (1986). *Wisdom: Explorations in adult competence.* Basel, Switzerland: Karger.

Honzik, M. P. (1983). Measuring mental abilities in infancy: The value and limitations. In M. Lewis (Ed.), *Origins of intelligence: Infancy and early childhood* (2nd ed.). New York: Plenum.

Honzik, M. P., Macfarlane, J. W., & Allen, L. (1948). The stability of mental test performance between two and eighteen years. *Journal of Experimental Education, 17,* 309–324.

Horn, J. L., & Cattell, R. B. (1967). Age differences in fluid and crystallized intelligence. *Acta Psychologica, 26,* 107–129.

Horn, J. L., & Noll, J. (1997). Human cognitive capabilities: Gf-Gc theory. In D. P. Flanagan, J. Genshaft, & P. L. Harrison (Eds.), *Contemporary intellectual assessment: Theories, tests, and issues.* New York: Guilford.

Howieson, N. (1981). A longitudinal study of creativity: 1965–1975. *Journal of Creative Behavior, 15,* 117–134.

Jaquish, G. A., & Ripple, R. E. (1981). Cognitive creative abilities and self-esteem across the adult life-span. *Human Development, 24,* 110–119.

Jarvik, L. F., & Bank, L. (1983). Aging twins: Longitudinal psychometric data. In K. W. Schaie (Ed.), *Longitudinal studies of adult psychological development.* New York: Guilford.

Jensen, A. R. (1969). How much can we boost IQ and scholastic achievement? *Harvard Educational Review, 39,* 1–123.

Jensen, A. R. (1977). Cumulative deficit in the IQ of blacks in the rural South. *Developmental Psychology, 13,* 184–191.

Jensen, A. R. (1980). *Bias in mental testing.* New York: Free Press.

Jensen, A. R. (1993). Why is reaction time correlated with psychometric *g*? *Current Directions in Psychological Science, 2,* 53–56.

Johansson, B., Zarit, S. H., & Berg, S. (1992). Changes in cognitive functioning of the oldest old. *Journal of Gerontology: Psychological Sciences, 47,* P75–P80.

Kail, R., & Salthouse, T. A. (1994). Processing speed as a mental capacity. *Acta Psychologica, 86,* 199–225.

Kaufman, A. S. (2000). Intelligence tests and school psychology: Predicting the future by studying the past. *Psychology in the Schools, 37,* 7–16.

Kaufman, A. S. (2001). WAIS-III IQs, Horn's theory, and generational changes from young adulthood to old age. *Intelligence, 29,* 131–167.

Kaufman, A. S., Kamphaus, R. W., & Kaufman, N. L. (1985). New directions in intelligence testing: The Kaufman Assessment Battery for Children (K-ABC). In B. B. Wolman (Ed.), *Handbook of intelligence.* New York: Wiley.

Kaufman, A. S., & Kaufman, N. L. (1983). *Kaufman Assessment Battery for Children.* Circle Pines, MN: American Guidance Service.

Kaufman, A. S., & Kaufman, N. L. (1997). The Kaufman Adolescent and Adult Intelligence Test. In D. P. Flanagan, J. L. Genshaft, & P. L. Harrison (Eds.), *Contemporary intellectual assessment: Theories, tests, and issues.* New York: Guilford.

Kleemeier, R. W. (1962). Intellectual change in the senium. *Proceedings of the Social Statistics Section of the American Statistical Association,* 290–295.

Klineberg, O. (1963). Negro–white differences in intelligence test performance: A new look at an old problem. *American Psychologist, 18,* 198–203.

Kogan, N. (1983). Stylistic variation in childhood and adolescence: Creativity, metaphor, and cognitive styles. In J. H. Flavell & E. H. Markman (Eds.), *Handbook of child psychology: Vol. 3. Cognitive development* (4th ed.). New York: Wiley.

Lazar, I., & Darlington, R. (1982). Lasting effects of early education: A report from the Consortium for Longitudinal Studies. *Monographs of the Society for Research in Child Development, 47*(2–3, Serial No. 195).

Lehman, H. C. (1953). *Age and achievement.* Princeton, NJ: Princeton University Press.

Lenhart, J. (1999, September 7). Young Mr. Smith goes to college. *Washington Post,* pp. A1, A10.

Lewontin, R. C. (1976). Race and intelligence. In N. J. Block & G. Dworkin (Eds.), *The IQ controversy.* New York: Pantheon.

Lidz, C. S. (1997). Dynamic assessment approaches. In D. P. Flanagan, J. Genshaft, & P. L. Harrison (Eds.), *Contemporary intellectual assessment: Theories, tests, and issues.* New York: Guilford.

Loehlin, J. C., Horn, J. M., & Willerman, L. (1997). Heredity, environment, and IQ in the Texas Adoption Project. In R. J. Sternberg & E. L. Grigorenko (Eds.), *Intelligence, heredity, and environment.* New York: Cambridge University Press.

Lopez, E. C. (1997). The cognitive assessment of limited English proficient and bilingual children. In D. P. Flanagan, J. Genshaft, & P. L. Harrison (Eds.), *Contemporary intellectual assessment: Theories, tests, and issues.* New York: Guilford.

Luckasson, R., Coulter, D. L., Polloway, E. A., Reiss, S., Schalock, R. L., Snell, M. E., Spitalnik, D. M., & Stark, J. A. (1992). *Mental retardation: Definition, classification, and systems of supports.* Washington, DC: American Association on Mental Retardation.

Maccoby, E. E. (2000). Parenting and its effects on children: On reading and misreading behavior genetics. *Annual Review of Psychology, 51,* 1–28.

MacPhee, D., Ramey, C. T., & Yeates, K. O. (1984). Home environmental and early cognitive development: Implications for intervention. In A. W. Gottfried (Ed.), *Home environment and early cognitive development: Longitudinal research.* Orlando, FL: Academic Press.

McCall, R. B. (1981). Nature–nurture and the two realms of development: A proposed integration with respect to mental development. *Child Development, 55,* 1–12.

McCall, R. B. (1983). A conceptual approach to early mental development. In M. Lewis (Ed.), *Origins of intelligence: Infancy and early childhood* (2nd ed.). New York: Plenum.

McCall, R. B., Applebaum, M. I., & Hogarty, P. S. (1973). Developmental changes in mental test performance. *Monographs of the Society for Research in Child Development, 38*(3, Serial No. 150).

McCall, R. B., & Carriger, M. S. (1993). A meta-analysis of infant habituation and recognition memory performance as predictors of later IQ. *Child Development, 64,* 57–79.

McCrae, R. R., Arenberg, D., & Costa, P. T., Jr. (1987). Declines in divergent thinking with age: Cross-sectional, longitudinal, and cross-sequential analyses. *Psychology and Aging, 2,* 130–137.

McGue, M., Bouchard, T. J., Jr., Iacono, W. G., & Lykken, D. T. (1993). Behavioral genetics of cognitive ability: A life span perspective. In R. Plomin & G. E. McClearn (Eds.), *Nature, nurture, and psychology.* Washington, DC: American Psychological Association.

Miller, J. G. (1997). A cultural-psychology perspective on intelligence. In R. J. Sternberg & E. L. Grigorenko (Eds.), *Intelligence, heredity, and environment.* New York: Cambridge University Press.

Miller, S. A. (1986). Parents' beliefs about their children's cognitive abilities. *Developmental Psychology, 22,* 276–284.

Moore, E. G. J. (1986). Family socialization and the IQ test performance of traditionally and transracially adopted black children. *Developmental Psychology, 22,* 317–326.

Morse, C. K. (1993). Does variability increase with age? An archival study of cognitive measures. *Psychology and Aging, 8,* 156–164.

Naglieri, J. A. (2001). Understanding intelligence, giftedness and creativity using the PASS theory. *Roeper Review, 23,* 151–156.

Naglieri, J. A., & Das, J. P. (1997). *Cognitive Assessment System.* Itasca, IL: Riverside.

Neisser, U., Boodoo, G., Bouchard, T. J., Jr., Boykin, A. W., Brody, N., Ceci, S. J., Halpern, D. F., Loehlin, J. C., Perloff, R., Sternberg, R. J., & Urbina, S. (1996). Intelligence: Knowns and unknowns. *American Psychologist, 51,* 77–101.

Nettelbeck, T., & Young, R. (1996). Intelligence and savant syndrome: Is the whole greater than the sum of the fragments? *Intelligence, 22,* 49–68.

Noble, K. D., Robinson, N. M., & Gunderson, S. A. (1993). All rivers lead to the sea: A follow-up study of gifted young adults. *Roeper Review, 15,* 124–130.

Nyborg, H., & Jensen, A. R. (2001). Occupation and income related to psychometric *g.* *Intelligence, 29,* 45–55.

Ochse, R. (1990). *Before the gates of excellence: The determinants of creative genius.* Cambridge, England: Cambridge University Press.

O'Connor, N., & Hermelin, B. (1991). Talents and preoccupations in idiot-savants. *Psychological Medicine, 21,* 959–964.

Oden, M. H. (1968). The fulfillment of promise: 40-year follow-up of the Terman gifted group. *Genetic Psychology Monographs, 77,* 3–93.

Ogbu, J. U. (1994). From cultural differences to differences in cultural frames of reference. In P. M. Greenfield & R. R. Cocking (Eds.), *Cross-cultural roots of minority child development.* Hillsdale, NJ: Erlbaum.

Okagaki, L., & Sternberg, R. J. (1993). Parental beliefs and children's school performance. *Child Development, 64,* 36–56.

Page, T. (1996, December 22). "Shine," brief candle. *Washington Post,* pp. G1, G10–G11.

Pasupathi, M., Staudinger, U. M., & Baltes, P. B. (2001). Seeds of wisdom: Adolescents' knowledge and judgment about difficult life problems. *Developmental Psychology, 37,* 351–361.

Patterson, C. J., Kupersmidt, J. B., & Vaden, N. A. (1990). Income level, gender, ethnicity, and household composition as predictors of children's school-based competence. *Child Development, 61,* 485–494.

Patton, J. R. (2000). Educating students with mild mental retardation. *Focus on Autism & Other Developmental Disabilities, 15,* 80–89.

Perkins, D. (1996). *Outsmarting IQ: The emerging science of learnable intelligence.* New York: Free Press.

Piaget, J. (1950). *The psychology of intelligence.* New York: Harcourt Brace & World.

Plomin, R. (1990). *Nature and nurture: An introduction to behavior genetics.* Pacific Grove, CA: Brooks/Cole.

Ramey, C. T., & Ramey, S. L. (1992). Effective early intervention. *Mental Retardation, 30,* 337–345.

Reiss, S. (1994). Issues in defining mental retardation. *American Journal of Mental Retardation, 99,* 1–7.

Renzulli, J. S. (1998). The three-ring conception of giftedness. In S. M. Baum, S. M. Reis, & L. R. Maxfield (Eds.), *Nurturing the gifts and talents of primary grade students.* Mansfield Center, CT: Creative Learning Press.

Reynolds, C. R., Chastain, R. L., Kaufman, A. S., & McLean, J. E. (1987). Demographic characteristics and IQ among adults: Analysis of the WAIS-R standardization sample as a function of the stratification variables. *Journal of School Psychology, 25,* 323–342.

Reznikoff, M., Domino, G., Bridges, C., & Honeyman, M. (1973). Creative abilities in identical and fraternal twins. *Behavior Genetics, 3,* 365–377.

Richards, R. (1996). Beyond Piaget: Accepting divergent, chaotic, and creative thought. In M. A. Runco (Ed.), *Creativity from childhood through adulthood: The developmental issues.* San Francisco: Jossey-Bass.

Robinson, N. M., & Janos, P. M. (1986). Psychological adjustment in a college-level program of marked academic acceleration. *Journal of Youth and Adolescence, 15,* 51–60.

Rodgers, J. L. (2001). What causes birth order–intelligence patterns? The admixture hypothesis, revived. *American Psychologist, 56,* 505–510.

Rodgers, J. L., Cleveland, H. H., van den Oord, E., & Rowe, D. C. (2000). Resolving the debate over birth order, family size, and intelligence. *American Psychologist, 55,* 599–612.

Rogers, M. T. (1986). *A comparative study of developmental traits of gifted and average children.* Unpublished doctoral dissertation, University of Denver.

Rose, S. A., & Feldman, J. F. (1997). Memory and speed: Their role in the relation of infant information processing to later IQ. *Child Development, 68,* 630–641.

Rose, S. A., Feldman, J. F., Wallace, I. F., & McCarton, C. (1989). Infant visual attention: Relation to birth status and developmental outcome during the first 5 years. *Developmental Psychology, 25,* 560–576.

Ross, R. T., Begab, M. J., Dondis, E. H., Giampiccolo, J. S., Jr., & Meyers, C. E. (1985). *Lives of the mentally retarded: A forty-year follow-up study.* Stanford, CA: Stanford University Press.

Rowe, D. C., Vesterdal, W. J., & Rodgers, J. L. (1999). Herrnstein's syllogism: Genetic and shared environmental influences on IQ, education, and income. *Intelligence, 26,* 405–423.

Runco, M. A. (1992). Children's divergent thinking and creative ideation. *Developmental Review, 12,* 233–264.

Russ, S. W. (1996). Development of creative processes in children. In M. A. Runco (Ed.), *Creativity from childhood through adulthood: The developmental issues.* San Francisco: Jossey-Bass.

Sacks, E. L. (1952). Intelligence scores as a function of experimentally established social relationships between child and examiner. *Journal of Abnormal and Social Psychology, 47,* 354–358.

Sameroff, A. J., Seifer, R., Baldwin, A., & Baldwin, C. (1993). Stability of intelligence from preschool to adolescence: The influence of social and family risk factors. *Child Development, 64,* 80–97.

Scarr, S., & Weinberg, R. A. (1983). The Minnesota adoption studies: Genetic differences and malleability. *Child Development, 54,* 260–267.

Schaie, K. W. (1983). The Seattle Longitudinal Study: A 21-year exploration of psychometric intelligence in adulthood. In K. W. Schaie (Ed.), *Longitudinal studies of adult psychological development.* New York: Guilford.

Schaie, K. W. (1989). The hazards of cognitive aging. *Gerontologist, 29,* 484–493.

Schaie, K. W. (1990). Intellectual development in adulthood. In J. E. Birren & K. W. Schaie (Eds.), *The handbook of the psychology of aging* (3rd ed.). San Diego: Academic Press.

Schaie, K. W. (1996). *Intellectual development in adulthood: The Seattle Longitudinal Study.* New York: Cambridge University Press.

Schaie, K. W., & Willis, S. L. (1986). Can decline in adult intellectual functioning be reversed? *Developmental Psychology, 22,* 223–232.

Schalock, R. L. (Ed.). (1999). *Adaptive behavior and its measurements: Implications for the field of mental retardation.* Washington, DC: American Association of Mental Retardation.

Schalock, R. L., Holl, C., Elliott, B., & Ross, I. (1992). A longitudinal follow-up of graduates from a rural special education program. *Learning Disability Quarterly, 15,* 29–38.

Schmidt, F. L., & Hunter, J. E. (1998). The validity and utility of selection methods in personnel psychology: Practical and theoretical implications of 85 years of research findings. *Psychological Bulletin, 124,* 262–274.

Shih, M., Pittinsky, T. L., & Ambady, N. (1999). Stereotype susceptibility: Identity salience and shifts in quantitative performance. *Psychological Science, 10,* 80–83

Shurkin, J. N. (1992). *Terman's kids: The groundbreaking study of how the gifted grow up.* Boston: Little, Brown.

Silverman, L. K., Chitwood, D. G., & Waters, J. L. (1986). Young gifted children: Can parents identify giftedness? *Topics in Early Childhood Special Education, 6,* 23–38.

Simonoff, E., Bolton, P., & Rutter, M. (1996). Mental retardation: Genetic findings, clinical implications and research agenda. *Journal of Child Psychology and Psychiatry and Allied Disciplines, 37,* 259–280.

Simonton, D. K. (1984). *Genius, creativity, and leadership: Historiometric inquiries.* Cambridge, MA: Harvard University Press.

Simonton, D. K. (1990). Creativity in the later years: Optimistic prospects for achievement. *Gerontology, 30,* 626–631.

Simonton, D. K. (1991). Career landmarks in science: Individual differences and interdisciplinary contrasts. *Developmental Psychology, 27,* 119–130.

Simonton, D. K. (1999). *Origins of genius: Darwinian perspectives on creativity.* New York: Oxford University Press.

Smith, J., & Baltes, P. B. (1990). Wisdom-related knowledge: Age/cohort differences in response to life-planning problems. *Developmental Psychology, 26,* 494–505.

Smith, K. E., Landry, S. H., & Swank, P. R. (2000). Does the content of mothers' verbal stimulation explain differences in children's development of verbal and nonverbal cognitive skills? *Journal of School Psychology, 38,* 27–49.

Sparrow, S. S., & Davis, S. M. (2000). Recent advances in the assessment of intelligence and cognition. *Journal of Child Psychology and Psychiatry, 41,* 117–131.

Spearman, C. (1927). *The abilities of man.* New York: Macmillan.

Staudinger, U. M., & Baltes, P. B. (1996). Interactive minds: A facilitative setting for wisdom-related performance? *Journal of Personality and Social Psychology, 71,* 746–762.

Staudinger, U. M., Smith, J., & Baltes, P. B. (1992). Wisdom-related knowledge in a life review task: Age differences and the role of professional specialization. *Psychology and Aging, 7,* 271–281.

Steele, C. M. (1997). A threat in the air: How stereotypes shape intellectual identity and performance. *American Psychologist, 52,* 613–629.

Steele, C. M. (1999). Thin ice: "Stereotype threat" and black college students. *Atlantic, 284,* 44–54.

Steele, C. M., & Aronson, J. (1995). Stereotype threat and the intellectual test performance of African Americans. *Journal of Personality and Social Psychology, 69,* 797–811.

Sternberg, R. J. (1985). *Beyond IQ: A triarchic theory of human intelligence.* Cambridge, MA: Cambridge University Press.

Sternberg, R. J. (1988). *The triarchic mind: A new theory of human intelligence.* New York: Viking.

Sternberg, R. J. (Ed.). (1990). *Wisdom: Its nature, origins, and development.* Cambridge, England: Cambridge University Press.

Sternberg, R. J. (1992). Ability tests, measurements, and markets. *Journal of Educational Psychology, 84,* 134–140.

Sternberg, R. J. (1997). Educating intelligence: Infusing the triarchic theory into school instruction. In R. J. Sternberg & E. L. Grigorenko (Eds.), *Intelligence, heredity, and environment.* New York: Cambridge University Press.

Sternberg, R. J. (Ed.). (1999). *Handbook of creativity.* New York: Cambridge University Press.

Sternberg, R. J. (2000). The concept of intelligence. In R. J. Sternberg (Ed.), *The handbook of intelligence* (pp. 3–15). New York: Cambridge University Press.

Sternberg, R. J., Grigorenko, E. L., & Bundy, D. A. (2001). The predictive value of IQ. *Merrill-Palmer Quarterly, 47,* 1–41.

Sternberg, R. J., & Lubart, T. I. (1996). Investing in creativity. *American Psychologist, 51,* 677–688.

Sternberg, R. J., Wagner, R. K., Williams, W. M., & Horvath, J. A. (1995). Testing common sense. *American Psychologist, 50,* 912–927.

Taylor, R. E., & Richards, S. B. (1991). Patterns of intellectual differences of black, Hispanic, and white children. *Psychology in the Schools, 28,* 5–9.

Terman, L. M. (1954). The discovery and encouragement of exceptional talent. *American Psychologist, 9,* 221–238.

Thorndike, R. L. (1997). The early history of intelligence testing. In D. P. Flanagan, J. L. Genshaft, & P. L. Harrison (Eds.), *Contemporary intellectual assessment: Theories, tests, and issues.* New York: Guilford.

Thorndike, R. L., Hagen, E. P., & Sattler, J. M. (1986). *The Stanford-Binet Intelligence Scale* (4th ed.). Chicago: Riverside.

Thurstone, L. L. (1938). *Primary mental abilities.* Chicago: University of Chicago Press.

Thurstone, L. L., & Thurstone, T. G. (1941). Factorial studies of intelligence. *Psychometric Monographs,* No. 2.

Thurstone, L. L., & Thurstone, T. G. (1948). *SRA Primary Mental Abilities, Ages 11–17, Form AM.* Chicago: Science Research Associates.

Tomlinson-Keasey, C., & Little, T. D. (1990). Predicting educational attainment, occupational achievement, intellectual skill, and personal adjustment among gifted men and women. *Journal of Educational Psychology, 82,* 442–455.

Torrance, E. P. (1969). *Creativity.* San Rafael, CA: Dimensions.

Torrance, E. P. (1975). Creativity research in education: Still alive. In I. A. Taylor & J. W. Getzels (Eds.), *Perspectives in creativity.* Chicago: Aldine-Atherton.

Torrance, E. P. (1988). The nature of creativity as manifest in its testing. In R. J. Sternberg (Ed.), *The nature of creativity: Contemporary psychological perspectives.* Cambridge, England: Cambridge University Press.

Treffert, D. A. (2000). *Extraordinary people: Understanding savant syndrome.* Available online: iUniverse.com

Turkheimer, E. (1991). Individual and group differences in adoption studies of IQ. *Psychological Bulletin, 110,* 392–405.

Vincent, K. R. (1991). Black/white IQ differences: Does age make the difference? *Journal of Clinical Psychology, 47,* 266–270.

Wallace, A. (1986). *The prodigy: A biography of William Sidis.* New York: Dutton.

Wallach, M. A., & Kogan, N. (1965). *Thinking in young children.* New York: Holt, Rinehart & Winston.

Weakliem, D., McQuillan, J., & Schauer, T. (1995). Toward meritocracy? Changing social-class differences in intellectual ability. *Sociology of Education, 68,* 271–286.

Wechsler, D. (1981). *Wechsler Adult Intelligence Scale–Revised.* New York: Psychological Corporation.

Wechsler, D. (1989). *WPPSI-R manual: Wechsler Preschool and Primary Scale of Intelligence–Revised.* San Antonio, TX: Psychological Corporation.

Wechsler, D. (1991). *Manual, WISC-III: Wechsler Intelligence Scale for Children–Third Edition.* San Antonio, TX: Psychological Corporation.

Weinberg, R. A., Scarr, S., & Waldman, I. D. (1992). The Minnesota transracial adoption study: A follow-up of IQ test performance at adolescence. *Intelligence, 16,* 117–135.

Whalley, L., & Deary, I. J. (2001). Longitudinal cohort study of childhood IQ and survival up to age 76. *British Medical Journal, 322,* 819–824.

Winner, E. (1996). *Gifted children: Myths and realities.* New York: Basic Books.

Yeates, K. O., MacPhee, D., Campbell, F. A., & Ramey, C. T. (1983). Maternal IQ and home environment as determinants of early childhood intellectual competence: A developmental analysis. *Developmental Psychology, 19,* 731–739.

Zajonc, R. B. (1976, April 16). Family configuration and intelligence. *Science, 192,* 227–236.

Zajonc, R. B. (2001). The family dynamics of intellectual development. *American Psychologist, 56,* 490–496.

Zigler, E. (1995). Can we "cure" mild mental retardation among individuals in the lower socioeconomic stratum? *American Journal of Public Health, 85,* 302–304.

Zigler, E., Abelson, W. D., Trickett, P. K., & Seitz, V. (1982). Is an intervention program necessary to improve economically disadvantaged children's IQ scores? *Child Development, 53,* 340–348.

Zigler, E., & Hodapp, R. M. (1991). Behavioral functioning in individuals with mental retardation. *Annual Review of Psychology, 42,* 29–50.

Chapter 10: Language and Education

Ablard, K. E., & Mills, C. J. (1996). Implicit theories of intelligence and self-perceptions of academically talented adolescents and children. *Journal of Youth and Adolescence, 25,* 137–148.

Acredolo, L., & Goodwyn, S. (1988). Symbolic gesturing in normal infants. *Child Development, 59,* 450–466.

Adams, M. J. (1990). *Beginning to read: Learning and thinking about print.* Cambridge, MA: MIT Press.

Adams, M. J., Treiman, R., & Pressley, M. (1998). Reading, writing, and literacy. In W. Damon (Editor-in-Chief), I. E. Sigel & K. A. Renninger (Vol. Eds.), *Handbook of child psychology: Vo. 4. Child psychology in practice* (5th ed., pp. 275–355). New York: Wiley.

Akhtar, N., Jipson, J., & Callanan, M. A. (2001). Learning words through overhearing. *Child Development, 72,* 416–430.

Amstutz, D. D., & Sheared, V. (2000). The crisis in adult basic education. *Education and Urban Society, 32,* 155–166.

Anderman, E. M., & Midgley, C. (1997). Changes in achievement goal orientations, perceived academic competence, and grades across the transition to middle-level schools. *Contemporary Educational Psychology, 22,* 269–298.

Anglin, J. M. (1993). Vocabulary development: A morphological analysis. *Monographs of the Society for Research in Child Development, 58*(Serial No. 10).

Arroyo, C. G., & Zigler, E. (1995). Racial identity, academic achievement, and the psychological well-being of economically disadvantaged adolescents. *Journal of Personality and Social Psychology, 69,* 903–914.

Au, R., Joung, P., Nicholas, M., Obler, L. K., Kass, R., & Albert, M. L. (1995). Naming ability across the adult life span. *Aging and Cognition, 2,* 300–311.

Bachman, J. G., & Schulenberg, J. (1993). How part-time work intensity relates to drug use, problem behavior, time use, and satisfaction among high school seniors: Are these consequences or merely correlates? *Developmental Psychology, 29,* 220–235.

Bandura, A. (1971). An analysis of modeling processes. In A. Bandura (Ed.), *Psychological modeling.* New York: Lieber-Atherton.

Barling, J., Rogers, K. A., & Kelloway, E. K. (1995). Some effects of teenagers' part-time employment: The quantity and quality of work make the difference. *Journal of Organizational Behavior, 16,* 143–154.

Baron, N. S. (1992). *Growing up with language: How children learn to talk.* Reading, MA: Addison-Wesley.

Barrett, M. (1995). Early lexical development. In P. Fletcher & B. MacWhinney (Eds.), *The handbook of child language* (pp. 362–392). Oxford: Blackwell.

Baruch, R. (1967). The achievement motive in women: Implications for career development. *Journal of Personality and Social Psychology, 5,* 260–267.

Bates, E., Marchman, V., Thal, D., Fenson, L., Dale, P., Reznick, J. S., Reilly, J., & Hartung, J. (1994). Developmental and stylistic variation in the composition of early vocabulary. *Journal of Child Language, 21,* 85–123.

Bates, E., O'Connell, B., & Shore, C. (1987). Language and communication in infancy. In J. D. Osofsky (Ed.), *Handbook of infant development* (2nd ed.). New York: Wiley.

Beal, C. R. (1990). The development of text evaluation and revision skills. *Child Development, 61,* 247–258.

Bear, M. F., Connors, B. W., & Paradiso, M. A. (2001). *Neuroscience: Exploring the brain* (2nd ed.). Lippincott, Williams & Wilkins.

Bellugi, U. (1988). The acquisition of a spatial language. In F. S. Kessel (Ed.), *The development of language and language researchers: Essays in honor of Roger Brown.* Hillsdale, NJ: Erlbaum.

Benedict, H. (1979). Early lexical development: Comprehension and production. *Journal of Child Language, 6,* 183–200.

Betts, J. R., & Shkolnik, J. L. (2000). The effects of ability grouping on student achievement and resource allocation in secondary schools. *Economics of Education Review, 19,* 1–15.

Birdsong, D. (1999). Introduction: Whys and why nots of the critical period hypothesis for second language acquisition. In D. Birdsong (Ed.), *Second language acquisition and the critical period hypothesis* (pp. 1–22). NJ: Erlbaum.

Bloom, L. (1970). *Language development: Form and function in emerging grammars.* Cambridge, MA: MIT Press.

Bloom, L. (1998). Language acquisition in its developmental context. In W. Damon (Editor-in-Chief), D. Kuhn & R. S. Siegler (Vol. Eds.), *Handbook of child psychology: Vol. 2. Cognition, perception, and language* (5th ed., pp. 309–370). New York: Wiley.

Bogenschneider, K. (1997). Parental involvement in adolescent schooling: A proximal process with transcontextual validity. *Journal of Marriage and the Family, 59,* 718–733.

Boggiano, A. K., & Katz, P. (1991). Maladaptive achievement patterns in students: The role of teachers' controlling strategies. *Journal of Social Issues, 47*(4), 35–51.

Bohannon, J. N., & Bonvillian, J. D. (2001). Theoretical approaches to language acquisition. In J. Berko-Gleason (Ed.), *The development of language* (5th ed., pp. 254–314). Needham Heights, MA: Allyn & Bacon.

Bohannon, J. N., & Stanowicz, L. (1988). The issue of negative evidence: Adult responses to children's language errors. *Developmental Psychology, 24,* 684–689.

Boloh, Y., & Champaud, C. (1993). The past conditional verb form in French children: The role of semantics in late grammatical development. *Journal of Child Language, 20,* 169–189.

Bowen, B. A. (1999). Four puzzles in adult literacy: Reflections on the national adult literacy survey. *Journal of Adolescent & Adult Literacy, 42,* 314–323.

Braddock, J. H., II, & McPartland, J. M. (1993). Education of early adolescents. *Review of Educational Research, 19,* 135–170.

Brookover, W., Beady, C., Flood, P., Schweitzer, J., & Wisenbaker, J. (1979). *School social systems and student achievement: Schools can make a difference.* New York: Praeger.

Brown, B. B., Mounts, N., Lamborn, S. D., & Steinberg, L. (1993). Parenting practices and peer group affiliation in adolescence. *Child Development, 64,* 467–482.

Brown, R. (1973). *A first language: The early stages.* Cambridge, MA: Harvard University Press.

Brown, R., Cazden, C., & Bellugi, U. (1969). The child's grammar from I–III. In J. P. Hill (Ed.), *Minnesota Symposia on Child Psychology* (Vol. 2). Minneapolis: University of Minnesota Press.

Brown, R., & Hanlon, C. (1970). Derivational complexity and order of acquisition. In J. R. Hayes (Ed.), *Cognition and the development of language.* New York: Wiley

Bruck, M. (1990). Word recognition skills of adults with childhood diagnoses of dyslexia. *Developmental Psychology, 26,* 439–454.

Bruck, M. (1992). Persistence of dyslexics' phonological awareness deficits. *Developmental Psychology, 28,* 874–886.

Bruer, J. T. (1999). *The myth of the first three years: A new understanding of early brain development and lifelong learning.* New York: Free Press.

Bruner, J. S. (1983). *Child's talk: Learning to use language.* New York: Norton.

Bryant, P. (1998). Sensitivity to onset and rhyme does predict young children's reading: A comment on Muter, Hulme, Snowling, and Taylor (1997). *Journal of Experimental Child Psychology, 71,* 39–44.

Burhans, K. K., & Dweck, C. S. (1995). Helplessness in early childhood: The role of contingent worth. *Child Development, 66,* 1719–1738.

Bus, A. G., & van Ijzendoorn, M. H. (1999). Phonological awareness and early reading: A meta-analysis of experimental training studies. *Journal of Educational Psychology, 91,* 403–414.

Bus, A. G., van Ijzendoorn, M. H., & Pellegrini, A. D. (1995). Joint book reading makes for success in learning to read: A meta-analysis on intergenerational transmission of literacy. *Review of Educational Research, 65,* 1–21.

Busch-Rossnagel, N. A. (1997). Mastery motivation in toddlers. *Infants and Young Children, 9,* 1–11.

Butler, R. (1990). The effects of mastery and competitive conditions on self-assessment at different ages. *Child Development, 61,* 201–210.

Butler, R. (1999). Information seeking and achievement motivation in middle childhood and adolescence: The role of conceptions of ability. *Developmental Psychology, 35,* 146–163.

Buysse, V., & Bailey, D. B. (1993). Behavioral and developmental outcomes in young children with disabilities in integrated and segregated settings: A review of comparative studies. *Journal of Special Education, 26,* 434–461.

Byrne, B. (1998). *The foundation of literacy: The child's acquisition of the alphabetic principle.* East Sussex, UK: Psychology Press.

Call, K. T., Mortimer, J. T., & Shanahan, M. (1995). Helpfulness and the development of competence in adolescence. *Child Development, 66,* 129–138.

Campbell, F. A., Pungello, E. P., Miller-Johnson, S., Burchinal, M., & Ramey, C. T. (2001). The development of cognitive and academic abilities: Growth curves from an early childhood educational experiment. *Developmental Psychology. 37,* 231–242.

Campbell, F. A., & Ramey, C. T. (1995). Cognitive and school outcomes for high-risk African-American students at middle adolescence: Positive effects of early intervention. *American Educational Research Journal, 32,* 743–772.

Carpenter, M., Nagell, K., & Tomasello, M. (1998). Social cognition, joint attention, and communicative competence from 9 to 15 months of age. *Monographs of the Society for Research in Child Development, 63*(Serial No. 255).

Ceci, S. J., & Williams, W. M. (1997). Schooling, intelligence, and income. *American Psychologist, 52,* 1051–1058.

Chall, J. S. (1967). *Learning to read: The great debate.* New York: McGraw-Hill.

Chen, C., & Stevenson, H. W. (1989). Homework: A cross-cultural examination. *Child Development, 60,* 551–561.

Chen, C., & Stevenson, H. W. (1995). Motivation and mathematics achievement: A comparative study of Asian-American, Caucasian-American, and east Asian high school students. *Child Development, 66,* 1214–1234.

Chomsky, N. (1968). *Language and mind.* New York: Harcourt Brace & World.

Chomsky, N. (1975). *Reflections on language.* New York: Pantheon Books.

Chomsky, N. (1995). *The minimalist program.* Cambridge: MIT Press.

Clark, H. H., & Clark, E. V. (1977). *Psychology and language: An introduction to psycholinguistics.* New York: Harcourt Brace Jovanovich.

Clarke-Stewart, K. A. (1998). Reading with children. *Journal of Applied Developmental Psychology, 19,* 1–14.

Coleman, J. (1961). *The adolescent society.* New York: Free Press.

Comer, J. P. (1997). *Waiting for a miracle: Why schools can't solve our problems—and how we can.* New York: Plume.

Cook, B. G., & Semmel, M. I. (1999). Peer acceptance of included students with disabilities as a function of severity of disability and classroom composition. *Journal of Special Education, 33,* 50–61.

Cooper, R. P., Abraham, J., Berman, S., & Staska, M. (1997). The development of infants' preference for motherese. *Infant Behavior and Development, 20,* 477–488.

Cooper, R. P., & Aslin, R. N. (1990). Preference for infant-directed speech in the first month after birth. *Child Development, 61,* 1584–1595.

Covington, M. V. (1998). *The will to learn.* New York: Cambridge University Press.

Covington, M. V. (2000). Goal theory, motivation, and school achievement: An integrative review. *Annual Review of Psychology, 51,* 171–200.

Crago, M. B., Allen, S. E., & Hough-Eyamir, W. P. (1997). Exploring innateness through cultural and linguistic variation. In M. Gopnik (Ed.), *The inheritance and innateness of grammars* (pp. 70–90). New York: Oxford University Press.

Cronbach, L. J., & Snow, R. E. (1977). *Aptitudes and instructional methods: A handbook for research on interactions.* New York: Irvington.

Dale, P. S. (1976). *Language development: Structure and function.* New York: Holt, Rinehart & Winston.

De Boysson-Bardies, B., Sagart, L., & Durand, C. (1984). Discernible differences in the babbling of infants according to target language. *Journal of Child Language, 11,* 1–16.

Deci, E. L., Koestner, R., & Ryan, R. M. (1999). A meta-analytic review of experiments examining the effects of extrinsic rewards on intrinsic motivation. *Psychological Bulletin, 125,* 627–668.

Deci, E. L., & Ryan, R. M. (1992). The initiation and regulation of intrinsically motivated learning and achievement. In A. K. Boggiano & T. S. Pittman (Eds.), *Achievement and motivation: A social-developmental perspective* (pp. 9–36). New York: Cambridge University Press.

Dinmore, I. (1997). Interdisciplinarity and integrative learning: An imperative for adult education. *Education, 117,* 452–468.

Duncan, H., & Dick, T. (2000). Collaborative workshops and student academic performance in introductory college mathematics courses: A study of a Treisman model math excel program. *School Science and Mathematics, 100,* 365–373.

Dweck, C. S., & Elliott, E. S. (1983). Achievement motivation. In E. M. Hetherington (Vol. Ed.; P. H. Mussen, General Ed.), *Handbook of child psychology: Vol. 4. Socialization, personality, and social development* (4th ed.). New York: Wiley.

Dweck, C. S., & Leggett, E. L. (1988). A social-cognitive approach to motivation and personality. *Psychological Review, 95,* 256–273.

Ebbeck, M. (1996). Parents' expectations and child rearing practices in Hong Kong. *Early Child Development and Care, 119,* 15–25.

Eccles, J. S., Lord, S., & Midgley, C. (1991). What are we doing to early adolescents? The impact of educational contexts on early adolescents. *American Journal of Education, 99,* 521–542.

Eccles, J. S., Midgley, C., Wigfield, A., Buchanan, C. M., Reuman, D., Flanagan, C., & Mac Iver, D. (1993). Development during adolescence: The impact of stage–environment fit on young adolescents' experiences in schools and in families. *American Psychologist, 48,* 90–101.

Ehri, L. C. (1999). Phases of development in learning to read words. In J. Oakhill & R. Beard (Eds.), *Reading development and the teaching of reading* (pp. 79–108). Oxford: Blackwell.

Eimas, P. D. (1975). Auditory and phonetic cues for speech: Discrimination of the (r-l) distinction by young infants. *Perception and Psychophysics, 18,* 341–347.

Elkind, D. (1987). *Miseducation: Preschoolers at risk.* New York: Knopf.

Elliot, A. J., & Church, M. A. (1997). A hierarchical model of approach and avoidance achievement motivation. *Journal of Personality and Social Psychology, 72,* 218–232.

Elliott, E. S., & Dweck, C. S. (1988). Goals: An approach to motivation and achievement. *Journal of Personality and Social Psychology, 54,* 5–12.

Ely, R. (2001). Language and literacy in the school years. In J. B. Gleason (Ed.), *The development of language* (5th ed., pp. 409–454). Boston: Allyn & Bacon.

Ensminger, M. E., & Slusarcick, A. L. (1992). Paths to high school graduation or dropout: A longitudinal study of a first-grade cohort. *Sociology of Education, 65,* 95–113.

Entwisle, D. R., & Alexander, K. L. (1992). Summer setback: Race, poverty, school composition, and mathematics achievement in the first two years of school. *American Sociological Review, 57,* 72–84.

Erdley, C. A., Loomis, C. C., Cain, K. M., & Dumas-Hines, F. (1997). Relations among children's social goals, implicit personality theories, and responses to social failure. *Developmental Psychology, 33,* 263–272.

Faust, M. A., & Glenzer, N. (2000). "I could read those parts over and over": Eighth graders rereading to enhance enjoyment and learning with literature. *Journal of Adolescent & Adult Literacy, 44,* 234–239.

Featherman, D. L. (1980). Schooling and occupational careers: Constancy and change in worldly success. In O. G. Brim, Jr., & J. Kagan (Eds.), *Constancy and change in human development.* Cambridge, MA: Harvard University Press.

Fenson, L., Dale, P. S., Reznick, J. S., Bates, E., Thal, D. J., & Pethick, S. J. (1994). Variability in early communicative development. *Monographs of the Society for Research in Child Development, 59*(Serial No. 242).

Fernald, A., Taeschner, T., Dunn, J., Papousek, M., & Fukui, I. (1989). A cross-language study of prosodic modifications in mothers' and fathers' speech to preverbal infants. *Journal of Child Language, 16,* 477–501.

Filipp, S. H. (1996). Motivation and emotion. In J. E. Birren, K. W. Schaie, R. P. Abeles, M. Gatz, & T. A. Salthouse (Eds), *Handbook of the psychology of the aging* (4th ed.). San Diego: Academic Press.

Fischer, R. B., Blazey, M. L., & Lipman, H. T. (1992). *Students of the third age.* New York: Macmillan.

Fisher, C., & Tokura, H. (1996). Acoustic cues to grammatical structure in infant-directed speech: Cross-linguistic evidence. *Child Development, 67,* 3192–3218.

Foorman, B. R. (1995). Research on ''The Great Debate'': Code-oriented versus whole language approaches to reading instruction. *School Psychology Review, 24,* 376–392.

Foorman, B. R., Francis, D. J., Fletcher, J. M., Schatschneider, C., & Mehta, P. (1998). The role of instruction in learning to read: Preventing reading failure in at-risk children. *Journal of Educational Psychology, 90,* 37–55.

Ford, M. E., & Thompson, R. A. (1985). Perceptions of personal agency and infant attachment: Toward a life-span perspective on competence development. *International Journal of Behavioral Development, 8,* 377–406.

Fordham, S., & Ogbu, J. U. (1986). Black students' school success: Coping with the "burden of 'acting white.'" *Urban Review, 18,* 176–206.

Fraser, B. J., Walberg, H. J., Welch, W. W., & Hattie, J. A. (1987). Synthesis of educational productivity research. *International Journal of Educational Research, 11,* 145–252.

Fuligni, A. J., & Stevenson, H. W. (1995). Time use and mathematics achievement among American, Chinese, and Japanese high school students. *Child Development, 66,* 830–842.

Fullilove, R. E., & Treisman, E. M. (1990). Mathematics achievement among African American undergraduates at the University of California, Berkeley: An evaluation of the mathematics workshop. *Journal of Negro Education, 59,* 463–478.

Gamoran, A., Porter, A. C., Smithson, J., & White, P. A. (1997). Upgrading high school mathematics instruction: Improving learning opportunities for low-achieving, low-income youth. *Educational Evaluation and Policy Analysis, 19,* 325–338.

Garner, R. (1999, November 15). Failing at four. *New York Times Magazine,* p. 26.

Ginsburg, G. S., & Bronstein, P. (1993). Family factors related to children's intrinsic/extrinsic motivational orientation and academic performance. *Child Development, 64,* 1461–1474.

Glasgow, K. L., Dornbusch, S. M., Troyer, L., Steinberg, L., & Ritter, P. L. (1997). Parenting styles, adolescents' attributions, and educational outcomes in nine heterogeneous high schools. *Child Development, 68,* 507–529.

Goldfield, B. A., & Reznick, J. S. (1996). Measuring the vocabulary spurt: A reply to Mervis and Bertrand. *Journal of Child Language, 23,* 241–246.

Goldfield, B. A., & Snow, C. E. (2001). Individual differences: Implications for the study of language acquisition. In J. B. Gleason (Ed.), *The development of language* (5th ed., pp. 315–346). Boston: Allyn & Bacon.

Goldwater, O. D., & Nutt, R. L. (1999). Teachers' and students' work-culture variables associated with positive school outcome. *Adolescence, 34,* 653–664.

Gopnik, A., & Choi, S. (1995). Names, relational words, and cognitive development in English and Korean speakers: Nouns are not always learned before verbs. In M. Tomasello & W. E. Merriman (Eds.), *Beyond names for things: Young children's acquisition of verbs* (pp. 83–90). Hillsdale, NJ: Erlbaum.

Gordon, P. (1990). Learnability and feedback. *Developmental Psychology, 26,* 217–220.

Gorey, K. M. (2001). Early childhood education: A meta-analytic affirmation of the short- and long-term benefits of educational opportunity. *School Psychology Quarterly, 16,* 9–30.

Goswami, U. (1999). Causal connections in beginning reading: The importance of rhyme. *Journal of Research in Reading, 22,* 217–241.

Gottfried, A. E., Fleming, J. S., & Gottfried, A. W. (1998). Role of cognitively stimulating home environment in children's academic intrinsic motivation: A longitudinal study. *Child Development, 69,* 1448–1460.

Gray-Little, B., & Carels, R. A. (1997). The effect of racial dissonance on academic self-esteem and achievement in elementary, junior high, and high school students. *Journal of Research on Adolescence, 7,* 109–131.

Greenberger, E., & Steinberg, L. (1986). *When teenagers work: The psychological and social costs of adolescent employment.* New York: Basic Books.

Greenfield, P. M., & Savage-Rumbaugh, E. S. (1993). Comparing communicative competence in child and chimp: The pragmatics of repetition. *Journal of Child Language, 20,* 1–26.

Grolnick, W. S., & Ryan, R. M. (1989). Parent styles associated with children's self-regulation and competence in school. *Journal of Educational Psychology, 81,* 143–154.

Hall, E. (2001). Babies, books and "impact": Problems and possibilities in the evaluation of a Bookstart project. *Educational Review, 53,* 57–64.

Hanushek, E. A. (1997). Assessing the effects of school resources on student performance: An update. *Educational Evaluation and Policy Analysis, 19,* 141–164.

Hanushek, E. A. (1998). *The evidence on class size: Occasional paper.* ERIC: 443158.

Harper, G., & Kember, D. (1986). Approaches to study of distance education students. *British Journal of Educational Technology, 17,* 211–212.

Harris, M. (1992). *Language experience and early language development: From input to uptake.* Hove, UK: Erlbaum.

Harter, S. (1981). A new self-report scale of intrinsic versus extrinsic orientation in the classroom: Motivational and informational components. *Developmental Psychology, 17,* 300–312.

Helmreich, R. L., Sawin, L. L., & Carsrud, A. L. (1986). The honeymoon effect in job performance: Temporal increases in the predictive power of achievement motivation. *Journal of Applied Psychology, 71,* 185–188.

Hirsch-Pasek, K., Golinkoff, R. M., & Hollich, G. (1999). Trends and transitions in language development: Looking for the missing piece. *Developmental Neuropsychology, 16,* 139–162.

Hoff, E. (2001). *Language development* (2nd ed.). Belmont, CA: Wadsworth.

Holahan, A., & Costenbader, V. (2000). A comparison of developmental gains for preschool children with disabilities in inclusive and self-contained classrooms. *Topics in Early Childhood Special Education, 20,* 224–235.

Hollich, G. J., Hirsch-Pasek, K., & Golinkoff, R. M. (2000). Breaking the language barrier: An emergentist coalition model for the origins of word learning. *Monographs of the Society for Research in Child Development, 65*(No. 262).

Hooker, K., & Siegler, I. C. (1993). Life goals, satisfaction, and self-rated health: Preliminary findings. *Experimental Aging Research, 19,* 97–110.

Houston, D. M., Jusczyk, P. W., Kuijpers, C., Coolen, R., & Cutler, A. (2000). Cross-language word segmentation by 9-month-olds. *Psychonomics Bulletin Review, 7,* 504–509.

Hunt, K. W. (1970). Syntactic maturity in schoolchildren and adults. *Monographs of the Society for Research in Child Development, 35*(1, Serial No. 134).

Hunt, P., & Goetz, L. (1997). Research on inclusive educational programs, practices, and outcomes for students with severe disabilities. *Journal of Special Education, 31,* 3–29.

Huttenlocher, J., Haight, W., Bryk, A., Seltzer, M., & Lyons, T. (1991). Early vocabulary growth: Relation to language input and gender. *Developmental Psychology, 27,* 236–244.

Hyson, M. C., Hirsch-Pasek, K., & Rescorla, L. (1989). *Academic environments in early childhood: Challenge or pressure?* Summary report to the Spencer Foundation.

Imel, S. (1996). Adult literacy education: Emerging directions in program development. ERIC Digest No. 179.

Jaffe, J., Beebe, B., Feldstein, S., Crown, C. L., & Jasnow, M. D. (2001). Rhythms of dialogue in infancy: Coordinated timing in development. *Monographs of the Society for Research in Child Development, 66*(No. 265).

Jia, G., & Aaronson, D. (1999). Age differences in second language acquisition: The dominant language switch and maintenance hypothesis. In A. Greenhill, H. Littlefield, & C. Tano (Eds.), *Proceedings of the 23rd Annual Boston University Conference on Language Development* (pp. 301–312). Somerville, MA: Cascadilla Press.

Johnson, D. W., Johnson, R. T., & Maruyama, G. (1983). Interdependence and interpersonal attraction among heterogeneous and homogeneous individuals: A theoretical formulation and a meta-analysis of the research. *Review of Educational Research, 53,* 5–54.

Johnson, J., & Newport, E. (1989). Critical period effects in second language learning: The influence of maturational state on the acquisition of English as a second language. *Cognitive Psychology, 21,* 60–99.

Jusczyk, P. W. (1999). How infants begin to extract words from speech. *Trends in Cognitive Science, 3,* 323–328.

Jusczyk, P. W., Houston, D. M., & Newsome, M. (1999). The beginnings of word segmentation in English-learning infants. *Cognitive Psychology, 39,* 159–207.

Kagan, J. (1998). *Three seductive ideas.* Cambridge, MA: Harvard University Press.

Kagan, J., & Moss, H. A. (1962). *Birth to maturity.* New York: Wiley.

Kaplan, D. S., Damphousse, K. R., & Kaplan, H. B. (1994). Mental health implications of not graduating from high school. *Journal of Experimental Education, 62,* 105–123.

Keller, H. (1954). *The story of my life.* New York: Doubleday.

Kemler Nelson, D. G., Hirsch-Pasek, K., Jusczyk, P. W., & Cassidy, K. W. (1989). How the prosodic cues in motherese might assist in language learning. *Journal of Child Language, 16,* 55–68.

Kemtes, K. A., & Kemper, S. (1997). Younger and older adults' on-line processing of syntactically ambiguous sentences. *Psychology and Aging, 12,* 362–371.

Kerka, S. (1995). Adult learner retention revisited. ERIC Clearinghouse on Adult, Career, and Vocational Education, Digest No. 166.

Kirsch, I. S., Jungeblut, A., Jenkins, L., & Kolstad, A. (1993). *Adult literacy in America: A first look at the results of the National Adult Literacy Survey.* Washington, DC: National Center for Education Statistics.

Klein, W. (1996). Language acquisition at different ages. In D. Magnusson (Ed.), *The lifespan development of individuals: Behavioral, neurobiological, and psychosocial perspectives: A synthesis.* Cambridge, England: Cambridge University Press.

Kopka, T. L. C., & Peng, S. S. (1993). *Adult education: Main reasons for participating.* Statistics in Brief NCES-93-451. Washington, DC: National Center for Education Statistics.

Krogh, K. M. (1985). Women's motives to achieve and to nurture in different life stages. *Sex Roles, 12,* 75–90.

Kulik, J. A., & Kulik, C. C. (1992). Meta-analytic findings on grouping programs. *Gifted Child Quarterly, 36,* 73–77.

Kulman, L. (1997, March 10). The prescription for smart kids. *U.S. News & World Report,* p. 10.

Ladd, G. W., Buhs, E. S., & Seid, M. (2000). Children's initial sentiments about kindergarten: Is school liking an antecedent of early classroom participation and achievement? *Merrill-Palmer Quarterly, 46,* 255–279.

Larson, R. W., & Verma, S. (1999). How children and adolescents spend time across the world: Work, play, and developmental opportunities. *Psychological Bulletin, 125,* 701–736.

Lemann, N. (1997, November). The reading wars. *Atlantic Monthly,* pp. 128–134.

Lenneberg, E. H. (1967). *Biological foundations of language.* New York: Wiley.

Lewis, B. A., & Thompson, L. A. (1992). A study of developmental speech and language disorders in twins. *Journal of Speech and Hearing Research, 35,* 1086–1094.

Lieven, E. V. M. (1994). Crosslinguistic and crosscultural aspects of language addressed to children. In C. Gallaway & B. J. Richards (Eds.), *Input and interaction in language acquisition.* Cambridge, England: Cambridge University Press.

Light, L. L. (1990). Interactions between memory and language in old age. In J. E. Birren & K. W. Schaie (Eds.), *The handbook of the psychology of aging* (3rd ed.). San Diego: Academic Press.

Locke, J. L. (1997). A theory of neurolinguistic development. *Brain and Language, 58,* 265–326.

Lonigan, C. J., Burgess, S. R., & Anthony, J. L. (2000). Development of emergent literacy and early reading skills in preschool children: Evidence from a latent-variable longitudinal study. *Developmental Psychology, 36,* 596–613.

Mac Iver, D. J., & Reuman, D. A. (1988, April). *Decision-making in the classroom and early adolescents' valuing of mathematics.* Paper presented at the annual meeting of the American Educational Research Association, New Orleans.

Mac Iver, D. J., Reuman, D. A., & Main, S. R. (1995). Social structuring of the school: Studying what is, illuminating what could be. *Annual Review of Psychology, 46,* 375–400.

MacKay, D. G., & Abrams, L. (1996). Language, memory, and aging: Distributed deficits and the structure of new-versus-old connections. In J. E. Birren & K. W. Schaie (Eds.), *Handbook of the psychology of aging* (4th ed). San Diego: Academic Press.

MacTurk, R. H., McCarthy, M. E., Vietze, P. M., & Yarrow, L. J. (1987). Sequential analysis of mastery behavior in 6- and 12-month-old infants. *Developmental Psychology, 23,* 199–203.

Maehr, M., & Meyer, H. (1997). Understanding motivation and schooling: Where we've been, where we are, and where we need to go. *Educational Psychology Review, 9,* 371–409.

Malatesta, C. Z., & Culver, L. C. (1984). Thematic and affective content in the lives of adult women. In C. Z. Malatesta & C. E. Izard (Eds.), *Emotion in adult development.* Beverly Hills, CA: Sage.

Manset, G., & Semmel, M. I. (1997). Are inclusive programs for students with mild disabilities effective? A comparative review of model programs. *Journal of Special Education, 31,* 155–180.

Maratsos, M. (1998). The acquisition of grammar. In W. Damon (Editor-in-Chief), D. Kuhn & R. S. Siegler (Vol. Eds.), *Handbook of child psychology: Vol. 2. Cognition, perception, and language* (5th ed., pp. 421–466). New York: Wiley.

Marcus, G. F., & Vijayan, S. (1999). Rule learning by seven-month-old infants. *Science, 283,* 77–80.

Martin, M. O., et al. (2000). *TIMSS 1999 International Science Report: Findings from IEA's Repeat of the Third International Mathematics and Science Study at the Eighth Grade.* Chestnut Hill, MA: Boston College.

Masataka, N. (1996). Perception of motherese in a signed language by 6-month-old deaf infants. *Developmental Psychology, 32,* 874–879.

Mayberry, R. I. (1994). The importance of childhood to language acquisition: Evidence from American Sign Language. In J. C. Goodman & H. C. Nusbaum (Eds.), *The development of speech perception: The transition from speech sounds to spoken words.* Cambridge, MA: MIT Press.

Mayes, L. C., & Zigler, E. (1992). An observational study of the affective concomitants of mastery in infants. *Journal of Psychology and Psychiatry, 4,* 659–667.

McAdams, P. P., de St. Aubin, E., & Logan, R. L. (1993). Generativity among young, middle, and older adults. *Psychology and Aging, 8,* 221–230.

McCaul, E. J., Donaldson, G. A., Coladarci, T., & Davis, W. E. (1992). Consequences of dropping out of school: Findings from high school and beyond. *Journal of Educational Research, 85,* 198–207.

McCormick, M. (1998). Mom's "BABY" vids sharpen new minds. *Billboard, 110,* 72–73.

McCune, L., Vihman, M. M., Roug-Hellichius, L. Delery, D. B., & Gogate, L. L. (1996). Grunt communication in human infants (*Homo sapiens*). *Journal of Comparative Psychology, 110*, 27–27.

McGhee-Bidlack, B. (1991). The development of noun definitions: A metalinguistic analysis. *Journal of Child Language, 18*, 417–434.

McGrath, E. P., & Repetti, R. L. (2000). Mothers' and fathers' attitudes toward their children's academic performance and children's perceptions of their academic competence. *Journal of Youth and Adolescence, 29*, 713–723.

McNeill, D. (1970). *The acquisition of language.* New York: Harper & Row.

Mehan, H., Villanueva, I., Hubbard, L., & Lintz, A. (1996). *Constructing school success: The consequences of untracking low-achieving students.* New York: Cambridge University Press.

Meier, R. P. (1991). Language acquisition by deaf children. *American Scientist, 79*, 69–70.

Mellinger, J. C., & Erdwins, C. J. (1985). Personality correlates of age and life roles in adult women. *Psychology of Women Quarterly, 9*, 503–514.

Mervis, C. B., & Johnson, K. E. (1991). Acquisition of the plural morpheme: A case study. *Developmental Psychology, 27*, 222–235.

Merzenich, M. M., Jenkins, W. M., Johnston, P., Schreiner, C., Miller, S. L., & Tallal, P. (1996). Temporal processing deficits of language-learning impaired children ameliorated by training. *Science, 271*, 77–81.

Messer, D. J., McCarthy, M. E., McQuiston, S., MacTurk, R. H., Yarrow, L. J., & Vietze, P. M. (1986). Relation between mastery behavior in infancy and competence in early childhood. *Developmental Psychology, 22*, 366–372.

Midgley, C., Feldlaufer, H., & Eccles, J. S. (1989). Student/teacher relations and attitudes toward mathematics before and after the transition to junior high school. *Child Development, 60*, 981–992.

Miller, A. (1985). A developmental study of the cognitive basis of performance impairment after failure. *Journal of Personality and Social Psychology, 49*, 529–538.

Moerk, E. L. (1989). The LAD was a lady and the tasks were ill-defined. *Developmental Psychology, 9*, 21–57.

Molfese, D. L. (2000). Predicting dyslexia at 8 years of age using neonatal brain responses. *Brain and Language, 72*, 238–245.

Morgan, G. A., MacTurk, R. H., & Hrncir, E. J. (1995). Mastery motivation: Overview, definitions, and conceptual issues. In R. H. MacTurk & G. A. Morgan (Eds.), *Mastery motivation: Origins, conceptualizations, and applications.* Norwood, NJ: Ablex.

Mortimer, J. T., Finch, M. D., Ryu, S., Shanahan, M. J., & Call, K. T. (1996). The effects of work intensity on adolescent mental health, achievement, and behavioral adjustment: New evidence from a prospective study. *Child Development, 67*, 1243–1261.

Myers, J., Jusczyk, P. W., Nelson, D. G. K., Charles-Luce, J., Woodward, A. L., & Hirsch-Pasek, K. (1996). Infants' sensitivity to word boundaries in fluent speech. *Journal of Child Language, 23*, 1–30.

Naigles, L. G., & Gelman, S. A. (1995). Overextensions in comprehension and production revisited: Preferential-looking in a study of dog, cat, and cow. *Journal of Child Language, 22*, 19–46.

National Center for Education Statistics. (1998). National Household Education Survey (NHES), "Adult Education Interview," 1991, 1995, 1999; Projections of Education Statistics to 2008 (NCES 98-016).

National Center for Education Statistics. (2001). *Drop Rates in the United States: 1999.* Available online: http://nces.ed.gov/pubs2001/dropout/HighSchoolRates3.asp

National Reading Panel. (1999). *Teaching children to read: An evidence-based assessment of the scientific literature on reading and its implications for reading instruction.* Washington, DC: National Institute of Child Health & Human Development.

Nelson, K. (1973). Structure and strategy in learning to talk. *Monographs of the Society for Research in Child Development, 38*(Serial No. 149).

Nelson, K., Hampson, J., & Shaw, L. K. (1993). Nouns in early lexicons: Evidence, explanations and implications. *Journal of Child Language, 20*, 61–84.

Neville, H. J., Coffey, S. A., Lawson, D. S., Fischer, A., Emmorey, K., & Bellugi, U. (1997). Neural systems mediating American Sign Language: Effects of sensory experience and age of acquisition. *Brain and Language, 57*, 285–308.

Newport, E. L. (1991). Contrasting conceptions of the critical period for language. In S. Carey & R. Gelman (Eds.), *The epigenesis of mind: Essays on biology and cognition.* Hillsdale, NJ: Erlbaum.

Nicholls, J. G., & Miller, A. T. (1984). Reasoning about the ability of self and others: A developmental study. *Child Development, 55*, 1990–1999.

Nippold, M. A., Hegel, S. L., Sohlberg, M. M., & Schwarz, I. E. (1999). Defining abstract entities: Development in pre-adolescents, adolescents, and young adults. *Journal of Speech, Language, and Hearing Research, 42*, 473–481.

Obler, L. K. (2001). Development and loss: Changes in the adult years. In J. B. Gleason (Ed.), *The development of language* (5th ed., pp. 455–488). Boston: Allyn & Bacon.

Obler, L. K., & Albert, M. L. (1985). Language skills across adulthood. In J. E. Birren & K. W. Schaie (Eds.), *Handbook of the psychology of aging* (2nd ed.). New York: Van Nostrand Reinhold.

Ochs, E. (1982). Talking to children in western Samoa. *Language in Society, 11*, 77–104.

Odden, A. (1990). Class size and student achievement: Research-based policy alternatives. *Educational Evaluation and Policy Analysis, 12*, 213–227.

O'Donnell, A. M., & O'Kelly, J. (1994). Learning from peers: Beyond the rhetoric of positive results. *Educational Psychology Review, 6*, 321–349.

Oliver, E. I. (1995). The writing quality of seventh, ninth, and eleventh graders, and college freshmen: Does rhetorical specification in writing prompts make a difference? *Research in the Teaching of English, 29*, 422–450.

Oller, D. K., & Eilers, R. E. (1988). The role of audition in infant babbling. *Child Development, 59*, 441–449.

Orth, L. C., & Martin, R. P. (1994). Interactive effects of student temperament and instruction method on classroom behavior and achievement. *Journal of School Psychology, 32*, 149–166.

Pan, B. A., & Gleason, J. B. (2001). Semantic development: Learning the meanings of words. In J. B. Gleason (Ed.), *The development of language* (5th ed., pp. 125–161). Boston: Allyn & Bacon.

Parker, F. L., Boak, A. Y., Griffin, K. W., Ripple, C., & Peay, L. (1999). Parent–child relationship, home learning environment, and school readiness. *School Psychology Review, 28*, 413–425.

Parnham, J. (2001). Lifelong learning: A model for increasing the participation of non-traditional adult learners. *Journal of Further and Higher Education, 25*, 57–65.

Pegg, J. E., Werker, J. F., & McLeod, P. J. (1992). Preference for infant-directed over adult-directed speech: Evidence from 7-week-old infants. *Infant Behavior and Development, 15*, 325–345.

Peisner-Feinberg, E. S., & Burchinal, M. R. (1997). Relations between preschool children's child-care experiences and concurrent development: The cost, quality, and outcomes study. *Merrill-Palmer Quarterly, 43*, 451–477.

Penner, S. G. (1987). Parental responses to grammatical and ungrammatical child utterances. *Child Development, 58*, 376–384.

Perfetti, C. A. (1999). Cognitive research and the misconceptions of reading education. In J. Oakhill & R. Beard (Eds.), *Reading development and the teaching of reading* (pp. 42–58). Malden, MA: Blackwell.

Peterson, P. L. (1977). Interactive effects of student anxiety, achievement orientation, and teacher behavior on student achievement and attitude. *Journal of Educational Psychology, 69*, 779–792.

Petitto, L. A., & Marentette, P. F. (1991). Babbling in the manual mode: Evidence for the ontogeny of language. *Science, 251*, 1493–1496.

Phelan, P., Yu, H. C., & Davidson, A. L. (1994). Navigating the psychosocial pressures of adolescence: The voices and experiences of high school youth. *American Educational Research Journal, 31*, 415–447.

Phillips, M. (1997). What makes schools effective? A comparison of the relationships of communitarian climate and academic climate to mathematics achievement and attendance during middle school. *American Educational Research Journal, 34*, 633–662.

Piaget, J. (1970). Piaget's theory. In P. H. Mussen (Ed.), *Carmichael's manual of child psychology* (Vol. 1). New York: Wiley.

Pine, J. M. (1994). The language of primary caregivers. In C. Gallaway & B. J. Richards (Eds.), *Input and interaction in language acquisition.* Cambridge, England: Cambridge University Press.

Pinker, S. (1994). *The language instinct: How the mind creates language.* New York: William Morrow.

Plomin, R. (1990). *Nature and nurture: An introduction to human behavioral genetics.* Pacific Grove, CA: Brooks/Cole.

Pomerantz, E. M., & Ruble, D. N. (1997). Distinguishing multiple dimensions of conceptions of ability: Implications for self-evaluation. *Child Development, 68*, 1165–1180.

Portes, A., & MacLeod, D. (1996). Educational progress of children of immigrants: The roles of class, ethnicity, and school context. *Sociology of Education, 69*, 255–275.

Quigley, B. A. (1997). *Rethinking literacy education: The critical need for practice-based change.* San Francisco: Jossey-Bass.

Quigley, B. A., & Uhland, R. L. (2000). Retaining adult learners in the first three critical weeks: A quasi-experimental model for use in ABE programs. *Adult Basic Education, 10,* 55–68.

Rapkin, B. D., & Fischer, K. (1992). Personal goals of older adults: Issues in assessment and prediction. *Psychology and Aging, 7,* 127–137.

Redding, R. E., Harmon, R. J., & Morgan, G. A. (1990). Maternal depression and infants' mastery behaviors. *Infant Behavior and Development, 13,* 391–395.

Reker, G. T., Peacock, E. J., & Wong, P. T. P. (1987). Meaning and purpose in life and well-being: A life-span perspective. *Journal of Gerontology, 42,* 44–49.

Reynolds, A. J., Mavrogenes, N. A., Bezruczko, N., & Hagemann, M. (1996). Cognitive and family-support mediators of preschool effectiveness: A confirmatory analysis. *Child Development, 67,* 1119–1140.

Reynolds, D. (1992). School effectiveness and school improvement: An updated review of the British literature. In D. Reynolds & P. Cuttance (Eds.), *School effectiveness: Research, policy, and practice.* London: Cassell.

Reznick, J. S., & Goldfield, B. A. (1992). Rapid change in lexical development in comprehension and production. *Developmental Psychology, 28,* 406–413.

Rimm-Kaufman, S., & Pianta, R. C. (1999). Patterns of family–school contact in preschool and kindergarten. *School Psychology Review, 28,* 426–438.

Rosenholtz, S. J., & Simpson, C. (1984). The formation of ability conceptions: Developmental trend or social construction? *Review of Educational Research, 54,* 31–63.

Roth, P. L., Bevier, C. A., Switzer, F. S., & Schippmann, J. S. (1996). Meta-analyzing the relationship between grades and job performance. *Journal of Applied Psychology, 81,* 548–556.

Ruble, D. N., Eisenberg, R., & Higgins, E. T. (1994). Developmental changes in achievement evaluation: Motivational implications of self–other differences. *Child Development, 65,* 1095–1110.

Rutter, M. (1983). School effects on pupil progress: Research findings and policy implications. *Child Development, 54,* 1–29.

Rutter, M., Maughan, B., Mortimore, P., Ouston, J., & Smith, A. (1979). *Fifteen thousand hours: Secondary schools and their effects on children.* Cambridge, MA: Harvard University Press.

St. John, N. H. (1975). *School desegregation: Outcomes for children.* New York: Wiley.

Salend, S. J. (1999). Facilitating friendships among diverse students. *Intervention in School and Clinic, 35,* 9–15.

Sargant, N., Field, J., Francis, H., Schuller, T., & Tuckett, A. (1997). *The learning divide.* Brighton, UK: National Organisation for Adult Learning.

Saxton, M. (1997). The contrast theory of negative input. *Journal of Child Language, 24,* 139–161.

Schaie, K. W. (1996). *Intellectual development in adulthood: The Seattle Longitudinal Study.* Cambridge, England: Cambridge University Press.

Schieffelin, B. B. (1986). *How Kaluli children learn what to say, what to do, and how to feel.* New York: Cambridge University Press.

Schneider, W., Roth, E., & Ennemoser, M. (2000). Training phonological skills and letter knowledge in children at risk for dyslexia: A comparison of three kindergarten intervention programs. *Journal of Educational Psychology, 92,* 284–295.

Seidman, E., Allen, L. R., Aber, J. L., Mitchell, C., & Feinman, J. (1994). The impact of school transitions in early adolescence on the self-system and perceived social context of poor urban youth. *Child Development, 65,* 507–522.

Senter, M. S., & Senter, R. (1997). Student outcomes and the adult learner. *Continuing Higher Education Review, 61,* 75–87.

Shanahan, M. J., Finch, M. D., Mortimer, J. T., & Ryu, S. (1991). Adolescent work experience and depressive affect. *Social Psychology Quarterly, 54,* 299–317.

Shaywitz, S. E., Fletcher, J. M., Holahan, J. M., Shneider, A. E., Marchione, K. E., Stuebing, K. K., Francis, D. J., Pugh, K. R., & Shaywitz, B. A. (1999). Persistence of dyslexia: The Connecticut Longitudinal Study at Adolescence. *Pediatrics, 104,* 1351–1359.

Simmons, R. G., & Blyth, D. A. (1987). *Moving into adolescence: The impact of pubertal change in school context.* New York: Aldine de Gruyter.

Singh, K., & Ozturk, M. (2000). Effect of part-time work on high school mathematics and science course taking. *Journal of Educational Research, 94,* 67–74.

Skinner, B. F. (1957). *Verbal behavior.* New York: Appleton-Century-Crofts.

Slavin, R. E. (1986). Cooperative learning: Engineering social psychology in the classroom. In R. S. Feldman (Ed.), *The social psychology of education: Current research and theory.* Cambridge, England: Cambridge University Press.

Slavin, R. E. (1989). Class size and student achievement: Small effects of small classes. *Educational Psychologist, 24,* 99–110.

Slobin, D. I. (1979). Psycholinguistics (2nd ed.). Glenview, IL: Scott, Foresman.

Smith, J. B. (1997). Effects of eighth-grade transition programs on high school retention and experiences. *Journal of Educational Research, 90,* 144–152.

Snow, C. E., Arlman-Rupp, A., Hassing, Y., Jobse, J., Joosken, J., & Vorster, J. (1976). Mother's speech in three social classes. *Journal of Psycholinguistic Research, 5,* 1–20.

Sommers, M. S. (1997). Speech perception in older adults: The importance of speech-specific cognitive abilities. *Journal of the American Geriatrics Society, 45,* 633–637.

Spence, J. T. (1985). Achievement American style: The rewards and costs of individualism. *American Psychologist, 40,* 1285–1295.

Spencer, P. E. (1996). The association between language and symbolic play at two years: Evidence from deaf toddlers. *Child Development, 67,* 867–876.

Stanovich, K. E. (1986). Matthew effects in reading: Some consequences of individual differences in the acquisition of literacy. *Reading Research Quarterly, 21,* 360–407.

Stanovich, K. E., & Stanovich, P. J. (1999). How research might inform the debate about early reading acquisition. In J. Oakhill & R. Beard (Eds.), *Reading development and the teaching of reading* (pp. 12–41). Oxford: Blackwell.

Steinberg, L. (1984). The varieties and effects of work during adolescence. In M. E. Lamb, A. L. Brown, & B. Rogoff (Eds.), *Advances in developmental psychology* (Vol. 3). Hillsdale, NJ: Erlbaum.

Steinberg, L., & Dornbusch, S. M. (1991). Negative correlates of part-time employment during adolescence: Replication and elaboration. *Developmental Psychology, 27,* 304–313.

Steinberg, L., Dornbusch, S. M., & Brown, B. B. (1992). Ethnic differences in adolescent achievement: An ecological perspective. *American Psychologist, 47,* 723–729.

Steinberg, L., Fegley, S., & Dornbusch, S. M. (1993). Negative impact of part-time work on adolescent adjustment: Evidence from a longitudinal study. *Developmental Psycholgy, 29,* 171–180.

Stephan, W. G. (1978). School desegregation: An evaluation of the predictions made in Brown vs. Board of Education. *Psychological Bulletin, 85,* 217–238.

Stevens, D. P., & Truss, C. V. (1985). Stability and change in adult personality over 12 and 20 years. *Developmental Psychology, 21,* 568–584.

Stevens, G. (1999). Age at immigration and second language proficiency among foreign-born adults. *Language in Society, 28,* 555–578.

Stevens, R. J., & Slavin, R. E. (1995). The cooperative elementary school: Effects on students' achievement, attitudes, and social relations. *American Educational Research Journal, 32,* 321–351.

Stevenson, H. W., Chen, C., & Lee, S. (1993). Mathematics achievement of Chinese, Japanese, and American children: Ten years later. *Science, 259,* 53–58.

Stevenson, H. W., & Lee, S. Y. (1990). Contexts of achievement: A study of American, Chinese, and Japanese children. *Monographs of the Society for Research in Child Development, 55*(1–2, Serial No. 221).

Stevenson, H. W., Lee, S. Y., & Stigler, J. W. (1986). Mathematics achievement of Chinese, Japanese, and American children. *Science, 231,* 693–699.

Stevenson, H. W., & Stigler, J. W. (1994). *The learning gap: Why our schools are failing and what we can learn from Japanese and Chinese education.* New York: Simon & Schuster.

Stevenson, H. W., Stigler, J. W., Lee, S. Y., Lucker, G. W., Litamura, S., & Hsu, C. (1985). Cognitive performance and academic achievement of Japanese, Chinese, and American children. *Child Development, 56,* 718–734.

Stigler, J. W., Lee, S. Y., & Stevenson, H. W. (1987). Mathematics classrooms in Japan, Taiwan, and the United States. *Child Development, 58,* 1272–1285.

Stine, E. A. L., Soederberg, L. M., & Morrow, D. G. (1996). Language and discourse processing through adulthood. In F. Blanchard-Fields & T. M. Hess (Eds.), *Perspectives on cognitive change in adulthood and aging.* New York: McGraw-Hill.

Stipek, D. J. (1984). The development of achievement motivation. In R. Ames & C. Ames (Eds.), *Research on motivation in education* (Vol. 1). Orlando, FL: Academic Press.

Stipek, D. J., Feiler, R., Daniels, D., & Milburn, S. (1995). Effects of different instructional approaches on young children's achievement and motivation. *Child Development, 66,* 209–223.

Stipek, D. J., & Gralinski, J. H. (1996). Children's beliefs about intelligence and school performance. *Journal of Educational Psychology, 88,* 397–407.

Stipek, D. J., & Mac Iver, D. J. (1989). Developmental change in children's assessment of intellectual competence. *Child Development, 60,* 521–538.

Stipek, D. J., Recchia, A., & McClintic, S. (1992). Self-evaluation in young-children. *Monographs of the Society for Research in Child Development, 57*(1, Serial No. 226).

Sudhalter, V., & Braine, M. D. S. (1985). How does comprehension of passives develop? A comparison of actional and experiential verbs. *Journal of Child Language, 12,* 455–470.

Sui-Chu, E. H., & Willms, J. D. (1996). Effects of parental involvement on eighth-grade achievement. *Sociology of Education, 69,* 126–141.

Suitor, J. J., & Reavis, R. (1995). Football, fast cars, and cheerleading: Adolescent gender norms, 1978–1989. *Adolescence, 30,* 265–272.

Tallal, P., Miller, S. L., Bedi, G., Byma, G., Wang, X., Nagarajan, S. S., Schreiner, C., Jenkins, W. M., & Merzenich, M. M. (1996). Language comprehension in language-learning impaired children improved with acoustically modified speech. *Science, 271,* 81–84.

Temple, E., Poldrack, R. A., Protopapas, A., Nagarajan, S., Salz, T., Tallal, P., Merzenich, M. M., & Gabrieli, J. D. (2000). Disruption of the neural response to rapid acoustic stimuli in dyslexia: Evidence from functional MRI. *Proceedings of the National Academy of Science, 97,* 13907–13912.

Thompson, J. R., & Chapman, R. S. (1977). Who is "Daddy" revisited? The status of two-year-olds' overextended words in use and comprehension. *Journal of Child Language, 4,* 359–375.

Toch, T., & Streisand, B. (1997, October 13). Does class size matter? *U.S. News & World Report,* pp. 22–29.

Tomasello, M. (1999). The human adaptation for culture. *Annual Review of Anthropology, 28,* 502–529.

Treiman, R. (2000). The foundations of literacy. *Current Directions in Psychological Science, 9,* 89–92.

Treiman, R., & Broderick, V. (1998). What's in a name? Children's knowledge about the letters in their own names. *Journal of Experimental Child Psychology, 70,* 97–116.

U.S. Bureau of the Census. (1997). *Statistical abstract of the United States* (117th ed.). Washington, DC: U.S. Government Printing Office.

U.S. Department of Education. (1997). Digest of Education Statistics, 1997. Washington D.C.: National Center for Education Statistics

Van Kleeck, A., Gillam, R. B., Hamilton, L., & McGrath, C. (1997). The relationship between middle-class parents' book-sharing discussion and their preschooler's abstract language development. *Journal of Speech, Language, and Hearing Research, 40,* 1261–1271.

Vellutino, F. R. (1991). Introduction to three studies on reading acquisition: Convergent findings on theoretical foundations of code-oriented versus whole language approaches

to reading instruction. *Journal of Educational Psychology, 83,* 437–443

Vellutino, F. R., Scanlon, D. M., Sipay, E. R., & Small, S. G. (1996). Cognitive profiles of difficult-to-remediate and readily remediated poor readers: Early intervention as a vehicle for distinguishing between cognitive and experiential deficits as basic causes of specific reading disability. *Journal of Educational Psychology, 88,* 601–638.

Veroff, J., Reuman, D., & Feld, S. (1984). Motives in American men and women across the adult life span. *Developmental Psychology, 20,* 1142–1158.

Wade, B., & Moore, M. (1998). An early start with books: Literacy and mathematical evidence from a longitudinal study. *Educational Review, 50,* 135–145.

Wang, M. C., Haertel, G. D., & Walberg, H. J. (1993). Toward a knowledge base for school learning. *Review of Educational Research, 63,* 249–294.

Weizman, A. O., & Snow, C. E. (2001). Lexical input as related to children's vocabulary acquisition: Effects of sophisticated exposure and support for meaning. *Developmental Psychology, 37,* 265–279.

Wenglinsky, H. (1998a). *Does it compute? The relationship between educational technology and student achievement in mathematics.* Princeton, NJ: Educational Testing Service.

Wenglinsky, H. (1998b). Finance equalization and within-school equity: The relationship between education spending and the social distribution of achievement. *Educational Evaluation and Policy Analysis, 20,* 269–283.

Whitehurst, G. J., & Lonigan, C. J. (1998). Child development and emergent literacy. *Child Development, 69,* 848–872.

Whitehurst, G. J., & Valdez-Menchaca, M. C. (1988). What is the role of reinforcement in early language acquisition? *Child Development, 59,* 430–440.

Wigfield, A., Eccles, J. S., Yoon, K. S., & Harold, R. D. (1997). Change in children's competence beliefs and subjective task values across the elementary school years: A 3-year study. *Journal of Educational Psychology, 89,* 451–469.

Woodward, A. L., & Markman, E. M. (1998). Early word learning. In W. Damon (Editor-in-Chief), D. Kuhn & R. S. Siegler (Vol. Eds.), *Handbook of child psychology: Vol. 2. Cognition, perception, and language* (5th ed., pp. 371–420). New York: Wiley.

Yarrow, L. J., Klein, R., Lomonaco, S., & Morgan, G. A. (1975). Cognitive and motivational development in early childhood. In B. Z. Friedlander, G. M. Sterritt, & G. E. Kirk (Eds.), *Exceptional infant: Assessment and intervention.* New York: Bruner/Mazel.

Yarrow, L. J., MacTurk, R. H., Vietze, P. M., McCarthy, M. E., Klein, R. P., & McQuiston, S. (1984). Developmental course of parental stimulation and its relationship to mastery motivation during infancy. *Developmental Psychology, 20,* 492–503.

Zigler, E., & Finn-Stevenson, M. (1993). *Children in a changing world: Developmental and social issues.* Pacific Grove, CA: Brooks/Cole.

Chapter 11: Self and Personality

Abraham, J. D., & Hansson, R. O. (1995). Successful aging at work: An applied study of selection, optimization, and compensation

through impression management. *Journal of Gerontology: Psychological Sciences, 50,* P94–P103.

Achenbaum, W. A., & Bengtson, V. L. (1994). Re-engaging the disengagement theory of aging: On the history and assessment of theory development in gerontology. *Gerontologist, 34,* 756–763.

Ackerman, S., Zuroff, D. C., & Moskowitz, D. S. (2000). Generativity in midlife and young adults: Links to agency, communion, and subjective well-being. *International Journal of Aging and Human Development, 50,* 17–41.

Adams, G. R., & Archer, S. L. (1994). Identity: A precursor to intimacy. In S. L. Archer (Ed.), *Interventions for adolescent identity development.* Thousand Oaks, CA: Sage.

Archer, S. L. (1982). The lower age boundaries of identity development. *Child Development, 53,* 1551–1556.

Archer, S. L. (1992). A feminist's approach to identity research. In G. R. Adams, T. P. Gullotta, & R. Montemayor (Eds.), *Adolescent identity formation* (Advances in Adolescent Development, Vol. 4). Newbury Park, CA: Sage.

Armstrong, P. I., & Crombie, G. (2000). Compromises in adolescents' occupational aspirations and expectations from grades 8 to 10. *Journal of Vocational Behavior, 56,* 82–98.

Arnett, J. J. (2000). Emerging adulthood: A theory of development from the late teens through the twenties. *American Psychologist, 55,* 469–480.

Asendorpf, J. B., Warkentin, V., & Baudonnière, P. M. (1996). Self-awareness and other-awareness: 2. Mirror self-recognition, social contingency awareness, and synchronic imitation. *Developmental Psychology, 32,* 313–321.

Atchley, R. C. (1976). *The sociology of retirement.* Cambridge, MA: Schenkman.

Avolio, B. J., & Sosik, J. J. (1999). A life-span framework for assessing the impact of work on white-collar workers. In S. L. Willis & J. D. Reid (Eds.), *Life in the middle: Psychological and social development in middle age.* San Diego: Academic Press.

Baltes, P. B., & Baltes, M. M. (1990). Psychological perspectives on successful aging: The model of selective optimization with compensation. In P. B. Baltes & M. M. Baltes (Eds.), *Successful aging: Perspectives from the behavioral sciences.* New York: Cambridge University Press.

Baltes, P. B., Lindenberger, U., & Staudinger, U. M. (1998). Life-span theory in developmental psychology. In W. Damon (Editor-in-Chief), R. M. Lerner (Vol. Ed.), *Handbook of child psychology: Vol. 1. Theoretical models of human development* (5th ed.). New York: Wiley.

Bandura, A. (1986). *Social foundations of thought and action: A social cognitive theory.* Englewood Cliffs, NJ: Prentice-Hall.

Barusch, A. S. (1997). Self-concepts of low-income older women: Not old or poor, but fortunate and blessed. *International Journal of Aging and Human Development, 44,* 269–282.

Beehr, T. A., Glazer, S., Nielson, N. L., & Farmer, S. J. (2000). Work and nonwork predictors of employee's retirement age. *Journal of Vocational Behavior, 57,* 206–225.

Bernal, M. E., & Knight, G. P. (1997). Ethnic identity of Latino children. In J. G. Garcia & M. C. Zea (Eds.), *Psychological interventions and research with Latino populations.* Boston: Allyn & Bacon.

Bertenthal, B. I., & Fischer, K. W. (1978). Development of self-recognition in the infant. *Developmental Psychology, 14,* 44–50.

Berzonsky, M. D., & Kuk, L. S. (2000). Identity status, identity processing style, and the transition to university. *Journal of Adolescent Research, 15,* 81–98.

Berzonsky, M. D., & Neimeyer, G. J. (1994). Ego identity status and identity processing orientation: The moderating role of commitment. *Journal of Research in Personality, 28,* 425–435.

Borkenau, P., Riemann, R., Angleitner, A., & Spinath, F. M. (2001). Genetic and environmental influences on observed personality: Evidence from the German Observational Study of Adult Twins. *Journal of Personality and Social Psychology, 80,* 655–668.

Brandtstädter, J., & Greve, W. (1994). The aging self: Stabilizing and protective processes. *Developmental Review, 14,* 52–80.

Bretz, R. D., & Judge, T. A. (1994). Person–organization fit and the theory of work adjustment: Implications for satisfaction, tenure, and career success. *Journal of Vocational Behavior, 44,* 32–54.

Brooks-Gunn, J., & Lewis, M. (1981). Infant social perception: Responses to pictures of parents and strangers. *Developmental Psychology, 17,* 647–649.

Brownell, C. A., & Carriger, M. S. (1990). Changes in cooperation and self/other differentiation during the second year. *Child Development, 61,* 1164–1174.

Buss, A. H., & Plomin, R. (1984). *Temperament: Early developing personality traits.* Hillsdale, NJ: Erlbaum.

Butler, R. (1990). The effects of mastery and competitive conditions on self-assessment at different ages. *Child Development, 61,* 201–210.

Butler, R., & Ruzany, N. (1993). Age and socialization effects on the development of social comparison motives and normative ability assessment in kibbutz and urban children. *Child Development, 64,* 532–543.

Butler, R. N. (1963). The life review: An interpretation of reminiscence in the aged. *Psychiatry, 26,* 65–76.

Butler, R. N. (1975). *Why survive? Being old in America.* New York: Harper & Row.

Carr, P. L., Ash, A. S., Friedman, R. H., Scaramucci, A., Barnett, R. C., Szalacha, L., Palepu, A., & Moskowitz, M. A. (1998). Relation of family responsibilities and gender to the productivity and career satisfaction of medical faculty. *Annals of Internal Medicine, 129,* 532–538.

Carstensen, L. L., & Freund, A. M. (1994). Commentary: The resilience of the aging self. *Developmental Review, 14,* 81–92.

Caspi, A. (1998). Personality development across the life course. In W. Damon (Editor-in-Chief), R. M. Lerner (Vol. Ed.), *Handbook of child psychology: Vol. 1. Theoretical models of human development* (5th ed.). New York: Wiley.

Caspi, A. (2000). The child is father of man: Personality continues from childhood to adulthood. *Journal of Personality & Social Psychology, 78,* 158–172.

Caspi, A., Elder, G. H., Jr., & Bem, D. J. (1987). Moving against the world: Life-course patterns of explosive children. *Developmental Psychology, 23,* 308–313.

Caspi, A., Elder, G. H., Jr., & Bem, D. J. (1988). Moving away from the world: Life-course patterns of shy children. *Developmental Psychology, 24,* 824–831.

Charles, S. T., Reynolds, C. A., & Gatz, M. (2001). Age-related differences and change in positive and negative affect over 23 years. *Journal of Personality & Social Psychology, 80,* 136–151.

Chess, S., & Thomas, A. (1984). *Origins and evolution of behavior disorders: From infancy to early adult life.* New York: Brunner/Mazel.

Chess, S., & Thomas, A. (1999). *Goodness of fit: Clinical applications from infancy through adult life.* Ann Arbor, MI: Edwards Brothers.

Christiansen, S. L., & Palkovitz, R. (1998). Exploring Erikson's psychosocial theory of development: Generativity and its relationship to parental identity, intimacy, and involvement with others. *Journal of Men's Studies, 7,* 133–156.

Clark, L. A., Kochanska, G., & Ready, R. (2000). Mother's personality and its interaction with child temperament as predictors of parenting behavior. *Journal of Personality and Social Psychology, 79,* 274–285.

Cooley, C. H. (1902). *Human nature and the social order.* New York: Scribner's.

Coopersmith, S. (1967). *The antecedents of self-esteem.* San Francisco: W. H. Freeman.

Costa, P. T., Jr., & McCrae, R. R. (1992). Trait psychology comes of age. In T. B. Sonderegger (Ed.), *Nebraska Symposium on Motivation: Vol. 39. Psychology and aging.* Lincoln: University of Nebraska Press.

Costa, P. T., Jr., & McCrae, R. R. (1994). Stability and change in personality from adolescence through adulthood. In C. F. Halverson, Jr., G. A. Kohnstamm, & R. P. Martin (Eds.), *The developing structure of temperament and personality from infancy to adulthood.* Hillsdale, NJ: Erlbaum.

Cote, J. E., & Levine, C. (1988). A critical examination of the ego identity status paradigm. *Developmental Review, 8,* 147–184.

Cox, T. H., & Harquail, C. V. (1991). Career paths and career success in the early career stages of male and female MBAs. *Journal of Vocational Behavior, 39,* 54–75.

Crain, R. M. (1996). The influence of age, race, and gender on child and adolescent multidimensional self-concept. In B. A. Bracken (Ed.), *Handbook of self-concept: Developmental, social, and clinical considerations.* New York: Wiley.

Cross, S. E. (2000). What does it mean to "know thyself" in the United States and Japan? The cultural construction of the self. In T. J. Owens (Ed.), *Self and identity through the life course in cross-cultural perspective.* Stamford, CT: JAI Press.

Cumming, E., & Henry, W. E. (1961). *Growing old: The process of disengagement.* New York: Basic Books.

Damon, W. (1994). *Greater expectations: Overcoming the culture of indulgence in America's homes and schools.* New York: Free Press.

Damon, W., & Hart, D. (1982). The development of self-understanding from infancy through adolescence. *Child Development, 53,* 841–864.

Damon, W., & Hart, D. (1988). *Self-understanding in childhood and adolescence.* New York: Cambridge University Press.

Davis-Kean, P. E., & Sandler, H. M. (2001). A meta-analysis of measures of self-esteem for young children: A framework for future measures. *Child Development, 72,* 887–906.

DeBerry, K. M., Scarr, S., & Weinberg, R. (1996). Family racial socialization and ecological competence: Longitudinal assessments of African-American transracial adoptees. *Child Development, 67,* 2375–2399.

DesRosiers, F., Vrsalovic, W. T., Knauf, D. E., Vargas, M., & Busch-Rossnagel, N. A. (1999). Assessing the multiple dimensions of the self-concept of young children: A focus on Latinos. *Merrill-Palmer Quarterly, 45,* 543–566.

DeVries, M. W. (1984). Temperament and infant mortality among the Masai of East Africa. *American Journal of Psychiatry, 141,* 1189–1194.

Digman, J. M. (1990). Personality structure: Emergence of the 5-factor model. *Annual Review of Psychology, 41,* 417–440.

DiLalla, L. F., Kagan, J., Reznick, S. J. (1994). Genetic etiology of behavioral inhibition among 2-year-old children. *Infant Behavior and Development, 17,* 405–412.

Doyle, A. B., Markiewicz, D., Brendgen, M., Lieberman, M., & Voss, K. (2000). Child attachment security and self-concept: Associations with mother and father attachment style and marital quality. *Merrill-Palmer Quarterly, 46,* 514–539.

Dyk, P. H., & Adams, G. R. (1990). Identity and intimacy: An initial investigation of three theoretical models using cross-lag panel correlations. *Journal of Youth and Adolescence, 19,* 91–110.

Eccles, J., Wigfield, A., Harold, R. D., & Blumefeld, P. (1993). Age and gender differences in children's self- and task perceptions during elementary school. *Child Development, 64,* 830–847.

Eder, R. A. (1989). The emergent personologist: The structure and content of $3^1/_2$-, $5^1/_2$-, and $7^1/_2$-year-olds' concepts of themselves and other persons. *Child Development, 60,* 1218–1228.

Ekerdt, D. J., Bossé, R., & Levkoff, S. (1985). Empirical test for phases of retirement: Findings from the Normative Aging Study. *Journal of Gerontology, 40,* 95–101.

Ekerdt, D. J., Kosloski, K., & DeViney, S. (2000). The normative anticipation of retirement by older adults. *Research on Aging, 22,* 3–22.

England, P., Reid, L. L., & Kilbourne, B. S. (1996). The effect of the sex composition of jobs on starting wages in an organization: Findings from the NLSY. *Demography, 33,* 511–521.

Erikson, E. H. (1963). *Childhood and society* (2nd ed.). New York: Norton.

Erikson, E. H. (1968). *Identity: Youth and crisis.* New York: Norton.

Erikson, E. H. (1982). *The life cycle completed: A review.* New York: Norton.

Erikson, E. H., Erikson, J. M., & Kivnick, H. Q. (1986). *Vital involvement in old age.* New York: Norton.

Etaugh, C., & Liss, M. B. (1992). Home, school, and playroom: Training grounds for adult gender roles. *Sex Roles, 26,* 129–147.

Field, D., & Millsap, R. E. (1991). Personality in advanced old age: Continuity or change?

Journal of Gerontology: Psychological Sciences, 46, P299–P308.

Fletcher, M. A. (2000, March 26). Putting value on self-worth: Studies challenge belief that black students' esteem enhances achievement. *Washington Post,* pp. A3, A17.

Flum, H., & Blustein, D. L. (2000). Reinvigorating the study of vocational research. *Journal of Vocational Behavior, 56,* 380–404.

Fox, N. A., Henderson, H. A., Rubin, K. H., Calkins, S. D., & Schmidt, L. A. (2001). Continuity and discontinuity of behavioral inhibition and exuberance: Psychophysiological and behavioral influences across the first four years of life. *Child Development, 72,* 1–21.

Freund, A. M., & Baltes, P. B. (1998). Selection, optimization, and compensation as strategies of life management: Correlations with subjective indicators of successful aging. *Psychology and Aging, 13,* 531–543.

Frey, K. S., & Ruble, D. N. (1985). What children say when the teacher is not around: Conflicting goals in social comparison and performance assessment in the classroom. *Journal of Personality and Social Psychology, 48,* 550–562.

Fry, P. S. (1992). Major social theories of aging and their implications for counseling concepts and practice: A critical review. *Counseling Psychologist, 20,* 246–329.

Gall, T. L., Evans, D. R., & Howard, J. (1997). The retirement adjustment process: Changes in the well-being of male retirees across time. *Journal of Gerontology: Psychological Sciences, 52,* P110–P117.

Gallup, G. G., Jr. (1979). Self-recognition in chimpanzees and man: A developmental and comparative perspective. In M. Lewis & L. A. Rosenblum (Eds.), *Genesis of behavior: Vol. 2. The child and its family.* New York: Plenum.

Gendell, M., & Siegel, J. S. (1996). Trends in retirement age in the United States, 1955–1993, by sex and race. *Journal of Gerontology: Social Sciences, 51,* S132–S139.

Giarrusso, R., Feng, D., Silverstein, M., & Bengtson, V. L. (2000). Self in the context of the family. In K. W. Schaie & J. Hendricks (Eds.), *The evolution of the aging self: The societal impact on the aging process.* New York: Springer.

Ginzberg, E. (1972). Toward a theory of occupational choice: A restatement. *Vocational Guidance Quarterly, 20,* 169–176.

Ginzberg, E. (1984). Career development. In D. Brown, L. Brooks, & Associates (Eds.), *Career choice and development.* San Francisco: Jossey-Bass.

Glick, M., & Zigler, E. (1985). Self-image: A cognitive-developmental approach. In R. L. Leahy (Ed.), *The development of the self.* Orlando, FL: Academic Press.

Gottfredson, L. S. (1996). Gottfredson's theory of circumscription and compromise. In D. Brown, L. Brooks, & Associates (Eds.), *Career choice and development* (3rd ed.). San Francisco: Jossey-Bass.

Gray-Little, B., & Hafdahl, A. R. (2000). Factors influencing racial comparisons of self-esteem: A quantitative review. *Psychological Bulletin, 126,* 26–54.

Grimsley, K. D. (2000, June 9). Panel asks why women still earn less. *Washington Post,* p. E3.

Grotevant, H. D., & Cooper, C. R. (1986). Exploration as a predictor of congruence in adolescents' career choices. *Journal of Vocational Behavior, 29,* 201–215.

Haan, N. (1981). Common dimensions of personality development: Early adolescence to middle life. In D. H. Eichorn, J. A. Clausen, N. Haan, M. P. Honzik, & P. H. Mussen (Eds.), *Present and past in middle life.* New York: Academic Press.

Hansson, R. O., DeKoekkoek, P. D., Neece, W. M., & Patterson, D. W. (1997). Successful aging at work: Annual review, 1992–1996: The older worker and transitions to retirement. *Journal of Vocational Behavior, 51,* 202–233.

Harris, J. R. (2000). Context-specific learning, personality, and birth order. *Current Directions in Psychological Science, 9,* 174–177.

Hart, D., & Fegley, S. (1997). Children's self-awareness and self-understanding in cultural context. In U. Neisser & D. A. Jopling (Eds.), *The conceptual self in context. Culture, experience, self-understanding.* Cambridge, UK: Cambridge University Press.

Harter, S. (1996). Historical roots of contemporary issues involving self-concept. In B. A. Bracken (Ed.), *Handbook of self-concept: Developmental, social, and clinical considerations.* New York: Wiley.

Harter, S. (1999). *The construction of the self: A developmental perspective.* New York: Guilford.

Harter, S., & Monsour, A. (1992). Development analysis of conflict caused by opposing attributes in the adolescent self-portrait. *Developmental Psychology, 28,* 251–260.

Harter, S., & Pike, R. (1984). The pictorial scale of perceived competence and social acceptance for young children. *Child Development, 55,* 1969–1982.

Hartup, W. W., & van Lieshout, C. F. M. (1995). Personality development in social context. *Annual Review of Psychology, 46,* 655–687.

Havighurst, R. J., Neugarten, B. L., & Tobin, S. S. (1968). Disengagement and patterns of aging. In B. L. Neugarten (Ed.), *Middle age and aging.* Chicago: University of Chicago Press.

Hedlund, B., & Ebersole, P. (1983). A test of Levinson's mid-life reevaluation. *Journal of Genetic Psychology, 143,* 189–192.

Heidrich, S. M. (1999). Self-discrepancy across the life span. *Journal of Adult Development, 6,* 119–136.

Helgeson, V. S., & Mickelson, K. (2000). Coping with chronic illness among the elderly: Maintaining self-esteem. In S. B. Manuck, R. Jennings, B. S. Rabin, & A. Baum (Eds.), *Behavior, health, and aging.* Mahwah, NJ: Erlbaum.

Hermans, H. J., & Oles, P. K. (1999). Midlife crisis in men: Affective organization of personal meanings. *Human Relations, 52,* 1403–1426.

Herzog, A. R., Kahn, R. L., Morgan, J. N., Jackson, J. S., & Antonucci, T. C. (1989). Age differences in productive activities. *Journal of Gerontology: Social Sciences, 44,* S129–S138.

Hill, S. D., & Tomlin, C. (1981). Self-recognition in retarded children. *Child Development, 52,* 145–150.

Hodgson, J. W., & Fischer, J. L. (1979). Sex differences in identity and intimacy development in college youth. *Journal of Youth and Adolescence, 8,* 37–50.

Hoffman, M. A., Levy-Shiff, R., & Malinski, D. (1996). Stress and adjustment in the transition to adolescence: Moderating effects of neuroticism and extroversion. *Journal of Youth and Adolescence, 25,* 161–175.

Holland, J. L. (1985). *Making vocational choices: A theory of vocational personalities and work environments* (2nd ed.). Englewood Cliffs, NJ: Prentice-Hall.

Jenkins, S. R. (1989). Longitudinal prediction of women's careers: Psychological, behavioral, and social-structural influences. *Journal of Vocational Behavior, 34,* 204–235.

Jones, C. J., & Meredith, W. (1996). Patterns of personality change across the life span. *Psychology and Aging, 11,* 57–65.

Jones, C. J., & Meredith, W. (2000). Developmental paths of psychological health from early adolescence to later adulthood. *Psychology and Aging, 15,* 351–360.

Kagan, J. (1989). Temperamental contributions to social behavior. *American Psychologist, 44,* 668–674.

Kagan, J. (1994). *Galen's prophecy: Temperament in human nature.* New York: Basic Books.

Kagan, J., & Moss, H. A. (1962). *Birth to maturity.* New York: Wiley.

Kerr, M., Lambert, W. W. Stattin, H., & Klackenberg-Larsson, I. (1994). Stability of inhibition in a Swedish longitudinal sample. *Child Development, 10,* 443–458.

Kohn, M. L., & Schooler, C. (1982). Job conditions and personality: A longitudinal assessment of their reciprocal effects. *American Journal of Sociology, 87,* 1257–1286.

Kroger, J. (1996). Identity, regression, and development. *Journal of Adolescence, 19,* 203–222.

Kroger, J. (1997). Gender and identity: The intersection of structure, content, and context. *Sex Roles, 36,* 747–770.

Lamborn, S. D., Mounts, N. S., Steinberg, L., & Dornbusch, S. M. (1991). Patterns of competence and adjustment among adolescents from authoritative, authoritarian, indulgent, and neglectful families. *Child Development, 62,* 1049–1065.

Leon, G. R., Gillum, B., Gillum, R., & Gouze, M. (1979). Personality stability and change over a 30-year period—middle age to old age. *Journal of Consulting and Clinical Psychology, 47,* 517–524.

Levinson, D. J. (1986). A conception of adult development. *American Psychologist, 41,* 3–13.

Levinson, D. J. (in collaboration with J. D. Levinson). (1996). *The seasons of a woman's life.* New York: Knopf.

Levinson, D. J., Darrow, C. N., Klein, E. B., Levinson, M. H., & McKee, B. (1978). *The seasons of a man's life.* New York: Ballantine.

Lewis, M., Alessandri, S. M., & Sullivan, M. W. (1990). Violation of expectancy, loss of control, and anger expressions in young infants. *Developmental Psychology, 26,* 745–751.

Lewis, M., & Brooks-Gunn, J. (1979). *Social cognition and the acquisition of self.* New York: Plenum.

Lewis, M., Sullivan, M. W., Stanger, C., & Weiss, M. (1989). Self-development and self-conscious emotions. *Child Development, 60,* 146–156.

Livesley, W. J., & Bromley, D. B. (1973). *Person perception in childhood and adolescence.* London: Wiley.

Livson, F. B. (1976). Patterns of personality in middle-aged women: A longitudinal study. *International Journal of Aging and Human Development, 7,* 107–115.

Livson, F. B. (1981). Paths to psychological health in the middle years: Sex differences. In

D. H. Eichorn, J. A. Clausen, N. Haan, M. P. Honzik, & P. H. Mussen (Eds.), *Present and past in middle life*. New York: Academic Press.

Loehlin, J. C., McCrae, R. R., Costa, P. T. Jr, & John, O. P. (1998). Heritabilities of common and measure-specific components of the Big Five personality factors. *Journal of Research in Personality. 32*, 431–453.

Luster, T., & McAdoo, H. P. (1995). Factors related to self-esteem among African American youths: A secondary analysis of the High/Scope Perry Preschool data. *Journal of Research on Adolescence, 5*, 451–467.

Magnus, K., Diener, E., Fujita, F., & Payot, W. (1993). Extraversion and neuroticism as predictors of objective life events: A longitudinal analysis. *Journal of Personality and Social Psychology, 65*, 1046–1053.

Marcia, J. E. (1966). Development and validation of ego identity status. *Journal of Personality and Social Psychology, 3*, 551–558.

Markstrom-Adams, C. (1992). A consideration of intervening factors in adolescent identity formation. In G. R. Adams, T. P. Gullotta, & R. Montemayor (Eds.), *Adolescent identity formation* (Advances in Adolescent Development, Vol. 4). Newbury Park, CA: Sage.

Markstrom-Adams, C., & Adams, G. R. (1995). Gender, ethnic group, and grade differences in psychosocial functioning during middle adolescence. *Journal of Youth and Adolescence, 24*, 397–417.

Markus, H. R., Mullally, P. R., & Kitayama, S. (1997). Self-ways: Diversity in modes of cultural participation. In U. Neisser & D. A. Jopling (Eds.), *The conceptual self in context. Culture, experience, self-understanding.* Cambridge, UK: Cambridge University Press.

Marsh, H. W., Craven, R., & Debus, R. (1999). Separation of competency and affect components of multiple dimensions of academic self-concept: A developmental perspective. *Merrill-Palmer Quarterly, 45*, 567–701.

Marshall, S. (1995). Ethnic socialization of African American children: Implications for parenting, identity development, and academic achievement. *Journal of Youth and Adolescence, 24*, 377–396.

Maziade, M., Caron, C., Côté, R., Merette, C., Bernier, H., Laplante, B., Boutin, P., & Thivierge, J. (1990). Psychiatric status of adolescents who had extreme temperaments at age 7. *American Journal of Psychiatry, 147*, 1531–1536.

McAdams, D. P., Hart, H. M., & Maruna, S. (1998). The anatomy of generativity. In D. P. McAdams & E. de St. Aubin (Eds.), *Generativity and adult development: How and why we care for the next generation.* Washington, DC: American Psychological Association.

McCrae, R. R., & Costa, P. T., Jr. (1990). *Personality in adulthood.* New York: Guilford.

McCrae, R. R., & Costa, P. T., Jr. (1997). Personality trait structure as a human universal. *American Psychologist, 52*, 509–516.

McCrae, R. R., Costa, P. T., Jr., De Lima, M. P., Simoes, A., Ostendorf, F., Angleitner, A., Marusic, I., Bratko, D., Caprara, G. V., Barbaranelli, C., Chae, J., & Piedmont, R. L. (1999). Age differences in personality across the adult life span: Parallels in five cultures. *Developmental Psychology, 35*, 466–477.

McCrae, R. R., Costa, P. T., Ostendorf, F., Angleitner, A., Hrebickova, M., Avia, M. D., Sanz, J., Sanchez-Bernardos, M. L., Kusdil, M. E., Woodfield, R., Saunders, P. R., & Smith, P. B. (2000). Nature over nurture: Temperament, personality, and life span development. *Journal of Personalty & Social Psychology, 78*, 173–186.

McGuire, S., Manke, B., Saudino, K. J., Reiss, D., Hetherington, E. M., & Plomin, R. (1999). Perceived competence and self-worth during adolescence: A longitudinal behavioral genetic study. *Child Development, 70*, 1283–1296.

McKeering, H., & Pakenham, K. I. (2000). Gender and generativity issues in parenting: Do fathers benefit more than mothers from involvement in child care activities? *Sex Roles, 43*, 459–480.

Mead, G. H. (1934). *Mind, self, and society.* Chicago: University of Chicago Press.

Meeus, W., Iedema, J., Helsen, M., & Vollebergh, W. (1999). Patterns of adolescent identity development: Review of literature and longitudinal analysis. *Developmental Review, 19*, 419–461.

Meilman, P. W. (1979). Cross-sectional age changes in ego identity status during adolescence. *Developmental Psychology, 15*, 230–231.

Mischel, W. (1973). Toward a cognitive social learning reconceptualization of personality. *Psychological Review, 80*, 252–283.

Mischel, W., & Shoda, Y. (1995). A cognitive-affective system theory of personality: Reconceptualizing situations, dispositions, dynamics, and invariance in personality structure. *Psychological Review, 102*, 246–268.

Mitchell, P. (1997). *Introduction to theory of mind: Children, autism, and apes.* London: Arnold.

Moen, P. (1992). *Women's two roles: A contemporary dilemma.* New York: Auburn House.

Molinari, V. (1999). Using reminiscence and life review as natural therapeutic strategies in group therapy. In M. Duffy (Ed.), *Handbook of counseling and psychotherapy with older adults.* New York: Wiley.

Molinari, V., & Reichlin, R. E. (1984–1985). Life review reminiscence in the elderly: A review of the literature. *International Journal of Aging and Human Development, 20*, 81–92.

Montemayor, R., & Eisen, M. (1977). The development of self-conceptions from childhood to adolescence. *Developmental Psychology, 13*, 314–319.

Moran, J. R., Fleming, C. M., Somervell, P., & Manson, S. M. (1999). Measuring bicultural ethnic identity among American Indian adolescents: A factor analytic study. *Journal of Adolescent Research, 14*, 405–426.

Morinaga, Y., Frieze, I. H., & Ferligoj, A. (1993). Career plans and gender-role attitudes of college students in the United States, Japan, and Slovenia. *Sex Roles, 29*, 317–334.

Mortimer, J. T., Finch, M. D., & Kumka, D. (1982). Persistence and change in development: The multidimensional self-concept. In P. B. Baltes & O. G. Brim, Jr. (Eds.), *Life-span development and behavior* (Vol. 4). New York: Academic Press.

Munro, G., & Adams, G. R. (1977). Ego-identity formation in college students and working youth. *Developmental Psychology, 13*, 523–524.

Offer, D., & Schonert-Reichl, K. A. (1992). Debunking the myths of adolescence: Findings from recent research. *Journal of the American Academy of Child and Adolescent Psychiatry, 31*, 1003–1013.

Oosterwegel, A., & Oppenheimer, L. (1993). *The self-system: Developmental changes between and within self-concepts.* Hillsdale, NJ: Erlbaum.

Palmore, E. B., Burchett, B. M., Fillenbaum, G. G., George, L. K., & Wallman, L. M. (1985). *Retirement: Causes and consequences.* New York: Springer.

Phillips, S. D. (1982). Career exploration in adulthood. *Journal of Vocational Behavior, 20*, 129–140.

Phinney, J. S. (1993). A three-stage model of ethnic identity development in adolescence. In M. E. Bernal & G. P. Knight (Eds.), *Ethnic identity: Formation and transmission among Hispanics and other minorities.* Albany: State University of New York Press.

Phinney, J. S. (1996). When we talk about American ethnic groups, what do we mean? *American Psychologist, 51*, 918–927.

Phipps, B. J. (1995). Career dreams of preadolescent students. *Journal of Career Development, 22*, 19–32.

Pinquart, M., & Sorensen, S. (2000). Influences of socioeconomic status, social network, and competence on subjective well-being in later life: A meta-analysis. *Psychology and Aging, 15*, 187–224.

Pipp, S., Easterbrooks, M. A., & Harmon, R. J. (1992). The relation between attachment and knowledge of self and mother in one-year-old infants to three-year-old infants. *Child Development, 63*, 738–750.

Pipp-Siegel, S., & Foltz, C. (1997). Toddlers' acquisition of self/other knowledge: Ecological and interpersonal aspects of self and other. *Child Development, 68*, 69–79.

Pomerantz, E. M., Ruble, D. N., Frey, K. S., & Grenlich, F. (1995). Meeting goals and confronting conflict: Children's changing perceptions of social comparison. *Child Development, 66*, 723–738.

Pratt, M. W., Norris, J. E., Arnold, M. L., & Filyer, R. (1999). Generativity and moral development as predictors of value-socialization narratives for young persons across the adult life span: From lessons learned to stories shared. *Psychology and Aging, 14*, 414–426.

Rapkin, B. D., & Fischer, K. (1992). Personal goals of older adults: Issues in assessment and prediction. *Psychology and Aging, 7*, 127–137.

Reznick, J. S., Kagan, J., Snidman, N., Gersten, M., Baak, K., & Rosenberg, A. (1986). Inhibited and uninhibited children: A follow-up study. *Child Development, 57*, 660–680.

Rhodes, S. R. (1983). Age-related differences in work attitudes and behavior: A review and conceptual analysis. *Psychological Bulletin, 93*, 328–367.

Roberts, B. W., & DelVecchio, W. F. (2000). The rank-order consistency of personality traits from childhood to old age: A quantitative review of longitudinal studies. *Psychological Bulletin, 126*, 3–25.

Roberts, R. E., Phinney, J. S., Masse, L. C., Chen, Y. R., Roberts, C. R., & Romero, A. (1999). The structure of ethnic identity of young adolescents from diverse ethnocultural groups. *Journal of Early Adolescence, 19*, 301–322.

Rochat, P., & Morgan, R. (1995). Spatial determinants of the perception of self-produced leg movements by 3- to 5-month-old infants. *Developmental Psychology, 31,* 626–636.

Roenkae, A., & Pulkkinen, L. (1995). Accumulation of problems in social functioning in young adulthood: A developmental approach. *Journal of Personality & Social Psychology, 69,* 381–391.

Rojewski, J. W., & Yang, B. (1997). Longitudinal analysis of select influences on adolescents' occupational aspirations. *Journal of Vocational Behavior, 51,* 375–410.

Rosenberg, S. D., Rosenberg, H. J., & Farrell, M. P. (1999). The midlife crisis revisited. In S. L. Willis & J. D. Reid (Eds.), *Life in the middle: Psychological and social development in middle age.* San Diego: Academic Press.

Rothbart, M. K., Ahadi, S. A., & Evans, D. E. (2000). Temperament and personality: Origins and outcomes. *Journal of Personality and Social Psychology, 78,* 122–135.

Rowe, D. C. (1994). *The limits of family influence: Genes, experience, and behavior.* New York: Guilford.

Ruble, D. N. (1983). The development of comparison processes and their role in achievement-related self-socialization. In E. T. Higgins, D. N. Ruble, & W. W. Hartup (Eds.), *Social cognition and social development: A sociocultural perspective.* New York: Cambridge University Press.

Ruth, J. E., & Coleman, P. (1996). Personality and aging: Coping and management of the self in later life. In J. E. Birren, K. W. Schaie, R. P. Abeles, M. Gatz, & T. A. Salthouse (Eds.), *Handbook of the psychology of aging* (4th ed.). San Diego: Academic Press.

Ryff, C. D. (1991). Possible selves in adulthood and old age: A tale of shifting horizons. *Psychology and Aging, 6,* 286–295.

Schaie, K. W., & Parham, I. A. (1976). Stability of adult personality traits: Fact or fable? *Journal of Personality and Social Psychology, 34,* 146–158.

Schmitz, S., Saudino, K. J., Plomin, R., Fulker, D. W., & DeFries, J. C. (1996). Genetic and environmental influences on temperament in middle childhood: Analyses of teacher and tester ratings. *Child Development, 67,* 409–422.

Schooler, C., Mulatu, M. S., & Oates, G. (1999). The continuing effects of substantively complex work on the intellectual functioning of older workers. *Psychology and Aging, 14,* 483–506.

Scott, W. A., Scott, R., & McCabe, M. (1991). Family relationships and children's personality: A cross-cultural, cross-source comparison. *British Journal of Social Psychology, 30,* 1–20.

Secord, P. F., & Peevers, B. H. (1974). The development and attribution of person concepts. In T. Mischel (Ed.), *Understanding other persons.* Totowa, NJ: Rowman & Littlefield.

Seibert, S. E., & Kraimer, M. L. (2001). The five-factor model of personality and career success. *Journal of Vocational Behavior, 58,* 1–21.

Seleen, D. R. (1982). The congruence between actual and desired use of time by older adults: A predictor of life satisfaction. *Gerontologist, 22,* 95–99.

Selman, R. L. (1980). *The growth of interpersonal understanding.* New York: Academic Press.

Shiner, R. L. (2000). Linking childhood personality with adaptation: Evidence for continuity and change across time into late adolescence. *Journal of Personality and Social Psychology, 78,* 310–325.

Shirk, S., & Harter, S. (1996). Treatment of low self-esteem. In M. A. Reineke, F. M. Dattilio, & A. Freeman (Eds.), *Cognitive therapy with children and adolescents: A casebook for clinical practice.* New York: Guilford.

Shoda, Y., & Mischel, W. (2000). Reconciling contextualism with the core assumptions of personality psychology. *European Journal of Personality, 14,* 407–428.

Shweder, R. A., Goodnow, J., Hatano, G., LeVine, R., Markus, H., & Miller, P. (1998). The cultural psychology of development: One mind, many mentalities. In W. Damon (Editor-in-Chief), R. M. Lerner (Vol. Ed.), *Handbook of child psychology: Vol. 1. Theoretical models of human development* (5th ed.). New York: Wiley.

Siegler, I. C., & Brummet, B. H. (2000). Associations among NEO personality assessments and well-being at mid-life: Facet-level analyses. *Psychology and Aging, 15,* 710–714.

Simmons, R. G., Burgeson, R., Carlton-Ford, S., & Blyth, D. A. (1987). The impact of cumulative change in early adolescence. *Child Development, 58,* 1220–1234.

Simonton, D. K. (1990). Creativity in the later years: Optimistic prospects for achievement. *Gerontologist, 30,* 626–631.

Sorensen, E. (1991). *Exploring the reasons behind the narrowing gender gap in earnings* (Urban Institute Report 1991–1992). Washington, DC: Urban Institute Press.

Spencer, M. B., & Markstrom-Adams, C. (1990). Identity processes among racial and ethnic minority children in America. *Child Development, 61,* 290–310.

Spokane, A. R., Meir, E. I., & Catalano, M. (2000). Person–environment congruence and Holland's theory: A review and reconsideration. *Journal of Vocational Behavior, 57,* 137–187.

Stein, J. A., & Newcomb, M. D. (1999). Adult outcomes of adolescent conventional and agentic orientations: A 20-year longitudinal study. *Journal of Early Adolescence, 19,* 39–65.

Steinberg, L., Dornbusch, S. M., & Brown, B. B. (1992). Ethnic differences in adolescent achievement: An ecological perspective. *American Psychologist, 47,* 723–729.

Stipek, D., Gralinski, H., & Kopp, C. (1990). Self-concept development in the toddler years. *Developmental Psychology, 26,* 972–977.

Super, D. E., Savickas, M. L., & Super, C. M. (1996). The life-span, life-space approach to careers. In D. Brown, L. Brooks, & Associates (Eds.), *Career choice and development* (3rd ed.). San Francisco: Jossey-Bass.

Szinovacz, M., & Ekerdt, D. J. (1995). Families and retirement. In R. Blieszner & V. H. Bedford (Eds.), *Handbook of aging and the family.* Westport, CT: Greenwood.

Taft, L. B., & Nehrke, M. F. (1990). Reminiscence, life review, and ego integrity in nursing home residents. *International Journal of Aging and Human Development, 30,* 189–196.

Thomas, A., & Chess, S. (1986). The New York Longitudinal Study: From infancy to early adult life. In R. Plomin & J. Dunn (Eds.), *The study of temperament: Changes, continuities, and challenges.* Hillsdale, NJ: Erlbaum.

Thompson, R. A. (1998). Early sociopersonality development. In W. Damon (Editor-in-Chief), N. Eisenberg (Vol. Ed.), *Handbook of child psychology: Vol. 3. Social, emotional, and personality development* (5th ed.). New York: Wiley.

Thorne, A., & Michaelieu, Q. (1996). Situating adolescent gender and self-esteem with personal memories. *Child Development, 67,* 1374–1390.

Tinsley, H. E. A. (2000). The congruence myth: An analysis of the efficacy of the person–environment fit model. *Journal of Vocational Behavior, 56,* 147–179.

Triandis, H. C. (1989). Self and social behavior in differing cultural contexts. *Psychological Review, 96,* 269–289.

Triandis, H. C. (1995). *Individualism and collectivism.* Boulder, CO: Westview.

Trzesniewski, K. H., Donnellan, M. B., & Robins, R. W. (2001, April). *Self-esteem across the lifespan: A meta-analysis.* Poster presented at the biennial meeting of the Society for Research in Child Development, Minneapolis.

Turk-Charles, S., & Carstensen, L. L. (1999). The role of time in the setting of social goals across the life span. In T. M. Hess & F. Blanchard-Fields (Eds.), *Social cognition and aging.* San Diego: Academic Press.

Twenge, J. M. (2000). The age of anxiety? Birth cohort change in anxiety and neuroticism, 1952–1993. *Journal of Personality and Social Psychology, 79,* 1007–1021.

Vaillant, G. E. (1977). *Adaptation to life.* Boston: Little, Brown.

Vaillant, G. E. (1983). Childhood environment and maturity of defense mechanisms. In D. Magnusson & V. L. Allen (Eds.), *Human development: An interactional perspective.* New York: Academic Press.

Vaillant, G. E., & Milofsky, E. (1980). Natural history of male psychological health: IX. Empirical evidence for Erikson's model of the life cycle. *American Journal of Psychiatry, 137,* 1348–1359.

van der Velde, M. E. G., Feij, J. A., & Taris, T. W. (1995). Stability and change of person characteristics among young adults: The effect of the transition from school to work. *Personality and Individual Differences, 18,* 89–99.

van Hoof, A. (1999). The identity status field re-reviewed: An update of unresolved and neglected issues with a view on some alternative approaches. *Developmental Review, 19,* 497–556.

Van Velsor, E., & O'Rand, A. M. (1984). Family life cycle, work career patterns, and women's wages at midlife. *Journal of Marriage and the Family, 46,* 365–373.

Verschueren, K., Buyck, P., and Marcoen, A. (2001). Self-representations and socioemotional competence in young children: A 3-year longitudinal study. *Developmental Psychology, 37,* 126–134.

Verschueren, K., Marcoen, A., & Schoefs, V. (1996). The internal working model of self, attachment, and competence in five-year-olds. *Child Development, 67,* 2493–2511.

Walls, R. T. (2000). Vocational cognition: Accuracy of 3rd-, 6th-, 9th-, and 12th-grade students. *Journal of Vocational Behavior, 56,* 137–144.

Warr, P. (1992). Age and occupational well-being. *Psychology and Aging, 7,* 37–45.

Waterman, A. S. (1982). Identity development from adolescence to adulthood: An extension of theory and a review of research. *Developmental Psychology, 18,* 341–358.

Waterman, A. S. (1992). Identity as an aspect of optimal psychological functioning. In G. R. Adams, T. P. Gullotta, & R. Montemayor (Eds.), *Adolescent identity formation* (Advances in Adolescent Development, Vol. 4). Newbury Park, CA: Sage.

Webster, J. D., & McCall, M. E. (1999). Reminiscence functions across adulthood: A replication and extension. *Journal of Adult Development, 6,* 73–85.

Whitbourne, S. K., & Tesch, S. A. (1985). A comparison of identity and intimacy statuses in college students and alumni. *Developmental Psychology, 21,* 1039–1044.

Wink, P. (1996). Transition from the early 40s to the early 50s in self-directed women. *Journal of Personality, 64,* 49–69.

Wong, P. T. P., & Watt, L. M. (1991). What types of reminiscence are associated with successful aging? *Psychology and Aging, 6,* 272–279.

Wrightsman, L. S. (1994). *Adult personality development: Vol. 1. Theories and concepts.* Thousand Oaks, CA: Sage.

Chapter 12: Gender Roles and Sexuality

Abrahams, B., Feldman, S. S., & Nash, S. C. (1978). Sex role self-concept and sex role attitudes: Enduring personality characteristics or adaptations to changing life situations? *Developmental Psychology, 14,* 393–400.

Alfieri, T., Ruble, D. N., & Higgins, E. T. (1996). Gender stereotypes during adolescence: Developmental changes and the transition to junior high school. *Developmental Psychology, 32,* 1129–1137.

Almli, C. R., Ball, R. H. & Wheeler, M. E. (2001). Human fetal and neonatal movement patterns: Gender differences and fetal-to-neonatal continuity. *Developmental Psychobiology, 38,* 252–273.

Althaus, F. (2001). Levels of sexual experience among U.S. teenagers have declined for the first time in three decades. *Family Planning Perspectives, 33,* 180.

Arber, S., & Ginn, J. (1991). *Gender and later life: A sociological analysis of resources and constraints.* London: Sage.

Archer, J. (1991). The influence of testosterone on human aggression. *British Journal of Psychology, 82,* 1–28.

Archer, J. (1996). Sex differences in social behavior: Are the social role and evolutionary explanations compatible? *American Psychologist, 51,* 909–917.

Bailey, J. M., Dunne, M. P., & Martin, N. G. (2000). Genetic and environmental influences on sexual orientation and its correlates in an Australian twin sample. *Journal of Personality and Social Psychology, 78,* 524–536.

Bailey, J. M., & Pillard, R. C. (1991). A genetic study of male sexual orientation. *Archives of General Psychiatry, 48,* 1089–1096.

Bailey, J. M., Pillard, R. C., Neale, M. C., & Agyei, Y. (1993). Heritable factors influence sexual orientation in women. *Archives of General Psychiatry, 50,* 217–223.

Bailey, J. M., & Zucker, K. J. (1995). Childhood sex-typed behavior and sexual orientation: A conceptual analysis and quantitative review. *Developmental Psychology, 31,* 43–55.

Baker, D. P., & Jones, D. P. (1992). Opportunity and performance: A sociological explanation for gender differences in academic mathematics. In J. Wrigley (Ed.), *Education and gender equality.* London: Falmer Press.

Barner, M. R. (1999). Sex-role stereotyping in FCC-mandated children's educational television. *Journal of Broadcasting & Electronic Media, 43,* 551–564.

Bandura, A. (1986). *Social foundations of thought and action: A social cognitive theory.* Englewood Cliffs, NJ: Prentice-Hall.

Banerjee, R. & Lintern, V. (2000). Boys will be boys: The effect of social evaluation concerns on gender-typing. *Social Development, 9,* 397–408.

Beal, C. R. (1994). *Boys and girls: The development of gender roles.* New York: McGraw-Hill.

Beitchman, J. H., Zucker, K. J., Hood, J. E., daCosta, G. A., & Akman, D. (1991). A review of the short-term effects of child sexual abuse. *Child Abuse & Neglect, 15,* 537–556.

Bem, S. L. (1974). The measurement of psychological androgyny. *Journal of Consulting and Clinical Psychology, 42,* 155–162.

Bem, S. L. (1975). Sex-role adaptability: One consequence of psychological androgyny. *Journal of Personality and Social Psychology, 31,* 634–643.

Bem, S. L. (1978). Beyond androgyny: Some presumptuous prescriptions for a liberated sexual identity. In J. A. Sherman & F. L. Denmark (Eds.), *The psychology of women: Future directions in research.* New York: Psychological Dimensions.

Bem, S. L. (1979). Theory and measurement of androgyny: A reply to the Podhazer-Tetenbaum and Locksley-Colten critiques. *Journal of Personality and Social Psychology, 37,* 1047–1054.

Bem, S. L. (1989). Genital knowledge and gender constancy in preschool children. *Child Development, 60,* 649–662.

Benbow, C. P., & Arjmand, O. (1990). Predictors of high academic achievement in mathematics and science by mathematically talented students: A longitudinal study. *Journal of Educational Psychology, 82,* 430–441.

Berenbaum, S. A., & Hines, M. (1992). Early androgens are related to childhood sex-typed toy preferences. *Psychological Science, 3,* 203–206.

Bergen, D. J., & Williams, J. E. (1991). Sex stereotypes in the United States revisited: 1972–1988. *Sex Roles, 24,* 413–424.

Bernstein, A. C., & Cowan, P. A. (1975). Children's concepts of how people get babies. *Child Development, 46,* 77–91.

Best, D. L., & Williams, J. E. (1993). A cross-cultural viewpoint. In A. E. Beall & R. J. Sternberg (Eds.), *The psychology of gender* (pp. 215–248). New York: Guilford Press.

Bianchi, S. M. (2000). Maternal employment and time with children: Dramatic change or surprising continuity? *Demography, 37,* 401–414.

Bianchi, S. M., Milkie, M. A., Sayer, L. C., & Robinson, J. P. (2000). Is anyone doing the housework? Trends in the gender division of household labor. *Social Forces, 79,* 191–228.

Bigler, R. S., & Liben, L. S. (1990). The role of attitudes and interventions in gender-schematic processing. *Child Development, 61,* 1440–1452.

Bjorkqvist, K. (1994). Sex differences in physical, verbal, and indirect aggression: A review of recent research. *Sex Roles, 30,* 177–188.

Blake, S. M., Simkin, L., Ledsky, R., Perkins, C., & Calabrese, J. M. (2001). Effects of a parent–child communications intervention on young adolescents' risk for early onset of sexual intercourse. *Family Planning Perspectives, 33,* 52–62.

Blakemore, J. E. O., LaRue, A. A., & Olejnik, A. B. (1979). Sex-appropriate toy preference and the ability to conceptualize toys as sex-role related. *Developmental Psychology, 15,* 339–340.

Boldizar, J. P. (1991). Assessing sex-typing and androgyny in children: The Children's Sex-Role Inventory. *Developmental Psychology, 27,* 505–515.

Botkin, D. R., Weeks, M. O., & Morris, J. E. (2000). Changing marriage role expectations: 1961–1996. *Sex Roles, 42,* 933–942.

Bradbard, M. R., Martin, C. L., Endsley, R. C., & Halverson, C. F. (1986). Influence of sex stereotypes on children's exploration and memory: A competence versus performance distinction. *Developmental Psychology, 22,* 481–486.

Breedlove, S. M. (1994). Sexual differentiation of the human nervous system. *Annual Review of Psychology, 45,* 389–418.

Brilleslijper-Kater, S. N., & Baartman, H. E. M. (2000). What do young children know about sex? Research on the sexual knowledge of children between the ages of 2 and 6 years. *Child Abuse Review, 9,* 166–182.

Brody, N. (1985). The validity of tests of intelligence. In B. B. Wolman (Ed.), *Handbook of intelligence.* New York: Wiley.

Brooks-Gunn, J., & Furstenberg, F. F., Jr. (1989). Long-term implications of fertility-related behavior and family formation on adolescent mothers and their children. In K. Kreppner & R. M. Lerner (Eds.), *Family systems and life-span development.* Hillsdale, NJ: Erlbaum.

Burn, S., O'Neil, A. K., & Nederend, S. (1996). Childhood tomboyishness and adult androgyny. *Sex Roles, 34,* 419–428.

Burnham, D. K., & Harris, M. B. (1992). Effects of real gender and labeled gender on adults perceptions of infants. *Journal of Genetic Psychology, 153,* 165–183.

Buss, A. H., & Perry, M. (1992). The aggression question. *Journal of Personality and Social Psychology, 63,* 452–459.

Buss, D. M. (1995). Psychological sex differences: Origins through sexual selection. *American Psychologist, 50,* 164–168.

Byne, W. (1994). The biological evidence challenged. *Scientific American, 270,* 50–55.

Byrnes, J. P., Miller, D. C., & Schafer, W. D. (1999). Gender differences in risk taking: A meta-analysis. *Psychological Bulletin, 125,* 367–383.

Cahan, S., & Ganor, Y. (1995). Cognitive gender differences among Israeli children. *Sex Roles, 32,* 469–484.

Caldera, Y. M., Huston, A.C., & O'Brien, M. (1989). Social interactions and play patterns of parents and toddlers with feminine, masculine, and neutral toys. *Child Development, 60,* 70–76.

Carter, D. B., & Patterson, C. J. (1982). Sex roles as social conventions: The development of children's conceptions of sex-role stereotypes. *Developmental Psychology, 18,* 812–824.

Centers for Disease Control. (1997). Youth risk behavior surveillance: National College Health Risk Behavior Survey—United States, 1995. *Morbidity and Mortality Weekly Reports, 46,* 1–56.

Clements, M. (1996, March 17). Sex after 65. *Parade Magazine,* pp. 4–6.

Coats, P. B., & Overman, S. J. (1992). Childhood play experiences of women in traditional and nontraditional professions. *Sex Roles, 26,* 261–271.

Colapinto, J. (1997, December 11). The true story of John Joan. *Rolling Stone,* pp. 54–97.

Cole, P. M., & Putnam, F. W. (1992). Effect of incest on self and social functioning: A developmental psychopathology perspective. *Journal of Consulting and Clinical Psychology, 60,* 174–184.

Colley, A., Griffiths, D., Hugh, M., Landers, K., & Jaggli, N. (1996). Childhood play and adolescent leisure preferences: Associations with gender typing and the presence of siblings. *Sex Roles, 35,* 233–245.

Comfort, A. (1974). Sexuality in old age. *Journal of the American Geriatrics Society, 22,* 440–442.

Condry, J., & Condry, S. (1976). Sex differences: A study in the eye of the beholder. *Child Development, 47,* 812–819.

Conrade, G., & Ho, R. (2001). Differential parenting styles for fathers and mothers: Differential treatment for sons and daughters. *Australian Journal of Psychology, 53,* 29–35.

Conway, M., & Vartanian, L. R. (2000). A status account of gender stereotypes: Beyond communality and agency. *Sex Roles, 43,* 181–199.

Cowan, C. P., Cowan, P. A., Heming, G., & Miller, N. B. (1991). Becoming a family: Marriage, parenting, and child development. In P. A. Cowan & M. Hetherington (Eds.), *Family transitions.* Hillsdale, NJ: Erlbaum.

Cowan, G., & Avants, S. K. (1988). Children's influence strategies: Structure, sex differences, and bilateral mother–child influences. *Child Development, 59,* 984–990.

Crick, N., & Bigbee, M. (1998). Relational and overt forms of peer victimization: A multiinformant approach. *Journal of Consulting and Clinical Psychology, 66,* 337–347.

Crockett, L. J., Bingham, C. R., Chopak, J. S., & Vicary, J. R. (1996). Timing of first sexual intercourse: The role of social control, social learning, and problem behavior. *Journal of Youth and Adolescence, 25,* 89–111.

Crooks, R., & Baur, K. (1999). *Our sexuality* (7th ed.). Pacific Grove, CA: Brooks/Cole.

Crouter, A. C., Manke, B. A., & McHale, S. M. (1995). The family context of gender intensification in early adolescence. *Child Development, 66,* 317–329.

Dabbs, J. M., & Morris, R. (1990). Testosterone, social class, and antisocial behavior in a sample of 4,462 men. *Psychological Science, 1,* 209–211.

Damon, W. (1977). *The social world of the child.* San Francisco: Jossey-Bass.

Daniluk, J. C. (1998). *Women's sexuality across the life span: Challenging myths, creating meanings.* New York: Guilford Press.

Darling, C. A., Davidson, J. K., & Passarello, L. C. (1992). The mystique of first intercourse among college youth: The role of partners, contraceptive practices, and psychological reactions. *Journal of Youth and Adolescence, 21,* 97–117.

Day, R. D., & Peterson, G. W. (1998). Predicting spanking of younger and older children by mothers and fathers. *Journal of Marriage & the Family, 60,* 79–92.

de Gaston, J. F., Jensen, L., & Weed, S. (1995). A closer look at adolescent sexual activity. *Journal of Youth and Adolescence, 24,* 465–479.

de Gaston, J. F., Weed, S., & Jensen, L. (1996). Understanding gender differences in adolescent sexuality. *Adolescence, 31,* 217–232.

Deaux, K., & Major, B. (1990). A social-psychological model of gender. In D. L. Rhode (Ed.), *Theoretical perspectives on sexual difference.* New Haven, CT: Yale University Press.

Deda, G., Caksen, H., Suskan, E., & Gumus, D. (2001). Masturbation mimicking seizure in an infant. *Indian Journal of Pediatrics, 68,* 779–781.

Deutsch, F. M. (1999). *Having it all: How equally shared parenting works.* Cambridge, MA: Harvard University Press.

Diamond, M., & Sigmundson, H. K. (1997). Sex reassignment at birth: Long-term review and clinical implications. *Archives of Pediatric and Adolescent Medicine, 151,* 298–304.

DiIorio, C., Dudley, W. N., Kelly, M., Soet, J. E., Mbwara, J., & Sharpe Potter, J. (2001). Social cognitive correlates of sexual experience and condom use among 13- through 15-year-old adolescents. *Journal of Adolescent Health, 29,* 208–216.

Dittman, R. W., Kappes, M. E., & Kappes, M. H. (1992). Sexual behavior in adolescent and adult females with congenital adrenal hyperplasia. *Psychoneuroendocrinology, 17,* 153–170.

Dreyer, P. H. (1982). Sexuality during adolescence. In B. B. Wolman (Ed.), *Handbook of developmental psychology.* New York: Wiley.

Dunne, M. P., Martin, N. G., Statham, D. J., Slutske, W. S., Dinwiddie, S. H., Bucholz, K. K., Madden, P. A. F., & Heath, A. C. (1997). Genetic and environmental contributions to variance in age at first sexual intercourse. *Psychological Science, 8,* 211–216.

Eagly, A. H. (1987). *Sex differences in social behavior: A social-role interpretation.* Hillsdale, NJ: Erlbaum.

Eagly, A. H., & Steffen, V. J. (1986). Gender and aggressive behavior: A meta-analytic review of the social psychological literature. *Psychological Bulletin, 100,* 309–330.

Eagly, A. H., & Steffen, V. J. (2000). Gender differences stem from the distribution of women and men into social roles. In C. Stangor (Ed.), *Stereotypes and prejudice: Essential readings* (pp. 142–160). Philadelphia: Taylor & Francis.

Eaton, W. O., & Enns, L. R. (1986). Sex differences in human motor activity level. *Psychological Bulletin, 100,* 19–28.

Eccles, J. S., Jacobs, J. E., & Harold, R. D. (1990). Gender role stereotypes, expectancy effects, and parents' socialization of gender differences. *Journal of Social Issues, 46,* 183–201.

Ehrhardt, A. A. (1985). The psychobiology of gender. In A. S. Rossi (Ed.), *Gender and the life course.* New York: Aldine.

Ehrhardt, A. A., & Baker, S. W. (1974). Fetal androgens, human central nervous system differentiation, and behavioral sex differences. In R. C. Friedman, R. M. Rickard, & R. L. Van de Wiele (Eds.), *Sex differences in behavior.* New York: Wiley.

Eichler, A., & Parron, D. L. (1987). *Women's mental health: Agenda for research.* Rockville, MD: National Institute of Mental Health.

Elias, J., & Gebhard, P. (1969). Sexuality and sexual learning in childhood. *Phi Delta Kappan, 50,* 401–405.

Ellis, L., Ames, M. A. Peckham, W., & Burke, D. M. (1988). Sexual orientation in human offspring may be altered by severe emotional distress during pregnancy. *Journal of Sex Research, 25,* 152–157.

Fabes, R. A., Eisenberg, N., & Miller, P. A. (1990). Maternal correlates of children's vicarious emotional responsiveness. *Developmental Psychology, 26,* 639–648.

Fagot, B. I. (1978). The influence of sex of child on parental reactions to toddler children. *Child Development, 49,* 459–465.

Fagot, B. I. (1985). Beyond the reinforcement principle: Another step toward understanding sex-role development. *Developmental Psychology, 21,* 1097–1104.

Fagot, B. I., & Hagan, R. (1991). Observation of parent reactions to sex-stereotyped behaviors: Age and sex effects. *Child Development, 62,* 617–628.

Fagot, B. I., & Leinbach, M. D. (1989). The young child's gender schema: Environmental input, internal organization. *Child Development, 60,* 663–672.

Fagot, B. I., & Leinbach, M. D. (1993). Gender-role development in young children: From discrimination to labeling. *Developmental Review, 13,* 205–224.

Fagot, B. I., Leinbach, M. D., & Hagan, R. (1986). Gender labeling and the adoption of sex-typed behaviors. *Developmental Psychology, 22,* 440–443.

Fagot, B. I., Leinbach, M. D., & O'Boyle, C. (1992). Gender labeling, gender stereotyping, and parenting behaviors. *Developmental Psychology, 28,* 225–230.

Feingold, A. (1988). Cognitive gender differences are disappearing. *American Psychologist, 43,* 95–103.

Feingold, A. (1992). Sex differences in variability in intellectual abilities: A new look at an old controversy. *Review of Educational Research, 62,* 61–84.

Feingold, A. (1994a). Gender differences in intellectual abilities: A cross-cultural perspective. *Sex Roles, 30,* 81–92.

Feingold, A. (1994b). Gender differences in personality: A meta-analysis. *Psychological Bulletin, 116,* 429–456.

Feldman, S. S., Biringen, Z. C., & Nash, S. C. (1981). Fluctuations of sex-related self-attributions as a function of stage of family life cycle. *Developmental Psychology, 17,* 24–35.

Felstein, I. (1983). Dysfunction: Origins and therapeutic approaches. In R. B. Weg (Ed.), *Sexuality in the later years: Roles and behavior.* New York: Academic Press.

Finkelhor, D., & Berliner, L. (1995). Research on the treatment of sexually abused children: A review and recommendations. *Journal of the American Academy of Child and Adolescent Psychiatry, 34,* 1408–1423.

Finkelhor, D., Hotaling, G. T., Lewis, I. A., & Smith, C. (1989). Sexual abuse and its relationship to later sexual satisfaction, marital status, religion, and attitudes. *Journal of Interpersonal Violence, 4,* 379–399.

Ford, C. S., & Beach, F. A. (1951). *Patterns of sexual behavior.* New York: Harper & Row.

Forrest, J. D., & Singh, S. (1990). The sexual and reproductive behavior of American women, 1982–1988. *Family Planning Perspectives, 22,* 206–214.

Frey, K. S., & Ruble, D. N. (1992). Gender constancy and the cost of sex-typed behavior: A test of the conflict hypothesis. *Developmental Psychology, 28,* 714–721.

Furnham, A., & Mak, T. (1999). Sex-role stereotyping in television commercials: A review and comparison of fourteen studies done on five continents over 25 years. *Sex Roles, 41,* 413–437.

Furstenberg, F. F., Jr., Brooks-Gunn, J., & Chase-Lansdale, L. (1989). Teenage pregnancy and childbearing. *American Psychologist, 44,* 313–320.

Furstenberg, F. F., Jr., Brooks-Gunn, J., & Morgan, S. P. (1987). *Adolescent mothers in later life.* New York: Cambridge University Press.

Galambos, N. L., Almeida, D. M., & Petersen, A. C. (1990). Masculinity, femininity, and sex role attitudes in early adolescence: Exploring gender intensification. *Child Development, 61,* 1905–1914.

Gandelman, R. (1992). *Psychobiology of behavioral development.* New York: Oxford University Press.

Garnets, L., & Kimmel, D. (1991). Lesbian and gay male dimensions of the psychological study of human diversity. In J. D. Goodchilds (Ed.), *Psychological perspectives on human diversity in America.* Washington, DC: American Psychological Association.

Giampaoli S. (2000). Epidemiology of major age-related diseases in women compared to men. *Aging, 12,* 93–105.

Goldman, R., & Goldman, J. (1982). *Children's sexual thinking: A comparative study of children aged 5 to 15 years in Australia, North America, Britain and Sweden.* London: Routledge and Kegan Paul.

Golombok, S., & Tasker, F. (1996). Do parents influence the sexual orientation of their children? Findings from a longitudinal study of lesbian families. *Developmental Psychology, 32,* 3–11.

Gordon, B. N., Schroeder, C. S., & Abrams, J. M. (1990). Children's knowledge of sexuality: A comparison of sexually abused and nonabused children. *American Journal of Orthopsychiatry, 60,* 250–257.

Green, R. (1987). *The "sissy boy syndrome" and the development of homosexuality.* New Haven, CT: Yale University Press.

Gutmann, D. (1987). *Reclaimed powers: Toward a new psychology of men and women in later life.* New York: Basic Books.

Gutmann, D. (1997). *The human elder in nature, culture, and society.* Boulder, CO: Westview.

Hall, J. A., & Halberstadt, A. G. (1980). Masculinity and femininity in children: Development of the Children's Personal Attributes Questionaire. *Developmental Psychology, 16,* 270–280.

Halpern, C. J. T., Udry, J. R., Suchindran, C., & Campbell, B. (2000). Adolescent males' willingness to report masturbation. *Journal of Sex Research* [Special Issue], *37,* 327–332.

Hamilton, V. L., Blumenfeld, P. C., Akoh, H., & Miura, K. (1991). Group and gender in Japanese and American elementary classrooms. *Journal of Cross-Cultural Psychology, 22,* 317–346.

Henker, B., & Whalen, C. K. (1989). Hyperactivity and attention deficits. *American Psychologist, 44,* 216–223.

Herdt, G., & Davidson, J. (1988). The Sambia "turnim-man": Sociocultural and cinical as-

pects of gender formation in male pseudo-hermaphrodites with 5-alpha-reductase deficiency in Papua New Guinea. *Archives of Sexual Behavior, 17,* 33–56.

Herdt, G., & McClintock, M. (2000). The magical age of 10. *Archives of Sexual Behavior, 29,* 587–606.

Hetherington, E. M., & Frankie, G. (1967). Effect of parental dominance, warmth, and conflict on imitation in children. *Journal of Personality and Social Psychology, 6,* 119–125.

Hill, J. P., & Lynch, M. E. (1983). The intensification of gender-related role expectations during early adolescence. In J. Brooks-Gunn & A. C. Petersen (Eds.), *Girls at puberty: Biological and psychosocial perspectives.* New York: Plenum.

Holt, C. L., & Ellis, J. B. (1998). Assessing the current validity of the Bem Sex-Role Inventory. *Sex Roles, 39,* 929–941.

Howes, C. (1988). Same- and cross-sex friends: Implications for interaction and social skills. *Early Childhood Research Quarterly, 3,* 21–37.

Hyde, J. S. (1984). How large are sex differences in aggression? A developmental meta-analysis. *Developmental Psychology, 20,* 722–736.

Hyde, J. S., Fennema, E., & Lamon, S. J. (1990). Gender differences in mathematics performance: A meta-analysis. *Psychological Bulletin, 107,* 139–155.

Hyde, J. S., & Linn, M. C. (1988). Gender differences in verbal ability: A meta-analysis. *Psychological Bulletin, 104,* 53–69.

Hyde, J. S., & Plant, E. A. (1995). Magnitude of psychological gender differences: Another side to the story. *American Psychologist, 50,* 159–161.

Imperato-McGinley, J., Peterson, R. E., Gautier, T., & Sturla, E. (1979). Androgens and the evolution of male gender identity among male pseudohermaphrodites with 5a-reductase deficiency. *New England Journal of Medicine, 300,* 1233–1237.

Intons-Peterson, M. J., & Reddel, M. (1984). What do people ask about a neonate? *Developmental Psychology, 20,* 358–359.

Jacklin, C. N. (1989). Male and female: Issues of gender. *American Psychologist, 44,* 127–133.

Jung, C. G. (1933). *Modern man in search of a soul* (W. S. Dell & C. F. Baynes, Trans.). New York: Harcourt, Brace.

Jussim, L., & Eccles, J. S. (1992). Teacher expectations II: Construction and reflection of student achievement. *Journal of Personality and Social Psychology, 63,* 947–961.

Kaplan, D. W., Feinstein, R. A., Fisher, M. M., Klein, J. D., Olmedo, L. F., Rome, E. S., & Yancy, S. (2001). Condom use by adolescents. *Pediatrics, 107,* 1463–1469.

Katz, P. A. (1986). Modification of children's gender-stereotyped behavior: General issues and research considerations. *Sex Roles, 14,* 591–602.

Katz, P. A., & Walsh, P. V. (1991). Modification of children's gender-stereotyped behavior. *Child Development, 62,* 338–351.

Kaye, R. A. (1993). Sexuality in the later years. *Aging and Society, 13,* 415–426.

Kendall-Tackett, K. A., Williams, L. M., & Finkelhor, D. (1993). Impact of sexual abuse on children: A review and synthesis of recent empirical studies. *Psychological Bulletin, 113,* 164–180.

Kerns, K. A., & Berenbaum, S. A. (1991). Sex differences in spatial ability in children. *Behavior Genetics, 21,* 383–396.

Kimura, D. (1992). Sex differences in the brain. *Scientific American, 267,* 119–125.

Kling, K. C., Hyde, J. S., Showers, C. J., & Buswell, B. N. (1999). Gender differences in self-esteem: A meta-analysis. *Psychological Bulletin, 125,* 470–500.

Klinger, L. J., Hamilton, J. A., & Cantrell, P. J. (2001). Children's perceptions of aggressive and gender-specific content in toy commercials. *Social Behavior and Personality, 29,* 11–20.

Knight, G. P., Fabes, R. A., & Higgins, D. A. (1996). Concerns about drawing causal inferences from meta-analyses: An example in the study of gender differences in aggression. *Psychological Bulletin, 119,* 410–421.

Kohlberg, L. (1966). A cognitive-developmental analysis of children's sex-role concepts and attitudes. In E. E. Maccoby (Ed.), *The development of sex differences.* Stanford, CA: Stanford University Press.

Kortenhaus, C. M., & Demarest, J. (1993). Gender role stereotyping in childrens literature: An update. *Sex Roles, 28,* 219–232.

Kovacs, D. M., Parker, J. G., & Hoffman, L. W. (1996). Behavioral, affective, and social correlates of involvement in cross-sex friendships in elementary school. *Child Development, 67,* 2269–2286.

Kuhn, D., Nash, S. C., & Brucken, L. (1978). Sex-role concepts of two- and three-year-olds. *Child Development, 49,* 445–451.

Laumann, E. O., Gagnon, J. H., Michael, R. T., & Michaels, S. (1994). *The social organization of sexuality: Sexual practices in the United States.* Chicago: University of Chicago Press.

Leaper, C. (1994). *Childhood gender segregation: Causes and consequences* (New Directions for Child Development, Vol. 65). San Francisco: Jossey-Bass.

Lee, V. E., & Bryk, A. S. (1986). Effects of single-sex secondary schools on student achievement and attitudes. *Journal of Educational Psychology, 78,* 381–395.

Lee, V. E., Marks, H. M., & Byrd, T. (1994). Sexism in single-sex and coeducational independent secondary school classrooms. *Sociology of Education, 67,* 92–120.

LePore, P. C., & Warren, J. R. (1997). A comparison of single-sex and coeducational Catholic secondary schooling: Evidence from the National Educational Longitudinal Study of 1988. *American Educational Research Journal, 34,* 485–511.

Leung, A. K. C., & Robson, W. L. M. (1993). Childhood masturbation. *Clinical Pediatrics, 32,* 238–241.

LeVay, S. (1996). *Queer science: The use and abuse of research into homosexuality.* Cambridge, MA: MIT Press.

Leve, L. D., & Fagot, B. I. (1997). Gender-role socialization and discipline processes in one- and two-parent families. *Sex Roles, 36,* 1–21.

Levy, G. D., Sadovsky, A. L., & Troseth, G. L. (2000). Aspects of young children's perceptions of gender-typed occupations. *Sex Roles, 42,* 993–1006.

Lewis, M., & Weinraub, M. (1979). Origins of early sex-role development. *Sex Roles, 5,* 135–153.

Liben, L. S., & Signorella, M. L. (1993). Gender-schematic processing in children: The role of initial interpretations of stimuli. *Developmental Psychology, 29,* 141–149.

Lobel, T., Slone, M., & Winch, G. (1997). Masculinity, popularity, and self-esteem among Israeli preadolescent girls. *Sex Roles, 36,* 395–408.

Lockheed, M. E. (1986). Reshaping the social order: The case of gender segregation. *Sex Roles, 14,* 617–628.

Loehlin, J. C. (1992). *Genes and environment in personality development* (Individual Differences and Development Series, Vol. 2). Newbury Park, CA: Sage.

Loewenstein, G., & Furstenburg, F. (1991). Is teenage sexual behavior rational? *Journal of Applied Social Psychology, 21,* 957–986.

Lorber, J. (1986). Dismantling Noah's ark. *Sex Roles, 14,* 567–580.

Lueptow, L. B., Garovich-Szabo, L., & Lueptow, M. B. (2001). Social change and the persistence of sex typing: 1974–1997. *Social Forces, 80,* 1–36.

Lytton, H. & Romney, D. M. (1991). Parents' differential socialization of boys and girls: A meta-analysis. *Psychological Bulletin, 109,* 267–296.

Maccoby, E. E. (1980). *Social development.* New York: Harcourt Brace Jovanovich.

Maccoby, E. E. (1998). *The two sexes: Growing up apart, Coming together.* Cambridge, MA: Harvard University Press.

Maccoby, E. E., & Jacklin, C. N. (1974). *The psychology of sex differences.* Stanford, CA: Stanford University Press.

Maccoby, E. E., & Jacklin, C. N. (1987). Gender segregation in childhood. In H. W. Reese (Ed.), *Advances in child development and behavior* (Vol. 20). Orlando, FL: Academic Press.

Marsh, H. W. (1989). Effects of attending single-sex and coeducational high schools on achievement, attitudes, behaviors, and sex differences. *Journal of Educational Psychology, 81,* 70–85.

Marsiglio, W., & Donnelly, D. (1991). Sexual relations in later life: A national study of married persons. *Journals of Gerontology: Social Sciences, 46,* S338–S344.

Martin, C. L. (1990). Attitudes and expectations about children with nontraditional gender roles. *Sex Roles, 22,* 151–165.

Martin, C. L., & Fabes, R. A. (2001). The stability and consequences of young children's same-sex peer interactions. *Developmental Psychology, 37,* 431–446.

Martin, C. L., & Halverson, C. F., Jr. (1981). A schematic processing model of sex typing and stereotyping in children. *Child Development, 52,* 1119–1134.

Martin, C. L., & Halverson, C. F., Jr. (1983). The effects of sex-typing schemas on young children's memory. *Child Development, 54,* 563–574.

Martin, C. L., & Halverson, C. F., Jr. (1987). The roles of cognition in sex-roles and sex-typing. In D. B. Carter (Ed.), *Current conceptions of sex roles and sex-typing: Theory and research.* New York: Preager.

Masters, W. H., & Johnson, V. E. (1966). *Human sexual response.* Boston: Little, Brown.

Masters, W. H., & Johnson, V. E. (1970). *Human sexual inadequacy.* Boston: Little, Brown.

McClintock, M. K., & Herdt, G. (1996). Rethinking puberty: The development of sexual attraction. *Current Directions in Psychological Science, 5,* 178–183.

McGhee, P. E., & Frueh, T. (1980). Television viewing and the learning of sex-role stereotypes. *Sex Roles, 6,* 179–188.

Meyer-Bahlburg, H. F. L., Ehrhardt, A. A., Rosen, L. R., & Gruen, R. S. (1995). Prenatal estrogens and the development of homosexual orientation. *Developmental Psychology, 31,* 12–21.

Miller, B. C., & Fox, G. L. (1987). Theories of adolescent heterosexual behavior. *Journal of Adolescent Research, 2,* 269–282.

Mills, C. J., Ablard, K. E., & Stumpf, H. (1993). Gender differences in academically talented young students' mathematical reasoning: Patterns across age and subskills. *Journal of Educational Psychology, 85,* 340–346.

Mischel, W. (1970). Sex-typing and socialization. In P. H. Mussen (Ed.), *Carmichael's manual of child psychology* (Vol. 2). New York: Wiley.

Mitchell, J. E., Baker, L. A., & Jacklin, C. N. (1989). Masculinity and femininity in twin children: Genetic and environmental factors. *Child Development, 60,* 1475–1485.

Moller, L. C., & Serbin, L. A. (1996). Antecedents of toddler gender segregation: Cognitive consonance, gender-typed toy preferences and behavioral compatibility. *Sex Roles, 35,* 445–460.

Money, J. (1985). Pediatric sexology and hermaphroditism. *Journal of Sex and Marital Therapy, 11,* 139–156.

Money, J. (1988). *Gay, straight, and in-between: The sexology of erotic orientation.* New York: Oxford University Press.

Money, J., & Ehrhardt, A. (1972). *Man and woman, boy and girl.* Baltimore: Johns Hopkins University Press.

Money, J., & Tucker, P. (1975). *Sexual signatures: On being a man or a woman.* Boston: Little, Brown.

Morrison, D. M. (1985). Adolescent contraceptive behavior: A review. *Psychological Bulletin, 98,* 538–568.

Munroe, R. H., Shimmin, H. S., & Munroe, R. L. (1984). Gender understanding and sex-role preferences in four cultures. *Developmental Psychology, 20,* 673–682.

Mussen, P. H., & Rutherford, E. (1963). Parent–child relations and parental personality in relation to young children's sex-role preferences. *Child Development, 34,* 589–607.

Myers, J. K., Weissman, M. M., Tischler, G. L., Holzer, C. E., III, Leaf, P. J., & Orvaschel, H. (1984). Six month prevalence of psychiatric disorders in three communities. *Archives of General Psychiatry, 41,* 959–967.

Nordvik, H., & Amponsah, B. (1998). Gender differences in spatial abilities and spatial activity among university students in an egalitarian educational system. *Sex Roles, 38,* 1009–1023.

Nowell, A., & Hedges, L. V. (1998). Trends in gender differences in academic achievement from 1960 to 1994: An analysis of differences in mean, variance, and extreme scores. *Sex Roles, 39,* 21–43.

O'Brien, M., Peyton, V., Mistry, R., Hruda, L., Jacobs, A., Caldera, Y., Huston, A., & Roy, C. (2000). Gender-role cognition in three-year-old boys and girls. *Sex Roles, 42,* 1007–1025.

Okami, P., Olmstead, R., & Abramson, P. R. (1997). Sexual experiences in early childhood: 18-year longitudinal data from the UCLA family lifestyles project. *Journal of Sex Research, 34,* 339–347.

Oliver, M. B., & Hyde, J. S. (1993). Gender differences in sexuality: A meta-analysis. *Psychological Bulletin, 114,* 29–51.

Parke, R. D. (1996). *Fatherhood.* Cambridge, MA: Harvard University Press.

Patterson, C. J. (1992). Children of lesbian and gay parents. *Child Development, 63,* 1025–1042.

Paul, J. P. (1993). Childhood cross-gender behavior and adult homosexuality: The resurgence of biological models of sexuality. *Journal of Homosexuality, 24,* 41–54.

Persson, G., & Svanborg, A. (1992). Marital coital activity in men at the age of 75: Relation to somatic, psychiatric, and social factors at the age of 70. *Journal of the American Geriatrics Society, 40,* 439–444.

Pomerleau, A., Bolduc, D., Malcuit, G., & Cossette, L. (1990). Pink or blue: Environmental gender stereotypes in the first two years of life. *Sex Roles, 22,* 359–367.

Ponton, L. (2001). *The sex lives of teenagers: Revealing the secret world of adolescent boys and girls.* New York: Plume.

Poulin-Dubois, D., Serbin, L. A., Kenyon, B., & Derbyshire, A. (1994). Infants' intermodal knowledge about gender. *Developmental Psychology, 30,* 436–442.

Powlishta, K. K. (2000). The effect of target age on the activation of gender stereotypes. *Sex Roles, 42,* 271–282.

Purifoy, F. E., Grodsky, A., & Giambra, L. M. (1992). The relationship of sexual daydreaming to sexual activity, sexual drive, and sexual attitudes for women across the life-span. *Archives of Sexual Behavior, 21,* 369–385.

Raz, S., Goldstein, R., Hopkins, T. L., Lauterbach, M. D., Shah, F., Porter, C. L., Riggs, W. W., Magill, L. H., & Sander, C. J. (1994). Sex differences in early vulnerability to cerebral injury and their neurobehavioral implications. *Psychobiology, 22,* 244–253.

Reid, P. T., & Trotter, K. H. (1993). Children's self-presentations with infants: Gender and ethnic comparisons. *Sex Roles, 29,* 171–181.

Reinisch, J. M., Sanders, S. A., Hill, C. A., & Ziemba-Davis, M. (1992). High-risk sexual behavior among heterosexual undergraduates at a midwestern university. *Family Planning Perspectives, 24,* 116.

Resnick, S. M., Berenbaum, S. A., Gottesman, I. I., & Bouchard, T. J. (1986). Early hormonal influences on cognitive functioning in congenital adrenal hyperplasia. *Developmental Psychology, 22,* 191–198.

Roberts, L. R., Sarigiani, P. A., Petersen, A. C., & Newman, J. L. (1990). Gender differences in the relationship between achievement and self image during early adolescence. *Journal of Early Adolescence, 10,* 159–175.

Robinson, C. C., & Morris, J. T. (1986). The gender-stereotyped nature of Christmas toys received by 36-, 48-, and 60-month-old children: A comparison between nonrequested vs. requested toys. *Sex Roles, 15,* 21–32.

Robinson, I., Ziss, K., Ganza, B., Katz, S., & Robinson, E. (1991). Twenty years of sexual revolution, 1965–1985: An update. *Journal of Marriage and the Family, 53,* 216–220.

Robinson, N. M., Abbott, R. D., Berninger, V. W. & Busse, J. (1996). The structure of abilities in mathematically precocious young children: Gender similarities and differences. *Journal of Educational Psychology, 88,* 341–352.

Robinson, P. K. (1983). The sociological perspective. In R. B. Weg (Ed.), *Sexuality in the later years: Roles and behavior.* New York: Academic Press.

Rosenwasser, S. M., Lingenfelter, M., & Harrington, A. F. (1989). Nontraditional gender role portrayals on television and children's gender role perceptions. *Journal of Applied Developmental Psychology, 10,* 97–105.

Ross, C. A., Miler, S. D., Bjornson, L., Reagor, P., Fraser, G. A., & Anderson, G. (1991). Abuse histories in 102 cases of multiple personality disorder. *Canadian Journal of Psychiatry, 36,* 97–101.

Rubin, J. Z., Provenzano, F. J., & Luria, Z. (1974). The eye of the beholder: Parents' views on sex of newborns. *American Journal of Orthopsychiatry, 44,* 512–519.

Rubinow, D. R., & Schmidt, P. J. (1996). Androgens, brain, and behavior. *American Journal of Psychiatry, 153,* 974–984.

Ruble, D. N., & Martin, C. L. (1998). Gender development. In W. Damon (Editor-in-Chief), N. Eisenberg (Vol. Ed.), *Handbook of child psychology: Vol. 3. Social, emotional, and personality development* (5th ed., pp. 933–1016). New York: Wiley.

Russell, A., Aloa, V., Feder, T., Glover, A., Miller, H., & Palmer, G. (1998). Sex-based differences in parenting styles in a sample with preschool children. *Australian Journal of Psychology, 50,* 89–99.

Rust, J., Golombok, S., Hines, M., Johnston, K., & Golding, J. (2000). The role of brothers and sisters in the gender development of preschool children. *Journal of Experimental Child Psychology, 77,* 292–303.

Sadker, M., & Sadker, D. (1994). *Failing at fairness: How America's schools cheat girls.* New York: Scribner's.

Savin-Williams, R. C. (1995). An exploratory study of pubertal maturation timing and self-esteem among gay and bisexual male youths. *Developmental Psychology, 31,* 56–64.

Schiavi, R. C., Schreiner-Engel, P., White, D., & Mandeli, J. (1991). The relationship between pituitary-gonadal function and sexual behavior in healthy aging men. *Psychosomatic Medicine, 53,* 363–374.

Serbin, L. A., Powlishta, K. K., & Gulko, J. (1993). The development of sex typing in middle childhood. *Monographs of the Society for Research in Child Development, 58*(2, Serial No. 232).

Serbin, L. A., Tonick, I. J., & Sternglanz, S. H. (1977). Shaping cooperative cross-sex play. *Child Development, 48,* 924–929.

Shaffer, D. R., Pegalis, L. J., & Cornell, D. P. (1992). Gender and self-disclosure revisited: Personal and contextual variations in self-disclosure to same-sex acquaintances. *Journal of Social Psychology, 132,* 307–315.

Shepard, R. N., & Metzler, J. (1971). Mental rotation of three-dimensional objects. *Science, 171,* 701–703.

Siegel, D. M., Klein, D. I., & Roghmann, K. J. (1999). Sexual behavior, contraception, and risk among college students. *Journal of Adolescent Health, 25,* 336–343.

Sieving, R. E., McNeely, C. S., & Blum, R. W. (2000). Maternal expectations, mother–child connectedness, and adolescent sexual debut. *Archives of Pediatrics and Adolescent Medicine, 154,* 809–816.

Sigelman, C. K., Carr, M. B., & Begley, N. L. (1986). Developmental changes in the influence of sex-role stereotypes on person perception. *Child Study Journal, 16,* 191–205.

Signorella, M. L., Bigler, R. S., & Liben, L. S. (1993). Developmental differences in children's gender schemata about others: A meta-analytic review. *Developmental Review, 13,* 147–183.

Signorella, M. L., Frieze, I. H., & Hershey, S. W. (1996). Single-sex versus mixed-sex classes and gender schemata in children and adolescents. *Psychology of Women Quarterly, 20,* 599–607.

Signorielli, N. (1990). Children, television, and gender roles. *Journal of Adolescent Health Care, 11,* 50–58.

Signorielli, N., & Kahlenberg, S. (2001). Television's world of work in the nineties. *Journal of Broadcasting & Electronic Media, 45,* 4–22.

Signorielli, N., & Lears, M. (1992). Children, television, and conceptions about chores: Attitudes and behaviors. *Sex Roles, 27,* 157–170.

Simon, W., & Gagnon, J. (1998). Psychosexual development. *Society, 35,* 60–67.

Slavkin, M., & Stright, A. D. (2000). Gender role differences in college students from one- and two-parent families. *Sex Roles, 42,* 23–37.

Smith, P. K., & Daglish, L. (1977). Sex differences in parent and infant behavior in the home. *Child Development, 48,* 1250–1254.

Smith, T. W. (1991). Adult sexual behavior in 1989: Number of partners, frequency of intercourse and risk of AIDS. *Family Planning Perspectives, 23,* 102–107.

Sneed, C. D., Morisky, D. E., Rotheram-Borus, M. J., Ebin, V., Malotte, C. K., Lyde, M., & Gill, J. K. (2001). "Don't know" and "didn't think of it": Condom use at first intercourse by Latino adolescents. *AIDS Care, 13,* 303–308.

Spence, J. T., & Hall, S. K. (1996). Children's gender-related self-perceptions, activity preferences, and occupational stereotypes: A test of three models of gender constructs. *Sex Roles, 35,* 659–691.

Spence, J. T., & Helmreich, R. L. (1978). *Masculinity and femininity: Their psychological dimensions, correlates, and antecedents.* Austin: University of Texas Press.

Sroufe, L. A., Bennett, C., Englund, M., Urban, J., & Shulman, S. (1993). The significance of gender boundaries in preadolescence: Contemporary correlates and antecedents of boundary violation and maintenance. *Child Development, 64,* 455–466.

Starr, B. D., & Weiner, M. B. (1981). *The Starr-Weiner report on sex and sexuality in the mature years.* New York: Stein & Day.

Stern, M., & Karraker, K. H. (1989). Sex stereotyping of infants: A review of gender labeling studies. *Sex Roles, 20,* 501–522.

Stevenson, M. R., & Black, K. N. (1988). Paternal absence and sex-role development: A meta-analysis. *Child Development, 59,* 793–814.

Stoddart, T., & Turiel, E. (1985). Children's concepts of cross-gender activities. *Child Development, 56,* 1241–1252.

Stumpf, H., & Stanley, J. C. (1996). Gender-related differences on the College Board's Advanced Placement and Achievement Tests, 1982–1992. *Journal of Educational Psychology, 88,* 353–364.

Taylor, M. G. (1996). The development of children's beliefs about social and biological aspects of gender differences. *Child Development, 67,* 1555–1571.

Thompson, S. K. (1975). Gender labels and early sex-role development. *Child Development, 46,* 339–347.

Thorne, B. (1993). *Gender play: Girls and boys in school.* New Brunswick, NJ: Rutgers University Press.

Trickett, P. K., & Putnam, F. W. (1993). Impact of child sexual abuse on females: Toward a developmental, psychobiological integration. *Psychological Science, 4,* 81–87.

Turner, P. J., & Gervai, J. (1995). A multidimensional study of gender typing in preschool children and their parents: Personality, attitudes, preferences, behavior, and cultural differences. *Developmental Psychology, 31,* 759–772.

Turner-Bowker, D. M. (1996). Gender stereotyped descriptors in children's picture books: Does "curious Jane" exist in the literature? *Sex Roles, 35,* 461–488.

Twenge, J. M. (1997). Changes in masculine and feminine traits over time: A meta-analysis. *Sex Roles, 36,* 305–325.

Updegraff, K., & McHale, S. M., & Crouter, A. C. (1996). Gender roles in marriage: What do they mean for girls' and boys' school achievement? *Journal of Youth and Adolescence, 25,* 73–88.

Urberg, K. A. (1979). Sex-role conceptualization in adolescents and adults. *Developmental Psychology, 15,* 90–92.

U.S. Department of Labor, Bureau of Labor Statistics. (2001). *Highlights of women's earnings in 2000* (Report 952). Washington, DC: Author.

Vobejda, B., & Havemann, J. (1997, May 2). Teenagers less sexually active in U.S. *Washington Post,* pp. A1, A12.

Voyer, D., Voyer, S., & Bryden, M. P. (1995). Magnitude of sex differences in spatial abilities: A meta-analysis and consideration of critical variables. *Psychological Bulletin, 117,* 250–270.

Wallen, K. (1996). Nature needs nurture: The interaction of hormonal and social influences on the development of behavioral sex differences in rhesus monkeys. *Hormones and Behavior, 30,* 364–378.

Warin, J. (2000). The attainment of self-consistency through gender in young children. *Sex Roles, 42,* 209–231.

Welch-Ross, M. K., & Schmidt, C. R. (1996). Gender-schema development and children's constructive story memory: Evidence for a developmental model. *Child Development, 67,* 820–835.

Wentzel, K. R. (1988). Gender differences in math and English achievement: A longitudinal study. *Sex Roles, 18,* 691–699.

Werner-Wilson, R. J. (1998). Gender differences in adolescent sexual attitudes: The influence of individual and family factors. *Adolescence, 33,* 519–531.

Whiting, B. B., & Edwards, C. P. (1988). *Children of different worlds: The formation of social behavior.* Cambridge, MA: Harvard University Press.

Widmer, E. D., Treas, J., & Newcomb, R. (1998). Attitudes toward nonmarital sex in 24 countries. *Journal of Sex Research, 35,* 349–358.

Williams, J. E., & Best, D. L. (1990). *Measuring sex stereotypes: A multination study* (rev. ed.). Newbury Park, CA: Sage.

Wink, P., & Helson, R. (1993). Personality change in women and their partners. *Journal* of *Personality and Social Psychology, 65,* 597–605.

Witt, S. (1997). Parental influence on children's socialization to gender roles. *Adolescence, 32,* 253–259.

Young, W. C., Goy, R. W., & Phoenix, C. H. (1964). Hormones and sexual behavior. *Science, 143,* 212–218.

Zick, C. D., & McCullough, J. L. (1991). Trends in married couples' time use: Evidence from 1977–78 and 1987–88. *Sex Roles, 24,* 459–487.

Chapter 13: Social Cognition and Moral Development

Ainlay, S. C., & Smith, D. R. (1984). Aging and religious participation. *Journal of Gerontology, 39,* 357–363.

Anderson, D. R., Huston, A. C., Schmitt, K. L., Linebarger, D. L., & Wright, J. C. (2001). Early childhood television viewing and adolescent behavior. *Monographs of the Society for Research in Child Development, 66*(1, Serial No. 264).

Anderson, K. E., Lytton, H., & Romney, D. M. (1986). Mothers' interactions with normal and conduct-disordered boys: Who affects whom? *Developmental Psychology, 22,* 604–609.

Badenes, L. V., Estevan, R. A. C., & Garcia Bacete, F. J. (2000). Theory of mind and peer rejection at school. *Social Development, 9,* 271–283.

Bandura, A. (1986). *Social foundations of thought and action: A social cognitive theory.* Englewood Cliffs, NJ: Prentice-Hall.

Bandura, A. (1991). Social cognitive theory of moral thought and action. In W. M. Kurtines & J. L. Gewirtz (Eds.), *Handbook of moral behavior and development: Vol. 1. Theory.* Hillsdale, NJ: Erlbaum.

Bandura, A., Caprara, G. V., Barbaranelli, C., Pastorelli, C., & Regalia, C. (2001). Sociocognitive self-regulatory mechanisms governing transgressive behavior. *Journal of Personality & Social Psychology, 80,* 125–135.

Bank, L., Marlowe, J., Reid, J., Patterson, G., & Weinrott, M. (1991). A comparative evaluation of parent-training interventions for families of chronic delinquents. *Journal of Abnormal Child Psychology, 19,* 15–33.

Baron-Cohen, S. (1995). *Mindblindness: An essay on autism and theory of mind.* Cambridge, MA: MIT Press.

Baron-Cohen, S., Leslie, A. M., & Frith, U. (1985). Does the autistic child have a "theory of mind"? *Cognition, 21,* 37-46.

Bartsch, K., & London, K. (2000). Children's use of mental state information in selecting persuasive arguments. *Developmental Psychology, 36,* 352–365.

Berkowitz, M. W., & Gibbs, J. C. (1983). Measuring the developmental features of moral discussion. *Merrill-Palmer Quarterly, 29,* 399–410.

Blanchard-Fields, F. (1986). Reasoning on social dilemmas varying in emotional saliency: An adult developmental perspective. *Psychology and Aging, 1,* 325–333.

Blanchard-Fields, F. (1996). Social cognitive development in adulthood and aging. In F. Blanchard-Fields & T. M. Hess (Eds.), *Perspectives on cognitive change in adulthood and aging.* New York: McGraw-Hill.

Blasi, A. (1980). Bridging moral cognition and moral action: A critical review of the literature. *Psychological Bulletin, 88,* 1–45.

Blazer, D., & Palmore, E. (1976). Religion and aging in a longitudinal panel. *Gerontologist, 16,* 82–85.

Bloom, P., & German, T. P. (2000). Two reasons to abandon the false belief task as a test of theory of mind. *Cognition, 77,* B25–B31.

Boom, J., Brugman, D., & van der Heijden, P. G. M. (2001). Hierarchical structure of moral stages assessed by a sorting task. *Child Development, 72,* 535–548.

Booth, W., & Snyder, D. (2001, March 7). Boy took gun from home. *Washington Post,* pp. A1, A12.

Bosacki, S. L. (2000). Theory of mind and self-concept in preadolescents: Links with gender and language. *Journal of Educational Psychology, 92,* 709–717.

Brabeck, M. (1983). Moral judgment: Theory and research on differences between males and females. *Developmental Review, 3,* 274–291.

Bretherton, I., & Beeghly, M. (1982). Talking about internal states: The acquisition of an explicit theory of mind. *Developmental Psychology, 18,* 906–921.

Brody, G. H., & Shaffer, D. R. (1982). Contributions of parents and peers to children's moral socialization. *Developmental Review, 2,* 31–75.

Bruggeman, E. L., & Hart, K. J. (1996). Cheating, lying, and moral reasoning by religious and secular high school students. *Journal of Educational Research, 89,* 340–344.

Burton, R. V. (1963). The generality of honesty reconsidered. *Psychological Review, 70,* 481–499.

Burton, R. V. (1976). Honesty and dishonesty. In T. Lickona (Ed.), *Moral development and behavior.* New York: Holt, Rinehart & Winston.

Burton, R. V. (1984). A paradox in theories and research in moral development. In W. M. Kurtines & J. L. Gewirtz (Eds.), *Morality, moral behavior, and moral development.* New York: Wiley.

Bushman, B., & Huesmann, L. R. (2001). Effects of televised violence on aggression. In D. G. Singer & J. L. Singer (Eds.), *Handbook of children and the media.* Thousand Oaks, CA: Sage.

Buss, D. M. (1999). *Evolutionary psychology: The new science of the mind.* Boston: Allyn & Bacon.

Bussey, K. (1992). Lying and truthfulness: Children's definitions, standards, and evaluative reactions. *Child Development, 63,* 129–137.

Campbell, R. L., & Christopher, J. C. (1996). Moral development theory: A critique of its Kantian presuppositions. *Developmental Review, 16,* 1–47.

Carpendale, J. I. M. (2000). Kohlberg and Piaget on stages and moral reasoning. *Developmental Review, 20,* 181–205.

Chandler, M., Fritz, A. S., & Hala, S. (1989). Small-scale deceit: Deception as a marker of two-, three-, and four-year-olds' early theories of mind. *Child Development, 60,* 1263–1277.

Chandler, M., Sokol, B. W., & Wainryb, C. (2000). Beliefs about truth and beliefs about rightness. *Child Development, 71,* 91–97.

Charman, T. (2000). Theory of mind and the early diagnosis of autism. In S. Baron-Cohen, H. Tager-Flusberg, & D. J. Cohen (Eds.), *Understanding other minds: Perspectives from developmental cognitive neuroscience* (2nd ed.). Oxford: Oxford University Press.

Coie, J. D., Dodge, K. A., Terry, R., & Wright, V. (1991). The role of aggression in peer relations: An analysis of aggression episodes in boys' play groups. *Child Development, 62,* 812–826.

Colby, A., & Kohlberg, L. (1987). *The measurement of moral judgment: Vol. 1. Theoretical foundations and research validation.* Cambridge, England: Cambridge University Press.

Colby, A., Kohlberg, L., Gibbs, J., & Lieberman, M. (1983). A longitudinal study of moral judgment. *Monographs of the Society for Research in Child Development, 48*(1–2, Serial No. 200).

Cole, P. M., Barrett, K. C., & Zahn-Waxler, C. (1992). Emotion displays in two-year-olds during mishaps. *Child Development, 63,* 314–324.

Courtin, C. (2000). The impact of sign language on the cognitive development of deaf children: The case of theories of mind. *Journal of Deaf Studies and Deaf Education, 5,* 266–276.

Crick, N. R., & Dodge, K. A. (1994). A review and reformulation of social information-processing mechanisms in children's social adjustment. *Psychological Bulletin, 115,* 74–101.

Crockenberg, S., & Litman, C. (1990). Autonomy as competence in 2-year-olds: Maternal correlates of child defiance, compliance, and self-assertion. *Developmental Psychology, 26,* 961–971.

Custer, W. L. (1996). A comparison of young children's understanding of contradictory representations in pretense, memory, and belief. *Child Development, 67,* 678–688.

Damon, W., & Hart, D. (1992). Self-understanding and its role in social and moral development. In M. H. Bornstein & M. E. Lamb (Eds.), *Developmental psychology: An advanced textbook.* Hillsdale, NJ: Erlbaum.

de Vries, B., & Walker, L. J. (1986). Moral reasoning and attitudes toward capital punishment. *Developmental Psychology, 22,* 509–513.

Dishion, T. J., Andrews, D. W., & Crosby, L. (1995). Antisocial boys and their friends in adolescence: Relationship characteristics, quality, and interactional process. *Child Development, 66,* 139–151.

Dishion, T. J., McCord, J., & Poulin, F. (1999). When interventions harm: Peer groups and problem behavior. *American Psychologist, 54,* 755–764.

Dodge, K. A. (1986). A social information processing model of social competence in children. In M. Perlmutter (Ed.), *Minnesota Symposia on Child Psychology* (Vol. 18). Hillsdale, NJ: Erlbaum.

Dodge, K. A. (1993). Social-cognitive mechanisms in the development of conduct disorder and depression. *Annual Review of Psychology, 44,* 559–584.

Dodge, K. A., & Price, J. M. (1994). On the relation between social information processing and socially competent behavior in early school-aged children. *Child Development, 65,* 1385–1397.

Dolen, L. S., & Bearison, D. J. (1982). Social interaction and social cognition in aging. *Human Development, 25,* 430–442.

Droege, K. L., & Stipek, D J. (1993). Children's use of dispositions to predict classmates' behavior. *Developmental Psychology, 29,* 646–654.

Dunn, J., Brown, J., Slomkowski, C., Tesla, C., & Youngblade, L. (1991). Young children's understanding of other people's feelings and beliefs: Individual differences and their antecedents. *Child Development, 62,* 1352–1366.

Dunn, J., Cutting, A. L., & Demetriou, H. (2000). Moral sensibility, understanding others, and children's friendship interactions in the pre-school period. *British Journal of Developmental Psychology, 18,* 159–177.

Eddy, J. M., & Chamberlain, P. (2000). Family management and deviant peer association as mediators of the impact of treatment condition on youth antisocial behavior. *Journal of Consulting and Clinical Psychology, 68,* 857–863.

Eddy, J. M., Leve, L. D., & Fagot, B. I. (2001). Coercive family processes: A replication and extension of Patterson's coercion model. *Aggressive Behavior, 27,* 14–25.

Eisenberg, N. (2000). Emotion, regulation, and moral development. *Annual Review of Psychology, 51,* 665–697.

Eisenberg, N., Fabes, R. A., Guthrie, I. K., Murphy, B. C., Maszk, P., Holmgren, R., & Suh, K. (1996). The relations of regulation and emotionality to problem behavior in elementary school children. *Development and Psychopathology, 8,* 141–162.

Elliott, D. S., & Ageton, S. S. (1980). Reconciling race and class differences in self-reported and official estimates of delinquency. *American Sociological Review, 45,* 95–110.

Elliott, D. S., Williams, K. R., & Hamburg, B. (1998). An integrated approach to violence prevention. In D. S. Elliott, B. A. Hamburg, & K. R. Williams (Eds.), *Violence in American schools: A new perspective.* New York: Cambridge University Press.

Emde, R. N., Biringen, Z., Clyman, R. B., & Oppenheim, D. (1991). The moral self of infancy: Affective core and procedural knowledge. *Developmental Review, 11,* 251–270.

Fischer, W. F. (1963). Sharing in pre-school children as a function of the amount and type of reinforcement. *Genetic Psychology Monographs, 68,* 215–245.

Flavell, J. H. (1985). *Cognitive development* (2nd ed.). Englewood Cliffs, NJ: Prentice Hall.

Flavell, J. H. (1999). Cognitive development: Children's knowledge about the mind. *Annual Review of Psychology, 50,* 21–45.

Fletcher, M. A., & Waxman, S. (2001, March 6). Boasts to friends went unbelieved. *Washington Post,* pp. A1, A4.

Fowler, J. W. (1981). *Stages of faith: The psychology of human development and the quest for meaning.* San Francisco: Harper & Row.

Fowler, J. W. (1991). The vocation of faith developmental theory. In J. W. Fowler, K. E. Nipkow, & F. Schweitzer (Eds.), *Stages of faith and religious development.* New York: Crossroad.

Fowles, D. C., & Kochanska, G. (2000). Temperament as a moderator of pathways to conscience in children: The contribution of electrodermal activity. *Psychophysiology, 37,* 788–795.

Freud, S. (1960). *A general introduction to psychoanalysis.* New York: Washington Square Press. (Original work published 1935)

Garbarino, J. (1999). *Lost boys: Why our sons turn violent and how we can save them.* New York: Free Press.

Gibbs, J. C., Potter, G. B., Barriga, A. Q., & Liau, A. K. (1996). Developing the helping skills and prosocial motivation of aggressive adolescents in peer group programs. *Aggression & Violent Behavior, 1,* 283–305.

Gilligan, C. (1977). In a different voice: Women's conceptions of self and morality. *Harvard Educational Review, 47,* 481–517.

Gilligan, C. (1982). *In a different voice: Psychological theory and women's development.* Cambridge, MA: Harvard University Press.

Gilligan, C. (1993). Adolescent development reconsidered. In A. Garrod (Ed.), *Approaches to moral development: New research and emerging themes.* New York: Teachers College Press.

Gnepp, J., & Chilamkurti, C. (1988). Children's use of personality attributions to predict other people's emotional and behavioral reactions. *Child Development, 59,* 743–754.

Gopnik, A., Capps, L., & Meltzoff, A. N. (2000). Early theories of mind: What the theory theory can tell us about autism. In S. Baron-Cohen, H. Tager-Flusberg, & D. J. Cohen (Eds.), *Understanding other minds: Perspectives from developmental cognitive neuroscience* (2nd ed.). Oxford: Oxford University Press.

Gralinski, J. H., & Kopp, C. B. (1993). Everyday rules for behavior: Mothers' requests to young children. *Developmental Psychology, 29,* 573–584.

Gregg, V., Gibbs, J. C., & Basinger, K. S. (1994). Patterns of developmental delay in moral judgment by male and female delinquents. *Merrill-Palmer Quarterly, 40,* 538–553.

Grizenko, N., Zappitelli, M., Langevin, J. P., Hrychko, S., El-Messidi, A., Kaminester, D., Pawliuk, N., & Stepanian, M. T. (2000). Effectiveness of a social skills training program using self/other perspective-taking: A nine-month follow-up. *American Journal of Orthopsychiatry, 70,* 501–509.

Grusec, J. E., Goodnow, J. J., & Kuczynski, L. (2000). New directions in analyses of parenting contributions to children's acquisition of values. *Child Development, 71,* 205–211.

Grusec, J. E., Kuczynski, L., Rushton, J. P., & Simutis, Z. (1979). Learning resistance to temptation through observation. *Developmental Psychology, 15,* 233–240.

Guerra, N. G., & Slaby, R. G. (1990). Cognitive mediators of aggression in adolescent offenders: 2. Intervention. *Developmental Psychology, 26,* 269–277.

Happe, F. G. E., Winner, E., & Brownell, H. (1998). The getting of wisdom: Theory of mind in old age. *Developmental Psychology, 34,* 358–362.

Harris, P. L. (1989). *Children and emotion: The development of psychological understanding.* Oxford, England: Basil Blackwell.

Hartshorne, H., & May, M. S. (1928–1930). *Studies in the nature of character: Vol. 1. Studies in deceit; Vol. 2. Studies in self-control; Vol. 3. Studies in the organization of character.* New York: Macmillan.

Hastings, P. D., Zahn-Waxler, C., Robinson, J., Usher, B., & Bridges, D. (2000). The development of concern for others in children with behavior problems. *Developmental Psychology, 36,* 531–546.

Helwig, C. C., Zelazo, P. D., & Wilson, M. (2001). Children's judgments of psychological harm in normal and noncanonical situations. *Child Development, 72,* 66–81.

Henrich, C. C., Brown, J. L., & Aber, J. L. (1999). Evaluating the effectiveness of school-based violence prevention: Developmental approaches. *Social Policy Report, 13*(Whole No. 3).

Hess, T. M. (1994). Social cognition in adulthood: Age-related changes in knowledge and processing mechanisms. *Developmental Review, 14,* 373–412.

Hess, T. M. (1999). Cognitive and knowledge-based influences on social representations. In T. M. Hess & F. Blanchard-Fields (Eds.), *Social cognition and aging.* San Diego: Academic Press.

Hilton, N. Z., Harris, G. T., & Rice, M. E. (2000). The functions of aggression by male teenagers. *Journal of Personality and Social Psychology, 79,* 988–994.

Hoffman, M. L. (1970). Moral development. In P. H. Mussen (Ed.), *Carmichael's manual of child psychology* (Vol. 2). New York: Wiley.

Hoffman, M. L. (2000). *Empathy and moral development: Implications for caring and justice.* Cambridge, England: Cambridge University Press.

Hudley, C., & Graham, S. (1993). An attributional intervention to reduce peer-directed aggression among African-American boys. *Child Development, 64,* 124–138.

Jackman, G. A., Farah, M. M., Kellermann, A. L., & Simons, H. K. (2001). Seeing is believing: What do boys do when they find a real gun? *Pediatrics, 107,* 1247–1250.

Jaffee, S., & Hyde, J. S. (2000). Gender differences in moral orientation: A meta-analysis. *Psychological Bulletin, 126,* 703–726.

Jagers, R. J., Bingham, K., & Hans, S. L. (1996). Socialization and social judgments among inner-city African-American kindergarteners. *Child Development, 67,* 140–150.

Jenkins, J. M., & Astington, J. W. (1996). Cognitive factors and family structure associated with theory of mind development in young children. *Developmental Psychology, 32,* 70–78.

Judy, B., & Nelson, E. S. (2000). Relationship between parents, peers, morality, and theft in an adolescent sample. *High School Journal, 83,* 31–42.

Kagan, J. (1981). *The second year: The emergence of self-awareness.* Cambridge, MA: Harvard University Press.

Keller, B. B., & Bell, R. Q. (1979). Child effects on adult's method of eliciting altruistic behavior. *Child Development, 50,* 1004–1009.

Kiesner, J., Dishion, T. J., & Poulin, F. (2001). A reinforcement model of conduct problems in children and adolescents: Advances in theory and intervention. In J. Hill & B. Maughan (Eds.), *Conduct disorders in childhood and adolescence.* New York: Cambridge University Press.

Kleiner, C., & Lord, M. (1999, November 22). The cheating game: "Everyone's doing it," from grade school to graduate school. *U.S. News & World Report,* pp. 54–66.

Kochanska, G. (1993). Toward a synthesis of parental socialization and child temperament in early development of conscience. *Child Development, 64,* 325–347.

Kochanska, G. (1995). Children's temperament, mothers' discipline, and security of attachment: Multiple pathways to emerging internalization. *Child Development, 66*, 597–615.

Kochanska, G. (1997). Multiple pathways to conscience for children with different temperaments: From toddlerhood to age 5. *Developmental Psychology, 33*, 228–240.

Kochanska, G., Casey, R. J., & Fukumoto, A. (1995). Toddlers' sensitivity to standard violations. *Child Development, 66*, 643–656.

Kochanska, G., Murray, K. T., & Coy, K. C. (1997). Inhibitory control as a contributor to conscience in childhood: From toddler to early school age. *Child Development, 68*, 263–277.

Kochanska, G., Murray, K. T., & Harlan, E. T. (2000). Effortful control in early childhood: Continuity and change, antecedents, and implications for social development. *Developmental Psychology, 36*, 220–232.

Koenig, A. L., Cicchetti, D., & Rogosch, F. A. (2000). Child compliance/noncompliance and maternal contributors to internalization in maltreating and nonmaltreating dyads. *Child Development, 71*, 1018–1032.

Kohlberg, L. (1963). The development of children's orientations toward a moral order: I. Sequence in the development of moral thought. *Vita Humana, 6*, 11–33.

Kohlberg, L. (1973). Continuities in childhood and adult moral development revisited. In P. B. Baltes & K. W. Schaie (Eds.), *Life-span developmental psychology: Personality and socialization.* New York: Academic Press.

Kohlberg, L. (1975, June). The cognitive-developmental approach to moral education. *Phi Delta Kappan,* pp. 670–677.

Kohlberg, L. (1981). *Essays on moral development: Vol. 1. The philosophy of moral development.* San Francisco: Harper & Row.

Kohlberg, L. (1984). *Essays on moral development: Vol. 2. The psychology of moral development.* San Francisco: Harper & Row.

Kruger, A. C. (1992). The effect of peer and adult–child transductive discussions on moral reasoning. *Merrill-Palmer Quarterly, 38*, 191–211.

Kruger, A. C., & Tomasello, M. (1986). Transactive discussions with peers and adults. *Developmental Psychology, 22*, 681–685.

Kurdek, L. A., & Krile, D. (1982). A developmental analysis of the relation between peer acceptance and both interpersonal understanding and perceived social self-competence. *Child Development, 53*, 1485–1491.

Laible, D. J., & Thompson, R. A. (2000). Mother–child discourse, attachment security, shared positive affect, and early conscience development. *Child Development, 71*, 1424–1440.

Lapsley, D. K. (1996). *Moral psychology.* Boulder, CO: Westview.

Lapsley, D. K., Harwell, M. R., Olson, L. M., Flannery, D., & Quintana, S. M. (1984). Moral judgment, personality, and attitude toward authority in early and late adolescence. *Journal of Youth and Adolescence, 13*, 527–542.

Legerstee, M., Barna, J., & DiAdamo, C. (2000). Precursors to the development of intention at 6 months: Understanding people and their actions. *Developmental Psychology, 36*, 627–634.

LeMare, L. J., & Rubin, K. H. (1987). Perspective taking and peer interaction: Structural and developmental analyses. *Child Development, 58*, 306–315.

Lemerise, E. A., & Arsenio, W. F. (2000). An integrated model of emotion processes and cognition in social information processing. *Child Development, 71*, 107–118.

Leslie, A. M. (1994). ToMM, ToBy, and agency: Core architecture and domain specificity in cognition and culture. In L. Hirschfeld & S. Gelman (Eds.), *Mapping the mind: Domain specificity in cognition and culture.* New York: Cambridge University Press.

Lewis, C., Freeman, N. H., Kyriakidou, C., Maridaki-Kassotaki, K., & Berridge, D. M. (1996). Social influences on false belief access: Specific sibling influences or general apprenticeship? *Child Development, 67*, 2930–2947.

Lillard, A. (1998). Ethno-psychologies: Cultural variations in theories of mind. *Psychological Bulletin, 123*, 3–32.

Livesley, W. J., & Bromley, D. B. (1973). *Person perception in childhood and adolescence.* London: Wiley.

Loeber, R., & Farrington, D. P. (2000). Young children who commit crime: Epidemiology, developmental origins, risk factors, early interventions, and policy implications. *Development and Psychopathology, 12*, 737–762.

Loeber, R., & Stouthamer-Loeber, M. (1998). Development of juvenile aggression and violence: Some common misconceptions and controversies. *American Psychologist, 53*, 242–259.

Lollis, S., Ross, H., & Leroux, L. (1996). An observational study of parents' socialization of moral orientation during sibling conflicts. *Merrill-Palmer Quarterly, 42*, 475–494.

Lytton, H. (1990). Child and parent effects in boys' conduct disorder: A reinterpretation. *Developmental Psychology, 26*, 683–697.

Lytton, H. (2000). Toward a model of family-environmental and child-biological influences on development. *Developmental Review, 20*, 150–179.

Margolin, G., & Gordis, E. B. (2000). The effects of family and community violence on children. *Annual Review of Psychology, 51*, 445–479.

Martin, G. B., & Clark, R. D., III. (1982). Distress crying in neonates: Species and peer specificity. *Developmental Psychology, 18*, 3–9.

Maughan, B. (2001). Conduct disorder in context. In J. Hill & B. Maughan (Eds.), *Conduct disorders in childhood and adolescence.* New York: Cambridge University Press.

Maughan, B., & Rutter, M. (2001). Antisocial children grown up. In J. Hill & B. Maughan (Eds.), *Conduct disorders in childhood and adolescence.* New York: Cambridge University Press.

McFadden, S. H. (1996). Religion, spirituality, and aging. In J. E. Birren & K. W. Schaie (Eds.), *Handbook of the psychology of aging* (4th ed.). San Diego: Academic Press.

Midlarsky, E., Kahana, E., Corley, R., Nemeroff, R., & Schonbar, R. A. (1999). Altruistic moral judgment among older adults. *International Journal of Aging and Human Development, 49*, 27–41.

Miles, D. R., & Carey, G. (1997). Genetic and environmental architecture of human aggression. *Journal of Personality and Social Psychology, 72*, 207–217.

Miller, P. A., Eisenberg, N., Fabes, R. A., & Shell, R. (1996). Relations of moral reasoning and vicarious emotion to young children's prosocial behavior toward peers and adults. *Developmental Psychology, 32*, 210–219.

Mitchell, P. (1997). *Introduction to theory of mind: Children, autism, and apes.* London: Arnold.

Moeller, T. G. (2001). *Youth aggression and violence.* Mahwah, NJ: Erlbaum.

Moffitt, T. E., & Caspi, A. (2001). Childhood predictors differentiate life-course persistent and adolescence-limited antisocial pathways among males and females. *Development and Psychopathology, 13*, 355–375.

Moshman, D. (1999). *Adolescent psychological development: Rationality, morality, and identity.* Mahwah, NJ: Erlbaum.

Nelson, K. (2000). Memory and belief in development. In D. L. Schacter & E. Scarry (Eds.), *Memory, brain, and belief.* Cambridge, MA: Harvard University Press.

Nelson, S. A. (1980). Factors influencing young children's use of motives and outcomes as moral criteria. *Child Development, 51*, 823–829.

Newton, P., Reddy, V., & Bull, R. (2000). Children's everyday deception and performance on false-belief tasks. *British Journal of Developmental Psychology, 18*, 297–317.

Nielsen, M., & Dissanayake, C. (2000). An investigation of pretend play, mental state terms and false belief understanding: In search of a metarepresentational link. *British Journal of Developmental Psychology, 18*, 609–624.

Niles, W. (1986). Effects of a moral development discussion group on delinquent and predelinquent boys. *Journal of Counseling Psychology, 33*, 45–51.

Nucci, L. P., & Nucci, M. S. (1982). Children's responses to moral and social conventional transgressions in free-play settings. *Child Development, 53*, 1337–1342.

Nucci, L. P., & Turiel, E. (1993). God's word, religious rules, and their relation to Christian and Jewish children's concepts of morality. *Child Development, 64*, 1475–1491.

O'Connor, T. G., Deater-Deckard, K., Fulker, D., Rutter, M., & Plomin, R. (1998). Genotype–environment correlations in late childhood and early adolescence: Antisocial behavioral problems and coercive parenting. *Developmental Psychology, 34*, 970–981.

Palmore, E. (1981). *Social patterns in normal aging: Findings from the Duke Longitudinal Study.* Durham, NC: Duke University Press.

Patterson, G. R., DeBaryshe, B. D., & Ramsey, E. (1989). A developmental perspective on antisocial behavior. *American Psychologist, 44*, 329–335.

Perner, J., Ruffman, T., & Leekam, S. R. (1994). Theory of mind is contagious: You catch it from your siblings. *Child Development, 65*, 1228–1238.

Perry, D. G., & Parke, R. D. (1975). Punishment and alternative response training as determinants of response inhibition in children. *Genetic Psychology Monographs, 91*, 257–279.

Peterson, C. C., Peterson, J. L., & Webb, J. (2000). Factors influencing the development of a theory of mind in blind children. *British Journal of Developmental Psychology, 18*, 431–447.

Peterson, C. C., & Siegal, M. (1999). Representing inner worlds: Theory of mind in autistic, deaf, and normal hearing children. *Psychological Science, 10,* 126–129.

Pettit, G. S., Polaha, J. A., & Mize, J. (2001). Perceptual and attributional processes in aggression and conduct problems. In J. Hill & B. Maughan (Eds.), *Conduct disorders in childhood and adolescence.* New York: Cambridge University Press.

Piaget, J. (1965). *The moral judgment of the child.* New York: Free Press. (Original work published 1932)

Pomerantz, E. M., & Saxon, J. L. (2001). Conceptions of ability as stable and self-evaluative processes: A longitudinal examination. *Child Development, 72,* 152–173.

Poulin, F., & Boivin, M. (2000). The role of proactive and reactive aggression in the formation and development of boys' friendships. *Developmental Psychology, 36,* 233–240.

Pratt, M. W., Diessner, R., Hunsberger, B., Pancer, S. M., & Savoy, K. (1991). Four pathways in the analysis of adult development and aging: Comparing analyses of reasoning about personal-life dilemmas. *Psychology and Aging, 4,* 666–675.

Pratt, M. W., Diessner, R., Pratt, A., Hunsberger, B., & Pancer, S. M. (1996). Moral and social reasoning and perspective taking in later life: A longitudinal study. *Psychology and Aging, 11,* 66–73.

Pratt, M. W., & Norris, J. E. (1999). Moral development in maturity. Life-span perspectives on the processes of successful aging. In T. M. Hess & F. Blanchard-Fields (Eds.), *Social cognition and aging.* San Diego, CA: Academic Press.

Pratt, M. W., Norris, J. E., Arnold, M. L., & Filyer, R. (1999). Generativity and moral development as predictors of value-socialization narratives for young persons across the adult life span: From lessons learned to stories shared. *Psychology and Aging, 14,* 414–426.

Repacholi, B. M., & Gopnik, A. (1997). Early reasoning about desires: Evidence from 14- and 18-month-olds. *Developmental Psychology, 33,* 12–21.

Rest, J., Narvaez, D., Bebeau, M. J., & Thoma, S. J. (1999). *Postconventional moral thinking. A neo-Kohlbergian approach.* Mahwah, NJ: Erlbaum.

Rowe, D. C., Almeida, D. M., & Jacobson, K. C. (1999). School context and genetic influences on aggression in adolescence. *Psychological Science, 10,* 277–280.

Ruble, D. N., & Dweck, C. S. (1995). Self-conceptions, person conceptions, and their development. In N. Eisenberg (Ed.), *Social development.* Thousand Oaks, CA: Sage.

Sacks, O. (1993, December 27). A neurologist's notebook: An anthropologist on Mars. *New Yorker,* pp. 106–125.

Scholl, B. J., & Leslie, A. M. (2001). Minds, modules, and meta-analysis. *Child Development, 72,* 696–701.

Selman, R. L. (1976). Social-cognitive understanding: A guide to educational and clinical experience. In T. Lickona (Ed.), *Moral development and behavior: Theory, research and social issues.* New York: Holt, Rinehart & Winston.

Selman, R. L. (1980). *The growth of interpersonal understanding.* New York: Academic Press.

Selman, R. L., Beardslee, W., Schultz, L. H., Krupa, M., & Podorefsky, D. (1986).

Assessing adolescent interpersonal negotiation strategies: Toward the integration of structural and functional models. *Developmental Psychology, 22,* 450–459.

Shweder, R. A., Mahapatra, M., & Miller, J. G. (1990). Culture and moral development. In J. W. Stigler, R. A. Shweder, & G. Herdt (Eds.), *Cultural psychology: Essays on comparative human development.* Cambridge, England: Cambridge University Press.

Simonoff, E. (2001). Genetic influences on conduct disorder. In J. Hill & B. Maughan (Eds.), *Conduct disorders in childhood and adolescence.* New York: Cambridge University Press.

Slaby, R. G., & Guerra, N. G. (1988). Cognitive mediators of aggression in adolescent offenders: 1. Assessment. *Developmental Psychology, 24,* 580–588.

Smetana, J. G. (1981). Preschool children's conceptions of moral and social rules. *Child Development, 52,* 1333–1336.

Smetana, J. G., Schlagman, N., & Adams, P. W. (1993). Preschool children's judgments about hypothetical and actual transgressions. *Child Development, 64,* 202–214.

Smithmyer, C. M., Hubbard, J. A., & Simons, R. F. (2000). Proactive and reactive aggression in delinquent adolescents: Relations to aggression outcome expectancies. *Journal of Clinical Child Psychology, 29,* 86–93.

Snarey, J. R. (1985). Cross-cultural universality of social-moral development: A critical review of Kohlbergian research. *Psychological Bulletin, 97,* 202–232.

Sodian, B. (1994). Early deception and the conceptual continuity claim. In C. Lewis & P. Mitchell (Eds.), *Children's early understanding of mind: Origins and development.* Hove, England: Erlbaum.

Stouthamer-Loeber, M. (1991). Young children's verbal misrepresentations of reality. In K. J. Rotenberg (Ed.), *Children's interpersonal trust.* New York: Springer-Verlag.

Strauss, V. (2001, May 8). No beating the problem of bullies: Stubborn, pervasive schoolyard behavior leaves long-term scars on perpetrators and victims. *Washington Post,* p. A11.

Symons, D. K., & Clark, S. E. (2000). A longitudinal study of mother–child relationships and theory of mind in the preschool period. *Social Development, 9,* 3–23.

Szarkowicz, D. L. (1999). Young children's false belief understanding during play. *Journal of Genetic Psychology, 160,* 243–254.

Tardif, T., & Wellman, H. M. (2000). Acquisition of mental state language in Mandarin- and Cantonese-speaking children. *Developmental Psychology, 36,* 25–43.

Taylor, M., & Carlson, S. M. (1997). The relation between individual differences in fantasy and theory of mind. *Child Development, 68,* 436–455.

Teichner, G., & Golden, C. J. (2000). The relationship of neuropsychological impairment to conduct disorder in adolescence: A conceptual review. *Aggression and Violent Behavior, 5,* 509– 528.

Tietjen, A. M., & Walker, L. J. (1985). Moral reasoning and leadership among men in a Papua New Guinea society. *Developmental Psychology, 21,* 982–992.

Tisak, M. S., & Tisak, J. (1990). Children's conceptions of parental authority, friendship, and sibling relations. *Merrill-Palmer Quarterly, 36,* 347–368.

Tomlinson-Keasey, C., & Keasey, C. B. (1974). The mediating role of cognitive development in moral judgment. *Child Development, 45,* 291–298.

Toner, I. J., Parke, R. D., & Yussen, S. R. (1978). The effect of observation of model behavior on the establishment and stability of resistance to deviation in children. *Journal of Genetic Psychology, 132,* 283–290.

Tremblay, R. E. (2000). The development of aggressive behaviour during childhood: What have we learned in the past century? *International Journal of Behavioral Development, 24,* 129–141.

Trevethan, S. D., & Walker, L. J. (1989). Hypothetical versus real-life moral reasoning among psychopathic and delinquent youth. *Development and Psychopathology, 1,* 91–103.

Turiel, E. (1978). The development of concepts of social structure: Social convention. In J. Glick & A. Clarke-Stewart (Eds.), *The development of social understanding.* New York: Gardner Press.

Turiel, E. (1983). *The development of social knowledge: Morality and convention.* Cambridge, England: Cambridge University Press.

Vinden, P. G., & Astington, J. W. (2000). Culture and understanding other minds. In S. Baron-Cohen, H. Tager-Flusberg, & D. J. Cohen (Eds.), *Understanding other minds: Perspectives from developmental cognitive neuroscience* (2nd ed.). Oxford: Oxford University Press.

Walker, J. S. (2000). Choosing biases, using power, and practicing resistance: Moral development in a world without certainty. *Human Development, 43,* 135–156.

Walker, L. J. (1980). Cognitive and perspective-taking prerequisites of moral development. *Child Development, 51,* 131–139.

Walker, L. J., Hennig, K. H., & Krettenauer, T. (2000). Parent and peer contexts for children's moral reasoning development. *Child Development, 71,* 1033–1048.

Walker, L. J., & Taylor, J. H. (1991). Family interactions and the development of moral reasoning. *Child Development, 62,* 264–283.

Walsh, C. (2000). The life and legacy of Lawrence Kohlberg. *Society, 37,* 36–41.

Wark, G. R., & Krebs, D. L. (1996). Gender and dilemma differences in real-life moral judgment. *Developmental Psychology, 32,* 220–230.

Watson, A. C., Nixon, C. L., Wilson, A., & Capage, L. (1999). Social interaction skills and theory of mind in young children. *Developmental Psychology, 35,* 386–391.

Wellman, H. M. (1990). *The child's theory of mind.* Cambridge, MA: MIT Press.

Wellman, H. M., & Bartsch, K. (1994). Before belief: Children's early psychological theory. In C. Lewis & P. Mitchell (Eds.), *Children's early understanding of mind: Origins and development.* Hove, England: Erlbaum.

Wellman, H. M., Cross, D., & Watson, J. (2001). Meta-analysis of theory-of-mind development: The truth about false-belief. *Child Development, 72,* 655–684.

Wellman, H. M., & Lagattuta, K. H. (2000). Developing understandings of mind. In S. Baron-Cohen, H. Tager-Flusberg, & D. J. Cohen (Eds.), *Understanding other minds: Perspectives from developmental cognitive neuroscience* (2nd ed.). Oxford: Oxford University Press.

Wellman, H. M., Phillips, A. T., & Rodriguez, T. (2000). Young children's understanding of perception, desire, and emotion. *Child Development, 71*, 895–912.

Wolff, M., Rutten, P., & Bayer, A. F., III. (1992). *Where we stand: Can America make it in the race for health, wealth, and happiness?* New York: Bantam Books.

Yeates, K. O., & Selman, R. L. (1989). Social competence in the schools: Toward an integrative developmental model for intervention. *Developmental Review, 9*, 64–100.

Young, G., & Dowling, W. (1987). Dimensions of religiosity in old age: Accounting for variation in types of participation. *Journal of Gerontology, 42*, 376–380.

Youngblade, L. M., & Dunn, J. (1995). Individual differences in young children's pretend play with mother and sibling: Links to relationships and understanding of other people's feelings and beliefs. *Child Development, 66*, 1472–1492.

Yuill, N. (1993). Understanding of personality and dispositions. In M. Bennett (Ed.), *The development of social cognition: The child as psychologist.* New York: Guilford.

Zahn-Waxler, C., Friedman, R. J., Cole, P. M., Mizuta, I., & Himura, N. (1996). Japanese and United States preschool children's responses to conflict and distress. *Child Development, 67*, 2462–2477.

Zahn-Waxler, C., Radke-Yarrow, M., & King, R. A. (1979). Child rearing and children's prosocial initiations toward victims of distress. *Child Development, 50*, 319–330.

Zahn-Waxler, C., Radke-Yarrow, M., Wagner, E., & Chapman, M. (1992). Development of concern for others. *Developmental Psychology, 28*, 126–136.

Chapter 14: Attachment and Social Relationships

Aboud, F. E., & Mendelson, M. J. (1996). Determinants of friendship selection and quality: Developmental perspectives. In W. M. Bukowski, A. F. Newcomb, & W. W. Hartup (Eds.), *The company they keep: Friendship in childhood and adolescence.* New York: Cambridge University Press.

Adams, R. G. (1985–1986). Emotional closeness and physical distance between friends: Implications for elderly women living in age-segregated and age-integrated settings. *International Journal of Aging and Human Development, 22*, 55–76.

Adams, R., & Laursen, B. (2001). The organization and dynamics of adolescent conflict with parents and friends. *Journal of Marriage and the Family, 63*, 97–110.

Ahnert, L., Rickert, H., & Lamb, M. E. (2000). Shared caregiving: Comparisons between home and child-care settings. *Developmental Psychology, 36*, 339–351.

Ainsworth, M. D. S. (1973). The development of infant–mother attachment. In B. M. Caldwell & H. N. Ricciuti (Eds.), *Review of child development research* (Vol. 3). Chicago: University of Chicago Press.

Ainsworth, M. D. S. (1979). Attachment as related to mother–infant interaction. In J. G. Rosenblatt, R. A. Hinde, C. Beer, & M. Busnel (Eds.), *Advances in the study of behavior* (Vol. 9). New York: Academic Press.

Ainsworth, M. D. S. (1989). Attachments beyond infancy. *American Psychologist, 44*, 709–716.

Ainsworth, M. D. S., Blehar, M., Waters, E., & Wall, S. (1978). *Patterns of attachment.* Hillsdale, NJ: Erlbaum.

Ajrouch, K. J., Antonucci, T. C., & Janevic, M. R. (2001). Social networks among blacks and whites: The interaction between race and age. *Journal of Gerontology: Social Sciences, 56*, S112–S118.

Anisfeld, E., Casper, V., Nozyce, M., & Cunningham, N. (1990). Does infant carrying promote attachment? An experimental study of the effects of increased physical contact on the development of attachment. *Child Development, 61*, 1617–1627.

Athey, I. (1984). Contributions of play to development. In T. D. Yawkey & A. D. Pelligrini (Eds.), *Child's play: Developmental and applied.* Hillsdale, NJ: Erlbaum.

Barnas, M. V., Pollina, L., & Cummings, E. M. (1991). Life-span attachment: Relations between attachment and socioemotional functioning in adult women. *Genetic, Social, and General Psychology Monographs, 117*, 175–202.

Barnes, K. E. (1971). Preschool play norms: A replication. *Developmental Psychology, 5*, 99–103.

Bartholomew, K., & Horowitz, L. M. (1991). Attachment styles among young adults: A test of a four-category model. *Journal of Personality and Social Psychology, 61*, 226–244.

Baydar, N., & Brooks-Gunn, J. (1991). Effects of maternal employment and child-care arrangements on preschoolers' cognitive and behavioral outcomes: Evidence from the children of the National Longitudinal Survey of Youth. *Developmental Psychology, 27*, 932–945.

Beckwith, L., Cohen, S. E., & Hamilton, C. E. (1999). Maternal sensitivity during infancy and subsequent life events relate to attachment representation at early adulthood. *Developmental Psychology, 35*, 693–700.

Begley, S. (1998, September 7). The parent trap. *Newsweek,* pp. 52–59.

Bell, K. L., & Calkins, S. D. (2000). Relationships as inputs and outputs of emotion regulation. *Psychological Inquiry, 11*, 160–163.

Bellanti, C. J., Bierman, K. L., & Conduct Problems Prevention Research Group (2000). Disentangling the impact of low cognitive ability and inattention on social behavior and peer relationships. *Journal of Clinical Child Psychology, 29*, 66–75.

Belsky, J., & Rovine, M. J. (1988). Nonmaternal care in the first year of life and the security of infant–parent attachment. *Child Development, 59*, 157–167.

Benenson, J. F., Apostoleris, N. H., & Parnass, J. (1997). Age and sex differences in dyadic and group interaction. *Developmental Psychology, 33*, 538–543.

Benoit, D., & Parker, K. C. (1994). Stability and transmission of attachment across three generations. *Child Development, 65*, 1444–1456.

Berman, W. H., & Sperling, M. B. (1991). Parental attachment and emotional distress in the transition to college. *Journal of Youth and Adolescence, 20*, 427–440.

Berndt, T. J. (1979). Developmental changes in conforming to peers and parents. *Developmental Psychology, 15*, 608–616.

Berndt, T. J., & Perry, T. B. (1990). Distinctive features and effects of early adolescent friendships. In R. Montemayor, G. R. Adams, & T. P. Gullotta (Eds.), *From childhood to adolescence: A transitional period.* Newbury Park, CA: Sage.

Biller, H. B. (1993). *Fathers and families: Paternal factors in child development.* Westport, CT: Auburn House.

Black, B., & Logan, A. (1995). Links between communication patterns in mother–child, father–child, and child–peer interactions and children's social status. *Child Development, 66*, 255–271.

Bowlby, J. (1960). Separation anxiety. *International Journal of Psychoanalysis, 41*, 89–113.

Bowlby, J. (1969). *Attachment and loss: Vol. 1. Attachment.* New York: Basic Books.

Bowlby, J. (1973). *Attachment and loss: Vol. 2. Separation.* New York: Basic Books.

Bowlby, J. (1980). *Attachment and loss: Vol. 3. Loss, sadness and depression.* New York: Basic Books.

Bowlby, J. (1988). *A secure base: Parent–child attachment and healthy human development.* New York: Basic Books.

Brendgen, M., Vitaro, F., & Bukowski, W. M. (2000). Deviant trends and early adolescents' emotional and behavioral adjustment. *Journal of Research on Adolescence, 10*, 173–189.

Bretherton, I. (1996). Internal working models of attachment relationships as related to resilient coping. In G. G. Noam & K. W. Fischer (Eds.), *Development and vulnerability in close relationships.* Mahwah, NJ: Erlbaum.

Bretherton, I., Stolberg, U., & Kreye, M. (1981). Engaging strangers in proximal interaction: Infants' social initiative. *Developmental Psychology, 17*, 746–755.

Bridges, L. J., & Grolnick, W. J. (1995). The development of emotional self-regulation in infancy and early childhood. In N. Eisenberg (Ed.), *Social development: Vol. 15. Review of personality and social psychology.* Thousand Oaks, CA: Sage.

Broberg, A. G., Wessels, H., Lamb, M. E., & Hwang, C. P. (1997). Effects of day care on the cognitive development of 8-year-olds: A longitudinal study. *Developmental Psychology, 33*, 62–69.

Brown, B. B. (1999). "You're going out with who?" Peer group influences on adolescent romantic relationships. In W. Furman, B. B. Brown, & C. Feiring (Eds.), *The development of romantic relationships in adolescence.* Cambridge, England: Cambridge University Press.

Brown, B. B., Feiring, C., & Furman, W. (1999). Missing the love boat: Why researchers have shied away from adolescent romance. In W. Furman, B. B. Brown, & C. Feiring (Eds.), *The development of romantic relationships in adolescence.* Cambridge, England: Cambridge University Press.

Brown, B. B., & Lohr, M. J. (1987). Peer-group affiliation and adolescent self-esteem: An integration of ego-identity and symbolic-interaction theories. *Journal of Personality and Social Psychology, 52*, 47–55.

Brown, B. B., Mory, M. S., & Kinney, D. (1994). Casting adolescent crowds in a relational perspective: Caricature, channel, and context. In R. Montemayor, G. R. Adams, & T. P. Gulotta (Eds.), *Personal relationships during adolescence.* Thousand Oaks, CA: Sage.

Brown, B. B., Mounts, N., Lamborn, S. D., & Steinberg, L. (1993). Parenting practices and peer group affiliation in adolescence. *Child Development, 64,* 467–482.

Brownell, C. A. (1986). Convergent developments: Cognitive-developmental correlates of growth in infant/toddler peer skills. *Child Development, 57,* 275–286.

Buhrmester, D. (1996). Need fulfillment, interpersonal competence, and the developmental contexts of early adolescent friendship. In W. M. Bukowski, A. F. Newcomb, & W. W. Hartup (Eds.), *The company they keep: Friendship in childhood and adolescence.* Cambridge, England: Cambridge University Press.

Buhrmester, D., & Furman, W. (1986). The changing functions of friends in childhood: A neo-Sullivanian perspective. In V. J. Derlega & B. A. Winstead (Eds.), *Friendship and social interaction.* New York: Springer-Verlag.

Bukowski, W. M., Sippola, L. K., & Newcomb, A. F. (2000). Variations in patterns of attraction to same and other-sex peers during early adolescence. *Developmental Psychology, 36,* 147–154.

Burchinal, M. R., Roberts, J. E., Riggins, R., Zeisel, S. A., Neebe, E., & Bryant, D. (2000). Relating quality of center-based child care to early cognitive and language development longitudinally. *Child Development, 71,* 339–357.

Campbell, F. A., & Ramey, C. T. (1994). Effects of early intervention on intellectual and academic achievement: A follow-up study of children from low-income families. *Child Development, 65,* 684–698.

Carlson, V., Cicchetti, D., Barnett, D., & Braunwald, K. (1989). Disorganized/disoriented attachment relationships in maltreated infants. *Developmental Psychology, 25,* 525–531.

Carstensen, L. L. (1992). Social and emotional patterns in adulthood: Support for socioemotional selectivity theory. *Psychology and Aging, 7,* 331–338.

Carstensen, L. L., Pasupathi, M., Mayr, U., & Nesselroade, J. R. (2000). Emotional experience in everyday life across the adult life span. *Journal of Personality and Social Psychology, 79,* 644–655.

Chen, X., Rubin, K. H., & Sun, Y. (1992). Social reputation in Chinese and Canadian children: A cross-cultural study. *Child Development, 63,* 1336–1343.

Christopher, J. S., Nangle, D. W., & Hansen, D. J. (1993). Social-skills interventions with adolescents: Current issues and procedures. *Behavior Modification, 17,* 314–338.

Cillessen, A. H., & Bukowski, W. M. (Eds.). (2000). *New direction for child and adolescent development: No. 88. Recent advances in the measurement of acceptance and rejection in the peer system.* San Francisco: Jossey-Bass.

Cillessen, A. H., van IJzendoorn, H. W., van Lieshout, C. F., & Hartup, W. W. (1992). Heterogeneity among peer-rejected boys: Subtypes and stabilities. *Child Development, 63,* 893–905.

Clark, K. E., & Ladd, G. W. (2000). Connectedness and autonomy support in parent–child relationships: Links to children's socioemotional orientation and peer relationships. *Developmental Psychology, 36,* 485–498.

Clarke-Stewart, A. (1993). *Daycare* (rev. ed.). Cambridge, MA: Harvard University Press.

Clarke-Stewart, K. A., Goossens, F. A., & Allhusen, V. D. (2001). Measuring infant–mother attachment: Is the Strange Situation enough? *Social Development, 10,* 143–169.

Coie, J. D., Dodge, K. A., & Coppotelli, H. (1982). Dimensions and types of social status: A cross-age perspective. *Developmental Psychology, 18,* 557–570.

Coie, J. D., Dodge, K. A., & Kupersmidt, J. B. (1990). Peer group behavior and social status. In S. R. Asher & J. D. Coie (Eds.), *Peer rejection in childhood.* Cambridge, England: Cambridge University Press.

Coie, J. D., Lochman, J. E., Terry, R., & Hyman, C. (1992). Predicting early adolescent disorder from childhood aggression and peer rejection. *Journal of Consulting and Clinical Psychology, 60,* 783–792.

Cole, P. M., Michel, M. K., & Teti, L. O. (1994). The development of emotion regulation and dysregulation: A clinical perspective. In N. Fox (Ed.), *The development of emotion regulation: Biological and behavioral considerations. Monographs of the Society for Research in Child Development, 59*(Nos. 2–3, Serial No. 240).

Colin, V. (1996). *Human attachment.* New York: McGraw-Hill.

Collins, W. A., Maccoby, E. E., Steinberg, L., Hetherington, E. M., & Bornstein, M. H. (2000). Contemporary research on parenting: The case for nature and nurture. *American Psychologist, 55,* 218–232.

Conger, R. D., Cui, M., Bryant, C. M., & Elder, G. H., Jr. (2000). Competence in early adult romantic relationships: A developmental perspective on family influences. *Journal of Personality and Social Psychology, 79,* 224–237.

Connidis, I. A., & Davies, L. (1992). Confidants and companions: Choices in later life. *Journal of Gerontology: Social Sciences, 47,* S115–S122.

Connolly, J. A., & Doyle, A. B. (1984). Relation of social fantasy play to social competence in preschoolers. *Developmental Psychology, 20,* 797–806.

Connolly, J. A., Furman, W., & Konarski, R. (2000). The role of peers in the emergence of heterosexual romantic relationships in adolescence. *Child Development, 71,* 1395–1408.

Cook, W. L. (2000). Understanding attachment security in family context. *Journal of Personality and Social Psychology, 78,* 285–294.

Cowan, P. A. (1997). Beyond meta-analysis: A plea for a family systems view of attachment. *Child Development, 68,* 601–603.

Cox, S. M., Hopkins, J., & Hans, S. L. (2000). Attachment in preterm infants and their mothers: Neonatal risk status and maternal representations. *Infant Mental Health Journal, 21,* 464–480.

Creasey, G., Kershaw, K., & Boston, A. (1999). Conflict management with friends and romantic partners: The role of attachment and negative mood regulation expectancies. *Journal of Youth and Adolescence, 28,* 523–543.

Crockenberg, S., & Litman, C. (1991). Effects of maternal employment on maternal and two-year-old child behavior. *Child Development, 61,* 930–953.

Crowell, J. A., Fraley, R. C., & Shaver, P. R. (1999). Measurement of individual differences in adolescent and adult attachment. In J. Cassidy & P. R. Shaver (Eds.), *Handbook of attachment: Theory, research, and clinical applications.* New York: Guilford.

Davies, P. T., & Windle, M. (2000). Middle adolescents' dating pathways and psychosocial adjustment. *Merrill-Palmer Quarterly, 46,* 90–118.

Dawson, G., & Ashman, S. B. (2000). On the origins of a vulnerability to depression: The influence of the early social environment on the development of psychobiological systems related to risk for affective disorder. In C. A. Nelson (Ed.), *Minnesota Symposium on Child Psychology: Vol. 31. The effects of early adversity on neurobehavioral development.* Mahwah, NJ: Erlbaum.

Deater-Deckard, K., & O'Connor, T. G. (2000). Parent–child mutuality in early childhood: Two behavioral genetic studies. *Developmental Psychology, 36,* 561–570.

de Jong-Gierveld, J. (1986). Loneliness and the degree of intimacy in interpersonal relationships. In R. Gilmour & S. Duck (Eds.), *The emerging field of personal relationships.* Hillsdale, NJ: Erlbaum.

DeRosier, M. E., Kupersmidt, J. B., & Patterson, C. J. (1994). Children's academic and behavioral adjustment as a function of the chronicity and proximity of peer rejection. *Child Development, 65,* 1799–1813.

De Wolff, M. S., & van Ijzendoorn, M. H. (1997). Sensitivity and attachment: A meta-analysis on parental antecedents of infant attachment. *Child Development, 68,* 571–591.

Dishion, T. J., Patterson, G. R., Stoolmiller, M., & Skinner, M. L. (1991). Family, school, and behavioral antecedents to early adolescent involvement with antisocial peers. *Developmental Psychology, 27,* 172–180.

Dodge, K. A., Coie, J. D., Pettit, G. S., & Price, J. M. (1990). Peer status and aggression in boys' groups: Developmental and contextual analysis. *Child Development, 61,* 1289–1309.

Dunn, J., & Hughes, C. (2001). "I got some swords and you're dead!": Violent fantasy, antisocial behavior, friendship, and moral sensibility in young children. *Child Development, 72,* 491–505.

Dunphy, D. C. (1963). The social structure of urban adolescent peer groups. *Sociometry, 26,* 230–246.

Eckerman, C. O., & Stein, M. R. (1990). How imitation begets imitation and toddlers' generation of games. *Developmental Psychology, 26,* 370–378.

Elicker, J., Englund, M., & Sroufe, L. A. (1992). Predicting peer competence and peer relationships in childhood from early parent–child relationships. In R. D. Parke & G. W. Ladd (Eds.), *Family–peer relationships: Modes of linkage.* Hillsdale, NJ: Erlbaum.

Ellis, S., Rogoff, B., & Cromer, C. C. (1981). Age segregation in children's social interactions. *Developmental Psychology, 17,* 399–407.

Fagot, B. I. (1997). Attachment, parenting, and peer interactions of toddler children. *Developmental Psychology, 33,* 489–499.

Fallon, B. J., & Bowles, T. V. (1997). The effect of family structure and family functioning on adolescents' perceptions of intimate time spent with parents, siblings, and peers. *Journal of Youth and Adolescence, 26,* 25–43.

Farver, J. A. M., Kim, Y. K., & Lee-Shin, Y. (2000). Within cultural differences: Examining individual differences in Korean American and European American preschoolers' social pretend play. *Journal of Cross-Cultural Psychology, 31,* 583–602.

Farver, J. A. M., & Shin, Y. L. (1997). Social pretend play in Korean and Anglo American preschoolers. *Child Development, 68,* 544–556.

Feeney, J. A., & Noller, P. (1996). *Adult attachment.* Thousand Oaks, CA: Sage.

Feinman, S. (1992). *Social referencing and the social construction of reality in infancy.* New York: Plenum.

Feiring, C. (1996). Concepts of romance in 15-year-old adolescents. *Journal of Research on Adolescence, 6,* 181–200.

Feiring, C. (1999). Other-sex friendship networks and the development of romantic relationships in adolescence. *Journal of Youth and Adolescence, 28,* 495–512.

Felton, B. J., & Berry, C. A. (1992). Do the sources of the urban elderly's social support determine its psychological consequences? *Psychology and Aging, 7,* 89–97.

Field, T. M. (1987). Affective and interactive disturbances in infants. In J. D. Osofsky (Ed.), *Handbook of infant development* (2nd ed.). New York: Wiley.

Finzi, R., Cohen, O., Sapir, Y., & Weizman, A. (2000). Attachment styles in maltreated children: A comparative study. *Child Psychiatry and Human Development, 31,* 113–128.

Fischer, C. S., & Phillips, S. L. (1982). Who is alone? Social characteristics of people with small networks. In L. A. Peplau & D. Perlman (Eds.), *Loneliness: A sourcebook of current theory, research and therapy.* New York: Wiley-Interscience.

Fischer, J. L., Sollie, D. L., Sorell, G. T., & Green, S. K. (1989). Marital status and career stage influences on social networks of young adults. *Journal of Marriage and the Family, 51,* 521–534.

Fisher, E. P. (1992). The impact of play on development: A meta-analysis. *Play and Culture, 5,* 159–181.

Fisher, L., Ames, E. W., Chisholm, K., & Savoie, L. (1997). Problems reported by parents of Romanian orphans adopted to British Columbia. *International Journal of Behavioral Development, 20,* 67–82.

Freud, S. (1930). *Three contributions to the theory of sex.* New York: Nervous and Mental Disease Publishing Company. (Original work published 1905)

Fuligni, A. J., & Eccles, J. S. (1993). Perceived parent–child relationships and early adolescents' orientation toward peers. *Developmental Psychology, 29,* 622–632.

Fuligni, A. J., Eccles, J. S., Barber, B. L., & Clenerts, P. (2001). Early adolescent peer orientation and adjustment during high school. *Developmental Psychology, 37,* 28–36.

Fuller, B., Holloway, S. D., & Liang, X. (1996). Family selection of child-care centers: The influence of household support, ethnicity, and parental practices. *Child Development, 67,* 3320–3337.

Furman, W., & Buhrmester, D. (1992). Age and sex differences in perceptions of networks of personal relationships. *Child Development, 63,* 103–115.

Furman, W., & Wehner, E. A. (1994). Romantic views: Toward a theory of adolescent romantic relationships. In R. Montemayor, G. R. Adams, & T. P. Gullotta (Eds.), *Personal relationships during adolescence: Vol. 6. Advances in adolescent development.* Thousand Oaks, CA: Sage.

Gandelman, R. (1992). *Psychobiology of behavioral development.* New York: Oxford University Press.

Gardner, M. (2001, May 30). Media's eye on moms. *Christian Science Monitor,* p. 12.

Garvey, C. (1990). *Play* (enlarged ed.). Cambridge, MA: Harvard University Press.

Gauvain, M., & Rogoff, B. (1989). Collaborative problem solving and children's planning skills. *Developmental Psychology, 25,* 139–151.

Gauze, C., Bukowski, W. M., Aquanassee, J., & Sippola, L. K. (1996). Interactions between family environment and friendship and associations with self-perceived well-being during early adolescence. *Child Development, 67,* 2301–2316.

George, T. P., & Hartmann, D. P. (1996). Friendship networks of unpopular, average, and popular children. *Child Development, 67,* 2301–2316.

Gest, S. D., Graham-Bermann, S. A., & Hartup, W. W. (2001). Peer experience: Common and unique features of number of friendships, social network centrality, and sociometric status. *Social Development, 10,* 23–40.

Goencue, A., Mistry, J., & Mosier, C. (2000). Cultural variations in the play of toddlers. *International Journal of Behavior Development, 24,* 321–329.

Goldberg, S., Perrotta, M., Minde, K., & Corter, C. (1986). Maternal behavior and attachment in low-birth-weight twins and singletons. *Child Development, 57,* 34–46.

Goldfarb, W. (1943). The effects of early institutional care on adolescent personality. *Journal of Experimental Education, 12,* 107–129.

Goldfarb, W. (1947). Variations in adolescent adjustment in institutionally reared children. *Journal of Orthopsychiatry, 17,* 449–457.

Gordon, D. E. (1993). The inhibition of pretend play and its implications for development. *Human Development, 36,* 215–234.

Gray, M. R., & Steinberg, L. (1999). Adolescent romance and the parent–child relationship. In W. Furman, B. B. Brown, & C. Feiring (Eds.), *The development of romantic relationships in adolescence.* Cambridge, England: Cambridge University Press.

Grolnick, W. S., Bridges, L. J., & Connell, J. P. (1996). Emotion regulation in two-year-olds: Strategies and emotional expression in four contexts. *Child Development, 67,* 928–941.

Grolnick, W. S., McMenamy J. M., & Kurowski, C. O. (1999). Emotional self-regulation in infancy and toddlerhood. In L. Balter & C. S. Tamis-LeMonda (Eds.), *Child psychology: A handbook of contemporary issues.* Philadelphia: Psychology Press/Taylor & Francis.

Grossmann, K., Grossmann, K. E., Spangler, S., Suess, G., & Unzner, L. (1985). Maternal sensitivity and newborn responses as related to quality of attachment in northern Germany. In I. Bretherton & E. Waters (Eds.), *Growing points of attachment theory. Monographs of the Society for Research in Child Development,* 50(1–2, Serial No. 209).

Gunnar, M. R. (1998). Quality of early care and buffering of neuroendocrine stress reactions: Potential effects on the developing human brain. *Preventive Medicine, 27,* 208–211.

Gunnar, M. R. (2000). Early adversity and the development of stress reactivity and regulation. In C. A. Nelson (Ed.), *Minnesota Symposium on Child Psychology: Vol. 31. The effects of early adversity on neurobehavioral development.* Mahwah, NJ: Erlbaum.

Gunnar, M. R., Bruce, J., & Grotevant, H. D. (2000). International adoption of institutionally reared children: Research and policy. *Development and Psychopathology, 12,* 677– 693.

Haight, W. L., Wong, X., Fung, H. H., Williams, K., & Mintz, J. (1999). Universal, developmental, and variable aspects of young children's play: A cross-cultural comparison of pretending at home. *Child Development, 70,* 1477–1488.

Hamm, J. V. (2000). Do birds of a feather flock together? The variable bases for African American, Asian American, and European American adolescents' selection of similar friends. *Developmental Psychology, 36,* 209–219.

Harlow, H. F., & Zimmerman, R. R. (1959). Affectional responses in the infant monkey. *Science, 130,* 421–432.

Harris, J. R. (1995). Where is the child's environment? A group socialization theory of development. *Psychological Review, 102,* 458–489.

Harris, J. R. (1998). *The nurture assumption: Why children turn out the way they do.* New York: Free Press.

Harris, J. R. (2000). Socialization, personality development, and the child's environments: Comment on Vandell (2000). *Developmental Psychology, 36,* 711–723.

Harris, P. L. (2000). Understanding emotion. In M. Lewis and J. M. Haviland-Jones (Eds.), *Handbook of emotions* (2nd ed.). New York: Guilford.

Harris, P. L., & Kavanaugh, R. D. (1993). Young children's understanding of pretense. *Monographs of the Society for Research in Child Development,* 58(1, Serial No. 181).

Harrist, A. W., Zaia, A. F., Bates, J. E., Dodge, K. A., & Pettit, G. S. (1997). Subtypes of social withdrawal in early childhood: Sociometric status and social-cognitive differences across four years. *Child Development, 68,* 278–294.

Hartup, W. W. (1996). The company they keep: Friendships and their developmental significance. *Child Development, 67,* 1–13.

Hartup, W. W., & Stevens, N. (1997). Friendships and adaptation in the life course. *Psychological Bulletin, 121,* 355–370.

Hatfield, E., & Rapson, R. L. (2000). Love and attachment processes. In M. Lewis and J. M. Haviland-Jones (Eds.), *Handbook of emotions* (2nd ed.). New York: Guilford.

Hay, D. F., Nash, A., & Pedersen, J. (1983). Interaction between six-month-old peers. *Child Development, 54,* 557–562.

Hazan, C., & Shaver, P. (1987). Romantic love conceptualized as an attachment process. *Journal of Personality and Social Psychology, 52,* 511–524.

Hazan, C., & Shaver, P. (1990). Love and work: An attachment-theoretical perspective. *Journal of Personality and Social Psychology, 59,* 270–280.

Hersch, P. (1998). *A tribe apart: A journey into the heart of American adolescence.* New York: Ballantine.

Hesse, E., & Main, M. (2000). Disorganized infant, child, and adult attachment: Collapse in behavioral and attentional strategies. *Journal of the American Psychoanalytic Association, 48,* 1097–1127.

Hetherington, E. M., Cox, M., & Cox, R. (1979). Play and social interaction in children following divorce. *Journal of Social Issues, 35,* 26–49.

Himes, C. L., & Reidy, E. B. (2000). The role of friends in caregiving. *Research on Aging, 22,* 315–336.

Hipwell, A. E., Goossens, F. A., Melhuish, E. C., & Kumar, R. (2000). Severe maternal psychopathology and infant–mother attachment. *Development and Psychopathology, 12,* 157–175.

Hodges, J., & Tizard, B. (1989). IQ and behavioural adjustment of ex-institutional adolescents. *Journal of Child Psychology and Psychiatry, 30,* 53–75.

Holden, C. (1996, November 15). Small refugees suffer the effects of early neglect. *Science, 274,* 1076–1077.

Howes, C. (1996). The earliest friendships. In W. M. Bukowski, A. F. Newcomb, & W. W. Hartup (Eds.), *The company they keep: Friendships in childhood and adolescence.* Cambridge, England: Cambridge University Press.

Howes, C., & Matheson, C. C. (1992). Sequences in the development of competent play with peers: Social and social pretend play. *Developmental Psychology, 28,* 961–974.

Howes, C., Phillips, D. A., & Whitebrook, M. (1992). Thresholds of quality: Implications for the social development of children in center-based child care. *Child Development, 63,* 449–460.

Howes, P., & Markman, H. J. (1989). Marital quality and child functioning: A longitudinal investigation. *Child Development, 60,* 1044–1051.

Ingrassia, M. (2000, April 12). Kids can adjust to a new home. *Newsday,* p. A41.

Ingrassia, M., & Springen, K. (1994, March 21). She's not Baby Jessica anymore. *Newsweek,* pp. 60–66.

Isabella, R. A. (1993). Origins of attachment: Maternal interactive behavior across the first year. *Child Development, 64,* 605–621.

Isabella, R. A., & Belsky, J. (1991). Interactional synchrony and the origins of infant–mother attachment: A replication study. *Child Development, 62,* 373–384.

Izard, C. E. (1982). *Measuring emotions in infants and children.* New York: Cambridge University Press.

Izard, C. E., & Ackerman, B. P. (2000). Motivational, organizational, and regulatory functions of discrete emotions. In M. Lewis and J. M. Haviland-Jones (Eds.), *Handbook of emotions* (2nd ed.). New York: Guilford.

Jacobsen, T., & Hofmann, V. (1997). Children's attachment representations: Longitudinal relations to school behavior and academic competency in middle childhood and adolescence. *Developmental Psychology, 33,* 703–710.

Jaffe, J., Beebe, B., Feldstein, S., Crown, C. L., & Jasnow, M. D. (2001). Rhythms of dialogue in infancy: Coordinated timing in development. *Monographs of the Society for Research in Child Development, 66*(2, Serial No. 265).

Jankowiak, W. R., & Fischer, E. F. (1992). A cross-cultural perspective on romantic love. *Ethnology, 31,* 149–155.

Johnson, C. L., & Troll, L. E. (1994). Constraints and facilitators to friendships in late late life. *Gerontologist, 34,* 79–87.

Johnson, W., Emde, R. N., Pannabecker, B., Stenberg, C., & Davis, M. (1982). Maternal perception of infant emotion from birth through 18 months. *Infant Behavior and Development, 5,* 313–322.

Jones, W. H., Hobbs, S. A., & Hockenbury, D. (1982). Loneliness and social skill deficits. *Journal of Personality and Social Psychology, 42,* 682–689.

Juffer, F., & Rosenboom, L. G. (1997). Infant–mother attachment of internationally adopted children in the Netherlands. *International Journal of Behavioral Development, 20,* 93–107.

Kagan, J. (1972). Do infants think? *Scientific American, 226,* 74–82.

Kahn, R. L., & Antonucci, T. C. (1980). Convoys over the life course: Attachment, roles, and social support. In P. B. Baltes & O. G. Brim, Jr. (Eds.), *Life-span development and behavior* (Vol. 3). New York: Academic Press.

Keller, H., & Scholmerich, A. (1987). Infant vocalizations and parental reactions during the first four months of life. *Developmental Psychology, 23,* 62–67.

Kendig, H. L., Coles, R., Pittelkow, Y., & Wilson, S. (1988). Confidants and family structure in old age. *Journal of Gerontology: Social Sciences, 43,* S31–S40.

Kenny, M. E. (1987). The extent and function of parental attachment among first-year college students. *Journal of Youth and Adolescence, 16,* 17–29.

Kenny, M. E., & Rice, K. G. (1995). Attachment to parents and adjustment in late adolescent college students: Current status, applications, and future considerations. *Counseling Psychologist, 23,* 433–456.

Kerns, K. A. (1996). Individual differences in friendship quality: Links to child–mother attachment. In W. M. Bukowski, A. F. Newcomb, & W. W. Hartup (Eds.), *The company they keep: Friendship in childhood and adolescence.* Cambridge, England: Cambridge University Press.

Kerns, K. A., Klepac, L., & Cole, A. K. (1996). Peer relationships and preadolescents' perceptions of security in the child–mother relationship. *Developmental Psychology, 32,* 457–466.

Kessen, W. (1975). *Childhood in China.* New Haven, CT: Yale University Press.

Klaus, H. M., & Kennell, J. H. (1976). *Maternal–infant bonding.* St. Louis: C. V. Mosby.

Kobak, R. R., Cole, H. E., Ferenz-Gilles, R., Fleming, W. S., & Gamble, W. (1993). Attachment and emotional regulation during mother–teen problem solving: A control theory analysis. *Child Development, 64,* 231–245.

Kochanska, G. (2001). Emotional development in children with different attachment histories: The first three years. *Child Development, 72,* 474–490.

Kohlberg, L. (1969). Stage and sequence: The cognitive-developmental approach to socialization. In D. A. Goslin (Ed.), *Handbook of socialization theory and research.* Chicago: Rand McNally.

Kopp, C. B. (1989). Regulation of distress and negative emotions: A developmental view. *Developmental Psychology, 25,* 343–354.

Krause, N. (1995). Negative interaction and satisfaction with social support among older adults. *Journal of Gerontology: Psychological Sciences, 50B,* P59–P73.

Krause, N., & Shaw, B. A. (2000). Giving social support to others, socioeconomic status, and changes in self-esteem in late life. *Journal of Gerontology: Social Sciences, 55,* S323–S333.

Ladd, G. W. (1999). Peer relationships and social competence during early and middle childhood. *Annual Review of Psychology, 50,* 333–359.

Laible, D. J., Carlo G., & Raffaelli, M. (2000). The differential relations of parent and peer attachment to adolescent adjustment. *Journal of Youth and Adolescence, 29,* 45–183.

Lamb, M. E., Sternberg, K. J., & Prodromidis, M. (1992). Nonmaternal care and the security of infant–mother attachment: A reanalysis of the data. *Infant Behavior and Development, 15,* 71–83.

Landreth, G., & Homeyer, L. (1998). Play as the language of children's feelings. In D. P. Fromberg & D. Bergen (Eds.), *Play from birth to twelve and beyond.* New York: Garland.

Lang, F. R., & Carstensen, L. L. (1994). Close emotional relationships in late life: Further support for proactive aging in the social domain. *Psychology and Aging, 9,* 315–324.

Lansford, J. E., Sherman, A. M., & Antonucci, T. C. (1998). Satisfaction with social networks: An examination of socioemotional selectivity theory across cohorts. *Psychology and Aging, 13,* 544–552.

Lapsley, D. K., Rice, K. G., & FitzGerald, D. P. (1990). Adolescent attachment, identity, and adjustment to college: Implications for the continuity of adaptation hypothesis. *Journal of Counseling and Development, 68,* 561–565.

Lempers, J. D., & Clark-Lempers, D. S. (1992). Young, middle and late adolescents' comparisons of the functional importance of five significant relationships. *Journal of Youth and Adolescence, 21,* 53–96.

Lester, B. M., Kotelchuck, M., Spelke, E., Sellers, M. J., & Klein, R. E. (1974). Separation protest in Guatemalan infants: Cross-cultural and cognitive findings. *Developmental Psychology, 10,* 79–85.

Levitt, M. J. (1991). Attachment and close relationships: A life-span perspective. In J. L. Gewirtz & W. M. Kurtines (Eds.), *Intersections with attachment.* Hillsdale, NJ: Erlbaum.

Levitt, M. J., Guacci-Franco, N., & Levitt, J. L. (1993). Convoys of social support in childhood and early adolescence: Structure and function. *Developmental Psychology, 29,* 811–818.

Levitt, M. J., Weber, R. A., & Guacci, N. (1993). Convoys of social support: An intergenerational analysis. *Psychology and Aging, 8,* 323–326.

Lewis, M. (2000). The emergence of human emotions. In M. Lewis and J. M. Haviland-Jones (Eds.), *Handbook of emotions* (2nd ed.). New York: Guilford.

Lewis, M., & Rosenblum, M. A. (1975). *Friendship and peer relations.* New York: Wiley.

Lindsey, E. W., & Mize, J. (2000). Parent–child physical and pretense play: Links to children's social competence. *Merrill-Palmer Quarterly, 46,* 565–591.

Lorenz, K. Z. (1937). The companion in the bird's world. *Auk, 54,* 245–273.

MacDonald, C. D., & Cohen, R. (1995). Children's awareness of which peers like them and which peers dislike them. *Social Development, 4,* 182–193.

Maestripieri, D. (2001). Is there mother–infant bonding in primates? *Developmental Review, 21,* 93–120.

Magai, C., Cohen, C., Milburn, N., Thorpe, B., McPherson, R., & Peralta, D. (2001). Attachment styles in older European American and African American adults. *Journal of Gerontology: Social Sciences, 56,* S28–S35.

Main, M., & Solomon, J. (1990). Procedures for identifying infants as disorganized/disoriented during the Ainsworth Strange Situation. In M. T. Greenberg, D. Cicchetti, & E. M. Cummings (Eds.), *Attachment in the preschool years: Theory, research, and intervention.* Chicago: University of Chicago Press.

Main, M., & Weston, D. R. (1981). The quality of the toddler's relationship to mother and to father: Related to conflict and the readiness to establish new relationships. *Child Development, 52,* 932–940.

Malatesta, C. Z., Culver, C., Tesman, J. R., & Shepard, B. (1989). The development of emotion expression during the first two years of life. *Monographs of the Society for Research in Child Development, 54*(1–2, Serial No. 219).

Malatesta, C. Z., Grigoryev, P., Lamb, C., Albin, M., & Culver, C. (1986). Emotional socialization and expressive development in preterm and full-term infants. *Child Development, 57,* 316–330.

Malik, N. M., & Furman, W. (1993). Practitioner review: Problems in children's peer relations: What can the clinician do? *Journal of Child Psychology and Psychiatry, 34,* 1303–1326.

Mangelsdorf, S. C. (1992). Developmental changes in infant–stranger interaction. *Infant Behavior and Development, 15,* 191–208.

Mangelsdorf, S. C., Gunnar, M., Kestenbaum, R., Lang, S., & Andreas, D. (1990). Infant proneness-to-distress temperament, maternal personality, and mother–infant attachment: Associations and goodness of fit. *Child Development, 61,* 820–831.

Mangelsdorf, S. C., Shapiro, J. R., & Marzolf, D. (1995). Developmental and temperamental differences in emotion regulation in infancy. *Child Development, 66,* 1817–1828.

Mayseless, O., Danieli, R., & Sharabany, R. (1996). Adults' attachment patterns: Coping with separations. *Journal of Youth and Adolescence, 25,* 667–690.

Mendes de Leon, C. F., Glass, T. A., Beckett, L. A., Seeman, T. E., Evans, D. A., & Berkman, L. F. (1999). Social networks and disability transitions across eight intervals of yearly data in the New Haven EPESE. *Journal of Gerontology: Social Sciences, 54,* S162–S172.

Mickelson, K. D., Kessler, R. C., & Shaver P. R. (1997). Adult attachment in a nationally representative sample. *Journal of Personality and Social Psychology, 73,* 1092–1106.

Mize, J., & Pettit, G. S. (1997). Mothers' social coaching, mother–child relationship style, and children's peer competence: Is the

medium the message? *Child Development, 68,* 312–332.

Morgan, G. A., & Ricciuti, H. N. (1969). Infants' responses to strangers during the first year. In B. M. Foss (Ed.), *Determinants of infant behavior* (Vol. 4). London: Methuen.

Mounts, N. S. (2001). Young adolescents' perceptions of parental management of peer relationships. *Journal of Early Adolescence, 21,* 92–122.

Mueller, E., & Lucas, T. (1975). A developmental analysis of peer interactions among toddlers. In M. Lewis & L. Rosenblum (Eds.), *Friendship and peer relations.* New York: Wiley.

Mueller, E., & Vandell, D. (1979). Infant–infant interaction. In J. Osofsky (Ed.), *Handbook of infant development.* New York: Wiley.

Murray, L., Fiori-Cowley, A., Hooper, R., & Cooper, P. (1996). The impact of postnatal depression and associated adversity on early mother–infant interactions and later infant outcome. *Child Development, 67,* 2512–2526.

Nation in brief. (2001, February 4). *Atlanta Constitution,* p. 6A.

Newcomb, A. F., & Bagwell, C. L. (1995). Children's friendship relations: A meta-analytic review. *Psychological Bulletin, 117,* 306–347.

NICHD Early Child Care Research Network. (1997). The effects of infant child care on infant–mother attachment security: Results of the NICHD Study of Early Child Care. *Child Development, 68,* 860–879.

Nicolich, L. M. (1977). Beyond sensorimotor intelligence: Assessment of symbolic maturity through analysis of pretend play. *Merrill-Palmer Quarterly, 23,* 89–99.

O'Connor, B. P. (1995). Family and friend relationships among older and younger adults: Interaction motivation, mood, and quality. *International Journal of Aging and Human Development, 40,* 9–29.

O'Connor, T. G., & Rutter, M. (2000). Attachment disorder behavior following early severe deprivation: Extension and longitudinal follow-up. *Journal of the American Academy of Child and Adolescent Psychiatry, 39,* 703–712.

Oden, S., & Asher, S. R. (1977). Coaching children in social skills for friendship making. *Child Development, 48,* 495–506.

Oppenheim, D., Koren-Karie, M., & Sagi, A. (2001). Mothers' empathic understanding of their preschoolers' internal experience: Relations with early attachment. *International Journal of Behavior Development, 25,* 16–26.

Oppenheim, D., Sagi, A., & Lamb, M. E. (1988). Infant–adult attachments on the kibbutz and their relation to socioemotional development 4 years later. *Developmental Psychology, 24,* 427–433.

Parker, J. G., & Asher, S. R. (1993). Friendship and friendship quality in middle childhood: Links with peer group acceptance and feelings of loneliness and social dissatisfaction. *Developmental Psychology, 29,* 611–621.

Parkhurst, J. T., & Asher, S. R. (1992). Peer rejection in middle school: Subgroup differences in behavior, loneliness, and interpersonal concerns. *Developmental Psychology, 28,* 231–241.

Parten, M. B. (1932). Social participation among preschool children. *Journal of Abnormal and Social Psychology, 27,* 243–269.

Passman, R. H. (1977). Providing attachment objects to facilitate learning and reduce distress: Effects of mothers and security blankets. *Developmental Psychology, 13,* 25–28.

Pettit, G. S., Clawson, M. A., Dodge, K. A., & Bates, J. E. (1996). Stability and change in peer-rejected status: The role of child behavior, parenting, and family ecology. *Merrill-Palmer Quarterly, 42,* 267–294.

Piaget, J. (1965). *The moral judgment of the child.* New York: Free Press. (Original work published 1932)

Pilisuk, M., & Minkler, M. (1980). Supportive networks: Life ties for the elderly. *Journal of Social Issues, 36*(2), 95–116.

Pinquart, M., & Sorensen, S. (2000). Influences of socioeconomic status, social network, and competence on subjective well-being in later life: A meta-analysis. *Psychology and Aging, 15,* 187–224.

Poehlmann, J., & Fiese, B. H. (2001). The interaction of maternal and infant vulnerabilities on developing attachment relationships. *Development and Psychopathology, 13,* 1–11.

Provence, S., & Lipton, R. C. (1962). *Infants in institutions.* New York: International Universities Press.

Pungello, E. P., & Kurtz-Costes, B. (1999). Why and how working women choose childcare: A review with a focus on infancy. *Developmental Review, 19,* 31–96.

Putallaz, M., & Wasserman, A. (1989). Children's naturalistic entry behavior and sociometric status: A developmental perspective. *Developmental Psychology, 25,* 297–305.

Rabiner, D. L., Keane, S. P., & MacKinnon-Lewis, C. (1993). Children's beliefs about familiar and unfamiliar peers in relation to their sociometric status. *Developmental Psychology, 29,* 236–243.

Reis, H. T., Lin, Y., Bennett, M. E., & Nezlek, J. B. (1993). Change and consistency in social participation during early adulthood. *Developmental Psychology, 29,* 633–645.

Reiss, D., with J. M. Neiderhiser, E. M. Hetherington, & R. Plomin. (2000). *The relationship code: Deciphering genetic and social influences on adolescent development.* Cambridge, MA: Harvard University Press.

Roberto, K. A., & Scott, J. P. (1986). Equity considerations in the friendships of older adults. *Journal of Gerontology, 41,* 241–247.

Rodkin, P. C., Farner, T. W., Pearl, R., & Van Acker, R. (2000). Heterogeneity of popular boys: Antisocial and prosocial configurations. *Developmental Psychology, 36,* 14–24.

Rook, K. S. (1984). Promoting social bonding: Strategies for helping the lonely and socially isolated. *American Psychologist, 39,* 1389–1407.

Rook, K. S. (1991). Facilitating friendship formation in late life: Puzzles and challenges. *American Journal of Community Psychology, 19,* 103–110.

Rothbaum, F., Weisz, J., Pott, M., Miyake, K., & Morelli, G. (2000). Attachment and culture: Security in the United States and Japan. *American Psychologist, 55,* 1093–1104.

Russakoff, D. (2000, July 6). A cost squeeze in child care: Families wonder where the aid is. *Washington Post,* pp. A1, A8.

Rutter, M. (1981). *Maternal deprivation revisited* (2nd ed.). New York: Penguin.

Ryalls, B. O., Gul, R. E., & Ryalls, K. R. (2000). Infant imitation of peer and adult models:

Evidence for a peer model advantage. *Merrill-Palmer Quarterly, 46,* 188–202.

Saarni, C. (1999). *The development of emotional competence.* New York: Guilford.

Santor, D. A., Messervey, D., & Kusumakar, V. (2000). Measuring peer pressure, popularity, and conformity in adolescent boys and girls: Predicting school performance, sexual attitudes, and substance abuse. *Journal of Youth and Adolescence, 29,* 163–182.

Scarr, S. (1997). Why child care has little impact on most children's development. *Current Directions in Psychological Science, 6,*143–148.

Scarr, S., & Eisenberg, M. (1993). Child care research: Issues, perspectives, and results. *Annual Review of Psychology, 44,* 613–644.

Schaffer, H. R. (2000). The early experience assumption: Past, present, and future. *International Journal of Behavior Development, 24,* 5–14.

Schaffer, H. R., & Emerson, P. E. (1964). The development of social attachments in infancy. *Monographs of the Society for Research in Child Development, 29*(3, Serial No. 94).

Schneider, B. H., Atkinson, L., & Tardif, C. (2001). Child–parent attachment and children's peer relations: A quantitative review. *Developmental Psychology, 37,* 86–100.

Sebald, H. (1986). Adolescents' shifting orientation toward parents and peers: A curvilinear trend over recent decades. *Journal of Marriage and the Family, 48,* 5–13.

Sharabany, R., Gershoni, R., & Hofman, J. E. (1981). Girlfriend, boyfriend: Age and sex differences in intimate friendship. *Developmental Psychology, 17,* 800–808.

Sharpsteen, D. J., & Kirkpatrick, L. A. (1997). Romantic jealousy and adult romantic attachment. *Journal of Personality and Social Psychology, 72,* 627–640.

Sherman, A. M., de Vries, B., & Lansford, J. E. (2000). Friendship in childhood and adulthood: Lessons across the life span. *International Journal of Aging & Human Development, 51,* 31–51.

Silverstein, M., & Waite, L. J. (1993). Are blacks more likely than whites to receive and provide social support in middle and old age? Yes, no, and maybe so. *Journal of Gerontology: Social Sciences, 48,* S212–S222.

Skolnick, A. (1986). Early attachment and personal relationships across the life course. In P. B. Baltes, D. L. Featherman, & R. M. Lerner (Eds.), *Life-span development and behavior* (Vol. 7). Hillsdale, NJ: Erlbaum.

Smith, P. K. (1978). A longitudinal study of social participation in preschool children: Solitary and parallel play reexamined. *Developmental Psychology, 14,* 517–523.

Sroufe, L. A. (1977). Wariness of strangers and the study of infant development. *Child Development, 48,* 1184–1199.

Sroufe, L. A. (1985). Attachment classification from the perspective of infant–caregiver relationships and infant temperament. *Child Development, 56,* 1–14.

Sroufe, L. A. (1996). *Emotional development: The organization of emotional life in the early years.* Cambridge, England: University of Cambridge Press.

Sroufe, L. A., Bennett, C., Englund, M. Urban, J., & Shulman, S. (1993). The significance of gender boundaries in preadolescence: Contemporary correlates and antecedents of boundary violation and maintenance. *Child Development, 64,* 455–466.

Sroufe, L. A., Egeland, B., & Carlson, E. A. (1999). One social world: The integrated development of parent–child and peer relationships. In W. A. Collins & B. Laursen (Eds.), *Minnesota Symposia on Child Psychology: Vol. 30. Relationships as developmental contexts.* Mahwah, NJ: Erlbaum.

Sroufe, L. A., Waters, E., & Matas, L. (1974). Contextual determinants of infant affectional response. In M. Lewis & L. A. Rosenblum (Eds.), *The origins of fear.* New York: Wiley.

Steele, H., Steele, M., Croft, C., & Fonagy, P. (1999). Infant–mother attachment at one year predicts children's understanding of mixed emotion at six years. *Social Development, 8,* 161–178.

Steele, H., Steele, M., & Fonagy, P. (1996). Associations among attachment classifications of mothers, fathers, and their infants. *Child Development, 67,* 541–555.

Steinberg, L., & Silverberg, S. B. (1986). The vicissitudes of autonomy in early adolescence. *Child Development, 57,* 841–851.

Stern, D. (1977). *The first relationship: Infant and mother.* Cambridge, MA: Harvard University Press.

Stevenson, M. B., VerHoeve, J. N., Roach, M. A., & Leavitt, L. A. (1986). The beginning of conversation: Early patterns of mother–infant vocal responsiveness. *Infant Behavior and Development, 9,* 423–440.

Stone, M. R., & Brown, B. B. (1999). Identity claims and projections: Descriptions of self and crowds in secondary school. In J. A. McLellan & M. J. V. Pugh (Eds.), *New directions for child and adolescent development: No. 84. The role of peer groups in adolescent social identity: Exploring the importance of stability and change.* San Francisco: Jossey-Bass.

Sullivan, H. S. (1953). The interpersonal theory of psychiatry. New York: Norton.

Suomi, S. J. (1997). Long-term effects of different early rearing experiences on social, emotional and physiological development in nonhuman primates. In M. S. Kesheven & R. M. Murra (Eds.), *Neurodevelopmental models of adult psychopathology.* Cambridge, England: Cambridge University Press.

Suomi, S. J. (1999). Developmental trajectories, early experiences, and community consequences: Lessons from studies with rhesus monkeys. In D. P. Keating & C. Hertzman (Eds.), *Developmental health and the wealth of nations: Social, biological, and educational dynamics.* New York: Guilford.

Suomi, S. J., & Levine, S. (1998). Psychobiology of intergenerational effects of trauma: Evidence from animal studies. In Y. Danieli (Ed.), *International handbook of multigenerational legacies of trauma.* New York: Plenum.

Swanson, K., Beckwith, L., & Howard, J. (2000). Intrusive caregiving and quality of attachment in prenatally drug-exposed toddlers and their primary caregivers. *Attachment and Human Development, 2,* 130–148.

Takahashi, K. (1990). Are the key assumptions of the "Strange Situation" procedure universal? A view from Japanese research. *Human Development, 33,* 23–30.

Terry, R., & Coie, J. D. (1991). A comparison of methods for defining sociometric status among children. *Developmental Psychology, 27,* 867–880.

Thompson, R. A. (1994). Emotion regulation: A theme in search of definition. In N. A. Fox (Ed.), *The development of emotion regulation: Biological and behavioral considerations. Monographs of the Society for Research in Child Development, 59*(Nos. 2–3, Serial No. 240).

Thorne, B. (1993). *Gender play: Girls and boys in school.* New Brunswick, NJ: Rutgers University Press.

Thurber, C. A. (1995). The experience and expression of homesickness in preadolescent and adolescent boys. *Child Development, 66,* 1162–1178.

Tronick, E. Z. (1989). Emotions and emotional communication in infants. *American Psychologist, 44,* 112–119.

Tucker, J. S., Schwartz, J. E., Clark, K. M., & Friedman, H. S. (1999). Age-related changes in the associations of social network ties with mortality risk. *Psychology and Aging, 14,* 564–571.

Turk-Charles, S., & Carstensen, L. L. (1999). The role of time in the setting of social goals across the life span. In T. M. Hess & F. Blanchard-Fields (Eds.), *Social cognition and aging.* San Diego: Academic Press.

Uchino, B. N., Cacioppo, J. T., & Keicolt-Glaser, J. K. (1996). The relationship between social support and physiological processes: A review with emphasis on underlying mechanisms and implications for health. *Psychological Bulletin, 119,* 488–531.

van den Boom, D. C. (1995). Do first-year intervention effects endure? Follow-up during toddlerhood of a sample of Dutch irritable infants. *Child Development, 66,* 1798–1816.

van IJzendoorn, M. H. (1995). Adult attachment representations, parental responsiveness, and infant attachment: A meta-analysis on the predictive validity of the Adult Attachment Interview. *Psychological Bulletin, 117,* 387–403.

van IJzendoorn, M. H., & De Wolff, M. S. (1997). In search of the absent father: Meta-analyses of infant–father attachment: A rejoinder to our discussants. *Child Development, 68,* 604–609.

van IJzendoorn, M. H., Goldberg, S., Kroonenberg, P. M., & Frenkel, O. J. (1992). The relative effects of maternal and child problems on the quality of attachment: A meta-analysis of attachment in clinical samples. *Child Development, 63,* 840–858.

van IJzendoorn, M. H., Juffer, F., & Duyvesteyn, M. G. C. (1995). Breaking the intergenerational cycle of insecure attachment: A review of the effects of attachment-based interventions on maternal sensitivity and infant security. *Journal of Child Psychology and Psychiatry and Allied Disciplines, 36,* 225–248.

van IJzendoorn, M. H., & Sagi, A. (1999). Cross-cultural patterns of attachment: Universal and contextual dimensions. In J. Cassidy & P. R. Shaver (Eds.), *Handbook of attachment.* New York: Guilford.

van IJzendoorn, M. H., Schuengel, C., & Bakermans-Kranenburg, M. J. (1999). Disorganized attachment in early childhood: Meta-analysis of precursors, concomitants, and sequelae. *Development and Psychopathology, 11,* 225–249.

Vandell, D. L. (2000). Parents, peer groups, and other socializing influences. *Developmental Psychology, 36,* 699–710.

Vandell, D. L., Wilson, K. S., & Buchanan, N. R. (1980). Peer interaction in the first year of life: An examination of its structure, content, and sensitivity to toys. *Child Development, 51*, 481–488.

Vaughn, B. E., Azria, M. R., Krzysik, L., Caya, L. R., Bost, K. K., Newell, W., & Kazura, K. L. (2000). Friendship and social competence in a sample of preschool children attending Head Start. *Developmental Psychology, 36*, 326–338.

Vaughn, B. E., Lefever, G. B., Seifer, R., & Barglow, P. (1989). Attachment behavior, attachment security, and temperament during infancy. *Child Development, 60*, 728–737.

Vivona, J. M. (2000). Parental attachment styles of late adolescents: Qualities of attachment relationships and consequences for adjustment. *Journal of Counseling Psychology, 47*, 316–329.

Vormbrock, J. K. (1993). Attachment theory as applied to wartime and job-related marital separation. *Psychological Bulletin, 114*, 122–144.

Walster, E., Walster, G. W., & Berscheid, E. (1978). *Equity: Theory and research.* Boston: Allyn & Bacon.

Waters, E., Merrick, S., Treboux, D., Crowell, J., & Albersheim, L. (2000). Attachment security in infancy and early adulthood: A twenty-year longitudinal study. *Child Development, 71*, 684–689.

Waters, E., Wippman, J., & Sroufe, L. A. (1979). Attachment, positive affect, and competence in the peer group: Two studies in construct validation. *Child Development, 50*, 821–829.

Webster, J. D. (1998). Attachment styles, reminiscence functions, and happiness in young and elderly adults. *Journal of Aging Studies, 12*, 315–330.

Weinfield, N. S., Sroufe, L. A., & Egeland, B. (2000). Attachment from infancy to early adulthood in a high-risk sample: Continuity, discontinuity, and their correlates. *Child Development, 71*, 695–702.

Weinfield, N. S., Sroufe, L. A., Egeland, B., & Carlson, E. A. (1999). The nature of individual differences in infant–caregiver attachment. In J. Cassidy & P. R. Shaver (Eds.), *Handbook of attachment: Theory, research, and clinical applications.* New York: Guilford.

Weinraub, M., & Lewis, M. (1977). The determinants of children's responses to separation. *Monographs of the Society for Research in Child Development, 42*(4, Serial No. 172).

Wilks, J. (1986). The relative importance of parents and friends in adolescent decision making. *Journal of Youth and Adolescence, 15*, 323–334.

Wolff, P. H. (1963). Observations on the early development of smiling. In B. M. Foss (Ed.), *Determinants of infant behavior* (Vol. 2). London: Methuen.

Woodward, L., Fergusson, D. M., & Belsky, J. (2000). Timing of parental separation and attachment to parents in adolescence: Results of a prospective study from birth to age 16. *Journal of Marriage and the Family, 62*, 162–174.

Youniss, J. (1980). *Parents and peers in social development: A Sullivan-Piaget perspective.* Chicago: University of Chicago Press.

Zaslow, M. (1980). Relationships among peers in kibbutz toddler groups. *Child Psychiatry and Human Development, 10*, 178–189.

Zeanah, C. H. (2000). Disturbances of attachment in young children adopted from institutions. *Journal of Developmental and Behavioral Pediatrics, 21*, 230–236.

Zimmer-Gembeck, M. J. (1999). Stability, change, and individual differences in involvement with friends and romantic partners among adolescent females. *Journal of Youth and Adolescence, 28*, 419–438.

Chapter 15: The Family

Agnew, R., & Huguley, S. (1989). Adolescent violence toward parents. *Journal of Marriage and the Family, 51*, 699–711.

Allen, K. R., Blieszner, R., & Roberto, K. A. (2000). Families in the middle and later years: A review and critique of research in the 1990s. *Journal of Marriage and the Family, 62*, 911–926.

Allen, K. R., Fine, M. A., & Demo, D. H. (2000). An overview of family diversity: Controversies, questions, and values. In D. H. Demo, K. R. Allen, & M. A. Fine (Eds.), *Handbook of family diversity.* New York: Oxford University Press.

Amato, P. R. (1993). Children's adjustment to divorce: Theories, hypotheses, and empirical support. *Journal of Marriage and the Family, 55*, 23–38.

Amato, P. R. (1996). Explaining the intergenerational transmission of divorce. *Journal of Marriage and the Family, 58*, 628–640.

Amato, P. R. (1999). The post divorce society: How divorce is shaping the family and other forms of social organization. In R. A. Thompson & P. R. Amato (Eds.), *The post divorce family: Children, parenting, and society.* Thousand Oaks, CA: Sage.

Amato, P. R. (2000). The consequences of divorce for adults and children. *Journal of Marriage and the Family, 62*, 1269–1287.

Ambert, A. (1992). *The effect of children on parents.* New York: Haworth.

Ambert, A. (1994). An international perspective on parenting: Social change and social constructs. *Journal of Marriage and the Family, 56*, 529–543.

Ammerman, R. T., & Patz, R. J. (1996). Determinants of child abuse potential: Contribution of parent and child factors. *Journal of Clinical Child Psychology, 25*, 300–307.

Anderson, K. E., Lytton, H., & Romney, D. M. (1986). Mothers' interactions with normal and conduct-disordered boys: Who affects whom? *Developmental Psychology, 22*, 604–609.

Aneshensel, C. S., Pearlin, L. I., Mullan, J. T., Zarit, S. H., & Whitlatch, C. J. (1995). *Profiles in caregiving: The unexpected career.* San Diego: Academic Press.

Aquilino, W. S. (1991). Predicting parents' experiences with coresident adult children. *Journal of Family Issues, 12*, 323–342.

Aquilino, W. S. (1997). From adolescent to young adult: A prospective study of parent–child relations during the transition to adulthood. *Journal of Marriage and the Family, 59*, 670–686.

Aquilino, W. S. (1999). Two views of one relationship: Comparing parents' and young adult children's reports of the quality of intergenerational relations. *Journal of Marriage and the Family, 61*, 858–870.

Arnett, J. J. (1995). Broad and narrow socialization: The family in the context of a cultural theory. *Journal of Marriage and the Family, 57*, 617–628.

Axinn, W. G., & Barber, J. S. (1997). Living arrangements and family formation attitudes in early adulthood. *Journal of Marriage and the Family, 59*, 595–611.

Bailey, J. M., Bobrow, D., Wolfe, M., & Mikach, S. (1995). Sexual orientation of adult sons of gay fathers. *Developmental Psychology, 31*, 124–129.

Barnett, R. C. (1994). Home-to-work spillover revisited: A study of full-time employed women in dual-earner couples. *Journal of Marriage and the Family, 56*, 647–656.

Barnett, R. C., Raudenbush, S. W., Brennan, R. T., & Pleck, J. H. (1995). Change in job and marital experiences and change in psychological distress: A longitudinal study of dual-earner couples. *Journal of Personality and Social Psychology, 69*, 839–850.

Baumrind, D. (1967). Child care practices anteceding three patterns of preschool behavior. *Genetic Psychology Monographs, 75*, 43–88.

Baumrind, D. (1977, March). *Socialization determinants of personal agency.* Paper presented at the biennial meeting of the Society for Research in Child Development, New Orleans.

Baumrind, D. (1991). Effective parenting during the early adolescent transition. In P. A. Cowan & M. Hetherington (Eds.), *Family transitions.* Hillsdale, NJ: Erlbaum.

Baydar, N., Hyle, P., & Brooks-Gunn, J. (1997). A longitudinal study of the effects of the birth of a sibling during preschool and early grade school years. *Journal of Marriage and the Family, 59*, 957–965.

Beaudry, M., Simard, M., Drapeau, S., & Charbonneau, C. (2000). What happens to the sibling subsystem following parental divorce? In C. Violato, E. Oddone-Paolucci, & M. Genuis (Eds.). *The changing family and child development.* Aldershot, England: Ashgate.

Bedford, V. H., Volling, B. L., & Avioli, P. M. (2000). Positive consequences of sibling conflict in childhood and adulthood. *International Journal of Aging & Human Development, 51*, 53–69.

Belsky, J. (1981). Early human experience: A family perspective. *Developmental Psychology, 17*, 3–23.

Belsky, J., & Isabella, R. A. (1985). Marital and parent–child relationships in family of origin and marital change following the birth of a baby: A retrospective analysis. *Child Development, 56*, 342–349.

Belsky, J., Lang, M. E., & Rovine, M. (1985). Stability and change in marriage across the transition to parenthood: A second study. *Journal of Marriage and the Family, 47*, 855–865.

Bengtson, V. (2001). Beyond the nuclear family: The increasing importance of multigenerational bonds. *Journal of Marriage and Family, 63*, 1–16.

Bengtson, V., Rosenthal, C., & Burton, L. (1990). Families and aging: Diversity and heterogeneity. In R. H. Binstock & L. K. George (Eds.), *Handbook of aging and the social sciences* (3rd ed.). San Diego: Academic Press.

Bengtson, V., Rosenthal, C., & Burton, L. (1996). Paradoxes of families and aging. In R. H. Binstock, L. K. George, V. W. Marshall, G. C. Myers, & J. H. Schulz (Eds.), *Handbook of aging and the social sciences* (4th ed.). San Diego: Academic Press.

Beyer, S. (1995). Maternal employment and children's academic achievement: Parenting styles as mediating variable. *Developmental Review, 15,* 212–253.

Beyers, W., & Goossens, L. (1999). Emotional autonomy, psychosocial adjustment and parenting: Interactions, moderating and mediating effects. *Journal of Adolescence, 22,* 753–769.

Bianchi, S. M. (2000). Maternal employment and time with children: Dramatic change or surprising continuity? *Demography, 37,* 401–414.

Biller, H. B. (1993). *Fathers and families: Paternal factors in child development.* Westport, CT: Auburn House.

Block, C. E. (2000). Dyadic and gender differences in perceptions of the grandparent–grandchild relationship. *International Journal of Aging and Human Development, 51,* 85–104.

Bolger, K. E., & Patterson, C. J. (2001). Developmental pathways from child maltreatment to peer rejection. *Child Development, 72,* 549–568.

Booth, A. (1999). Causes and consequences of divorce: Reflections on recent research. In R. A. Thompson & P. R. Amato (Eds.), *The post divorce family: Children, parenting, and society.* Thousand Oaks, CA: Sage.

Booth, A., & Amato, P. R. (2001). Parental predivorce relations and offspring postdivorce well-being. *Journal of Marriage and the Family, 63,* 197–212.

Booth, A., & Johnson, D. (1988). Premarital cohabitation and marital success. *Journal of Family Issues, 9,* 255–272.

Boykin-McElhaney, K., & Allen, J. P. (2001). Autonomy and adolescent social functioning: The moderating effect of risk. *Child Development, 72,* 220–235.

Brody, E. M. (1985). Parent care as a normative family stress. *Gerontologist, 25,* 19–29.

Brody, E. M. (1990). *Women in the middle: Their parent-care years.* New York: Springer.

Brody, E. M., Johnsen, P. T., & Fulcomer, M. C. (1984). What should adult children do for elderly parents? Opinions and preferences of three generations of women. *Journal of Gerontology, 39,* 736–746.

Brody, E. M., Litvin, S. J., Hoffman, C., & Kleban, M. H. (1992). Differential effects of daughters' marital status on their parent care experiences. *Gerontologist, 32,* 58–67.

Brody, G. H., & Stoneman, Z. (1996). A risk-amelioration model of sibling relationships: Conceptual underpinnings and preliminary findings. In G. H. Brody (Ed.), *Sibling relationships: Their causes and consequences.* Stamford, CT: Ablex.

Brooks-Gunn, J., Britto, P. R., & Brady, C. (1999). Struggling to make ends meet: Poverty and child development. In M. E. Lamb (Ed.), *Parenting and child development in "nontraditional" families.* Mahwah, NJ: Erlbaum.

Bryant, W. K., & Zick, C. D. (1996). An examination of parent–child shared time. *Journal of Marriage and the Family, 58,* 227–237.

Bryson, K., & Casper, L. M. (1999). Coresident grandparents and grandchildren. *Current Population Reports,* P23-198.

Buehler, C. A., Hogan, M. J., Robinson, B. E., & Levy, R. J. (1985–1986). The parental divorce transition: Divorce-related stressors and well-being. *Journal of Divorce, 9,* 61–81.

Bugental, D. B. (2001). *Parental cognitions as predictors of dyadic interaction with very young children.* Paper presented at the biennial

meeting of the Society for Research in Child Development, Minneapolis.

Bugental, D. B., Lewis, J. C., Lin, E., Lyon, J., & Kopeikin, H. (1999). In charge but not in control: The management of teaching relationships by adults with low perceived power. *Developmental Psychology, 35,* 1367–1378.

Buhrmester, D., & Furman, W. (1990). Perceptions of sibling relationships during middle childhood and adolescence. *Child Development, 61,* 1387–1398.

Burchinal, M. R., Follmer, A., & Bryant, D. M. (1996). The relations of maternal social support and family structure with maternal responsiveness and child outcomes among African-American families. *Developmental Psychology, 32,* 1073–1083.

Burr, J. A., & Mutchler, J. E. (1999). Race and ethnic variation in norms of filial responsibility among older persons. *Journal of Marriage and the Family, 61,* 674–687.

Burton, L. M. (1990). Teenage childrearing as an alternative life-course strategy in multigenerational black families. *Human Nature, 1,* 123–143.

Burton, L. M. (1996). The timing of childbearing, family structure, and the role responsibilities of aging black women. In E. M. Hetherington & E. A. Blechman (Eds.), *Stress, coping, and resiliency in children and families.* Mahwah, NJ: Erlbaum.

Cabrera, N. J., Tamis-LeMonda, C. S., Bradley, R. H., Hofferth, S., & Lamb, M. E. (2000). Fatherhood in the twenty-first century. *Child Development, 71,* 127–136.

Carstensen, L. L., Levenson, R. W., & Gottman, J. M. (1995). Emotional behavior in long-term marriages. *Psychology and Aging, 10,* 140–149.

Caspi, A., Herbener, E. S., & Ozer, D. J. (1992). Shared experiences and the similarity of personalities: A longitudinal study of married couples. *Journal of Personality and Social Psychology, 62,* 281–291.

Chan, C. G., & Elder, G. H., Jr. (2000). Matrilineal advantage in grandchild–grandparent relations. *Gerontologist, 40,* 179–190.

Chao, R. K. (1994). Beyond parental control and authoritarian parenting style: Understanding Chinese parenting through the cultural notion of training. *Child Development, 65,* 1111–1119.

Chao, R. K. (2000). Cultural explanations for the role of parenting in the school success of Asian-American children. In R. D. Taylor & M. C. Wang (Eds.), *Resilience across contexts: Family, work, culture, and community.* Mahwah, NJ: Erlbaum.

Chase-Lansdale, P. L., Cherlin, A. J., & Kiernan, K. E. (1995). The long-term effects of parental divorce on the mental health of young adults: A developmental perspective. *Child Development, 66,* 1614–1634.

Cherlin, A., & Furstenberg, F. F., Jr. (1986). *The new American grandparent: A place in the family, a life apart.* New York: Basic Books.

Cherlin, A. J., Furstenberg, F. F., Jr., Chase-Lansdale, P. L., Kiernan, K. E., Robins, P. K., Morrison, D. R., & Teitler, J. O. (1991). Longitudinal studies of effects of divorce on children in Great Britain and the United States. *Science, 252,* 1386–1389.

Chipperfield, J. G., & Havens, B. (2001). Gender differences in the relationship between marital status transitions and life satisfaction in

later life. *Journal of Gerontology: Psychological Sciences, 56,* P176–P186.

Cicchetti, D., & Barnett, D. (1991). Attachment organization in maltreated preschoolers. *Development and Psychopathology, 3,* 397–411.

Cicirelli, V. G. (1982). Sibling influence throughout the life span. In M. E. Lamb & B. Sutton-Smith (Eds.), *Sibling relationships: Their nature and significance across the lifespan.* Hillsdale, NJ: Erlbaum.

Cicirelli, V. G. (1991). Sibling relationships in adulthood. *Marriage and Family Review, 16,* 291–310.

Cicirelli, V. G. (1993). Attachment and obligation as daughters' motives for caregiving behavior and subsequent effect on subjective burden. *Psychology and Aging, 8,* 144–155.

Cicirelli, V. G. (1995). *Sibling relationships across the life span.* New York: Plenum.

Clyburn, L. D., Stones, M. J., Hadjistavropoulos, T., & Tuokko, H. (2000). Predicting caregiver burden and depression in Alzheimer's disease. *Journal of Gerontology: Social Sciences, 55,* S2–13.

Collins, W. A., Maccoby, E. E., Steinberg, L., Hetherington, E. M., & Bornstein, M. H. (2000). Contemporary research on parenting: The case for nature and nurture. *American Psychologist, 55,* 218–232.

Coltrane, S. (2000). Research on household labor: Modeling and measuring the social embeddedness of routine family work. *Journal of Marriage and the Family, 62,* 1208–1233.

Conger, R. D., Conger, K. J., Elder, G. H., Jr., Lorenz, F. O., Simons, R. L., & Whitbeck, L. B. (1992). A family process model of economic hardship and adjustment of early adolescent boys. *Child Development, 63,* 526–541.

Conger, R. D., Patterson, G. R., & Ge, X. (1995). It takes two to replicate: A mediational model for the impact of parents' stress on adolescent adjustment. *Child Development, 66,* 80–97.

Conner, K. A. (2000). *Continuing to care: Older Americans and their families.* New York: Falmer Press.

Connidis, I. A. (1994). Sibling support in older age. *Journals of Gerontology, 49,* S309–S317.

Coohey, C., & Braun, N. (1997). Toward an integrated framework for understanding child physical abuse. *Child Abuse and Neglect, 21,* 1081–1094.

Cook, W. L. (2001). Interpersonal influence in family systems: A social relations model analysis. *Child Development, 72,* 1179–1197.

Cooney, T. M., & Smith, L. A. (1996). Young adults' relations with grandparents following recent parental divorce. *Journal of Gerontology: Social Sciences, 51,* S91–S95.

Coontz, S. (2000). Historical perspectives on family diversity. In D. H. Demo, K. R. Allen, & M. A. Fine (Eds.), *Handbook of family diversity.* New York: Oxford University Press.

Cowan, C. P., & Cowan, P. A. (2000). *When partners become parents: The big life change for couples.* Mahwah, NJ: Erlbaum.

Cox, M. J., Owen, M. T., Henderson, V. K., & Margand, N. A. (1992). Prediction of infant–father and infant–mother attachment. *Developmental Psychology, 28,* 474–483.

Cox, M. J., Paley, B., Burchinal, M., & Payne, C. C. (1999). Marital perceptions and interactions across the transition to parenthood.

Journal of Marriage and the Family, 61, 611–625.

Crnic, K., & Booth, C. (1991). Mothers' and fathers' perceptions of daily hassles of parenting across early childhood. *Journal of Marriage and the Family, 53,* 1042–1050.

Crouch, J. L., & Behl, L. E. (2001). Relationships among parental beliefs in corporal punishment, reported stress, and physical child abuse potential. *Child Abuse and Neglect, 25,* 413–419.

Darling, N., & Steinberg, L. (1993). Parenting style as context: An integrative model. *Psychological Bulletin, 113,* 487–496.

Darwish, D., Esquivel, G. B., Houtz, J. C., & Alfonso, V. C. (2001). Play and social skills in maltreated and non-maltreated preschoolers during peer interactions. *Child Abuse and Neglect, 25,* 13–31.

Deater-Deckard, K., Dodge, K. A., Bates, J. E., & Pettit, G. S. (1996). Physical discipline among African American and European American mothers: Links to children's externalizing behaviors. *Developmental Psychology, 32,* 1065–1072.

DeMaris, A., & MacDonald, W. (1993). Premarital cohabitation and marital instability: A test of the unconventionality hypothesis. *Journal of Marriage and the Family, 55,* 399–407.

Demo, D. H., & Allen, K. R. (1996). Diversity within lesbian and gay families: Challenges and implications for family theory and research. *Journal of Social and Personal Relationships, 13,* 415–434.

Demo, D. H., Allen, K. R., & Fine, M. A. (Eds.). (2000). *Handbook of family diversity.* New York: Oxford University Press.

Demo, D. H., & Cox, M. J. (2000). Families with young children: A review of research in the 1990s. *Journal of Marriage and the Family, 62,* 876–895.

Deutsch, F. M. (2001). Equally shared parenting. *Current Directions in Psychological Science, 10,* 25–28.

Dickson, F. C. (1995). The best is yet to be: Research on long-lasting marriages. In J. T. Wood & S. Duck (Eds.), *Under-studied relationships: Off the beaten track.* Thousand Oaks, CA: Sage.

Dilworth-Anderson, P., & Burton, L. M. (1996). Rethinking family development: Critical conceptual issues in the study of diverse groups. *Journal of Social and Personality Relationships, 13,* 325–334.

Downey, D. B., Ainsworth-Darnell, J. W., & Dufur, M. J. (1998). Sex of parent and children's well-being in single parent households. *Journal of Marriage and the Family, 60,* 878–893.

Doyle, A. B., Markiewicz, D., Brendgen, M., Lieberman, M., & Voss, K. (2000). Child attachment security and self-concept: Associations with mother and father attachment style and marital quality. *Merrill-Palmer Quarterly, 46,* 514–539.

Dunn, J. (1993). *Young children's close relationships: Beyond attachment.* Newbury Park, CA: Sage.

Dunn, J., & Kendrick, C. (1982). *Siblings: Love, envy, and understanding.* Cambridge, MA: Harvard University Press.

Dunn, J., Slomkowski, C., & Beardsall, L. (1994). Sibling relationships from the preschool period through middle childhood and early

adolescence. *Developmental Psychology, 30,* 315–324.

Duvall, E. M. (1977). *Marriage and family development* (5th ed.). Philadelphia: J. B. Lippincott.

Dwyer, J. W., & Coward, R. T. (1991). A multivariate comparison of the involvement of adult sons versus daughters in the care of impaired parents. *Journal of Gerontology: Social Sciences, 46,* S259–S269.

Eckenrode, J., Laird, M., & Doris, J. (1993). School performance and disciplinary problems among abused and neglected children. *Developmental Psychology, 29,* 53–62.

Egeland, B. (1979). Preliminary results of a prospective study of the antecedents of child abuse. *International Journal of Child Abuse and Neglect, 3,* 269–278.

Egeland, B., Jacobvitz, D., & Sroufe, L. A. (1988). Breaking the cycle of abuse. *Child Development, 59,* 1080–1088.

Egeland, B., Sroufe, L. A., & Erickson, M. (1983). The developmental consequences of different patterns of maltreatment. *International Journal of Child Abuse and Neglect, 7,* 459–469.

Ehrle, G. M. (2001). Grandchildren as moderator variables in the family, social, physiological, and intellectual development of grandparents who are raising them. In E. L. Grigorenko & R. J. Sternberg (Eds.), *Family environment and intellectual functioning: A life-span perspective.* Mahwah, NJ: Erlbaum.

El-Khorazaty, M. N. (1996). Twentieth-century family life cycle and its determinants in the United States. *Journal of Family History, 22,* 70–109.

Emery, R. E. (1999). Post divorce family life for children: An overview of research and some implications for policy. In R. A. Thompson & P. R. Amato (Eds.), *The post divorce family: Children, parenting, and society.* Thousand Oaks, CA: Sage.

Emery, R. E., & Laumann-Billings, L. (1998). An overview of the nature, causes, and consequences of abusive family relationships: Toward differentiating maltreatment and violence. *American Psychologist, 53,* 121–135.

Emery, R. E., Laumann-Billings, L., Waldron, M. C., Sbarra, D. A., & Dillon, P. (2001). Child custody mediation and litigation: Custody, contact, and coparenting 12 years after initial dispute resolution. *Journal of Counseling and Clinical Psychology, 69,* 323–332.

Emery, R. E., & Tuer, M. (1993). Parenting and the marital relationship. In T. Luster & L. Okagaki (Eds.), *Parenting: An ecological perspective.* Hillsdale, NJ: Erlbaum.

Fagot, B. I., & Kavanaugh, K. (1993). Parenting during the second year: Effects of children's age, sex, and attachment classification. *Child Development, 64,* 258–271.

Fingerman, K. L. (2000). "We had a nice little chat": Age and generational differences in mothers' and daughters' descriptions of enjoyable visits. *Journal of Gerontology: Psychological Sciences, 55,* P95–P106.

Fingerman, K. L., & Bermann, E. (2000). Applications of family systems theory to the study of adulthood. *International Journal of Aging and Human Development, 51,* 5–29.

Finkelhor, D., & Dziuba-Leatherman, J. (1994). Victimization of children. *American Psychologist, 49,* 173–183.

Flaks, D. K., Ficher, I., Masterpasqua, F., & Joseph, G. (1995). Lesbians choosing moth-

erhood: A comparative study of lesbian and heterosexual parents and their children. *Developmental Psychology, 31,* 105–114.

Fox, B. (2001a). As times change: A review of trends in personal and family life. In B. J. Fox (Ed.), *Family patterns, gender relations* (2nd ed.). Don Mills, Ontario: Oxford University Press.

Fox, B. (2001b). Reproducing difference: Changes in the lives of partners becoming parents. In B. J. Fox (Ed.), *Family patterns, gender relations* (2nd ed.). Don Mills, Ontario: Oxford University Press.

Forgatch, M. S., & DeGarmo, D. S. (1999). Parenting through change: An effective prevention program for single mothers. *Journal of Consulting and Clinical Psychology, 67,* 711–724.

Fuhrman, T., & Holmbeck, G. N. (1995). Contextual-moderator analysis of emotional autonomy and adjustment in adolescence. *Child Development, 66,* 793–811.

Fuligini, A. J. (1998). Authority, autonomy, and parent–adolescent conflict and cohesion: A study of adolescents from Mexican, Chinese, Filipino, and European backgrounds. *Developmental Psychology, 34,* 782–792.

Fuller-Thomson, E., Minkler, M., & Driver, D. (1997). A profile of grandparents raising grandchildren in the United States. *Gerontologist, 37,* 406–411.

Furman, W., & Buhrmester, D. (1985a). Children's perceptions of the personal relationships in their social networks. *Developmental Psychology, 21,* 1016–1024.

Furman, W., & Buhrmester, D. (1985b). Children's perceptions of the qualities of sibling relationships. *Child Development, 56,* 448–461.

Furman, W., & Buhrmester, D. (1992). Age and sex differences in perceptions of networks of personal relationships. *Child Development, 63,* 103–115.

Gadsen, V. (1999). Black families in intergenerational and cultural perspective. In M. E. Lamb (Ed.), *Parenting and child development in "non traditional" families.* Mahwah, NJ: Erlbaum.

Gagnon, M. D., Hersen, M., Kabacoff, R. I., & Vanhasselt, V. B. (1999). Interpersonal and psychological correlates of marital dissatisfaction in late life: A review. *Clinical Psychology Review, 19,* 359–378.

Galinsky, E. (1999). *Ask the children: What America's children really think about working parents.* New York: William Morrow.

Gallagher, S. K., & Gerstel, N. (2001). Connections and constraints: The effects of children on caregiving. *Journal of Marriage and the Family, 63,* 265–275.

Garbarino, J. (1992). *Children and families in the social environment* (2nd ed.). New York: Aldine de Gruyter.

Garcia, M. M., Shaw, D. S., Winslow, E. B., & Yaggi, K. E. (2000). Destructive sibling conflict and the development of conduct problems in young boys. *Developmental Psychology, 36,* 44–53.

Gaugler, J. E., Davey, A., Pearlin, L. I., & Zarit, S. H. (2000). Modeling caregiver adaptation over time: The longitudinal impact of behavior problems. *Psychology and Aging, 15,* 437–450.

Ge, X., Best, K. M., Conger, R. D., & Simons, R. L. (1996). Parenting behaviors and the occurrence and co-occurrence of adolescent depressive symptoms and conduct problems. *Developmental Psychology, 32,* 717–731.

Giarrusso, R., Feng, D., Silverstein, M., & Bengtson, V. L. (2000). Self in the context of the family. In K. W. Schaie & J. Hendrick (Eds.), *The evolution of the aging self: The societal impact on the aging process.* New York: Springer.

Gigy, L., & Kelly, J. B. (1992). Reasons for divorce: Perspectives of divorcing men and women. *Journal of Divorce and Remarriage, 18,* 169–187.

Gil, D. G. (1970). *Violence against children.* Cambridge, MA: Harvard University Press.

Gilbert, N. (1997). *Combatting child abuse: International perspectives and trends.* New York: Oxford University Press.

Glasgow, K. L., Dornbusch, S. M., Troyer, L., Steinberg, L., & Ritter, P. L. (1997). Parenting styles, adolescents' attributions, and educational outcomes in nine heterogeneous high schools. *Child Development, 68,* 507–529.

Glick, P. C. (1989). Remarried families, stepfamilies, and stepchildren: A brief demographic profile. *Family Relations, 38,* 24–47.

Goldberg, W. A., Greenberger, E., & Nagel, S. K. (1996). Employment and achievement: Mothers' work involvement in relation to children's achievement behaviors and mothers' parenting behaviors. *Child Development, 67,* 1512–1527.

Golombok, S., & Tasker, F. (1996). Do parents influence the sexual orientation of their children? Findings from a longitudinal study of lesbian families. *Developmental Psychology, 32,* 3–11.

Gottman, J., M., & Levenson, R.W. (1992). Marital processes predictive of later dissolution: Behavior, physiology, and health. *Journal of Personality and Social Psychology, 63,* 221–233.

Gottman, J. M., & Levenson, R. W. (2000). The timing of divorce: Predicting when a couple will divorce over a 14-year period. *Journal of Marriage and the Family, 62,* 737–745.

Gottman, J. M., & Notarius, C. I. (2000). Decade review: Observing marital interaction. *Journal of Marriage and the Family, 62,* 927–947.

Graefe, D. R., & Lichter, D. T. (1999). Life course transitions of American children: Parental cohabitation, marriage, and single motherhood. *Demography, 36,* 205–217.

Greenberger, E., O'Neil, R., & Nagel, S. K. (1994). Linking workplace and homeplace: Relations between the nature of adults' work and their parenting behaviors. *Developmental Psychology, 30,* 990–1002.

Greene, A. L., & Boxer, A. M. (1986). Daughters and sons as young adults: Restructuring the ties that bind. In N. Datan, A. L. Greene, & H. W. Reese (Eds.), *Life-span developmental psychology: Intergenerational relations.* Hillsdale, NJ: Erlbaum.

Grych, J. H., & Fincham, F. D. (1992). Interventions for children of divorce: Toward greater integration of research and action. *Psychological Bulletin, 111,* 434–454.

Hagestad, G. O. (1985). Continuity and connectedness. In V. L. Bengtson & J. F. Robertson (Eds.), *Grandparenthood.* Beverly Hills, CA: Sage.

Haskett, M. E., Johnson, C. A., & Miller, J. W. (1994). Individual differences in risk of child abuse by adolescent mothers: Assessment in the perinatal period. *Journal of Child Psychology and Psychiatry, and Allied Disciplines, 35,* 461–476.

Heaton, T. B., Jacobson, C. K., & Holland, K. (1999). Persistence and change in decisions to remain childless. *Journal of Marriage and the Family, 61,* 531–539.

Hernandez, D. J. (1997). Child development and the social demography of childhood. *Child Development, 68,* 149–169.

Hetherington, E. M. (1981). Children and divorce. In R. W. Henderson (Ed.), *Parent–child interaction: Theory, research and prospects.* New York: Academic Press.

Hetherington, E. M. (1989). Coping with family transitions: Winners, losers, and survivors. *Child Development, 60,* 1–14.

Hetherington, E. M., Bridges, M., & Insabella, G. M. (1998). What matters? What does not? Five perspectives on the association between marital transitions and children's adjustment. *American Psychologist, 53,* 167–184.

Hetherington, E. M., Clingempeel, W. G., & Associates. (1992). Coping with marital transitions. *Monographs of the Society for Research in Child Development, 57*(2–3, Serial No. 227).

Hetherington, E. M., Cox, M., & Cox, R. (1982). Effects of divorce on parents and children. In M. E. Lamb (Ed.), *Nontraditional families.* Hillsdale, NJ: Erlbaum.

Hetherington, E. M., & Jodl, K. M. (1994). Stepfamilies as settings for child development. In A. Booth & J. Dunn (Eds.), *Stepfamilies: Who benefits? Who does not?* Hillsdale, NJ: Erlbaum.

Hetherington, E. M., & Kelly, J. (2002). *For better or for worse: Divorce reconsidered.* New York: W. W. Norton.

Hetherington, E. M., & Stanley-Hagen, M. (2000). Diversity among stepfamilies. In D. H. Demo, K. R. Allen, & M. A. Fine (Eds.), *Handbook of family diversity.* New York: Oxford University Press.

Hewlett, B. S. (1992). Introduction. In B. S. Hewlett (Ed.), *Father–child relations: Cultural and biosocial contexts.* New York: Aldine de Gruyter.

Hill, R., & Rodgers, R. H. (1964). The developmental approach. In H. Christensen (Ed.), *Handbook of marriage and the family.* Chicago: Rand-McNally.

Hock, E., Eberly, M., Bartle-Haring, S., Ellwanger, P., & Widaman, K. F. (2001). Separation anxiety in parents of adolescents: Theoretical significance and scale development. *Child Development, 72,* 284–298.

Hoffman, L. W. (2000). Maternal employment: Effects of social context. In R. D. Taylor & M. C. Wang (Eds.), *Resilience across contexts: Family, work, culture, and community.* Mahwah, NJ: Erlbaum.

Holden, G. W., & Miller, P. C. (1999). Enduring and different: A meta-analysis of the similarity in parents' child rearing. *Psychological Bulletin, 125,* 223–254.

Howe, N., Aquan-Assee, J., Bukowski, W. M., Rinaldi, C. M., & Lehoux, P. M. (2000). Sibling self-disclosure in early adolescence. *Merrill-Palmer Quarterly, 46,* 653–671.

Howe, N., & Ross, H. S. (1990). Socialization, perspective-taking, and the sibling relationship. *Developmental Psychology, 26,* 160–165.

Huston, T. L., & Schwartz, P. (1995). The relationships of lesbians and gay men. In J. T. Wood & S. Duck (Eds.), *Under-studied relationships: Off the beaten track.* Thousand Oaks, CA: Sage.

Huston, T. L., Caughlin, J. P., Houts, R. M., Smith, S. E., & George, L. J. (2001). The connubial crucible: Newlywed years as predictors of marital delight, distress, and divorce. *Journal of Personality and Social Psychology, 80,* 237–252.

Huston, T. L., McHale, S. M., & Crouter, A. C. (1986). When the honeymoon's over: Changes in the marriage relationship over the first year. In R. Gilmour & S. Duck (Eds.), *The emerging field of personal relationships.* Hillsdale, NJ: Erlbaum.

Ingoldsby, B. B., & Smith, S. (1995). *Families in multicultural perspective.* New York: Guilford.

Jacobson, K. C., & Crockett, L. J. (2000). Parental monitoring and adolescent adjustment: An ecological perspective. *Journal of Research on Adolescence, 10,* 65–97.

Johnson, C. L. (2000). Perspectives on American kinship in the later 1990s. *Journal of Marriage and the Family, 62,* 623–639.

Johnson, C. L., & Troll, L. (1996). Family structure and the timing of transitions from 70 to 103 years of age. *Journal of Marriage and the Family, 58,* 178–187.

Johnson, M. P., & Ferraro, K. J. (2000). Research on domestic violence in the 1990s: Making distinctions. *Journal of Marriage and the Family, 62,* 948–963.

Jonsson, J. O., & Gahler, M. (1997). Family dissolution, family reconstitution, and children's educational careers: Recent evidence for Sweden. *Demography, 34,* 277–293.

Kalmuss, D., Davidson, A., & Cushman, L. (1992). Parenting expectancies, experiences, and adjustment to parenthood: A test of the violated expectations framework. *Journal of Marriage and the Family, 54,* 516–526.

Kaufman, J., & Zigler, E. (1989). The intergenerational transmission of child abuse. In D. Cicchetti & V. Carlson (Eds.), *Child maltreatment: Theory and research on the causes and consequences of child abuse and neglect.* New York: Cambridge University Press.

Keller, B. B., & Bell, R. Q. (1979). Child effects on adult's method of eliciting altruistic behavior. *Child Development, 50,* 1004–1009.

Kempe, R. S., & Kempe, C. H. (1978). *Child abuse.* Cambridge, MA: Harvard University Press.

Kerr, M., & Stattin, H. (2000). What parents know, how they know it, and several forms of adolescent adjustment: Further support for a reinterpretation of monitoring. *Developmental Psychology, 36,* 366–380.

King, V., & Elder, G. H. (1995). American children view their grandparents: Linked lives across three rural generations. *Journal of Marriage and the Family, 57,* 165–178.

Kitson, G. C. (1992). *Portrait of divorce: Adjustment to marital breakdown.* New York: Guilford.

Kitson, G. C., Babri, K. B., & Roach, M. J. (1985). Who divorces and why: A review. *Journal of Family Issues, 6,* 255–293.

Kitzmann, K. M. (2000). Effects of marital conflict on subsequent triadic family interactions and parenting. *Developmental Psychology, 36,* 3–13.

Klein, D. M., & White, J. M. (1996). *Family theories: An introduction.* Thousand Oaks, CA: Sage.

Klimes-Dougan, B., & Kistner, J. (1990). Physically abused preschoolers' responses to peers' distress. *Developmental Psychology, 26,* 599–602.

Kline, M., Tschann, J. M., Johnston, J. R., & Wallerstein, J. S. (1989). Children's adjustment in joint and sole physical custody families. *Developmental Psychology, 25,* 430–438.

Kobak, R. R., Cole, H.E., Ferenz-Gilles, R., Fleming, W. S., & Gamble, W. (1993). Attachment and emotional regulation during mother–teen problem solving: A control theory analysis. *Child Development, 64,* 231–245.

Koestner, R., Zuroff, D. C., & Powers, T. A. (1991). Family origins of adolescent self-criticism and its continuity into adulthood. *Journal of Abnormal Psychology, 100,* 191–197.

Kohn, M. L. (1969). *Class and conformity: A study of values.* Homewood, IL: Dorsey Press.

Korbin, J. E. (2001). Context and meaning in neighborhood studies of children and families. In A. Booth, & A. C. Crouter (Eds.), *Does it take a village? Community effects on children, adolescents, and families.* Mahwah, NJ: Erlbaum.

Kurdek, L. A. (1991a). Correlates of relationship satisfaction in cohabiting gay and lesbian couples: Integration of contextual investment and problem-solving models. *Journal of Personality and Social Psychology, 61,* 910–922.

Kurdek, L. A. (1991b). The relations between reported well-being and divorce history, availability of a proximate adult, and gender. *Journal of Marriage and the Family, 53,* 71–78.

Kurdek, L. A. (1995). Lesbian and gay couples. In A. R. Augelli & C. J. Patterson (Eds.), *Lesbian and gay identities over the life span: Psychological perspectives on personal, relational, and community processes.* New York: Oxford University Press.

Kurdek, L. A. (1999). The nature and predictors of the trajectory of change in marital quality for husbands and wives over the first 10 years of marriage. *Developmental Psychology, 35,* 1283–1296.

Lachs, M. S., Williams, C., O'Brien, S., Hurst, L., & Horwitz, R. (1997). Risk factors for reported elder abuse and neglect: A nine-year observational cohort study. *Gerontologist, 37,* 469–474.

Lamborn, S. D., Mounts, N. S., Steinberg, L., & Dornbusch, S. M. (1991). Patterns of competence and adjustment among adolescents from authoritative, authoritarian, indulgent, and neglectful families. *Child Development, 62,* 1049–1065.

Lamborn, S. D., & Steinberg, L. (1993). Emotional autonomy redux: Revisiting Ryan and Lynch. *Child Development, 64,* 483–499.

Larson, R. W., Richards, M. H., Moneta, G., Holmbeck, G., & Duckett, E. (1996). Changes in adolescents' daily interactions with their families from ages 10 to 18: Disengagement and transformation. *Developmental Psychology, 32,* 744–753.

Lee, G. R., Netzer, J. K., & Coward, R. T. (1995). Depression among older parents: The role of intergenerational exchange. *Journal of Marriage and the Family, 57,* 823–833.

Lerner, J. V., & Noh, E. R. (2000). Maternal employment influences on early adolescent development: A contextual view. In R. D. Taylor & M. C. Wang (Eds.), *Resilience across contexts: Family, work, culture, and community.* Mahwah, NJ: Erlbaum.

Lerner, M. J., Somers, D. G., Reid, D., Chiriboga, D., & Tierney, M. (1991). Adult children as caregivers: Egocentric biases in judgments of sibling contributions. *Gerontologist, 31,* 746–755.

Lerner, R. M., Sparks, E. E., & McCubbin, L. D. (2000). Family diversity and family policy. In D. H. Demo & K. R. Allen (Eds.), *Handbook of family diversity.* New York: Oxford University Press.

Leventhal, J. M. (2001). The prevention of child abuse and neglect: Successfully out of the blocks, *Child Abuse and Neglect, 25,* 431–439.

Levinson, D. (1989). *Family violence in cross-cultural perspective.* Newbury Park, CA: Sage.

Levy-Shiff, R. (1994). Individual and contextual correlates of marital change across the transition to parenthood. *Developmental Psychology, 30,* 591–601.

Leyendecker, B., & Lamb, M. E. (1999). Latino families. In M. E. Lamb (Ed.), *Parenting and child development in "nontraditional" families.* Mahwah, NJ: Erlbaum.

Li, L. W., Seltzer, M. M., & Greenberg, J. S. (1999). Change in depressive symptoms among daughter caregivers: An 18-month longitudinal study. *Psychology and Aging, 14,* 206–219.

Lillard, L. A., & Panis, C. W. A. (1996). Marital status and mortality: The role of health. *Demography, 33,* 313–327.

Litwak, E. (1960). Geographic mobility and extended family cohesion. *American Sociological Review, 25,* 385–394.

Lustig, J. L., Wolchik, S. A., & Braver, S. L. (1992). Social support in chumships and adjustment in children of divorce. *American Journal of Community Psychology, 20,* 393–399.

Lye, D. N. (1996). Adult child–parent relationships. *Annual Review of Sociology, 22,* 79–102.

Lytton, H. (2000). Toward a model of family-environmental and child-biological influences on development. *Developmental Review, 20,* 150–179.

Maccoby, E. E. (1980). *Social development.* San Diego: Harcourt Brace Jovanovich.

Maccoby, E. E., & Martin, J. A. (1983). Socialization in the context of the family: Parent–child interaction. In E. M. Hetherington (Ed.; P. H. Mussen, General Ed.), *Handbook of child psychology: Vol. 4. Socialization, personality, and social development* (4th ed.). New York: Wiley.

Mackey, R. A., & O'Brien, B. A. (1995). *Lasting marriages: Men and women growing together.* Westport, CT: Praeger.

MacPhee, D., Fritz, J., & Miller-Heyl, J. (1996). Ethnic variations in personal social networks and parenting. *Child Development, 67,* 3278–3295.

Maier, E. H., & Lachman, M. E. (2000). Consequences of early parental loss and separation for health and well-being in midlife. *International Journal of Behavioral Development, 24,* 183–189.

Main, M. & George, C. (1985). Responses of abused and disadvantaged toddlers to distress in agemates: A study in the day-care setting. *Developmental Psychology, 21,* 407–412.

Main, M., & Weston, D. R. (1981). The quality of the toddler's relationship to mother and to father: Related to conflict and the readiness to establish new relationships. *Child Development, 52,* 932–940.

Malinosky-Rummell, R., & Hansen, D. J. (1993). Long-term consequences of childhood physical abuse. *Psychological Bulletin, 114,* 68–79.

Margolin, G., & Gordis, E. B. (2000). The effects of family and community violence on children. *Annual Review of Psychology, 51,* 445–479.

Markides, K. S., Boldt, J. S., & Ray, L. A. (1986). Sources of helping and intergenerational solidarity: A three-generations study of Mexican Americans. *Journal of Gerontology, 41,* 506–511.

Marsiglio, W., Amato, P., Day, R. D., & Lamb, M. E. (2000). Scholarship on fatherhood in the 1990s and beyond. *Journal of Marriage and the Family, 62,* 1173–1191.

McCloskey, L. A., Figueredo, A. J., & Koss, M. P. (1995). The effects of systematic family violence on children's mental health. *Child Development, 66,* 1239–1261.

McGuire, S., Manke, B., Eftekhari, A., & Dunn, J. (2000). Children's perceptions of sibling conflict during middle childhood: Issues and sibling (dis)similarity. *Social Development, 9,* 173–190.

McHale, S. M., Updegraff, K. A., Helms-Erikson, H., & Crouter, A. C. (2001). Sibling influences on gender development in middle childhood and early adolescence: A longitudinal study. *Developmental Psychology, 37,* 115–125.

McHale, S. M., Updegraff, K. A., Jackson-Newsom, J., Tucker, C. J., & Crouter, A. C. (2000). When does parents' differential treatment have negative implications for siblings? *Social Development, 9,* 149–172.

McKeering, H., & Pakenham, K. I. (2000). Gender and generativity issues in parenting: Do fathers benefit more than mothers from involvement in child care activities? *Sex Roles, 43,* 459–480.

McLoyd, V. C. (1990). The impact of economic hardship on black families and children: Psychological distress, parenting, and socioemotional development. *Child Development, 61,* 311–346.

McLoyd, V. C., Cauce, A. M., Takeuchi, D., & Wilson, L. (2000). Marital processes and parental socialization in families of color: A decade review of research. *Journal of Marriage and the Family, 62,* 1070–1093.

McLoyd, V. C., Jayaratne, T. E., Ceballo, R., & Borquez, J. (1994). Unemployment and work interruption among African-American single mothers: Effects on parenting and adolescent socioemotional functioning. *Child Development, 65,* 562–589.

Mekos, D., Hetherington, E. M., & Reiss, D. (1996). Sibling differences in problem behavior and parental treatment in nondivorced and remarried families. *Child Development, 67,* 2148–2165.

Menaghan, E. G., & Lieberman, M. A. (1986). Changes in depression following divorce: A panel study. *Journal of Marriage and the Family, 48,* 319–328.

Miller, N. B., Cowan, P. A., Cowan, C. P., Hetherington, E. M., & Clingempeel, W. G. (1993). Externalizing in preschoolers and early adolescents: A cross-study replication of a family model. *Developmental Psychology, 29,* 3–18.

Monk, T. H., Essex, M. J., Smider, N. A., Klein, M. H., Lowe, K. K., & Kupfer, D. (1996). The impact of the birth of a baby on the time structure and social mixture of a couple's daily life and its consequences for well-being. *Journal of Applied Social Psychology, 26,* 1237–1258.

Moorehouse, M. J. (1991). Linking maternal employment patterns to mother–child activities and children's school competence. *Developmental Psychology, 27,* 295–303.

Morrison, D. R., & Coiro, M. J. (1999). Parental conflict and marital disruption: Do children benefit when high-conflict marriages are dissolved? *Journal of Marriage and the Family, 61,* 626–637.

Mylod, D. E., Whitman, T. L., & Borkowski, J. G. (1997). Predicting adolescent mothers' transition to adulthood. *Journal of Research on Adolescence, 7,* 457–478.

Neville, B., & Parke, R. D. (1997). Waiting for paternity: Interpersonal and contextual implications of the timing of fatherhood. *Sex Roles, 37,* 45–59.

Nock, S. L., & Kingston, P. W. (1988). Time with children: The impact of couples' work-time commitment. *Social Forces, 67,* 59–85.

Nydegger, C. N. (1986). Asymmetrical kin and the problematic son-in-law. In N. Datan, A. L. Greene, & H. W. Reese (Eds.), *Life-span developmental psychology: Intergenerational relations.* Hillsdale, NJ: Erlbaum.

Oates, R. K., & Bross, D. C. (1995). What have we learned about treating child physical abuse? A literature review of the last decade. *Child Abuse and Neglect, 19,* 463–473.

O'Brien, M. (1996). Child-rearing difficulties reported by parents of infants and toddlers. *Journal of Pediatric Psychology, 21,* 433–446.

O'Connor, T. G., Caspi, A., DeFries, J. C., & Plomin, R. (2000). Are associations between parental divorce and children's adjustment genetically mediated? An adoption study. *Developmental Psychology, 36,* 429–437.

O'Connor, T. G., Deater-Deckard, K., Fulker, D., Rutter, M., & Plomin, R. (1998). Genotype–environment correlations in late childhood and early adolescence: Antisocial behavioral problems and coercive parenting. *Developmental Psychology, 34,* 970–981.

Offer, D., Ostrov, E., & Howard, K. I. (1981). *The adolescent: A psychological self-portrait.* New York: Basic Books.

Ogbu, J. U. (1981). Origins of human competence: A cultural-ethological perspective. *Child Development, 52,* 413–429.

Ogbu, J. U. (1994). From cultural differences to differences in cultural frames of reference. In P. M. Greenfield & R. R. Cocking (Eds.), *Cross-cultural roots of minority child development.* Hillsdale, NJ: Erlbaum.

Ostwald, S. K., Hepburn, K. W., Caron, W., Burns, T., & Mantell, R. (1999). Reducing caregiver burden: A randomized psychoeducational intervention for caregivers of persons with dementia. *Gerontologist, 39,* 299–309.

Oyserman, D., Radin, N., & Benn, R. (1993). Dynamics in a three-generational family: Teens, grandparents, and babies. *Developmental Psychology, 29,* 564–572.

Palkovitz, R. (1996). Parenting as a generator of adult development: Conceptual issues and implications. *Journal of Social and Personal Relationships, 13,* 571–592.

Parke, R. D. (1996). *Fatherhood.* Cambridge, MA: Harvard University Press.

Parke, R. D., & Sawin, D. B. (1976). The father's role in infancy: A reevaluation. *Family Coordinator, 25,* 365–371.

Patterson, C. J. (1995). Lesbian and gay parenthood. In M. H. Bornstein (Ed.), *Handbook of parenting: Vol. 3. Status and social conditions of parenting.* Mahwah, NJ: Erlbaum.

Patterson, C. J. (2000). Family relationships of lesbians and gay men. *Journal of Marriage and the Family, 62,* 1052–1069.

Paveza, G. J., Cohen, D., Eisdorfer, C., Freels, S., Semla, T., Ashford, J. W., Gorelick, P., Hirschman, R., Luchins, D., & Levy, P. (1992). Severe family violence and Alzheimer's disease: Prevalence and risk factors. *Gerontologist, 32,* 493–497.

Perez-Granados, D. R., & Callanan, M. A. (1997). Conversations with mothers and siblings: Young childrens' semantic and conceptual development. *Developmental Psychology, 33,* 120–134.

Perry-Jenkins, M., Repetti, R. L., & Crouter, A. C. (2000). Work and family in the 1990s. *Journal of Marriage and the Family, 62,* 981–998.

Peters, A., & Liefbroer, A. C. (1997). Beyond marital status: Partner history and well-being in old age. *Journal of Marriage and the Family, 55,* 687–699.

Peterson, C. C. (1999). Grandfathers' and grandmothers' satisfaction with the grandparenting role: Seeking new answers to old questions. *International Journal of Aging and Human Development, 49,* 61–78.

Pettit, G. S., Laird, R. D., Bates, J. E., & Dodge, K. A. (1997). Patterns of after-school care in middle childhood: Risk factors and developmental outcomes. *Merrill-Palmer Quarterly, 43,* 515–538.

Phares, V. (1999). *"Poppa" psychology: The role of fathers in children's mental well-being.* Westport, CT: Praeger.

Pianta, R., Egeland, B., & Erickson, M. F. (1989). The antecedents of maltreatment: Results of the Mother–Child Interaction Research Project. In D. Ciccetti & V. Carlson (Eds.), *Child maltreatment: Theory and research on the causes and consequences of child abuse and neglect.* Cambridge, England: Cambridge University Press.

Pinto, A., Folkers, E., & Sines, J. O. (1991). Dimensions of behavior and home environment in school-age children: India and the United States. *Journal of Cross-Cultural Psychology, 22,* 491–508.

Rank, M. R. (2000). Poverty and economic hardship in families. In D. H. Demo, K. R. Allen, & M. A. Fine (Eds.), *Handbook of family diversity.* New York: Oxford University Press.

Reese-Weber, M. (2000). Middle and late adolescents' conflict resolution skills with siblings: Associations with interparental and parent–adolescent conflict resolution. *Journal of Youth and Adolescence, 29,* 697–711.

Reiss, D., with J. M. Neiderhiser, E. M. Hetherington, & R. Plomin. (2000). *The relationship code: Deciphering genetic and social influences on adolescent development.* Cambridge, MA: Harvard University Press.

Rempel, J. (1985). Childless elderly: What are they missing? *Journal of Marriage and the Family, 47,* 343–348.

Robins, R. W., Caspi, A., & Moffitt, T. E. (2000). Two personalities, one relationship: Both partners' personality traits shape the quality of their relationship. *Journal of Personality and Social Psychology, 79,* 251–259.

Rohner, R. P. (1998). Father love and child development: History and current evidence. *Current Directions in Psychological Science, 7,* 157–161.

Rollins, B. C., & Feldman, H. (1970). Marital satisfaction over the family life cycle. *Journal of Marriage and the Family, 32,* 20–28.

Ross, H. G., & Milgram, J. I. (1982). Important variables in adult sibling relationships: A qualitative study. In M. E. Lamb & B. Sutton-Smith (Eds.), *Sibling relationships: Their nature and significance across the lifespan.* Hillsdale, NJ: Erlbaum.

Rothbaum, R., Pott, M., Azuma, H., Miyake, K., & Weisz, J. (2000). The development of close relationships in Japan and the United States: Paths of symbiotic harmony and generative tension. *Child Development, 71,* 1121–1142.

Rubinstein, R. L., Alexander, R. B., Goodman, M., & Luborsky, M. (1991). Key relationships of never married, childless older women: A cultural analysis. *Journal of Gerontology: Social Sciences, 46,* S270–S277.

Ruggles, S. (1994). The origins of African-American family structure. *American Sociological Review, 59,* 136–151.

Russell, R. J., & Wells, P. A. (1991). Personality similarity and quality of marriage. *Personality and Individual Differences, 12,* 407–412.

Sameroff, A. (1975). Early influences on development: Fact or fancy? *Merrill-Palmer Quarterly, 21,* 263–294.

Sanchez, L., & Thomson, E. (1997). Becoming mothers and fathers: Parenthood, gender, and the division of labor. *Gender & Society, 11,* 747–772.

Savin-Williams, R. C., & Esterberg, K. G. (2000). Lesbian, gay, and bisexual families. In D. H. Demo, K. R. Allen, & M. A. Fine (Eds.), *Handbook of family diversity.* New York: Oxford University Press.

Scarr, S., & McCartney, K. (1983). How people make their own environments: A theory of genotype→environment effects. *Child Development, 54,* 424–435.

Schaefer, E. S. (1959). A circumplex model for maternal behavior. *Journal of Abnormal and Social Psychology, 59,* 226–235.

Schinke, S. P., Schilling, R. F., II., Barth, R. P., Gilchrist, L. D., & Maxwell, J. S. (1986). Stress-management intervention to prevent family violence. *Journal of Family Violence, 1,* 13–26.

Scott, W. A., Scott, R., & McCabe, M. (1991). Family relationships and children's personality: A cross-cultural, cross-source comparison. *British Journal of Social Psychology, 30,* 1–20.

Seccombe, K. (2000). Families in poverty in the 1990s: Trends, causes, consequences, and lessons learned. *Journal of Marriage and the Family, 62,* 1094–1113.

Seltzer, J. A. (2000). Families formed outside of marriage. *Journal of Marriage and the Family, 62,* 1247–1268.

Seltzer, M. M., & Li, L. W. (2000). The dynamics of caregiving: Transitions during a three-year prospective study. *Gerontologist, 40,* 165–178.

Shanas, E. (1980). Older people and their families: The new pioneers. *Journal of Marriage and the Family, 42,* 9–15.

Sherrod, K. B., O'Connor, S., Vietze, P. M., & Altemeier, W. A., III. (1984). Child health and maltreatment. *Child Development, 55,* 1174–1183.

Shonk, S. M., & Cicchetti, D. (2001). Maltreatment, competency deficits, and risk for academic and behavioral maladjustment. *Developmental Psychology, 37,* 3–17.

Silverberg, S. B., & Steinberg, L. (1990). Psychological well-being of parents with early adolescent children. *Developmental Psychology, 26,* 658–666.

Silverstein, M., Chen, X., & Heller, K. (1996). Too much of a good thing? Intergenerational social support and the psychological well-being of older parents. *Journal of Marriage and the Family, 58,* 970–982.

Simons, R. L., Robertson, J. F., & Downs, W. R. (1989). The nature of the association between parental rejection and delinquent behavior. *Journal of Youth and Adolescence, 18,* 297–310.

Simons, R. L., Whitbeck, L. B., Beaman, J., & Conger, R. D. (1994). The impact of mothers' parenting, involvement by nonresidential fathers, and parental conflict on the adjustment of adolescent children. *Journal of Marriage and the Family, 56,* 356–374.

Sirignano, S. W., & Lachman, M. E. (1985). Personality change during the transition to parenthood: The role of perceived infant temperament. *Developmental Psychology, 21,* 558–567.

Smetana, J. G. (2000). Middle-class African American adolescents' and parents' conceptions of parental authority and parenting practices: A longitudinal investigation. *Child Development, 71,* 1672–1686.

Sorensen, E. (1997). A national profile of nonresident fathers and their ability to pay child support. *Journal of Marriage and the Family, 59,* 785–797.

Span, P. (2000, August 27). Home alone. *Washington Post Magazine,* pp. 12–15, 24–25.

Steinberg, L. (2002). *Adolescence* (6th ed.). Boston: McGraw-Hill.

Steinberg, L., Darling, N. E., & Fletcher, A. C., in collaboration with B. B. Brown & S. M. Dornbusch. (1995). Authoritative parenting and adolescent adjustment: An ecological journey. In P. Moen, G. H. Elder, Jr., & K. Luscher (Eds.), *Examining lives in context: Perspectives on the ecology of human development.* Washington, DC: American Psychological Association.

Steinberg, L., & Morris, A. (2000). Adolescent development. *Annual Review of Psychology, 52,* 83–110.

Stemp, P. S., Turner, J., & Noh, S. (1986). Psychological distress in the postpartum period: The significance of social support. *Journal of Marriage and the Family, 48,* 271–277.

Stephens, M. A., & Franks, M. M. (1995). Spillover between daughters' roles as caregiver and wife: Interference or enhancement? *Journal of Gerontology: Psychological Sciences, 50,* P9–P17.

Stephens, M. A., Townsend, A. L., Martire, L. M., & Druley, J. A. (2001). Balancing parent care with other roles: Interrole conflict of adult daughter caregivers. *Journal of Gerontology: Psychological Sciences, 56,* P24–P34.

Stewart, R. B., & Marvin, R. S. (1984). Sibling relations: The role of conceptual perspective-taking in the ontogeny of sibling caregiving. *Child Development, 55,* 1322–1332.

St. George, D. (2001, June 8). A child's unheeded cry for help. *Washington Post,* pp. A1, A20–A21.

Stith, S. M., Rosen, K. H., Middleton, K. A., Busch, A. L., Lundeberg, K., & Carlton, R. P.

(2000). The intergenerational transmission of spouse abuse: A meta-analysis. *Journal of Marriage and the Family, 62,* 640–654.

Straus, M. A., & Gelles, R. J. (1986). Societal change and change in family violence from 1975 to 1985 as revealed by two national surveys. *Journal of Marriage and the Family, 48,* 465–479.

Straus, M. A., & Gelles, R. J. (Edited with C. Smith). (1990). *Physical violence in American families: Risk factors and adaptations to violence in 8,145 families.* New Brunswick, NJ: Transaction Publishers.

Suitor, J. J. (1991). Marital quality and satisfaction with the division of household labor across the family life cycle. *Journal of Marriage and the Family, 53,* 221–230.

Sweet, J. A., & Bumpass, L. L. (1987). *American families and households.* New York: Russell Sage Foundation.

Szinovacz, M. E., DeViney, S., & Atkinson, M. P. (1999). Effects of surrogate parenting on grandparents' well-being. *Journals of Gerontology: Social Sciences, 54,* S376–S388.

Taeuber, C. (1990). Diversity: The dramatic reality. In S. A. Bass, E. A. Kutza, & F. M. Torres-Gil (Eds.), *Diversity in aging.* Glenview, IL: Scott, Foresman.

Taylor, R. D., Jacobson, L., Rodriguez, A. U., Dominguez, A., Cantic, R., Doney, J., Boccuti, A., Alejandro, J., & Tobon, C. (2000). Stressful experiences and the psychological functioning of African-American and Puerto Rican families and adolescents. In R. D. Taylor & M. C. Wang (Eds.), *Resilience across contexts: Family, work, culture, and community.* Mahwah, NJ: Erlbaum.

Taylor, R. L. (2000). Diversity within African-American families. In D. H. Demo, K. R. Allen, & M. A. Fine (Eds.), *Handbook of family diversity.* New York: Oxford University Press.

Teachman, J. D. (2000). Diversity of family structure: Economic and social influences. In D. H. Demo, K. R. Allen, & M. A. Fine (Eds.), *Handbook of family diversity.* New York: Oxford University Press.

Teti, D. M., Sakin, J. W., Kucera, E., & Corns, K. M. (1996). And baby makes four: Predictors of attachment security among preschool-age firstborns during the transition to siblinghood. *Child Development, 67,* 579–596.

Thompson, R. A., & Amato, P. R. (1999). The post divorce family: An introduction to the issues. In R. A. Thompson & P. R. Amato (Eds.), *The post divorce family: Children, parenting, and society.* Thousand Oaks, CA: Sage.

Thomson, E., & Colella, U. (1992). Cohabitation and marital stability: Quality or commitment. *Journal of Marriage and the Family, 54,* 259–267.

Umberson, D. (1992). Relationships between adult children and their parents: Psychological consequences for both generations. *Journal of Marriage and the Family, 54,* 664–674.

Umberson, D., & Slaten, E. (2000). Gender and intergenerational relationships. In D. H. Demo, K. R. Allen, & M. A. Fine (Eds.), *Handbook of family diversity.* New York: Oxford University Press.

U.S. Census Bureau. (2000). *Statistical abstract of the United States: 2000.* Washington, DC: U.S. Government Printing Office.

van Ijzendoorn, M. H. (1992). Intergenerational transmission of parenting: A review of studies in nonclinical populations. *Developmental Review, 12,* 76–99.

Vobejda, B. (1998, May 28). Traditional families hold on: Statistics show a slackening of 1970s, '80s social trends. *Washington Post,* p. A2.

Volling, B. L., & Belsky, J. (1992). The contribution of mother–child and father–child relationships to the quality of sibling interaction: A longitudinal study. *Child Development, 63,* 1209–1222.

Vondra, J., & Belsky, J. (1993). Developmental origins of parenting: Personality and relationship factors. In T. Luster & L. Okagaki (Eds.), *Parenting: An ecological perspective.* Hillsdale, NJ: Erlbaum.

Waite, L. J., & Gallagher, M. (2000). *The case for marriage: Why married people are happier, healthier, and better off financially.* New York: Doubleday.

Wallerstein, J. S., & Blakeslee, S. (1989). *Second chances: Men, women, and children a decade after divorce.* New York: Ticknor & Fields.

Wang, H. Y., & Amato, P. R. (2000). Predictors of divorce adjustment: Stressors, resources, and definitions. *Journal of Marriage and the Family, 62,* 655–668.

Ward, R. & Spitze, G. (1992). Consequences of parent–adult child coresidence. *Journal of Family Issues, 13,* 533–572.

Weisner, T. S., & Gallimore, R. (1977). My brother's keeper: Child and sibling caretaking. *Current Anthropology, 18,* 169–190.

Weiss, L. H., & Schwarz, J. C. (1996). The relationship between parenting types and older adolescents' personality, academic achievement, adjustment, and substance use. *Child Development, 67,* 2101–2114.

Whipple, E. E., & Richey, C. A. (1997). Crossing the line from physical discipline to child abuse: How much is too much? *Child Abuse and Neglect, 21,* 431–444.

Whitbeck, L. B., Hoyt, D. R., & Huck, S. M. (1994). Early family relationships, intergenerational solidarity, and support provided to parents by their adult children. *Journals of Gerontology, 49,* S85–S94.

White, K., Speisman, J. C., & Costos, D. (1983). Young adults and their parents: Individuation to mutuality. In H. D. Grotevant & C. R. Cooper (Eds.), *Adolescent development in the family* (New Directions for Child Development, No. 22). San Francisco: Jossey-Bass.

White, L., & Edwards, J. N. (1990). Emptying the nest and parental well-being: An analysis of national panel data. *American Sociological Review, 55,* 235–242.

White, L., & Rogers, S. J. (1997). Strong support but uneasy relationships: Coresidence and adult children's relationships with their parents. *Journal of Marriage and the Family, 59,* 62–76.

White, L., & Rogers, S. J. (2000). Economic circumstances and family outcomes: A review of the 1990s. *Journal of Marriage and the Family, 62,* 1035–1051.

Widmayer, S., & Field, T. (1980). Effects of Brazelton demonstrations on early interactions of preterm infants and their teen-age mothers. *Infant Behavior and Development, 3,* 79–89.

Wiehe, V. R. (1996). *Working with child abuse and neglect.* Thousand Oaks, CA: Sage.

Wolchik, S. A., West, S. G., Sandler, I. N., Tein, J. Y., Coatsworth, D., Lengua, L., Weiss, L., Anderson, E. R., Greene, S. M., & Griffin, W. A. (2000). An experimental evaluation of theory-based mother and mother–child programs for children of divorce. *Journal of Consulting and Clinical Psychology, 68,* 843–856.

Wolf, R. S. (2000). Elder abuse. In V. B. Van Hasselt & M. Hersen (Eds.), *Aggression and violence: An introductory text.* Needham Heights, MA: Allyn & Bacon.

Wolfner, G. D., & Gelles, R. J. (1993). A profile of violence toward children: A national study. *Child Abuse and Neglect, 17,* 197–212.

Woodward, L., Fergusson, D. M., & Belsky, J. (2000). Timing of parental separation and attachment to parents in adolescence: Results of a prospective study from birth to age 16. *Journal of Marriage and the Family, 62,* 162–174.

Yates, M. E., Tennstedt, S., & Chang, B. H. (1999). Contributors to and mediators of psychological well-being for informal caregivers. *Journal of Gerontology: Psychological Sciences, 54,* P12–P22.

Youn, G. Y., Knight, B. G., Jeong, H. S., & Benton, D. (1999). Differences in familism values and caregiving outcomes among Korean, Korean American, and White American dementia caregivers. *Psychology and Aging, 14,* 355–364.

Chapter 16: Developmental Psychopathology

Achenbach, T. M. (1982). *Developmental psychopathology* (2nd ed.). New York: Wiley.

Achenbach, T. M., & Edelbrock, C. S. (1978). The classification of child psychopathology: A review and analysis of empirical efforts. *Psychological Bulletin, 85,* 1275–1301.

Aldwin, C. M. (1994). *Stress, coping, and development.* New York: Guilford.

Allen, A. (2001, May 8). Memory lapse or Alzheimer's? *Washington Post/Health,* pp. 10–14.

American Psychiatric Association. (1994). *Diagnostic and statistical manual of mental disorders: DSM-IV* (4th ed.). Washington, DC: Author.

Asarnow, J. R., Jaycox, L. H., & Tompson, M. C. (2001). Depression in youth: Psychosocial interventions. *Journal of Clinical Child Psychology, 30,* 33–47.

Bacskai, B. J., Kajdasz, S. T., Christie, R. H., Carter, C., Games, D., Seubert, P., Schenk, D., & Hyman, B. T. (2001). Imaging of amyloid-beta deposits in brains of living mice permits direct observation of clearance of plaques with immunotherapy. *Nature Medicine, 7,* 369–372.

Bailey, A., Lecouteur, A., Gottesman, I., Bolton, P., Simonoff, E., Yuzda, E., & Rutter, M. (1995). Autism as a strongly genetic disorder: Evidence from a British twin study. *Psychological Medicine, 25,* 63–77.

Bailey, A., Phillips, W., & Rutter, M. (1996). Autism: Towards an integration of clinical, genetic, neuropsychological, and neurobiological perspectives. *Journal of Child Psychology and Psychiatry and Allied Disciplines, 37,* 89–126.

Bailey, C. E. (Ed.). (2000). *Children in therapy: Using the family as a resource.* New York: W. W. Norton.

Baldwin, R. C. (2000). Poor prognosis of depression in elderly people: Causes and actions. *Annals of Medicine, 32,* 252–256.

Barkley, R. A. (1997). Behavioral inhibition, sustained attention, and executive functions: Constructing a unifying theory of ADHD. *Psychological Bulletin, 121,* 65–94.

Barkley, R. A. (2000). Genetics of childhood disorders: XVII. ADHD, Part 1: The executive functions and ADHD. *Journal of the American Academy of Child and Adolescent Psychiatry, 39,* 1064–1068.

Barkley, R. A., Fischer, M., Edelbrock, C., & Smallish, L. (1991). The adolescent outcome of hyperactive children diagnosed by research criteria: Mother–child interactions, family conflicts and maternal psychopathology. *Journal of Child Psychology and Psychiatry and Allied Disciplines, 32,* 233–255.

Baron-Cohen, S. (2000). Theory of mind and autism: A fifteen year review. In S. Baron-Cohen, H. Tager-Flusberg, & D. J. Cohen (Eds.), *Understanding other minds: Perspectives from developmental cognitive neuroscience* (2nd ed.). Oxford: Oxford University Press.

Bauchner, H. (1996). Failure to thrive. In R. E. Behrman, R. M. Kliegman, & A. M. Arvin (Eds.), *Nelson textbook of pediatrics* (15th ed.). Philadelphia: W. B. Saunders.

Beck, C., Cody, M., Souder, E., Zhang, M. L., & Small, G. W. (2000). Dementia diagnostic guidelines: Methodologies, results, and implementation costs. *Journal of the American Geriatrics Society, 48,* 1195–1203.

Bemporad, J. R. (1979). Adult recollections of a formerly autistic child. *Journal of Autism and Developmental Disorders, 9,* 179–197.

Bergem, A. L. M., Engedal, K., & Kringlen, E. (1997). The role of heredity in late-onset Alzheimer disease and vascular dementia: A twin study. *Archives of General Psychiatry, 54,* 264–270.

Berman, A. L., & Jobes, D. A. (1991). *Adolescent suicide: Assessment and intervention.* Washington, DC: American Psychological Association.

Biederman, J., Faraone, S., Milberger, S., Guite, J., Mick, E., Chen, L., Mennin, D., Marrs, A., Oullette, C., Moore, P., Spencer, T., Norman, D., Wilens, T., Kraus, I., & Perrin, J. (1996). A prospective 4-year follow-up study of attention-deficit hyperactivity and related disorders. *Archives of General Psychiatry, 53,* 437–446.

Biederman, J., Milberger, S., Faraone, S. V., Kiely, K., Guite, J., Mick, E., Ablon, S., Warburton, R., & Reed, E. (1995). Family-environment risk factors for attention-deficit hyperactivity disorder: A test of Rutter's indicators of adversity. *Archives of General Psychiatry, 52,* 464–470.

Black, M. M., Hutcheson, J. J., Dubowitz, H., & Berenson-Howard, J. (1994). Parenting style and developmental status among children with nonorganic failure to thrive. *Journal of Pediatric Psychology, 19,* 689–707.

Blazer, D. G. (1993). *Depression in late life.* St. Louis: Mosby.

Blazer, D. G. (1996). Epidemiology of psychiatric disorders in late life. In E. W. Busse & D. G. Blazer (Eds.), *Textbook of geriatric psychiatry* (2nd ed.). Washington, DC: American Psychiatric Press.

Blazer, D. G., & Koenig, H. G. (1996). Mood disorders. In E. W. Busse & D. G. Blazer (Eds.),

Textbook of geriatric psychiatry (2nd ed.). Washington, DC: American Psychiatric Press.

Boise, L., Camicioli, R., Morgan, D. L., Rose, J. H., & Congleton, L. (1999). Diagnosing dementia: Perspectives of primary care physicians. *Gerontologist, 39,* 457–464.

Boris, N. W., & Zeanah, C. H. (1999). Disturbances and disorders of attachment in infancy: An overview. *Infant Mental Health Journal, 20,* 1–9.

Bowers, W. A., Evans, K., & Van Cleve, L. (1996). Treatment of adolescent eating disorders. In M. A. Reineke, F. M. Dattilio, & A. Freeman (Eds.), *Cognitive therapy with children and adolescents: A casebook for clinical practice.* New York: Guilford.

Bradley, J. D. D., & Golden, C. J. (2001). Biological contributions to the presentation and understanding of attention-deficit/hyperactivity disorder: A review. *Clinical Psychology Review, 21,* 907–929.

Bristol, M. M., Cohen, D. J., Costello, E. J., Denckla, M., Eckberg, T. J., Kallen, R., Kraemer, H. C., Lord, C., Maurer, R., Mcilvane, W. J., Minshew, N., Sigman, M., & Spence, M. A. (1996). State of the science in autism: Report to the National Institutes of Health. *Journal of Autism and Developmental Disorders, 26,* 121–154.

Brown, D. (2000, March 26). Autism's new face. *Washington Post,* pp. A1, A12.

Brownell, K. D., & Napolitano, M. A. (1995). Distorting reality for children: Body size proportions of Barbie and Ken dolls. *International Journal of Eating Disorders, 18,* 295–298.

Buhrmester, D., Camparo, L., Christensen, A., Gonzales, L. S., & Hinshaw, S. P. (1992). Mothers and fathers interacting in dyads and triads with normal and hyperactive sons. *Developmental Psychology, 28,* 500–509.

Bulik, C. M., Sullivan, P. F., Wade, T. D., & Kendler, K. S. (2000). Twin studies of eating disorders: A review. *International Journal of Eating Disorders, 27,* 1–20.

Butters, M. A., Becker, J. L., Nebes, R. D., Zmuda, M. D., Mulsant, B. H., Pollock, B. G., & Reynolds, C. F. (2000). Changes in cognitive functioning following treatment of late-life depression. *American Journal of Psychiatry, 157,* 1949–1954.

Cantwell, D. P. (1996). Attention deficit disorder: A review of the past 10 years. *Journal of the American Academy of Child and Adolescent Psychiatry, 35,* 978–987.

Carmelli, D., Swan, G. E., Kelly-Hayes, M., Wolf, P. A., Reed, T., & Miller, B. (2000). Longitudinal changes in the contribution of genetic and environmental influences to symptoms of depression in older male twins. *Psychology and Aging, 15,* 505–510.

Caspi, A., Moffitt, T. E., Newman, D. L., & Silva, P. A. (1996). Behavioral observations at age 3 years predict adult psychiatric disorders: Longitudinal evidence from a birth cohort. *Archives of General Psychiatry, 53,* 1033–1039.

Charman, T. (2000). Theory of mind and the early diagnosis of autism. In S. Baron-Cohen, H. Tager-Flusberg, & D. J. Cohen (Eds.), *Understanding other minds: Perspectives from developmental cognitive neuroscience* (2nd ed.). Oxford: Oxford University Press.

Clark, L. A., Watson, D., & Reynolds, S. (1995) Diagnosis and classification of psychopathology: Challenges to the current system and future directions. *Annual Review of Psychology, 46,* 121–153.

Clark, W. R. (1999). *A means to an end: The biological basis of aging and death.* New York: Oxford University Press.

Committee on Adolescence. (1996). *Adolescent suicide* (Group for the Advancement of Psychiatry, Report No. 140). Washington, DC: American Psychiatric Press.

Compas, B. E., Connor, J. K., & Hinden, B. R. (1998). New perspectives on depression during adolescence. In R. Jessor (Ed.), *New perspectives on adolescent risk behavior.* Cambridge, England: Cambridge University Press.

Connor, M. (1998). A review of behavioral early intervention programs for children with autism. *Educational Psychology in Practice, 14,* 109–117.

Coyne, J. C., & Whiffen, V. E. (1995). Issues in personality as diathesis for depression: The case of sociotropy–dependency and autonomy–self-criticism. *Psychological Bulletin, 118,* 358–378.

Creskoff, N., & Haas, A. (1999). Oral-motor skills and swallowing. In D. B. Kessler & P. Dawson (Eds.), *Failure to thrive and pediatric undernutrition: A transdisciplinary approach.* Baltimore: Paul H. Brookes.

Crijnen, A. A. M., Achenbach, T. M., & Verhulst, F. C. (1997). Comparisons of problems reported by parents of children in 12 cultures: Total problems, externalizing, and internalizing. *Journal of the American Academy of Child and Adolescent Psychiatry, 36,* 1269–1277.

Cummings, E. M., Davies, P. T., & Campbell, S. B. (2000). *Developmental psychopathology and family process: Theory, research, and clinical implications.* New York: Guilford.

Cyranowski, J. M., Frank, E., Young, E., & Shear, M. K. (2000). Adolescent onset of the gender difference in lifetime rates of major depression: A theoretical model. *Archives of General Psychiatry, 57,* 21–27.

Cytryn, L., & McKnew, D. H., Jr. (1996). *Growing up sad: Childhood depression and its treatment.* New York: W. W. Norton.

Dawson, G., & Ashman, S. B. (2000). On the origins of a vulnerability to depression: The influence of the early social environment on the development of psychobiological systems related to risk for affective disorder. In C. A. Nelson (Ed.), *Minnesota Symposium on Child Psychology: Vol. 31. The effects of early adversity on neurobehavioral development.* Mahwah, NJ: Erlbaum.

Deater-Deckard, K. (2001). Annotation: Recent research examining the role of peer relationships in the development of psychopathology. *Journal of Child Psychiatry and Allied Disciplines, 42,* 565–579.

Dominy, N. L., Johnson, W. B., & Koch, C. (2000). Perception of parental acceptance in women with binge-eating disorder. *Journal of Psychology, 134,* 23–36.

Donenberg, G., & Baker, B. L. (1993). The impact of young children with externalizing behaviors on their families. *Journal of Abnormal Child Psychology, 21,* 179–198.

Doyle, A. E., Biederman, J., Seidman, L. J., Weber, W., & Faraore, S. V. (2000). Diagnostic efficiency of neuropsychological test scores for discriminating boys with and without attention deficit-hyperactivity disorder. *Journal of Consulting and Clinical Psychology, 68,* 477–488.

Eating disorders rise with arrival of TV. (1999, June 11). *Chronicle of Higher Education,* p. A22.

Falcon, L. M., & Tucker, K. L. (2000). Prevalence and correlates of depressive symptoms among Hispanic elders in Massachusetts. *Journal of Gerontology: Social Sciences, 55,* S108–S116.

Field, T. (1995). Infants of depressed mothers. *Infant Behavior and Development, 18,* 1–13.

Filipek, P. A., Accardo, P. J., Ashwal, S., & Baranek, G. T. (2000). Practice parameter: Screening and diagnosis of autism: Report of the Quality Standards Subcommittee of the American Academy of Neurology and the Child Neurology Society. *Neurology, 55,* 468–479.

Fischer, K. W., Ayoub, C., Singh, I., Noam, G., Maraganore, A., & Raya, P. (1997). Psychopathology as adaptive development along distinctive pathways. *Development and Psychopathology, 9,* 749–779.

Fischer, M., Barkley, R. A., Edelbrock, C. S., & Smallish, L. (1990). The adolescent outcome of hyperactive children diagnosed by research criteria: II. Academic, attentional, and neuropsychological status. *Journal of Consulting and Clinical Psychology, 58,* 580–588.

Folkman, S., Lazarus, R. S., Pimley, S., & Novacek, J. (1987). Age differences in stress and coping processes. *Psychology and Aging, 2,* 171–184.

Frank, E., & Young, E. (2000). Pubertal changes and adolescent challenges: Why do rates of depression rise precipitously for girls between the ages of 10 and 15 years old? In E. Frank (Ed.), *Gender and its effects on psychopathology.* Washington, DC: American Psychiatric Press.

Garber, J. (1984). The developmental progression of depression in female children. In D. Cicchetti & K. Schneider-Rosen (Eds.), *Childhood depression* (New Directions for Child Development, No. 26). San Francisco: Jossey-Bass.

Garber, J., & Flynn, C. (2001). Vulnerability to depression in childhood and adolescence. In R. E. Ingram & J. M. Price (Eds.), *Vulnerability to psychopathology: Risk across the lifespan.* New York: Guilford.

Garber, J., Weiss, B. & Shanley, N. (1993). Cognitions, depressive symptoms, and development in adolescents. *Journal of Abnormal Psychology, 102,* 47–57.

Gard, M. C. E., & Freeman, C. P. (1996). The dismantling of a myth: A review of eating disorders and socioeconomic status. *International Journal of Eating Disorders, 20,* 1–12.

Gardner, L. J. (1972). Deprivation dwarfism. *Scientific American, 227,* 76–82.

Gardner, R. A. (1993). *Psychotherapy with children.* Northvale, NJ: Jason Aronson.

Garland, A., & Zigler, E. (1993). Adolescent suicide prevention: Current research and social policy implications. *American Psychologist, 48,* 169–182.

Garmezy, N. (1994). Reflections and commentary on risk, resilience, and development. In R. J. Haggerty, L. R. Sherrod, N. Garmezy, & M. Rutter (Eds.), *Stress, risk and resilience in children and adolescents: Processes, mechanisms, and interventions.* Cambridge, England: Cambridge University Press.

Gatz, M., Popkin, S. J., Pino, C. D., & VandenBos, G. R. (1985). Psychological interventions in

older adults. In J. E. Birren & K. W. Schaie (Eds.), *Handbook of the psychology of aging* (2nd ed.). New York: Van Nostrand Reinhold.

Ge, X. J., Lorenz, F. O., Conger, R. D., Elder, G. H., & Simons, R. L. (1994). Trajectories of stressful life events and depressive symptoms during adolescence. *Developmental Psychology, 30,* 467–483.

Gelfand, D. M., Teti, D. M., Seiner, S. A., & Jameson, P. B. (1996). Helping mothers fight depression: Evaluation of a home-based intervention program for depressed mothers and their infants. *Journal of Clinical Child Psychology, 25,* 406–422.

Gillberg, C., & Steffenburg, S. (1987). Outcome and prognostic factors in infantile autism and similar conditions: A population-based study of 46 cases followed through puberty. *Journal of Autism and Developmental Disorders, 17,* 273–287.

Gillick, M. R. (1998). *Tangled minds: Understanding Alzheimer's disease and other dementias.* New York: Penguin.

Girard, C. (1993). Age, gender, and suicide: A cross-national analysis. *American Sociological Review, 58,* 553–574.

Goodman, S. H., & Gotlib, I. H. (1999). Risk for psychopathology in the children of depressed mothers: A developmental model for understanding mechanisms of transmission. *Psychological Review, 106,* 458–490.

Gordon, R. A. (2000). *Eating disorders: Anatomy of a social epidemic* (2nd ed.). Oxford, England: Blackwell.

Gorman, J., Leifer, M., & Grossman, G. (1993). Nonorganic failure to thrive: Maternal history and current maternal functioning. *Journal of Clinical Child Psychology, 22,* 327–336.

Gotlib, I. H., & Hammen, C. L. (1992). *Psychological aspects of depression: Toward a cognitive–interpersonal integration.* Chichester, England: Wiley.

Graham, C. A., & Easterbrooks, M. A. (2000). School-aged children's vulnerability to depressive symptomatology: The role of attachment security, maternal depressive symptomatology, and economic risk. *Development and Psychopathology, 12,* 201–213.

Grayson, D. A., Mackinnon, A., Jorm, A. F., Creasey, H., & Broe, G. A. (2000). Item bias in the Center for Epidemiologic Studies Depression Scale: Effects of physical disorders and disability in an elderly community sample. *Journal of Gerontology: Psychological Sciences, 55,* P273–P282.

Green, W. H. (1986). Psychosocial dwarfism: Psychological and etiological considerations. In B. B. Lahey & A. E. Kazdin (Eds.), *Advances in clinical child psychology* (Vol. 9). New York: Plenum.

Greene, R. W., Biederman, J., Faraone, S. V., Sienna, M., & Garcia-Jetton, J. (1997). Adolescent outcome of boys with attention-deficit/hyperactivity disorder and social disability: Results from a 4-year longitudinal follow-up study. *Journal of Consulting and Clinical Psychology, 65,* 758–767.

Gresham, F. M., & MacMillan, D. L. (1998). Early intervention project: Can its claims be sustained and it effects replicated? *Journal of Autism and Developmental Disorders, 28,* 5–13.

Grober, E., & Kawas, C. (1997). Learning and retention in preclinical and early Alzheimer's disease. *Psychology and Aging, 12,* 183–188.

Gurland, B. (1991). Epidemiology of psychiatric disorders. In J. Sadavoy, L. W. Lazarus, & L. F. Jarvik (Eds.), *Comprehensive review of geriatric psychiatry.* Washington, DC: American Psychiatric Press.

Hall, G. S. (1904). *Adolescence* (2 vols). New York: Appleton.

Hammen, C., & Compas, B. E. (1994). Unmasking unmasked depression in children and adolescents: The problem of comorbidity. *Clinical Psychology Review, 14,* 585–603.

Hammen, C., Henry, R., & Daley, S. (2000). Depression and sensitization to stressors among young women as a function of childhood adversity. *Journal of Consulting and Clinical Psychology, 68,* 782–787.

Happé, F. G. E. (1994). Annotation: Current psychological theories of autism: The "theory of mind" account and rival theories. *Journal of Child Psychology and Psychiatry and Allied Disciplines, 35,* 215–229.

Harley, J. P., Ray, R. S., Tomasi, L., Eichman, P. L., Matthews, C. G., & Chun, R. (1978). Hyperkinesis and food additives: Testing the Feingold hypothesis. *Pediatrics, 61,* 818–828.

Hart, E. L., Lahey, B. B., Loeber, R., Applegate, B., & Frick, P. J. (1995). Developmental change in attention-deficit hyperactivity disorder in boys: A four-year longitudinal study. *Journal of Abnormal Child Psychology, 23,* 729–749.

Heffer, R. W., & Kelley, M. L. (1994). Nonorganic failure to thrive: Developmental outcomes and psychosocial assessment and intervention issues. *Research in Developmental Disabilities, 15,* 247–268.

Hendrie, H. C. (2001). Exploration of environmental and genetic risk factors for Alzheimer's disease: The value of cross-cultural studies. *Current Directions in Psychological Science, 10,* 98–101.

Heston, L. L., & White, J. A. (1991). *The vanishing mind: A practical guide to Alzheimer's disease and other dementias.* New York: W. H. Freeman.

Hill, P. (1993). Recent advances in selected aspects of adolescent development. *Journal of Child Psychology and Psychiatry and Allied Disciplines, 34,* 69–99.

Hinz, L. D., & Williamson, D. A. (1987). Bulimia and depression: A review of the affective variant hypothesis. *Psychological Bulletin, 102,* 150–158.

Hofstra, M. B., Van der Ende, J., & Verhulst, F. C. (2000). Continuity and change of psychopathology from childhood into adulthood. *Journal of the American Academy of Child and Adolescent Psychiatry, 39,* 850–858.

Hooper, S. R., & Tramontana, M. G. (1997). Advances in the neuropsychological bases of child and adolescent psychopathology: Proposed models, findings, and ongoing issues. In T. H. Ollendick & R. J. Prinz (Eds.), *Handbook of adolescent health risk behavior.* New York: Plenum.

Horwitz, A. V., & White, H. R. (1987). Gender role orientations and styles of pathology among adolescents. *Journal of Health and Social Behavior, 28,* 158–170.

Howieson, D. B., Dame, A., Camicioli, R., Sexton, G., Payami, H., & Kaye, J. A. (1997). Cognitive markers preceding Alzheimer's dementia in the healthy oldest old. *Journal of the American Geriatrics Society, 45,* 584–589.

Howlin, P, Mawhood, L., & Rutter, M. (2000). Autism and developmental receptive language disorder—A follow-up comparison in early adult life: II. Social, behavioral, and psychiatric outcomes. *Journal of Child Psychology and Psychiatry and Allied Disciplines, 41,* 561–578.

Hsu, L. K. G. (1990). *Eating disorders.* New York: Guilford.

Hutcheson, J. J., Black, M. M., & Starr, R. H., Jr. (1993). Developmental differences in interactional characteristics of mothers and their children with failure to thrive. *Journal of Pediatric Psychology, 18,* 453–466.

Ialongo, N. S., Edelsohn, G., & Kellam, S. G. (2001). A further look at the prognostic power of young children's reports of depressed mood. *Child Development, 72,* 736–747.

Ingram, J. L., Stodgell, C. J., Hyman, S. L., Figlewicz, D. A., Weitkamp, L. R., & Rodier, P. M. (2000). Discovery of allelic variants of HOXA1 and HOXB1: Genetic susceptibility to autism spectrum disorders. *Teratology, 62,* 393–405.

Ingram, R. E., & Price, J. M. (2001). The role of vulnerability in understanding psychopathology. In R. E. Ingram & J. M. Price (Eds.), *Vulnerability to psychopathology: Risk across the lifespan.* New York: Guilford.

Jacobvitz, D., & Sroufe, L. A. (1987). The early caregiver–child relationship and attention-deficit disorder with hyperactivity in kindergarten: A prospective study. *Child Development, 58,* 1496–1504.

Jensen, P. S. (2000). Current concepts and controversies in the diagnosis and treatment of attention-deficit/hyperactivity disorder. *Current Psychiatry Reports, 2,* 102–109.

Jensen, P. S., Bhatara, V. S., Vitiello, B., Hoagwood, K., Feil, M., & Burke, L. B. (1999). Psychoactive medication prescribing practices for U.S. children: Gaps between research and clinical practice. *Journal of the American Academy of Child and Adolescent Psychiatry, 38,* 557–565.

Jensen, P. S., Hinshaw, S. P., Swanson, J. M., Greenhill, L. L., Conners, C. K., Arnold, L. E., Abikoff, H. B., Elliott, G., Hechtman, L., Hoza, B., March, J. S., Newcorn, J. H., Severe, J. B., Vitiello, B., Wells, K., & Wigal, T. (2001). Findings from the NIMH Multimodal Treatment Study of ADHD (MTA): Implications and applications for primary care providers. *Journal of Developmental and Behavioral Pediatrics, 22,* 60–73.

Jessor, R. (Ed.). (1998). *New perspectives on adolescent risk behavior.* Cambridge, England: Cambridge University Press

Johnson, C. L., Stuckey, M. K., Lewis, L. D., & Schwartz, D. M. (1982). Bulimia: A descriptive survey of 316 cases. *International Journal of Eating Disorders, 2,* 3–16.

Johnson, J. G., Cohen, P., Kasen, S., Smailes, E., & Brook, J. (2001). Association of maladaptive parental behavior with psychiatric disorder among parents and their offspring. *Archives of General Psychology, 58,* 453–460.

Kameguchi, K., & Murphy-Shigematsu, S. (2001). Family psychology and family therapy in Japan. *American Psychologist, 56,* 65–70.

Kanner, L. (1943). Autistic disturbances of affective contact. *Nervous Child, 2,* 217–250.

Kaplan, H. I., & Sadock, B. J. (1998). *Synopsis of psychiatry: Behavioral sciences/clinical psychiatry* (8th ed.). Baltimore: Williams & Wilkens.

Karel, M. J., & Hinrichsen, G. (2000). Treatment of depression in late life: Psychotherapeutic interventions. *Clinical Psychology Review, 20,* 707–729.

Kasl-Godley, J., & Gatz, M. (2000). Psychosocial interventions for individuals with dementia: An integration of theory, therapy, and a clinical understanding of dementia. *Clinical Psychology Review, 20,* 755–782.

Kaslow, N., Mintzer, M. B., Meadows, L. A., & Grabill, C. M. (2000). A family perspective on assessing and treating childhood depression. In C. E. Bailey (Ed.), *Children in therapy: Using the family as a resource.* New York: W. W. Norton.

Kaszniak, A. W. (1990). Psychological assessment of the aging individual. In J. E. Birren & K. W. Schaie (Eds.), *The handbook of the psychology of aging* (3rd ed.). San Diego: Academic Press.

Kazdin, A. E. (2000). *Psychotherapy for children and adolescents: Directions for research and practice.* New York: Oxford University Press.

Keel, P. K., & Fulkerson, J. A. (2001). Vulnerability to eating disorders in childhood and adolescence. In R. E. Ingram & J. M. Price (Eds.), *Vulnerability to psychopathology: Risk across the lifespan.* New York: Guilford

Keel, P. K., & Mitchell, J. E. (1997). Outcome in bulimia nervosa. *American Journal of Psychiatry, 154,* 313–321.

Kendall, P. C. (2000). *Childhood disorders.* East Sussex, UK: Psychology Press.

Kent, A., & Waller, G. (2000). Childhood emotional abuse and eating psychopathology. *Clinical Psychology Review, 20,* 887– 903.

Kerr, M. A., Black, M. M., & Krishnakumar, A. (2000). Failure-to-thrive, maltreatment and the behavior and development of 6-year-old children from low-income, urban families: A cumulative risk model. *Child Abuse and Neglect, 24,* 587–598.

Kessler, R. C. (2000). Gender differences in major depression: Epidemiological findings. In E. Frank (Ed.), *Gender and its effects on psychopathology.* Washington, DC: American Psychiatric Press.

Kessler, R. C., Avenevoli, S., & Merikangas, K. R. (2001). Mood disorders in children and adolescents: An epidemiologic perspective. *Biological Psychiatry, 49,* 1002–1014.

Kessler, R. C., McGonagle, K. A., Zhao, S., Nelson, C. B., Hughes, M., Eshleman, S., Wittchen, H. U., & Kendler, K. S. (1994). Lifetime and 12-month prevalence of DSM-III-R psychiatric disorders in the United States. Results from the National Comorbidity Study. *Archives of General Psychiatry, 51,* 8–19.

Koegel, R. L., Koegel, L. K., & McNerney, E. K. (2001). Pivotal areas in intervention for autism. *Journal of Clinical Child Psychology, 30,* 19–32.

Kosky, R. (1983). Childhood suicidal behavior. *Journal of Child Psychology and Psychiatry and Allied Disciplines, 24,* 457–468.

Kovacs, M., & Goldston, D. (1991). Cognitive and social cognitive development of depressed children and adolescents. *Journal of the American Academy of Child and Adolescent Psychiatry, 30,* 388–392.

La Rue, A., Dessonville, C., & Jarvik, L. F. (1985). Aging and mental disorders. In J. E. Birren &

K. W. Schaie (Eds.), *Handbook of the psychology of aging* (2nd ed.). New York: Van Nostrand Reinhold.

Lester, D. (1994). Are there unique features of suicide in adults of different ages and developmental stages? *Omega, 29,* 337–348.

Levenkron, S. (2000). *Anatomy of anorexia.* New York: W. W. Norton.

Levy, F., Hay, D. A., McStephen, M., Wood, C., & Waldman, I. (1997). Attention-deficit hyperactivity disorder: A category or a continuum? Genetic analysis of a large-scale twin study. *Journal of the American Academy of Child and Adolescent Psychiatry, 36,* 737–744.

Lewinsohn, P. M., Rohde, P., Seeley, J. R., & Baldwin, C. L. (2001). Gender differences in suicide attempts from adolescence to young adulthood. *Journal of the American Academy of Child and Adolescent Psychiatry, 40,* 427–434.

Lieberman, M. A. (1983). Social contexts of depression. In L. D. Breslau & M. R. Haug (Eds.), *Depression and aging: Causes, care, and consequences.* New York: Springer.

Lopez, S. R., & Guarnaccia, P. J. J. (2000). Cultural psychopathology: Uncovering the social world of mental illness. *Annual Review of Psychology, 51,* 571–598.

Lovaas, O. I. (1987). Behavioral treatment and normal educational and intellectual functioning in young autistic children. *Journal of Consulting and Clinical Psychology, 55,* 3–9.

Lovaas, O. I., Smith, T., & McEachin, J. J. (1989). Clarifying comments on the young autism study: Reply to Schopler, Short, and Mesibov. *Journal of Consulting and Clinical Psychology, 57,* 165–167.

Luk, S-L. (1996). Cross-cultural aspects. In S. Sandberg (Ed.), *Hyperactivity disorders of childhood.* Cambridge, England: Cambridge University Press.

Martin, M, Grunendahl, M., & Martin, P. (2001). Age differences in stress, social resources, and well-being in middle and old age. *Journal of Gerontology: Psychological Sciences, 56,* P214–P222.

McLanahan, S. S., & Sorensen, A. B. (1985). Life events and psychological well-being over the life course. In G. H. Elder, Jr. (Ed.), *Life course dynamics: Trajectories and transitions, 1968–1980.* Ithaca, NY: Cornell University Press.

Meador, K. G., & Davis, C. D. (1996). Psychotherapy. In E. W. Busse & D. G. Blazer (Eds.), *Textbook of geriatric psychiatry* (2nd ed.). Washington, DC: American Psychiatric Press.

Meeks, S., Murrell, S. A., & Mehl, R. C. (2000). Longitudinal relationships between depressive symptoms and health in normal older and middle-aged adults. *Psychology and Aging, 15,* 100–109.

Mesman, J., Bongers, I. L., Koot, H. M. (2001). Preschool developmental pathways to preadolescent internalizing and externalizing problems. *Journal of Child Psychology and Psychiatry and Allied Disciplines, 42,* 679–689.

Milich, R., & Pelham, W. E. (1986). Effects of sugar ingestion on the classroom and play-group behavior of attention deficit disordered boys. *Journal of Consulting and Clinical Psychology, 54,* 714–718.

Miller, E., & Morris, R. (1993). *The psychology of dementia.* Chichester, England: Wiley.

Minuchin, S., Rosman, B. L., & Baker, L. (1978). *Psychosomatic families: Anorexia nervosa in context.* Cambridge, MA: Harvard University Press.

Morgan, D., Diamond, D. M., Gottschall, P. E., Ugen, K. E., Dickey, C., Hardy, J., Duff, K., Jantzen, P., DiCarlo, G., Wilcock, D., Connor, K., Hatcher, J., Hope, C., Gordon, M., & Arendash, G. W. (2000). A beta peptide vaccination prevents memory loss in an animal model of Alzheimer's disease. *Nature, 408,* 982–985.

Morris, J. C., Storandt, M., Miller, J. P., McKeel, D., Price, J. L., Rubin, E. H., & Berg, L. (2001). Mild cognitive impairment represents early-stage Alzheimer disease. *Archives of Neurology, 58,* 397–410.

Mulsant, B. H., & Ganguli, M. (1999). Epidemiology and diagnosis of depression in late life. *Journal of Clinical Psychiatry, 60*(Suppl. 20), 9–15.

Murnen, S. K., & Smolak, L. (1997). Femininity, masculinity and disordered eating: A meta-analytic review. *International Journal of Eating Disorders, 22,* 231–242.

Myers, J. K., Weissman, M. M., Tischler, G. L., Holzer, C. E., III, Leaf, P. J., & Orvaschel, H. (1984). Six-month prevalence of psychiatric disorders in three communities. *Archives of General Psychiatry, 41,* 959–967.

National Institute on Aging. (2000). *Progress report on Alzheimer's disease 2000: Taking the next steps* (NIH Publication No. 00-4859). [Available online at http://www.alzheimers.org/pubs/prog00.htm]

Nesse, R. M. (2000). Is depression an adaption? *Archives of General Psychiatry, 57,* 14–20.

Nolen-Hoeksema, S. (1990). *Sex differences in depression.* Stanford, CA: Stanford University Press.

Nolen-Hoeksema, S., & Girgus, J. S. (1994). The emergence of gender differences in depression during adolescence. *Psychological Bulletin, 115,* 424–443.

Nolen-Hoeksema, S., Larson, J., & Grayson, C. (1999). Explaining the gender difference in depressive symptoms. *Journal of Personality and Social Psychology, 77,* 1061–1072.

Nourhashemi, F., Gillette-Guyonnet, S., Andrieu, S., Ghisolfi, A., Ousset, P. J., Grandjean, H., Grand, A., Pous, J., Vellas, B., & Albarede, J. L. (2000). Alzheimer disease: Protective factors. *American Journal of Clinical Nutrition, 71,* 643S–649S.

Offer, D., & Schonert-Reichl, K. A. (1992). Debunking the myths of adolescence: Findings from recent research. *Journal of the American Academy of Child and Adolescent Psychiatry, 31,* 1003–1013.

Okie, S. (2001, May 8). Confronting Alzheimer's: Promising vaccine targets ravager of minds. *Washington Post,* pp. A1, A4.

Pearlin, L. I. (1980). Life strains and psychological distress among adults. In N. J. Smelser & E. H. Erikson (Eds.), *Themes of work and love in adulthood.* Cambridge, MA: Harvard University Press.

Pearson, J. L. (2000). Preventing late life suicide: National Institutes of Health initiatives. *Omega, 42,* 9–20.

Perner, J., & Lang, B. (2000). Theory of mind and executive function: Is there a developmental relationship? In S. Baron-Cohen, H. Tager-Flusberg, & D. J. Cohen (Eds.), *Understanding other minds: Perspectives from developmental cognitive neuroscience* (2nd ed.). Oxford: Oxford University Press.

Peskind, E. R., & Raskind, M. A. (1996). Cognitive disorders. In E. W. Busse & D. G. Blazer (Eds.), *Textbook of geriatric psychiatry* (2nd ed.). Washington, DC: American Psychiatric Press.

Petersen, A. C., Compas, B. E., Brooks-Gunn, J., Stemmler, M., Ey, S., & Grant, K. E. (1993). Depression in adolescence. *American Psychologist, 48,* 155–168.

Phares, V. (1999). *"Poppa" psychology: The role of fathers in children's mental well-being.* Westport, CT: Praeger.

Plassman, B. L., Havlik, R. J., Steffens, D. C., Helms, M. J., Newman, T. N., Drosdick, D., Phillips, C., Gau, B. A., Welsh-Bohmer, K. A., Burke, J. R., Guralnik, J. M., & Breitner, J. C. (2000). Documented head injury in early childhood and risk of Alzheimer's disease and other dementias. *Neurology, 55,* 1158–1166.

Pratico, D., & Delanty, N. (2000). Oxidative injury in diseases of the central nervous system: Focus on Alzheimer's disease. *American Journal of Medicine, 109,* 577–585.

Quay, H. C., Routh, D. K., & Shapiro, S. K. (1987). Psychopathology of childhood: From description to validation. *Annual Review of Psychology, 38,* 491–532.

Rappley, M. D., Mullan, P. B., Alvarez, F. J., Eneli, I. U., Wang, J., & Gardiner, J. C. (1999). Diagnosis of attention-deficit/hyperactivity disorder and use of psychotropic medication in very young children. *Archives of Pediatrics and Adolescent Medicine, 153,* 1039–1045.

Regier, D. A., Boyd, J. H., Burke, J. D., Rae, D. F., Myers, J. K., Kramer, M., Robins, L. N., George, L. K., Karno, M., & Locke, B. Z. (1988). One-month prevalence of mental disorders in the United States. *Archives of General Psychiatry, 45,* 977–986.

Reinherz, H. Z., Giaconia, R. M., Hauf, A. M. C., Wasserman, M. S., & Silverman, A. B. (1999). Major depression in the transition to adulthood: Risks and impairments. *Journal of Abnormal Psychology, 108,* 500–510.

Reiss, D., with J. M. Neiderhiser, E. M. Hetherington, & R. Plomin. (2000). *The relationship code: Deciphering genetic and social influences on adolescent development.* Cambridge, MA: Harvard University Press.

Ricciardelli, L. A., & McCabe, M. P. (2001). Children's body image concerns and eating disturbance: A review of the literature. *Clinical Psychology Review, 21,* 325–344.

Riddle, M. A., Kastelic, E. A., & Frosch, E. (2001). Pediatric psychopharmacology. *Journal of Child Psychology and Psychiatry and Allied Disciplines, 42,* 73–90.

Riley, K. P., Snowdon, D. A., Saunders, A. M., Roses, A. D., Mortimer, J. A., & Nanayakkara, N. (2000). Cognitive function and apolipoprotein E in very old adults: Findings from the Nun Study. *Journal of Gerontology: Social Sciences, 55,* S69–S75.

Robins, L. N., & Regier, D. A. (Eds.). (1991). *Psychiatric disorders in America: The Epidemiologic Catchment Area Study.* New York: Free Press.

Rodier, P. M. (2000). The early origins of autism. *Scientific American, 282,* 56–63.

Rodin, J., Striegel-Moore, R. H., & Silberstein, L. R. (1990). Vulnerability and resilience in the age of eating disorders: Risk and protective factors for bulimia nervosa. In J. Rolf, A. S. Masten, D. Cicchetti, K. H. Nuechterlein, & S. Weintraub (Eds.), *Risk and protective factors in the development of psychopathology.*

Cambridge, England: Cambridge University Press.

Rosenthal, P. A., & Rosenthal, S. (1984). Suicidal behavior by preschool children. *American Journal of Psychiatry, 141,* 520–525.

Rotheram-Borus, M. J., Piacentini, J., Cantwell, C., Belin, T. R., & Song, J. W. (2000). The 18-month impact of an emergency room intervention for adolescent female suicide attempters. *Journal of Consulting and Clinical Psychology, 68,* 1081–1093.

Rovner, S. (1994, March 29). An Alzheimer's journal. *Washington Post Health,* pp. 12–15.

Rudolph, K. D., Hammen, C., Burge, D., Lindberg, N., Herzberg, D., & Daley, S. E. (2000). Toward an interpersonal life-stress model of depression: The developmental context of stress generation. *Development and Psychopathology, 12,* 215–234.

Rutter, M. (1996). Developmental psychopathology: Concepts and prospects. In M. Lenzenweger & J. Havgaard (Eds.), *Frontiers of developmental psychopathology.* New York: Oxford University Press.

Rutter, M. (2000). Psychosocial influences: Critiques, findings, and research needs. *Development and Psychopathology, 12,* 375–405.

Rutter, M., & Schopler, E. (1987). Autism and pervasive developmental disorders: Concepts and diagnostic issues. *Journal of Autism and Developmental Disorders, 17,* 159–186.

Rutter, M., & Sroufe, L. A. (2000). Developmental psychopathology: Concepts and challenges. *Development and Psychopathology, 12,* 265–296.

Sameroff, A. J. (2000). Developmental systems and psychopathology. *Development and Psychopathology, 12,* 297–312.

Schachar, R. J., Tannock, R., Cunningham, C., & Corkum, P. V. (1997). Behavioral, situational, and temporal effects of treatment of ADHD with methylphenidate. *Journal of the American Academy of Child and Adolescent Psychiatry, 36,* 754–763.

Schenk, D., Barbour, R., Dunn, W., Gordon, G., Grajeda, H., Guido, T., Hu, K., Huang, J., Johnson-Wood, K., Khan, K., Kholodenko, D., Lee, M., Liao, Z., Lieburg, I., Motter, R., Mutter, L., Soriano, F., Shopp, G., Vasquez, N., Vandevert, V., Walker, S., Wogulis, M., Yednock, T., Games, D., & Seubert, P. (1999). Immunization with amyloid-beta attenuates Alzheimer-disease-like pathology in PDAPP mouse. *Nature, 400,* 173–177.

Scogin, F., & McElreath, L. (1994). Efficacy of psychosocial treatments for geriatric depression: A quantitative review. *Journal of Consulting and Clinical Psychology, 62,* 69–74.

Scott, J., Clark, C., & Brady, M. P. (2000). *Students with autism: Characteristics and instructional programming for special educators.* San Diego: Singular.

Selkoe, D. J. (1997). Alzheimer's disease: From genes to pathogenesis. *American Journal of Psychiatry, 154,* 1198.

Shaffer, D., & Pfeffer, C. R. (2001). Practice parameters for the assessment and treatment of children and adolescents with suicidal behavior. *Journal of the American Academy of Child and Adolescent Psychiatry, 40,* 24S–51S.

Sharpe, T. M., Killen, J. D., Bryson, S. W., Shisslak, C. M., Estes, L. S., Gray, N., Crago, M., & Taylor, C. G. (1998). Attachment style and weight concerns in preadolescent and adolescent girls. *International Journal of Eating Disorders, 23,* 39–44.

Shute, N. (2001, January 15). Children in anguish: A call for better treatment of kids' mental ills. *U.S. News & World Report,* p. 42.

Shute, N., Locy, T., & Pasternak, D. (2000, March 6). The perils of pills. *U.S. News & World Report,* pp. 45–50.

Sigman, M., & Capps, L. (1997). *Children with autism: A developmental perspective.* Cambridge, MA: Harvard University Press.

Silver, L. B. (1992). *Attention-deficit hyperactivity disorder: A clinical guide to diagnosis and treatment.* Washington, DC: American Psychiatric Press.

Sines, J. O. (1987). Influence of the home and family environment on childhood dysfunction. In B. B. Lahey & A. E. Kazdin (Eds.), *Advances in clinical child psychology* (Vol. 10). New York & London: Plenum.

Smolak, L., & Levine, M. P. (1996). Adolescent transitions and the development of eating problems. In L. Smolak, M. P. Levine, & R. Striegel-Moore (Eds.), *The developmental psychopathology of eating disorders: Implications for research, prevention, and treatment.* Mahwah, NJ: Erlbaum.

Snowdon, D. A. (1997). Aging and Alzheimer's disease: Lessons from the Nun Study. *Gerontologist, 37,* 150–156.

Spitz, R. A. (1946). Anaclitic depression: An inquiry into the genesis of psychiatric conditions in early childhood: II. *Psychoanalytic Study of the Child, 2,* 313–342.

Sprich, S., Biederman, J., Crawford, M. H., Mundy, E., & Faraone, S. V. (2000). Adoptive and biological families of children and adolescents with ADHD. *Journal of the American Academy of Child and Adolescent Psychiatry, 39,* 1432–1437.

Sroufe, L. A. (1997). Psychopathology as an outcome of development. *Development and Psychopathology, 9,* 251–268.

Sroufe, L. A., & Rutter, M. (1984). The domain of developmental psychopathology. *Child Development, 55,* 17–29.

Stapley, J. C., & Haviland, J. M. (1989). Beyond depression: Gender differences in normal adolescents' emotional experiences. *Sex Roles, 20,* 295–308.

Steinberg, L., & Avenevoli, S. (2000). The role of context in the development of psychopathology: A conceptual framework and some speculative propositions. *Child Development, 71,* 66–74.

Strauss, J., Muday, T., McNall, K., & Wong, M. (1997). Response style theory revisited: Gender differences and stereotypes in rumination and distraction. *Sex Roles, 36,* 771–792.

Strober, M. (1986). Psychopathology in adolescence revisited. *Clinical Psychology Review, 6,* 199–209.

Strober, M., Freeman, R., Lampert, C., Diamond, J., & Kaye, W. (2000). Controlled family study of anorexia nervosa and bulimia nervosa: Evidence of shared liability and transmission of partial syndromes. *American Journal of Psychiatry, 157,* 393–401.

Sullivan, P. F., Neale, M. C., & Kendler, K. S. (2000). Genetic epidemiology of major depression: Review and meta-analysis. *American Journal of Psychiatry, 157,* 1552–1562.

Tager-Flusberg, H. (2000). Language and understanding minds: Connections in autism. In S. Baron-Cohen, H. Tager-Flusberg, & D. J. Cohen (Eds.), *Understanding other minds: Perspectives from developmental cognitive neuroscience* (2nd ed.). Oxford: Oxford University Press.

Tanzi, R. E., & Parson, A. B. (2000). *Decoding darkness: The search for the genetic causes of Alzheimer's disease.* Cambridge, MA: Perseus.

Teeter, P. A. (1998). *Interventions for ADHD: Treatment in developmental context.* New York: Guilford.

Teicher, M. H., Anderson, C. M., Polcari, A., Glod, C. A., Maas, L. C., & Renshaw, P. F. (2000). Functional deficits in basal ganglia of children with attention-deficit/hyperactivity disorder shown with functional magnetic resonance imaging relaxometry. *Nature Medicine, 6,* 470–473.

Thelen, M. H., Powell, A. L., Lawrence, C., & Kuhnert, M. E. (1992). Eating and body image concerns among children. *Journal of Clinical Child Psychology, 21,* 41–46.

Todd, R. D. (2000). Genetics of childhood disorders: XXI. ADHD, Part 5: A behavioral genetic perspective. *Journal of the American Academy of Child and Adolescent Psychiatry, 39,* 1571–1573.

U.S. Bureau of the Census. (1996). *Statistical abstract of the United States* (116th ed.). Washington, DC: U.S. Government Printing Office.

U.S. Bureau of the Census. (2000). *Statistical abstract of the United States: 2000* (120th ed.). Washington, DC: U.S. Government Printing Office.

van IJzendoorn, M. H., & Bakermans-Kranenburg, M. J. (1996). Attachment representations in mothers, fathers, adolescents, and clinical groups: A meta-analytic search for normative data. *Journal of Consulting and Clinical Psychology, 64,* 8–21.

Vannatta, R. A. (1996). Risk factors related to suicidal behavior among male and female adolescents. *Journal of Youth and Adolescence, 25,* 149–160.

Vink, T., Hinney, A., van Elburg, A. A., van Goozen, S. H., Sandkuji, L. A., Sinke, R. J., Herpertz-Dahlmann, B. M., Hebebrand, J., Remschmidt, H., van Engeland, H., & Adan, R. A. (2001). Association between an agouti-related protein gene polymorphism and anorexia nervosa. *Molecular Psychiatry, 6,* 325–328.

Volkmar, F. R. (2001). Pharmacological interventions in autism: Theoretical and practical issues. *Journal of Clinical Child Psychology, 30,* 80–87.

Volkmar, F. R., Cook, Jr, E. J., Pomeroy, J., Realmuto, G., Tanguay, P., & the Work Group on Quality Issues. (1999). Practice parameters for the assessment and treatment of children, adolescents, and adults with autism and other pervasive developmental disorders. *Journal of the American Academy of Child and Adolescent Psychiatry, 38,* 32S–54S.

Wagner, B. M. (1997). Family risk factors for child and adolescent suicidal behavior. *Psychological Bulletin, 121,* 246–298.

Wagner, K. D., & Ambrosini, P. J. (2001). Childhood depression: Pharmacological therapy/treatment. *Journal of Clinical Child Psychology, 30,* 88–97.

Wallander, J. L., & Hubert, N. C. (1985). Long-term prognosis for children with attention deficit disorder with hyperactivity (ADD/H). In B. B. Lahey & A. E. Kazdin (Eds.),

Advances in clinical child psychology (Vol. 8). New York: Plenum.

Ward, M. J., Lee, S. S., & Lipper, E. G. (2000). Failure-to-thrive is associated with disorganized infant–mother attachment and unresolved maternal attachment. *Infant Mental Health Journal, 21,* 428–442.

Weiss, G., & Hechtman, L. T. (1993). *Hyperactive children grown up* (2nd ed.). New York: Guilford.

Weisz, J. R., McCarty, C. A., Eastman, K. L., Chaiyasit, W., & Suwanlert, S. (1997). Developmental psychopathology and culture: Ten lessons from Thailand. In S. S. Luthar, J. A. Burack, D. Cicchetti, & J. R. Weisz (Eds.), *Developmental psychopathology: Perspectives on adjustment, risk and disorder.* Cambridge, England: Cambridge University Press.

Weisz, J. R., & Weiss, B. (1993). *Effects of psychotherapy with children and adolescents* (Vol. 27, Developmental Clinical Psychology and Psychiatry Series). Newbury Park, CA: Sage.

Wender, P. H. (1995). *Attention-deficit hyperactivity disorder in adults.* New York: Oxford University Press.

Weyandt, L. L. (2001). *An ADHD primer.* Boston: Allyn & Bacon.

Whalen, C. K., Henker, B., Buhrmester, D., Hinshaw, S. P., Huber, A., & Laski, K. (1989). Does stimulant medication improve the peer status of hyperactive children? *Journal of Consulting and Clinical Psychology, 57,* 545–549.

Whitbeck, L. B., Hoyt, D. R., Simons, R. L., Conger, R. D., Elder, G. H., Jr., Lorenz, F. O., & Huck, S. (1992). Intergenerational continuity of parental rejection and depressed affect. *Journal of Personality and Social Psychology, 63,* 1036–1045.

Wildes, J. E., Emery, R. E., & Simons, A. D. (2001). The roles of ethnicity and culture in the development of eating disturbance and body dissatisfaction: A meta-analytic review. *Clinical Psychology Review, 21,* 521–551.

Williams, G. J., Power, K. G., Millar, H. R., Freeman, C. P., Yellowlees, A., Dowds, T., Walker, M., Campsie, L., MacPherson, F., & Jackson, M. A. (1993). Comparison of eating disorders and other dietary/weight groups on measures of perceived control, assertiveness, self-esteem, and self-directed hostility. *International Journal of Eating Disorders, 14,* 27–32.

Williams, M. E. (1995). *The American Geriatrics Society's complete guide to aging and health.* New York: Harmony Books.

Windle, R. C., & Windle, M. (1997). An investigation of adolescents' substance use behaviors, depressed affect, and suicidal behaviors. *Journal of Child Psychology and Psychiatry and Allied Disciplines, 38,* 921–929.

Wolfe, R., Morrow, J., & Fredrickson, B. L. (1996). Mood disorders in older adults. In L. L. Carstensen, B. A. Edelstein, & L. Dornbrand (Eds.), *The practical handbook of clinical gerontology.* Thousand Oaks, CA: Sage.

Wonderlich, S., Klein, M. H., & Council, J. R. (1996). Relationship of social perceptions and self-concept in bulimia nervosa. *Journal of Consulting and Clinical Psychology, 64,* 1231–1237.

Wright, C., & Birks, E. (2000). Risk factors for failure to thrive: A population based survey. *Child: Care, Health, and Development, 26,* 5–16.

Yirmiya, N., Solomonica-Levy, D., Shulman, C., & Pilowsky, T. (1996). Theory of mind abilities in individuals with autism, Down syndrome, and mental retardation of unknown etiology: The role of age and intelligence. *Journal of Child Psychology and Psychiatry and Allied Disciplines, 37,* 1003–1014.

Zahn-Waxler, C., Klimes-Dougan, B., & Slattery, M. J. (2000). Internalizing problems of childhood and adolescence: Prospects, pitfalls, and progress in understanding the development of anxiety and depression. *Development and Psychopathology, 12,* 443–466.

Zarit, S. H., Eiler, J., & Hassinger, M. (1985). Clinical assessment. In J. E. Birren & K. W. Schaie (Eds.), *Handbook of the psychology of aging* (2nd ed.). New York: Van Nostrand Reinhold.

Zeanah, C. H., Boris, N. W., & Scheeringa, M. S. (1997). Psychopathology in infancy. *Journal of Child Psychology and Psychiatry and Allied Disciplines, 38,* 81–99.

Chapter 17: The Final Challenge: Death and Dying

Adams, D. W., & Deveau, E. J. (1986). Helping dying adolescents: Needs and responses. In C. A. Corr & J. N. McNeil (Eds.), *Adolescence and death.* New York: Springer.

Adams, D. W., & Deveau, E. J. (1987). When a brother or sister is dying of cancer: The vulnerability of the adolescent sibling. *Death Studies, 11,* 279–295.

Applebaum, D. R., & Burns, G. L. (1991). Unexpected childhood death: Posttraumatic stress disorder in surviving siblings and parents. *Journal of Clinical Child Psychology, 20,* 114–120.

Ariès, P. (1981). *The hour of our death* (H. Weaver, Trans.). New York: Knopf. (Original work published 1977)

Aspinall, S. Y. (1996). Educating children to cope with death: A preventive model. *Psychology in the Schools, 33,* 341–349.

Baer, W. M., & Hanson, L. C. (2000). Families' perception of the added value of hospice in the nursing home. *Journal of the American Geriatrics Society, 48,* 879–882.

Balk, D. E., & Corr, C. A. (2001). Bereavement during adolescence: A review of research. In M. S. Stroebe, R. O. Hansson, W. Stroebe, & H. Schut (Eds.), *Handbook of bereavement research: Consequences, coping, and care.* Washington, DC: American Psychological Association.

Bankoff, E. A. (1983). Aged parents and their widowed daughters: A support relationship. *Journal of Gerontology, 38,* 226–230.

Berger, A. S. (1993). *Dying and death in law and medicine: A forensic primer for health and legal professionals.* Westport, CT: Praeger.

Bertman, S. L. (1991). Children and death: Insights, hindsights, and illuminations. In D. Papadatou & C. Papadatos (Eds.), *Children and death.* New York: Hemisphere.

Bluebond-Langner, M. (1977). Meanings of death to children. In H. Feifel (Ed.), *New meanings of death.* New York: McGraw-Hill.

Bodnar, A. G., Oullette, M., Frolkis, M., Holt, S. E., Chiu, C., Morin, G. B., Harley, C. B., Shay, J. W., Lichsteiner, S., & Wright, W. E. (1998). Extension of life-span by introduction of telomerase into normal human cells. *Science, 279,* 349–352.

Bodnar, J. C., & Kiecolt-Glaser, J. K. (1994). Caregiver depression after bereavement: Chronic stress isn't over when it's over. *Psychology and Aging, 9,* 372–380.

Bohannon, J. R. (1990–1991). Grief responses of spouses following the death of a child: A longitudinal study. *Omega, 22,* 109–121.

Bonanno, G. A. (2001). Introduction: New direction in bereavement research and theory. *American Behavioral Scientist, 44,* 718–725.

Bonanno, G. A., & Field, N. P. (2001). Examining the delayed grief hypothesis across 5 years of bereavement. *American Behavioral Scientist, 44,* 798–816.

Bonanno, G. A., & Kaltman, S. (1999). Toward an integrative perspective on bereavement. *Psychological Bulletin, 125,* 760–776.

Bonanno, G. A., & Kaltman, S. (2000). The varieties of grief experience. *Clinical Psychology Review, 21,* 705–734.

Bower, A. R. (1997). The adult child's acceptance of parent death. *Omega, 35,* 67–96.

Bowlby, J. (1980). *Attachment and loss: Vol. 3. Loss, sadness and depression.* New York: Basic Books.

Brent, S. B., Speece, M. W., Lin, C. G., Dong, Q., & Yang, C. M. (1996). The development of the concept of death among Chinese and U.S. children 3–17 years of age: From binary to "fuzzy" concepts? *Omega, 33,* 67–83.

Caddell, D. P., & Newton, R. R. (1995). Euthanasia: American attitudes toward the physician's role. *Social Science and Medicine, 40,* 1671–1681.

Cantor. N. L. (2001). Twenty-five years after Quinlan: A review of the jurisprudence of death and dying. *Journal of Law, Medicine, and Ethics, 29,* 182–196.

Capron, A. M. (1999). The bifurcated legal standard for determining death: Does it work? In S. J. Youngner, R. M. Arnold, & R. Schapiro (Eds.), *The definition of death: Contemporary controversies.* Baltimore: Johns Hopkins University Press.

Carr, D., House, J. S., Kessler, R. C., Nesse, R. M., Sonnega, J., & Wortman, C. (2000). Marital quality and psychological adjustment to widowhood among older adults: A longitudinal analysis. *Journal of Gerontology: Social Sciences, 55,* S197–S207.

Carr, D., House, J. S., Wortman, C., Neese, R., & Kessler, R. C. (2001). Psychological adjustment to sudden and anticipated spousal loss among older widowed persons. *Journal of Gerontology: Social Sciences, 56,* S237–S248.

Chochinov, H. M., Tataryn, D., Clinch, J. J., & Dudgeon, D. (1999). Will to live in terminally ill. *Lancet, 354,* 816–819.

Clark, D. C., Pynoos, R. S., & Goebel, A. E. (1994). Mechanisms and processes of adolescent bereavement. In R. J. Haggerty, L. R. Sherrod, N. Garmezy, & M. Rutter (Eds.), *Stress, risk, and resilience in children and adolescents: Processes, mechanisms, and interventions.* Cambridge, England: Cambridge University Press.

Clark, W. R. (1999). *A means to an end: The biological bases of aging and death.* New York: Oxford University Press.

Cleiren, M. P. H. D. (1993). *Bereavement and adaptation: A comparative study of the aftermath of death.* Washington, DC: Hemisphere.

Colburn, D. (1995, December 5). The grace of a "good death" escapes many. *Washington Post Health,* p. 7.

Compas, B. E., Connor-Smith, J. K., Saltzman, H., Thomsen, A. H., & Wadsworth, M. E. (2001). Coping with stress during childhood and adolescence: Problems, progress, and potential in theory and research. *Psychological Bulletin, 127,* 87–127.

Connor, S. R. (2000). Hospice care and the older person. In A. Tomer (Ed.), *Death attitudes and the older adult: Theories, concepts, and applications.* Philadelphia: Brunner-Routledge.

Cook, A. S., & Dworkin, D. S. (1992). *Helping the bereaved: Therapeutic interventions for children, adolescents, and adults.* New York: Basic Books.

Corr, C. A. (1993). Coping with dying: Lessons that we should and should not learn from the work of Elisabeth Kübler-Ross. *Death Studies, 17,* 69–83.

Corr, C. A. (1995). Entering into adolescent understanding of death. In E. A. Grollman (Ed.), *Bereaved children and teens.* Boston: Beacon Press.

Corr, C. A., & Corr, D. M. (1992). Children's hospice care. *Death Studies, 16,* 431–449.

Cristofalo, V. J. (1996). Ten years later: What have we learned about human aging from studies of cell cultures? *Gerontologist, 36,* 737–741.

Cytron, B. D. (1993). To honor the dead and comfort the mourners: Traditions in Judaism. In D. P. Irish, K. F. Lundquist, & V. J. Nelson (Eds.), *Ethnic variations in dying, death, and grief: Diversity in universality.* Washington, DC: Taylor & Francis.

Davies, B. (1995). Toward siblings' understanding and perspectives of death. In E. A. Grollman (Ed.), *Bereaved children and teens.* Boston: Beacon Press.

Davis, C. G., & Nolen-Hoeksema, S. (2001). Loss and meaning: How do people make sense of loss? *American Behavioral Scientist, 44,* 726–741.

DeBusk, F. L. (1972). The Hutchinson-Gilford progeria syndrome: Report of 4 cases and review of the literature. *Journal of Pediatrics, 80,* 697–724.

DeFrain, J. D., Jakub, D. K., & Mendoza, B. L. (1991–1992). The psychological effects of sudden infant death on grandmothers and grandfathers. *Omega, 24,* 165–182.

DeFrain, J., Taylor, J., & Ernst, L. (1982). *Coping with sudden infant death.* Lexington, MA: Lexington Books.

DeGarmo, D. S., & Kitson, G. C. (1996). Identity relevance and disruption as predictors of psychological distress for widowed and divorced women. *Journal of Marriage and the Family, 58,* 983–997.

Dijkstra, I. C., & Stroebe, M. S. (1998). The impact of a child's death on parents: A myth (not yet) disproved? *Journal of Family Studies, 4,* 159–185.

Dowdney, L. (2000). Annotation: Childhood bereavement following parental death. *Journal of Child Psychology and Psychiatry and Allied Disciplines, 41,* 819–830.

Emanuel, E. J. (2001). Euthanasia: Where the Netherlands leads will the world follow? *British Medical Journal, 322,* 1376–1377.

Essa, E. L., & Murray, C. I. (1994). Young children's understanding and experience with death. *Young Children, 49,* 74–81.

Faulkner, K. W. (1997). Talking about death with a dying child. *American Journal of Nursing, 97,* 64, 66, 68–69.

Field, N. P., & Bonanno, G. A. (2001). The role of blame in adaptation in the first 5 years following the death of a spouse. *American Behavioral Scientist, 44,* 764–781.

Field, N. P., Nichols, C., Holen, A., & Horowitz, M. J. (1999). The relation of continuing attachment to adjustment in conjugal bereavement. *Journal of Consulting & Clinical Psychology, 67,* 212–218.

Field, N. P., Sturgen, S. E., Puryear, R., Hibbard, S., & Horowitz, M. J. (2001). Object relations as a predictor of adjustment in conjugal bereavement. *Development and Psychopathology, 13,* 399–412.

Florian, V., & Kravetz, S. (1985). Children's concepts of death: A cross-cultural comparison among Muslims, Druze, Christians, and Jews in Israel. *Journal of Cross-Cultural Psychology, 16,* 174–189.

Folkman, S., & Moskowitz, J. T. (2000). Positive affect and the other side of coping. *American Psychologist, 55,* 647–654.

Fry, P. S. (1997). Grandparents' reactions to the death of a grandchild: An exploratory factor analytic study. *Omega, 35,* 119–140.

Furman, E. (1984). Children's patterns in mourning the death of a loved one. In H. Wass & C. A. Corr (Eds.), *Childhood and death.* Washington, DC: Hemisphere.

Glaser, B. G., & Strauss, A. L. (1968). *Time for dying.* Chicago: Aldine.

Goodkin, K., Baldewicz, T. T., Blaney, N. T., Asthana, D., Kumar, M., Shapshak, P., Leeds, B., Burkhalter, J. E., Riggs, D., Tyll, M. D., Cohen, J., & Zheng, W. L. (2001). Physiological effects of bereavement and bereavement support group interventions. In M. S. Stroebe, R. O. Hansson, W. Stroebe, & H. Schut (Eds.), *Handbook of bereavement research: Consequences, coping, and care.* Washington, DC: American Psychological Association.

Graham-Pole, J., Wass, H., Eyberg, S., Chu, L., & Olejnik, S. (1989). Communicating with dying children and their siblings: A retrospective analysis. *Death Studies, 13,* 463–483.

Grbich, C., Parker, D., & Maddocks, I. (2001). The emotions and coping strategies of caregivers of family members with a terminal cancer. *Journal of Palliative Care, 17,* 30–36.

Green, B. L., Krupnick, J. L., Stockton, P., Goodman, L., Corcoran, C., & Petty, R. (2001). Psychological outcomes associated with traumatic loss in a sample of young women. *American Behavioral Scientist, 44,* 817–837.

Grollman, E. A. (1995). Explaining death to young children: Some questions and answers. In E. A. Grollman (Ed.), *Bereaved children and teens.* Boston: Beacon Press.

Haas-Hawkings, G., Sangster, S., Ziegler, M., & Reid, D. (1985). A study of relatively immediate adjustment to widowhood in later life. *International Journal of Women's Studies, 8,* 158–166.

Harlow, S. D., Goldberg, E. L., & Comstock, G. W. (1991). A longitudinal study of the prevalence of depressive symptomatology in elderly widowed and married women. *Archives of General Psychiatry, 48,* 1065–1068.

Harman, D. (2001). Aging: An overview. In S. C. Park, E. S. Hwang, H. Kim, & W. Park (Eds.), *Annals of the New York Academy of Sciences: Vol. 928. Molecular and cellular interactions in senescence.* New York: New York Academy of Sciences.

Harris, T., & Bifulco, A. (1991). Loss of parent in childhood, attachment style, and depression in adulthood. In C. M. Parkes, J. Stevenson-Hinde, & P. Marris (Eds.), *Attachment across the life cycle.* London: Tavistock/Routledge.

Harvey, J. H. (2001). The psychology of loss as a lens to a positive psychology. *American Behavioral Scientist, 44,* 817–837.

Hayflick, L. (1976). The cell biology of human aging. *New England Journal of Medicine, 295,* 1302–1308.

Hayflick, L. (1994). *How and why we age.* New York: Ballantine.

Hays, J. C., Kasl, S. V., & Jacobs, S. C. (1994). The course of psychological distress following threatened and actual conjugal bereavement. *Psychological Medicine, 24,* 917–927.

Herkert, B. M. (2000). Communicating grief. *Omega, 41,* 93–115.

Hinton, J. (1975). The influence of previous personality on reactions to having terminal cancer. *Omega, 6,* 95–111.

Hodes, R. J., McCormick, A. M., & Pruzan, M. (1996). Longevity assurance genes: How do they influence aging and life span? *Journal of the American Geriatrics Society, 44,* 988–991.

Hoffman, S. I., & Strauss, S. (1985). The development of children's concepts of death. *Death Studies, 9,* 469–482.

Irish, D. P., Lundquist, K. F., & Nelson, V. J. (1993). *Ethnic variations in dying, death, and grief: Diversity in universality.* Washington, DC: Taylor & Francis.

Jacobs, S. C., Kosten, T. R., Kasl, S. V., Ostfeld, A. M., Berkman, L., & Charpentier, P. (1987–1988). Attachment theory and multiple dimensions of grief. *Omega, 18,* 41–52.

Janssen, H. J. E. M., Cuisinier, M. C. J., & Hoogduin, K. A. L. (1996). A critical review of the concept of pathological grief following pregnancy loss. *Omega, 33,* 21–42.

Kaminer, H., & Lavie, P. (1993). Sleep and dreams in well-adjusted and less adjusted Holocaust survivors. In M. S. Stroebe, W. Stroebe, & R. O. Hansson (Eds.), *Handbook of bereavement: Theory, research, and intervention.* Cambridge, England: Cambridge University Press.

Kaplan, R. M., & Erickson, J. (2000). Quality adjusted life expectancy for men and women in the United States. In S. B. Manuck, R. Jennings, B. S. Rabin, & A. Baum (Eds.), *Behavior, health, and aging.* Mahwah, NJ: Erlbaum.

Kastenbaum, R. J. (1998). *Death, society, and human experience* (6th ed.). Boston: Allyn & Bacon.

Kastenbaum, R. (2000). *The psychology of death.* New York: Springer.

Kinsella, K., & Gist, Y. J. (1998, October). Gender and aging: Mortality and health. *International Brief, IB/98-2.* Washington, DC: U.S. Census Bureau.

Kissane, D. W., Bloch, S., Onghena, P., McKenzie, D. P., Snyder, R. D., & Dowe, D. L. (1996). The Melbourne Family Grief Study: II. Psychosocial morbidity and grief in bereaved families. *American Journal of Psychiatry, 153,* 659–666.

Klapper, W., Parwaresch, R., & Krupp, G. (2001). Telomere biology in human aging and aging syndromes. *Mechanisms of Ageing and Development, 122,* 695–712.

Klass, D. (2001). Continuing bonds in the resolution of grief in Japan and North America. *American Behavioral Scientist, 44,* 742–763.

Knight, J. A. (2000). The biochemistry of aging. *Advances in Clinical Chemistry, 35,* 1–62.

Koocher, G. P. (1973). Childhood, death, and cognitive development. *Developmental Psychology, 9,* 369–375.

Koocher, G. P. (1974). Talking with children about death. *American Journal of Orthopsychiatry, 44,* 404–411.

Kübler-Ross, E. (1969). *On death and dying.* New York: Macmillan.

Kübler-Ross, E. (1974). *Questions and answers on death and dying.* New York: Macmillan.

Lane, M. A., Black, A., Handy, A., Tilmont, E. M., Ingram, D. K., & Roth, G. S. (2001). Caloric restriction in primates. In S. C. Park, E. S. Hwang, H. Kim, & W. Park (Eds.), *Annals of the New York Academy of Sciences: Vol. 928. Molecular and cellular interactions in senescence.* New York: New York Academy of Sciences.

Leahy, J. M. (1992–1993). A comparison of depression in women bereaved of a spouse, child, or a parent. *Omega, 26,* 207–217.

Lee, C., Klopp, R. G., Weindruch, R., & Prolla, T. A. (1999). Gene expression profile of aging and its retardation by caloric restriction. *Science, 285,* 1390–1393.

Lee, G. R., DeMaris, A., Bavin, S., & Sullivan, R. (2001). Gender differences in the depressive effect of widowhood in later life. *Journal of Gerontology: Social Sciences, 56,* S56–S61.

Lehman, D. R., Davis, C. G., DeLongis, A., Wortman, C. B., Bluck, S., Mandel, D. R., & Ellard, J. H. (1993). Positive and negative life changes following bereavement and their relations to adjustment. *Journal of Social and Clinical Psychology, 12,* 90–112.

Lehman, D. R., Ellard, J. H., & Wortman, C. B. (1986). Social support for the bereaved: Recipients' and providers' perspectives on what is helpful. *Journal of Consulting and Clinical Psychology, 54,* 438–446.

Lehman, D. R., Wortman, C. B., & Williams, A. F. (1987). Long-term effects of losing a spouse or child in a motor vehicle crash. *Journal of Personality and Social Psychology, 52,* 218–231.

Lesher, E. L., & Bergey, K. J. (1988). Bereaved elderly mothers: Changes in health, functional activities, family cohesion, and psychological well-being. *International Journal of Aging and Human Development, 26,* 81–90.

Levy, L. H., Martinkowski, K. S., & Derby, J. F. (1994). Differences in patterns of adaptation in conjugal bereavement: Their sources and potential significance. *Omega, 29,* 71–87.

Lieberman, M. A., & Videka-Sherman, L. (1986). The impact of self-help groups on the mental health of widows and widowers. *American Journal of Orthopsychiatry, 56,* 435–449.

Lohnes, K. L., & Kalter, N. (1994). Preventive intervention groups for parentally bereaved children. *American Journal of Orthopsychiatry, 64,* 594–603.

Lopata, H. Z. (1996). *Current widowhood: Myths and realities.* Thousand Oaks, CA: Sage.

Lund, D. A., Dimond, M. F., Caserta, M. S., Johnson, R. J., Poulton, J. L., & Connelly, J. R. (1985–1986). Identifying elderly with coping difficulties after two years of bereavement. *Omega, 16,* 213–224.

Ly, D. H., Lockhart, D. J., Lerner, R. A., & Schultz, P. G. (2000). Mitotic misregulation and human aging. *Science, 287,* 2486–2492.

Malmstrom, M., Sundquist, J., Bajekal, M., & Johansson, S. E. (1999). Ten-year trends in all-cause mortality and coronary heart disease mortality in socio-economically diverse neighbourhoods. *Public Health, 113,* 279–284.

Maraniss, D., Hull, A., & Schwartzman, P. (2001, September 30). The days after. *Washington Post,* pp. A1, A18.

Martikainen, P., & Valkonen, T. (1996). Mortality after the death of a spouse: Rates and causes of death in a large Finnish cohort. *American Journal of Public Health, 86,* 1087–1093.

Maurer, A. (1961). The child's knowledge of non-existence. *Journal of Existential Psychiatry, 2,* 193–212.

McCarthy, E. P., Phillips, R. S., Zhong, Z., Drew, R. E., & Lynn, J. (2000). Dying with cancer: Patients' function, symptoms, and care preferences as death approaches. *Journal of the American Geriatrics Society, 48,* S110–S121.

McGoldrick, M., Almeida, R., Hines, P. M., Garcia-Preto, N., Rosen, E., & Lee, E. (1991). Mourning in different cultures. In F. Walsh & M. McGoldrick (Eds.), *Living beyond loss: Death in the family.* New York: W. W. Norton.

McKinlay, E. (2001). Within the circle of care: Patient experiences receiving palliative care. *Journal of Palliative Care, 17,* 22–29.

Medina, J. J. (1996). *The clock of ages: Why we age, how we age, winding back the clock.* Cambridge, England: Cambridge University Press.

Medvedev, Z. A. (1991). The structural basis of aging. In F. C. Ludwig (Ed.), *Life span extension: Consequences and open questions.* New York: Springer.

Metcalf, P., & Huntington, R. (1991). *Celebrations of death: The anthropology of mortuary ritual* (2nd ed.). Cambridge, England: Cambridge University Press.

Meydani, M. (2001). Nutrition interventions in aging and age-associated disease. In S. C. Park, E. S. Hwang, H. Kim, & W. Park (Eds.), *Annals of the New York Academy of Sciences: Vol. 928. Molecular and cellular interactions in senescence.* New York: New York Academy of Sciences.

Mishara, B. L. (1999a). Conceptions of death and suicide in children ages 6–12 and their implications for suicide prevention. *Suicide & Life-Threatening Behavior, 29,* 105–118.

Mishara, B. L. (1999b). Synthesis of research and evidence on factors affecting the desire of terminally ill or seriously chronically ill persons to hasten death. *Omega, 39,* 1–70.

Moore, M., & Carr, A. (2000). Depression and grief. In A. Carr (Ed.), *What works with children and adolescents? A critical review of psychological interventions with children, adolescents, and their families.* Florence, KY: Taylor & Francis/Routledge.

Moss, M. S., Moss, S. Z., Rubinstein, R., & Resch, N. (1993). Impact of elderly mother's death on middle age daughters. *International Journal of Aging and Human Development, 37,* 1–22.

Murray, J. A., Terry, D. J., Vance, J. C., Battistutta, D., & Connolly, Y. (2000). Effects of a program of intervention on parental distress following infant death. *Death Studies, 24,* 275–305.

Najman, J. M., Vance, J. C., Boyle, F., Embleton, G., Foster, B., & Thearle, J. (1993). The impact of a child death on marital adjustment. *Social Science and Medicine, 37,* 1005–1010.

Nolen-Hoeksema, S., Larson, J., & Bishop, M. (2000). Predictors of family members' satisfaction with hospice. *Hospice Journal, 15,* 29–48.

Nolen-Hoeksema, S., McBride, A., & Larson, J. (1997). Rumination and psychological distress among bereaved partners. *Journal of Personality and Social Psychology, 72,* 855–862.

Noppe, I. C. (2000). Beyond broken bonds and broken hearts: The bonding of theories of attachment and grief. *Developmental Review, 20,* 514–538.

Noppe, I. C., & Noppe, L. D. (1997). Evolving meanings of death during early, middle, and later adolescence. *Death Studies, 21,* 253–275.

Noppe, L. D., & Noppe, I. C. (1996). Ambiguity in adolescent understandings of death. In C. A. Corr & D. E. Balk (Eds.), *Handbook of adolescent death and bereavement.* New York: Springer.

Norris, F. H., & Murrell, S. A. (1990). Social support, life events, and stress as modifiers of adjustment to bereavement by older adults. *Psychology and Aging, 5,* 429–436.

O'Connor, B. P., & Vallerand, R. J. (1998). Psychological adjustment variables as predictors of mortality among nursing home residents. *Psychology and Aging, 13,* 368–374.

O'Halloran, C. M., & Altmaier, E. M. (1996). Awareness of death among children: Does a life-threatening illness alter the process of discovery? *Journal of Counseling and Development, 74,* 259–262.

Oltjenbruns, K. A. (2001). Developmental context of childhood: Grief and regrief phenomena. In M. S. Stroebe, R. O. Hansson, W. Stroebe, & H. Schut (Eds.), *Handbook of bereavement research: Consequences, coping, and care.* Washington, DC: American Psychological Association.

Osterweis, M., Solomon, F., & Green, M. (Eds.). (1984). *Bereavement: Reactions, consequences, and care.* Washington, DC: National Academy Press.

Parkes, C. M. (1991). Attachment, bonding, and psychiatric problems after bereavement in adult life. In C. M. Parkes, J. Stevenson-Hinde, & P. Marris (Eds.), *Attachment across the life cycle.* London: Tavistock/Routledge.

Parkes, C. M. (1996). *Bereavement: Studies of grief in adult life* (3rd ed.). London: Routledge.

Parkes, C. M. (2000). Comments on Dennis Klass' article "Developing a cross-cultural model of grief." *Omega, 41,* 323–326.

Parkes, C. M., & Weiss, R. S. (1983). *Recovery from bereavement.* New York: Basic Books.

Perry, H. L. (1993). Mourning and funeral customs of African Americans. In D. P. Irish, K. F. Lundquist, & V. J. Nelson (Eds.), *Ethnic variations in dying, death, and grief: Diversity in universality.* Washington, DC: Taylor and Francis.

Quill, T. E. (1993). *Death and dignity: Making choices and taking charge.* New York: W. W. Norton.

Ragow-O'Brien, D., Hayslip, B., & Guarnaccia, C. A. (2000). The impact of hospice on attitudes toward funerals and subsequent bereavement adjustment. *Omega, 41,* 291–305.

Rando, T. A. (1986). A comprehensive analysis of anticipatory grief: Perspectives, processes, promises, and problems. In T. A. Rando (Ed.), *Loss and anticipatory grief.* Lexington, MA: Lexington Books.

Rando, T. A. (1991). Parental adjustment to the loss of a child. In D. Papadatou & C.

Papadatos (Eds.), *Children and death*. New York: Hemisphere.

Raphael, B. (1983). *The anatomy of bereavement*. New York: Basic Books.

Raphael, B., Minkov, C., & Dobson, M. (2001). Psychotherapeutic and pharmacological intervention for bereaved persons. In M. S. Stroebe, R. O. Hansson, W. Stroebe, & H. Schut (Eds.), *Handbook of bereavement research: Consequences, coping, and care*. Washington, DC: American Psychological Association.

Raveis, V. H., Siegel, K., & Karus, D. (1999). Children's psychological distress following the death of a parent. *Journal of Youth & Adolescence, 28,* 165–180.

Ringler, L. L., & Hayden, D. C. (2000). Adolescent bereavement and social support: Peer loss compared to other losses. *Journal of Adolescent Research, 15,* 209–230.

Robinson-Whelen, S., Kiecolt-Glaser, J. K., & Glaser, R. (2000). Effects of chronic stress on immune function and health in the elderly. In S. B. Manuck, R. Jennings, B. S. Rabin, & A. Baum (Eds.), *Behavior, health, and aging*. Mahwah, NJ: Erlbaum.

Rosenblatt, P. C. (1993). Cross-cultural variation in the experience, expression, and understanding of grief. In D. P. Irish, K. F. Lundquist, & V. J. Nelson (Eds.), *Ethnic variations in dying, death, and grief: Diversity in universality*. Washington, DC: Taylor and Francis.

Rosenblatt, P. C. (2001). A social constructionist perspective on cultural differences in grief. In M. S. Stroebe, R. O. Hansson, W. Stroebe, & H. Schut (Eds.), *Handbook of bereavement research: Consequences, coping, and care*. Washington, DC: American Psychological Association.

Roth, G. S., Ingram, D. K., & Lane, M. A. (2001). Caloric restriction in primates and relevance to humans. In S. C. Park, E. S. Hwang, H. Kim, & W. Park (Eds.), *Annals of the New York Academy of Sciences: Vol. 928. Molecular and cellular interactions in senescence*. New York: New York Academy of Sciences.

Rubin, S. S., & Malkinson, R. (2001). Parental response to child loss across the life cycle: Clinical and research perspectives. In M. S. Stroebe, R. O. Hansson, W. Stroebe, & H. Schut (Eds.), *Handbook of bereavement research: Consequences, coping, and care*. Washington, DC: American Psychological Association.

Saldinger, A., Cain, A. Kalter, N., & Lohnes, K. (1999). Anticipating parental death in families with young children. *American Journal of Orthopsychiatry, 69,* 39–48.

Sanchez, L., Fristad, M., Weller, R. A., Weller, E. B., & Moye, J. (1994). Anxiety in acutely bereaved prepubertal children. *Annals of Clinical Psychiatry, 6,* 39–43.

Sanders, C. M. (1979–1980). A comparison of adult bereavement in the death of a spouse, child and parent. *Omega, 10,* 303–322.

Saunders, C. (1977). Dying they live: St. Christopher's Hospice. In H. Feifel (Ed.), *New meanings of death*. New York: McGraw-Hill.

Scharlach, A. E., & Fredriksen, K. I. (1993). Reactions to the death of a parent during midlife. *Omega, 27,* 307–319.

Schonfeld, D. J., & Kappelman, M. (1990). The impact of school-based education on the young child's understanding of death.

Developmental and Behavioral Pediatrics, 11, 247–252.

Schulz, R., & Aderman, D. (1974). Clinical research and the stages of dying. *Omega, 5,* 137–143.

Schulz, R., & Beach, S. R. (1999). Caregiving as a risk factor for mortality: The caregiver health effects study. *Journal of the American Medical Association, 282,* 2215–2219.

Schulz, R., & Schlarb, J. (1987–1988). Two decades of research on dying: What do we know about the patient? *Omega, 18,* 299–317.

Seale, C. (1991). A comparison of hospice and conventional care. *Social Science and Medicine, 32,* 147–152.

Shapiro, E. R. (2001). Grief in interpersonal perspective: Theories and their implications. In M. S. Stroebe, R. O. Hansson, W. Stroebe, & H. Schut (Eds.), *Handbook of bereavement research: Consequences, coping, and care*. Washington, DC: American Psychological Association.

Shaver, P. R., & Tancredy, C. M. (2001). Emotion, attachment, and bereavement: A conceptual commentary. In M. S. Stroebe, R. O. Hansson, W. Stroebe, & H. Schut (Eds.), *Handbook of bereavement research: Consequences, coping, and care*. Washington, DC: American Psychological Association.

Shneidman, E. S. (1973). *Deaths of man*. New York: Quadrangle.

Shneidman, E. S. (1980). *Voices of death*. New York: Harper & Row.

Shuchter, S. R., & Zisook, S. (1993). The course of normal grief. In M. S. Stroebe, W. Stroebe, & R. O. Hansson (Eds.), *Handbook of bereavement: Theory, research, and intervention*. Cambridge, England: Cambridge University Press.

Siebold, C. (1992). *The hospice movement: Easing death's pains*. New York: Twayne.

Siegel, K., Karus, D., & Raveis, V. H. (1996). Adjustment of children facing the death of a parent due to cancer. *Journal of the American Academy of Child and Adolescent Psychiatry, 35,* 442–450.

Silverman, P. R. (1981). *Helping women cope with grief* (Sage Human Services Guide No. 25). Beverly Hills, CA: Sage.

Silverman, P. R. (2000). *Never too young to know: Death in children's lives*. New York: Oxford University Press.

Silverman, P. R., & Worden, J. W. (1993). Children's reactions to the death of a parent. In M. S. Stroebe, W. Stroebe, & R. O. Hansson (Eds.), *Handbook of bereavement: Theory, research, and intervention*. Cambridge, England: Cambridge University Press.

Slaughter, V., Jaakkola, R., & Carey, S. (1999). Constructing a coherent theory: Children's biological understanding of life and death. In M. Siegal & C. C. Peterson (Eds.), *Children's understanding of biology and health*. Cambridge, England: Cambridge University Press.

Speece, M. W., & Brent, S. B. (1984). Children's understanding of death: A review of three components of a death concept. *Child Development, 55,* 1671–1686.

Speece, M. W., & Brent, S. B. (1992). The acquisition of a mature understanding of three components of the concept of death. *Death Studies, 16,* 211–229.

Sprang, G., & McNeil, J. (1995). *The many faces of bereavement*. New York: Brunner/Mazel.

Stambrook, M., & Parker, K. C. H. (1987). The development of the concept of death in childhood: A review of the literature. *Merrill-Palmer Quarterly, 33,* 133–157.

Stepp, L. S. (2001, November 2). Children's worries take new shape. *Washington Post,* pp. C1, C4.

Stevens, M. M., & Dunsmore, J. C. (1996). Adolescents who are living with a life-threatening illness. In C. A. Corr & D. E. Balk (Eds.), *Handbook of adolescent death and bereavement*. New York: Springer.

Stillion, J. M., & McDowell, E. E. (1996). *Suicide across the life span: Premature exits* (2nd ed.). Washington, DC: Taylor & Francis.

Stroebe, M. (2001a). Bereavement research and theory: Retrospective and prospective. *American Behavioral Scientist, 44,* 854–865.

Stroebe, M. (2001b). Gender differences in adjustment to bereavement: An empirical and theoretical review. *Review of General Psychology, 5,* 62–83.

Stroebe, M., Gergen, M. M., Gergen, K. J., & Stroebe, W. (1992). Broken hearts or broken bonds. *American Psychologist, 47,* 1205–1212.

Stroebe, W., & Schut, H. (2001). Risk factors in bereavement outcome: A methodological and empirical review. In M. S. Stroebe, R. O. Hansson, W. Stroebe, & H. Schut (Eds.), *Handbook of bereavement research: Consequences, coping, and care*. Washington, DC: American Psychological Association.

The, A., Hak, T., Koeter, G., & van der Wal, G. (2000). Collusion in doctor–patient communication about imminent death: An ethnographic study. *British Medical Journal, 321,* 1376–1381.

Trueheart, C. (1997, August 5). Champion of longevity ends her reign at 122. *Washington Post,* pp. A1, A12.

Tyson-Rawson, K. J. (1996). Adolescent responses to the death of a parent. In C. A. Corr & D. E. Balk (Eds.), *Handbook of adolescent death and bereavement*. New York: Springer.

Umberson, D., & Chen, M. D. (1994). Effects of a parent's death on adult children: Relationship salience and reaction to loss. *American Sociological Review, 59,* 152–168.

Umberson, D., Wortman, C. B., & Kessler, R. C. (1992). Widowhood and depression: Explaining long-term gender differences in vulnerability. *Journal of Health and Social Behavior, 33,* 10–24.

Urofsky, M. I. (1993). *Letting go: Death, dying, and the law*. New York: Charles Scribner's Sons.

U.S. Agency for International Development. (2000, July). *New data shows tremendous impact of AIDS on developing world*. Available online: http://www.usaid.gov/press/releases/2000/pr000710.html

U.S. Bureau of the Census. (2000). *Statistical abstract of the United States: 2000* (120th ed.). Washington, DC: U.S. Government Printing Office.

Van Eerdewegh, M. M., Clayton, P. J., & Van Eerdewegh, P. (1985). The bereaved children: Variables influencing early psychopathology. *British Journal of Psychiatry, 147,* 188–194.

Waechter, E. H. (1984). Dying children: Patterns of coping. In H. Wass & C. A. Corr (Eds.), *Childhood and death*. Washington, DC: Hemisphere.

Walford, R. L. (1983). *Maximum life span.* New York: Norton.

Wass, H. (1991). Helping children cope with death. In D. Papadatou & C. Papadatos (Eds.), *Children and death.* New York: Hemisphere.

Wenestam, C., & Wass, H. (1987). Swedish and U.S. children's thinking about death: A qualitative study and cross-cultural comparison. *Death Studies, 11,* 99–121.

Wickens, A. P. (1998). *The causes of aging.* Amsterdam: Harwood Academic Publishers.

Wikan, U. (1988). Bereavement and loss in two Muslim communities: Egypt and Bali compared. *Social Science and Medicine, 27,* 451–460.

Wikan, U. (1991). *Managing turbulent hearts.* Chicago: University of Chicago Press.

Wilmoth, J. R., Deegan, L. J., Lundstrom, H., & Horiuchi, S. (2000). Increase of maximum life-span in Sweden, 1861–1999. *Science, 289,* 2366–2368.

Wolfe, J., Grier, H. E., Klar, N., Levin, S. B., Ellenbogen, J. M., Salem-Schatz, S., Emanuel, E. J., & Weeks, J. C. (2000). Symptoms and suffering at the end of life in children with cancer. *New England Journal of Medicine, 342,* 326–333.

Worchel, F. F., Copeland, D. R., & Barker, D. G. (1987). Control-related coping strategies in pediatric oncology patients. *Journal of Pediatric Psychology, 12,* 25–38.

Worden, J. W., & Silverman, P. S. (1993). Grief and depression in newly widowed parents with school-age children. *Omega, 27,* 251–261.

Worden, J. W., & Silverman, P. R. (1996). Parental death and the adjustment of school-age children. *Omega, 33,* 91–102.

Worthen, L. T., & Yeatts, D. E. (2000–2001). Assisted suicide: Factors affecting public attitudes. *Omega, 42,* 115–135.

Wortman, C. B., & Silver, R. C. (1989). The myths of coping with loss. *Journal of Consulting and Clinical Psychology, 57,* 349–357.

Wortman, C. B., & Silver, R. C. (2001). The myths of coping with loss revisited. In M. S. Stroebe, R. O. Hansson, W. Stroebe, & H.

Schut (Eds.), *Handbook of bereavement research: Consequences, coping, and care.* Washington, DC: American Psychological Association.

Zick, C.D., & Holden, K. (2000). An assessment of the wealth holdings of recent widows. *Journal of Gerontology: Social Sciences, 55,* S90–S97.

Zisook, S., & Shuchter, S. R. (1991). Depression through the first year after the death of a spouse. *American Journal of Psychiatry, 148,* 1346–1352.

Zisook, S., & Shuchter, S. R. (2001). Treatment of the depressions of bereavement. *American Behavioral Scientist, 44,* 782–797.

Epilogue: Fitting the Pieces Together

Baltes, P. B. (1987). Theoretical propositions of life-span developmental psychology: On the dynamics between growth and decline. *Developmental Psychology, 23,* 611–626.

Baltes, P. B., Lindenberger, U., & Staudinger, U. M. (1998). Life-span theory in developmental psychology. In W. Damon (Editor-in-Chief), R. M. Lerner (Vol. Ed.), *Handbook of child psychology: Vol. 1. Theoretical models of human development* (5th ed.). New York: Wiley.

Baltes, P. B., Smith, J., & Staudinger, U. M. (1992). Wisdom and successful aging. In T. B. Sonderegger (Ed.), *Nebraska Symposium on Motivation: Vol. 39. Psychology and aging.* Lincoln: University of Nebraska Press.

Bronfenbrenner, U., & Morris, P. A. (1998). The ecology of developmental processes. In W. Damon (Editor-in-Chief), R. M. Lerner (Vol. Ed.), *Handbook of child psychology: Vol. 1. Theoretical models of human development* (5th ed.). New York: Wiley.

Chess, S., & Thomas, A. (1999). *Goodness of fit: Clinical applications from infancy through adult life.* Ann Arbor, MI: Edwards Brothers.

Eccles, J. S., Midgley, C., Wigfield, A., Buchanan, C. M., Reuman, D., Flanagan, C., & Mac Iver, D. (1993). Development during adolescence: The impact of stage–environment fit on young adolescents' experiences in schools

and in families. *American Psychologist, 48,* 90–101.

Flavell, J. H., Miller, P. H., & Miller, S. A. (1993). *Cognitive development.* Englewood Cliffs, NJ: Prentice Hall.

Harris, J. R., Pedersen, N. L., McClearn, G. E., Plomin, R., & Nesselroade, J. R. (1992). Age differences in genetic and environmental influences for health from the Swedish Adoption/Twin Study of Aging. *Journal of Gerontology: Psychological Sciences, 47,* P213–P220.

Kwon, Y., & Lawson, A. (2000). Linking brain growth with the development of scientific reasoning ability and conceptual change during adolescence. *Journal of Research in Science Teaching, 37,* 44–62.

Lerner, R. M., & Kauffman, M. B. (1985). The concept of development in contextualism. *Developmental Review, 5,* 309–333.

Morse, C. K. (1993). Does variability increase with age? An archival study of cognitive measures. *Psychology and Aging, 8,* 156–164.

Schaie, K. W. (1996). *Intellectual development in adulthood: The Seattle Longitudinal Study.* New York: Cambridge University Press.

Thompson, R. A., & Nelson, C. A. (2001). Developmental science and the media: Early brain development. *American Psychologist, 56,* 5–15.

Werner, H. (1957). The concept of development from a comparative and organismic point of view. In D. B. Harris (Ed.), *The concept of development: An issue in the study of human behavior.* Minneapolis: University of Minnesota Press.

Name Index

Beach, F. A., 331
Beach, S. R., 477
Beal, C. R., 254, 312, 323, 324
Beardsley, T., 65
Bearison, D. J., 346
Bear, M. F., 255
Bearsall, L., 412
Beauchamp, G. K., 150
Beaudry, M., 424
Beck, C., 457
Beck, J., 94
Beck, M., 83
Becker Burwell, 449
Becker, J. B., 127
Beckwith, L., 380, 395
Bedford, V. H., 412, 418
Beeghly, M., 93, 342
Beehr, T. A., 307
Begley, N. L., 318
Begley, S., 75, 373
Behl, L. E., 428
Behrend, D. A., 187
Beilin, H., 183
Beitchman, J. H., 333
Bell, K. L., 375
Bell, R. Q., 355, 409
Bell, Terrel, 249
Bellanti, C. J., 388
Bellinger, D., 94
Bellugi, U., 255, 259
Belsky, J., 55, 380, 383, 390, 402,
    411, 414, 415, 424, 427
Bem, D. J., 291
Bem, S. L., 322, 326, 328, 329, 330
Bemis, A., 129
Bemporad, J. R., 438
Benbow, C. P., 240, 323
Benda, B. B., 38
Benedict, H., 250
Benenson, J. F., 385
Benes, F. M., 114
Bengston, V. L., 11
Bengtson, V., 405, 419
Bengtson, V. L., 307, 308
Benn, R., 417
Benoit, D., 396
Benson, B., 45
Benson, J. B., 170
Benson, P., 69
Berenbaum, S. A., 314, 320
Berg, C. A., 205, 214, 230
Bergamasco, N. H. P., 150
Berg, S., 231
Berg, W. K., 147
Bergem, A. L. M., 456
Bergeman, C. S., 74
Bergen, D. J., 313
Berger, A. S., 460
Bergey, K. J., 478
Berk, L. E., 186, 187
Berkowitz, M. W., 360
Berliner, L., 333
Berman, A. L., 450, 451
Berman, W. H., 390
Bermann, E., 402
Bernal, M. E., 295
Berndt, T. J., 390, 392
Bernieri, F., 68
Bernstein, A. C., 331
Berry, C. A., 396
Berry, J. W., 152
Berscheid, E., 396
Berson, E. L., 157
Bertenthal, B. I., 119, 120, 144, 284
Bertman, S. L., 478

Berzonsky, M. D., 296
Bess, F. H., 149
Best, D. L., 213, 313
Betts, J. R., 266
Beyer, S., 422
Beyers, W., 413
Bianchi, S. M., 328, 405, 422
Bidell, T., 170
Biederman, I., 206
Biederman, J., 442, 443
Bifilco, A., 475
Bigbee, M., 314
Biggs, J., 212
Bigler, R. S., 317, 330
Biller, H. B., 384, 405, 406
Billing, L., 93
Binet, Alfred, 39, 222, 223
Bingham, K., 359
Birdsong, D., 258
Biringen, Z. C., 329
Birks, E., 440
Birren, J. E., 135, 136, 232
Bisanz, J., 192
Bishop, J. A., 53
Bishop, J. E., 63
Bishop, M., 482
Bivens, J. A., 187
Bjork, 199
Bjorklund, D. F., 173, 194, 197, 198,
    199, 200, 201, 203, 204
Bjorkqvist, K., 314
Black, B., 388
Black, J. E., 112, 114, 136
Black, K. N., 322
Black, M. M., 440
Blackburn, J. A., 180, 182, 186
Blake, S. M., 335
Blakemore, J. E. O., 317
Blanchard-Fields, F., 210, 211, 346
Blasi, A., 354, 356
Blass, E. M., 149
Blazer, D., 362
Blazer, D. G., 452, 453, 454
Blazey, M. L., 277
Bliesnzer, R., 419, 421
Block, C. E., 417
Block, J., 243
Block, J. H., 243
Bloom, L., 252, 254, 256
Bloom, P., 342
Bluebond-Langner, M., 473
Blum, R. W., 335
Blustein, D. L., 296
Blyth, D. A., 129, 130, 271
Bodnar, A. G., 465
Bodnar, J. C., 481
Bodrova, E., 184, 185-186, 187
Bogenschneider, K., 267
Boggiano, A. K., 263
Bohannon, J. N., 254, 255, 256, 257
Bohannon, J. R., 478
Boise, L., 457
Boivin, M., 357
Boldizar, J. P., 318, 328, 330
Boldt, J. S., 419
Bolger, K. E., 428
Boller, K., 195, 196, 201
Boloh, Y., 254
Bolton, P., 239
Bonanno, G. A., 470-471, 476, 478,
    479, 480
Bondareff, W., 114
Bongers, I. L., 447
Bonvillian, J. D., 254, 255, 256, 257
Boodman, S. G., 123

Boom, J., 362
Booth, A., 421, 424
Booth, C., 415
Booth, W., 340
Borch, K., 96
Boris, N. W., 440, 441
Borkenau, P., 301
Borkowski, J. G., 415
Bornstein, M. H., 151, 226
Borton, R. W., 151
Bosacki, S. L., 343
Bossé, R., 307
Boston, A., 395
Botkin, D. R., 313
Bottino, P. J., 60, 61
Botuck, S., 151
Botwinick, J., 208
Bouchard, C., 126
Bouchard, T. J., Jr., 52, 66, 68,
    69, 71
Boudreau, J. P., 122
Bouldin, P., 171
Bowen, B. A., 277
Bowen, R., 179
Bower, A. R., 478
Bower, T. G. R., 120, 146, 151
Bowers, W. A., 450
Bowlby, J., 371-372, 376, 381, 382,
    385, 395, 396, 399, 470, 471,
    479, 480
Bowles, T. V., 389
Boxer, A. M., 418
Boykin-McElhaney, K., 410
Brabeck, M., 366
Brabyn, J., 155, 156
Bracha, H. S., 71
Brackett, D., 149
Brackshaw, E., 15
Bradbard, M. R., 326
Braddick, O., 170
Braddock, J. H., II, 271
Bradley, J. D. D., 443
Bradley, R. H., 100, 234-235, 235,
    236
Brady, C., 408
Brady, M. P., 438
Braine, M. D. S., 254
Brainerd, C. J., 202
Bralic, I., 127
Brambilla, D. J., 133
Brandtstädter, J., 299
Brauer, S., 135
Braun, N., 427
Braver, S. L., 425
Bray, N. W., 198, 205
Brazelton, T. Berry, 100
Breedlove, S. M., 319, 320, 321
Bremner, J. D., 207
Brendgen, M., 392
Brent, S. B., 472, 473
Bretherton, I., 342, 372, 377
Brewster, K. L., 17-18
Bridges, L. J., 375, 380
Bridges, M., 423
Brilleslijper-Kater, S. N., 331
Bristol, M. M., 439
Britt, G. C., 100
Britto, P. R., 408
Broberg, A. G., 235, 383
Broderick, V., 264
Brody, E. B., 228
Brody, E. M., 419, 420
Brody, G. H., 355, 412
Brody, J. A., 133
Brody, N., 219, 228, 324

Bromley, D. B., 287, 288, 291, 344
Bronfenbrenner, U., 13-14, 25, 42-
    44, 43, 45, 46, 47, 48, 81, 99,
    403, 494
Bronstein, P., 263
Brookover, W., 267
Brooks-Gunn, J., 24, 46, 100, 103,
    127, 238, 284, 287, 334, 335,
    383, 408, 409, 411
Bross, D. C., 429
Broughton, J. M., 151
Brown, A. L., 198, 199, 204, 205
Brown, B. B., 271, 274, 289, 391,
    392, 393
Brown, D., 7, 90, 438
Brown, E., 144
Brown, H. S., 97
Brown, J. L., 115, 360
Brown, R., 253, 255
Brownell, C. A., 285, 385
Brownell, H., 346
Brownell, K. D., 449
Browning, Robert, 489
Bruce, J., 382
Brucken, L., 316
Bruck, M., 203, 265
Bruer, J. T., 260
Bruggeman, E. L., 366
Brugman, D., 362
Brummett, B. H., 308
Bruner, J. S., 183-184, 185, 256
Bryan, J., 211
Bryant, D. M., 403
Bryant, P., 264
Bryant, W. K., 422
Bryden, M. P., 314
Bryk, A. S., 324
Bryson, K., 417
Buchanan, C. M., 127
Buchanan, N. R., 385
Buchner, D. M., 135
Buehler, C. A., 425
Bugental, D. B., 428
Buhrmester, D., 372, 385, 389, 390,
    411, 412, 418, 442
Buhs, E. S., 263
Bukowski, W. M., 388, 392
Bulcroft, R. A., 128
Bulik, C. M., 449
Bull, R., 343
Bumpass, L. L., 421
Bundy, D. A., 227
Burack, 154
Burchinal, M. R., 260, 383, 403
Burgess, S. R., 264
Burhans, K. K., 262
Burnham, D. K., 316
Burn, S., 318, 319
Burns, G. L., 478
Burns, G. W., 60, 61
Burr, J. A., 419
Burton, L., 405, 419
Burton, L. M., 7, 403, 417, 419
Burton, R. V., 119, 120, 351, 354,
    355
Bus, A. G., 264, 265
Busch-Rossnagel, N. A., 259, 260
Bushman, B., 15, 359
Bushnell, E. M., 122
Bushnell, E. W., 151
Buss, A. H., 69, 285, 286, 314
Buss, D. M., 53, 54, 320, 358
Bussey, K., 353
Butcher, P. R., 143, 153
Butler, R., 263, 288

Butler, R. N., 303
Butterfield, S. A., 124
Butters, M. A., 454
Buyck, P., 288
Buysse, V., 269
Byne, W., 334
Byrd, J. E., 91
Byrd, T., 324
Byrne, B., 264
Byrnes, J. P., 192, 193, 205, 314

C

Cabrera, N. J., 405, 406, 422
Cacioppo, J. T., 397
Caddell, D. P., 462
Cahan, S., 313
Cairns, R. B., 8, 9, 48
Calder, Y. M., 316
Caldwell, B. M., 234-235, 235
Caldwell, P., 98
Calkins, S. D., 375
Call, K. T., 274
Callanan, M. A., 255, 412
Camp, C. J., 209, 213
Campbell, F. A., 69, 227, 260, 261, 383
Campbell, K., 75
Campbell, S. B., 434
Campbell, V. A., 155, 162
Campione, J. C., 223
Campos, J. J., 119, 144
Canfield, R. L., 147
Cantor, N. L., 462
Cantrell, P. J., 317
Cantwell, D. P., 443
Capelli, C. A., 177
Caplan, L. J., 209
Capps, L., 342, 437
Capron, A. M., 461
Capute, A. J., 85
Carels, R. A., 268
Carey, G., 358
Carey, S., 472
Carlesimo, G. A., 207
Carlo, G., 393
Carlson, B. M., 65
Carlson, E. A., 389
Carlson, S. M., 171, 343
Carlson, V., 380
Carlton, M. P., 187
Carmelli, D., 436
Carpendale, J. I. M., 349, 353
Carpenter, M., 251
Carper, R., 110
Carr, A., 483
Carr, D., 481
Carr, M. B., 318
Carr, P. L., 306
Carrera, M., 41
Carriger, M. S., 226, 285
Carroll, J. B., 220
Carskadon, M. A., 128, 129
Carsrud, A. L., 275
Carsten, O., 158
Carstensen, L. L., 299, 308, 394, 418
Carter, D. B., 317
Carter, S. L., 96
Cartwright, B. S., 171
Case, R., 184, 197, 198, 228
Casey, B. J., 113
Casey, R. J., 351
Casper, L. M., 417
Caspi, A., 182, 287, 290, 291, 301, 359, 418, 447
Cassel, W. S., 203

Cassidy, D. J., 199
Castro, a., 97
Catalano, M., 298
Cattell, R. B., 219
Cavanaugh, J. C., 206, 209, 211
Cazden, C., 255
Ceci, S. J., 202, 203, 229, 230, 275
Census Bureau, U.S., 6, 24, 275, 403, 404, 405, 413, 418, 421, 450, 451, 463, 466
Centers for Disease Control, 335
Centerwall, S. A., 74
Centerwall, W. R., 74
Cernoch, J. M., 150
Chall, J. S., 265
Chalmers, B., 98
Chamberlain, G., 94
Chamberlain, P., 361
Champaud, C., 254
Chance, G., 146
Chan, C. G., 417
Chandler, M., 342, 353
Chandler, M. J., 88, 96, 232
Chandler, S., 99
Chang, B. H., 420
Chao, R. K., 410
Chapman, A. J., 176
Chapman, L. L., 99
Chapman, M., 175
Chapman, R. S., 251
Charles, S. T., 304
Charlesworth, W. R., 8
Charman, T., 342, 438
Charness, N., 244
Chase, W. G., 206
Chase-Lansdale, L., 335
Chase-Lansdale, P. L., 24, 424
Chassin, L., 127
Chen, C., 273
Chen, D., 149
Chen, J. Q., 220
Chen, M. D., 479, 481
Chen, X., 389, 419
Chen, Y., 210
Chen, Z., 204
Cheng, A. K., 149
Cherlin, A., 416, 417
Cherlin, A. J., 424
Cherry, K. E., 136, 207, 211
Chess, S., 286, 287, 494
Chi, M. T. H., 200, 205, 206
Chilamkurti, C., 344
Chinsky, J. M., 198
Chipperfield, J. G., 418
Chiriboga, C. A., 93
Chitwood, D. G., 240
Chiu, S., 187
Chochinov, H. M., 462
Choi, S., 252
Chomsky, N., 253, 255
Choudhury, N., 154
Christiansen, S. L., 303
Christofalo, V. J., 131
Christopher, J. S., 398
Chukwu, Nkem, 83
Church, M. A., 262
Cicchetti, D., 355, 428
Cicero, T. J., 93
Cicirelli, V. G., 418, 420, 426
Cillessen, A. H., 388, 389
Clark, C., 438
Clark, D. C., 475
Clark, D. O., 132
Clark, E. V., 251, 254
Clark, H. H., 251, 254

Clark, J. L., 152
Clark, K. E., 384
Clark, L. A., 286, 442
Clark, R., 96
Clark, R. D., III, 352
Clark, S. E., 343-344
Clark, W. R., 455, 465, 467, 468
Clarke, S. C., 96
Clarke-Stewart, K. A., 260, 264, 381, 382, 383
Clark-Lempers, D. S., 389
Clarkson, B. H., 135
Clarkson, M. G., 147
Clayton, P. J., 481
Clayton, V. P., 232
Cleckner-Smith, C. S., 132
Cleiren, M. P. H. D., 478, 480
Clements, M., 336, 337
Clifton, R. K., 195
Clinton, Bill, 2
Clyburn, L. D., 420
Cnattingius, S., 93
Coats, P. B., 323
Cobb, R. W., 158
Cobliner, W. G., 41
Cohen, B. B., 103
Cohen, M., 204
Cohen, R., 388
Cohen, S. E., 395
Coie, J. D., 357, 388, 389
Coiro, M. J., 424
Colapinto, J., 321
Colbert, K. K., 182
Colburn, D., 92, 152, 161, 482
Colby, A., 347, 348, 352, 356, 360, 362
Cole, A. K., 384
Cole, P. M., 332, 333, 351, 375
Cole, T. R., 6
Colella, U., 421
Coleman, J., 271
Coleman, L. J., 240
Coleman, P., 299
Coley, J. D., 206
Coley, R. L., 24
Colin, V., 380, 381, 382, 394
Colley, A., 324
Collins, Francis, 56
Collins, W. A., 76, 373, 411
Coltrane, S., 422
Columbo, J., 225
Comer, J. P., 267
Comfort, A., 336
Committee on Adolescence, 433
Commons, M. L., 180, 181
Compas, B. E., 450, 474
Comstock, G. W., 477
Condon, J. T., 132
Condry, J., 316
Condry, S., 316
Conger, R. D., 396, 408
Connell, J. P., 375
Conner, K. A., 416, 419, 420, 426
Connidis, I. A., 397, 418
Connolly, J. A., 387, 391
Connolly, K. J., 152, 153
Connor, J. K., 450
Connor, M., 439
Connor, S. R., 482
Connors, B. W., 255
Conrade, G., 323
Conway, M., 313
Coohey, C., 427
Cook, A. S., 461, 463
Cook, B. G., 269

Cook, C. A., 156
Cook, W. L., 384, 411
Cooke, L. M., 53
Cooley, C. H., 284
Cooney, T. M., 417
Coontz, S., 6, 402
Cooper, C. R., 296, 298
Cooper, P. J., 99
Cooper, R. P., 148, 256
Coopersmith, S., 289, 290
Copeland, D. R., 474
Coppotelli, H., 388
Corcoran, J., 45, 46
Coren, S., 112
Cornelius, S. W., 182
Cornell, D. P., 330
Cornwell, G. T., 24, 30
Corr, C. A., 469, 475, 482
Corr, D. M., 482
Corwin, J., 160
Costa, P. T., Jr., 30, 245, 282, 300, 301, 304
Costenbader, V., 269
Costos, D., 419
Cote, J. E., 296
Cotterell, J. L., 43
Coughlin, J. F., 158
Council, J. R., 449
Courage, M. L., 196, 201, 203
Courchesne, E., 114
Courtin, C., 344
Couzin, J., 63, 75
Covington, M. V., 262, 263
Cowan, C. P., 328, 414, 415
Cowan, G., 314
Cowan, P. A., 328, 331, 384, 414, 415
Coward, R. T., 419
Cowart, B. J., 160
Cox, M., 387, 424
Cox, M. J., 405, 406, 414, 415, 425
Cox, R., 387, 424
Cox, S. M., 380
Cox, T. H., 306
Coy, K. C., 351, 355
Coyle, T. R., 199
Coyne, J. C., 435
Crago, M. B., 255
Crain, W., 185
Craven, R., 288
Creasey, G., 395
Creehan, P. A., 91, 97
Cregger, M. E., 208
Creskoff, N., 440
Creusere, M. A., 177
Crews, F., 30, 31
Crick, N. R., 314, 356, 357
Crijnen, A. A. M., 441
Cristofalo, V. J., 466
Crnic, K., 415
Crockenberg, S., 235, 351, 383
Crockett, L. J., 335, 422
Crombie, G., 297, 298
Cromer, C. C., 385
Cronbach, L. J., 267
Crook, T. H., 209
Crooks, R., 331
Crosby, L., 358
Cross, C. E., 9
Cross, D., 343
Cross, S. E., 298
Crouch, J. L., 428
Crouter, A. C., 81, 319, 323, 414, 421
Crowell, J. A., 394, 395

Goebel, A. E., 475
Goencue, A., 387
Goethe, Johann, 245
Goetz, L., 269
Gold, E. B., 133
Goldberg, A. P., 131, 135, 136
Goldberg, E. L., 477
Goldberg, G. R., 88
Goldberg, S., 380
Goldberg, W. A., 422
Golden, C. J., 358, 443
Goldfarb, W., 382
Goldfield, B. A., 251, 252
Goldhaber, D. E., 37, 44
Goldman, A., 30
Goldman, J., 331
Goldman, R., 331
Goldsmith, M., 202
Goldston, D., 445
Goldwater, O. D., 267
Golinkoff, R. M., 250, 251
Golombok, S., 83, 333, 422
Goltzman, D., 131
Golub, M., 88
Goodkin, K., 477, 483
Goodman, G. S., 202, 203
Goodman, S. H., 441
Goodnow, J. J., 355
Goodship, Daphne, 52
Goodwyn, S., 251
Goossens, F. A., 381
Goossens, L., 212, 413
Gopnik, A., 183, 252, 342, 343
Gordis, E. B., 357, 358, 428
Gordon, B. N., 331
Gordon, D. E., 387
Gordon, D. H., 178
Gordon, L. L., 202
Gordon, P., 41, 257
Gordon, R. A., 448, 449, 450
Gorey, K. M., 260
Gorman, J., 440
Gorman, K. S., 154
Gortmaker, S. L., 123
Goswami, U., 264
Gotlib, I. H., 3, 99, 441, 444
Gottesman, I. I., 70
Gottfredson, L. S., 297
Gottfried, A. E., 236, 263
Gottfried, A. W., 227, 235, 236, 240, 263
Gottlieb, G., 41, 53, 55, 58, 68, 76, 104
Gottlob, L. R., 157
Gottman, J. M., 414, 418, 423
Gould, D. C., 134
Goy, R. W., 320
Graber, J. A., 128, 129, 130
Graber, M., 170
Grady, J. G., 206
Graefe, D. R., 421
Graf, P., 193, 233
Graham-Bermann, S. A., 389
Graham, C. A., 445
Graham-Pole, J., 478
Graham, S., 361
Gralinski, H., 287
Gralinski, J. H., 263, 351
Grandin, T., 342
Gray, A., 134
Gray, J. T., 201
Gray, M. R., 392
Gray, S. W., 226
Gray, W. M., 179
Gray-Little, B., 268, 292, 295
Grayson, C., 453

Grayson, D. A., 452
Grbich, C., 470
Green, B. L., 477
Green, C. R., 207
Green, M., 474
Green, R., 333
Green, W. H., 440
Greenberger, E., 273, 422
Greenberg, J. S., 420
Greenberg, R. P., 30
Greene, A. L., 418
Greene, J. G., 134
Greene, K., 179
Greene, R. W., 442
Greenfield, P. M., 256
Greenough, W. T., 112, 114
Greenspan, S. I., 139
Gregg, V., 356
Gresham, F. M., 439
Greve, W., 299
Grigorenko, E. L., 227
Grilo, C. M., 71, 123
Grimsley, K. D., 305
Grizenko, N., 345
Grober, E., 455
Grodsky, A., 336
Grodstein, F., 134
Grollman, E. A., 472
Grolnick, W. S., 263, 375, 380
Grontved, A. M., 161
Grossman, G., 440
Grossman, J. A., 132
Grossmann, K., 381
Gross, S., 223
Grotevant, H. D., 296, 298, 382
Gruber, R., 115
Gruber-Baldini, A. L., 232
Grunendahl, M., 452
Grusec, J. E., 355
Grych, J. H., 425
Guacci, N., 370
Guacci-Franco, N., 370
Guarnaccia, C. A., 482
Guarnacia, P. J. J., 434
Guerra, N. G., 357, 360
Guilford, J. P., 219, 242
Guinsburg, R., 150
Gul, R. E., 385
Gulko, J., 316
Gunderson, S., 242
Gunnar, M. R., 382, 384
Gunnarson, A. D., 152
Guralnick, M. J., 227
Gurland, B., 456
Gusella, James, 63
Gutmann, D., 328-329
Guttentag, R. E., 208, 210
Guyer, B., 98, 103

H

Haan, N., 300
Haas, A., 440
Haas-Hawkings, G., 480
Haber, D., 122, 123, 130, 136
Hack, M., 85, 103
Haddow, J. F., 107
Haertel, G. D., 266
Hafdahl, A. R., 292, 295
Hagan, R., 317
Hagberg, J. M., 131, 135, 136
Hagen, E. P., 223
Hagestad, G. O., 417
Hahn, C., 83
Haight, W. L., 387
Hainline, L., 141, 142, 143, 151
Haith, M. M., 144, 170, 226

Hala, S., 342
Halberstadt, A. G., 328
Hale, S., 135, 210
Hales, D., 107
Hall, C. S., 27
Hall, E., 260
Hall, G. Stanley, 8, 9, 292, 293, 447
Hall, J. A., 328
Hall, J. G., 108
Hall, L. K., 209
Hall, S. K., 330
Halpern, C. J. T., 334
Halpern, S. H., 97
Halverson, C. F., Jr., 315, 326, 327
Halverson, H. M., 120
Hamburg, B., 361
Hamilton, C. E., 395
Hamilton, J. A., 317
Hamilton, V. L., 324
Hamm, J. V., 390
Hammen, C. L., 3, 436, 444
Hammer, M., 211
Hammond, N. R., 203
Hampson, J., 251
Hanlon, C., 255
Hans, S. L., 359, 380
Hansen, D., 87
Hansen, D. J., 398, 428
Hanson, L. C., 482
Hansson, R. O., 306, 307
Hanushek, E. A., 266
Happé, F. G. E., 346, 438
Harkness, S., 101-102
Harlan, E. T., 351
Harley, J. P., 443
Harley, K., 202
Harlow, H. F., 379
Harlow, S. D., 477
Harman, D., 463, 467, 468
Harman, S. M., 132
Harmon, R. J., 260, 284
Harold, R. D., 315
Harper, G., 277
Harper, S., 131
Harquail, C. V., 306
Harrington, A. F., 325
Harrington, D. M., 242, 243
Harrington, L. C., 97
Harris, Eric, 340
Harris, G. T., 358
Harris, J. R., 70, 71, 131, 283, 372, 373, 494
Harris, M., 256, 257
Harris, M. B., 316
Harris, M. J., 68
Harris, P. L., 342, 375, 387
Harris, T., 475
Harrist, A. W., 388
Hart, B., 30
Hart, D., 287, 288, 291, 298, 356
Hart, E. L., 444
Hart, H. M., 303
Hart, K. J., 366
Hart, M. A., 87
Harter, S., 269, 281, 284, 287, 288, 289, 290, 291, 292, 293, 295
Hartman, B. T., 160
Hartmann, D. P., 391
Hartshorne, H., 354
Hartup, W. W., 171, 291, 389, 390
Harvey, J. H., 480
Hasher, L., 157
Haskell, W. L., 122
Haskett, M. E., 427, 428
Hassinger, M., 453

Hastings, P. D., 356
Hatch, T., 173
Hatcher, R. P., 100
Hatfield, E., 395
Hattie, J., 212
Haug, K., 91
Haught, P. A., 211
Hauspie, R. C., 117
Havemann, J., 335
Havens, B., 418
Havighurst, R. J., 307
Haviland, J. M., 453
Hawley, R. S., 56, 57, 61, 62, 63, 64, 65, 74, 76
Hay, D. F., 385
Hayden, D. C., 475
Hayes, N. L., 111
Hayes, R., 184, 188
Hayflick, L., 465
Hayne, H., 196
Hays, J. C., 481
Hayslip, B., 482
Hayward, C., 129, 130
Hazan, C., 395, 396
Heaton, T. B., 404, 421
Hechtman, L. T., 442
Hedges, L. V., 313, 314
Hedlund, B., 304
Heffer, R. W., 440
Heidrich, S. M., 299
Heikkinen, R., 122
Helfgott, David, 244
Helgeson, V. S., 299
Heller, K., 419
Hellige, J. B., 112
Helmreich, R. L., 275, 328
Helms, J. E., 236, 237
Helson, R., 329
Helwig, C. C., 353
Hencke, R. W., 170
Henderson, C. R., Jr., 87
Henderson, J. E., 131
Hendrie, H. C., 455, 456
Henig, R. M., 59
Henker, B., 314
Hennig, K. H., 363
Henrich, C. C., 360
Henry, R., 436
Henry, W. E., 307
Herbener, E. S., 418
Herbert, Barbara, 52
Herbert, J., 196
Herdt, G., 108, 321, 331, 332
Herkert, B. M., 481
Herkowitz, J., 130
Herman-Giddens, M. E., 125
Hermans, H. J., 304
Hermelin, B., 221
Hermer, L., 145
Hernandez, D. J., 403, 405
Hernandez, E., 31
Herrnstein, R. J., 236-237, 238
Hersch, P., 6, 392
Hersh, R. E., 205
Hershey, S. W., 324
Hertzog, C., 209
Herzog, A. R., 307
Hespos, S. J., 147
Hess, T. M., 209, 211, 346
Hesse, E., 379
Heston, L. L., 70, 454, 456
Hetherington, E. M., 76, 323, 387, 404, 423, 424, 425, 426
Hetu, R., 159
Hewlett, B. S., 406
Hickey, P. R., 150

Mendes de Leon, C. F., 397
Mendoza, B. L., 478
Mennella, J. A., 150
Menon, B. K., 96
Meredith, W., 300
Merikangas, K. R., 445
Mervis, C. B., 253
Merzenich, M. M., 266
Meschke, L. L., 45
Mesman, J., 447
Messer, D. J., 260
Messervey, D., 393
Metcalf, P., 461
Metcalfe, J., 205
Metress, E. K., 130
Metress, S. P., 130
Metzler, J., 314
Metz, M. E., 134
Metzoff, A. N., 195
Meydani, M., 467
Meyer, H., 249
Meyer-Bahlburg, H. F. L., 333
Miceli, P. J., 103
Michaelieu, Q., 290
Michelangelo, 245
Michel, M. K., 375
Mickelson, K., 299
Mickelson, K. D., 396
Midgley, C., 270, 271
Midlarsky, E., 366
Miles, D. R., 358
Milgram, J. I., 418
Milich, R., 443
Miller, A., 134, 262
Miller, A. T., 262
Miller, B. C., 45, 332
Miller, D. C., 314
Miller, E., 456
Miller, Ella, 2, 4, 6
Miller, J. A., 74
Miller, J. G., 222, 364, 365
Miller, J. L., 147
Miller, J. W., 427
Miller, K. F., 166, 204
Miller, N. B., 408
Miller, P. A., 314, 366
Miller, P. C., 408
Miller, P. H., 25, 40, 154, 183, 198-199, 205, 493
Miller, P. M., 101
Miller, S. A., 183, 199, 235, 493
Miller-Heyl, J., 410
Milloy, M., 2
Mills, C. J., 263, 314
Millsap, R. E., 301
Milofsky, E., 303
Minard, K. L., 115
Miner, M. H., 134
Minkler, M., 398, 417
Minkov, C., 482-483
Minuchin, S., 449
Mischel, W., 282, 283, 323
Mishara, B. L., 462, 472
Mishra, G. D., 91
Mistry, J., 387
Mitchell, J. E., 320, 450
Mitchell, L. A., 320
Mitchell, P., 284, 342, 343
Miyawaki, K., 147
Mize, J., 356, 388
Moen, P., 6, 306
Moerk, E. L., 256
Moffitt, T. E., 359, 418
Mohr, P. E., 148
Molfese, D. L., 112, 265

Molfese, V. J., 235
Molina, B. S. G., 127
Molina, G. B., 38, 46
Molinari, V., 304
Moller, L. C., 318
Mollnow, E., 93, 94
Molnar, A. M., 84
Mondloch, C. J., 151
Money, J., 319, 320, 321, 322, 327, 333
Monk, C., 88
Monk, T. H., 414
Monsour, A., 291, 292
Montemayor, R., 291
Montgomery, A., 134
Moore, E. G. J., 237, 238
Moore, J. W., 4
Moore, K. L., 89
Moore, M., 260, 483
Moore, M. K., 151, 170, 194, 195
Moore, S. M., 127
Moorehouse, M. J., 422
Moran, J. R., 295
Morelli, G. A., 101
Morgan, D., 456
Morgan, G. A., 259, 260, 377
Morgan, M., 135
Morgan, R., 283
Morgan, S. P., 46, 335
Mori, C. A., 56, 57, 61, 62, 63, 64, 65, 74, 76
Morinaga, Y., 298
Morrell, R. W., 213
Morris, A., 412
Morris, J., 94
Morris, J. C., 207, 455
Morris, J. E., 313
Morris, J. T., 325
Morris, P. A., 43, 494
Morris, R., 320, 456
Morrison, D. M., 41, 335
Morrison, D. R., 424
Morrongiello, B. A., 146
Morrow, D., 206, 209, 254
Morrow, J., 452
Morse, C. A., 114, 134
Morse, C. K., 231, 494
Mortensen, P. B., 70
Mortimer, J. T., 274, 300, 301
Morton, M. R., 136
Mory, M. S., 391
Moshman, D., 366
Mosier, C., 387
Moskowitz, D. S., 303
Moskowitz, J. T., 480, 481
Moss, H. A., 275, 291
Moss, M. S., 479
Mueller, E., 385
Muir, D. W., 141, 142, 146, 150
Mulatu, M. S., 306
Mullally, P. R., 298, 299
Mulsant, B. H., 452
Munro, G., 296
Munroe, R. H., 326
Munroe, R. L., 12, 326
Murnen, S. K., 449
Murphy, C., 160
Murphy, D. R., 210
Murphy, G. L., 209
Murphy, S. L., 98, 103
Murphy, W. E., 157
Murphy-Shigematsu, S., 434
Murray, C., 236-237, 238
Murray, C. I., 473
Murray, I., 98
Murray, J. A., 483

Murray, K. T., 351, 355
Murray, L., 99, 380, 381
Murray, M. P., 135
Murrell, S. A., 452, 480
Mussen, P. H., 323
Must, A., 123
Mutchler, J. E., 419
Mwamwenda, B. A., 178
Mwamwenda, T. S., 178
Myers, B. J., 100
Myers, J., 250
Myers, J. K., 314, 452
Myers, R. E., 97
Myers, S. E., 97
Myerson, J., 135
Mylod, D. E., 415

N

Nagel, S. K., 422
Nagell, K., 251
Naglieri, J. A., 224
Nahom, A., 135
Naigles, L. G., 252
Najman, J. M., 99, 478
Nakagawa, N., 177
Nanez, J. E., 144
Nangle, D. W., 398
Napolitano, M. A., 449
Narasimham, G., 178
Narayan, M., 207
Nash, A., 385
Nash, S. C., 316, 329
National Academy of Sciences, 128, 129
National Center for Education Statistics, 274, 277
National Center for Health Statistics, 113, 123, 125
National Institute on Aging, 161, 454, 455-456
National Institute on Deafness and Other Communication Disorders, 159, 161
National Institutes of Health, 129, 148
National Reading Panel, 265
National Sleep Foundation, 129
Neale, M. C., 71, 436
Neale, N. G., 71
Nederend, S., 318
Needham, A., 145
Nehrke, M. F., 304
Neiderhiser, J. M., 76
Neiderman, D., 170
Neimark, E. D., 180
Neimeyer, G. J., 296
Neisser, U., 201, 228–229, 234, 237, 238
Nelson, C. A., 194, 196, 493
Nelson, E. S., 366
Nelson, K., 195, 202, 251, 252, 343
Nelson, S. A., 353
Nelson, V. J., 461
Nesbitt, T. S., 87
Nesse, R. M., 434
Nettelbeck, T., 221
Netzer, J. K., 419
Neugarten, B. L., 4, 307
Neville, B., 406
Neville, H. J., 259
Newcomb, A. F., 389, 392
Newcomb, M. D., 303
Newcomb, R., 332
Newcombe, N. S., 201, 202
Newell, A., 192
Newell, M., 90

Newman, C., 170
Newport, E. L., 257
Newsome, M., 250
Newstead, A. H., 135
Newton, P., 343
Newton, R. R., 462
NICHD Early Child Care Research Network, 382, 383
Nicholls, J. G., 262
Nichols, M., 83
Nicolich, L. M., 386
Nielsen, M., 343
Nikolic, J., 179
Niles, W., 360
Nilsson, M., 112
Nippold, M. A., 254
Noble, K. D., 242
Nock, S. L., 422
Noh, E. R., 422
Noh, S., 415
Nolen-Hoeksema, S., 453, 479, 480, 481, 482
Noll, J., 219, 220, 230
Noller, P., 394, 396
Noppe, I. C., 470, 474, 475, 479, 480
Noppe, L. D., 475
Nordentoft, M., 91
Nordin, S., 160
Nordvik, H., 314
Norman, A., 202
Normile, D., 75
Norris, F. H., 480
Norris, J. E., 346, 361
Norris, L., 210
Northern, J. L., 159
Notarius, C. I., 414
Nourhashemi, F., 456
Nowakowski, R. S., 111
Nowell, A., 313, 314
Nsamenang, A. B., 101
Nucci, L. P., 354
Nucci, M. S., 354
Nutt, R. L., 267
Nyborg, H., 229, 230
Nydegger, C. N., 413

O

Oates, G., 306
Oates, R. K., 429
Obler, L. K., 254
O'Boyle, C., 323
O'Brien, B. A., 416
O'Brien, M., 316, 318, 415
O'Brien, W. H., 134
Ochs, A. L., 135
Ochs, E., 257
Ochse, R., 243
O'Connell, B., 251
O'Connell, C. M., 93
O'Connor, B. P., 179, 397, 469
O'Connor, N., 221
O'Connor, T. G., 75, 358, 380, 382, 409, 424
Odden, A., 266
O'Dempsey, T. J. D., 98
Oden, M. H., 241, 242
Oden, S., 398
O'Donnell, A. M., 269
O'Donnell, E. M., 130
O'Donoghue, G. M., 149
Offer, D., 292, 413, 448
Ogbu, J. U., 7, 237, 271, 410
O'Grady, J. P., 96
O'Halloran, C. M., 473
O'Hara, M. W., 99

Shaffer, D. R., 224, 330, 355
Shakespeare, William, 489
Shanahan, M., 274
Shanahan, M. J., 4, 274
Shanas, E., 419
Shanley, N., 450
Shannon, E., 142
Shapiro, E. R., 476
Shapiro, J. R., 375
Shapiro, S. K., 444
Sharabany, R., 390, 391
Sharpe, P. A., 122
Sharpe, T. M., 449
Sharpsteen, D. J., 395
Shaver, P. R., 395, 396, 480
Shaw, B. A., 396
Shaw, C., 133
Shaw, L. K., 251
Shayer, M., 186
Shaywitz, S. E., 265
Sheared, V., 277
Sheiner, E., 97
Shepard, R. J., 122
Shepard, R. N., 314
Sherman, A. M., 394, 396
Sherrod, K. B., 427
Shiffrin, R. M., 192, 193
Shih, M., 238
Shiloh, S., 63
Shimamura, A. P., 211
Shimmin, H. S., 326
Shin, Y. L., 387
Shiner, R. L., 291
Ship, J. A., 160
Shirk, S., 290
Shkolnik, J. L., 266
Shneidman, E. S., 469
Shoda, Y., 282, 283
Shonk, S. M., 428
Shore, C., 251
Shuchter, S. R., 476, 477, 480, 483
Shukla, D., 179
Shumway-Cook, A., 135
Shurkin, J. N., 242
Shute, N., 446
Shweder, R. A., 298, 364, 365
Sibulesky, L., 157
Sidis, William, 241
Siebold, C., 482
Siegal, M., 344
Siegel, A. C., 119, 120
Siegel, D. M., 334
Siegel, J. S., 307
Siegel, K., 474, 475, 481
Siegler, 200
Siegler, I. C., 275, 308
Siegler, R. S., 167, 203, 204
Sieving, R. E., 335
Sigafoos, A. D., 194
Sigelman, C. K., 318
Sigman, M. D., 226, 437
Sigmundson, H. K., 321
Signorella, M. L., 317, 324, 327
Signorielli, N., 325
Silberstein, L. R., 449
Silva, P. A., 127
Silver, L. B., 442
Silver, R. C., 471, 477, 479
Silverberg, S. B., 392, 415
Silverman, L. K., 240
Silverman, P. R., 473, 474, 475, 476, 478, 481, 483
Silverman, P. S., 481
Silverstein, M., 396, 419
Simion, Theodore, 222

Simmons, R. G., 129, 130, 271, 292
Simon, H. A., 192
Simon, T. J., 147
Simon, W., 331, 334
Simonoff, E., 239, 358
Simons, A. D., 449
Simons, R. F., 357
Simons, R. L., 411, 425
Simonton, D. K., 242, 243, 244, 245, 305
Simpson, C., 270
Simpson, K. R., 91, 97
Simpson, L., 103
Sines, J. O., 410, 445
Singer, D. G., 14, 15, 171
Singer, J. L., 14, 15, 171
Singer, L. T., 93
Singh, B., 132
Singh, K., 274
Singh, S., 45, 46, 334, 335
Sinnott, J., 180, 181, 182
Sippola, L. K., 392
Sirignano, S. W., 415
Sivak, M., 158
Skinner, B. F., 25, 34-36, 37, 38, 45, 47, 48, 192, 206, 255
Skolnick, A., 384-385
Slaby, R. G., 357, 360
Slaten, E., 419
Slater, A., 142, 144, 195
Slattery, M. J., 444
Slaughter, V., 472
Slavin, R. E., 266, 269
Slavkin, M., 330
Sliwinski, M., 135
Slobin, D. I., 253
Slomkowski, C., 412
Slone, M., 330
Slotkin, T. A., 92
Slusarcick, A. L., 274
Smagorinsky, P., 185
Small, B. J., 211
Smart, J. L., 112
Smetana, J. G., 354, 413
Smiley, S. S., 204
Smith, A. D., 207, 208, 209, 211
Smith, B., 149
Smith, D. F., 92
Smith, D. R., 362
Smith, E. G., 147
Smith, G. E., 206
Smith, J., 209, 212, 233, 493
Smith, J. B., 272
Smith, K. E., 235
Smith, L. A., 417
Smith, L. B., 120, 122, 140
Smith, M. L., 12
Smith, P. K., 316, 386
Smith, R. S., 102
Smith, S., 413
Smith, T., 439
Smith, T. W., 333, 336
Smithmyer, C. M., 357
Smolak, L., 449, 450
Smoll, F. L., 130
Smotherman, W. P., 81, 85, 86, 100
Snarey, J. R., 362, 364
Sneed, C. D., 335
Snow, C. E., 252, 257
Snow, R. E., 267
Snow, T. K., 130
Snowdon, D. A., 455
Snyder, D., 340
Snyder-Keller, A., 93

Society for Research in Child Development, 20
Sodian, B., 199, 343
Soederberg, L. M., 208, 254
Sokol, B. W., 353
Solomon, F., 474
Solomon, J., 379
Somers-Smith, M. J., 95
Somerville, S. C., 198
Sommers, M. S., 254
Somsen, R. J. M., 113
Son, L. K., 205
Sophian, C., 196
Sorensen, A. B., 4, 452
Sorensen, E., 306, 425
Sorensen, S., 308, 397
Sorenson, L. C., 96
Sosik, J. J., 306
Soussignan, R., 150
South, S. J., 45
Spanier, G. B., 45
Span, P., 415
Sparks, E. E., 409
Sparling, P. B., 130
Sparrow, S. S., 223
Spear, L. P., 113, 125
Spearman, C., 219
Speece, M. W., 472
Speisman, J. C., 419
Spelke, E. S., 140, 144, 145
Spence, J. T., 275, 328, 330
Spence, M. J., 148
Spencer, M. B., 295
Spencer, P. E., 259
Sperling, M. B., 390
Spiby, H., 87
Spilich, G. J., 205
Spirduso, W. W., 135
Spitze, G., 416
Spitz, R. A., 440
Spokane, A. R., 298
Sprang, G., 478
Spreen, O., 88
Sprich, S., 443
Springen, K., 370, 399
Springer, Jim, 52
Springer, S., 112
Squire, L. R., 193
Squires, S., 6
Sroufe, L. A., 318, 374, 375, 377, 378, 381, 383, 384, 389, 427, 434, 435, 443
Stager, C. L., 151
Stambrook, M., 473
Stanley-Hagan, M., 426
Stanley, J. C., 314, 315
Stanner, S. A., 88
Stanovich, K. E., 178, 264
Stanovich, P. J., 264
Stanowicz, L., 257
Stapley, J. C., 453
Starr, B. D., 335-336
Starr, R. H., Jr., 440
State, M. W., 70
Stattin, H., 129, 413
Staudinger, U. M., 3, 209, 232, 233, 491, 493
Staudt, J., 180, 181
Steele, C. M., 237, 238
Steele, H., 396
Steele, M., 396
Steffenburg, S., 439
Steffen, V. J., 314, 315
Stein, A. H., 13, 14
Stein, J. A., 303
Stein, J. H., 127

Stein, M. R., 385
Stein, Z., 88
Stein, Z. A., 88, 102
Steinberg, E. P., 83
Steinberg, L., 55, 127, 271, 273, 274, 289, 392, 407, 409, 410, 412, 413, 415, 436, 437
Steinberg, S., 98
Steiner, J. E., 149
Stelmach, G. E., 124, 135
Stemp, P. S., 415
Stephan, W. G., 268
Stephens, B. R., 143
Stephens, M. A., 420
Stepp, L. S., 473
Stern, D., 376
Stern, M., 316, 322
Sternberg, K. J., 383
Sternberg, R. J., 218, 221-222, 222, 225, 227, 232, 234, 242, 243
Sternglanz, S. H., 330
Stevens, D. P., 275
Stevens, G., 258
Stevens, M. M., 475
Stevens, N., 389, 390
Stevens, R. J., 269
Stevenson, H. W., 263, 273
Stevenson, M. B., 376
Stevenson, M. R., 322
Stewart, R. B., 412
Stigler, J. W., 263, 273
Stillion, J. M., 460, 462
Stine, E. A. L., 254
Stine-Morrow, E. A. L., 208
Stipek, D. J., 260, 262, 263, 268, 269, 270, 287, 344
Stith, S. M., 427
Stoddart, T., 318
Stohr, Oscar, 52
Stolberg, U., 377
Stone, E. J., 123
Stone, M. R., 391
Stone, R., 94
Stoneman, Z., 412
Stones, M. J., 135
Stoolmiller, M., 66
Storandt, M., 213
Stouthamer-Loeber, M., 343, 359
Stratton, K., 92
Straus, M. A., 36, 426
Strauss, A. L., 469
Strauss, J., 453
Strauss, S., 472
Strauss, V., 359
Strayer, F. F., 54
Streisand, B., 266
Streissguth, A. P., 91, 92, 93
Streri, A., 151
Striegel-Moore, R. H., 449
Stright, A. D., 330
Strigini, P., 62, 94
Strober, M., 448, 449
Stroebe, M. S., 477, 478, 479, 480
Stroebe, W., 478, 480, 481
Strutt, G. F., 153
Stumpf, H., 314, 315
Styles, I., 228
Sudhalter, V., 254
Sugden, D., 124, 130
Sui-Chu, E. H., 267
Suitor, J. J., 271, 416
Sullivan, H. S., 31, 372, 389, 390
Sullivan, M. W., 283
Sullivan, P. F., 436, 445
Sun, R., 24, 30
Sun, Y., 389

Subject Index

American Psychological Association, 9, 20
American Sign Language (ASL), 258–259
Amnesia, 193
Amniocentesis, 63, 65
Amnion, 84
Amorality, 350–351
Anal stage, 29, 30
Androgenized females, 320
Androgens, 107, 126
Androgyny, 328, 330
Androgyny shift, 329
Anencephaly, 108
Anger, and death, 468–469
Anorexia nervosa, 127, 448
A, not B, error, 170
Anoxia, 96
Anticipatory grief, 470
Antiepileptic drugs, 93
Antioxidants, 467
Antisocial behavior, 356–360
Apgar test, 97, 98
Aptitude-treatment interaction (ATI), 267
ART (assisted reproduction technologies), 83
Artificial insemination, 83
Asian Americans
    aging parents and, 419–420
    death and dying and, 461, 463
    eating disorders and, 449
    education and, 269
    ethnic identity and, 295
    IQ scores and, 237, 238
    life-span development and, 7
ASL (American Sign Language), 258–259
Aspirin, 93
Assimilation, 167, 168
Assisted reproduction technologies (ART), 83
Assisted suicide, 462
Associative play, 386
Athletic competence, 288
ATI (aptitude-treatment interaction), 267
Attachment
    adolescents and, 390
    adults and, 394–396
    attachment theory, 371–372
    bereavement experience and, 470–471
    children and, 385
    first relationship and, 375–378
    implications of, 381–385
    infants and, 372, 375–385
    quality of, 378–381
Attachment theory, 371–372
Attention
    adolescents and, 154–155
    adolescent sleep deprivation and, 129
    adults and, 157, 159
    children's development of, 153–154
    joint attention, 251, 284, 342
Attention-deficit hyperactivity disorder, 441–444
Attention span, 153, 154
Attribution of hostile intent, 357
Authoritarian parenting, 407, 408, 409
Authoritative parenting, 407, 408, 410, 413

Authority and social-order-maintaining morality, 348
Autism, 340, 341, 342, 437–439
Autobiographical memory, 201–203
Automatization, 198, 201, 222
Autonomy, 413
Autonomy versus shame and doubt, 29, 32, 282, 302
Autosomes, 57, 58
Average class size, 266
Avoidant attachment, 378–379, 380, 384, 385, 395
Axons, 108, 111

B
Babbling, 250
Babinski reflex, 115, 116
Baby biographies, 8–9
Baby boom generation, 6
Babysitters, 377
Bandura's social learning theory, 36–38, 46, 282–283, 323–325, 350
Bargaining, 469
Basic gender identity, 325
Bayley Scales of Infant Development, 225, 226
Bayley Scales of Mental and Psychomotor Development, 120
Beanpole family, 405
Beginning of thought, 168, 169
Behavioral conduct, 288
Behavioral enactment, 357
Behavioral genetics, 64–76, 373
Behavioral inhibition, 285, 286, 351
Behavioral observations, 11–12
Behavioral schemes, 168
Behavioral states, of infants, 115, 117
Behaviorism, 33, 192, 255, 434. See also Classical conditioning; Operant conditioning
Belief-desire psychology, 343
The Bell Curve (Herrnstein & Murray), 236–237
Bereavement experience, 470–471, 474–475, 476, 481–483
Beta-amyloid, 454, 456
Big Five personality dimensions, 282, 300–301
Bioecological approach, 42–44, 403
Biological aging, 3
Biological causality, and death, 472
Biosocial theory, 319–322
Birth order, 236
Blank slate, 26, 139
Blastula, 84
Bodily-kinesthetic intelligence, 220
Brain
    aging brain and, 114
    biological evolution and, 53
    early brain development and, 108–112
    intelligence and, 227
    language development and, 258
    later brain development, 112–114
    perceptual development and, 151–152
    prenatal period and, 85
Brain growth spurt, 111
Brazelton Neonatal Behavioral Assessment Scale, 100

Breathing reflex, 115, 116
Breech presentation, 96
Bronfenbrenner's bioecological approach, 42–44, 403
Brown v. Board of Education of Topeka (1954), 268
Bulimia nervosa, 448–449

C
Career-related motivation, 275
Career. See Vocation
Caregiver burden, 420
Carriers, 60
CAS (Cognitive Assessment System), 224, 225
Cataracts, 155, 157, 158
Catch-up growth, 117
Categorical self, 284
Cause-and-effect relationship
    correlational method and, 14–15
    experimental method and, 13
Centenarians, 2
Centration, 171
Cephalocaudal principle, 117, 119
Cerebral cortex, 108, 110, 112
Cerebral palsy, 96, 103
Cesarean section, 96–97
Characteristics of Giftedness Scale, 240
Chicken pox, 91
Child abuse, 5–6, 355, 380, 387, 426, 427, 428, 430, 440, 451
Childbirth process, 95
Child-directed speech, 256
Child effects model, 409, 415, 445
Childhood amnesia, 201, 202, 203
Childless married couples, 421
Child-rearing family, 415
Children. See also Preschool children
    achievement motivation and, 262–264
    attachment and, 385
    attention-deficit hyperactivity disorder, 441–444
    autobiographical memory and, 201–203
    bereavement and, 474, 481
    cognitive development and, 167, 170–175, 490
    creativity and, 242–244
    death and dying and, 472–475
    depression and, 444–445, 446, 447
    development psychopathology and, 441–447
    dying child and, 473–474, 478
    education and, 261–268
    effective schools and, 266–268
    family and, 404–412
    gender roles and, 316–318
    historical changes in childhood, 5–6
    intelligence and, 227–229
    language development and, 253–254
    memory and, 197–201
    models of influence in family, 409, 411
    moral development and, 352–356
    naturalistic observation and, 11
    parenting styles and, 407–409
    perception and, 153–154

    personality development and, 290–291, 491
    physical activity and, 122–123
    physical behavior of, 123–124
    physical development and, 122–124, 490
    plasticity and, 9
    problem solving and, 203–204
    psychotherapy for, 445, 446
    reading and, 264–266
    self and, 287–288
    self-esteem and, 288–290
    sexuality and, 331–333
    sibling relationships and, 411–412
    social relationships and, 385–389, 491
    steady growth of, 123
    thyroid deficiency and, 107
    trends in development, 488, 490
Child sexual abuse, 30–31, 332–333, 451
Chlamydia, 91
Chorion, 84
Chorionic villus sampling (CVS), 63, 65
Chromosome abnormalities, 61–63
Chromosomes, 55–57, 312, 319–320
Chronic grief, 479
Chumships, 372
Chunking, 198, 200
Circadian rhythms, 128
Clarification of goals, 357
Classical conditioning, 33–34, 37
Classification, 173
Class inclusion, 173, 175, 176
Climacteric, 134
Clinical method, 166
Cliques, 391
Cloning, 75
Cocaine, 93–94
Cochlear implants, 149, 152, 161
Codominance, 60
Coercive family environments, 358, 361, 373
Cognition, 166
Cognitive Assessment System (CAS), 224, 225
Cognitive development
    adolescents and, 175–180, 490
    adults and, 180–182, 490
    attachment and, 380
    children and, 167, 170–175, 490
    developmental psychopathology and, 434
    gender roles and, 325–326
    identity and, 296
    infants and, 167, 168–170, 490
    information-processing approach compared to Piaget's theory, 194, 196, 197, 203, 204, 205
    Kohlberg's moral reasoning theory and, 347–349, 352, 356, 360, 362–366
    peers and, 372
    Piaget's theory of, 38–41, 46, 47, 166–168, 183–184, 276, 352–354
    role-taking skills and, 345
    self-awareness and, 284, 287
    stages of cognitive development, 39–40, 168–180, 183

Drugs, and prenatal environment, 90–94
DSM-IV, 433–434
Dual-career families, 421–422
Dynamic assessment, 223–224
Dynamic systems approach, 120–122
Dyslexia, 265–266

E

Easiness/difficultness, 286
Easy temperament, 286, 383
Eating disorders, 441, 448–450
Echolalia, 437
Eclectic, 48, 495
Economic goal, 101
Education
    achievement motivation and, 263–264
    adolescents and, 268–275
    adults and, 275–277
    children and, 261–268
    computers and, 270
    effective schools and, 266–268
    infants and, 259–261
    single-sex education, 324
    social experience and, 363
    theory/research contributions and, 276
Educational Testing Service, 270
Ego, 28–29, 30, 281
Egocentrism, 171, 174, 183, 186
Ego virtues, 33
Elaboration, 198, 245
Elder abuse, 426
Electra complex, 30, 322, 347
Elimination disorders, 441
Embryonic period, 84
Emergent literacy, 264–265
Emotional development
    infants and, 374–375, 384
    play and, 387
Emotionality, 285, 286
Emotional lability, 129
Emotional support, 412
Emotion regulation, 375
Empathy, 346, 352, 366
Empiricists, 139
Empty nest, 415–416
Encephalocele, 108
Encoding, 193, 198, 357
Endocrine glands, 107
Endocrine system, physical development and, 107–108
Environment, definition of, 81
Environmental hazards
    Down syndrome and, 62
    hemophilia and, 61
    prenatal environment and, 94
Environmental influences
    attention-deficit hyperactivity disorder and, 443
    bioecological approach and, 43–44, 45
    contextual/systems theories and, 42, 43–44, 45, 47, 48
    creativity and, 244
    development process and, 4
    development theories and, 26
    estimating influences of, 67
    gene/environment correlations and, 73–76, 235, 301, 358
    gene/environment interactions, 53, 58, 72, 76
    genetics and, 64–68
    goodness of fit and, 286–287

individual differences and, 68–72
    intelligence and, 64, 167, 218, 226
    IQ scores and, 234–236, 238–239
    language development and, 256–257
    learning theories and, 45, 46, 48
    perinatal environment and, 94–99
    personality development and, 283, 301, 308
    physical/sexual maturation and, 127
    postnatal environment and, 99–104
    prenatal environment and, 82–94
    sociocultural perspective and, 42, 45
Epistemology, 166
Equilibrium, 168
Equity, 396
Erectile dysfunction, 134
Erikson's psychosocial theory, 29, 31–33, 46, 47, 232
Estrogen, 107, 108, 126, 132
Ethics
    cloning and, 75
    experimental method and, 14
    rights of research participants and, 19–20
Ethnic identity, 295, 296
Ethology, evolution theory and, 53–54
Eugenics, 76
European Americans
    academic achievement and, 274
    aging parents and, 419–420
    attachment and, 396
    death and dying and, 461
    eating disorders and, 448–449
    education and, 268
    ethnic identity and, 295
    family and, 403
    IQ scores and, 227, 235, 236, 237, 238, 239
    life expectancy and, 463
    life-span development and, 7
    menopause and, 133
    parenting and, 410, 413
    sexual maturation and, 125
    socioemotional selectivity theory and, 394
Euthanasia, 461, 462
Evocative gene/environment correlations, 73
Evoked potentials, 140
Evolutionary psychology, 53, 54–55, 320, 434
Evolution theory
    Darwin and, 52–53
    modern evolutionary perspectives and, 53–55
Executive control processes, 194
Executive functions, 438, 442
Exosystems, 43, 44, 45
Expansion, 257
Experiential component, and triarchic theory of intelligence, 221, 222
Experimental breeding, 65
Experimental control, 13
Experimental method, 13–14, 15

Experiments, 13
Expertise
    adults and, 205–206
    in domain of knowledge, 180, 181
    memory and, 200
Explanation goal, and life-span development, 8
Explicit memory, 193–194, 201, 208
Exploratory behavior, 378
Expressive style, 252
Extended family household, 403
Externalizing problems, 441, 447
External memory aids, 211
Extinction, 35
Extraversion, 282
Eye-blink reflex, 115, 116
Eye-hand coordination, 124
Eyewitness memory, 202–203

F

Factor analysis, 219, 220, 282
Failure to thrive, 440, 441
False belief tasks, 340, 341, 343, 344
Falsifiable theories, 24–25
Family. See also Fathers; Mothers; Parents
    adolescents and, 412–413
    adults and, 413–421
    attention-deficit hyperactivity disorder and, 443
    childless married couples and, 421
    children and, 407–412
    depression and, 451
    diversity in, 405, 421–426
    divorce and, 423–425
    dual-career families, 421–422
    eating disorders and, 449
    evolutionary psychology and, 54
    family violence, 426–430
    gay/lesbian families, 422
    gene/environment correlation and, 76
    infants and, 405–407
    IQ scores and, 236
    personality traits and, 69–70
    physical/sexual maturation and, 127
    remarriage/reconstituted families and, 426
    singles and, 421
    as system, 402–405
Family life cycle, 403, 404, 418, 476
Family studies, 66, 68
Family Support Act of 1988, 425
Family systems theory, 402
Family violence, 426–430
Fantasy stage of vocational development, 297, 298
FAS (fetal alcohol syndrome), 92–93, 102
Fathers. See also Family; Mothers; Parents
    attachment and, 379
    divorce and, 424, 425
    family as system and, 405–407
    perinatal environment and, 99
    prenatal environment and, 91, 94
    speech recognition and, 148
Fear of drop-offs, 144
Fearful working model, 395
Feeding and eating disorders, 441

Fertilization, 82
Fetal alcohol syndrome (FAS), 92–93, 102
Fetal death, 87
Fetal period, 84–86
Finality, death and, 472
Fine motor skills, 119
First trimester, 84
First words, 251–252
Fixation, 29, 30
Fluid intelligence, 219–220, 230, 236
Flynn effect, 236
Food additives, 443
Food recognition, 162
Forceps, 96
Forebrain, 108, 110
Foreclosure status, 293, 294, 296
Formal operations stage
    cognitive development and, 39, 40, 167, 175–180
    death and, 475
    depression and, 450
    play and, 387
    postconventional morality and, 363
Fraternal twins, 57, 65–71
Free radical theory, 467, 468
Freud's psychosexual theory, 27–31, 46, 47, 281–282, 322–323, 331, 346–347, 370, 379
Friendships, 389, 390, 396
Full alphabetic phase, 264
Functional grammar, 252
Fuzzy-trace memory, 202

G

Gay/lesbian families, 422
Gender bias, 364–366
Gender consistency, 325
Gender differences
    aggressive behavior and, 12
    assumptions concerning, 312
    depression and, 450, 452, 453
    gender roles and, 312–315
    life expectancy and, 464
    longitudinal/cross-sectional design and, 16–18
    vocational development and, 305–306
Gender identity, 316, 319, 325
Gender intensification, 318–319
Gender-role norms, 313
Gender roles
    adolescents and, 130, 298, 318–327
    adults and, 303, 305–306, 327–330
    attitudinal/behavioral change and, 330
    children and, 316–318
    definition of, 312–313
    gender-role development theories, 319–327
    giftedness and, 242
    infants and, 315–316
    male/female differences, 312–315
Gender-role stereotypes, 313, 315, 316–317, 405
Gender schemata, 326
Gender schema theory, 326–327
Gender segregation, 317–318, 385
Gender stability, 325
Gender typing, 313, 327

Intelligence (continued)
　　IQ scores and, 234–239
　　measurement of, 222–225
　　Piaget on, 166–167, 218, 245
　　psychometric approach to,
　　　219–220, 245
　　Sternberg's triarchic theory of,
　　　221–222
　　Vygotsky on, 184, 245
Intelligence quotient (IQ), 223
Interactionist perspective, and lan-
　　guage development,
　　256–257
Internalizing problems, 441
Internally consistent theories, 24
Internal working models, 372
Interpersonal intelligence, 220
Interpretation, 357
Interviews, 11
Intimacy and self-disclosure, 390
Intimacy versus isolation, 29, 32,
　　282, 302–303
Intonation, 250
Intrapersonal intelligence, 220
Intrinsic motivation, 263
Intuitive theories, 145, 341
Invariant sequence of cognitive de-
　　velopment, 167, 347
In vitro fertilization (IVF), 83
Involved grandparents, 417
IQ (intelligence quotient), 223
IQ scores, 66, 68–69
　　adolescents and, 228
　　adults and, 229–232
　　children and, 227–229
　　creativity and, 242
　　distribution of, 223
　　factors influencing, 234–239
　　giftedness and, 240–242
　　mental retardation and, 240
IQ tests, 39, 220
Ironic statements, 177
Irreversibility, and death, 472
IVF (in vitro fertilization), 83

J
Joint attention, 251, 284, 342

K
Karyotype, 57, 58
Kaufman Assessment Battery for
　　Children, 223
Klinefelter syndrome, 62–63, 75
Knowledge base, 200, 205, 209

L
LAD (language acquisition device),
　　255, 256
Lamaze method, 87
Language, mastery of, 249–250
Language acquisition device
　　(LAD), 255, 256
Language development
　　before first words, 250–251
　　critical period and, 257–259
　　first words and, 251–252
　　interactionist perspective and,
　　　256–257
　　later development of, 254
　　learning perspective and,
　　　254–255
　　nativist perspective and,
　　　255–256
　　Piaget on, 256, 259
　　telegraphic speech and,
　　　252–254

Vygostky on, 256
Latchkey children, 422
Latency period, 29, 30, 331
Lateralization, 112
Learned helplessness orientation,
　　262
Learning, developmental process
　　and, 4
Learning abilities, infants and, 117
Learning disorders, 441
Learning goals, 262–263
Learning perspective, language de-
　　velopment and, 254–255
Learning Potential Assessment
　　Device, 223
Learning theories
　　classical conditioning and,
　　　33–34
　　environmental influences and,
　　　45, 46, 48
　　operant conditioning and,
　　　34–36, 47
　　social learning theory and,
　　　36–38, 47
　　strengths/weaknesses of, 37–38
Lens changes (vision), 156–157
Lesbian/gay families, 422
Liberal bias, 364
Libido, 29
Life expectancy, 6, 463–465
Life review, 303–304
Life span
　　historical changes and, 4–6, 8,
　　　494
　　models of, 3
　　periods of, 4
Life-span development
　　current perspectives on, 9–10
　　definition of development, 2–3
　　developmental processes and,
　　　3–4, 491
　　developmental research and,
　　　10–19
　　goals of study, 8
　　issues of, 19–20
　　origins of, 8–9
　　views of life span, 4–8
Life-span perspective, 9
Life structure, 304
Linguistic intelligence, 220
Literacy
　　adults and, 275, 277
　　emergent literacy, 264–265
Living Will, 462
Locomotor development, of in-
　　fants, 118–120
Logical-mathematical intelligence,
　　220
Logical reasoning, 174
Longevity, 467
Longitudinal design, 16, 17–18
Long-term memory, 193, 194
Looking-glass self, 284
Love withdrawal, 355
Low birth weight babies, 102–103

M
Macrosystems, 43, 44, 45, 99, 428
Major depressive disorder, 433
Maladaptiveness, 433
Male climacteric, 134
MA (mental age), 223
Manipulating objects, 120
Marijuana, 93
Marriage, 413–414, 417–418
Marriage postponement, 403–404

Masked depression, 444
Mastery motivation, 259–260, 274
Mastery orientation, 262
Math education, 272–273
Mathematical ability, 314
Mating strategy, 54–55
Maturation, 3, 226
Maximum life span, 465
Medications, and perinatal envi-
　　ronment, 97
Meiosis, 55, 56
Melatonin production, 128
Memory
　　adolescents and, 204–205
　　adults and, 206–211
　　children and, 197–201
　　improvement of, 212–213
　　infants and, 194–196
　　information-processing ap-
　　　proach and, 192–194
Memory strategies, 198–199, 200,
　　205, 209–210, 212–213
Menarche, 125, 127, 133
Menopause, 133–134, 336
Mental age (MA), 223
Mental representation, 170
Mental retardation, 239–240, 439,
　　441
Mental scale, 225
Mercy-killing dilemma, 349
Mesosystems, 43, 44, 45
Meta-analysis, 11–12
Metacognition
　　metamemory and, 199, 200,
　　　205, 209
　　private speech and, 187
Metalinguistic awareness, 254
Metamemory, 199, 200, 205, 209
Method of loci, 212
Microsystems, 43, 44, 45
Midbrain, 108, 110
Middle-aged adults
　　death and, 477, 478
　　Erikson on, 32, 303
　　gender roles and, 328–329
　　historical changes in, 6
　　memory and, 213, 214
　　middle generation squeeze,
　　　419–421
　　physical activity and, 123
　　sense of taste and, 160
　　trends in development, 489,
　　　490
　　vision and, 156
Middle generation squeeze,
　　419–421
Middle schools, 271
Midlife crisis, 31, 304, 415
Migration of neurons, 111
Mild cognitive impairment, 207,
　　455
Minnesota Twin Study, 71
Miseducation: Preschoolers at Risk
　　(Elkind), 260
Mitosis, 55
Models, 36–37, 355
Modified extended family, 419
Moodiness, 129
Moral affect, 346–347
Moral behavior, 350, 354–356
Moral development
　　adolescents and, 356–360
　　adults and, 360–362
　　children and, 352–356
　　infants and, 350–352

Kohlberg's theory of, 347–349,
　　362–366
　　moral affect and, 346–347
　　moral behavior and, 350
　　moral reasoning and, 347–349,
　　　352, 356, 360, 362–366
Morality, 346
Morality of care, 365
Morality of contract, individual
　　rights, and democratically
　　accepted law, 348
Morality of individual principles of
　　conscience, 348–349
Morality of justice, 365
Moral reasoning, 347–349, 352,
　　356, 360, 362–366
Moral rules, 354
Moral socialization, 351–352,
　　354–355
Moratorium period, 293
Moratorium status, 293, 294, 296
Moro reflex, 116
Morphology, 249
Mothers. *See also* Family; Fathers;
　　Parents
　　attachment and, 379
　　autism and, 438
　　depression of, 441
　　emotional development and,
　　　374
　　failure to thrive and, 440
　　family as system and, 405–407
　　infant depression and, 440
　　IQ scores and, 235, 239
　　perinatal environment and,
　　　98–99
　　prenatal environment and,
　　　86–94, 87–88
　　speech recognition and,
　　　147–148
Motivation
　　adults and, 275
　　children and, 262–264
　　creativity and, 244
　　infants and, 259–260
　　IQ scores and, 237–238
　　memory and, 211
　　occupational success and, 228
Motor scale, 225
Motor skill disorder, 441
Motor skills
　　adults and, 135
　　of children, 124
　　of infants, 120–122
Mourning, 470
Multigeneration families, 405
Multimodal Treatment of
　　Attention-Deficit
　　Hyperactivity Disorder
　　Study, 444
Multiple births, 83
Multiple classification, 174
Multiple intelligences theory,
　　220–221, 243
Muscular dystrophy, 61
Musical intelligence, 220
Mutations, 61
Myelin, 85, 108
Myelination, 108, 112, 113

N
Narcotics, 93
Native Americans
　　death and dying and, 463
　　ethnic identity and, 295
　　IQ scores and, 237

Plasticity
   of brain, 111–112, 114
   childhood and, 9
   in development, 493
   intelligence and, 232
Play, 386–388
Playful interaction, 406
Pleasant stimulus, 35
Pleasure principle, 28
PMS (premenstrual syndrome), 132
Pollutants, and prenatal environment, 94
Polygenic inheritance, 61
Polygenic traits, 61
Population, 19
Positive punishment, 35
Positive reinforcement, 34–35
Postconventional morality, 348, 349, 362–363
Postformal thought, 180
Postnatal depression, 98–99
Postnatal environment
   early socialization and, 99–102
   risk and resilience in, 102–104
Posttraumatic stress disorder, 333
Power assertion, 355
Pragmatics, 249–250, 254
Preconventional morality, 348, 349, 354–357
Preference for novelty, 226
Preferential looking, 140
Prelinguistic sounds, 250–251
Premature babies, 103
Premenstrual syndrome (PMS), 132
Prenatal environment
   mothers' state and, 86–88
   prenatal stages and, 82–86
   risk and resilience in, 102–104
   teratogens and, 88–94
Prenatal screening, 63, 64–65
Prenatal stages, 82–86
Preoccupied working model, 395
Preoperational stage
   cognitive development and, 39, 40, 167,
      171–173
   concrete operational stage compared to, 174
   death and, 473
Pre-retirement phase, 307
Presbycusis, 159
Presbyopia, 156
Preschool children
   creativity and, 243
   death and, 472, 473, 474
   early education and, 260–261
   early intervention for, 226–227
   moral reasoning and, 352
   moral rules and, 354
   Piaget's theory and, 173
   self-concept and, 287
   theory of mind and, 343
   trends in development, 486, 488, 490
Pretend play, 342, 386–387, 474
Preterm infants, 100
Primary circular reactions, 168, 169
Primary mental abilities, 219
Primitive reflexes, 115, 116
Private speech, 186–188
Problem solving
   adults and, 211–215
   children and, 203–204
   formal operations stage and, 175, 177
   infants and, 197
   information-processing approach and, 194
Prodigies, 243–244
Progeria, 466
Progesterone, 107, 108, 126, 132
Programmed theories of aging, 465–466
Project Head Start, 228–229, 261
Proliferation of brain cells, 110–111

Prosocial behavior, 346–347, 352
Protection from harm, 20
Protective factors, 102, 447
Protest phase, 381
Proximodistal principle, 117, 119, 120
Psychoanalytic theory
   attachment and, 379
   developmental psychopathology and, 434
   Freud and, 27–31, 46, 47
   gender roles and, 322–323
   moral affect and, 346–347
   personality development and, 281–282
   sexuality and, 331
   social relationships and, 370
Psychobiology, 53, 55
Psychological disorders, and individual differences, 70–71
Psychometric approach, 219–220, 256
   personality development and, 282
Psychopathology. See Development psychopathology
Psychosexual theory, of Freud, 29
Psychosocial development
   early adult intimacy and, 302–303
   Erikson's theory of, 29, 31–33, 46, 47, 232
   middle age generativity and, 303
   old age integrity and, 303–304
   path to adulthood and, 302
   personality development and, 281–282
   systematic changes/continuities and, 3
Puberty, 124, 127, 128, 129, 271
Punishment, 35–36, 355, 428
Punishment-and-obedience orientation, 348
Pupil changes (vision), 155–156
Pupillary reflex, 116

Q

Qualitative changes, 27
Quantitative changes, 27
Quasi-experiments, 14, 15
Questionnaires, 9, 11

R

Racial/ethnic differences, IQ scores and, 236–239
Racial integration, 268–269
Radiation, and prenatal environment, 94
Random assignment, 13
Random samples, 19
Reaction time, 124, 135
Reading, children and, 264–266
Realistic stage of vocational development, 297,
   298
Recall memory, 193, 196, 198, 208
Recessive genes, 59–60
Reciprocal determinism, 37, 70
Reciprocal influence, 43, 81
Recognition memory, 193, 195, 198, 208
Reconstituted families, 404, 426
Referential style, 252
Reflexes, and infants, 115, 116
Regression, 30
Regulator genes, 58
Rehearsal, 198
Reinforcement, 34–35, 355
The Relationship Code (Reiss, Neiderhiser,
   Hetherington, & Plomin), 76
Relativistic thinking, 180–181
Religious faith, 361–362, 473, 480
Remarriage/reconstituted families, 404, 426
Remote grandparents, 416
REM sleep, infants and, 115
Reorganization, bereavement and, 470
Reorientation phase of retirement, 307
Repetitive, stereotyped behavior, 437–438
Reproductive technologies, 83
Research designs, 15–19

Research ethics, 19–20
Research methods, 13–15
Reserve capacity, 131
Resilience, and postnatal environment, 102–104
Resistant attachment, 378, 379, 384, 385, 395
Response decision, 357
Response search, 357
Response to novelty, 222
Responsive environment, 260
Retinal changes, 157
Retinitis pigmentosa, 157
Retirement, 307
Retrieval, 193
Retrieval strategies, 199
Reversibility, 171, 174
Rhythmic stereotypies, 120
Rights of research participants, 19–20
Risks
   adolescents and, 113
   gender differences and, 314
   postnatal environment and, 102–104
Role reversal, 419
Role-taking skills, 345
Rooting reflex, 116
Rubella, 89–90, 91
Rule assessment approach, 203
Rules as sacred, 353–354
Rumination, 453

S

Samples, 19
Savant syndrome, 220–221, 438
Scaffolding, 256
Schemes, 166–167
Schizophrenia, 70, 75
Scholastic competence, 288
Science education, 272–273
Scientific method, 10
Scripts, 202
Secondary circular reactions, 168, 169
Second language learning, 257–258
Second trimester, 85
Secular trend, physical/sexual maturation and,
   126
Secure attachment, 378, 379, 385, 395
Secure base, 378, 396, 405
Secure working model, 395
Selective attention, 153
Selective breeding, 65
Selective optimization with compensation,
   306–307
Self
   adolescents and, 291–292
   adults and, 298–300
   children and, 287–288
   conceptualization of, 281
   cultural differences and, 298, 299
   infants and, 283–285
Self-actualization goal, 101
Self-concept, 281, 287
Self-conscious emotions, 374
Self-esteem
   adolescents and, 292–293
   boosting, 290
   children and, 288–290
   family violence and, 427
   gender differences and, 314
   multidimensional/hierarchical nature of, 288,
      289
   older adults and, 299
   self-perception and, 281
Self-fulfilling prophecies, 323
Self-recognition, 284
Self-reports, 11
Semantics, 249, 254, 255
Semenarche, 125, 127

Credits

These pages constitute an extension of the copyright page. We have made every effort to trace the ownership of all copyrighted material and to secure permission from copyright holders. In the event of any question arising as to the use of any material, we will be pleased to make the necessary corrections in future printings. Thanks are due to the following authors, publishers, and agents for permission to use the material indicated.

Tables, Figures, and Cartoons

Chapter 1. **5:** © The New Yorker Collection 2000 Alex Gregory from cartoonbank.com. All Rights Reserved. **11:** From "Stratum Contrasts and Similarities in Attitudes toward Death," by V. L. Bengston, J. B. Cuellar, and P. K. Ragan, 1977, *Journal of Gerontology*, 32. Reprinted by permission.

Chapter 3. **57:** Adapted from "For DNA, a defining moment. With code revealed, challenge will be to find its meaning and use," *The Washington Post*, May 23, 2000, p. A16. **67:** From "EAS Temperaments During the Last Half of the Life Span: Twins Reared Apart and Twins Reared Together" by R. Plomin, et al. from *Psychology and Aging*, 3, 1988. Copyright 1988 by The American Psychological Association. Reprinted by permission.

Chapter 4. **86:** From "Fetal Neurobehavioral Development" by J. A. DiPietro, et al. from *Child Development*, 67. © 1996 Society for Research in Child Development, Inc. Reprinted by permission. **89:** Adapted from *The Developing Human*, by K. L. Moore, 1988 (4th ed.). Philadelphia, W. B. Saunders. Reprinted by permission. **94:** Adapted with permission from "Longitudinal analyses of prenatal and postnatal lead exposure and early cognitive development" by D. Bellinger, et al. from *The New England Journal of Medicine*, 316, 1987. Copyright © 1987 by Massachusetts Medical Society. All rights reserved.

Chapter 5. **120:** Adapted with permission from A. C. Siegel & R. V. Burton (1999). "Effects of baby walkers on motor and mental development in human infants." *Journal of Developmental and Behavioral Pediatrics, 20*, p. 355–361. **121:** From "Walking infants adapt locomotion to changing body dimensions." *Journal of Experimental Psychology: Human Perception and Performance, 26*, p. 1148–1166. Copyright 2000 by The American Psychological Association. Reprinted by permission.

Chapter 6. **141:** Adapted with permission from Schiffman, *Sensation and Perception, 5/e*, p. 295, Fig 11.4. Copyright © 2000 John Wiley & Sons, Inc. **143:** From *Handbook of Child Psychology: Vol. 2 Infancy and Developmental Psychology, 4/e*, edited by Paul Henry Mussen. Copyright ©1983 by John Wiley & Sons, Inc. Adapted with permission. **143:** Adapted from "Pattern Perception in Infancy" by P. Salapatek from *Infant Perception: From Sensation to Cognition, Vol. 1* edited by L. B. Cohen and P. Salapatek. Copyright © 1975 by Academic Press, Inc. Reprinted by permission. **146:** Reprinted with permission from *Nature*, 358, "Addition and Subtraction by Human Infants" by K. Wynn, 1992, p. 749–750. Copyright 1992 Macmillan Magazines Limited. **153:** From "Human Figure Drawings by Schooled and Unschooled Children in Papua New Guinea" by M. Matthew and K. J. Connolly from *Child Development*, 67. © 1996 Society for Research in Child Development, Inc. Reprinted by permission. **158:** Insurance Institute of Highway Safety. **162:** "Food Recognition by the Elderly" by S. Schiffman, 1977, *Journal of Gerontology*, 32. Reprinted by permission.

Chapter 7. **181:** Data from "Individual Differences in College Students' Performance on Formal Operations Tasks," by R. De Lisi and J. Staudt, 1980, *Journal of Applied Developmental Psychology, 1*, p. 163–174.

Chapter 8. **193:** Adapted from "Human Memory: A Proposed System and Its Control Processes" by R. C. Atkinson and R. M. Shiffrin from *The Psychology of Learning and Motivation: Advances in Research and Theory* edited by K. W. Spence and J. T. Spence, Vol. 2, 1968. Copyright © 1968 by Academic Press. Reprinted by permission. **200:** Adapted from "Knowledge Structures and Memory Development" by M. T. H. Chi from *Children's Thinking: What Develops?* edited by R. Siegler. Copyright 1978 by Lawrence Erlbaum Associates, Inc. Reprinted by permission. **201:** From "Childhood Amnesia and the Beginnings of Memory for Four Early Life Events" by J. A. Usher and U. Neisser, 1993, *Journal of Experimental Psychology: General, 122*, p. 155–165. Copyright 1993 by the American Psychological Association. Reprinted by permission. **204:** From *Emerging Minds: The Process of Change in Children's Thinking* by Robert S. Siegler. Copyright © 1996 by Oxford University Press, Inc. Used by permission of Oxford University Press, Inc. **210:** From "Aging free from negative stereotypes: Successful memory in China and among the American deaf" by B. Levy and E. Langer, *Journal of Personality and Social Psychology, 66*, 1994. Copyright © 1994 by the American Psychological Association. Reprinted by permission. **212:** Adapted from "Further Testing of Limits of Cognitive Plasticity: Negative Age Differences in a Mnemonic Skill Are Robust" by P. B. Baltes and R. Kliegl, 1992. *Developmental Psychology, 28*, p. 121–125. Copyright 1992 by the American Psychiatric Association. Reprinted by permission. **214:** From "Effects of Contextual Organization on Spatial Memory of Middle-Aged and Older Women" by K. J. Waddell and B. Rogoff, 1981, *Developmental Psychology, 17*, p. 878–885. Copyright 1981 by the American Psychological Association. Reprinted by permission.

Chapter 9. **224:** From *Developmental Psychology: Childhood and Adolescence, 4/e* by D. R. Shaffer, p. 334, Brooks/Cole Publishing Company, 1996. Reprinted by permission. **229:** Reprinted from *Intelligence, 29*, H. Nyborg & A. R. Jensen, Fig 1, p. 15, copyright © 2001, with permission from Elsevier Science." **230:** From "Schooling, intelligence, and income" by S. J. Ceci and W. M. Williams (1997) in *American Psychologist, Vol. 53*, p. 1056. Copyright © 1997 by the American Psychological Association. Reprinted by permission. **231:** Reprinted from *Intelligence, 29*, A. S. Kaufmann (2001), Table 2, p. 140, copyright © 2001, with permission from Elsevier Science." **235:** Adapted from B. M. Caldwell and R. H. Bradley, *Manual for the HOME Observation for Measurement of the Environment*, 1984. Little Rock: University of Arkansas Press. Adapted by permission of the authors. **238:** From "Stereotype Threat and the Intellectual Test Performance of African Americans" by C. M. Steele and J. Aronson, *Journal of Personality and Social Psychology, 69*, 1995. Copyright © 1995 by the American Psychological Association. Reprinted by permission. **243:** Figure adapted from *Modes of Thinking in Young Children* by Michael A. Wallach and Nathan Kogan, copyright © 1965. Reprinted with permission of Wadsworth, a division of Thomson Learning. **244:** Data from "Creative Productivity between the Ages of 20 and 80 Years" by W. Dennis, 1966, *Journal of Gerontology, 21*, p. 2. Reprinted by permission.

Chapter 10. **251:** From B. A. Pan & J. B. Gleason, "Semantic development: Learning the meaning of words." In J. K. Gleason (ed.), *The Development of Language, 4/e*. Copyright © 2001 by Allyn & Bacon. Reprinted by permission. **252:** From L. Fenson, P. S. Dale, J. S. Reznick, E. Bates, D. Thal, S. J. Pethick (1994), "Variability in early communicative development." *Monographs of the Society for Research in Child Development*, No. 242, V. 59, no. 5. **253:** From *Psycholinguistics, 2/e* by Dan I. Slobin. Copyright © 1979, 1974 by Scott, Foresman and Company. Reprinted by permission of Addison Wesley Longman, Inc. **261:** From Campbell, F. A., et al. (2001) The development of cognitive and academic abilities: Growth curves from an early childhood educational experiment. *Developmental Psychology, Vol. 37* (March 2001), p. 231–242. Copyright © 2001 by the American Psychological Association. Reprinted by permission. **266:** From Jean Berko-Gleason,

Development of Language, Table 10.4, p. 434. Copyright © 2001 by Allyn & Bacon. Reprinted by permission. **272:** From Martin, et al. (2000). TIMSS 1999 International Science Report: Findings from IEA's Repeat of the Third International Mathematics and Science Study at the Eighth Grade. Exhibit 1.1. Chestnut Hill, MA: Boston College, Figure 2. Reprinted with permission.

Chapter 11. **292:** From S. Harter (1999). *The construction of the self: A developmental perspective.* Guilford Publications, p. 70. **294:** Adapted with permission from "Cross-Sectional Age Changes in Ego Identity Status during Adolescence" by P. W. Meilman, 1979, *Developmental Psychology, 15,* p. 230–231. Copyright 1979 by the American Psychological Association. **299:** From "Possible Selves in Adulthood and Old Age: A Table of Shifting Horizons" by C. D. Ryff, 1991, *Psychology and Aging,* p. 286–295. Copyright by the American Psychological Association. Reprinted by permission. **306:** Copyright 1987, G. B. Trudeau. Reprinted with permission of Universal Press Syndicate. All rights reserved.

Chapter 12. **314:** From "Mental Rotation of Three-Dimensional Objects" by R. N. Shepard, and J. Metzler, 1971, *Science, 17,* p. 701–703. Copyright 1971 by the American Association for the Advancement of Science. **317:** Calvin and Hobbes © 1995 Watterson. Distributed by Universal Press Syndicate. Reprinted with permission. All rights reserved. **317:** Figure from "Gender Segregation in Childhood" by Maccoby and Jacklin in *Advances in Child Development and Behavior,* Volume 20, edited by H. Reese, copyright © 1987 by Academic Press, reproduced by permission of the publisher. **320:** *From Man and Woman, Boy and Girls,* by J. Money and A. Ehrhardt, 1972, Johns Hopkins University Press. Reprinted by permission. **326:** Adapted from "The Roles of Cognition in Sex-Roles and Sex Typing" by C. L. Martin and C. F. Halverson, Jr. in *Current Conceptions of Sex Roles and Sex-Typing: Theory and Research* edited by D. B. Carter. Copyright 1987 by Bruce Carter. Reprinted by permission.

Chapter 13. **356:** From "A Longitudinal Study of Moral Judgment" by A. Colby, L. Kohlberg, J. Gibbs, and M. Lieberman, 1983, *Monographs of the Society for Research in Child Development, 48* (Nos. 1–2 serial No. 200). © 1983 by The Society for Research in Child Development, Inc. Reprinted by permission. **365:** From "Culture and Moral Devlopment" by R. A. Shweder, M. Mahapatra, and J. G. Miller in *Cultural Psychology Essays on Comparative Human Development* edited by J. W. Stigler, R. A. Shweder, and G. Herdt. Reprinted by permission of Cambridge University Press.

Chapter 14. **386:** Adapted from "Preschool Play Norms: A Replication" by K. E. Barnes, 1971, *Developmental Psychology, 5,* p. 99–103. Copyright 1971 by the American Psychological Association. Reprinted by permission. **391:** From "Girlfriend, Boyfriend: Age and Sex Differences in Intimate Friendship" by R. Sharabany, R. Gershoni, and J. E. Hofman, 1981, *Developmental Psychology, 17,* p. 800-808. Copyright 1981 by the American Psychological Association. Reprinted by permission. **391:** From "The Social Structure of Urban Adolescent Peer Groups" by D. C. Dunphy, 1963, *Sociometry, 26,* p. 230-246. Reprinted by permission.

Chapter 15. **402:** From "Early Human Experience: A Family Perspectives" by J. Belsky, 1981, *Developmental Psychology, 17,* p. 3–23. Copyright 1981 by the American Psychological Association. Reprinted by permission. **404:** From E. M. Duvall, *Marriage and Family Development,* 1978. Copyright © 1978 by J. B. Lippincott Company. Reprinted by permission of Harper and Row, Publishers, Inc. **408:** From "A Family Process Model of Economic Hardship and Adjustment of Early Adolescent Boys" by R. D. Conger, K. J. Conger, G. H. Elder, Jr., F. O. Lorenz, R. L. Simons, and L. B. Whitbeck, 1992, *Child Development, 63,* p. 526–541. Copyright 1992 by The Society for Research in Child Development, Inc. Adapted by permission. **416:** © The New Yorker Collection 2000 Barbara Smaller from cartoonbank.com. All Rights Reserved. **423:** Adapted from "Reasons for Divorce: Perspectives of Divorcing Men and Women" by L. Gigy and J. B. Kelly, *Journal of Divorce and Remarriage,* Vol. 18, 1992. Copyright © 1992 The Hawthorne Press, Inc. Reprinted by permission. **428:** Adapted from "Responses of Abused and Disadvantaged Toddlers to Distress in Agemates: A Study in the Day-Care Setting" by M. Main and C. George, 1985, *Developmental Psychology, 21,* p. 407–412. Copyright 1985 by the American Psychological Association. Reprinted by permission.

Chapter 16. **435:** From "Psychopathology as an outcome of development" by L. A. Sroufe, *Development and Psychopathology,* Vol. 9, 1997. Reprinted by permission of Cambridge University Press. **436:** From R. E. Ingram & J. M. Price (2001). The role of vulnerability in understanding psychopathology. In R. E. Ingram & J. M. Price (eds.) *Vulnerability to psychopathology: Risk across the lifespan.* Guilford Publications, 2001. **443:** © 1993 John McPherson/Dist. by Universal Press Syndicate. **451:** From Lewinsohn, P. M., Rohde, P., Seeley, J. R., & Baldwin, C. L. (2001) "Gender differences in suicide attempts from adolescence to young adulthood" in *Journal of the American Academy of Child and Adolescent Psychiatry, 40,* p. 427–434.

Chapter 17. **471:** Adapted with permission from G. A. Bonanno and S. Kaltman (2000). "The varieties of grief experience," *Clinical Psychology Review, 21,* p. 705–734. **476:** Adapted from C. M. Parkes, *Bereavement: Studies of Grief in Adult Life (3rd ed.).* London: Routledge, Appendix Table 3. **477:** Reprinted from *Omega 29,* L. H. Levy, et al., "Differences in Patterns of Adaptation in Conjugal Bereavement," p. 71–87. Copyright 1994, with permission from Elsevier Science.

Photographs

Chapter 1. **1:** Joel Gordon **2:** James A. Parcell / *The Washington Post* **3:** David Young-Wolff / PhotoEdit **5:** Henry Lillie Pierce Fund, Courtesy, Museum of Fine Arts, Boston **7:** AP / Wide World Photos **8:** Bettmann / CORBIS **13:** Michael Newman / PhotoEdit **17:** Lewis W. Hine / CORBIS **19:** Bob Daemmrich / Stock, Boston

Chapter 2. **23:** © Laura Dwight / CORBIS **24:** www.teenpregnancy.org **28:** UPI-Bettmann / CORBIS **31:** UPI-Bettmann / CORBIS **33:** Underwood & Underwood / Bettmann - CORBIS **35:** Rick Friedman / Stockphoto.com **36:** L.A. Cicero / Stanford University News Service **37:** Jim Pickerell / Stock Connection / PictureQuest **39:** Yves DeBraine / Stockphoto.com **40:** Bob Daemmrich / Stock, Boston **42:** Ria-Novosti / Sovfoto **43:** Cornell University

Chapter 3. **51:** Myrleen Ferguson / PhotoEdit **52:** Christopher Brown / Stock, Boston **54:** © John Cancalosi / Stock, Boston **54:** © Picture Press / CORBIS **58:** both, CNRI / Science Photo Library / Photo Researchers, Inc. **59:** Mike Blanpied **60:** Photo Researchers, Inc. **62:** Stockphoto.com / Cindy Karp **64:** SuperStock **67:** Getty Images / Yellow Dog Productions **70:** Stockphoto.com / Richard Hirneisen **73:** Tim Pannell / CORBIS **77:** Courtesy of Professor Karl Fredga, Uppsala University

Chapter 4. **80:** © Laura Dwight / PhotoEdit **81:** © David Young-Wolff / PhotoEdit **84:** Nestle / Petit Format / Photo Researchers, Inc. **85:** Petit Format / Nestle / Science Source / Photo Researchers, Inc. **85:** Photo Lennart Nilsson / Albert Bonniers Forlag AB, *A Child Is Born,* Dell Publishing Company **86:** Photo Lennart Nilsson / Albert Bonniers Forlag AB, *A Child Is Born,* Dell Publishing Company **90:** © Bryn Colton, Assignments Photographers / CORBIS **92:** © David H. Wells / CORBIS **96:** © Vince Streano / CORBIS **97:** © Vince Streano / CORBIS **101:** P. Amranand / SuperStock **104:** © Annie Griffiths Belt / CORBIS

Chapter 5. **106:** © Laura Dwight / CORBIS **113:** Benelux Press / Index Stock Imagery / PictureQuest **114:** © Gary A. Conner / PhotoEdit **116:** Paul Conklin / PhotoEdit **116:** © Spencer Grant / Stock, Boston **116:** © Jennie Woodcock; Reflections Photolibrary / CORBIS **119:** © Bill Horsman / Stock, Boston **121:** © Laura Dwight / CORBIS **122:** Bob Daemmrich / Stock, Boston **124:** Dennis MacDonald / PhotoEdit **125:** David Young-Wolff / PhotoEdit, Inc. **128:** © Paul A. Souders / CORBIS **131:** © Bob Daemmrich / Stock. Boston **133:** AP / Wide World Photos

Chapter 6. **138:** Stockphoto.com / Jim Sugar **139:** Al Cook / Stock, Boston **142:** © Laura Dwight / CORBIS **144:** Mark Richards / PhotoEdit **145:** © Laura Dwight / CORBIS **150:** Gail Meese **151:** David Young-Wolff / PhotoEdit **154:** David Young-Wolff / PhotoEdit **156:** Gail Meese **159:** David Young-Wolff / PhotoEdit

Chapter 7. **165:** Jim Corwin / Stock, Boston **167:** Don Smetzer / PhotoEdit **169:** © Laura Dwight / CORBIS **169:** © Brent Jones/ Stock, Boston Inc./ PictureQuest **174:** both, © Laura Dwight / CORBIS **176:** © Jeffry W. Myers/CORBIS **178:** © Dana White / PhotoEdit **179:** © Michael Newman / PhotoEdit, Inc. **182:** Charles Thatcher / Getty Images **184:** Sidney Bahrt / Photo Researchers, Inc. **185:** © Laura Dwight / CORBIS

Chapter 8. **191:** © Paul Conklin / PhotoEdit **195:** From A.N. Meltzoff & M.K. Moore (1977). "Imitation of facial and manual gestures by human neonates." *Science,* 198, 75-78. **196:** Courtesy Carolyn Rovee-Collier **197:** © Laura Dwight / CORBIS **200:** © Richard Hutchings / PhotoEdit **202:** © Jeff Greenberg / PhotoEdit **206:** Simon Fraser / Science Photo Library / Photo Researchers, Inc. **209:** © Gary Conner / PhotoEdit / PictureQuest

Chapter 9. **217:** © David Young-Wolff / PhotoEdit **218:** AP / Wide World Photos **220:** Pam Driscol Gallery, CO **222:** Bill Lai / Index Stock Imagery **226:** © Michael Newman / PhotoEdit, Inc. **233:** © Picture Finders Ltd. / eStock Photography / PictureQuest **237:** © Barbara Stitzer / PhotoEdit **240:** © Tony Freeman / PhotoEdit, Inc. **241:** Harvard University Archives

TO THE OWNER OF THIS BOOK:

I hope that you have found *Life-Span Human Development,* Fourth Edition, useful. So that this book can be improved in a future edition, would you take the time to complete this sheet and return it? Thank you.

School and address: _____

_____

Department: _____

Instructor's name: _____

1. What I like most about this book is: _____

_____

_____

2. What I like least about this book is:_____

_____

_____

3. My general reaction to this book is:_____

_____

_____

4. The name of the course in which I used this book is: _____

_____

5. Were all of the chapters of the book assigned for you to read? _____

   If not, which ones weren't? _____

6. In the space below, or on a separate sheet of paper, please write specific suggestions for improving this book and anything else you'd care to share about your experience in using this book.

_____

_____

_____

_____

_____

_____

OPTIONAL:

Your name: _____ Date: _____

May we quote you, either in promotion for *Life-Span Human Development,* Fourth Edition, or in future publishing ventures?

Yes: _____ No: _____

Sincerely yours,

Carol Sigelman and Elizabeth Rider

FOLD HERE

BUSINESS REPLY MAIL

FIRST CLASS   PERMIT NO. 34   BELMONT, CA

POSTAGE WILL BE PAID BY ADDRESSEE

ATTN: Edith Beard Brady, Psychology Publisher

WADSWORTH/THOMSON LEARNING
10 DAVIS DRIVE
BELMONT, CA   94002-9801

FOLD HERE